W9-BSK-159

40th Edition • 1995

THE
BOWKER
ANNUAL

Library and
Book Trade Almanac™

Editor • Catherine Barr
Consultant • Jane Williams

R.R. Bowker®
A Reed Reference Publishing Company
New Providence, New Jersey

Published by R. R. Bowker,
a Reed Reference Publishing Company
Copyright © 1995 by Reed Elsevier Inc.
All rights reserved
Printed and bound in the United States of America
Bowker® is a registered trademark of Reed Reference Publishing, a Division of
Reed Elsevier Inc.
The Bowker Annual Library and Book Trade Almanac™ is a trademark of Reed
Elsevier Properties Inc., used under license.

International Standard Book Number 0–8352–3613–7
International Standard Serial Number 0068–0540
Library of Congress Catalog Card Number 55–12434

No part of this publication may be reproduced or transmitted in any form or by
any means, or stored in any information storage and retrieval system, without
prior written permission of R. R. Bowker, 121 Chanlon Road, New Providence,
NJ 07974.

No copyright is claimed for articles in this volume prepared by U.S. government
employees as part of their official duties. Such articles are in the public domain
and can be reproduced at will.

ISBN 0 - 8352 - 3613 - 7

9 780835 236133

Contents

Part 1
Reports from the Field

Part 2
Legislation, Funding, and Grants

Part 3
Library/Information Science
Education, Placement, and Salaries

Part 4
Research and Statistics

Library Research and Statistics

Book Trade Research and Statistics

Part 5
Reference Information

Part 6
Directory of Organizations

Preface

Welcome to this, the 40th, edition of *The Bowker Annual*. This almanac has evolved and grown over the years, but its intent remains to provide you with a mix of analysis and practical information on the library and publishing world. Although there is a natural temptation in these exciting years of technological innovation to focus on electronic issues and the "Information Superhighway," we continue to bring you details on everything from legislation, funding, and education to average book prices, sales statistics, and best book lists of interest to every librarian, publisher, and bookseller.

Four of our Special Reports this year focus on library networking and the impact of new technologies, with contributions on the growth of civic or community networks in the United States by R. Kathleen Molz; on the delivery of library services through campus networks by Judy Montgomery and Katherine Kott; on library cooperation and networking developments by JoAn S. Segal; and on the federal national information infrastructure (NII) initiative by Toni Carbo Bearman and David A. Wallace. You will also find an account of the Library of Congress's digitization program under the Federal Agency and Federal Library Reports.

A fifth Special Report, by Prudence Dalrymple, covers library and information education from the standpoint of quality assurance.

Along with the customary reports from federal agencies and federal libraries are two new contributions—from the Government Printing Office and the National Library of Education.

In addition to the above features, Part 2 brings you news roundups from *Library Journal*, *School Library Journal*, and *Publishers Weekly* and accounts of the Frankfurt Book Fair and of 1994 activities of national library associations and the International Federation of Library Associations and Institutions. Finally, Ken Haycock updates us on "Trends and Issues in Library and Information Services in Canada."

Part 2, Legislation, Funding, and Grants, covers legislation proposed and enacted during 1994 that is of particular interest to librarians and publishers and reports on funding and grants programs conducted by the National Endowment for the Humanities, the Council on Library Resources, and the U.S. Department of Education.

Part 3 offers professional information for librarians: a guide to employment sources, statistics on salaries, a list of accredited master's degree programs, and scholarship sources and award recipients.

Part 4 reports on research taking place in the library field and gathers together all the statistics needed to predict library expenditures and justify budgets: average acquisition expenditures, price indexes, construction costs, prices of books and other materials, and so forth. Chandler Grannis, who contributed statistics to the *Annual* from its inception, has retired. We have been very fortunate that William Lofquist of the U.S. Department of Commerce has taken over the task of updating the import/export figures; Gary Ink of *Publishers Weekly* continues to oversee the title output tables.

Part 5 brings together basic reference information: publishers' toll-free numbers, ISBN and ISSN tips, best book lists, bestseller lists, and literary prizes. Part 6, the Directory of Organizations, gives contact names, E-mail addresses, phone and fax numbers, and other details on library and book trade organizations both in the United States and abroad.

Finally, you'll find a list of National Information Standards Organization (NISO) standards, a calendar of events, a list of acronyms, and indexes by organization and subject.

Compiling the *Annual* is a complex task. Thanks are owed to Jane Williams of the National Commission on Libraries and Information Science, consultant editor; to Nancy Mink, editorial assistant, and Nancy Bucenec, production editor; and to all who contributed articles and answered questionnaires. We hope you find this 40th edition as invaluable as its forerunners, and, as always, we would be glad to hear your comments or suggestions for future editions.

Catherine Barr
Editor

Part 1
Reports from the Field

News of the Year

LJ News Report: Public Libraries Meet Fiscal Reality Head On

Evan St. Lifer

Senior Editor/News, *Library Journal*

Ever since local governments were forced five or so years ago to exact the first wave of deep cuts on shell-shocked library systems, librarians have remained sanguine that an economic turnaround would eventually return them to the heady days of the mid-1980s, when 10 percent budget jumps were more the rule than the exception.

While the "wait till next year" mentality still exists in some libraries, an increasing number of librarians have come to realize that the most recent period of fiscal conservatism is not the downside of a finite economic cycle but rather the new economic reality. Pundits can no longer cite stagflation as the culprit: The economy is performing at fairly robust levels bolstered by the lowest unemployment rate in almost six years.

In case there was any question about how the nation's voters felt about paying taxes, the November 8 elections provided a stiff answer: Americans practically tripped over each other to get to the polls to vote primarily for the Republican's antitax, too-much-Washington platform. Republican upstarts, who had hopped the conservative gravy train shrewdly engineered by recently anointed House Speaker Newt Gingrich, were on the winning end of one of the largest congressional house cleanings in the nation's history.

While it remains to be seen whether Republican control of Congress for the first time in four decades is an aberration, the same cannot be said for public libraries' fiscal realities.

So far, public libraries have met the challenge of having to operate in a more stringent economic milieu head-on, according to *Library Journal*'s fifth annual Budget Report. Despite finding themselves increasingly having to fight harder for their piece of the local pie, the majority of libraries continue to post positive budgetary gains.

How have public libraries (PLs) fared during the country's fiscal belt-tightening, which began during 1990–1991? Over the five-year period, 85 percent of

Research was conducted by the staff of Cahners Research Department: Catherine Hoey, Research Director; Sandy Gettenberg, Research Assistant; tabulations done by Laura Girmscheid, Tabulations Supervisor.

Note: Adapted from *Library Journal*, January 1995.

PLs responding to *LJ*'s 1995 Budget Survey have seen their total budgets increase, with growth averaging a healthy 7 percent per year. Broken down even further, respondents saw their materials budgets increase at a rate of more than 8 percent per year, salaries at 7 percent annually. While the numbers don't bespeak the dire financial straits in which some libraries find themselves—or even the angst that most public librarians endure until funds are found and the budget okayed—they do serve as a national gauge indicating that library service remains an essential priority in most of our nation's communities.

Two of the prime indicators of a public library's fiscal health—staff and hours—offer encouraging signs despite the tough economic climate. While the majority of respondents said their staffs remained unchanged from FY 1993/1994 to FY 1994/1995, 27 percent of libraries said they had staff increases, while only 10 percent said they endured cuts. More than two-thirds of libraries didn't add or cut hours, but of those that did, 13 percent increased hours, while almost 5 percent decreased.

The breakdown of public libraries' funding sources has changed little since last year: 47.46 percent of libraries' funding comes from local resources; 29.42 percent from the county; 13.3 percent from the state; 3.1 percent from fees and fines; 1.07 percent from fund raising; 1.4 percent from federal funding; and 4.23 percent from other sources.

LJ's New Approach

LJ, in conjunction with its research arm, Cahners Research, surveyed 1,624 public libraries (selected from R. R. Bowker's *American Library Directory* database) from across the country. We received 511 responses, for a response rate of 32 percent, matching last year's strong return.

As part of our ongoing effort to better articulate the issues facing public libraries of similar size and scope, we broke down the size classifications even further than in past years. We divided public libraries into the following groups by population served: fewer than 10,000; 10,000–24,999; 25,000–49,999; 50,000–99,999; 100,000–999,999; and one million or more.

Libraries fall under the headings Smaller, Medium, and Larger public libraries, rather than into the state-by-state and regional categories used by *LJ* in previous years. Recognizing that public libraries are also confronted with a host of jurisdictional issues, we are working with our research department to create a formula that would classify libraries by type (e.g., city, county, district, and regional PLs) in addition to size.

Election Day's Upside

Election day wasn't exclusively reserved for Republican gains in Congress: November 8 also provided an encouraging sign for libraries. Two-thirds of public library bond/tax referenda on the ballot were approved by voters. Even the seismic shift in Congress may not be all that bad. After all, Gingrich, Washington's newest power broker and a budding sci-fi author, is reputed to be a devoted fan of libraries. Whether librarians become devoted fans of Gingrich's in 1995 remains to be seen.

Smaller Public Libraries

Although *LJ*'s Budget Survey provides just a glimpse of what types of budgetary gains and losses smaller libraries across the country are experiencing, the news is encouraging for the public libraries serving fewer than 10,000, nonetheless. They saw their median total budgets climb 8 percent for FY 1994/1995, from $89,100 to $96,600. The jump represents the largest increase in total budget among all six library categories. Salary budgets increased by 7 percent, while materials jumped an encouraging 11 percent.

Staffing and hours were indicative of the smallest libraries' positive progression. While the bulk of responding libraries reported no changes in staffing or hours, of those that did, more than twice as many reported staff increases (13 percent) as reported staff decreases (6 percent). Similarly, 8 percent increased hours, while only 2 percent cut back.

Asked to give his outlook for the future, Karl Aroma of the Rumford (ME) PL (population served: 8,891) said, "Things seem to be improving," despite the library receiving the same budget for FY 1995 as it had in FY 1994.

Helen King of the Altamont (NY) Free Library, which serves a patron base of about 1,500, said she was "exploring alternative sources of funding from the private sector." King reported healthy gains in the library's materials (30 percent) and salaries budgets (14 percent), with a modest increase in total budget (3 percent). Hay Memorial Library, Sacketts Harbor, NY, finds itself with a jurisdictional problem: The library, serving about 3,000, has received support from the village but not the town, explained librarian Toni Ellenger. The staff would like to move the library to a newer facility but needs more fiscal backing. Still, the library was able to post a 10 percent gain in its total budget, a slight increase in salaries and an impressive 30 percent increase in materials.

Two other small libraries—Millinocket (ME) Memorial Library and Jamestown (NC) PL—are just simply trying to dodge debilitating losses. Jamestown's Mary Hamil said her library (population served: 6,000) "desperately needs more money," after shooting a budgetary blank by not gaining anything in FY 1995, while Millinocket (population served: 6,780) saw its budget shrink by 16 percent in FY 1994/1995.

For some libraries, a budget increase is a matter of survival. For others, it may prevent them from keeping up with technology, a concern expressed by Dorothy Aye, Lyon County Library District, Allen, KS.

The next largest size library category, those PLs that serve a population ranging from 10,000 to 24,999, realized more modest budgetary gains: up 4 percent in total budgets, up 7 percent in materials, and an increase of 6 percent in salaries.

The subtle increase in hours for the 10,000–24,999 group was similar to that of the under-10,000 group: 8 percent said they added hours while only 2 percent said they cut back. Libraries showed very promising signs of growth in terms of staffing, with 25 percent of respondents increasing staff and only 4 percent decreasing.

Some libraries have characterized their fiscal situations as "stable." Steven Read of the McPherson (KS) PL (population served: 12,400) said he "felt optimistic" about his library's fiscal situation. Read can justify his instincts with the

Table 1 / **Smaller Public Libraries (fewer than 10,000–24,999): A Snapshot Changes in Budget for FY 1994 to FY 1995**

Library	Per Capita	Materials	Salary	Total Budget
Halstead Public Library, KS (2,021)*	$12.37	NC	NC	NC
Samuel H. Wentworth Library, NH (4,100)	11.22	11%	5%	7%
Webster Addison PL, Webster Springs, WV (4,100)	3.50	NC	NC	NC
Lake Park PL, FL (6,704)	24.91	21%	8%	3%
West Long Branch PL, NJ, (7,800)	23.72	17%	-3%	8%
Franklin PL, NH, (8,300)	20.24	NC	4%	3%
Rumford PL, ME (8,891)	17.71	NC	1%	1%
Farmville PL, NC (9,000)	17.78	6%	-19%	6%
Rogers Memorial Library, Southampton, NY (12,000)	49.33	4%	6%	6%
Wayland Free PL, MA (12,000)	35.42	16%	14%	6%
McPherson PL, KS (12,400)	21.94	9%	8%	7%
Sewickley PL, PA (14,600)	30.13	NC	4%	NC
Auburn PL, MA (15,086)	23.46	NC	4%	3%
Ethelbert B. Crawford PL, Monticello, NY (16,500)	11.58	34%	3%	14%
John R. Kaufman Jr. PL, Sanbury, PA (16,717)	10.38	-40%	8%	-2%

*Population served
NC=No change
Source: *Library Journal* Budget Report 1995

library's 7 percent increase in total budget, 9 percent jump in materials, and 8 percent jump in salaries. Carbondale (PA) PL (population served: 12,000) is "stable at the moment," according to Ann Muldoon, but heads into 1995 with exactly the same budget as it did last year.

Medium-Size Public Libraries

The smaller of the medium-sized libraries, those in the 25,000–49,999 group, showed a modest gain of 3 percent in total budget and a 6 percent increase each in materials and salaries budgets. While 19 percent reported that they had increased hours and only 4 percent reported cutting them, staffing was less encouraging: 21 percent had new hires, but almost 13 percent of respondents said they endured staff cuts. The Westerly (RI) PL (population served: 28,000)—with its healthy total budget increase of 9 percent, a hefty jump in materials (40 percent), and a 7 percent increase in salaries—is an unusual, yet thought-provoking, model. Unlike most other PLs, only 28 percent of its funding is local—much of the rest comes from an endowment. The library is owned and operated by the nonprofit library association of Westerly.

Although Mississippi libraries traditionally are among the lowest-ranking libraries in terms of per capita support—the state averages just over $8 per capita—there are some exceptions. Rising property values in Vicksburg, MS, have allowed the Warren County Vicksburg PL (population served: 48,000) to increase its per capita support to $11.12. The library's total budget increased by

Table 2 / Medium Public Libraries (fewer than 25,000–99,999): A Snapshot
Changes in Budget for FY 1994 to FY 1995

Library	Per Capita	Materials	Salary	Total Budget
Northlake PL District, IL (25,741)*	$34.95	-3%	-8%	-28%
J. Blackstone Memorial Library, Branford, CT (27,510)	22.01	2%	3$	4%
Smyrna PL, Georgia (32,000)	13.47	21%	8%	3%
Chesterfield County Library, SC (38,577)	5.71	NC	11%	6%
Sweetwater County Library System, WY (41,500)	58.6	-4%	1%	1%
East Providence PL, RI (52,000)	18.83	-13%	9%	-4%
Jefferson Township, IN (53,449)	22.54	5%	5%	5%
Ashtabula County District Library, OH (63,000)	17.12	5%	1%	-1%
Champaign PL, IL (63,502)	45.08	-13%	9%	-4%
Fargo PL, ND (74,111)	13.63	5%	1%	-1%
Missoula PL, MT (82,000)	9.76	7%	5%	12%
Tangipahoa Parish Library, LA (85,709)	11.38	2%	-2%	1%
Deschutes County PL System, Bend, OR (89,500)	11.49	8%	13%	11%
Davenport PL, IA (95,333)	21.30	1%	5%	4%
River Bluffs Regional Library, MO (97,715)	20.46	9%	4%	7%

*Population served
NC=No change
Source: *Library Journal* Budget Report 1995

about 5 percent, its salaries by 13 percent, while materials remained static. The neighboring Hancock (MS) Library System (population served: 31,000) has an even more impressive per capita expenditure of $21.65, with a 10 percent increase in its total budget, a 14 percent increase in salaries, and a 7 percent jump for materials.

Libraries in the 50,000–99,999 group surveyed by *LJ* had a standard 5 percent increase across the board for materials, salaries, and total budgets. One-quarter of all responding institutions reported an increase in staffing: 10 percent had cuts. Service hours were less volatile, with three times as many libraries saying they had increased hours (12 percent) as those that reported decreases (4 percent).

LJ found a number of responding libraries in this population group winning the budget battle. In comparing some of the successful PLs with some of those that have struggled, it became evident that those library administrators garnering higher budget increases and more per capita funding were able to accomplish their goals, i.e., form a new taxing district, cultivate stronger voter support at the polls, become more politically prominent in the community, etc. While libraries that continue to struggle may be dealing with financial realities that transcend their ability to change them—such as state or regional woes or a locally depressed economy—they are only beginning to set goals similar to those above. Kay Runge, director of the Davenport (IA) PL (population served: 95,333), is up against a millage level in her municipality "that has been frozen at $8.10 per $1,000 of assessed valuation." Her library "is investigating" getting a special levy put on the ballot in 1996. With a simple majority vote, the special levy would add 27¢ per $1,000. Davenport, with a better-than-average per capita expenditure of $21.30, saw its total budget increase by only 4 percent.

The director of the Redford Township (MI) Library (population served: 54,362) said his institution is "fiscally sound for the next 15 years," after a ballot issue was passed that will yield the library almost $900,000 annually. Redford Township had gains in total (9 percent), salaries (6 percent), and materials (14 percent) budgets. Aggressive growth is keeping the Kenosha (WI) PL (population served: 84,394) well funded with $39 per capita and a slight 3.5 percent increase that has allowed the library to keep pace with inflation.

While most libraries look forward to ballot issues as a means to raise much-needed revenue, Daniel Pauli at the Missoula (MT) PL (population served: 82,000) is worried that two pending ballot issues "may have a negative effect on our local government's ability to raise revenue." Nevertheless, for a PL with a low per capita ($9.76), Missoula more than held its own heading into 1995, with increases of 12 percent, 7 percent, and 5 percent in total, materials, and salaries.

Despite the Bloomington PL's strong per capita of $36, a 5 percent increase in its total budget, and a 42 percent increase in its total budget since 1990, officials have said that "public library funding must come from sources other than property tax if our libraries are to hold their own." They also expressed concern that a municipal levy would never increase above the current 1.5 percent rate.

Other libraries in the category were less fortunate: Union City (NJ) PL (population served: 58,000) saw its total budget drop 13 percent. "Unless we obtain major funding we will cease to exist," said a Union City librarian. Also absorbing cuts were the Hammond (IN) PL (population served: 84,234), down 3 percent, and the Ashtabula County (OH) District Library (population served: 63,000), down 1.5 percent—a rarity for an Ohio PL. Ohio PLs are generally regarded as among the country's best-supported libraries.

Larger Public Libraries

The next largest public library group, 100,000–999,999, encompasses a broad and eclectic range of PLs that could easily have been divided in half or in thirds. In fact, the smaller libraries in the group—those serving around 100,000—more closely resemble in operation and administration their large counterparts in the medium-sized category. As a group, this category showed a 5 percent gain in both total and materials budgets and a 6 percent increase in salary. Hiring was on an upswing, with one-third of all libraries in the group reporting an increase, while only 10 percent had cuts. Hours were up marginally, with 14 percent saying they had increased hours and 6 percent reporting cutbacks.

Looking at libraries in the low-100,000s, cities such as Las Cruces, NM (population served: 135,000), Decatur, AL (Wheeler Basin Regional Library; population served: 192,622), and Allentown, PA (population served: 109,000), have been hard-pressed to fund their PLs adequately. "Ours is an aging, changing, and stricken city," said Kathryn Stephanoff in Allentown. "If we believe in the value of our service [and we do], we must look for different funding arrangements." Stephanoff said the library, with a per capita of $16.77, has been suc-

Table 3 / Larger Public Libraries (100,000+): A Snapshot
Changes in Budget for FY 1994 to FY 1995

Library	Per Capita	Materials	Salary	Total Budget
Livonia PL, MI (100,850)*	$36.39	-22%	10%	4%
Sioux Falls Library, SD (112,000)	23.57	5%	4%	12%
Branigan Memorial Library, Las Cruces, NM (135,000)	8.42	-12%	14%	6%
Lincoln City Libraries, NE (200,000)	21.35	4%	9%	7%
Jackson Hinfs Library System, MS (350,000)	5.71	20%	1%	NC
Mobile PL, AL (389,234)	11.79	13%	3%	5%
Denver PL (497,204)	43.56	10%	14%	19%
Cuyahoga County PL, OH (607,909)	65.73	23%	10%	25%
Milwaukee PL (602,684)	29.51	3%	6%	11%
Hennepin County Library, Minnetonka, MN (664,048)	36.11	1%	1%	1%
Enoch Pratt Free Library, Baltimore (736,014)	20.19	7%	7%	3%
San Antonio PL, TX (1,200,000)	10.00	8%	22%	29%
Broward County PL, Ft. Lauderdale, FL (1,371,435)	21.94	4%	3%	4%
Queens Borough PL, Jamaica, NY (1,950,000)	27.98	-7%	7%	8%
County of Los Angeles PL (3,320,330)**	19.34	560%	-1%	27%

*Population served
NC=No change
**Material budget slashed by 600% over FY's 1991 to 1993
Source: *Library Journal* Budget Report 1995

cessful in selling "contract services" to a neighboring municipality and "must continue developing arrangements that add value."

Still other libraries anticipate being in a tenuous situation, no matter how well things are going in the present. Charleston, West Virginia's Kanawha County PL (population served: 207,619) reported a 13 percent total budget increase, as well as gains in materials (7 percent) and salaries (6 percent). Yet because the area is in the final year of a three-year property reevaluation, librarians are concerned that the flat local economy threatens the library's recently enhanced fiscal situation. Livonia (MI) PL (population served: 100,850) serves as another example: Despite impressive per capita funding of $36.39, library administrators are concerned that recent legislation capping property taxes will have a negative impact on future budgets.

Libraries that would engender envy among their financially beleaguered counterparts include Montana's Parmly Billings Library (population served: 113,419), with an unexceptional per capita of $14.30 but a whopping 31 percent jump in total budget and a five-mill dedicated levy for operations passed in April 1994; and Lawrenceville, N.J.'s Mercer County Library (population served: 120,800), which has a huge $59.55 per capita and saw its total budget jump 16 percent.

Success stories among libraries serving a population in the mid-100,000s aren't too hard to find: Can anyone top king-of-the-hill Cuyahoga County (OH)

PL (population served: 607,909)? Besides seeing its per capita jump about as high as or higher than some libraries—more than $16 to a lofty $65.73— Cuyahoga's total budget grew by 25 percent to almost $40 million. Although dwarfed by Cuyahoga's seemingly endless support, Omaha PL (population served: 418,935) did have a good year, with its budget surging 25 percent. Administrators there are seeking to establish a county library first, then a district library, based in Omaha. Denver PL (population served: 497,204) also had a very strong year that included an almost 20 percent increase in total budget to coincide with the opening of its new main library. Support for libraries is strong and steady in the Mile High City, with a per capita of $43.56. Recently, dollars have been especially tight for libraries in Austin, TX (population served: 477,227), Mobile, AL (population served: 389,234), and Hennepin County, Minnetonka, MN (population served: 664,048).

As libraries inch closer to the one million–plus population served, the sizes of the increases tend to be less pronounced, based on the data *LJ* received from its survey respondents. The Columbus (OH) Metropolitan Library (population served: 708,000), the St. Louis County Library (population served: 843,638), and Baltimore's Enoch Pratt Free Library (population served: 736,014) had respective total budget increases of 3 percent, 0.5 percent, and 3 percent.

The largest libraries, those that serve populations of one million or more, had increases of 1 percent for total budgets, 6 percent for materials budgets, and 4 percent for salaries, and almost all of those *LJ* surveyed posted gains. Those that hired were nearly triple those that fired—57 percent versus 21 percent. And hours were also up, with 29 percent of respondents adding hours and 14 percent cutting back.

The New York Public Library (population served: 3,070,302) saw its budget rise by $2 million, or 2.5 percent, to $83.2 million. However, NYPL officials are concerned, as are their New York City counterparts, about how the city's $2 billion budget deficit will affect them. Still, they're committed to retaining the recently restored six-day-a-week service.

SLJ News Report: Buckle Up for a Ride Through the Year's Disappointments and Victories

Renée Olson

News and Features Editor, *School Library Journal*

Bette Davis would have called it a bumpy year for youth services librarians, especially those drenched in Georgia and Texas or shaken in Los Angeles.

But, while many are juggling shiny CD-ROMs and skillfully navigating the information highway, others are witness to a somber trend: the increasing number of children being killed.

Note: Adapted from *School Library Journal*, December 1994.

Today, for many children forced to grow up well before their time, survival is a more pressing issue than education. In June, Marion Wright Edelman, founder of the Children's Defense Fund, shared with the audience at ALA's opening session in Miami Beach a tragic statistic: 25 children, or a full classroom, die violently every two days in the United States.

Three months after the ALA meeting, the country read about 11-year-old Robert Sandifer, who, after murdering the "wrong" child on Chicago's South Side, was killed by his own gang members, who feared he would talk to police. Chilling stories like this are rare; but during the past six years, there has been a significant increase in the most violent types of juvenile crime: murder, rape, robbery, and aggravated assault, according to a recent article in *Time*.

The true madness about all this is that children who live under a constant threat of violence are also the least likely to have easy access to books and computers, the tools for a decent education.

There are some who would argue that the situation is hopeless. In their new book *The Bell Curve: Intelligence and Class Structure in American Life*, authors Charles Murray and the late Richard Herrnstein dust off the old argument that intelligence is linked to race and that bad genetics may cancel out environmental influences like education. On October 20, William Safire, the on-again, off-again conservative and *New York Times* columnist, opted not to condemn outright the authors' findings. He did, however, reject the notion that anyone is bound to a particular class for life and offered as a cure what every youth services librarian already knows: "Early reading training . . . may shrink the gaps within and between groups. And the computer, while no leveler, can provide online access to creative communities far beyond the dangerous neighborhood."

Lip Service Instead of Cash

Bill Clinton made all the right noises this year about the importance of education and technology, but then he failed to give librarians what they needed to move forward. His budget did not provide earmarked funds for school library materials in the Elementary and Secondary Education Act (ESEA), nor did it fund the Library Services and Construction Act (LSCA) even at last year's level. "It was a very tough year for us," said Mary Costabile, assistant to the director of ALA's Washington Office. The 103rd Congress, however, did restore funding of various levels to both bills.

For the first time since the 1970s, school librarians convinced lawmakers to add language to ESEA to earmark funds for school library materials. Congress failed to appropriate the proposed $200 million for it, yet those who pushed for the language were ecstatic to see it survive what *Education Week* called "an all-out effort [by Republicans] . . . to smother several pending bills" just before midterm elections.

Several portions of ESEA were subject to contentious debate. The House and Senate differed as to what formula should be used to distribute Chapter 1, now called Title 1, funds—more than half the total ESEA budget—to communities with certain percentages of disadvantaged students.

Costabile felt that senators spent more time on the issue than necessary, using it as a screen to impede the bill's passage. It was "part of a larger Republican opposition to pass anything," she said. "On Monday [October 3], it didn't look as though we had enough votes for cloture [to bring an end to the debate]," said Costabile. Other controversial issues that threw ESEA on thin ice included school prayer and materials and programs with sexual content.

A Balancing Act

Lawmakers aren't the only ones made uneasy by books and videos with sexual content. Two parents in Springfield, Oregon, complained to the city council a year ago that their children had borrowed R-rated videos from the public library. Eager to solve the problem, the council decided that children under 16 would not be allowed to take out those videos.

The move drew fire from some residents concerned about intellectual freedom; one person contacted the American Civil Liberties Union, which in turn called the Motion Picture Association of America (MPAA), the group that hands out ratings. MPAA wrote Springfield's mayor, advising him that the ratings are completely voluntary and cannot be used in a legal sense. After a review of the policy by the city's legal counsel, the library decided to keep the age restriction.

Another age-related issue emerged in March when the St. Louis Public Library (SLPL) began offering parents two types of library cards for children under 18: restricted and unrestricted. Those parents opting for the restricted card (there were 14 as of September) deny their children the opportunity to check out materials from the adult collection. Although the majority of large metropolitan libraries are not as conservative in their approach, St. Louis's new policy is actually less restrictive than the one it replaced, which barred everyone under 18 from checking out adult materials. In a letter to *SLJ*, Leslie Edmonds Holt, director of SLPL's youth services, defended the policy as a way to give parents choices.

"Parental rights," used as a political tool, enjoyed a renaissance this year. First employed in two 1920s Supreme Court cases, the concept is now being used by groups to launch challenges to books and videos. In many cases, lobbyists bank on the idea that more people will sympathize with the personal-rights angle than with a conservative mindset. Of the People, a Virginia-based parental-rights lobby, introduced vague legislation in several states this year designed to strengthen the parental voice when it comes to challenging assigned classroom reading and materials in school and public libraries.

A Chancy Busine$$

Libraries are finding that lottery money, when added to budgets, can have a Jekyll and Hyde personality. Georgia saw the Dr. Jekyll side this year when its state lottery dropped a small windfall—$17,500—on each public library and school. Many librarians used the funds to buy automated circulation systems and CD-ROM packages, said Joellen Ostendorf, assistant director of the state library. Ostendorf, who oversaw the public library portion of the project, said that all 254 public libraries in the state—even the smallest—are now automated.

"We hope [it will] be ongoing," said Ostendorf when asked if libraries could count on a check next year.

South Dakota's video lottery, on the other hand, may turn out to be Mr. Hyde. This summer, the state library, which serves as a public library for 200,000 in small communities, received word that it could close this fall because the state's video lottery—the source of nearly a fifth of its budget—had been outlawed. As of this writing, residents had not yet voted on the lottery's constitutionality. If it is abolished, State Librarian Jane Kolbe will cut books and films, but not staff. She now advises against relying on lottery funds, yet she admits it was tempting because the money "seemed to keep on coming."

Lawmakers Hang Up on Reform

"I can't find anyone in this house or anywhere [who] was against this bill," FCC commissioner Andrew Barrett told the *Atlanta Journal-Constitution*, referring sarcastically to the unwillingness on the part of lawmakers and lobbyists to take responsibility for the painful death of federal telecommunications law reform, in late September. This was the first major attempt at an overhaul since the original Communications Act of 1934.

"I haven't found anybody that didn't support it. I'm trying to figure out why the hell it died," said Barrett.

Observers blamed the demise of the Communications Act of 1994 on various segments of the telephone industry, including regional Bell companies, that were threatened financially by the reforms.

Under the bill, telecommunications providers would have had to reserve 5 percent of network capacity at cost or less for public and nonprofit libraries, educational institutions at all levels, and other, similar nonprofits. The legislation would have also required companies to provide the same institutions with "universal service," defined nebulously as "telecommunications and information services." The money to cover expenses would come out of a pot to which all telecommunications providers would contribute.

This year's reform would have hastened the complete reordering of the country's telecommunications. Cable companies are eager to jump into telephone service and phone companies are eying cable. Two companies in New York City—Nynex and Liberty Cable Television—are already offering a trial package combining cable with local and long-distance phone service. Price, naturally, will help determine who will be the important players. A better rate from a cable company convinced schools in Alabama to go with a cable provider for their network after they found that North Carolina schools were paying the phone company nearly four times as much for fewer hours of service, according to *Multichannel News*.

In other telecommunications news, a survey sent out by Rep. Edward J. Markey (D-Mass.) at the very end of 1993 found that most major phone companies have reservations about providing schools with free links to advanced networks. Markey, who chairs the House Telecommunications and Finance Subcommittee, found that, of the companies who responded, only Bell Atlantic would offer free service. GTE and Nevada Bell opposed free service, and Bell

South, SW Bell, US Sprint, and US West wanted to look at the issue. According to Nynex's statement, free digital links are "not in [the] long-term public interest. The public would ultimately pay, and it would lead to hospitals, government, etc., demanding free access."

Instability Is Certain

The year 1995—the midpoint of the decade—promises the kind of technological chaos from which great things emerge. Internet roadmaps and navigators, both online and on paper, will continue to swamp the market, and new computer operating systems like IBM's Warp and Microsoft's Windows '95 (formerly Chicago) will come complete with connections to the information highway.

The crucial issue here, however, is not how quickly businesses will pave the way for librarians; it's whether librarians—including youth librarians—will pave the way for others. Who else will make sure that children won't be left by the side of the road?

Telecommunications news will continue to fascinate, if not produce migraines. Sen. Ernest F. Hollings (D-S.C.), architect of 1994's telecommunications reform, will reintroduce his bill in 1995, and Vice President Gore announced a Telecommunications Summit in Washington in early 1995.

The legislation to watch in 1995 will once again be ESEA. Now that $200 million of earmarked funds for school libraries is on the books, the trick will be to get Congress to appropriate the funds. Even before November's elections, Carol Henderson, executive director of ALA's Washington Office, admitted it will be an uphill battle.

With Republicans fixed on capturing the presidency in 1996, they're apt to block all Democratic initiatives, the way they did with ESEA this fall. Children, and library funding, are likely to fall victims to party politics unless youth services librarians demand results instead of rhetoric.

A Spin Through the Year's Stories

Books for Croatia

"We're happy that the books arrived," said Fred Giordano, director of the New City (NY) Public Library, referring to a shipment of books he organized this spring for children in war-torn Croatia. Spurred on by a call for help in a library newsletter, Giordano asked his children's room staff to choose picture and elementary-level books on understanding other ethnic groups. The local Rotary, of which Giordano is a member, footed the bill. The books are sorely needed; more than 100 libraries have been damaged during the war.

More Schools Travel on the Infobahn

More K–12 schools are using Internet than commercial online services. A survey by Quality Education Data, Inc., a division of Peterson's, found that 12.8 percent of, or 19,967, schools are using Internet. Only 5,000 use Prodigy; 4,000 are America Online users.

Heroine of the Year

Gwen Page, children's librarian at the Salt Lake City Public Library, kept a cool head when she and others were taken hostage for five hours by a gunman on a Saturday morning in March. Page, who allowed other hostages to be released before her, felt that security training gave her the skills to manage a dangerous situation.

Privatizing Internet

One year ago, Al Gore assured the country that government would insist on an information highway "safety net" so that schools and libraries would not be driven off the road by high prices. His pledge might be harder to keep now. In October [1994], four commercial network hubs—San Francisco, Chicago, Washington, D.C., and Pennsauken, N.J.—replaced a group of regional Internet providers, according to the *New York Times*. How will greater commercialization of Internet affect prices and access? Observers say it's too early to tell.

The Online Mall

At the same time that library advocates are trying not to be run off the highway, marketers are setting up camp. In October [1994], the *New York Times* reported that Don Logan, the president and CEO of Time Inc., told the Association of National Advertisers that marketers should stop thinking about Internet as the "'Information Superhighway' and start thinking about it as the 'Marketing Superhighway.'"

Baby Be Mine

Librarians in five communities around the country (as yet to be named) will team up with health care providers to reach at-risk parents-to-be this spring as part of a new program called Born to Read. Hillary Rodham Clinton agreed to be honorary chair. Sponsored by the American Library Association's Association for Library Service to Children (ALSC), the five model partnerships will each receive $30,000 from the Prudential Foundation.

A Remarkable Sum

Library Journal tells us that if public libraries could get their hands on just what American spent on [legal] gambling in 1992, they could say goodbye to budget worries for the next 75 years (that is, figuring 1992 funding levels). The pot? $330 billion, according to the State of Colorado's Library Research Service.

No Tricycles on Info Highway?

Ameritech, a regional Bell headquartered in Chicago, pledged this year to provide free fiber optic cabling to schools and libraries in its area. The company made the offer in exchange for fewer government regulations, according to the *Milwaukee Sentinel*. Yet, when Ameritech prepared a list of institutions eligible for cabling, elementary schools were not included. A spokesperson for the company told the paper that Ameritech didn't originally intend to include the younger set, but it looks like the company will bend to pressure from lawmakers and educators.

Reversing the Trend

In contrast to news during the recession, residents in many communities—from Delaware to Montana—have said yes to tax increases for new public libraries or services. In St. Louis, voters raised the library's budget by $4.5 million to add, among other things, children's materials and more deliveries to day care centers. Branches of the Los Angeles Public Library also saw an increase in their budgets, but those in the county library underwent huge cuts when Governor Pete Wilson shifted $2.6 billion to public schools.

Barney Sales Slump

Those seeking relief from Barney plush toys, bed sheets, and books are in luck: Sales of the purple dinosaur's merchandise tumbled to $30 million this year, down from $130 million the year before, according to the *New York Times*. Barney has little chance of disappearing, however; his television show, videos, a magazine, and a movie deal are all going strong.

Start Them Early

The growing field of multimedia-equipped day care centers means that some children will come to school computer-ready. In Great Falls, Virginia, a company called Computertots sends instructors and CD-ROMs to day care facilities and kindergartens; and in Los Angeles, a company called Futurekids does likewise, according to *CD-ROM World*. One Computertots instructor, as she boots up the computer, has her class sing this techno-tune (sung to "Frère Jacques"): "Disc is loading / Disc is loading / Drive to RAM / Drive to RAM / Busy light is burning / Busy light is burning / When it's gone / Then we're on."

PW News Reports, 1994, and Outlook 1995

The Changing Face of Print

Paul Hilts
Multimedia News/Technology Editor, *Publishers Weekly*

Book publishing stands today on the brink of changes as important to its business as anything since the introduction of independent booksellers at the beginning of this century. The change involves the economies of how books are printed and distributed, and thus affects the foundation of the publishing business. What is driving the publishing business toward this change is a combination of fiscal

Note: Adapted from *Publishers Weekly,* January 2, 1995.

necessity and the introduction of digital printing presses and computer-to-plate (CTP) production systems.

The book publishing industry has been tied throughout this century to a policy of printing many more copies than were needed, often exceeding 50 percent more than demand, then storing and distributing remaining copies. This is because until now the cost of setting up presses to print a book, and the unpredictability of demand, meant that the only way to keep costs down was to use the longest print run possible.

Though digital presses are only one year old, introduced at the end of 1993, and integrated computer-to-plate systems are just being introduced now in such places as R. R. Donnelley & Sons, the long-term objective is already becoming clear: distributing printing away from a few centralized plants, and eliminating warehousing of titles. The idea of all-digital delivery is not new in other areas of publishing, such as magazines and newspapers, where stocking inventories was impossible. *Newsweek* and *USA Today* have been delivering their contents to widely separated printing plants via satellite for years. But the costs involved in long-term storage of books have been called into question only in the last few years, as publishers looked for places to cut costs in this thin-margin business. The evils of warehouses were amply demonstrated in Baker & Taylor's unfortunate loss of an entire facility's inventory in the Northridge, California, earthquake a year ago.

The fiscal necessity of eliminating these dangers and costs has finally been linked to the physical possibility of new methods of printing, via digital systems. In CTP production, the publisher assembles all text, art, and layout in computer files, which are sorted at the printer, and can then be used to drive either imagesetters making printing plates for conventional offset presses or direct-imaging electronic presses.

Benny Landa, founder of Indigo, Israel, and developer of the E-Print 1000 electronic printer, describes the change: "Today you print and then distribute. Tomorrow, you'll distribute and then print. Instead of having one press on the East Coast and one on the West Coast, each producing a half-million copies, you'll have presses in 200 cities, each producing 5,000 copies. You produce only the quantities you need, just in time, instead of carrying them in your inventory."

Digital printing isn't just trading offset presses for digital ones, though, says Charles Pesko, president of industry consultant Charles A. Pesko Ventures. "It's a whole different way of doing business. You don't just take one of these products, put it on the floor next to a conventional press and run it in a regular production mode. Instead of printing in Boston and distributing to my 50 sales offices in the United States, we can distribute the information electronically, via modem, to a printer that is near the local sales office and have it printed there. This is the FTD concept of print. We've done away with inventory, trucking, and distribution."

Also, according to Landa, long runs are not needed to bring the cost per copy down. Because digital presses don't use plates, and there is no waste of paper and ink getting up to speed, the cost-per-unit is pretty much the same for two copies or 2,000. "Setup for traditional processes like gravure is very expensive, so that once you've made the plates and readied the press, you need to do a very long run for the unit cost to be viable. With Indigo, on the other hand, you have no investment in plates or tooling—and no make-ready time."

R. R. Donnelley has demonstrated such a system this fall in its Crawfordsville, Indiana, plant, using files from Macmillan's Alpha Books division to operate both Creo platesetters for standard web presses and, at the same time, a Xeikon DCP-1 electronic printer.

At the Seybold Conference in San Francisco last September, Donnelley Executive Vice President Rory J. Cowan introduced the Donnelley Digital Architecture (DDA) system, integrating computer functions for editorial, production, file storage, electronic distribution, and printing. At the same time, Cowan announced the formation of a new Digital Division to handle the business of information management and fulfillment in digital publishing.

The brain of DDA is a computer running PowerBase, Donnelley's "bundle of software services," based on the Oracle large-computer database. PowerBase keeps track of the form of a publisher's submission, electronic or otherwise, and the final desired size and type of output (number of copies of a book or CD-ROM, or floppy disk or online distribution), then matches this with the number and type of presses available, and controls the production steps necessary for each type of press or outputter.

The Digital Division, based in a leased 60,000-square-foot facility in Memphis, Tennessee, will use "the industry's most advanced digital presses and a new transaction management system" to manage customers' information in whatever way they want to distribute it, Cowan said. The Memphis plant contains at least 14 Xeikon and two Indigo E-Print 1000 electronic printers, and two Heidelberg GTO-DI electronic direct-imaging sheetfed presses, and will concentrate on jobs with runs of fewer than 5,000. Memphis is connected to Donnelley's clients and other manufacturing facilities through Donnelley's high-speed electronic communications system.

The Memphis facility is also situated next to FedEx's home distribution center, and at the crossroads of several highway and rail systems, assuring fastest distribution after printing, often within 24 hours.

According to Mary Lee Schneider, marketing manager for the Digital Division, "companies warehouse print materials to ensure responsiveness to unpredictable demand. Our solution is a virtual local production resource that reduces warehouse and inventory-carrying costs. The Digital Division provides the advantages of centralized information management with all the benefits of distributed print."

Still, because it is a single printing plant, Memphis represents a transition between old systems and new. In the ideal future distributed printing system, the PowerBase files would drive Xeikons and Creos all over the country (or around the world). There might be four small print shops in Manhattan printing on Xeikons, supplying all the books ordered in the New York City area, while sheetfed presses in Boston and Phoenix take care of their states' orders. Both Donnelley and Arcata (now Quebecor) had built distribution centers near, but not in, printing plants; this sort of regional substation may become much more important as the new distribution channels develop.

Donnelley's chairman, John Walter, has been quoted as saying that the new technology, such as the computer-to-plate system, is "redefining the production process" and that he expects dramatic changes in the printing business to continue. Walter said that by using the Digital Division, book publishers can reduce inventories by promising 24-hour turnaround on orders, and that "theoretically, you can go from printer to retailer, thus collapsing an entire distribution channel [meaning wholesalers]."

Barbara Shetter, vice president of Donnelley's Digital Division, describes the initial growth of the digital printing market. "The rate of growth for on-demand print is likely to be four to six times faster than the traditional print market growth," she predicts. Should Ingram be looking for a new line of business?

Shetter doesn't think digital distributed printing will wipe out the traditional market—yet. "What we see happening is a realignment along segment lines," says Shetter. "The traditional long-run component will still be there, along with a short-run component for quality four-color products. Some of these products will be similar, but they will also complement each other. We may, for example, use short-run technology to print advance copies of a book in small quantities before the initial print run is produced in larger quantities on other presses."

What makes the change to digital and distributed printing likely is that, between rising costs of paper, labor, shipping, and warehousing, and the crushing need to stop waste and increase profit margins, what had been merely a nice idea a few years ago is now not only possible, but is the best hope for publishers to find real savings.

Spotlight '94: The Great Viacom Battle for Paramount

It started September 12, 1993, and ended, more or less, on February 15, 1994, with Viacom's purchase of Paramount, including all its publishing interests—formerly known, and now known again, as Simon & Schuster. The initial bid was for $8.2 billion, but the deal eventually closed for $9.7 billion—the extra $1.5 billion inspired by a bidding war as Barry Diller and QVC joined the battle. Viacom gained a key ally in January when it undertook to merge with Blockbuster, and the war finally ended when Diller decided he didn't want to go any higher, calling it quits with the memorable line: "They won. We lost. Next."

Viacom took control of Paramount March 12, and the merger was officially concluded in early July, when the Paramount and Viacom boards both approved the transaction; Blockbuster shareholders approved the merger agreement in September, finally creating a mega-company that had pro forma sales of $9.3 billion in 1993.

The big bundle didn't stay wrapped for long. Viacom made a deal to sell Madison Square Garden Network and its sports teams in the fall, and more wheeling and dealing is expected. As for book publishing, S&S got its name back, President Richard Snyder got shown the door, the integration of Macmillan was completed, and the divestiture of some "non-core businesses" began, with new S&S President John Newcomb insisting that trade publishing would remain a significant part of the picture.

Soaring Paper Costs Push Retail Prices

Sally Taylor

Far East Correspondent, *Publishers Weekly*

Hoping for a prosperous 1995? Better think twice. World paper demand outstripped supply in 1994, causing the commodity price of pulp to more than double, according to Rob Gallen, executive editor of *Pulp & Paper Week*. The supply of book papers tightened very quickly, and there is little relief in sight. Most mills are already running at or near capacity and only one new uncoated free-sheet paper machine is scheduled for startup before 1997, said the American Forest & Paper Association (AFPA) in its December 1994 forecast.

With a tight market, the faster the world economy grows in 1995, the faster paper prices are likely to rise. Publishers are very nervous about what this will mean for retail prices.

"It's a cycle," explains Ralph Bowen, who is director of purchasing for the book group operations at Quebecor, America's second-largest book printer. "Every four to seven years, the paper market gets tight and the prices skyrocket, then you have more capacity, and prices drop. Now the market is tightening, a little faster than it did in 1989–1990 and in 1982–83. It means book publishers are going to have to plan ahead. The lead time for paper availability is going to be greater, especially in the lower grades."

Bob Severud, senior vice president at Lindenmeyr P&S Book Publishing Papers, which sells to book publishers and printers nationally, says he has seen prices on uncoated book paper go up 35 percent on average in the last six months, and he expects prices will continue upward, with more increases in 1995, if the economy stays strong.

Mike Ducey, who covers the paper industry for *Graphic Arts Monthly*, says he has spoken to more than 80 paper manufacturers in the last two months and he has no doubts about paper prices going up in 1995, probably by another 25 percent and at least to 1989 price levels. He thinks they will increase incrementally until the third quarter, then taper off.

How Elastic Is Demand?

Grant Mcguire, president of the Book Publishing Services Division of R. R. Donnelley, says the rate of increase depends on demand. "We can look at the past and try to guess at what the current shortage will do to paper prices. But we do think there will be significant price increases next year [1995], 15 percent on the low side. It could be double that on the high side. My belief is the mills will invest in new equipment, but the investment is so large that it tends not to be made until supplies tighten up, so you end up with two to three years of tight paper."

He continues: "The thing we can't determine is how tight the market will be next year. We haven't got a gauge of how elastic demand is. As paper costs are passed through, you may see a decrease in demand for some products, such as catalogs and direct mail sales, especially with the postal increases in January. It's a question of how strong the economies remain and how price sensitive are all the various uses of paper."

Another part of the supply/demand formula is the varying costs of making different kinds of paper. There are only so many machine hours in a paper mill's day and many end products compete on a profitability standpoint for those machine hours.

"Some mills in down markets jump into book paper production and will be the first to leave when demand increases and they can make more value-added products," warns Severud. "Remember, the book industry is only 4 percent to 5 percent of the printing and writing papers business."

Why haven't paper companies been adjusting production better in anticipation of this jump in demand? It isn't that easy, according to Diehl Jenkins, president of Pratt Paper, a book papers distribution firm headquartered in Boston. Before paper companies spend new income on developing new capacity, they need to pay down their debts. A number of new plants came on line in the early 1990s that increased the supply just when the world economy stalled and demand tapered off, forcing paper prices way below the 1989 high.

"American book paper manufacturers have borrowed money," says Jenkins, "and they are now over-leveraged."

A new plant would cost $1.2 billion minimum, according to Tom Norris, president of P. H. Gladfelter Company, a major book papers manufacturer in Spring Grove, Pennsylvania, and would take two to three years to come on line, if it passed current government regulations. That means we could be at the year 2000 before we will see appreciable increases in book paper supplies. Meanwhile, prices will rise.

In addition, last year AFPA announced its intention that by the year 2000 half the paper used in America would be recycled (currently, about 40 percent of paper gets recycled). By reclaiming large amounts of used paper, it was thought, excess demand could be met. Unfortunately, because fine book papers use much more virgin pulp than recycled papers use, while highly profitable paperboard uses high proportions of recycled material, all the increase in raw material went to lower grades of paper, and supply of pulp stayed tight.

What to Do?

"Before the paper price increases came along, paper was already roughly 50 percent of our production costs," says Mcguire at Donnelley. "So we are pretty focused already on trying to reduce waste. Paper price increases and the lack of availability will push all of us much harder to manage the supply chain carefully."

If publishers follow such principles as substituting paper, reducing trim sizes, and avoiding large print runs in 1995, the paper supply might be sufficient to meet demand and prices won't rise too much. But that is not likely. Some U.S. publishers printing in Asia, where paper shortages became evident early in 1994, started stockpiling last summer for the Christmas demand. Now they are nervous about what paper prices will be when their current supplies run out. They will be sorely tempted to stockpile again.

The current paper crisis is a good argument for short runs, according to Bob Kreger at BookCrafters. "In our business, it is faster and faster turnarounds," he says, and to help turnaround time, BookCrafters has just invested in a new short-run web press from the United Kingdom.

Others have little choice on paper usage. Textbook publishers have inescapable seasonal demands, and large states like California and Texas are already preparing for their schools' paper needs next year. Mass market titles demand long print runs to reduce unit costs and earn back high advances. For example, Tom Clancy's latest title had a two million first print run just before Christmas, as specified by the author's contract.

The next six months will be a period of adjustment for many book publishers, paper merchants predict. Partnerships with suppliers are going to be important, as paper people suddenly seem to be holding all the cards.

"Over the past several years it seems that certain publishers got what they wanted," says Pratt's Diehl Jenkins. "Now paper costs are up, publishers' costs are up, distribution costs are up. We are going to have to work together."

Tom Norris of Gladfelter agrees. "The world economies are in a growth cycle now. At the bottom of this is that market pulp prices have increased substantially through '94 and our guess is they will continue upward, though not at the rate of '94. Having a good relationship with a supplier will be most important over the long term."

David AvRutick, vice president of publishing administration for HarperCollins North America, agrees. "Over the last five years we have stuck by our regular paper suppliers. Now they won't forget us."

How Bad Will It Be?

Book publishers have good reason to be nervous and, while no one likes to talk about it yet, book retailers should expect to see increases in book prices in 1995.

Publishers will have to pass the added paper costs on to the end consumer. Paper represents some 40 percent to 60 percent of production costs. If the retail book price is normally five times the cost of printing, paper, and production, that means a 20 percent increase in paper price should create up to a 10 percent increase in retail price.

Joseph L. Dionne, chairman and CEO of McGraw-Hill, says he expects manufacturing costs, including printing, paper, postage, and other forms of distribution, to increase 8 percent to 9 percent in 1995, meaning "about $30 million more than normal" in costs for the company.

"We're going to deal with this situation aggressively," he promises. "First, we will pass along as much of the price increase as we can. Where appropriate we will reduce the trim size of our publications. We will consider reducing the weight of the stock and look for alternative grades. We will also re-evaluate the use of color." And, in tune with times, Dionne mentions one more strategy: "We will look for alternative means of delivering our products."

Spotlight '94: Multimedia Joint Ventures

As publishers pondered how best to enter the electronic world in 1994, collaborations with existing multimedia operations seemed to many to be the most promising route, and there was a steady rattle of such announcements throughout the year.

Random House was the most active publisher in lining up such joint ventures, especially in the trade area. During the year Random announced agreements with Humongous Entertainment to develop nonfiction children's CD-ROMs; an alliance (and equity investment) with Knowledge Adventure to develop children's reference materials for ages seven and up; and increased its equity stake in Worldview Systems, a provider of electronic destination information, working with Fodor's. In 1993 it had pioneered in its deal with Broderbund.

Two other heavyweight teamings both involved Microsoft: one with Reader's Digest that will have Microsoft publish a limited number of CD-ROMs based on RD reference books, and an agreement with Scholastic for multimedia titles based on the latter's Magic School Bus series.

In one of the most ambitious joint ventures of the year, Simon & Schuster signed an agreement under which it will invest at least $50 million in Davidson & Associates to develop multimedia products for both the education and consumer markets. Time Life expanded an agreement with IVI Publishing through which IVI became the exclusive digital publisher for all Time Life health and medical content. In an intra-company agreement, Warner Books agreed to distribute titles from Time Warner Interactive (TWI), while Time Warner Electronic Publishing and TWI agreed to jointly develop multimedia products.

Meanwhile, a foreign investor, Germany's Holtzbrinck group (which already owns Henry Holt and has now taken over FSG), took an equity stake in Voyager.

Books Wherever You Look

John Mutter
Executive Editor, Bookselling, *Publishers Weekly*

As recently as five years ago the major channels of distribution for trade books were easily summed up: at that time, most general books were sold through chain mall bookstores, independent bookstores, college bookstores, supermarkets and drugstores, and book clubs.

But now, just five years before the millennium, book retailing has changed—and continues to change—dramatically.

Part of the change is attributable to the growth of chain superstores, the first of which appeared only in 1990. Of course, independents near chain superstores have been hurt. Some have closed; others take many months or years to climb back to pre-superstore sales levels. Ironically, the once-omnipotent chain mall stores are in disarray: Crown announced last month that it will close more than 100 of its smaller mall outlets, or some 43 percent of its stores; Waldenbooks, which is in the process of closing 200 stores, is being absorbed into Borders; B. Dalton Bookseller's share of sales within the Barnes & Noble empire is constantly decreasing. As predicted by many, even by the heads of some bookstore chains, the chains have devoured their young.

But there are other causes besides the growth of chain superstores sparking change in bookselling: New technology and cross-media synergy are remaking book distribution. Suddenly books are being sold in the most unlikely places and in ways unimaginable just a few years ago.

Several online bookstores, including the Online Bookstore and the Internet Bookstore, have appeared on Internet and various commercial online services. BookZone has opened as a "virtual" bookstore, offering books and related services around the clock. For $129 a year, publishers can list their titles; users can "stroll" down aisles delineated by category and read descriptions, excerpts, reviews, etc.

Book Stacks Unlimited has more than 250,000 books available for ordering. It also has a reader's conference "area," called Biblio-Tech, where users can browse and chat.

BiblioBytes has pushed the virtual envelope further than its competitors. On Internet it offers titles from a variety of publishers that users can download in their entirety into their own computers. In the near future, books may be downloaded in a similar way via interactive cable TV.

Books are appearing with regularity on TV shopping networks, where, in some cases, thousands of copies are sold at a time. Earlier this year, *In the Kitchen with Bob* (Morrow), a cookbook by QVC announcer Bob Bowersox, demonstrated the power of the selling medium. Helped by an audience familiar with Bowersox, QVC sold over 150,000 copies of the book in one day. In a related development, TV infomercials have become another significant outlet for selling books.

In a more traditional retail setting (they are at least in buildings!), bestsellers have found a home in warehouse clubs such as PriceCostco and Sam's, which are often the single-largest buyers of a bestseller's printing. Usually 200 to 300 different titles are available in these stores, often at discounts of 49 percent and more. As one measure of the size of this market, the warehouse clubs' main supplier, Advanced Marketing Services (AMS), has estimated that in 1993 three publishers accounted for 38 percent of its $250 million in revenues—or about $100 million. (AMS also sells significant amounts of books to electronics and computer superstores and through its own factory outlet stores.)

In part because of the warehouse club's dominance of the bestseller business, chain superstores are buying more of a range of titles, cutting into independents' traditional turf. In a continued blurring of what constitutes a bookstore, the chain superstores are selling more and more nonbook products, from music to food. For example, all new Borders stores are called Borders Books & Music, have coffee bars, and sell music CDs, videotapes, and other products. New Barnes & Noble superstores sell music and have the obligatory coffee bars. Even venerable Waterstone's Booksellers, which has had a strong emphasis on books, has started to sell music and opened a coffee bar in its Chicago store.

Specialty bookstores that concentrate in a particular area have proliferated. Many of them stock even more nonbook items proportionally than chain superstores. For example, travel bookstores like Powell's in Portland, Oregon, and

Travel Fest in Austin, Texas, carry luggage, videos, and travel accessories—and even handle travel reservations.

Bookstores opened in conjunction with other businesses seem to be getting ever more eccentric. There are now several bookstore/hair salons. A few bookstores and inns share space. A bookstore/car wash operates in Los Angeles.

Conversely, more and more books are being sold in stores with roots in other media. For example, Musicland, the owner of Musicland and Sam Goody music stores, which sold no books in 1991, now is a powerhouse in the book industry. In 1992, the company founded Media Play and On Cue, which sell a mix of media, including books, music, videos, software, and other entertainment products. (Media Plays are 40,000 to 50,000 square feet; On Cues are about 6,000.) Opening as fast as book superstores, Media Play and On Cue now sell at least $10 million worth of books a year, a number that should multiply several times over during the next few years.

Similarly, in the last several years, new all-media educational/entertainment chains have thrived. Zany Brainy, which is geared to children, now has almost 20 booming stores between Atlanta and New York. Learningsmith, which is more educational and has products for "learners of all ages," has almost 20 stores around the country, some of which have partnerships with local PBS TV stations.

Stores that are devoted to a specific subject and happen to carry books as part of the product mix are also becoming more significant outlets for books. For example, the Nature Company sells titles of relevant environmental interest. Likewise, such once-unlikely bookselling sites as gardening stores, kitchen-supply retailers, and knitting shops are selling more books than ever.

It's no wonder that special sales, once considered unimportant, are now key to many publishers, wholesalers, and retailers.

Ron Smith, owner of BookWorld Services, Sarasota, Florida, which is a distributor for more than 100 middle-sized publishers and which has an 800-number credit card service used by some 200 publishers, is one of the many wholesalers and distributors with a growing special-markets operation. In the past year, "We're selling a lot more to specialized gay and lesbian outlets and health food outlets, as well as to museum and nature stores," he said. BookWorld still sells millions of dollars' worth of titles through bookstores, but for middle-sized publishers, nontraditional markets are "the dazzling white hope," as he put it.

For booksellers, particularly independents, the proliferation of book-distribution channels may seem disheartening. But booksellers would be well advised simply to join the fray. The National Association of College Stores has the right idea: It wants its members to be at the center of the electronic revolution, even if this means that the campus store of the future may not technically be a bookstore.

Consider also the example of the Future Fantasy Bookstore, Palo Alto, California, the science fiction and fantasy bookstore with over 10,000 titles. Last year, it began selling books on Internet, and is receiving orders from around the world. Internet sales now account for fully 20 percent of the store's sales.

Booksellers can also send out information on Internet, as Booksmith in San Francisco does. Soon bookstores with a sophisticated book printer like Xerox's DocuTech will be able to "stock" more than a million titles in less than 1,000 square feet of space.

Meanwhile, booksellers have plenty of opportunities to sell outside the store—at book fairs, to businesses, to schools. Wit & Wisdom Booksellers, Lawrenceville, New Jersey, has tried various imaginative out-of-store promotions. It has advertised titles related to movie features in the lobby of a local theater, advertised business books in limos, and "traded" space for services with neighboring businesses.

Also, booksellers and others should remember that book distribution seems clear and stable only in retrospect. In the 1980s, independents seemed invincible. A decade earlier, everyone feared that chain mall bookstores would wipe out independents. In the 1960s, department store book departments were still the single most important outlet for general books. And it wasn't that long ago that peddlers were the main booksellers.

Spotlight '94: ABA's Year of Living Dangerously

Whatever kind of year it may have been for independent booksellers, with many of them struggling with fierce competition from the growing ranks of chain superstores and other book outlets, it was a bold and risky one for their association.

For the first time, the American Booksellers Association (ABA) didn't manage its own trade show. Instead Reed's Association Expositions & Services put on the convention, a big, crowded affair in Los Angeles that broke records for both attendance and exhibit space. It was also the year ABA jolted the book world by filing an antitrust suit against five publishers. In terms of internal ABA politics, it was a master stroke: Independent booksellers, who in 1993 had roundly criticized the board for not doing enough to fight chains, were won over. In the wider book world, however, the suit felt like a slap in the face, especially for the defendants, some of whom wondered why they had never heard complaints from ABA before the suit was filed. Other publishers threatened to reduce their presence at the show.

In a move that would have been unheard-of had the event been held a year before, no heads of publishing houses bothered to attend the October grand opening of ABA's spiffy new headquarters, which is set among sylvan acres in New York's upscale Westchester County and features a remodeled mansion and associated outbuildings that will serve as association offices, a library, and an educational center. Several attendees commented on the contrast between the wealthy association and the tenuous situation of many of its members, who may be putting too much faith in what promises to be a protracted and expensive lawsuit.

Special Reports

Civic Networks in the United States

R. Kathleen Molz

Professor of Public Affairs
Graduate Program in Public Policy and Administration
School of International and Public Affairs
Columbia University, New York

This is the latest in a sequence of *Bowker Annual* Special Reports dealing with computer/communications technologies and their effects on the library community. In the 1991 edition, Clifford A. Lynch addressed the topic "Visions of Electronic Libraries"; Charles McClure et al. examined the virtual library and the relationship between Internet and the emerging National Research and Education Network in 1993; and in 1994 staff members of the U.S. National Commission on Libraries and Information Science commented on libraries and the national information infrastructure (NII)—sometimes referred to as the Information Superhighway.

It is perhaps unfortunate that the continuing, albeit uneven, trajectory of federal government policy toward the Information Superhighway anticipated in some of the previous articles has been subjected to a number of political actions that may defer its development or dramatically alter its course. Almost all major bills aimed at rewriting the nation's telecommunications laws failed to pass in the 103rd Congress. This failure was ascribed to disagreements between the competing cable and telephone industries, each of which wished to encroach on the markets of the other. In the long run, however, potential losers were not just the billion-dollar entertainment, cable, and telephone industries but the American consumers who use the schools, libraries, and medical clinics identified by President Clinton in his 1994 State of the Union Address: "We must also work with the private sector to connect every classroom, every clinic, every library, every hospital in America into a national Information Superhighway by the year 2000." Also contributing to the uncertain future of the "seamless web of communications networks," to use another phrase mentioned in Clinton administration documents, is the emergence of a Republican majority in both houses of the 104th Congress while the executive branch remains under the aegis of a Democratic president. Whether agreement can be reached on the development of a telecommunications infrastructure that will accommodate the educational, research, and information needs of its noncommercial users as well as those of private sector enterprises is an issue that is still unresolved.

This article does not deal specifically with the development of national policy but rather with the emergence of a grass-roots phenomenon that has made excellent use of some elements of the nation's telecommunications infrastructure to serve as the base for the conduct of local and community affairs. The nomenclature for these local information and knowledge webs is not exactly precise. Sometimes called civic networks, they are also referred to as community networks, electronic commons, or—in the case of networks affiliated with the National Public Telecomputing Network (NPTN)—they are Free-Nets. Seattle resident Douglas Schuler of Computer Professionals for Social Responsibility, who is writing a book about community networks, provides the following definition:

> A community network is a computer-based electronic network that provides a wide range of community-based information and services to people in a community for little or no cost. Although not a requirement, these systems are generally administered by non-profit groups or government agencies. Extra attention is paid to providing access to people who traditionally have little or no acces s to electronic information and services. Generally, community networks are activist-oriented—they have been established primarily to meet social needs rather than financial goals. Outreach to the community and feedback from the community are vital to the system.[1]

Early Networking Efforts

The origins of computer networking date back to 1969, when the ARPAnet, the precursor of today's Internet, linked four computers—three in California and one in Utah. This first American computer network, underwritten by the Department of Defense's Advanced Research Projects Agency (ARPA), reached personnel primarily engaged in research in the emerging field of internetworking. Over the past 25 years, a number of developments have occurred, resulting in the development of an electronic metanetwork capable of international linkages. Internet—in part a derivative of the former ARPAnet (which ceased to exist in 1990)—today plays host to over two million computers with host users numbering in the multiple millions.

Earlier electronic innovations—such as the Computer Bulletin Board System in Chicago and the Old Colorado City Electronic Cottage, pioneered by David R. Hughes—were formed in the late 1970s and early 1980s. Bulletin board systems are low-cost, relatively simple computer-based services that permit E-mail and other forms of message exchange and allow the downloading and uploading of data files. The movement toward a more sophisticated form of community networking gained prominence following a 1984 experiment by Tom Grundner of Case Western Reserve University's Department of Family Medicine. He initiated a single-phone-line computerized bulletin board system called St. Silicon's Hospital and Information Dispensary. The system facilitated the deposit of questions regarding health care from area residents, who could use their home, school, or business computers to call the electronic dispensary. Replies from a board-certified physician were received within 24 hours. The experiment proved so successful that AT&T, the Ohio Bell Telephone Company, and the University Hospitals of Cleveland cooperated in expanding the project.

Dr. Grundner then began to design a community computer system with ten incoming phone lines. The system was intended to provide community information in such areas as law, government, medicine, the arts and sciences, and education. In addition, free E-mail services were provided for residents of northeastern Ohio. Called the Cleveland Free-Net,[2] the system was dedicated by Ohio's governor and Cleveland's mayor on July 16, 1986. The following year, the Youngstown (Ohio) Free-Net began operation, becoming the second Free-Net system. In 1988, the Big Sky Telegraph (a Free-Net in Dillon, Montana) went online on the first day of January. Begun by a pioneer in this area—Frank Odasz, a professor at Western Montana College—this rural telecomputing testbed initially offered an online course via modem to rural K–12 teachers, many of whom held their classes in one- or two-room schools.

Free-Net Movement

With enhanced telecommunications capabilities, the Cleveland Free-Net was further expanded in 1989, the year that marked Dr. Grundner's establishment of the National Public Telecomputing Network (NPTN), headquartered in Cleveland, to serve as the information center of the emerging Free-Net movement. Through its national office, NPTN has aided 47 communities in the United States and in ten countries abroad to build local Free-Nets. Citizen organizing committees are working to found additional networks in over 130 other communities.

In accessing a Free-Net, a user dials directly onto the system or through an Internet account. Registered users have electronic mail addresses and can send E-mail to users of the network and to addressees worldwide through Internet. Most Free-Nets are menu driven so that new users can easily navigate through the network's offerings. Bulletin boards, forums or sessions where users can chat together, and file transfer functions are among the most frequent services offered.

In the fall of 1994, NPTN was the recipient of a $447,955 grant from the Commerce Department's Telecommunications and Information Infrastructure Assistance Program (TIIAP) to fund 30 electronic community networks in rural areas, affording citizens free or low-cost access to E-mail, a range of information services, and access to Internet. The process to select eligible rural communities was begun in January 1995. In acknowledging the grant, which when matched with local funds will amount to approximately $900,000, Dr. Grundner said: "This will go a long way toward separating the rural-urban issue from debates about the 'information haves' and 'have-nots.'"[3]

Another national organization concerned with issues of equitable access to computing technologies is Playing to Win (PTW), which originated in New York City as a local nonprofit organization affording technical assistance in the teaching of computer skills to other nonprofits and the Harlem Community Computing Center. Realizing that their largely poor and isolated clients needed opportunities to share resources and information with others, PTW's designers expanded the original enterprise into a membership organization with affiliates scattered along the East Coast, serving similarly disadvantaged persons. In addition, Playing to Win has international affiliates in Poland, Ireland, and El Salvador. Network affiliates are housed in a variety of settings, including church basements, child-care centers, and multiservice agencies. Although the affiliates offer job counseling, teaching of word-processing skills, literacy programs, and service to seniors, some of them have unique missions. For example, the Fortune Society, located in New York City's Greenwich Village, serves a clientele of former offenders, offering adult-literacy and job-training programs. Another affiliate, the Somerville (Massachusetts) Community Computing Center, is situated in a largely working-class community in which many new immigrants reside. A large percentage of the center's users are out of work and use the center to prepare employment résumés. As with PTW, the Somerville Center was begun with the mission of providing socioeconomically disadvantaged people with access to computer-related technologies. Electronic linkages among Playing to Win's affiliates permit staff members to exchange ideas and information with one another and provide an opportunity to try out new approaches to serving their respective customers.

Support Covers Broad Spectrum

Not all community networks are affiliates or members of larger organizations. Many were erected under the sponsorship of governmental entities, local schools, hospitals, public libraries, and newly formed nonprofit corporations, while others sprang from the cooperative "town-gown" efforts of local community groups and academic institutions. Diamond Bar City Online was established by the City of Diamond Bar, California, in part to reduce the number of vehicular trips made by local residents in conducting business with their government and thereby to reduce air pollution in southern California. Diamond Bar residents can electronically file a building permit application, access city zoning and land use information, enroll in recreation classes, leave electronic messages for members of the City Council or city departments, and peruse the City Council agenda and other public documents. INFO/CAL, administered by the Data Center of the California Health and Welfare Agency, makes use of kiosks to provide daily information on available jobs, material on family and child-care issues, information about such transportation opportunities as ride-sharing and car registration, and miscellaneous other items. Thousands of users have registered with California's Santa Monica PEN (Public Electronic Network), a network operated by the city government that affords residents the opportunity to take part in conferences dealing with civic matters such as crime, education, homelessness, and the environment. Hundreds of these electronic conferences are run concurrently, and participants choose the one in which they would like to participate. Some conferences are operated like interactive bulletin boards where individuals can respond to the posted messages, while others are moderated, with respondents submitting questions to a moderator.

Inspired by the efforts of the local public librarian, a multi-organizational consortium—including among others the City of Springfield (Illinois), the local schools, the public library, and a regional medical center—brought about the creation of ORION (Ozark Regional Information On-Line Network). As described by ORION's proponent, librarian Annie Linnemeyer, a civic network serves to provide needed public information to ordinary citizens. The local public library was also a vital force in the creation of the Seattle (Washington) Community Network and in the founding of Charlotte's WEB, which serves the City of Charlotte and Mecklenburg County in North Carolina.

Local community networks that have been aided by academic institutions located in their environs include Blacksburg (Virginia) Electronic Village, which began operation in 1993 in an effort to link Blacksburg residents with students, staff, and faculty of the Virginia Polytechnic Institute and State University. Bell Atlantic–Virginia was also a major partner in this endeavor. From the university's perspective, one of the advantages of the network was the linkage to the campus of off-campus students; from the community's perspective, the advantage was educational and informational enrichment. With the support of the academic computing services of the University of Illinois at Urbana-Champaign, Prairienet, launched by two library and information science faculty members of the university, provides access to bulletin boards, electronic mail, and Internet. The statewide university system's library catalog is online, along with a number of lists of community and recreational events. The University of Maryland is facilitating the development of SAILOR, the Maryland statewide project designed to connect local public libraries and some colleges to Internet.

Revenue for these initiatives comes from an aggregate of sources, including government, private foundations, corporate contributions from local telephone companies and other businesses, individual gifts in cash or kind (such as volunteer work on the network), and, in some cases, user fees. For example:

- Big Sky Telegraph was begun with support from the M. J. Murdoch Charitable Trust and US West
- Although operated by the College of Agricultural Sciences at Pennsylvania State University, PEN Pages receives the majority of its funds from the Pennsylvania State Legislature
- Santa Monica PEN is funded by local government
- Bell Atlantic was generous in its support of Blacksburg Electronic Village
- Northcoast Electronic Town, located in northern California, is an example of a for-profit network supported by the private resources of its founder

Free-Net Information Menus

One of the main functions of these networks is the provision of information covering a wide range of topics and interests. Almost all supply some form of a calendar of events for visitors to the community as well as its residents. Another frequent feature is a listing of community organizations, identifying specific agencies and supplying information about them. The remaining informational spectrum is broad, including material about health, schooling, employment, job opportunities, consumer and business information, and governmental information embracing local, state, and federal levels. Library involvement in these networks differs from community to community; but in general public librarians have played prominent roles as community advocates for the development of these networks, have used their physical facilities to house network terminals, have served on network boards of directors, and, in company with many of their academic librarian colleagues, have made available their online cataloging data as an item on the networks' menus. In the case of several networks—Buffalo Free-Net, Charlotte's WEB, ORION, Prairienet, and the Seattle Community Net—librarians or library school faculty played active roles as network founders.

The Town Hall Concept

In addition to providing information, these community networks supply a means by which residents can communicate with one another. Electronic forums, discussion groups, and opportunities for informal chats about local issues of concern have given rise to the concept of these networks as electronic town halls or as the commons of early New England towns. Information technology consultant Nancy Willard, who is writing a book about community networking, explains:

> Community networks are not just "on-ramps to the information highway," they are the local "commons." They provide an electronic location for community access to the vast amount of public interest information available within the community through various agencies, organizations, and individuals, as well as the opportunity to discuss community affairs online. Community networks are also not just a service that is provided "for" a community, they are a service created "by" a community.[4]

Steve Cisler of Apple Computer, Inc., a frequent contributor to *Library Journal*, expresses a similar concept a little differently:

> The information contained in such [community] networks as well as the relationships that form between the participants make up what I call an electronic greenbelt to reinforce and add value to the community. These communities do include a variety of other interest groups whose needs and interests transcend the geographic boundaries of the town, region, or state. The decisions these communities have made are similar, in some ways, to what happened with the spread of electrical networks a century ago.[5]

Because of its potential for the enhancement of the democratic experience, community networking has been increasingly recognized by governmental circles. A modest indication of this was revealed when the TIIAP (Telecommunications and Information Infrastructure Assistance Program) awards were announced by the U.S. Department of Commerce on Oct. 13, 1994. Of the 92 grants awarded to telecommunications initiatives for education, libraries, arts and culture, science, health, government, and other categories, the largest category to receive federal assistance was "community information."

Among the largest of the grants in this category was the previously mentioned award to the National Public Telecomputing Network for its series of model demonstrations in 30 rural communities. Other awardees were Charlotte's WEB in North Carolina, a community network with considerable involvement from the local public library; LatinoNet, a project of the Hispanic Community Fund of the Bay Area in San Francisco; an Information Technology Initiative in New York City to create an information infrastructure for five pilot settlement houses; the Rhode Island Network (RINET), which sought funding to extend its services to municipalities, nonprofits, and state agencies; and a telecommunications network in St. Louis, Missouri, set up under the aegis of the Grace Hill

Neighborhood Services to facilitate communications for residents in five low-income communities. Federal funding for these efforts amounted to over $7 million, nearly one-third of the total amount for all categories ($24 million).

Government Involvement

State governments are increasingly becoming involved as key partners in the emerging networked environment. Hawaii FYI is a nonprofit organization established in 1988 by the Hawaii State Legislature in an effort to offset the geographical distance between Hawaii and the U.S. mainland. Its mission is to promote the development of an information industry in the state and to facilitate Hawaiians' access to a wide range of information sources, including Internet. Full-text editions of proposed state legislation, resolutions, committee reports, and hearing notices, as well as the text of local Honolulu legislation and resolutions, are made available.

The Iowa Communications Network is a publicly financed fiber-optic network capable of transporting voice, data, and video signals statewide at the speed of light. The network links Iowa's schools, public universities, community colleges, independent colleges, government offices, and libraries. Each Iowan is within 20 minutes of an end-user site.

Library leaders in Maryland anticipate that a telecommunications network linking libraries in all of the state's 23 counties will be in place by the end of 1995. Serving as the operational center for the project is the Enoch Pratt Free Library in Baltimore City, which is the Maryland State Library Resource Center. The system is an extension of the telecommunications backbone established by the University of Maryland to connect its 13 campuses.

In October 1994, the first state-supported gopher service in Massachusetts, the Massachusetts Library and Information Network, became operational. It is expected that the network will eventually provide comprehensive access to a wide range of government information and selected Internet resources, including indexes, abstracts, and other databases. Another Massachusetts initiative, the creation of MassNet, an umbrella nonprofit organization created to boost economic growth in the Massachusetts region, was launched in January 1995. Among the first volunteers to serve as advisers to the project were Rosabeth Moss Kanter of the Harvard Business School and Representative Ed Markey, former chair of the U.S. House of Representatives Telecommunications Subcommittee. MassNet was partially inspired by Smart Valley, an electronic community in California's Silicon Valley with extensive ties to that region's telecommunications industries.

Although some of these state-based networks cover a far larger geographic area than is normally implied by the use of the words "civic" and "community," they are instrumental in making linkages to local communities possible and in enriching the body of intellectual resources available to them. Many other states are in the process of implementing a statewide network or are in the process of planning for one.

Support from Public-Interest Groups

No account of the civic networking movement would be complete without some recognition of at least a few of the public-interest groups that have been established to serve as the movement's advocates. Prominent among these is the Center for Civic Networking, headquartered in Cambridge, Massachusetts, with an office in Washington, D.C. In 1993, the center, under the leadership of Director Miles R. Fidelman, initiated its program with an invitational conference, "From Electronic Townhalls to Civic Networks: Democratic Reform for the 21st Century." An outcome of that conference was the publication, also in 1993, of a position paper, *A National Strategy for Civic Networking: A Vision of Change*, highlighting the need for a civic vision of the national information infrastructure and proposing a policy agenda for the development of the civic networking movement. (References to this and other statements are provided in the bibliography that concludes this article.) More recently, the center has cooperated with other public-interest groups to sponsor public forums on community networking and related topics, and it has dedicated considerable energy to supporting the Cambridge community as a civic networking testbed. On February 1, 1995, Fidelman announced an experiment in creating a vehicle for daily civic communication. Although compared to the "walking bell-ringer of old," *The Cambridge Town Crier*, a daily electronic newsletter, takes its place in the information age, bringing to its subscribers late-breaking news about civic events and local issues.

The Morino Institute, incorporated in 1994 in Virginia, is dedicated to helping individuals and communities work toward social change through the power of information and the potential of electronic communications. Its four key areas of interest are:

- An educational and communications program to aid individuals and communities in the use of electronic communications
- A collaborative pilot and research program to explore the use of electronic technology for social change
- A community service fellowship program to sponsor the work of outstanding individuals
- A community works program to make information about the institute available

On May 5, 1994, institute chair and principal donor Mario Morino presented a well-received paper, "Assessment and Evolution of Community Networking," at the Apple Conference on Building Community Computing Networks, held in Cupertino, California. The Morino Institute is currently compiling an authoritative list of community-based networks.

Also concerned with the development of civic networking is the Corporation for Public Broadcasting, which, in cooperation with the US West Foundation, has granted awards for community computer networking projects across the nation. The primary purpose of the programmatic activity supported by these two organizations is the linkage of a local public radio or television station with such institutions as schools, libraries, museums, local governments, and medical centers to build a community-based telecommunications infrastructure. The program is known as Community-Wide Education and Information Services (CWEIS). In 1994, 12 projects were selected for funding from among 90 proposals submitted by local stations in 38 states. Among the awardees were a Free-Net in Omaha, Nebraska; the San Francisco CityLink Bridge; a network serving the Detroit metropolitan area; and other initiatives in Alaska, Colorado, Indiana, Massachusetts, Minnesota, South Carolina, Virginia, and Washington.

The Telecommunications Policy Roundtable (TPR)—a public interest coalition now including more than 200 nonprofit, consumer, labor, and civil rights groups concerned with Information Superhighway issues—was formed in 1992 and meets monthly in Washington, D.C. Among its members are the national associations of television and computer professionals, librarians, educators, and representatives of the mass media. Included among the participants are several organizations linked to the library and information science communities: the American Association of Law Libraries, American Library Association, American Society for Information Science, Association of Research Libraries, Coalition for Networked Information, Council on Library Resources, Libraries for the Future, Medical Library Association, and Special Libraries Association. Also participating is the Benton Foundation, headquartered in Washington, D.C. With support from the John D. and Catherine T. MacArthur Foundation, the Benton Foundation has created the Communications Policy Project to strengthen public-interest advocacy in communications policy. The Benton Foundation's chair is Charles Benton, who served from 1978 to 1982 as chair of the U.S. National Commission on Libraries and Information Science and from 1982 to 1985 as one of its members.

On October 26, 1993, the Telecommunications Policy Roundtable, which promotes the concept of a public lane or right-of-way on the Information Superhighway, put forth a statement of principles that should govern the public policy agenda for the development of the national information infrastructure. Included are:

1 Universal access: *All people should have affordable access to the information infrastructure.*
2 Freedom to communicate: *The information infrastructure should enable all people to effectively exercise their fundamental right to communicate.*
3 Vital civic sector: *The information infrastructure must have a vital civic sector at its core.*
4 Diverse and competitive marketplace: *The information infrastructure should ensure competition among ideas and information providers.*
5 Equitable workplace: *New technologies should be used to enhance the quality of work and to promote equity in the workplace.*
6 Privacy: *Privacy should be carefully protected and extended.*
7 Democratic policy making: *The public should be fully involved in policy making for the information infrastructure.*

Chapters of this national coalition are located in other communities in the United States. One of them, the Telecommunications Policy Roundtable–Northeast (TPR-NE), maintains its own listserv (**tpr-ne@mitvma.bitnet**) and makes available current information on the telecommunications infrastructure.

Financial Struggles—Present and Future

The burgeoning phenomenon of community or civic networking is not without its problems. Accounts of the creation of these emerging webs in which citizen endeavors predominate tend to reflect the high degree of enthusiasm and tenacity of purpose that brought them into being. At the same time, a sizable number of these networks, especially those in smaller communities, tend to operate on the proverbial shoestring and ongoing financial support remains a persistent problem. Some of these networks operate without any paid employees and depend on the goodwill of local citizens who volunteer their time or rely on the part-time efforts of personnel attached to government agencies, academic institutions, and other organizations. A survey of 24 network directors, conducted by Columbia University graduate students in the spring of 1994, revealed that nine of the respondents had no full-time employees and only one employed ten or more persons.[6]

Exacerbating the financial issue is the changing dimension of the public policy framework that will shape the future of the communications infrastructure. During 1995, the U.S. Commerce Department will again make available Information Superhighway grants amounting to $64 million, a figure more than double the 1994 appropriation of $26 million. When one considers, however, that the 1994 requests made of the Commerce Department amounted to $560 million in federal funds, a figure that does not reflect the local matching efforts required of the proposals, the contrast between the projected demand and the availability of funds to support it is rather staggering. Nonetheless, as the rapid growth of these virtual communities attests, the die is case for the further development of citizen participation in the emerging electronic revolution. The future of the civic networks may still be uncertain, but at present they are very much alive in cyberspace.

Notes

1. E-mail message from Joan Fanning <joanfann@u.washington.edu> and Doug Schuler <comnets@u.washington.edu> to: Multiple recipients of list communet<communet@uvmvm.bitnet> Friday, 12 Aug. 1994.

2. "Free-Net" is a registered service mark of the National Public Telecomputing Network (NPTN).

3. E-mail press release "NPTN Rural Information Network" to: Multiple recipients of list communet <communet@uvmvm.bitnet>. Thursday, 13 Oct. 1994.

4. Nancy Willard <willard@edlane.lane.edu>, "Community Networks Overview." To:Multiple recipients of list communet <communet@uvmvm. bitnet>. Friday, 10 June 1994.

5. Steve Cisler, "Community Computer Networks: Building Electronic Greenbelts," Cupertino, CA, June 1993, p. 1.

6. R. Kathleen Molz, "Civic Networking in the United States: A Report by Columbia University Students," *Internet Research* 4 (Winter 1994): 58.

References

Center for Civic Networking. *A National Strategy for Civic Networking: A Vision of Change* (Oct. 1993). Gopher URL: gopher://gopher.civic. net:2400/; web URL: http://www.civic.net:2401/.

Cisler, Steve. *Community Computer Networks: Building Electronic Greenbelts* (Cupertino, CA, June 1993). This essay is available for anonymous ftp from ftp.apple.com in the alug/communet directory in ASCII, Word, and PostScript.

———. "Can We Keep Community Networks Running?" *Computer-Mediated Communication Magazine* 2 (Jan. 1, 1995). The article is also on the World-Wide Web. URL: http://www.rpi.edu/~decemj/cmc/mag/1995/jan.cisler.html.

"Civic Networks." In "Communications as Engagement: The Millennium Report to the Rockefeller Foundation." October 1944. URL:http://www.cdinet.com/Millenium/Resource/network.html.

"COMMUNET: Community and Civic Network Discussion List" is an excellent source of ongoing information on community networks. To subscribe, send an E-mail message to listserv@uvmvm.uvm.edu (or listserv@uvmvm.bitnet) with the single-line message: subscribe communet.

Mattison, David. "Librarians and the Free-Net Movement." *Internet Librarian* 14 (May 1994): 46–50, 52.

Molz, R. Kathleen. "Civic Networking in the United States: A Report by Columbia University Students." *Internet Research* 4 (Winter 1994): 52–62.

Morino, Mario. "Assessment and Evolution of Community Networking." Paper presented at the Apple Conference on Building Community Computing Networks, Cupertino, CA, May 5, 1994. Available in ASCII text on the WELL gopher. URL: gopher://gopher.well.com/11/Community/com-munets/morino.

The Morino Institute. "Directory of Public Access Networks." On Feb. 9, 1995, the Morino Institute announced a pre-release of an online directory of over 200 public-access networks in the United States. The pre-release period will continue for several months as the institute continues to collect information. General release of the directory was scheduled for May 3, 1995, at which time the institute plans to publish the first edition of a hard copy version of the directory. The pre-release version is available on the World-Wide Web: URL://www.morino.org/pand.htm.

National Public Telecomputing Network. Information about the national association of Free-Nets is available on the World-Wide Web. URL: http://www.nptn.org/.

Schuler, Doug. The results of a survey conducted by Doug Schuler of community-oriented computer networks in the United States and Canada are accessible through ftp [ftp.cs.washington.edu; logon: anonymous; cd to: community networks].

Library Services on Campus Networks

Judy Montgomery

Associate Librarian for Public Services
Bowdoin College Library

Katherine Kott

Automated Services Librarian
Ladd Library, Bates College

College and university libraries in the United States have effectively incorporated the use of technology and networking into their operations since the early 1970s. At that time, efforts were focused on the automation of technical processing functions including cataloging, serials control, and, to some degree, acquisitions. The development of national bibliographic databases by OCLC (Online Computer Library Center), RLIN (Research Libraries Information Network), and WLN (Washington Library Network) provided thousands of libraries with shared, online access to MARC (machine-readable cataloging) records and reduced the need for performing original cataloging at each individual institution. The locally customized, machine-readable records created through these utilities would later form the foundation of many library online catalogs. Development of a national union catalog of holdings information, a byproduct of shared cataloging, facilitated future automation of interlibrary loan processing for participating libraries.

The next decade saw increased attention to computerized, mediated reference service available within the library. Online searching of commercial information services such as Dialog and BRS (Bibliographic Retrieval Services) became a regular reference practice. Stand-alone CD-ROM indexes began replacing or supplementing standard print sources. Libraries automated the processing of interlibrary loan requests as the demand for these services increased. During this time, pioneers such as the University of California, Penn State, Northwestern, Dartmouth, and Ohio State provided public access to local bibliographic information through online public access catalogs (OPACs). At the same time, campus computing organizations began to shift emphasis from centralized mainframe-based computing, to more distributed systems, placing computers on the desktops of many faculty and staff.[1]

Up to this point, technology in libraries was used primarily to automate existing services and did not change the traditional role of the library and librarian. It is the extension of the library through the technology of wide-area networks and the growth in the number of online catalogs publicly accessible through these networks that has challenged librarians to conceptualize new ways to deliver library services in a distributed environment.

The addition of networked microcomputers on student and faculty desktops opens an array of new research opportunities. As libraries provide greater online access to bibliographic information for local and remote collections, subject-related indexes, and full-text databases, information seekers who formerly scheduled their research around library hours can now expect 24-hour access to many of these services. But while library users are freed from the restrictions of time and place, they frequently face unanticipated difficulties.

For many researchers comfortable with the traditional organization of library collections, the proliferation of information on the network—and the often chaotic nature of the organization of this information—presents a new set of challenges. For the novice user of technology, accustomed to working with information in print, hardware and software used to access networked resources can be a barrier to effective information retrieval.

Unmediated use of library resources empowers faculty and students to seek solutions to their own information needs. At the same time, "we are adding to the complexity of choice [the user must make] in deciding which system contains the information desired, and each generation of computer-based information tools, while claiming user friendliness, requires new levels of expertise."[2]

Librarians are faced with many of the same challenges that confront the library user. In the past, keeping up with technological change was the responsibility of the small number of librarians who were trained to do mediated searches or charged with operating automated systems within the library. The shift to delivering library services on the network, the quantity and variety of information resources, and the diversity of user interfaces to electronic sources now require all librarians to have a greater understanding of and facility with technology.

Above all, in the face of constant technological change, librarians must begin "reconceptualizing . . . the library" to meet the new needs and expectations of its users.[3] This article will identify some of the ways in which librarians are reshaping library services in response to this changing environment.

The Role of the Library in the Scholarly Process

In her article "Regrowing Staff: Managerial Priority for the Future of University Libraries," Lois Jennings makes the following observation about the role of libraries:

> The traditional business of a university library has been to identify, acquire, organize, locate, and distribute information and knowledge from external sources that are relevant to its university's mission and goals and that benefit staff and students.[4]

Continuing to define the library in this manner has become impossible. Traditional roles of librarians and other stakeholders in the scholarly process are less well defined as librarians participate more actively in electronic publishing. The Office of Research and Special Projects at OCLC is engaged in ongoing projects to find ways to meld the tools of librarianship—cataloging and the MARC record—with the world of electronic publishing and hypertext—SGML (Standard Generalized Markup Language) and HTML (Hypertext Markup Language). These projects build on librarians' traditional skills in selecting, describing, and organizing material and extend them beyond the local collection to networked resources. The lines become even more blurred as libraries and librarians take a more active role in the creation of material beyond the traditional pathfinders and bibliographic guides. At North Carolina State University, Carolyn Argentati, head of the Natural Resources Library, describes her participation in the

"Student-Driven, Information-Rich Undergraduate Education Project," a partnership between the libraries, the Computing Center, and the College of Forest Resources. "I participate on the project team to identify and make available relevant information sources from the network and from our collection, and to assist in planning and *production* [emphasis added] of multimedia training modules that we produce."[5]

A further blurring of the traditional division of responsibility for production, acquisition, and organization of scholarly communication can be seen in such projects as the Scholarly Communications Project at Virginia Polytechnic and State University, where the technical director, James Powell, works in the library, coordinating experiments with producing, distributing, and archiving electronic information. Electronic book projects at the University of Virginia and the University of Tennessee involve collaboration between the university presses and the libraries. In the networked electronic environment, the time from creation to publication is compressed, so that what was once a linear process must now become collaborative and interactive to be effective. Possibilities for self-publishing are also greater on the net, calling into question the time-tested process of refereed journal publishing so pivotal in academic tenure and promotion processes, and making the librarian's traditional task of evaluating resources through "authentication" of particular editions of books more of a challenge.

Reference Services

The increase in new electronic information resources delivered to library clients at remote locations via a campus network and new methods of electronic communication have engendered new needs on the part of information users and new models for delivering effective and appropriate reference service. Students and faculty seem increasingly interested in unmediated access to reference resources and many libraries are responding by expanding the number of databases available on the campus network. While telephone reference has long been a function of most reference desks, requests for assistance from library users not physically in the building were the exception and not the rule. Reference librarians now frequently provide instruction in the use of these databases to library clients working on their personal workstations in their offices or rooms. Librarians visit faculty in their offices to provide instruction and research assistance and ensure that the services are accessible on the client's own hardware and software. Reference librarians are fielding more questions related to hardware, software, and network problems encountered while using networked resources.

On many campuses, including Indiana University, North Carolina State University, and Purdue University, virtual reference desks supplement traditional services.[6] Reference questions, literature search requests, and client feedback are transmitted electronically to many libraries. This increase in electronic communication does not seem to have translated into a decrease in the number of face-to-face reference interactions. Librarians must find ways to fairly integrate electronic reference queries with traditional walk-in services.

Electronic Resources

Researchers now have a wide selection of electronically delivered resources to aid them in their work. Faculty and students are free to access these information resources from their desktop workstations and, in many cases, to download needed information for future use. Networks have made possible a "location independence" for information users and have eliminated the physical constraints of local collections.[7]

Libraries have developed electronic gateways to commercially produced indexes and full-text databases through their library or campus-wide information systems (CWIS). E-journal publishing, while initially slow to develop, now seems to be on the rise. Many E-text projects such as the Gutenberg Project, the University of Virginia Library's Electronic Text Center, the UMLibText project at the University of Michigan, Rutgers's Inventory of Machine-Readable Texts in the Humanities, and the Center for Electronic Texts in the Humanities established jointly by Princeton University and Rutgers University are identifying, developing, and disseminating full-text resources to the larger scholarly community.[8]

Librarians, faculty, and students regularly take advantage of information sources on Internet to answer questions on which information may not be available in their own collections. Access to databases and full-text archives via gopher and World-Wide Web increase access to timely information on current news events, new legal decisions and legislative initiatives, the latest in scientific discoveries, and a host of other topics. Easy access to remote library catalogs, locally produced indexes and full-text databases, and campus-wide information systems provides local information not previously obtainable without traveling to remote sites.

Several critical questions face librarians as they strive to develop, manage, and integrate the use of these new electronic materials into already existing print collections. New criteria for the selection of commercially produced databases must include consideration of quality of information, coverage period, ease of use and appropriateness of search interfaces, hardware and software requirements and costs, and electronic method of database delivery to library users. Stronger collaboration must be fostered between librarians, publishers, and system vendors. The development and implementation of a common user interface for use with a variety of electronic resources, such as that offered through the Z39.50 protocol, will continue to be an important goal. The viability of the campus network and the accessibility of computers and printers play a central role in electronic collection development decision-making.

In the past, library users have assumed that reference sources chosen for inclusion in library collections had been judged as the best, most authoritative source on a given topic. As collections incorporate the vast resources available on Internet, this assumption is no longer true. Researchers now have access to masses of information about which questions of quality and authority of the information and consistency of accessibility are not immediately answerable. Librarians and computer professionals are supporting efforts to develop local and national organizational tools and structures that provide road maps to available Internet resources.

To aid in collection development, many libraries have provided electronic forms for the transmission of acquisition requests and recommendations from faculty via the campus network. Up-to-date information on the status of ordered library materials is available in many library catalogs. Lists of recent library acquisitions are now available for browsing on campus-wide information systems.

Interlibrary Loan/Document Delivery

The development of campus networks and the introduction of Internet as a means of transmitting digitized text and images has had a profound effect on almost every aspect of document delivery services in libraries. Students and faculty are interested in transmitting their loan requests to the library via the campus network with a minimum of data rekeying. Libraries are providing electronic request forms on their online catalogs and CWIS. At Colorado State University, bibliographic information can be transferred from the CARL database to an online form and E-mailed to the library. At the University of Maine, students and faculty can place an electronic request for materials available at another campus through their library catalog.

As user expectations rise for timely delivery of high-quality, low-cost printed and digitized text, libraries are investigating and implementing multifaceted document delivery systems incorporating interlibrary loan with commercial methods of document delivery. Many of the newly marketed online reference database services, such as FirstSearch (OCLC), CARL Uncover (CARL), and Eureka (RLG), have incorporated online document ordering and transmission into their products. Payment is made through use of a credit card or by debiting an on-deposit account, and can be initiated by library staff or the end user. Other electronic reference services such as Lexis-Nexis, Dialog, and Information Access Company's ASAP databases are providing library clients with direct access to full-text with printing and downloading capabilities. Library clients can also subscribe to electronic table of contents services and receive lists of articles included in specific journals via E-mail.

The sharing of detailed holdings information made available through online catalogs has enhanced collaborative borrowing agreements. Online access to serial union lists allows librarians to check holdings information of consortia members and broadens access to periodicals collections.

Libraries are also pursuing new methods of transmitting requested interlibrary loan material to other libraries. Ariel (Research Libraries Group Inc.) is a menu-driven software product that facilitates the scanning and digitizing of text and images and the transmission of this electronic information via Internet to any library that has implemented a like system. Articles are then printed on a high-quality laser printer and delivered to the requester.

Electronic Reserves

While most libraries have focused their attention on automating the processing of library reserve materials, providing online access to bibliographic information about them, and automating checkout procedures through their library OPACs, a handful have begun to provide student access to the full text of reserve readings in electronic format via their campus networks. In 1992 the Association of Research Libraries (ARL) introduced an initiative to explore alternative methods for the delivery of reserve materials electronically through the Reserve Materials Publishing Project. ARL's objective was to measure faculty and student acceptance of this concept, explore related copyright issues, and "develop a prototype and vision for providing [high-quality] instructional support materials [cost effectively] within an electronic environment."[9]

In response, Colorado State University began a pilot project to do just that. The project goal was "to enable a student to access the reserve list on CARL, [CSU's] online catalog; choose an item identified as being available electronically; pull the text up on their own PC or a CARL PC terminal; and either read, print, or download the text."[10] The materials, which were limited to course notes, syllabi, and solutions that were not copyrighted, would be available 24 hours a day at no cost to the student. Faculty would be able to submit reserve lists to the library electronically.

CSU's final evaluation of its project helps to identify several key issues of general concern to others interested in implementing a similar service. Both students and faculty who participated in the project were pleased with the results and seemed eager to extend the service to include copyrighted works. However, copyright status for electronically produced materials made available for educational use is still unclear and continues to create a major barrier against the widespread implementation of electronic reserve services. Other challenges include finding ways to deliver graphic materials across the campus network, assuring students of adequate access to computer and printing facilities in remote locations and linking these local scanning projects to libraries' integrated library systems.

Imaging

Connection to the campus network and to Internet offers particularly exciting opportunities to libraries with archival and other special collections. Digitizing photographs, maps, and documents can be an effective means of preserving fragile collections while extending access by delivering these images using such tools as Web browsers. For example, desktop browsers such as Mosaic and Netscape allow the student in the Northeast to travel to the Mission Churches of the Sonoran Desert, through the University of Arizona's collection of digitized photographs on the World-Wide Web. Libraries delivering image collections via the network are often making primary research material available to a much broader range of researchers than have had access to these special collections in the past.

Library Instruction

Librarians must be creative when confronted with the need to communicate to remote users about accessing and using new services. Library instruction held in the library is still necessary and appropriate to teach about traditional local print collections. In addition, networked resources require classes taught outside the library in collaboration with faculty and computing colleagues. Twenty-four-hour access requires availability of help when staff are not present; information professionals therefore are challenged to think of new ways to create and promote such tools as online help sheets and tutorials. Librarians see an increased role for themselves in helping users develop the critical thinking skills needed to evaluate and sift through the wealth of electronic resources confronting them on the network.

In many places, librarians and computing professionals teach courses that cover Internet resources collaboratively, with the computing professional typically covering the "technical" part and the librarian having responsibility for "content." A few places that are at the forefront of developing interactive learning modules on the network, such as Johns Hopkins's Welch Medical Library, actually have self-paced instructional programs on the World-Wide Web. These developments have occurred through a combination of user-initiated requests for help in using networked services, and recognition by librarians that the one-on-one instructional model that was typical when library patrons came into the library to use a closely defined collection on the premises is not sustainable in the networked environment. Much of current work in this area emphasizes user-initiated learning following the "just in time" model to address the need for training when staff is not present. Here again, being connected to the network gives the impetus for change, and offers the tools for providing the necessary services to meet users' needs.

Communications

For librarians, being on the network enables closer communication with colleagues, both in the library profession and in related areas. Many librarians stressed the value of improved communications in the electronic environment in response to a listserv query initiated as part of this research. Several respondents mentioned the ease with which they are able to communicate with faculty, especially as they work together to design library instruction and develop library collections.

Access to electronic mail in the library can also break down barriers that are sometimes a result of hierarchies or functional divisions. While librarians might be hesitant to make a formal appointment with a busy administrator or faculty colleague to discuss an issue or ask a question, E-mail can often make the necessary link in a less intrusive way.

Restrictions of time and place are minimized as more communication is done on the campus network. In the case of faculty on sabbatical and students studying abroad, Internet becomes an extension of the campus network. Sharing information with colleagues in other parts of the country or world has become much easier as electronic "conferences" take place on listservs and librarians use lists to get help with difficult reference questions or policy issues. Conference planning with colleagues in other places, for those meetings that still occur "actually" rather than "virtually," is often undertaken without leaving the office.

Karen Campbell describes her experience planning a conference while working at MIT:

> When I was asked to help plan a professional society annual meeting in 1993, I could not have found the time, had it not been for the fact that virtually all the planning was done over E-mail. In addition, by the time I went to the conference (my first), I was familiar with many of the participants, from the society's listserv, which made it much easier to get to know them in person and gain insight from their experiences.[11]

Conclusion

Clearly, "reconceptualizing the library" means fostering the new collaborative relationships librarians are forming with their colleagues who teach, do research and generate scholarly information, and administer the network and other campus computer services. In addition, as a result of what Lois Jennings calls the "scholar's workstation environment," libraries have a new mission based on this "shift in values from":

> (1) collection building in anticipation of needs to collection building to meet identified essential needs, (2) ownership of information to access to information on demand, (3) the library as a physical entity to the library as an information system accessible from the client's multifunctional workstation, (4) the library as the provider of external information to the library as an intermediary facilitating access for the individual to campus information and external information, and (5) large central databases to distributed databases with mechanisms to make them widely accessible to students and staff. The shift will be made all the more complex by the presence of a transition period that is unlikely to end. University libraries will be servicing both the traditional information gathering behavior of students and academic staff as well as their new needs as they participate in the scholar's workstation environment."[12]

The prospect of an unending transition period means that the "reconceptualization" process itself must be an ongoing one. Perhaps the biggest change caused by linking to the campus network is a change in culture from the relatively predictable, controlled environment of the traditional college or university library to the dynamic and volatile world of the campus network and beyond.

Notes

1. Carolyn Arms, ed. *Campus Strategies for Libraries and Electronic Information* (Bedford, MA: Digital Press, 1990).
2. Janice Simmons-Welburn, "New Technologies and Reference Services," *RQ* 33, no. 1 (Fall 1993): 17.
3. Lois Jennings, "Regrowing Staff: Managerial Priority for the Future of University Libraries," *Public-Access Computer System Review* 3, no. 3 (1992): 5. To retrieve this article, send the following E-mail message to listserv@uhupvm1 or listserv@uhupvm1.uh.edu: GET JENNINGS PRV3N3 F=MAIL.
4. Ibid., p. 6.
5. "Re: How has the network changed service?" E-mail message from Carolyn Argentati, North Carolina State University, Natural Resources Library, Raleigh, North Carolina (Feb. 28, 1995).

6. "Innovative Internet Applications," WWW page, http://frank.mtsu.edu/kmiddlet/libweb/reference.html, Ken Middleton, Todd Library, Middle Tennessee State University.

7. Janice Simmons-Welburn, op. cit., p. 18.

8. *Information Technology and Libraries*, 13, no. 1 (March 1994). Articles on several of these projects, as well as an excellent bibliography, are included in this issue.

9. Halcyon R. Enssle. "Reserve On-line: Bringing Reserve into the Electronic Age," *Information Technology and Libraries* 13, no. 3 (September 1994): 197.

10. Ibid., p. 197.

11. "Re: How has the network changed service?" E-mail message from Karen Campbell, Hamline University, Bush Memorial Library, Saint Paul, Minnesota (Jan. 30, 1995).

12. Lois Jennings, op. cit., p. 7.

Library Cooperation and Networking, 1994

JoAn S. Segal

Vintage Ventures, Boulder, Colorado

The continued development of statewide consortia linking local systems and thus providing access to bibliographic and other data in electronic form, as well as creating new document delivery infrastructures, has given libraries multiple options for procuring bibliographic records, electronic data files, and document delivery services. It also sets the stage for a potential fragmentation of cooperative programs or for added ways to cooperate. The widespread adoption of Internet as an operational reality in a wide variety of types and sizes of libraries characterized 1994. This article addresses developments within networks at various levels, followed by discussion of the key issues involved in library networking and future trends.

National Networks

It was a year of innovation, realization of the fruits of planning, and unprecedented growth for the two major national networking organizations: OCLC (Online Computer Library Center) and RLG (Research Libraries Group).

OCLC

K. Wayne Smith, OCLC's president and chief executive officer, reminded readers in his year-end newsletter editorial that OCLC has been planning its work and working its plan.[1] Referring to the OCLC Strategic Planning document of 1991, he pointed out that three white papers—on telecommunication (August 1992), on cataloging (November 1993), and on resource sharing (December 1994)—have

Readers who are unfamiliar with the history and philosophy of library cooperation and networking might wish to refer to *The Bowker Annual Library and Book Trade Almanac*, 39th edition, 1994, pages 49–53, for a discussion of these issues.

responded to the plan's three priorities. The first of the white papers documents the improved connectivity to OCLC via Internet and links with local systems. The cataloging paper focused on alternative ways to create and deliver cataloging records and on increased availability of the records. The resource-sharing paper announced the integration of interlibrary loan with FirstSearch and new document delivery options. The OCLC Board of Trustees has set three new priorities for the next time period—enhancing PRISM, expanding internationally, and growing Reference Services—OCLC announced strong financial results from the 1994 fiscal year.

Cataloging. The original OCLC product/service, cataloging, has become a broad group of offerings including Retrocon and Techpro, a service for cataloging items for libraries of all types and sizes, and specialized cataloging systems like CJK Plus, for creating records for East Asian languages. Quality control of the database is a high priority; the recent completion of the Automatic Authority Control project corrected 5 million name and subject headings. Maintenance, education, upgrading, and publication of the Dewey Decimal Classification is also a major operation of the Dublin, Ohio-based cooperative.

Reference services. These have taken on increased importance in OCLC's planning. The highly successful databases EPIC (for information professionals) and FirstSearch (for end users) have been enhanced by the provision of Internet accessibility. (See Carol Tenopir's impressive analysis of FirstSearch.[2]) The Boston Spa became a supplier in 1994.[3] Elsevier's GeoBASE database became available on FirstSearch and EPIC.[4]

Interlibrary loan and document delivery. The OCLC ILL PRISM Transfer Service was introduced as a way to streamline the processing of interlibrary loan requests in libraries, where patrons are permitted to make such requests via the library's local system. Instead of rekeying requests into the OCLC System, staff members can now transfer requests directly to OCLC.[5] At the request of the OCLC Users Council, OCLC will develop a reimbursement system for lenders.[6] An arrangement with UMI made it possible to receive items by fax in less than an hour, and certain business documents were promised in half-an-hour turnaround time.[7]

Electronic publishing. OCLC's activities in this area have gradually established it as a significant player in this arena. The first effort of the Electronic Journals Online service, jointly with the American Association for the Advancement of Science (AAAS), was the *Online Journal of Current Clinical Trials*, which became the first electronic journal to be included in the *Index Medicus*. Although AAAS has since sold the journal to a commercial publisher, the cooperative publishing venture will continue. *The Online Journal of Knowledge Synthesis for Nursing* began publication in 1994, and OCLC has announced a cooperative venture with Elsevier that will result in publication in 1995 of more than 30 electronic journals in various areas of the sciences. Not only is OCLC in the forefront in publishing electronically, it has been negotiating and finalizing agreements with prestigious publishers, enhancing software to provide desirable features for users, and loading collections of journals to increase information acquisition and access. With its acquisition of Information Dimensions Inc., OCLC has also obtained the means to organize information for its electronic publishing activity and to assist libraries in bringing order to new types of publications.[8]

Communication and access. Internet access for all reference databases has been provided for some time. For nearly a year, libraries have been trying out Internet as a way to access the PRISM service for cataloging and interlibrary loan.[9] A World-Wide Web Mosaic home page was mounted September 26.[10] OCLC Gateway Software was successfully implemented at three sites to connect non-OCLC terminals and workstations on a campus or local network to OCLC and other services.[11] Internet has helped OCLC and its member libraries reach a new audience of end users with new products and technologies.[12]

Educational activities. A highly successful symposium on the future of technical processing was held during the ALA Midwinter Meeting in Los Angeles. Well-known librarians offered their views of what is to come; participants had an opportunity to discuss the immense professional ramifications of the changing nature of technical services in the new electronic age.[13] Proceedings of the symposium were also published in both paper and electronic forms.[14] On October 4, OCLC hosted a video conference on the emerging electronic, digital library. More than 20,000 people at 700 sites (including most of the OCLC regional networks) saw the program, in which Sidney Verba offered the keynote address and a panel of seven librarians discussed the implications for librarianship of upcoming changes in technology and answered questions called in by viewers.[15]

Research. Terry Noreault was named OCLC's director of research and special projects. In an interview, he noted that three major areas of work are database quality, networked information services, and applied information about libraries and the OnLine Union Catalog (OLUC).[16] The office also offers grants of up to $10,000 to faculty members in schools of library and information service.[17]

Other activities. In the fall, it was announced that OCLC had been awarded some $62,000 under the College Library Technology and Cooperation program of the U.S. Department of Education, to build a catalog of Internet resources. The volunteer effort, to which OCLC is committing another $45,000, will involve librarians identifying, selecting, and cataloging computer files available via Internet.[18]

Further expansion of the OCLC network to school libraries was reported to be having beneficial results on students' searching, thus reinforcing their positive attitudes toward their media centers.[19]

OCLC's international activities have also continued to grow. User groups in Europe and Japan held meetings to hear reports and news about OCLC, to discuss common concerns, and to entertain ideas about the electronic library of the future.[20, 21]

Governance. The OCLC Users Council met January 9–11 to hear reports and discuss OCLC electronic publishing activities; May 22–24 on the topic of knowledge management; and October 2–4 on building the electronic library. On October 4, the group participated in the OCLC video conference mentioned above. The council elected Bill Potter and Ellen Waite to six-year terms on the OCLC board of directors.

Statistics. At year end OCLC had almost 20,000 participating libraries; its database had over 31 million records and 539 million holding/location listings; over 55 million interlibrary requests had been recorded on the system.

RLG

An important article detailing the history, products, service programs, and future possibilities of RLG was published by two of its principals, with contributions by other major staff members.[22] The authors cover changes in membership structure intended to encourage a variety of types and sizes of libraries and related organizations to become members. They report both successes and failures in attempts to lead members of the research community toward increased cooperation with each other and relate their plans for responding to the new needs and expectations arising on campuses. Excellent sidebars depict:

- RLIN, the major bibliographic database underlying RLG's shared cataloging efforts, including its architecture
- CitaDel Service, RLG's citation and document delivery program
- ARIEL, its advanced document transmission software
- Eureka, the search service designed for patron use
- Zephyr, a server that facilitates searching RLIN and CitaDel from non-RLG terminals
- Archival programs
- Special files
- JACKPHY-Plus, a program for cataloging and reference in languages in non-roman scripts
- Collaborative preservation

The piece constitutes a first-rate reference for all aspects of RLG activity.

1994 developments. Eureka—a "user-friendly" search service aimed at allowing patrons to gain access to the RLIN database and to obtain copies through the CitaDel citations and delivery service—was developed and underwent user trials in 1993–1994.[23] The "Rutgers Inventory of Machine-Readable Texts in the Humanities" was added to the RLIN database, allowing access to these electronic texts.[24] Another addition to the CitaDel service will be the *U.S. Government Periodicals Index*, which covers more than 5,500 articles published between October 1993 and March 1994.[25] The publication *Electronic Access to Information: A New Service Paradigm* covered the research and teaching missions of RLG members.[26] It was announced that eight members of RLG would each select from their collections 1,000 photographs that depict "the urban landscape," to develop and test a system for digitizing images for future sharing of such unique materials.[27] RLG had a big jump in membership (to 143) in the 1993–1994 year.[28] It was also announced in the fall of 1994 that RLG would keep its 1995 pricing structure at the current level.[29]

WLN

Continued growth and development characterized 1994 for WLN (the Western Library Network). New features included a graphical user interface (GUI) for the Windows environment for LaserCat, the CD-ROM database of 4 million USMARC cataloging records.[30] It was announced at the end of the year that the *WLN Participant* (WLN's newsletter) was to be divided into two separate quarterly publications, one consisting of analytical articles discussing innovative applications in various WLN libraries and the other focusing on technical updates and developments of concern to customers.[31] WLN also announced that its Conspectus software would be available through PALINET.[32]

Regional Networks

AMIGOS

Important developments at AMIGOS included the initiation of the Internet Service, which provides access, training, and user support; the expansion of the Preservation Service, which now includes site surveys and enhanced training; and the implementation of a planning process (Plan 2000) that led to the discontinuance of 7 lesser-used services while adding some 18 new ones (6 from OCLC). The analytic process established in 1994 will routinely provide information for decision support regarding the viability of continuing, expanding, reducing, or eliminating products and services.[33] Spring and fall membership conferences provide regular opportunities for continuing education for members; recent topics have included TQM (total quality management), electronic journals and the library, telecommunications,[34] preservation, the psychology of change, and violence in the library.[35] The AMIGOS Consulting Service became fully operational; a major 1994 activity was the Tex-Share Planning Project, which focused on innovative uses of technology to provide information and ways of sharing information housed in Texas libraries.[36]

BCR

The state of Nevada became a member of BCR on July 1, 1994, bringing to six the number of state members.[37] The BCR Internet server, **BCR.org**, was implemented[38] to provide better service to member libraries and to ease communication between members and staff. Efforts to improve print publications resulted in a new format for *Action for Libraries* and a number of attractive new brochures.[39] A major program on interlibrary loan (ILL) and document delivery brought well-known ILL librarian Mary Jackson and others to BCR for a workshop in the spring of 1994. Cost comparisons between traditional ILL and document delivery services indicate a trade-off between ILL staff time and commercial charges, including copyright and delivery costs. Libraries need to integrate the two methods into the service operation to provide users with what they need, workshop speakers indicated.[40] Celebrating its 60th anniversary, BCR continued to enjoy growth in numbers of institutions (now 457), training offerings (227), and financial equity (up $94,000 to $1.4 million).[41]

Table 1 / Bibliographic Databases

Database	Characteristics
OCLC, Online Computer Library Center	Serves 20,000 libraries of all types; largest database; has own national telecommunications network.
RLIN, the Research Libraries Information Network	Online library service of the Research Libraries Group. Targeted to research libraries, has own national telecommunications network.
WLN, the Western Library Network	Regional database for Northwest U.S. & Canada known for quality and authority control. Formerly part of Washington State Library, now independent.

Table 2 / OCLC Regional Networks (Independent or State-Operated)

Network	Chief Area Served	Status
AMIGOS	TX, AZ, NM, OK	Independent
BCR	CO, UT, WY, KS, IA, NV	Independent
CAPCON	Washington DC Metro area	Independent
FEDLINK	Federal libraries anywhere	U.S. government
ILLINET	IL	State library supported
INCOLSA	IN	State agency
MINITEX	MN, SD, ND	Independent, some state support
MLC (Michigan Library Consortium)	MI	Independent
MLNC (Missouri Library Network Corporation)	MO	Independent
Nebraska Library Commission (NEBASE)	NE	State library supported
NELINET	New England	Independent
OCLC–Asia Pacific	Asia	OCLC Service Center
OCLC–Europe	Europe	OCLC Service Center
OHIONET	OH	Independent
PACNET	WA, OR, CA	OCLC Service Center
PALINET	Eastern PA, NJ, DE, MD	Independent
PRLC (Pittsburgh Regional Library Center)	Western PA, WV	Independent
SOLINET	AR, VA, NC, SC, FL, GA, AL, MS, LA, KY, TN	Independent
SUNY/OCLC	NY	Part of State Univ. of NY
Utlas	Canada	Independent
WILS	WI	Independent

Note: These networks provide various services, both cooperative (group buying plans) and automated (reference services, PCs, CD-ROM applications, and Internet services in addition to OCLC), and training. The particular mix of services varies.

CAPCON

Growth in the CAPCON network, especially in Internet services and training activities, has resulted in an increase in staff to 15 from 11.[42]

INCOLSA

INCOLSA marked its 20th anniversary with a celebration on April 21. The anniversary brochure *Twenty Successes to Celebrate* noted growth in members and staff, and observed that its members have cataloged or converted some 10 million holdings in the OCLC OnLine Union Catalog.[43] Executive Director Barbara Markuson, who has headed the operation for all its 20 years, is a national leader in library networking and cooperation.

MINITEX

MINITEX, which focuses on interlibrary cooperation, passed its 25th anniversary in 1994 with a celebration during the Minnesota Library Association conference in October.[44] The network added several new products and services. It made available the Chadwyck-Healey CD-ROM version of the *English Poetry Full Text Database*;[45] it loaded Ariel for Windows to transmit documents to certain of its libraries;[46] it expanded its overnight delivery system to include additional cities;[47] and it added increased access to IAC's InfoTrac databases.[48] MINITEX also held a workshop on the future of interlibrary loan and document delivery.[49]

NELINET

Marshall Keys's usual lucid financial report indicated continued financial success, bringing the fund balance (equity) to almost $700,000 at the end of FY 1993. There are 520 members in the network.[50]

OHIONET

The network celebrated the burning of the mortgage on its building in September.[51] The annual program meeting focused on multitype cooperation in Ohio.[52] The Internet service exceeded expectations, with addition of such features as additional USENET newsgroups, a signature file feature on the menu, file management software improvements, a directory of staff in member libraries, the OHIONET publications and workshop calendar, and an online calendar of Ohio continuing-education events.[53] A third annual Internet conference was held in March.[54]

SOLINET

Kate Nevins, formerly OCLC vice president for member services, became executive director upon Frank Grisham's retirement in May.[55] A long-range strategic plan for the years 1994/1995–1996/1997 was approved by the board March 3, 1994. The document incorporates a "Vision for Change," a sweeping commitment to "contribute to the economic development, educational enhancement, and overall quality of life" in the Southeast.[56] A summary of reference products and services filled the September/October issue of the newsletter *SOLINEWS*; this included the SOLINET Internet gopher, FirstSearch, reference tools available through the discounted cooperative-purchase plan, and reference workshops.[57] SOLINET received a Department of Commerce grant (through the National Telecommunications and Information Administration) to explore electronic access to government information and library special collections in the Southeast. It increased partnerships with libraries, consortia, academic institutions, and businesses to facilitate access to information, and it experienced an increased demand from libraries for training in management decision making, new technologies, and information access tools.[58] A major milestone was reached as the balance sheet at the end of FY 1994 indicated SOLINET had finally recovered from its decision some 15 years ago to pursue a capital-intensive plan for library automation in the region.[59]

WILS

Entering the world of distance learning, WILS (Wisconsin Inter Library Services) conducted several training sessions via the Picture-tel compressed video. In one session, instructors in different locations were viewed by participants at four sites. One workshop had kickoff and wrap-up sessions via compressed video, with self-paced coursework in between via electronic mail. WILS is now considered a leader in Wisconsin in this technology, and the potential is considered very good for future training using distance learning. Locally, WILS has become the lender for all interlibrary loans from the University of Wisconsin at Madison. This has made good use of the WILS staff and their skills and has enhanced the university's services. Like other networks, WILS has also found an increased demand for Internet training and has responded to demand for such training, not only from libraries, but from educational institutions in the state.[60] Through an LSCA (Library Services and Construction Act) grant, WILS offered a series of preservation-related workshops at a minimal cost and in geographic proximity to a large number of libraries of all types to facilitate and encourage preservation education and training for Wisconsin. Two hundred people participated and gave the sessions "rave reviews."[61] The New Technologies Information program continues to be an unusual and valuable service.[62]

State Networks

Several recently announced state networks include libraries. The Iowa Communications Network links schools and colleges, including their libraries. The North Carolina Information Highway—which uses sophisticated technology for voice, video, and data—will include libraries in the linkages. NYSERNET began as a library networking agent and is now serving as the link to Internet for New York State. The Utah Electronic Highway for Education links schools and colleges, with development planned for secondary schools; and the state library plans to tap into this network for the use of all libraries in the state.[63]

OhioLINK, a statewide academic library automation project, has been described in some detail by David Kohl.[64] The security of such networks was called into question after OhioLINK suffered a network crash due to hackers in

August.[65] Cooperative storage of little-used materials began in Ohio with the opening of the Northeastern Ohio Cooperative Regional Library Depository.[66]

The State Library of Pennsylvania's Library Development Division set up a model program through Mansfield University to develop a cooperative CD-ROM network providing dial-up access to bibliographic databases and training to school librarians and teachers, including installing six periodical indexes.[67] ACCESS PENNSYLVANIA gave junior high school students access to library resources via local area networks, CD-ROM, and a dedicated optical file server.[68]

The Iowa Library Information Project is designed to link the libraries of the state's three public universities and eventually all the libraries in the state.[69] A $2.5 million federal grant will finance a two-year research and demonstration project to provide a statewide network using Internet, the Iowa Communications network, and the Extension EXNET ICN/frame relay network, with a point of presence in each of Iowa's 99 counties and local dial-in connections through local telephone companies.[70] The network will provide access to online resources from libraries throughout the state, including Internet access, state documents, and magazine indexes.

Wyoming libraries have begun to move to their second-generation statewide circulation system, with interlibrary loan features, OPACs (online public access catalogs) for libraries in larger population centers, and links to all other systems operating within the state.[71]

Colorado will expand access to ACLIN (Access Colorado Library and Information Network), the statewide online library network, with funding from a U.S. Department of Education grant. The expansion will include increased dial-up coverage, additional telephone lines, more databases, training of resource people throughout the state, and the establishment of policies to ensure the public has free access to appropriate information.[72]

The Nevada Academic Libraries Information System (NALIS) provides local and remote networked information resources to faculty, students, and citizens of Nevada, using the existing telecommunications infrastructure on the campuses, and builds on the library automation programs already present in the libraries.[73] The libraries of the six campuses of the University and Community College System of Nevada worked with the system's computer service to develop the project.

The Minnesota State University System's Project for Automated Library Systems (MSUS/PALS) includes 53 state universities, community colleges, private colleges, and state library agencies, and some 130 academic, public, and special libraries. Not only catalog searching, but E-mail, inventory control, circulation, interlibrary loan, serials control, and acquisitions are now available on the system.[74]

Center for Networked Information

The fall meeting of the Center for Networked Information (CNI) involved research librarians addressing copyright issues and the management and negotiation of site licenses within the framework of constant growth. Participants reportedly were optimistic about what seems to be an unthreatened period of expansion for networking.[75]

Other Library Cooperation and Networking Activities

Founded more than 30 years ago, the Committee on Inter-Institutional Cooperation (CIC) includes in extensive programs of cooperation the University of Chicago, the University of Illinois at Chicago, the University of Illinois at Urbana, the University of Iowa, the University of Michigan, the University of Minnesota, the University of Wisconsin–Madison, Indiana University, Michigan State University, Northwestern University, Ohio State University, Pennsylvania State University, and Purdue University. A recent grant of $1.2 million from the U.S. Department of Education will allow the libraries of these institutions to organize themselves as a "Virtual Electronic Library." The combined library holdings are over 56 million volumes; they also have strong subject collections. As a result of the project, users at one library will be able to search ("seamlessly") the catalogs of all the CIC libraries and request materials without the mediation of library staff.[76]

A new interlibrary loan code has been released, providing general guidelines for requesting and supplying materials between libraries.[77] Cooperative reference services were explored by Carl Orgren, who interviewed librarians involved in such services.[78] The Basic Health Sciences Library Network is an interlibrary loan network crossing state lines and operating without fees or federal funding.[79]

Key Issues in Networking

Interlibrary Loan and Document Delivery

Interlibrary cooperation had its origins in interlibrary loan; even shared cataloging through OCLC was first seen as a mechanism by which library holdings could be made available so that interlibrary loans would be made easier. The demand for journal articles and other library materials uncovered through database searches has greatly increased the necessity to provide material not held by the user's library and has led to new and innovative methods. A key issue is the question of how to integrate commercial systems into library operations to satisfy the user's need.[80] Ease of use and speed are criteria for selecting commercial document delivery services to complement traditional interlibrary loan operations. Five models for integration of the two systems were posited by Mary Jackson.[81] These include the "last resort" model, where a commercial service is used only after all other options have been exhausted; the "first resort" model, where speed of processing and delivery are the primary considerations; the "table-of-contents" model, where end users have access to a table-of-contents database and may order directly; the "user-dependent" model, in which certain classes of users are eligible for the service; and the "full-text" model, an extremely expensive option, but one that enables end users to bypass library staff for many of their needs.

Levels of Networking

The issue of the appropriate levels for certain networking activities has never been fully addressed. Although it has generally been agreed that a national (perhaps even a multinational) bibliographic database is desirable, we continue to have multiple players at the national level: OCLC and RLIN, with the Library of Congress (always a potential competitor to both of these) and WLN a strong presence. Regional networks, many of whom have allied themselves with OCLC to provide its products and services, also offer their member libraries assistance with reference services, Internet access, group purchasing discounts on all kinds of products, and all aspects of computerization. Some of the OCLC-affiliated networks operate in a single state; the agent may or may not be the state library. Networks are operated by state libraries for a variety of purposes; they may provide a statewide bibliographic database (often created with a subset of the OCLC database representing the libraries in the state); they may serve as statewide consortia linking local systems to provide access to electronic data and to establish the infrastructure for document delivery. In some of these activities, they may be in competition with national or regional networks.

An increased interest in scanning and digitization for possible sharing of information gave rise to other types of networking and cooperation. An example of this trend is the decision of the CIC libraries to create a virtual electronic library among themselves. Substantial funding from the U.S. Department of Education will support this exciting development. But how will the project impinge on other library networking and cooperation activities? Without a consideration of the overlapping activities of all these levels of networking, without the setting of criteria as to what is appropriate at various levels, how can the best interests of library cooperation and networking be served? Should such criteria be taken into consideration in the allocation of government funding?

Preservation and Conservation

Regional network directors report that libraries want more assistance with preservation and conservation. The continued deterioration of library materials, together with the uncertainty about the life of the media onto which the content is being transferred, increase the importance of librarians' decisions to preserve at least the content if not also the physical form of their library's materials.

Late in the year, OCLC reasserted its demand for contracts with the regional networks, enjoining them from pursuing certain lines of business. At this writing, no reaction had been reported. (In the early 1980s OCLC's requirements for contracts with its networks engendered much debate; the matter was delicately put to rest.) However, the regional networks in general desire to enhance and strengthen their relationship with OCLC. They have a commitment to a national bibliographic database, to shared cataloging, and to the many OCLC products and services that form an important part of their offerings.

Internet

The year 1994 saw increasingly widespread use of Internet for library cooperation and networking but also growing activity on the part of individual libraries,
not necessarily in concert with other libraries, to deepen and enhance the services
they provide to their users. The explosive growth in Internet use for interlibrary
loan, cooperative reference, and cataloging seemed additional to the use of other
communication modes. Whitney and Glogoff note the rapidity of change, point-
ing out that it is little more than a year since the early gophers appeared and that
the national information infrastructure (NII) legislation was only signed into law
in 1993.[82]

The role of libraries and their networks in the development of Internet and
NII continues to be a prime issue. Library staff need technical assistance and
training for various aspects of Internet use and management of the new technology. Some directors are concerned at the amount of time staff must now spend
using Internet; the question of the quality of information available from this
source is of utmost importance in maintaining the reputation of libraries as
sources of reliable facts and knowledge. Projects like that of OCLC in creating a
catalog of Internet resources need to be supplemented by research into the merits
of such resources and the efficiency of their use.

Financing Cooperative Activities

Networking activities have sometimes been touted as a way to save money.
Experienced networkers know this oversimplification is inaccurate. Cooperation
does increase the resources available and does make it possible to give more
users access to more information, but it is not necessarily a panacea in times of
retrenchment. The question of how to pay for new services, while continuing to
provide existing services that are still needed, faced libraries and regional networks in 1994. Even in corporate situations, the decision to discontinue a product
or service is traumatic. In the world of libraries and their networks, where all services are perceived as beneficial and cannot be judged on a financial basis only,
such decisions are of unprecedented difficulty. Library networks need to
acknowledge that they must move forward and at the same time let go of the
past. Some networks (e.g., AMIGOS) have begun to take steps in this direction.

Regional Network Issues

Changes in the ways libraries use online systems and the development of "virtual
libraries" have made old network fiscal and legal arrangements outdated; new
contracting and service arrangements are becoming necessary. Internet use creates a large demand for training and technical assistance, but there is little opportunity for networks to generate sufficient revenue to support such service.

The networks are continually evolving to new offerings for full text, digitization, and Internet in response to libraries' needs. To do so, many networks
have entered into partnerships with vendors, other networks, state libraries, and
consortia to improve service to their members. The risks and complexity of these

partnerships are of constant concern to network managers and governance bodies. Further proliferation of options for libraries to procure bibliographic records, electronic data files, and document delivery services tests library loyalty to their regional networks. Keeping ahead of the competition while anticipating library needs is a challenge of serious proportions.

Tight library budgets have combined with changing library needs to make the financial viability of regional networks even more uncertain. For instance, networks that have long offered group discounts to members for a variety of products from vendors are finding that the ongoing fragmentation of the automation market is making it harder to get such discounts. When they do negotiate discounts, they are often smaller than in the past. The seeking of grant funding for network activities must be carried out carefully so as not to compete with member libraries.

All these issues are driven by the needs of the member libraries, who are the networks' "customers." This creates a further need for gathering more information about library needs through market analysis and improved communication tools. This means networks must help libraries define their role in the electronic information era and figure out how they can best support libraries in the transition to that new role. Some of the networks are discovering their own headquarters' technology needs updating, another costly aspect of providing a leadership role.

National Information Infrastructure

Implications of a national information infrastructure (NII) for libraries are manifold, but the role of libraries is still uncertain. As the various forces in the federal government jockey for position, they sometimes forget libraries have already established themselves as a presence on Internet, with library networks providing servers, training, and technical assistance. Some public libraries have become the de facto suppliers of Internet services in their communities. The Pike's Peak Library District in Colorado, for example, provides free Internet access to all users through its MAGGNET service. Fortunately, at least one librarian was chosen to serve on the NII Advisory Council. [See the Special Report by Toni Carbo Bearman and David Wallace on the activities of the NII Advisory Council—*Ed.*]

The effect of the Republican victory in November 1994 is likely to be felt by libraries in a number of ways. Their victory may weaken any program (such as NII) advocated by the White House. Networking application bills are not likely to be brought up again,[83] and further commercialization of the network is possible under Republican domination.

The U.S. Postal Service announced it is planning to work with libraries in the pilot test of Citizen Kiosks for "networking government service information through the Internet and other value-added networks." No funding mechanism for the kiosks has yet been determined.[84] Librarians testified in October before a House Science, Space, and Technology Subcommittee hearing on Internet access, promoting libraries as a means for rural Americans to get cheaper access to Internet.[85]

As summarized by Dennis Reynolds,[86] a May U.S. Commerce Department report identified four roles for libraries and librarians in the electronic information society. First characterizing the traditional library role as that of a "safety net" or "information equalizer," the report sees a second role for libraries in training and instruction or use of electronic networks and information. Third, the library would have a role in organizing and classifying networked information, and, finally, libraries would have a special role in the archiving and preserving of electronic data.

Internet

The incorporation of Internet into the work of librarians has caused an explosion of conferences and printed materials on the topic. Some examples are Meckler's Internet World and Document Delivery World, now held annually in December,[87] OHIONET's Annual Internet Conference,[88] NCLIS's publication *Public Libraries and the Internet*,[89] and an article in *Minnesota Media*, the journal for school library and media specialists in Minnesota.[90] The American Library Association debuted its own gopher in the spring.[91] In fact, it is impossible to open any library-related publication without finding information on resources available in specific fields,[92,93] lists of listservs, articles about how to "get on" Internet,[94] threats to Internet security,[95] possible future billing systems,[96] and a bevy of related topics.

As stated in previous editions of the *Bowker Annual*, the term *network* may have several different meanings and connotations in the library world. As we see the incorporation of this international linking tool into the daily work flow of more and more librarians, we come to still another kind of meaning. Internet may connect individual librarians with other individual librarians, libraries, and nonlibrary resources. Although it may play a role in connecting libraries for cooperative purposes, it is in fact a specific kind of tool for certain subsets of library activity and we need to give some thought to how we incorporate it into the broader sense of library networking and cooperation.

Future of Information Networks

Continuities

The need for links with others to share work and information will militate for the continuation of library networks structured much as they are today, probably for at least another decade or two. Librarians will continue to join networks that are effective in helping them use technology to share this work and make these links.

In a recent article, Liz Bishoff, OCLC vice president for member relations, suggested these links need to be broadened to include not only libraries and networks but publishers, bookstores, video outlets, and telecommunications and cable companies.[97] Using OCLC as an example, she shows how a network can position itself to serve end users in an environment where it must compete with organizations not previously seen as providing similar services. One advantage of libraries and their networks, she says, is the "means of delivering . . . universal service," one of the prerequisites demanded by the Clinton administration for the new industry. Another competitive advantage library organizations can bring to such alliances is the equivalent of public service announcements—namely the databases, OPACs, abstracting and indexing files, and digitized image databases they have developed. They can provide customer support and training, and finally, they can assist in integrating traditional print and audiovisual media with the emerging electronic information.

Networks will increasingly turn to their members and customers to help them decide which services and products to provide. The customer service philosophy is growing in importance, according to reports from network directors.

Networks will need to be even more involved in work on the many standards that will enable the development of the National Information Infrastructure. Networks can play a significant role in educating their members, coalescing agreement, and seeing that the new standards are implemented.

Possible Discontinuities

Although the idea of shared cataloging is widely accepted, cooperative activities continue to be jeopardized by institutions that will not accept others' work, by failure to load locally produced records into a national database such as OCLC's, and by a concentration on local, rather than universal, library interests. But many libraries seem not to agree that a national database is of value. They fear the loss of autonomy and control that comes with any cooperative agreements. Many are in a mode of "inventing their own"—making their mark on the library world by doing something creative for a specific library or small group of libraries, rather than working within existing agreements to the benefit of a larger cooperative.

Some librarians fear that the increased use of electronic media and networked information will erode the traditional library. One role for library networks must be in helping librarians deal with these media. But they must also recognize that networked information and services alter the market for networks themselves. Many networks are heavily involved in helping their members get access to Internet and learn how to "navigate" it. Some have begun to offer this training to nonlibrarians. OCLC has already targeted end users.

New Predictions

The end user will eventually become independent of librarian mediation for many transactions but will need librarians for more difficult transactions and for guidance and training. Librarians will be even more involved with copyright issues as new storage and access methods change the traditional ways a user receives intellectual content.

Two interesting papers address possible alternative futures. B. G. Leonard suggests that future academic library information resource budgets may be redirected away from print and into more cooperative arrangements.[98] Thomas J. Dorst predicts that users will fund resource sharing "at the point of transaction, as they pay for access to information, rather than institutions paying for ownership of information."[99]

The rise in the price of materials, compounded by the increase in the amount of material and information available in various formats, has altered in a major way the role of large university and research libraries. Over time, they will be able to acquire less and less of the "total" information output of the world, author Brian Hawkins points out.[100] The solution he proposes is a national electronic library with free access, an academic orientation, developed cooperatively with commercial interests, and aggressive in advancing experimentation—especially with multi- and hypermedia formats. He suggests a nonprofit corporate model for the project and proposes a business plan based on volunteerism, on institutional (vs. individual) payment for access, on using the existing infrastructure, and on the development of technical standards and advanced searching tools.

Conclusion

The increased use of Internet by librarians and library users is having a significant impact on how librarians do their work and what services they need from their networking agencies. The realization that libraries have competitors in providing information to the public is driving them in new directions as quickly as they can move. As the U.S. institutionalizes the national information infrastructure, the role for libraries will become clearer, but librarians must take the lead in seeing that their potential in the electronic information society is appreciated and exploited.

Notes

1. K. Wayne Smith, "Planning Our Work and Working Our Plan," *OCLC Newsletter*, no. 212 (November/December 1994): 3.

2. Carol Tenopir, "A Second Look at FirstSearch," *Library Journal* 119, no. 8 (November 1, 1994): 30, 32.

3. "British Library Document Supply Centre Now a Document Supplier on the FirstSearch Catalog," *OCLC Newsletter*, no. 207 (January/February 1994): 30.

4. "GEOBASE Included on OCLC Services," *Library Journal* 119, no. 15 (September 1994): 27.

5. "OCLC ILL PRISM Transfer Service Streamlines the Interlibrary Loan Process," *OCLC Newsletter*, no. 211 (September/October 1994): 43.

6. "OCLC Will Develop ILL Reimbursement System," *Information Today* 11, no. 4 (April 1994): 5.

7. *What's New at OCLC* (Dublin, OH: OCLC, 1994).

8. Andrea Keyhani, "OCLC Electronic Publishing: Creating New Pathways to Information," *OCLC Newsletter*, no. 211 (September/October 1994): 15–29.

9. "OCLC to Test Internet Access to PRISM," *Information Today* 11, no. 4 (April 1994): 68.

10. "OCLC World-Wide Web Server Offers Information, Documentation and More," *OCLC Newsletter* (November/December 1994): 5.

11. "OCLC Gateway Software Is Now Available," *OCLC Newsletter*, no. 210 (July/August 1994): 34.

12. T. Storcy, "The Internet and OCLC: Broadening Access to the World's Information," *Reference Librarian*, no. 41–42 (1994): 375–385.

13. Phil Schieber, "Symposium on the Future of Technical Processing Draws SRO Audience in Los Angeles," *OCLC Newsletter*, no. 207 (January/February 1994): 32.

14. "The Future Is NOW: Changing Library Paradigms," *Computers in Libraries* 14, no. 5 (May 1994): 43.

15. "OCLC Sponsors International Videoconference," *Advanced Technology/Libraries* 23, no. 11 (November 1994): 1, 2.

16. Mark Crook, "Terry Noreault Discusses the OCLC Office of Research," *OCLC Newsletter,* no. 210 (July/August 1994): 18–19.

17. Keith Shafer, "OCLC Awards Three Research Grants," *OCLC Newsletter,* no. 212 (November/December 1994): 18–19.

18. "OCLC Gets 62K for Internet Project," *Library Journal* 119, no. 17 (October 15, 1994): 15.

19. P. M. Anker, "OCLC Group Access in High Schools," *Computers in Libraries* 14, no. 3 (March 1994): 18–20.

20. "Librarians from 11 Countries Across Europe Attended the OCLC Europe User's Forum on April 14," photo caption, *OCLC Newsletter,* no. 210 (July/August 1994): 16.

21. "Third Japan OCLC Users Meeting Draws More than 300 Librarians," *OCLC Newsletter,* no. 210 (July/August 1994): 17.

22. James Michalko and John Haeger, "The Research Libraries Group: Making a Difference," *Library Hi Tech* 12, no. 2 (1994): 7–32.

23. H. Hannon, "Eureka Opens New Door to RLG's Scholarly Resources," *Computers in Libraries* 14, no. 1 (January 1994): 16–20.

24. A. Hoogcarspel, "Rutgers Inventory of Machine-Readable Texts in the Humanities: Cataloging and Access," *Information Technology and Libraries* 13, no. 1 (March 1994): 27–34.

25. "Government Periodicals," *Library Journal* 119, no. 17 (October 15, 1994): 20.

26. Nancy Melin Nelson, "The Future Is Now: Changing Library Paradigms," *Computers in Libraries* 14, no. 5 (May 1994): 4–6.

27. "RLG to Digitize the 'Urban Landscape,'" *American Libraries* 25, no. 2 (February 1994): 157.

28. "'93 Year Good to RLG," *American Libraries* 25, no. 4 (April 1994): 446.

29. "RLG Holds Rates for 1995 Services," *Library Journal* 119, no. 17 (October 15, 1994): 19–20.

30. "WLN LaserCat gets GUI," *American Libraries* 25, no. 4 (April 1994): 446.

31. Correspondence from WLN to those receiving the WLN Participant.

32. "WLN Conspectus Software Available Through PALINET," *Information Today* 11, no. 7 (July/August 1994): 41.

33. Bonnie Juergens, "Letter from the Executive Director," *Annual Report 1994* (Dallas: AMIGOS, 1994), p. 3.

34. "Telecommunications and Information: The Commercial Perspective," *¿Que Pasa?* 15, no. 2 (April 1994): 1.

35. "AMIGOS 1994 Fall Conference Examines These Changing Times," *¿Que Pasa?* 15, no. 4 (October 1994): 1, 6.

36. "Tex-Share Planning Project Underway," news release, AMIGOS, February 23, 1994.

37. "Nevada Hailed as New BCR Member State," *Action for Libraries* 20, no. 9 (September 1994): 2.

38. "BCR to Install Internet Server, Broaden Services to Member Libraries," *Action for Libraries* 20, no. 5 (May 1994): 1–2.

39. "Program Highlights," *BCR Annual Report 1994,* p. 1.

40. "Cost, Convenience, Quick Access to Define Future of Document Delivery," *Action for Libraries* 20, no. 7 (July 1994): 1, 2.

41. "FY 1993–1994: Expanding BCR Services on the Internet," *BCR Annual Report 1994,* p. 3.

42. Personal communication with Dennis Reynolds, CAPCON director, January 1995.

43. "INCOLSA Celebrates Its 20th Anniversary," *OCLC Newsletter,* no. 210 (July/August 1994): 5.

44. "Help Celebrate MINITEX's 25th Anniversary," *MINITEX Messenger* 12, no. 1 (August 29, 1994): 1.

45. "MINITEX Helps Arrange Access to English Poetry Full Text Database," *MINITEX Messenger* 12, no. 2 (October 17, 1994): 1.

46. "MINITEX Loads Ariel for Windows," *MINITEX Messenger* 12, no. 2 (October 17, 1994): 3.

47. "Expansion of MINITEX Overnight Delivery System," *MINITEX Messenger* 12, no. 2 (October 17, 1994): 3.

48. "MINITEX Library Information Network Expands Access to IAC's InfoTrac Databases," *Information Today* 11, no. 9 (October 1994): 41.

49. "MINITEX Librarians Discuss Trends in Managing ILL," *MINITEX Messenger* 11, no. 9 (June 22, 1994): 2–6.

50. "Finances in Plain English IV," *NELINET Liaison* 16, no. 2 (February 1994): 1–7.

51. Michael P. Butler, "Business Meeting Notes," *OHIONETwork* 16, no. 10 (October 1994): 1.

52. "OHIONET Annual Program Meeting," *OHIONETwork* 16, no. 7 (July 1994): 1.

53. Michael P. Butler, "A Note from the Executive Director," *OHIONETwork* 16, no. 6 (June 1994): 1.

54. "Third Annual Internet Conference," *OHIONETwork* 16, no. 3 (March 1994): 1.

55. Larry P. Alford, "Message from the New Board Chair," *SOLINEWS* 21, no. 4 (July/August 1994): 1.

56. "SOLINET's Long Range Strategic Plan FY1994/95–FY1996/97," *SOLINEWS* 21, no. 4 (July/August 1994): 7.

57. "Finding Answers to Reference Needs with SOLINET," *SOLINEWS* 21, no. 5 (September/October 1994): 1–7.

58. Personal communication with Kate Nevins, January 11, 1995.

59. Larry Alford, "SOLINET Reaches Major Milestone," *SOLINEWS* 21, no. 5 (September/October 1994): 8.

60. Personal communication with Kathy Schneider, February 6, 1995.

61. "WISPPR," in *WILS Annual Report,* 1993–94, p. 7.

62. "New Technologies Information," in *WILS Annual Report,* 1993–94, p. 6.

63. "Some Examples of State Networks," *Chronicle of Higher Education* 41, no. 16 (December 14, 1994): A22.

64. David F. Kohl, "OhioLINK: A Statewide System Raises New Issues and Opportunities for Cooperation," *RSR Reference Services Review* 22, no. 2 (1994): 27–29.

65. "OhioLINK Tightens Security after Hackers Cause a Network Crash," *American Libraries* 25, no. 9 (October 1994): 806.

66. "Little-Used Books Get a New Home," *Chronicle of Higher Education* 40, no. 28 (March 16, 1994): A6.

67. A. L. Garretson, "A Cooperative CD-ROM Network: School Libraries and Mansfield University," *Computers in Libraries* 14, no. 2 (February 1994): 42–45.

68. M. A. Brenner, "The ACCESS PENNSYLVANIA Reference Center: Swatara Junior High School's 'Biggest Bang for the Buck,'" *Computers in Libraries* 14, no. 3 (March 1994): 12–16.

69. "Iowa's Libraries Plan New Computer Network," *Information Today* 11, no. 3 (March 1994): 4.

70. "Colorado, Iowa State Libraries Receive Grants to Expand Information Networks," *Action for Libraries* 20, no. 12 (December 1994): 1–2.

71. Personal correspondence with C. Walters and J. Krois, April 1994.

72. Ibid.

73. Carol A. Parkhurst, "The Nevada Academic Libraries Information System: An Application of Internet Services," *Reference Librarian*, no. 41–42 (1994): 333–345.

74. M. S. Barnett, "MSUS/PALS: Building a Regional Information Infrastructure," *Library Hi Tech* 12, no. 1 (1994): 7–34.

75. Tom Gaughan, "Manifest Destiny at Disney World," *American Libraries* 26, no. 1 (January 1995): 82, 84.

76. Thomas L. Shaughnessy, "Libraries Organize as a Virtual Electronic Library," *LibraryLine* 5, no. 2 (March 1994): 1–2.

77. "National Interlibrary Loan Code for the United States," *RQ* 33, no. 4 (Summer 1994): 477–479.

78. Carl Orgren, "Cooperative Reference Service," *Reference Librarian*, no. 43 (1994): 63–70.

79. L. Friedman et al. "A Unique Approach to Multi-State Networking: BHSL," *Special Libraries* 85, no. 3 (Summer 1994): 183–194.

80. Sandra Salazar Sternfield, "Cost, Convenience, Quick Access to Define Future of Document Delivery," *Action for Libraries* 20, no. 7 (July 1994): 1–2.

81. Mary Jackson, "Integrating ILL with Document Delivery: Five Models," *Wilson Library Bulletin* 68, no. 1 (September 1993): 76–78.

82. Gretchen Whitney and Stuart Glogoff, "Automation for the Nineties: A Review Article," *Library Quarterly* 64, no. 3 (1994): 319–331.

83. Gordon Flagg, "*American Libraries* Washington Wire," *American Libraries* 26, no. 1 (January 1995): 8.

84. Leonard Kniffel, "Post Office Says Libraries Will Be 'Citizen Kiosk' Sites," *American Libraries* 25, no. 11 (December 1994): 974.

85. Gordon Flagg, "American Libraries Washington Wire," *American Libraries* 25, no. 11 (December 1994): 976.

86. Dennis Reynolds, "Libraries and the NII Highlighted in Commerce Department Report," *¿Qué Pasa?* 15, no. 4 (October 1994): 3.

87. "Document Delivery/Internet Event Has Strong 2d Year," *Library Journal* 119, no. 1 (January 1994): 33.

88. "Much Ado About Something," March 25, 1994. Flyer from OHIONET.

89. "Public Libraries and the Internet," *Library Journal* 119, no. 15 (September 15, 1994): 50.

90. Don E. Descy, "Let's Talk About the Internet," *Minnesota Media* (Fall 1993): 24–25, 34–36.

91. "ALA Gopher Debuts," *American Libraries* 25, no. 6 (June 1994): 588.

92. "The U.S. Department of Education has Established an 'On-line Library' of Reports, Statistics, and Legislation Related to Education," *Chronicle of Higher Education* 40, no. 39 (June 1, 1994): A18.

93. Julie Kelly, "Bio-Medical Library Gopher Opportunities," *Library Line* 5, no. 6 (November 1994): 1–2.

94. Jean Armour Polly, "Connecting to the Global Internet," *Library Journal* 119, no. 1 (January 1994): 38, 40.

95. David L. Wilson, "Threats to Internet Security," *Chronicle of Higher Education* 40, no. 30 (March 30, 1994): A22, A26.

96. David L. Wilson, "Carnegie Mellon to Test Computerized Billing System for Internet," *Chronicle of Higher Education* 40, no. 33 (April 20, 1994): A33.

97. Liz Bishoff, "Does Organizational Networking Have a Future in a Competitive Environment?" *American Libraries* 25, no. 11 (December 1994): 990–991.

98. B. G. Leonard, "The Metamorphosis of the Information Resources Budget," *Library Trends* 42, no. 3 (Winter 1994): 490–498.

99. Thomas J. Dorst, "Cooperative Collection Management at the Crossroads: Is There a New Social Paradigm for Resources Sharing?" *Illinois Libraries* 76, no. 2 (Spring 1994): 97–100.

100. Brian L. Hawkins, "Planning for the National Electronic Library," *EDUCOM Review* 29, no. 3 (May–June 1994): 19–29.

National Information Infrastructure

Toni Carbo Bearman

Dean, University of Pittsburgh School of Library and Information Science
Member, NII Task Force

David A. Wallace

Research Associate for Information Policy

A national information infrastructure (or "Information Superhighway") was proposed by Vice President Al Gore when he was a senator from Tennessee. Gore's father, when he was in the U.S. Senate, had envisioned a nation linked by a federal highway system for the transport of goods; the future vice president foresaw a nation linked by a convergence of technologies for the transfer of information and for improved communications among people. One of the first acts of the Clinton Gore administration was to call for the development of a national information infrastructure (NII) as part of a larger, global information infrastructure (GII). Commerce Secretary Ron Brown, under the oversight of Vice President Gore, was given responsibility for translating the vision into reality, determining the role of the U.S. government, and bringing together leaders and resources from the public and private sectors to develop a vision and strategies.

Defining NII

The national information infrastructure consists of many different components:

- **People** to create, publish, organize, preserve, manage, and use information; to develop applications and services; to design and implement policies and standards; and to educate and train individuals for all aspects of NII
- **Information content** in all formats and media, including text, still and moving images, numeric files, sound recordings, archival records, museum collections, and other evidence of all kinds
- **Hardware and other physical components**, including computers, monitors, input devices, printers, telephones, fax machines, compact disks, video and audio media, cameras, televisions, cable and other wires,

switches, satellites, microwave nets, optical fiber transmission lines, and other devices yet to be invented

- **Software and news groups** such as file transfer protocol (ftp), gophers, USENET News, Wide Area Information Servers (WAIS), the World-Wide Web (WWW) with Mosaic and HyperText Markup Language (HTML), and many others yet to be developed
- **Standards, codes, regulations, and other policies** to facilitate, interconnect, provide interoperability, ensure privacy, protect security, provide for appropriate compensation to owners of intellectual property, protect the integrity of data, promote ethical practices, and ensure true universal access and service

NII builds on many existing services and mechanisms, such as Internet, Free-Nets, satellite systems, cable services and networks, entertainment networks and services, satellite systems, and commercial services and networks (e.g., America Online, Prodigy, and shopping services).

Principles and Goals

The Clinton-Gore administration developed a series of nine principles and goals to guide the government's work on building the information infrastructure:

- Promote private sector investment
- Extend the "universal service" concept to ensure that information resources are available to all at affordable prices
- Act as a catalyst to promote technological innovation and new applications
- Promote seamless, interactive, user-driven operation of the infrastructure
- Ensure information security and network reliability
- Improve management of the radio frequency spectrum
- Protect intellectual property rights
- Coordinate with other levels of government and with other nations
- Provide access to government information and improve government procurement

The administration decided to concentrate on three strategies:

- Establishing an interagency Information Infrastructure Task Force
- Establishing a private sector Advisory Council on NII
- Strengthening and streamlining federal communications and information policy-making agencies, such as the National Telecommunications and Information Administration (NTIA), the Office of Information and Regulatory Affairs within the Office of Management and Budget (OMB), and the Federal Communications Commission (FCC)

Information Infrastructure Task Force

The Information Infrastructure Task Force (IITF) was charged with articulating and implementing the administration's NII vision, working with the private sector to develop comprehensive telecommunications and information policies that best meet the needs of both the agencies and the nation, and helping to build consensus on thorny policy issues to enable agencies to make and implement policy more quickly and effectively. IITF established three major committees with a series of working groups under each. Two of the committees, one on applications and technology and one on telecommunications, were located within the Department of Commerce, under the directors of the National Institute on Standards and Technology (NIST) and NTIA, respectively. The third committee, on information policy, fell under the Office of Management and Budget.

These committees have published several major documents in draft form for public comment, including: *Putting the Information Infrastructure to Work, The Information Infrastructure: Reaching Society's Goals,* and *Intellectual Property and the National Information Infrastructure* (also known as the "green paper"). They have also held a series of open hearings, received hundreds of comments on the drafts, and worked with numerous federal agencies, the Advisory Council, state and local governments, and a wide range of industry, professional, and consumer groups to elicit comments and opinions.

NII Advisory Council

Early in 1994, the administration appointed 37 members to the Advisory Council to represent different industries in the information and telecommunications field, representatives of state and local governments, and individuals from various public interests.

The Advisory Council first met on February 19, 1994, and is expected to conclude its work in December 1995. The council is charged with advising the Secretary of Commerce on a national strategy for promoting the development of information infrastructure and addressing issues including: 1) the appropriate roles of the private and public sectors; 2) developing a vision for both public and commercial applications; 3) the impact of current and proposed regulatory regimes on its evolution; 4) national strategies for maximizing both the benefits of NII and for interconnection and interoperability of networks, and for developing and demonstrating specific applications; 5) national security, emergency preparedness, system security, and network protection implications; 6) international concerns; 7) universal access and service; and 8) privacy, security, and copyright.

Working Groups and Outreach Activities

The Advisory Council has divided its activities into six major areas:

- Outreach to the public to identify the concerns and ideas of the American people
- A public awareness program to educate the general population as to what NII is and what it can do

- A global information infrastructure working group
- Three "Mega-Projects on Vision and Goals Driven by Specific Applications, Universal Access and Service, and Privacy, Security and Intellectual Property"

Mega-Project One concentrated its efforts in the first year on Lifelong Learning, including libraries and training, and Electronic Commerce. In 1995 it will complete these projects and also address Government Information and Services, Public Safety, and Health Care. For each application area, the Mega-Project is identifying its vision for the national infrastructure, developing a series of principles, describing key issues to be addressed (including the national interests to be served, public and private sector concerns, and international implications), describing "best practices," and recommending specific actions for the government and guideposts to measure implementation of the strategies.

Mega-Project Two has focused on Universal Access and Service. It has developed a set of principles on these and has also compiled an "environmental scan," illuminating where things currently stand on a host of issues connected with universal access and service.

Mega-Project Three has concentrated on Intellectual Property and Privacy and Security. Aside from developing principles in these areas, Mega-Project Three has also taken primary responsibility for drafting the Advisory Council's response to the "green paper," as well as cosponsoring public meetings on the security issues associated with finance and insurance, and education and health.

In other work, the Advisory Council has submitted letters to Secretary Brown assessing the administration's NII activities and provided recommendations on global infrastructure issues to be addressed by the U.S. delegation to the Group of 7 Conference in Brussels, Belgium. The Advisory Council also developed a draft of its first official report to Secretary Brown, highlighting the fundamental principles developed by the Advisory Council. The Advisory Council will submit its final report to Secretary Brown at its last official meeting on December 13, 1995, in Washington, D.C.

As its work winds down over the upcoming year, the Advisory Council will address challenges for implementing the national infrastructure, such as identifying the public's needs, articulating a clear vision, determining what already exists, identifying successful projects, identifying roles of the public and private sectors, building new partnerships, determining who pays, strengthening human resources, and defining and teaching new mediacy skills. The Advisory Council will also explore fundamental challenges that must be tackled, such as focusing on societal interests, creating and maintaining an ethical environment, and distinguishing among value, cost, and price.

Advisory Council Members

Members of the NII Advisory Council are: Morton Bahr (President, Communications Workers of America, AFL-CIO), Toni Carbo Bearman (Dean and Professor, University of Pittsburgh School of Library and Information Science), Marilyn Bergman (President, American Society of Composers), Bonnie Bracey (Teacher, Ashlawn Elementary School), John F. Cooke (Executive Vice President, Corporate Affairs,

Walt Disney Co.), Esther Dyson (EDventure Holdings Inc.), William C. Ferguson (Chairman and CEO, NYNEX Corporation), Craig Fields (Chairman and CEO, Microelectronics and Computer Technology Corporation), R. Jack Fishman (President, Lakeway Publishers Inc. and Editor/Publisher, *Citizen-Tribune*), Lynn Forester (President and CEO, FirstMark Holdings Inc.), Carol Fukunaga (Hawaii State Senator), Jack Golodner (President, Department for Professional Employees, AFL-CIO), Eduardo L. Gomez (President and General Manager, KABQ Radio), Haynes G. Griffin (President, Vanguard Cellular Systems Inc.), LaDonna Harris (President and Founder, Americans for Indian Opportunity), George Heilmeier (President and CEO, Bellcore), Susan Herman (General Manager, Los Angeles Department of Telecommunications), James Houghton (Chairman and CEO, Corning Incorporated), Stanley S. Hubbard (Chairman and CEO, Hubbard Broadcasting), Robert Johnson (President, Black Entertainment Television), Robert E. Kahn (President, Corporation for National Research Initiatives), Deborah Kaplan (Vice President, World Institute on Disability), Mitchell Kapor (Chairman of the Board, Electronic Frontier Foundation Inc.), Delano Lewis (President and CEO, National Public Radio), Alex J. Mandl (Executive Vice President, AT&T, and CEO, Communications Services Group), Ed McCracken (Chairman and CEO, Silicon Graphics), Nathan Myhrvold (Senior Vice President, Advanced Technology, Microsoft Corporation), N. M. (Mac) Norton Jr. (Attorney at Law, Wright, Lindsey & Jennings), Vance K. Opperman (President, West Publishing Company), Jane Smith Patterson (Adviser to the Governor for Policy, Budget & Technology, State of North Carolina), Frances W. Preston (President and CEO, Broadcast Music Inc.), Bert C. Roberts Jr. (Chairman and CEO, MCI Communications Corporation), John Sculley (CEO, Sculley Communications Inc.), Joan Smith (Chairman, Oregon Public Utility Commission), Al Teller (Executive Vice President, MCA Incorporated, and Chairman, MCA Music Entertainment Group), Laurence Tisch (President and CEO, CBS Incorporated) and Jack Valenti (CEO and President, Motion Picture Association of America).

Electronic Access

Electronic access to information about the Advisory Council and about NII in general is available by connecting to the following:

Information Infrastructure Task Force (IITF) World-Wide Web URL **gopher://
iitf.doc.gov/**

IITF Gopher Server: gopher, telnet (login=gopher), or anonymous ftp to **iitf.doc.gov**

IITF Bulletin Board: Dial by modem to 202-501-1920. Modem communication parameters should be set at no parity, 8 data bits, and one stop (N,8,1). Modem speeds up to 14,400 baud are supported.

Fedworld: Telnet to **fedworld.doc.gov** or dial by modem to 703-321-8020.

Quality Assurance in the Library and Information Professions

Prudence W. Dalrymple, Ph.D.

Director, Office for Accreditation
American Library Association

Society establishes a system of checks and balances to ensure that the goods and services provided to its citizens are of sufficient quality and integrity to protect the welfare of the public. It may also work to assure access to goods and services and to ensure that entry into a profession is not restricted. Quality assurance systems can take many forms, but one of the oldest and most respected in the United States is peer review or self-regulation, referred to here as credentialing. In education and the professions, accreditation and certification provide an overall system of credentialing and regulation that serves multiple constituents by attesting that an institution or individual practitioner has met standards agreed upon in the designated field. The overall process of credentialing addresses both individuals and institutions; it may be mandatory or voluntary. Credentialing may focus on basic eligibility to practice, on maintaining or updating knowledge and skills, or on professional development.

The purpose of this special report is to provide an overview of issues of credentialing in the field of library and information studies (LIS), with the aim of enabling the reader to analyze and understand current questions of quality assurance, professional stature, and public accountability for the library and information professions.

Credentialing: Accreditation and Certification

The term credentialing refers to the process of self-regulation in which interests in professions, businesses, or other fields of endeavor band together to exercise certain controls for the betterment of society at large.[1] When credentialing focuses on institutions, it is known as accreditation; when credentialing addresses the individual practitioner, it is called certification. In the field of library and information studies, accreditation of educational programs to prepare librarians for entry-level employment has been administered by the American Library Association (ALA) since 1924; graduation from an ALA-accredited program is a nearly universal requirement for employment in a library. Certification, on the other hand, addresses ability to practice and may require examinations or continuing education. Although it is widespread among many professions, it is not a typical feature of the library and information professions in the United States. The Medical Library Association's credentialing program, in existence since the late 1970s, is a notable exception.

Credentialing Programs

Credentialing programs are usually carried out by agencies in the private sector and are voluntary. Licensure, on the other hand, is implemented by governmental agencies, usually at the state level, and is a requirement for practice. While some states require licensure or certification for librarians, it is by no means universal and varies by type of library.

Because credentialing programs require an individual or institution to meet a threshold level of competence or quality, credentialing programs are vulnerable to charges of being restrictive or discriminatory. While their intent is clearly to foster improvement as well as to attest to the ability to meet minimal standards, both certification and accreditation have been accused of stifling innovation, rewarding mediocrity, and discouraging a pluralistic approach to education. In order to reduce the abuse of power among credentialing agencies, both private and governmental processes have been established to promulgate standards of good practice and to sanction agencies that are not in compliance. The structures for this oversight and regulation function are being reorganized and are the subject of a section of this report.

The system of quality assurance in higher education has evolved so that it now consists of these components: standards, self-study, a site visit, a public decision, and ongoing monitoring. Accreditation has always been voluntary and self-regulating, private and non-governmental. Yet as the environment of higher education faces changing demographics, budgetary pressures, new technology, and political pressure, the process and structures of accreditation are evolving.

Certification Programs

Certification programs are frequently combined with licensing procedures that enable an individual to practice his or her profession. Certification is conducted by a the private sector through a certification board. Increasingly, these boards find it advisable to separate themselves from a parent professional association to minimize concerns over restraint of trade (access to practice). Certification may be awarded for a specific period of time and may require re-examination, mandatory continuing education, or both. There is growing interest in utilizing a variety of ways to provide evidence of continued professional development such as portfolio review and self-assessment, in addition to the traditional CE courses. Such a broadened approach also reduces the opportunity for a "closed loop" between the educational provider and the certifying body.

Certification can also provide an alternate mode of entry into a profession when the traditional educational requirements have not been met. This can be accomplished through credential review, which can be provided through a separate organization and is a service offered to graduates of non-U.S. educational systems, graduates of unaccredited programs, or those seeking to determine whether they possess "equivalent" knowledge and skills.

Current Issues in Quality Assurance

The need for quality assurance in education and professional practice is as strong today as it was a century ago when the system of accreditation began. Indeed, the technological and social changes now under way have many parallels with those during the transition to the 20th century. Professions such as library and information studies (LIS) must address their responsibility to society by ensuring that those professionals charged with facilitating intellectual participation in today's changing world do indeed possess the qualifications to perform their jobs. Such an undertaking involves a number of issues affecting both individuals and institutions. Some of these issues are addressed in the sections that follow.

Public Interest and the Profession

Quality assurance is a joint enterprise whose stakeholders consist of educators, members of the profession, and the public. Accreditation and certification boards are composed of representatives from each of these sectors. Both educators and practitioners sit on accreditation and certification boards, serve as peer evaluators on accreditation teams, and contribute their leadership to the associations that financially support the accreditation and certification boards. Additional involvement comes from alumni, employers, and colleagues of the graduates. In the library and information professions, ALA is engaged in an ongoing discussion with other LIS associations to explore ways in which these "sister societies" can formally participate in the accreditation process. Finally, the public who interact with LIS professionals are under-represented stakeholders whose participation is increasingly important. Two of the 12 members of ALA's Committee on Accreditation, for example, serve in the public interest; some accreditation agencies now invite public representatives to serve on their evaluation teams.

In professional education, credentialing provides a forum through which various constituencies can join a discussion of the knowledge and skills needed for professional practice. This discussion can and should be a shared responsibility of all stakeholders. In 1994 the H. W. Wilson Foundation and ALA joined together with six LIS societies to sponsor an international teleconference aimed at increasing awareness and understanding of accreditation among both LIS professionals and the LIS educational community.

The question of public accountability in LIS raises additional challenges. While the public to whom the professional education program may be accountable is relatively easy to identify (students and employers, for example), demonstrating professional accountability to the public at large is a less tractable problem and one that has not been fully addressed profession-wide.

How shall LIS demonstrate its commitment to ongoing quality assurance for the professional services rendered? Certification for librarians and other information professionals has been proposed, explored, and rejected several times in recent decades. Yet it is an idea that refuses to disappear completely. And as technology transforms the information professions, the need to warrant currency of professional knowledge and skills after graduation from an accredited program becomes more apparent. As calls continue to be sounded for certification, as they most certainly will be, it will be worth watching to see whether they will gain broad support.

Accountability and Assessment

A central issue in quality assurance today is assessment. The term "assessment" connotes appraising whether or not an individual or institution meets the standards set for it. This strict definition of assessment is far more summative, suggesting a pass/fail approach that is less prevalent today. Permeating most accreditation and certification standards today is an emphasis on continuous planning and evaluation, setting objectives and assessing progress toward goals.

Assessment is sometimes equated with accountability, but to do so is to miss an important distinction. Assessment can be done internally and is indeed compatible with peer review, self-study, and an openness to diverse approaches in professional education. In today's environment, accountability frequently suggests adherence to requirements established by an external body and may mandate specific levels of achievement on particular tests. For example, the process undertaken by ALA's Committee on Accreditation does indeed involve a summative decision that determines compliance with standards; but it is clear that the standards themselves encourage innovation and diverse approaches to achievement. Certification programs like those of the Medical Library Association's Academy of Health Information Professionals also stress goal setting and monitoring progress toward achievement.

Accountability requires that an individual or institution deliver on a promise. Assessment can be useful in demonstrating accountability because it can show to what degree an individual or institution exceeds or falls short of meeting its publicly stated goals. Accreditation, by encouraging self-reflection and -assessment, should focus on outcomes and results and should embody values that are central to the academic enterprise: freedom of inquiry, objectivity in methods and deliberation, open access to information, respect for diversity of background.[2] These values thrive in an atmosphere of scholarly inquiry and collegiality.

ALA's current *Standards for Accreditation of Master's Programs in Library and Information Studies* place great emphasis on ongoing planning and evaluation that involves assessing the outcomes of educational programs. With funding provided by the U.S. Department of Education, the Office for Accreditation initiated a project to introduce outcomes assessment into LIS accreditation through seminars and the publication of a resource manual (see References at the end of this article). One aim of these materials is to provide an incentive for LIS programs to create a shared body of knowledge and experience that demonstrates how the process of setting educational objectives can result in observable outcomes. Despite the political appeal of being able to demonstrate educational accomplishment, critics question the use of outcomes assessment at the post-baccalaureate level, fearing that it restricts academic freedom and creates pressures to focus on easily achieved outcomes rather than more important and complex goals. Professional education, however, is thought by some to be more amenable to outcomes assessment because of its emphasis on acquiring an acknowledged set of knowledge and skills.

Confidentiality and Disclosure

Even a casual perusal of the media over the last several years underscores the perception that the public's trust in many of society's institutions has eroded. Higher education and the professions are no exception. Accreditation has addressed this concern in two ways: greater disclosure of accreditation action and greater public participation on accreditation boards. Believing that the public has a right to information concerning institutional quality, ALA's Committee on Accreditation changed its policies in 1993 to encourage more public disclosure about accredited status on the part of the accredited institutions and the committee itself. Beginning with the accreditation decisions made in 1995, the committee implemented its policy of making these decisions, and the document that describes the accredited status of the programs, a public document whose broad distribution is encouraged.

On the other hand, the committee recognizes that in order for a review process to retain its credibility and for the accreditation review to result in real institutional improvement, schools must be assured that they can engage in candid assessment of their strengths and weaknesses without fear of reprisal. One way that this can be accomplished is by ensuring that accreditation decisions are diagnostic, not prescriptive. That is, both the external review panel and the Committee on Accreditation must refrain from dictating to the school how it should conduct its educational program, and must recognize a diversity of educational approaches. The ability to analyze and evaluate educational performance is a skill not easily acquired, and recruiting, selecting, and appointing individuals from education, the profession, and the public to perform these tasks is daunting. Furthermore, striking a balance between the competing agendas of public disclosure and confidentiality is an ongoing question requiring thoughtful deliberation and continual re-examination.

While the LIS professions have had little experience with individual certification, the problem of public censure of professionals such as attorneys and physicians illustrates that similar tensions exist for individual credentialing.

Peer Review and Credibility

The accreditation procedures currently practiced by ALA's committee differ from those in the past by encouraging the external review panel to provide the school with collegial advice and counsel aimed at improvement. This "formative" or "developmental" aspect of accreditation is best undertaken in an atmosphere of mutual trust among peers. The school has, after all, invested time, money, and effort in preparing itself for an intensive review aimed not only at meeting standards but also at institutional improvement. In most well-established professions such as LIS, the number of programs seeking accreditation for the first time is small; thus, the ongoing monitoring and developmental functions of accreditation take on more importance, and the recent revisions in ALA's accreditation process reflect that emphasis.

Despite this emphasis on collegiality, accreditation's commitment to peer review can contribute to the perception that it is an "old boys' (or old girls') club" where educators from a relatively small population review one another, with little motivation to question the status quo. One way to address this perception is through involving reviewers from outside academe such as practitioners and the public. Indeed, both accreditation boards such as the Committee on Accreditation and the external review panels themselves are composed of individuals selected from academia, from the profession, and, in the case of ALA's committee, from the public at large.

Academics, however, may question whether this practice strays too far from true "peer review" while those outside academia may value accountability over peer review and collegiality. And of course, human nature being what it is, determining who is a peer of whom can be a delicate negotiation.

A process in which value is added through self-reflection as well as peer review and consultation is so central to accreditation that it is unlikely to disappear any time soon, but striking a balance among all interested parties is a challenge not only for individual accreditation agencies, but also for society as it examines the future role of accrediting agencies themselves.

Regulating Accrediting Bodies

A similar dilemma is reflected in current discussions about regulating accrediting bodies. Agencies administering accreditation programs typically share common concerns, conduct research, provide professional development, and speak to policy issues in accreditation. Since 1938 a number of organizations have served this purpose, most recently the Council on Postsecondary Accreditation (COPA). These accreditation organizations also developed a system of peer review and self-regulation, known as recognition. COPA, for example, established standards of good practice for accreditors intended to maintain and improve accrediting practices, to respect institutional autonomy, to ensure that accreditation of a particular field met a societal need, and to protect the public interest. When COPA dissolved in 1993, several organizations were created to assume its functions. One of these groups, the National Policy Board, is working to design a new umbrella organization. The details and composition of this structure were yet to be determined as this article went to press, but many of the issues under discussion are the same as those that affect the accreditation process and, indeed, are characteristic of credentialing in general.

Certification processes are also subject to review by oversight agencies, of which there are several with different constituencies, jurisdictions, and missions. Because librarians and information professionals are not now involved in certification, a detailed discussion of these oversight agencies is not included here.

Technological and Social Change

Evidence of the impact of technological change on the library and information professions is pervasive. Many graduate programs are engaged in curriculum reform, some with substantial grant support. The impact that these curricula will have on the other accredited LIS programs, and indeed on LIS accreditation and the *Standards for Accreditation* themselves, could be profound. Given the present pace of technological and social change, it seems unlikely that another 20 years will pass before the *Standards* will be revised; indeed, the Committee on Accreditation has made a commitment to review the *Standards* on a regular basis. Such a commitment is not only good accrediting practice, it is also necessary to ensure that accredited programs educate their students to practice in a rapidly changing world.

Monitoring how those graduates continue to perform over the course of their careers is the function of an individual credentialing process. While professional associations and graduate programs alike provide opportunities for the LIS professional to keep abreast of developments in digital information management, telecommunications, and other topics, there is currently little to distinguish those

LIS professionals who have achieved and maintain expertise in these areas from those who do not possess a minimum level of skill. Nor is this lack of incentive for professional development confined to technological skill. Few sectors of librarianship provide incentive or reward for systematic continuing education or certification of professional competency. When accreditation and certification are partnered, they can create a system of quality assurance that serves not only employers of new graduates but also members of the public. Together, accreditation of the first professional degree and certification of ongoing professional competence could provide a system of credentialing that assures that the quality of service is not compromised due to rapid and uneven adoption of technological and social change.

Governmental Regulation and Globalization

The private, voluntary system of credentialing and self-regulation known as accreditation and certification has, until recently, been unique in the world. Most educational systems in other nations are controlled by ministries of education; the U.S. system of accreditation and regulation by organizations in the private sector has existed for nearly a century. With the expansion of higher education following World War II and the increased availability of federal student aid funds, however, the federal government sought a way to ensure that student loan funds were being disbursed to bona fide educational institutions that could warrant that their graduates had indeed received the education and training that they purchased. Accreditation provided such a warrant, and so the secretary of education established a list of agencies whose accreditation could be consulted as a criterion when dispensing student loan funds. Starting in 1952 the secretary of education began to recognize accrediting agencies, including ALA.

With the reauthorization of the Higher Education Act in 1992, however, a number of regulations were changed to restrict the scope of the secretary's recognition powers to agencies whose accreditation was necessary to establish eligibility for student loan funds. Since ALA's *Standards* require U.S. programs to be located in regionally accredited institutions, ALA falls outside the secretary's scope of authority under the new regulations.

Restricting the federal government's direct oversight of accreditation activities has not eliminated the role of governmental interest in quality assurance activities in the professions, however. Both the General Agreement on Tariffs and Trade and the North American Free Trade Agreement address the globalization of education and the mobility of professionals both to and from the United States.

Assuring the quality of services delivered by professionals while avoiding undue restrictions on trade is a topic of increasing importance. At recent meetings sponsored by the Center for Quality Assurance in International Education, of which ALA is a member, discussions have focused on mechanisms for reciprocity and for assisting other nations to establish quality assurance models. As globalization of LIS education progresses through distance learning, the importance of addressing such issues will become even clearer.

Summary

During the past three years, the quality assurance process for higher education and the professions has being undergoing a profound transformation. Fundamental values such as accountability, assessment, peer review, confidentiality, regulation, and recognition have been challenged due to a changing climate of opinion and technological transformation. Accrediting agencies such as ALA's Committee on Accreditation have coped with these challenges by themselves engaging in reflective self-study, planning, evaluation, and change, and by participating in organizations committed to peer review, standards of good practice, and ongoing monitoring. In order to maintain and improve its ability to provide expertise to those seeking information and resources, the LIS professions must continue to explore ways to demonstrate that commitment through responsive and viable credentialing programs that strengthen the profession while serving the public interest.

Notes

1. Jacobs, Jerald A. *Certification and Accreditation Law Handbook.* Washington, D.C.: American Society of Association Executives, 1992, p. 1.
2. Ewell, Peter T. "A Matter of Integrity: Accountability and the Future of Self-Regulation." *Change* 26:6 (November/December 1994): 24–29.

References

Accreditation under the 1992 Standards for Accreditation of Master's Programs in Library and Information Studies: An Overview. Chicago, IL: American Library Association, 1994. Committee on Accreditation, 1994.

Standards for Accreditation of Master's Programs in Library and Information Studies. Chicago, IL: American Library Association, 1992.

Publications describing the accreditation policies and procedures are available from the Office for Accreditation, American Library Association, 50 E. Huron St., Chicago, IL 60611.

International Reports

International Federation of Library Associations and Institutions

Nancy D. Anderson

Mathematics Librarian and Professor of Library Administration
University of Illinois at Urbana–Champaign

Founded in 1927, the International Federation of Library Associations and Institutions (IFLA) has moved from a primarily European-focused organization to one that is truly international. Its membership is made up of 127 associations, 941 institutions, 214 personal affiliates, and 29 sponsors. While IFLA found itself much more financially sound in 1994, it continued to focus on fiscal and membership concerns. The annual conference, in Havana, Cuba, was attended by nearly 1,500 delegates from 80 countries.

Organization

IFLA consists of 32 sections (or standing committees) and 14 roundtables that funnel information to eight divisions. Section and roundtable members are elected by association and institutional members, and every two years—in odd-numbered years—section members elect section officers who, in turn, elect division officers. Division chairpersons form the Professional Board, which oversees the program activities of the organization. The Executive Board—which is responsible for general policy, management, finance, and external communications—is also elected every two years.

Underlying the activities of the sections are IFLA's five core programs: Universal Availability of Publications (UAP), Universal Bibliographic Control International MARC (UBCIM), Universal Dataflow and Telecommunications (UDT), Preservation and Conservation (PAC), and Advancement of Librarianship in the Third World (ALP). The Professional Board is considering a recommendation to create a sixth core program: the Promotion of Literacy and Reading Through Libraries.

To inform divisions, sections, and roundtables of one another's activities, IFLA prepares a Medium-Term Program (MTP) every six years. Once a year the standing committees of the sections, the roundtable executive committees, and the coordinating boards of the divisions are asked to update their work plans and approve them at the IFLA annual conference. This information is then compiled, published, and distributed to IFLA officers and other interested individuals. In this way, all IFLA professional groups are kept up to date on one another's work and can note opportunities for cooperative action.

The UDT Core Program, working with the staff at SilverPlatter, has established the IFLA-L listserv. IFLA members are already finding it extremely useful for posting plans on upcoming conference workshops and open sessions. Also, IFLA documents have been compiled and are currently available via anonymous ftp (file transfer protocol) from SilverPlatter's file server.

Annual Conference

The annual IFLA conference is the highlight of the association's activities. The 1994 (60th) general conference was held in Havana August 21–27 with the theme "Libraries and Social Development." The first IFLA conference in Latin America, it drew 1,479 delegates from 80 nations. More than 100 of these were librarians from the United States, the second-largest delegation after Cuba—and this was despite the uncertainties involved in making travel arrangements (most Americans are prevented from general contact with Cuba by the U.S. Treasury Department's "trading with the enemy" regulations).

Upon arrival, delegates were whisked to their generally well-maintained tourist hotels. Many were able to watch from their windows as desperate Cubans left their country on rafts. Delegates were further saddened to realize that their Cuban colleagues, already enduring severe rationing of consumer goods, agreed to further cuts in food and fuel so that no one at the conference would suffer inconvenience. In response to the warmth and courtesy of their hosts, most American delegates signed a statement calling for the "normalization" of relations between the United States and Cuba and an end to the trade embargo. Prospects appear good for continuing the dialogue begun in Havana between American and Cuban librarians.

In contrast to the human tragedy being played out outside the conference, delegates enjoyed meeting colleagues in some 56 workshops, 186 contributed-paper sessions, and 37 poster sessions. The Palacio de las Convenciones offered the best facilities of any IFLA conference yet. Delegates were touched by the beautiful keynote address of Cuban poet Cintio Vitier. The Guest Lecture Series addressed the role of national libraries in the social and economic evolution of Latin American societies. A very popular workshop, Telecommunication Options for the '90s, developed themes on Internet that had interested delegates at the Barcelona conference a year earlier. Visits to libraries were scheduled daily, and receptions were held each evening. A complete listing of the conference papers is available from IFLA headquarters, and copies of the papers are available from the regional clearinghouses.

Each IFLA conference produces a number of resolutions, and the 60th annual conference was no exception. The Pre-Session Seminar "Libraries for Literacy in Geographically and Socially Isolated Communities," held in Matanzas, August 15–19, recommended that IFLA give priority to the establishment of a program to promote literacy. The Roundtable for the Management of Library Associations urged IFLA to support actions related to its signing in October 1994 of the Tokyo Resolution of the International Federation for Information and Documentation

(FID). The Roundtable on Mobile Libraries resolved that IFLA provide roundtables with copies of their own publications on a sale-or-return basis. The Section on Government Information and Official Publications presented a resolution on UNESCO depository libraries, expressing concern that UNESCO has recently reduced the number of depository libraries to one per country and asking that the organization provide up to 10 depositories in the largest countries, based on demographic and geographic needs.

1995 Conference

IFLA's sections and roundtables are planning a full program for the 1995 Council and General Conference in Istanbul, Turkey, August 17–26. Its theme is "Libraries of the Future." Several sections are planning programs on aspects of electronic publishing; council elections will be held. An official Pre-Session Seminar, Influencing the Decision Makers, will be held in Ankara August 16–19.

Future Conferences

Considering the current commitments and focusing on the growth in interest in the conference, IFLA's Executive Board, in its April 1994 meeting, firmly committed itself to offering a yearly conference. Conferences are planned for Beijing in 1996, Copenhagen in 1997, Amsterdam in 1998, Bangkok in 1999, and Edinburgh (celebrating IFLA's 75th anniversary) in 2002. The Executive Board further decided to keep the well-established August meeting time. Changes in the length and character of the opening session were made, making the UNESCO contribution more issue oriented and inviting addresses from the International Council on Archives, International Publishers Association, and FID only in Council years.

Other Activities

In April 1993 the Professional Board, Core Program directors, and senior IFLA staff held a retreat in The Hague, Netherlands, called IFLA Trends. The topic of the retreat was "Developing a Strategic View of IFLA's Program Objectives." Building on the results achieved in 1993, Trends 2 was held in April 1994 to develop an action plan and timetable for the important issues affecting the future development of IFLA, focusing on the role of the Professional Board in determining program priorities and strategies. Some of the proposed actions coming from Trends 2 discussions include strengthening communication between IFLA and national association members, restructuring financial allotments of sections and roundtables to favor project funding, defining responsibilities of standing committee members, and establishing criteria for review of IFLA groups.

IFLA groups hold a lively series of meetings throughout the year. Those held since mid-1993 include the following. Universal Bibliographic Control—The Second International Seminar, organized by IFLA and the National Library of Romania, was held in Bucharest on August 11–14, 1993. The IFLA Section of

Libraries for the Blind held an "Expert Meeting" in Barcelona, Spain, August 16–19, 1993. IFLA was one of several cosponsors of the Central European Conference and Exhibition for Academic Libraries and Informatics held in Vilnius, Lithuania, September 27–29, 1993. The IFLA Seminar "Preservation of Maps and Other Spatial Information" was organized in Moscow, September 26–October 1, 1993, by the IFLA Section of Geography and Map Libraries and the IFLA Section on Conservation. The UBCIM Core Program, in collaboration with the Regional Office for Africa, organized a UBC/UNIMARC workshop for francophone Africans in Dakar, Senegal, November 22–26, 1993. IFLA's UAP Core Program was among those cosponsoring the First International Conference on Grey Literature held in Amsterdam, Netherlands, December 13–15, 1993. (Grey literature is semi-published material, such as internal documents, theses, and technical reports, which are not formerly published or available commercially and are consequently difficult to trace bibliographically.)

The ALP Program sponsored a Workshop to Identify and Assess Need in Indochina and Formulate Project Proposals, June 2–4, 1994. The Division of Bibliographic Control and the IFLA UBCIM Program held a UBCIM/UNIMAR Seminar at the Lietuvos Nacionaline Martyno Mazvydo Biblioteka (National Library of Lithuania) in Vilnius, June 2–4, 1994.

Awards and Grants

In 1994 IFLA again awarded the Gustav Hoffmann Study Grant, the successor award to its Martinus Nijhoff Study Grant; it is offered by K. G. Saur. It allows a librarian in a country where librarianship is a newly developing profession to study an issue in one or more countries in Western Europe. The winner was Catherine Muyawala, librarian of Small Industries Development Organization in Lusaka, Zambia, to study constraints on the flow of information to small and medium-scale industries.

Juries for the Guust van Wesemael Literacy Prize, the Hans-Peter Geh Study Grant, and the Dr. Shawky Salem Training Grant had not made a decision at the time of this writing.

Recent Publications

Each year, IFLA sections and core programs offer a growing number of useful professional publications. During the past year, the following were published:

- *The Advancement of Librarianship: A Workshop to Identify and Assess Needs in South-East Asia and to Formulate Proposals*, ed. by Pensri Guaysuwan for the IFLA ALP Program and IFLA Regional Standing Committee for Asia and Oceania. Bangkok, Thailand: Thammasat University Press.
- *Automated Systems for Access to Multilingual and Multiscript Library Materials: Proceedings of the Second IFLA Satellite Meeting, Madrid, August 18–19, 1993*, ed. by Sally H. McCallum and Monica Ertel for the Section on Library Services to Multicultural Populations and the Section

on Cataloging. Munich, Germany: K. G. Saur (IFLA Publications, No. 70). ISBN 3-598-21797-8.

- *Cataloging of the Hand Press: A Comparative and Analytical Study of Cataloging Rules and Formats Employed in Europe*, prepared by Henry L. Snyder and Heidi L. Hutchinson. Munich, Germany: K. G. Saur (IFLA/Saur Professional Library Series, No. 1). ISBN 3-598-23400-7.

- *Communications, Content Creation, and Dissemination of Information: Selected Internet Projects*. Ottawa, Canada: IFLA UDT Program Office (UDT Series on Data Communication Technologies and Standards for Libraries, No. 7).

- *Directory of Government Documents Specialists*, compiled by Siegfried Detemple for the Section on Government Information and Official Publications. Berlin, Germany: Staatsbibliothek zu Berlin.

- *Directory of Special Collections in Western Europe*, ed. by Alison Gallico for the IFLA Office for International Lending. London, UK: Bowker-Saur.

- *Document Supply in Eastern Europe*. Papers from a workshop held in conjunction with the Third International Interlending and Document Supply Conference. Ed. by Graham Cornish and Sara Gould. Boston Spa, Wetherby, England: IFLA Office for UAP. ISBN 0-7123-2109-8.

- *Global Perspectives on Preservation Education*, ed. by Michele Valerie Cloonan under the auspices of the PAC Core Program. Munich, Germany: K. G. Saur (IFLA Publications, No. 69). ISBN 3-598-21796-X.

- *Government Publications Collections in Libraries: Status, Problems and Recommendations for an Undervalued Resource*, Papers from an IFLA seminar held in London, August 12–14, 1987, ed. by Alfred Kagan for the Section on Government Information and Official Publications. Berlin, Germany: Staatsbibliothek zu Berlin.

- *Interlending and Document Supply for Developing Countries: Papers from the IFLA Pre-Session Seminar on Interlending and Document Supply, Paris, August 1989*, ed. by Graham P. Cornish and Sara Gould. Boston Spa, Wetherby, England: IFLA UAP Core Program.

- *Interlending and Document Supply: Proceedings of the Third International Conference Held in Budapest, March 1993*, ed. by Andrew J. Swires for the IFLA Core Program for the Universal Availability of Publications. Boston Spa, Wetherby, England: IFLA Offices for UAP and International Lending. ISBN 0-7123-2108-X.

- *Models for Open Systems Protocol Development: A Technical Report*, compiled and ed. by Liv Holm under the auspices of the Section on Information Technology. Ottawa, Canada: IFLA UDT Program Office (UDT Series on Data Communication Technologies and Standards for Libraries, No. 6).

- *Recommendations pour la construction et l'equipement de bibliobus*, trans. of Mobile Library Guidelines by Mireille Fayret and Remi Sagna and issued under the auspices of the Roundtable on Mobile Libraries. The

Hague, Netherlands: IFLA (IFLA Professional Reports, No. 40). ISBN 90-70916-50-90.

- *Report on the Project to Assess the Acquisitions Needs of University Libraries in Developing Countries*, by G. G. Allen and P. Katris under the auspices of the IFLA Section on University Libraries and Other General Research Libraries. Odense, Denmark: Odense University.

- *Status, Image and Reputation of Librarianship: A Report of Empirical Research Undertaken on Behalf of IFLA's Roundtable for the Management of Library Associations*, by Hans Prins and Wilco de Gier under the IFLA logo. The Hague, Netherlands: Nederlands Bibliotheek and Lectuur Centrum.

- *The Status, Reputation and Image of the Library and Information Profession: Proceedings of the IFLA Pre-Session Seminar, Delhi, 24–28 August 1992*, ed. by Russell Bowden and Donald Wijasuriya under the auspices of the IFLA Roundtable for the Management of Library Associations. Munich, Germany: K. G. Saur (IFLA Publications, No. 68). ISBN 3-598-21795-1.

- *Survival under Adverse Conditions: Proceedings of the African Library Science Journals Workshop.* Ed. by Michael Wise, Chair of the Roundtable of Editors of Library Journals. The Hague, Netherlands: IFLA (IFLA Professional Reports, No. 38). ISBN 90-70916-48-8.

- *UNIMARC and CDS/ISIS: Proceedings of the Workshops Held in Budapest, 21-22 June 1993 and Barcelona, 26 August 1993*, ed. by Marie-France Plassard and Marvin Holdt. Munich, Germany: K. G. Saur (UBCIM Publications, New Series, No. 13). ISBN 3-598-11210-6.

- *Workshop on Access to Third World Journals and Conference Proceedings.* Boston Spa, Wetherby, England: IFLA UAP Core Program. ISBN 0-7123-2091-1.

- *Young People and Reading: International Perspectives.* Papers presented at the 1991 Moscow Conference Workshop of the Section of Children's Libraries and the Roundtable on Research in Reading. Ed. by Adele M. Fasick. The Hague, Netherlands: IFLA (IFLA Professional Reports, No. 39). ISBN 90-70916-49-5.

Frankfurt Book Fair, 1994:
It Still Confounds the Naysayers

Herbert R. Lottmann

International Correspondent, *Publishers Weekly*

John F. Baker

Editorial Director, *Publishers Weekly*

For years, incredulous book traders have been predicting the inevitable demise of the leviathan of book fairs. Frankfurt, the feeling went, is too confusing and unfriendly to users—much too expensive as well. Regional and specialized fairs and technological advances that expedite negotiations (such as the fax) made all that discomfort and expense unnecessary.

Seemingly, the naysayers were wrong again, and they knew it, for they patently joined the crush at the 46th Frankfurt Book Fair (October 5–10), helping to break all records—6,332 individual exhibitors, 4,087 of them from outside Germany, and more than 100 participating nations spread over 1.4 million square feet of exhibition space. The U.S. contingent—containing some of the naysayers—was larger than ever (756 exhibiting logos), with nearly every prominent head of house visible on the floor.

All this in a business climate not conducive to optimism—but no longer gloomy. "No particular country is suffering particularly," observed Jonas Modig of Sweden's trade imprint Wahlström & Widstrand. "Markets are stable. This is a low-key fair, but that's the way it should be." Most visitors were prepared to say that this had been another "quiet" fair, before going on to enumerate results justifying and rewarding their presence. If big books were absent from some of the expected sources, they did arrive from unexpected places (like France, with memoirs of Brigitte Bardot, still more photographs of Claudia Schiffer, and a posthumous Jules Verne). The collective energies in action at the mobbed Literary Agents Center suggested that if the figures could be added up (obviously, they can't be), the 1994 Frankfurt fair would turn out to have been among the best in decades. Of course, a whole new fair had been appended to the print book fair, ostensibly centered in a separate exhibition hall for electronic books, although much of the action took place on and among the stands of traditional book publishers.

Taking the Temperature

Everybody spent a day or so taking each other's temperature. "The Germans are embarrassed," said Munich agent Michael Meller, "because they don't have any problems. The recession was too short to hurt publishers, and now they're having their best year ever."

Thanks to the strong yen and the irresistibility of translated books, Japanese publishers were buying as many rights as before, and Tokyo agent Tom Mori of Tuttle-Mori was ready with figures showing that an American book right for his

Note: Adapted from *Publishers Weekly*, October 24, 1994.

country could sell better in Japan than at home. Milan agent Susanna Zevi thought the Italian scene "not brilliant" for rights, and for the moment Italian originals (like the Pope's) are driving the market. She found a reluctance to bid on proposals, a hankering after backlist potential.

For a view of how American publishing is perceived from the outside, there can't be a better source than the New York–based scouts who report to the rest of the world on a regular basis. Todd Siegal of Franklin & Siegal covers U.S. production for many foreign trade leaders in their respective countries. Siegal's clients may be confused by the rapid changes in U.S. publishing personnel, but they are excited by the emergence of new imprints for quality fiction and nonfiction. On the other hand, foreign readers are tired of stereotyped thrillers ("and serial killers") that call for high advances not justified by quality. Give them an old-fashioned saga anytime, or a good woman's read.

Siegal's foreign contingent was particularly interested in recent nonfiction breakthroughs (such as Bantam's *Life-giver*, about melatonin, sold on proposal to Germany for $100,000, and *Mindhunter*, for which prime publisher S&S paid $1.1 million—also on proposal). Franklin & Siegal clients go for American books in science and biography, but also for novelizations and other tie-ins.

Bustle on the British Floor

The British floor in Hall 4 was notably more bustling than the American ground floor below it, and publishers like Penguin, HarperCollins, and Warner—who took advantage of their international outreach to locate there—enjoyed much heavier traffic. Bill Strachan of Henry Holt was one of many visiting Americans who spent much of his time up there. "They have more rights to sell than we do, they bring larger contingents than us, and they seem to have a greater interest in selling," he reported.

Penguin's Peter Mayer found this a "strange" fair, one at which he spent much of the time on the phone or at the fax machine rather than, as usual, looking at books and meeting editors. He welcomed the electronic revolution as "an addition rather than a subtraction," but he sees it, for people at his level in publishing, as essentially "blessing the projects of others. The higher up you are, the harder you have to work at keeping the basic business going, which is books." He had just come from a meeting of world publishers of Microsoft founder Bill Gates's book about the future. The book has been rescheduled for spring, Mayer said, and he expects a first U.S. printing to run about 500,000.

Morgan Entrekin at Grove Atlantic reported a less pressured fair than in past years, "probably because we're in a better financial situation." He found much foreign interest in *Bongwater*, which he described as a "grunge" novel by Michael Homburg, already sold in Australia and Italy, and with an auction for German rights upcoming. Suzanne Allen, rights director at Newmarket Press, was taking advantage of foreign interest in movie tie-ins with a special catalog listing some of the firm's upcoming tie-ins, including *Little Women*, *Mary Shelley's Frankenstein*, *Camilla*, *Only You*, and *First Knight*.

Will Schwalbe, making his first fair appearance as William Morrow's new editorial director, found he was selling rather than buying. With new bestsellers in Sidney Sheldon and Richard Bach, a hit British novel, *Green River Rising*, and a new Deborah Tannen on the way, he felt his house was on much stronger ground than in some years. He also rejoiced in the international success of new Asian fiction, a particular passion of his: "It's great to see everyone catching up, especially with Chinese work." His was one of several suggestions that publishers overseas were hungry for more than conventional works. Michael Ayrton and Ira Silverberg at Serpent's Tail, who have a previously unpublished William Burroughs novel, had interested no fewer than 12 foreign publishers. "I sense a boredom with middlebrow writing, to the point that many hitherto conservative publishers are taking an interest in more daring work," explained Silverberg. At the New Press, André Schiffrin found he was selling a lot of backlist titles. "Publishers are consolidating their lists, looking for material they feel they must have. There's been so much of a general retreat in recent years that now they seem to be interested in acting like publishers again." He also found an interest in new formats. "Many can't afford the research and development costs for CD-ROM, but they want something out of the ordinary"—like his press's Portfolio art series, which he is now extending to cover European art museums.

Interest in New Formats

New formats were also booming at Hyperion, where Bob Miller has world rights in the interactive game Myst, which, he says, has sold 750,000 copies worldwide, only one-third of them in the United States. In a co-venture with Andrews & McMeel, he is also doing a "magic eye" Disney book in which licensed Disney characters will be placed against the exciting three-dimensional backgrounds that are currently the rage.

Frankfurt is also the scene for a handful of stellar author appearances, and the most spectacularly orchestrated this year was that of General Colin Powell, brought over by Random House to recruit foreign publishers for his untitled memoir (due in autumn 1995)—and without a written proposal.

Although preceded by a reputation as "camera shy," the former chief of staff lent himself to an exhausting series of meetings with potential publishers, under the watchful eyes of Random's Alberto Vitale, Harold Evans, and Wanda Chappell, vice president and director of subsidiary rights. Powell first met foreign publishers at a party, then a more select group at a dinner; the next day, in a Random booth, he received interested publishers individually at 15-minute intervals.

Then there were the unexpected books—of the kind Abrams's Paul Gottlieb discovered when he was invited to Russia to preview 70 masterpiece paintings seized by the Red Army from German collections and not seen since; some were among the best work of the likes of Cézanne, Monet, and Van Gogh. On the eve of the fair, the *New York Times* front-paged the finding, the story was faxed to Gottlieb, and copublishing rights became just about the hottest ticket in town. Another unexpected book was the stunningly illustrated *Diary of Frida Kahlo*—Diego Rivera's wife and Trotsky's lover—for which Gottlieb won a New York auction and was busily auctioning in turn.

Obviously, being upmarket didn't stop a publisher from making money. Hubert Nyssen of France's small and provincial Actes Sud was learning that, with the unexpurgated diaries of Russian dancer Vaslav Nijinksy (which Farrar, Straus & Giroux preempted for the United States). New York agent Roslyn Targ came to Frankfurt with a manuscript by Nazipo Maraire, a Zimbabwean author (now studying neurosurgery at Yale). Titled *Zenzele, A Letter for My Daughter*, it had been sold to U.S. Crown and the U.K.'s Weidenfeld & Nicolson (among others) just before the fair; at Frankfurt, deals were consummated with major houses in Germany, the Netherlands, Norway, Sweden, and Brazil.

The Multimedia Puzzler

The electronics hall was a bigger-than-ever deal, having doubled its exhibit space since the fair opened its doors to multimedia last year. It was difficult to figure out quite what was happening there, however. (The real multimedia creators—like Dorling Kindersley, Voyager, and Byron Preiss—chose to show in their national halls among the book publishers, where one was most likely to come upon projects ripe for plucking.) And if visitors were confused, so were some of the exhibitors. "We don't know why we came," the executive of a leading European group confessed. "We were told that the fair was going electronic, so we brought electronics." "We're still trying to figure out why we're here," another famous name admitted, though in his case it turned out to be worthwhile, for he was discussing program content with potential licensees from a number of countries.

So it seemed to make sense to tour the exhibits with the fair's marketing director, Sigrid Moritz, and Christian Spanik, the multimedia expert who helped put the show together. At the Rowohlt stand, multimedia manager Ralph Möllers figured that he was spending 10 percent of his time with foreign colleagues interested in licensing Rowohlt's CD-ROMs or house-produced adaptations, the rest with German booksellers.

Frankfurt kept the ball rolling with a five-day program of electronics seminars and workshops—in English for the international trade, in German to educate its own bookselling community.

Frankfurt is more a fair for promotion than order-taking, but the promotion can be fruitful. For German publishers, who sell year-round to their booksellers at strictly controlled terms, there are no "ABA specials" at Frankfurt. Concerning U.S. books, *PW*'s reporter caught up with the team from France's Brentano's, a large one, including company chair Maurice Darbelay and Anne Warter, in charge of Brentano's Nouveau Quartier Latin wholesale-retail operation for foreign-language books. "We come to Frankfurt mainly to renew contacts," Darbelay explained, "as well as to meet new publishers." With Brentano's buyer Susan Rosenberg, he was also scouting for fiction and general nonfiction—from the United States principally. "Whether or not the French want to admit it," says Rosenberg, "American culture is what they look for." That can mean sports and crafts as well as literature and music—the criterion being newness, and "new" means the United States.

New Players to Watch

PW came across a small new packaging operation that happens to be part of one of Italy's leading publishing groups, the $1.68 billion De Agostini group (which makes 70 percent of its sales outside Italy). Knowing that truly international publishing must begin with English, the group recruited Simon McMurtrie, 28, who earned his stripes as publisher of Reed Illustrated Books. He joined De Agostini just a year ago and now operates De Agostini Editions with a London-based team of nine. The first list of eight titles covers a broad range of subjects, from family problems to how-to and animals. McMurtrie will publish when possible with one or more of the group's own imprints and play the field after that. Joanna Everard is rights director out of London; another staffer, Erica Marcus, works out of New York with major trade houses.

Another New York venture discovered during Frankfurt week is Rowohlt U.S., an imprint of the parent company in Germany, to be run in America's publishing capital by Rowohlt's well-known publisher, Michael Naumann. The plan is to do a dozen books the first year, Rowohlt-type upscale writers, Americans among them, but also the Germans and Danes and Hungarians that Americans seldom translate. Naumann will get an office at Henry Holt (which, like Rowohlt, is a Holtzbrinck company). It seemed the first time in a long time that a European was going to the United States to publish.

Many guests at the traditional S. Fischer Verlag reception—held on the eve of the fair at its Frankfurt headquarters—went on to a 10 p.m. reception thrown by Arnulf Conradi, publisher at Fischer as recently as the 1993 Frankfurt fair, now launching his own publishing house. Conradi's Berlin Verlag, with offices in an old house in that city, will publish some of the authors he took with him and others in the Conradi-Fischer style (Margaret Atwood, Nadine Gordimer, and Richard Ford, Batya Gur and Sami Michael, Robert K. Massie and Richard Sennett).

The Germans had other news to bite on. There was a stir when Bertelsmann announced with pride that its paperback imprint Goldmann was now Germany's number one—a fact contested by Heyne, holder of that title, and whose publisher Hans-Peter Übleis could produce a survey giving his house—with its 600 paperbacks, 70 hardcovers annually— 16 percent of the total market, to Goldmann's 13 percent. The context is a strong book market for both hard- and softcover books and higher list prices the public seems to have accepted.

The Presence from the East

Clearly, Frankfurt's management had won its wager with the East. Visitors in the recent past may have seen the fair's Eastern European sector as an object of charity; this year, their displays, on the lower level of Hall 3, looked very much like the rest of the fair. There were 181 individual stands (including nine national collectives), 55 of which were subsidized to a greater or lesser degree, while 35 publishers were brought to the fair by Frankfurt's management. There was a round of panels during the three fair days reserved for trade professionals, the subjects including such burning issues as the competing Eastern fairs, the question of how rights are sold there, and the "near-criminal practices" in some of the new nations. Frankfurt was also administering an AAP-sponsored intern program for Eastern European publishing people working with U.S. firms, under the direction of Robert Baensch.

Frankfurt will continue to play godfather to the East, but to a lesser extent in future years. The East-West center itself is to be replaced by a North-South project (South meaning undeveloped); it's because, says Frankfurt's Barbel Becker, Eastern Europe is ready to enter the real world. This truth was confirmed by Lynn Franklin, who announced the opening of an agency in Prague to handle translation rights for American publishers and agents in Russia and Central Europe.

A Meeting Place

Bringing together as it does the makers and shakers of the book world, the Frankfurt fair is an obvious site for the assemblies and congresses of the principal organization in the field. Thus, the executive bodies and theme committees of the International Publishers Association (IPA) all convene during fair week. This year, IPA also mounted an electronic-publishing workshop, with case studies presented by leading content providers and software makers. At an October 6 press conference, IPA Vice President Philip Attenborough, deputy chair of Hodder Headline (U.K.), hailed the application for membership from the newly united Publishers Association of South Africa, representing "that country's reestablishment within the world publishing community." Sigmund Stromme of Norway's Cappelen, chair of IPA's Freedom to Publish Committee, denounced the unofficial death sentence against Bangladeshi writer Taslima Nasrin, the fatwa still in force against the life of Salman Rushdie, and the imprisonment of dissident publishers in Turkey. In a surprise appearance (accompanied by two bodyguards and German police), publisher William Nygaard of Norway's Aschehoug—Rushdie's Norwegian publisher and victim of a shooting just after last year's Frankfurt—made a strong case for renewed protests against Iran's death threat to Rushdie.

Once again, the Frankfurt fair and AAP cohosted a meeting of international-rights directors on the afternoon preceding the opening of the fair; this time, the focus was "The Emerging Markets of the Pacific Rim." Publisher Ernst Klett again sponsored an international meeting of educational publishers, which heard media consultant Stephan Götz warn that European educational publishers will have to join the technological revolution or see their share of the school market fall into the hands of U.S. publishers taking advantage of the faster development of electronic publishing in the United States. He estimated sales of CD-ROMs this year at 100 million units worldwide.

Even a fair-goer jaded by summit meetings is likely to be impressed by the annual gathering of STM, the International Group of Scientific, Technical, and Medical Publishers. This year's 26th general assembly brought together 270 executives from the high end of the publishing communities of the United States, Europe, Japan, and everywhere else professional publishing is done.

The Frankfurt assembly chose a new chairman for STM in the person of John Dill, president and CEO of the Times Mirror group's health-science imprint Mosby in St. Louis. In all, the group now counts 117 members representing 269 imprints in 20 countries. Herman Frank of Elsevier Science, chair of STM's Innovations Committee (which had long been pushing for a commitment to CD-ROM), read an advertisement for a traditional Swiss watch company boasting that it had never made a quartz watch and never will. "Perhaps there would be an STM publisher to say, 'We never published an electronic product and never will,'" added Frank. "Well, that publisher will be very famous, and very small."

Brazil Bounces Back

Each year, Frankfurt spotlights a national culture; it was Brazil this time, around which 300 activities—performances, exhibitions, lectures—were staged inside the fairgrounds and out. More than 60 authors were on hand for readings and panels. As always, book trade professionals tended to ignore the public-oriented events—their Brazil consists of a few major players at Frankfurt fairs, such as Sergio Machado of Record, Paolo Rocco of Rocco, Siciliano's Pedro Paolo de Sena Madureira, and Luis Schwartz of Companhia das Letras. Any one of them was ready to tell of a new Brazil, where inflation that previously ran at up to 50 percent a month has been reduced to 1 percent to 2 percent, putting the country (for the first time in recent history) in a position to realize its powerful potential as a book market.

The German Booksellers Peace Prize went to Jorge Semprun, Spanish author long exiled in France, who returned to be a minister of culture. One writer who didn't make it to the fair was the besieged Bangladeshi novelist Taslima Nasreen, who had been booked to appear at the stand of her German publisher; after France refused her a visa, she decided to remain in her temporary exile in Sweden.

But the stern businesslike side of the fair has to relax sometimes. Cologne-born U.S. publisher Werner Mark Linz of Continuum threw his own party to celebrate surviving 40 consecutive Frankfurt fairs (he began at age 19, as an apprentice at Germany's Herder). The Janklow & Nesbit team staged a power breakfast for Peter Arnett and his publishers (*Live from the Battlefield*). Harper hosted a lively party for the impressive Anthony Quinn (*Self Portrait*) at the German Film Museum.

For the 25th anniversary of the fair's technical director, Franz-Josef Fenke, his colleagues held a stand party—except it was the kind of stand everybody fears to have: upside down, ceiling lights on the floor, floor cabinets overhead, books and posters turned on their heads—a reminder that for a fair this size, complaints about amenities are rare, though, ironically, this year saw a major mixup by the furniture contractors that delayed the opening of a number of stands.

Speaking of amenities, Frankfurt has more and more of them, inside and outside the fairgrounds, but they come dearly, with unbelievable hotel rates (hiked at fair time), taxis strategically absent at the times and places of one's choosing. Yet no one would think of skipping the punishment.

Next time, come disguised as an airplane pilot. One of the main fair hotels offers special discounts to flight crews, though it probably won't apply during fair time—which next year runs October 11–16.

Trends and Issues in Library and Information Services in Canada, 1994

Ken Haycock

School of Library, Archival and Information Studies
University of British Columbia
Vancouver, British Columbia

Trends and issues in Canada in 1994 appear to be consistent with previous annual reports: budget reductions, automation of functions and services, preservation of resources, lobbying for tax and copyright exemptions for libraries, services to special client groups, the need for improved advocacy and marketing, the impact of information technology on services, and equitable access. The immediate focus or demand changes each year.

Information Technology

The federal government appointed an Information Highway Advisory Council, which includes two information professionals. The main issues facing the council are how to use the "Information Superhighway" to improve the growth and competitiveness of Canadian business, how to assure that Canadians have universal access to essential services at reasonable cost, how to achieve an appropriate balance between competition and regulation, and how to promote the development and distribution of Canadian culture and content. The Canadian Library Association (CLA) has worked closely with several of the council's working committees.

Government continues, through its agencies, to improve options and opportunities on the Information Superhighway. CANARIE (the Canadian Network for the Advancement of Research, Industry, and Education), for example, called for proposals to develop advanced communication applications, particularly in the areas of technology development and diffusion. CISTI (the Canadian Institute for Scientific and Technical Information) initiated 12 projects to support the electronic library in six categories: user interfaces, database creation, network and standards development, futuristic demonstrations, marketing, and services development.

The National Library of Canada (NLC) continued its development and testing of Phase I of AMICUS, the replacement system for DOBIS, the library's 15-year-old computing platform and bibliographic system, with a relational database management system, full-text management software, and a suite of applications using client-server technology. A national resource-sharing strategy discussion paper was released by NLC for discussion and debate; priority issues were identified and solutions are now being developed.

NLC established its bilingual gopher server, which handles over 15,000 accesses a week. This resource maintains links to all Canadian Internet sites, identifies libraries within those sites, and monitors both federal and provincial government Internet services and information. The library is also piloting a project involving electronic journals and representative documents on Internet to ascertain policy implications and organizational responsibilities. NLC published a list of Dial-up Internet Access Providers in Canada.

Internet training is ubiquitous across Canada and many librarians are founding members of the "Freenets" being established from coast to coast.

Information Access and Rights

Information policy meetings and summits have been held nationally and provincially in Canada in the past two years. Both national and provincial associations are developing opportunities for public and professional consultation on information policy issues, particularly in reviewing proposed and emerging federal government information policy priorities, debate over who controls "the pipe," meeting the demand for public information, and equitable access principles. The Coalition for Public Information, an amalgam of associations and other groups initiated by the Ontario Library Association and now jointly sponsored with the Canadian Library Association, has prepared an action agenda to encourage public forums and discussion around the issues outlined in their discussion paper "Future-Knowledge: A Public Policy Framework for the Information Highway."

Copyright continues to be an issue as librarians wait for Phase 2 of the Copyright Act to be declared; at present there are no explicit exemptions for libraries although "fair dealing" applies to libraries, archives, and schools; there is no clear definition of fair dealing except that copying must be for private study, research, criticism, review, or newspaper summary.

Revised statutes and regulations were also introduced to require Canadian publishers, including the government, to deposit two copies of publications with NLC rather than one; this move will make resources more available and result in considerable savings for NLC.

The Don't Tax Reading Coalition continues its efforts to have the Goods and Services Tax, the first federal tax in Canada applied to reading materials, removed from Canadian reading materials.

A national Information Rights Week, initiated by the British Columbia Library Association, is now celebrated across the country in April to focus on information policy issues.

Services to Exceptional Customers

The National Library of Canada continued its adaptive technology program whereby libraries are provided with funds to improve services to handicapped users. The Department of Heritage contributed funds to the Canadian National Institute for the Blind (CNIB) to support the production of multicultural heritage books in Braille and on tape for the blind and visually impaired, while Ronald McDonald Children's Charities of Canada funded a new PrintBraille collection of 140 children's books, with print and Braille versions side by side for parent and child to share. NLC also produced *Federal Government Publications Issued in Alternative Format, 1981–1992* to assist libraries in providing access to government information.

Due to budget reductions, NLC's Multilingual Biblioservice shifted its focus to providing a clearinghouse and advisory service with short-term backup resources for libraries unable to meet changing community needs. In some major urban areas public libraries provide growing multilingual and multicultural services and are finding alternate sources of revenue to enhance relations and services with community groups. In Vancouver, for example, the Vancouver Public Library has sponsored a Chinese Gallery and Reading Room for its new Central Library (opening in 1995), with $200,000 raised through private fund-raising then matched by the Hong Kong Bank of Canada. This is a clear trend and becoming an important role for directors and trustees.

Marketing

Provincial library associations, systems, and staff are focusing more on the importance of advocacy and marketing. Provincial library weeks are held in some provinces, notably Saskatchewan and Ontario. Freedom to Read Week is celebrated nationally in February, by declaration of the national Book and Periodical Development Council, of which the Canadian Library Association is a founding member. Information Rights Week is held in April.

Canadian Children's Book Week is celebrated in November, with the assistance of a kit prepared by the Canadian Children's Book Center and NLC's Read Up On It kit, with 20,000 copies distributed for use in schools and public libraries and available in electronic format to 4,000 schools. The Canadian School Library Association has also developed a reading promotion poster, highlighting a Canadian Olympic athlete.

The Library Association of Alberta, long a leader in library marketing, developed Libraries Count: Influencing the Political Process, a kit for library workers and trustees. The Association for Teacher-Librarianship in Canada prepared an advocacy disk of resources for its members to use in marketing efforts.

Provincial Outlook

In the Atlantic provinces development is uneven, with significant budget reductions in some areas and notable successes in others. In Nova Scotia a strategic planning report is to be released shortly. In the meantime the good news is that the federal secretary of state for multiculturalism and citizenship provided major grants for literacy collections for the regional libraries systems; the bad news is that the province has witnessed serious cutbacks in school library services. However, the government has recently announced its intention to reinstate the provincial coordinator of school libraries position and to re-examine earlier decisions to shift responsibility for school library services from schools to regional public library systems and to replace teacher-librarians with library technicians.

In Prince Edward Island, on the other hand, consolidations and restructuring of public agencies have not adversely affected libraries; indeed, school libraries, after years of effective advocacy by teacher-librarians, are experiencing renewed support and leadership. New Brunswick's Library Review Task Force highlighted the need to automate the library system, leading to an innovative pilot project with the federal and provincial governments and the New Brunswick Library Services to complete retrospective conversion of records of the public library system through a guaranteed income for older people (over 55) who have exhausted other options for re-employment. Newfoundland is now awaiting government response to its provincial report on the Newfoundland Library System.

Quebec is challenged by the replacement of retiring librarians with city managers and library technicians but the provincial library association is commencing a million-dollar marketing campaign this year.

The Ontario strategic plan has a focal point—One Place to Look—and the Ontario government is providing funding to increase automation of collections for improved services and the development of INFO (Information Network for Ontario) for libraries to access the new provincial database on CD-ROM. Network development will include access to government information and other public information databases, resource sharing for public libraries, and partnership of public and corporate sectors and government. Public libraries have also been selected as sites for access to the provincial Environmental Registry, with information on acts, policies, regulations, and appeals, through the INFO Workstations. The Provincial Library Review Task Force is reviewing user fees, governance, and the deconditionalizing of grants, but the provincial legislature recently endorsed municipal library boards as the best model for public library governance.

Manitoba, like other jurisdictions, noted government fascination with new technology. Six provincial library associations sponsored a joint conference on the virtual library and convinced government to acknowledge the need for organized and local content on the Information Superhighway. Libraries suddenly became viewed as an asset rather than a liability and a new Linking Libraries Initiative was undertaken. The Public Library Advisory Board report was released and money allocated for a province-wide computer network to enhance efficient use of library resources, particularly in rural areas where a 30 percent budget increase was introduced. The Manitoba Library Consortium Inc., established in 1992, now includes 25 library systems (academic, public, special, school) and sponsors Library Express, a priority interlibrary loan and courier service.

Saskatchewan residents with visual disabilities who are registered with their local library can borrow talking books from any branch in the province, extending a noted feature of the provincial library system whereby any citizen can borrow from any public library; branches can also borrow blocks of talking books from the provincial library. A Multitype Library Development Advisory Committee has been established to build on the Saskatchewan Union Catalogue on CD-ROM, which includes public, academic, government, and special libraries with some school library representation.

In Alberta library services are free, as in every other province, but libraries can charge for a library card, and the Edmonton Public Library is now doing just that—at $12 per card—as a result of reduced funding. The Alberta Public Library Review Task Force has been established to gather information across the province and to make recommendations on organizational issues and funding structures for the delivery of services.

The Library Association of Alberta has initiated both the Alberta Libraries ASAP (Alberta Strategic Alliance for Planning) process and a provincial public library marketing implementation plan. As a result of work by the University of Alberta and University of Calgary libraries, the Alberta Health Knowledge Network has been created through external funding from the Alberta Heritage Foundation for Medical Research, matched by consortium members; this joint project of the faculties of medicine, hospitals, and libraries will provide access through campus networks and dial-in access to health knowledge databases for health professionals from libraries, offices, laboratories, and homes.

A new Library Act proclaimed in British Columbia provides for the establishment of public library boards and regional library district boards, defining membership, terms, rules, and operational guidelines.

InterLINK, an umbrella organization serving 12 public library systems in the Lower Mainland, was also established, replacing the former Greater Vancouver Library Federation. The British Columbia Library Association has been a leader in providing forums on the public's right to information. A newly named Yukon Library and Information Network organized opportunities for resource sharing and continuing education of members, and the Northwest Territories is undertaking a review of community libraries and access to information in the North.

Public, Academic, Special, and School Libraries

Public libraries are giving more attention to planning for the future and focusing on the customer, through marketing studies and focus groups to find out what customers want. In times of fiscal restraint there is also increased interest in self-service technologies and options such as dial-in access to catalogs and databases, telephone renewals, and automated message services for overdue and reserved items. More "friends" groups are being established, fund-raising activities started, and improved marketing programs implemented. Some systems, such as the Calgary Public Library, have instituted a Business Information Service, providing specialized services on a fee basis while "basic" services are still free. The Canadian Association of Public Libraries continues to lobby the National Library for the reinstatement of the children's literature consultant position, eliminated as a result of fiscal restraint.

In universities, journal price increases have led to the cancellation of thousands of titles, almost 1,600 at the University of British Columbia (UBC) alone. More systems are seeking joint partnerships such as the University of Alberta Libraries pilot project with ISM Library Information Services and Coutts Library Services to provide an efficient and cost-effective solution to providing 6,000 shelf-ready English-language monographs. The Council of Prairies and Pacific University Libraries (COPPUL) is purchasing electronic information resources collectively for members, and a number of university library systems have been successful in obtaining external grants for scholarly research collections through the Social Sciences and Humanities Research Council's support to specialized collections program. Dalhousie also obtained grants from the United States

Information Agency for American studies. The University of Lethbridge obtained more than $4 million for its Library Information Network Center. Some universities, such as the Technical University of Nova Scotia, are introducing a fee-based Library Research Service for "beyond the basics" support. The University of British Columbia library preservation microfilming project under the Canadian Cooperative Preservation Project filmed more than 100 reels related to education and sessional papers in British Columbia.

New buildings include Queen's University's new Central Library Complex with two complementary central library buildings, UBC's new Education Library, and the University of Alberta's innovative and award-winning Book and Record Depository (BARD), a climate-controlled state-of-the-art high-density facility with capacity for 3.2 million volumes and more than 8 kilometers of archives, maps, and aerial photos.

Through its unique network of chapters across the country, the Canadian Association of Special Libraries and Information Services provided innumerable opportunities for continuing education of members, focusing especially on creating value-added information services, electronic access, and repackaging services such as competitive intelligence for marketing. Special libraries were also included for the first time in the National Core Library Statistics Program Advisory Committee established by NLC to determine the best means of ensuring the development, coordination, collection, and implementation of national core library statistics.

School libraries have faced tough times, and the Canadian School Library Association (CSLA) has established a committee with the Canadian Association of Children's Librarians to study the impact of school library funding cuts on public library services. CSLA has also established a joint task force on education for teacher-librarianship with the Association for Teacher-Librarianship in Canada. In spite of tough times there were bright spots for teacher-librarians. They were able to exhibit strong teaching and partnership skills, particularly in integration of electronic information in the curriculum. In this regard the government of Manitoba joined most other provinces in issuing a position statement and guidelines on the role of the school library resource center and the teacher-librarian in resource-based learning. Through a strategic planning and priority setting exercise, the Canadian Library Association discontinued *CM: A Reviewing Journal of Canadian Materials for Young People*, Canada's only national evaluation tool for Canadian materials. CSLA continued its series of teleconferences on a variety of topics.

Education

The national Alliance of Libraries, Archive and Records Management (ALARM), an Industrial Adjustment Service committee of the federal Department of Human Resource Development, was created jointly by the Industrial Adjustment Service, the Canadian Library Association, the Council of Canadian Archives, the Association of Records Managers and Administrators, and the Canadian Union of Public Employees, with representation from several other associations. It is developing a human resource strategy for the information sector, examining the impact of political, regulatory, economic, and technological forces on people who work in this sector. Supported by government funding, ALARM has produced a consultation document to generate discussion among those who work with the selection, acquisition, dissemination, and preservation of information, and plans to identify the nature of the workforce in ten years, to the extent possible. Issues identified to date include technological change, the need to attract more extroverted and politically proactive workers, credibility within the parent organizations, and the need for a better reflection of the cultural and ethnic diversity of communities in the information workforce.

The graduate program in library and information studies at Dalhousie University—the only ALA-accredited program in Atlantic Canada—was threatened with closure but remains open within the Faculty of Management. McGill, like other schools, is seeking alternate sources of revenue. Toronto made changes to its curriculum and changed the name of the Faculty of Library and Information Science to the Faculty of Information Studies; the master's degrees in library science and in information science were discontinued, being replaced by a Master of Information Studies [M.I.St.], with specializations in librarianship, archival studies, and information science. Western Ontario gained unconditional government approval for its graduate degrees based on the scholarly record of the program. Alberta sponsored programs to encourage alumni and student networking. And British Columbia introduced its revised curriculum and an external Board of Visitors, with government and business representation.

All schools report that graduates are finding an increasing number of professional positions outside traditional librarianship.

A national Northern Exposure to Leadership institute brought together 24 recently graduated librarians, nominated and selected for their leadership potential, with leaders/mentors to explore issues in leadership and library and information services in Canada. Funded by Ameritech Library Services, the program was modeled to some extent on the American Snowbird program and was an intensely emotional and motivating experience for those involved.

Emerging Trends

Partnership is the new pattern of development: partnerships with other institutions to share resources; partnerships with business and industry to support and exploit those resources; partnerships with government to make libraries the primary information access point for citizens; partnerships with colleagues and citizens to advocate for libraries and librarians through their associations. Training continues to be the most urgent issue in Canadian librarianship—more training in newer technologies and more training in advocating the importance of the work of information professionals. The newer challenges include acquiring, organizing, preserving, storing, and accessing electronic publications; balancing the increased commercialization of information; government (at all levels) cost-recovery initiatives, providing Canadian content for the Information Superhighway and the need for equitable access to information.

Federal Agency
and Federal Library Reports

National Commission on Libraries
and Information Science

1110 Vermont Ave. N.W., Suite 820, Washington, DC 20005-3522
202-606-9200, FAX 202-606-9203
Internet: py_nclis@inet.ed.gov; jw_nclis@inet.ed.gov

Jane Williams
Research Associate

Commission Members

In late 1993 President Clinton appointed Jeanne Hurley Simon of Illinois to the National Commission on Libraries and Information Science (NCLIS) for a term ending July 19, 1997, replacing J. Michael Farrell. The Senate confirmed her nomination on November 20. That same day, the President named Simon to chair the commission. The Senate received four more nominations on November 22: Martha Gould, Frank Lucchino, Bobby Roberts, and Gary Sudduth.

On February 2 the Senate received the nomination of Robert Willard, director of government marketing for Mead Data Central in Dayton, Ohio, to replace James Lyons. The Senate confirmed these five nominations on April 14, 1994.

On July 12 the President submitted to the Senate the appointment of Joel Valdez, the senior vice president for business affairs at the University of Arizona. On October 7 the Senate confirmed his appointment, replacing Ben Chieh-Liu.

Continuing commissioners are NCLIS Vice Chair Elinor Swaim, Shirley Adamovich, Daniel Casey, Carol DiPrete, Norman Kelinson, Kay Riddle, and Barbara Taylor. Winston Tabb represents the Librarian of Congress, a permanent NCLIS member.

Budget and Staffing

NCLIS staff remained at five full-time permanent employees, along with contractual staff dealing primarily with the Library Statistics Program. Peter R. Young continued as executive director.

The NCLIS budget for FY 1994 was $904,000, up from the appropriation of $889,000 for FY 1993. The commission held planning meetings in March and

July 1994. The March sessions in Atlanta coincided with the Public Library Association conference, at which the preliminary results of the study of public libraries and Internet were announced. NCLIS met in conjunction with the Mountain Plains Library Association and held a hearing in Nevada, October 25–27, 1994.

Along with all other federal agencies, NCLIS participated in and was affected by the initiatives of the National Performance Review (NPR), begun in September 1993 to cut costs and improve services. In December 1993 NCLIS submitted a streamlining plan and in August 1994 submitted a discussion draft of a customer service plan.

Support for Executive and Legislative Branches

During the year the commission developed and strengthened working relationships with officials in the executive and legislative branches so that NCLIS had opportunities for timely input in national policies affecting library and information services. Chairperson Simon kept an active schedule of appointments and consultations with many officials in the federal government, meeting with some of them several times over the year. She met with people in various offices of the Executive Office of the President, Department of Commerce, Department of Education, National Archives and Records Administration, National Corporation for Public and Community Service, National Institute for Literacy, National Library of Medicine, and National Science Foundation.

Simon and her staff also met with members and staff of the congressional committees concerned with appropriations, education, information policy, libraries, telecommunications, and other technology, as well as with officials in agencies of the legislative branch, such as the Government Printing Office and the Library of Congress.

Part of NCLIS's 1994 contribution to reauthorization of the Library Services and Construction Act (LSCA) was two policy analyses of the recommendations from the conference as well as a March 1994 snapshot of the status of implementation of the recommendations. NCLIS also participated in a task force on LSCA reauthorization coordinated by the American Library Association.

Commissioners and staff made or maintained contacts with national library and information organizations. NCLIS also expanded its base from which to understand policy issues and formulate advice to include consultations with different or new nonprofits such as Libraries for the Future, the Center for Civic Networking, and the Benton Foundation.

NCLIS reviewed and responded to memoranda from the Legislative Reference Division of the Office of Management and Budget (OMB) regarding reauthorization of the Elementary and Secondary Education Act, the Government Reform and Savings Act, Goal 2000, Office of Educational Research and Improvement reauthorizations, and Education Research and Statistics reauthorizations.

The commission answered questions and provided background for staff and members of Congress on a variety of subjects, mostly related to libraries in a networked, electronic environment; libraries in support of education; and the status of training and education for library and information services. Likewise, the reports from commission activities related to libraries and education were distributed to appropriate congressional committees and discussed with them.

In addition to OMB and congressional inquiries, other entities have solicited suggestions on draft documents, regulations, and other items. Examples of these opportunities in 1994 were the draft reports of the National Information Infrastructure Advisory Council and the Information Infrastructure Task Force. [For further information on NII activities, see the special report earlier in Part 1—*Ed.*]

Library and Information Services in a Networked Environment

In 1993 NCLIS named Charles R. McClure, professor at Syracuse University's School of Information Studies, the first NCLIS distinguished researcher, to examine the impacts of networking on libraries and information services.

McClure's work for the commission was later refined and extended to include a survey and analysis of public libraries and Internet, for which the co-principal investigators were McClure and Douglas L. Zweizig, professor at the School of Library and Information Studies, University of Wisconsin–Madison. Syracuse Ph.D. student John Carlo Bertot and others analyzed the survey results, of which selected findings were as follows:

- 20.9 percent of U.S. public libraries are connected to Internet.
- Public library access to Internet is not equitable.
- Public libraries serving larger communities are likelier to have access to Internet than public libraries serving smaller communities.
- There are regional variations in public libraries' connectivity to Internet.
- Public libraries are using Internet services to answer reference inquiries, access federal information resources, and perform interlibrary loan transactions.
- There are wide variations in public libraries' Internet costs. Libraries for small populations report annual costs of $412. Libraries for larger populations report annual costs of $14,697.
- Federal assistance for connecting public libraries to Internet is required.

Vice President Gore met with NCLIS on July 29, 1994, and called for "a concerted effort to ask the questions and to inventory the challenges and to come up with the best answers" regarding libraries and the national information infrastructure (NII).

In response, the commission conducted briefings in Washington, D.C., on September 21–22, 1994. The first day featured directors and other officials of 15 state library agencies, who briefed commissioners on the status of statewide library networks and plans for connecting libraries to Internet. On September 22 the commissioners, Charles McClure, representatives of Congress and the administration, and other key representatives from the library and information services communities examined the federal role relating to libraries and the Information Superhighway.

The following points emerged from discussion at the briefing on the federal role:

- Better program coordination is needed among federal agencies to provide support to libraries for Internet access.
- Libraries need to partner with other service agencies developing network services at the state and local levels.
- Additional studies are needed on the status of library networking, especially for academic and school libraries.
- An analysis of federal programs relating to libraries and networking is needed.
- Further work is needed to clarify what libraries require in order to take full advantage of the benefits of Internet/NII, especially in light of plans for LSCA reauthorization.
- There is a need to clarify the vision of library involvement in the Information Superhighway.
- The question of whether the safety-net role limits libraries in providing a full range of networking services needs to be resolved.

Libraries and Education

In early December 1993 NCLIS concluded its series of regional briefings and forums on library and information services and literacy programs for children and youth with events in Des Moines. (Earlier forums were held in May 1993 in Boston and in September 1993 in Sacramento.) The forums served as the basis for the commission to advise the Clinton administration and the Congress on formulating national programs and plans for young people. NCLIS published and distributed the proceedings of each briefing and forum.

In 1993 the commission launched a cooperative project with the American Library Association's Office of Research and Statistics and the American Association of School Librarians to collect selected statistics from a sample of school library media centers in 12 states. This 1993–1994 joint project was designed to obtain current information for activities related to the legislation cited above, because the National Center for Education Statistics (NCES) last collected statistics on school library media centers in 1985. Also, results of NCES's fall 1994 survey are not expected until late 1995.

The survey report was published and distributed in June 1994 and reprinted in September. The following summarizes some of the survey's findings:

- Many school libraries are poorly equipped to support instruction.
- One-half of elementary school libraries buy less than one book per student per year.

- One-half of secondary school libraries buy less than 0.33 books per student per year.
- Almost no school libraries have access to Internet.
- There is a wide variance in average annual funding for school libraries.
    —Elementary school libraries receive from $15 to $58,874 per year.
    —Secondary school libraries receive from $155 to $100,810 per year.
- In 31 percent of elementary school libraries, the latest world atlas available has a copyright date before 1990.
- In 21 percent of secondary school libraries, the latest world atlas available has a copyright date before 1990.
- Much work is needed to provide opportunities for school library media specialists to work more closely with classroom teachers.

Library Statistics

For the sixth consecutive year, NCLIS and the National Center for Education Statistics operated the Library Statistics Program through an interagency agreement. The original component of the Library Statistics Program is the Federal-State Cooperative System for public library data (FSCS). The training workshop for state data coordinators is the major yearly event for the public library component of the Library Statistics Program. The December 1993 workshop (the sixth annual workshop) included territorial representatives for the first time.

NCES published *Public Libraries in the United States: 1992* in August 1994. Within the past three years, 75 percent of the states have submitted their public library data to NCES by the July 31 deadline and the quality and completeness of the data required no follow-up by NCES.

A pilot test of the survey of state library agencies was conducted to prepare for the actual fall 1994 survey. Planning and development took place for collection of 1994 data on academic libraries. Progress with the Department of Education's 1994 School and Staff Survey (to include school library media centers) was reviewed with the Statistical Committee of the American Association of School Librarians.

On May 16–17, 1994, NCLIS and NCES co-sponsored the second annual Forum on Library and Information Services Policy. The 1994 forum focused on policy issues related to the role of libraries in NII and statistical indicators needed to measure the effective involvement of libraries. NCLIS issued the proceedings of the forum in September 1994. NCES also helped support the September briefings on libraries and the Information Superhighway.

International Activities

The commission completed its ninth year of cooperation with the Department of State to coordinate and monitor proposals for International Contributions for Scientific, Educational and Cultural Activities (ICSECA) funds and to disburse the funds. The allocation for ICSECA, included in the State Department's

International Organizations and Programs account, was formerly under International Conventions and Scientific Organizations Contributions (ICSOC). Seven projects received a total of $175,000.

Commission staff continued to host orientation and information-sharing sessions for librarians and other officials visiting the United States, usually under the auspices of the U.S. Information Agency or Meridian House International. Executive Director Young met with visitors from France, Hungary, and China in FY 1994.

Publications

Annual Report 1992–1993. April 1994.

Briefing and Open Forum on Children and Youth Services: Redefining the Federal Role for Libraries (Sacramento, CA). December 1993.

Briefing and Open Forum on Children and Youth Services: Redefining the Federal Role for Libraries (Des Moines, IA). February 1994.

Libraries and the National Information Infrastructure: Proceedings of the 1994 Forum on Library and Information Services Policy. September 1994.

Library and Information Services Policy: A Forum Report. (Forum held September 23–24, 1993). 1994.

Lynch, Mary Jo, Pamela Kramer, and Ann Weeks. *Public School Library Media Centers in 12 States: Report of the NCLIS/ALA Survey.* June 1994.

McClure, Charles R., John Carlo Bertot, and Douglas L. Zweizig. *Public Libraries in the Internet: Study Results, Policy Issues, and Recommendations.* June 1994.

McCook, Kathleen de la Peña. *Toward a Just and Productive Society.* 1994.

Walsh, Taylor. *The National Information Infrastructure and the Recommendations of the 1991 White House Conference on Library and Information Services.* 1994.

At the time this report was written, copies of all the above were available free from NCLIS.

Conclusion

Continuation of programs in education and the information infrastructure, involvement with such legislative matters as the reauthorization of the Library Services and Construction Act, celebration of the commission's 25th year, exploration of new efforts in research, analysis, and statistics, and having a budget of $901,000 with which to work are among the challenges and assets in 1995 for the National Commission on Libraries and Information Science.

National Technical Information Service

Technology Administration
U.S. Department of Commerce, Springfield, VA 22161
703-487-4650

Thomas N. King
Marketing Specialist
Marketing Communications

In 1995 the National Technical Information Service (NTIS) marks 50 years of service as the central resource for U.S. government scientific, technical, engineering, and business-related information. Its collection also includes similar information from foreign governments and from domestic and foreign nongovernment sources.

NTIS's predecessor agency, the Publications Board, was established at the end of World War II by President Harry Truman to evaluate and disseminate scientific and technical information documents seized from enemy nations. Congress later ordered the Department of Commerce to operate the board as a clearinghouse to collect and distribute scientific and technical information from domestic and foreign sources. In 1970 the agency was formally renamed the National Technical Information Service.

NTIS is a self-supporting federal agency within the U.S. Department of Commerce's Technology Administration. All costs associated with collecting, abstracting, indexing, archiving, reproducing, and disseminating the information that NTIS houses are paid for by sales of its products and services. Expenditures for NTIS salaries, marketing, postage, and all other operating costs are also funded by sales revenues.

Each year NTIS adds more than 78,000 new titles to its collection of approximately 2.5 million products. The collection includes technical reports, periodicals, databases, computer software, diskettes, CD-ROMs, audiocassettes, videotapes, and online services.

Reinventing Government

The Clinton administration's plans for reinventing government have created new opportunities for NTIS. Not only is NTIS working to meet the president's goal of making government work better, cost less, and better serve its customers, but the agency is also assisting other agencies to meet these objectives. Three of NTIS's recent initiatives in this area include its merger with the National Audiovisual Center and its expanded work on FedWorld and the Continuous Acquisition and Life-Cycle Support (CALS) Information Center.

National Audiovisual Center

On October 1, 1994, the National Audiovisual Center joined NTIS to consolidate most of the U.S. government's activity in the duplication and distribution of audio, visual, and multimedia products. The merger provides the opportunity to make federally produced media products available to a wider audience. The National Audiovisual Center has served as a central information and distribution source for federal multimedia programs since its creation as part of the National Archives and Records Administration in 1969.

Its collection contains more than 9,000 government-produced audiovisual and multimedia products in a wide range of formats, grouped by more than 600 individual subject headings, representing over 200 federal agencies and their bureaus. The range of subject areas includes foreign-language training, occupational safety and health, law enforcement training, fire service training, history, science, medical training, business and economics, agriculture, and natural resources.

The merger of NTIS and the National Audiovisual Center, two government agencies with overlapping missions, creates a more efficient organization. Because the process also included the transfer of personnel, NTIS and its customers will benefit by this exchange of expertise.

FedWorld®

NTIS's FedWorld is an expanding electronic access point to locate, research, and acquire U.S. and foreign government scientific, technical, and business information. With more than 140,000 registered subscribers, FedWorld's user base continues to grow at a rate of 10 percent a month.

FedWorld brings more than 130 federally operated online computer systems together for entry through a single gateway. Simply by connecting to FedWorld through Internet or via a modem, users have access to these systems without leaving FedWorld.

Thousands of time-sensitive government information resources—such as inventories of published reports, databases, software, bulletin board systems, and contacts for information providers—are housed on FedWorld. Current FedWorld features include walk-you-through prompts, a simple online help system, and electronic mail services.

An Internet World-Wide Web (WWW) server was recently added to the FedWorld network. This new server makes accessing information easier and faster. It also lists government Web servers by subject and provides a path through which users can link up to other U.S. government servers. In addition, NTIS has added an Internet file transfer protocol (ftp) server that allows users to obtain files from the FedWorld online system.

Users can shop for popular NTIS products online through the FedWorld marketplace. Depending on the item, customers may order products in paper form, on computer disk, or by downloading an electronic version to their computer. Here is a partial product listing of downloadable FedWorld files:

- Transcripts of White House press conferences, briefings, remarks by the president, and executive orders
- The General Agreement on Tariffs and Trade (GATT) documents
- Dozens of catalogs listing thousands of U.S. government publications
- Listings of federal job openings across the nation

FedWorld offers subscription service to databases and file collections from many U.S. government agencies.

In 1994 NTIS was awarded the first annual Federal Applications Medal for Excellence (FAME), cosponsored by *Government Computer News* and several other leading private-sector publications. The award was for providing online scientific, technical, and business information to industry and government through FedWorld.

The award honors individuals, agencies, and contractors who have contributed toward fulfillment of National Performance Review objectives. NTIS was also selected for the FOSE award, which goes to the top FAME award recipient.

FedWorld received the Commerce Department's Customer Service Excellence Award for Putting Customers First in November 1994. The award honors those employees, teams, and organizations that have put into action their commitment to improve customer service. The four award categories—Cutting Red Tape, Putting Customers First, Empowering Employees, and Cutting Back to Basics—mirror the four major themes of the reinventing effort.

To connect to FedWorld by modem: Set modem parity to none, data bits to 8, and stop bits to 1. Set terminal emulation to ANSI. Set duplex to full. Then set your communication software to dial FedWorld at 703-321-8020.

To connect to FedWorld via Internet: Telnet to **fedworld.gov**. For Internet file transfer protocol (ftp) services, connect to **ftp.fedworld.gov**. For World-Wide Web services, point your Mosaic client or other browser to **http://www.fedworld.gov**.

Access is free of charge. For more information on FedWorld, call 703-487-4608.

Continuous Acquisition and Life-Cycle Support Information Center

The Continuous Acquisition and Life-Cycle Support (CALS) Information Center was formed in 1991 and is operated with the support of the Office of the Secretary of Defense. CALS was originally conceived by the Department of Defense and private industry as a strategy to streamline acquisition of weapons systems. It has since become a major government and industry initiative to speed the transition from a paper-intensive environment to a highly automated and integrated operation. The CALS Information Center promotes the widespread understanding, acceptance, and use of CALS principles through an effective flow of CALS-related technical information. The center provides a public source of CALS-related information, including standards and specifications, technical reports, training materials, computer datafiles, and the CALS electronic bulletin board system.

The CALS electronic bulletin board provides the CALS community with a vehicle to exchange information, to post and read bulletins, and to download files containing data or the full text of reports. To access the CALS bulletin board, users must first connect to FedWorld, choose Research, Technical and Education Mall from the main FedWorld menu, and then select option "A" for the CALS Database.

For more information about the CALS Information Center, call 703-487-4650 and ask for PR-898.

Sources of Information

U.S. Government

More than 200 U.S. government agencies and bureaus contribute to the NTIS collection, including the National Aeronautics and Space Administration, the Environmental Protection Agency, the National Institute of Standards and Technology, the National Institutes of Health, and the departments of Agriculture, Commerce, Defense, Energy, Health and Human Services, Interior, Labor, and Transportation.

Until recently, NTIS relied upon voluntary transfers by federal agencies to ensure the comprehensiveness of its collection. However, with the passage of the American Technology Preeminence Act (ATPA) of 1991 (Public Law 102-245) NTIS's wealth of information has increased dramatically. ATPA requires all federal agencies to submit their federally funded scientific, technical, and engineering information products to NTIS within 15 days of the date the product is made publicly available. Consequently, NTIS can provide its customers with timely access to a more diverse and practical range of information.

The primary purposes of ATPA are to assist U.S. industries to accelerate the development of new processes and products and to assist the United States in maintaining a leading economically competitive position worldwide. Under ATPA, information products are technical reports, articles, papers, and books; regulations, standards, and specifications; charts, maps, and graphs; software; data collections, datafiles, and data compilations software; audio and video products; technology application assessments; training packages; and other federally owned or originated technologies.

NTIS–Agency Partnerships

Federal agencies are struggling to improve customer service at a time of budget and staff cutbacks. While an agency's involvement with a product often ends when the product is turned over to NTIS, these are examples of mutually beneficial partnerships:

The White House. NTIS continues to offer a full range of services to disseminate White House publications and information to the public rapidly. The cooperative agreement between NTIS and the White House benefits both parties because the White House can provide the American public with timely exposure to important documents and NTIS can market the information in user-friendly formats to meet customer needs. With FedWorld's electronic capabilities and NTIS's fax management services, customers have quick access to many health care, National Performance Review, and North American Free Trade Agreement (NAFTA) publications.

Since the partnership's inception, several government offices have taken advantage of NTIS's services. For example, the Office of Intergovernmental Affairs at the White House used NTIS's fax capabilities to notify more than 500 government officials about business-related opportunities. In addition, at the request of the NAFTA Office at the White House, NTIS faxed daily updates on the NAFTA proceedings to 900 broadcast fax recipients.

Department of Labor. The Department of Labor (DOL) Davis-Bacon Wage Determination Act Database in its traditional paper format exceeds 4,000 pages, with hundreds of additional pages of updates each week. Increased costs of the paper product and customer demand drove the Labor Department to ask NTIS to make a digital version of the Davis-Bacon Database available on FedWorld. The result was a FedWorld subsystem that is accessed by subscribers. For less than the cost of the paper document, a subscriber can search the database for specific data. Updates can be found and searched within seconds, and the electronic data are immediately available.

Food and Drug Administration. NTIS and the Food and Drug Administration (FDA) have been information partners for the past 20 years. FDA places numerous information products with NTIS for sales and marketing, order fulfillment, and distribution to the many health professionals and pharmaceutical and food companies throughout the world. Having NTIS manage its information products has relieved FDA of a substantial workload.

Environmental Protection Agency. The Office of Emergency and Remedial Response (OERR), the Superfund management office within the Environmental Protection Agency (EPA), and NTIS have also formed a partnership. In 1990 OERR faced a rapidly increasing demand for free documents and an impending reduction in available printing funds. At the same time, OERR was committing increasing staff time to respond to requests under the Freedom of Information Act.

Through its partnership with NTIS, OERR now provides service and products to EPA personnel and EPA-sponsored clients through a document management center. NTIS performs reproduction, distribution, inventory management, and public access services. By concentrating its resources to serve its mission and by channeling public inquiries and Freedom of Information Act requesters to NTIS, OERR has eliminated significant costs and has been able to reallocate staff in order to support primary program initiatives. Now, those seeking Superfund information can locate it in one place, as soon as it becomes available.

Worldwide

NTIS is the leading U.S. government agency in international technical and business information exchange. It actively acquires and distributes information produced by a large number of foreign government departments and other organizations. In 1994, nearly 30 percent of NTIS's total product offerings came from international organizations and 81 foreign countries, including Canada, the United Kingdom, Japan, Western Europe, the nations of the former Soviet Union, and other Eastern European countries. These products address such topics as technology transfer, tariffs, export markets, all fields of science and technology, and international economics and politics.

NTIS continues to negotiate agreements to increase the number and scope of reports from major industrialized countries, as well as from newly industrialized countries producing advanced technologies. NTIS is working with existing sources to focus its acquisition efforts on topics of major interest to NTIS customers.

In May 1994 NTIS hosted an executive communication exchange meeting for 17 prominent Japanese business executives who were visiting the United States to study American information systems. Participants included senior-level executives from Sony Corp., Toshiba Corp., and Fuji Electronics Corp.

NTIS cosponsors highly successful conferences with the Japan Information Center of Science and Technology on accessing Japanese scientific and technical information. A conference in Boston in July 1994 addressed how small- and medium-sized companies acquire and use such information.

Joint Ventures

The National Technical Information Act of 1988 authorized NTIS to work with private industry to build strategic alliances through contracts or cooperative agreements with the private sector, individuals, firms, or other organizations. As a result, NTIS established its Joint Ventures Program, which allows it to enter into joint ventures with businesses to create new information products from U.S. government-produced data and software. In addition, NTIS is looking for partnerships that will open new channels of sales and distribution for U.S. government information products. For more information about joint ventures with NTIS, call 703-487-4785.

Accessing the NTIS Collection

Standard Reference Tools

A number of reference tools provide access to information about the NTIS collection. These tools come in the form of databases, reports, announcements, and catalogs. The major information vehicles include the following:

NTIS Bibliographic Database. When a government agency or its contractor submits a report or other product to NTIS, information on the item is entered into the NTIS Bibliographic Database and remains permanently available. The database can be accessed through a number of commercial online vendors, which are listed in the free *NTIS Catalog of Products and Services.* To obtain a catalog, call 703-487-4650 and request PR-827.

Government Reports Announcements and Index. This journal lists summaries of U.S. government research reports and surveys, regulations, handbooks, directories, and recently developed computer software and data files, on a twice-monthly basis. It is indexed by keyword, personal and corporate author, government/contract grant number, and report number. A six-volume, hardbound cumulative annual index is also available.

NTIS Catalog of Products and Services. This free catalog, arranged by subject category, features more than 250 of NTIS's most popular products including health care, business, and the environment. To order this catalog, call 703-487-4650 and request PR-827.

Competitive Intelligence Tracking Tools. The Foreign Broadcast Information Service (FBIS) Daily Reports contain news accounts, commentaries, and government statements. The material is gathered from foreign broadcasts, press agency transmissions, newspapers, and periodicals released within the previous 48 to 72 hours. *FBIS Daily Reports*, published Monday through Friday, include political, military, economic, environmental, and sociological news, as well as scientific and technical data and reports. Areas covered include Eastern Europe, China, East Asia, the Near East and South Asia, Latin America, Central Eurasia (including Russia and the independent states), Western Europe, and sub-Saharan Africa.

A new monthly publication, *Science and Technology Perspectives*, reports on leading-edge scientific, technological, and industrial developments throughout the world. *Science and Technology Perspectives* covers eight high-tech fields in the context of government policy, technological advancement, marketing strategies, and technology transfer issues.

Joint Publications Research Service Reports provide translations of articles and reports from publications around the world. The reports are available by specific country or region and by topics within regions. The translated articles cover the political, economic, and military aspects of each particular country, region, or topic. They contain information that is less time-sensitive than the *FBIS Daily Reports*.

Dispatch is a weekly bulletin published by the Department of State. It provides a diverse compilation of major speeches, congressional testimony, policy statements, fact sheets, and other foreign policy information. Contents include profiles of countries currently in the news, lists of ambassadorial appointments, treaty actions, and updates on current events worldwide and on public and private-sector assistance to Eastern and Central Europe.

For more information, call the NTIS Subscription Section at 703-487-4630.

Customized Research Tools

NTIS Published Search™. Published Search is a joint-venture product from NTIS and NERAC Inc. A *Published Search* is an exclusively prepared bibliography providing the latest research data on a specific subject from both U.S. government and worldwide sources. Each bibliography contains 50 to 250 abstracts of reports and studies available from a preselected individual database source. More than 30 specialty databases are currently included in the *Published Search* program. These information abstracts offer a quick and inexpensive way to determine which items are needed. For titles of the latest searches, contact NTIS Research Services at 703-487-4780 or search the NTIS Bibliographic Database. To order a *Published Search*, call the NTIS Sales Desk at 703-487-4650. Direct online access to the NTIS Bibliographic Database may be arranged through commercial services, which are listed in the *NTIS Catalog of Products and Services*, PR-827.

NTIS Alerts. Approximately 1,500 new titles are added to the NTIS collection every week. *NTIS Alerts* were developed to provide an efficient and timely way to stay in touch with the latest research, technologies, and studies available from NTIS. The *Alerts* feature concise, easy-to-read summaries with subheadings that help identify essential information quickly. NTIS prepares a list of topic search criteria that are run against all new studies and research and development reports in 26 subject areas. The relevant material is then formatted twice a month.

Annual indexes are available for many of the prepackaged *Alerts*. Indexes convert the *NTIS Alerts* into a valuable reference tool.

Because information needs vary, *NTIS Alerts* can also be customized to focus only on specific topics. The user can choose from among 200 topics to tailor a subscription. For more information on *NTIS Alerts*, call 703-487-4650 and request PR-797.

Selected Research in Microfiche. The wide range of options available accommodates virtually any microform need. *Selected Research in Microfiche (SRIM)* automatically sends subscribers microfiche copies of full texts of reports. There are 350 subject areas to choose from; a subject area can be customized to meet the user's needs. As new reports enter the collection in the chosen field, microfiche copies are immediately sent to users. Customers often receive documents before their availability is officially announced.

SRIM is particularly valuable for corporate and special libraries, especially those that need immediate access to new information or need a complete collection on a particular topic. Call 703-487-4630 to start your subscription or to request free brochure PR-271. NTIS also offers a custom SRIM service. Individuals interested in this service should contact an NTIS subject specialist at 703-487-4640. A custom SRIM profile will be created to capture only those technical reports in the customer's field of interest.

Seminars and Conferences

NTIS understands the importance of communication with the agencies and customers it serves. For several years, NTIS has organized a Users Conference to provide current and potential customers the opportunity to learn more about its new products and services. At the most recent conference, held November 9, 1994, speakers discussed such topics as customer service, new developments, and the future at NTIS.

NTIS addresses the needs of the agencies it serves through its Managing Smarter seminars. A Managing Smarter seminar was held October 18, 1994, at the Department of Commerce Auditorium, Washington, D.C. NTIS staff provided guidance to federal agency attendees on such issues as implementing National Performance Review objectives, FedWorld applications, the NTIS Bibliographic Database, electronic media production services, audiovisual services, and the Freedom of Information Act.

Key NTIS Telephone Numbers

Technical Reports and Computer Products

Sales Desk—Regular service	703-487-4650
Sales Desk—Rush service	1-800-553-NTIS
Fax	703-321-8547
To verify receipt of a fax	703-487-4679
TDD (for the hearing impaired)	703-487-4639
Subscription Section	703-487-4630
Military Publications	703-487-4684

The Sales Desk, Subscription Section, and Military Publications are open 8:30 A.M. to 5:00 P.M., Eastern time, Monday through Friday.

Other Assistance

For help in identifying a title for sale	703-487-4780
For help in tracing an order	703-487-4660
For help with NTIS Deposit Accounts	703-487-4064
For help with invoices	703-487-4770
NTIS Online Searching Help Desk	703-487-4640
FedWorld Help Desk	703-487-4608

National Archives and Records Administration

Seventh and Pennsylvania Ave. N.W., Washington, DC 20408
202-501-5400

Lori A. Lisowski

Policy and IRM Services

The National Archives and Records Administration (NARA), an independent federal agency, identifies, preserves, and makes available records that document the origins and evolution of the U.S. government and the history of the American people across three centuries. NARA is singular among the world's archives as a unified federal institution that accessions and preserves materials from all three branches of government. NARA assists federal agencies in documenting their activities, administering records management programs, scheduling records, and retiring noncurrent records to federal records centers. NARA also manages the Presidential Libraries system; assists the National Historical Publications and Records Commission in its grant program for state and local records and edited publications of the papers of prominent Americans; and publishes the laws, regulations, presidential documents, and other official notices of the federal government. NARA constituents include the federal government, the public, the media, the archival community, and a broad spectrum of professional associations and researchers in such fields as history, political science, law, library and information services, and genealogy.

The size and breadth of NARA's holdings are staggering. Together, NARA's 32 facilities hold approximately 20 million cubic feet of original textual material documenting the activities of the federal government. In addition, NARA has extensive multimedia collections including 9 million aerial photographs; 7 million still pictures; more than 4 million maps, charts, and architectural and engineering plans; more than 310,000 motion picture, sound, and video recordings; almost 300,000 microforms; and 6,000 computer data sets.

Table 1 / Dates for Moving Textual Records,
by Cluster

Cluster	Timeframe
Air Force	July–Sept. 1995
Defense	Oct. 1995–March 1996
Education	June–Sept. 1995
Executive Office of the President and presidential agencies	April–June 1995
General government	Oct. 1994–April 1995
Health	April–July 1995
Housing	Sept.–Oct. 1995
Justice	Nov. 1994–May 1995
Labor	Sept. 1994–April 1995
Modern Army	April 1995–March 1996
Science	Dec. 1994–April 1995
State/foreign relations	Sept. 1994–April 1995
Treasury	April–Dec. 1995

Securing the means to open the archives to a wider public in an era of tight budgets and accelerating technological change presents the agency with a formidable challenge. During 1994, in conjunction with the National Performance Review and other government-wide improvement initiatives, NARA focused on innovation in delivering access to federal records, rethinking internal processes to serve customers more effectively, and creating a leaner organization that will concentrate on core functions. NARA plans to expand these efforts, capitalizing on the skills and knowledge of its staff and developing partnerships with other institutions.

Records and Access

Archives II

The formal dedication of NARA's state-of-the-art archival facility, located on 33 acres in College Park, Maryland, was held on May 12, 1994. The new building houses a research complex, 21 stack areas with a total capacity of 2 million square feet, preservation and conservation laboratories, administrative offices, and conference facilities. Movement of records from the National Archives Building in downtown Washington, D.C., and the Washington National Records Center in Suitland, Maryland, began in November 1993, and the move will continue until 1996. All nontextual records, as well as several clusters of textual records, have been moved to Archives II. Table 1 shows the remaining records clusters moving to Archives II. Each cluster should be closed to the public for only a few weeks while the records are being transported. NARA is planning special reference services for researchers during the move. Although much of the archives' holdings will be consolidated at College Park, the following clusters of records will be stored in the National Archives Building: genealogy, American Indian, District of Columbia, New Deal/Great Depression, World War I agencies, maritime, old Army, old Navy, judicial, and general records of the U.S. government.

CLIO

CLIO is the NARA gopher available via Internet. Construction of the gopher began in May 1994, and the gopher is now accessed almost 250 times an hour, or 6,000 times a day, by people outside NARA. CLIO—found at **gopher.nara.gov** and its associated World-Wide Web site at **www.nara.gov**—offers immediate access to more than 300 files that include publications, digital photographs, and pointers to related Internet resources.

Fax-on-Demand

This is an interactive fax retrieval system in which a single digital copy of a document is stored on the hard drive of a computer, where it can be selected and retrieved by any customer with access to a fax machine. The system was set up in November 1993 and since March 1994 has received more than 7,000 calls. There is no charge for the service except for any long-distance telephone charges the user may incur. Documents are updated or added regularly and include General Information Leaflets, press releases, training bulletins, records finding aids, regional archives and Presidential Library fact sheets, NARA library news, preservation reports, and *Federal Register* notices. The system can be reached at 301-713-6905.

PRESIDENT

The University of North Carolina (UNC), in coordination with the Office of Presidential Libraries, is developing an online Internet database called PRESIDENT that will include finding aids for library holdings and actual documents and photographs from library collections. During 1994 Presidential Libraries have been loading information onto the UNC system, and the university hopes to make the information available to the public by the end of 1995. Individual libraries have also been collaborating with local universities to put facility information and historical materials on Internet. The Ford Library and the University of Michigan have developed a multimedia presentation titled "A Day in the Life of a President;" the Roosevelt Library and Marist College are producing "FDR Day by Day," a multimedia presentation of President Franklin D. Roosevelt's life and times; and the Johnson Library and the University of Texas have made oral histories, photographs, speeches, and other information available online.

Online Federal Register

The *Federal Register,* which is the daily newspaper of the federal government, includes notices of meetings, regulations, reorganizations, and other governmental activities of wide interest to the public. Publication and distribution of the *Federal Register* is the responsibility of the Government Printing Office (GPO), and it has made electronic access to the *Federal Register* one of the keystones of its own electronic delivery system: GPO ACCESS. Free access to the full text of the electronic version of the *Federal Register* is available through federal depository libraries, or an electronic subscription may be purchased from GPO (as well as from some commercial vendors). The full text of the *United States Government Manual,* another publication of the Office of the Federal Register, is available on Internet through the University of Michigan and is accessible via CLIO.

Electronic Access Project

To more systematically explore the information needs of citizens in a location remote from a NARA facility, NARA is working with a team of research scientists from the National Institute of Standards and Technology (NIST). During the summer of 1994 the NIST team interviewed and surveyed a select group of individuals in Nebraska to determine what government information Nebraskans need, when they need it, and in what formats they need it. The project authors will assess NARA's existing and planned online and digital resources and systems to see how they must be modified or improved if NARA is to address the identified customer information needs. The report will also include recommendations on the criteria NARA should follow in selecting material to digitize for access, and perhaps eventually for preservation, and will offer suggestions as to future initiatives and pilot projects NARA may wish to undertake. The final report of the project should serve as a blueprint for further NARA activities on the "Information Superhighway."

Declassification

On November 17, 1994, President Clinton signed Executive Order 12937 calling for the bulk declassification of almost 44 million pages of security-classified records at NARA. This order covers approximately 14 percent of NARA's holdings of classified materials and is the largest single group of classified records to be declassified by NARA. The records include about 21 million pages of records from World War II and 23 million pages of records from the postwar period through the Vietnam War era. Almost all of this material is available for research in the Washington, D.C., area. A small amount of material will be withheld under exemptions of the Freedom of Information Act.

Silvio O. Conte Federal Records Center and Regional Archives

The dedication of the Silvio O. Conte Federal Records Center and Regional Archives took place August 15, 1994, in Pittsfield, Massachusetts. The 133,440-square-foot facility contains warehouse space for the storage of noncurrent federal records and office and public spaces. The regional archives will focus on collections of NARA microfilm publications of interest to genealogists. There are now 15 centers in the nationwide Federal Records Center System and 13 archives in the Regional Archives System.

Bush Presidential Library and Museum

The groundbreaking for the George Bush Presidential Library and Museum was held November 30, 1994, in College Station, Texas. The library, which is expected to be completed in 1997, will be built with private funds on 90 acres of land on the campus of Texas A&M University. After construction, the operation and funding of the library will be assumed by NARA. The Bush Presidential Materials Project, composed of NARA staff, currently oversees the storage and preservation of the records of the Bush presidency. The future Bush Library will join ten other libraries and projects covering the records of each president since Herbert Hoover at sites around the country.

Truman Presidential Library and Museum

On April 20, 1994, the Truman Library and the Truman Library Institute for National and International Affairs announced plans for a major renovation of the library's museum to begin in 1994 and to be completed in conjunction with the observance of the 50th anniversary of Harry S. Truman's presidency, 1945–1953. The renovation will include the construction of a new Presidential Gallery for the permanent exhibition on the Truman Administration as well as video screens and interactive software to help tell the Truman story to a new generation of visitors.

Customer Service

Centers Information Processing System (CIPS)

CIPS allows federal agencies to make electronic reference requests for records stored at a Federal Records Center. CIPS improves customer service by reducing reference preparation time and cost, delivery delays, and turnaround times. Begun as a pilot project in October 1993, CIPS now processes more than 50,000 electronic requests each month, and turnaround times have been reduced to 2 to 3 days from the former 10 to 12 days. NARA's service improvement allows other federal agencies to provide faster service to their public customers as well. On December 1, the Office of Federal Records Centers was awarded a 1994 Federal Technology Leadership Award for CIPS.

Technology to Enhance Reference Customer Satisfaction (TERCS)

The Fort Worth Federal Records Center has improved service for customers needing information from civil and criminal court cases. Center staff will research and provide copies of records directly to the public in response to telephone and fax requests. Previously, all requests were submitted to the originating court, which then requested the files for processing.

The Pacific Southwest Regional Archives in Laguna Niguel, California, is making federal census indexes and Social Security death indexes available on CD-ROM to improve service for genealogical and other researchers. Many regional archives do not have a complete set of census indexes, and those that are available are often complicated and cumbersome to use.

Both of these pilot projects have been praised by staff and the public for their resulting improvements in customer service. The Fort Worth pilot project will be expanded to include other records centers in 1995.

Organizational Changes

Restructuring

On October 1, 1994, NARA restructured its staff services units. The key changes included the creation of a Professional Development and Training staff within the Office of the Archivist, the abolishment of the Office of Management and Administration, and the establishment of two service units to support NARA's program offices. The service units are Administrative Services, and Policy and Information Resources Management Services. The reorganization will result in stronger and more efficient partnerships between NARA's operating units and staff services units at lower costs, and enhanced support, tools, and training for all NARA staff.

Buyouts

To help the agency meet the administration's streamlining goals, NARA offered early retirement and buyouts to all eligible employees in the spring and summer of 1994. More than 170 employees took advantage of the offer, enabling the agency to exceed its personnel reduction goals for the next two years.

Administration

NARA employs approximately 2,880 people, of whom 1,900 are full-time permanent staff members. For fiscal year 1994, the National Archives' budget was $190 million, with $5.25 million to support the National Historic Publications and Records Commission. An annual description of the activities and finances of NARA can be found in the *Annual Report of the National Archives*. For a copy of the report or for further information about NARA, call the public affairs staff at 202-501-5525.

United States Information Agency Library and Book Programs

Bureau of Information
301 Fourth St. S.W., Washington, DC 20547
202-619-4915

The United States Information Agency (USIA), an independent organization within the executive branch, is responsible for the U.S. government's overseas information, educational exchange, and cultural programs. The work of the agency is carried out by a staff of foreign service officers assigned to U.S. missions abroad and by a professional staff of career civil servants in Washington, D.C. Known abroad as the United States Information Service (USIS), the agency has more than 200 posts in 146 countries that are grouped in six geographic areas: Africa; Western Europe; Eastern Europe and the Newly Independent

States; East Asia and the Pacific; the American Republics; and North Africa, the Near East, and South Asia. Posts in these areas report to area offices in Washington, D.C.

History of USIS Library Programs

Today's worldwide system of USIS libraries evolved from a matrix of programs. First, in Latin America, came libraries associated with President Franklin Roosevelt's "Good Neighbor" program. In 1941 the coordinator of inter-American affairs, Nelson Rockefeller, contracted with the American Library Association (ALA) to establish and operate a library in Mexico City, the now-famous Biblioteca Benjamin Franklin. Under similar contracts, ALA opened and operated on behalf of the U.S. government two other libraries in Latin America: in Managua, Nicaragua (1942), and Montevideo, Uruguay (1943).

Beginning in 1942 the Office of War Information (OWI) began to establish reference libraries as part of its overseas information program. These were separate and distinct from U.S. Embassy reference libraries at the outset. Later, parts of many embassy collections were turned over to USIS libraries. The American Library in London started operations in December 1942 and officially opened in April 1943. The London library was the first overseas library directly under U.S. government control. Between 1942 and 1945 OWI established libraries in 40 more locations throughout the world. In 1945 the Department of State assumed responsibility for overseas libraries.

Shortly after World War II the U.S. military government began opening Information Center (Amerika Häuser) libraries and reading rooms in Germany, throughout the American Zone, and in the major cities of the British and French zones. At the same time Information Center libraries were started under the auspices of the United States Forces in Austria, Japan, and Korea. The State Department assumed responsibility for these centers when civilian control was restored in each country. Nine centers came under the department's auspices in January 1949, and ten centers in Austria were added in 1950. These centers were initially transferred to the State Department and finally, on August 1, 1953, to the newly created United States Information Agency. Since that time USIS libraries and information resource centers have been opened in virtually every country with which the United States maintains diplomatic relations.

Library Programs

More than 5 million patrons visited the more than 160 USIS libraries that were in operation worldwide during 1994.

USIS library services and holdings vary significantly from country to country, depending on the objectives of the USIS post (the public affairs office of the U.S. Embassy), the information needs of audiences served, and the communications environment in the host country. All USIS libraries, however, perform two mutually supportive functions: to provide the latest and most accurate information about U.S. government policies and to serve as continuing sources of informed commentary on the origin, growth, and development of American social, political, economic, and cultural life.

As greater emphasis is placed on outreach and reference/research services for foreign opinion leaders, USIS librarians increasingly work as subject specialists with direct electronic access to the wealth of information sources in the United States. In recent years more than 100 USIS libraries in Europe, Latin America, Asia, Africa, and the Near East have begun accessing online databases (principally DIALOG, NEXIS, LEGI-SLATE, and the in-house public affairs database PDQ).

At the same time, USIS libraries are giving increased attention in their circulating collections to long-term objectives, including improved understanding of American intellectual and cultural history, American economic and social institutions, and American political traditions. With collections ranging in size from several hundred to more than 30,000 volumes, USIS libraries seek to provide a balanced cross section of outstanding American contributions in the social sciences and humanities, often in places where such access is extremely limited or virtually nonexistent.

USIS also provides substantial support for more than 50 libraries located in binational centers in about 20 countries. The USIS-supported libraries, as distinct from USIS libraries, operate under the direction of an indigenous organization rather than a USIS post. USIS support usually consists of donations of materials and services or a grant of funds for rent, materials, and staff.

With the exception of the large USIS library programs in Brazil, Germany, India, and Mexico, USIS libraries and information resource centers abroad are managed by librarians from the host country who provide a vital link between the objectives of the USIS information program and the needs of the local audience. They are assisted by a team of 20 American library professionals who are stationed in all parts of the world and visit USIS local libraries to ensure their effective management, promote new resources and technologies, and help the libraries and posts define their roles in relation to the foreign policy of the United States.

A major reorganization of USIA's Washington headquarters in 1994 closed the Library Programs Division and devolved greater authority for library and information resource center programs to USIS posts abroad. USIA Washington continues to operate one of the federal government's most dynamic special libraries, each year fielding about 18,000 requests for information, half from USIA Washington staff and half from overseas posts. The headquarters library maintains 50,000 books, 800 journals, and 1,000 online text sources, allowing staff to respond to a wide range of complex bibliographic and information queries. USIA headquarters is also responsible for assuring the proper training of field librarians.

Public Diplomacy Query Database

USIA also produces and maintains a family of databases called Public Diplomacy Query (PDQ), to index, store, and make available to USIS libraries most program and foreign policy materials acquired and produced by USIA. PDQ is available online and via CD-ROM.

Library Fellows Programs

In 1987 USIA and the American Library Association inaugurated an annual Library Fellows program, which enables U.S. librarians with special expertise to serve in institutions abroad for periods ranging from three months to a year. The general objectives of the program are to improve host country or regional access to important information from and about the United States and to establish wherever possible ongoing linkages between American library professionals and institutions and their overseas counterparts in the interest of improving mutual understanding.

Under the terms of the program, which is administered by the American Library Association through a grant from USIA, prospective host institutions abroad are invited to submit proposals through local USIS posts. Project proposals are evaluated and ranked by a committee convened by USIA, after which the American Library Association announces the positions available and oversees the recruitment and selection of candidates.

Typical Library Fellow projects include planning automation of library functions in a national library, developing an American studies collection in an academic library, designing programs for teaching library skills to children and young adults through public library systems, establishing the organizational framework for a national law library, centralizing cataloging and technical services in an academic library, conducting an assessment of public library networking requirements, or managing a retrospective bibliographic conversion project.

In 1993 the Fellows program was expanded to a two-way exchange, with librarians from foreign institutions coming to libraries in the United States for periods of several months to carry out prearranged programs designed to broaden their professional skills and strengthen their roles as participants in the steadily growing worldwide movement toward free access to information.

For more information on USIA library programs, write to the Information Resources Division (I/R), Office of Information, USIA, Washington, DC 20547.

Book Programs

USIA also supports the publication of American books abroad, both in English and in translation. The agency, through its field posts abroad, works with publishers to produce a variety of translated books in the humanities and social sciences that reflect a broad range of American thought and serve to explain American life and institutions.

Through programs of book translation and through a variety of seminars, conferences, and short-term professional publishing workshops, USIA seeks to encourage respect for and adherence to international standards of intellectual property rights protection. The agency works closely on this issue both with foreign governments and with domestic and foreign nongovernment organizations.

American publishers seeking additional information about the agency's book program should direct their inquiries to the Publications Section, I/RP, Office of Information Resources, Bureau of Information, USIA, 301 Fourth St. S.W., Washington, DC 20547. Foreign publishers should turn for assistance to the Public Affairs Office of the U.S. Embassy in their country.

National Center for Education Statistics Library Statistics Program

U.S. Department of Education, Office of Educational Research and Improvement
555 New Jersey Ave. N.W., Washington, DC 20208-5652

Adrienne Chute
Library Statistics Program

The mandate of the National Center for Education Statistics (NCES) to collect library statistics is included in the National Education Statistics Act of 1994 (PL 103-382). NCES regularly collects and disseminates statistical information on public, academic, and elementary and secondary school libraries. These data provide the only current, comprehensive, national data on the status of libraries. They are used by federal, state, and local officials, professional associations, and local practitioners for planning, evaluation, and policy making. These data are also available to researchers and educators to analyze the state of the art of librarianship and to improve its practice.

Public Libraries

Descriptive statistics for nearly 9,000 public libraries are collected and disseminated annually through a voluntary census, the Public Libraries Survey. The survey is conducted by NCES through the Federal-State Cooperative System (FSCS) for public library data. In 1994 FSCS completed its sixth data collection.

FSCS is an example of the synergy that can result from combining federal/state cooperation with state-of-the-art technology. FSCS was the first national NCES data collection in which the respondents supplied the data electronically. It was also edited and tabulated completely in machine-readable form. All six data collections have been collected electronically. The software—the most recent version is called DECPLUS—is cost-effective and has improved data quality.

The 50 states and the District of Columbia participate in data collection. Beginning in 1993 the following territories also joined FSCS: Guam, Northern Marianas, Palau, Puerto Rico, and the U.S. Virgin Islands. During 1994, for the collection of 1993 data, the respondents were nearly 9,000 public libraries, identified by state library agencies, in the 50 states, the District of Columbia, and several of the territories. In general, both unit response and response to specific items are very high and item response rates have increased annually. Efforts to improve FSCS data quality are ongoing. Over the past several years the clarity of FSCS definitions, software, and tables has been significantly improved.

At the state level and in the territories, FSCS is administered by data coordinators, appointed by each state or territory's chief officer of the state library agency. FSCS is a working network. An annual training conference is provided for the state data coordinators and a steering committee that represents them is active in the development of the Public Libraries Survey and its software.

Note: Jeffrey Williams and Elizabeth Gerald, Library Statistics Program, contributed to this article.

Technical assistance to states is provided by phone and in person by state data coordinators and by NCES staff and contractors. NCES also works cooperatively with the National Commission on Libraries and Information Science (NCLIS), the Chief Officers of State Library Agencies (COSLA), the American Library Association (ALA), and the U.S. Department of Education's Library Programs Office.

Data files on diskette that contain 1992 data on about 9,000 responding libraries were made available in 1994. These 1992 data were also aggregated to state and national levels in an E.D. TABS, an NCES publication designed to present major findings with minimal statistical analyses. The Public Libraries Survey collects data on staffing; type of governance; type of administrative structure; service outlets; operating income and expenditures; size of collection; service measures such as reference transactions, interlibrary loans, circulation, public service hours, library visits, circulation of children's materials, children's program attendance, and interlibrary relationship; and other data items. The 1993 FSCS data were collected in July 1994, with release of these data scheduled for spring 1995. The 1994 data will be collected in August 1995, with release scheduled for summer 1996.

Additional information on FSCS may be obtained from Adrienne Chute (202-219-1772), Education Surveys Division, National Center for Education Statistics, Room 311A, 555 New Jersey Ave. N.W., Washington, DC 20208-5652.

The following are highlights from E.D. TABS Public Libraries in the United States: 1992, released in May 1994.

- 8,946 public libraries (administrative entities) were reported in the 50 states and the District of Columbia in 1992 (Table 1).
- Nearly 71 percent of the population of legally served areas in the United States was served by 957 (nearly 11 percent) public libraries. Each of these public libraries has a legal service area population of 50,000 or more (Tables 1A and 1B).
- 1,463 public libraries (over 16 percent) reported one or more branch library outlets, with a total of 7,035 branches. The total number of central library outlets reported was 8,837. The total number of stationary outlets reported (central library outlets and branch library outlets) was 15,872. Nearly 10 percent of reporting public libraries had one or more bookmobile outlets, with a total of 1,066 (Table 2).
- Over 81 percent of public libraries had only one service outlet (Table 17).
- Nearly 57 percent of public libraries were governed by a municipal government; almost 12 percent by a county/parish; nearly 10 percent by a nonprofit association or agency; over 6 percent by a library district; over 5 percent had multijurisdictional governance under an intergovernmental agreement; over 3 percent were governed by a school district; and over 1 percent by a combination of school/public or academic/public libraries. For over 5 percent of public libraries, their governance did not fit into any of these categories (Table 16).

- Public libraries reported that nearly 79 percent of total operating income of nearly $5.0 billion came from local sources, 12 percent from the state, 1 percent from federal sources, and over 8 percent from other sources, such as gifts and donations, service fees, and fines (Table 5).
- Per capita operating income from local sources was under $3 for over 14 percent of public libraries, $3 to $14.99 for nearly 54 percent and $15 or more for 32 percent. Per capita income from local sources varies considerably, with a percentage distribution of about 10 percent in each of 10 categories reported (Table 6).
- Total operating expenditures for public libraries were over $4.5 billion in 1992. Of this, nearly 65 percent was for paid full-time-equivalent (FTE) staff and over 15 percent for the library collection (Table 7). The average U.S. per capita operating expenditure was $18.73. The highest state average per capita operating expenditure was $35.81 and the lowest was $7.45 (Table 14).
- Over 42 percent of public libraries reported operating expenditures of less than $50,000 in 1992. Nearly 38 percent expended between $50,000 and $399,999, and over 20 percent exceeded $400,000 (Table 8).
- Public libraries reported a total of 109,933 paid FTE staff (Table 3).
- Nationwide, public libraries reported over 642.6 million book and serial volumes in their collections, or 2.7 volumes per capita. By state, the number of volumes per capita ranged from 1.6 to 5.5 (Table 11).
- Nationwide, public libraries reported collections of over 22.6 million audio materials, about 532,000 films, and nearly 6.8 million video materials (Table 11).
- Total nationwide circulation of library materials was over 1.5 billion or 6.4 per capita. Highest statewide circulation per capita was 11.7 and lowest was 3.2 (Table 15).
- Nationwide, nearly 6.8 million library materials were loaned by public libraries to other libraries (Table 15).

The numbers and percentages in the highlights above are based entirely on reporting public libraries. The percentage of public libraries not responding to a given item varied across states, ranging from 0.9 to 100 percent. There was no imputation for public libraries that did not respond or for items left blank. Thus, unless the response rate to a particular item was 100 percent, totals are probably underestimates. Readers are urged to take response rates into account when making inferences or forming conclusions. Per capita figures in these highlights are based not on the total population of the nation or state but on their total unduplicated population of legal service areas. Population of legal service area means the population of those areas in the state or nation where public library service is available. It does not include the population of unserved areas.

Academic Libraries

NCES surveyed academic libraries on a three-year cycle between 1966 and 1988. Since 1988, the Academic Libraries Survey (ALS) has been a component of the Integrated Postsecondary Education Data System (IPEDS) and is on a two-year cycle. ALS provides data on about 3,500 academic libraries. In aggregate, these data provide an overview of the status of academic libraries nationally and statewide.

The survey collects data on the libraries in the entire universe of accredited higher education institutions and on the libraries in nonaccredited institutions with a program of four years or more. ALS produces descriptive statistics on academic libraries in postsecondary institutions in the 50 states, the District of Columbia, and the outlying areas.

NCES has developed IDEALS, a software package for states to use in submitting ALS data to NCES. Its model was DECTOP, the predecessor of DEC-PLUS, the software developed for the collection of public library data in the FSCS program. IDEALS was used by 45 states in the collection of 1992 data.

ALS, using FSCS as a model, has established a steering committee, composed of representatives of the academic library community. Its mission is to improve data quality and the timeliness of data collection, processing, and release. This network of academic library professionals works closely with state IPEDS coordinators (representatives from each state who work with NCES to coordinate the collection of IPEDS data from postsecondary institutions in each of their states). NCES also works cooperatively with ALA, NCLIS, the Association of Research Libraries, the Association of College and Research Libraries, and numerous academic libraries in the collection of ALS data. ALS collects data on total operating expenditures, full-time-equivalent library staff, service outlets, total volumes held at the end of the fiscal year, circulation, interlibrary loans, public service hours, gate count, reference transactions per typical week, and online services.

The following are highlights from *E.D. TABS Academic Libraries: 1992*, released in November 1994.

- In 1992, total operating expenditures for libraries at the 3,274 institutions of higher education totaled $3.6 billion (Table 1A).
- The three largest individual expenditure items for all academic libraries were salaries and wages, $1.9 billion (51.8 percent); current serial subscription expenditures, $639 million (17.5 percent); and print material expenditures, $421 million (11.5 percent) (Tables 2A and 3A).
- The libraries of the 500 doctoral-granting institutions (15.3 percent of the total institutions) accounted for $2.3 billion, or 62 percent of the total operating expenditure dollars at all college and university libraries. This included $1.1 billion for salaries and wages, $467 million current serial subscription expenditures, and $253 million print material expenditures (Tables 2B and 3B).

- The number of volumes held at all academic libraries at the end of FY 1992 totaled about 749 million (Table 5A).
- Libraries at institutions granting doctoral degrees held about 471 million volumes, or 63 percent of the total volumes held (Table 5B).
- The total number of full-time-equivalent (FTE) staff members in college and university libraries equaled 96,000, including about 26,000 librarians and other professional staff, 40,000 other paid staff, 29,000 student assistants, and 404 staff who contributed their services (Table 4A).
- Libraries at institutions granting doctoral degrees accounted for 52,000, or half of all, FTE staff at all academic libraries. This included about 14,000 librarians and other professional staff, 24,000 other paid staff, 14,000 student assistants, and 128 staff who contributed their services (Table 4B).
- Academic libraries had 229 million circulation transactions; 78.8 percent from general collections, and 21.2 percent from reserve collections (Table 9A).
- Libraries at institutions granting doctoral degrees accounted for more than half of this total circulation with 129 million circulation transactions (Table 9B).

Additional information on academic library statistics may be obtained from Jeffrey Williams, Education Surveys Division, National Center for Education Statistics, 320A, 555 New Jersey Ave. N.W., Washington, DC 20208-5652 (202-219-1362).

School Library Media Centers

A national survey of school library media centers was conducted in school year 1993–1994, the first since school year 1985–1986.

In 1991, a small amount of data on school libraries was collected as embedded items from a sample of public and private elementary and secondary schools as part of the NCES 1990–1991 Schools and Staffing Survey (SASS). Data collected included number of students served; number of professional staff and aides; number of full-time-equivalent (FTE) librarians/media specialists; number of vacant positions, positions abolished, and approved positions; and amount of librarian input in establishing curriculum. NCES released a short report on these data in November 1994.

In addition, in 1991, as a separate part of the same SASS, NCES field-tested two new, more comprehensive, questionnaires for school libraries. One questionnaire covered the school library media center and the other the school library media specialist. A statistics committee has been established by the American Association of School Librarians to work with the federal government on the statistical needs and concerns of the school library media center community. The committee evaluated the results of the field test and helped to revise collection procedures and both the school library media center questionnaire and the school library media specialist questionnaire for the full-scale survey. NCES, with the assistance of the U.S. Bureau of the Census, conducted this survey as part of the

1994 SASS. Release of these data is scheduled for 1995. The school library media specialist questionnaire will provide a nationwide profile of the school library media specialist workforce. The school library media center questionnaire will provide a national picture of school library collections, expenditures, technology, and services. This effort will be used to assess the status of school library media centers nationwide and to assess the federal role in their support.

Additional information on school library media center statistics may be obtained from Jeffrey Williams, Postsecondary Education Statistics Division, National Center for Education Statistics, 320A, 555 New Jersey Ave. N.W., Washington, DC 20208-5652 (202-219-1362).

Federal Libraries and Information Centers Survey

The Federal Library Survey is designed to obtain data on the mission and function, administrative and managerial components (e.g., staff size and expenditures), information resources (e.g., collection size), and services of federal libraries and information centers. The Federal Library Survey is a cooperative effort between NCES and the staff of the Federal Library and Information Center Committee (FLICC) of the Library of Congress. The survey will establish a nationwide profile of federal libraries and information centers, update statistics from previous surveys, and provide estimates of how these facilities have changed.

The survey was pretested in 1993 and 1994 with the full-scale survey scheduled for 1995. Release of these data is scheduled for late 1995.

Plans for the Library Statistics Program

NCES plans to continue collecting the Public Library Survey. NCES has annually funded technical assistance to states for library data collection. To enhance the Public Libraries Survey, NCES developed the first comprehensive public library universe file (PLUS) and merged it with DECTOP into a revised software package called DECPLUS. DECPLUS was used to collect 1992 and 1993 data and will be used for future data collections. DECPLUS collects identifying information on all known public libraries and their outlets, all state libraries, and some library systems, federations, and cooperatives. This resource is now available for use in drawing samples for special surveys on such topics as literacy, access for the disabled, library construction, and the like. A mechanism to track changes was established beginning with DECPLUS. Closings, additions, and mergers of public libraries and public library service outlets, for example, are tracked in a historical file.

Several topical surveys are also under way. In 1993, under the sponsorship of Library Programs, NCES conducted two fast-response surveys—on public library services to children and on services to young adults. The results are expected to be available in 1995. NCES has also sponsored a project through the American Institutes for Research to develop the first index of inflation for public libraries. A report of the project will be available in 1996. FSCS is also exploring the potential of software, including mapping software, to make customized analysis of public library data available to data users.

Public library questions are also being included as parts of other NCES surveys. For example, questions about purposes for which households use public libraries and about barriers to use are being pretested as part of an expanded household screener for the NCES Household Survey. The full-scale study is planned for 1996, with data available in 1997. FSCS also plans to include some library-oriented questions on the Early Childhood Survey, planned for 1998.

NCES pretested a survey on state library agencies in 1994 and collected data in late 1994. Release of these data is scheduled for 1995. The state library survey is a cooperative effort between NCES and COSLA.

NCES has also fostered the use and analysis of FSCS data. A Data Use Subcommittee of the FSCS Steering Committee has been addressing the dissemination, use, and analysis of FSCS data. Data dissemination has also been broadened with electronic release of the data and E.D. TABS on Internet. In addition, an information service called the National Data Resource Center (NDRC) has been set up. NDRC helps customers obtain reports and data files and also responds to requests for tabulations and limited analysis on the library and other NCES studies and surveys.

The collection of academic library data through IPEDS will also be continued. NCES plans to improve the quality of the data by promoting the use of IDEALS software for data collection. New data elements focusing on electronic access and other new technologies may be added to the survey. The ALS reports will contain more detailed analyses of the data.

Several questions about the role of academic libraries in distance education are planned as part of another survey sponsored by the National Institute on Postsecondary Education. The survey is called the Survey on the Instructional Uses of New Technologies and will be conducted under NCES's Postsecondary Education Quick Information System (Peqis).

NCES will continue school library data collection through SASS.

NCES is also laying the groundwork for an Interlibrary Cooperation Survey. NCES plans to pretest this survey in 1996.

The Library Statistics Program also sponsors activities that cut across all types of libraries. For example, in 1993, NCES sponsored an invitational forum on policy analysis using library data from all types of libraries. The 1994 forum focused on electronic technology. The 1995 forum topic is "Changes in Library and Information Services in the Next Five Years." Since 1993, NCES has also sponsored the attendance of FSCS state data coordinators at NCES training opportunities, including the semiannual Cooperative System Fellows Program, the Management Information Systems Conference, and the Summer Data Conference.

Publications

Public Libraries in Forty-Four States and the District of Columbia: 1988; An NCES Working Paper (November 1989). o.p.

E.D. TABS: Academic Libraries: 1988 (September 1990). o.p.

E.D. TABS: Public Libraries in Fifty States and the District of Columbia: 1989 (April 1991). o.p.

E.D. TABS: Public Libraries in the U.S.: 1990 (June 1992). o.p.

E.D. TABS: Academic Libraries: 1990 (December 1992). o.p.

Survey Report: School Library Media Centers in the United States: 1990–1991 (November 1994). For sale through the Government Printing Office, No. 065-000-00715-1.

E.D. TABS: Public Libraries in the United States: 1991 (April 1993). o.p.

Report on Coverage Evaluation of the Public Library Statistics Program (June 1994). Prepared for NCES by the Governments Division, Bureau of the Census. Government Printing Office, No. 065-00-00662-6. $11.

Report on Evaluation of Definitions Used in the Public Library Statistics Program (1995). Prepared for NCES by the Governments Division, Bureau of the Census. Government Printing Office, No. 065-000-00736-3. $6.00.

E.D. TABS: Public Libraries in the United States: 1992 (August 1994). Government Printing Office, No. 065-000-00670-7. $7.

Data Comparability and Public Policy: New Interest in Public Library Data. Papers presented at meetings of the American Statistical Association. Working Paper No. 94-07. NCES, November 1994.

E.D. TABS: Academic Libraries: 1992 (November 1994). Government Printing Office, No. 065-000-00717-7. $3.75.

More recent publications may be available through the Superintendent of Documents, Government Printing Office. Write to: New Orders, Box 371954, Pittsburgh, PA 15250-7954. Credit card orders may be placed by fax at 202-512-2264.

Data Files Released on Diskette

Public Libraries in Forty-Four States and the District of Columbia: 1988 (March 1990).

Public Libraries in Fifty States and the District of Columbia: 1989 (May 1990).

Academic Libraries: 1988 (October 1990).

Public Libraries Data 1990 (July 1992).

Academic Libraries: 1990 (February 1993).

The NCES data files above are generally available on computer diskette through the U.S. Department of Education, Office of Educational Research and Improvement, Data Systems Branch, 555 New Jersey Ave. N.W., Washington, DC 20208-5725.

Public Libraries Data 1992 (September 1994). For sale through Government Printing Office, No. 065-000-00675-8. $15.

Academic Libraries: 1992 (November 1994). Available through NDRC.

The NCES data files above are generally available through the Government Printing Office, 202-512-1530. They are also available through the National Data Resource Center (NDRC), 703-845-3151, at no charge. Send two DOS formatted high-density 3.5-inch diskettes and a self-addressed diskette mailer. NDRC also responds to requests for tabulations and limited analysis of NCES studies and surveys.

Electronic Releases of Publications and Data Files

OERI Toll-Free Electronic Bulletin Board System (EBBS)

E.D. TABS: Public Libraries: 1990 (March 1992)

E.D. TABS: Public Libraries in the United States: 1991 (March 1993)

E.D. TABS: Public Libraries in the United States: 1992 (May 1994)

For more information, call 202-219-1547.

Internet

Public Libraries Data 1989 (December 1994)

Public Libraries Data 1990 (November 1994)

E.D. TABS: Public Libraries in the United States: 1991 (March 1993)

Public Libraries Data 1991 (November 1993)

E.D. TABS: Public Libraries in the United States: 1992 (August 1994)

Public Libraries Data 1992 (September 1994)

E.D. TABS: Academic Libraries: 1992 (November 1994)

Academic Libraries Data 1992 (November 1994)

DECPLUS Software

DECPLUS Manual

The reports and data files listed above are available on Internet. To reach the U.S. Department of Education/OERI gopher server, point to <gopher.ed.gov> and follow this menu path:

Select Educational Research, Improvement, and Statistics (OERI & NCES)/ Then select National Center for Education Statistics (NCES)/ Then select either NCES Publications & Reports, NCES Tabulations and (Special) Tables, or NCES Data (surveys and raw data)/

Each data file and report is preceded by an accompanying descriptive readme file, designated by the descriptor "About." Each readme file, the report, and the data files may be downloaded.

For more information about obtaining reports and data files through Internet, GPO, or NDRC, contact NDRC. Send your request by Internet to: ndrc@pcci.com; or send a fax to 703-820-7465; or write to NDRC at 1900 Beauregard St., Suite 200, Alexandria, VA 22311; or call 703-845-3151.

Library of Congress

Washington, DC 20540
202-707-5000

The Library of Congress (LC), the world's largest library, was founded in 1800 to serve the research needs of the U.S. Congress. Over the years, it has expanded its mission to serve not only the legislative branch but also other branches of government, libraries everywhere, the scholarly community, the American people, and the world.

In 1994 LC employed a staff of approximately 4,600 organized into seven service units, working primarily in the institution's three buildings on Capitol Hill, Washington, D.C. The library also has a storage facility in Landover, Maryland, and in 1994 began developing additional off-site storage at Fort Meade, Maryland. There are also six overseas field offices that specialize in the acquisition of foreign books, documents, and serial publications.

LC operated under strong budgetary restraints in fiscal year (FY) 1994 (October 1, 1993–September 30, 1994), when appropriations available for obligation totaled $331.9 million, nearly $2.5 million less than the amount available in FY 1993. In response to this, the library, as of March 6, 1994, began closing all buildings to the public on Sundays throughout the year. In 1993, the library had closed general reading rooms on Tuesday and Friday evenings and on Sundays between Memorial Day and Labor Day.

LC's appropriations available for obligation for FY 1995, as approved by Congress in July, totaled $348.5 million, an increase of 5.4 percent from 1994. (LC had asked for $358 million for the year.)

Hiram Logan Davis, formerly director of libraries at Michigan State University, East Lansing, became Deputy Librarian of Congress in July 1994. As chief operating officer, Davis supervises day-to-day internal operations, and LC's seven service unit heads report to him.

Services to Congress, 1994

In serving Congress, LC provides impartial, analytical research reports and information on public policy issues. In 1994 LC's Congressional Research Service (CRS) provided Congress with more than 600,000 products and customized responses to requests from members and committees. The year also marked the beginning of the ninth decade of CRS service to Congress.

In 1914 an appropriation amendment introduced by Senator Robert La Follette of Wisconsin was approved by the 63rd Congress with a provision to establish a Legislative Reference Division within LC. The amendment enabled the Librarian for the first time to "gather, classify, and make available . . . data for or bearing upon legislation, and to render such data serviceable to Congress and committees and members thereof." Librarian of Congress James H. Billington joined Daniel P. Mulhollan, who became director of CRS in January 1994, in greeting members of Congress and other guests at a celebration of the 80th anniversary of CRS on July 26 in the Great Hall of the Thomas Jefferson Building.

Services to the Nation, 1994

The Copyright Office administers U.S. copyright laws and actively promotes international protection for intellectual property created by U.S. citizens. In 1994 it processed more than 620,000 claims for copyright registration and answered 400,000 requests for information. Marybeth Peters, a 28-year veteran of the Copyright Office, was appointed Register of Copyrights in July.

LC's National Library Service for the Blind and Physically Handicapped in 1994 distributed more than 21 million items—including books and periodicals in braille and on tape, as well as its own publications—to more than 750,000 persons. This service is provided through 147 regional and subregional libraries and two distribution centers at no cost to users. In 1994 LC launched a major public information program to expand its services to the blind and physically handicapped.

LC also provided bibliographic records and related products to libraries and information centers in the 50 states and all five territories and the Commonwealth of Puerto Rico. This cataloging would have cost these institutions $336 million in 1994 had they done the work themselves.

LC in 1994 responded to more than 1.4 million requests for reference and research assistance from scholars and other researchers and welcomed 830,865 visitors and users of its collections. It also provided more than 36,000 free interlibrary loans to researchers throughout the country through their public, university, or state libraries. The Law Library served more than 135,000 users, supplying research in more than 200 foreign jurisdictions to Congress, the judiciary, and federal agencies, as well as providing public access to its collections.

The library's Japan Documentation Center became fully operational with the appointment in March of its first director, Ichiko Morita, formerly of the Ohio State University faculty. An acquisitions office in Tokyo had opened earlier. The center was established in 1992 in response to a congressional directive to enhance current Asian collections in order to keep Congress well informed. The center is focusing on the acquisition of hard-to-find reports and other documents issued by the Japanese government and private research centers on political, economic, legal, and policy issues.

Although initiated to meet the needs of Congress, the center, part of LC's Asian Division, makes its holdings available to executive branch agencies, educational institutions, business researchers, and others. The center is funded in part by a grant from the Japan Foundation's Center for Global Partnership.

LC's American Folklife Center pursued its work to "preserve and present" American folklife in cooperative programs, including cultural documentation in Paterson, New Jersey, and a field school on "Documenting Traditional Culture." From June through September, center staff members studied occupational culture in Paterson, the nation's first planned industrial center, for the National Park Service's Urban History initiative. From July 9 to 22, staff conducted classes in Colorado Springs and Crestone, Colorado, in cooperation with Colorado College and the University of New Mexico, for teachers and students interested in community-based cultural documentation projects.

In July, under a National Endowment for the Humanities grant awarded to the Dance Coalition, an archivist began two years' work in the American Folklife

Center archiving dance and dance-related collections. In 1994, processing was completed on the Paul Bowles Moroccan Music and Dance Collection; the Gothland, North Yorkshire, Sword Dance Photograph Collection; the Diana Cohen Hopi Religion Collection; and the Agnes Bellinger Tlingit Collection.

Electronic Access

During 1994 LC made major strides in setting in motion the development of the National Digital Library. In October, the Librarian announced plans to form a coalition of major institutions to convert important collections to digital formats. The coalition plans to have digitized 5 million images by the year 2000, making them available worldwide over computer networks. The coalition also will work to resolve copyright issues.

LC plans to digitize core collections, which will be made available freely to all. As the year ended, 60 Americana collections were being considered for digitization.

At an October 13 ceremony, James Billington announced gifts of $13 million to support the program. Grants of $5 million each from John Kluge and from the Lucile and David Packard Foundation are earmarked for a major program to digitize LC's historical collections in the public domain. Kluge is chair and president of Metromedia and chair of LC's private-sector advisory group, the James Madison Council; David Packard is a founder of the Hewlett-Packard Co. Also announced was a $3 million grant from the W. K. Kellogg Foundation to help LC identify instructional uses of digital library materials.

October 13 also saw the opening of the Digital Library Visitors' Center, where visitors are given hands-on demonstrations of digital library products and computer networking. The center, located in the James Madison Memorial Building, initially was open by appointment only. It was expected to open to the public at large in January 1995.

LC's computerized databases, containing 26 million bibliographic records and a wealth of other information including images from exhibitions, text of some LC publications, and copyright records, have been available online on Internet since 1993. The Internet telnet address is **locis.loc.gov**; the numeric address is **140.147.254.3**.

Another electronic offering, the Library of Congress News Service, is a free service available online. Its offerings include:

- Items of interest to the media, such as upcoming conferences, exhibition openings, major acquisitions, and other announcements, as well as features suitable for reprinting in other publications
- Information of particular interest to librarians, such as availability of Cataloging Distribution Service products, news from Collections Services, new LC publications, changes in LC procedures in cataloging and other areas, major personnel appointments, and professional meetings
- A calendar of events
- Information on current LC job openings

- Instructions for downloading information from the News Service to personal computers. The News Service will allow 30 minutes of access per call. The telephone number is 202-707-3854.

Poetry Programs, 1994

Pulitzer Prize-winning poet Rita Dove began her second year as Poet Laureate Consultant in Poetry and opened LC's 1994–1995 literary season October 6 with the lecture "A Handful of Inwardness: The World in the Poet," which is to be published in one volume with "Stepping Out: The Poet in the World," her concluding lecture of the 1993–1994 literary year.

Ms. Dove, who is Commonwealth Professor of English at the University of Virginia, Charlottesville, presided over an innovative year of literary programs. She traveled widely in an effort to encourage the growing general interest in poetry. Most of the library's 1994 poetry programs, which are free, had overflow attendance, and the videotape "A Conversation with Poet Laureate Rita Dove" proved very popular.

One notable poetry program honored the memory of poet William Stafford, consultant in poetry 1970–1971, who died August 28, 1993.

LC in September hosted the 60th anniversary celebration of the Academy of American Poets, at which the first Dorothea Tanning Prize of $100,000 was presented to poet W. S. Merwin. Tanning, an artist and widow of surrealist Max Ernst, gave $2 million to the academy to establish the annual prize to recognize outstanding and proven mastery in the art of poetry. It is the largest literary prize in the United States.

On October 27 LC's own poetry prize, the Rebekah Johnson Bobbitt National Poetry Prize, was awarded to A. R. Ammons for his book *Garbage*, published by W. W. Norton in 1993. The $10,000 prize is given every two years for the best book of poetry by an American published during the previous two years. Bobbitt was the sister of the late President Lyndon B. Johnson.

International Visitors, 1994

While LC traditionally hosts visits by scholars and others from around the world, 1994 was a notable year for distinguished visitors.

On September 28, President Bill Clinton and Russian President Boris Yeltsin opened the exhibition "In the Beginning Was the Word: The Russian Church and Native Alaskan Cultures," which continued at LC through December 31. The exhibition, based on the archives of the Russian Orthodox Greek Catholic Church in Alaska, a part of LC's collections, focused on the religious, educational, social, and linguistic relationships between the Alaskan, Aleutian, and Kuril Islands natives of the 19th and early 20th centuries and the Russian Orthodox Church.

Another head of state, South African President Nelson Mandela, visited LC October 4 for a reception in his honor given by the Congressional Black Caucus.

It was the South African president's first official visit to Washington since his election in April.

Emperor Akihito and Empress Michiko of Japan were given a royal welcome when they visited June 14. Six members of Congress joined LC officials in welcoming the royal couple to the sparkling, newly renovated Great Hall in the Thomas Jefferson Building and guiding them to an array of LC treasures, including the first copy, in Lincoln's hand, of the Gettysburg address. The empress visited the Children's Literature Center to talk about children's books.

Preservation

Seeking to extend its leadership in preservation of library materials, on March 14 LC hosted 75 preservation specialists from libraries, museums, and other institutions to ask for advice on taking its preservation program into the 21st century. Preservation is one of the major focuses of LC's strategic plan for the year 2000. The March 14 advisory session was one of a series that started in December 1993 for staff members and others under the direction of Diane Nester Kresh, now director of preservation and national preservation program officer.

In January the Librarian appointed a special committee and four task forces to assist him in planning a national film preservation program as mandated by the National Film Preservation Act of 1992. The special committee is assisting in securing funding for preservation, and the task forces are addressing preservation issues, public access and educational use, public-private cooperation, and public awareness. Composed of representatives from the motion picture industry, archives, and the educational community, the groups immediately began working to develop the framework for a coordinated national film preservation program.

The National Film Preservation Board advises the Librarian on selection of films for the National Film Registry and other matters. Films must be at least ten years old for selection for the registry and are chosen because they are culturally, historically, or aesthetically significant. LC encourages preservation of registry films and the National Film Registry Seal may be exhibited only on films that meet the same standards as those in LC's collections.

Films selected for the registry in 1994, bringing the total to 150, were:

The African Queen (1951)

The Apartment (1960)

The Cool World (1963)

A Corner in Wheat (1909)

E.T.: The Extra-Terrestrial (1982)

The Exploits of Elaine (1914)

Force of Evil (1948)

Freaks (1932)

Hell's Hinges (1916)

The Hospital (1971)

Invasion of the Body Snatchers (1956)

The Lady Eve (1941)

The Louisiana Story (1948)

The Manchurian Candidate (1962)

Marty (1955)

Meet Me in St. Louis (1944)

Midnight Cowboy (1969)

A Movie (1958)

Pinocchio (1940)

Safety Last (1923)

Scarface (1932)

Snow White (1933)

Tabu (1931)

Taxi Driver (1976)

Zapruder Film (1963)

During 1994 LC celebrated the "Cinema's First Century" with a yearlong series of films dating from 1893 to the present. Films were shown most week-nights throughout the year in the Mary Pickford Theater in the Madison Building. Mary Pickford Theater films are free and open to the public.

Library of Congress Associates

The year saw formation of the Library of Congress Associates and the publication of the first issue of the bimonthly *Civilization: The Magazine of the Library of Congress*. The associates group is made up of men and women who are interested in LC's collections and exhibitions and the well-being of the institution.

The associates receive special weekly tours and discounts in LC's gift shop and buffet dining room as well as a subscription to *Civilization*, which made its debut in November. The magazine draws heavily on LC's unmatched collections of more than 108 million items. Each issue contains a calendar of upcoming events at LC and at other libraries around the country. *Civilization* is published by a partnership controlled by L.O.C. Corporation, based in New York City, under license by the library. Its editorial offices are in Washington, D.C. For information about Library of Congress Associates membership, call 1-800-829-0427.

Additional Sources of Information

The Library of Congress Information Bulletin, published biweekly, and a catalog of publications, *Library of Congress Publications in Print*, issued biennially, are available free to libraries from the Library of Congress, Office Systems Services, Printing and Processing Section, Washington, DC 20540-5446.

Library of Congress telephone numbers for public information:

Main switchboard   202-707-5000

Copyright information   202-707-3000

Copyright hotline (to order forms)	202-707-9100
Directions to the library	202-707-4700
Employment information	202-707-4315
LC News Service (computer access)	202-707-3854
Mary Pickford Theater	202-707-5677
National Reference Service	202-707-5522
Poetry and literature programs	202-707-5394
Reading room hours and locations	202-707-6400
Research information	202-707-6500
Sales shop	202-707-0204
Visitor services (including tours and exhibitions)	202-707-8000

The National Digital Library Program

Guy Lamolinara
Public Affairs Specialist, Library of Congress

In 1990 the Library of Congress (LC) embarked on a test program to bring the riches of its collections to all Americans—not just those able to travel to one of LC's three buildings on Capitol Hill.

That project, called American Memory, has become the foundation on which LC is building the National Digital Library Program—a cooperative effort that plans to digitize up to 5 million items from the collections of LC and other major institutions by the year 2000. Selections from American Memory's digitized collections are available worldwide over Internet and on disk at 44 test sites across the country.

The core of the digital library will initially consist of American historical collections but contemporary materials will also be important. At LC, 200 collections have been nominated for digitization—photographs, sound recordings, documents, printed matter, and motion pictures that represent the nation's memory.

In order for this digital library to be national, even international, in scope, leaders of the library, education, information, technology, and philanthropic communities will guide the effort in concert with LC. Priorities for digitizing these 200 collections will be made by subject matter scholars within and outside the library.

For the National Digital Library to be a valuable research and learning resource, it must offer services as well as collections. The library envisions playing a leading role in the development of new ways to describe, preserve, and deliver digital items.

Because it is home to the U.S. Copyright Office, LC will construct new models and mechanisms to protect intellectual property rights in the digital environment and has embarked on a number of pilot projects in that regard. The collections digitized thus far are in the public domain or those for which it has obtained the proper permissions.

The library's National Preservation Program also has implications in the digital arena. Digitized formats can make rare and fragile materials available to the public. However, the perpetuity of digital files is not guaranteed and LC is exploring preservation technologies that will assure that these digital files are available for future generations.

Online Use of Primary-Source Materials

Educators are increasingly structuring lessons and assignments on the use of primary-source materials. Textbooks are being supplemented by videos, sound recordings, manuscripts, and other non-book materials.

From 1991 to 1993 LC conducted an evaluation at the 44 American Memory sites, which include libraries in 16 K–12 schools and 18 colleges and universities across the country. The results showed that the digitized collections encouraged students to think more creatively and independently and reduced their reliance on textbooks.

In October 1994 LC accepted a $3 million grant from the W. K. Kellogg Foundation to enable it to continue to identify educational uses for digitized materials. LC also received in October $5 million each from the Lucile and David Packard Foundation and from John Kluge, president of Metromedia. These funds were earmarked primarily for the digitization of American historical materials from LC collections. In January 1995 the digital library effort received a pledge of $1.5 million from Bell Atlantic.

LC will request an additional congressional appropriation of $3 million for each of the next five fiscal years, beginning with fiscal 1996, for its digital library initiative. The library plans to raise a total of $45 million from the private sector during the same period. These funds will enable LC to digitize up to 5 million items by 2000, in collaboration with other research institutions.

Many digitized collections of the National Digital Library will be available at no cost in unenhanced form to Internet users. The private sector will be able to take these offerings and tailor them to suit the needs of the marketplace; LC will not grant exclusive rights to any of its collections.

The Digital Library Visitors' Center

In October 1994 LC opened its Digital Library Visitors' Center as a place where members of Congress and their staff could see demonstrations of the digital initiatives. The center was expected to open to the general public in early 1995.

Digitization activities focus not only on LC's collections but also on the services the library provides to Congress and the nation, such as legislative information, cataloging, and copyright registration. The 15 workstations in the Visitors' Center offer the following LC initiatives.

American Memory

So far, more than 300,000 items from more than two dozen collections on American culture and history in the public domain have been digitized in this initial project. Until recently, American Memory was only available on disk at 44 test sites across the United States. LC is in the process of making selections from those collections more widely available over Internet.

Six photographic, motion picture, and manuscript collections from American Memory are available via LC's World-Wide Web server (Uniform Resource Locator: http://www.loc.gov):

- Selected Civil War Photographs from the Library of Congress, 1861–1865
- Early Films of San Francisco Before and After the Earthquake and Fire, 1897–1907
- Life History Manuscripts from the Folklore Project, WPA Federal Writers' Project, 1936–1939
- Color Photographs from the Farm Security Administration and the Office of War Information, ca. 1938–1944
- Films of President William McKinley and the Pan-American Exposition, 1901
- Early Films of New York City, 1897–1906

THOMAS

An online resource for congressional information about the workings of the U.S. Congress, THOMAS organizes electronic information in one place. Available on the World-Wide Web and via telnet, THOMAS debuted January 5, 1995, as an initiative of the 104th Congress (World-Wide Web URL: http://thomas.loc.gov; telnet URL: thomas.loc.gov; login as thomas). It contains the full text of bills of the 103rd and 104th Congress and the *Congressional Record*, as well as links to other legislative information resources.

Online Exhibitions

Not everyone can visit Washington to see LC exhibitions, which are on view for relatively short periods. Over the past several years, the library has therefore been making images and accompanying text from its major exhibitions available over Internet, where they can be viewed from across the country or around the globe, increasing their longevity and outreach. The library is the only national cultural institution with eight major exhibitions online:

- Rome Reborn: The Vatican Library and Renaissance Culture
- Selections from the African-American Mosaic
- 1492: An Ongoing Voyage
- Revelations of the Russian Archives
- The Dead Sea Scrolls: The Ancient Library of Qumran and Modern Scholarship
- In the Beginning Was the Word: The Russian Church and Native Alaskan Cultures
- The Gettysburg Address: Words That Shaped America
- Temple of Liberty: Building the Capitol for a New Nation

Internet Access to LC Databases

The Library of Congress provides Internet access to more than 40 million computerized records of books, bill summaries, copyright registrations, and summaries of foreign laws. LC's gopher, LC MARVEL, organizes some of the library's digital offerings, along with resources from other government agencies and institutions around the world. The library's World-Wide Web server also offers access to additional resources and makes them available to users with appropriate browser software.

Global Legal Information Network

The Global Legal Information Network (GLIN) is a cooperative international network in which foreign national institutions contribute their statutes to a database at LC's Law Library, which in turn shares access with the international community. This project is in its early stages, with tests being conducted with several nations.

Electronic Cataloging in Publication (CIP)

In 1993 LC initiated a project that tests the feasibility of the transmission of electronic manuscripts over Internet. Currently, printed galleys must be mailed. The University of New Mexico Press, University of South Carolina, and HarperCollins have sent digital texts for cataloging in the CIP program. Capturing the information from the electronic text ensures a high degree of accuracy and reduces cataloging time and publishers' costs.

Copyright Imaging System

The Copyright Office at LC receives nearly 700,000 applications each year. Library patrons can now search records online, and retrieve and print digital images of copyright applications, which are scanned and stored on disks. The system is the key to a paperless office, allowing data to be stored efficiently. The system also produces printed registration certificates.

Electronic Copyright Management System

In 1993 the Copyright Office began working with the Corporation for National Research Initiatives (CNRI) on the development of a testbed system to determine the feasibility of receiving machine-readable copyright registrations, deposits, and copyright transfer documents over Internet. CNRI is developing the system under contract with the Advanced Research Projects Agency and the Library of Congress, which will allow copyright applicants to prepare registrations and deposits in digital form, to "sign" digitally their submissions and to send them to the Copyright Office electronically.

Country Studies

LC provides access to a series of books prepared by its Federal Research Division under the Country Studies/Area Handbook Program sponsored by the Department of the Army. Most books in the series deal with a particular foreign country, describing and analyzing its systems and institutions. The Ethiopia country study is available on the LC World-Wide Web server. The gopher at the University of Missouri at Saint Louis makes available country studies on Egypt, Indonesia, Israel, Japan, the Philippines, Singapore, Somalia, South Korea, and Yugoslavia.

Center for the Book

John Y. Cole
Director, Center for the Book
Library of Congress

With its network of 29 affiliated state centers and 134 organizations serving as national reading-promotion partners, the Center for the Book is one of the Library of Congress's most dynamic outreach projects. Since 1977, when it was created by Librarian of Congress Daniel J. Boorstin, the center has used the prestige and resources of the Library of Congress (LC) to stimulate public interest in books, reading, and libraries and to encourage the study of books and the print culture.

The center is a successful public-private partnership; LC supports its four full-time positions, but its program and the programs of its state affiliates are funded largely through contributions from individuals, corporations, and foundations.

Highlights

Significant Center for the Book activities in 1994 included the addition of three states—Idaho, Louisiana, and Vermont—to the center's national network of state affiliates; the addition of ten national civic and educational organizations to the reading-promotion partnership program; successful "Library-Head Start Partnership" workshops in California, Virginia, and Kansas that brought together more than 150 Head Start teachers and librarians who serve children to plan family literacy projects; a planning conference for a new library-museum-Head Start partnership project; participation in the 1994 Frankfurt Book Fair and the 60th International PEN Congress, held in Prague; and the announcement of a $1 million endowment from the Annenberg Foundation that will establish an endowment for the Center for the Book beginning in 1996; his will be named the Daniel and Ruth Boorstin Trust for the Center for the Book, honoring the center's founder.

Themes

The center establishes national reading-promotion themes to stimulate interest and support for reading and literacy projects that benefit all age groups. Used by state centers, national organizational partners, and hundreds of schools and libraries across the nation, each theme reminds Americans of the importance of books, reading, and libraries in today's world. "Books Change Lives," the theme for 1993–1994, continued to be the centerpiece for most of the center's reading-promotion activities in 1994. The new theme for 1995–1996, "Shape Your Future—READ!" was introduced at the end of the year.

Reading-Promotion Partners

The center's organizational partnership program grew to 134 partners in 1994. Private and governmental organizations become reading-promotion partners of the Library of Congress by agreeing to participate in each year's reading-promotion campaign. They publicize the national promotion theme, develop their own projects, or make an in-kind or financial contribution to support the effort.

New organizational partners for 1994 included the American Association of Community Colleges, the Association of Junior Leagues International, the Auxiliary of the National Rural Letter Carriers, Boy Scouts of America, Boys and Girls Clubs of America, the Corporation for Public Broadcasting, Washington Independent Writers, and the Weekly Reader Corporation.

On January 19, 1994, organizational partners gathered at LC to share ideas about using the "Books Change Lives" theme. Examples of projects developed by partners included the restocking of a flood-devastated library in Kansas by American Mensa Ltd.; a student essay contest in the Dallas/Fort Worth area sponsored by the North Texas Association of the Phi Beta Kappa Society, with a $1,000 scholarship as the prize, plus the gift of $500 worth of books to the winner's school library; promotion of "Books Change Lives" projects and materials by the National Council of Negro Women at all seven of its annual "Black Family Reunion Celebrations" in 1993; and the issuing by the U.S. Postal Service of a poster honoring four new 29-cent stamps featuring favorite childhood books and the "Books Change Lives" campaign.

State Centers

When James H. Billington became Librarian of Congress in 1987, the Center for the Book had ten affiliated state centers. The number of state centers increased dramatically in subsequent years, and at the end of 1994 there were 29. The three newest centers are Idaho, located at the Hemingway Western Studies Center at Boise State University; Louisiana, a part of the Louisiana State Library; and Vermont, which grew out of the Vermont Reading Project in Chester. The oldest state center, Florida, celebrated its tenth anniversary in February.

Each state center works with LC to promote books, reading, and libraries as well as the state's own literary and intellectual heritage. Each develops and funds its own operation and projects, using LC promotion themes when appropriate and occasionally hosting LC traveling exhibits. When its application is approved, a state center is granted affiliate status for three years. Renewals are for three-year periods.

In 1994, eight states (Colorado, Florida, Iowa, Michigan, Minnesota, North Dakota, Oklahoma, Pennsylvania) hosted the LC traveling exhibition "Language of the Land" and developed programming around it. The exhibit "Bonfire of

Liberties: Censorship of the Humanities" was seen in Minnesota, Nebraska, and Wisconsin.

On April 18, 1994, representatives from 26 state centers participated in an idea-sharing session at LC. During the panel discussions, the state center representatives reviewed such topics as how to recruit and motivate effective board members, networking opportunities, and fund-raising techniques. Growing interest in electronic communication and production techniques was explored, as well as the importance of maintaining databases of information. State center projects considered included Alaska's two-day celebration of Alaskan authors and literature; Arizona's authors-interview program on local public television and its writers-in-the-classroom project; Colorado's first and very successful Rocky Mountain Book Festival; Idaho's book arts exhibit and celebration; Iowa's program on censorship; Minnesota's use of CD-ROM technology to capture the state's literary heritage; Oklahoma's annual book award ceremony; and Virginia's use of teleconferencing in its programming, particularly an event that featured Rita Dove, Poet Laureate Consultant in Poetry at the Library of Congress for 1993–1995.

Projects

The "Literary Heritage of the States" project, funded with a grant from the Lila Wallace-Reader's Digest Fund, reached across the country with its traveling exhibit "Language of the Land: Journeys into Literary America." The colorful exhibit, which appeared at eight state centers, explores the nation's rich literary heritage through maps from LC's collection, photographs, and quotations from writers. It was developed by the center in collaboration with LC's Interpretive Programs Office and its Geography and Map Division.

The Library-Head Start Partnership project, funded with a transfer of funds from the U.S. Department of Health and Human Services to the Center for the Book, ended the second phase with the completion of three regional workshops. Implemented in collaboration with the Association for Library Service to Children (ALSC), a division of the American Library Association, the Library-Head Start project was designed to demonstrate in communities nationwide how libraries that serve children and Head Start programs can work together in family literacy projects. The regional workshops, hosted by affiliated state centers in California, Kansas, and Virginia, featured a 40-minute video produced by the Center for the Book and discussed development of plans for operating Library-Head Start Partnerships productively in each state.

To mark the 200th anniversary of LC, the Center for the Book launched a project that will feature symposia, lectures, and publications—both popular and scholarly—about the Library and its history.

Outreach

In 1994, the Center for the Book prepared 12 reading lists for the Library of Congress/CBS Television "Read More About It" book project. The 30-second messages appeared during several major prime-time telecasts, including the

Super Bowl and the U.S. Open tennis championship. The project is now in its 15th season; messages have been telecast since 1979 on more than 400 CBS Television programs.

Four issues of the newsletter *Center for the Book News* were prepared and distributed in 1994. The first issue of *Partners Update*, a newsletter for reading-promotion partners, was produced. A handbook describing the activities of the state centers was produced and distributed. The December 1993 issue of *Wilson Library Bulletin* featured a three-page article about the state centers. The November/December 1993 issue of *Humanities*, a bimonthly review published by the National Endowment for the Humanities (NEH), featured a conversation between NEH Chair Sheldon Hackney and Center for the Book Director John Cole about literacy, technology, and the future of the book.

Events

Sponsorship of significant events and meetings at LC and around the country is an important way that the Center for the Book accomplishes its mission. Recent examples of events at LC include "Adult Literacy and Technology" and "Interpreting the National Adult Literacy Survey," symposia sponsored with the National Center on Adult Literacy; "From Gutenberg to William Gibson: Revolutions in Knowledge from the Renaissance into the 21st Century," lectures by historians Elizabeth L. Eisenstein and Richard W. Bulliet, sponsored with Columbia University Press and Houghton Mifflin Co.; "Textbook Development and Western Assistance in Russia and the Newly Independent States," a symposium co-sponsored with PUBWATCH, one of the center's reading-promotion partners; "Book and Publishing History," the second annual conference of the Society for the History of Authorship, Reading, and Publishing, which featured the presentation of 81 scholarly papers about different aspects of book and publishing history; "What Books Live?," a symposium honoring Librarian of Congress Emeritus Daniel J. Boorstin on his 80th birthday; and "Amassing American Stuff," a program at LC that focused on the New Deal art collections of the Library of Congress: manuscripts, music, prints, photographs, posters, recordings, folklife and theater materials, and first-person narratives.

Publications

Center for the Book publications in 1994 included *The Politics of Silence*, a lecture by National Book Award winner Paul Monette, sponsored with the National Book Foundation; *Thomas Jefferson: A List of Books for Young Readers*; *Capital Libraries and Librarians: A Brief History of the District of Columbia Library Association, 1894–1994*, by John Y. Cole; and a reprint of the center's most popular publication, *Reading for Survival* by John D. MacDonald, which was originally published in 1987 in collaboration with the Florida Center for the Book. The theme of the essay, in Mr. MacDonald's words, is "the terrible isolation of the nonreader, his life without meaning or substance because he cannot comprehend the world in which he lives."

Federal Library and Information Center Committee

Library of Congress, Washington, DC 20540
202-707-4800

Susan M. Tarr
Executive Director

During fiscal year 1994, the Federal Library and Information Center Committee (FLICC) worked to meet the changing professional and service needs of the federal library and information center community. FLICC provided a forum for examining information's role in "reinventing" government, and FLICC working group initiatives updated federal library personnel standards, monitored federal depository library developments, and prepared the nationwide survey of federal libraries and information centers. FLICC's cooperative network, FEDLINK, continued to enhance its fiscal operations, saving member agencies an estimated $12.1 million in discounts and contracting cost avoidance. FEDLINK Network Operations (FNO) expanded its ambitious training program to include Internet training for federal librarians.

FLICC submitted its formal proposed reorganization plan to the Constituent Services Service Unit at the Library of Congress (LC) in May 1994. In April 1994 Mary Berghaus Levering, FLICC executive director since 1989, was appointed to the new position of deputy registrar of copyrights by Librarian of Congress James H. Billington. Louis R. Mortimer, chief of the Federal Research Division, Constituent Services, was assigned to serve collateral duties as acting FLICC executive director. Joseph W. Price—acting FLICC director after Levering was detailed in August 1993 to the Copyright Office to assist its operation during a transition period—retired from LC in April 1994. Joseph S. Banks, FEDLINK business manager, served during Levering's detail as acting FEDLINK director. In November 1994 Susan M. Tarr, chief of the Cataloging Distribution Service at LC since 1986, was named FLICC executive director by the Librarian of Congress.

The FLICC Personnel Working Group completed a successful five-year project in July 1994 with release by the Office of Personnel Management (OPM) of classification standards for the GS-1410 Librarian Series and GS-1412 Technical Information Services Series. With the earlier release of classification standards for the Library Technician Series, GS-1411, and of qualification standards for all three series, the FLICC Personnel Working Group's work with OPM brought federal library classification standards into the electronic age.

The FLICC Federal Depository Library Working Group—established in 1993 in response to proposed changes in the Federal Depository Library Program (FDLP) of the Government Printing Office (GPO)—researched the important role federal libraries have played in making government information available and alerted federal libraries to the challenges facing the program. Federal libraries gained representation on the Depository Library Council, the body that advises GPO on the conduct of FDLP.

The FLICC Statistics Working Group, in concert with the National Center for Education Statistics (NCES), tested and refined the nationwide survey of federal libraries and information centers developed to update the 1978 survey.

The 1994 Annual FLICC Forum on Federal Information Policies, "Information's Role in Reinventing Government: Delivery of Government Information," examined the administration's move to reinvent government and the effect of the National Performance Review (NPR), National Information Infrastructure Initiative, and related executive and legislative actions on the delivery of government information. The program stressed the role of federal librarians and other information professionals in serving the needs of the public.

In FY 1994 the FEDLINK ALIX electronic bulletin board was connected to Internet to provide direct Internet access to federal librarians. ALIX also became available from the LC Marvel gopher menu. The ALIX Fiscal System (ALIX-FS) was enhanced to enable FEDLINK members to download and import OCLC usage data. The FEDLINK Library Network News listserv (FEDLIB-L) was implemented to distribute FEDLINK information to a wider audience. Overall, FEDLINK conducted training for 978 federal librarians and federal library technicians nationwide. To meet the demand for Internet training, FEDLINK offered an Internet overview, workshops, and advanced classes that constituted 28 of the 110 FEDLINK training classes during the fiscal year.

At the end of FY 1994 FEDLINK Fiscal Operations (FFO) reconciled the FY 1994 transfer pay service dollar obligation, requiring no temporary obligation for the second year in a row. FFO earned discounts in excess of the amount of interest paid to FEDLINK vendors, reconciled FEDLINK accounts from FY 1990, worked to integrate FEDLINK's management system with the library's new Federal Financial System (FFS) automated accounting system, and completed the selection of a FEDLINK member services supervisor. An interagency agreement (IAG) established for the National Agricultural Library (NAL) project in Egypt expanded the business volume of the FEDLINK program.

Quarterly Membership Meetings

At the first FY 1994 FLICC Quarterly Membership Meeting in December 1993, Harold Relyea, Congressional Research Service (CRS), explained the status and effect of the National Performance Review (NPR). John Chambers and Sarah C. Jones of the Joint Committee on Printing and Bruce McConnell of the Office of Management and Budget discussed NPR initiatives affecting GPO. The second meeting, in February 1994, featured Forrest Gale of the Defense Systems Management College, who presented the report "Quality of Information—A New Paradigm." At the May meeting, Levering discussed "Copyright and Librarians: A Summary of Today's Issues." During the September meeting, Blane Dessy, acting director, National Library of Education, described the establishment of the agency. Doria Grimes (National Oceanic and Atmospheric Administration, federal library delegate) and Davis McCarn (user representative for federal librarians) reported on the activities of the White House Conference on Library and Information Services Task Force.

Working Groups

Education Working Group

The FLICC Education Working Group planned and organized education programs of importance to federal librarians and information specialists on topics that addressed the Federal Depository Library Program, binding issues, information technology, access to federal libraries, and collections maintenance. In addition to the Annual FLICC Forum on Federal Information Policies, FLICC sponsored 26 programs that attracted a total of 900 federal librarians. Programs in the "Great Escapes" series were conducted at various federal libraries and agencies, including the National Technical Information Service, the Pentagon Library, the Justice Department Library, and the Naval Research Library.

Federal Depository Library Working Group

The FLICC Federal Depository Library Working Group focused on the role of federal depository libraries in the Federal Depository Library Program and presented a paper to the Federal Depository Conference on the important role federal libraries have played in making government information available and alerting federal libraries to the challenges facing FDLP. Federal libraries gained representation on the Depository Library Council, the body that advises the Public Printer on conduct of FDLP, with the appointment of Phyllis Christenson, Government Accounting Office, and Dan Clemmer, State Department and chair of the working group.

Finance Working Group

The FLICC Finance Working Group produced the FY 1995 FLICC budget, which ultimately held FEDLINK service fees to FY 1994 levels.

Membership and Governance Working Group

The FLICC Membership and Governance Working Group was reactivated in FY 1994 to review the FLICC nominating process and reexamine the FLICC bylaws, which have been in operation for three years.

Nominating Working Group

The FLICC Nominating Working Group conducted the annual FLICC three-phase election process under the FLICC Bylaws.

Personnel Working Group

The FLICC Personnel Working Group continued working with OPM to achieve final approval and release of the classification standards for the GS-1410 Librarian Series and GS-1412 Technical Information Services Series that OPM placed on hold in September 1993. The group met with OPM officials in November 1993 to obtain final approval of both series standards. On July 1, 1994, OPM officially issued the two standards.

Policy Working Group

Harold Relyea briefed the FLICC Policy Working Group on H.R. 3400, the Congressional Reform and Savings Act of 1993.

Preservation and Binding Working Group

Prior to merging with the FLICC Preservation Working Group, the FLICC Binding Working Group planned educational programs for federal library personnel that included a workshop on in-house use of protective enclosures, tours of the GPO binder facility, and a luncheon discussion on binding training opportunities. The Preservation Working Group developed a recommended statement in support of the government policy promoting the use of acid-free paper by federal agencies. In the spring of 1994 the Binding Working Group recommended merging with the Preservation Working Group because of their overlapping interests and programs. In May 1994 the combined group held the first of three meetings concerned with program planning and support for projects in progress.

Reference/Public Services Working Group

The FLICC Reference/Public Services Working Group sponsored a public access workshop to increase awareness of federal collections and access policies in major agency libraries. The session addressed library holdings, special collections, physical access policies, and electronic resource availability, and confirmed the considerable variance in access policies for federal employees and the general public.

Statistics Working Group

Organized in FY 1991 to update the 1978 federal library statistics prepared by FLICC, the FLICC Statistics Working Group continued working with the National Center for Education Statistics and the Bureau of the Census to develop an updated survey that also would include federal information centers. The group analyzed the results of a September 1993 survey pretest, revised the survey questionnaire, and tested the questionnaire in September 1994 in a limited sampling of 50 federal libraries and information centers. The revised final survey was targeted for a mailing in January 1995 to about 1,500 federal libraries and information centers.

Publications and Education

The FLICC Publications and Education Office (FPE) continued to provide communications and education outreach to the federal library and information center community by issuing FLICC and FEDLINK publications and administrative reports, organizing educational events and technical programs, coordinating more than 50 meetings of the FLICC working groups, and providing logistical, program development, and organizational support for the quarterly meetings of the FLICC membership and bimonthly meetings of the FLICC Executive Board.

FPE maintained an ambitious publications schedule despite staffing short-ages, producing ten issues of *FEDLINK Technical Notes*, including two double issues for the months of October/September 1993 and July/August 1994; and three issues of the *FLICC Newsletter*, Fall 1993, Winter 1993, and a double issue for Spring/Summer 1994.

FPE's annual publications included the *FY95 FEDLINK Services Registration Package*; the *FY95 FEDLINK Serials Registration Package*; the *FY94 FEDLINK Services Directory Data Sheets*; the 1994 FLICC Annual Forum Summary and Papers, *Information's Role in Reinventing Government: Delivering Government Information*; and the Summary of Conference Proceedings, *Federal Librarians in the 21st Century: Changing Roles in the Electronic Age*.

FPE also produced the FY 1994 FLICC management reports—including the FLICC monthly, quarterly, and annual reports, as well as the minutes of the FLICC quarterly membership meetings and the bimonthly executive board meet-ings—and worked in conjunction with the FLICC Education Working Group on FLICC education seminars and programs.

FEDLINK

In FY 1994, 974 federal agencies received cost-effective access to an array of automated information retrieval services for online research, cataloging, and interlibrary loan (ILL) through FEDLINK (Federal Library and Information Network). FEDLINK member agencies also procured publications, serials, and books through FEDLINK in FY 1994 via LC/FEDLINK contracts with major vendors.

The FEDLINK Advisory Council (FAC) formed a marketing committee to assist FEDLINK in determining market strategies, approved the FY 1995 FEDLINK fee structure, initiated discussion on ways to extend FAC membership in the field, and worked with the FLICC Membership and Governance Working Group to clarify the FLICC Bylaws.

At the October 1993 FEDLINK Membership Meeting, Carol A. Risher, vice president of copyright and new technology at the Association of American Publishers, and attorney Patrice A. Lyons presented "Copyright in the Electronic Environment." At the May 1994 meeting, Tom Bagg—systems engineer, National Institute for Standards and Technology (NIST)—discussed "The Dilemma of Preservation vs. Access." Sami Klein, NIST, presented the FY 1995 FLICC/ FEDLINK proposed budget, and FLICC staff provided updates on pro-grams and activities. FEDLINK network librarians Erik Delfino and Meg Williams presented the workshop "Using FEDLINK's Electronic Publications ALIX, ALIX-FS, and Internet."

FY 1994 was a year of transition for the Internet Planning Group (IPG), which recommended the creation of a FLICC working group to address automa-tion issues with the IPG as a task force. The executive board addressed the con-cept during FY 1994. An ad hoc group of federal librarians met in February and March 1994 to discuss issues and strategies for Internet training in federal agencies.

FEDLINK Network Operations

FEDLINK Network Operations (FNO) functioned as the regional library network for 825 Online Computer Library Center (OCLC) member federal libraries during FY 1994. FNO conducted training events in the Washington, D.C., area and nationally, and provided daily technical and program support to all federal libraries and information centers. FNO staff prepared solicitations and other required contract documents for LC Contracts and Logistics Services in support of the FEDLINK procurement program for information products and services; served on the Technical Evaluation Review Panels to evaluate vendor responses; and served as the Contract Officer Technical Representatives for the awarded FEDLINK contracts. FNO also provided other direct assistance in the planning and operation of the FLICC and FEDLINK programs.

OCLC Network Activity

During the first quarter of the fiscal year, FEDLINK network librarians conducted an open forum on format integration to identify training needs and expectations and provided needed updates. In the second quarter, OCLC began a one-year pilot of PRISM Internet access and FNO coordinated a national library training program for GPO at the request of OCLC. In the third quarter, the OCLC/FEDLINK basic ordering agreements (BOAs) instituted cost savings for the majority of FEDLINK OCLC members with decreases in charges for cataloging, ILL, and telecommunications. Billing for maintenance of OCLC equipment was moved from the FEDLINK agreement to direct arrangements between members and OCLC. FNO and OCLC assisted members with the transition. FEDLINK assisted the National Oceanic and Atmospheric Administration mini-network in securing a $22,000 savings in OCLC local database creation through project coordination. In the fourth quarter, FNO announced changes in OCLC services for FEDLINK users, reprogrammed the OCLC cataloging profiles of two OCLC mini-networks—the U.S. Information Agency and the Veterans Administration—and hosted the final meeting of the OCLC/Network User Support Task Force, which drafted "A Common Vision and Strategic Plan for User Support by Regional Networks and OCLC."

FEDLINK Training

Again in FY 1994 approximately one-half of FEDLINK's 978 trainees received instruction outside the Washington, D.C., area. FEDLINK conducted regional and on-site training in Alaska, California, Florida, Missouri, Nebraska, New Jersey, New Mexico, North Dakota, Washington, and West Virginia. FEDLINK provided Internet instruction for 118 federal librarians from the Air Force at the American Library Association annual meeting in Miami. Overall, FNO conducted a total of 110 classes, including 71 OCLC classes and 28 Internet classes.

FEDLINK OCLC Member Activity

FEDLINK OCLC members during the reporting period July 1993–June 1994 continued trends recorded in the previous year with dramatic increases in two areas: shared online cataloging transactions and EPIC Online Union Catalog (OLUC) displays.

OCLC online ILL activity showed the following changes: Total requests and referrals (borrowing activity) dropped 3.5 percent, from 303,362 to 292,817, while total lending credits (lending activity) increased about 1 percent, from 160,810 to 161,950, and total union list holdings displays continued to rise by 15.7 percent, from 43,000 to 49,746.

OCLC cataloging activity included the following: Total master records created by FEDLINK libraries in 1994 decreased 9.1 percent, from 66,335 to 60,291; while total online cataloging activity (adding symbols to records) rose 26 percent, from 512,557 to 645,919; and total offline retrospective conversion (Microcon) rose 163 percent, from 22,103 to 58,199. Total MARC records recorded to tape decreased 55 percent as a direct result of cancellation in July 1993 of the FLICC tape, which comprised over 1 million records annually. Discounting the FLICC tape, total MARC records ordered directly by members climbed 5.7 percent, from 745,226 to 787,517.

OCLC Reference Services (EPIC) statistics again rose sharply, as total EPIC OLUC (database 23) displays climbed 38.9 percent, from 101,705 in June 1993 to 141,313 in June 1994.

Library Automation Resource Service

Through its Library Automation Resource Service (LARS), FNO offered expert counsel to federal librarians in the application of automation and telecommunications in their library environment. LARS continued to focus on introducing Internet to federal librarians, and 385 federal librarians participated in the extensive FNO Internet training program that included 18 two-day workshops, one advanced class, and nine half-day overviews. FNO also conducted Internet training in the field to meet member needs.

Support for ALIX remained a priority during FY 1994. In November 1993 ALIX-FS was reorganized to display summary account balance information by fiscal year. A feature that enables users to download and import OCLC usage data into various database management packages was loaded on ALIX-FS in February. In August 1994 ALIX was connected to Internet for direct access by federal libraries and became available from the LC Marvel gopher menu. FY 1994 ALIX usage statistics reveal 28,000 total calls to ALIX from 4,000 registered users; FY 1994 ALIX-FS statistics showed 2,500 calls from 280 users. A total of 800 log-ons were registered to ALIX via Internet following implementation on August 15, 1994. In February 1994 FEDLINK implemented FEDLIB-L to distribute FEDLINK information, calendars, and news from member libraries. A total of 300 subscribers registered in the first month.

FEDLINK Procurement Program

FEDLINK analyzed the discounts offered through LC/FEDLINK BOAs (basic ordering agreements) and typical contracting costs for information procurements to assess the cost effectiveness of the FEDLINK procurement vehicle. A brief review of FY 1993 invoices suggested that FEDLINK BOA discounts ranged from 0 percent to 57 percent of commercial rates and saved members at least $2.3 million in service dollars. Analysis of comparable contracting costs for establishing 87 BOAs and providing competition for 403 individual serials orders over $25,000 suggested that FEDLINK's centralized contracting activity saved the government approximately $9.8 million in cost avoidance (estimating $20,000 per contracting action). Thus, through discounts and contracting cost avoidance alone—not considering FEDLINK's invoice processing, education, and other services—the FEDLINK program saved $12.1 million, an amount nearly triple the FEDLINK annual operating budget.

FEDLINK Fiscal Operations

FEDLINK Fiscal Operations (FFO) establishes federal agencies' membership in FEDLINK, determines FEDLINK service fees for members, prepares member IAGs (interagency agreements) and IAG amendments, FEDLINK vendor delivery orders, and administers FEDLINK member accounts, including processing all FEDLINK vendor invoices and generating individual FEDLINK member account statements. FY 1994 represented another successful year of operating performance for the FEDLINK program.

FFO reconciled the FY 1994 transfer pay service dollar obligations to the FEDLINK SYMIN signed IAG database, the Financial Services Directorate (LC/FSD) Budget Office billed report, and LC/C&L deliver order database; no temporary obligation was necessary for FY 1994. FFO processed 7,739 member service transaction requests representing $54.5 million of transactions for the current year and $3.4 million for the prior year (experiencing a low 1.7 percent error rate for processing member service transaction requests), and processed 513 requests by members to move their prior multiyear funds across fiscal year boundaries (representing a contracting volume of $3 million composed of 1,026 delivery orders). FFO also earned discounts in excess of the amount of interest remitted to FEDLINK vendors for the late payment of invoices in the amount of $4,056, representing a turnaround in performance from FY 1992, when FFO experienced interest payment net of discounts in the amount of $38,360.

FFO and LC/FSD reconciled FEDLINK's accounts from FY 1990; FEDLINK ensured that administrative expenditures/obligations did not exceed program fee projections; FFO and the SYMIN team worked closely with LC/FSD and LC/C&L to integrate FEDLINK's financial management system with FFS; FFO worked to resolve all issues concerning the IAG established for the U.S. Agency for International Development and NAL joint venture to establish a National Agricultural Library in Egypt, a project representing new business volume for the FEDLINK program.

Summary Statistics

FEDLINK processing statistics show the significant volume of both current and prior-year IAG, delivery order, invoice, and statement transactions handled during FY 1994.

FFO processed FY 1994 registrations from federal libraries, information centers and other federal offices, resulting in 944 signed FY 1994 IAGs, compared to 892 basic IAGs in FY 1993. In addition, FFO processed 2,167 IAG amendments (1,326 FY 1994 and 841 prior-year adjustments) for agencies that added, adjusted, or terminated service funding. These IAGs and IAG amendments represented 3,446 individual service requests to begin, renew, convert, or cancel service from 93 FY 1994 FEDLINK vendors. FFO executed service requests by generating delivery orders that were issued to vendors by LC/C&L. Delivery orders represented $50.7 million in FY 1994 and prior-year transfer pay service dollars. For FY 1994 alone, FEDLINK processed approximately $54.5 million in service dollars for 2,824 transfer pay accounts and approximately $60 million in service dollars for 350 direct pay accounts. FY 1994 activities represented a total of 3,174 FEDLINK agency accounts.

On behalf of transfer pay users, FFO processed 60,985 invoices for payment during FY 1994 for both current and prior-year orders. Vendor payments from agencies' FY 1994 transfer pay accounts totaled $30 million. FFO continued to maintain open accounts for three prior years for members using book and serial services or paying publications service invoices based on the order date and invoice items.

Summary

During FY 1994, FLICC and its components FNO and FFO continued to refine structure and programming to serve the federal library and information center community and forwarded the formal FLICC-proposed reorganization to Constituent Services in May.

FLICC worked to meet the professional needs of its members by sponsoring a forum that examined information's role in "reinventing" government, successfully working to update the federal librarian classification standards, monitoring federal depository library challenges, and testing and refining the nationwide survey that will be used to update the 1978 federal library and information center statistics.

The FEDLINK procurement program provided discounts and contract cost avoidance that saved federal libraries an estimated $12.1 million, an amount approximately three times greater than FEDLINK's annual operating budget. FNO conducted 110 training classes, including 71 OCLC classes and 28 Internet classes, attended by 978 librarians and library technicians nationwide. The FEDLINK ALIX electronic bulletin board was connected to Internet to provide direct Internet access to federal librarians.

During another successful year of operating performance for the FEDLINK program, FFO continued to provide initiative and leadership in financial management.

National Agricultural Library

U.S. Department of Agriculture, NAL Bldg., Beltsville, MD 20705
Internet: agref@nalusda.gov

Brian Norris
Public Affairs Officer

Change and accomplishment highlighted 1994 for the National Agricultural Library (NAL). The following are some of the significant activities in which NAL was involved during the year.

NAL to Merge with Agricultural Research Service

NAL will be merged into the U.S. Department of Agriculture's Agricultural Research Service (ARS) under a total reorganization of the department proposed by then-Secretary Mike Espy, approved by Congress, and signed by the president in October 1994. Plans called for the reorganization to take effect on December 1, 1994. With the merger, NAL will remain a national library and will retain its organizational identity; however, it will report to the director of the Agricultural Research Service rather than to the Assistant Secretary, Science and Education, USDA.

André Named New Director Following Howard's Retirement

Pamela André, formerly NAL's associate director for automation, was named NAL director in November 1994, replacing Joseph H. Howard, who retired earlier in the year. André had served as acting director of the library since Howard's retirement.

As NAL's associate director for automation, André was instrumental in the success of the National Agricultural Text Digitizing Program, in which selected portions of the NAL collection are placed on compact discs and distributed to land-grant university libraries nationwide.

André has also held positions as assistant chief of the MARC Editorial Division of the Library of Congress (LC), as a member of the management team of the LC Optical Disk Pilot Project, and as a computer systems analyst at LC. She has a master's degree in library science from the University of Maryland.

NAL Commits to Electronic Library Goal

On January 1, 1995, electronic information became the "preferred medium" for library materials in an effort to make NAL's services and collection available in various electronic formats worldwide.

NAL is making this commitment because of a belief that the current paper-based information delivery system is inadequate to keep pace with the needs of modern agriculture.

The "electronic library" goal was set in Electronic Information Initiative—Phase I, undertaken by NAL as part of a strategic plan to guide operations into the next century. The overall purpose of the initiative is to research, plan, and implement a systematic program of managing data in electronic form.

The statement of commitment to this goal says: "Increasingly, information is produced in digitized form, and with recent telecommunications innovations and the Internet, the resources available to the computer-literate researcher are expanding exponentially. . . . The NAL is taking the initiative in a systematic program of managing data in electronic form and establishing strategies for collecting, storing and distributing U.S. agricultural information in electronic form."

Jefferson Letters Found in NAL Collection

Eleven letters signed by Thomas Jefferson were found among old NAL files in late summer 1993. The letters date from April 24, 1786, to October 20, 1819, and include requests to Jefferson for appointments to federal agricultural offices, letters from Jefferson transferring "millet seed" and "succory seed" to acquaintances in the United States, and a letter to Jefferson from "Lord Sheffield" of the Board of Agriculture in London, England, commenting on Jefferson's invention of a farming tool. The letters were found in files of agricultural materials dating from the 1940s that had recently been sent to NAL by the USDA Economic Research Service.

NAL Aids Agricultural Libraries in Central Europe

NAL continues its efforts to forge lasting ties with agricultural libraries in the recently reorganized Central European countries. NAL has helped these agricultural libraries with gifts of books and journals, internships at NAL for their librarians, assistance in writing grant proposals, and expertise in setting up electronic information management systems.

NAL began cultivating relationships with Central European countries in 1991 when the library arranged and sponsored a conference in Beltsville, Maryland. Representatives from six countries attended. Assisting NAL in this activity was Associates of the National Agricultural Library, Inc. (a nonprofit "friends-of-the-library" group). A second conference was held in Budapest, Hungary, in the fall of 1992; a third conference in Radzikow, Poland, a year later; and another in Nitra, Slovakia, this past fall.

Countries participating in the conferences and exchanging agricultural information with NAL include Albania, Belarus, the Czech Republic, Estonia, Hungary, Latvia, Lithuania, Poland, Romania, Russia, Slovakia, Slovenia, and Ukraine.

NAL Seeks Relations with Latin American Libraries

Early in 1994 representatives from agricultural organizations in South American and Caribbean countries joined with NAL personnel in Washington, D.C., and

Beltsville, Maryland, for a workshop on agricultural information transfer and networking. The workshop focused on improving and strengthening the exchange of agricultural information between the United States and countries represented at the workshop. These countries were Argentina, Brazil, Chile, Colombia, Costa Rica, the Dominican Republic, El Salvador, Mexico, Nicaragua, Paraguay, Peru, Trinidad and Tobago, and Venezuela. Joining NAL and the foreign officials were representatives from U.S. organizations, public and private, that work with agricultural information. Canadian and British agricultural information specialists also attended.

The workshop produced an outline for a comprehensive regional plan for agricultural infrastructure development that will improve national systems and enhance regional and international cooperation, communications, and coordination. The plan is intended to overcome technological isolation and develop structures that can provide cost-effective access to information.

NAL Participates in National Cataloging Program

NAL has been selected to participate in the National Coordinated Cataloging Program (NCCP), a cooperative cataloging program of the Library of Congress (LC) in which selected libraries produce full, high-quality cataloging for the LC database and bibliographic utility (OCLC). NAL began full participation in 1993 and has contributed hundreds of records to the program since that time.

Unified Agricultural Thesaurus Progresses

NAL continues to be a key player in the international effort to produce a Unified Agricultural Thesaurus (UAT). This project will improve worldwide access to agricultural information through an improved thesaurus system. NAL, CAB International (CABI), and the Food and Agricultural Organization (FAO) of the United Nations are working to develop classified versions of both the thesaurus used by FAO (AGROVOC) and the CAB Thesaurus used by CABI and NAL. This is the first step in unifying the thesauri.

NAL, CABI, and FAO agreed on a thesaurus classification structure as the basis of this classification effort. An outline was presented at a policy meeting of the project partners in Bonn, Germany, and will be a component in Zentralstelle für Agrardokumentation und Information's agricultural expert system, AGRIRES.

Thesaurus management software to support the project is being developed in conjunction with the Canadian International Development Research Centre (IDRC). Representatives of NAL, FAO, CABI, and IDRC met in Rome to discuss the management software, and specifications were reviewed, amended, and accepted by NAL and CABI.

NAL/Land-Grants Cooperate to Add State Publications to Database

More than 45,000 citations for state-produced agricultural publications have been added to NAL's AGRICOLA database as a result of cooperation between land-grant universities and NAL under the NAL/Land-Grant University State Agricultural Publications Program.

The program has seen significant growth in recent years. In 1990 the program was expanded to include citations for agricultural theses and dissertations. In 1991 Colorado State University, Louisiana State University, and the universities of Maine, Maryland, Minnesota, and New Hampshire joined the University of Florida, the University of Nebraska, and the Massachusetts Institute of Technology in contributing citations of current research materials.

In 1992 the University of Arkansas and the University of Kentucky became participants. Recently, Ohio State and Texas A&M Universities renewed their participation in the Cooperative Cataloging Program, and the University of Nevada and Virginia State University and Polytechnic Institute began contributing records.

NAL Continues Aid to Egyptian Library

A project begun in 1990 to assist the government of Egypt in establishing an Egyptian National Agricultural Library (ENAL) has seen further development recently as groups of Egyptians visited NAL for training in library procedures, collection development, and management, including selecting and ordering monographs and serials for the core collection of the new Cairo library. NAL sorted, stored, and edited information into reports for the Egyptians, using database management systems.

NAL has also assisted ENAL in procuring electronic library systems, including microcomputer workstations, a CD-ROM development system, and an integrated library system.

NAL Improves Service to USDA Researchers

Throughout the year, NAL and the Agricultural Research Service continued to cooperate to improve information services to USDA researchers. NAL and the University of California at Davis, Shields Library, completed a remote-user evaluation study. The resultant report focuses on USDA researchers' use of NAL, USDA field libraries, and cooperating land-grant university libraries. It includes strategies to improve delivery of information services to USDA scientists.

NAL Strengthens Ties to Black Colleges and Universities

In an effort to improve cooperation and strengthen partnerships with historically black colleges and universities, NAL has provided internships in the Public Services Division for individuals from such institutions. A member of the staff of John B. Watson Memorial Library, University of Arkansas at Pine Bluff, trained for six weeks at NAL. A student majoring in agribusiness at the University of Maryland-Eastern Shore trained for several months. The interns received extensive orientation to NAL programs, services, and technology, and practical experience in public service operations.

In a related activity, members of the 1890 Land-Grant and Tuskegee Institute Library Directors' Association met with the NAL director and key library staff during an association meeting in Washington, D.C. NAL staff provided technology demonstrations and program updates.

NAL Serves as USDA Grants Cooperator

NAL continued to serve as a USDA "agency cooperator" for several grants awarded under USDA's 1890 Institutions Capacity Building Grants Program. The program advances the teaching and research capacity of 1890 land-grant universities and Tuskegee Institute. Projects covered by the grants and assisted by NAL are:

- "Building Human Capital in Foods and Nutrition," Tennessee State University
- "Strengthening Enrollment Using Shared Resources and Distance Delivery," North Carolina A&T State University
- "Enhancing Library Services in Support of the Degree Program in Regulatory Science," University of Arkansas

The program is administered by USDA's Cooperative State Research Service and requires coordination with one or more USDA agencies in developing and implementing projects. The "agency cooperator" role further strengthens USDA ties to 1890 institutions.

USDA Plant Genome Database

NAL is playing a key role in the USDA National Genetics Resources Program, a cooperative effort of the Agricultural Research Service, the Cooperative State Research Service, and NAL to incorporate germ plasm conservation and five genome research programs (plant, tree, animal, insect, and microorganism).

NAL is responsible for data gathered from the genome research programs and from the international research community and stored in a master database. The users for this information are plant breeders and molecular geneticists.

The Plant Genome Database (PGD) evolved from the design and development stage to full production. The database consists of genome data from five species groups—wheat, maize, soybean, pine, and Arabidopsis—as well as relevant bibliographic data from AGRICOLA.

Interactive access to PGD is provided via Internet. The database provides links to other relevant databases, such as DNA and protein sequence databases, and ARS's Germplasm Resources Information Network (GRIN).

The database will expand to include data from solanaceous crop plants, rice, cotton, and ultimately about 70 important crops. A CD-ROM release of the PGD is also planned.

Food Labeling Education Information Center Established

Established as part of the Nutrition Labeling and Education Act of 1990, the FDA/USDA Food Labeling Education Information Center, located at NAL, is in full swing. The center is a cooperative effort between NAL's Food and Nutrition Information Center (FNIC), the USDA Food Safety Inspection Service, and the Food and Drug Administration (FDA).

A cornerstone of the center's activities is a database of new food-labeling education activities and materials developed by the private and public sectors. Center staff provide technical assistance nationwide in an effort to assist the consumer in understanding and using the new food labels.

NAL Linked with National Food Service Institute

Authorized under the Child Nutrition Women, Infant, and Children Reauthorization Act of 1989, the National Food Service Management Institute (NFSMI) has a Trust Fund Cooperative Agreement with NAL linking the resources of NAL's Food and Nutrition Information Center with NFSMI at the University of Mississippi in Oxford. An NFSMI nutritionist has been assigned to FNIC's offices, and reference calls to the institute's toll-free number are automatically switched to FNIC for response. NAL also provides document delivery services to NFSMI clientele.

United States and Japan Exchange Aquaculture Information

NAL's Aquaculture Information Center (AIC) coordinated an international effort to provide aquaculture documents to Japan for a meeting of the United States/Japan Natural Resources—Aquaculture Panel. Materials were collected through the Joint Subcommittee on Aquaculture, which involves 23 federal agencies. Japan provided 65 titles in return, which AIC added to the NAL collection of aquaculture materials.

Biomonitoring Database Produced with NAL Help

In cooperation with NAL's Biotechnology Information Center (BIC), the National Biological Impact Assessment Program at USDA's Cooperative State Research Service released a CD-ROM Biomonitoring Database. The database contains biosafety information on the release of genetically engineered organisms into the environment.

Composed of full-text environmental assessments produced by USDA's Animal and Plant Health Inspection Service, the database is intended to provide scientific risk assessment information to the biotechnology research community, state and local governments, public interest groups, and the interested public. BIC assisted in collecting records for the database, in obtaining copyright clearances, and in producing and distributing the CD-ROM.

AGRICOLA Continues to Grow

There are now well over three million records in NAL's AGRICOLA (AGRICultural OnLine Access) bibliographic database. (The three-million mark was reached in the summer of 1993.) AGRICOLA is the backbone of the NAL collection and consists of records for literature citations of journal articles, monographs, theses, patents, software, audiovisual materials, serials, and technical reports relating to all aspects of agriculture. It is a catalog and index to the NAL collections.

Since 1984 AGRICOLA has been expanded to include materials collected by and input from cooperating institutions. The database has been available on magnetic tape since 1970. Tapes are updated monthly. Coverage of AGRICOLA is international, with records representing materials in more than 65 languages from more than 160 countries. About 65 percent of the records are for English-language documents.

ISIS Strides On

The Integrated System for Information Services (ISIS), NAL's online union catalog, continues to grow. It contains more than 333,800 indexing records and 533,400 cataloging records. In addition to NAL citations, the database includes machine-readable citations from the National Arboretum and USDA's ARS Regional Research Center Libraries.

NAL's Indexing Branch has begun using the ISIS Journal Indexing Subsystem to input current indexing records. This enables searchers to retrieve AGRICOLA journal citations two to six weeks earlier than previously possible. It will also result in a cost savings to NAL because two processing systems will no longer be needed.

NAL Conducts Animal Welfare Courses

NAL's Animal Welfare Information Center (AWIC) continued to offer a unique training course on meeting the information needs of those using animals in research, teaching, and testing. The two-day workshop includes an overview of the Animal Welfare Act, a review of the alternatives concept, an introduction to NAL, AWIC, and other information organizations, instruction on the use of information databases, and online searching exercises.

Last year AWIC conducted a total of eight workshops reaching 170 professionals. The workshops were held at NAL, two pharmaceutical companies, an Animal and Plant Health Inspection Service regional conference, Georgetown University, and a National Institutes of Health training workshop.

Workshop participants included representatives from the Office of Animal Care and Use of the Food and Drug Administration, the National Institutes of Health, the Humane Society of the United States, and the office of the National Animal Care Coordinator for the Agricultural Research Service.

Internet Aids in Document Delivery

NAL's Document Delivery Services Branch (DDSB) began accepting Internet requests for information about NAL holdings, collection access, and document delivery services. NAL's Circulation and Access Section receives messages addressed to **circinfo@nalusda.gov** and responds with holdings information or policy statements. Also, the Circulation and Access Section regularly reviews several Internet listservs, responding to requests for help in locating materials in the library.

By sending an Internet message to NAL, Internet users may request information on titles in the NAL collection (journal, article, book, translation, audiovisual, and other media or types); on how to borrow the title or obtain a photocopy; and on NAL and USDA services, programs, and policies.

Interlibrary Borrowing Improvements

There have been important changes in NAL's Interlibrary Borrowing (ILB) Section. ILB is responsible for obtaining materials for USDA researchers that are not available from the NAL collection.

Traditionally, the borrowing process had been time-consuming, with ILB transmitting requests to other libraries and then waiting to receive the material via regular mail. NAL has reduced the time required to obtain and deliver documents by using private companies that specialize in rapid document delivery. Agreements with these companies permit online ordering of journal articles and delivery of the articles via telefacsimile, usually within 24 hours.

Also, agreements were negotiated with certain publishers to scan and retain articles in electronic format. These agreements permit delivery of materials in about six hours. NAL has also worked out an arrangement that allows ILB to order documents and have them faxed directly to the patron.

Another step that has improved services is the purchase of an electronic document transmission and receipt workstation. The workstation consists of a scanner, a high-quality laser printer, and a DOS-based microcomputer. The system allows the operator to scan documents and transmit them via Internet to other sites.

Electronic Access to Youth Development Information Available

NAL's Youth Development Information Center (YDIC) has established an information resource on Internet called CYFERNET (Child, Youth and Family Education and Research Network). It incorporates file server and gopher computer technologies. Last year, the CYFERNET gopher logged over 400 accesses per month.

CYFERNET contains curricula and program support materials of interest to child, youth, and family development professionals. Program support materials are gleaned by YDIC from federal, state, and nonprofit organizations using Internet.

YDIC, using CYFERNET, is helping to establish "networks for action" within the youth and family development community of the land-grant university system. These networks will be composed of four or more universities collaborating through Internet on common projects.

Electronic Bulletin Board Gives Access to NAL

ALF (Agricultural Library Forum), NAL's computerized bulletin board that provides remote access to library services and products, continued to improve its service.

Internet users were given ALF access when the National Technical Information Service of the U.S. Department of Commerce announced that FedWorld bulletin boards would allow dial-out via its gateway system. [See the National Technical Information Service article for more information—*Ed.*]

ALF usage increased immediately, and NAL increased the size of the current-user file to accommodate extra callers. After connecting to FedWorld via telnet or direct dial, users may connect to any of more than 100 federal bulletin board systems and database services, including ALF. A Small Business Administration bulletin board also includes ALF as a dial-out option.

Several hundred bibliographic and full-text NAL documents are loaded on ALF, including NAL Quick Bibliography titles, special reference briefs, NAL news releases, and special publications from NAL information centers, as well as a number of calendars and resource lists.

Callers to ALF during the year totaled over 50,000, and there are currently more than 200 files on ALF for user access. More than 20 subboards exist covering various special-interest topics.

NAL Collects Materials on New Food Pyramid

The USDA's Human Nutrition Information Service and NAL's Food and Nutrition Information Center (FNIC) signed a memorandum of understanding calling for the agencies to work together to build a database of educational materials on USDA's new Food Guide Pyramid. USDA developed the Food Guide Pyramid to provide the public with basic information on good nutrition and healthful diets. All materials acquired under this agreement become part of the NAL collection, and appropriate items are listed on AGRICOLA.

NAL Increases Coverage of Plant Genetics

In support of USDA's Plant Genome Research Program, NAL's Indexing Branch increased coverage of plant genetics literature in AGRICOLA. Since the initiation of the Plant Genome Research Program in 1990, AGRICOLA has accumulated over 25,000 citations related to molecular genetics. This is an increase of 240 percent in the number of citations added during the year over those added in 1990. The percentage of genetics and breeding citations that have full abstracts increased from just 20 percent in 1990 to over 50 percent.

More than 5,000 citations in AGRICOLA are identified as containing molecular-sequence data. Efforts continue to enhance access to plant genetics information in AGRICOLA by improving NAL's indexing vocabulary in this area.

NAL Conducts Food Irradiation Study

NAL'S Food and Nutrition Information Center is conducting a study on providing international access to food irradiation materials. The library has converted to another software package, an NAL-produced CD-ROM containing thousands of pages of unpublished food irradiation research materials, improving its usefulness.

Also, FNIC contacted a food irradiation expert to evaluate thousands of documents on food irradiation research conducted by the U.S. Army in the 1950s and 1960s. The materials are being scanned for a series of CD-ROMs.

Germany, France, and other countries have indicated an interest in providing documents to an international center for food irradiation information to be located at NAL. NAL is seeking funding for this center. The United Nations' International Consultative Group for Food Irradiation and the USDA Food Safety and Inspection Service strongly support this project.

NAL Computer Network Grows

NALnet, the NAL computer network, experienced dramatic growth. Of note is the transition of NAL Internet mail service to Cliff, the NAL Sun SPARC2 UNIX workstation. All NAL staff needing mail access received accounts on Cliff, and training sessions in using the service were held. Staff use is high and growing.

NAL uses PINE mail software for its Internet mail service, and NAL staff use such tools as gopher and WAIS to search remote information systems through Internet.

In addition, the NALnet backbone has been extended. Fiber optic cable now connects the NAL computer room to 11 strategic hub locations throughout the library. From these hubs, it is possible to extend copper wire to the desktop of each NAL employee.

In collaboration with the National Science Foundation, Iowa State University, and the USDA Extension Service, NAL has launched an initiative to deploy a system for managing electronic information in agriculture. A pilot project known as AgNIC (Agricultural Network Information Center), which will implement the initiative, is being developed by NAL as part of this effort.

Text-Digitizing Program Enters Seventh Year

The National Agricultural Text Digitizing Program (NATDP), shepherded by NAL, continued to produce and distribute CD-ROMs of important agricultural literature. Planning is also underway to upgrade NATDP's optical scanning and optical character recognition (OCR) system.

NATDP began in 1987 as a study by NAL and more than 40 land-grant university libraries to evaluate the use of optical scanning and OCR in the library environment. An evaluation report, "National Agricultural Text Digitizing Project: Toward the Electronic Library," was completed and published in November 1992.

Since NATDP became a fully operational program, several discs have been produced, including Aquaculture II, completed in late 1992, containing more than 6,500 pages of full text and images from selected noncopyrighted materials; a disc containing the papers of famed agricultural scientist George Washington Carver (selected from Tuskegee Institute's collection); and Food Irradiation I, completed in 1993 and containing nearly 5,100 images (this is the first of six or seven food irradiation CD-ROMs).

Scanning and indexing for a second Agronomy Journal CD-ROM was completed, and disc premastering is under way. It will be published as a cooperative effort between NAL and the American Society of Agronomy. This will be the final database scanned with the original NATDP system, used since January 1988. A new scanning and OCR system was selected in 1993.

Future discs will include other volumes of the *Agronomy Journal*, the food irradiation series mentioned above, and a series containing the *American Journal of Agricultural Economics* to be produced with the Foundation of the American Agricultural Economics Association.

Home-Landscaping Disc Developed

NAL, the University of Florida Institute for Food and Agricultural Sciences (IFAS), and the Michigan State University Cooperative Extension Service, after a three-year development and evaluation period, released the final version of "Plant It!–CD," an interactive multimedia CD-ROM for home landscaping.

Nearly 1,000 U.S. plants are described in detail on the disc, accompanied by full-color photographs, printable landscape designs, and materials on backyard composting, attracting birds, and so on.

The preliminary version of the disc was released in January 1993 to 200 evaluation sites nationwide. The disc, which became available commercially in late 1993, is distributed by IFAS.

Networking Information Available Through Image Transfer

NAL, the University of Pittsburgh School of Library and Information Sciences, and the Michigan State University Cooperative Extension Service began a project to examine the use of images in information retrieval.

A database of 2,000 digitized images of rare botanical prints plus horticultural pests and diseases was produced and made accessible from a server in Pittsburgh. Local-network testing began prior to making the system available on the Internet. A telecommunications protocol was designed to maximize the use of the network server during interactive sessions.

After the database is searched, images can be downloaded for preview in thumbnail sizes and requested in high resolution and full color in a choice of formats. NAL is developing a CD-ROM version of the database. Once the online version is fully operational and accessible at test sites, Internet access will be available.

System Links Sites for Statistical Tracking

The second phase of a USDA aquaculture evaluation study funded by NAL's Aquaculture Information Center (AIC) was initiated. As part of the study, AIC established Aquaforum, an electronic communications system that includes a statistical database, a private E-mail module, and a hypertext module. Through Aquaforum, aquaculture information sites in the United States entered reference statistics to an AIC file server to track and profile services provided by the sites and AIC.

Participating were Auburn University, Iowa State University, Louisiana State University, University of Delaware, University of Hawaii, and Washington State Department of Agriculture. In addition, the University of Hawaii received data from a subsystem that linked remote Pacific sites. This data was included in Aquaforum.

Analysis of the data will assist in identifying strengths and weaknesses in information delivery programs and in improving aquaculture information services.

NAL Materials Help Celebrate Smokey the Bear Anniversary

Materials from the NAL collection are the basis for a national exhibit commemorating the 50th anniversary of Smokey the Bear. NAL assisted coordinators of the exhibit in searching the vast collection of Smokey the Bear materials given to NAL by the USDA Forest Service. Items in the collection include artwork, comic books, coloring books, dolls and other toys, recordings, and video materials. The Smokey the Bear Exhibit toured nationally throughout 1994.

National Library of Medicine

8600 Rockville Pike, Bethesda, MD 20894
301-496-6308
Internet: publicinfo@occshost.nlm.nih.gov

Robert Mehnert
Public Information Officer

The 100,000th user joined MEDLINE, the National Library of Medicine's online network, early in 1995. The milestone marked an increase of nearly 30 percent for the year; in fact, more users joined in 1994 than in the first 17 years of the network's operation.

MEDLINE continued to grow in other ways. Added during the fiscal year (FY) ending September 30, 1994, were 368,000 references, most with abstracts. The MEDLINE database, which began in 1971, is updated weekly; in most cases, references are added within 30 days of a journal issue arriving at the library.

It is estimated that NLM's 50 databases contain almost 20 million records, including not only the latest in published medical findings but historical materials dating back to the eleventh century.

Internet continues to be the fastest-growing route of access to NLM's databases. From virtually no Internet users three years ago, some 25 percent of network users now come to NLM via Internet. In addition, the library continues to expand the information it makes available via Internet using such vehicles as telnet, file transfer protocol (ftp), gopher, and Mosaic (NLM's home page on the World-Wide Web is **http://www.nlm.nih.gov/**). NLM believes Internet is so vital for the health sciences that it continues to support an "Internet connections" grant program. This is an interagency program with the National Science Foundation that provides grant funds to encourage hospitals and other institutions to connect to Internet.

Fixed-fee and flat-rate plans for accessing NLM online databases are expanding rapidly. There are about 25 plans in place, and many more are under consideration. They range in size and scope from the entire National Institutes of Health (NIH) to individual hospitals, universities, and commercial organizations. The largest university program, at the University of Illinois, has five sites with a potential of 75,000 users.

Publications

NLM has published the fifth edition of the *National Library of Medicine Classification* (available from the Superintendent of Documents, U.S. Government Printing Office). Prepared under the direction of Christa F. B. Hoffmann, head of NLM's Cataloging Section, and Wen-min Kao, principal cataloger, who served as editor, the fifth edition supersedes the revised edition published in 1981. The new edition contains close to 4,000 classification numbers and more than 18,000 index terms. Approximately 300 new classification numbers have been added, including new form numbers that are repeated in the applicable schedules across the entire classification scheme.

The full text of many NLM publications is now available directly to Internet users. These publications may be downloaded at no cost via Internet in two ways: through the NLM gopher and via ftp. The NLM gopher (**gopher.nlm.nih.gov**) provides menu-driven access and allows users to browse publications, search them by textword, and transfer them over Internet for local use. File transfer protocol (ftp to **nlmpubs.nlm.nih.gov** and login as anonymous) provides similar access, with an index file in each directory to provide information about the files in that directory. Among the NLM publications so available: the *NLM News, Gratefully Yours*, the monthly *AIDS Bibliography*, and the library's fact sheets.

Table 1 / Selected NLM Statistics*

Library Operation	Volume
Collection (book and nonbook)	5,016,000
Serial titles received	23,250
Articles indexed for MEDLINE	368,000
Circulation requests filled	410,000
For interlibrary loan	230,000
For on-site users	180,000
Computerized searches (all databases)	6,890,000

*For the year ending September 30, 1994.

New Databases

The NLM online network logged 6.9 million searches in FY 1994, 15 percent more than 1993 and by far the highest number ever recorded. Part of the reason, of course, is that there are more users. But two other factors were influential. In January 1994 the library announced that its four databases containing HIV/AIDS information would henceforth be free to all users. Their use immediately doubled. Also, two new databases joined the NLM online family: HSTAR and HSTAT.

These databases are coordinated by a new component of the library: the National Information Center on Health Services Research and Health Care Technology. HSTAR (Health Services/Technology Assessment Research) contains about 1.5 million post-1984 references on research related to health services—cost, access, and quality, including practice guidelines and technology assessment.

The other new database, HSTAT (Health Services/Technology Assessment Text), is noteworthy in that it contains not references and abstracts but the full texts of clinical practice guidelines issued by the Agency for Health Care Policy and Research (AHCPR) and NIH consensus statements and technology assessments. Further, the AHCPR guidelines are presented not only in a form for physicians and health professionals but also in an abbreviated form written in language understandable by the layperson. This is a considerable departure from the nature of most other databases on NLM's system. Like the HIV/AIDS databases, HSTAT is provided to network users without charge via telnet (**text.nlm.nih.gov**), anonymous ftp, gopher, and Mosaic.

Another new database, retrievable only via the World-Wide Web, is *Images from the History of Medicine*. This is a collection of 60,000 historical images from NLM's History of Medicine Division that may be viewed using a browser such as Mosaic. The pictures are caricatures, photographs, fine prints, ephemera, portraits, and illustrations drawn from the books and journals held by NLM. An interactive online order form that will allow users to request high-quality photographic copies is being planned.

High Performance Computing and Communications

NLM continues to provide facilities for the High Performance Computing and Communications (HPCC) National Coordination Office. NLM's director, Donald A. B. Lindberg, is also head of that office. The HPCC initiative is a major interagency program that involves ten federal agencies, including all the major science agencies. The goal of the program is to develop computers with scalable performance up to a trillion operations per second (tera-op machines) and a digital network capable of transmitting a billion bits per second. The present Internet and the federally funded high-speed backbone (the National Research and Education Network, or NREN) are the forerunners of the more extensive system of the future.

High-performance computers and high-speed computer networks are key technologies for the future of biomedical science. Grand challenges in biomedicine—such as the analysis of the human genome, prediction of biological structure and function from genetic code, and rational drug design—require new and faster computers, advanced software, a national research and education computer network, and expanded training of scientists in the use of computer-based tools.

In April 1994 NLM funded ten projects designed to help physicians practice better medicine by utilizing advanced computing and networking capabilities along the "Information Superhighway." These, and one funded in 1993, amount to an expenditure of $26 million over three years. The projects are funding such HPCC health care applications as test bed networks to share information resources, computerized patient records and medical images, telemedicine projects to provide consultation and medical care to patients in rural areas, and advanced computer simulations of human anatomy for training via "virtual surgery." The projects will also grapple with such thorny issues as how to store, access, and transmit patient medical records while protecting their accuracy and privacy.

The development of a system of computerized medical records is seen as crucial if we are to be successful in applying the latest in computer and communications technology to medical care. Although much work has been done on electronic patient records, no fully satisfactory system exists as yet. In September 1994 the library made five awards, totaling $1.5 million, to conduct research in such areas as developing clinical medical terminology and vocabularies, automated tools to support health services research, and Internet access to multimedia electronic medical records systems. The library is funding these projects jointly with the Agency for Health Care Policy and Research.

Visible Man

For the last three years NLM has been supporting a project to create two three-dimensional, computer-generated human beings—male and female. The Visible Man was introduced to the world at a meeting of radiologists in Chicago on November 28, 1994. The project is managed and funded by NLM; work was carried out by scientists at the University of Colorado Health Sciences Center in Denver.

The Visible Man was created with digitized data compiled from the body of a 39-year-old who had willed his body to science. The body was imaged from head to toe using CT, MRI, and x-rays. It was then frozen and photographed in 1,800 millimeter-thin slices. The digital photographs were processed in an imaging computer system along with data acquired from the radiologic studies. The resulting data set is immense—15 gigabytes—and would take up to two weeks of uninterrupted Internet time to transmit in its entirety.

This is the first time such detailed information about an entire human body has been compiled, and there are many uses envisioned for the data set. For example, it will be a powerful tool for introducing students to the human body, planning surgery, explaining physical processes to patients, and designing artificial joints and other fabricated body parts. Comparable work on a Visible Woman is to be completed in 1995.

Another area of science that is tied intimately with HPCC is that of biotechnology. The National Center for Biotechnology Information, a research component of NLM, creates and maintains systems for storing, analyzing, and retrieving information on molecular biology, biochemistry, and genetics. Since October 1992, when the center assumed responsibility for the GenBank DNA sequence database, the number of entries has more than doubled to some 200,000 sequences from 5,000 different organisms. Each day, the center's computers handle some 10,000 searches of GenBank from remote users.

Another research component, the Lister Hill National Center for Biomedical Communications, is responsible for coordinating the HPCC-related projects described earlier; conducts research in expert systems, medical linguistics, and other aspects of biomedical communications; and operates a hands-on facility called the Learning Center for Interactive Technology.

Outreach

Outreach to the health science community remains one of the library's highest priorities. The information services offered, if they are to be of maximum benefit, need to be made widely known to physicians and other health professionals. A key to all of NLM's outreach efforts is the cooperation of the eight Regional Medical Libraries and the 4,100 members of the National Network of Libraries of Medicine. Some 50 major exhibits and hundreds of training sessions, workshops, and demonstrations are conducted under the auspices of the Regional Medical Libraries.

On January 21, 1994, NLM for the first time used an interactive satellite link for its annual update session with the members of the National Network of Libraries of Medicine. A three-hour broadcast focused on changes in the Medical Subject Headings vocabulary, MEDLINE changes and enhancements, and anticipated new databases and online services. Videocassette copies of the broadcast were later sent to each Regional Medical Library for distribution at no cost throughout the network.

In 1994 a number of NLM's outreach efforts emphasized HIV/AIDS information services. NLM and NIH sponsored a June 1993 conference on AIDS information services, from which a report with a number of recommendations emanated. One result was a press conference held by NLM in conjunction with the January 1994 NLM Board of Regents meeting, at which it was announced that four of NLM's databases containing AIDS-related information would be free to all users. Other recommendations in the report had to do with reaching out to groups that have not traditionally used NLM's services: public libraries and community groups of various kinds. In May 1994 NLM announced it would make small awards (up to $25,000) to local organizations (forming partnerships was encouraged) to enable them to purchase computer and telecommunication equipment and to gain training in the use of NLM's and other databases. NLM was able to fund 19 of 87 applications.

NLM has a long-standing outreach program in toxicology and environmental health with the historically black colleges and universities (HBCUs). That program has been expanded to include HIV/AIDS, the impact of which has been especially severe in communities of color. The project involves providing training to health professionals affiliated with the HBCUs in the use of NLM's databases as well as other electronic resources. It also involves identifying community health professionals and providing them with training and access.

An unusual outreach effort in 1994 was the library's "adoption" of Coolidge High School, a public high school in Washington, D.C. Under the partnership, Coolidge students are being exposed to a variety of NLM programs, including the library's online databases, use of Internet, biotechnology, computer science, and engineering. A number of students enrolled in a special summer program at NLM, and NLM has provided equipment, connections, and training to a computer laboratory at the high school.

Outreach has been a high priority of NLM's Board of Regents since 1989, when a special planning panel under the leadership of Michael E. DeBakey, published *Improving Health Professionals' Access to Information*. This report has served the library as a blueprint for outreach ever since. This year, another planning-panel report was being prepared under the auspices of the board on the subject "Education and Training of Health Science Librarians." The report is scheduled for release in 1995.

New Regents

Michael E. DeBakey, M.D., who is chancellor of the Baylor College of Medicine in Houston, was appointed by the secretary of health and human services in 1994 to a second four-year term on the board (he served on the first board in 1956). Also appointed regents were Marion J. Ball, ED.D., vice president for information services, University of Maryland at Baltimore, and George H. Nolan, M.D., director, Obstetric Division of Maternal-Fetal Medicine, Henry Ford Hospital, Detroit. H. Kenneth Walker, M.D., was elected chair of the board of regents at the May 1994 meeting.

Administration

NLM sponsors a Library Associate Program, open to practicing librarians and library school students who will have a master's degree in library/information science by August preceding the year of their training. The program is a one-year traineeship that orients those chosen (four or five a year) to the major programs and services of NLM and provides opportunities for independent projects.

As part of its continuing efforts to diversify its workforce, NLM has established a Minority Applicant Locator File. The database especially targets six federal position series in the areas of librarianship, technical information, computers, and office automation. As vacancies occur in these series, potential applicants whose records are in the database are notified.

For the year ending September 30, 1994, NLM had an appropriated budget of $118,019,000 and a full-time staff of 596.

Educational Resources Information Center

ERIC Processing and Reference Facility
1301 Piccard Drive, Suite 300, Rockville, MD 20850-4305
301-258-5500, 800-799-3742, FAX 301-948-3695
Internet: ericfac@inet.ed.gov

Ted Brandhorst
Director

ERIC Program Office

The ERIC Program Office resides within the U.S. Department of Education's Office of Educational Research and Improvement (OERI). OERI is the research arm of the department and contains, among other units, the National Center for Education Statistics (NCES) and the National Library of Education. With the legislative reauthorization of OERI in 1994 and its subsequent reorganization, ERIC was shifted within OERI from its Office of Research to the newly defined National Library of Education (NLE), and during 1995 will continue its mission within that new organizational context.

ERIC Contract Competitions

Contracts for operation of the ERIC clearinghouses and other components are periodically competed and awarded on the basis of technical and cost proposals submitted. During 1994 the contract for the operation of the ERIC Processing and Reference Facility was competed, with an award made on June 16, 1994, to Computer Sciences Corporation (CSC). The contract for ACCESS ERIC was scheduled to be competed during the first quarter of 1995 and the contract for the ERIC Document Reproduction Service (EDRS) later in 1995. The contracts for the 16 ERIC clearinghouses were awarded in 1993 and generally extend for a five-year period (through 1997).

ERIC Director

Robert Stonehill, director of ERIC from 1988 to 1994, ushered ERIC into the age of Internet and began a number of initiatives calculated to move ERIC onto the "Information Superhighway" (e.g., ACCESS ERIC, books and nonprint media in the database, toll-free national 800 numbers, Internet connectivity for all components, Adjunct Clearinghouses, AskERIC Internet-based question-answering service, ERIC Digests in full text, *The ERIC Review*, International ERIC, reference and referral databases online, and so on). Stonehill left ERIC late in 1994 to head up the department's larger and more substantially funded Educational Laboratory Program. The ERIC director position was vacant in early 1995, with a search for a successor under way.

One of Stonehill's last official acts as director of ERIC was to write the introduction to the *ERIC Annual Report, 1994*. Because this introduction reflects both his sense of ERIC's major recent accomplishments and his vision of ERIC's future, it is appropriate that it be reproduced here in its entirety:

> More than 20 years after providing the world's first online database, ERIC has again become a recognized leader in using state-of-the-art technology to support teaching and learning. Historically recognized as an online database primarily used by librarians and scholars, ERIC has evolved into a national network of resources and services available "at the desktop" to educators, policymakers, and parents. There are two facets to this evolution: enhancing access to ERIC information and enhancing the information itself.
>
> **Enhancing Access.** In the last decade, ERIC has expanded from a system that produced one online database to a system that produces a wide variety of online and CD-ROM resources. Online access to ERIC information, previously provided only by costly commercial services, is now available through ERIC components, libraries, universities, and government agencies—often for free. But most important, the advent and increasing availability of advanced telecommunications and electronic storage and retrieval systems—and especially the explosive growth of the Internet—have dramatically expanded the ways in which users can now have low-cost, on-demand access to ERIC information.
>
> These developments, when coupled with other initiatives such as obtaining toll-free 800 numbers and Internet addresses for each ERIC component, establishing ACCESS ERIC as a contact point for new users, and creating an active ERIC Partners program, have resulted in a dramatic upsurge in the use of ERIC resources and in requests for ERIC services over the past 5 years. In 1987, we estimated that the total online usage of the ERIC database amounted to 100,000 hours per year. Now, combining online database use (which has expanded beyond the traditional commercial vendors, such as Dialog, to include services such as America Online and CompuServe) with CD-ROM and Internet use, it is estimated that ERIC resources are being accessed at a rate as much as 20 times greater than that of the mid-1980s.
>
> Despite these impressive gains, we have only begun to realize the potential of a universally accessible National Information Infrastructure, or Information Superhighway. Today, we estimate that perhaps 10 to 15 percent of the nation's 2.5 million teachers are connected to the Internet at their schools (although the National Education Association reports that approximately two-thirds of its members have computers and modems at home); tomorrow, we expect all schools, teachers, and students to have full access to information resources located throughout the world. As a first step towards accommodating this dramatically increased demand for information, ERIC is planning to provide direct, state-of-the-art, user-friendly access to the ERIC database and the AskERIC Virtual Library with technical support and the capability to host hundreds of simultaneous users.

Enhancing the Information. For the first 20 years of its existence, ERIC concentrated on building its bibliographic database, which now contains summaries of approximately 850,000 documents and journal articles. While the database in many ways is still the cornerstone of ERIC's information network, ERIC has been steadily diversifying its products and services—usually in response to user requests.

Examples of these current and future improvements include:

- The development, by ACCESS ERIC, of a series of reference and referral databases, including annual editions of a *Directory of Education-Related Information Centers, Calendar of Education-Related Conferences,* and a *Directory of ERIC Information Service Providers.*
- The expansion of the ERIC database to include commercially published books, machine-readable data files, and multimedia products.
- The establishment of AskERIC, which now includes online question-answering services, the AskERIC Virtual Library, an extensive National Parent Information Network, and an active research and development program applying emerging technologies to the dissemination of education information.
- The provision of full-text access to the materials indexed in the ERIC database, beginning with the ERIC Digests Online file. ERIC Digests—short summaries of research and developments in education—are already available in full text on the Internet and in the online and CD-ROM versions of the ERIC database. Beginning in 1995, ERIC will begin providing experimental, full-text, online access to new documents indexed in the database.
- The expansion of ERIC's role in providing Internet access to third-party information, such as the ETS Test Collection database, CNN Newsroom and Discovery Channel materials, PBS's Newton's Apple and Academy One lesson plans, and more.

In identifying and adopting new strategies for providing a full range of education materials and services, we have begun to understand that the next immediate challenge for ERIC is to provide on-demand, free or low cost, electronic access to a wide variety of materials in many formats (including video, audio, and hypermedia). We have taken the first steps, but much remains to be done.

Fortunately, ERIC will have new allies in meeting these challenges. In March 1994, Congress authorized the establishment of the National Library of Education. ERIC, in conjunction with other key information and technology programs, will be instrumental in the development of the new Library. As it evolves, the Library will become the U.S. Department of Education's one-stop information service where print and online information resources, reference and referral services, and information technology applications will be carefully crafted to meet the needs and demands of educators, students, and parents. Everyone at ERIC looks forward to participating in this venture.

ERIC Annual Report

The *ERIC Annual Report* ("summarizing the recent accomplishments of the Educational Resources Information Center") is produced by the ERIC Program Office, with the assistance of ACCESS ERIC. It is the best single source of current summary information, both statistical and narrative, about ERIC. Copies are available free of charge from ACCESS ERIC (1-800-538-3742). The report is also placed in the ERIC database and microfilmed for archival purposes. Prior reports have the following accession numbers in the ERIC database:

1988	ED-313 057
1989	ED-322 934
1990–1991	ED-344 615
1992	ED-359 989
1993–1994	In process

ERIC Component	800 Number	Internet Address
ERIC Program Office (Dept. of Ed.)		
Office of Educational Research and Improvement (OERI)	—	eric@inet.ed.gov
ACCESS ERIC	800-538-3742	acceric@inet.ed.gov
ERIC Document Reproduction Service (EDRS)	800-443-3742	edrs@inet.ed.gov
ERIC Processing and Reference Facility	800-799-3742	ericfac@inet.ed.gov
Oryx Press	800-279-6799	arhjb@asuvm.inre.asu.edu
ERIC Clearinghouse on/for:		
Adult, Career, and Vocational Education (CE)	800-848-4815	ericacve@magnus.acs.ohio-state.edu
Assessment and Evaluation (TM)	800-464-3742	eric_ae@cua.edu
Community Colleges (JC)	800-832-8256	eeh3rie@mvs.oac.ucla.edu
Counseling and Student Services (CG)	800-414-9769	ericcass@iris.uncg.edu
Disabilities and Gifted Education (EC)	800-328-0272	ericec@inet.ed.gov
Educational Management (EA)	800-438-8841	ppiele@oregon.uoregon.edu
Elementary and Early Childhood Education (PS)	800-583-4135	ericeece@ux1.cso.uiuc.edu
Higher Education (HE)	800-773-3742	eriche@inet.ed.gov
Information and Technology (IR)	800-464-9107	eric@ericir.syr.edu
Languages and Linguistics (FL)	800-276-9834	jeannie@cal.org
Reading, English, and Communication (CS)	800-759-4723	ericcs@ucs.indiana.edu
Rural Education and Small Schools (RC)	800-624-9120	u56d9@wvnvm.wvnet.edu
Science, Mathematics, and Environmental Education (SE)	800-276-0462	ericse@osu.edu
Social Studies/Social Science Education (SO)	800-266-3815	ericso@ucs.indiana.edu
Teaching and Teacher Education (SP)	800-822-9229	jbeck@inet.ed.gov
Urban Education (UD)	800-601-4868	cue_eric@columbia.edu
Adjunct ERIC Clearinghouses on:		
Chapter 1 (Compensatory Education)	800-456-2380	—
Clinical Schools	800-822-9229	iabdalha@inet.ed.gov
Consumer Education	—	cse_bonner@emunix.emich.edu
ESL Literacy Education	—	ncle@cal.org
Test Collection	—	mhalpern@rosedale.org
United States–Japan Studies	—	risinger@ucs.indiana.edu

Database Size and Growth

The ERIC database consists of two files: *Resources in Education (RIE)* and *Current Index to Journals in Education (CIJE)*. The ED records announced in

RIE represent documents; they are approximately 1,800 characters long on average. The EJ records announced in *CIJE* represent journal articles; they are approximately 650 characters long on average. Overall, the ERIC database through 1994 contains 366,092 records for documents and 488,942 records for journal articles, for a grand total of 855,034 bibliographic records. Approximately 13,000 document records and 20,000 article records are added annually, for a total of 33,000 records per year. Overall, the ERIC database through 1994 is approximately 980 million bytes in size and growing at a rate of around 35 million bytes per year.

	Number of Records		
File	1966–1993	1994	Total
Resources in Education (RIE)–ED Records	353,419	12,673	366,092
Current Index to Journals in Education (CIJE)–EJ Records	468,113	20,829	488,942
Total	821,532	33,502	855,034

ERIC Document Reproduction Service

The ERIC Document Reproduction Service (EDRS) is the document delivery arm of ERIC and handles all subscriptions for ERIC microfiche and on-demand requests for reproduced paper copy or microfiche. During 1994 the volume of standing order customers (SOCs) subscribing to the total ERIC microfiche collection (about 12,750 titles, or 17,000 fiche cards, for approximately $2,500 annually) rose to 967. SOCs include more than 100 overseas addresses.

EDRS prices were increased effective January 1, 1995, as follows:

Product	1995 Prices*
Microfiche (price per card)**	$0.130
Monthly subscription	
(approximate annual cost $2,500)	$0.266 (silver)
Back collections (1966–previous month)	$0.153
Clearinghouse collections	$0.020
On-demand documents	
Per title (up to 5 fiche = 480 pages)	$1.30
Each additional fiche (96 pages)	$0.25
Reproduced paper copies	
First 1–25 pages	$3.85
Each 25-page increment (or part thereof)	$3.85
1994 Cumulative indexes on microfiche	$75.00
(Subject, author, title, institution, descriptor, and identifier indexes)	

*Prices do not include shipping. Prices are valid for calendar 1995.

**Diazo, unless other specified.

Types of Users Who Contact ERIC Components (1990–1993)

ERIC clearinghouses and support components keep records of the types of users who contact them for information. The pie chart below shows the relative percentages of several types of users; however, it is important to note that these statistics are based primarily on users who call, write, or visit. Data are not available on the thousands of users who send E-mail requests, visit ERIC exhibits at conferences, search the print indexes or ERIC database, or access ERIC information on computer networks.

Total = approximately 493,00

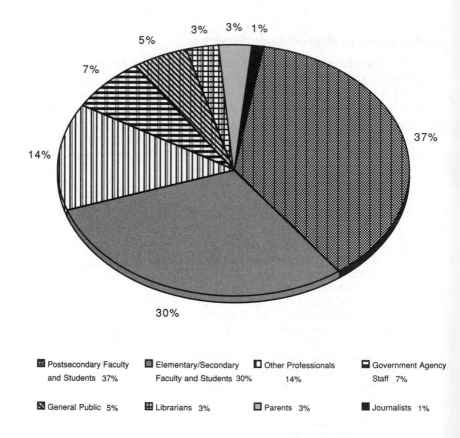

| Postsecondary Faculty and Students 37% | Elementary/Secondary Faculty and Students 30% | Other Professionals 14% | Government Agency Staff 7% |
| General Public 5% | Librarians 3% | Parents 3% | Journalists 1% |

Adjunct ERIC Clearinghouses

Adjunct ERIC clearinghouses are organizations that, at no cost to ERIC, cooperate with ERIC to help provide improved coverage of a particular area of the educational literature. During 1993, two new adjunct clearinghouse arrangements were announced: Clinical Schools (adjunct to the ERIC Clearinghouse on Teaching and Teacher Education) and Law-Related Education (adjunct to the ERIC Clearinghouse on Social Studies/Social Science Education).

Full names and addresses for all ERIC components, including the adjunct clearinghouses, can be found readily in ERIC Ready Reference 6 and in ERIC's standard informational brochures, such as the *Pocket Guide to ERIC* and *All About ERIC*.

ERIC Digests

ERIC Digests (two-page concentrated treatments of key education topics, with suggestions for further reading) are extremely popular and over the past few years have supplanted many longer monographic types of publications. The ERIC clearinghouses each produce approximately eight to ten digests per year for a system-wide total of around 130 to 150 annually. Because of their brevity, digests are ideally suited to full-text processing, and through 1994 a total of 1,300 digests have been converted to full text and added in this form to the ERIC bibliographic database. These digests are identifiable in online and CD-ROM retrieval systems by accessing Publication Type Code 073 ("ERIC Digests [selected] in full text") and Publication Type Code 074 ("NonERIC Digests [selected] in full text").

Books in ERIC

Education-related commercially available books were permitted into the ERIC database beginning in 1993. They can be identified by accessing Publication Type Code 010 ("Books"). Since that time, there has been a gradual increase in the volume of such items processed by the ERIC clearinghouses. During 1994, a total of 1,083 items classified as "Books" were entered into the ERIC database.

National Parent Information Network

The ERIC Clearinghouse on Elementary and Early Childhood Education (ERIC/PS) at the University of Illinois at Urbana–Champaign has received a major equipment grant from Apple Computer to create a World-Wide Web (WWW) server on Internet devoted to child development and the care, education, and parenting of children from birth through early adolescence.

ERIC/PS will use the server as a new home for the National Parent Information Network (NPIN), a national resource for parents and those who support them. Currently, NPIN is located on Prairienet (the East Central Illinois Free-Net), where programmers have begun the development of a Mosaic interface to NPIN. (To try NPIN at its current location, telnet to prairienet.org. or gopher to gopher.prairienet.org, or, to try out the Mosaic interface, URL:http://www. prairienet.org/htmls/eric/npin/npinhome.html.)

The Apple equipment grant also will be used to support other activities on Internet pertaining to young children. In addition to discussion groups and forums on topics of interest to early-childhood educators, parents, and policy-makers, and PARENTS AskERIC—a service that taps the resources of ERIC to respond to parents' questions—other collections of information specifically related to the development, care, and education of children from birth through eight years of age are planned. For more information, contact ERIC/PS at 1-800-583-4135; E-mail: ericeece@ux1.cso.uiuc.edu.

Concerns About Online Vendor Copyright Notices

In May 1994 Dialog began to include the following notice just above each ERIC citation resulting from a Dialog search: "Copyright Format Only/1994 Dialog Info. Svc./All Rts. Reserv."

ERIC reacted with concern that this "format only" copyright notice will leave users with the impression that they can only copy ERIC citations if they pay Dialog and, as a result, will inhibit users from the free and easy duplication of ERIC search results for educational applications.

In response to these concerns, Dialog will include a notice in its terms and conditions booklet under the entry for ERIC that will also be used online when users seek HELP for ERIC's terms and conditions, and that ERIC can distribute widely among users. This notice is as follows:

> ERIC is a Federal Government database sponsored by the U.S. Department of Education and in the public domain. ERIC encourages the widespread dissemination and use of its bibliographic data, particularly for educational purposes. The ERIC database is not copyrighted by the Government and there are no special terms or conditions restricting ERIC's use. Users who have obtained ERIC bibliographic data via computer searches may without restriction reproduce additional photocopies of such ERIC citations/abstracts.

Finding the ERIC Database on Internet

Finding and accessing the ERIC database on Internet is not always as easy as following the instructions in the most recent *Internet Access Points to ERIC* networker issue. The locations offering access to outsiders and the instructions for accessing these locations change often. The ERIC Clearinghouse on Assessment and Evaluation (ERIC/TM) now offers a "Search ERIC" pointer on its Internet gopher site that automatically leads users to several locations on Internet that currently offer access to the ERIC database. To access this point, gopher to gopher.cua.edu and choose "Special Resources."

If you have questions about the ERIC/TM gopher site, contact: ERIC/TM, Catholic University of America, 210 O'Boyle Hall, Washington, DC 20064-4035; 202-319-5120; 800-464-3742; fax 202-319-6692; Internet: eric_ae@cua.edu.

International Bibliography of Higher Education

The International Bibliography of Higher Education (HEDBIB) is a joint effort of Unesco (the United Nations Educational, Scientific, and Cultural Organization) and the International Association of Universities (IAU). The objective is eventually to have contributions from every country. Meanwhile, ERIC is a major contributor to HEDBIB, as it appears that approximately 20 percent of ERIC citations may be relevant to higher education, as broadly defined for HEDBIB's purposes. ERIC has developed a HEDBIB search profile and periodically retrieves relevant citations, converts them to HEDBIB format, and transmits them to IAU for inclusion in HEDBIB. Currently, HEDBIB is available on a CD-ROM along with 15 other Unesco databases. For further information contact Claudine Langlois, Head, Unesco Information Centre on Higher Education, International Association of Universities, 1 rue Miollis, 75732 Paris, Cedex 15, France; 011-33-1-45-68-25-45; fax 011-33-1-47-34-767; Internet: iau@citi2.fr or trace@citi2.fr.

The Top Dozen ERIC Documents Ordered from EDRS in 1994 (Paper Copies)

Title	ED Number	Clearinghouse
1 Teaching Mathematics with Understanding to Limited English Proficient Students	ED 322 284	Urban Education
2 Methodologies of Reading and Writing in Kindergarten	ED 302 834	Reading, English, and Communication
3 Violence Prevention for Young Adults	ED 356 441-2	Counseling and Student Services
4 Teaching History in the Elementary School	ED 292 749	Social Studies/Social Science Education
5 Indians of Washington State	ED 259 853	Rural Education and Small Schools
6 Teaching a Second Language	ED 195 165	Languages and Linguistics
7 Must They Wait Another Generation? Hispanics and Secondary School Reform	ED 273 705	Urban Education
8 A Student Outcomes Model for Community Colleges—Measuring Institutional Effectiveness	ED 349 072	Community Colleges
9 Understanding and Conducting Qualitative Research	ED 300 937	Disabilities and Gifted Education
10 Teaching Technical Writing in the Secondary School	ED 243 111	Reading, English, and Communication
11 What Young Adolescents Want from Out-of-School Programs	ED 358 180	Urban Education
12 Institutional Effectiveness and Student Success	ED 356 843	Community Colleges

United States Government Printing Office

North Capitol and H Streets N.W., Washington, DC 20401
202-512-1991
Internet: gpo5@access.digex.net

Francis W. Biden
Director, Office of Congressional, Legislative and Public Affairs

The United States Government Printing Office (GPO) produces or procures printed and electronic publications for Congress and the agencies of the federal government. GPO also disseminates printed and electronic government information to the public through the Superintendent of Documents' sales and depository library programs.

GPO is a part of the legislative branch. It began operations in accordance with Congressional Joint Resolution 25 of June 23, 1860. Its activities are outlined and defined in the public printing and documents statutes of Title 44 of the U.S. Code.

GPO's primary facility is in Washington, D.C. Across the country, 5 field printing offices, 14 regional procurement offices, 6 satellite procurement facilities, a major distribution facility, a retail sales branch, and 24 bookstores complete the GPO printing and sales structure.

Printing

GPO executes orders for printing and binding placed by Congress and the departments and establishments of the federal government. It also furnishes blank paper, inks, and similar supplies to all government agencies on order.

GPO's annual revenues from printing and binding exceeded $724 million during fiscal year (FY) 1994. More than $526 million of that revenue covers printing and binding services, which GPO procures from commercial firms throughout the country. The remainder of the revenue represents the volume of work actually completed in GPO's central office and field facilities. Over 250,000 orders for internal production or commercial procurement are processed each year.

GPO invites bids from commercial suppliers on a wide variety of printing and binding services, awards and administers contracts, and maintains liaison between ordering agencies and contractors.

Printing and binding processes used are electronic photocomposition; linotype and hand composition; letterpress printing and photopolymer platemaking; offset photography, stripping, platemaking, and press; and manual and machine bookbinding.

The best-known ongoing effort of GPO is production of the *Congressional Record*, the printed compilation of each daily session of Congress. Manuscript copy is received at GPO's central office each day until midnight, with delivery of the printed *Record* back to Congress before it convenes the next day. Another important daily publication of the central office is the *Federal Register*, a compilation of presidential proclamations, executive orders, and federal agency regulations.

Two of GPO's field printing facilities are recognized for their specialized efforts. The Chicago plant produces the *Commerce Business Daily (CBD)* each business day. *CBD* is a listing of the goods and services being contracted by the government from the private sector. GPO's Denver Field Printing Plant is equipped and staffed to handle classified printing needs. Documents up to and including those at the "Secret" classification level can be produced in the recently updated full-service facility.

GPO employs state-of-the-art technology to provide the products traditionally demanded by its federal agency clients. In addition to GPO's high-end electronic photocomposition system, 33 offset presses and 19 letterpresses are in operation, supported by more than 150 bindery machines, including cutters, folders, sewing machines, adhesive binders, and stitchers. GPO uses approximately 100 million pounds of paper each year, part for production purposes and part sold to agencies as blank paper.

GPO is a highly versatile printing facility. It produces cut forms, perfect-bound books, and leather-bound volumes. Money, bonds, and postage stamps are produced at the Bureau of Engraving and Printing, which is part of the Department of the Treasury. GPO does, however, produce millions of passports and postal cards each year.

Superintendent of Documents

Although the original job of GPO was to handle printing, responsibility for the sale and distribution of government documents was added in 1895. Today, through its documents program, GPO disseminates one of the largest volumes of informational literature in the world, distributing more than 100 million government publications every year through a variety of channels.

Library Programs

Most publications produced by GPO are available to the public for reference through nearly 1,400 depository libraries in the United States and its possessions. Depository libraries are public, academic, or other types of libraries that are designated by members of Congress or by law as official depositories. The Federal Depository Library Program is administered by the Library Programs Service, under the Superintendent of Documents.

Participating libraries receive government information products at no cost in return for providing free public access to federal information. The information products are sent to depositories in a variety of formats, including paper, microfiche, and CD-ROM.

Each year, most federal depository libraries select titles from a list of more than 7,000 information product categories. These libraries are known as selective depositories. In addition, 53 regional depository libraries receive every government information product distributed through the depository program and are responsible for retaining this material permanently.

Most states have a single regional depository library and several selective depositories, with the number depending on the number of congressional districts in the state. Selective depositories obtain needed information products as interlibrary loans from regional depositories.

In 1994 more than 17 million copies of 44,600 titles were distributed to depository libraries through the Superintendent of Documents. In addition, approximately 500,000 U.S. Geological Survey maps, 63,000 Defense Mapping Agency maps, and 2.1 million U.S. Department of Energy microfiche publications were distributed to depository libraries.

Among the other programs administered by the Library Programs Service is the Cataloging and Indexing Program, which provides bibliographic control of most of the materials disseminated to the depository libraries. The Cataloging Branch manages this program by supplying descriptive and subject cataloging records for the government documents acquired by the Library Programs Service. The cataloging records are published in the *Monthly Catalog of U.S. Government Publications*, and worldwide dissemination of cataloging records takes place in all media.

The Depository Administration Branch acquires government documents, determines the format of publications distributed to depository libraries (i.e., paper, microfiche, or electronic media), assigns Superintendent of Documents classification numbers, and provides administrative support to the distribution function of the Federal Depository Library Program. It also acts as the documents distribution agent to the foreign libraries in the International Exchange Service Program, on behalf of the Library of Congress.

The Depository Distribution Division performs all functions relating to receipt, storage, allotment, and shipment of publications distributed to depository libraries.

The Depository Services Staff within the Library Programs Service focuses on the functioning of individual depository libraries and their relation to each other and to GPO. It administers the designation and termination of depository libraries and changes of status of existing depositories. A primary responsibility is to monitor the condition of depository libraries through periodic inspection visits and a biennial survey.

Sales

The sales program currently offers for public sale more than 12,000 federal information products on a wide array of subjects. These are sold principally by mail order and through bookstores across the country. In FY 1994 the sales program generated over $80 million in revenues. The program operates on a cost-recovery basis, without the use of tax dollars. The average price of a government publication sold by GPO is $11.00. Some of the best sellers are *Federal Benefits for Veterans and Dependents, 1994; Statistical Abstract of the United States, 1994; General Industry Digest; Uniform Crime Reports for the United States, 1993;* and *County and City Data Book, 1994.*

Publications for sale include single-issue items such as books, forms, posters, pamphlets, and maps. Subscription services, for multiple-issue products—such as dated periodicals and magazines and basic-and-supplement services involving an initial volume and supplemental issues—are also offered. A growing selection of electronic information products—including CD-ROMS, computer diskettes, and magnetic tapes—are now available in the sales program.

In addition to telephone, mail, and fax order services, GPO sells federal information products through government bookstores. Certain consumer-oriented publications are also sold through the Consumer Information Center, which GPO operates on behalf of the General Services Administration.

Government Bookstores

A nationwide network of 24 government bookstores ensures broad distribution of sales program information products. Publications of particular public interest are made available in government bookstores when they are released, but the bookstores can order any government information product currently offered for sale and have it sent directly to a customer. Customers can place orders by phone, mail, or fax.

Catalogs

GPO publishes a variety of free catalogs to increase public awareness of and access to federal information products. The catalogs are mailed to prospective customers on targeted internal and leased mailing lists and to people who request information on federal information products, and they include hundreds of products on a vast array of subjects. The free catalogs include:

- U.S. Government Information: new and popular information products of interest to the general public
- New Information: bimonthly listing of new titles; distributed to librarians and other information professionals
- U.S. Government Subscriptions: periodicals and other subscription services in the SuDocs Sales Program
- Subject Bibliographies (SBs): nearly 200 listings, each containing titles relating to a single subject or field of interest
- Subject Bibliography Index: lists all SB subject areas
- Catalog of Information Products for Business: the largest catalog for business audiences
- Selling to the Government: information products on business opportunities with the federal government; distributed to small businesses
- U.S. Government Publications about Military History: distributed through special-interest mailing lists
- Environmental Science and Methods: information products for scientists, environmental professionals, and businesses needing current information on environmental regulation

Publication Reference File

The Superintendent of Documents issues the GPO Sales Publication Reference File (PRF), a guide to current information products offered for sale that provides author, title, and subject access. It is available on subscription and is issued in 48X microfiche format or on machine-readable magnetic tape. The microfiche service consists of bimonthly mailings of the complete master file and monthly mailings of a single fiche containing new information products. The magnetic tape service provides biweekly mailings of the complete file.

The file is also available online as a component of the DIALOG Information Retrieval System (File 166). This service offers online ordering, retrieval, and research capabilities.

Monthly Catalog of U.S. Government Publications

The Monthly Catalog of U.S. Government Publications is the most comprehensive listing of publications issued by more than 250 federal departments and agencies within the legislative, judicial, and executive branches. More than 2 million bibliographic records have been published in the *Monthly Catalog*. Data include the official title, series, author, and publisher. Entries are indexed by subject, title, author, and series.

The cataloging records are also disseminated for online use within approximately 17,000 libraries in the United States and overseas via OCLC. The *Monthly Catalog* is available from the Superintendent of Documents and is online as a component of the DIALOG Information Retrieval System (File 66). It can also be accessed through many commercial databases and electronic products.

Consumer Information Catalog

The Consumer Information Center, a separately funded operation of the U.S. General Services Administration, publishes the *Consumer Information Catalog* four times a year. Established in 1970, the Consumer Information Center helps federal agencies develop, promote, and distribute consumer information. GPO provides order processing and distribution services to the Consumer Information Center. Millions of orders are processed by GPO each year at the Public Documents Distribution Center, Pueblo, CO 81009.

Electronic Publishing and Dissemination

GPO's Office of Electronic Information Dissemination Services (EIDS) helps federal agencies disseminate their publications through several electronic formats, including:

- Online via Internet
- Compact disc-read-only memory (CD-ROM)
- Computer diskette
- Magnetic tape
- Electronic bulletin board

EIDS guides agencies through all phases of electronic publishing, from product design and configuration through replication and dissemination. Information specialists are available for free consultations with agency publishers and program staff, providing expert advice on:

- The electronic format that best matches the information
- Selecting CD-ROM software
- Publishing schedules, including premastering, mastering, replication, and shipping
- User support services

GPO Access

GPO provides free public access to important federal information over a unique online delivery system called GPO Access, created by law in 1993 and launched in June 1994. Free use of the system is available through the Federal Depository Library Program administered by GPO. Access is provided on-site at depository libraries, off-site through gateways established by these libraries, or by existing state or local public networks acting as gateways in cooperation with a depository library.

The full text of the *Federal Register*, *Congressional Record*, and all published versions of congressional bills are available on the day of publication. The *Register* and *Record* include complete text and graphics. Exact copies of the bills can be reproduced on the user's own printer. The U.S. Code database, containing the text of laws in effect as of January 1994, was added late in 1994, and other databases continue to be added.

The public can access this information by visiting a depository library or calling from their home or business through a growing number of gateways. GPO is working to establish gateways in all 50 states. Gateway users can access the information free, 24 hours a day, seven days a week.

In December 1994 GPO Access received a Federal Technology Leadership Award, which is presented annually for mission effectiveness, cost effectiveness, and service to the public.

GPO Access is more than just an online database. Under the GPO Electronic Information Access Enhancement Act of 1993 (PL 103-40), the Superintendent of Documents is required to:

- Maintain an electronic directory of federal electronic information (the Locator Service)
- Provide a system of online access to the *Congressional Record*, the *Federal Register*, and other appropriate publications (the Online Service)
- Operate an electronic storage facility for federal electronic information (the Storage Facility)

Collectively, along with the Federal Bulletin Board, these facilities are referred to as GPO Access. The GPO Access system manages the flow of information throughout its life cycle. The cycle begins with creation of the document or database, includes its reproduction in print or electronic formats, involves dissemination to appropriate audiences, and continues with storage during periods of declining use. Ultimately the information will be turned over to the National Archives for preservation as historical records.

Important Facts About GPO Access

- GPO Access is economical because it utilizes the existing Federal Depository Library Program and includes as partners state and local online networks. The depositories and their local network partners contribute both personnel and computer resources.
- The system emphasizes community initiatives and depends on local library and educational leaders to promote its use.
- Members of the House and Senate designate depository libraries in their state and districts. There is at least one depository in every congressional district and nearly 1,400 federal depositories nationwide.
- PL 103-40 requires that the GPO Access system be made available to depository libraries without charge. Others may access the information at the incremental cost of dissemination.
- GPO's Locator Service will include descriptive information on federal information products held by all depository libraries in any format: paper, microfiche, or electronic. The locator will refer users to the nearest depository library holding the desired information. The locator will also identify a gateway to other government information locators created by federal agencies. Use of the GPO Locator Service is free. The locator will go online in 1995.
- GPO Access information is official and complete. GPO guards the integrity of the databases to ensure against unauthorized changes in text or graphics.
- GPO uses Internet for dissemination. Although there are costs to obtain an Internet connection, these costs are not distance sensitive and do not disadvantage rural areas. Once connected, users may search as much or as long as they wish.
- Individuals who do not have Internet connections may use the GPO Access system from their home or office through their personal computer, phone, and modem, placing calls through the nearest participating depository library or its state or local network partner. These "gateways" connect with the GPO computers over Internet.
- GPO Access also includes the Federal Bulletin Board maintained by GPO. The bulletin board offers over 6,000 files from more than 25 agencies and organizations in all three branches of the federal government.
- The Storage Facility will supplement and complement the Online Service and the Federal Bulletin Board. It will provide access to both image and full-text electronic files on demand. Information in the Storage Facility will normally be of a final nature, requiring no update. On-demand elec-

tronic access provided by this facility may ultimately replace much of the paper and microfiche currently being sent to depository libraries, offering significant cost savings.

- GPO will continually update and improve its databases, software systems, and operations. The law creating GPO Access requires consultation with users and the private sector to assess the quality and usefulness of the system.

- GPO in 1995 will begin using Standard Generalized Markup Language (SGML) to produce the *Federal Register* and *Congressional Record*. The SGML-tagged databases can be converted to any format—paper, online, or CD-ROM. Utilization of SGML will allow users of the electronic databases to more easily identify the precise information they want. It will reduce searching time and improve the precision of results. (For instance, SGML permits the user searching the *Congressional Record* to ask for instances in which a member of Congress speaks on a topic, rather than all instances in which a member's name and the topic occur somewhere in the same day's *Record*.)

National Library of Education

555 New Jersey Ave. N.W., Washington, DC 20208-5721
202-219-1692
Internet: library@inet.ed.gov

The new National Library of Education (NLE) is the largest federally funded library in the world devoted solely to education. An expansion of the former U.S. Department of Education Research Library, NLE houses on-site more than 200,000 books and about 750 periodical subscriptions in addition to studies, reports, ERIC microfiche, and CD-ROM databases. It holds books on education, management, public policy, and related social sciences; dictionaries, encyclopedias, handbooks, directories, abstracts, indexes, and legal and other research sources in print and CD-ROM; current and historical journals and newsletters; and more than 450,000 microforms.

Special collections include rare books published before 1800, mostly in education; historical books from 1800 to 1964; early American textbooks, 1775–1900; modern American textbooks, 1900–1959; U.S. Department of Education reports, bibliographies, and studies; archived speeches, policy papers, and reports; and children's classics.

Mission

The mission of the National Library of Education is to ensure the improvement of educational achievement at all levels by becoming a principal center for the collection, preservation, and effective use of research and other information related to education. NLE will promote widespread access to its materials, expand coverage of all education issues and subjects, and maintain quality control. NLE will also participate with other major libraries, schools, and educational centers across the United States in providing a network of national education resources.

Organizational Structure

Under the recent reorganization of the Office of Educational Research and Improvement (OERI), the director of the National Library of Education reports to the assistant secretary of OERI. NLE is composed of three divisions: Reference and Information Services, Collection and Technical Services, and Resource Sharing and Cooperation.

History

The U.S. Department of Education was established by an act of Congress in 1867 for the purpose of

> collecting such statistics and facts as shall show the condition and progress of education in the several states and territories, and of diffusing information as shall aid in the establishment and maintenance of efficient school systems and otherwise promote the cause of education throughout the country. (14 Stat. L. 434, 39th Congress, 1867)

The prominent educator Henry Barnard was named commissioner of education. After one year of independent operation, however, the Department of Education was transferred to the Department of the Interior, where it was known as the Bureau of Education. When Barnard, who was interested in establishing an education library, resigned as commissioner in 1870, he left his own extensive private collection of books on education with the bureau. During the 70 years of its operation in the Department of the Interior, the Bureau of Education administered an independent library serving the specialized needs of its employees.

In 1939, the Bureau of Education became one of the five constituent agencies of the new Federal Security Agency, forerunner of the Department of Health, Education, and Welfare (HEW). The Bureau of Education Library then became part of the Federal Security Agency library, which eventually became the HEW library.

As a result of a management study of the HEW library conducted in 1973, which recommended decentralization of the library, the education collection was transferred to the newly established (1972) National Institute of Education (NIE). NIE agreed to maintain an educational research library in an effort to fulfill its mandate to "provide leadership in the conduct and support of scientific inquiry in the education process" (Education Amendments of 1972, U.S. Code, vol. 20, Sect. 1221 (a), 1972).

From 1973 to 1985, the NIE Educational Research Library was the recipient of several fine education collections, including the education and library and information science collections of the HEW library, the library of the Center for Urban Education (formerly in New York City), the National Education

Association library, the Community Services Administration library, and the former Central Midwest Regional Education Laboratory (CEMREL) library.

A major reorganization of the Office of Education Research and Improvement, which had included NIE as a component, occurred in October 1985. The name of the library was changed to U.S. Department of Education Research Library, and it was operated as part of Information Services, one of the five units of OERI. More recently, it operated under OERI's Library Programs.

In March 1994 Congress authorized the establishment of the National Library of Education, with specific charges. By law, two other units in OERI—the former Education Information Branch and the former Education Information Resources Division—have joined forces with the library staff to form NLE, boosting services to department employees and other clients. Although ERIC (the Educational Resources Information Center) is not yet officially part of NLE, the library works in partnership with this major program that serves the community, government, and the general public with ready access to education information nationwide.

This new designation as National Library and expansion of functions meant a broader range of services and a larger staff. NLE now has 42 staff members compared to the former Education Research Library's staff of 7.

Functions

NLE provides a central location within the federal government for information about education; provides comprehensive reference services on education to employees of the U.S. Department of Education and its contractors and grantees, other federal employees, and members of the public; and promotes cooperation and resource sharing among providers and repositories of education information in the United States.

Major Themes and Goals

The major themes and goals of NLE are to establish and maintain a one-stop central information and referral service to respond to telephone, mail, electronic, and other inquiries from the public on:

- Programs and activities of the U.S. Department of Education
- ERIC resources and services of the 16 clearinghouses and ERIC Support Components, including the ERIC database's more than 850,000 records of journal articles, research reports, curriculum and teaching guides, conference papers, and books
- U.S. Department of Education publications
- Research and referral services available to the public, including ERIC, the OERI Institutes, and the national education dissemination system
- Statistics from the National Center for Education Statistics

- Referrals to additional sources of information and expertise about educational issues available through educational associations and foundations, the private sector, colleges and universities, libraries, and bibliographic databases

In addition, NLE aims to:

- Provide for the delivery of a full range of reference services on subjects related to education, including specialized subject searches; search and retrieval of electronic databases; document delivery by mail and fax; research counseling, bibliographic instruction, and other training; interlibrary loan services; and selective information dissemination
- Promote greater cooperation and resource sharing among libraries and archives with significant collections in education by establishing networks; developing a National Union List of education journals held by education libraries throughout the United States; developing directories and indexes to textbook and other specialized collections held by education libraries; and cooperating to preserve, maintain, and promote access to educational items of special historical value or interest

Current Activities

During its first few months, the library has focused on the selection of the National Library of Education Task Force and planning for its spring meeting, budgeting, establishing Collection Assessment and Collection Development Policies, producing a commemorative poster, designing outreach and promotion programs, setting up and monitoring an 800 toll-free customer service line, and establishing near- and long-term goals and objectives.

The library is also providing legislative reference services through a branch library in the department's headquarters building. Further, NLE is establishing liaisons with the OERI Institutes and other offices within OERI, planning for the opening of an NLE Reading Room in the headquarters office building, participating in the orientation of new department employees, and undergoing an internal management review and evaluation.

Future Plans

NLE's plans include:

- Establishing a networking/resource-sharing program
- Developing a three-year plan to eliminate the arrearage of uncataloged books and other materials in the library's collection and to preserve and maintain their usability
- Establishing an NLE presence on Internet through INet, the U.S. Department of Education's Internet, and ERIC
- Initiating a digitization program
- Carrying out a functional analysis of the library

Publications

NLE's primary publication is *New at NLE*, a bimonthly recent acquisitions list of the library's circulating and noncirculating collections, and those of the Technology Resources Center, and INet. Flyers and other informational material are available on request.

Primary Collections

NLE's primary collections include its circulating, reference, serials, and microform collections. The circulating collection includes primarily books in the field of education published since 1965. The broad coverage of the collection includes not only education but such related areas as law, public policy, economics, urban affairs, sociology, history, philosophy, and library and information science. The reference collection includes current dictionaries, general and specialized encyclopedias, handbooks, directories, major abstracting services, newspapers and journals related to education and the social sciences, and indexes.

Current periodical holdings number more than 750 English-language journals and newsletters. The collection includes nearly all of the primary journals indexed by *Current Index to Journals in Education (CIJE)* and *Education Index*. The library subscribes to eight major national newspapers and maintains back issues of four national newspapers on microform.

The microform collection consists of more than 450,000 items, including newspapers, the *Federal Register, Congressional Record, Newsbank*, college catalogs, the William S. Gray Collection on Reading, the Kraus Curriculum Collection, and various education and related journals. It also includes the complete microfiche collection of the ERIC system, a program funded by the U.S. Department of Education. NLE's ERIC collection contains complete sets of the ERIC indexes and recent ERIC clearinghouse publications and products. Research publications are in varied formats: bibliographies, state-of-the-art papers, reviews, and information analyses in the 16 areas of education currently covered by the ERIC system.

Special Collections

The earliest volumes of NLE's special collections date to the 15th century and include books about education, early American textbooks, and children's books. Some restoration has taken place; items are housed in controlled space, and a catalog—*Early American Textbooks, 1775–1900*—has been issued. This collection began with Henry Barnard's private collection of American schoolbooks, was nurtured by Commissioner John Eaton during his tenure (1870–1886), and was further enriched by several private donors. Other special collections maintained by the library are (1) material from the former National Institute of Education, the former U.S. Office of Education, and the U.S. Department of Education, including reports, studies, manuals, and other documents; (2) archives of the former U.S. Office of Education and National Institute of Education, including speeches, policy papers, and other documents; and (3) the historical collection of

Kathryn Heath, former employee of the Office of Education, and Elaine Exton, a local education writer.

Interlibrary Loan

NLE offers an active interlibrary loan (ILL) service and is a member of the Online Computer Library Center (OCLC). Through this database, library staff can tap the resources of a large number of research library collections throughout the United States and draw on their holdings, as well as offering ILL service to other libraries.

Technology Resources

NLE's Technology Resources Center offers an opportunity to explore what is available in technology, use the equipment, and look at programs designed to be used in classrooms. The center has computer programs, CD-ROMs, videotapes, and videodiscs. It offers a range of hardware and software for all levels of education and training.

The center is open to visits from all educators, researchers, administrators, curriculum specialists, teachers, librarians, and anyone else interested in the effective use of technology in education and training. Publishers of computer materials have provided over 400 programs from preschool to postgraduate levels. The collection of computer programs is strong in science, reading, mathematics, and word processing. Programs on art, music, science, biology, history, mathematics, chemistry, and employment skills are included. Many of the titles are chosen from programs listed by the Association for Supervision and Curriculum Development's "Only the Best."

Equipment represents state-of-the-art computer technology available for use in schools. Included are Apple, IBM, and Compaq systems, as well as Kodak Photo CD and Philips Full-Motion CDi systems. Several models of CD-ROM units are demonstrated for both MS-DOS and Macintosh. Interactive videodiscs using computers and bar code readers are also shown; and videotape, electronic mail, online data services (including Internet), and closed-captioned decoders are all on display.

The center provides monthly programs on the use of technology in education. Special presentations and demonstrations are arranged on request. Tours of the facilities and demonstrations of materials are given for visiting educators and the public. Center staff work with school systems, software publishers, and vendors to arrange special demonstrations related to individual school system needs.

Copies of commercially published software evaluations and an index of software programs are available for use in the center. Software lists from state and local education agencies are welcomed. The center does not evaluate, recommend, or endorse hardware or software, nor does it lend software or equipment. Equipment is used solely for demonstration.

OERI Online Access

NLE maintains an electronic repository of education information and provides public access through several electronic networks:

- EDWeb. An Internet-based service of NLE's INet system, EDWeb makes information available through World-Wide Web, gopher, and ftp servers.
- OERI Toll-Free Bulletin Board System. The bulletin board provides access to much of the same information as EDWeb for educators who do not yet have access to Internet.
- GTEnet. NLE posts education information on the GTE Educational Services Network (GTEnet).

How to Access the U.S. Department of Education via Internet

The U.S. Department of Education maintains several types of Internet servers and tries to make all its holdings accessible to the public through the channels commonly used by educators.

- World-Wide Web. The World-Wide Web Server can be accessed at URL (uniform resource locator) **http://www.ed.gov/**.
- Gopher. The gopher server's address is **gopher.ed.gov** or you may select **North America—>USA—>General—>U.S. Department of Education** from the All/Other Gophers menu on your system.
- FTP. FTP users can access the information by ftping to **ftp.ed.gov** (log on anonymous).
- E-mail. E-mail users can get the catalog and instructions for using the mail server by sending E-mail to **almanac@inet.ed.gov**. In the body of the message, type: send catalog<M>; avoid the use of signature blocks.

The library does not offer public access gopher or WWW clients. You must either have an appropriate gopher or WWW client, such as NCSA Mosaic or Lynx, at your site or be able to telnet to a public access client elsewhere. You cannot access our public servers by telneting to our site; you will be denied telnet access. Gopher and Mosaic/Lynx are the preferred access methods. Our ftp directories remain somewhat cryptic and the E-mail server is by its very nature a slow method to get documents.

Questions and Comments

Suggestions or questions about the contents of the WWW, gopher, ftp, and mail servers should be directed to one of the following:

E-mail: inetmgr@inet.ed.gov
                 gopheradm@inet.ed.gov
                 wwwadmin@inet.ed.gov

Telephone:	202-219-1547
Fax:	202-219-1817
Mail:	INet Project Manager
	U.S. Department of Education
	Office of Educational Research
	and Improvement
	National Library of Education/RSCD
	555 New Jersey Ave. N.W., Rm. 214
	Washington, DC 20208-5725

How to Access the OERI Toll-Free Bulletin Board System

Virtually any computer with telecommunications software can be used to access the OERI Toll-Free Bulletin Board System. The toll-free number is 1-800-222-4922; within Washington, D.C., call 202-219-1511.

For any computer, the following parameters should be set in the communications software before you dial the bulletin board:

* Speed up to 14,400 baud
* 8 data bits
* 1 stop bit
* No parity
* Full duplex

Please be patient; the system is extremely busy. Call 202-219-1526 with any system access problems.

How to Find Out What's New Online

The INet World-Wide Web, gopher, ftp, and E-mail servers are continuously updated with new press releases, grant announcements, publication summaries, full-text documents, and statistical data sets. New material on major U.S. Department of Education initiatives such as Goal 2000, School-to-Work, Technology, and ESEA Schoolwides is added frequently.

To find new items on the INet World-Wide Web Server, select **What's New** near the top of the home page to display a list of recent additions.

To find new items on the gopher server, follow the path:

What's New in This Gopher/
What's New (Format: nn=#days back or mm/dd/yy=since date)<?>

and enter a search string in one of the formats indicated (e.g., "7 days" or "12/31/94"). The gopher will quickly build and present to you a menu of items added or changed during that time.

To find new items on the OERI Toll-Free Bulletin Board System, type **L** to select [L]ibraries from the main menu. Then type **D mm/dd/yy** where mm/dd/yy represents the cutoff date for files listed (e.g., **D 12/25/94** would list files added or modified since December 25, 1994).

NLE Telephones

(Area Code 202)

Library Administration	219-1884
Reference/Research/Statistics	219-1692
Outside Washington, D.C., area	1-800-424-1616
	(fax) 219-1696
Circulation/Interlibrary loan	219-2238
Collection Development/Technical Services	219-1883
Legislative Reference Service	401-1045
	(fax) 401-9023
Technology Resources Center	219-1699
Data Tape Sales	219-1522
ACCESS ERIC	1-800-LET-ERIC

National Association Reports

American Library Association

50 E. Huron St., Chicago, IL 60611
312-944-6780, 800-545-2433

Arthur Curley
President

Founded in 1876, the American Library Association (ALA) is the chief advocate for the people of the United States to achieve and maintain high-quality library and information services—whether by protecting the right to read, educating librarians, or making information accessible to everyone.

ALA is the oldest and largest library association in the world, its 55,000-plus members are primarily librarians but also trustees, publishers, and other friends of libraries. Priority areas of concern are access to information, legislation and funding, intellectual freedom, public awareness, personnel resources, and library services, development, and technology.

The association encompasses 11 membership divisions: the American Association of School Librarians, the American Library Trustee Association, the Association for Library Collections and Technical Services, the Association for Library Service to Children, the Association of College and Research Libraries, the Association of Specialized and Cooperative Library Agencies, the Library Administration and Management Association, the Library and Information Technology Association, the Public Library Association, the Reference and Adult Services Division, and the Young Adult Library Services Association.

In addition to its headquarters in Chicago, ALA maintains an office in Washington, D.C., and an editorial office in Middletown, Connecticut, for *Choice*, a review journal for academic libraries.

Conferences and Programs

ALA holds two major membership meetings each year: an annual conference and a midwinter business meeting. The 113th Annual Conference, held June 23–30, attracted 12,627 members, exhibitors, and guests to Miami Beach. "Customer Service: The Heart of the Library" was the conference theme selected by 1993–1994 ALA President Hardy Franklin.

Keynote speakers Marian Wright Edelman, founder and director of the Children's Defense Fund, and Deborah Prothrow-Stith, an expert on teen violence, denounced the violence that is claiming so many young lives and praised librarians for their efforts to reach out to teens. Franklin recognized ten libraries for their exemplary youth-service programs with $500 awards provided by the Margaret A. Edwards Trust. The award-winning libraries are profiled in *Excellence in Library Services to Young Adults: The Nation's Top Programs*, published by ALA Editions.

In his inaugural speech, 1994–1995 ALA President Arthur Curley began his term with an emphasis on libraries as a fundamental American value. "While times have changed," he said, "what people want from their libraries has not."

Former U.S. President Jimmy Carter and longtime library advocate Virginia Mathews were awarded ALA's highest honor in Miami Beach, when they were named Honorary Members.

Earlier in the year almost 11,000 librarians, exhibitors, and other guests attended the Midwinter Meeting February 4–10 in Los Angeles, where they toured the newly restored and remodeled Los Angeles Main Library.

The largest library education program ever, a teleseminar titled "Achieving Breakthrough Service" was broadcast live May 12 to some 12,000 library staff, trustees, and others at more than 400 sites in the United States, Canada, and Puerto Rico. A first-ever teleconference, sponsored by ALA's Committee on Accreditation and the H. W. Wilson Foundation on September 8, focused on preparing library educators to implement new standards for the accreditation of master's programs in library and information science.

ALA's Public Library Association (PLA) observed its 50th anniversary by hosting its fifth—and largest—national conference March 22–26 with some 5,806 participants gathered in Atlanta. The American Association of School Librarians (AASL) met in Indianapolis November 9–13 for its seventh national conference, which drew 3,126 school library media specialists, educators, exhibitors, and guests.

Upcoming conferences include the 1995 ALA Annual Conference, scheduled June 22–29, in Chicago, and the ALA Midwinter Meeting, January 19–25, 1996, in San Antonio. The Library Administration and Management Association and the Library and Information Technology Association will hold their first joint division conference in 1996.

Issues

The emergence of the "Information Superhighway" has raised many wide-ranging issues of special concern to the nation's libraries and librarians. These range from concerns about public access and telecommunications rates for libraries to intellectual property rights.

In a January 11 speech at the University of California at Los Angeles, Vice President Gore challenged telephone and cable companies to provide free electronic links to every classroom, library, and health clinic by the year 2000. In his State of the Union Address, President Clinton also urged that every classroom and library be part of the "Information Superhighway." These and other nods to libraries are the kind of recognition ALA's Washington Office pushes hard to achieve.

At an April 19 Senate hearing, ALA President Hardy Franklin and librarians from across the country testified about how services in their libraries were enhanced by electronic data transmission. Timed to coincide with National Library Week and National Library Legislative Day, the hearing was chaired by library supporter Senator Paul Simon (D-Ill.), who warned: "If in creating the superhighway we do not include public libraries as an integral part at the start, the superhighway will bypass and shut out many of our citizens." In addition to live testimony, electronic input from ALA members increased the timeliness and effectiveness of the Washington Office's responses to issues in 1994.

ALA played a key role developing public interest principles endorsed by the Telecommunications Policy Roundtable, a new coalition of more than 60 non-profit, consumer, labor, and civil rights organizations. The principles address policy development in the areas of the First Amendment, privacy, intellectual property, ubiquity, universal and equitable access, and interoperability.

In November, ALA joined with four national education groups to propose an innovative plan to use price-cap regulation formulas to promote investment by local telephone companies in connecting schools and libraries to the nation's electronic information network.

Elaine Albright, chair of the ALA Legislative Committee's subcommittee on telecommunications testified before the Commerce, Science, and Transportation Committee in support of preferential telecommunications rates for libraries, hospitals, and educational institutions. "If Congress provides incentives to the marketplace as an engine of investment and economic growth, it should balance this by extracting support of public interest goals," Albright told the committee chaired by Senator Ernest Hollings (D-S.C.).

Several national information infrastructure bills that were stalled or died at the end of the congressional session had useful provisions—thanks, in part, to ALA's efforts. These included provisions in support of networking applications for education, libraries, and government information as well as preferential telecommunications rates for libraries and educational institutions.

Resolutions in support of public access and intellectual property principles in the development of the information highway were among actions taken by the ALA Council in 1994. A resolution on telecommunications policy, forwarded to Congress, recommends that any new telecommunications legislation should

- Ensure public access to telecommunications services
- Reduce barriers by employing preferential rates, set-asides, least-cost access, universal service contributions, and other approaches
- Include a process to assess and review the impact of change in the regulatory environment on public interests, including libraries, education, and state and local government
- Ensure open data network standards that will allow open access and interoperability and avoid control of access by a few

ALA also went on record as opposing legislation that would "fundamentally alter" the U.S. Copyright Act of 1976 and supporting intellectual property principles as guaranteed by "fair use" and other library provisions of the Copyright Act in development of the "Information Superhighway."

In other actions, the ALA Council

- Endorsed a revision of the federal Library Services and Construction Act (LSCA), due to "sunset" in 1995, with a special emphasis on improving library services so that "all people have convenient and appropriate access to information via new and emerging technologies"
- Urged the National Commission on Libraries and Information Science to conduct a survey to identify states without mandates for the use of permanent paper for state and local documents of enduring value

Also in 1994, the ALA Executive Board reaffirmed the position it had taken a year earlier barring future meetings in Colorado after passage of legislation that denied antidiscrimination protection based on sexual preference. The board voted to move the 1995 Midwinter Meeting from Cincinnati to Philadelphia after the Ohio city passed similar legislation.

In a survey conducted as part of an ALA self-study, members cited the following as their chief concerns: open access to information, including electronic information; legislation and funding for libraries; intellectual freedom; information technology; and public relations, as a means of raising visibility for libraries.

Washington Report

Author and illustrator David Macaulay was among school library supporters who testified before the Senate Subcommittee on Education, Arts, and Humanities in support of funding for school libraries as part of the reauthorization of the Elementary and Secondary Education Act (ESEA). "There are countless chilling statistics to document the cutbacks, closing, and basic disintegration of the American library system both in and out of schools. At this point, only a major national commitment will turn the tide," said Macaulay. Congress approved the act in October with a new program authorizing aid for school library media resources. Part of the Improving America's Schools Act, the new program could, when funded, provide up to $200 million for school library resources. The provision for school library funding was part of the omnibus children and youth literacy initiative, the top recommendation of the 1991 White House Conference on Library and Information Services.

Federal library programs received $144 million for FY 1995, $2 million less than the previous year, but 40 percent more than the administration requested. Two programs for college library technology and research libraries were eliminated due to pressure from Vice President Gore's reinventing government proposals, but most of the funds were switched to other library programs.

"Give libraries more money—not less—so they can buy more books and computers and more people can get smarter," was the message delivered by 9-year-old Alexandria Johnson in an April 22 visit with President Clinton during National Library Week. She was accompanied by ALA President Franklin and Executive Director Peggy Sullivan. Alexandria was selected for the presidential visit for having written one of the most inspirational letters received during ALA's Libraries Change Lives campaign.

Intellectual Freedom

Daddy's Roommate by Michael Willhoite, a picture book designed to help children understand a nontraditional family setting, once again topped the list of the year's "most challenged" books in 1994, according to the ALA Office for Intellectual Freedom (OIF), the library censorship monitoring group. It was also the "most challenged" book in 1993. Other most-challenged titles include *Forever* by Judy Blume, *More Scary Stories to Tell in the Dark* by Alvin Schwartz, *Bridge to Terabithia* by Katherine Paterson, *The Chocolate War* by Robert Cormier, and *The New Joy of Gay Sex* by Charles Silverstein.

Alvin Schwartz was the most-challenged author in 1994, with three titles on the list. Other authors on this list include Michael Willhoite, Stephen King, V. C. Andrews, and Maurice Sendak.

ALA recorded a total of 760 challenges to school, school library, and public library materials in 1994, an 8 percent increase over 1993. Two-thirds occurred in schools, with the majority challenging school library materials.

The annual Banned Books Week "Celebrating the Freedom to Read" resource kits prepared by OIF helped libraries and other agencies across the country call attention to the dangers of censorship. The event—cosponsored by the American Booksellers Association, the American Booksellers Foundation for Free Expression, the Association of American Publishers, the American Society of Journalists and Authors, and the National Association of College Stores—will take place September 23–30, 1995.

In 1994 the Intellectual Freedom Committee adopted *Guidelines for the Development and Implementation of Policies, Regulations and Procedures Affecting Access to Library Materials, Services and Facilities*.

The 1994 Freedom to Read Honor Roll award went to the late musician Frank Zappa, a tireless opponent of censorship who remembered ALA in his will.

Children's Book and Media Awards

Lois Lowry's *The Giver* won the 1994 Newbery Medal for "the most distinguished contribution to American literature for children." The Caldecott Medal for "the most distinguished American picture book for children" went to *Grandfather's Journey*, illustrated by Allen Say. The awards are presented annually by ALA's Association for Library Service to Children.

The 1994 Coretta Scott King Awards for outstanding children's books by African American authors and illustrators whose works promote understanding and appreciation of all cultures went to Angela Johnson for *Toning the Sweep* and to Tom Feelings for illustrating *Soul Looks Back in Wonder*.

The Andrew Carnegie Medal for Excellence in Children's Video went to Rawn Fulton, producer-director of *Eric Carle: Picture Writer*, a 27-minute video that looks into the studio of the creator of *The Very Hungry Caterpillar* and other books.

Farrar, Straus and Giroux, publisher of *The Apprentice* by Pilar Molina Llorente, received the 1994 Mildred L. Batchelder Award for the most outstanding foreign-language children's book subsequently published in English in the

United States. Translated by Robin Longshaw, the book was originally published in Spanish under the title *El aprendiz*. Walter Dean Myers, author of *Hoops, Motown and Didi, Fallen Angels,* and other works for teens, received the Margaret A. Edwards Award for his lifetime contribution to literature for young adults. The award is sponsored by *School Library Journal* and administered by ALA's Young Adult Library Services Association.

Public Awareness

A first national attempt to gauge customer satisfaction with libraries found library users giving high marks both to their libraries and their librarians. More than 90 percent said they were satisfied with services at their local library, with about three-quarters claiming to be very or extremely satisfied. Virtually all of the respondents (95 percent) found library staff to be helpful, with 84 percent describing them as very or extremely helpful.

ALA developed a questionnaire intended to provide a national "snapshot" of library customer satisfaction. This questionnaire was administered by some 600 public, school, and college libraries during National Library Week, April 17–23, 1994. A total of 147,000 library users—primarily adult users of public libraries—took advantage of the opportunity to give feedback. "Any business would be proud to have this high level of customer satisfaction," said ALA President Hardy Franklin in announcing the results. "We are a service-driven profession."

More than 20,000 testimonials were received in support of the National Library Week theme, "Libraries Change Lives." They included the following:

- "As an independent technical consultant, access to library services literally makes it possible for me to stay in business!"
- "Growing up poor, Puerto-Rican, and familyless, drugs and gangs offered nothing to rescue my self-esteem. Librarians taught me to read books rather than dwell on destructive anger."
- "The library was an essential partner in my successful job search."
- "In 1990 I was injured in a car accident. The library's medical reference helped me understand the doctors' vague explanations, reducing my anxieties."

The comments were put to use in testimony before Congress, news releases, postcards, and other promotional materials for libraries. An exhibit featuring photos and comments from such well-known library users as President Clinton, author Erma Bombeck, and athlete Bo Jackson made its debut at a National Library Week reception hosted by ALA and the Center for the Book at the Library of Congress. Guest of honor author Sidney Sheldon, one of those featured in the exhibit, praised librarians for their role in promoting literacy and intellectual freedom and called the lack of federal government funding for libraries "a disgrace."

A proposal to train and mobilize a nationwide network of library advocates was selected to receive the $10,000 World Book/ALA Goal Award. The proposal was submitted by ALA President-Elect Arthur Curley's Special Committee on

Public Awareness, the Chapter Relations Office, the Public Information Office, and the Washington Office. Thirty-five presenters, trained at the 1994 ALA Annual Conference, began conducting programs at state and regional library conferences in the fall.

ALA's acclaimed celebrity READ poster series celebrated its tenth anniversary in 1994 with singer Michael Bolton, actors Edward James Olmos and Marlee Matlin, and producer/director Spike Lee lending their support. Elvis Presley belatedly joined the READ poster lineup via a 1962 photograph that shows "The King" reading. Andrew Shue, teen heartthrob and spokesperson for the World Cup USA, appeared on a poster bearing the message "Use your head, READ."

McDonald's restaurants joined with ALA for a second year to sponsor a national summer reading program designed to encourage families to read together. The 1994 program, "Reading Is a Magic Trip," featured the Magic School Bus. McDonald's provided a free starter kit of materials to all 16,000 public libraries in the United States.

ALA's efforts to reach wider audiences both within and outside the library community were intensified in 1994 when news releases and many other publications went electronic. News releases became available through the ALANEWS listserv, and the "Libraries Change Lives" campaign went online with the addition of two electronic mailboxes to receive statements of support. The ALA gopher was established on Internet, and ALA became host to more than 20 Internet public listservs and electronic journals by the end of the year and published a guide titled What's Up with the ALA Gopher and ALA Listservs?

ALA's flagship magazine, *American Libraries*, went online with an electronic companion offering a sneak preview of print issues. A wide range of office and division publications also became available electronically, ranging from the ALAWON, an irregularly published newsletter of the Washington Office, to the C&RL NewsNet, an abridged electronic version of *C&RL* (College and Research Libraries) *News*.

Special Projects

ALA and its divisions continue to develop a wide array of programs, exhibits, and activities to support libraries as centers for culture, literacy, and learning, often with the help of major foundations and corporations.

First Lady Hillary Rodham Clinton will serve as honorary chair for "Born to Read: How to Nurture a Love for Learning in Your New Babies," a three-year demonstration project administered by ALA's Association for Library Service to Children and funded with a $560,000 grant from the Prudential Foundation. The program will support development of five model projects designed to promote partnerships between librarians and health care providers to reach out to low-literate expectant mothers and help them raise children who are "born to read."

ALA received major grants totaling nearly $1 million from the National Endowment for the Humanities for three new traveling exhibitions. "The Many Realms of King Arthur," sponsored in cooperation with the Newberry Library in Chicago and the New York Public Library, began a two-year tour of 64 public and academic libraries in November. "Beyond Category: The Musical Genius of Duke Ellington," based on the Smithsonian's National Museum of American History exhibition, will tour 30 libraries in 1995–1997. A third exhibition, "A More Perfect Union: Japanese Americans and the U.S. Constitution," also based on a Smithsonian exhibition, is in the planning stage.

The DeWitt Wallace–Reader's Digest Fund awarded a total of $100,000 in 1994 to five communities as part of the National Library Power Program. The program has awarded $45 million in 30 cities since 1988, with the goal of changing teaching and learning by making the school library media center the heart of the education process. ALA's American Association of School Librarians provides leadership and technical support to Library Power sites.

In its seventh year, the Library Fellows program, supported by the United States Information Agency, placed nine U.S. library professionals in assignments in countries including Uganda, Costa Rica, Saudi Arabia, and Cambodia. The program also welcomed its first group of international library fellows, who came to the United States for three to ten months to work in American libraries.

Other program highlights:

- Independent analysis of ALA's "Writers Live at the Library" program found that library-sponsored programs featuring writers can have a significant impact on libraries and community cultural life. The pilot project, funded with a 1991 grant from the Lila Wallace–Reader's Digest Fund, funded literary events attended by some 20,000 people at 19 public libraries in Illinois, Michigan, and Wisconsin. Participating authors include Pulitzer Prize-winning poet Gwendolyn Brooks, best-selling mystery writer Walter Mosley, and National Book Award winner Larry Heinemann.

- "Read to Someone You Love. Literacy Begins at Home," a traveling exhibit that encourages parents, caregivers, and children to share the pleasures of reading, began traveling to 56 libraries in the Mid-Atlantic region, participants in the Bell Atlantic/ALA Family Literacy Project. The project, established in 1989, provides training and support for programs that bring parents and children together to build reading and literacy skills. The Bell Atlantic Foundation has awarded more than $1 million in grants since 1989.

Officers and Staff

Arthur Curley, director of the Boston Public Library, assumed the 1994–1995 presidency of ALA at the end of the 1994 Annual Conference in Miami Beach. Betty J. Turock—chair of the Department of Library and Information Studies and director of the master's in library science program at Rutgers University in New Jersey—is vice president/president-elect.

Elizabeth Martinez, formerly librarian for the Los Angeles Public Library, was named the sixth executive director of ALA, effective August 15. She succeeded Peggy Sullivan, a past president of ALA, who served two years as executive director.

In October, Martinez presented "ALA Goal 2000," a five-year plan "to position the association for the Information Age." The plan, endorsed unanimously by the ALA Executive Board, calls for an expanded Washington, D.C., office and establishment of an Office for Information Technology Policy in Washington to increase ALA's ability to influence national policy and legislation that affect libraries and public access to information. The plan also calls for association-wide activities to focus on a single theme over the next five years and creation of an independent, charitable foundation called the Fund for America's Libraries to raise money in support of ALA Goal 2000 and other areas of concern.

Carol Henderson was named executive director of the ALA Washington Office in February 1994 after serving as deputy director since 1979. She succeeded Eileen Cooke, who retired at the end of 1993 after 30 years of service. Lynne Bradley was selected deputy director. Other ALA appointments included Margaret Monsour, deputy executive director of the Reference and Adult Services Division; Tina Roose, deputy executive director of the Association of Specialized and Cooperative Library Agencies; and Kay Tavill, assistant director of the Chapter Relations Office.

Publishing Highlights

Marking its 100th year of providing major book resources for the library community, ALA's general publishing program changed its name from ALA Books to the broader ALA Editions. Under the new name, ALA will focus on products in various formats with immediate applications to state-of-the-art library services and management.

Among the 34 titles published in 1994 were *The Internet Troubleshooter: Help for the Logged-On and Lost*, by Nancy R. John and Edward J. Valauskas, and *Guide to Technical Services Resources*, edited by Peggy Johnson.

ALA Editions also published *The Big Book of Library Grant Money: Profiles of 1,471 Private and Corporate Foundations and Direct Corporate Givers Receptive to Library Grant Proposals*. The book was prepared by the Taft Group, one of the nation's leading compilers of private-funding information. *The Whole Library Handbook 2: Current Data, Professional Advice, and Curiosa about Libraries and Library Services*, compiled by George Eberhart, continued a tradition of timely and comprehensive information in its second edition.

ALA Editions marked the 25th anniversary of the annual Coretta Scott King Awards with publication of *The Coretta Scott King Awards*, edited by Henrietta Smith, with annotations for each award recipient since 1969 and a representation of all winning illustrators by one of their award-winning works. Also, for the first time ever, ALA brought together the annual Best Books for Young Adults lists in a compilation by Betty Carter titled *Best Books for Young Adults: The Selection, the History, the Romance*, which contains all the selections since the founding of the list in 1966.

Special Libraries Association

1700 18th St. N.W., Washington, DC 20009-2508
202-234-4700, FAX 202-265-9317

Mark S. Serepca
Director, Public Relations

Headquartered in Washington, D.C., the Special Libraries Association (SLA) is an international organization serving more than 14,000 special librarians and information managers, brokers, and consultants. As the second-largest library and information-related association in North America, SLA provides a variety of programs and services in the areas of professional development, public relations, research, specialized publications, government relations, and career and employment services.

More than 50 percent of the association's members are employed by corporations, with the remainder at government agencies, museums, associations, universities, hospitals, and other organizations with specialized information needs.

At year-end 1994, SLA had 56 regional chapters in the United States, Canada, the Caribbean, the Pacific, Europe, and the Middle East; 28 subject-area divisions; and seven special-interest caucuses.

Association activities are developed with specific direction toward achieving SLA's strategic goals, which are to advance the leadership role of its members in putting knowledge to work for the benefit of decision makers in their organizations and the general public and to shape the destiny of the information society.

Highlights of 1994

In the past year, two technological developments have dominated the evolution of the information profession. They are also having a profound impact upon SLA, by challenging its ability to react to and shape change.

First is the unprecedented growth of Internet. Used mainly by a handful of defense-oriented researchers in the early 1970s, this international network of roughly 30,000 computer networks now connects well over 20 million users in more than 145 countries and is doubling in size every year.

Today, Internet has transcended information industry boundaries to become an international pop phenomenon, used not only for the exchange of information but also for personal correspondence, advertising, and even dating. The use of the network has become so widespread that *USA Today* has published an article on Internet etiquette (called *netiquette*)—complete with a list of "dos and don'ts."

At any local bookstore, there are now several shelves of publications about Internet, with provocative titles ranging from *The Internet Guide for Dummies* to *Zen and the Art of Internet*. It is becoming such an integral part of society that one Washington, D.C., columnist wrote that *Time* magazine should have named Internet as its "Person of the Year."

In response to the growing importance of Internet as a communications vehicle, SLA began publishing E-mail addresses as well as telephone and fax numbers in *Who's Who in Special Libraries*.

Professional Development

In addition, Internet is becoming a dominant focus of SLA's professional development programming. What was traditionally the SLA Winter Education Conference was reshaped into InfoTech '94, a program with a strong technological theme and exhibits. InfoTech was extremely well received, and—not surprisingly—the most popular sessions focused on Internet. Because of the continuing strong interest in information technology, this will again be the theme for the 1995 Winter Education Conference, to be held in Raleigh, North Carolina, in January.

At SLA's Annual Conference in Atlanta, nine divisions pooled their resources to offer a series of informative workshops on topics ranging from the basic functions to advanced applications. Attendance at these sessions and at the continuing-education courses on information technology was at peak capacity.

Internet is also prominent on SLA's list of new publications. Last year, SLA published *The Internet and Special Librarians*. It sold 1,100 copies in the first six months and has continued to be a best-seller. In the planning stage is another book, *Users Guide to Internet by Subject*, which will be a must for navigating Internet.

Of course, Internet also impacts SLA at the chapter and division level, where numerous units have set up their own listservs. These listservs facilitate communication not only among members but among members and nonmembers with similar interests.

Creative Information Pathways

The second technological development having a significant impact on the association is the "Information Superhighway." Although essentially a North American undertaking, this process will affect SLA's membership worldwide. (Information has become an international commodity.) The Information Superhighway is getting almost as much media coverage as Internet. For now, the media's fascination is focused on the entertainment aspects of the new information infrastructure, especially interactive television.

SLA supports the establishment of a new national information infrastructure that can provide universal access to all segments of society and has joined with more than 60 diverse public interest groups to found the Telecommunications Policy Roundtable.

Enhancing the Profession's Image

In SLA's dealings with the Clinton administration, the association has made it clear that the role of the information professional is a crucial one and must not be overlooked by policymakers. Not only will special librarians continue to perform their traditional functions of collecting, analyzing, packaging, and disseminating information, but they will also become educators in the new networked environment.

Special librarians will help end users increase their awareness of what is available over the networks and work with them to improve their information retrieval skills. They will teach their clients how to use highway off-ramps to places other than Hollywood or the shopping networks.

SLA has also reminded the administration and Congress that attention must be given to the information that is being carried by the new networks as well as to the telecommunications systems themselves. They should not focus solely on the process and take the integrity of the information on the system for granted.

Because of the importance of the Information Superhighway, it has become the topic of numerous workshops and continuing-education courses at SLA's annual conference. In addition, SLA made this the focus of its 1994 State-of-the-Art Institute, which was held in November in Washington, D.C.

The 1994 institute covered a variety of critical issues, such as federal legislation, regulatory developments, business initiatives, and technological innovations. The program, which was sponsored by Disclosure (a provider of public company information), brought together more than 100 senior-level information professionals, business leaders, and government officials for an informative and educational series of addresses, workshops, and networking opportunities.

One of SLA's newest and most exciting publications is *Mastering Information in the New Century*. This book, written by futurists Marvin J. Cetron and Owen Davies, provides an excellent analysis of how economic, political, and societal trends, including the development of the information infrastructure, have been affecting the value of information. In addition, there is a thought-provoking, comprehensive set of trends and predictions.

Although Internet and the Information Superhighway were dominant forces impacting SLA programs in 1994, there were many other important association activities.

Government and Public Relations

SLA's government relations staff and Copyright Committee have been closely monitoring the progress—or lack of progress—in the *American Geophysical Union* vs. *Texaco* copyright case. In October 1994 the U.S. Appeals Court for the Second Circuit rejected Texaco's claim of fair use. However, Texaco is expected to file a petition for a rehearing. Regardless of the outcome of the appeal, it is likely that this case will ultimately go to the Supreme Court for final disposition.

Library Legislative Day—which occurs during National Library Week and has become a focal point for SLA's government relations program—took place on April 19 in Washington, D.C. The day's activities included briefings by congressional staff, meetings with members of Congress, and a congressional reception on Capitol Hill.

Another important SLA event during National Library Week is International Special Librarians Day. This public relations event provides an opportunity for members to gain recognition for their contributions to their organization and to society. The theme for 1994 was "Building a Better World with Information."

Also as part of the public relations program, SLA produced two new brochures, *Edges* and *Power*, which explain the role of the profession and the value of the information that special librarians provide. Copies were distributed to a large, diverse audience, including CEOs at hundreds of large companies and business editors at major newspapers and magazines.

Publications and Marketing

In the area of nonserial publications, SLA has been extremely busy, producing 16 new titles since the beginning of 1993. New editions of two SLA mainstay publications—*Guide to Special Issues and Indexes of Periodicals*, fourth edition, and *Directory of Business and Financial Information Services*, ninth edition—were released after much anticipation. Also completed was *Libraries and Copyright: A Guide to Copyright Law in the 1990s*, written by two experts in the copyright field.

By publishing information kits, professional papers from the Annual Conference, the proceedings of the State-of-the-Art Institute, and other specialized publications as well as books, the nonserial publications program ensures a balance of products available to meet the broad range of member needs.

SLA is doing a better job of analyzing its potential purchasers and marketing its publications, and sales are soaring. In 1994 sales exceeded the association's initial projection by 62 percent.

In the area of professional development, SLA is stepping up its production of self-study programs, which provide a convenient, self-paced, cost-effective means of developing or upgrading critical skills and knowledge.

Among the new titles is *Communicating with Library Users*, which guides the special librarian toward a better understanding of the library patron. Through examples and exercises, this workbook offers techniques that librarians can adopt for effective interaction at the desk and beyond.

Even more recently completed is *Legal Research for Non-lawyers*. The workbook is designed to help students analyze the facts and identify the issues involved in a legal research project, determine the required research tools, and effectively use the tools.

Also forthcoming is a series of miniworkbooks called the Career Management Series, which will address a variety of topics related to job searching, resume writing, interviewing, and managing one's career after finding a job.

In another move to make professional development more accessible to the membership, SLA worked with six chapters to offer locally the same continuing-education courses that were offered at the Annual Conference.

Research

While SLA is localizing some of its educational offerings, its research program is going international with the development of a worldwide survey of the modern information professional. The purpose of the survey, being conducted in cooperation with the International Federation for Information and Documentation, is to provide a baseline inventory of the knowledge, competencies, and skills of modern information professionals, including an analysis of the operational contexts within which they function.

To assist in the process, a random sample of 5 percent of SLA members will receive the survey form. The findings will be analyzed and the results disseminated widely. It is expected that the study will validate the emergence of the modern information professional as a critically important major new occupational category whose services are essential to all levels and sectors of societies around the world.

To support research that will further the strategic objectives of the association, SLA has a special grant program. In 1994 the Research Committee selected Raya Fidel and Michael Crandall as recipients of the Steven I. Goldspiel Research Grant. Their proposal is titled "Users' Choice of Filtering Methods for Electronic Text."

Internal Operations

SLA pays close attention not only to membership-oriented programs but to internal operations. A new telephone system was installed in 1994 to improve communications with members and others. SLA headquarters also has begun providing membership data to its chapters and divisions electronically. This will enhance record-keeping and communication with members.

The chapters and divisions will also be among the beneficiaries of the dues increase that was approved in 1994 by a wide margin; a portion of this increase will go to support additional chapter and division services.

Association of Research Libraries

21 Dupont Circle N.W., Washington, DC 20036
202-296-2296

Duane E. Webster
ARL Executive Director

The Association of Research Libraries (ARL) represents the 119 principal research libraries that serve major research institutions in the United States and Canada. ARL's mission is to shape and influence forces affecting the future of research libraries in the process of scholarly communication. ARL programs and services promote equitable access to and effective use of recorded knowledge in support of teaching, research, scholarship, and community service. The association articulates the concerns of research libraries and their institutions, forges coalitions, influences information policy development, and supports innovation and improvement in research library operations.

ARL fulfills its mission through programs and services that include Federal Relations and Information Policy, Access and Technology, Collections Services, the Office of Scientific and Academic Publishing, Statistics and Measurement, Minority Recruitment and Retention, the Office of Management Services, the Coalition for Networked Information, the Office of Research and Development, and Communications.

Federal Relations and Information Policy

The Federal Relations and Information Policy Program monitors activities resulting from legislative, regulatory, or operating practices and programs of various international and domestic government agencies and other relevant bodies on matters of concern to research libraries. It analyzes and responds to federal programs and issues, including information policy, networking and telecommunications, privacy, preservation, and higher education, with an emphasis on issues relating to networking, intellectual property, and dissemination of government information.

During 1994 ARL actively participated in information policy debates. ARL has focused on responding to and shaping legislative initiatives, with particular emphasis on telecommunications restructuring efforts as part of the national information infrastructure (NII) initiatives, implementing agency programs, such as the Government Printing Office's Access Program, and monitoring and influencing congressional appropriations. With regard to copyright and intellectual property, ARL has concentrated on reviewing and responding to the administration's recommendations regarding revisions to the 1976 Copyright Act and related NII efforts. This included drafting an ARL statement of principles on intellectual property and designing strategies to respond to specific legal challenges, including the Texaco fair-use case. Additionally, this program manages the ARL GIS (Geographic Information System) Literacy Project.

Copyright and intellectual property issues commanded much attention during 1994. At its May meeting, the membership of the association endorsed *Intellectual Property: An ARL Statement of Principles, Affirming the Rights and Responsibilities of the Research Library Community in the Area of Copyright.* These principles have since been endorsed by the American Library Association (ALA), the American Association of Law Libraries, CAUSE, and the National Humanities Alliance; other groups within the scholarly community are also considering endorsement. The association also became involved in a number of activities in response to the publication of the NII draft report "Intellectual Property and the National Information Infrastructure" by the NII Information Infrastructure Task Force (IITF) Working Group on Intellectual Property Rights. ARL submitted a response to this draft report.

ARL joined with over 100 nonprofit groups in support of provisions in S. 1822 that promote public access rights in a deregulated telecommunications environment. ARL, with others in the library and higher education community, has focused on issues relating to ensuring affordable and predictable access to telecommunications services. Specifically, this has included developing a "suggested approaches" paper with ALA, promoting the provision of preferential rates for both interstate and intrastate services, and promoting eligibility of libraries and educational institutions at all levels for these services.

ARL responded to the IITF report "Putting the Information Infrastructure to Work." The draft report includes a series of chapters on NII applications, including NII and libraries. ARL's response focused on issues relating to digitization of research resources, federal research and development activities, and new directions for federal library support.

Phase III (Canada) of the ARL GIS Literacy Project is under way. The project seeks to educate librarians and users about GIS as well as to develop GIS capabilities in research libraries. ARL continues to participate in discussions and conferences related to the development of a national spatial data standard.

Access and Technology

The Access and Technology Program of ARL addresses the myriad issues related to the ARL mission of enhancing access to scholarly information resources. The work of three ARL groups contributed to this capability in the previous six months: the Committee on Access to Information Resources, the Working Group on Scientific and Technical Information (STI), and the ARL Steering Committee for the Coalition for Networked Information. In addition, this program encompasses the relationship established among ARL, EDUCOM, and CAUSE—the HEIRAlliance, or Higher Education Information Resources Alliance—and ARL support for the Association of American Universities Task Force on a National Strategy to Manage STI.

Current activity within the Committee on Access to Information Resources and the Subcommittee on ILL (interlibrary loan) and Document Delivery focuses on the committee's agenda in support of resource sharing in an electronic environment. The Subcommittee on ILL and Document Delivery maintains an active and visible program to encourage developments to improve ILL systems and operations. The program is encompassed in the North American ILL/DD (NAILDD) Project. NAILDD Project activities have included orchestrating discussions with a wide variety of vendors and system providers to enlist their participation in a Developers/Implementors Group (DIG) to collaborate on implementing elements of the "ideal" ILL system. DIG facilitates the development of technologies that will meet the three priorities that surfaced in subcommittee discussions: a management system, an accounting system, and interconnectivity and linkages among systems. Steady progress has been reported in DIG by members who announced products that take steps toward meeting the project's technical objectives.

In July the ARL board formally adopted a statement developed by the Access Committee that presents a consensus view about the future direction of research library access and delivery services. The need for such a statement grew from DIG discussions, and at the committee's winter retreat that called for a shared understanding to guide vendor and library planning. *Information Access and Delivery Services: A Strategic Direction for Research Libraries* describes an environment in which users may exercise choice and responsibility and in which libraries serve as sources for comprehensive collections, centers of instruction and advice, and providers of gateway services to other libraries or information sources. The statement was posted on the ARL gopher, distributed on a number of electronic lists, and published in the September 1994 issue of the ARL newsletter.

Other activities undertaken by the Access Committee included working in collaboration with ARL's Statistics and Measurements Committee to consider if there are new measures that may provide incentives for change. Additionally, a workshop, Transforming the Reserve Function, sponsored by ARL and the National Association of College Stores (NACS), was conducted twice in 1994. A number of ARL institutions were represented by staff from both the library and the college store. Additional meetings on the topic were planned for early spring 1995.

In December HEIRAlliance prepared and distributed another briefing paper in the series *What Presidents Need to Know*. HEIRAlliance Executive Strategies Report No. 5 was *What Presidents Need to Know . . . about the AAU Action Agenda for University Libraries*. This series of reports is available through the CAUSE office in Boulder, Colorado.

Collection Services

The Collection Services Program addresses the broad issues facing research libraries in the areas of collection management and preservation. Two ARL Committees govern the capability: Research Collections and Preservation of Research Library Materials. The association's collection development efforts are directed toward fulfilling the program objective and supporting member libraries' efforts to develop and maintain research collections, both individually and in the aggregate. Strategies to accomplish the objective include promoting government and foundation support for collections of national importance in the United States and Canada; improving the structures and processes for effective cooperative collection development programs; providing collection management consultation throughout the Collection Analysis Program; and developing and operating collection management training programs.

The preservation efforts support the strategic program objective of promoting and coordinating member libraries' programs to preserve their collections. Strategies in pursuit of this objective include strengthening and encouraging broad-based participation in national preservation efforts in the United States and Canada; supporting the development of preservation programs within member libraries; supporting effective bibliographic control of preservation-related processes; encouraging the development of preservation information resources; and monitoring technological developments that may have an impact on preservation goals.

Initiatives undertaken by the Research Collections Committee in 1995 included oversight of the Foreign Acquisitions Project and the ARL/AAU demonstrations projects and examination of service models for the collection and distribution of foreign materials. A central focus of the committee's work was the examination of service models for the collection and distribution of foreign materials. The committee is also exploring the implications of electronic information in developing research collections.

Central to the work of the Preservation of Research Library Materials Committee was the consideration of an ARL action plan for preservation. Elements of this plan include the development of cost models for preservation decision making, establishment of a mechanism for codifying successful strategies for capturing and managing digitized information, participation in the development of standards critical to the preservation of research library collections, and support for preservation-related scientific research. The National Register of Microform Masters (NRMM) Serials RECON Project, a multiyear effort currently undertaking the conversion of about 30,000 serials reports into machine-readable records, is a separately funded project monitored by the preservation capability.

Office of Scientific and Academic Publishing

The objective of the Office of Scientific and Academic Publishing (OSAP) is to maintain and improve scholars' access to information. OSAP undertakes activities to understand and influence the forces affecting the production, dissemination, and use of scholarly and scientific information. The office seeks to promote innovative, creative, and alternative ways of sharing scholarly findings, particularly through championing newly evolving electronic techniques for recording and disseminating academic and research scholarship. The office also maintains a continuing educational outreach to the scholarly community in order to encourage a shared "information conscience" among all participants in the scholarly publishing chain: academics, librarians, and information producers. OSAP receives guidance through the work of the ARL Committee on Scholarly Communication.

As part of its interest in the newly emerging Internet scholarly communications movement, the office produced the fourth edition of the *Directory of Electronic Journals, Newsletters, and Academic Discussion Lists*, some 70 percent larger in both coverage and level of sophistication. An abridged version of this book is available on the ARL gopher. The OSAP director moderates an Internet conference, NewJour-L, which serves as a supplement between *Directory* editions.

The Association of American University Presses (AAUP) and ARL held their fourth joint Symposium on Electronic Publishing, "Filling the Pipeline and Paying the Piper," in November 1994. The proceedings of the second joint AAUP/ARL Symposium on Electronic Publishing were published in February 1994.

In May ARL published *Association of American Universities: Reports of the Three Task Forces*. AAU and ARL, at their respective spring 1994 membership meetings, endorsed a common action agenda that emerged from the completed Research Libraries Project. An AAU/ARL Coordinating Committee has been established to promote implementation of the recommendations and agenda. The main thrusts are to improve access and delivery of international research resources; introduce more competition and cost-based pricing into the marketplace, particularly for STI materials; ensure that network policies are in place to take advantage of the many needs they can serve and opportunities they offer; and build academic consensus on intellectual property matters.

Statistics and Measurement

The Statistics and Measurement Program describes and measures the performance of research libraries and their contribution to teaching, research, scholarship, and community service. The work of the ARL Statistics and Measurement Committee is covered by this program. The ARL board added an objective to the ARL Strategic Program Objectives at its July 1994 meeting to emphasize the increased importance of this area.

Strategies to accomplish this objective include

- Collecting, analyzing, and publishing quantifiable information about library collections, personnel, and expenditures, as well as expenditures and indicators of the nature of a research institution
- Developing new ways to describe and measure traditional and networked information resources and services
- Developing mechanisms to assess the relationship between campus information resources and high-quality research, the teaching environment, and, in general, the production of scholars and researchers
- Providing customized, confidential analysis of data for peer comparisons
- Developing a leadership role in the testing and application of academic research library statistics for North American institutions of higher education
- Collaborating with other national and international library statistics programs and accreditation agencies

In 1994 the Andrew W. Mellon Foundation awarded a grant to the Statistics and Measurement Program to develop an in-house data analysis and statistical consulting capability. The award was used to purchase and lease statistical software and hardware. This will enable ARL to provide customized data analysis and prepare reports and custom-made charts and graphs to members.

Publication of data will continue to be a central focus. The program produces two major publications annually, the *ARL Annual Salary Survey* and *ARL Statistics*. The 1993 *ARL Annual Salary Survey* presents trends in professional positions and salaries for fiscal year 1994, with special sections on minority librarians, Canadian librarians, and librarians in ARL university law and medical libraries. In 1993 the average salary for all ARL university librarians was $43,075 ($45,336 for men and $41,777 for women). The median professional salary was $25,834, and for minority librarians (about 11.3 percent of ARL's U.S. university librarians) the average salary was $40,680 overall. The 1992–1993 *ARL Statistics* presents data on ARL member libraries in the areas of collections, staffing, expenditures, and ILL. Findings from 1992–1993 data indicate that total library expenditures for ARL libraries were over $2.1 billion.

Library materials accounted for 28 percent, at just under $589 million; salaries and wages 52 percent, at just under $1.1 billion, and other operating expenditures, which include automation costs, 19 percent, at $418 million. These data are also available in machine-readable form.

The year 1994 saw the first electronic publication of ARL statistics on the World-Wide Web. Featuring reports on 48 data categories for the 108 university and 11 nonuniversity ARL members, the electronic publication is accompanied by fully documented descriptions of the 1992–1993 data files. It also provides selected graphs and maps.

Minority Recruitment and Retention

The Minority Recruitment and Retention Program is charged with increasing the number of minorities recruited and retained by ARL Libraries. To this end, program staff work closely with a broad range of libraries, graduate library education programs, and other library associations to promote minority student awareness of opportunities presented by research library careers. Over the past four years ARL has actively pursued issues relating to the underrepresentation of minorities in research libraries, and during 1994 the association promoted this to ARL library personnel and the broader research library community. A five-year plan was presented at the fall 1994 membership meeting. The current focuses are supporting libraries in the development of local, regional, and national minority recruitment initiatives; strengthening relationships with other library organizations; and engaging in dialogues about incorporating minority recruitment and retention strategies within library education programs.

Office of Management Services

The ARL Office of Management Services (OMS), celebrating its 25th anniversary in 1995, serves as a bridge between the business world and the world of academic and research libraries. Constantly seeking concepts and techniques with the potential to contribute to the effective management of libraries, the primary responsibility of OMS is to stay abreast of current management theory and practice. OMS provides consulting, training, and information services on the management of human and material resources in libraries.

The OMS Training and Staff Development Program offers institutes and workshops designed to strengthen the organizational, analytical, creative, and interpersonal skills of library staff. It seeks to promote personal responsibility for improvements in library services and programs and for effective individual performance. The institutes, designed to strengthen leadership skills and professional performance, are conducted by OMS staff with the assistance of librarians who have completed training and consultation skills programs with OMS. In 1994 over 800 library staff attended OMS training institutes and workshops. Three new programs were designed and offered in 1994: Women in Library Leadership Institute, Management Skills Institute for Library Personnel Officers, and Facilitation Skills Workshop.

The OMS Information Services Program gathers, analyzes, and distributes information on contemporary library management techniques, conducts surveys and analytical reviews, and answers inquiries on library issues and trends. The overall goals of the program: to identify expertise and encourage its exchange; to promote experimentation and innovation; to improve performance; and to facilitate the introduction of change. These goals are accomplished through an active publication and information service program whose principal components are the Systems and Procedures Exchange Center (SPEC), the OMS Occasional Paper Series, the Quick-SPEC survey service, and the new OMS Conference Program.

OMS publications in 1994 included SPEC Kits on strategies for obtaining funding for new library space, electronic journals in ARL libraries, reference service policies, document delivery services, and user surveys. Occasional Paper No. 16, *Resource Strategies in the 90's: Trends in ARL University Libraries*, was published in March 1994.

The OMS Consulting Service Program is designed to facilitate change in libraries. OMS provides a wide range of consulting services, incorporating new research on service delivery, marketing, and organizational effectiveness. Using an assisted self-study approach, the Consulting Service Program helps libraries investigate current practices and future trends, develop workable plans for collection management, technical and public services, leadership development, organizational screening, and organizational review and design. In 1994 the services of this program focused on facilitation of management retreats, organizational review and design, and strategic planning.

The newest OMS service is the Diversity Program. Begun in 1990 as a research and development project, this program seeks to respond to rapidly changing demographics by encouraging an awareness of human differences that leads to a value of and respect for these differences. It assists libraries in the development of workplace environments that welcome, develop, foster, and support diversity. Presentations, consultation, and training are all offered as part of this program. A special effort has been made to use a partnership approach to work with other organizations within the field of librarianship and higher education to support the goals of this program.

Coalition for Networked Information

The Coalition for Networked Information (CNI) was founded in March 1990 to help realize the promise of advanced networks and high-performance computing for information access and delivery. The coalition was established by three associations: ARL, CAUSE, and EDUCOM. ARL promotes equitable access and effective use of recorded knowledge supporting teaching, research, and scholarship. CAUSE and EDUCOM are dedicated to introducing, using, and managing information technology and related research resources in general and higher education. CNI promotes the creation of and access to information resources in networked environments in order to enrich scholarship and enhance intellectual productivity.

A task force of institutions and organizations able and willing to contribute resources and attention to the mission of the coalition was created in 1990 and continues to grow. This task force now provides a common vehicle by which over 190 institutions and organizations pursue a shared vision of information management and how it must change in the 1990s to meet the social, educational, and economic opportunities and challenges of the 21st century. Members of the task force include higher education institutions; publishers; network service providers; computer hardware, software, and systems companies; library networks and organizations; and public and state libraries.

Office of Research and Development

The Office of Research and Development (ORD) consolidates the administration of grants and grant-supported projects administered by ARL. The major goal within ORD is to promote the ARL research agenda by identifying and developing projects in support of the research library community's mission. ORD also works to develop funding support for those projects. Another part of this capability is the ARL Visiting Program Officer project. This project provides ARL staff and staff from member libraries with the opportunity to collaborate on programs of interest to the association. There were eight Visiting Program Officers in 1994—contributing to the ARL/AAU Latin American Demonstration Project, the Latin American Studies Assessment project, the review of government information access and dissemination programs, total quality management (TQM) and continuous improvement in research libraries, the ARL Foreign Acquisitions Project, demographic characteristics of library professionals, and interlibrary loan and document delivery.

Among the funded projects in 1994:

- ARL, in conjunction with the Library of Congress, administered a project funded by the National Endowment for the Humanities to convert into machine-readable records approximately 529,000 monographic reports that represent the records for microform masters held by libraries, archives, publishers, and other producers. NEH will also support another ARL project to convert serials records in the National Register of Microform Masters (NRMM), this activity in conjunction with Harvard University Library, the Library of Congress, and the New York Public Library.
- Under the Scholarship, Research Libraries, and Foreign Publishing in the 1990s Project, and with the support of the Andrew W. Mellon Foundation, ARL is developing "projects" to provide a clearer understanding of the forces influencing North American research libraries' ability to build collections of foreign materials.
- The Japan-U.S. Friendship Commission awarded ARL a grant to develop pilot projects to assist Japanese studies librarians to test different approaches to information access and provision. This is a joint project with the National Coordinating Committee for Japanese Library Resources (NCC).

- The North American Interlibrary Loan and Document Delivery Project is supplemented with support from the H. W. Wilson Foundation and the Council for Library Resources.
- ARL was awarded a grant from OCLC in partial support for the preparation of the second edition of *Preservation Microfilming: A Guide for Librarians and Archivists*. It will be published in 1995.

Communications and External Relations

The ARL Communications Program has as its goal the education of academic communities regarding research library issues as well as influencing policy and decision makers within higher education and other fields related to research and scholarship. Through the ARL newsletter and press releases, members of the library, higher education, and scholarly communication communities are apprised of current developments of importance to research libraries and are informed of ARL positions on issues that affect the research library community.

Issues 171–177 of *ARL: A Bimonthly Newsletter of Research Library Issues and Actions* were published in 1994. Jaia Barrett, director of the Office of Research and Development, and Lallie D. Leighton, publications program assistant, served as editor and managing editor, respectively. The newsletter addressed such key topics as NII and intellectual property, campus seminars on scholarly communication, geographic information systems, the AAU/ARL action agenda, and future directions of library and access delivery services. The newsletter also contained regular reports from each area of ARL, including a feature listing recent additions to the ARL gopher.

ARL's presence on Internet strengthened in 1994 with establishment of the ARL gopher in February and a World-Wide Web server in June. Key documents and a number of ARL publications are now available electronically. Additionally, a new electronic information service for research and academic libraries, ARL-Announce, was established in December 1994.

Minutes/Proceedings of Membership Meetings

Gateway to the Pacific Rim: Information Resources for the 21st Century, Minutes of the 122nd Meeting (May 1993, Honolulu), *The Emerging Information Infrastructure: Players, Issues, Technology and Strategies, Proceedings from the 123rd Meeting, Part I* (October 1993, Washington, D.C.), and *Transitions and Transformations: Proceedings from the 123rd Meeting, Part II*, were published in February, April, and August 1994, respectively.

Relations with the Scholarly Community and External Groups

Activities at the executive level in 1994 included meetings with, among others, the National Humanities Alliance, the Association of American Universities, and the American Council of Learned Societies.

Association Governance and Membership Activities

The spring ARL Membership Meeting was held in Austin, Texas, May 18–20, 1994. The theme, "The Research Library the Day After Tomorrow," explored the emerging technological environment in which academic and research libraries now operate and the implications for the development of future library programs and services. The program was hosted by the University of Texas Libraries.

The fall ARL Membership Meeting was held in Washington, D.C., October 19–21. The theme, "Renewing the ARL Agenda," investigated ARL's programmatic agenda in relation to the organization's capabilities and committees. Both meetings included reports and discussions on the AAU Research Libraries Project.

At the conclusion of the ARL Business Meeting in October, ARL President John Black, University of Guelph, handed the gavel over to President-Elect Jerry D. Campbell, Duke University. During the business meeting, three directors were elected to serve three-year terms on the ARL Board: Nancy Eaton, Iowa State University; James Neal, Indiana University; and Barbara von Whaled, State University of New York at Buffalo. The two directors whose board terms ended at this meeting—Sul Lee, University of Oklahoma, and Susan Nutter, North Carolina State University—were acknowledged.

Standing committees in 1994 included Information Policies, Access to Information Resources, Research Collections, Preservation of Research Library Materials, Management of Research Library Resources, Minority Recruitment and Retention, Scholarly Communication, and Statistics and Measurement. Advisory committees and project groups include the Ad Hoc Working Group on Copyright Issues, the Firm Subscription Prices Working Group, the Working Group on Networked Resources, the Advisory Committee on the Office of Management Services, the Working Group on Scientific and Technical Information, and the AAU/ARL Research Libraries Coordinating Committee.

Association of American Publishers

220 E. 23 St., New York, NY 10010
212-689-8920

1718 Connecticut Ave. N.W., Washington, DC 20009
202-232-3335

Judith Platt
Director of Communications and Public Affairs

The Association of American Publishers (AAP), with more than 200 members located in every region of the United States, is the principal trade association of the book publishing industry.

AAP members publish hardcover and paperback books in every field, including general fiction and nonfiction; poetry; children's books; textbooks; Bibles and other religious books; reference works; scientific, medical, technical, professional, and scholarly books and journals; and classroom instructional and testing materials. Members of the association also produce computer software and electronic products and services, such as online databases, CD-ROM, and CD-I.

The association's highest priorities are:

- Serving as the industry's voice in Washington, D.C., and throughout the country
- Safeguarding the rights of creators through ongoing efforts to protect copyright in all media, at home and abroad
- Expanding domestic and foreign markets for American books, journals, and electronic publishing products
- Defending freedom of expression, at home and abroad
- Providing information to the AAP membership to aid them in understanding and utilizing the new information technologies
- Informing AAP member publishers on legislative, regulatory, and policy issues that affect the business of publishing
- Offering practical educational programs to assist members

The association is structured to serve both the general and specific interests of its members.

AAP's core programs, carried out under the guidance of standing committees, deal with issues that affect all publishers, such as copyright, freedom of expression, tax and trade policy, education and library funding, and new technology.

The association's six divisions—General Publishing, Paperback Publishing, School, Higher Education, Professional and Scholarly Publishing, and International—deal with specific market areas. Each division operates under the guidance of its own executive body, within policy guidelines set by AAP's 20-member board of directors. Members of the board are elected to four-year terms, under a chairperson who serves for two years. Jack Hoeft, president and CEO of Bantam Doubleday Dell Publishing Group, began his two-year term of office as AAP chair on April 1, 1994. Ambassador Nicholas A. Veliotes is president of the association.

AAP maintains two offices, in New York and Washington, D.C., with a total of approximately 40 professional and support staff members.

Highlights of 1994

- Jack Hoeft was elected AAP chair and initiated a strategic review to ensure AAP is targeting its resources to the highest priorities: government relations, copyright, new technology, and education.
- Book sales rose 6.6 percent to $18 billion in 1993.
- Publishers won two important copyright victories in Texaco and Michigan Document Services cases.
- AAP established new committees to handle electronic publishing, new media issues, and shifting resources to these issues.

- AAP appointed its first full-time director of copyright education, carrying the copyright message to campuses nationwide.
- The Professional and Scholarly Publishing Division (PSP) published a white paper on Internet publishing and surveyed library acquisitions of electronic products.
- The School Division worked successfully to improve instructional-materials funding in key states.
- AAP opened a new front in its antipiracy war with successful raids in Puerto Rico.
- AAP joined in a challenge to FDA policy restricting medical publishing.
- AAP responded to the Clinton administration's "green paper" on copyright and the National Information Infrastructure (NII) and brought First Amendment issues to the fore in NII deliberations.
- AAP put forward U.S. publishers' views on the Global Information Infrastructure to the European Commission.
- The Rushdie Defense Committee marked the 2,000th day of the fatwa (death sentence).
- The School Division developed model legislation to serve visually handicapped students.
- The Higher Education Division (HED) strategic review generated a study of faculty and student views on textbooks and exploration of the changing college market.
- The General Publishing Division (GPD) Children's Publishing Committee "Teachers as Readers" project expanded to 800 reading groups in all 50 states.
- Pubnet continued impressive growth and instituted technical improvements.
- The International Division completed a second successful year of the Eastern European intern program at Frankfurt.
- AAP received an unprecedented visit from a Cuban publishing delegation and explored possible exchanges of book exhibits.
- The GDP initiated support for "Reach Out and Read," an innovative literacy initiative spearheaded by pediatricians.
- Among those honored in 1994: children's book publisher Margaret McElderry received the Curtis Benjamin Award; John Davis (Paramount Publishing) was HED's James F. Leisy Award winner; *Buildings of the United States* (Oxford University Press) won PSP's R. R. Hawkins Award; Steven Vana-Paxhia (InfoSoft) won the Pubnet Recognition Award.
- AAP held its 24th annual meeting in Puerto Rico.

Government Relations

The AAP Washington office is the industry's front line on matters pertaining to federal legislation and government policy. The Washington staff keeps the membership informed about developments on Capitol Hill and in the agencies of the Executive Branch. The Washington office serves as the industry's voice, communicating publishers' views and concerns to members of Congress, government officials, and the media.

A number of AAP member houses maintain a corporate presence in Washington, either through their own offices or through representation by Washington legal counsel. This AAP Washington Representatives Group, which meets at the AAP Washington office to share information and coordinate legislative strategy, is a valuable resource for the association.

AAP maintains a Political Action Committee, allowing industry members to take an active part in the political process by supporting Senate and House candidates of both parties who share the industry's concerns on such issues as First Amendment rights, education and library funding, and copyright protection.

Core Committees

Copyright Committee

The Copyright Committee coordinates AAP efforts to protect and strengthen intellectual property rights and to enhance public awareness of the importance of copyright. Edward Stanford (St. Martin's Press) is chairman of the committee.

The year 1994 brought victory for the publishers in two important copyright infringement suits.

In a resounding defense of copyright, a federal judge in Michigan reaffirmed the need to comply with U.S. law in the preparation of "course packs" used in teaching college courses. The decision was handed down June 9 in the copyright infringement suit filed by three U.S. publishers against Michigan Document Services (MDS) and its owner, James Smith. In finding willful infringement, the judge enjoined MDS from reproducing any of the plaintiffs' existing or future copyrighted works and awarded statutory damages in the amount of $30,000 and attorney's fees, later set at $326,000.

In October a federal appellate court ruled in the publishers' favor in the copyright infringement suit against Texaco. The ruling upheld the July 1992 ruling by Federal Judge Pierre Leval that unauthorized photocopying by employees of Texaco of single copies of copyrighted articles in scientific and technical journals was not fair use under U.S. law.

The year also saw the appointment of Jill Braaten as AAP's first full-time director of copyright compliance (later redesignated director of copyright education). Braaten's mandate is to encourage compliance with the copyright law in the academic community and the copying facilities that serve it. In 1994 Braaten visited 40 colleges and universities, speaking with information providers on and off campus, including libraries, copy centers, bookstores, and, increasingly, academic computing centers. Her discussions focused on the copyright ramifications of the services they provide. As part of the campaign to raise public awareness, AAP developed a new copyright graphic that stresses the connection between copyright and creativity, which is being offered free of charge to individuals and organizations wishing to incorporate it into their own materials.

Much of the Copyright Committee's energy in 1994 was devoted to legislative issues, analyzing proposals before Congress with specific reference to their copyright implications, and advising the AAP board and membership on appropriate industry responses. These legislative issues are covered in detail in Part 2 of the *Bowker Annual*. [See the article titled "Legislation and Regulations Affecting Publishing in 1994"—*Ed.*]

AAP also provided copyright leadership in the international community, participating in a number of international symposia during the year, including the International Publishers Association Third Copyright Symposium, held in Turin, Italy, in May.

In January 1994 the Copyright Committee established a special Digital Technology Subcommittee (later reconstituted as a full AAP core committee) to work on copyright issues in the context of the digital environment, with special emphasis on the Clinton administration's efforts to promote the National Information Infrastructure (NII). In April AAP issued a Statement on Document Delivery and in June a Statement on Scanning. Both papers were developed by the Digital Technology Subcommittee. Working through the subcommittee, the Copyright Committee guided AAP deliberations on the "green paper," the report of the Working Group on Intellectual Property Rights of the president's NII Task Force, crafting AAP's formal response to the Green Paper September 7 and its subsequent testimony at public hearings. The copyright ramifications of NII and the emerging Global Information Infrastructure will continue to be of paramount concern to the AAP membership. On the international front, in July AAP filed a statement on "Copyright and Related Rights in the Information Society" with the Commission of the European Community.

In alliance with other copyright industry organizations and publishers around the world, AAP was working to ensure that when the world's leading industrial nations (the so-called Group of 7) met in Brussels in February 1995 to discuss the information society, a prominent place on the agenda would be given to protection of copyright.

The committee's two Rights and Permissions Advisory Committees continued to sponsor workshops on the east and west coasts. Two seminars were held in San Francisco, one in Washington, D.C., and one in New York City in 1994. The seminars looked at rights in the electronic age, copyright ownership in the digital environment, and the role of permissions professionals in the context of the new information technologies.

AAP filed an *amicus* brief in the U.S. Court of Appeals for the Fifth Circuit supporting the constitutionality of the 1990 federal law that precludes states and state agencies (such as universities) from using the "sovereign immunity" provision of the 11th Amendment to protect themselves from monetary damages when they are found to have infringed copyright.

Freedom to Read Committee

The Freedom to Read Committee coordinates AAP's efforts to promote and protect First Amendment rights and intellectual freedom. In fulfilling its mandate, the committee provides guidance on possible AAP intervention in First

Amendment court cases, lobbies on free-expression issues at the national and state level, and conducts educational programs. The committee works closely with allied organizations—such as the Intellectual Freedom Committee of the American Library Association and the American Booksellers Foundation for Free Expression—and coordinates AAP participation as a member of the Media Coalition, a group of trade associations formed to defend First Amendment rights. Lisa Drew (Lisa Drew Books/Scribner's) is committee chairperson.

Responding to concerns raised by AAP's Professional and Scholarly Publishing Division, the committee coordinated AAP participation in a "citizen's petition" to the U.S. Food and Drug Administration, challenging FDA's attempts to regulate publication and distribution of medical textbooks and journal articles dealing with "off-label" uses of certain drugs (uses for which the FDA has not given formal approval). When FDA failed to respond to the petition, suit was filed in federal court, which the government tried to have dismissed because other remedies had not been exhausted. AAP joined other media and free-expression organizations in an *amicus* brief opposing dismissal of the suit on the grounds that, as an abridgement of free speech, FDA's actions can be challenged without the need to exhaust other remedies.

In 1994 the committee began to focus on the First Amendment and free-speech implications of the "Information Superhighway." Heather Grant Florence (Bantam Doubleday Dell), former committee chair, testifying at a special forum in Washington on NII security issues, warned that First Amendment considerations might get lost "in the understandable effort to get ahead of the new technology curve." She stated: "As we move from the NII to the Global Information Infrastructure, America's unique commitment to free speech and press must be preserved and should remain a bellwether of greater freedom around the world." The committee is planning to hold a joint conference in 1995 with ALA and the Thomas Jefferson Center for Free Expression to address some of these concerns.

The committee supported a proposal by the Small Business Administration to repeal its "opinion molder" rule, which had prevented publishers and other small businesses engaged in production and distribution of media from obtaining SBA loan guarantees. The 40-year-old regulation was repealed.

AAP again participated in the observance of Banned Books Week— Celebrating the Freedom to Read, an annual event spotlighting the problem of book censorship. Among the materials available was a Resource Guide published by ALA providing an annotated list of book challenges in 1993–1994.

The committee was involved in a number of court cases with First Amendment implications during the year:

- Late in 1993, AAP, joined by New Orleans librarians, filed an *amicus* brief in the Fifth Circuit protesting the order of a district court judge that author Joseph Bosco turn over notes and tapes used in the writing of *Blood Will Tell* (Morrow), a nonfiction account of a murder. In January the Louisiana State Court of Appeals upheld the right of book authors to the same First Amendment protections that Louisiana grants to journalists and returned the case to the trial court to determine whether other conditions for limited shield protection had been met.

- In a ruling that First Amendment advocates found profoundly disturbing, the U.S. Court of Appeals for the District of Columbia (with a strong dissent by its then chief judge, Abner Mikva) reinstated a defamation suit brought against the *New York Times* by author Dan Moldea, who claimed that the review cast doubt upon his journalistic competence. AAP joined with PEN American Center in an *amicus* brief calling for a rehearing by the full court and an affirmation of Judge Mikva's dissent. The brief asserts that, while no author or publisher enjoys a negative or inaccurate review, a libel suit is not the proper response. The brief states that "the threat of libel litigation will chill the creation and publication of meaningful literary criticism. . . ." In a highly unusual move, the appellate court reversed itself and dismissed the suit, saying that its earlier ruling had been "misguided."

- Author Ronald J. Watkins—whose contempt citation for refusing to turn over to a federal district court research materials used in writing a book was overturned by the U.S. Court of Appeals for the Ninth Circuit—found himself back in district court in Arizona fighting a new subpoena. Again cited for contempt, Watkins saw his case go back to the Ninth Circuit. The Freedom to Read Committee has provided moral and practical support for Watkins through his long fight in defense of the rights of investigative journalists.

- On June 15 the Ninth Circuit Court of Appeals upheld a lower court ruling in *Brown* v. *Woodland Unified School District,* rejecting the claim of a group of right-wing activist parents in California that the *Impressions* reading series (published by Harcourt Brace) and related classroom activities promoted the religion of Wicca (witchcraft) in violation of the First Amendment's separation clause. AAP and a dozen education and library organizations had filed an *amicus* brief in the case in the fall of 1992, opposing the parents' challenge.

- The threat of excessive punitive-damage awards—a concern for publishers in libel suits—was diminished by a U.S. Supreme Court decision handed down in June. The court struck down an amendment to the Oregon State Constitution that prohibited review of punitive-damage awards, stating that a mechanism for reviewing potentially excessive judgments must be available. Although it was not a publishing case, its implications for libel litigation caused AAP and a number of journalism and media groups to file an *amicus* brief asking that the Oregon statute be struck down.

- AAP, joined by the Authors Guild, PEN American Center, and a number of media organizations, filed an *amicus* brief in New York State's highest court in *Armstrong* v. *Simon & Schuster,* a case involving "libel by innuendo" (a libel action based not on the actual statements in a text but on an implication or impression allegedly arising out of otherwise truthful statements). While supporting the publisher, the brief goes beyond the specific facts of the case to articulate a clear test for dealing with claims of "libel by innuendo."

- In November the U.S. Supreme Court heard oral arguments in a case challenging the 1989 Ethics Reform Act, which bars federal employees from receiving money for outside speeches and writings, even if they have nothing to do with the employee's work. AAP, the ALA-affiliated Freedom to Read Foundation, PEN American Center, and others joined in an *amicus* brief asking that the law be struck down because it infringes on the free speech rights of government workers, publishers, librarians, and the public.

International Freedom to Publish Committee

AAP's International Freedom to Publish (IFTP) Committee defends and promotes freedom of written communication worldwide. The committee monitors human rights issues and provides moral support and practical assistance to publishers and authors outside the United States who are denied basic freedoms. The committee carries on its work in close cooperation with other human rights groups, including Human Rights Watch and PEN International. Wendy Wolf (Penguin USA) is committee chairperson.

AAP has long favored passage of legislation to encourage free trade in ideas. Major provisions of the Free Trade in Ideas legislation were incorporated into the Foreign Relations Authorization Act for fiscal year 1994–1995. [This is discussed more fully in the section dealing with legislation affecting publishing in Part 2 of this volume—*Ed.*]

Approaching the 2,000th day of the fatwa (death sentence) pronounced against author Salman Rushdie by the Ayatollah Khomeini on publication of Rushdie's *Satanic Verses,* AAP, PEN American Center, and the other organizations comprising the U.S. Committee for the Defense of Salman Rushdie distributed a statement over Internet urging U.S. citizens to write Congress in support of a resolution condemning the fatwa and calling for its repudiation. Citizens of other countries were urged to contact officials of their own governments.

In 1994 the committee lent its support to efforts by PEN Canada, the Canadian Book and Periodicals Council's Free Expression Committee, and others opposing the seizure by Canadian Customs of books, magazines, and other sexually explicit materials in the wake of the Canadian Supreme Court's *Butler* decision. The *Butler* decision, which was grounded in antipornography theories espoused by U.S. law professor Catherine MacKinnon, sets forth the controversial viewpoint that sexually explicit materials, by virtue of their very existence, may degrade women and cause harm to society. According to a report issued by the Human Rights Watch/Free Expression Project in early 1994, the *Butler* decision has had a repressive effect and instead of fulfilling its intent of promoting gender equality, has been used to weaken fundamental liberties, particularly those of women and gay men. The Little Sisters Book Store, a feminist bookstore in Canada, is involved in a lawsuit aimed at ending the Canadian Customs seizures. The committee provided some modest financial support to Little Sisters.

In June a delegation of Cuban publishers paid an unprecedented visit to the AAP New York office to discuss the possibility of exchanging book exhibits and establishing publishing ties between the United States and Cuba. In December three committee members—Roland Algrant (Hearst), Jack Macrae (Henry Holt), and Fred Perkins (McGraw-Hill)—visited Havana to explore the possibility of a U.S. book exhibit and program of activities in Havana in the spring of 1995.

Plans for an IFTP mission to the People's Republic of China in 1994 had to be canceled because of the Chinese government's failure to issue the necessary visas. The committee will revisit the issue in 1995.

The committee continued to voice protests on behalf of writers, journalists, and publishers who have been denied basic freedom of expression. Letters were sent to the President and Prime Minister of Bangladesh and to the Bangladeshi Ambassador, protesting the persecution of writer Taslima Nasreen and the filing of criminal charges against four editors of a Bangladeshi newspaper; the President of Kenya and other government officials, protesting the government's ban on Kenneth Matiba's book *Kenya: Return to Reason* and the imprisonment of journalists Bedan Mbugua and Davad Makali; Chinese government officials, protesting the imprisonment of publisher Liu Taiheng, the detention of dissident Zhou Guoqiang, the reimprisonment of writer Li Guiren, and the ongoing harassment of dissident writer Wei Jingsheng; the president of South Korea, regarding the arrest of publisher Park Chi-Kwan and the ongoing detention of 13 writers, publishers, and editors being held under the National Security Law; the Prime Minister of Turkey and other government officials, protesting the detention of publisher Recep Marasli and continuing attacks against journalists and violations of press freedom; the Indonesian Ambassador, regarding the revocation of publishing licenses for three publications; the Israeli Ambassador, protesting attacks by Israeli soldiers against the press in Jericho, Gaza, and the West Bank; the Ambassador of Mauritania, regarding the seizure and suspension of the newspaper *Le Calame*; the Mexican Ambassador, regarding the murder of news editor Jorge Martin Dorantes; and the Pakistani Ambassador, regarding charges of blasphemy pending against five Ahmadi journalists.

The committee makes small grants to assist publishers overseas. In 1994 a grant went to the FAMA Foundation, a group of Sarajevans in exile in Zagreb, for publication of its *Sarajevo Survival Guide,* a "guidebook" to living in war-torn Sarajevo. The book's proceeds will be used to assist FAMA in its work of promoting and sustaining the cultural life of Sarajevo. A grant also went to Radio B92 of Belgrade for use in its Apatrides project, which publishes works of writers exiled from the former Yugoslavia.

Committee for Managing Diversity

The Committee for Managing Diversity develops programs to foster understanding of the growing diversity in our nation's population and to aid publishers in successfully managing that diversity. Jim Martin (Harcourt Brace) and Lolita Chandler (McGraw-Hill) cochaired the committee during 1994.

The committee seeks to offer AAP member publishers meaningful assistance in identifying and establishing long-term, sustainable publishing industry diversity programs.

The committee maintains connections with various groups having a similar focus, including Black Women in Publishing, a professional development group.

During 1994 the committee participated in two events designed to provide minority students with information on career opportunities in publishing.

- The *Newsday* Opportunity Conference brought more than 250 minority students and recent college graduates from all over the country together with a variety of print media organizations, including more than 40 daily newspapers.

- The committee participated for the first time in the *New York Times* Diversity Challenge Job Fair, held in conjunction with the newspaper's special section on workplace diversity (in which AAP advertised on behalf of its members). The fair drew several thousand job seekers, many with an interest in book publishing. At the AAP booth, representatives from member houses and AAP staff met with hundreds of job seekers and distributed copies of AAP's popular *Introduction to Book Publishing* handbook. Based on interviews at the fair, the committee established a résumé file as a resource for AAP member companies.

New Technology Committee

Virtually all of AAP's programs are beginning to have a new technological component. The association's sharpened focus in the area of new media and electronic publishing resulted in the establishment of several new AAP committees in 1994 and the reorganization and renaming of the original New Technology Committee.

- The Committee on New Media, chaired by Randi Benton (Random House), deals with CD-ROM issues related to products and markets, market trends, and relationships with booksellers
- The Committee on Enabling Technologies, chaired by Time King (John Wiley & Sons), focuses on publishing in the electronic networked environment and is charged with considering a model (or models) for a copyright management system.
- The Digital Technology Committee, chaired by Richard Rudick (John Wiley & Sons), was originally set up as a special subcommittee of the Copyright Committee. Since January 1994 the group has been working on copyright issues in the context of the digital environment, with special emphasis on the National Information Infrastructure and the Global Information Infrastructure.
- The Electronic Development and Production Committee (formerly called the New Technology Committee), chaired by Paul Constantine (John Wiley & Sons), focuses on technology and standards for creating electronic products and on publishing applications of SGM (standard general mark-up language).

The Digital Technology Committee devoted much of its time and attention to the preliminary report of the NII Task Force Working Group on Intellectual Property (the "green paper"), articulating AAP's response both to the report and to the comments submitted by other groups. In its formal statement, AAP stressed the need to allow licensing and permissions arrangements across NII to be a natural outgrowth of innovative marketplace solutions rather than government-imposed strictures. The committee was also responsible for drafting AAP's statement "Copyright and Related Rights in the Information Society," which was filed with the Commission of the European Communities in the summer of 1994. A main point of this position paper is the assertion that fundamental principles of existing intellectual property law, particularly copyright law, work well on a national and international basis.

The Committee on Enabling Technologies is exploring the publishing industry's requirements for a copyright management system with universal applicability in an electronic network environment to protect the integrity of copyrighted works utilized in this environment, to provide automated billing and tracking, and to collect compensation for electronic use and reuse of copyrighted material.

As a first step, the committee embarked on a project to identify the features and functions that the publishing community sees as essential to such a system; to catalog existing technologies and those being developed by vendors; and to compare the industry's requirements with what exists, to determine which technologies, if any, require further development in order to meet realistic goals.

Following this initial study, the committee will look into possible investment in developing additional technologies to ensure the availability of one or more systems to meet the industry's needs.

In late 1994 the committee issued a Request for Proposal to carry out the initial study.

Postal Committee

The Postal Committee coordinates AAP activity in the area of postal rates and regulations. It monitors developments at the U.S. Postal Service (USPS) and the independent Postal Rate Commission and intervenes on the industry's behalf in formal proceedings before the commission. The committee also directs AAP lobbying activities on postal issues. Stephen Bair (Time Life Books) continued to serve as chair during 1994.

Early in 1994 the U.S. Postal Service sought a 10.3 percent across-the-board rate increase. AAP and other groups representing major mailers supported the across-the-board increase as a way of avoiding the costs of litigation associated with a typical postal rate filing and of spreading the increases equitably among the various classes of mailers. However, the Postal Rate Commission put forward its own recommendations, adjusting many USPS proposals and raising the rates for classes used by commercial mailers, including fourth class. The new rate schedule, effective January 1, 1995, substantially increases the rates used by publishers for distributing professional and scholarly publications, posing a particularly difficult situation for journal publishers that are unable to fold the increase into previously set subscription prices.

The financial condition of the USPS is expected to worsen as Congress and the administration try to impose extraordinary financial burdens on it to alleviate federal budget problems, and this in turn may well generate additional postal rate increases in 1995.

Divisions

General Publishing Division

The General Publishing Division (GPD) represents publishers of fiction, nonfiction, poetry, children's literature, reference, and religious books. Its programs strive to broaden the audience for consumer books and are often carried out in conjunction with other AAP divisions. GPD maintains close ties with the book-selling and library communities, wholesalers, and authors' groups through a number of joint liaison committees. It provides major support for literacy programs, for the National Book Awards, and for the reading-promotion efforts of the Center for the Book in the Library of Congress. Peter Osnos (Random House) chaired the committee during 1994.

Marking the 1994 celebration of National Book Week, GPD joined with PEN American Center to sponsor "The Book/Movie Connection," a symposium exploring the relationship between American letters and American cinema. Janet Maslin, chief film critic for the *New York Times*, served as moderator.

The division again sponsored its popular educational roundtable series, the Publishers Forum Luncheons. Programs in 1994 covered such topics as multimedia marketing, global publishing opportunities, ethnic marketing, and corporate social responsibility.

GPD cosponsored the program "Selecting Products in Electronic Formats" at the 1994 summer meeting of the American Library Association (ALA).

The AAP Reading Initiative, a project of GPD's Children's Publishing Committee, works to promote the use of children's literature in school classrooms. Its Teachers as Readers (TAR) project engages teachers, school administrators, and others in the world of contemporary children's trade books. More than 800 Teachers as Readers groups have been set up in all 50 states, the District of Columbia, and Guam. The project has now been endorsed by eight major educational organizations, including ALA, the International Reading Association (IRA), and the National Council of Teachers of English. IRA is producing a staff training video on Teachers as Readers, which will be available during the 1994–1995 school year. In 1994 TAR initiated an electronic pilot project to enable teachers across the country to talk about children's books via computer network.

For the third consecutive year, GPD, along with the American Booksellers Association (ABA) and the Book Industry Study Group, has underwritten a comprehensive survey of American consumer book-buying behavior.

To promote the concept of books as gifts, the division initiated a contest to design a logo that will help consumers identify a variety of trade books as gift items. Using the new logo as its centerpiece, GPD plans to launch a marketing campaign with the help of ABA and other industry organizations, by Mother's Day 1995.

In the area of literacy, GPD agreed to collaborate on an innovative early-childhood literacy program, Reach Out and Read, developed by the pediatric staff at Boston City Hospital. A major initiative to take the program nationwide will be launched in 1995.

Higher Education Division

The Higher Education Division (HED) is concerned with the publishing and marketing of textbooks and related multimedia materials for post-secondary education. The division works to enhance the perceived value of instructional materials from college publishers and to protect and expand intellectual property rights within the college marketplace. HED serves as a link among publishers, college bookstores, faculty, and students, working in close cooperation with the National Association of College Stores. Jeff Sund (Richard D. Irwin) chaired the division in 1994.

New media in the higher education marketplace and intellectual property in the information age were the subjects of the division's annual meeting held in Boston, May 9–11.

In 1994 the division formed a Permissions Procedures Committee to further simplify the process of requesting and granting permissions among publishers as they move into the digital environment. The committee will field the first comprehensive market research on custom publishing early in 1995.

HED heads of house met in Boston in June for the second strategic planning session in as many years. Two primary areas emerged as the focus of divisional activities in the coming months: research into student and faculty attitudes regarding teaching materials, and research on the evolution of new forms of text materials. As one of its first major projects, the division's Faculty Relations Committee conducted a survey of faculty and student perceptions regarding the value of textbooks. Survey results, which will provide a baseline for future AAP studies, were widely reported in the fall of 1994. In November 1994 the division issued a Request for Proposal for a broad-ranging research project exploring possible changes in the business of college publishing over the next ten years.

The division worked closely with AAP's new director of copyright education to carry the association's copyright message to college campuses throughout the country.

The division's James Leisy Award for distinguished contributions to college publishing went to John Davis, who began a four-decade publishing career as a sales representative at Prentice Hall and went on to become president of the Higher Education Division at Paramount Publishing.

For the 18th year, the division sponsored Pubcenter at the annual meeting and Campus Market Expo (CAMEX) of the National Association of College Stores, held in Orlando, Florida, in 1994. AAP participation went beyond the usual exhibits to include panel discussions on changing student attitudes toward textbooks and on the division's "Invest in Your Future" marketing campaign.

International Division

The membership of the International Division (ID) reflects the full range of general AAP membership in terms of size and market. Alun Davies (Bantam Doubleday Dell) is the committee chairperson.

The division is concerned with marketing American books and related products overseas through direct sales, copublishing ventures, sales of English-language and translation rights, and the promotion of English as a second language. ID sponsors educational programs to help publishers strengthen their international capability and assists U.S. publishers in participating at international book fairs. The division serves as liaison with various agencies involved in promoting American books overseas (including the State and Commerce Departments, the U.S. Information Agency, and the World Bank).

Through its International Copyright Protection Committee, the division seeks to secure overseas markets by promoting effective international protection for U.S. copyrights and dismantling market barriers.

Inside Export, the ID newsletter, reports on specific trade opportunities for American publishers. The newsletter is available by subscription to publishers who are not ID members.

The division sponsors a major seminar for publishers attending the American Booksellers Association convention. As the international component of the ABA meeting has grown, interest in the ID seminar has intensified and it has become one of the best-attended events at the meeting. The 1994 program explored the book/movie connection from an international perspective.

The division's Professional Development Committee sponsored Legal Tips from the Pros, a seminar covering some of the legal implications of acquisition.

The division continued, for a second year, cosponsorship with the Frankfurt Fair Organization of an internship program that brings publishers from Eastern Europe to the fair, giving them an opportunity to work at U.S. publishing stands.

In 1994 ID published a new guide for buying and selling translation rights in the United States. *Focus on Rights: A Basic Guide for Buying and Selling Translation Rights in the U.S.* is aimed at publishers in developing markets, especially those of Eastern and Central Europe.

Among the foreign visitors to AAP in 1994 was a delegation of Russian copyright specialists who came to learn about U.S. copyright enforcement methods.

The division again sponsored an international rights directors' meeting at Frankfurt, this year focusing on the emerging markets of the Pacific Rim.

Antipiracy: The International Copyright Protection Committee

The committee operates under the administrative umbrella of the International Division, and its activities are coordinated with AAP's domestic copyright program. The committee works with other U.S. copyright industries in the International Intellectual Property Alliance to focus U.S. government attention on efforts to protect American copyrights overseas and eliminate market access barriers for U.S.-copyrighted works. The International Copyright Protection Committee coordinates AAP's overseas copyright enforcement campaign, which is now operating in Indonesia, Japan, Korea, Malaysia, Puerto Rico, Singapore, and Taiwan.

AAP participated in the alliance's filing to the U.S. Trade Representative targeting countries whose failure to protect American copyrights warrants special attention under the Special 301 provisions of the Omnibus Trade and Competitiveness Act of 1988 [see the article on legislation and regulations affecting publishing in Part 2—*Ed.*]

AAP's vigorous antipiracy enforcement campaign continued to bring pressure on international pirates responsible for the unauthorized duplication and sale of AAP members' books, journals, and software. In the ten years since its inauguration, the enforcement program has produced impressive results.

In February 1994 AAP action resulted in the arrest in Seoul, South Korea, of four people charged with duplicating and selling some 7,000 unauthorized copies of medical reference texts published by AAP members. A raid in Taiwan netted 400 pirated books published by AAP members. AAP representatives, together with government enforcement officers, carried out raids on photocopying shops in Malaysia. In August raids were carried out against 14 copyright pirates in Puerto Rico, resulting in the seizure of masters used to produce illegal copies of books published by AAP members. Copyright infringement suits against the pirates were subsequently filed. (Book piracy in Puerto Rico costs authors and publishers $4 million to $5 million annually and siphons off an estimated 40 percent of legitimate book sales. By mid-January 1995, 11 of the pirates agreed to settle the charges against them, and criminal actions had been initiated against the others.

AAP broke new ground in 1994 by filing copyright infringement suits on behalf of two of its members in China. The suits are seen as test cases of China's willingness to fulfill its international obligations by enforcing criminal penalties for copyright violations.

Paperback Publishing Division

Concentrating on issues of special concern to mass market paperback publishers, the Paperback Publishing Division (PPD) works to expand the market for paperback books. Carole Baron (Bantam Doubleday Dell) chaired the division in 1994. The division works with the General Publishing Division in support of reading promotion and literacy programs, including support for the National Book Foundation.

In 1994 the division launched a new initiative to increase the value of rack-size paperback books in the retail marketplace.

The division sponsors the Fall Book Previews video program at the annual meeting and exhibit of the National Association of College Stores.

The Rack Clearance Center, now entering its 17th year of operation, serves as liaison between participating publishers and wholesalers, auditing reimbursement claims for mass market paperback book racks installed in retail locations. The center currently processes claims for 44 publishers/imprints.

Professional and Scholarly Publishing Division

The Professional and Scholarly Publishing Division (PSP) is concerned with the publication of technical, scientific, medical, and scholarly materials. Division members produce books, journals, computer software, databases, and CD-ROM and CD-I products. Professional societies and university presses play an important role in the division. Robert Grand (CRC Press) is division chairperson.

The division publishes a quarterly newsletter, the *PSP Bulletin*.

Registration for the division's 1994 annual meeting in Washington, D.C., almost doubled that of the previous year. With Nobel laureate Arno Penzias as keynote speaker, the meeting again featured a new technology services exhibit and, for the first time, an Internet room. Outstanding achievements in professional and scholarly publishing were honored at the annual awards banquet; the R. R. Hawkins Award went to Oxford University Press for *Buildings of the United States, Volumes 1–4*.

PSP and the Council on Library Resources (CLR) established a Joint Working Group on Professional/Scholarly Information in the Electronic Age. With funding from PSP and CLR, the group met for several sessions to explore their respective roles in adding value to information in an electronic environment. A report will be issued.

The division published *Promises and Pitfalls—An AAP/PSP Briefing Paper on Internet Publishing*, which explores some of the issues in the emergence of distributed network publishing.

PSP continued to sponsor educational workshops and seminars. Sessions in 1994 covered the global picture for journal sales and the marketing of professional publications.

The division conducted a new survey on library acquisitions of electronic products. Survey results were published in the fall of 1994.

School Division

The School Division is concerned with publishing for the elementary and secondary school (K–12) market. The division works to enhance the role of instructional materials in the education process, to secure increased funding for these materials, and to simplify the procedures under which educational materials are "adopted" by various states. The division serves as a bridge between the publishing industry and the education community. It works for the cause of education at the state and local level and maintains an effective lobbying network in key adoption states. Al Bursma (D. C. Heath) chaired the division in 1994.

With *Electronic Learning* magazine, the division sponsored a second conference on multimedia. The meeting, Multimedia: The Next Step, was held in Atlanta in February and featured sessions on platforms, patents, the emerging vocational education market, and Texas state technology adoptions.

The division sponsored a two-day conference in Chicago on national standards, to discuss the status, projected completion date, and probable content of new standards for American education. In November the division vice president participated in a press conference at the U.S. Supreme Court accompanying the release of new voluntary national standards for teaching civics and government, emphasizing the vital role of publishers in disseminating the new standards. The division planned to hold a conference in early 1995 on the published humanities standards.

One of the most important issues facing the division's Committee on Serving Disabled Students is enactment by a growing number of states of legislation governing the rights of sight-impaired students to the same instructional materials as those used by sighted classmates. Working with AAP's Washington staff and Senator Bob Dole's office, the committee played a key role in drafting proposed federal legislation to help meet the needs of visually handicapped students by establishing a national repository of electronic files for the production of Braille editions of textbooks.

Reforming the instructional-materials adoption process and securing full funding for instructional materials in the states has been the focus of much School Division activity during the past year. Division publishers, working with AAP staff and local press, were instrumental in raising public awareness of the crisis in funding for the purchase of instructional materials in Texas. As a result, the Texas legislature and the governor approved an additional $28.8 million in emergency funds to purchase textbooks in 1994. In September the Texas State Board of Education voted to request full funding for the state's instructional-materials purchases in 1995. The state board also adopted new rules governing the submission, review, and marketing of instructional materials.

The division's Professional Development Committee sponsored a series of conferences on meeting the needs of the middle school market, held in conjunction with the National Middle Schools Association.

School Division legislative advocates in California worked with California State Assemblyman Cruz Bustamante to gain passage of an instructional-materials incentive bill. The bill—which creates an incentive program enabling local school districts to provide up-to-date instructional materials to each student in each subject and sets up local accountability mechanisms—was signed into law by Governor Pete Wilson in September.

The division worked closely with the AAP Washington staff on a host of federal legislative initiatives of concern to educational publishers [see the article on legislation affecting publishing in Part 2—*Ed.*]

Some of the division's most important work is carried on at the state level to provide legislators with a better understanding of the importance of instructional materials and the need to preserve the integrity of the funding for these materials. The division's work in three key states—Florida, California, and Texas—produced significant results in 1994.

In the wake of an essentially flat state instructional-materials fund for the past three years, there are indications that the situation may be improving in California. The California legislature increased the fund by $9.1 million. In Florida, the appropriation for instructional materials was increased by 7.5 percent.

The AAP School Division, the National Association of State Textbook Administrators, and the Book Manufacturers Institute compose the Advisory Commission on Textbook Specifications (ACTS). ACTS sets acceptable manufacturing standards for "el-hi" textbooks; adoption states and many large school districts use the standards as baseline specifications to ensure quality and durability of print materials used in schools.

Administrative Committees

Three administrative committees direct and coordinate AAP member services. They are:

Compensation Survey Committee

This committee coordinates and supervises preparation of the *AAP Survey of Compensation and Personnel Practices in the Publishing Industry*. Published every two years (a *Survey* was published in 1993), the report is designed to provide members of the association with current and accurate information on prevailing compensation levels for representative management and professional positions in the book publishing industry. The survey is prepared by Organization Resources Counselors, Inc., a compensation firm with extensive experience in the book publishing industry. Christine Names (Random House) chairs the committee.

Lawyers Committee

The Lawyers Committee is composed of both in-house and outside counsel of AAP member companies. It meets quarterly to discuss legal issues under review in the committees and divisions. Ellis Levine (Random House) is committee chairperson.

Statistics Committee

The Statistics Committee oversees the preparation of monthly and annual statistics reports published by AAP. The committee coordinates the efforts of the various divisional statistics committees as they update and modify data for their various market segments. The AAP industry report includes information on sales, operating costs, inventory turnover, and accounts receivable aging. The Statistical Service Center, an independent consulting firm, collects and analyzes data under procedures guaranteed to protect confidentiality. William Grace (D. C. Heath) chaired the committee in 1994.

Pubnet

The year 1994 brought continued growth for Pubnet, AAP's electronic database interchange service for book ordering. More than 2,800 bookstores and some 75 publishers are now on the system. Pubnet's managing director, John Zotz, served as chair of the Pubnet Executive Committee following Steven Vana-Paxhia's departure from Macmillan.

Originally established to serve the college publishing community, Pubnet has successfully expanded in recent years to trade, mass market, and university press publishing. Key trade book wholesalers and vendors for the academic library market are Pubnet customers.

The number of orders processed on the network grew by more than 28 percent, from 530,490 in 1993 to more than 682,000 in 1994.

In conjunction with General Electric Information Systems, Pubnet inaugurated a Marketing Agency Program with third-party bookstore inventory systems, bringing systems such as Wordstock, Riverview, Computac, Booklog, and IBID into the process of marketing Pubnet to bookstores.

Steven R. Vana-Paxhia, who left Macmillan to become president of InfoSoft International, received the Pubnet Recognition Award for his part in the creation and implementation of Pubnet. The award was presented during the Higher Education Division's annual meeting in Boston.

The Pubnet annual meeting in June featured ten roundtable sessions on topics ranging from Pubnet*Express to Pubnet's role in the international marketplace.

In 1994 Pubnet made important technological changes, switching traffic on the network to the ANSI X12 format, making Pubnet compatible with other industries trading electronic data. The move is designed to increase the efficiency of electronic trading by putting the industry on a single format.

Late in 1994 Pubnet began exploring a possible connection with Canadian Telebook Agency. Such a connection would enable Canadian booksellers to order electronically from eligible U.S. publishers through Pubnet.

Literacy

A major focus of the association's work is to encourage reading and literacy in the United States. The association participated in the first International

Publishers Association Reading Seminar, held in Frankfurt October 5, reporting on publisher-supported reading-promotion efforts in the United States.

AAP is a member of the national network of Reading Promotion Partners supporting the work of the Center for the Book in the Library of Congress. The association also provides funding for the annual observance of National Book Week in January, which serves to focus national attention on reading and books through the staging of book-related events. AAP has provided support for special literacy projects in cooperation with the International Reading Association and Reading Is Fundamental, and this year it undertook support for Reach Out and Read, a new initiative pioneered at Boston City Hospital that seeks to integrate literacy training and reading promotion into pediatric well-baby care.

Communications and Public Affairs

The AAP communications and public affairs program is responsible for creating and disseminating information reflecting the concerns of AAP members and providing an accurate picture of the association and its activities. The program furnishes information and offers industry views on major issues to the trade press and other media and to the general public, focusing attention on the ways in which the association serves its members and advances the cause of publishing in the United States.

The association's newsletter, the AAP *Monthly Report*, covers AAP initiatives, core committee and divisional activities, legislative and regulatory developments, activity in the courts, and international developments of interest to members. Supplementing this primary newsletter, several AAP divisions and Pubnet issue newsletters of interest to their special constituencies.

American Booksellers Association

828 S. Broadway, Tarrytown, NY 10591
914-591-2665

Carol Miles
Director of Research

The capstone of 1994 activities of the American Booksellers Association (ABA) was the October 24 dedication to its member booksellers of the new national headquarters in Tarrytown, New York. Sharing the podium with ABA President Avin Mark Domnitz of Harry W. Schwartz Bookshops (Milwaukee, Wisconsin), Executive Director Bernie Rath referred to the potential of the facilities to become "a book institute to advance the professional development of all in the industry—booksellers, publishers, writers, editors, and librarians." Other participants in the program included New York State's lieutenant governor, the

Westchester County Executive, and six ABA past presidents serving between 1980 and mid-1994. The 10.3-acre property—which was toured by several hundred booksellers, publishers, authors, and other industry members—includes the Moller House (containing ABA's book industry library of more than 4,000 volumes), an administration building housing staff, and the G. Royce Smith Education Center, named in honor of ABA's executive director from 1972 to 1984. The center is being used for a variety of industry educational initiatives, including selected booksellers' schools and seminars of various types.

The policy set by the ABA Board of Directors guiding 1994 initiatives mandated continuing emphasis on the four major themes of the strategic plan approved in 1993:

1 To create and provide access to information, knowledge, and tools to support business success for member booksellers
2 To promote efficient operation and standardization within the industry
3 To fight encroachments against free expression and to build the widest possible market for books
4 To ensure a fair and nondiscriminatory trade environment

Based on the findings of a special task force that had been appointed by the board in 1993 to work with ABA legal counsel and staff to implement those portions of the strategic plan that deal with ensuring a fair and nondiscriminatory trade environment, ABA announced at its annual convention in Los Angeles that it had filed an antitrust lawsuit on May 27 against five publishers, charging them with price discrimination, promotional allowance discrimination, and illegally favoring certain kinds of retail booksellers. The complaint, approved unanimously by the ABA Board of Directors, named Penguin USA, St. Martin's Press, Houghton Mifflin, Rutledge Hill Press, and Hugh Lauter Levin Associates. Six bookstores are co-plaintiffs with ABA in the lawsuit.

U.S. Commerce Department figures indicate that retail sales for bookstores increased 6 percent over 1992, reaching an estimated $9 billion in 1993, and that the market for adult books continued to increase in 1993, with unit purchases up 10 percent over the previous year, according to NPD estimates in the *1993 Consumer Research Study on Book Purchasing*. However, many booksellers continued to express concern about the challenges posed by changing distribution patterns, particularly as influenced by the trade environment. In fact, the NPD study—conducted for ABA, the Association of American Publishers, and the Book Industry Study Group—shows rapid growth from 1991 through 1993 in book purchases at warehouse clubs, used-book stores, and miscellaneous nonbookstore outlets (including department stores, hobby stores, stationery/card/gift shops, newsstands, toy stores, variety stores, books ordered direct from the manufacturer, and so forth). Over that period, the market share for adult books purchased at independent bookstores dropped eight percentage points, from 32 percent in 1991 to 24 percent in 1993. The warehouse club and miscellaneous "all other" groupings, in contrast, each gained three share points (up to 6 percent and 10 percent, respectively), while used-book stores increased by 2 percentage points (reaching 5 percent in 1993). Bookstore chains, on the other hand, increased their share one percentage point, from 22 percent in 1991 to 23 percent in 1993.

Membership

Total membership in the association at the end of 1994 stood at 8,382. Bookstore members numbered 5,113. The increase in the latter number over the previous year is largely attributable to an 8 percent increase in the number of member bookstore businesses (i.e., main stores/headquarters), up to 4,319 in 1994 from 4,000 in 1993.

ABA's five specialty membership segments (Scientific/Technical/Professional, Science Fiction, Travel, African-American, and Gay/Lesbian) enjoyed expanded coverage through tabloid-sized quarterly newsletters designed and produced by ABA's periodicals publishing division. In addition, various roundtables and other sessions arranged with the assistance of ABA were held during the 1994 ABA Convention and Trade Exhibit in Los Angeles. In addition to roundtables, the Scientific/Technical/Professional group sponsored an entire day of panels relating to its specialty, while the African-American booksellers group held a half-day conference on marketing and business development.

Two new group programs were introduced in 1994, both intended to bring the benefits of group buying power to member bookstores. On the one hand, a competitive bank card–processing program was made available to the membership, while on the other hand ABA was able to offer a cost-saving long-distance service. The new services join a previously introduced low-cost group business insurance program.

1994 Convention and Trade Exhibit

The theme of ABA's annual Convention and Trade Exhibit, held in Los Angeles May 28–31, was "Booksellers Make a Difference." The event broke all previous convention attendance records. A total of 38,000 booksellers, exhibitors, trade visitors, and members of the press attended the four-day event. The trade show was the first to be managed by Reed Exhibition Companies' Association Exposition Services of Stamford, Connecticut. ABA and Reed Exhibition Companies, a division of Reed Publishing (USA) Inc., formed a joint venture company in 1993 called Booksellers Show Associates (BSA)—in which ABA holds majority interest—for the purpose of ownership and operation of the ABA trade show. The convention portion, however, continues to be managed by ABA.

The ever popular educational component of the 1994 ABA convention was, as always, organized by ABA's Department of Professional Development and Education. The educational offerings included roundtables and more than 50 workshops, panels, and seminars on a wide variety of topics as diverse as expanding audio sales, competitive marketing, literature of the Los Angeles rebellion, and understanding and using financial documents. Among the highlights were an all-day workshop on producing effective newsletters and a three-part series on new media, conducted for booksellers with varying levels of knowledge and experience.

As always, large numbers of adult- and juvenile-book authors were in attendance. While many autographed their latest books, a selected few were speakers at four book-and-author breakfasts, two reading rooms, and a special session showcasing local authors called "Los Angeles: My Unique Literary Landscape." Speakers at these events included Jerry Pinkney, Pat Conroy, Archbishop Desmond Tutu, Joyce Carol Oates, E. Annie Proulx, Walter Mosley, Anna Quindlen, and Michael Crichton.

A wide variety of convention events honored outstanding achievements in the book community. Prominent among them were the American Booksellers Book of the Year (ABBY) awards. The ABBY award honors the titles that booksellers most enjoyed hand-selling during the previous year. The fourth annual ABBY award in the adult trade category went to Laura Esquivel for *Like Water for Chocolate*, published by Doubleday & Company. Esquivel was present to accept her award and thank booksellers for their support. The ABBY honor books for 1994 (in alphabetical order) were *All the Pretty Horses* by Cormac McCarthy; *Having Our Say* by Sarah Delany and A. Elizabeth Delany with Amy Hearth; *Pigs in Heaven* by Barbara Kingsolver; and *Smilla's Sense of Snow* by Peter Hoeg. The second annual children's ABBY award went to Janell Cannon for *Stellaluna*, published by Harcourt Brace & Company. Cannon also was at the convention to accept her ABBY. In addition, Ed Elrod of the Ventura Book Store in Ventura, California, arrived fresh from the International Congress of Young Booksellers in Elspeet, Netherlands, to thank ABA for the Charley Haslam International Scholarship that enabled him to attend this important international bookselling event.

American Booksellers Foundation for Free Expression

During its fifth year of operation, the American Booksellers Foundation for Free Expression (ABFFE) continued its vigorous efforts to oppose censorship and to support free expression. The 1994 ABA Convention and Trade Exhibit once again provided an opportunity for ABFFE to sponsor a timely discussion of a current First Amendment topic. The program, "Murder, Mayhem, and the Media," addressed concerns about potential regulations dealing with violence in the media and featured Susan Estrich, Robert Evans, John Irving, Tony Kushner, Walter Mosley, Nadine Strossen, and Grant Tinker. Earlier in the year, ABFFE signed an anticensorship statement on TV violence that appeared as a full-page advertisement in the *Washington Post*.

In another 1994 initiative, ABFFE successfully opposed constitutional amendments on the ballots in Colorado and Oregon that would have chilled the availability in those states of otherwise constitutionally protected material. ABFFE joined in a series of *amicus* briefs defending the rights of booksellers and others to sell controversial, although First Amendment-protected, materials. In one case, the U.S. Supreme Court ruled that it was unconstitutional for retailers to be prosecuted unless it could be shown that they knew in advance that the material sold was illegal.

ABFFE continued to work with the Rushdie Defense Committee, USA. The fifth anniversary of the fatwa (the Iranian death sentence) against Salman Rushdie was observed on February 14, 1994, the unhappy occasion being marked by the distribution of over 200,000 flyers in support of Rushdie to bookstores all across the country. ABFFE also appealed to the U.S. State Department, urging that Gerry Adams of Ireland's Sinn Fein be allowed to visit the United States to talk about his new books. In addition, ABFFE joined with others in protesting the decision by the California Department of Education to censor several works by Alice Walker.

ABFFE also developed a series of educational brochures on various First Amendment/free expression topics. Written by ABFFE board members, they include *Questions and Answers about Free Expression, Hate Speech and Politically Correct Speech,* and *Obscenity and Pornography.* ABFFE continued its sponsorship of Banned Books Week and once again made materials for this annual observance available to all ABA member bookstores.

Other 1994 initiatives included continuing support of litigation by the Little Sisters' Bookshop in Vancouver, British Columbia, challenging the right of Canadian customs to seize books at the border, and the conversion of ABFFE's quarterly newsletter *Free Expression* to a tabloid format. Finally, ABFFE continued to work closely with the Free Expression Network, the National Coalition Against Censorship, and the Media Coalition (chaired throughout 1994 by ABFFE's president) to support First Amendment matters.

Government Affairs

ABA's Government Affairs Department's efforts in 1994 focused on how the various health care reform initiatives proposed by President Clinton and Congress would affect the operations of retail bookstores. Because many booksellers were concerned about government mandates, the ABA Board of Directors adopted a resolution supporting health care reform, "provided that the peculiar needs and concerns of small retail businesses were taken into account." To that end, ABA joined the Small Business Coalition for Health Care Reform and worked closely with the Clinton administration and congressional leaders of both parties. Booksellers were also encouraged to participate in the state meetings being held around the country in preparation for the 1995 White House Conference on Small Business.

Both the outgoing and incoming ABA presidents met with various congressional leaders in a series of meetings in Washington, D.C., and also were among those participating in the quadrennial presentation of books, on behalf of U.S. bookstores, for the White House Library. The presentation to President Clinton was made in the Oval Office on April 15. The Government Affairs Department was successful in its multiyear fight to seek repeal of the so-called opinion-molder rule of the Small Business Administration (SBA). This rule had effectively disqualified many bookstores from eligibility for SBA loans; its repeal guaranteed that bookstores could compete effectively with other small businesses for SBA-guaranteed loans.

Education and Professional Development

In addition to the extensive educational program provided at the convention, ABA's Department of Education and Professional Development also provided six bookseller schools at various levels and four one-day seminars, in keeping with the educational mandates contained in the strategic plan. These educational events took place in various cities around the country, often in conjunction with regional trade shows or in tandem with the annual ABA Convention and Trade Exhibit. Highlights of 1994 included the first Prospective Booksellers School held at ABA's new G. Royce Smith Education Center; a special one-day seminar designed especially for publishers; and ABA's first booksellers school centering on the single topic of visual merchandising.

With sponsorship and funding from the Soros Open Society Foundation, ABA once again participated in providing training to booksellers in Eastern Europe. Booksellers schools were conducted by volunteer faculty members in both Romania and Bulgaria during 1994. The Education Department also continued to provide videotapes to members for in-store staff training throughout the year.

Publications

The ABA Publications Department stepped up its efforts to provide booksellers with a wide range of informational and practical books and periodicals. In 1994 the association introduced the *ABA Book Buyer's Handbook* in electronic (Windows) format to increase the usefulness of this directory for many bookstores; the print version continued to be available and to grow. The 1994–1995 edition contains more than 2,000 vendor listings, together with distribution and ISBN indexes and updated information on sources of supply for many products.

Booksellers Publishing Inc. (BPI), the book publishing subsidiary of ABA, continued to expand its list of professional titles for people in the book community. New additions to the list of BPI's Booksellers House imprint in 1994 included a reprint of *Wise Men Fish Here*, a biography of Frances Steloff, founder of the Gotham Book Mart in New York City; and *Cody's Books: The Life and Times of a Berkeley Bookstore*, an autobiography of the founders of the renowned California bookstore. BPI also published a new edition of *ABACUS Expanded*, containing results of ABA's annual financial survey of member bookstores compiled by the ABA Research Department. The 1994 edition, based on 1992 operations, contains data supplied by more than 200 ABA-member independent booksellers doing business in 242 locations and offers a range of new tables and operating ratios. Also in 1994, BPI began distribution of *Small Store Survival: Success Strategies for Illinois Retailers*, a new book from the Illinois Retail Merchants Association. The book uses case studies, statistical analyses, and self-assessment surveys to examine what independent retailers are doing—right and wrong—and what stores can do to increase profits.

A major event of 1994 for ABA's Publications Department was the April 11th launching of a new, expanded weekly to replace its newsletter *ABA Newswire*. In tabloid format, the new *Bookselling This Week* brings readers more news, expanded features and guest columns, extensive coverage of books in the media, author tours, and late-breaking announcements. Building on the popularity of *Bookselling This Week*'s eye-catching tabloid format, the association's specialty newsletters—for members of specialty membership segments interested in scientific and technical, African-American, science fiction, gay and lesbian, or travel bookselling—were expanded and redesigned as well. ABFFE's quarterly newsletter *Free Expression* was similarly revamped and will be inserted quarterly into *Bookselling This Week*.

For *American Bookseller* magazine, 1994 was a year of innovation, both editorially and graphically. Graphically, *American Bookseller* showed readers a bold new look with a revamped cover design that features full-color photographs of booksellers. Editorially, the magazine's renewed emphasis on covering the business of bookselling was reflected in both the introduction of new departments and new editorial treatment of feature articles.

Several new departments were introduced in 1994. A new column titled "Between Us" was created as a forum for industry commentary, and the contributions ranged from the candid observations of literary agent Tom Wallace regarding the consolidation of publishing to the more evocative reflections of bookseller Ethan Gilsdorf on the multifaceted relationships between booksellers and customers. "Omnibus" first appeared in the May issue and has since provided timely, four-color monthly coverage of intriguing projects from a number of innovative publishers—both large and small—as well as current events in publishing, from clever promotions to noteworthy releases. "Check It Out," a monthly listing of promotional materials available from publishers, has garnered wide support from publishers and positive feedback from readers. Coverage of key trends in feature articles was completely overhauled in 1994, with an emphasis on shorter, more focused articles on trends, together with expanded coverage of proven marketing ideas and tested titles. As ever, interviews with key publishing figures—such as the ever candid Tom Peters on competition and Roger Straus on the history and sale of Farrar, Straus and Giroux—brought a different perspective to *American Bookseller*'s editorial content.

With a view to the coming millennium, the magazine has also endeavored to share a vision of the future of bookselling with its readers. A special section, "Shaping the Future: The Bookselling Industry Meets the 21st Century," which was included with the September issue, sought to answer vital questions regarding the destiny of the book, drawing upon contributions (via Internet) from a variety of publishing industry voices. In addition, the magazine played a leading role in exploring the burgeoning Information Superhighway for booksellers. With an eye toward providing booksellers with the information they need to operate successfully and profitably, *American Bookseller* launched a new "Pick of the List" feature: "Booksellers Choice: New Media," which provided reviews by technologically savvy booksellers of the best in bookstore-appropriate CD-ROMs.

Finally, as always, the *Bookstore Source Guide*, a directory to everything a bookstore needs, except books; the *Bookstore Merchandising Calendar*; and excerpts from other ABA publications—including Booksellers House's *Wise Men Fish Here* and BPI's *1994 ABACUS Expanded* and forthcoming *Manual on Bookselling*—rounded out the editorial contributions of *American Bookseller* to the book publishing and bookselling industry in 1994.

Research

With the debut of *Bookselling This Week* in April 1994, the research department increased its preparation of bookselling-related statistical information for dissemination to members. In addition to monthly release of current retail census figures on bookstore sales, the department developed monthly figures collected by the U.S. Department of Commerce on personal consumption expenditures on books and maps for quarterly publication. The research staff regularly identified and prepared material for the weekly "In Fact..." feature and also developed tables and graphics to be used in articles summarizing key findings of the 1992 Census of Retail Trade for each state and region. (The department is presenting detailed state results by region in monthly articles appearing in *American Bookseller* starting in November 1994.)

Using data on consumer book purchasing collected and tabulated by the NPD Group for ABA, AAP, and the Book Industry Study Group (BISG), the Research Department developed outlet market share findings by state and region, as well as for the entire United States. These results were presented to the regional booksellers associations at their 1994 winter gathering in Napa, California, as well as to the advisory council of the New England Booksellers Association (NEBA) and at NEBA's 1994 fall trade show in Boston. Also presented at both the NEBA show and the 1994 ABA Convention and Trade Exhibit in Los Angeles were findings from a new consumer study of comparative bookstore shopping experiences (independent, regular chain store, chain superstore), conducted for ABA by the Wirthlin Group. The findings of the shopping study were also incorporated in materials prepared by the Wallis Group for use by booksellers during National Independent Bookstore Week. In addition, highlights of the findings of both of these studies were presented in *Bookselling This Week*.

The 1994 ABACUS study included in-depth treatment of the financial implications for booksellers of including varying proportions of used book sales in the product mix and also compared the results of bookstores selling predominantly new books with the results of those selling mainly used books. Other additions in 1994 included employee productivity information based on full-time equivalency, inventory shrinkage as a percentage of sales, length of time in business, and two new ratios: return on equity and the margin of safety. The full range of study results was made available to the membership in an *American Bookseller* excerpt, as well as in BPI's *1994 ABACUS Expanded*.

Two major ongoing studies continued during 1994. The Gallup Organization collected benchmark data for ABA on numerous facets of consumer book-buying and will continue tracking the information on a quarterly basis for annual compilation. Second, Industry Insights conducted a benchmark study of member satisfaction and needs; these results will also be tracked annually henceforth. Work also continued on the direct marketing study sponsored jointly by ABA and AAP's Professional and Scholarly Publishing (PSP) Division. It is anticipated that results from all three of these studies will be released in 1995.

Other initiatives of the ABA Research Department during 1994 included design and data collection for a study of bookseller involvement in audio, video, and multimedia sales; the development and implementation of a computerized index of resource materials contained in the department's files; and the introduction of two new Information Modules developed by the research staff, titled "Audio, Video, and Multimedia Books" and "Statistical Overview of Retail Bookselling" (joining the previously developed "Opening a Bookstore" and "Children's Bookselling" modules).

In addition to responding to a large number of requests for statistical information, the department also continues to manage the ABA library. Following its move into the Moller House in the fall of 1994, the state-of-the-art facility has added *Books in Print* (R. R. Bowker) and numerous other directories in electronic format to its holdings. The library is open by appointment. Finally, the Fall 1994 issue of *Publishing Research Quarterly* contained an article prepared by the department titled "Bookselling Research: An Overview of the Past and Priorities for the Future."

Industry Relations

The year was one of growth and innovation in the area of industry relations. In late 1993 the Publisher Relations Committee delivered a questionnaire to publishers seeking detailed information on policies and procedures in the hope of publishing a supplement to the *ABA Book Buyer's Handbook*. Insufficient information was received, however, for publication of a supplemental handbook. Therefore, still wishing to impart the data gathered to the membership, the committee decided to present the information in a series of articles in *Bookselling This Week*. The series, "In Plain Terms," was prepared by Industry Relations staff and has appeared biweekly since August 1994. Individual articles have covered such topics as distribution center discounts, book club discounts, and the advance shipment of new releases. In the spring of 1994 the Publisher Relations Committee visited small and mid-sized publishers in Atlanta and Washington, D.C., and scientific and technical publishers in New York and New Jersey. A wide range of topics was covered during the visits, including paperwork, returns, cooperative advertising, and the level playing field.

One of the inaugural events held at the new G. Royce Smith Education Center in the fall of 1994 was ABA's first-ever seminar designed specifically for publishers. The program for the seminar, titled "The Bookselling Process: A Cooperative Venture," grew out of ABA's Publisher Intern Program and was a joint project of Industry Relations and Education Department staff. Conducted by an outstanding roster of bookselling educators, the event was so well received that plans are being made for other publisher-specific seminars to be held in the future.

Also in the fall of 1994, ABA exhibited at all ten regional trade shows. In addition, members of the ABA Executive Committee spoke on panels at nine of the ten shows, answering questions from booksellers on a variety of topics.

Other Activities

Booksellers Order Service (BOS), a wholly owned subsidiary of ABA, continued to offer advantageously priced products to bookstores (shipped freight free) that could be sold or used by booksellers in their day-to-day operations. New products introduced during calendar 1994 included booklites, batteries, and bulbs and hand-painted animal bookmarks. Another innovation was a special program featuring Booksellers Choice Classics, available on both cassette and CD. Other items that BOS continues to stock include an expanded line of 3M security strips;

adult gift-wrapping paper with a book design; children's gift-wrapping paper by renowned children's illustrator Thacher Hurd; and photo-degradable plastic and paper bags imprinted with BOS's definition of a book on one side and of a bookstore on the other. Additional products made available by BOS include gift certificates, heavyweight canvas totebags (plain or imprinted with the store's logo); lightweight cotton totebags; recycled paper shopping bags; and book slogan T-shirts (with or without imprinted bookstore name and logo).

Throughout 1994 the Industry Standardization Committee concentrated its efforts on achieving the objectives detailed in ABA's strategic plan under the goal stating, "Booksellers, publishers and wholesalers will benefit from efficient operations and industry standardization." In some cases, internal monitoring was required, e.g., determining that all ABA-member bookstores continue to have Standard Address Numbers (SANs). In other cases, the group worked with ABA's Publisher Relations Committee and/or the Book Industry Systems Advisory Committee (BISAC) to encourage implementation of board-approved standards for routine communications—to the mutual benefit of all—between members of the book industry, for example the "hard copy" standard for statement/remittance advice and the strippable indicator and Bookland EAN on cover four of all mass market paperbacks. The committee was also instrumental in developing an electronic data interchange (EDI) seminar for senior publishing executives held on April 13. Titled "EDI—A Look at the Future," the session was jointly sponsored by ABA, AAP, and BISG. The committee also organized and moderated a well-attended 1994 ABA convention workshop titled "EDI or Die."

Early in 1994 ABA created an in-house marketing function to develop programs designed to assist bookstores in meeting today's marketplace challenges. A major achievement of the first year's activity was the coordination of ABA's first annual National Independent Bookstore Week. Created and implemented by the Wallis Group of Tulsa, Oklahoma, the campaign was launched November 5. With the help of a media relations program to spread the word and a kit containing extensive how-to tips, bookmarks, a poster, and other collateral materials, bookstores across the nation united to "Celebrate Your Independents" by hosting in-store and community-based events. Other initiatives include the development and sale of low-cost marketing aids such as "Sale Price" stickers. Furthermore, "Check It Out," a new column that premiered in the September 1994 issue of *American Bookseller*, provides publishers with an opportunity to publicize title-specific promotional materials that booksellers can order for use in their stores. Potentially beneficial to both publishers and booksellers, one goal of "Check It Out" is that it become the source that booksellers will turn to when making marketing decisions. Finally, a consolidated ABA catalog was designed and published for the first time, for the convenience of members. The catalog contains descriptions of all products offered by ABA and its subsidiaries and includes a detachable order form.

As 1994 drew to a close, ABA was actively pursuing the development of an online service through which its members will be able to communicate and interact electronically with each other, association staff, other industry professionals, and the book-buying public.

Part 2
Legislation, Funding, and Grants

Legislation

Legislation and Regulations Affecting Libraries in 1994

Carol C. Henderson
Executive Director, Washington Office, American Library Association

Anne H. Heanue
Associate Director, Washington Office, American Library Association

Voters brought about a dramatic power shift in Congress in the November 8 elections, moving control of both Houses to the Republicans. With the White House and Capitol Hill controlled by different parties, the Clinton administration will have a difficult time getting its initiatives through Congress. The outlook for library and information issues in the next two years is uncertain.

During its second year in office, the administration carried on its ambitious technology plan and national information infrastructure (NII) agenda. The administration continued to highlight the role of libraries in its NII documents and speeches, and it included in its budget request to Congress funds for libraries to make their resources available electronically. However, funding for two small library programs was lost in the appropriations process.

The major legislative achievement of the year was enactment of new legislation authorizing assistance for school library media resources. School library champions in Congress worked for almost three years to ensure that provisions for assistance for school library resources would be included in the law (P.L. 103-382) signed by the president on October 20. Several parts of the Omnibus Children and Youth Initiative from the 1991 White House Conference were enacted in the reauthorization of the Elementary and Secondary Education Act.

Funding

The Clinton administration's fiscal year (FY) 1995 budget request of February 7 contained both good news and bad news for library programs. A funding level of $83,277,000 was requested for Library Services and Construction Act (LSCA) Title I public library services. Funding of $19.7 million was requested for LSCA Title III, interlibrary cooperation, a level that "would enable the States to expand their networking capabilities and library participation in development of the national information infrastructure." This request followed up on the president's State of the Union address, which described extending the information infrastructure to every school and library. However, all other LSCA programs—public library construction, foreign-language materials, and library literacy programs— were recommended for zero funding. Additionally, the administration's budget would have eliminated all Higher Education Act (HEA) library programs ($17.4 million).

During the annual National Library Week Library Legislative Day on April 19, at least 500 library supporters came to Capitol Hill to make the case for continued library funding. On April 22, 9-year-old Alexandria Johnson visited the White House and told President Clinton: "Give libraries more money—not less— so they can buy more books and computers and more people can get smarter." Alexandria was accompanied by her mother, American Library Association (ALA) President Hardy Franklin, and Executive Director Peggy Sullivan.

After a concerted ALA Washington Office and grassroots campaign that involved helping library champions Rep. Major Owens (D-N.Y.), Rep. Jack Reed (D-R.I.), Rep. Pat Williams (D-Mont.), and Rep. Dale Kildee (D-Mich.), 111 members of Congress signed a letter to House appropriators. Subsequently, LSCA and HEA library programs received $144,161,000 in FY 1995. That total is 40 percent higher than the Clinton administration requested, but $2 million less than FY 1994.

Reflecting the intense pressure to streamline and "reinvent" government, two of the smaller library programs—HEA II-A college library technology and cooperation grants and HEA II-C strengthening research library resources—were not funded at all. However, most of the funds were transferred to increased levels of funding in two other library programs: LSCA III interlibrary cooperation and resource sharing and HEA II-B research and demonstrations.

Copyright and Intellectual Property Issues

IITF "Green Paper"

In July, the administration's Information Infrastructure Task Force (IITF) Working Group on Intellectual Property Rights, chaired by Patent and Trademark Commissioner Bruce A. Lehman, issued *Intellectual Property and the National Information Infrastructure*, a preliminary draft "green paper" for public comment. The report recommended several changes in copyright law that, taken together, would be a major expansion of proprietors' rights without any corresponding protection of user privileges, such as fair use and library and classroom uses. For information that existed only in electronic formats, the proposed amendments could provide unprecedented exclusive control over the right to read, listen to, or view copyrighted material.

ALA's response to the report was coordinated by the Committee on Legislation's Ad Hoc Subcommittee on Copyright, chaired by Edward J. Valauskas. ALA's views—submitted in a September 2 letter from Arthur Curley, 1994–1995 ALA president—were summarized in three key statements:

- Expanded limitations must accompany expanded rights. No expansion of copyright holders' rights to include electronic transmission should be

Table 1 / Appropriations for Federal Library and Related Programs
(figures in thousands)

Library Programs	FY 1994 Appropriation	FY 1995 Clinton Request	FY 1995 House	FY 1995 Senate	FY 1995 Appropriation
El/Sec Education Act I—Chap. 2 (incl. school libraries)	$369,500	$ 0	$ 0†	$ 0†	$347,250
GPO Superintendent of Documents	29,082	33,900	30,600	32,207	32,207
Higher Education Act	17,443	0	4,916	13,186	11,416
Title II-A, College Library Technology and Cooperation	3,873	0	0	0	0
II-B, Library Education	4,960	0	4,916	4,916	4,916
II-B, Research and Demonstrations	2,802	0	0	8,270	6,500
II-C, Improving Access to Research Library Resources	5,808	0	0	0	0
VI, Section 607 Foreign Research Materials	0	0	0	0	0
Library of Congress	330,864	358,000	344,428	348,855	348,480‡
Library Services and Construction Act	128,866	102,976	111,080	134,372	132,745
Title I, Public Library Services	83,227	83,227	83,482	83,227	83,227
II, Public Library Construction	17,792	0	0	17,792	17,792
III, Interlibrary Cooperation	19,749	19,749	19,572	25,327	23,700
IV, Indian Library Services*	—	—	—	—	—
V, Foreign Language Materials	0	0	0	0	0
VI, Library Literacy Programs	8,098	0	8,026	8,026	8,026
National Agricultural Library	18,155	19,528	17,845	18,307	18,307
National Commission on Libraries and Information Science	904	901	901	901	901
National Library of Medicine and MLAA	119,981	135,330	123,274	127,274	126,274

† Both House and Senate passed $667,548,000 for a combination of Chapter 2 and a new professional development program for teachers and other school personnel.
‡ Includes authority to obligate $25.2 million in receipts.
* Funded at 2% of appropriations for LSCA I, II, and III.

Table 1 / Appropriations for Federal Library and Related Programs *(cont.)*
(figures in thousands)

Library Programs	FY 1994 Appropriation	FY 1995 Clinton Request	FY 1995 House	FY 1995 Senate	FY 1995 Appropriation
Library-Related Programs					
Adult Education and Literacy	$ 304,908	$ 322,541	$ 303,690	$ 302,235	$ 302,235
Bilingual, Immigrant, Refugee Education	227,431	253,920	247,572	238,082	245,200
ESEA Title I, Disadvantaged Children	6,901,304	7,568,129	7,235,363	7,223,119	7,222,430
ESEA Title II, Eisenhower Professional Development	250,998	0	0†	0†	320,300
ESEA Title III, Educational Technology	0	0	30,000	50,000	40,000
ESEA Title III pt. 3, Star Schools	25,944	25,944	29,711	33,000	30,000
Education of Handicapped Children (state grants)	2,858,973	3,045,425	3,858,973	3,045,425	2,998,812
Educational Research	78,000	87,450	81,082	83,000	86,200
Even Start	91,373	118,000	102,024	102,024	102,024
Goals 2000	105,000	708,000	388,400	428,400	403,400
HEA Title III, Developing Institutions	212,870	219,805	232,854	222,967	229,656
HEA Title IV-C, College Work-Study	616,508	716,508	616,508	616,508	616,508
HEA Title VI, International Education	0	0	0	5,000	3,000
Inexpensive Book Distribution (RIF)	10,300	10,300	10,208	10,300	10,300
National Archives and Records Administration	190,232	194,638	194,638	200,238	195,238
National Center for Education Statistics	77,850	101,805	80,920	80,920	80,920
National Endowment for the Arts	170,228	170,100	167,678	161,596	167,678
National Endowment for the Humanities	177,491	177,383	177,383	177,383	177,383
National Historical Pubs. and Records Commission	5,250	4,000	7,000	5,000	9,000
NTIA Information Infrastructure Grants	26,000	99,988	70,000	52,000	64,000
Postsecondary Education Improvement Fund	16,872	20,326	16,723	18,364	17,543
VISTA Literacy Corps (Corp. for Nat'l and Community Service)	5,009	5,600	5,024	5,600	5,020

enacted without enactment of corresponding limitations on those rights in areas such as fair use, classroom use, and library use. Marginalizing these interests, now protected in the Constitution and the Copyright Act, will not maintain balance. Further, the library provisions of the copyright law should be strengthened to allow preservation activities that use electronic or other appropriate technologies as they emerge.

- A new CONTU is needed. ALA urged the working group to recommend to Congress enactment of a new National Commission on New Technological Uses (CONTU) of copyrighted works. The complexity of the copyright problems raised by the NII technology surpasses those of photocopying and early computer technologies that led Congress to create CONTU 1974. A new CONTU is needed to conduct studies, compile data, and better justify needed changes in copyright law, both to ensure public access to material disseminated via NII and to respect the rights of owners of copyrighted works.

A series of working group hearings on the draft report was held in three American cities. Valauskas testified in Chicago on September 14; ALA's testimony was endorsed by six library and related organizations. Other hearings were held in Los Angeles on September 16 and in Washington, D.C., on September 22 and 23. Additionally, ALA and the Association of Research Libraries on October 21 submitted reply comments on the working groups' draft report.

Fair Use Conferences

The "green paper" also resulted in a series of invitational conferences on educational and library fair use in the NII context. The purpose was to attempt to develop guidelines for such fair uses. Several such conferences, organized by the Patent and Trademark Office, were held and proved useful for improving understanding among library and educational practitioners and print, electronic, software, and other publishers, as well as authors; but at year's end the process was still in the preliminary stages.

Texaco Fair Use Case

On October 28, the U.S. Court of Appeals for the Second Circuit issued a decision in the long-awaited fair use case appeal, *American Geophysical Union* v. *Texaco Inc.*, affirming the original decision that the copying at issue was not fair use. The lawsuit was initiated in 1985 by a group of publishers with copyrights in scientific and technical journals that were registered by the Copyright Clearance Center (CCC). The publishers filed a class action against Texaco for making routine photocopies from these journals without paying CCC more than minimal payments.

The issue was whether photocopies of eight articles from the *Journal of Catalysis* made by one of Texaco's scientists for future reference constituted fair use when Texaco had paid for subscriptions to that publication. ALA's *amicus curiae* brief filed in March 1993 maintained that the original opinion did not consider the likely effect on libraries and their users.

ALA, represented by attorney Susan Braden of Ingersoll and Bloch Chartered, filed an *amicus curiae* brief supporting Texaco's petition for rehearing *en banc* (in full court) of the decision in this case. On December 23, the Second Circuit denied Texaco's petition for rehearing. At the same time, the court modified its earlier opinion with amendments that seem to be directed at avoiding the appearance of conflict with a Supreme Court decision, *Campbell* v. *Acuff-Rose Music Inc.*, 114 S. Ct. 1164 (1994).

Government Information Policy

Electronic Records

On December 13, 1994, ALA joined as a plaintiff in *American Historical Association et al.* v. *Peterson*. The suit seeks to block an agreement between Don Wilson, former Archivist of the United States, and former President George Bush granting Wilson control over electronic records created by officials of the White House and the Office of Policy Development during Bush's administration. Plaintiffs charge that an agreement between the former archivist and Bush unlawfully seeks to deny the public and historians access to government records.

Government Information Locator Service (GILS)

The Office of Management and Budget (OMB) established a Government Information Locator Service (GILS) through OMB Bulletin 95-01 on December 7. Designed to help the public and federal agencies locate and access information throughout the U.S. government, GILS is accessible through Internet in various ways.

In its October comments to OMB on a draft of the bulletin, ALA asked that Internet access to GILS be provided free to depository libraries and that access be made available for use by the American public at no charge. OMB responded by telling agencies to provide direct Internet library access to the GILS core library records.

GPO Access Act

In June the Government Printing Office (GPO) rolled out the GPO Access system, meeting its requirement to implement P.L. 103-40, the GPO Electronic Information Access Enhancement Act, within a year of enactment. ALA helped to develop the law and get it enacted. Databases available on the system include the *Congressional Record and Index*, the *Federal Register*, Congressional Bills, the History of Bills, and the Unified Regulatory Agenda. In October GPO announced the first two sites giving the public free access to the Access system. Off-site callers can retrieve this information through the Columbia Online Information Network (COIN) located at the Daniel Boone Regional Library in Columbia, Missouri, or through the Seattle Public Library's QUEST System. Other depository library gateways will gradually provide free public access through the GPO Access Act. Free electronic searches are already available to walk-in patrons of many of the 1,400 depository libraries located in congressional districts around the nation.

GPO Access also includes the GPO Locator and Federal Bulletin Board and eventually will provide access to the GPO IDEA storage facility.

GPO Funding

The Senate included $1.5 million to implement the GPO Access Act in H.R. 4454, the Legislative Branch funding bill, on June 16. ALA helped to spark an outcry from constituents that convinced senators to restore the $1.5 million the House had cut. The Senate passed $32,207,000 for the GPO Superintendent of Documents operation; the House later agreed, and this amount was signed into law.

In a September 8 letter, ALA President Arthur Curley urged President Clinton to reconsider the restrictive interpretations announced as he signed the Legislative Branch funding bill into law. The letter said restricting procurement through GPO to documents intended primarily for distribution to and use by the general public is contrary to law and would reduce the availability of items to the public through depository libraries.

In an October 4 letter in response to Curley, President Clinton said the administration agreed to maintain the status quo regarding current printing and duplicating arrangements for the current fiscal year and would work with Congress on a legislative approach to these issues.

[For more information on GPO activities, see the GPO report in Part 1.—Ed.]

NPR Support Services Report

ALA publicized widely and sought input from the library field on the implications of the accompanying report of the administration's National Performance Review about Reinventing Support Services. The accompanying report was dated September 1993 but issued a year later. Although the report recognized the key role depository libraries play in providing printed government publications and information to the public, it ignored the fact that depositories have been making government information available to the public in electronic formats since 1988.

Paperwork Reduction Act

The Senate on October 6 passed S. 560, a five-year reauthorization of the Paperwork Reduction Act, but the House did not act and the measure died. S. 560 was a compromise bill approved in August by the Governmental Affairs Committee after what committee chair Senator John Glenn (D-Ohio) called "long and difficult negotiations." While most of the bill focused on OMB's regulatory review and paperwork clearance responsibilities, some sections concerned dissemination of government information, but these were not as controversial to the library community as past versions.

In June then-ALA President Hardy Franklin wrote a letter to the Senate committee offering recommendations for improving a draft bill from Senator Glenn. Franklin also wrote to Senator Sam Nunn (D-Ga.), sponsor of S. 560, stating that his bill was unacceptable without changes to ensure equitable, timely, and ready public access to government information.

Postal Service Kiosk Project

The U.S. Postal Service (USPS) announced on October 20 a pilot project to test kiosks as a delivery vehicle to provide electronic access to government information and services, including purchase of stamps and other services for a fee. Libraries could be among the sites to be tested.

In a statement by ALA President Arthur Curley, ALA proposed that public libraries be designated as trial sites for the postal kiosks. Curley said he was optimistic that the Clinton administration and the USPS will recognize that it makes good sense to build on the system that is already there. The ALA Washington Office was working at year's end to assist libraries interested in being designated test sites.

Library of Congress

Budget

The Library of Congress requested $358 million in FY 1995. When Congress passed H.R. 4454, Legislative Branch Appropriations for FY 95, it approved a 5.44 percent increase in the Library of Congress budget, or a net appropriation of $323.2 million. In addition to this total, the library has authority to retain $24.3 million in receipts. Some 395 positions have been cut at the library since 1992 because of funding cuts. Early in 1994, due to budgetary pressures, the library announced further reductions in reading rooms hours.

Financial Reform Bill

A minimal and remedial financial reform bill was drafted by the Library of Congress to replace the Library of Congress Fund Act. The bill addresses accounting weaknesses identified by the General Accounting Office, the need for revolving fund authority, and other technical amendments. The Library of Congress Financial Reform Act of 1994 was introduced by Representative Charles Rose (D-N.C.) and Senator Claiborne Pell (D-R.I.) as H.R. 4945 and S. 2419, but the bills died when Congress adjourned without taking action.

The ALA Committee on Legislation concluded that the new draft focused only on current operations and services and removed the issues that had caused concern in the library community relating to S. 345. On June 29 the ALA Council adopted a resolution supporting the bill and encouraging prompt enactment by Congress.

Lobbying by Nonprofits

Through Independent Sector, a coalition of nonprofit groups to which ALA belongs, the Washington Office continued to participate in activities related to revision of the law governing lobbying by nonprofits. The Lobbying Disclosure Act, S. 349, was defeated in the Senate on October 7. Questions were raised concerning a provision that would have required many groups, including nonprofits, to provide the names and addresses of persons who contributed money to organizations to lobby on their behalf. Some helpful modifications were made in the legislation before it came to the Senate floor as a result of requests by a coalition that included Independent Sector, but the measure continued to require disclosure that would have been a burden to nonprofits.

LSCA Reauthorization

A one-year extension of the Library Services and Construction Act (LSCA) was passed as part of the Senate bill reauthorizing the Elementary and Secondary Education Act, agreed to by the House, and enacted as part of P.L. 103-382. With the automatic one-year extension that applies as part of the General Education Provisions Act, this action authorizes LSCA through FY 1996.

Jan Moltzan and Joan Ress Reeves, who together chair the ALA Committee on Legislation Ad Hoc Subcommittee on LSCA Reauthorization, also cochair an interassociation Task Force on LSCA Reauthorization (with representatives from the Committee on Legislation, Association of Specialized and Cooperative Library Agencies, Chief Officers of State Library Agencies, Public Library Association, Urban Libraries Council, and the National Commission on Libraries and Information Science, and with observers from the Department of Education's Office of Library Programs).

The task force, with much input from the library community, developed a consensus proposal for a major revision and renewal of LSCA, with an emphasis on technology and special services (outreach). A document outlining this proposal was distributed widely throughout the library community in May by the Washington Office, and it was discussed at the Miami Annual Conference in June. A resolution based on the proposal was adopted by the ALA Council on June 29.

Since then, the LSCA task force—with the help of attorneys and the Washington Office, and with informal advice from congressional staff—has worked to draft a bill based on the policy directions approved by the parent organizations of task force members.

National Information Infrastructure

National information infrastructure (NII) initiatives have taken place on a number of fronts. Following are highlights of selected administration and congressional activities as well as activities initiated by ALA or made in response to government initiatives.

Administration

White House

The administration's various NII initiatives were articulated in a series of speeches by Vice President Gore and Secretary of Commerce Brown. Two noteworthy goals were laid out:

- By the year 2000 all of the classrooms, libraries, hospitals, and clinics in the United States will be connected to NII.

* Telecommunications regulatory reform should include preferential rates for libraries and schools and should include the concept of the public right-of-way.

NII Advisory Council

Secretary of Commerce Brown made appointments to the administration's U.S. Advisory Council on NII. The sole librarian on the council is Toni Carbo Bearman, Dean, School of Library and Information Science, University of Pittsburgh, and former executive director, U.S. National Commission on Libraries and Information Science. [For more information on the activities of this council, see the Special Report in Part 1.—*Ed.*]

NII Task Force

The various committees and working groups of the administration's Information Infrastructure Task Force (IITF) were active in meetings, hearings, and issuance of reports. Among the most relevant reports were *Putting the Information Infrastructure to Work*, with a chapter on "Libraries and the NII," by the IITF Committee on Applications and Technology, and *Intellectual Property and the National Information Infrastructure*, the preliminary draft report of the IITF Working Group on Intellectual Property Rights.

Administration Outreach Efforts

The administration engaged in a variety of outreach activities, including high-level briefings for interested communities and seeking public input to some working group activities. "Shaping the National Information Infrastructure" was a Public Interest Summit on March 29 and included a keynote speech by Vice President Gore.

National Telecommunications and Information Administration

The National Telecommunications and Information Administration (NTIA) (part of the Commerce Department) made $26 million available in matching grants to help nonprofit entities, including libraries, to connect to electronic networks and to deliver social and governmental services and information.

NTIA held a series of field hearings on the concept of universal service and initiated an inquiry on universal service and open access to the telecommunications network, with public comment due December 14. In connection with the inquiry, a virtual conference was scheduled for the week of November 14–18 to solicit additional public input. Libraries were encouraged to make their facilities available to the public for the virtual conference.

Congress

Telecommunications Deregulation

Both the House and Senate worked on major revisions of telecommunications regulatory policy. The House passed a package, H.R. 3626, the Antitrust and Communications Reform Act. In the Senate, the Commerce Committee approved S. 1822, the Communications Act of 1994, but industry and partisan disagreements kept it from a floor vote.

Although there were substantial differences between H.R. 3626 and S. 1822, under specific conditions and timings both would:

- Allow regional Bell telephone companies to enter previously prohibited lines of business, such as long distance, cable TV service, and electronic publishing
- Open up local phone service to competition from cable companies, long-distance companies, or other competitors
- Allow imposition of common-carrier obligations and universal service requirements

ALA was successful at getting substantial (although not all) favorable concepts and explanatory language included in these bills. The House passed the Antitrust and Communications Reform Act and the National Communications and Competition and Information Infrastructure Act on June 28 and then combined the bills into one measure (H.R. 3626). The combined House-passed bill included preferential rates for libraries in three separate provisions. However, one of these was limited to provision of noncommercial services to the general public, and another excluded, for the most part, higher education institutions.

On August 11 the Senate Commerce, Science and Transportation Committee approved a substitute version of S. 1822, the Communications Act of 1994, and the final version and report were issued in late September. Soon after, the bill was declared dead by its sponsor, Senator Ernest Hollings (D-S.C.). Key provisions of the committee bill included:

- Preferential rate provisions for libraries and other nonprofits (combining concepts from the original S. 1822 with concepts from S. 2195, the National Public Telecommunications Infrastructure Act introduced by Senator Daniel Inouye, D-Hawaii)
- Reservation of up to 5 percent of capacity for eligible entities (public and nonprofit libraries, educational institutions, and certain nonprofits) at incremental cost-based rates for delivery of information services to the general public
- Advanced services to be provided at preferential rates (although, for the most part, higher education institutions were excluded)

Measures that would support network applications for education (especially K–12), health care, libraries, and government information stalled in House-

Senate conference and died as the session ended. H.R. 820, the National Competitiveness Act, incorporated the networking applications provisions passed by the House in July 1993 as H.R. 1757 and by the Senate in March 1994 as S. 4 (Title VI). The bills defined the National Research and Education Network as a program with three components:

- Networking research and development
- Experimental testbed networks
- Network access support

A connections program at the National Science Foundation (NSF) would foster local networks in communities for connecting libraries and other entities to each other and to Internet. Training programs would include training of librarians as well as librarians training the public in the use of networked resources. Activities would be authorized at NSF and several other federal agencies.

American Library Association

The ALA Washington Office participated in numerous high-level briefings and meetings sponsored by the Clinton administration and initiated other meetings with a variety of administration officials. Critical issues addressed included universal service, preferential rates, and reservation of capacity for library and public uses.

ALA, working with the Association of Research Libraries (ARL), developed a paper proposing several approaches to implementing the administration's goal of connecting every library to NII. This paper, "Suggested Approaches to Implement the Administration Goal of Connecting to the NII Every Library, School, Hospital and Clinic," was shared widely with administration officials, congressional offices, and other organizations. Features of this proposal included

- Preferential rates for libraries, an approach incorporated by the administration in its telecommunications white paper as well as in House and Senate legislation
- Reservation of capacity
- Requiring universal service contributions for public networking

Statement of Principles

ALA—with the Washington Office, the ALA Committee on Legislation's telecommunications subcommittee, and the Library and Information Technology Association (LITA) unit of ALA providing coordination—spearheaded joint library association development of a set of "Principles for the Development of the NII." ALA voted to support these principles in February; the principles cover First Amendment, privacy, intellectual property, ubiquity, equitable access, and interoperability. The principles were widely disseminated to Washington policy-

Table 2 / Status of Legislation of Interest to Librarians

(103rd Congress, 2nd Session, Convened: January 25, 1994, Adjourned: December 1, 1994)

Legislation	House Introduced	House Hearings	House Reported by Subcommittee	House Committee Report No.– H. Rept. 103-	House Floor Action	Senate Introduced	Senate Hearings	Senate Reported by Subcommittee	Senate Committee Report No.– S. Rept. 103-	Senate Floor Action	Conference Report– H. Rept. 103-	Final Passage	Public Law– PL 103-
Arts and Humanities Reauthorization	H.R. 2351	•	•	186	•	S. 1218	•	•	182	•			
Communications and Antitrust Reform	H.R. 3626	•	•	559	•								
Communications Act of 1994						S. 1822	•						
Communications Act Reform	H.R. 3636	•	•	560	•		•						
Copyright Reform Act	H.R. 897	•	•	388	•	S. 373	•						
Depository Library Restructuring	H.R. 3400, t. xiv	•		366	•	H.R. 3400, t. xiv	•						
El/Sec School Library Media Act	H.R. 1151					S. 266	•						
Electronic FOIA	H.R. 4917					S. 1782	•	•	none	•			
Electronic Library Act						S. 626	•						
Emergency Book Fund Act	H.R. 2256												
ESEA Reauth. (Improve America's Schools Act)	H.R. 6	•	•	425	•	S. 1513	•	•	292	•	761		382
Goals 2000 Educate America	H.R. 1804	•	•	168	•	S. 1150	•	•	85	•	446	•	227
HBCU Restoration of Historic Buildings	H.R. 2921	•	•	398	•	H.R. 2921	•	•	279	•	398	•	
Head Start Reauthorization	H.R. 4250	•	•	483, pt 1	•	S. 2000	•	•	251	•	497	•	252
Improvement of Information Access Act	H.R. 629												
LC Financial Reform Act	H.R. 4945												
Lobbying Disclosure Act	H.R. 823	•	•	none	•	S. 2419	•	•	37	•			
National Competitiveness Act	H.R. 820	•	•	77	•	S. 4	•		113	•			
Networking Applications Bills	H.R. 1757	•	•	173	•	S. 4	•		113	•			

Table 2 / Status of Legislation of Interest to Librarians *(cont.)*
(103rd Congress, 2nd Session, Convened: January 25, 1994, Adjourned: December 1, 1994)

Legislation	House					Senate					Final Action		
	Introduced	Hearings	Reported by Subcommittee	Committee Report No.—H. Rept. 103-	Floor Action	Introduced	Hearings	Reported by Subcommittee	Committee Report No.—S. Rept. 103-	Floor Action	Conference Report—H. Rept. 103-	Final Passage	Public Law—PL 103-
NHPRC Reauthorization	H.R. 2139	•	•	215	•	S. 314	•	•	145	•		•	262
NTIA Pilot Projects	H.R. 2639	•	•	325	•								
National Public Telecommunications Infrastructure Act		•				S. 2195	•	•					
Organization of Congress	H.R. 3801					S. 1824	•	•	297				
Paperwork Reduction Act	H.R. 2995					S. 560	•	•	392	•			
Privacy Protection Act						S. 1735	•						
Technology for Education Act	H.R. 2728	•				S. 1040	•		234				
Appropriations													
Agriculture FY 1995	H.R. 4554	•	•	542	•	H.R. 4554	•	•	290	•	734	•	330
Commerce, Justice, State FY 1995	H.R. 4603	•	•	552	•	H.R. 4603	•	•	309	•	708	•	317
Interior FY 1995	H.R. 4602	•	•	551	•	H.R. 4602	•	•	294	•	740	•	332
Labor-HHS-ED FY 1995	H.R. 4606	•	•	553	•	H.R. 4606	•	•	318	•	733	•	333
Legislative branch FY 1995	H.R. 4454	•	•	517	•	H.R. 4454	•	•	293	•	567	•	283
Treasury, Postal FY 1995	H.R. 4539	•	•	534	•	H.R. 4539	•	•	286	•	741	•	329

For free copies of bills, reports, and laws, write: House Document Rm., B-18 Annex No. 2, Washington, DC 20515; Senate Document Rm., B-04 Hart, Washington, DC 20510.

makers and were well received. An expansion of the intellectual property princi-ples, developed by ARL, was endorsed by ALA in June.

FCC and School/Library Connections

To speed up the connection of libraries to NII, ALA joined with four national education groups to present the Federal Communications Commission (FCC) with an innovative plan to use regulatory policy to benefit the public without raising prices. ALA urged FCC to redirect a small portion of funds available through price cap regulation formulas to pay for investments made by local tele-phone companies in educational and library infrastructure in their territories. If the proposal were adopted, up to $300 million a year could be made available for connecting libraries and schools.

NTIA Universal Service Inquiry

On behalf of ALA, the Washington Office, together with its educational organi-zation partners, submitted to the NTIA (National Telecommunications and Information Administration) the coalition's proposal to use a portion of funds available under price cap regulation as investment funds to connect schools and libraries to NII. The document was submitted to NTIA in response to its Notice of Inquiry on Universal Service and Open Access Issues, announced in September with comments due by December 14.

Postal Rate Case—Library Rate

The U.S. Postal Service (USPS) Board of Governors in December, and the Postal Rate Commission (PRC) in November, approved a large increase in the library postal rate, effective January 1, 1995. As recommended by the independent PRC, the USPS Board of Governors made only minor changes from the rates proposed in March by USPS staff.

For the fourth-class library rate, the new rates are 69.9 percent higher than the previous rates, a marginal improvement over the 73.7 percent requested by USPS. A typical three-pound library rate package increases from $1.14 to $1.96. Overall, postal rates increased an average of 10 percent, so the result for the library rate was way out of line and very disappointing. The library rate is used for books-by-mail programs to reach isolated and homebound users, for delivery of books reserved by users, and for interlibrary loans. However, the majority of library rate use is by schools and colleges for shipment of educational materials.

School Library Media Bill/ESEA Reauthorization

The major legislative achievement of the year was enactment of new legislation authorizing assistance for school library media resources. This result was the cul-mination of several years of effort by school library media specialists across the country, as well as by other librarians, state library agencies, and the ALA

Washington Office. It was also due to the remarkable and persistent leadership of the two sponsors of the original Elementary and Secondary School Library Media Act: Representative Jack Reed (D-R.I.) and Senator Paul Simon (D-Ill.).

The bill was incorporated in different House and Senate versions in the larger Improving America's Schools Act, a five-year reauthorization of the Elementary and Secondary Education Act. The final version (H.R. 6) was signed into law in October. It implements the school library portion of the omnibus children and youth literacy initiative that was the top priority recommendation of the 1991 White House Conference on Library and Information Services.

P.L. 103-382 includes much of interest to librarians, but four key provisions are specifically helpful to school library media specialists:

- Elementary and Secondary School Library Media Resources Program, ESEA Title III, part F. Authorizes $200 million for (FY) 1995 and such sums as necessary for the following four fiscal years. However, this program has no actual funding in FY 1995. When funded, this program would provide assistance for the acquisition of school library media resources for the use of students, library media specialists, and teachers in elementary/secondary schools.

- Chapter 2 school block grant. Retained as ESEA Title VI, Innovative Education Program Strategies, with support for library services and instructional and media materials as an eligible use of funds. Actual FY 1995 funding was $347.3 million.

- Technology for Education, ESEA Title III. School libraries and school library media specialists have been integrated into Title III so that school library media centers are eligible for technology assistance and school library media specialists are eligible for technology training. Public libraries may be eligible for partnership activities with schools. Actual FY 1995 funding for ESEA III technology programs was $40 million.

- School Facilities Infrastructure Improvement Act, ESEA Title XII. Proposed by Senator Carol Moseley-Braun (D-Ill.), the program provides assistance for the improvement of public elementary/secondary facilities or school library media centers. Actual funding for FY 1995 was $100 million.

Legislation and Regulations Affecting Publishing in 1994

Judith Platt

Director of Communications and Public Affairs
Association of American Publishers

Copyright

Copyright Reform Act of 1993

A significant outcome of the 103rd Congress was the fact that the Copyright Reform Act of 1993 was not passed. This legislation, introduced early in 1993 by Senators Dennis DeConcini (D-Ariz.) and Orrin Hatch (R-Utah) (S. 373) and Representative William Hughes (D-N.J.) (H.R. 897), proposed, among other things, repeal of Section 412 of the Copyright Act (which requires timely registration as a condition for the award of statutory damages and attorney's fees in copyright infringement suits).

Because registration is voluntary under U.S. copyright law, the Copyright Act contains incentives to encourage copyright owners to register their works, and Section 412 is generally recognized as the most important of these incentives. Registration and its accompanying deposit requirement are essential to the integrity of the Library of Congress's vast collections, to the public record of registrations maintained by the Copyright Office, and to the scholars, researchers, and members of Congress who use these collected works and registration records.

The Association of American Publishers (AAP) worked with a broad coalition of librarians, historians, authors, and others to oppose outright repeal. This opposition was based on two points: (1) that repeal would do serious harm to the Library of Congress's collections and the public record of registered works; and (2) that because it would mean universal eligibility for statutory damages and attorney's fees, repeal of Section 412 would have a dramatic chilling effect on the use of pre-existing materials (photos, letters, diaries) by scholars, journalists, and other authors and their publishers.

Throughout the debate, AAP argued that the concerns voiced by those advocating repeal of Section 412 could be addressed through nonlegislative means— changes in the Copyright Office's registration and deposit regulations. The Copyright Office is now in the process of reviewing its regulations, and it is hoped that this will result in administrative action that renders further efforts to repeal Section 412 unnecessary.

Education

Elementary and Secondary Education Act Reauthorization

Legislation providing a six-year extension for programs carried out under the Elementary and Secondary Education Act (ESEA) of 1965 was approved by Congress and signed by the president (the Improving America's Schools Act).

The final bill contained funding of $347 million for a new Chapter 2 block grant program, designated as the Targeted Assistance Program. Retaining Chapter 2, which provides support for library services and the purchase of instructional materials, was a victory for AAP and a coalition of allied organizations that fought to retain the program in the face of administration efforts to scuttle it and attempts in the Senate to divert a substantial portion of its funds elsewhere.

Goal 2000

President Clinton signed the Goal 2000: Educate America Act into law on March 31, 1994, just under the wire for an April 1 appropriations deadline. Among its provisions, the new law allows states to adopt "opportunity to learn" standards, which could well increase the demand for high-quality, up-to-date instructional materials.

Intellectual Freedom

Helms Amendment to ESEA

Early in August, during floor debate on the Elementary and Secondary Education Act, Senators Jesse Helms (R-N.C.) and Robert Smith (R-N.H.) succeeded in having language added to the bill stipulating that local educational agencies receiving funds under ESEA were prohibited from carrying out programs or activities having "either the purpose or effect of encouraging or supporting homosexuality as a positive lifestyle alternative." A similar provision was added to the House-passed bill. Joining a number of organizations—including PEN American Center and the American Library Association—AAP expressed to members of Congress its opposition, arguing that in addition to contravening a long-established policy of noninterference by the federal government in local curriculum decisions, the Helms amendment was viewpoint-based suppression of speech, violating the First Amendment. The amendment was dropped from the bill in conference and in its place the conferees adopted general language barring the use of federal funds for programs that "promote sexual activity."

Repeal of SBA "Opinion Molder" Rule

For the first time in more than 40 years, small book publishers and distributors became eligible for federal Small Business Administration (SBA) loan guarantees. On July 15, 1994, SBA officially repealed its "opinion molder" rule, which, since 1953, had precluded assistance to firms engaged in "creation, origination, expression, dissemination, propagation, or distribution of ideas, values, thoughts, opinions, or similar intellectual property." AAP had long called for repeal of this rule and was among the organizations filing comments in support of SBA's action.

Free Trade in Ideas

Major provisions of Representative Howard Berman's (D-Calif.) "Free Trade in Ideas" bill were incorporated into the fiscal year 1994–1995 Foreign Relations Authorization Act and signed into law in April 1994. The new law clarifies the

"Berman Amendment" to the 1988 Omnibus Trade Act, which among other things prohibits the Executive Branch from regulating the import and export of books, publications, films, and other informational materials. The new law also includes a statement of congressional intent prohibiting restrictions on travel by U.S. citizens for informational, educational, religious, cultural, and humanitarian purposes and for public performances and exhibitions. Travel restrictions to Cuba were grandfathered into the legislation, but the Clinton administration made a commitment to give immediate approval to travel connected with trade in publications and other cultural and informational materials.

FDA Regulation of Medical Publishing

Early in 1994, AAP signed on to an *amicus* brief challenging attempts by the federal Food and Drug Administration (FDA) to regulate publication and distribution of medical textbooks, peer-reviewed medical journal articles, and other materials dealing with "off-label" uses of FDA-approved drugs (uses for which FDA has not given approval). The brief was filed in support of a "citizen's petition" originated by the Washington Legal Foundation. When FDA failed to respond to the petition, the foundation filed suit in federal court. The government responded by asking dismissal of the suit because other available remedies had not been exhausted. AAP, the Media Institute, and a host of other groups joined in an *amicus* brief opposing dismissal on the grounds that, as an abridgement of protected speech, FDA's actions can be challenged without the need to exhaust other remedies.

Trade

General Agreement on Tariffs and Trade

As its last major act, the 103rd Congress approved U.S. participation in the expanded General Agreement on Tariffs and Trade (GATT), soon to become the World Trade Organization (WTO). More than seven years in the making, the new GATT accord provides a trade framework for 124 participating nations. Most significantly for publishers, it establishes a high level of protection for intellectual property, including copyrights. AAP and the other copyright industry organizations comprising the International Intellectual Property Alliance played a key role in initiating U.S. government efforts to include intellectual property rights within the scope of GATT for the first time in history. Although the final TRIPS (Trade Related Intellectual Property Rights) portion of GATT was not all that AAP had hoped it would be (the agreement gives long transitions to developing countries to improve their laws, among other shortcomings), the positive effects outweigh the shortcomings.

A significant provision of the GATT implementing legislation grants "retroactive" protection, restoring copyright protection in the United States to certain foreign works that had fallen into the public domain. AAP worked successfully with the administration and Congress to build safeguards into the legislation to help protect the interests of and minimize the risks for publishers who use recaptured public domain works.

"Special 301" Provisions of the U.S. Trade Act

Under the "Special 301" provisions of the Omnibus Trade and Competitiveness Act of 1988, the U.S. Trade Representative (USTR) is required to identify foreign countries where abuses of U.S. intellectual property rights are particularly egregious and to set in motion an accelerated process for correcting these abuses. AAP, through the International Intellectual Property Alliance (IIPA), provides data on copyright piracy and market access barriers for U.S. copyrighted works to aid USTR in identifying problem areas. In February 1994 IIPA identified 32 countries whose failure to protect U.S. copyrights poses significant problems for U.S. industries. Estimated trade losses due to piracy in these 32 countries cost the U.S. economy more than $6.2 billion in 1993. IIPA identified China as its highest priority, asking USTR to designate the nation as a Priority Foreign Country for its failure to enforce its copyright laws. This designation took effect on June 20, and on December 31, 1994, U.S. Trade Representative Mickey Kantor announced preparation of a list of punitive tariffs involving Chinese exports to the United States valued at more than $2.8 billion a year. Kantor indicated that he would make a final determination regarding trade sanctions in early 1995.

The Information Superhighway

National Information Infrastructure

The Clinton administration's plans and policies regarding creation of a national information infrastructure (NII) continue to be an area of major interest for publishers.

On July 7, 1994, the Working Group on Intellectual Property Rights of the President's NII Task Force issued its "green paper," a preliminary report on its findings with respect to the protection of intellectual property in NII's digital environment. Issuance of the green paper set in motion a process of public hearings and conferences in which AAP has been a major participant. At a series of public hearings held around the country, AAP and its member publishers put forth the industry's views and concerns. AAP has also been a participant in ongoing deliberations mandated by the green paper to explore the parameters of "fair use" in the context of the digital networked environment. [For more information on the NII task force, see the Special Report earlier in Part 1.—*Ed.*]

In addition to intellectual property protection issues, AAP is looking at NII in the context of First Amendment and free speech concerns. Heather Grant Florence (Bantam Doubleday Dell), a former chair of the AAP Freedom to Read Committee, spoke on First Amendment issues at a special Security Issues forum in Washington in July.

Telecommunications Policy

Although the 103rd Congress failed to pass major telecommunications legislation dealing with the operations of the Regional Bell Operating Companies (RBOCs), a good deal of time and energy was spent in hearings and committee deliberations. Included in the legislative proposals were provisions designed to prevent the RBOCs from using their market power to compete unfairly in the area of electronic publishing services. AAP's major concern was that the legislation, as originally introduced in the House, defined "electronic publishing" narrowly and might have been interpreted to exclude the electronic publishing activities of AAP members, thus cutting AAP member publishers off from legislative safeguards. AAP, working with the Association of American University Presses and others, succeeded in having a more comprehensive definition of electronic publishing incorporated in committee.

Failure of the 103rd Congress to act on the legislation was not good news for publishers. At present, as a result of action by the federal courts, the RBOCs are free to enter into electronic publishing services. Without legislation, there are no safeguards in place against anticompetitive behavior. Republicans are expected to try to enact a major telecommunications bill in 1995, and AAP will continue its efforts to ensure that it contains a definition of electronic publishing comprehensive enough to protect its members' interests.

Funding Programs and Grant-Making Agencies

National Endowment for the Humanities

Old Post Office, 1100 Pennsylvania Ave. N.W., Washington, DC 20506
202-606-8438

Thomas C. Phelps
Humanities Project in Libraries and Archives

The National Endowment for the Humanities (NEH) is an independent grant-making agency of the federal government, created by Congress in 1965. It supports exemplary work to advance and disseminate knowledge in all the disciplines of the humanities. Endowment support is intended to complement and assist private and local efforts and to serve as a catalyst to increase nonfederal support for projects of high quality. Although the activities funded by the endowment vary greatly in cost, in numbers of people involved, and in their specific intents and benefits, all activities have in common two requirements for funding: significance to learning in the humanities and excellence in conception.

In general terms, NEH supports research, education, and public understanding of the humanities through grants to individuals, organizations, and institutions. The endowment's outreach mission is to ensure that all the American people participate fully in the humanities. Through outreach and grant-making activities, NEH provides information about its grant opportunities, promotes participation in NEH-funded projects and programs, and encourages examination of the diversity and richness of the American cultural heritage.

NEH grant-making operations are conducted through four major divisions: the Division of Public Programs, the Division of Preservation and Access, the Division of Research Programs, and the Division of Education Programs. Other grants are made through the Federal/State Partnership, which supports humanities councils in the 50 states, the District of Columbia, Puerto Rico, the U.S. Virgin Islands, the Northern Mariana Islands, American Samoa, and Guam. Grants are also made to nonprofit institutions interested in developing new sources of long-term support for educational, scholarly, preservation, and public programs in the humanities through Challenge Grant Opportunities.

Division of Public Programs

The division of Public Programs endeavors to fulfill NEH's mandate to foster public appreciation and understanding of the humanities. It includes programs that assist institutions and organizations—such as public, college and university, and special libraries and library associations—in developing projects for presentation to general public audiences. The division's mission is "to enrich individual lives, enhance the common good, and promote effective citizenship by enabling people to assess ideas and values." The goals are "to give access to public humanities programs to all Americans, to offer excellence in programming, to exhibit national leadership in the realm of public humanities, and to encourage the educational role of cultural institutions and organizations."

The division is composed of four programs: Museums and Historical Organizations, Media, Public Humanities Projects, and Libraries and Archives. The single program within the division that supports libraries directly is Humanities Projects in Libraries and Archives, although other programs offer indirect support.

Humanities Projects in Libraries and Archives encourages all types of libraries to plan and present humanities programs in many different formats. Libraries and archives acquire and preserve records of the world's cultural heritage and make them accessible to everyone in many forms using various technologies and varieties of public service. Beyond their intrinsic importance as repositories of resources vital to scholars, libraries and archives also offer settings to which different audiences may be drawn to learn about the humanities. These institutions may also create programs to reach those far outside their walls, perhaps to inner-city or isolated rural sites through larger statewide, regional, or national projects. Above all, libraries, archives, and other community and cultural organizations that may join them as cosponsors of programs must create welcoming environments to challenge the minds of those not enrolled in educational institutions; exploration of the varieties of human experience can and should be a lifelong pursuit open to all. Humanities Projects in Libraries and Archives supports programs designed to stimulate public understanding of the humanities disciplines as tools that anyone may use to interpret and illuminate what it means to be human, through activities based on books and other resources available from libraries and archives.

Project and program formats vary, encompassing such activities as reading and media discussion groups; lecture series; live or broadcast conferences for laypersons; professional development seminars for those who will lead public programs (including archivists and librarians); and interpretive exhibitions of books, documents, manuscripts, or other library or archival materials. Professionals in the field are encouraged to work together with humanities scholars, public programming or media or exhibition specialists, community groups, and leaders of other types of cultural institutions. Previously underserved audiences can be reached when organizations with different constituencies combine forces to design and offer programs. Partnerships might unite, among others, such institutions as public, academic, or special libraries; archives, museums, and historical societies; civic groups, community centers, churches, or retirement communities. Project activities may take place at locations other than libraries or archives so long as library and archival resources provide the intellectual substance of the programs.

Applicants for support of such projects are urged to consider carefully the most appropriate means of implementing their programs in libraries and archives and to discuss them with NEH staff. Projects should involve librarians and the active collaboration of scholars from the appropriate disciplines of the humanities during both the planning and presentation of the programs. Programs should create an opportunity for thoughtful examination of scholarship or a dialogue between the scholarly community and the public based on the existing collection of humanities resources held in libraries and archives. Programs should include the active use of such collections and fulfill those parts of any library's mission having to do with the education of constituent users. Humanities Projects in Libraries and Archives also encourages libraries to design out-of-school projects for young people. By involving youth in projects, libraries can help them to acquire and apply new knowledge and skills in the disciplines of the humanities. Projects for this age group are intended to encourage a lifelong interest in the humanities on the part of young people by introducing them to the range of resources and activities in the humanities that are available to them through collections found in libraries and archives.

The following are examples of such projects:

- Based on the successful, NEH-supported exhibition at the Newberry Library, the American Library Association (ALA) received an award of $375,000 to mount a traveling panel exhibition and develop thematic units for reading and discussion programs at 45 libraries throughout the country. Two stories—historian Frederick Jackson Turner's account of free land and the peaceful settlement of the West and Buffalo Bill Cody's interpretation in his Wild West Show of the violent conquest of the West—were the focus of the traveling exhibition. The exhibition examines how a belief in the significance of the frontier emerged as an all-important part of American identity. Using the two stories as its organizational basis, the exhibition explains how the stories merged, passed into history, and still occupy an enduring and influential place in our national memory. There will be curriculum guides and training sessions for site librarians as well as reading and discussion programs of such books as Faragher's biography *Daniel Boone*; Russell's *The Lives and Legends of Buffalo Bill*; Slotkin's *Gunfighter Nations: The Myth of the Frontier in Twentieth-Century America*; and Turner's essay "The Significance of the Frontier in American History."
- Reading and discussion programs in libraries on all of the Hawaiian Islands about tradition, story, values, and language found in children's literature are supported by a grant of $165,000. The programs center on such themes as sharing traditions, telling stories, and using language. At libraries in Hawaii, scholars from various humanities disciplines work with parents, grandparents, guardians, and children, as well as teachers, caregivers, and librarians, to discover how values inherent in children's literature are expressed and how they in turn broaden and enrich everyday

activities. In Hawaii, these programs naturally bring together people of diverse backgrounds to read and discuss such works as *St. George and the Dragon*, *Saturnalia*, and *Night Journey*, as well as works by Newbery Award-winning author Paul Fleishman and by Caldecott Medal-winning illustrator Trina Schart Hyman, both of whom will be guest speakers at the programs.

- The Four County Library System in Vestal, New York, received an award of $190,000 in support of book and video discussion programs about American economic, social, and intellectual life in the 20th century. Themes at these programs in libraries throughout the state of New York include, among others, "Religion and the Search for Values," "Rediscovering the Landscape," "Being American," "Working Lives," "Twentieth Century Immigration," "Literature of the '20s and '30s," and "Literary Outsiders: Contemporary Voices." Most of these programs take place in libraries in isolated rural locations.

Division of Preservation and Access

Grants are made from this division to institutions for projects that will preserve and increase the availability of resources important for research, education, and public programming in the humanities. Resources may include books, journals, newspapers, manuscripts and other archival materials, maps, photographs, film, sound recordings, and objects of material culture held by libraries, archives, museums, historical organizations, and other repositories.

The division accepts applications that address problems of preservation and access from a variety of perspectives. Support may be sought for:

- Microfilming projects conducted by individual libraries and archives or by institutions acting as a consortium
- The conservation treatment of endangered materials where conversions to a more stable medium is not appropriate
- Projects to preserve material-culture collections
- Projects that will provide intellectual access to textual and nontextual collections
- Education and training projects on a regional or national level
- The work of regional preservation services
- The preparation of statewide preservation plans
- Research and demonstration projects to improve procedures and technology
- Projects involving issues of national significance to the library and archives field

Proposals may combine preservation and access activities.

Through awards from this division, NEH established the National Heritage Preservation Program to support efforts to stabilize material culture collections important to the humanities through the appropriate housing and storage of objects, improved climate control, and the installation of security, lighting, and fire prevention systems. Grants are also available to establish regional or national training programs for the care and conservation of material-culture collections, as well as for projects that will document collections significant to the humanities.

Support for access projects can involve the arrangement and description of archival and manuscript collections; archival surveys; the cataloging of graphic, film, sound, or artifact collections; the bibliographic control of printed works; the microfilming of collections in non-U.S. repositories; the preparation of oral histories; and the exploration of issues that have a national impact on the library and archival fields.

These are some examples:

- The Amigos Bibliographic Council Inc. received $498,247 to support the Regional Field Service Program, which provides surveys of preservation needs, workshops and seminars, and technical consultations to libraries and archives in the Southwest.

- About 6,800 titles of newspapers in Boston repositories are being catalogued and made available in the OCLC (Online Computer Library Center) database because of a $304,057 grant made to the Boston Public Library to support the further implementation of the U.S. Newspaper Program in Massachusetts.

- To support planning for Michigan's participation in the U.S. Newspaper Project, the Library of Michigan in Lansing was awarded $32,354. With this support, repositories in the state will be surveyed for their newspaper holdings, and the staff of the library will develop a plan for cataloguing and microfilming them.

- The arrangement and description of the archives of the Pullman Palace Car Company, 1865–1981, which include the personal and financial papers of George M. Pullman, will be completed with support in the amount of $231,222 awarded to the Newberry Library in Chicago.

- The Pittsburgh Regional Library Center was awarded $86,880 to support a regional preservation services program, which will provide educational and information services for libraries and archives in western Pennsylvania, West Virginia, and western Maryland.

- Preservation microfilming of 10,350 brittle volumes and repair of 3,000 additional books from the library's collections of political and intellectual history and Slavic and East European literatures was initiated by the University of Michigan libraries with an award of $970,502 from NEH.

Division of Research Programs

The Division of Research Programs provides support for the preparation for publication of editions, translations, and other important works in the humanities; the preparation of reference materials; the conduct of large or complex interpretive studies; research conferences; and research opportunities offered through independent research centers (many of which are libraries) and scholarly organizations. The Editions, Translations, and Reference Materials Programs within the division are of particular interest to libraries and librarians.

The Editions Program supports various stages in the preparation of authoritative and annotated editions of works and documents valuable to both scholars and general readers and generally accessible through libraries. The Translations Program supports individual or collaborative projects to translate into English works that provide insight into the history, literature, philosophy, and artistic achievements of other cultures. The Reference Materials Program supports the preparation of works that will enhance the availability of information and research materials, such as dictionaries, atlases, encyclopedias, concordances, reference grammars, databases, text bases, and other projects that will provide essential scholarly tools for libraries.

These are examples of projects that won grants:

- The preparation of a catalog of 300 medieval and Renaissance manuscripts in the Plimpton Collection was supported by a grant of $89,760 to the Columbia University Library.
- With a grant of $28,160, Stanford University planned and presented a conference to enhance access to Russian archives through the Research Libraries Information Network.
- An online bibliography of published works for theater research, a comprehensive database of references to current theater-related periodicals and books published around the world was supported with a grant of $140,000 to the CUNY/Brooklyn College Library.
- The University of California at Riverside Library was awarded $600,000 to support the continued preparation of the *Eighteenth-Century Short-Title Catalogue*, which records all publications produced in Great Britain and its dependencies during the years 1701–1800.

Division of Education

Libraries may receive Division of Education Programs grants directly or may be part of a college or university effort to strengthen teaching in the humanities. Direct grants to libraries usually support humanities institutes at which elementary and secondary school teachers or college and university faculty use the library's resources as part of a program of study directed by recognized scholars.

Office of Challenge Grants

Libraries are eligible for support within the Challenge Grant Program. By inviting libraries to appeal to a broader funding public, challenge grants assist them to increase long-term financial stability and capital support and thereby improve the quality of humanities activities and collections. To receive each federal dollar, a challenge grant recipient must raise $3 to $4 from nonfederal funding sources. Both federal and nonfederal funds may be used to support the costs of renovation and construction and the purchase of equipment and the acquisition of collections. Funds may also be invested in interest-bearing accounts to ensure annual revenues to support educational programs in the humanities in perpetuity. Awards in this category are limited to two per institution; second awards require the 4:1 match.

These are examples:

- The Wittenberg University Library in Springfield, Ohio, received a $200,000 challenge grant to support collection development and cataloging to establish an endowment for humanities acquisitions in the university library.
- The New Orleans Public Library received a $200,000 challenge grant to support the endowment of acquisitions in Louisiana history, culture, and literature, ethnic history and culture, and literary criticism, as well as to support public programs such as exhibits and reading and discussion programs.
- An endowment for five research fellowships, two internships in archival conservation and management, and staff positions was supported by a $1,000,000 challenge grant to the New York State Archives.
- The Corpus Christi (TX) Public Library received a $75,000 challenge grant to support an endowment for the acquisition of humanities materials.

Office of Federal/State Partnership

NEH Endowment annually makes awards to state humanities councils in the 50 states, the District of Columbia, Puerto Rico, the U.S. Virgin Islands, Guam, American Samoa, and the Northern Marianas. The state councils, in turn, award grants to institutions and organizations within each state or territory according to guidelines and application deadlines determined by each council. Most grants are for projects that promote or foster public understanding and appreciation of the humanities. Many awards are made to libraries for such projects. Guidelines and application deadlines may be obtained by contacting the appropriate state or territorial council directly. A list of state councils follows.

Office of Publications and Public Affairs

For publications or information about any NEH divisions, offices, or programs, contact the Public Information Office at 1100 Pennsylvania Ave., N.W., Room 407, Washington, DC 20506 (202-606-8438).

State Humanities Councils

Alabama Humanities Foundation
2217 Tenth Ct. S.
Birmingham, AL 35205
205-930-0540

Alaska Humanities Forum
430 W. Seventh Ave., Suite 1
Anchorage, AK 99501
907-272-5341

Arizona Humanities Council
Ellis-Shackelford House
1242 N. Central Ave.
Phoenix, AZ 85004
602-257-0335

Arkansas Humanities Council
10816 Executive Center Dr., Suite 310
Little Rock, AR 72211-4383
501-221-0091

California Council for the Humanities
312 Sutter St., Suite 601
San Francisco, CA 94108
415-391-1474

Colorado Endowment for the Humanities
1623 Blake St., Suite 200
Denver, CO 80202
303-573-7733

Connecticut Humanities Council
41 Lawn Ave., Wesleyan Sta.
Middletown, CT 06459
203-685-2260

Delaware Humanities Forum
1812 Newport Gap Pike
Wilmington, DE 19808-6179
302-633-2400

D.C. Community Humanities Council
1331 H St. N.W., Suite 902
Washington, DC 20005
202-347-1732

Florida Humanities Council
1514 1/2 E. Eighth Ave.
Tampa, FL 33605-3708
813-272-3473

Georgia Humanities Council
50 Hurt Plaza S.E., Suite 440
Atlanta, GA 30303-2936
404-523-6220

Hawaii Committee for the Humanities
First Hawaiian Bank Bldg.
3599 Wai'alae Ave., Rm. 23
Honolulu, HI 96816
808-732-5402

Idaho Humanities Council
217 W. State St.
Boise, ID 83702
208-345-5346

Illinois Humanities Council
618 S. Michigan Ave.
Chicago, IL 60605
312-939-5212

Indiana Humanities Council
1500 N. Delaware St.
Indianapolis, IN 46202
317-638-1500

Iowa Humanities Board
Oakdale Campus N210 OH
Univ. of Iowa
Iowa City, IA 52242
319-335-4153

Kansas Humanities Council
112 S.W. Sixth Ave., Suite 210
Topeka, KS 66603
913-357-0359

Kentucky Humanities Council
417 Clifton Ave.
Univ. of Kentucky
Lexington, KY 40508-3406
606-257-5932

Louisiana Endowment for the Humanities
1001 Howard Ave., Suite 3110
New Orleans, LA 70113
504-523-4352

Maine Humanities Council
371 Cumberland Ave.
Portland, ME 04112
207-773-5051

Maryland Humanities Council
601 N. Howard St.
Baltimore, MD 21201-4585
410-625-4830

Massachusetts Foundation for the Humanities
One Woodbridge St.
South Hadley, MA 01075
413-536-1385

Michigan Humanities Council
119 Pere Marquette Dr., Suite 3B
Lansing, MI 48912-1231
517-372-7770

Minnesota Humanities Commission
26 E. Exchange St., Lower Level S.
Saint Paul, MN 55101
612-224-5739

Mississippi Humanities Council
3825 Ridgewood Rd., Rm. 311
Jackson, MS 39211
601-982-6752

Missouri Humanities Council
911 Washington Ave., Suite 215
Saint Louis, MO 63101-1208
314-621-7705

Montana Committee for the Humanities
Box 8036, Hellgate Sta.
Missoula, MT 59807
406-243-6022

Nebraska Humanities Council
Lincoln Center Bldg., Suite 225
215 Centennial Mall S.
Lincoln, NE 68508
402-474-2131

Nevada Humanities Committee
Box 8029
Reno, NV 89507
702-784-6587

New Hampshire Humanities Council
19 Pillsbury St.
Box 2228
Concord, NH 03302-2228
603-224-4071

New Jersey Committee for the Humanities
390 George St., Suite 602
New Brunswick, NJ 08901-2019
908-932-7726

New Mexico Endowment for the Humanities
Onate Hall, Rm. 209
Univ. of New Mexico
Albuquerque, NM 87131
505-277-3705

New York Council for the Humanities
198 Broadway, 10th fl.
New York, NY 10038
212-233-1131

North Carolina Humanities Council
425 Spring Garden St.
Greensboro, NC 27401
910-334-5325

North Dakota Humanities Council
2900 Broadway E., Suite 3
Box 2191
Bismarck, ND 58502
701-255-3360

Ohio Humanities Council
695 Bryden Rd.
Box 06354
Columbus, OH 43206-0354
614-461-7802

Oklahoma Foundation for the Humanities
Festival Plaza
428 W. California, Suite 270
Oklahoma City, OK 73102
405-235-0280

Oregon Council for the Humanities
812 S.W. Washington St., Suite 225
Portland, OR 97205
503-241-0543

Pennsylvania Humanities Council
320 Walnut St., Suite 305
Philadelphia, PA 19106
215-925-1005

Rhode Island Committee for the Humanities
60 Ship St.
Providence, RI 02903
401-273-2250

South Carolina Humanities Council
1200 Catawba St.
Columbia, SC 29250
803-771-8864

South Dakota Humanities Council
Box 7050, Univ. Sta.
Brookings, SD 57007
605-688-6113

Tennessee Humanities Council
1003 18th Ave. S.
Nashville, TN 37202
615-320-7001

Texas Committee for the Humanities
Banister Pl. A
3809 S. Second St.
Austin, TX 78704
512-440-1991

Utah Humanities Council
350 S. 400 E., Suite 110
Salt Lake City, UT 84111-2946
801-531-7868

Vermont Council on the Humanities
Main St., Box 58
Hyde Park, VT 05655
802-888-3183

Virginia Foundation for the Humanities and
Public Policy
145 Ednam Dr.
Charlottesville, VA 22903-4629
804-924-3296

Washington Commission for the Humanities
615 Second Ave., Suite 300
Seattle, WA 98104
206-682-1770

West Virginia Humanities Council
723 Kanawha Blvd., E. Suite 800
Charleston, WV 25301
304-346-8500

Wisconsin Humanities Council
802 Regent St.
Madison, WI 53715
608-262-0706

Wyoming Council for the Humanities
Box 3643, Univ. Sta.

Laramie, WY 82071-3643
307-766-6496

American Samoa
American Samoa Humanities Planning Group
Box 1935
Department of Education
Pago Pago, AS 96799
684-633-4255

Guam Humanities Council
Renaissance Plaza
272 W. Rte. 8, Suite 2A
Barrigada, GU 96921
671-734-1713

Commonwealth of the Northern Mariana
Islands Council for the Humanities
AAA 3394, Box 10001
Saipan, MP 96950
670-235-4785

Fundación Puertorriqueña de las
Humanidades
Box S-4307
Old San Juan, PR 00904
809-721-2087

Virgin Islands Humanities Council
Box 1829
Saint Thomas, VI 00803-1829
809-776-4044

Council on Library Resources, 1994

1400 16th St. N.W., Suite 510, Washington, DC 20036
202-483-7474

Ellen B. Timmer
Publications Consultant

The Council on Library Resources (CLR) is an exempt operating foundation established in 1956 to "aid in the solution of library problems; to conduct research in, develop, and demonstrate new techniques and methods; and to disseminate through any means the results thereof." The council awards grants and contracts to institutions and individuals, with the objective of helping to find solutions to the generic problems of libraries and information services. In addition, as an operating foundation, the council directs its own projects. It often performs a catalytic role by bringing individuals and organizations together to define problems and help determine priorities for action in the council's areas of interest. Areas currently receiving the most attention include human resources, the economics of information services, infrastructure, and access and processing. In addition to the general program grants, the council continues to sponsor the CLR Fellows program and the Cooperative Research program, both of which encourage research projects and the development of research skills by individual professionals.

Support is not provided for construction or renovation, collection acquisitions, routine operating costs, activities judged to be of limited influence, or work that essentially repeats previous research. CLR does not fund indirect costs or, with rare exceptions, equipment purchases.

The board of directors consists of individuals from libraries, academic institutions, the business community, and the professions. As of June 30, 1994, council officers were Martin M. Cummings, chairperson; William N. Hubbard, Jr., vice chairperson; W. David Penniman, president; and Mary Agnes Thompson, secretary and treasurer. (In late 1994 it was announced that Deanna B. Marcum would succeed David Penniman.) During the fiscal year ending June 30, 1994, the council received support for its activities from the William and Flora Hewlett Foundation, the W. K. Kellogg Foundation, and the Andrew W. Mellon Foundation.

Highlights of FY 1994

As indicated by its name, the Council on Library Resources is primarily concerned with helping libraries make optimum use of their resources in order to provide the best service possible to their users. The council considers the term "library" to include any institution concerned with management, stewardship, and support of the delivery of information resources. Increasing economic and technological challenges compel the leaders and staff of those institutions to take a new look at how they can efficiently manage the resources available to them, no matter how extensive or limited those resources may be. In FY 1994 CLR took a look at some of the changes occurring to library resources, including new formats of materials; the globalization and commercialization of information services; increased use of contracted services; self-sufficient and demanding users; a changing workforce; a wide variety of information delivery systems; an increasing number of networks and collaborative activities (along with a need for space to accommodate these activities); the increasing importance of systems rather than buildings; and a decreased availability of funds coupled with an increased demand for accountability. Although there are many kinds of "library resources" the council has chosen to direct its energies to four areas of library resources: human resources, economic resources, community resources (i.e., infrastructure), and resources of services (access and processing). Our distinctive challenge is to provide support to the library community in general to address the changing nature of those resources in broad, but useful, terms. The following four sections describe CLR's current program areas and discuss some of the grants awarded or active in FY 1994.

Human Resources

The focus of the council's human resources program is to encourage the development of the next generation of leaders who will build and manage the information support systems needed by society. In addition, the council continues to look for ways to assist current library leaders to transform their institutions in response to the changing needs of their communities. This program area emphasizes leadership and management development, recruitment, education (including continuing education), and research.

With support from the W. K. Kellogg Foundation, the council is embarking on a major program to address information services leadership issues for the future. The Kellogg Foundation is supporting more than three years of CLR efforts to build networks, foster dialogue, and develop leaders within the library and information science community. This program is just beginning and will attempt to articulate the role and function of libraries within the evolving information infrastructure, identify how best to train library leaders to participate in and influence public dialogue, and explore the educational issues related to developing new leaders. The program will identify innovative individuals and programs and will encourage the transfer of successful efforts to other environments. Planned program activities include convening meetings and developing human networks to share information about common problems and possible solutions. Leadership development planning activities such as mentor, fellowship, and recruitment programs will also take place.

New college library directors are learning from the experience of seasoned directors by participating in the CLR-supported College Library Director Mentor Program. The new directors also benefit from the camaraderie fostered by the program. Through the efforts of the Leadership Committee of the College Libraries Section, Association of College and Research Libraries, 15 pairs of mentors and new directors took part in the program during 1993–1994. Program coordinator is Larry Hardesty, director of library services, Eckerd College. The council provided financial resources for the first two years of the College Library Director Mentor Program and, in the spring of 1994, approved a grant to extend the program for two more years.

Activities in the area of library and information science education included publication of the analytical bibliography *The Future of Education for Librarianship: Looking Forward from the Past,* produced by the Palmer School of Library and Information Science, Long Island University (Anne Woodsworth, principal investigator), with CLR support. The bibliography addresses topics such as accreditation, curriculum, continuing education, interdisciplinary linkages, international perspectives, recruitment, specialization, technology, and theory versus practice. The analysis of the literature revealed a lack of vision regarding the future of education for the field.

The Graduate School of Library and Information Studies at Queens College/City University of New York completed a CLR-funded series of seminars/workshops on multiculturalism and diversity in libraries. The purpose of the workshops was to gather library and information science professionals and educators to discuss the implications of social change on the clientele, operations, services, and collections of libraries and information centers. The seminar discussions did not result in suggestions for significant changes in the curriculum, but rather suggestions for the addition of multicultural elements to the existing curriculum.

The council received several reports on CLR-supported research projects. Topics included equal opportunity and affirmative-action guidelines; a methodology analyzing the degree of similarities in job content of positions in libraries and academic computing centers; a series of interactive training modules in preservation management for use in Southeast Asia and the Pacific regions; an overview of the field of preservation education; and standards for ethical conduct for rare-book librarians.

Economic Data

The council's economics program serves as a focal point for the investigation and discussion of how libraries can allocate their financial resources to maximize the benefits of the services provided. Determining how best to invest limited resources is a major challenge for libraries today. The desire to provide new services, the multiple formats for information delivery, and the need to update or acquire new technologies to meet service demands continue to put a strain on library budgets. In addition, the price escalation of scholarly journals, particularly in the science and technology fields, has contributed in large measure to the economic crisis faced by many libraries.

The studies in the economics program area continue the focus on microeconomic issues. The topics addressed in the 1994 program included document delivery, serial pricing, costs of networked information, cost/benefit analyses, and assessment. The council continues to emphasize the application of total quality management tools for the improvement of library operations.

The North American Interlibrary Loan and Document Delivery (NAILDD) Project was launched by the Association of Research Libraries (ARL) as one response to the need to reconceptualize interlibrary loan and document delivery services. CLR provided partial support for an ARL Visiting Program Officer to coordinate the initiative. The ARL Committee on Access to Information Resources is spearheading the effort in collaboration with a broad group of library vendors, software developers, document delivery suppliers, and libraries. The project seeks to promote developments that will facilitate the delivery of materials to users at costs that are sustainable to libraries.

The State University of New York University Center Libraries at Albany, Binghamton, Buffalo, and Stony Brook are studying the costs of access compared with the costs of ownership for selected high-cost research journals. The CLR-funded study is using a theoretical economic model that will help to determine cost savings, financial efficiency, and economic efficiency of local ownership compared with document delivery via a consortium of the SUNY University Center Libraries or commercial supply/delivery services. The study will use the economic models and data collected to develop two cost-benefit analyses of document delivery.

The Coalition for Networked Information (CNI) is investigating the life cycle of the scholarly and scientific communication process to identify the cost centers that will be most affected by the increased significance of networks and networked information. They also will recommend some strategies for measuring those effects over time. The cost center analysis and measurement strategies developed for this study will serve as a baseline for tracking trends in the scholarly communication process.

Investigators at the School of Communication, Information and Library Studies, Rutgers University, are developing guidelines and a workbook to enable other libraries inexpensively to survey the positive impacts (i.e., benefits) they have on their communities of users. This CLR-supported research study is breaking new ground by developing a taxonomy, or classification, of benefits in a language that users themselves provide. The analysis of the interviews with faculty members and students is providing the necessary working language upon which the taxonomy will be based.

A seminar on assessment factors for academic libraries was sponsored by the Graduate School of Library and Information Science, University of Texas; Texas A&M University; and CLR. Assessment was defined as affixing a value for the purpose of determining how well libraries are meeting the needs of their users. The purpose of the meeting was to identify those factors that are not solely quantitative in nature. A preliminary list of assessment factors was identified and is being further developed by meeting participants.

With a grant from the council, the Association of Research Libraries is testing the applicability of benchmarking methodologies in an academic library environment by examining three interlibrary loan subprocesses: borrowing, lending, and delivery. A smallscale study of three institutions will lead to the development of a dynamic model of procedures that can be refined or adapted by other members of the academic library community.

The First International Conference on TQM and Academic Libraries was held in April and was sponsored by the ARL's Office of Management Services and the Wayne State University Libraries, with some support from CLR. More than 140 participants attended the conference to learn from experts and to exchange ideas about how best to implement continuous improvement methods in academic libraries.

Infrastructure

Infrastructure resources are those systems, services, and facilities that are drawn upon to help libraries and other information services operate more efficiently and effectively. Through its infrastructure program area, CLR tries to establish continuing communication and cooperation among the various information systems and services that support our libraries and to ensure that economic, sociopolitical, technical, and legal changes do not inhibit library functions or access to information by individuals and groups. The council is interested particularly in finding the key points at which it can help strengthen the information infrastructure.

The council continued its activities this year to encourage a national engineering information initiative (NEII). This initiative is intended to improve access to engineering information in libraries and specialized information services in the United States. Although some progress has been made, it was decided that an organization other than CLR would be better equipped to lead this effort. However, the council did fund some specific projects related to the NEII efforts. For example, the Cornell University Engineering Library is maintaining servers for engineering information on Internet. Project ICE (Internet Connections for Engineering) is organizing network resources for easy browsing and searching and making them accessible via gopher and World-Wide Web Internet servers. This project is intended to help demonstrate the range and accessibility of information available to the engineering community.

The Aerospace Knowledge Diffusion Research Project is investigating the production, transfer, and use of scientific and technical information (STI) for aerospace engineering. The project is providing descriptive and analytical data regarding the flow of SI at the individual, organizational, national, and international levels. A portion of the work is being conducted with CLR funding by the Center for Survey Research at Indiana University. The results will provide valuable baseline data about needs, preferences, and expectations regarding technical communication and library use.

Investigators from the University of Tennessee Center for Information Studies are examining the topic of information needs and information-seeking habits in engineering. They are developing an annotated bibliography, to be published by the council, that will provide documentation on the use of information by engineers and scientists.

Several years ago, CLR made four strategic planning grants to Columbia University, Harvard University, the State University of New York University Center Libraries, and the Triangle Research Libraries Network as part of the program "Setting Library Policies and Priorities in Research Universities." In the fall of 1993, with most of the projects nearing completion, the council convened a meeting of project participants to discuss the outcomes of their planning activities. An evening group discussion concentrated on how the results of the planning activity have changed the way the libraries operate. A second group discussion focused on the planning activity itself and how it was conducted within the institutions. Some of the benefits of the planning process include an acknowledgment of the leadership role that librarians can take in institutional planning and the ability to strengthen each library's relationship with its administration.

The results of the strategic planning grants made by the council to research libraries demonstrate the importance of intra-institutional planning. In Maryland, Towson State University is beginning a strategic planning process to integrate information resources within the campus planning context, focusing on information management and literacy. Included in the planning process is an assessment and documentation of the information needs of and current technologies available to the campus community, a definition of strategies for developing the information resources and technologies of the university, and establishment of a feedback and planning process for adjusting strategies as needs and technologies change.

Representatives of national library and information associations met in September 1993 to discuss their common interests in policy issues related to the national information infrastructure (NII). The group reached consensus on some key principles related to First Amendment, privacy, intellectual property, ubiquity, equitable access, and interoperability issues. The representatives agreed that libraries will play several key roles in the evolving national information infrastructure, including providing and consuming information, protecting public access, and serving as a source for public access. CLR provided support for the production and distribution of the brochure *Principles for the Development of the National Information Infrastructure* and the meeting's proceedings.

To address tensions between librarians and publishers over the costs of scholarly communication, a Joint Working Group on Professional and Scholarly Information in the Electronic Age was established by CLR and the Association of American Publishers (AAP) to discuss the functions that publishers and librarians perform, how each group adds value to the information it handles, how key economic issues challenge both old and new ways of doing business, and how electronic delivery of information may change traditional roles and economics. The Joint Working Group hopes that one result of these deliberations will be a wider and more complete understanding by all segments of the academic community of the roles and tasks undertaken by publishers and librarians.

A CLR-funded survey of the attitudes of municipal and county officials toward public libraries in the areas of services, value, and funding will be conducted by the Library Research Center, University of Illinois at Urbana-Champaign. This will be a national survey, based on a stratified random sample of municipal officials, and should provide the library community with useful information about issues of funding for library services by local government entities.

CLR's support for the Robert Vosper IFLA Fellows Program took on special significance with the death of Robert G. Vosper in May 1994. Dr. Vosper, a long-time member of the council's board of directors and an honorary fellow of IFLA (International Federation of Library Associations and Institutions), was pleased to have his name linked to a program that focused on supporting library leadership at the international level and was proud of the accomplishments of those selected to participate in the program. Project reports were received in 1994 on preservation education, cataloging in publication, and Western literature availability in Polish libraries.

Access and Processing

Throughout its history, CLR has continually sought ways to improve the methods by which libraries acquire, organize, store, retrieve, reproduce, and make available information for efficient use by the communities they serve. CLR considers library resources to consist not only of collections of materials but also of information services; both are used to help users answer questions and solve problems or to assist users in professional or personal development. CLR's access and processing program looks for new approaches to enhance access to information and encourages improvement in the internal processes performed by libraries so that the resources invested in libraries are used more efficiently and effectively.

CLR contracted with the University of Michigan School of Information and Library Studies to conduct an analytical review of the literature. The purpose of the review was to note the trends, topics, issues, and concerns identified by the many individuals writing about the library of the future. Included in the report, *Analytical Review of the Library of the Future* (published by the council), is a collection of definitions, overviews of current technologies and tools, a discussion of digital library models, brief descriptions of some active projects, and a concluding section that discusses the future. Because a review of this type could never be entirely comprehensive, the document was made available both in print and electronically, with the expectation that readers would continue to add their own references to the bibliography.

Researchers at Indiana University of Pennsylvania completed a CLR-supported research project concerned with developing an online catalog search system that incorporates aids for clustering and organizing useful retrieval sets. With each step of the project, the feasibility of the concept of clustering has been tested and the limitations imposed by different hardware and software configurations have been examined. The final report recommends that systems can improve subject access for the user with the following techniques: increased use of classification systems and associated data, weighting terms by the strength of their contribution to the "aboutness" of an item, filtering, faceting based on subdivision of subject headings, truncation options, and sorting options.

Researchers at the University of California, Santa Cruz, reported on the results of their CLR-supported study to analyze search behavior of remote users of the University of California MELVYL® Library System. Transaction logs provided data on the number and type of searches done by remote users, their choice of search mode, the database selected, the number of retrievals, the number and type of errors, and their use of help functions. Although brief known-item searching seemed to be effective for 40 percent of the users, the remaining 60 percent conducted longer search sessions that did not appear to be as successful. The investigators concluded that more and better design elements that guide or lead users are needed. Research in this area continues this year with an examination of the behavior of in-library users of public access catalogs.

A report by the Japan Information Access Project on access to and use of Japanese information argues that yesterday's conventional wisdom suggesting a lack of interest in Japanese information has been replaced, and today's users, who are discipline oriented, recognize that information from Japan is a part of the larger corpus of knowledge. The report includes an essay, recommendations, and selected papers from a symposium on Japanese Information: Access, Use and Demand, held February 25, 1992, with partial support from the council.

In February 1993, a Cooperative Cataloging Council (CCC) was formed and charged itself to develop a useful strategic plan for increasing the effectiveness of cooperative cataloging among the nation's libraries. CCC established issue-oriented task groups to focus on specific goals and/or objectives defined by the CCC members; the council provided support for their meetings. The task force reports and subsequent discussions with CCC have led to a new, shared vision for cooperative cataloging. A strategic plan for the next five years was developed and was widely disseminated to the library community. CCC is working on governance issues and has established additional task forces to address specific questions; active monitoring is under way by members.

At the University of California, Riverside, a CLR-supported study analyzed the varying catalog rules used to create bibliographic records for materials of the Hand Press Era, 1450–1825. This study was conducted to determine the feasibility of creating a cooperative European database and union catalog of such materials. Twenty-eight members of the Consortium of European Research Libraries selected the Research Libraries Group to supply database support for this union catalog.

At the Institute of Arctic and Alpine Research, University of Colorado, CLR supported the development of a plan for distributing the responsibilities among libraries and information providers to provide access to polar literature. The plan was needed to address the problem of uneven bibliographic coverage of the literature. Included in the plan are a final core list of polar-regions journals, results of analysis of the library catalog statistics and overlapping coverage in databases, and recommendations for action. As a result of the project, negotiations are already under way to reduce duplication in the indexing of the literature.

A Robert Vosper IFLA Fellow surveyed CIP (cataloging in publication) programs in several countries to investigate their progress over the last 20 years, the nature of the bibliographic data being recorded, and what trends can be determined for the future. Although national bibliographic agencies play a valuable role by continuing to contribute standardized bibliographic descriptions, the increase of publications in both scope and format creates a large demand on their services and strains their resources. The report notes that progress in automation and telecommunications technologies may provide a means to decentralize some of the CIP responsibilities and includes a suggested plan for implementation of a CIP program in Romania.

Another study conducted under the auspices of the council's IFLA Vosper Fellows Program includes the results of an investigation of the availability of Western periodical literature in Polish research libraries from 1980 to 1991. Although most collections were small, they did seem to meet their users' needs. Bibliographic access was found to be unsatisfactory, and recommendations for technical, political, and management improvements are included in the final report.

The Working Group on Form and Genre Vocabularies meets annually to continue the process of rationalization of form and genre terminologies in major thesauri. CLR is providing partial support for these meetings, which are being held in August of each year at the offices of the Art and Architecture Thesaurus (AAT). Participants include representatives of the major published vocabularies that include form and genre terms.

Under the direction of the unified Agricultural Thesaurus Project Team (with membership from the National Agricultural Library and international organizations), a study was conducted with CLR support to determine the means to solve the problems of duplication of effort in thesaurus maintenance and the complexity of searching agricultural materials. An analysis of existing systems was conducted, and the report includes a recommendation for a new system and a proposed governance structure to manage a unified thesaurus.

Cornell University has been producing high-resolution digital copies of original images held in their Division of Rare and Manuscript Collections. To investigate how such images can be included in the research and teaching process, CLR is providing partial support for the development of a multimedia collection access tool. The project will support the design and development of remote access to these images by faculty, staff, and students and will evaluate the effectiveness of such access. While some projects utilize single-purpose applications, this project proposes to address the potential of the digital library, not by prescribing the application, but by letting the users themselves explore the variety of information resources available to create their own compositions.

CLR supported the development at Northwestern University of a prototype workstation that provides an academic library user with easier access to multiple databases. The investigators report that while technical limitations can be overcome, a significant investment in hardware would be required. Access to resources available over Internet can be managed, but major difficulties arise in accessing remote CD-ROM databases due to their multiple formats and retrieval systems.

Further information about other new and ongoing grants can be found in CLR's *38th Annual Report* for FY 1994.

Grants and Contracts Over $5,000, FY 1994

Association of Research Libraries, Washington, D.C.
    Benchmarking pilot project $17,540

Coalition for Networked Information, Washington, D.C.
    To establish an analytical framework and baseline
    for networked information resources and services $25,000

Cornell University Engineering Library, Ithaca, N.Y.
    Managing engineering information resources on Internet $14,000

Cornell University Library, Ithaca, N.Y.
    Development of a multimedia collection access tool $24,677

Eckerd College, St. Petersburg, Fla.
    College library director mentor program (1994–1996) $22,600

Indiana University, Bloomington, Ind.
    NASA knowledge diffusion research project $9,568

Library and Information Technology Association,
    American Library Association, Chicago, Ill.
    Forum in telecommunications and information
    infrastructure policy issues $15,000

Towson State University, Towson, Md.
    Strategic planning for information resources $10,000

University at Albany Foundation, Albany, N.Y.
    Study of costs and benefits of access compared
    to ownership costs for high-cost research journals $54,012

University of Illinois, The Library Research Center, Urbana, Ill.
    Study of attitudes of municipal and county
    officials toward public libraries $12,000

U.S. Department of Education
Library Programs, 1994

555 New Jersey Ave. N.W., Washington, DC 20208-5571
202-219-2293, FAX 202-219-1725

Ray M. Fry
Director, Library Programs
Office of Educational Research and Improvement
U.S. Department of Education

The U.S. Department of Education's Office of Library Programs contributes to the improvement of the nation's libraries and library education by administering the ten programs under the Library Services and Construction Act (LSCA) and the Higher Education Act, Title II (HEA II). The programs

- Promote resource sharing and cooperation among all types of libraries by facilitating development and access to information that permit individuals to find and use books and other materials from libraries across the country
- Assist state library agencies in improving local library services for all citizens, with a focus on underserved populations such as the handicapped and disadvantaged
- Support local and state efforts to construct new public library facilities and upgrade existing ones
- Improve library services to native populations—Indian tribes, Alaskan native villages, and Hawaiian natives—through basic and special projects
- Support adult literacy programs conducted by state library agencies and local public libraries
- Strengthen major research libraries, including those of postsecondary institutions, by helping them improve access to important collections, preserve deteriorating materials, and acquire unique, distinctive, and specialized materials
- Advance the education of librarians through fellowships and training institutes
- Encourage colleges and universities to promote and develop exemplary uses of technology for resource sharing and networking
- Fund research and demonstration projects on library and information science issues

In addition to administering LSCA and HEA II, Library Programs provides leadership to the library community by

Note: The following Library Programs' staff assisted in writing and/or compiling data for this article: Christina Dunn, Beth Fine, Clarence Fogelstrom, Donald Fork, Jane Heiser, Barbara Humes, Neal Kaske, Robert Klassen, Carol Cameron Lyons, Linda Miles, Evaline Neff, Jan Owens, Trish Skaptason, and Louise Sutherland.

- Planning for library development
- Implementing federal policies and programs
- Providing guidance and technical assistance to grant recipients
- Promoting the evaluation of library programs
- Recognizing exemplary library programs
- Conducting research to address national issues
- Interpreting federally funded library activities to library and nonlibrary audiences
- Integrating the contributions of libraries into the framework of the National Education Goals

In FY 1994, the Office of Library Programs undertook an important special project to conduct a national assessment of the role of school and public libraries in education reform. A $1.3 million contract, funded under the Secretary's Fund for Innovation in Education, was awarded to Westat Inc., which is conducting the study in cooperation with the American Library Association (ALA).

The purpose of this study is to find out how school and public libraries are performing as education providers and how well they are responding to the country's urgent demands for school improvement. It is intended to inform researchers, policymakers, and practitioners on six key issues:

- To what extent are school and public libraries contributing to education reform and to what extent can they contribute?
- What programs and services are school and public libraries providing to meet the needs of preschool and elementary and secondary (K–12) education providers?
- How well do these services and programs meet the needs of preschool and K–12 education providers?
- Do school and public libraries have the capacity—human and information resources, technology, and facilities—to adequately respond to identified needs and support systemic reform?
- What new technologies are promoting student opportunity to learn by improving services and resources in school and public libraries?
- What can we learn from successful school and public library programs and services designed to support preschool and K–12 education? Can these programs serve as models for the improvement of all school and public libraries? What are the barriers to effective services and programs?

In response to the need for data on these issues, the study will undertake a national assessment of the current and evolving role of school and public libraries in support of the National Education Goals and case studies of selected programs that support the goals. This combination of quantitative and qualitative data should provide a rich portrait of school and public libraries, providing current and reliable information about how they are performing and are able to perform within the education system. The study will give special consideration to the issue of how school and public libraries can best serve the needs of disadvantaged students.

In addition, the Office of Library Programs continued the Evaluating Federally Funded Library Programs project, a contract started in 1992 with the University of Wisconsin–Madison, to train state library personnel in planning and evaluation; commissioned eight papers on public library services to the aging; and entered into a cooperative agreement with the Library of Congress to conduct a program promoting reading to young people. (These agreements are further described under HEA II-B, Research and Demonstration Program.)

Higher Education Act (HEA, PL 99-498)

Title II of the Higher Education Act has been the backbone of federal financial assistance to college and university libraries for more than two decades. With the continuing expansion of information resources and the increasing demands on higher education libraries, Title II has been an important factor in helping these libraries to preserve, acquire, and share resources; to train and retrain personnel; and to use new technologies to improve services. In 1986 HEA Title II was reauthorized and some parts rewritten to accommodate further change, including establishment of the College Library Technology and Cooperation Grants program (HEA II-D; now HEA II-A). In 1987 these amendments were implemented fully through revisions in the regulations and development of new regulations for the II-D program. Changes in HEA Title II under the 1992 reauthorization reflect a new emphasis on the electronic networked environment. Changes include:

- Under Library Education, Research, and Development (HEA II-B), "Library Career Training" became "Library Education and Human Resource Development," with a focus on meeting critical needs, such as minority recruitment. Determining critical needs in library education and research priorities requires the Secretary to consult with library and information science professional bodies.
- "Strengthening Research Library Resources" (HEA II-C) was changed to "Improving Access to Research Library Resources." The new title reflects the new emphasis on access.
- Part D under HEA Title II, College Library Technology and Cooperation Grants program, became Part A.
- "Strengthening Library and Information Science Programs and Libraries in Historically Black Colleges and Universities and Other Minority-Serving Institutions" (HEA II-D) was added as a new part. However, no funds were appropriated for its administration.

The 1992 amendments were implemented in FY 1993 through revisions in the regulations.

College Library Technology and Cooperation Grants Program (HEA, Title II-A)

The College Library Technology and Cooperation Grants Program, HEA Title II-A (formerly HEA Title II-D), was added to the Higher Education Act when the law was reauthorized in 1986. The program awards grants to institutions of higher education for technological equipment to enhance resource-sharing activities among colleges and universities. In FY 1994, the seventh year of program funding, $3,873,000 was appropriated for Title II-A.

In addition to encouraging resource-sharing projects among libraries of institutions of higher education, this program promotes innovative research and demonstration projects that meet special needs in utilizing technology to enhance library services. Grants are awarded in four categories:

- Networking grants to plan, develop, acquire, maintain, or upgrade technological equipment necessary to organize, access, or utilize material in electronic formats and to participate in electronic networks for sharing of library resources
- Combination grants to establish and strengthen joint-use library facilities, resources, or equipment for the accessing and sharing of library and information resources
- Services to Institutions grants to establish, develop, or expand programs or projects that improve information services provided to institutions of higher education
- Research and Demonstration grants to conduct research or demonstration projects that improve information services to meet specialized national or regional needs in using technology to enhance library and information services such as through the National Research and Education Network (NREN)

In FY 1994, the College Library Technology and Cooperation Grants Program awarded 38 grants (28 new, 10 continuation) totaling $3,873,000 to institutions in 20 states and the District of Columbia. Of the total amount, $2,714,125 supported 28 new grants and $1,098,662, 10 continuation grants. Of the 10 continuation awards, 6 were Research and Demonstration projects.

Awards promote networking and resource-sharing activities and were made primarily to academic libraries, although state and public libraries and other nonprofit organizations are eligible.

A total of 235 applications, requesting $26,261,951, were received for the FY 1994 competition. Table 1 reports the number of new awards made and applications received for each of the four grant categories.

The projects funded in FY 1994 demonstrate the broad range of resource sharing through technology. The following represent each category of grants:

Networking. Drake University (Des Moines, Iowa) will use its $26,525 grant to begin the first part of a three-year project to institute a public bulletin board service through which Iowa libraries will gain greater access to the University Law Library's collection. Using a fax/scanner, the library will provide five new services: conversion of primary and secondary legal materials into electronic format for file transfer or faxing; 24-hour electronic communications with the University Law Library faculty and staff for those institutions without Internet access; creation of a public electronic forum for Iowa libraries interested in legal reference services and legal research; enhancement of existing photocopying and interlibrary loan service through the use of an online order and billing system; and creation of a public file exchange system whereby Iowa libraries will be able to upload electronic files for information exchange with other institutions.

Combination. The $200,000 grant to San Diego State University (California), in cooperation with Grossmont-Cuyamac Community College District, will establish a library resource-sharing network among four campuses. By allowing access to and delivery of the holdings of the participating institutions and the resources of Internet, the network will provide a valuable supplement to local library holdings currently available to faculty and students. It will also facilitate local campus outreach programs to underserved populations. The project will establish initial network linkages, allow formation of a joint-use Library/Academic Support Information System, and provide personnel to install and develop the system. The university will create a model of cooperation that can be expanded to other community college districts in San Diego and Imperial Valley counties.

Services to Institutions. The grant of $62,000 to OCLC (Online Computer Library Center Inc.) initiates a nationwide, coordinated effort among libraries and institutions of higher education to create, implement, test, and evaluate a searchable database of USMARC format bibliographic records, complete with electronic location and access information (USMARC field 856), for Internet-accessible materials. In a volunteer effort, libraries participating in this project—in cooperation with representatives from their host institutions—will identify, select, and catalog Internet-accessible electronic information objects. OCLC will provide cataloging guidelines and Help Desk support (phone and online) to all participants; create a database of all records produced in this venture and provide general Internet access to it; test the technical feasibility of using coded information in the bibliographic record (field 856) to provide direct user access to the remotely accessible objects; and evaluate the success of this project.

Research and Demonstration. Researchers at the School of Information Studies, Syracuse University (New York), will use their $140,834 grant to assess the impacts of Internet/National Research and Education Network (NREN) networking on the academic institution. Despite the fact that many institutions of higher education have been connected to Internet and the evolving NREN, there is little knowledge of how such connections have affected the institutions. This study will identify and describe the impacts of network access and use via exploratory, qualitative design, based on multiple data collection activities. Key components of the academic networked environment will be defined and indicators of the effects of networked information services and resources on academic institutions will be developed. Results of this study will enable members of the academic community to better describe, measure, and justify the development of the academic networked environment. Using the tools developed, academic deci-

Table 1 / Applications Received and FY 1994 Awards by Category, College Library Technology and Cooperation Grants Program

	Networking	Combination	Services to Institutions	Research and Demonstration
Number of awards	10	11	2	5
Total dollars awarded	$471,635	$1,567,000	$201,656	$473,834
Average award	$47,164	$142,455	$100,828	$94,767
Applications received	137	51	11	36
Total dollars requested	$6,513,301	$ 11,425,834	$1,663,877	$6,658,939
Average request	$47,542	$224,036	$151,262	$184,971

sion makers will be better able to determine the degree to which access to, and use of, national networking has affected teaching, research, learning, and service at their particular institutions.

Table 2 lists projects funded under each category.

Library Education and Human Resource Development Program (HEA, Title II-B)

The Library Education and Human Resource Development Program (Title II-B of the Higher Education Act) authorizes a program of federal financial assistance to institutions of higher education and other library organizations and agencies to assist in training persons in library and information science and to establish, develop, and expand programs of library and information science. Grants are made for fellowships and traineeships at the master's and doctoral levels. Grants may also be used to assist in covering the costs of institutes, or courses, to upgrade the competencies of persons serving in all types of libraries, information centers, or instructional materials centers offering library and information services, and of those serving as educators.

In FY 1994, Congress appropriated $4,960,000 for the HEA II-B, Library Education and Human Resource Development Program. Sixty-four fellowship awards were made to 37 institutions to support 167 fellowships (18 new doctoral, 95 continuing doctoral, and 54 master's). The total of all grants was $3,843,661. Stipends were $14,000 for all fellowship candidates, based on economic need. For each fellowship, institutions received $8,000 for master's-level and $10,000 for doctoral-level studies.

Areas of study reflect the Secretary's priorities:

- Master's level studies support four areas of study where there are currently shortages of trained library personnel: children's and young adult services; science reference; school library media; and cataloging.
- Doctoral fellowships support candidates who will teach in some area of library and information science or engage in library planning, evaluation, and research.

Table 2 / College Library Technology and Cooperation Grants Program Projects Funded under HEA Title II-A, Summary Listing for FY 1994

	City	State	Funds Granted
Networking			
Spring Hill College[1]	Mobile	AL	$49,000
Trinity College[1]	Washington	DC	50,000
Drake University	Des Moines	IA	26,525
State Community College[1]	East Saint Louis	IL	49,307
Southwestern College	Winfield	KS	48,600
Western Michigan University	Kalamazoo	MI	49,941
Blue Ridge Community College	Flat Rock	NC	49,809
Middlesex County College[1]	Edison	NJ	50,000
Middlesex County College[1,2]	Edison	NJ	50,000
Cleveland College of Jewish Studies	Beachwood	OH	48,453
(mean award size $47,164)		Subtotal	$471,635
Combination			
San Diego State University	San Diego	CA	200,000
Maharishi International University	Fairfield	IA	95,000
University of Iowa	Iowa City	IA	170,000
University of Kentucky Research Foundation	Lexington	KY	118,000
Montana State University	Billings	MT	178,000
Davidson County Community College	Lexington	NC	210,000
SUNY Research Foundation	New Paltz	NY	70,000
Ohio State University Research Foundation	Columbus	OH	181,000
Oklahoma State University	Stillwater	OK	117,000
Portland State University	Portland	OR	94,000
University of Wyoming	Laramie	WY	134,000
(mean award size $142,455)		Subtotal	$1,567,000
Services to Institutions			
Westchester Academic Libraries	Elmsford	NY	139,656
OCLC Online Computer Library Center	Dublin	OH	62,000
(mean award size $100,828)		Subtotal	$201,656
Research and Demonstration			
University of California	Berkeley	CA	48,000
University of California	Irvine	CA	122,000
University of Maine	Orono	ME	115,000
University of New Mexico	Albuquerque	NM	48,000
Syracuse University	Syracuse	NY	140,834
(mean award size $94,767)		Subtotal	$473,834
Noncompeting Continuations			
Arizona State University	Tempe	AZ	$4,882
University of California	Berkeley	CA	83,485
Georgetown University	Washington	DC	86,667
Center for Research Libraries	Chicago	IL	49,508
University of Illinois	Champaign	IL	494,950
University of Michigan	Ann Arbor	MI	58,000
University of Michigan	Ann Arbor	MI	65,099
Penn Valley Community College	Kansas City	MO	32,562
Oregon State University	Corvallis	OR	113,793
University of Tennessee	Knoxville	TN	109,716
(mean award size $109,866)		Subtotal	$1,098,662
		Award total	$3,812,787
		Reviewers expenses	$60,213
		Grand total	$3,873,000

[1] Developing institutions
[2] Competed in FY 1993 and funded in FY 1994.

Table 3 shows the Library Education and Human Resource Development fellowship grants awarded in FY 1994.

Between 1966 and 1994, institutions of higher education were awarded a total of 5,267 awards: 1,474 doctoral, 282 post-master's, 3,365 master's, 16 bachelor's, and 53 associate's fellowships; and 77 traineeships. Table 4 reviews the fellowship program's history.

In FY 1994, the Library Education and Human Resource Development Program made awards totaling $1,083,179 to support institutes or training workshops primarily for school and public librarians. Sixteen institute grants were awarded to institutions of higher education and library organizations. These grants, training approximately 1,700 participants, ranged from $29,154 to $125,000.

The institutes represent a variety of subject matter and approaches. However, all address at least one of the Secretary's priorities:

- Areas of library specialization where there are currently shortages, such as school media, children's services, young adult services, science reference, and cataloging
- Serving the information needs of people who are elderly, illiterate, disadvantaged, or residents of rural America

Because libraries are in a unique position to aid community efforts in support of the National Education Goals, the Secretary invited applicants to tie their proposals to the goals. Many of the institutes also reflect this commitment particularly in the areas of:

- Preparing children to learn in school
- Helping students to achieve in mathematics and science and other challenging subjects
- Improving the public library as a center for lifelong learning for adults

Since the utilization of information technologies will play a key role in how well libraries will serve Americans' information needs, many of the institutes place heavy emphasis on training and retraining in information technology and management to improve services, especially in K-12 programs. Table 5 shows institute grants awarded in FY 1994.

Library Research and Demonstration Program (HEA, Title II-B)

The Library Research and Demonstration Program (Title II-B of the Higher Education Act) authorizes grants and contracts for research and demonstration projects related to the improvement of libraries, training in librarianship, and the dissemination of information derived from these projects. Table 6 presents a chronological funding history of the program.

Title II, Part B, of the Higher Education Act was amended by the Higher Education Amendments of 1986. In 1987, by statutory mandate, "information

Table 3 / HEA Title II-B, Library Education and Human Resource Development Program, FY 1994 Fellowship Grantees

Grantee	Number and Level	Area of Study
New Awards		
Catholic University	2 master's	Children and young adult services; academic, law, and special librarianship
Clark Atlanta University	1 master's	Services to ethnically and racially diverse populations
Drexel University	2 doctoral	Information resource management
Florida State University	1 doctoral	Children and young adult services; library education and research
Indiana University	1 doctoral	Children and youth services; handicapped services; adult services; literacy
InterAmerican University of Puerto Rico	2 master's	Services to Hispanic populations
Long Island University	2 master's	Archives management; children and young adult services; school library media
Ohio University	1 master's	School llibrary media
Rutgers University	3 master's	School library media; children and young adult services
	1 doctoral	Research in human information-seeking behavior
Simmons College	3 master's	Services to ethnically diverse communities
St. John's University	2 master's	School library media
SUNY at Albany	1 doctoral	Research in information transfer
Syracuse University	2 doctoral	Information transfer; library education and research
Texas Woman's University	3 master's	Children and young adult services; cataloging; science reference
	2 doctoral	Library education and research
University of Alabama	2 doctoral	Information studies; research in youth services
University of California, Los Angeles	2 master's	School library media; children and young adult services; science reference
University of Central Arkansas	3 master's	School library media
University of Houston, Clear Lake	3 master's	School library media
University of Illinois	2 master's	Youth services; science reference
University of Iowa	3 master's	School library media; children and young adult services
University of Maryland	2 master's	Children and young adult services; school library media; science reference
	1 doctoral	Youth services; archival studies; information technology; literacy
University of Michigan	1 master's	School library media; science and engineering reference
	1 doctoral	New techniques of information acquisition, transfer, and communication
University of Missouri	2 master's	School library media; children's services; science reference; cataloging
University of Oklahoma	3 master's	Science reference services to children and young adults

Table 3 / HEA Title II-B, Library Education and Human Resource
Development Program, FY 1994 Fellowship Grantees (cont.)

Grantee	Number and Level		Area of Study
University of Pittsburgh	2	doctoral	Research; library education-cataloging; information storage and retrieval
University of South Carolina	3	master's	Children and young adult services
University of South Florida	1	master's	School library media; children's services; cataloging
University of Texas	1	doctoral	Research in school readiness; cataloging; health and engineering reference
University of Wisconsin, Milwaukee	3	master's	Children and young adult services; science reference; cataloging
	3	master's	
	1	doctoral	Children and young adult services; library education and research
Wayne State University	2	master's	Children and young adult services; cataloging
Continuation Fellowships			
Drexel University	5	doctoral	Library education and research; administration
Florida State University	4	doctoral	Children and young adult services
Rutgers University	5	doctoral	Library education, research, planning, and evaluation
SUNY at Albany	3	doctoral	Library education and research
Texas Woman's University	6	doctoral	Library education
University of Alabama	2	doctoral	Information studies; library education and research
University of Arizona	4	doctoral	Library planning, evaluation, and research
University of California, Berkeley	5	doctoral	Library education
	4	doctoral	Research in new technologies
	2	doctoral	Management of libraries, networks, and consortia
University of California, Los Angeles	5	doctoral	Library education, planning, evaluation, and research
University of Illinois	2	doctoral	Library education; children and young adult services; school library media
University of Michigan	1	doctoral	Library education and research
University of North Carolina	6	doctoral	Library education and research
University of Pittsburgh	4	doctoral	Library education and research
	4	doctoral	Library administration, education, and research
University of North Texas	6	doctoral	Library education; medical informatics
	4	doctoral	Library education; management
	4	doctoral	Library education
	5	doctoral	Library education and research; management
University of Texas	4	doctoral	Library education, planning, and research
	5	doctoral	Library planning, evaluation, and research
University of Wisconsin, Madison	2	doctoral	Library research and management
	3	doctoral	Library education; financial management

Table 4 / HEA, Title II-B, Library Education
Fellowship/Trainee Program, Academic Years 1966–1994

| Academic Year | Insti-tutions | Funding | Fellowship/Traineeship | | | | | | FY |
			Doctoral	Post-Master's	Master's	Bachelor's	Associate's	Trainee-ship	
1966/67	24	898,941	52	25	62	0	0	0	1966
1967/68	38	3,733,250	116	58	327	0	0	0	1967
1968/69	51	5,102,690	168	47	494	0	0	0	1968
1969/70	56	4,477,400	193	30	379	0	0	0	1969
1970/71	48	3,038,060	171	15	200	0	0	20	1970
1971/72	20	1,461,374	116	6	0	0	0	20	1971
1972/73	15	520,574	39	3	0	0	0	20	1972
1973/74	33	1,420,980	21	4	145	0	20	14	1973
1974/75	50	1,361,130	21	3	168	0	5	3	1974
1975/76	22	896,760	27	6	94	0	0	0	1975
1976/77	12	353,200	5	3	43	0	0	0	1976
1977/78	37	1,023,350	18	3	134	0	5	0	1977
1978/79	33	1,198,450	25	9	139	10	5	0	1978
1979/80	36	1,054,550	19	4	134	2	3	0	1979
1980/81	32	667,000	17	5	72	0	7	0	1980
1981/82	34	667,000	13	2	59	0	5	0	1981
1982/83	33	639,050	13	2	56	0	3	0	1982
1983/84	33	640,000	8	7	56	4	0	0	1983
1984/85	39	638,800	5	4	67	0	0	0	1984
1985/86	37	636,100	11	4	57	0	0	0	1985
1986/87	38	612,200	14	3	51	0	0	0	1986
1987/88	27	542,200	10	5	45	0	0	0	1987
1988/89	18	282,800	9	0	14	0	0	0	1988
1989/90	15	277,600	10	0	12	0	0	0	1989
1990/91	20	404,400	10	2	21	0	0	0	1990
1991/92	21	644,000	24	3	23	0	0	0	1991
1992/93	38	4,999,800	104	12	300	0	0	0	1992
1993/94	47	3,870,400	122	17	159	0	0	0	1993
1994/95	37	3,843,661	113	0	54	0	0	0	1994
Totals		45,905,720	1,474	282	3,365	16	53	77	

Table 5 / HEA, Title II-B, Library Education and Human Resource Development FY 1994 Institute Awards

Grantee	Award Amount	Project Title
California		
San Jose State University	$51,997	Information Needs and Behaviors of Diverse Populations: Research and Methodology
University of California at Berkeley	109,035	Institute for the Recruitment, Education, and (Re)Training of Minorities in Academic Libraries
Colorado		
Colorado Department of Education	83,833	Information Literacy and Standards-Based Education: Tools for Library Media Specialists
Illinois		
College of DuPage	125,000	National Institute for Library Personnel
Illinois State Library	40,000	Institute in Introductory Librarianship
Louisiana		
Louisiana State University	29,154	Louisiana Public Libraries Electronic Access Seminar
Mississippi		
University of Southern Mississippi	46,393	Transforming Information: Getting Librarians Involved with Technology and Instruction
Missouri		
University of Missouri	91,650	Library Leadership Education Action Project
Montana		
Montana State University	65,340	Science and Math Curriculum Applications Update for Rural School Library Media Specialists
Montana State University	00,402	Tribal College Librarians Professional Development Institute
New York		
New York Public Library	90,623	The Library as a Resource for Adult New Readers: An NYPL Staff Development Institute
State University of New York at Buffalo	45,000	Institute for Training Urban and Rural Librarians to Develop and Use Community Information Resources Within a Community Information Computer System
North Carolina		
University of North Carolina at Chapel Hill	79,986	Information Highway Training Initiative
Ohio		
Kent State University	72,182	Library Partnerships for Preschoolers: School Readiness 2000
Oklahoma		
University of Oklahoma	33,158	Tribal Librarians' Summer Institute for School Readiness
Pennsylvania		
Pennsylvania State University	83,366	Pennsylvania Library Institute: Meeting the Informational and Educational Needs of Special Populations

technology" was deleted from the list of authorized research and demonstration subjects. This amendment precludes research on or about information technology but allows use of technology to accomplish the goals of a research or demonstration project.

In FY 1994 Congress appropriated $2,802,400 for the HEA II-B, Research and Demonstration Program. Funds supported one grant, two contracts, and eight commissioned papers.

- From the 21 applicants requesting more than $56 million under the Library Research and Demonstration Program Statewide Multitype Library Network and Database competition, one grant of $2,480,000 was awarded to the Colorado Department of Education's State Library and Adult Education Office to expand electronic library networking statewide. The Colorado State Library proposed to build on its strong statewide network, Access Colorado Library and Information Network (ACLIN), which is already online, to improve free public access to information and library resources. Working with academic, public, school, and special libraries, it will add new databases and create one comprehensive network.

- The contract with the University of Wisconsin–Madison ($281,789) begun in FY 1992 to provide training for state library agency personnel in planning and evaluating federally funded library programs, was continued. Training is designed to strengthen state library agencies' capabilities in evaluating projects, demonstrating greater accountability for federal funds, and identifying and disseminating information about effective programs.

  In FY 1994, the contractor presented regional workshops in Connecticut, Illinois, Indiana, and Arizona, and refined the two draft manuals, creating one document that both introduces participants to the TELL IT! Evaluation Process and provides materials and guidance for trainers in the TELL IT! framework. The contractor also entered into two subcontracts with the American Library Association: one to develop a manual on the topic of evaluating young adult programming in public libraries and the other to conduct a workshop on applying the TELL IT! model to the accreditation process for library education programs. The latter was undertaken in concert with the introduction of the new ALA accreditation standards.

- The $25,000 contract (cooperative agreement) with the Library of Congress, Center for the Book, supported developing "Leaders Are Readers," a demonstration program to promote reading to young people. The project includes a national planning conference at the Library of Congress to discuss materials and publications to support the project; a book about Thomas Jefferson that emphasizes the crucial role of reading, books, and libraries in individual development and in the creation of our democracy; and reading lists for young people.

- In preparation for the White House Conference on Aging (scheduled for May 1995), eight papers, totaling $7,500, were commissioned on public library services to the aging. The papers represented a broad spectrum of public library services, including an introduction to public library services to the aging; exemplary programs; library cooperation with other agencies; intergenerational programs; services to the homebound, institutionalized, and disabled; information networking; services to the aging in multicultural communities; and the aging as a resource for providing youth services.

Table 6 / HEA Title II-B, Library Research and Demonstration Program, 1967–1994

Fiscal Year	Appropriation	Grants and Contracts Obligations	Number of Grants and Contracts
1967	$3,550,000	$3,381,052	38
1968	3,550,000	2,020,942	21
1969	3,000,000	2,986,264	39
1970	2,171,000	2,160,622	30
1971	2,171,000	2,170,274	18
1972	2,750,000	2,748,953	31
1973	1,785,000	1,784,741	24
1974	1,425,000	1,418,433	20
1975	1,000,000	999,338	19
1976	1,000,000	999,918	19
1977	1,000,000	995,193	18
1978	1,000,000	998,904	17
1979	1,000,000	980,563	12
1980	1,000,000 *	319,046	4
1981	1,000,000 *	239,954	2 contracts
			10 commissioned papers
1982	1,000,000 *	243,438	1 contract
1983	1,000,000 *	237,643	4 contracts
1984	1,000,000 *	250,764	3 contracts
1985	1,000,000 *	360,000	3 contracts
1986	1,000,000 *	378,000	3 contracts
1987	1,000,000 *	336,522	3 grants
			2 contracts
1988	718,000 *	306,303	5 grants
1989	709,000 *	297,325	5 grants
1990	855,000 *	285,000	5 grants
1991	976,000 *	320,753	4 grants
			2 commissioned papers
			1 contract
1992	325,000	324,894	2 contracts
1993	2,802,400	2,802,400	1 grant
			1 contract
1994	2,802,400	2,802,400	1 grant
			2 contracts
			8 commissioned papers

Includes the II-B training appropriation

Improving Access to Research Library Resources Program (HEA, Title II-C)

Title II-C of the Higher Education Act, Improving Access to Research Library Resources Program (formerly Strengthening Research Library Resources Program), promotes quality research and education throughout the United States by awarding funds to research libraries to make accessible collections that are rare, exclusively held, and of interest to a national research audience. This is achieved by making the content and location of the materials known through machine-readable catalog records contributed to national databases; and by making handling and perusal of the materials possible through conservation of the physical items and preservation of their intellectual content. The program also funds the acquisition of rare and unique research materials to fill gaps and strengthen existing collections.

In authorizing the Improving Access to Research Library Resources Program, Congress recognized that expansion of educational and research programs, together with the rapid increase in the production of recorded knowledge, places unprecedented demands on major research libraries by requiring programs and services beyond their financial capability. Authorized funding activities include:

- Creating and making available machine-readable catalog records via nationwide databases
- Acquiring specialized rare material to enhance or complete a library collection that may be a focus for national or international research
- Preserving collections of unique materials for scholarly use via microfilming, encapsulation, deacidification, and other chemical and manual processes
- Developing improved methods and procedures to provide bibliographic access, enhance collections, and meet preservation needs
- Demonstrating the cost benefits and advantages of cooperative cataloging ventures among major research libraries

Major research libraries are defined as public or private nonprofit institutions that contribute significantly to higher education and research, with unique collections containing material that is not widely available but is in substantial demand by researchers and scholars not connected with the institution and of national or international significance for research.

An amendment regarding eligibility (as a major research library) was added in 1986 with the reauthorization of the Higher Education Act. It permits institutions that do not qualify as a major research library under the criteria listed in the program regulations to provide information or documentation to demonstrate the national or international significance for scholarly research of the collection described in the grant application. This amendment allows the applicant's project to be evaluated if the collection is of national or international significance.

During the 17 years of program operation, $98,977,348 has been awarded to acquire rare and unique materials; to augment special collections in demand by researchers and scholars; to preserve fragile and deteriorating materials not generally available elsewhere; and to provide access to research collections by converting bibliographic information into machine-readable form and entering the records into national databases. Overall, 1,517 applications have been received and 587 funded.

In FY 1994, 77 applications requesting more than $11.9 million were received. With an allotment of $5,808,160, 31 new and 7 continuation grants were awarded, supporting projects at 37 institutions. Bibliographic control again emerged as the major activity in FY 1994, accounting for 67 percent of the funds. Preservation was second, accounting for 31 percent, and collection development accounted for 2 percent.

Following are examples of FY 1994 funded projects:

- The Center for Research Libraries in Chicago will use its $195,335 grant to increase researchers' access to monographs on the sciences and technology published by the Russian Academy of Sciences (RAS). The focus of the project is to catalog 30,800 titles (published from 1966 through 1991) held by few, if any, other libraries in North America and to widely disseminate bibliographic information about these materials. Staff working at the center will catalog these titles using the OCLC bibliographic database. The center's bibliographic records also will be loaded into the Research Libraries Group's Research Libraries Information Network (RLIN) on a regular basis. The catalog records will be added to the center's online public access catalog (OPAC), which is available through Internet. This project will significantly enlarge the availability of RAS resources that are easily obtainable through interlibrary loan from the center.

- The Henry E. Huntington Library in San Marino, California, will use the $178,412 grant it received to preserve and provide national access to the visual materials in the Otis R. Marston Collection, a unique resource that documents the history and exploration of the Colorado and Green river basins. The library will make preservation copies of 41,000 photographs and will write these images to a series of Kodak Photo CDs to provide improved research access to the collection. Sub-collection level MARC records will be created and distributed via the appropriate bibliographic utilities. A local Item-level computer database will also be prepared and made available to researchers.

- The Chicago Historical Society's grant of $115,920 will preserve and make readily available to researchers manuscript collections that illuminate major, national civil liberties and civil rights issues of the mid- and late-20th century. The 25 manuscript collections to be processed document activities in Chicago both when events focused national attention on the city and as the long-term trends of the civil rights movement and of civic activism shaped the fabric of life in this metropolitan area.

Table 7 analyzes FY 1994 grant awards by major activity and Table 8 summarizes Improving Access to Research Library Resources Program grant activities since FY 1978.

Table 7 / HEA, Title II-C, Improving Access to Research Library Resources Program FY 1994 Grants by Major Activity

Institute	Total	Bibliographic Control	Preservation	Collection Development
Brooklyn Historical Society	$123,340	$92,524	$30,816	$0
Brown University	118,431	118,431	0	0
Center for Research Libraries	228,646	228,646	0	0
Center for Research Libraries	195,335	195,335	0	0
Chicago Historical Society	115,920	92,736	23,184	0
Columbia University	63,840	63,840	0	0
Cornell University	192,780	71,778	121,002	0
Cornell University	192,418	10,069	182,349	0
Duke University	161,127	161,127	0	0
Folger Shakespeare Library	94,699	44,468	50,231	0
Georgetown University	44,216	44,216	0	0
Harvard University	622,710	622,710	0	0
Huntington Library	178,412	32,828	145,584	0
Iowa State University	44,361	44,361	0	0
Indiana University	339,463	69,920	240,322	29,221
Jewish Theological Seminary	52,102	34,734	17,368	0
Newberry Library	89,555	89,555	0	0
New York Public Library	141,819	141,175	644	0
Northwestern University	64,307	64,307	0	0
Ohio University	144,014	41,614	102,400	0
Princeton University	99,225	99,225	0	0
Rutgers University	94,013	54,215	39,798	0
Rutgers University	66,211	54,251	11,960	0
State Historical Society of Wisconsin	92,275	54,153	38,122	0
SUNY/Binghamton	97,231	0	97,231	0
University of California, Berkeley	226,290	46,689	179,601	0
University of California, Davis	306,025	34,873	271,152	0
University of California, Los Angeles	143,502	143,502	0	0
University of California, Riverside	358,289	358,289	0	0
University of Chicago	145,320	28,930	25,570	90,820
University of Chicago	105,332	79,717	25,615	0
University of Chicago	74,756	53,306	21,450	0
University of Nevada, Reno	162,414	162,414	0	0
University of North Carolina	111,207	110,162	1,045	0
University of Oklahoma	145,348	145,348	0	0
University of Texas, Austin	80,600	66,561	14,039	0
University of Virginia	123,621	123,621	0	0
Winterthur Museum Library	138,111	0	138,111	0
Total	$5,777,265	$3,879,630	$1,777,594	$120,041

Table 8 / HEA, Title II-C, Improving Access to Research Library Resources Program, Summary of Funding, by Major Activity, FYs 1978–1994

Fiscal Year	Total Funding	Bibliographic Control	Percent of Funding	Preservation	Percent of Funding	Collection Development	Percent of Funding
1978	$4,999,996	$2,864,339	57	$1,340,554	27	$795,103	16
1979	6,000,000	3,978,366	66	1,393,201	23	628,433	11
1980	5,992,268	4,345,765	73	805,383	13	841,120	14
1981	6,000,000	4,249,840	71	1,298,542	22	451,618	7
1982	5,760,000	4,042,549	70	1,521,258	27	196,193	3
1983	6,000,000	4,738,575	79	909,612	15	351,813	6
1984	6,000,000	4,526,772	76	1,044,973	17	428,255	7
1985	6,000,000	4,236,695	70	1,729,997	29	33,308	(*)
1986	5,742,000	4,429,374	77	1,122,409	20	190,217	3
1987	6,000,000	4,732,543	79	1,202,696	20	64,761	1
1988	5,744,000	4,804,408	84	850,570	15	89,022	1
1989	5,675,000	4,674,002	82	591,729	11	409,269	7
1990	5,738,000	5,141,888	90	510,255	9	85,857	1
1991	5,854,924	4,447,920	76	851,780	15	555,224	9
1992	5,855,000	4,720,805	81	766,648	13	367,547	6
1993	5,808,160	5,052,594	87	639,491	11	116,075	2
1994	5,808,000**	3,879,630	67	1,777,594	31	120,041	2
Total	$98,977,348	$74,866,065		$18,356,692		$5,723,856	

* Less than 1 percent.
** Total appropriation $5,808,000; total money used for grants $5,777,265.

Library Services and Construction Act

Library Services for Indian Tribes and Hawaiian Natives Program (LSCA, Title IV)

LSCA Title IV discretionary grants awarded in FY 1994 will improve public library services to 240 Indian Tribes and Alaska Native Villages and to approximately 170,000 Hawaiian Natives. Funds are being used in 25 states to support a variety of activities, including salaries and training of library staff, purchase of library materials, and the renovation or construction of library facilities.

Since FY 1985, 2 percent of the appropriations for LSCA Titles I, II, and III has been set aside as the available funding for LSCA Title IV (1.5 percent for Indian Tribes and 0.5 percent for Hawaiian Natives). Only Indian Tribes and Alaska Native Villages that are federally recognized and organizations serving Hawaiian Natives that are recognized by the governor of Hawaii are eligible to participate in the program. For the past ten years, Alu Like Inc. has been the only organization recognized to apply for the Hawaiian Native set-aside.

Two types of grants are awarded—Basic Grants and Special Projects Grants. The Basic Grant is noncompetitive, and if an Indian Tribe or Alaska Native Village is eligible and pursues authorized activities, funding is guaranteed. In FY 1994 the established Basic Grant for Indian Tribes and Alaska Native Villages was $3,774; Alu Like Inc. received the entire Hawaiian Native set-aside of $603,840.

These funds continue to be used to support projects emphasizing outreach, collection development, and training of Hawaiian Natives for librarianship.

Indian Tribes are using the majority of the 1994 Basic Grant funds to support library personnel and purchase library materials. For example, the Pueblo of Pojoaque in Santa Fe, New Mexico, will use its $3,774 basic grant to enhance the library's attraction for children through expansion of its existing Children's and Young Adult Collection. The Pueblo will not only acquire additional books and periodicals, but will start an audiotape collection for youngsters. Some funds will also be used to purchase such materials as posters, bookmarks, and flyers that will promote library services to the entire community. In Valley Center, California, the La Jolla Band of Indians will hire a full-time librarian who will establish and promote resource sharing by working closely with the tribe's education program, the San Diego Library, and other Indian Reservation Libraries. Hours will be expanded so that children can obtain reference materials after school and learn of the library's value as an information resource center.

The Native Village of Kivalina, Alaska—isolated in the deep bush area where jobs are scarce and subsistence hunting remains essential to survival—is recording elders in their native language on the traditional making of hunting gear and clothing for arctic survival. Accounts, which will be compiled into a reference book for school children and the general public, will cover weapons, transportation modes, game-stalking techniques, migration of Eskimos with animals, seasons, clothing materials and patterns, and other information relevant to hunting.

The Hawaiian Native Library Project is using its $603,840 Basic Grant to support several different projects. Alu Like Inc. places a strong emphasis on outreach activities, which include cultural presentations for the entire family. Materials used to supplement these presentations are linked to the Hawaii State Public Library system, thus encouraging library use. In certain targeted communities programs are being conducted to encourage reading and basic literacy skills, while fostering lifelong learning and regular library use. In addition, public service announcements are being aired to inform Hawaiian Natives about the services and resources they can find in libraries, and training is provided for them in library and information services.

Forty-four percent of the eligible Indian Tribes and Alaska Native Villages applied for and received Basic Grants. Approximately $900,000 was awarded under the Basic Grant Program (Table 9); the remaining $895,242 was used for Special Projects grants.

Although the Special Projects Program supports the same types of activities as the Basic Grant Program, the two programs differ sharply in the amount of support and the required effort for funding. All Special Projects proposals are reviewed for quality of project, scored, and then ranked on a competitive basis.

Each grantee is required to have a librarian, provide a long-range program of three to five years, and contribute a minimum of 20 percent of the total project costs. Twelve Indian Tribes in eight states successfully competed for Special Projects funds, with awards ranging from $38,558 to the Oneida Indian Nation of New York for the employment and training of a library assistant to $106,323 to the Crow Tribe of Indians in Montana to support automation of the Crow Tribal Library at Little Big Horn College.

In Oklahoma, the Wyandotte Tribe will use its first Special Projects grant of $68,428 to hire a librarian and to expand public library services to the community

An initial assessment of tribal library needs will be conducted, materials will be purchased, and a computer software package for library management will be installed.

Another first-time grantee, the Red Cliff Band of Lake Superior Chippewa in Bayfield, Wisconsin, received $79,804 for renovation of a building for use as a public library by its 1,535 tribal members. Funds will also support staff salaries, the acquisition of computers, furniture, and office machines, and the purchase of books, magazines, and historical documents.

Table 10 shows grants made under the Special Projects Program in FY 1994.

Foreign–Language Materials Acquisition Program (LSCA, Title V)

The Foreign–Language Materials Acquisition Program, Title V of LSCA, was established to support state and local public library efforts to develop foreign-language materials collections to serve the needs of their communities. Although the program was established in 1984, no funds were appropriated until FY 1991. The program was funded for the next two fiscal years; however, no funds were appropriated in FY 1994.

Table 9 / LSCA Title IV, Library Services for Indian Tribes and Hawaiian Natives Program, Basic Grant Awards, FY 1994

State	Number of Awards	Amount
Alabama	1	$3,774
Alaska	55	252,858
Arizona	12	45,288
California	39	158,508
Connecticut	1	3,774
Florida	2	7,548
Hawaii	1	603,840
Idaho	1	3,774
Louisiana	2	7,548
Michigan	6	22,644
Minnesota	1	3,774
Mississippi	1	3,774
Missouri	1	3,774
Montana	7	26,418
Nebraska	3	11,322
Nevada	6	22,644
New Mexico	14	52,836
New York	3	11,322
North Carolina	1	3,774
North Dakota	4	15,096
Oklahoma	22	86,802
Oregon	8	30,192
South Dakota	5	18,870
Texas	2	7,548
Washington	19	71,706
Wisconsin	8	30,192
Total	225 *	$1,509,600

*Five awards serve more than one Indian Tribe. A total of 240 Tribes and one Hawaiian Native organization received Basic Grants.

Table 10 / LSCA, Title IV, Library Services for Indian Tribes and Hawaiian Natives Program, Special Projects Awards, FY 1994

State/Tribe	Federal Funds
Michigan	
Hannahville Indian Community, Wilson	$69,309
Montana	
Chippewa Cree Tribe, Box Elder	60,606
Crow Tribe of Indians, Crow Agency	106,323
New Mexico	
Pueblo of Santa Clara, Espanola	55,044
New York	
Oneida Indian Nation of New York, Oneida	38,558
North Dakota	
Devils Lake Sioux Tribe, Fort Totten	94,241
Oklahoma	
Cherokee Nation, Tahlequah	81,215
Wyandotte Tribe	68,428
Washington	
Nisqually Indian Tribe	89,258
Shoalwater Bay Indian Tribe, Tokeland	93,755
Wisconsin	
Lac Courte Oreilles Tribe, Hayward	63,146
Red Cliff Band of Lake Superior Chippewa, Bayfield	79,804

Library Literacy Program (LSCA, Title VI)

Title VI of the Library Services and Construction Act authorizes a discretionary grant program to support adult literacy programs in state and local public libraries. The program received an appropriation of $8,098,000 for FY 1994.

Under the Library Literacy Program, state and local public libraries may apply directly to the U.S. Department of Education for grants of up to $35,000. State libraries may use grants to coordinate and plan library literacy programs and to train librarians and volunteers to carry out such programs. Local public libraries may use grants to promote use of voluntary services of individuals, agencies, and organizations in literacy programs and to acquire library materials, use library facilities, and train volunteers for the programs.

In FY 1994, LSCA Title VI awarded 244 grants totaling over $8 million to 231 local public libraries and 13 state libraries. The grants were reviewed by a panel of 86 literacy experts representing local and state libraries, literacy councils, state departments of education, institutions of higher education, and private or other literacy efforts. Grants ranged in size from $3,517 to the maximum amount of $35,000. The average amount was $32,994. Grantees planned and coordinated literacy activities with literacy councils, schools, private agencies, and other literacy providers in the state or community. They were also encouraged to coordinate literacy activities with recipients of grants under Title I of the Library Services and Construction Act.

The Library Literacy Program supported coordinating and planning library literacy programs, training volunteers as tutors, recruiting adult literacy students to participate, and purchasing books, videocassettes, and other teaching materials. In most projects, adults are taught literacy skills, usually by trained volunteers in a one-to-one or small group setting. Instruction is provided in libraries, businesses, homes, and other non-school environments. Teaching methods are usually based on those developed by Laubach and Literacy Volunteers of America, the two national volunteer tutoring literacy organizations. Computer-assisted instruction, family literacy, and job and life skills instruction are offered by most of the projects. Specific projects funded in FY 1994 follow.

- The Fulton County Library in Pennsylvania received $8,440 to coordinate a workplace literacy project to teach basic skills for the workplace. In 1990 the library set up a Workplace Computer System covering such topics as career planning, job search strategies, small business management, and vocational schools and colleges. However, the library and employment and training staff soon realized that the residents most in need of vocational assistance did not have the basic skills required to use the resources. With this project, the library will teach basic skills to adults and will instruct library, literacy, and employment agency staff in effective use of materials and equipment. The library will work with the county literacy coalition, literacy council volunteers, and instructors from the local vocational/technical school and employment and training agencies.
- The "Library/Literacy Link" project at the Tacoma Public Library in Washington, funded at $34,426, is designed to enhance and enrich adult literacy students' educational opportunities and experiences by linking current adult literacy program instruction with the resources of the library. Library staff and staff of the local literacy provider will survey the literacy students to determine how they have used libraries, for what purposes, any barriers they have encountered, and what type of experiences they have had. This information will be used to design a training program and to make any adjustments in how the library serves adult literacy students. Under the project, adult literacy students will also learn to use and access computer technology at a local library and at a large community-based literacy site in the city. Adult literacy students, literacy program staff, and library personnel will receive specialized training that will enable them to effectively use the computer and library resources for adult literacy instruction. In addition, the local literacy coalition will help disseminate information about the services and resources available to all the literacy programs in the city.
- The East Providence Public Library in Rhode Island received $31,852 to collaborate with the Visiting Nurses Association to assemble and deliver library/learning kits to low-literate new mothers in the hospital; to present, with the help of a local medical clinic, two six-week workshops on basic family health care; and to present two seven-week reading discussion series designed to give adult new readers an opportunity to share insights and explore the meaning of the material they have read.

- The Monroe County and Peterstown Public Libraries in West Virginia have designed "In Our Own Voice," an intergenerational whole-language adult literacy program that strives to combat adult illiteracy in their rural Appalachian community. The libraries received a joint grant of $70,000 in 1994 to expand the program by developing an innovative curriculum for tutoring mathematics, an area in which few of their volunteer tutors felt comfortable and for which no training program was available. They will develop pilot modules for training tutors to teach math to adult students and to teach parents ways to support their children's learning of math competencies.

See Table 11 for a complete list of FY 1994 grantees under the Library Literacy Program.

Table 11 / Library Literacy Program Grants, FY 1994

Alabama
Anniston and Calhoun County Library
Anniston
Bonnie Seymour, 205-548-2686
Award amount: $26,955

Foley Public Library
Foley
Susan A. Wolfe, 205-943-7665
Award amount: $35,000

Mobile Public Library
Mobile
Dean Soldner, 205-434-5176
Award amount: $34,989

Pickens County Cooperative Library
Carrollton
Lori Ward Smith, 205-367-2142
Award amount: $32,000

Prichard Public Library
Prichard
Beatrice Morse, 205-452-7847
Award Amount: $35,000

Alaska
Fairbanks North Star Borough Public Library
Fairbanks
Greg Hill, 907-459-1020
Award amount: $34,991

Arizona
Camp Verde Public Library
Camp Verde
Dane Bullard, 602-567-6631
Award amount: $34,780

Chandler Public Library
Chandler
Karen Drake, 602-786-2312
Award amount: $34,198

Flagstaff City/Coconino Public Library
Flagstaff
Kay Whitaker, 602-779-7670
Award amount: $11,000

Gila County Library District
Miami
Mary Kostanski, 602-425-7265
Award amount: $21,561

Arkansas
Arkansas State Library
Little Rock
John A. Murphey, Jr., 501-682-1526
Award amount: $35,000

Jonesboro Public Library
Jonesboro
Phyllis Burkett, 501-935-2114
Award amount: $35,000

California
Alameda County Library ESOL (English for
    Speakers of Other Languages) Tutoring
Fremont
Sherry Drobner, 510-745-1484
Award amount: $35,000

Alameda County Library Small Group
    Tutoring
Fremont
Sherry Drobner, 510-745-1484
Award amount: $34,938

Alameda County Library Tutoring in Jails
    Fremont
Sherry Drobner, 510-745-1484
Award amount: $34,993

Auburn-Placer County Library
Auburn
Delana Rudd, 916-889-4114
Award amount: $35,000

Benicia Public Library
Benicia
Susan Lynn, 707-746-4341
Award amount: $32,200

Blanchard Community Library
Santa Paula
Elaine Hunt, 805-525-2384
Award amount: $17,076

Camarena Memorial Library
Calexico
Sandra Trawler, 619-357-2170
Award amount: $35,000

Chula Vista Public Library Model Writing
    Project
Chula Vista
Meg Schofield, 619-425-4784
Award amount: $34,986

Chula Vista Public Library Adult Dyslexia
    Chula Vista
Meg Schofield, 619-425-4784
Award amount: $34,720

Colton Public Library
Colton
Mary Ann Ponder, 909-370-5170
Award amount: $24,642

Contra Costa Public Library
Pleasant Hill
Bonnie Bjerre, 519-646-6358
Award amount: $16,211

Coyote Valley Tribal Community Library
    Redwood Valley
Judy Fisch, 707-485-8723
Award amount: $35,000

El Dorado County Library
Placerville
Marilyn Crouch, 916-621-5546
Award amount: $26,009

Huntington Beach Library Family Literacy
    Project
Huntington Beach
Ronald Hayden, 714-960-8836
Award amount: $34,832

Huntington Beach Library Adult Literacy
    Services
Huntington Beach
Linda Light, 714-375-5102
Award amount: $35,000

Lake County Library
Lakeport
Dallas Cook, 707-263-7633
Award amount: $35,000

Marin County Free Library
San Rafael
Barbara Hughes, 415-499-6051
Award amount: $35,000

Menlo Park Public Library
Menlo Park
Judith Wilczak, 415-321-8818
Award amount: $25,400

Monterey County Free Libraries Project
    Long Valley
Salinas
Karen J. Albertus, 408-899-0417
Award amount: $24,596

Monterey County Free Libraries Project
    Nueros Horizontes
Salinas
Karen J. Albertus, 408-899-0417
Award amount: $33,199

Napa City-County Library
Napa
Thomas G. Trice, 707-253-4283
Award amount: $35,000

National City Public Library
National City
Russell Hamm, 619-474-2129
Award amount: $21,060

Orange County Public Library
Santa Ana
Scott Cheney, 714-566-3070
Award amount: $34,818

Orland Free Library
Orland
Gloria Manezes, 916-865-7175
Award amount: $34,121

Redwood City Public Library
Redwood City
David Miller, 415-780-7077
Award amount: $35,000

Salinas Public Library
Salinas
Marie E. Roddy, 408-758-7340
Award amount: $32,418

San Bernardino County Library
San Bernardino
Lucy Johnson-Sims, 909-387-5730
Award amount: $34,649

San Francisco Public Library Project
Read–Adult Learner Support
San Francisco
Ana Linder, 415-557-4388
Award amount: $34,997

San Francisco Public Library Project
Read–Tutor Support
San Francisco
Ana Linder, 415-557-4388
Award amount: $29,058

San Jose Public Library
San Jose
Ruth Kohan, 408-277-3230
Award amount: $34,987

San Rafael Public Library with Marin County
Free Library
San Rafael
Barbara Barwood, 415-485-3318
Award amount: $35,000

Santa Clara County Library with four other
libraries Computer-Aided Literacy
San Jose
Taylor Willingham, 408-262-1349
Award amount: $174,557

Santa Clara County Library Project Enable
San Jose
Taylor Willingham, 408-262-1349
Award amount: $34,989

Sonoma County Library
Santa Rosa
Donna Champion, 707-544-2622
Award amount: $14,119

Stockton-San Joaquin County Public Library
Santa Rosa
Pat Tobert, 209-941-2778
Award amount: $23,443

Upland Public Library
Upland
Marie Boyd, 909-931-4202
Award amount: $35,000

Ventura County Library Service Agency Pro-
ject Special Help
Ventura
Pat Flanigan, 805-652-6294
Award amount: $34,560

Ventura County Library Service Agency
Write to Read
Ventura
Pat Flanigan, 805-652-6294
Award amount: $34,953

Ventura County Library Service Agency Pro-
ject Publish
Ventura
Pat Flanigan, 805-652-6294
Award amount: $17,820

Willows Public Library
Willows
Susan Domenighini, 916-934-7413
Award amount: $33,200

Colorado
Basalt Regional Library
Basalt
Jean Winkler, 303-927-4311
Award amount: $11,025

Canon City Public Library
Canon City
Gary Shook, 719-269-9011
Award amount: $35,000

Colorado Department of Education State
Library
Denver
Mary Willoughby, 303-866-6743
Award amount: $35,000

Eagle Valley Library District
Eagle
Charyln Canada, 303-328-6273
Award amount: $35,000

Fort Collins Public Library
Fort Collins
Linda Saferite, 303-221-6742
Award amount: $35,000

Garfield County Public Library
New Castle
Stephen J. Thomas, 303-984-3121
Award amount: $35,000

The Heginbotham Library
Holyoke
Dorothy Ortner, 303-854-2594
Award amount: $35,000

Mesa County Public Library District
Grand Junction
Caryl LaDuke, 303-245-5522
Award amount: $35,000

Security Public Library
Security
Barbara Garvin, 719-392-4443
Award amount: $20,711

Sterling Public Library
Sterling
Connie Nicely, 303-522-2023
Award amount: $22,130

Upper San Juan Library District
Pagosa Springs
Gloria G. Macht, 303-264-2835
Award amount: $34,867

Connecticut
Bugbee Memorial Library
Danielson
Marie C. Chartier, 203-774-9429
Award amount: $35,000

Connecticut State Library
Hartford
Patricia Owens, 203-566-2712
Award amount: $32,500

Meriden Public Library
Meriden
Brenda Vumbaco, 203-235-1714
Award amount: $34,950

Willimantic Public Library
Willimantic
Theodore Perch, 203-423-6182
Award amount: $35,000

Delaware
Corbit-Calloway Memorial Library
Odessa
Susan Menei, 302-378-8838
Award amount: $15,602

Kent County Department of Library Services
Dover
Martha Hadaway, 302-736-2265
Award amount: $35,000

Wilmington Institute Library
Wilmington
Carmen Knox, 302-658-5624
Award amount: $35,000

District of Columbia
District of Columbia Public Library
Washington, DC
Marcia Harrington, 202-727-1101
Award amount: $35,000

Florida
Calhoun County Public Library System with
    two other libraries
Blountstown
Rita Maupin, 904-674-5200
Award amount: $102,393

Columbia County Public Library
Lake City
Eileen Brunner, 904-758-1018
Award amount: $17,717

Florida State Library
Tallahassee
Betty Scott, 904-487-2651
Award amount: $35,000

Gadsden County Public Library
Quincy

Jane Mock, 904-627-7106
Award amount: $34,895

Manatee County Public Library System
Bradenton
John Van Berkel, 813-748-5555
Award Amount: $35,000

New Port Richey Public Library
New Port Richey
Susan Dillinger, 813-841-4548
Award amount: $35,000

Wilderness Coast Public Libraries with two
other libraries
Crawfordville
Cheryl Turner, 904-926-4571
Award amount: $105,000

Georgia
Athens Regional Library System
Athens
Susan Colegrove, 796-613-3650
Award amount: $34,997

Chattooga County Library System
Summerville
Susan Stewart, 706-857-2553
Award amount: $35,000

Conyers-Rockdale Library System
Conyers
Deborah Manget, 404-388-5041
Award amount: $13,157

Lake Blackshear Regional Library
Americus
Jane Hendrix, 912-924-8091
Award amount: $35,000

Ocumulgee Regional Library
Eastman
Dottie Welch, 912-374-4711
Award amount: $35,000

Peach Public Libraries Byron Public Library
Branch
Fort Valley
Gilda Stanberry-Cotney, 912-825-8540
Award amount: $21,305

Peach Public Libraries
Fort Valley
Gilda Stanberry-Cotney, 912-825-8540
Award amount: $30,402

Sara Hightower Regional Library
Rome
Carrol Maloof, 706-236-4617
Award amount: $34,861

Screven-Jenkins Regional Library
Sylvania
Sandra Lively, 706-236-4617
Award amount: $16,130

Southwest Georgia Regional Library
Bainbridge
Susan Whittle, 912-248-2665
Award amount: $34,500

Hawaii
Hawaii State Public Library System Hilo
Public Library
Hilo
Maile Williams, 808-933-4650
Award amount: $28,670

Hawaii State Public Library System Kailua-
Kona Public Library
Kailua-Kona
Michael Hayley, 808-329-2196
Award amount: $33,940

Hawaii State Public Library System Molokai
Public Library
Kaunakakai
Sri P. Tencate, 808-553-5483
Award amount: $10,348

Hawaii State Public Library System Pahoa
Public & School Library
Pahoa
Laura Ashton, 808-965-8574
Award amount: $26,030

Hawaii State Public Library System
Waimanalo Public & School Library
Waimanalo
Helen Kahn, 808-259-9926
Award amount: $35,000

Idaho
Clearwater Memorial Public Library
Clearwater
Jill Lynch, 208-476-3411
Award amount: $32,390

East Bonner County Library
Sandpoint
James Murray, 208-263-6930
Award amount: $35,000

Illinois
Chicago Public Library
Chicago
Maribel Pelayo, 312-747-4162
Award amount: $20,620

Rockford Public Library
Rockford
Marcia Cook, 815-965-6731
Award Amount: $24,730

St. Charles Public Library
St. Charles
Peg Coker, 708-584-2811
Award amount: $20,002

Indiana
Anderson City, Anderson, Stony Creek and
   Union Townships' Public Library
Anderson
Donna Cumberland, 317-641-2462
Award amount: $35,000

Johnson County Public Library
Franklin
Rose Marie Stiffler, 317-738-2833
Award amount: $32,799

Knox County Public Library
Vincennes
Emily Cooper Bunyan, 812-886-4380
Award amount: $33,200

Lowell Public Library
Lowell
Virginia Maravilla, 219-696-7704
Award amount: $34,692

Vigo County Public Library
Terre Haute
Katherine Hackleman, 812-232-1113
Award amount: $34,882

Iowa
Davenport Public Library
Davenport
Mary Heinzman, 319-326-7841
Award amount: $33,118

Decorah Public Library
Decorah
Paula Gardner, 319-382-3717
Award amount: $34,763

Kansas
Coffeyville Public Library

Coffeyville
Karyl Buffington, 316-251-1370
Award amount: $3,517

Johnson County Library
Shawnee Mission
Linda Springer, 913-967-8600
Award amount: $35,000

Kentucky
Breathitt County Public Library
Jackson
Jeanette Shouse, 606-666-5541
Award amount: $34,960

Breckinridge County Public Library
Hardinsburg
Jade Meador, 502-756-2323
Award amount: $35,000

Greenup County Public Library
Greenup
Dorothy Griffith, 606-473-6514
Award amount: $11,400

Jackson County Public Library District
McKee
Betty Bingham, 606-287-8113
Award amount: $28,651

Laurel County Public Library
London
Lori Schecter, 606-864-5759
Award amount: $35,000

Pike County Public Library District
Elkhorn City
Jeffrey Plymale, 606-754-5451
Award amount: $35,000

Rhett Brown Memorial Library
Sandy Hook
Wanda Oliver, 606-738-5796
Award amount: $35,000

Louisiana
Calcasieu Parish Public Library
Lake Charles
Linda Carlberg, 318-437-3485
Award amount: $35,000

New Orleans Public Library
New Orleans
Gertiana Williams, 504-596-2601
Award amount: $25,279

Ouachita Parish Public Library
Monroe
Ben Brady, 318-327-1490
Award amount: $35,000

Terrebonne Parish Library
Houma
Margaret Shaffer, 504-876-5861
Award amount: $34,964

Maine
Sanford Library Association
Sanford
Kenneth Scott, 207-324-4714
Award amount: $35,000

Maryland
Anne Arundel County Public Library
Annapolis
Betty Morganstern, 410-222-7371
Award amount: $30,944

Massachusetts
Berkshire Athanaeum with two other libraries
Pittsfield
Ronald Lathum, 413-499-9484
Award amount: $73,348

Cary Memorial Library
Lexington
Donna Salacuse, 617-862-3706
Award amount: $34,960

Chicopee Public Library
Chicopee
Michael Barron, 413-594-6679
Award amount: $34,700

Fall River Public Library
Fall River
Regina Slezak, 508-324-2700
Award amount: $34,794

Haverhill Public Library
Haverhill
Virginia Behan, 508-373-1588
Award amount: $30,410

Hudson Public Library with Marlborough
   Public Library
Hudson
Patricia Desmond, 508-568-9644
Award amount: $31,690

Morrill Memorial Library
Norwood
Bettina Blood, 617-769-0200
Award amount: $34,963

Plymouth Public Library
Plymouth
Mary Anne Odell, 508-830-4260
Award amount: $33,703

Springfield Library and Museum Association
Springfield
Janet Kelly, 413-788-8806
Award amount: $35,000

Vineyard Haven Public Library with two
   other libraries
Vineyard Haven
Marjorie Convery, 508-696-4211
Award amount: $12,917

Watertown Free Public Library
Watertown
Susan Viskin, 617-924-8797
Award amount: $35,000

Michigan
Adrian Public Library
Adrian
Jule Fosbinder, 517-265-7525
Award amount: $35,000

Bay County Library System
Bay City
K. Lynn Derck, 517-894-2837
Award amount: $24,139

Dearborn Department of Libraries
Dearborn
R. Patrick Coady, 313-943-2037
Award amount: $35,000

Grand Rapids Public Library
Grand Rapids
Robert Raz, 616-456-3623
Award amount: $33,605

Greenville Public Library
Greenville
Virginia Schantz, 616-754-6359
Award amount: $32,635

Jackson District Library
Jackson

Joy Rosynek, 517-788-4317
Award amount: $35,000

Kalamazoo Public Library
Kalamazoo
Mary Doud, 616-342-9837
Award amount: $35,000

Library Cooperative of Macomb
Mt. Clemens
Marsha DeVergilio, 313-286-2750
Award amount: $35,000

Mitchell Public Library
Hillsdale
Diana Pierson, 517-437-2581
Award amount: $35,000

Ypsilanti District Library
Ypsilanti
Donna DeButts, 313-482-0565
Award amount: $34,888

Minnesota
Anoka County
Blaine
Sally Manler, 612-571-1934
Award amount: $18,401

Mississippi
Bolivar County Library
Cleveland
Ronnie W. Wisc, 601-843-2774
Award amount: $35,000

Elizabeth Public Library
Grenada
Hardy McElwain, 601-226-2072
Award amount: $35,000

First Regional Library
Hernando
James Anderson, 601-226-2072
Award amount: $32,240

Madison County–Canton Public Libraries
Canton
Beverly Herring, 601-859-3202
Award amount: $35,000

Sunflower County Library
Indianola
Sara Jump, 601-887-2641
Award amount: $30,087

Missouri
Dunklin County Library
Kennett
Benny Freeman, 314-888-3561
Award amount: $35,000

Montana
Big Horn County Public Library
Hardin
Betty Cheeseman, 406-665-1808
Award amount: $33,880

Bitterroot Public Library
Hamilton
Nansu Haynes, 406-363-1670
Award amount: $34,486

Butte-Silver Bow Public Library
Butte
Ann Drew, 406-723-7905
Award amount: $35,000

Confederated Salish & Kootenai Tribes
Pablo
Stacy Gordon, 406-675-4800
Award amount: $34,651

Havre-Hill County Library
Havre
Bonnie Williamson, 406-256-2123
Award amount: $29,378

Montana State Library Commission
Helena
Darlene Staffeldt, 406-265-4073
Award amount: $35,000

Rocky Boy Community Public Library
Box Elder
Peggy Nagel, 406-395-4313
Award amount: $34,840

Nebraska
Columbus Public Library
Columbus
Robert Trautwein, 402-564-7116
Award amount: $32,410

Nevada
Las Vegas-Clark County Library District
Las Vegas
Caron Schwahn, 702-382-3493
Award amount: $34,048

Nevada State Library and Archives
Carson City
Emmy Bell, 702-687-8340
Award amount: $35,000

New Hampshire
Carpenter Memorial Library
Pittsfield
Leslie Vogt, 603-435-8406
Award amount: $32,430

Concord Public Library
Concord
Louis Ungarelli, 603-225-8671
Award amount: $34,962

Fuller Public Library
Hillsboro
Tamara McClure, 603-464-3595
Award amount: $34,880

New Hampshire State Library Connections
Concord
Christie Sarles, 603-271-2866
Award amount: $34,825

New Hampshire State Library Read to Me
Concord
Christie Sarles, 603-271-2866
Award amount: $34,955

New Hampshire State Library Project SCIT
Concord
Art Ellison, 603-271-6698
Award amount: $35,000

New Jersey
Camden County Library with the Camden
    Free Public Library
Voorhees
Sivya Romisher, 609-772-1636
Award amount: $63,244

Irvington Public Library
Irvington
Lorelei McConnell, 201-372-6400
Award amount: $35,000

Jersey City Public Library
Jersey City
Annie Kessler, 201-547-4518
Award amount: $35,000

Old Bridge Public Library with 23 other
    libraries
Old Bridge

Elissa Director, 908-679-1004
Award amount: $90,000

Paterson Free Public Library Adult Basic Literacy
Paterson
Kwaku Ameabeng, 201-357-3013
Award amount: $35,000

Paterson Free Public Library
Literacy for Non-English Speakers
Paterson
Kwaku Ameabeng, 201-357-3013
Award amount: $35,000

Westwood Free Public Library
Westwood
Leonard LoPinto, 201-664-0583
Award amount: $30,000

New Mexico
Belen Public Library
Belen
Boleslo Lovato, 505-758-3063
Award amount: $35,000

Harwood Public Library
Taos
Tracy McCallum, 505-758-3063
Award amount: $35,000

Socorro Public Library
Socorro
Valerie Moore, 505-835-4659
Award amount: $17,334

New York
Brentwood Public Library
Brentwood
Doris Lewis Sargent, 516-273-7883
Award amount: $35,000

Brooklyn Public Library
Brooklyn
Susan O'Connor, 718-780-7819
Award amount: $35,000

Chemung-Southern Tier Library System
Corning
Mary Passage, 607-962-3141
Award amount: $34,266

Mastics-Moriches-Shirley Community
    Library
Shirley

Denise Boinay, 516-399-1511
Award amount: $34,987

Nassau Library System
Uniondale
Dorothy Puryear, 516-292-8920
Award amount: $35,000

Onondaga County Public Library
Syracuse
Sharon Nottingham, 315-448-4700
Award amount: $25,297

Queens Borough Public Library
Jamaica
Catherine Kavenaugh, 718-990-0800
Award amount: $35,000

Wyandanch Public Library
Wyandanch
Rita Liversedge, 516-643-4848
Award amount: $35,000

North Carolina
Ashe County Public Library
West Jefferson
Cheryl Earnhardt, 919-246-2041
Award amount: $35,000

Transylvania County Library
Brevard
Mark Brevard, 704-884-3151
Award amount: $26,575

Ohio
Toledo-Lucas County Public Library
Toledo
Pat Lora, 419-259-5262
Award amount: $33,850

Oklahoma
Buckley Public Library
Poteau
Elizabeth Neff, 918-647-3833
Award amount: $24,042

Elk City Carnegie Library
Elk City
Pat Sprowls, 405-247-0136
Award amount: $34,810

Lawton Public Library
Lawton
Marion F. Donaldson, 405-581-3450
Award amount: $31,000

Oklahoma Department of Libraries
Oklahoma City
Leslie Gelders, 405-521-2502
Award amount: $29,725

Southern Prairie Library System
Altus
Katherine Hale, 405-477-2890
Award amount: $34,996

Oregon
Eugene Public Library
Eugene
Sandra Carrick, 503-687-5450
Award amount: $34,800

Oregon State Library
Salem
Mary Ginnane, 503-378-2112
Award amount: $34,992

Pennsylvania
Bayard Taylor Memorial Library
Kennett Square
Alice Peters, 215-444-2988
Award amount: $24,005

Crawford County Federated Library System
Meadville
Mary Lindquist, 814-337-7323
Award amount: $34,800

Fulton County Library
McConnellsburg
Bernice Crouse, 717-485-5327
Award amount: $8,440

State Library of Pennsylvania
Harrisburg
Elizabeth Funk, 717-783-5732
Award amount: $34,735

Free Library of Philadelphia
Philadelphia
Nancy Laskowski, 215-686-5346
Award amount: $35,000

Rhode Island
Coventry Public Library
Coventry
Deborah Barchi, 401-822-9100
Award amount: $21,279

East Providence Public Library
East Providence

Eileen Socha, 401-434-2719
Award amount: $31,852

Providence Public Library Family Literacy
Providence
Roseanne Trissler, 401-455-8041
Award amount: $34,997

Providence Public Library Family Writing
Centers
Providence
Roseanne Trissler, 401-455-8041
Award amount: $35,000

Westerly Public Library
Westerly
Regan Robinson, 401-596-9411
Award amount: $16,858

Woonsocket Harris Public Library
Woonsocket
Kathy Ellen Bullard, 401-769-9044
Award amount: $19,800

Texas
Andrews County Library
Andrews
Cindy Tochterman, 915-524-1432
Award amount: $34,975

Commerce Public Library
Commerce
Rebecca Goughnor, 903-886-3721
Award amount: $33,650

Decatur Public Library
Decatur
Mary McClure, 817-627-5512
Award amount: $34,329

Delta County Public Library
Cooper
Cindy Switzer, 903-395-4575
Award amount: $35,000

Emily Fowler Public Library
Denton
Mary Cresson, 903-395-4574
Award amount: $34,033

Fort Bend County Libraries
Richmond
Linda Behling, 713-341-2640
Award amount: $33,300

Fort Worth Public Library
Fort Worth
Connie Barnes, 817-624-7350
Award amount: $28,756

Franklin County Public Library
Mt. Vernon
Jean Shelby, 903-537-4916
Award amount: $35,000

Lubbock City-County Library
Lubbock
Jeffrey Rippel, 806-767-2822
Award amount: $33,399

Plano Public Library System
Plano
Anne Womack, 214-578-7175
Award amount: $35,000

San Antonio Public Library Bazan Branch
San Antonio
Mary L. Cantu, 210-223-5687
Award amount: $35,000

San Antonio Public Library Collins Garden
Branch
San Antonio
Mary L. Cantu, 210-223-5687
Award amount: $35,000

Smithville Public Library
Smithville
Karen Bell, 512-237-2707
Award amount: $30,007

Sterling Municipal Library
Baytown
Jane Brody, 713-427-7331
Award amount: $35,000

Tom Green County Library System
San Angelo
D. Karen Vavricka, 915-655-7321
Award amount: $35,000

Weslaco Public Library
Weslaco
Michael Fisher, 210-968-4533
Award amount: $35,000

Utah
Brigham City Library
Brigham City
Claudia Oyler, 801-723-5891
Award amount: $13,165

Davis County Library
Farmington
Louise Pollard, 801-451-2322
Award amount: $11,312

Logan Library
Logan
Nancy Steinhoff, 801-753-5064
Award amount: $29,500

Provo City Library
Provo
Norma Henrie, 801-379-6667
Award amount: $35,000

Vermont
Cobleigh Public Library
Lyndonville
Pat Hazelhurst, 802-626-5475
Award amount: $32,385

Virginia
Arlington County Department of Libraries
Arlington
Neil Phillips, 703-358-6336
Award amount: $32,896

Caroline Library, Inc.
Bowling Green
Kay Brooks, 804-633-5455
Award amount: $30,729

Central Rappahannock Regional Library
Fredericksburg
Nancy Buck Schiff, 703-372-1144
Award amount: $32,000

Jefferson-Madison Regional Library
Charlottesville
Karen Morris, 804-971-7151
Award amount: $34,444

Smyth-Bland Regional Library
Marion
Judith A. Taminger, 703-783-7950
Award amount: $35,000

Southside Regional Library
Boydton
Nancy Tippens, 804-676-2006
Award amount: $22,602

Washington County Public Library
Abingdon
Charlotte Lewis, 703-676-6222
Award amount: $33,869

Washington
Nisqually Indian Tribe Community Library
Olympia
Maria Fletter, 206-456-5221
Award amount: $35,000

Tacoma Public Library
Tacoma
Susan Hardie, 206-591-5611
Award amount: $34,426

West Virginia
Greenbrier County Public Library with six
other libraries
Lewisburg
Ann Farr, 304-645-2350
Award amount: $48,052

Hamlin-Lincoln County Public Library System
Hamlin
Margaret Smith, 304-824-5481
Award amount: $20,125

Martinsburg-Berkeley County Public Library
Martinsburg
Margaret Batten, 304-267-8933
Award amount: $35,000

Monroe County Library with Peterson Public
Library
Union
Judith Azulay, 304-772-3038
Award amount: $70,000

Randolph County Library
Elins
Jane Fair, 304-636-1121
Award amount: $16,000

Summers County Public Library
Hinton
Myra Zeigler, 304-466-4490
Award amount: $29,151

Wisconsin
Berlin Public Library
Berlin
Carol Frank, 414-361-2650
Award amount: $29,578

Mauston Public Library
Mauston
Kathleen Manders, 608-847-4454
Award amount: $9,977

Milwaukee County Federated Library System
Milwaukee
Doris Nix, 414-286-3211
Award amount: $33,725

Milwaukee Public Library
Milwaukee
Marcy Nagy, 414-286-3070
Award amount: $35,000

Wyoming
Converse County Public Library
Douglas
Sandra Johnson, 307-358-3644
Award amount: $24,090

Total number of awards:	244
Total award amount:	$8,050,4507

LSCA State-Administered Programs

More than 80 percent of the Office of Library Program's funding is allocated under the LSCA state-administered programs (Titles I, II, and III). Analysis of the state reports indicates that the funds are used in the following ways (with a breakdown by percentage).

Public Library Services (LSCA, Title I)

- To upgrade local public library services—41 percent
- To improve services to targeted populations—32 percent
- To strengthen state library administrative agencies to improve statewide public library services—15 percent
- To improve services for targeted institutions—12 percent

Public Library Construction (LSCA, Title II)

- To remodel buildings—64 percent
- To build additions—23 percent
- To construct new public libraries—13 percent

Interlibrary Cooperation and Resources Sharing (LSCA, Title III)

To operate library networks—36 percent

- To plan new networking activities such as Internet—31 percent
- To promote resource-sharing activities among public, academic, school, and special libraries—21 percent
- To increase the technological capacity of interlibrary cooperative efforts—11 percent
- To promote preservation of fragile library materials—1 percent

In FY 1995 the funds appropriated for these programs totaled $122,224,620. Table 12 gives a state-by-state breakdown for LSCA Titles I, II, and III.

Highlights

In order to provide a more focused perspective for these state-administered grants, the state library administrative agency reports were reviewed primarily for FY 1993 to identify some of the innovative activities and trends in support of improved public library services for these selected LSCA categories.

Support for Targeted Populations: The Disabled (LSCA, Title I)

Nearly all states and most outlying areas provide services on a statewide or territorial basis through a regional library for the blind and physically handicapped. Regional libraries serve as service and distribution centers for audio-recorded materials and playback equipment available from the National Library Service (NLS) of the Library of Congress. In addition to services provided on a statewide basis, many states use LSCA funds to reach persons whose disabilities prevent them from coming to a library by funding projects at the local level.

The types of services supported on a statewide basis include books and magazines recorded on disk, cassette, and magnetic tape, along with appropriate playback equipment; materials in braille; and automation of collection inventories, patron records, and loans. Projects at the area and community levels focus on outreach activities, such as visits to shut-ins, programs for the deaf and hearing-impaired, summer reading programs for children, and radio reading services. In-house services include assistive devices for the visually and hearing-impaired, and publications in formats other than in standard print.

Major trends continue to include:

- Automation of records concerning users, materials, equipment, and circulation, enabling the libraries to serve increasing numbers of users with the same or fewer staff
- Greater use of assistive devices such as reading machines (print-to-voice), print-to-braille, magnifiers and screen enlargers, Closed-Circuit Television Systems (CCTV), text on computer screen to either large print, voice, or braille for the visually impaired, radio reading programs for the blind, and page turners for the physically handicapped. Also included are telecommunication devices for the deaf (TDDs) and closed captioned video/television programs for the hearing-impaired
- Projects whose specific purpose is to comply with the requirements of the Americans With Disabilities Act (ADA)
- Disabilities awareness and sensitivity training for library staff.

The sum of federal, state, and local funds expended for services to the disabled in FY 1993 was $31.6 million. Of this amount, $5.8 million came from federal funds. Table 13 shows the state-by-state breakout of expenditures for the Blind and Physically Handicapped.

A sampling of LSCA-funded projects for the disabled illustrates some of the innovative services provided.

Newport Beach (CA) Public Library. Newport Responds for Access. This library was one of seven chosen in the state library competitive grant program entitled Public Library Models for Americans with Disabilities Act (ADA) Compliance. The project objectives were to provide (1) a combined screen image magnifying terminal with speech synthesizer for access by visually impaired persons to the library's online catalog; (2) a personal reading machine for print materials; (3) a TDD telecommunication link to reference, book renewals, and other library services accessible by telephone for the hearing impaired; (4) wireless receivers for use in the public meeting room; (5) adjustable walking assis-

Table 12 / Funding for LSCA Titles I, II, and III, FY 1995

State	Title I	Title II	Title III
Alabama	$ 1,334,988	$ 294,108	$ 377,414
Alaska	362,422	127,778	88,285
Arizona	1,267,036	282,487	357,213
Arkansas	857,228	212,401	235,383
California	8,660,825	1,546,989	2,555,267
Colorado	1,166,685	265,325	327,380
Connecticut	1,088,437	251,943	304,118
Delaware	389,834	132,466	96,435
District of Columbia	356,810	126,818	86,617
Florida	3,908,174	734,180	1,142,381
Georgia	2,075,146	420,692	597,451
Hawaii	517,603	154,317	134,418
Idaho	497,951	150,956	128,576
Illinois	3,370,994	642,311	982,686
Indiana	1,748,659	364,855	500,392
Iowa	962,856	230,465	266,785
Kansas	886,052	217,330	243,952
Kentucky	1,227,096	275,656	345,339
Louisiana	1,364,447	299,146	386,172
Maine	535,998	157,463	139,887
Maryland	1,545,919	330,182	440,120
Massachusetts	1,829,847	378,740	524,527
Michigan	2,769,238	539,397	803,793
Minnesota	1,424,612	309,436	404,058
Mississippi	916,414	222,523	252,978
Missouri	1,618,828	342,651	461,795
Montana	427,556	138,917	107,649
Nebraska	635,691	174,513	169,524
Nevada	576,515	164,392	151,932
New Hampshire	505,057	152,171	130,688
New Jersey	2,335,938	465,293	674,980
New Mexico	638,207	174,943	170,272
New York	5,133,010	943,654	1,506,505
North Carolina	2,082,747	421,992	599,711
North Dakota	372,123	129,437	91,169
Ohio	3,206,706	614,214	933,845
Oklahoma	1,076,007	249,817	300,423
Oregon	1,021,899	240,563	284,337
Pennsylvania	3,466,128	658,581	1,010,967
Rhode Island	471,090	146,362	120,591
South Carolina	1,187,493	268,883	333,566
South Dakota	393,933	133,167	97,653
Tennessee	1,582,217	336,390	450,911
Texas	5,088,099	935,974	1,493,153
Utah	704,108	186,214	189,863
Vermont	356,062	126,690	86,395
Virginia	1,959,526	400,918	563,079
Washington	1,624,637	343,645	463,522
West Virginia	693,416	184,385	186,684

Table 12 / Funding for LSCA Titles I, II, and III, FY 1995 *(cont.)*

State	Title I	Title II	Title III
Wisconsin	1,565,717	333,568	446,005
Wyoming	327,477	121,802	77,897
American Samoa	52,680	22,168	13,769
Guam	76,096	26,173	20,731
Northern Marianas	51,750	22,010	13,493
Palau	44,099	20,701	11,219
Puerto Rico	1,154,778	263,288	323,840
Virgin Islands	67,599	24,720	18,205
Total	$ 81,562,460	$ 17,436,160	$ 23,226,000

tance devices; (6) staff sensitivity training that was videotaped for dissemination to individuals and libraries, and for orientation for new staff; and (7) publicity. As a result of this grant, the library reached all three major categories of disability (visual, hearing, and physically challenged) to benefit users in adjoining communities who lacked access to reading machines, TDDs, or large print catalog terminals.

Leon County (FL) Public Library. Library Services and Materials for People with Disabilities. Print materials were made accessible to persons with visual impairments through the use of the Reading Edge machine, closed circuit television, or a word processing workstation in the library. More than 400 titles were added to the large type collection. Hearing-impaired persons benefited from 140 new closed captioned videos and interpreters at some library programs. Also added were a manual wheelchair, an electric scooter and a modem that was attached to the visually impaired word processing station. Staff members were given disabilities awareness training through viewing and discussion of the *People First* video. Later, when the staff were tested to determine levels of awareness, 92 percent of the answers on the test were correct.

Massachusetts. Braille and Talking Book Library. Talking Book Outreach. Workshops on ADA were conducted for libraries in three regions of the state with over 100 library staff members participating. As a result of workshop participation, a comprehensive resource directory for use by public library staff was developed; the Braille and Talking Book Library revised its application for services as part of an outreach campaign to increase patron registration; and a brochure describing the services was published in French and Spanish, and its contents recorded in English and Spanish for distribution to prospective patrons. Libraries also reported a 12 percent increase in Talking Book service patrons. Twelve additional public libraries signed up for Talking Book deposit collections—a 15 percent increase. Nearly all of the workshop attendees reported that they had a better understanding of how ADA affects the operation of their libraries and gave the workshops an excellent rating. The workshop format was so successful that the Perkins School for the Blind brought the presenter back to Massachusetts to give a fourth ADA workshop attended by another 28 librarians, thus bringing critical information about ADA to more than 130 libraries in the state.

Chemung-Southern Tier (NY) Library System. Access and Authenticity: Historic Library Buildings; Resolving Physical Access and Historic Preservation Issues in Public Library Buildings (a publication of this project). The purpose of

Table 13 / LSCA Title I Expenditures for the Blind
and Physically Handicapped, FY 1993

	Federal	State	Local	Total	Population Served
Alabama	$32,882	$423,984	$16,541	$473,407	4,460
Alaska	0	77,229	0	77,229	746
Arizona	3,941	430,714	0	434,655	13,881
Arkansas	126,316	181,199	0	307,515	2,522
California	186,112	1,098,745	2,175,350	3,460,216	40,123
Colorado	118,612	208,464	0	327,076	16,474
Connecticut	269,399	171,705	0	441,104	8,500
Delaware	72,108	45,227	0	117,335	1,435
District of Columbia	24,829	107,855	0	132,684	17,000
Florida	327,843	559,787	102,171	989,801	232,881
Georgia	76,938	1,017,519	0	1,094,457	12,883
Hawaii	949	470,255	0	471,204	2,462
Idaho	19,300	206,154	0	225,454	3,650
Illinois	154,712	2,177,134	0	2,331,846	21,490
Indiana	316,111	187,216	0	503,327	12,864
Iowa	47,155	8,408	0	55,563	8,015
Kansas	122,499	469,543	0	592,042	14,771
Kentucky	89,995	200,000	0	289,995	5,561
Louisiana	171,398	221,778	0	393,176	4,830
Maine	150,467	116,638	0	267,105	3,200
Maryland	100,979	429,021	0	530,000	6,000
Massachusetts	29,350	962,916	0	992,266	20,130
Michigan	415,096	484,106	0	899,202	27,377
Minnesota	16,633	340,865	0	357,498	7,511
Mississippi	35,494	177,214	0	212,708	2,983
Missouri	95,451	287,506	0	382,957	13,928
Montana	105,869	42,165	0	148,034	2,500
Nebraska	86,944	381,342	0	468,286	4,564
Nevada	83,228	44,766	0	127,994	3,521
New Hampshire	50,169	128,877	0	179,046	2,900
New Jersey	571,244	261,428	0	832,672	15,000
New Mexico	0	145,581	0	145,581	3,015
New York	468,851	1,429,108	0	1,897,959	47,579
North Carolina	63,477	709,597	0	773,074	9,617
North Dakota*	0	0	0	0	2,204
Ohio	284,332	1,654,783	29,092	1,968,207	20,140
Oklahoma	25,179	0	0	25,179	12,000
Oregon	5,917	240,235	0	246,152	13,093
Pennsylvania	17,113	2,063,000	0	2,080,113	34,189
Rhode Island	104,438	330,939	0	435,377	2,000
South Carolina	118,765	596,975	11,091	726,831	9,261
South Dakota*	174,781	85,299	0	260,080	3,390
Tennessee	186,536	639,490	0	826,026	9,950
Texas	0	1,194,684	0	1,194,684	24,475
Utah	109,100	189,111	0	298,211	6,352
Vermont	44,760	2,251	0	47,011	1,884
Virginia	0	143,361	0	143,361	8,861
Washington	158,161	1,228,533	0	1,386,694	40,804
West Virginia	67,127	144,860	0	211,987	4,074
Wisconsin	53,345	548,725	0	602,070	15,277
Wyoming	0	55,383	0	55,383	1,200
Guam	3,000	29,535	0	32,535	16
Puerto Rico	37,412	73,272	0	110,684	964
Virgin Islands	14,460	49,552	0	64,012	200
Total	$ 5,838,777	$ 23,474,034	$ 2,334,245	$ 31,647,065	804,707

*Figures for South Dakota include North Dakota

the project was to select and survey five Carnegie-era (1880–1925) libraries in the system area for historic architectural features/layout and access obstacles. A database of all Carnegie-funded libraries in New York state was assembled. Carnegie-Mellon School of Architecture fifth-year students surveyed the five project libraries and translated the data into a computer format. A design charrette was held to compile detailed analysis and recommendations for each of the project libraries, and cost estimates for the project work were prepared for each library by the project architect. Another accomplishment of the project was the production of five logos in electronic format, five sets of plans, five 3-D computer-based models, two computer-based slide-shows, and one 3-D model on a self-contained runtime demonstration disk. In terms of user satisfaction and user success, outcomes for *Access and Authenticity* are primarily long-term, to be used as a planning tool. Short-term outcomes sought to demonstrate that physical access and aesthetic historic preservation can be compatible, and to set in motion more dialogue between library planners and the New York State Historic Preservation Office to prevent past impasses. Results of the project show that a bridge between library overseers and historic preservation officials has been built.

De Forest (WI) Public Library. Special Services for Children with Special Needs. The mission of this project was to increase family literacy by providing materials and information that will encourage parents and children to read and learn together, to enable the parents of middle and high school students who are cognitively and emotionally disabled to participate more fully in the remediation of their children, and to involve these children in library programs. The key activity was the creation and use of Busy Bags (multimedia kits based on a student interest inventory) for each ESEA (Elementary and Secondary Education Act) Chapter One student in the school district. The students were invited to assist in the creation of the kits and 52 Keepers (one-way learning activity kits) to be used weekly by parents with their children. The Busy Bags also contained Hal's Pals Dolls, designed to illustrate a variety of disabilities. Chapter One teachers brought the children in small groups to the library where all of them were issued library cards. Of the 102 children in the program, 98 percent used their cards independently of school activities. The teachers, in turn, logged the public library book use and found a correlation between improved performance and book use.

As the project evolved, the students expanded their personal use of the library and more ways were found to include them in other library activities. Some of the more profoundly disabled students were able to assist at pre-school story hours by manipulating puppets that illustrated a story. This required some rehearsal and a show of courage to perform, but they did well. A permanent display area set aside for adaptive art created by the special needs students generated positive community response. The circulation of 450 Busy Bags was 100 percent per month. The 52 Keepers on topics such as math, science, writing, and social studies were provided on a first-come, first-serve basis. Seventy-five families signed a contract to participate in program activities with their children.

As the year progressed, the school district increased its participation by providing transportation for the students, its special education instructors or aides to supervise the students, and its expert task analysis of the assembled projects. Finally, as part of this project, the Summer Reading Program was modified to count time spent being read to as pages read.

Support for Targeted Populations: Literacy (LSCA, Title I)

State reports for FY 1993 indicated a small decrease in the expenditure of LSCA funds for literacy, continuing a downward trend that started in 1988. The federal funds expended dropped from almost $2.6 million in FY 1992 to a little over $2.3 million. State and local expenditures showed a substantial increase, from $4.8 million to $6.2 million. Federal support for those with limited-English-speaking proficiency increased to $1.6 million in FY 1993 from a little over $1 million in the previous fiscal year, while state and local support more than doubled, from $41,700 in 1992 to more than $85,000 in 1993. However, these figures reflect the uneven nature of state and local support. Illinois, New Jersey, and California showed high levels of LSCA and state support for literacy. While local funds are not required to be reported and are rarely submitted, there appears to be increased support from agencies such as the United Way and a variety of combined charity campaigns.

The amount that states spend in any one category varies widely and is determined by the needs and priorities of each state. In FY 1993 each state spent on the average of 2.8 percent of its LSCA Title I funds on literacy and 1.42 percent for limited-English speakers. (Table 14 presents a state-by-state breakout for expenditures for the limited-English-speaking and Table 15 shows expenditures for literacy.) The following states far exceeded the national average expenditures in FY 1993:

Limited-English-Speaking		Literacy	
State	Percent	State	Percent
IL	10	DC	49
NC	10	IL	12
DC	5	MA	9
MA	5	ID	8
CA	4	NJ	6
NJ	4	TX	6

There is also increasing literacy activity and spending in several other categories funded by LSCA Title I funds. Family literacy activities were supported under Title I categories for inadequate services, disadvantaged, institutionalized, and child-care centers. Other programs were found under Title I categories for the elderly, populations without services, community information and referral centers, construction and technology (LSCA Title II), and resource sharing (LSCA Title III).

State library agencies continue to be aggressive in using LSCA funds to leverage other federal, state, and local funds. In addition, support for literacy activities seems to be broadening to include family literacy programs in libraries, child care centers, limited-English-speaking environments, and prisons. The following state programs illustrate some of these trends.

Table 14 / LSCA Title I Expenditures for the Limited-English-Speaking, FY 1993

	Federal	State	Local	Total
Alabama	$0	$0	$0	$0
Alaska	0	0	0	0
Arkansas	0	0	0	0
Arizona	0	0	0	0
California	303,871	0	0	303,871
Colorado	20,633	0	0	20,633
Connecticut	0	0	0	0
Delaware	0	0	0	0
District of Columbia	18,849	28,703	0	47,552
Florida	34,770	0	11,590	46,360
Georgia	0	0	0	0
Hawaii	0	0	0	0
Idaho	0	0	0	0
Illinois	321,388	0	0	321,388
Indiana	0	0	0	0
Iowa	3,057	0	0	3,057
Kansas	0	0	0	0
Kentucky	0	0	0	0
Louisiana	16,061	11,759	0	27,820
Maine	0	0	0	0
Maryland	30,199	0	0	30,199
Massachusetts	119,131	0	0	119,131
Michigan	58,184	0	0	58,184
Minnesota	0	0	0	0
Mississippi	0	0	0	0
Missouri	0	0	0	0
Montana	0	0	0	0
Nebraska	0	0	0	0
Nevada	2,500	0	0	2,500
New Hampshire	0	0	0	0
New Jersey	115,000	0	0	115,000
New Mexico	0	0	0	0
New York	140,556	0	0	140,556
North Carolina	202,709	0	31,097	233,886
North Dakota	0	0	0	0
Ohio	8,081	66	0	8,147
Oklahoma	0	0	0	0
Oregon	15,789	0	0	15,789
Pennsylvania	0	0	0	0
Rhode Island	0	0	0	0
South Carolina	0	0	0	0
South Dakota	0	0	0	0
Tennessee	0	0	0	0
Texas	141,979	0	0	141,979
Utah	0	0	0	0
Vermont	0	0	0	0
Virginia	25,564	0	0	25,564
Washington	17,649	0	0	17,649
West Virginia	0	0	0	0
Wisconsin	0	0	0	0
Wyoming	0	0	0	0
American Samoa	0	0	0	0
Guam	2,000	2,000	0	4,000
Northern Marianas	0	0	0	0
Palau	0	0	0	0
Puerto Rico	2,984	0	0	2,984
Virgin Islands	0	0	0	0
Total	$1,601,034	$42,528	$42,687	$1,686,249

Table 15 / LSCA Title I Expenditures for Literacy, FY 1993

	Federal	State	Local	Total
Alabama	$2,234	$0	$3,322	$5,556
Alaska	0	0	0	0
Arkansas	0	0	0	0
Arizona	0	0	0	0
California	155,911	0	0	155,911
Colorado	0	0	0	0
Connecticut	25,000	0	0	25,000
Delaware	12,292	8,838	0	21,130
District of Columbia	169,111	98,530	0	267,641
Florida	23,520	0	7,840	31,360
Georgia	10,000	0	0	10,000
Hawaii	29,615	0	0	29,615
Idaho	45,759	0	0	45,759
Illinois	391,214	4,907,072	0	5,298,286
Indiana	12,007	0	0	12,007
Iowa	0	0	0	0
Kansas	49,834	0	0	49,834
Kentucky	41,685	0	0	41,685
Louisiana	19,273	14,111	0	33,384
Maine	0	0	0	0
Maryland	3,150	0	0	3,150
Massachusetts	198,896	0	0	198,896
Michigan	25,138	0	0	25,138
Minnesota	0	0	0	0
Mississippi	4,998	0	0	4,998
Missouri	9,910	0	0	9,910
Montana	0	0	0	0
Nebraska	0	0	0	0
Nevada	6,000	0	0	6,000
New Hampshire	0	0	0	0
New Jersey	194,373	1,154,886	0	1,349,259
New Mexico	0	0	0	0
New York	289,761	0	0	289,761
North Carolina	10,409	0	0	10,409
North Dakota	0	0	0	0
Ohio	22,017	66	0	22,083
Oklahoma	54,034	0	0	54,034
Oregon	0	0	0	0
Pennsylvania	0	0	0	0
Rhode Island	10,746	13,946	0	24,692
South Carolina	29,701	2,471	15,953	48,125
South Dakota	1,334	4,243	0	5,577
Tennessee	99,823	0	0	99,823
Texas	279,744	0	0	279,744
Utah	31,000	0	0	31,000
Vermont	0	0	0	0
Virginia	46,578	0	0	46,578
Washington	0	0	0	0
West Virginia	0	0	0	0
Wisconsin	32,388	0	0	32,388
Wyoming	0	0	0	0
Guam	0	0	0	0
Puerto Rico	0	0	0	0
Virgin Islands	0	0	0	0
Total	$2,337,455	$6,204,163	$27,115	$8,568,73؛

- The Illinois Secretary of State/Librarian has identified literacy as a major program for his administration with emphasis on family literacy. The initial literacy efforts were started in FY 1986 with LSCA funds and in succeeding years were supported primarily with state funds. In FY 1993 approximately $4.9 million of state funds was appropriated to combat illiteracy. Currently 12 percent of LSCA funds are targeted for family literacy grants. The state has used the approach of coordinating and developing new programs statewide, providing regional workshops for local libraries on the role of libraries in the literacy effort and working with local community organizations to identify needs for literacy projects to be funded with state or federal funds.

  In FY 1993 the Illinois State Library Advisory Committee made family literacy a new priority. Using approximately $400,000 in LSCA funds, 14 projects were funded. The projects, using a variety of names—Reading as Families Together (RAFT), Families Learning Together, Family Magic, Serving the Deserving/A Family Affair, express the common goal of serving disadvantaged parents and children-at-risk and breaking the cycle of illiteracy. *The Role of Illinois Libraries in Family Literacy: An Initial Look at Library Involvement in Family Literacy Programs* was produced as part of the effort. The 75-page report provides a summary of the role of libraries in developing and implementing family literacy programs in Illinois; examines the differences and similarities of the programs throughout the state; provides useful and practical information about the programs; and makes preliminary recommendations on program development and growth.

  While several of the above programs targeted the category of limited-English speaking, the state also used 10 percent of its LSCA funds to meet the need for materials and programs aimed at those who speak other languages. "We Speak Your Language," a project sponsored by the Chicago Public Library, produced a videotape introducing the American public library and provided multimedia materials for the study of English. The video, produced in Spanish, Polish, Korean and Chinese, shows that a library is an informational place for all citizens. The tape is generic so that it can be used by any library.

  The Portage-Cragin Branch of the Chicago Public Library established a reference and referral center for Polish-language materials. An 800-number telephone line was installed and directories of Polish American organizations and collections were produced. The North Suburban Library System designed a project called Beyond the Library Card: A Partnership to Design an English as a Second Language Library Curriculum to link ESL teachers and classes with the library. Components include teacher notes, reading passages, cultural comparison activities, language practice activities, "Information Gaps," games, and home activities. The Adult Learning Resource Center added a workshop based on the library curriculum; it is being offered to the state's 1,500 ESL teachers.

- The IDAHO State Library combined its Summer Reading and Literacy programs into one unit called the Statewide Reading Program. Using 8 percent of its LSCA funds, the library planned and coordinated the summer program, which attracted 85 public libraries and approximately 15,000 children; employed a special projects coordinator to provide support for local literacy projects, the Idaho Coalition for Adult Literacy and the Boise State University Adult Learning Center; and supported local literacy projects through competitive subgrants. The Boise Public Library purchased materials for its Literacy Lab, which offers a wide range of learning opportunities for adults and a family literacy program of classes for low-income adults and their 3- to 5-year-old children. These services and materials included reading readiness software designed for pre-school use; story hours; activities to practice small motor skills; and a listening center with music and books. Parents learned basic parenting skills, and how to choose books and read to their children; and were encouraged to "volunteer" in their child's classroom once a month. The Caldwell Public Library bought high interest/low vocabulary reading materials and books with tapes to support the adult new readers in the community. The Preston Carnegie Library used its grant to buy materials and equipment, implement a volunteer tutor training program, and publicize the program through multimedia advertising.

- Massachusetts used 10 percent of its LSCA funds to support literacy and 5 percent for limited-English-speaking categories. Also, it used more than $70,000 under the inadequate services category in Title I to fund literacy-related services such as the Massachusetts Family Reading Project. Over 350 public libraries and 53,485 children participated in this summer reading program and 189 child-care providers and librarians attended special continuing education workshops. Two smaller literacy-related programs were also funded under this category: Whole Language at Home and at School, which produced language theme-based kits for children in kindergarten through grade 3 and offered instruction to parents in their use; and Learning All the Time, which created a supportive environment where parents and children could use materials and computer-assisted programs to learn together.

- Fifteen subgrants were made to a wide variety of programs under the literacy and limited-English-speaking Title I categories. For example, the LIFT (Literacy Involves Families Together) project at the Morrill Memorial Library provided active support for adult learners and their children through a series of structured activities based in the library, workshops, and the production of learning packets. The New Visions for New Learners book discussion group at the Palmer Public Library helped to broaden adult learners' skills as they read and discussed American history and autobiography with the assistance of their tutors. West Springfield Public Library established a program called ESL for Those at Home, helping over 80 non-English speakers (Russian, Polish, Vietnamese, Chinese and Spanish) learn English. The Lawrence Public Library conducted a Library ESL/Job Survival Skills Literacy program of interactive lessons combining digitized video and movies with voice-annotated text, to teach listening skills needed for job interviews, employability skills, and writing and reading comprehension.

- The District of Columbia continued to use the largest portion of its LSCA funds for literacy activities (49 percent for literacy and 5 percent for limited-English-speaking categories under Title I), reaching over 75,000 people. The program, housed in the Adult Basic Education Office at the Martin Luther King Library, is totally integrated into the service goals of the library. This year the library noted an increase in the number of technical assistance requests from city literacy providers, as well as an increase in the number of requests for the Spanish-speaking and literacy-related videos. LSCA funds were used to expand and enhance collections at 10 branch libraries, offer training to individuals and community organizations, and publish a bi-monthly newsletter. LSCA funds also were used for a model literacy center and the printing of Remembering Washington, a "best-seller" authored and edited by participants in the Never Too Old to Learn Program. This oral history program also produced a tutor manual to accompany the text.

Support for Targeted Populations: The Elderly (LSCA, Title I)

Since 1971 when library services to the elderly was added under Title I, projects under this category funded in whole or in part with LSCA funds have been tracked. The sum of federal, state, and local funds expended for services to the elderly in FY 1992 was $2.1 million. Of this amount, $1.7 million came from LSCA funds. In FY 1993 $1.4 million was expended on services to the elderly; of this $1.14 million came from LSCA funds, representing approximately 2.56 percent of the total funding under Title I. Table 16 provides a state-by-state breakout of expenditures for the elderly.

Projects support programs for materials in special formats, special interests or needs of the elderly, and materials or programs presented or delivered in settings outside the public library, such as where the elderly live and congregate. In 1990 a new category was added under Title I for intergenerational services; this category also has implications for the elderly.

About half of elderly projects (59) supported the acquisition of large-print books. The increased popularity of these books, coupled with improved typesetting methods, has increased the number of titles available and brought their pricing in line with other comparable library books. Some projects funded by the Maine State Library provided such books, circulating them either to individuals or libraries for short-term loans or in rotating sets to local libraries for longer periods of time.

As the elderly population becomes more technologically sophisticated, audio materials, which were once unappreciated by this age group, appear to be increasingly popular. There were 35 projects related to books on tape and 23 projects related to the purchase of films and videos. Books and magazines of special interest to the elderly also remain popular; there were 18 projects related to books and magazines of special interest to the elderly; popular subjects were health issues, crafts, and travel. For example, the Pittsburgh-Camp County (TX) Library combined the purchase of audio materials, books, and magazines for use by the elderly.

Eighteen projects supporting the purchase and use of multisensory kits as an aid in life review and stimulation of the senses were supported under LSCA. The Atchison (KS) Public Library purchased Bi-Folkal kits and used them and a "Kansas Kit" for programming. These proved so popular that a kit is being produced on Atchison County. The Seattle Public Library produced kits aimed at reaching the Japanese and Chinese communities in nursing homes, retirement homes, and senior centers.

Thirty-five projects involved special programming on travel, retirement, and health issues, while only two book-talk programs were offered. Twenty projects were designed as intergenerational programs that included read-aloud sessions, storytelling, and study assistance. While bringing satisfaction to both generations, these programs were primarily designed to use senior volunteers to improve the reading and language skills of school age and pre-school children. For example, Los Angeles Public Library's popular Grandparents and Books project is now being carefully replicated throughout the state. The DeKalb County (GA) Public Library System's successful Building Blocks on Wheels program has been reaching over 50 families a month through homeless shelters, public health clinics, and high school parenting classes.

The awareness of transportation problems encountered by the elderly has generated a number of projects designed to bring books and other materials directly to them. Rotating and deposit collections at sites such as nursing homes and senior centers were mentioned in 27 projects. Books were delivered to the elderly in 19 projects, while similar services to group sites were mentioned in 23 projects. Bookmobiles were used in 7 of these projects. Libraries also have continued to support books-by-mail programs. Some libraries have reported having difficulty in obtaining approval for free postage for large-print books. The Kentucky Department for Libraries and Archives had such a problem, but resolved it and used the additional funds to buy more large-print books!

Twenty-eight of the LSCA projects showed increased cooperation with other service agencies within the community. In addition, training of service workers was mentioned in 21 projects. For example, a Mississippi Library Commission project trained local library staff in using new technology in service delivery; the Aurora (CO) Public Library trained seniors in the art of storytelling; the Mount Clemens (MI) Public Library trained senior volunteers in the use of computers; and the Mid-York (NY) Library System produced training kits for all senior citizen caregivers to the elderly.

Support to Targeted Institutions: Major Urban Resource Libraries (MURLs) (LSCA, Title I)

Funding support for Major Urban Resource Libraries (MURLs) was first authorized under LSCA in 1977. The provision requires that when the total appropriation for LSCA Title I exceeds $60 million, states must initiate a MURLs program. To be eligible, a city must have a population of at least 100,000 and the library must provide services or access to its collection beyond its traditional service area.

Table 16 / LSCA Tilte I Expenditures for the Elderly, FY 1993

	Federal Funds		State	Local
	Carry Over	Current		
Alabama	$229	$89	$0	$0
Alaska	0	0	0	0
Arkansas	0	0	0	0
Arizona	0	0	0	0
California	299,429	0	0	0
Colorado	8,620	2,874	0	0
Connecticut	0	0	0	0
Delaware	0	6,582	0	0
District of Columbia	1,234	0	104,663	0
Florida	0	0	0	0
Georgia	48,574	0	0	0
Hawaii	9,960	0	0	0
Idaho	5,475	0	0	0
Illinois	103,765	0	0	0
Indiana	0	4,527	0	0
Iowa	1,175	0	0	0
Kansas	25,000	0	0	0
Kentucky	54,208	11,160	0	0
Louisiana	0	12,045	8,819	0
Maine	0	448	42,790	0
Maryland	25,075	5,625	0	0
Massachusetts	0	41,537	0	0
Michigan	35,471	5,272	0	0
Minnesota	0	11,700	0	0
Mississippi	1,548	0	3,451	0
Missouri	48,915	3,483	0	0
Montana	5,435	0	0	14,560
Nebraska	0	0	0	0
Nevada	0	0	0	0
New Hampshire	1,401	464	0	0
New Jersey	0	0	0	0
New Mexico	0	0	0	0
New York	34,736	6,131	0	0
North Carolina	49,021	0	0	0
North Dakota	0	0	0	0
Ohio	14,980	1,404	176	13,631
Oklahoma	0	0	0	0
Oregon	4,210	0	0	0
Pennsylvania	45,115	0	0	0
Rhode Island	1,578	3,319	23,303	0
South Carolina	1,503	35,700	4,789	25,400
South Dakota	12,414	5,838	15,645	0
Tennessee	54,550	0	0	0
Texas	167,359	0	0	0
Utah	11,500	0	0	0
Vermont	0	0	0	0
Virginia	27,601	0	0	0
Washington	46,986	26,317	0	0
West Virginia	0	0	0	0
Wisconsin	83,286	0	0	0
Wyoming	0	0	0	0
Guam	0	0	0	0
Puerto Rico	0	0	0	0
Virgin Islands	0	0	0	0
Total	$1,230,353	$184,515	$203,636	$53,591

When the law was initially passed there had been some confusion in determining whether a major urban resource library included the population of the library's service area or just the population of the city in which the library was located. Sections 3(14) and 102(c)(2) of LSCA ultimately defined the MURL in terms of the city.

The state library administrative agency determines which cities qualify as a MURL. From FY 1992 to FY 1994, 39 states and Puerto Rico had eligible cities over 100,000 population. Delaware, District of Columbia, Maine, Montana, New Hampshire, North Dakota, South Carolina, Vermont, West Virginia, and Wyoming had no cities with populations over 100,000. The Bureau of Census population counts for 1993 indicated that there were 194 eligible American cities with population over 100,000 (excluding the District of Columbia) and six cities in Puerto Rico.

Table 17 shows the amount expended for MURLs from FY 1979 through FY 1993 and the amount reserved by the states in FY 1994. Table 18 provides a state-by-state breakout of MURLs expenditures for FY 1992 and FY 1993 and funds reserved for FY 1994.

The following projects are representative.

California. California is an example of a state that has developed an innovative MURLs program. A designated MURL in the state had to serve as one of the resource centers for the California Library Services Act (CLSA) system and participate in the CLSA database and statewide interlibrary loan programs. It also had to file a Regional Area Collection Development Plan, prepared in cooperation with neighboring libraries and systems and based on a needs assessment of libraries and users within the region. The MURL funds were then used for the purchase of materials and their processing along with other related activities described in their collection development plan.

In FY 1993 the California State Library sponsored a seminar on the regional collection development plans with its 44 MURL libraries. They used two state-of-the-art toolkits for collection evaluation: the Pacific Northwest Collection Development (PNCD) plan (a multistate effort) and the Research Libraries Group Conspectus (a national program). The two-day conference laid the groundwork for all of these libraries to launch needs assessment, develop pilot projects, and identify regional cooperative approaches. A second seminar was held in spring 1994 to integrate the progress achieved at the regional level. Planners were to draft purpose statements, goals, and define objectives for a Statewide Cooperative Collection Development Program.

The Orange County Public Library at Anaheim targeted purchases in business reference and technology for users in Northern Orange County including personal and corporate finance, investment corporate directories, export/import and banking. Business reference accounts for one-half of questions asked at the Central Library. All MURL libraries in Orange County now meet regularly to coordinate selection decisions on a regional basis.

The Kern County Public Library in Bakersfield purchased subscriptions to business and medical journals; reference materials in business, medicine, law, world affairs, and multiculturalism; and microform subscriptions to key out-of-

Table 17 / Major Urban Resource Libraries (MURLs) Expenditures for FYs 1979–1993, Amount Reserved for FY 1994

FY 1979	$1,666,225
FY 1980	$1,722,990
FY 1981	$1,776,609
FY 1982*	$0
FY 1983*	$0
FY 1984	$2,142,102
FY 1985	$4,256,151
FY 1986	$4,231,144
FY 1987	$4,921,172
FY 1988	$4,857,391
FY 1989	$5,086,800
FY 1990	$5,393,628
FY 1991	$5,460,369
FY 1992	$5,804,659
FY 1993	$6,013,781
FY 1994	$6,444,853
Total	$59,777,874

*In FY 1982 and FY 1983, the Title I appropriation was $60,000,000. Therefore, states did not reserve funds for MURLs.

state newspapers. Materials on employment received especially heavy use during the grant period. MURL materials were consulted to answer inquiries from 24 branches and from other types of libraries in the region.

The San Bernardino County Public Library purchased materials in career/education, especially job searching; business and government; and current events/contemporary issues. CD-ROM periodical indexes such as Infotrac were purchased covering all major subject priorities. As a result of strengthening the reference collection, only 85 out of 109,124 inquiries received in 1991/1992 had to be forwarded to the system reference center.

In cooperation with nearby MURL libraries in the County of Los Angeles and the cities of El Monte, Glendale, Pasadena, and Pomona, Los Angeles Public Library identified the first steps to coordinate collection development on a regional basis. The top priority was to purchase resources on employment and business development in the Los Angeles basin.

The priority for expenditure at the Oakland Public Library was the development of an ethnic collection. The MURL grant was used to expand the library's emphasis on serving new immigrants beyond the ongoing programs for its Latin American and Asian branches. Subjects covered include English as a second language, citizenship, non-English-language materials, ethnic video and music, and materials on African Americans, Asian Americans, Hispanics (Latinos), and Native Americans. The Oakland ethnic collection is one of the identified critical areas in the San Francisco Bay Area Regional Collection Development Plan.

New York. The New York state MURLs added materials and equipment to strengthen and expand collections that were available to users outside their immediate service area. The Albany Public Library used its MURL funds to

Table 18 / Major Urban Resource Libraries (MURLs) Expenditures for FYs 1992, 1993, and Funds Reserved for FY 1994

State	FY 1992	FY 1993	FY 1994 (Reserved)
Alabama	$40,130	$126,639	$173,360
Alaska	18,392	19,888	19,888
Arizona	177,291	120,226	157,900
Arkansas	20,000	20,000	20,000
California	1,036,023	1,117,838	1,095,635
Colorado	195,682	195,682	154,393
Connecticut	55,235	52,935	52,935
Delaware	0	0	0
District of Columbia	0	0	0
Florida	202,380	202,374	402,760
Georgia	73,680	74,160	74,000
Hawaii	38,878	38,829	79,448
Idaho	18,190	18,200	36,400
Illinois	284,996	284,945	284,945
Indiana	110,719	110,719	110,719
Iowa	27,586	27,573	27,237
Kansas	60,761	60,761	70,178
Kentucky	45,688	45,688	45,688
Louisiana	184,262	184,262	184,262
Maine	0	0	0
Maryland	67,099	67,099	65,757
Massachusetts	87,864	83,823	83,823
Michigan	172,649	172,625	172,656
Minnesota	56,195	54,492	54,492
Mississippi	17,578	17,192	17,192
Missouri	96,664	91,141	97,422
Montana	0	0	0
Nebraska	47,908	46,420	44,847
Nevada	34,000	34,769	34,769
New Hampshire	0	0	0
New Jersey	68,006	68,006	68,006
New Mexico	0	33,842	67,684
New York	739,725	725,533	720,455
North Carolina	89,300	93,890	90,715
North Dakota	0	0	0
Ohio	233,167	192,732	234,072
Oklahoma	60,270	80,439	132,794
Oregon	9,912	57,709	104,568
Pennsylvania	302,809	302,809	302,809
Rhode Island	13,826	13,859	13,859
South Carolina	0	0	0
South Dakota	0	8,817	8,820
Tennessee	132,000	132,000	132,000
Texas	628,752	623,304	627,109
Utah	25,000	25,000	25,000
Vermont	0	0	0
Virginia	135,600	135,602	135,602
Washington	0	75,742	90,660
West Virginia	0	0	0
Wisconsin	98,580	71,933	23,810
Wyoming	0	0	0
Guam	0	0	0
Northern Marianas	0	0	0
Puerto Rico	97,862	104,284	106,184
Virgin Islands	0	0	0
Total	$5,804,659	$6,013,781	$6,444,853

acquire video, book, and microfilm materials in the areas of substance abuse and health issues, parenting, employment skills and job hunting, multicultural awareness, arts and literature, finance and small business development, the American justice system, and consumer issues. The library also purchased archival microfilm subscriptions to the *Albany Times Union, Wall Street Journal, Christian Science Monitor,* and the *New York Times.*

The Buffalo and Erie County Public Library strengthened heavily used special collections. Over 1,200 volumes and 59 audiovisual items were purchased for the collections in art, computers, genealogy, disabilities, international trade and travel, medical books for the layperson, and job hunting videos. Feedback from the subject specialists indicated a significant improvement in library service. Testimonials from a number of area residents indicated that having more current materials purchased with MURLs money had made the library a much more valuable resource.

The New York Public Library used a Gallup Study as an evaluative tool for defining its needs. The results indicated that the staff's perceptions of use patterns and needs were very much in agreement with the public's perception of services. Areas where perceptions differed will be used as places to finetune the service. MURL funds provided two new databases in the History and Social Services Department, 40 audiovisual items, 46 periodical subscriptions on CD, and 346 periodical subscriptions. In addition, over 970 print items were purchased.

The Onondaga County Syracuse Public Library reviewed, updated, and expanded indexes and general reference, education and careers, science and technology, and history and genealogy holdings. The library tested OCLC First Search with an eye to purchasing blocks of searches from OCLC rather than investing in print copies of the indexes. With MURL funds they were able to buy "Help Wanted" and a microfiche publication that compiled help-wanted ads from the Sunday papers of 64 cities.

The Queens Borough Public Library bought over 3,000 books and nearly 900 audiovisual items. About 38 percent of its MURL funding was spent for the Instant Image project designed to store, retrieve, and print 55,000 photographs from the local history collection of the Long Island Division.

In the Yonkers Public Library the MURL funds were used to purchase specialized reference sources not readily available in other public libraries. Use of these unique resources enabled the staff to answer patrons' business and technical questions by telephone, fax, and in person. The "phonefiche" collection is a service constantly used by both telephone and walk-in patrons.

Support to Targeted Institutions: Metropolitan Libraries (LSCA, Title I)

Under LSCA, states may provide funds to cities to strengthen metropolitan public libraries serving as state-defined national or regional resource centers. This provision allows the states to determine which libraries have the capacity to serve as such resource centers without the 100,000 population requirement used for MURLs.

The amount expended for this activity from FY 1984 through FY 1993 and the amount reserved for FY 1994 are shown in Table 19. Table 20 provides a state-by-state breakout for FY 1992 and FY 1993 and funds reserved for FY 1994.

As in preceding years, the LSCA funds made a significant impact on strengthening public library collections. The reports continued to show increased purchases of compact disk recordings, videotapes, computers, microform readers and printers, videotape recorders, and other applicable technologies. The following projects are representative.

California. The California State Library addressed its need for regional resource centers in the state's long-range plan by noting that the regional reference centers would be the backup resource for referral of questions from the California Library Services Act (CLSA) system reference centers, which, in turn, back up the local public libraries. California has funded this third-level reference referral program with LSCA funds since 1969 and has been engaged in an extensive planning process to develop the CLSA State Reference Centers since 1985. LSCA funds have been used to provide continuity in the provision of third-level reference referral services. They have also been used to field-test alternative methods of strengthening and improving reference services throughout California. The State of California Answering Network (SCAN) at the Los Angeles Public Library (LAPL) is supported as an overall backup for questions from the state's system reference centers. SCAN's mission is to provide California residents with responses to advanced inquiries by tapping the rich resources of LAPL and the University of California at Los Angeles Library, among other resources. The goal set by SCAN is to respond to any reference query referred by a California public library. In fulfilling this mission, the SCAN staff provide service to all 15 of California's cooperative system reference centers.

A second state grant was made to the Metropolitan Cooperative Library System in the Los Angeles area to field-test alternative methods for organizing reference service. California's public library systems have also voluntarily arrived at standard definitions for reference service over the past four years. The new system enables them to collect and aggregate it from the local level, allowing a much more detailed and accurate picture of the information needs of California's library users on an ongoing basis.

Florida. In Florida the Jacksonville Public Library used its FY 1993 funds to make revisions to the library system's interlibrary loan policy and procedures. These revisions allow the branch libraries to turn reserve requests for materials that have been declared lost or missing into interlibrary loan requests. This process appears seamless to the customer as no contact is made unless information needs to be verified. This policy change allows customers to obtain needed material more quickly as the library staff fills out and submits all necessary forms without the customer needing to make a second request.

Support for Public Library Construction (LSCA, Title II)

In FY 1992 the states obligated more than $16.8 million in LSCA funds for public library construction projects. Funding included more than $8.2 million from the total FY 1992 appropriation of $16.4 million and $13.4 million carried over from the previous years' allotments. This left $8.1 million from the FY 1992

Table 19 / Metropolitan Public Libraries Serving as National or Regional Resource Centers, Expenditures for FYs 1984–1993, Amount Reserved for FY 1994

FY 1984	$2,726,236
FY 1985	$3,571,713
FY 1986	$3,514,961
FY 1987	$2,959,216
FY 1988	$2,972,531
FY 1989	$2,892,955
FY 1990	$2,623,184
FY 1991	$2,613,508
FY 1992	$3,249,556
FY 1993	$3,506,013
FY 1994	$3,412,736
Total	$34,042,609

allotment and over $4.8 million of carryover funds available for approved projects in FY 1993.

During the same year, 33 states completed 112 public library construction projects involving Title II funds. Table 21 lists the completed projects. There were 15 fewer completed projects than in FY 1991. The combined LSCA, state, and local funding for these projects totaled $58.7 million with 18.3 percent coming from Title II funds.

When compared with expenditures for FY 1991, there was a 20 percent decrease in the amount of LSCA funds used to support these local projects. During the same period there was an increase of 100 percent in state matching funds. The combined state and local matching funds totaled more than $47.9 million or 81 percent of the total costs for all completed public library construction projects in FY 1992. Of this amount, local contributions made up the largest percentage with 68 percent of the funds.

Support for Preservation (LSCA, Title III)

As allowed under Section 305 of Title III, a number of states developed statewide preservation cooperation plans and initiated several major projects in FY 1993. In many instances, the state librarian coordinated and supported conservation and preservation of records throughout their state and provided technical assistance to their local public libraries.

The District of Columbia Public Library used Title III funds to support a Local History Resource Sharing Project, which was expanded to include the microfilming of valuable local resources. Included was an oral history project that resulted in the first publication of a D.C. neighborhood history.

The Nevada State Library provided continued support for a preservation program coordinated with the University of Nevada, Reno, to film most of Nevada's newspapers.

Massachusetts funded three projects that allowed previously inaccessible historical collections to be accessed by the public. In Newburyport, a collection of genealogy, local, and maritime history was cataloged and entered into the

Table 20 / Metropolitan Public Libraries Serving as National or Regional Resource Centers, Expenditures for FYs 1992, 1993, and Funds Reserved for FY 1994

State	FY 1992	FY 1993	FY 1994
Alabama	$ 7,950	$0	$0
Alaska	0	0	0
Arizona	0	0	0
Arkansas	0	0	0
California	722,200	882,165	821,185
Colorado	1,092,792	1,092,792	1,092,792
Connecticut	0	0	0
Delaware	0	0	0
District of Columbia	123,126	71,628	72,149
Florida	302,500	302,500	302,500
Georgia	0	0	0
Hawaii	0	0	0
Idaho	0	0	0
Illinois	0	0	0
Indiana	0	0	0
Iowa	0	0	0
Kansas	16,592	16,592	0
Kentucky	0	0	0
Louisiana	0	0	0
Maine	0	0	0
Maryland	0	0	0
Massachusetts	0	0	0
Michigan	160,762	231,380	65,084
Minnesota	301,672	339,000	350,810
Mississippi	0	0	0
Missouri	0	0	0
Montana	0	0	0
Nebraska	0	0	0
Nevada	34,000	0	18,000
New Hampshire	0	0	0
New Jersey	74,007	0	0
New Mexico	0	0	0
New York	0	0	0
North Carolina	198,365	354,895	475,126
North Dakota	0	0	0
Ohio	0	0	0
Oklahoma	0	0	0
Oregon	0	0	0
Pennsylvania	0	0	0
Rhode Island	0	0	0
South Carolina	0	0	0
South Dakota	0	0	0
Tennessee	215,590	215,061	215,090
Texas	0	0	0
Utah	0	0	0
Vermont	0	0	0
Virginia	0	0	0
Washington	0	0	0
West Virginia	0	0	0
Wisconsin	0	0	0
Wyoming	0	0	0
Guam	0	0	0
Puerto Rico	0	0	0
Virgin Islands	0	0	0
Total	$3,249,556	$3,506,013	$3,412,736

Table 21 / LSCA Title II Construction Projects Completed in FY 1992

	Project	Federal	State	Local	Total
Alabama	Jackson P.L.	$112,500	$0	$180,035	$292,535
	Guntersville P.L.	100,000	0	122,273	222,273
Alaska		0	0	0	0
Arizona		0	0	0	0
Arkansas	Arkansas State Library	27,639	0	70,496	98,135
California	Nevada County Library	994,500	0	1,219,325	2,213,825
	El Segundo P.L.	158,727	0	3,834,325	3,993,052
Colorado	Limon P.L. (A)	2,760	0	3,420	6,180
	Limon P.L. (B)	41,400	0	48,600	90,000
	Limon P.L. (C)	5,110	0	6,000	11,110
	Limon P.L. (D)	50,000	0	398,448	448,448
	Burlington P.L.	70,000	0	248,633	318,633
	Co State Library (Admin)	36,085	0	0	36,085
	Mancos P.L.	57,000	0	61,650	118,650
	Lake City P.L.	15,000	0	16,320	31,320
	Nucla P.L.	2,000	0	5,100	7,100
Connecticut	Shelton	100,000	350,000	642,466	1,092,466
Delaware		0	0	0	0
District of Columbia		0	0	0	0
Florida	East Naples Br. Lib.	200,000	0	515,500	715,500
	DeLand Area P.L.	200,000	70,000	2,248,102	2,518,102
	Englewood Charlotte P.L.	200,000	0	219,423	419,423
Georgia		0	0	0	0
Hawaii	Salt Lake Moanalua P.L.	135,050	6,896,597	0	7,031,647
Idaho		0	0	0	0
Illinois		0	0	0	0
Indiana	Greenwood	198,051	0	2,001,949	2,200,000
Iowa	Edgewood P.L.	89,000	0	278,085	367,085
	Rock Valley P.L.	111,036	0	490,964	602,000
Kansas		0	0	0	0
Kentucky		0	0	0	0
Louisiana	Ascension	143,122	0	779,579	922,701
	Morton P.L.	80,000	0	129,302	209,302
Maine	Patten Free	6,452	0	8,513	14,965
	Madawaska	137,640	0	137,640	275,280
	Maine	9,800	0	0	9,800
Maryland	Cecil County P.L.	50,000	0	78,500	128,500
Massachusetts	Plympton P.L.	100,000	193,910	163,449	457,359
Michigan	Brigeport P.L.	120,000	0	495,000	615,000
	Grand Rapids P.L.	77,320	81,347	13,156	171,823
	Cadillac Wexford P.L.	20,600	0	35,555	56,155
	South Haven	95,000	0	297,200	392,200
Minnesota	Foley P.L.	108,062	0	217,288	325,350
	Hector P.L.	72,701	0	147,607	220,308
	Hinckley P.L.	65,922	0	135,447	201,369
	Hoyt Lakes P.L.	162,987	0	464,753	627,740
	Madelia Lib.	155,204	0	315,385	470,589
	Stewartville P.L.	171,600	0	368,619	540,219

Table 21 / LSCA Title II Construction Projects Completed in FY 1992 *(cont.)*

	Project	Federal	State	Local	Total
Missippi	Morton P.L.	80,000	0	129,302	209,302
Missouri	Rolla	23,590	0	28,468	52,058
	Flat River	63,359	0	63,363	126,722
	Grundy	47,500	0	47,500	95,000
	Douglas	47,500	0	47,235	94,735
	St. Louis	150,000	0	342,587	492,587
Montana		0	0	0	0
Nebraska		0	0	0	0
Nevada		0	0	0	0
New Hampshire	South Hampton	25,000	0	25,000	50,000
	Tucker Free	40,000	0	64,000	104,000
	Wilton	8,700	0	8,800	17,500
	Manchester	50,000	0	50,000	100,000
	New Hampshire	6,197	28,200	0	34,397
New Mexico		0	0	0	0
New Jersey	Bloomfield P.L.	45,000	0	144,136	189,136
New York	Rockville Centre	39,096	0	3,280,000	3,319,096
	Canajoharie	192,192	0	1,197,299	1,389,491
	Floral Park	13,128	0	38,461	51,589
	Southhold Free	189,245	0	1,241,658	1,430,903
	Barnevald	6,608	0	12,272	18,880
	Crosby	1,114	0	2,068	3,182
	Massena	1,890	0	3,600	5,490
	New City	3,334	0	6,192	9,526
	Tonawanda	3,500	0	6,500	10,000
	Finkelstein	28,490	0	52,910	81,400
	Kent	29,750	0	55,502	85,252
	Katonah	47,124	0	87,516	134,640
	Riverhead	4,375	0	12,100	16,475
	Raquette	994	0	1,845	2,839
	Western Town	9,415	0	17,485	26,900
North Carolina	Macon County	80,000	164,500	418,454	662,954
	Bethel	85,000	0	103,031	188,031
North Dakota	Casselton P.L.	27,500	0	27,500	55,000
	Minot P.L.	33,123	0	33,123	66,246
	Walhalla P.L..	350	0	350	700
	Divide County Lib.	238	0	238	476
Ohio		0	0	0	0
Oklahoma	Stanley Tubbs Mem. Lib.	60,000	0	60,000	120,000
	Jim Lucas Mem. Lib.	108,663	0	312,387	421,050
	Pratt Branch Lib.	50,000	0	146,400	196,400
	Weatherford P.L.	123,887	0	123,887	247,774
	Chandler P.L.	75,000	0	74,975	149,975
Oregon		0	0	0	0
Pennsylvania	Lackawanna	400,000	0	838,420	1,238,420
	Adams	400,000	0	471,259	871,259
	Bradford	400,000	0	1,648,718	2,048,718
	Dauphin	400,000	0	886,120	1,286,120
	Indiana	178,955	0	240,964	419,919

Table 21 / LSCA Title II Construction Projects Completed in FY 1992 *(cont.)*

	Project	Federal	State	Local	Total
	Palmerton	130,149	0	229,145	359,294
	Peoples	233,170	0	233,170	466,340
Rhode Island	Providence	2,314	0	2,314	4,628
	Providence	144,106	0	149,628	293,734
South Carolina		0	0	0	0
South Dakota		0	0	0	0
Tennessee	Bolivar/Hardeman Cnty	107,811	35,784	76,604	220,199
	Sullivan Cnty P.L..	100,000	35,784	187,226	323,010
Texas		0	0	0	0
Utah	Salt Lake	48,060	0	109,796	157,856
	Milford	19,000	0	36,016	55,016
	Uintah	150,000	0	312,491	462,491
Vermont	Richmond	100,000	0	184,168	284,168
Virginia	Rappahannock Cnty	140,998	0	463,386	604,384
	Rockingham Pub. Lib.	59,689	0	110,524	170,213
Washington	Spokane Cnty Lib.	250,000	0	297,059	547,059
	Timberland Reg. Lib.	242,292	0	2,385,959	2,628,251
	Sno-Isle	107,118	0	374,618	481,736
West Virginia	Bolivar	39,000	0	46,376	85,376
	Phillippi	148,861	0	149,861	298,722
	Stephenson	200,000	0	391,955	591,955
	WVa St. Library Comm	14,898	0	0	14,898
Wisconsin	Aram	125,000	0	475,000	600,000
	Brillion	73,637	0	171,822	245,459
	Columbus	10,000	0	237,114	247,114
	Johnson Creek	101,068	0	235,826	336,894
	Racine	125,000	0	4,451,085	4,576,085
Wyoming	Goshen County Lib.	4,234	0	6,351	10,585
	Sublette County Lib.	37,200	0	61,074	98,274
Guam		0	0	0	0
Puerto Rico		0	0	0	0
Virgin Islands		0	0	0	0
Total		$10,775,690	$7,856,122	$40,128,300	$58,760,112

MVLC automated resource sharing network database and into OCLC. In Westborough, materials and items documenting the town's history back to 1659 were cataloged and conserved to allow for public access. In Fitchburg, town annual reports, as well as early editions of the local newspapers, were collated and microfilmed.

Other states focused on developing statewide preservation plans and training opportunities so that coordinated efforts could be supported with Title III funds in subsequent years. For example, Florida conducted a series of preservation-related workshops and developed an RFP for continuing education experiences that could be replicated at various locations around the state. The winning proposal included such topics as Administrative Issues in Preservation, Preservation of Collections in a Hostile Environment, Library Binding, and Book Repair and Mending. Over 270 people participated in the series at five different locations.

Support for Technology and Networks (LSCA Title III)

In FY 1993 the states successfully planned and carried out many projects that took advantage of new technological advances in the fields of telecommunications and information retrieval. Many of these projects were supported in whole or in part by funds authorized under Title III. Some states elected to use their Title III funds along with Titles I and II for these purposes. This pooling of funds allowed many states to initiate a number of major statewide technology-related projects. In FY 1993 Title III funds totaled $17.5 million with $6.4 million used for projects to establish, expand, and operate local, regional, and interstate cooperative networks of libraries. Other uses included:

- $5.5 million for planning and taking other steps leading to the development of cooperative library networks
- $3.7 million for resource sharing purposes
- $1.9 million to develop the technological capacity of libraries for interlibrary cooperation and resource sharing
- More than $97,000 to develop statewide preservation cooperative plans

Nearly $8.2 million was reported as state and local matching funds even though this is not required under Title III. Most often the state funding decisions seemed to be result from initial library efforts to convert bibliographic records into machine-readable formats, to automate interlibrary loan procedures, and to establish statewide lists and databases of periodical and book holdings that could be shared cooperatively.

Tennessee. The Tennessee State Library and Archives reported using Title III funds to support several beginning automation efforts, including cataloging materials purchased by 12 multi-county regional libraries using the AGILE system; and creating a statewide database, TELINET, that has been expanded to include OCLC searches and interlibrary loan using the IMPACT ILL subsystem.

Connecticut. Connecticut used its Title III funds to support ongoing development of a statewide database and continued planning toward the implementation of a fully automated statewide library and information services network by the year 2000.

Florida. Recognizing the developmental aspect of improving library services through technology, the Florida State Library has used Title III funds for several years to provide library technology subgrants. A basic part of the program was an automation planning grant that allowed each public library at a certain stage of readiness to contract with the best consultants available in the field to determine the appropriate course of action. Following this planning phase, there was a year or more in which the library had to devote its efforts to the conversion of the data before the installation of a system could be requested from the state. An installation phase was defined to take place over a one- to two-year period. This planning approach to statewide automation has helped Florida move toward one of its key long-range statewide objectives.

Vermont. Vermont built on the success of the Vermont Automated Libraries System (VALS), extending its capabilities as an online library holdings list to include full-text access to such state government databases as human service information, Supreme Court opinions, legislative bills, and the state's open competitive bid system. In FY 1993 Vermont allowed full access to Internet for all local libraries that were able to connect online to the VALS system. This provided access for the smallest rural libraries of the state to worldwide information sources at no cost to the local library.

West Virginia. The West Virginia Library Commission also reported that Internet access had been provided to over 90 public libraries on its statewide automation network along with E-mail capabilities among 137 sites. In addition, dial-up access to Family Matters, a statewide information and referral database was made available to participating libraries on the network, as well as to local residents with a computer and modem.

Rhode Island. The Rhode Island Department of State Library Services reported that it continued planning for a statewide electronic library network to be called the Ocean State FreeNet. As a preliminary step, the department opened an electronic library building, the Library of Rhode Island (LORI), serving staff of member libraries of the Rhode Island Library Network. LORI began operation in January 1993 and had over 200 registered users by the end of the fiscal year.

LORI provides for local E-mail, searchable local data files, topical discussion forums, online help screens, and access to Internet. Users can reach the system through dial-up and through a shared telecommunications system used by the public library consortium called CLAN. A special tariff filed by NYNEX with the Rhode Island Public Utilities Commission provided for the free installation and use of local dial-up lines to call authorized in-state Internet access points at nonprofit schools, and public, institutional, and academic libraries. Besides conducting surveys and planning for future enhancements to the network, team members also identified future training and support needs and continued to work with other agencies within the state to plan for future improvements such as shared telecommunications access on a statewide basis.

Other states initiated Internet access or connections to other electronic resources.

New York. Following priorities published in *The Electronic Doorway Library: Meeting the Information Needs of the People of New York,* New York public libraries were urged to participate in networking to obtain and share basic materials and information. Besides support for individual projects such as OCLC Group Access Capability, regional CD-ROM databases, telefacsimile transmission among libraries, and access to document delivery vendors, the program also supported the basic access to Internet. Two test projects allowing for free access to state and national resources available through Internet, were made available through the NYSILL telecommunications network, which was recently expanded to include direct access to all 44 school library systems in the state. In addition, an electronic communication system, NYLINE, supported by LSCA funds, carried information about statewide library developments to public library systems, reference and research library resources systems, school library systems, and central public libraries. Participants have 24-hour-a-day access to electronic mail and bulletin board information as well as electronic interfaces to telefacsimile and worldwide telex services.

Nebraska. The Nebraska Library Commission served as the lead agency in the overall development and management of the Nebraska Development Information Partnership and its online system, Nebraska Online. As a part of this major statewide initiative, economic development needs were met by providing electronic access to a services directory, an electronic mail service, a conferencing service, and a gateway bulletin board. As part of a separate project, services were provided to Nebraska libraries needing access to shared international databases (OCLC), state databases (NEON), and the statewide resource-sharing network.

Part 3
Library/Information Science Education, Placement, and Salaries

Guide to Employment Sources in the Library and Information Professions

Margaret Myers
Director, Office for Library Personnel Resources
American Library Association

This guide updates the listing in the 1994 Bowker Annual with information on new services and changes in contacts and groups previously listed. The sources given primarily assist professionals in obtaining positions, although a few assist paraprofessionals, who tend, however, to be recruited through local sources.

General Sources of Library and Information Jobs

Library Literature

Many national, regional, and state library journals and newsletters carry classified ads of library job vacancies and positions wanted. Association members can sometimes list a position-wanted ad free in association publications. *American Libraries, Chronicle of Higher Education, College & Research Libraries News, Library Journal*, and *Library Hotline* regularly carry listings of available positions. State and regional library association newsletters, state library journals, foreign library periodicals, and other types of periodicals that carry such ads are listed in later sections of this guide.

Newspapers

In addition to the regular classifieds, the *New York Times* Sunday Week in Review includes a special section of jobs for librarians. Local newspapers—particularly the larger city Sunday editions, such as the *Washington Post, Los Angeles Times*, and *Chicago Tribune*—often carry listings for both professional and paraprofessional positions in libraries.

Internet

The many library-related electronic listservs on Internet often post library job vacancies, and there are a growing number of general online job search bulletin boards that may include library- and information-related job notices. This guide includes information on electronic access where available. A useful resource is

Note: The author wishes to thank Maxine Moore, OLPR administrative assistant, for her help in gathering and compiling updated information.

Copyright © 1995 by the American Library Association. All rights reserved except those that may be granted by Sections 107 and 108 of the Copyright Revision Act of 1976. Printed in the United States of America.

"Library Jobs and Employment: A Guide to Internet Resources," compiled by Jeffery C. Lee, Texas Woman's University, and posted on the University of Michigan gopher (gopher.lib.umich.edu.) under "What's New & Featured Resources/Clearinghouse for Subject-Oriented Internet Resources Guides (UM/All Guides/Library Employment; J. Lee; v.1.1; 1/29/95; URL: http://www.lib.umich.edu/chhome.html).

A guide to other types of employment information on Internet is available on the same gopher clearinghouse: "Job Searching & Employment; P. Ray, B. Taylor." Several articles in the fall 1994 *Journal of Career Planning and Employment* discuss "Career Counseling in Cyberspace" and "The Job Search Goes Computer."

Library Joblines

Library joblines, or job hotlines, provide recorded telephone messages of job openings in a specific geographic area. Most tapes are changed once a week, although a listing may sometimes be carried for several weeks. The information is fairly brief and the cost of calling is borne by the individual job seeker, but a jobline provides a quick and up-to-date listing of vacancies that is not usually possible with printed listings or journal ads.

Most joblines only carry listings for their state or region, although some occasionally accept out-of-state positions if there is room on the tape. A few list technician and other paraprofessional positions, but the majority include only professional jobs. Callers sometimes find that the jobline doesn't answer; this usually means that the tape is being changed or that there are no new jobs for that period. The classified section of *American Libraries* carries jobline numbers periodically as space permits.

The following joblines are in operation:

Jobline Sponsor	Job Seekers (To Hear Job Listings)	Employers (To Place Job Listings)
American Association of Law Libraries	312-939-7877	53 W. Jackson Blvd., Suite 940, Chicago, IL 60604. 312-939-4764; FAX 312-431-1097
Arizona Department of Library, Archives and Public Records (Ariz. libraries only)	602-275-2325	Research Div., 1700 W. Washington, Phoenix, AZ 85007 FAX 602-255-4312
British Columbia Library Association (B.C. listings only)	604-430-6411	Jobline, 110-6545 Bonsor Ave., Burnaby, BC V51 1H3, Canada.
California Library Association	916-443-1222 818-797-4602 (identical listings)	717 K St., Suite 300D1, Sacramento, CA 95814-3477. 916-447-8541

Jobline Sponsor	Job Seekers (To Hear Job Listings)	Employers (To Place Job Listings)
California Media and Library Educators Association	415-697-8832	1499 Old Bayshore Hwy., Suite 142, Burlingame, CA 94010. 415-692-2350
Cleveland (OH) Area Metropolitan Library System Job Listing Service	216-921-4702	CAMLS, 20600 Chagrin Blvd., Suite 500, Shaker Heights, OH 44122.
Colorado State Library[1] (includes paraprofessionals)	303-866-6741	Jobline, 201 E. Colfax, 3rd fl., Denver, CO 80203-1704. 303-866-6732, FAX 303-866-6940; also via Libnet
Connecticut Library Association	203-645-8090 (24 hours)	Box 1046, Norwich, CT 06360.
Delaware Division of Libraries (Del., N.J., and Pa. listings)	800-282-8696 (in-state) 302-739-4748 (out-of-state)	43 S. Dupont Hwy., Dover, DE 19901.
Drexel University College of Information Studies	215-895-1672	College of Information Studies, Philadelphia, PA 19104. 215 895-2478D
State Library of Florida	904-488-5232	R. A. Gray Bldg., Tallahassee, FL 32399-0251. 904-487-2651
Library Jobline of Illinois[2]	312-828-0930 (professional) 312-828-9198 (support staff)	Illinois Library Assn., 33 W. Grand, Suite 301, Chicago, IL 60610. 312-644-1896; $40/2 weeks
Indiana Statewide Library Jobline	317-926-6561	Central Indiana ALSA, 1100 W. 42 St., Indianapolis, IN 46208.
State Library of Iowa (professional jobs in Iowa; only during regular business hours)	515-281-6788	East 12 & Grand, Des Moines, IA 50319.
Kansas State Library Jobline (also includes paraprofessional and out-of-state)	913-296-3296	c/o Jana Ealy, 3rd fl., State Capitol, Topeka, KS 66612.
Kentucky Job Hotline	502-564-3008 (24 hours)	Dept. for Libs. and Archives, Box 537, Frankfort, KY 40602. 502-875-7000
Long Island (NY) Library Resources Council Jobline	516-632-6658	516-632-6650; FAX 516-632-6662
Maryland Library Association	410-685-5760 (24 hours)	115 W. Franklin St., Baltimore, MD 21201. 410-727-7422 (Mon.–Fri., 9:30 A.M.–2:30 P.M.)
Medical Library Association Jobline	312-553-4636 (24 hours)	6 N. Michigan Ave., Suite 300, Chicago, IL 60602. 312-419-9094
Metropolitan Washington (D.C.) Council of Governments Library Council	202-962-3712	777 N. Capitol St. N.E., Suite 300, Washington, DC 20002. 202-962-3200

Jobline Sponsor	Job Seekers (To Hear Job Listings)	Employers (To Place Job Listings)
Michigan Library Association	517-694-7440	1000 Long Blvd., Suite 1, Lansing, MI 48911. 517-694-6615 ($40/week)
Missouri Library Association Jobline	314-442-6590	1306 Business 63 S., Suite B, Columbia, MO 65201-8404. 314-449-4627
Mountain Plains Library Association[3]	605-677-5757	c/o I. D. Weeks Library, University of South Dakota, Vermillion, SD 57069. 605-677-6082, FAX 605-677-5488
Nebraska Job Hotline (in-state and other openings during regular business hours)	402-471-2045 800-307-2665 (in-state)	Nebraska Library Commission, 1200 N St. 120, Lincoln, NE 68508-2023.
New England Library Jobline (New England jobs only)	617-738-3148	GSLIS, Simmons College, 300 The Fenway, Boston, MA 02115.
New Jersey Library Association	609-695-2121	Box 1534, Trenton, NJ 08607; nonmembers $25/4 weeks
New York Library Association	518-432-6952 800-232-6952 (in-state)	252 Hudson Ave., Albany, NY 12210-1802. 518-432-6952 (members $15/3 months, nonmembers $25/3 months)
North Carolina State Library (professional jobs in N.C. only)	919-733-6410	Division of State Library, 109 E. Jones St., Raleigh, NC 27601-2807. 919-733-2570
Ohio Library Council	614-225-6999	35 E. Gay St., Suite 305, Columbus, OH 43215. 614-221-9057; FAX 614-221-6234
Oklahoma Department of Libraries Jobline (5:00 P.M.–8:00 A.M., Monday–Friday and all weekend)	405-521-4202	200 N.E. 18 St., Oklahoma City, OK 73105. 405-521-2502
Oregon Library Association (Northwest listings only)	503-585-2232	Oregon State Library, State Library Bldg., Salem, OR 97310. 503-378-4243
Pacific Northwest Library Association[4]	206-543-2890	c/o Graduate School of Library and Information Science, University of Washington, FM-30, Seattle, WA 98195. 206-543-1794
Pennsylvania Jobline[5]	717-234-4646	Pennsylvania Library Assn., 1919 N. Front St., Harrisburg, PA 17102. 717-233-3113 (weekly fee for non-members)
Pratt Institute SILS Job Hotline	718-636-3742	SILS, Brooklyn, NY 11205. 718-636-3702

Jobline Sponsor	Job Seekers (To Hear Job Listings)	Employers (To Place Job Listings)
University of South Carolina College of Library and Information Science (no geographic restrictions)	803-777-8443	University of South Carolina, Columbia, SC 29208. 803-777-3858
Special Libraries Association	202-234-3632	1700 18th St. N.W., Washington, DC 20009. 202-234-4700
Special Libraries Association, New York Chapter	212-740-2007	David Jank, FIND/SVP, 625 Ave. of the Americas, New York, NY 10011. FAX 212-645-7681
Special Libraries Association, San Andreas-San Francisco Bay Chapter	415-856-2140	415-858-4070; FAX 415-858-4043
Special Libraries Association, Southern California Chapter	818-795-2145	818-302-8966; FAX 818-302-8015
Texas Library Association Job Hotline (24 hours; Texas listings only)	512-328-0651	3355 Bee Cave Rd., Suite 401, Austin, TX 78746. 512-328-1518
Texas State Library Jobline (Texas listings only)	512-463-5470	Library Development, Box 12927, Austin, TX 78711. 512-463-5447
Virginia Library Association Jobline (Virginia libraries only)	703-519-8027	669 S. Washington St., Alexandria, VA 22314.
University of Toronto Faculty of Information Studies	416-978-7073	416-978-3035; FAX 416-978-5762
University of Western Ontario School of Library and Information Science	519-661-3543	GSLIS, London, ON N6G 1H1, Canada. 519-661-2111 Ext. 8494

1. Weekly printed listing sent on receipt of stamps and mailing labels.
2. Cosponsored by the Special Libraries Association Illinois Chapter and the Illinois Library Association.
3. 800-356-7820 available from all MPLA states, 10:00 P.M.–8:00 A.M., Sunday–Thursday; 5:00 P.M. Friday–5:00 P.M. Sunday (includes listings for the states of Arizona, Colorado, Kansas, Montana, Nebraska, Nevada, North Dakota, Oklahoma, South Dakota, Utah, and Wyoming, and paid listings from out-of-region institutions—$10/week).
4. Alaska, Alberta, British Columbia, Idaho, Montana, Oregon, and Washington; includes both professional and paraprofessional jobs.
5. Sponsored by the Pennsylvania Library Association; also accepts paraprofessional out-of-state listings.

Specialized Library Associations and Groups

Advanced Information Management

444 Castro St., Suite 320, Mountain View, CA 94041 (415-965-7799). This placement agency, with offices in Southern California (900 Wilshire Blvd., Suite 1424, Los Angeles, CA 90017; 213-243-9236) as well as in the San Francisco Bay area, specializes in library and information personnel. It offers professional librarians and paraprofessionals work on a temporary, permanent, or contract basis in special, public, and academic libraries. It also places consultants on special projects in libraries or as managers of library development projects. There is no fee for applicants.

American Association of Law Libraries Career Hotline

53 W. Jackson Blvd., Suite 940, Chicago, IL 60604 (312-939-4764). The hotline (312-939-7877) is a 24-hour-a-day recording updated each Friday at noon and available as an index in geographic order of positions currently available in full text in the AALL Job Data Base. Any interested person may receive the complete Job Data Base free on request. Ads may also be viewed on AALLNET, an Internet bulletin board. To access AALLNET type: telnet lawlib.wuacc.edu and login as aallnet. To list a position, contact AALL, Placement Assistant (FAX 312-431-1097).

American Libraries "Career LEADS"

c/o *American Libraries*, 50 E. Huron St., Chicago, IL 60611. Classified job listings are published in each monthly issue of *American Libraries*. Some 100 job openings are grouped by type, and "Late Job Notices" are added near press time. Subsections are Positions Wanted, Professional Exchange, Requests for Proposals, Librarians' Classified, joblines, and regional salary scales." *American Libraries* ConsultantBase" (see below) appears four times a year.

American Libraries "Career LEADS EXPRESS"

c/o Georgia Okotete, 50 E. Huron St., Chicago, IL 60611. Advance galleys (3–4 weeks) of classified job listings with approximately 100 "Positions Open" to be published in the next issue of *American Libraries* are sent about the 17th of each month. Galleys do not include editorial corrections and late changes, but they do include some "Late Job Notices." For each month, send a $1 check made out to AL EXPRESS and a self-addressed, standard business-size envelope (4 x 9) with 55 cents postage.

American Libraries ConsultantBase (CBase)

This *AL* service helps match professionals offering library/information expertise with institutions. Published quarterly, CBase appears in the "Career LEADS" section of *AL*'s January, April, June, and October issues. Rates: $4.50/line (classified); $45/inch (display). Inquiries should be made to Jon Kartman, LEADS Editor, *American Libraries*, 50 E. Huron St., Chicago, IL 60611 (312-280-4211).

American Library Association, ASCLA/SLAS State Library Consultants to Institutional Libraries Discussion Group

This group compiles a list of job openings in institutional libraries throughout the United States and its territories. Send self-addressed, stamped envelope(s) to Institutional Library Jobline, c/o Gloria Spooner, State Library of Louisiana, Box 131, Baton Rouge, LA 70821-0131. Send job listings to the same address, or call 504-342-4931 or FAX 504-342-3547. Listings appear for one month unless resubmitted.

American Library Association, Association of College and Research Libraries

50 E. Huron St., Chicago, IL 60611-2795 (312-280-2513). Classified advertising appears each month in *College & Research Libraries News*. Ads are also posted

to C&RL NewsNet, an abridged electronic edition of *C&RL News* accessible on Internet through the gopher server at the University of Illinois at Chicago. You can connect your favorite gopher client directly to host gopher.uic.edu 70. Select "The Library" from the menu and "C&RL NewsNet" from the next menu.

American Library Association, Office for Library Personnel Resources

50 E. Huron St., Chicago, IL 60611 (312-280-4277). A placement service is provided at each annual conference (June or July) and midwinter meeting (January or February). Request job seeker or employer registration forms before the conference. Those unable to attend a conference can register with the service and have job or applicant listings sent directly to them from the conference site for a fee. Handouts on interviewing, preparing a résumé, and other job-seeking information are available from the ALA Office for Library Personnel Resources.

ALA divisions also usually have a placement service at national conferences. See *American Libraries* "Datebook" for dates of upcoming divisional conferences (not held every year).

American Society for Information Science

8720 Georgia Ave., Suite 501, Silver Spring, MD 20910-3602 (301-495-0900). ASIS operates an active placement service at annual meetings (usually October). Locales change. All conference attendees (both ASIS members and nonmembers), as well as ASIS members who cannot attend the conference, are eligible to use the service to list or find jobs. The service accepts listings from employers who cannot attend the conference, arranges interviews, and sponsors special seminars. Throughout the year, job openings are listed in *ASIS JOBLINE*, a monthly publication sent to all members and available to nonmembers on request.

Art Libraries Society/North America (ARLIS/NA)

c/o Executive Director, 4101 Lake Boone Trail, Suite 201, Raleigh, NC 27607 (919-787-5181; FAX 919-787-4916). *ARLIS/NA UPDATE* (6 issues a year) lists jobs for art librarians and slide curators, and the society maintains a job registry at its headquarters. Any employer may list a job with the registry, but only members may request job information.

Asian/Pacific American Libraries Newsletter

c/o Anna Wang, Ohio State University, 124 Main Library, 1858 Neil Ave. Mall, Columbus, OH 43210-1286 (614-292-6151). This quarterly newsletter includes some job ads. It is free to members of the association.

Association for Educational Communications and Technology

Placement and Referral Service, 1025 Vermont Ave., Suite 820, Washington, DC 20005 (202-347-7834, FAX 202-347-7839). A referral service is available free to AECT members. The placement center at the annual conference is free to all conference registrants. Members, upon request, also receive a free monthly newsletter of job vacancies.

Association for Library and Information Science Education

4101 Lake Boone Trail, Raleigh, NC 27606 (919-787-5181). ALISE provides a placement service for library and information science faculty and administrative positions at its annual conference in January or February.

C. Berger and Company

327 E. Gundersen Dr., Carol Stream, IL 60188 (708-653-1115, 800-382-4222; FAX 708-653-1691 or Internet c-berg@dupagels.lib.il.us.). CBC conducts nationwide executive searches to fill permanent management, supervisory, and director positions in libraries, information centers, and related firms. It also supplies special, academic, and public libraries in Illinois, Indiana, Pennsylvania, Texas, and Wisconsin with temporary professional personnel and clerks to work under contract or for short- or long-term assignments. In addition, CBC offers library and records management consulting services and provides staff to manage projects for clients.

Black Caucus Newsletter

c/o George C. Grant, Editor, Rollins College, 1000 Holt Ave., Suite 2654, Winter Park, FL 32789 (407-646-2676, FAX 407-646-1515). Published bimonthly by Four-G Publishers, this newsletter lists paid advertisements for job vacancies and complementary brief summaries of others, as well as news reports, biographies, essays, and book reviews of interest to members. Free to members; $10/year to others.

Canadian Association of Special Libraries and Information Services/Ottawa Chapter Job Bank

c/o CASLIS Job Bank Coordinator, 266 Sherwood Dr., Ottawa, ON K1Y 3W4, Canada. Job seekers should send a résumé; employers who want to list a job should call 613-728-9982.

Canadian Library Association

200 Elgin St., Suite 602, Ottawa, ON K2P 1L5, Canada (613-232-9625). This national association operates a Jobmart at its annual conference in June and publishes classified job ads in *Feliciter*.

Catholic Library Association

9009 Carter St., Allen Park, MI 48101. Personal and institutional members can advertise for jobs or list job openings (up to 35 words) free in *Catholic Library World* (4 issues/year). Others should contact the advertising coordinator for rates.

Chinese-American Librarians Association Newsletter

c/o Vicki Toy-Smith, Getchell Library 322, Reno, NV 89557. (702-784-4692; FAX 702-784-1751). The association newsletter issued in February, June, and October includes job listings. Free to members.

Council on Library/Media Technicians, Inc.

c/o Ruth A. Tolbert, Membership Chairperson, Central Indiana ALSA, 1100 W. 42 St., Suite 305, Indianapolis, IN 46208. *COLT Newsletter* appears bimonthly in *Library Mosaics*. Dues: personal: U.S., $25, foreign, $50; students: $20; institutions: U.S., $50, foreign, $75.

Gossage Regan Associates, Inc.

25 W. 43 St., New York, NY 10036 (212-869-3348, FAX 212-997-1127). Gossage Regan Associates is a full-service library personnel and consulting firm that places librarians and information managers in permanent positions nationwide. The emphasis, however, is on the New York metropolitan area, where the agency is the leading provider of temporary professional and support personnel to libraries. Other services include executive search for library directors, division heads, and information vice presidents and managers, and information management consultation.

Indiana Jobline, Central Indiana Area Library Services Authority

1100 W. 42 St., Suite 305, Indianapolis, IN 46208 (317-926-6561). Libraries may access this computer-based listing of job openings in all types of libraries in Indiana through telex or other electronic communication system by calling 317-924-9584. A printed job listing is available on request.

Labat-Anderson, Inc.

2200 Clarendon Blvd., Suite 900, Arlington, VA 22201 (703-525-9400). Labat-Anderson supports various federal agencies in 27 states, with most positions located in the Washington, D.C., area. Résumés with cover letters are accepted from librarians with an ALA-accredited MLS and from records managers for part-time and full-time employment.

The Library Co-Op, Inc.

3840 Park Ave., Suite 107, Edison, NJ 08820 (908-906-1777, 800-654-6275). This employment agency supplies permanent and temporary personnel and consultants to work in a variety of information settings, from library moving to database management, catalog maintenance, reference, retrospective conversion, and more. The agency recently formed a new division, ABCD Filing Services, and hired two specialists in space planning. Another new division, LAIRD Consulting, provides a full range of automation expertise for hardware, software, LANs, and WANs.

Library Management Systems

16027 Ventura Blvd, Suite 612, Encino, CA 91436 (818-789-3141; 800-567-4669; FAX 818-789-6815). Established in 1983 to provide contract library services and personnel to public and special libraries and businesses, Library Management Systems organizes and manages small to medium-sized special libraries and designs and implements major projects such as retrospective data conversions, automation studies, reference services, and records management.

LMS provides cataloging outsourcing services off-site as well as contract staffing to all kinds of information centers. LMS has 75 librarians and library assistants on call for long- and short-term projects and provides permanent placement at all levels.

Library Mosaics

Box 5171, Culver City, CA 90231 (310-410-1573). This bimonthly magazine accepts job listings for library/media technicians but does not handle correspondence relating to advertised jobs.

Medical Library Association

6 N. Michigan Ave., Suite 300, Chicago, IL 60602-4805 (312-419-9094). *MLA News* (10 issues/year, June/July and November/December combined issues) lists positions wanted and available in its "Employment Opportunities" column. The position-available rate is $2.75/word for nonmembers and for advertisements received through an employment or advertising agency or other third party. Up to 50 words are free for MLA members; each additional word is $2.40. Both members and nonmembers may rerun ads once in the next consecutive issue for $25. Positions-available advertisements must list a minimum salary; a salary range is preferred. Positions-wanted rates are $1.50/word for nonmembers; 100 free words for members and $1.25 for each additional word. Advance mailing of "Employment Opportunities" is available for six months for a prepaid fee: MLA members, $15; nonmembers, $25. MLA also offers a placement service at its annual conference each spring. Job advertisements received for publication in *MLA News* are posted to the MLANET Jobline the week of receipt. The jobline can be accessed 9:00 A.M. to 5:00 P.M. Central Time by calling 312-419-9094, Ext. 343; for 24-hour access, call 312-553-4636. In the MLA jobline, positions are categorized by type, salary range, and regional area.

Pro Libra Associates Inc.

6 Inwood Place, Maplewood, NJ 07040 (201-762-0070, 800-262-0070). A multi-service agency, Pro Libra specializes in consulting, personnel, and project support for libraries and information centers.

REFORMA, National Association to Promote Library Service to the Spanish-Speaking

Box 832, Anaheim, CA 92815-032. Employers wishing to send direct mailings to the REFORMA membership (600+) may obtain mailing labels arranged by zip code for $100 per set. For those who want to mail job fliers to REFORMA Executive Board members, a set of mailing labels is available for $5. Contact Al Milo, 714-738-6383. Job ads are also published quarterly in the *REFORMA Newsletter*. For rate information, contact Felipe Ortego, 915-837-2132.

Society of American Archivists

600 S. Federal, Suite 504, Chicago, IL 60605 (312-922-0140). The bimonthly *Archival Outlook* (sent only to members) contains features about the archival profession and other timely topics, such as courses in archival administration,

meetings, and professional opportunities (job listings). The "SAA Employment Bulletin" is a bimonthly listing of job opportunities available to members by subscription for $24/year and to nonmembers for $10/issue. Prepayment is required.

Special Libraries Association

1700 18th St. N.W., Washington, DC 20009-2508 (202-234-4700 Ext. 627; FAX 202-265-9317). SLA operates a telephone jobline called SpeciaLine, 202-234-3632, available 24 hours a day, seven days a week. Most SLA chapters have employment chairpersons who provide referral services for employers and job seekers. Several SLA chapters have joblines. The association's monthly newsletter, *The SpeciaList*, carries classified advertising, and SLA offers an employment clearinghouse and career advisory service at the annual conference in June. SLA also provides a discount to members using the résumé evaluation service offered through Advanced Information Management. "Guide to Career Opportunities," a resource kit is available for $20 (SLA members, $15). "Getting a Job: Tips and Techniques" is free to unemployed SLA members. The SLA Job Bulletin Board is a computer listserv organized by Indiana University staff. Subscribe by sending the message "subscribe SLAJOB first name, last name" to listserv@iubvm. ucs.indiana.edu.

Tuft & Associates Inc.

1209 Astor St., Chicago, IL 60610 (312-642-8889, FAX 312-642-8883). Specialists in nationwide executive searches for administrative posts in libraries and information centers.

State Library Agencies

Some state library agencies issue lists of job openings within their area. These include Colorado (via listserv and Denver Free-Net, send SASE for access); Indiana (monthly on request); Iowa (*Joblist*, monthly on request); Massachusetts (*Massachusetts Position Vacancies*, monthly, sent to all state public libraries and to interested individuals on a one-time basis); Mississippi (*Library Job Opportunities*, monthly); and Ohio (*Library Opportunities in Ohio*, sent monthly to accredited library education programs and to interested individuals on request).

The Georgia, Nebraska, North Carolina, Oklahoma, Pennsylvania, South Carolina, and Texas state libraries have an electronic bulletin board service that lists job openings in each state. Georgia can be accessed via Internet (telnet to gcedunet.peachnet.edu) or modem (912-453-1897; in-state 800-642-7375). Nebraska can be accessed via Nebraska Online (402-471-4020, 800-307-2665 in Nebraska). North Carolina can be accessed nationally by Internet. South Carolina can be accessed in-state by users of the South Carolina Library Network. Oklahoma access via computer and modem is 405-524-4089. Texas can be accessed in-state and nationally via Internet (link.tsl.texas.gov).

On occasion, state library newsletters or journals list vacancies. These include Alabama (*Cottonboll*, quarterly); Alaska (*Newspoke*, bimonthly); Arizona (*Arizona Libraries Newsweek*); Indiana (*Focus on Indiana Libraries*, 11/year);

Iowa (*Joblist*); Kansas (*Kansas Libraries*, monthly); Louisiana (*Library Communique*, monthly); Missouri (*Show-Me Libraries*, semiannual); Nebraska (*Overtones*, quarterly); New Hampshire (*Granite State Libraries*, bimonthly); New Mexico (*Hitchhiker*, weekly); Utah (*Directions for Utah Libraries*, monthly); and Wyoming (*Outrider*, monthly).

Many state library agencies do not have formal placement services but refer applicants informally when they know of vacancies. The following states primarily make referrals to public libraries: Alabama, Alaska, Arizona, Arkansas, California, Georgia, Louisiana, Pennsylvania, South Carolina (institutional also), Tennessee, Utah, Vermont, and Virginia. Those that refer applicants to all types of libraries are Alaska, Delaware, Florida, Idaho, Illinois, Kansas, Kentucky, Maine, Maryland, Mississippi, Montana, Nebraska, Nevada (largely public and academic), New Hampshire, New Mexico, North Carolina, North Dakota, Ohio, Pennsylvania, Rhode Island, South Dakota, West Virginia (on Pennsylvania Jobline, public, academic, and special), and Wyoming.

The following state libraries post job notices for all types of libraries on a bulletin board: California, Connecticut, Florida, Georgia, Illinois, Indiana, Iowa, Kentucky, Michigan, Montana, Nevada, New Jersey, New York, North Carolina, Ohio, Oklahoma, Pennsylvania, South Carolina, South Dakota, Utah, and Washington. [For the addresses of state agencies, see Part 6 of the *Bowker Annual—Ed.*]

State and Regional Library Associations

State and regional library associations often make referrals, run ads in association newsletters, or operate a placement service at annual conferences. Some also sponsor joblines. The following associations refer applicants when they know of jobs: Arkansas, Delaware, Hawaii, Louisiana, Michigan, Nevada, Pennsylvania, South Dakota, Tennessee, and Wisconsin.

Although listings are infrequent, the following association newsletters and journals do announce job vacancies: Alabama (*Alabama Librarian*, 7/year); Alaska (*Newspoke*, bimonthly); Arizona (*Newsletter*, 10/year); Arkansas (*Arkansas Libraries*, 6/year); Connecticut (*Connecticut Libraries*, 11/year); Delaware (*Delaware Library Association Bulletin*, 3/year); District of Columbia (*Intercom*, 11/year); Florida (*Florida Libraries*, 10/year); Indiana (*Focus on Indiana Libraries*, 11/year); Iowa (*Catalyst*, 6/year); Kansas (*KLA Newsletter*, 6/year); Minnesota (*MLA Newsletter*, 10/year); Missouri (bimonthly); Mountain Plains (*MPLA Newsletter*, bimonthly, lists vacancies and positions wanted for individuals and institutions); Nebraska (*NLAQ*); Nevada (*Highroller*, 4/year); New Hampshire (*NHLA Newsletter*, 6/year); New Jersey (*NJLA Newsletter*, 10/year); New Mexico (shares notices via State Library's *Hitchhiker*, weekly); New York (*NYLA Bulletin*, 10/year; free for institutional members; $25/week, $40/2 weeks for others); Ohio (*ACCESS*, monthly); Oklahoma (*Oklahoma Librarian*, 6/year); Rhode Island (*RILA Bulletin*, 6/year); South Carolina (*News and Views*); South Dakota (*Book Marks*, bimonthly); Tennessee (*TLA*

Newsletter); Vermont (*VLA News*, 10/year); Virginia (*Virginia Librarian*, quarterly), and West Virginia (*West Virginia Libraries*, 6/year).

At their annual conference, the following associations have some type of placement service, although it may only consist of bulletin board postings: Alabama, California, Connecticut, Georgia, Idaho, Illinois, Indiana, Kansas, Louisiana, Maryland, Massachusetts, Mountain Plains, New England, New Jersey, New York, North Carolina (biennial), Oregon, Pacific Northwest, Pennsylvania, South Dakota, Southeastern, Tennessee, Texas, Vermont, and Wyoming.

The following associations have no placement service at this time: Kentucky, Middle Atlantic Regional Library Federation, Midwest Federation, Minnesota, Mississippi, Montana, Nebraska, Nevada, New Mexico, North Dakota, Ohio, Oklahoma, Utah, West Virginia, and Wisconsin. [State and regional association addresses are listed in Part 6 of the *Bowker Annual—Ed.*]

The Pacific Northwest Library Association (PNLA) offers an electronic source for job postings in addition to its voice jobline. The listserv PNLA-L includes job postings in the PNLA region in addition to postings on other library issues. Send the following message: subscribe PNLA-L YOUR NAME to listserv@wln.com. Questions may be addressed to list owner Bruce Ziegman at ziegman@fvrl.lib.wa.us or phone 360-699-8810.

Library and Information Science Programs

Library and information science programs offer some type of service for current students as well as alumni. Most schools provide job-hunting and résumé-writing seminars. Many invite outside speakers who represent different types of libraries or recent graduates who relate career experiences. Faculty members or a designated placement officer offer individual advisory services or résumé critiques.

Of the ALA-accredited programs, the following handle placement activities through the library school: Alabama, Albany, Alberta, British Columbia, Buffalo (compiles annual graduate biographical listings), Dalhousie, Drexel, Hawaii, Illinois, Kent State, Louisiana, McGill, Michigan, Missouri, Pittsburgh (Department of Library Science only), Pratt, Puerto Rico, Queens, Rhode Island, Rosary, Rutgers, Saint John's, South Carolina, Syracuse, Tennessee, Texas–Austin, Toronto, UCLA (compiles graduate profile booklets), Western Ontario, Wisconsin–Madison, and Wisconsin–Milwaukee.

Although the central university placement center handles placement activities for California–Berkeley and Emporia, in most cases faculty in the library school still counsel job seekers informally.

Some schools handle placement services in a cooperative manner; in most cases, the university placement center sends out credentials and the library school posts or compiles the job listings. Such schools include Alabama, Albany, Arizona, Buffalo, Catholic, Clarion, Florida State, Illinois, Indiana, Iowa, Kent State, Kentucky, Long Island, Maryland, Montreal, North Carolina–Chapel Hill, North Carolina–Greensboro, North Carolina Central, North Texas, Oklahoma,

Pittsburgh, Queens, Saint John's, San Jose, Simmons, South Florida, Southern Connecticut, Southern Mississippi, Syracuse, Tennessee, Texas Woman's, Washington, Wayne State, and Wisconsin–Milwaukee.

Schools vary as to whether they distribute placement credentials free, charge a general registration fee, or request a fee for each file or set of credentials sent out.

Schools that post job notices for review but do not issue printed lists include Alabama, Alberta, Arizona, British Columbia, Buffalo, Catholic, Clark–Atlanta, Dalhousie, Drexel, Florida State, Hawaii, Kent State, Kentucky, Louisiana, Maryland, McGill, Montreal, North Carolina–Chapel Hill, North Carolina–Greensboro, North Carolina Central, Oklahoma, Puerto Rico, Queens, Rutgers, Saint John's, San Jose, Simmons, South Carolina, Southern Mississippi, Syracuse (general postings), Tennessee, Texas Woman's, Toronto, UCLA, Washington, Wayne State, Western Ontario, and Wisconsin–Madison.

In addition to posting job vacancies, some schools offer printed listings, joblines, or database services:

- Albany (job placement bulletin free to School of Information Science and Policy students; $15/year for others)
- British Columbia (uses British Columbia Library Association Jobline, 604-430-6411)
- Buffalo (to subscribe to the listserv for entry-level N.Y. state positions, send the following message: SUBSCRIBE LIBJOB-L first name last name to listserv@ubvm.cc.buffalo.edu)
- California–Berkeley (weekly out-of-state job list and jobline free to students and graduates for six months after graduation; $55 annual fee for University of California alumni; call 510-642-3283)
- Clarion (free with SASE to alumni)
- Dalhousie (listserv for Atlantic Canada jobs, send message: sub list-joblist to mailserv@ac.dal.ca)
- Drexel (job hotline listing local jobs only, changed each Monday, 215-895-1672)
- Emporia (weekly bulletin of school, university, and public jobs; separate bulletin for special libraries positions; $15.71/6 months for Emporia graduates; $30 plus tax/6 months for others)
- Florida State
- Hawaii
- Illinois (8 issues by mail for $4 and 8 No. 10 SASEs to alumni; $8 and 8 SASEs to nonalumni; also free online placement JOBSearch database on campus and via dial access through Internet: telnet alexia.lis.uiuc.edu, login; jobs, password: Urbaign)
- Indiana (free for one year following graduation; alumni and others may send SASEs)
- Iowa ($15/year for registered students and alumni)
- Michigan (free for one year following graduation; all other graduates, $15/year for 24 issues; $20 for others)

- Missouri (Library Vacancy Roster, monthly printout, $2/issue, with minimum of 6 issues, to anyone)
- North Texas ($5/6 months, students and alumni)
- Oklahoma
- Pittsburgh (free online placement to alumni)
- Pratt (free to students and alumni for full-time or part-time professional positions only)
- Rhode Island (monthly, $5/year)
- Rosary (*Placement News* every 2 weeks, free for 6 months following graduation, $15/year for students and alumni, $25 to others; *Placement News* is also on Lincolnet and can be accessed by telephone)
- Simmons operates the New England Jobline, which announces professional vacancies in New England, 617-521-2815
- South Florida (in cooperation with ALIS; $10/year)
- Southern Connecticut (printed listing twice a month, mailed to students and alumni free; also on gopher at scsu.ctstateu.edu)
- Syracuse (lists selected jobs online through electronic mail to students)
- Texas–Austin (semimonthly *Placement Bulletin*, including "Classifacts," free to students and alumni for one year following graduation, $17/6 months and $30/year thereafter; Austin/Central Texas Area Job-Hunters' List—full job descriptions—$16/6 months, $26/year; some job listings are carried on Internet, other listings are available only to students and recent graduates)
- Washington operates Pacific Northwest Library Association jobline, which announces professional vacancies, 206-543-2890
- Wisconsin–Madison (now sends listings from Wisconsin and Minnesota to Illinois for its JOBSearch and placement bulletin)
- Wisconsin–Milwaukee sends selected jobs online through electronic mail to students
- Western Ontario operates the SLIS (School of Library and Information Science) Jobline, which announces openings for professionals, 519-661-3543; to list positions, 519-661-2111, Ext. 8495

Employers often list jobs only with schools in their geographic area; some library schools give nonalumni information in person regarding specific locales, but are not staffed to handle mail requests. Schools that allow librarians in the area to view listings are Alabama, Albany, Alberta, Arizona, British Columbia, Buffalo, California–Berkeley, Catholic, Clarion, Clark–Atlanta, Dalhousie, Drexel, Emporia, Florida State, Hawaii, Illinois, Indiana, Iowa, Kent State, Kentucky, Louisiana, Maryland, McGill, Michigan, Missouri, Montreal, North Carolina–Chapel Hill, North Carolina–Greensboro, North Carolina Central, North Texas, Oklahoma, Pittsburgh, Pratt, Puerto Rico, Queens, Rhode Island, Rosary, Rutgers, Saint John's, San Jose, Simmons, South Carolina, South Florida, Southern Connecticut, Southern Mississippi, Syracuse, Tennessee, Texas–Austin, Texas Woman's, Toronto, UCLA, Washington, Wayne State, Western Ontario, Wisconsin–Madison, and

Wisconsin–Milwaukee. [For a list of accredited library schools, see later in Part 3. For information on the placement services of other library education programs, contact the school directly—*Ed.*]

Federal Library Jobs

To be considered for employment in many federal libraries, an applicant must establish civil service eligibility and be placed on the Office of Personnel Management (OPM) register in the appropriate geographic area. As of November 1987, OPM terminated its nationwide register and each office in the OPM network became responsible for hiring librarians in its area.

Eligibility can be established by meeting education and/or experience requirements and submitting appropriate forms to OPM during designated "open" periods. Interested applicants should contact their local Federal Job Information/ Testing Center (FJI/TC) periodically to find out when the next open period will be and to obtain the proper forms. FJI/TCs are listed under "U.S. Government" in metropolitan telephone directories. Current library job openings in the Washington, D.C., area are listed on a recorded phone message with other federal jobs (202-606-2700; press 1, 2, 406). You may obtain additional information on jobs nationwide by visiting the FJI/TC in your area and using its touch screen computer.

The Federal Library and Information Center Committee operates a federal library electronic bulletin board listing professional and paraprofessional positions (telnet alix.loc.gov3000). Federal jobs are posted on the Dartmouth College FEDJOBSlist. Send message to listserv@dartcms1 with command INDEX FED-JOBS; to get the librarian and government documents openings use command SEND LIBRARY TXT. The publication *Washington Online: How to Access the Government's Electronic Bulletin Boards* by Bruce Maxwell (Washington, D.C., Congressional Quarterly, 1995) lists services that may include library jobs among other government positions.

Applications are evaluated by the grade(s) for which applicants are qualified. Information on beginning salary levels can be obtained from FJI/TC. To qualify for librarian positions, applicants must possess a master's degree in library science, a fifth-year bachelor's degree in library science, or 30 semester hours of graduate study in library science. (Candidates who have a combination of education and/or experience may qualify to take the written subject-matter test, which is administered in the Washington, D.C., metropolitan area. To be considered for librarian positions and testing outside the D.C. metropolitan area, contact the nearest FJI/TC.)

The OPM office that maintains the register refers candidates but does not hire and therefore is unaware of a vacancy until an agency requests candidates to fill it. Applications are evaluated according to the agency's requirements. OPM refers only the most qualified candidates.

In addition to filing the appropriate forms, applicants can contact federal agencies directly. More than half the vacancies occur in the Washington, D.C., area. Most positions are in three agencies: the Army, Navy, and Veterans Administration.

The Department of Veterans Affairs (VA) employs more than 350 professional librarians at 176 health care facilities throughout the United States and Puerto Rico. Although most VA positions require training in medical librarianship, many entry-level GS-9 positions require no previous experience; each GS-11/13 position requires specific experience. The VA has examining authority for library positions throughout the agency. This register is open continuously. To receive information and application forms, contact the VA Special Examining Unit, Box 24269, Richmond, VA 23224. For a copy of the current job vacancy list, call 202-233-2820 Monday–Friday, 8:00 A.M.–4:30 P.M. (Eastern Time).

Some "excepted" agencies are not required to hire through usual OPM channels. Although these agencies may require the standard forms, they maintain their own employee selection policies and procedures. Agencies with positions outside the competitive civil service include the Board of Governors of the Federal Reserve System, Central Intelligence Agency, Defense Intelligence Agency, Department of Medicine and Surgery, Federal Bureau of Investigation, Foreign Service of the United States, General Accounting Office, Library of Congress, National Science Foundation, National Security Agency, Tennessee Valley Authority, U.S. Nuclear Regulatory Commission, U.S. Postal Service, judicial branch of the government, legislative branch of the government, U.S. Mission to the United Nations, World Bank, International Finance Corporation, International Monetary Fund, Organization of American States, Pan American Health Organization, and United Nations Secretariat.

The Library of Congress (LC), the world's largest and most comprehensive library, administers its own merit selection system. Job classifications, pay, and benefits are the same as in other federal agencies, and job qualifications generally correspond to those required of the U.S. Office of Personnel Management. LC does not use registers but announces vacancies as they become available. A separate application must be submitted for each position. Announcements for most professional positions stating required qualifications and ranking criteria are widely distributed and remain posted for a minimum of 30 days. The Library of Congress Human Resources Operations Office is located in the James Madison Memorial Bldg., 101 Independence Ave. S.E., Washington, DC 20540 (202-707-5620).

Additional Sources: General and Specialized Jobs

Affirmative Action Register

8356 Olive Blvd., Saint Louis, MO 63132. The goal of the register is to "provide female, minority, handicapped, and veteran candidates with an opportunity to learn of professional and managerial positions throughout the nation and to assist employers in implementing their Equal Opportunity Employment programs." The monthly bulletin is distributed free to leading businesses, industrial and academic institutions, and more than 4,000 agencies that recruit qualified minorities and women, as well as to all known professional organizations for women, minorities, and the handicapped; placement offices; newspapers; magazines; rehabilitation facilities; and more than 8,000 federal, state, and local governmental employment units. The bulletin's total readership is more than 3.5 million (audited). Individual mail subscriptions are available for $15 a year (free to libraries on request). Almost every issue has library job listings.

Chronicle of Higher Education

1255 23rd St. N.W., Suite 700, Washington, DC 20037 (202-466-1055, FAX 202-296-2691). Forty-eight issues a year with breaks in August and December. This publication lists a variety of library positions each week, including administrative and faculty jobs. Job listings are searchable by specific categories, keywords, or geographic locations on Internet (gopher at Chronicle, merit.edu or World-Wide Web at **http://chronicle.merit.edu**).

National Faculty Exchange

4656 W. Jefferson, Suite 140, Fort Wayne, IN 46804. This program brokers the exchange of faculty and staff at U.S. institutions. Librarians interested in participating should ascertain whether their academic institution is a member.

Additional Sources: School Libraries

School librarians often find that the channels for locating positions in education, such as contacting county or city school superintendent offices, are of more value than the usual library channels. Primary sources include university placement offices, which carry listings for a variety of school system jobs, and local information networks of teachers and library media specialists. A list of teachers' agencies may be obtained from the National Association of Teachers' Agencies, Sandra R. Alexander, CPC, Treas., c/o G. A. Agency, 104 S. Central Ave. Valley Stream, NY 11580-5442 (516-568-8871).

Overseas

Opportunities for employment in foreign countries are limited, and interested candidates should investigate the immigration policies of individual countries. Employment for Americans is virtually limited to U.S. government libraries, libraries of U.S. firms doing worldwide business, and American schools abroad. Library journals from other countries sometimes list job vacancies. Some individuals have obtained jobs by contacting foreign publishers or vendors directly. Non-U.S. government jobs usually call for foreign-language fluency. "Job Hunting in the UK" by Diane Brooks, *Canadian Library Journal*, 45:374–378 (December 1988), offers advice for those interested in the United Kingdom. *Career Opportunities for Bilinguals and Multilinguals: A Directory of Resources in Education, Employment and Business* by Vladimir F. Wertsman (Scarecrow

Press, 1991, ISBN 0-8108-2439-6, $35) includes contact names for foreign employment and business resources. "International Jobs" by Wertsman (*RQ*, Fall 1992, pp. 14–19) provides a listing of library resources for finding jobs abroad.

Council for International Exchange of Scholars

3007 Tilden St. N.W., Suite 5M, Washington, DC 20008-3097 (202-686-7877). CIES administers U.S. government Fulbright awards for those wishing to lecture at universities or do advanced research abroad; usually 10 to 15 awards are made to specialists in library science each year. In addition, many countries offer research or lecture awards for which specialists in library and information science may apply. Open to U.S. citizens with university or college teaching experience. Several opportunities exist for professional librarians as well. Applications and information may be obtained, beginning each year in March, directly from CIES. The worldwide application deadline is August 1.

Department of Defense, Dependents Schools

2461 Eisenhower Ave., Alexandria, VA 22331-1100. With overall management and operational responsibilities for the education of dependent children of active-duty U.S. military personnel and DOD civilians stationed in foreign areas, this agency is responsible for teacher recruitment. Write for the complete application brochure. The latest edition of *Overseas Opportunities for Educators* provides information on employment opportunities in about 225 schools worldwide operated for the children of U.S. military and civilian personnel stationed overseas.

International Association of School Librarianship

Box 1486, Kalamazoo, MI 49005. Informal contacts can be established through this group.

International Schools Services

Box 5910, Princeton, NJ 08543 (609-452-0990). This private, not-for-profit organization, founded in 1955, serves U.S. schools, other than Department of Defense schools, overseas. These include international elementary and secondary schools that enroll children of businessmen and -women and diplomats living abroad. ISS services to overseas schools include recruitment and recommendation of personnel, curricular and administrative guidance, purchasing, and facility planning. ISS also publishes a comprehensive directory of overseas schools and a bimonthly newsletter, *NewsLinks*, for those interested in the intercultural educational community. Write for information regarding these publications and other services.

Library Fellows Program

c/o Robert P. Doyle, American Library Association, 50 E. Huron St., Chicago, IL 60611 (312-280-3211). ALA administers a grant from the U.S. Information Agency for a program that places American library and book service professionals in institutions overseas for several months to one year. Assignments vary depending on the projects requested by host countries. Candidates should have foreign-language skills, technical expertise, and international interests or expertise. Positions are announced in January, interviews are held in April, and fellows start assignments in mid-September. A similar program places midlevel librarians from other countries in U.S. libraries for three to ten months. Non-U.S. librarians interested in participating should contact the public affairs or cultural affairs officer at the U.S. Embassy in their country.

Peace Corps

1990 K St. N.W., 9th fl., Washington, DC 20526. The Peace Corps needs professionals with experience in medicine, agriculture, automated systems, cataloging and technical services. Write for a brochure and application form.

U.S. Information Agency

Special Services Branch, USIA, 301 Fourth St. S.W., Washington, DC 20547 USIA, known overseas as the U.S. Information Service (USIS), seeks librarians with an MLS and at least four years' experience for regional library officer positions. Candidates must have a master's degree in librarianship from an ALA accredited graduate library program, proven administrative ability, and the skills to coordinate the overseas USIS library program with other USIS information functions in various cities worldwide. Practical experience in at least one of the major functional areas of adult library services is required. Other relevant experience could include cooperative library program development, community outreach, public affairs, project management, and personnel training. USIA maintains about 160 libraries in nearly 90 countries, with 1 million books and about 400 local library staff. Libraries provide reference service and publications about the United States for foreign audiences. U.S. citizenship is required. Benefits include overseas allowances and differentials where applicable, vacation, term life insurance, and medical and retirement programs. To apply, send the standard U.S. government application (SF171), official transcripts, and 1,000-word autobiographical statement to USIA, Foreign Service Recruitment Officer, Office of Personnel, M/PDP Personnel Br., Rm. 518, 301 Fourth St. S.W., Washington, DC 20547.

Overseas Exchange Programs

Most exchanges are handled by direct negotiation between interested parties. A few libraries have established exchange programs for their own staff. To facilitate exchange arrangements, the *IFLA Journal* (issued February, May, August and November) lists individuals wishing to exchange their position for one outside their country. Listings must include the following information: full name, address, present position, qualifications (with year obtained), language abilities, and preferred country, city, library, and type of position. Send to International Federation of Library Associations and Institutions Secretariat, Box 95312, 250 The Hague, Netherlands.

The ALA International Relations Committee/International Relations Round Table (IRC/IRRT) Joint Committee on International Exchange is developing database of U.S. and international libraries and librarians interested in international study or exchanges. The committee welcomes requests for information and for inclusion in the database by all countries, although initially the focus will be on Eastern and Central Europe, the former Soviet Union, and Asia. The committee can be contacted by writing to Lucinda Covert-Vail, Bobst Library, New York University, 70 Washington Sq., New York, NY 10012.

The two-page "Checklist for Preparing for an International Exchange," prepared by the ALA International Relations Committee/International Relations Round Table (IRC/IRRT), is available from the ALA Office for Library Personnel Resources (OLPR) or the ALA International Relations Committee. Also available from OLPR is a short bibliography on international exchanges. Under the auspices of the IRC/IRRT Joint Committee on International Exchange of Librarians and Information Professionals, Linda E. Williamson wrote *Going International: Librarians' Preparation Guide for a Work Experience/Job Exchange Abroad* (1988, 74 pp., ISBN 0-8389-7268-3, $15 from ALA Order Services, 50 E. Huron St., Chicago, IL 60611).

LIBEX Bureau for International Staff Exchange

c/o A. J. Clark, Information and Library Studies Library, University of Wales, Aberystwyth (formerly College of Librarianship Wales Library), Llanbadarn Fawr, Aberystwyth, Dyfed SY23 3AS, Wales (Tel. 0970-622417, FAX 0970-622190, E-mail ilslib@aber.ac.uk). LIBEX assists in two-way exchanges for British librarians wishing to work abroad and for librarians from the United States, Canada, the European Community, the Commonwealth, and many other countries who wish to work in Britain.

Using Information Skills in Nonlibrary Settings

Information professionals have shown a great deal of interest in "alternative careers" and in using information skills in a variety of settings. These jobs are not usually found through regular library placement channels, although many library schools are trying to generate such listings for students and alumni. Listings for jobs that require information management skills may not specifically call for librarians, so job seekers may need to use ingenuity to find them. Some librarians offer their services on a free-lance basis to businesses, alternative schools, community agencies, legislators, and the like; these opportunities are usually not advertised but are found through contacts developed over time. A number of businesses that broker information have developed from individual free-lance experiences. Small companies or other organizations often need a one-time service for organizing files or collections, bibliographic research for special projects, indexing or abstracting, compiling directories, or consulting work.

Bibliographic networks and online database companies are using librarians as information managers, trainers, researchers, systems and database analysts, and online services managers. Jobs are sometimes advertised in library network newsletters or data-processing journals. Librarians can be found working in law firms as litigation case supervisors (organizing and analyzing records for legal cases); in publishing companies as sales representatives, marketing directors, editors, and computer services experts; in community agencies as adult education coordinators, volunteer administrators, and grant writers.

The classifieds in *Publishers Weekly* and *National Business Employment Weekly* may lead to information-related positions. One might also consider reading the Sunday classified sections in metropolitan newspapers to locate job descriptions under a variety of job titles calling for information skills.

The *Burwell Directory of Information Brokers* is an annual publication that lists information brokers, free-lance librarians, independent information specialists, and institutions that provide services for a fee. Individuals do not need to pay to be listed; the 1994 directory is available from Burwell Enterprises, 3724 FM 1960 Rd. W., Suite 214, Houston, TX 77068 (713-537-9051, FAX 713-537-8332). It is supplemented by the bimonthly *Information Broker*, a newsletter that includes articles by, for, and about individuals and companies in the fee-based information field, with book reviews, a calendar of events, and issue-oriented articles.

The Independent Librarians Exchange Round Table is a unit within the American Library Association that serves as a networking source for owners of information businesses, consultants, and those who work for a company that provides support services to libraries or other information services outside traditional library settings. The membership fee is $8, in addition to ALA dues, and includes the newsletter *ILERT Alert*. At the 1993 ALA annual conference, ILERT sponsored the program "Jobs for Indexers," which is available on cassette ALA332 for $24 from Teach 'em Inc., 160 E. Illinois St., Chicago, IL 60611 (800-224-3775).

The Association of Independent Information Professionals, not affiliated with ALA, was formed in 1987 for individuals who own and operate for-profit information companies. Contact Marilyn Levine, 2266 N. Prospect Ave., Suite 314, Milwaukee, WI 53202.

A growing number of publications describe opportunities for librarians in the broader information arena. "You Can Take Your MLS Out of the Library," by Wilda W. Williams (*Library Journal*, Nov. 1994, pp. 43–46); "Information Entrepreneurship: Sources for Reference Librarians" by Donna Gilton (*RQ*, Spring 1992, pp. 346–355); "Information Brokering: The State of Art" by Alice Sizer Warner (*Wilson Library Bulletin*, April 1989, pp. 55–57); and "The Information Broker: A Modern Profile" by Mick O'Leary (*Online*, November 1987, pp. 24–30), provide an overview of information brokerage. *The Information Broker's Handbook* by Sue Rugge and Alfred Glossbrenner (Blue Ridge Summit, PA: Windcrest/McGraw-Hill, 1992, 379 pp., ISBN 0-8306-3798-2) covers the market for information, getting started, pricing and billing, and more. *Mind Your Own Business: A Guide for the Information Entrepreneur* by Alice Sizer Warner (New York: Neal-Schuman, 1987, 165 pp., ISBN 1-55570-014-4) describes planning for and managing an information business, including marketing, sales, and record keeping. *Opening New Doors: Alternative Careers for Librarians*, edited by Ellis Mount (Washington, DC: Special Libraries Association, 1993), provides profiles of librarians who are working outside libraries. *Extending the Librarian's Domain: A Survey of Emerging Occupation Opportunities for Librarians and Information Professionals* by Forest Woody

Horton, Jr. (Washington, DC: Special Libraries Association, 1994) explores information job components in a variety of sectors.

New Options for Librarians: Finding a Job in a Related Field, edited by Betty-Carol Sellen and Dimity S. Berkner (New York: Neal-Schuman, 1984, 300 pp., ISBN 0-918212-73-1, $27.95), covers how to prepare for and initiate a job search and examines career possibilities in publishing, public relations, abstracting and indexing, association work, contract service companies, information management, and more. Also included is a survey of librarians working in related fields and an annotated bibliography. The survey results are summarized in "Librarians in Alternative Work Places" (*Library Journal* 110, February 15, 1985), pp. 108–110.

Guide to Careers in Abstracting and Indexing by Wendy Wicks and Ann Marie Cunningham (Philadelphia: NFAIS, 1992, 126 pp.) is available for $25 from the National Federation of Abstracting and Information Services, 1518 Walnut St., Philadelphia, PA 19102 (215-893-1561). The American Society of Indexers, Box 386, Port Aransas, TX 78373 (512-749-4052), has a number of publications that would be useful for individuals who are interested in indexing careers. Send for membership and publication information.

Careers in Information, edited by Jane F. Spivack (Boston: G. K. Hall, 1982, ISBN 0-914236-83-0), includes chapters on the work of information specialists, entrepreneurship in the information industry, and information professionals in the federal government, as well as guidance on finding a job and information on placements and salaries for the broader information field in addition to librarianship. "Atypical Careers and Innovative Services in Library and Information Science," edited by Walter C. Allen and Lawrence W. S. Auld, composes the entire issue of *Library Trends* 32 (Winter 1984). It focuses on new directions with potential employment opportunities for librarians and some of the implications for the changing role of the information professional.

Although out of print, some earlier publications are still useful sources: *What Else You Can Do with a Library Degree,* edited by Betty-Carol Sellen (New York: Neal-Schuman and Gaylord Brothers, 1979); *The Information Brokers: How to Start and Operate Your Own Fee-Based Service* by Kelly Warnken (New York: Bowker, 1981); and *Careers in Other Fields for Librarians . . . Successful Strategies for Finding the Job* by Rhoda Garoogian and Andrew Garoogian (Chicago: ALA, 1985). Chapters in the latter book include bridging traditional and nontraditional employment; opportunities in business, government, education, and entrepreneurship; and employment techniques (where to look for jobs, résumés and letters, and interviewing). Of particular interest is the chapter describing the process of translating traditional library tasks and skills into new types of job responsibility. Scattered throughout are sample job descriptions in other fields that incorporate information functions.

Temporary/Part-Time Positions

Working as a substitute librarian or in temporary positions may be an alternative career path or interim step while looking for a regular job. This type of work can provide valuable contacts and experience. Organizations that hire library workers for part-time or temporary jobs include Pro Libra Associates, Inc., 6 Inwood Place, Maplewood, NJ 07040 (201-762-0070); C. Berger and Co., 327 E. Gundersen Dr., Carol Stream, IL 60188 (708-653-1115, 800-382-4222); Gossage Regan Associates, Inc., 25 W. 43 St., New York, NY 10036 (212-869-3348); The Library Co-Op, Inc., 3840 Park Ave., Suite 107, Edison, NJ 08820 (908-906-1777, 800-654-6275); Library Management Systems, 16027 Ventura Blvd., Suite 612, Encino, CA 91436 (818-789-3141, 800-567-4669), and Advanced Information Management, 444 Castro St., Suite 320, Mountain View, CA 94041 (415-965-7799) or 900 Wilshire Blvd., Suite 1424, Los Angeles, CA 90017 (213-243-9236).

Part-time jobs are not always advertised, and they are often found by canvassing local libraries and leaving applications.

Job Hunting in General

Wherever information needs to be organized and presented to patrons in an effective, efficient, and service-oriented fashion, professional librarians can apply their skills. However, one must be prepared to invest considerable time, energy, imagination, and money to create or obtain a satisfying position in a conventional library or other type of information service. Usually, one job-hunting method or source is not enough.

"How to Find a Job Online" by Ann J. Van Camp, *Online* 12 (July 1988): 26–34, offers guidance on databases that might lead to library or information-related positions.

Public and school library certification requirements often vary from state to state; contact the state library agency for such information. Certification requirements are summarized in *Certification of Public Librarians in the United States* (4th ed., 1991), available from the ALA Office for Library Personnel Resources. A summary of school library/media certification requirements by state is included in *Requirements for Certification of Teachers, Counselors, Librarians and Administrators for Elementary and Secondary Schools*, published annually by the University of Chicago Press. "School Library Media Certification Requirements: 1992 Update" by Patsy H. Perritt also provides this information. [See the 1993 edition of *The Bowker Annual—Ed.*] For information on a specific state, contact the state supervisors of school library media services. [For a list of the state supervisors, see Part 6 of the *Bowker Annual—Ed.*]

Civil service requirements—be they on the local, county, or state level—can add another layer of procedures to the job search. Some civil service jurisdictions require written and/or oral examinations; others assign a ranking based on a review of credentials. Jobs are usually filled from a list of qualified candidates. Because the exams are held only at certain times and a variety of jobs can be filled from a single list of applicants (e.g., all Librarian I positions, regardless of type of function), candidates should be certain that the library of interest falls under civil service regulations.

For a position in a specific specialty or geographic area, remember those reference skills to ferret information from directories and other tools regarding local industries, schools, subject collections, and the like. Directories such as the *American Library Directory, Subject Collections, Directory of Special Libraries and Information Centers, and Directory of Federal Libraries*, as well as state directories and directories for other special subject areas, can provide a wealth of information for job seekers. "The Job Hunter's Search for Company Information" by Robert Favini (*RQ*, Winter 1991, pp. 155–161) lists general reference business sources that might also be useful for librarians seeking employment in corporations. Some state employment offices will include library listings as part of their job services department. Some students have pooled resources to hire a clipping service for a specific period to get classified ads for a particular geographic area.

For information on other job-hunting and personnel matters, request a checklist of materials from the ALA Office for Library Personnel Resources, 50 E. Huron St., Chicago, IL 60611.

Placements and Salaries, 1993:
Placements Up, But Full-Time Jobs Are Scarce

Fay Zipkowitz

Associate Professor, Graduate School of Library and Information Studies
University of Rhode Island, Kingston

The 43rd annual Placements and Salaries survey reveals a distressing trend: a doubling—to nearly 20 percent—of the number of part-time and nonprofessional placements of library school graduates. That is to say, of the 2,536 1993 library school graduates who got jobs, one out of every five has been unable to find a full-time position. They are working at the margins of the profession, in temporary professional positions (267 graduates, 10.5 percent) or in nonprofessional library jobs (235 graduates, 9 percent), as indicated in Table 1.

The difference from this year to last is stunning. In 1993, of 1,646 placements in library positions reported, there were barely 4 percent (62 graduates) in temporary professional positions and 6 percent (96 graduates) in nonprofessional library positions.

Contributing to this unhealthy situation is new graduates' refusal or inability to move away from the state or region where they received their library degrees. Placement officers nationwide commented on the difficulty of placing people who are not mobile and are unable to move into regions where there are few or no library schools and more job openings (e.g., the Great Plains). In locales where there have been massive cutbacks, such as California, new librarians may find themselves competing with those who've been laid off and have years of experience. That can be devastating for a new entrant to the field.

The statistics on placement by location (see Tables 7 and 8) support the impressions of library placement officers: 71 percent of graduates were placed in the same state or district as their library schools; an additional 14 percent were placed in the same region. Last year these percentages were 73 percent and 12 percent, respectively—not much change. For minority placements last year, 65 percent of graduates stayed in the same states or districts and 9 percent in the same region. This year, the numbers are 72 percent and 7 percent, respectively.

The Big Picture

This year's survey encompasses the entire 50 accredited, operational library schools in the United States. The program at Northern Illinois University has graduated its last class and closed its doors, thus no report was available. The University of California at Berkeley did not admit any new students this past academic year, but both UC-Berkeley and UCLA are still operating and possibly moving in new directions. This report includes the University of Puerto Rico for the first time. A special thanks to all the participating schools for their efforts in gathering the data about their graduates.

Note: Adapted from *Library Journal*, October 15, 1994.

Table 1 / Status of 1993 U.S. Graduates, Spring 1994*

	Number of Schools Reporting	Graduates Total	Not in Lib. Positions			Employment Unknown			Perm. Prof. Positions			Temp. Prof. Positions			Nonprof. Lib. Positions			Total in Lib. Positions		
			Women	Men	Total	Women	Men	Total	Women	Men	Total	Women	Men	Total	Women	Men	Total	Women	Men	Total
Northeast	16	1,532	97	34	131	364	105	534	494	150	644	57	17	74	47	7	54	598	174	772
Southeast	12	753	33	4	37	127	36	161	281	71	352	29	4	33	28	2	30	338	77	415
Midwest	12	1,407	60	14	74	81	20	172	466	115	581	53	17	70	63	14	77	582	146	728
Southwest	5	475	27	5	32	52	14	66	209	58	267	13	6	19	17	7	24	239	71	310
West	5	587	27	5	32	176	21	197	160	30	190	57	14	71	36	14	50	253	58	311
All Schools	50	4,754	244	62	306	800	195	1,130	1,610	424	2,034	209	58	267	191	44	235	2,010	526	2,536

*For an explanation of why the figures in these tables do not always add up to the Total columns, see "The Big Picture."

Table 2 / Placements and Full-Time Salaries of 1993 U.S. Graduates: Summary by Region

	Total Placements	Number of Reported Salaries			Low Salary		High Salary		Average Salary			Median Salary		
		Women	Men	Total	Women	Men	Women	Men	Women	Men	Total	Women	Men	Total
Northeast	781	439	114	555	$13,440	$14,100	$65,000	$80,000	$28,672	$29,620	$28,851	$27,000	$27,000	$27,000
Southeast	416	270	61	331	13,200	14,100	39,000	43,164	24,525	25,558	24,716	24,000	25,000	24,100
Midwest	736	376	105	480	12,000	15,000	64,132	50,000	26,207	26,364	26,241	25,200	25,500	25,300
Southwest	314	188	55	243	12,400	13,000	43,000	48,000	25,421	25,032	25,640	25,000	24,120	25,000
West	305	144	35	179	18,000	20,000	72,000	50,000	30,978	30,779	30,939	30,000	30,000	30,000
Combined	2,552	1,417	370	1,788	$12,000	$13,000	$72,000	$80,000	$27,031	$27,454	$27,116	$28,000	$28,000	$26,000

Forty-seven schools provided information on salaries and placements for most of their 1993 graduates. As in previous reports, the completeness and accuracy of individual data vary among and within the institutional reports. For example, gender and type of placement might have been reported, but not a salary figure; or, salary, gender, and type of library may have been reported but not location or type of assignment. There are some graduates for whom no specific information was available, but they are included in the totals of graduates nonetheless. Three institutions (two Midwest, one Southeast) did not report any individual data for graduates but did provide summary data on the total numbers of graduates, on gender, and on minority status when that information was available to them. We therefore have a highly accurate picture of the 4,754 recipients of the first professional degree (not including an unknown number from Northern Illinois). The ratio of women to men is still no surprise—80 percent to 20 percent.

Salaries Inch Up

The average salary overall was $27,116, a gain of $450 over last year's average salary. The average reported salary for minorities was $27,865, a gain of $326. The average salary for men was $423 higher than for women; last year the difference was $263. The median salary difference is more dramatic: last year it was $300 more for men than women—this year the men's median is $2,000 more (see Table 2). The difference may be skewed by men with significant professional experience adding the MLS degree and returning to a position that was already highly paid. Nevertheless, this figure bears watching.

In Table 9, Average Salary Index, we have attempted to provide a longitudinal view of the purchasing power of the average beginning salary from one annual group of graduates to another. For the base period of 1982–1984, which the Bureau of Labor Statistics uses for the current Consumer Price Index, the average beginning salary was $17,693. In the intervening years the CPI has risen 44.4 percent, compared to the average beginning professional salary, which has risen 53.3 percent. Thus, the average salary for a newly graduated MLS placed in 1993 had 6.2 percent more purchasing power (153.3 to 144.4) than the average salary of a 1982–84 graduate.

Men Creeping Up in Academe

Table 3 displays, among other salient data, the number of placements by gender and type of library. Not surprisingly, school libraries have the highest percent of female placements: 93 percent. Public libraries, special libraries, and the varied types clustered together in the "Other" category all have nearly the same distribution as the population of new graduates: 80 percent female and 20 percent male placements. Only in college and university libraries do we see a significant representation of male placements; in academe, the placement ratio is 69 percent women to 31 percent men, about 7 percent more men than last year's figure.

(text continues on p. 391)

Table 3 / Placements by Type of Library of 1993 U.S. Graduates by School

School	Public			Elementary & Secondary			College & University			Special			Other			Total		
	Women	Men	Total	Women	Men	Total	Women	Men	Total	Women	Men	Total	Women	Men	Total	Women	Men	Total
Alabama	13	3	16	12	0	12	8	3	11	6	0	6	1	0	1	43	6	49
Arizona	9	2	11	8	0	8	8	3	11	4	2	6	1	1	2	30	8	38
Calif., Berkeley	11	2	13	1	1	2	10	6	16	10	2	12	10	2	12	42	13	55
Calif., Los Angeles	7	0	7	2	0	2	9	5	14	7	0	7	4	0	4	29	5	34
Catholic	5	1	6	4	0	4	3	1	4	9	2	11	7	2	9	28	6	34
Clarion	15	5	21	5	0	5	8	1	9	1	0	1	0	0	0	29	6	36
Clark Atlanta	0	0	0	0	0	0	0	0	0	0	0	0	0	0	0	0	0	0
Drexel	6	1	7	5	0	5	11	5	16	12	2	14	5	2	7	39	10	49
Emporia	0	0	0	0	0	0	0	0	0	0	0	0	0	0	0	0	0	0
Florida State	12	3	15	5	2	7	4	4	8	2	3	5	3	1	4	26	13	39
Hawaii	12	2	14	16	1	17	7	3	10	8	3	11	2	2	4	47	13	60
Illinois	0	0	0	0	0	0	0	0	0	0	0	0	0	0	0	0	0	0
Indiana	47	9	56	10	1	11	23	6	29	4	0	4	3	0	3	101	17	118
Iowa	19	1	20	8	1	9	8	6	14	3	1	4	2	0	2	40	10	50
Kent	45	7	52	11	0	11	8	9	17	9	5	14	2	1	3	75	22	97
Kentucky	13	1	14	9	0	9	14	9	23	5	2	7	3	1	4	45	14	59
Long Island	7	6	14	7	0	7	5	0	5	5	0	5	0	0	0	24	6	31
Louisiana State	11	4	15	8	0	8	14	3	17	5	1	6	3	1	4	41	9	50
Maryland	7	0	7	9	1	10	9	4	13	10	4	14	5	2	7	44	11	55
Michigan	14	7	21	6	0	6	13	3	16	10	0	10	4	1	5	47	11	58
Missouri	14	3	17	6	0	6	9	8	17	9	4	13	2	0	2	41	15	56
N.C., Central	8	1	9	12	2	14	5	4	9	5	0	5	0	0	0	30	7	37
N.C., Chapel Hill	7	0	7	5	0	5	9	3	12	8	2	10	8	1	9	37	6	43
N.C., Greensboro	8	3	11	20	1	21	4	4	8	5	1	6	0	0	0	37	9	46
North Texas	13	4	17	13	1	14	13	5	18	14	3	17	2	1	3	56	14	70
Oklahoma	3	5	8	18	1	19	10	8	18	3	1	4	1	0	1	35	15	50

Table 3 / Placements by Type of Library of 1993 U.S. Graduates by School (cont.)

School	Public			Elementary & Secondary			College & University			Special			Other			Total		
	Women	Men	Total	Women	Men	Total	Women	Men	Total	Women	Men	Total	Women	Men	Total	Women	Men	Total
Pittsburgh	13	5	18	6	2	8	12	7	19	6	4	10	9	4	13	46	22	68
Pratt	10	4	14	2	0	2	2	1	3	10	8	18	3	4	7	27	17	44
Puerto Rico	0	0	0	2	0	2	1	0	1	1	0	1	0	0	0	4	0	4
Queens	19	4	23	4	1	5	7	0	7	5	2	7	2	0	2	37	7	44
Rhode Island	19	2	21	14	0	14	10	1	11	3	1	4	3	1	4	49	5	54
Rosary	31	4	35	20	2	22	12	10	22	10	1	11	3	3	6	76	20	96
Rutgers	16	5	21	9	1	10	8	2	10	4	0	4	13	3	16	53	13	66
St. John's	11	2	13	2	0	2	3	2	5	9	2	11	0	0	0	25	6	31
San Jose	26	2	28	10	1	11	15	4	19	13	2	15	0	0	0	65	10	75
Simmons	20	2	22	9	0	9	24	3	27	26	4	30	11	0	11	90	9	99
South Carolina	9	4	13	26	3	29	10	6	16	4	0	4	2	0	2	51	13	64
South Florida	9	2	11	6	0	6	4	1	5	2	0	2	3	1	4	24	4	28
Southern Connecticut	9	3	12	8	0	8	5	0	5	8	0	8	0	2	2	30	5	35
Southern Mississippi	7	1	8	4	2	6	8	3	11	3	0	3	1	0	1	23	6	29
SUNY-Albany	13	2	15	5	1	6	8	5	13	5	1	6	7	3	10	38	12	50
SUNY-Buffalo	14	8	22	14	1	15	8	5	13	6	0	6	6	0	6	48	14	62
Syracuse	1	2	3	6	0	6	6	5	11	4	2	6	3	2	5	20	11	31
Tennessee	2	1	3	9	0	9	7	2	9	2	0	2	1	0	1	21	3	24
Texas, Austin	21	9	30	15	0	15	20	16	36	13	4	17	11	1	12	80	30	110
Texas Woman's	13	0	13	7	0	7	7	1	8	5	0	5	2	0	2	34	1	35
Washington	18	3	21	6	1	7	6	2	8	22	5	27	0	0	0	52	11	63
Wayne State	26	3	29	12	2	14	7	1	8	8	0	8	3	0	3	56	6	62
Wisconsin, Madison	10	3	13	4	2	6	12	3	15	7	2	9	2	1	3	35	11	46
Wisconsin, Milwaukee	11	7	18	23	2	25	28	11	39	5	1	6	1	0	1	68	21	89
Total	634	148	784	423	33	456	442	194	636	335	77	412	154	43	197	2,018	503	2,523

Table 4 / Placements and Full-Time Salaries of 1993 U.S. Graduates by School

School	Total Placements	Salaries Women	Salaries Men	Salaries Total	Low Salary Women	Low Salary Men	High Salary Women	High Salary Men	Average Salary Women	Average Salary Men	Average Salary Total	Median Salary Women	Median Salary Men	Median Salary Total
Alabama	49	38	3	41	$13,700	$22,600	$32,740	$25,900	$22,754	$24,500	$22,882	$22,175	$25,000	$22,800
Arizona	38	13	2	15	21,000	22,000	33,000	28,000	25,846	25,000	25,733	25,000	25,000	25,000
Calif., Berkeley	55	22	6	28	24,000	23,000	48,000	41,323	30,979	33,005	31,413	29,500	32,600	30,300
Calif., Los Angeles	34	23	3	26	23,000	25,000	46,000	35,052	31,543	29,016	31,252	31,000	27,000	31,000
Catholic	34	25	5	30	14,000	14,700	42,500	30,000	29,462	25,220	28,755	29,500	27,000	29,500
Clarion	36	21	6	28	15,000	16,800	32,000	34,000	23,944	23,960	23,840	24,500	23,000	23,400
Drexel	49	30	9	39	15,000	23,000	54,000	56,000	28,686	34,191	29,956	26,200	28,000	27,000
Florida State	39	21	13	34	18,767	14,400	30,000	36,000	23,691	25,408	24,348	23,000	26,000	23,900
Hawaii	60	44	12	56	14,784	20,000	54,000	42,000	28,096	28,813	28,242	27,350	29,966	28,000
Indiana	118	85	16	101	13,000	16,900	41,249	32,000	23,818	23,553	23,859	24,000	24,000	24,000
Iowa	50	26	5	31	17,500	22,000	44,000	32,000	26,924	26,840	26,911	26,000	27,000	26,000
Kent State	97	53	14	56	14,500	19,300	49,700	50,000	25,036	24,914	25,385	24,500	25,200	24,750
Kentucky	59	44	14	58	16,000	17,300	39,400	39,800	26,289	28,464	26,814	26,250	28,000	26,730
Long Island	31	23	6	30	13,600	26,280	46,000	36,250	29,892	29,372	29,719	31,000	28,500	30,000
Louisiana State	50	36	8	44	18,000	16,500	33,000	30,000	24,967	23,727	24,742	25,000	24,500	25,000
Maryland	55	34	10	44	14,000	16,305	45,000	35,000	26,248	26,083	26,210	26,362	28,000	26,499
Michigan	58	47	11	58	17,200	22,000	38,500	32,000	26,037	26,309	26,089	25,000	25,800	25,150
Missouri	56	31	14	45	16,000	19,000	40,000	42,000	24,387	26,174	24,943	23,600	24,561	24,000
N.C., Central	37	28	7	35	17,000	17,172	29,000	36,000	23,934	27,525	24,652	24,750	28,000	25,000
N.C., Chapel Hill	43	27	3	30	18,500	24,000	36,400	43,164	25,667	32,055	26,306	25,500	29,000	25,500
N.C., Greensboro	46	34	7	41	15,000	16,800	34,000	30,000	25,114	22,900	24,736	24,460	23,500	24,000
North Texas	70	51	13	64	15,000	13,000	35,500	48,000	25,787	26,616	25,955	25,500	25,500	25,500
Oklahoma	50	31	12	43	13,000	16,500	31,000	40,000	23,935	23,483	23,809	24,000	22,500	24,000
Pittsburgh	68	20	8	28	15,000	23,000	40,000	30,000	25,150	27,125	25,714	26,250	27,000	27,000
Pratt	44	25	14	39	16,800	25,000	45,000	53,000	29,879	33,643	31,230	26,800	30,500	28,000
Puerto Rico	4	4	0	4	13,200	—	16,920	—	15,030	—	15,030	15,000	—	15,000
Queens	44	33	6	39	17,500	26,000	53,278	36,000	29,832	31,117	30,029	27,000	32,000	28,000

Table 4 / Placements and Full-Time Salaries of 1993 U.S. Graduates by School *(cont.)*

School	Total Placements	Placements Women	Placements Men	Placements Total	Low Salary Women	Low Salary Men	High Salary Women	High Salary Men	Average Salary Women	Average Salary Men	Average Salary Total	Median Salary Women	Median Salary Men	Median Salary Total
Rhode Island	54	30	3	33	17,800	19,000	48,000	31,000	26,735	25,233	26,610	26,000	25,700	26,669
Rosary	96	37	12	49	17,600	15,093	46,000	36,000	27,025	24,693	26,454	26,500	25,000	26,000
Rutgers	66	40	10	50	16,900	25,000	65,000	80,000	35,913	40,975	36,044	32,693	38,150	33,250
St. John's	31	19	4	23	15,600	17,500	45,000	31,000	29,641	23,575	28,586	26,808	22,900	26,800
San Jose	75	44	7	51	15,120	24,200	72,000	50,000	31,301	34,457	31,734	29,500	35,000	30,000
Simmons	99	61	6	67	13,000	25,000	38,000	34,000	25,368	28,523	25,650	26,100	28,569	26,280
South Carolina	64	47	13	60	13,000	21,600	39,000	36,000	25,166	26,678	25,493	25,000	25,800	25,000
South Florida	28	22	3	25	17,600	19,000	33,000	23,000	24,850	21,000	24,388	23,500	21,000	23,000
So. Connecticut	35	26	4	30	18,800	26,800	46,000	35,500	30,367	29,825	30,295	28,000	28,500	28,000
So. Mississippi	29	13	5	18	14,000	17,000	36,000	27,000	25,523	21,672	24,453	26,000	20,000	25,000
SUNY-Albany	50	31	7	38	15,000	19,200	41,000	33,000	26,240	26,457	26,280	26,000	26,000	26,000
SUNY-Buffalo	62	39	12	51	13,000	23,000	39,000	38,000	25,945	27,301	26,264	26,300	26,000	26,290
Syracuse	31	10	5	15	24,860	20,000	44,000	36,900	30,609	28,480	29,899	29,600	26,500	29,200
Tennessee	24	18	3	21	17,500	22,000	31,102	23,500	24,807	22,767	23,899	25,000	22,800	23,000
Texas, Austin	110	60	26	86	19,500	20,000	43,000	32,878	29,968	24,922	26,349	24,750	26,050	25,700
Texas Woman's	35	31	1	32	14,800	26,000	33,000	26,000	23,700	26,000	23,346	23,429	26,000	23,850
Washington	63	36	9	45	15,000	14,000	46,000	34,519	27,530	26,913	27,407	26,640	28,000	26,500
Wayne State	62	32	6	38	13,200	14,040	64,132	32,000	27,483	25,007	27,092	26,901	26,000	26,901
Wisconsin, Madison	46	22	9	31	16,224	15,000	45,000	35,000	27,209	24,790	26,506	25,500	23,500	25,000
Wisconsin, Milwaukee	89	27	9	36	13,000	14,000	35,000	42,000	26,004	27,500	26,378	26,700	25,800	26,700

Table 5 / Special Placements, 1993

	Women	Men	Total
Government jurisdictions (U.S.)			
National libraries	3	1	4
State & provincial libraries	6	1	7
Armed Services libraries (domestic)	2	1	3
Overseas agencies (incl. Armed Services)	0	0	0
Other government agencies (except USVA hospitals)	4	3	7
Library science			
Post-MLS studies or advanced academic studies	19	5	24
Teaching library & information studies	0	1	1
Other			
Architecture	10	7	17
Art and/or museum library	9	2	11
Audiovisual and media centers	26	1	27
Bibliographic instruction	6	2	8
Booktrade sales (retail and/or wholesale)	2	0	2
Commercial enterprises (finance, industrial, insurance,etc.)	10	7	17
Correctional institutions	2	1	3
Databases (publishing, servicing)	7	3	10
Freelance consultants & information brokers	10	3	13
Genealogical libraries & services	0	0	0
Government documents	5	3	8
Historical agencies and archives	4	2	6
Hospitals (incl. USVA hospitals)	2	1	3
Indexing & abstracting	1	1	2
Information services (nonlibrary)	10	0	10
International relations (area studies, agencies)	2	0	2
Law libraries (incl. academic, bar association, etc.)	34	8	42
Library services to the handicapped	1	0	1
Maps	1	0	1
Medicine (incl. nursing schools)	31	9	40
Music, theater, motion picture, dance	1	2	3
Networks and consortia	2	0	2
Outreach activities and services	6	2	8
Pharmaceutical	2	1	3
Professional associations	0	0	0
Rare books, manuscripts, archives	7	1	8
Records management	2	1	3
Religion (seminaries, theological schools)	4	2	6
Science and technology (incl. R&D)	18	2	20
Social sciences	0	0	0
Spanish-speaking centers	0	0	0
Suppliers & vendors (nonautomation)	0	0	0
Systems, automation (incl. vendors)	15	14	29
Technical writing & documentation	2	0	2
Youth/young adult services	52	4	56
Total special placements	318	91	409

Table 6 / Salaries of Minority Placements by Type of Library, 1993

	Number	Percent of Total	Low Salary	Average Salary	High Salary
Academic	85	31.1	$13,000	$26,372	$46,000
Public	76	27.8	18,400	27.089	44,000
School	30	11.0	14,400	30,844	45,000
Special	45	16.5	19,000	29,366	54,000
Other	18	6.6	14,000	27,934	33,000
Total	273	100.0	$13,000	$27,865	$54,000

Table 7 / 1993 Graduates, Placement by Location

Library School Location	Number of Graduates Placed	Placed in Same State (as library school)	Placed in Same Region (as library school)	Placed in Other Regions					
				Northeast	Southeast	Midwest	Southwest	West	Foreign Jurisdiction
Alabama	49	37	9	0	—	0	1	1	1
Arizona	38	17	3	1	2	5	9	0	1
California	180	157	7	10	1	0	3	0	2
Connecticut	35	25	9	0	0	0	0	1	0
Dist. of Columbia	33	14	2	0	17	0	0	0	0
Florida	67	52	7	3	0	1	2	1	1
Hawaii	59	49	6	1	1	0	1	0	1
Illinois	97	89	3	0	3	0	1	0	1
Indiana	115	64	34	4	4	0	5	3	1
Iowa	49	24	15	4	1	0	3	2	0
Kentucky	56	20	11	6	17	0	1	0	1
Louisiana	49	34	8	1	0	2	3	1	0
Maryland	55	25	15	0	12	1	0	1	1
Massachusetts	98	72	17	0	2	0	1	2	4
Michigan	120	83	14	10	8	0	4	1	0

Mississippi	29	14	8	2	0	1	0	2	2
Missouri	62	40	12	2	3	0	3	1	1
New Jersey	50	33	14	0	1	2	0	0	0
New York	300	247	33	0	6	4	1	4	5
North Carolina	127	96	14	11	0	3	2	0	1
Ohio	96	86	1	5	2	0	0	0	2
Oklahoma	49	41	1	1	1	2	0	3	0
Pennsylvania	164	104	33	0	9	8	4	4	2
Rhode Island	54	17	33	0	0	3	0	0	1
South Carolina	66	41	16	4	0	3	0	2	0
Tennessee	24	17	5	0	0	1	0	0	1
Texas	223	175	9	8	15	10	0	5	1
Washington	63	52	0	5	1	4	1	0	0
Wisconsin	139	88	11	4	2	0	5	5	24
Total	2,546	1,313	350	82	108	50	50	39	54
Percentage	—	71%	14%	3%	4%	2%	2%	2%	2%

Table 8 / 1993 Minority Graduates, Placement by Location

Library School Location	Number of Graduates Placed	Placed in Same State (as library school)	Placed in Same Region (as library school)	Placed in Other Regions					
				Northeast	Southeast	Midwest	Southwest	West	Foreign Jurisdiction
Alabama	5	2	1	0	0	0	0	1	1
Arizona	6	0	2	0	1	0	0	2	1
California	18	17	0	1	0	0	0	0	0
Florida	5	4	0	0	0	0	1	0	1
Hawaii	38	33	3	1	1	0	0	0	1
Indiana	6	4	1	0	1	0	0	0	0
Iowa	3	1	1	0	0	0	1	0	1
Kentucky	3	1	1	1	0	0	0	0	0
Louisiana	12	10	0	1	0	1	0	0	0
Maryland	6	4	0	0	2	0	0	0	0
Massachusetts	3	3	0	0	0	0	0	0	0
Michigan	8	7	0	1	0	0	0	0	0
Mississippi	8	5	0	2	0	1	0	0	0
Missouri	8	4	1	1	1	0	0	0	1
New Jersey	7	6	0	0	1	0	0	0	0
New York	39	35	2	0	0	0	0	1	1
North Carolina	13	8	0	2	0	2	0	0	1
Ohio	6	3	0	2	0	0	0	0	1
Oklahoma	7	5	0	0	1	1	0	0	0
Pennsylvania	16	2	5	0	3	2	2	1	1
South Carolina	5	4	0	0	0	1	0	0	0
Texas	24	20	0	1	1	1	0	0	1
Washington	6	5	0	0	0	1	0	0	0
Wisconsin	7	4	0	0	0	0	1	1	0
Total	259	187	17	13	11	10	5	6	10
Percentage	—	72%	7%	5%	4%	4%	2%	2%	4%

**Table 9 / Average Salary Index
Starting Library Positions, 1985–1993***

	Library Schools	Average Beginning Salary	Dollar Increase in Average Salary	Beginning Index	BLS-CPI
1985	58	$19,753	$962	111.6	109.3
1986	54	20,874	1,121	118.0	110.5
1987	55	22,247	1,373	125.7	115.4
1988	51	23,491	1,244	132.8	120.5
1989	43	24,581	1,090	138.9	124.0
1990	38	25,306	725	143.0	130.7
1991	46	25,583	277	144.6	136.2
1992	41	26,666	1,083	150.7	140.5
1993	50	27,116	450	153.3	144.4

*The U.S. Bureau of Labor Statistics' present Consumer Price Index is based on the average price data from 1982–1984 as equaling 100. The average beginning professional salary from that period was $17,693 and is used as the equivalent base of 100 for salary data.

Job Postings and Placements

Job listings were a wash, with 14 schools indicating that listings were up from 1992, and 14 saying they were down; five indicated no change. One school stated that it encouraged the use of Internet listings and relied less on traditional postings. Of those schools that reported on whether they saw salaries going up or down from 1992, 14 reported that salaries were up, 7 said they were down, and 12 said they were about the same.

Five institutions reported major difficulty in placing 1993 graduates compared to 1992, but 35 reported that they had no greater difficulty. Seven schools saw the demand for academic librarians decrease, while 5 reported a lower demand for school library media specialists. Subject areas for which there was demand but not enough candidates included languages, music, computer expertise (including programming), math, medicine, and sciences and technology. Five schools also listed cataloging and advanced cataloging as areas in demand but ones that their students could not fill. "We offer the courses but few students take them," said one placement officer.

Clearly we have not made great gains in placements or in average salaries during the last year. The economy is still hampering job searches and creating a disturbing move toward fewer full-time placements, with temporary and nonprofessional library placements on the rise. Many placement officers noted students' reluctance to give information until they had full-time work, with the common plaint being, "I'm still out here looking."

Table 10 / Comparison of Salaries by Type of Library, 1993

	Total Placements	Salaries Women	Salaries Men	Salaries Total	Low Salary Women	Low Salary Men	High Salary Women	High Salary Men	Average Salary Women	Average Salary Men	Average Salary Total	Median Salary Women	Median Salary Men	Median Salary Total
Public libraries														
Northeast	239	143	43	188	$13,000	$14,100	$44,000	$44,500	$26,010	$27,441	$26,320	$26,300	$26,800	$26,800
Southeast	107	76	18	94	13,700	16,500	34,000	36,000	23,486	23,399	23,469	23,750	22,800	23,500
Midwest	274	172	37	209	13,000	14,000	39,400	42,000	24,458	23,724	24,328	24,900	24,000	24,743
Southwest	79	44	16	60	18,000	18,000	33,000	27,000	24,181	23,001	23,866	24,000	23,560	24,000
West	85	41	8	49	15,000	26,200	72,000	37,000	28,244	27,806	28,173	28,000	29,250	28,500
All public	784	478	120	600	13,000	14,000	72,000	44,500	25,057	25,209	25,085	25,000	26,000	25,286
School libraries														
Northeast	116	95	7	102	16,000	25,000	56,455	44,500	30,056	30,914	30,115	29,350	27,000	29,350
Southeast	120	99	9	108	13,000	21,000	39,000	30,000	24,706	24,044	24,651	24,000	24,000	24,000
Midwest	118	74	8	82	14,500	20,650	64,132	42,000	29,758	28,919	29,676	27,550	25,750	27,500
Southwest	64	50	2	52	15,000	24,000	43,000	29,000	26,968	33,500	26,950	26,000	33,500	26,000
West	41	32	3	35	16,500	14,000	45,000	50,000	31,491	41,333	31,506	30,578	31,000	31,000
All school	459	350	29	379	13,000	14,000	64,132	50,000	28,170	28,805	28,157	27,000	25,000	27,000
College/university libraries														
Northeast	171	93	29	122	13,440	19,000	46,000	50,100	26,164	28,582	26,739	26,000	28,000	26,200
Southeast	107	56	32	84	14,000	16,800	35,000	36,000	24,192	24,426	24,937	24,000	25,006	25,000
Midwest	201	83	45	128	13,000	17,000	45,000	42,000	24,506	26,489	25,203	25,000	27,000	28,300
Southwest	91	44	24	68	13,000	13,000	33,500	40,000	24,160	24,881	24,418	24,400	24,750	26,000
West	67	28	9	37	14,784	20,000	47,000	38,000	28,279	28,776	28,400	27,500	27,000	27,000
All academic	637	304	135	439	13,000	13,000	47,000	50,100	25,253	26,792	25,727	25,000	26,000	25,300
Special libraries														
Northeast	155	98	22	120	13,000	16,305	65,000	53,000	30,373	29,538	30,220	28,900	29,000	29,000
Southeast	50	32	6	38	15,000	22,500	36,000	30,000	25,887	24,167	25,997	26,000	26,500	26,000
Midwest	86	50	13	63	13,200	20,000	40,000	39,800	26,610	27,885	26,873	26,500	26,936	26,500
Southwest	49	36	6	42	14,800	22,000	36,500	48,000	26,288	30,417	26,826	27,000	26,000	27,000
West	72	49	11	60	15,000	22,080	54,000	35,000	30,078	29,144	29,907	29,000	30,000	30,000
All special	412	264	58	322	13,000	16,305	65,000	53,000	28,536	28,878	28,598	28,000	28,000	28,000
Other libraries														
Northeast	79	32	11	43	15,500	22,700	45,000	56,000	28,738	34,745	30,275	27,500	32,000	29,530
Southeast	25	16	3	19	18,900	14,400	36,400	21,915	26,012	19,105	24,921	26,200	21,000	26,000
Midwest	31	15	5	20	14,000	15,000	35,000	50,000	23,260	31,200	25,245	25,000	29,000	25,000
Southwest	20	12	3	15	19,500	20,000	35,000	28,000	25,424	25,333	25,406	24,500	28,800	29,000
West	36	17	6	23	24,000	24,200	48,000	41,232	30,358	33,005	31,049	28,000	32,800	29,000

Accredited Master's Programs in Library and Information Studies

This list of graduate programs accredited by the American Library Association was issued in fall 1994. The list of accredited programs is updated semiannually in the spring and fall and is available from the ALA Committee on Accreditation. A list of more than 200 institutions offering both accredited and non-accredited programs in librarianship appears in the 47th edition of the *American Library Directory* (R. R. Bowker, 1994).

Northeast: Conn., D.C., Md., Mass., N.J., N.Y., Pa., R.I.

Catholic University of America, School of Lib. and Info. Science, Washington, DC 20064. Elizabeth S. Aversa, Dean. 202-319-5085.

Clarion University of Pennsylvania, College of Communication, Computer Info. Science, and Lib. Science, Clarion, PA 16214. Rita Rice Flaningam, Dean. 814-226-2328.

Drexel University, College of Info. Studies, Philadelphia, PA 19104. Richard H. Lytle, Dean. 215-895-2474.

Long Island University, Palmer School of Lib. and Info. Science, Brookville, NY 11548. Anne Woodsworth, Dean. 516-299-2855.

Pratt Institute, School of Info. and Lib. Science, Brooklyn, NY 11205. S. M. Matta, Dean. 718-636-3702.

Queens College, City University of New York, Grad. School of Lib. and Info. Studies, 254 Rosenthal Lib., Flushing, NY 11367. Marianne Cooper, Dir. 718-997-3790.

Rutgers University, School of Communication, Info., and Lib. Studies, 4 Huntington St., New Brunswick, NJ 08903. Betty J. Turock, Chair and Program Dir. 908-932-7917.

Saint John's University, Div. of Lib. and Info. Science, 8000 Utopia Pkwy., Jamaica, NY 11439. James A. Benson, Dir. 718-990-6200.

Simmons College, Grad. School of Lib. and Info. Science, Boston, MA 02115-5898. James M. Matarazzo, Dean. 617-521-2805.

Southern Connecticut State University, School of Lib. Science and Instructional Technology, New Haven, CT 06515. Edward C. Harris, Dean. 203-392-5781.

State University of New York at Albany, School of Info. Science and Policy, Albany, NY 12222. Vincent Aceto, Interim Dean. 518-442-5115.

State University of New York at Buffalo, School of Info. and Lib. Studies, Buffalo, NY 14260. George S. Bobinski, Dean. 716-645-2412.

Syracuse University, School of Info. Studies, 4-206 Center for Science and Technology, Syracuse, NY 13244-4100. Jeffrey Katzer, Interim Dean. 315-443-2911.

University of Maryland, College of Lib. and Info. Services, College Park, MD 20742. Ann E. Prentice, Dean. 301-405-2033.

University of Pittsburgh, School of Lib. and Info. Science, Pittsburgh, PA 15260. Toni Carbo Bearman, Dean. 412-624-5230.

University of Rhode Island, Grad. School of Lib. and Info. Studies, Rodman Hall, Kingston, RI 02881-0815. 401-792-2947.

Southeast: Ala., Fla., Ga., Ky., La., Miss., N.C., S.C., Tenn., P.R.

Clark Atlanta University, School of Lib. and Info. Studies, Atlanta, GA 30314. Charles D. Churchwell, Dean. 404-880-8697.

Florida State University, School of Lib. and Info. Studies, Tallahassee, FL 32306-2048. F. William Summers, Dean. 904-644-5775.

Louisiana State University, School of Lib. and Info. Science, Baton Rouge, LA

70803. Bert R. Boyce, Dean. 504-388-3158.

North Carolina Central University, School of Lib. and Info. Sciences, Box 19586, Durham, NC 27707. Benjamin F. Speller, Jr., Dean. 919-560-6485.

University of Alabama, School of Lib. and Info. Studies, Tuscaloosa, AL 35487-0252. Philip M. Turner, Dean. 205-348-4610.

University of Kentucky, School of Lib. and Info. Science, Lexington, KY 40506-0039. Donald O. Case, Dir. 606-257-8876.

University of North Carolina, School of Info. and Lib. Science, Chapel Hill, NC 27599-3360. Barbara B. Moran, Dean. 919-962-8366.

University of North Carolina, Dept. of Lib. and Info. Studies, Greensboro, NC 27412. Marilyn L. Miller, Chair. 910-334-3477.

University of Puerto Rico, Escuela Graduada de Bibliotecologia y Ciencia de la Información, Box 21906, San Juan, PR 00931-1906. Mariano A. Maura, Dir. 809-763-6199.

University of South Carolina, College of Lib. and Info. Science, Columbia, SC 29208. Fred W. Roper, Dean. 803-777-3858.

University of South Florida, School of Lib. and Info. Science, Tampa, FL 33620-7800. Kathleen de la Peña McCook, Dir. 813-974-3520.

University of Southern Mississippi, School of Lib. and Info. Science, Hattiesburg, MS 39406. Joy Greiner, Dir. 601-266-4228.

University of Tennessee, Knoxville, School of Info. Sciences, Knoxville, TN 37996-4330. José-Marie Griffiths, Dir. 615-974-2148.

Midwest: Ill., Ind., Iowa, Kan., Mich., Mo., Ohio, Wis.

Emporia State University, School of Lib. and Info. Management, Emporia, KS 66801. Martha L. Hale, Dean. 316-341-5203.

Indiana University, School of Lib. and Info. Science, Library 011, Bloomington, IN 47405-1801. Blaise Cronin, Dean. 812-855-2018.

Kent State University, School of Lib. and Info. Science, Kent, OH 44242. Rosemary R. DuMont, Dean. 216-672-2782.

Rosary College, Grad. School of Lib. and Info. Science, River Forest, IL 60305. Michael E. D. Koenig, Dean. 708-524-6844.

University of Illinois, Grad. School of Lib. and Info. Science, 501 East Daniel, Champaign, IL 61820. Leigh Estabrook, Dean. 217-333-3281.

University of Iowa, School of Lib. and Info. Science, Iowa City, IA 52242-1420. Carl F. Orgren, Dir. 319-335-5707.

University of Michigan, School of Info. and Lib. Studies, Ann Arbor, MI 48109-1092. Daniel E. Atkins, Dean. 313-764-9376.

University of Missouri, Columbia School of Lib. and Info. Science, Columbia, MO 65211. Thomas R. Kochtanek, Acting Dean. 314-882-4546.

University of Wisconsin–Madison, School of Lib. and Info. Studies, Helen C. White Hall, 4217, 600 North Park St., Madison, WI 53706. James Krikelas, Interim Dir. 608-263-2900.

University of Wisconsin–Milwaukee, School of Lib. and Info. Science, 2400 E. Hartford Ave., Enderis Hall 1110, Milwaukee, WI 53211. Mohammed M. Aman, Dean. 414-229-4707.

Wayne State University, Lib. and Info. Science Program, 106 Kresge Library, Detroit, MI 48202. Robert P. Holley, Dir. 313-577-1825.

Southwest: Ariz., Okla., Tex.

Texas Woman's University, School of Lib. and Info. Studies, Denton, TX 76204-0905. Keith Swigger, Dean. 817-898-2602.

University of Arizona, School of Lib. Science, Tucson, AZ 85719. Charlie D. Hurt, Dir. 602-621-3565.

University of North Texas, School of Lib. and Info. Sciences, Denton, TX 76203. Raymond F. von Dran, Dean. 817-565-2445.

University of Oklahoma, School of Lib. and Info. Studies, Norman, OK 73019-0528. June Lester, Dir. 405-325-3921.

University of Texas at Austin, Grad. School of Lib. and Info. Science, Austin, TX 78712-1276. Brooke E. Sheldon, Dean. 512-471-3821.

West: Calif., Hawaii, Wash.

San Jose State University, School of Lib. and Info. Science, San Jose, CA 95192-0029. Stuart A. Sutton, Dir. 408-924-2492.

University of California at Berkeley, School of Lib. and Info. Studies, Berkeley, CA 94720-4600. Nancy Van House, Acting Dean. 510-642-9980.

University of California at Los Angeles, Grad. School of Education and Info. Studies, 405 Hilgard Ave., Los Angeles, CA 90024-1520. Marcia J. Bates, Chair. 310-825-8799.

University of Hawaii, School of Lib. and Info. Studies, Honolulu, HI 96822. Miles M. Jackson, Dean. 808-956-7321.

University of Washington, Grad. School of Lib. and Info. Science, 133 Suzzallo, FM-30, Seattle, WA 98195. Phyllis Van Orden, Dir. 206-543-1794.

Canada

Dalhousie University, School of Lib. and Info. Studies, Halifax, NS B3H 4H8. Louis Vagianos, Interim Dir. 902-494-3656.

McGill University, Grad. School of Lib. and Info. Studies, Montreal, PQ H3A 1Y1. J. Andrew Large, Dir. 514-398-4204.

Université de Montréal, Ecole de Bibliothe-conomie et des Sciences de l'Information, Montreal, PQ H3C 3J7. Gilles Deschatelets, Dir. 514-343-6044.

University of Alberta, School of Lib. and Info. Studies, Edmonton, AB T6G 2J4. Sheila Bertram, Dir. 403-492-4578.

University of British Columbia, School of Lib., Archival, and Info. Studies, Vancouver, BC V6T 1Z1. Ken Haycock, Dir. 604-822-2404.

University of Toronto, Faculty of Info. Studies, Toronto, ON M5S 1A1. Adele M. Fasick, Dean. 416-978-3202.

University of Western Ontario, Grad. School of Lib. and Info. Science, London, ON N6G 1H1. Jean Tague-Sutcliffe, Dean. 519 661-3542.

Library Scholarship Sources

For a more complete list of scholarships, fellowships, and assistantships offered for library study, see *Financial Assistance for Library and Information Studies*, published annually by the American Library Association.

American Association of Law Libraries. (1) A varying number of scholarships of a minimum of $1,000 for graduates of an accredited law school who are degree candidates in an ALA-accredited library school; (2) a varying number of scholarships of varying amounts for library school graduates working on a law degree, non-law graduates enrolled in an ALA-accredited library school, and law librarians taking a course related to law librarianship; (3) the George A. Strait Minority Stipend of $3,500 for an experienced minority librarian working toward an advanced degree to further a law library career. For information, write to: Scholar-ship Committee, AALL, 53 W. Jackson Blvd., Suite 940, Chicago, IL 60604.

American Library Association. (1) The David H. Clift Scholarships of $3,000 for a varying number of U.S. or Canadian citizens who have been admitted to an ALA-accredited library school. For information, write to: Staff Liaison, Clift Scholarship Jury, ALA, 50 E. Huron St., Chicago, IL 60611; (2) the Louise Giles Minority Scholarship of $3,000 for a varying number of minority students who have been admitted to an ALA-accredited library school. For information, write to: Staff Liaison, Giles Minority Scholarship Jury, ALA, 50 E. Huron St., Chicago, IL 60611.

ALA/American Association of School Librarians. The AASL School Librarians Workshop Scholarship of $2,500 for a candidate admitted to a full-time ALA-accredited MLS or school library media program. For information, write to: AASL/ALA, 50 E. Huron St., Chicago, IL 60611.

ALA/Association for Library Service to Children. (1) The Bound to Stay Bound Books Scholarship of $5,000 each for two students who are U.S. or Canadian citizens, who have been admitted to an ALA-accredited program, and who will work with children in a library for one year after graduation; (2) the Frederic G. Melcher Scholarship of $5,000 each for two U.S. or Canadian citizens admitted to an ALA-accredited library school who plan to work with children in school or public libraries for two years after graduation. For information, write to: Executive Director, ALSC/ALA, 50 E. Huron St., Chicago, IL 60611.

ALA/Association of College and Research Libraries and the Institute for Scientific Information. (1) The ACRL Doctoral Dissertation Fellowship of $1,000 for a student who has completed all coursework and submitted a dissertation proposal that has been accepted, in the area of academic librarianship; (2) the Samuel Lazerow Fellowship of $1,000 for research in acquisitions or technical services in an academic or research library; (3) the ACRL and Martinus Nijhoff International West European Specialist Study Grant pays travel expenses, room, and board for a ten-day trip to the Netherlands and two other European countries for an ALA member; selection is based on proposal outlining purpose of trip. For information, write to: Althea Jenkins, ACRL/ALA, 50 E. Huron St., Chicago, IL 60611.

ALA/Government Documents Round Table. The David Rozkuszka Scholarship of $3,000 for a student currently working in a library who has been accepted to an ALA-accredited program and is committed to government documents. For information, write to: Jan Swanbeck, George Smathers Library School, University of Florida, Gainesville, FL 32611-2048.

ALA/International Relations Committee. The Bogle International Library Travel Fund grant of $500 for a varying number of ALA members to attend a first international conference. For information, write to: Robert P. Doyle, ALA, 50 E. Huron St., Chicago, IL 60611.

ALA/Library and Information Technology Association. Three LITA Scholarships in library and information technology of $2,500 each for students (two of whom are minority students) who have been admitted to an ALA-accredited program in library automation and information science. For information, write to: LITA/ALA, 50 E. Huron St., Chicago, IL 60611.

ALA/New Members Round Table. EBSCO/NRMT Scholarship of $1,000 for a U.S. or Canadian citizen who is a member of the ALA New Members Round Table. Based on financial need, professional goals, and admission to an ALA-accredited program. For information, write to: Monika Antonelli, 208 1/2 Ave. D, Denton, TX 76201-5713.

ALA/Public Library Association. The New Leaders Travel Grant Study Award of up to $1,500 for a varying number of PLA members with five years' or less experience. For information, write to: PLA/ALA, 50 E. Huron St., Chicago, IL 60611.

American-Scandinavian Foundation. Fellowships and grants for 25 to 30 students, in amounts from $2,500 to $15,000, for advanced study in Denmark, Finland, Iceland, Norway, or Sweden. For information, write to: Exchange Division, American-Scandinavian Foundation, 725 Park Ave., New York, NY 10021.

Association for Library and Information Science Education. (1) A varying number of research grants of up to $2,500 each for members of ALISE; and (2) the Jane Anne Hannigan Research Award of $500 for an untenured faculty member or doctoral student. For information, write to: Sally Nicholson, Executive Director, Association for Library and Information Science Education, 4101 Lake Boone Trail, Raleigh, NC 27607.

Association of Jewish Libraries. The May K. Simon Memorial Scholarship Fund offers a varying number of scholarships of at least $500 each for MLS students who plan to work as Judaica librarians. For information, write to: Sharona R. Wachs, Association of Jewish Libraries, 1000 Washington Ave., Albany, NY 12203.

Association of Seventh-Day Adventist Librarians. The D. Glenn Hilts Scholarship of $1,000 to a member of the Seventh-Day Adventist Church in a graduate library program. For information, write to: Ms. Foutz, Association of Seventh-Day Adventist Librarians, 3800 S. 48 St., Lincoln, NE 68506.

Beta Phi Mu. (1) The Sarah Rebecca Reed Scholarship of $1,500 for a person accepted in an ALA-accredited library program; (2) the Frank B. Sessa Scholarship of $750 for a Beta Phi Mu member for continuing education; (3) the Harold Lancour Scholarship of $1,000 for study in a foreign country related to the applicant's work or schooling. For information, write to: Blanche Woolls, Executive Secretary, Beta Phi Mu, School of Library and Information Science, University of Pittsburgh, Pittsburgh, PA 15260.

Canadian Association of Law Libraries. The Diana M. Priestly Scholarship of $2,000 for a student with previous law experience or for entry to an approved Canadian law school or accredited Canadian library school. For information, write to: Suzan Hebditch, Chair, Scholarship Committee, Canada Department of Justice, 211 Bank of Montreal Bldg., 10199 101st St., Edmonton, AB T5J 3Y4, Canada.

Canadian Federation of University Women. Alice E. Wilson Award of $1,000 for a Canadian citizen or permanent resident with a BA degree or equivalent accepted into a program of specialized study. For information, write to: Canadian Federation of University Women, 297 Dupuis St., Suite 308, Ottawa, ON K1L 7H8, Canada.

Canadian Health Libraries Association. The Student Paper Prize is a scholarship of $300 to a student or recent MLIS graduate or library technician; topic of paper must be in health or information science. For information, write to: Student Paper Prize, Canadian Health Libraries Association/

ABSC, Box 94038, 3332 Yonge St., Toronto, ON M4N 3R1, Canada.

Canadian Library Association. (1) The Howard V. Phalin–World Book Graduate Scholarship in Library Science of $2,500; (2) the CLA Dafoe Scholarship of $1,750; and (3) the H. W. Wilson Scholarship of $2,000. Each scholarship is given to a Canadian citizen or landed immigrant to attend an accredited Canadian library school; the Phalin scholarship can also be used for an ALA-accredited U.S. school. For information, write to: CLA Membership Services Department, Scholarships and Awards Committee, 200 Elgin St., Suite 602, Ottawa, ON K2P 1L5, Canada.

Catholic Library Association. The World Book, Inc., Grant of $1,500 is divided among no more than four CLA members for workshops, institutes, etc. For information, write to: Jean R. Bostley, SSJ Scholarship Committee, St. Joseph Central High School Library, 22 Maplewood Ave., Pittsfield, MA 01201.

Chinese American Librarians Association. The Sheila Suen Lai Scholarship of $500 for a Chinese descendant who has been accepted in an ALA-accredited program. For information, write to: Ling H. Jeng, School of Library and Information Science, University of Kentucky, 502 King Library S., Lexington, KY 40506-0039.

Church and Synagogue Library Association. The Muriel Fuller Memorial Scholarship of $131.54 for a correspondence course offered by the University of Utah Continuing Education Division. Open to CSLA members only. For information, write to: CSLA, Box 19357, Portland, OR 97280-0357.

Sandra Garvie Memorial Fund. A scholarship to a student for $1,000 to pursue a course of study or research on library information aspects of public legal education. For information, write to: Sandra Garvie Memorial Fund, c/o Director, Legal Research Centre, 10049 81st Ave., Edmonton, AB T6E 1W7, Canada.

Massachusetts Black Librarians' Network. Two scholarships of at least $500 and $1,000 for a minority student entering an ALA-accredited master's program in library science, with no more than 12 semester hours toward a degree. For information, write to: Pearl Mosley, Chair, Massachusetts Black Librarians' Network, 27 Beech Glen St., Roxbury, MA 02119.

Medical Library Association. (1) A scholarship of $2,000 for a person entering an ALA-accredited library program, with no more than one-half of the program yet to be completed; (2) a scholarship of $2,000 for a minority student for graduate study; (3) a varying number of Research, Development and Demonstration Project Grants of $100–$1,000 for U.S. or Canadian citizens who are ALA members; (4) Continuing Education Grants of $100–$500 for U.S. or Canadian citizens who are ALA members; (5) the Cunningham Memorial International Fellowship of $3,000 plus travel expenses for a foreign student for postgraduate study in the United States; (6) the MLA Doctoral Fellowship of $1,000 for postgraduate work in medical librarianship or information science. For information, write to: Professional Service Area, Medical Library Association, 6 N. Michigan Ave., Suite 300, Chicago, IL 60602.

Mountain Plains Library Association. (1) A varying number of grants of up to $600 each; and (2) a varying number of grants of up to $150 each for MPLA members with at least two years of membership for continuing education. For information, write to: Joseph R. Edelen, Jr., MPLA Executive Secretary, I. D. Weeks Library, University of South Dakota, Vermillion, SD 57069.

REFORMA, the National Association to Promote Library Services to the Spanish-Speaking. A varying number of scholarships of $1,000 each to attend an ALA-accredited school. For information, write to: Luis Chaparro, Learning Resources Center, El Paso Community College, Box 20500, El Paso, TX 79998.

Society of American Archivists. The Colonial Dames Awards are two grants of $1,200 each for specific types of repositories and collections. For information, write to: Debra Mills, Society of American Archivists, 600 S. Federal St., Suite 504, Chicago, IL 60605.

Southern Regional Education Board. For residents of Arkansas, Georgia, Kentucky, Louisiana, Maryland, Mississippi, Oklahoma, South Carolina, Tennessee, Texas, Virginia, and West Virginia, (1) a varying number of grants of varying amounts to cover in-state tuition for graduate or postgraduate study in an ALA-accredited library school; (2) Tuition Aid for Graduate Library Education, a varying number of scholarships of varying amounts to cover in-state tuition. For information write to: Southern Regional Education Board, 592 Tenth St. N.W., Atlanta, GA 30318-5790.

Special Libraries Association. (1) Two $6,000 scholarships for students interested in special-library work; (2) the Plenum Scholarship of $1,000 and (3) the ISI Scholarship of $1,000, each also for students interested in special-library work; (4) two Affirmative Action Scholarships of $6,000 each for minority students interested in special-library work; (5) two Pharmaceutical Division Stipend Awards of $750 and $250 for students with an undergraduate degree in chemistry, life sciences, or pharmacy entering or enrolled in an ALA-accredited program. For information on the first four scholarships, write to: Laura Devlin, Manager of Membership Development, Special Libraries Association, 1700 18th St. N.W., Washington, DC 20009; for information on the Pharmaceutical Stipend, write to: Susan E. Katz, Awards Chair, Knoll Pharmaceuticals Science Information Center, 30 N. Jefferson St., Whippany, NJ 07981.

Library Scholarship and Award Recipients, 1994

Library awards are listed by organization. An index listing awards alphabetically by title follows this section.

American Association of Law Libraries (AALL)

AALL Scholarships. *Offered by:* AALL; Matthew Bender & Company; Columbia University Law School Library; Information America; Mead Data Central; Thomson Professional Publishing; and/or West Publishing Company. *Winners:* (Type I: Library Degree for Law School Graduates) Kenneth Kozlowski, Kristina Kulhman, Maurine Mattson, Karen Papasodora, Henry Robb, Mary Rose Schoenmaker, Kristin Standaert; (Type II: Law Degree for Library School Graduates) Jodi Dobozin; (Type III: Library Degree for Non–Law School Graduates) Shannon S. Burchard, Donna de Jong, Steven Klukowski, Jana Maryska, Julia Overstreet, Susan Ryan, Constance Smith, Lisa Stillwell, Kathryn Zimmerman; (Type IV: Meira Pimsleur Scholarship) Dale Deegan; (Type V: George A. Strait Minority Stipend) Jessie Lois Cranford, Sheilla Desert, Kumar Percy, Bernadette Powell, Kimberly Sean Snoddy, Ruth Sumuel.

Joseph L. Andrews Bibliographical Award. For significant contribution to legal bibliographical literature. *Winner:* Fred Shapiro for *The Oxford Dictionary of American Legal Quotations* (Oxford University Press, 1993).

Marian Gould Gallagher Distinguished Service Award. To recognize extended and sustained service to law librarianship, for exemplary service to the association, or for contributions to the professional literature. *Winners:* Jack S. Ellenberger, Elizabeth Finley, Diana Vincent-Daviss.

Law Library Journal Article of the Year Award. *Winner:* Donald Jack Dunn for "Why Legal Research Skills Declined, or When Two Rights Make a Wrong," 85 *Law Library Journal* 49 (1993).

Law Library Publication Award. To recognize achievements in in-house, user-orient-

ed library materials that are outstanding in quality and significance. *Winner:* Cadwalader, Wickersham & Taft.

American Library Association (ALA)

ALA/Mecklermedia Library of the Future Award ($2,500). For a library, consortium, group of librarians, or support organization for information technology in a library setting. *Donor:* Mecklermedia Corporation. *Winner:* University of Iowa Libraries.

Hugh C. Atkinson Memorial Award ($2,000). For outstanding achievement (including risk taking) by academic librarians that has contributed significantly to improvements in library automation, management, and/or development or research. *Offered by:* ACRL, ALCTS, LAMA, and LITA divisions. *Winner:* Dorothy Gregor.

Carroll Preston Baber Research Grant ($7,500). For innovative research that could lead to an improvement in library services to any specified group(s) of people. *Donor:* Eric R. Baber. *Winner:* Not awarded in 1994.

Beta Phi Mu Award ($500). For distinguished service in library education. *Donor:* Beta Phi Mu International Library Science Honorary Awards Committee. *Winner:* Dr. Jane Robbins.

David H. Clift Scholarship ($3,000). To a worthy U.S. or Canadian citizen to begin an MLS degree in an ALA-accredited program. *Donor:* Scholarship endowment interest. *Winner:* Zoe Butler.

Melvil Dewey Medal. To an individual or group for recent creative professional achievement in library management, training, cataloging and classification, and the tools and techniques of librarianship. *Donor:* OCLC/Forest Press Inc. *Winner:* Frank Grisham.

Tom and Roberta Drewes Scholarship. To a library support staffer who wishes to attend a master's program. *Winner:* June M. Rutkowski.

EBSCO ALA Conference Sponsorships. To allow librarians to attend ALA's Midwinter Meetings and Annual Conferences. *Donor:* EBSCO. *Winners:* Teresa Day, Linda Horiuchi, Loretta Lafferty, Dr. Fannette Thomas, Beth Ann Zambella.

Equality Award ($500). To an individual or group for an outstanding contribution that promotes equality of women and men in the library profession. *Donor:* Scarecrow Press. *Winner:* Lotsee Patterson.

Loleta D. Fyan Award ($10,000). For projects in public library development. *Winners:* Middle County Public Library (Centereach, NY) and Onondaga Public Library (Syracuse, NY).

Gale Research Company Financial Development Award ($2,500). To a library organization for a financial development project to secure new funding resources for a public or academic library. *Donor:* Gale Research Company. *Winner:* Staunton (VA) Public Library.

Grolier Foundation Award ($1,000). For stimulation and guidance of reading by children and young people. *Donor:* Grolier Foundation. *Winner:* Jane Botham.

G. K. Hall Award for Library Literature ($500). For outstanding contribution to library literature issued during the three years preceding presentation. *Donor:* G. K. Hall & Company. *Winner:* Hazel Rochman for *Against Borders* (ALA Booklist).

Honorary ALA Membership. *Winners:* Virginia Mathews, President Jimmy Carter.

Miriam Hornback Minority Scholarship ($3,000). For library support staff or ALA staff to begin an MLS degree in an ALA-accredited program. *Donor:* ALA Scholarship Endowment Committee. *Winner:* Nina Lindsay.

Tony Leisner Scholarship ($3,000). For a library support staff person to enter a master's library program. *Winner:* Not given in 1994.

Joseph W. Lippincott Award ($1,000). To a librarian for distinguished service to the profession. *Donor:* Joseph W. Lippincott, Jr. *Winner:* Frank Kurt Cylke.

Bessie Boehm Moore Award ($1,000). Presented to a public library that has developed an outstanding and creative program for public library services to the aging. *Donor:* Bessie Boehm Moore. *Winner:* Decorah (IA) Public Library.

Herbert W. Putnam Honor Award ($500). To an American librarian of outstanding ability, for travel, writing, or other use to improve service to the library profession or society. No award until 1996.

H. W. Wilson Library Periodical Award ($1,000). To a library, library group, or association for a periodical making a contribution to librarianship. *Donor:* H. W. Wilson Company. *Winner:* Colorado Library Association for *Colorado Libraries*, edited by Nancy Carter and Melinda Chesbro.

H. W. Wilson Library Staff Development Grant ($2,500). To a library organization for a program to further its goals and objectives. *Donor:* H. W. Wilson Company. *Winner:* Newport News (VA) Public Library System.

World Book–ALA Goal Awards ($8,000). To ALA units for the advancement of public, academic, or school library service and librarianship through support of programs that implement the goals and priorities of ALA. *Donor:* World Book Inc. *Winner:* ALA Special Committee on Public Awareness for "Library Advocacy Now: Mobilizing Support for Libraries—An American Value."

American Association of School Librarians (AASL)

AASL ABC/Clio Leadership Grant (up to $1,750). For planning and implementing leadership programs at state, regional, or local levels to be given to school library associations that are affiliates of AASL. *Donor:* ABC/Clio. *Winner:* Alaska Association of School Librarians.

AASL Distinguished School Administrator Award ($2,000 and plaque). For expanding the role of the library in elementary and/or secondary school education. *Donor:* Social Issues Resources Series, Inc. *Winner:* James Enochs, Supt., Modesto (CA) City Schools.

AASL/Highsmith Research Grant (up to $5,000). To conduct innovative research aimed at measuring and evaluating the impact of school library media programs on learning and education. *Donor:* Highsmith Company Inc. *Winners:* Kathleen Garland, "The Information Search Process: A Study of Cognitive Strategies for Teaching Higher Level Thinking Skills"; Roberta Ponis, Dian Walster, and Lynda Welborn, "Information Literacy Standards—Alternative Assessments."

AASL Information Plus Continuing Education Scholarship ($500). To a school library media specialist, supervisor, or educator to attend an ALA or AASL continuing education event. *Donor:* Information Plus. *Winner:* Linda de Lyon Friel.

AASL Intellectual Freedom Award ($2,000 to recipient, $1,000 to media center of recipient's choice). For a school library media specialist who has upheld principles of intellectual freedom. *Donor:* Social Issues Resources Series Inc. (SIRS). *Winner:* Ruth Dishnow.

AASL School Librarian's Workshop Scholarship ($2,500). To a full-time student preparing to become a school library media specialist at the preschool, elementary, or secondary level. *Donor:* Library Learning Resources. *Winner:* Ginger Searey.

Distinguished Service Award, AASL/Baker & Taylor ($3,000). For outstanding contributions to librarianship and school library development. *Donor:* Baker & Taylor Books. *Winner:* Lucille C. Thomas.

Emergency Librarian Publication Award ($500). For an outstanding publication in school librarianship to be given to a school library association affiliated to AASL. *Donor: Emergency Librarian. Winner:* Washington Library Media Association.

Frances Henne Award ($1,250). To a school library media specialist with five or fewer years in the profession to attend an AASL regional conference or ALA Annual Conference for the first time. *Donor:* R. R. Bowker Company. *Winner:* Robert Craig Bunch.

Microcomputer in the Media Center Award ($1,000 to the specialist and $500 to the library). To library media specialists for innovative approaches to microcomputer applications in the school library media center. *Donor:* Follett Software Company. *Winner:* Becky Mather.

National School Library Media Program of the Year Award (up to $3,000). To school districts and a single school for excellence and innovation in outstanding library media programs. *Donor:* AASL and Encyclopaedia Britannica Companies. *Winners:* (Single School District) tie/co-winners, Providence Senior High School, Charlotte, NC; Lakeview Elementary School, Neenah, WI; (Small School District), Duneland School Corp., Chesterton, IN.

American Library Trustee Association (ALTA)

ALTA/Gale Outstanding Trustee Conference Grant Award ($750). *Donor:* Gale Research Company. *Winners:* Marina Gagic, Kenneth Perez.

ALTA Major Benefactors Honor Award. To individual(s), families, or corporate bodies that have made major benefactions to public libraries. *Winners:* Not awarded in 1994.

Literacy Award. To a library trustee or an individual who in a volunteer capacity has made a significant contribution to addressing the illiteracy problem in the United States. *Winner:* Phyllis Kline.

Trustee Citations. To recognize public library trustees for individual service to library development on the local, state, regional, or national level. *Winners:* Herbert Davis, Gloria Twine Chisum.

Armed Forces Libraries Round Table

Armed Forces Library Achievement Citation. For contributions toward development of interest in libraries and reading in armed forces library service and organizations. Candidates must be members of the Armed Forces Libraries Round Table. *Winner:* Nellie Stricklan.

Armed Forces Library Certificate of Merit. To librarians or "friends" who are members of AFLRT who provide an exemplary program to an Armed Forces library. *Winner:* Daniel Jones.

Armed Forces Library Newsbank Scholarship Award ($1,000 to the school of the recipient's choice). To members of the Armed Forces Libraries Round Table who have given exemplary service in the area of library support for off-duty education programs in the armed forces. *Donor:* Newsbank Inc. *Winner:* Nova Maddox.

Association for Library Collections and Technical Services (ALCTS)

Hugh C. Atkinson Memorial Award. *See under* American Library Association.

Best of "LRTS" Award. To the author(s) of the best paper published each year in the division's official journal. *Winners:* Angela Giral, Arlene Taylor.

Margaret Mann Citation. To a cataloger or classifier for achievement in the areas of cataloging or classification. *Winner:* Carol Ann Mandel.

Esther J. Piercy Award ($1,500). To a librarian with fewer than ten years' experience for contributions and leadership in the field of library collections and technical services. *Donor:* Yankee Book Peddler. *Winner:* Nancy Elkington.

Resources Section

Blackwell/North America Scholarship Award. To the author(s) of an outstanding monograph, published article, or original paper on acquisitions, collection development, or areas of resources development in libraries ($2,000 to library school of winner's choice). *Donor:* Blackwell/North America. *Winners:* Joel S. Rutstein, Anna L. DeMiller, Elizabeth A. Fuseler.

Serials Section

Bowker/Ulrich's Serials Librarianship Award ($1,500). For contribution to serials librarianship in areas of professional association, participation, library education, serials literature, research, or development of tools leading to better understanding. *Donor:* R. R. Bowker Company/Ulrich's. *Winner:* Tina Feick.

First Step Award, Serials Section/Wiley Professional Development Grant ($1,500). For librarians new to the serials field to attend ALA's Annual Conference. *Donor:* John Wiley & Sons. *Winner:* H. Charlene Chon-Chou.

Association for Library Service to Children (ALSC)

ALSC/Book Wholesalers Summer Reading Program Grant ($3,000). To an ALSC member for implementation of an outstanding public library summer reading program for children. *Donor:* Book Wholesalers Inc. *Winner:* Emily Fowler Public Library, Denton, TX.

ALSC/Econo-Clad Literature Program Award ($1,000). To an ALSC member who has developed and implemented an outstanding library program for children involving reading and the use of literature, to attend an ALA conference. *Donor:* Econo-Clad Books. *Winner:* Vaunda M. Nelson.

May Hill Arbuthnot Honor Lecturer 1995. To invite an individual of distinction to prepare and present a paper that will be a significant contribution to the field of children's literature and that will subsequently be published in *Journal of Youth Services in Libraries. Winner:* Leonard Everett Fisher.

Mildred L. Batchelder Award (citation). To an American publisher of an English-language translation of a children's book originally published in a foreign language in a foreign country. *Winner: The Apprentice* by Pilar Molina Llorente (Farrar, Straus & Giroux).

Bound to Stay Bound Books Scholarship ($5,000). Two awards for study in the field of library service to children toward the MLS or beyond in an ALA-accredited program. *Donor:* Bound to Stay Bound Books. *Winners:* Roberta Lee Pierce, Martin Juan Rivera, Sr.

Randolph Caldecott Medal. *See* "Literary Prizes, 1994" by Gary Ink.

Andrew Carnegie Medal. To U.S. producer of the most distinguished video for children in the previous year. *Donor:* Carnegie Corporation of New York. *Winner:* Rawn

Fulton for "Eric Carle: Picture Writer" (Searchlight Films).

Distinguished Service to ALSC Award ($1,000). To recognize significant contributions to, and an impact on, library services to children and/or ALSC. *Winner:* Carolyn W. Field.

Frederic G. Melcher Scholarship ($5,000). To students entering the field of library service to children for graduate work in an ALA-accredited program. *Winners:* Andrea Michelle Chambers, Evi Klett.

John Newbery Medal. *See* "Literary Prizes, 1994" by Gary Ink.

Putnam and Grosset Book Group Awards ($600). To children's librarians in school or public libraries with ten or fewer years of experience to attend ALA Annual Conference for the first time. Must be a member of ALSC. *Donor:* Putnam and Grosset Book Group. *Winners:* Abbey-jo Rehling, Leslie Page, Cecilia Swanson, Vera Flores.

Laura Ingalls Wilder Award (medal, triennially). To an author or illustrator whose works have made a lasting contribution to children's literature. *Winner:* Not awarded in 1994.

Association of College and Research Libraries (ACRL)

ACRL Academic or Research Librarian of the Year Award ($3,000). For outstanding contribution to academic and research librarianship and library development. *Donor:* Baker & Taylor. *Winner:* Irene Braden Hoadley.

ACRL Doctoral Dissertation Fellowship ($1,000). To a doctoral student in the field of academic librarianship whose research indicates originality, creativity, and interest in scholarship. *Winner:* Not awarded in 1994.

ACRL/EBSS Distinguished Education and Behavioral Sciences Librarian Award (citation). To an academic librarian who has made an outstanding contribution as an education and/or behavioral sciences librarian through accomplishments and service to the profession. *Sponsor:* Association of College and Research Libraries. *Winner:* Mary Ellen Collins.

Hugh C. Atkinson Memorial Award. *See under* American Library Association.

EBSCO Community College Learning Resources Achievement Awards ($500). Two awards to individuals, groups, or institutions to recognize significant achievement in the areas of programs and leadership. *Donor:* EBSCO Subscription Services. *Winners:* Imogene Book, Ed Rivenburgh.

Samuel Lazerow Fellowship for Research in Acquisitions or Technical Services ($1,000). To foster advances in acquisitions or technical services by providing librarians a fellowship for travel or writing in those fields. *Sponsor:* Institute for Scientific Information (ISI). *Winner:* Kuang-Hwei (Janet) Lee-Smeltzer.

Katharine Kyes Leab and Daniel J. Leab *American Book Prices Current* Exhibition Catalogue Awards. For the three best catalogs published by American or Canadian institutions in conjunction with exhibitions of books and/or manuscripts. *Winners:* (First Division) "Reconstructing a Medieval Library: Fragments from Lambach," Beinecke Rare Book and Manuscript Library, Yale University; (Second Division) "Human Documents: Tom Phillipps's Art of the Page," Department of Special Collections, Van Pelt-Dietrich Library, University of Pennsylvania; (Third Division) "Picturing Britain: Time and Place in Image and Text, 1700–1850," Special Collections, University of Chicago Library; (Honorable Mention) "About Faces: Historic and Contemporary Issues in Type Design," Printing and Graphic Arts Department of Houghton Library, Harvard University.

Martinus Nijhoff International West European Specialist Study Grant. Supports research pertaining to West European studies, librarianship, or the book trade. Focus on acquisitions, organization, or use of library materials. *Sponsor:* Martinus Nijhoff International. *Winner:* Stephen Lehmann.

Oberly Award for Bibliography in the Agricultural Sciences. Biennially, for the best English-language bibliography in the field of agriculture or a related science in the preceding two-year period. *Donor:* Eunice

R. Oberly Fund. *Winner:* Awarded in odd-numbered years.

K. G. Saur Award for Best *College and Research Libraries* Article ($500 to each author). To author(s) to recognize the most outstanding article published in *College and Research Libraries* during the preceding year. *Donor:* K. G. Saur. *Winner:* Ross Atkinson for "Networks, Hypertext, and Academic Information Services: Some Longer-Range Implications."

Bibliographic Instruction Section (BIS)

Bibliographic Instruction Publication of the Year Award. *Winners:* Not awarded in 1994.

Miriam Dudley Bibliographic Instruction Librarian Award ($1,000). For contribution to the advancement of bibliographic instruction in a college or research institution. *Donor:* Mountainside Publishing. *Winner:* Cerise Oberman.

Association of Specialized and Cooperative Library Agencies (ASCLA)

ASCLA Exceptional Service Award. To recognize effective programming, pioneering activity, or significant research in service to special populations. *Winner:* Joanne Crispen.

ASCLA Leadership Achievement Award. To recognize leadership and achievement in the areas of consulting, multitype library cooperation, and state library development. *Winner:* Clarence Walters.

ASCLA/National Organization on Disability Award. To institutions or organizations that have made the library's total service more accessible through changing physical and/or additional barriers. *Donor:* National Organization on Disability, funded by J. C. Penney. *Winner:* Broward County Library, Fort Lauderdale, FL.

ASCLA Professional Achievement Award. For professional achievement within the areas of consulting, networking, statewide services and programs. *Winner:* Sandra M. Cooper.

ASCLA Service Award. For outstanding service and leadership to the division. *Winner:* Stephen Prine.

Section on Library Service to the Blind and Physically Handicapped

Francis Joseph Campbell Citation. For contribution of recognized importance to library service for the blind and physically handicapped. *Winner:* Richard C. Peel.

Federal Librarians Round Table (FLRT)

Federal Librarians Achievement Award. For leadership or achievement in the promotion of library and information science in the federal community. *Winner:* Louise Nyce.

Government Documents Round Table (GODORT)

James Bennett Childs Award. To a librarian or other individual for distinguished lifetime contributions to documents librarianship. *Winner:* Sandra Peterson.

CIS/GODORT/ALA Documents to the People Award ($2,000). To an individual, library, organization, or noncommercial group that most effectively encourages or enhances the use of government documents in library services. *Donor:* Congressional Information Service Inc. (CIS). *Winner:* Gary Cornwell.

Bernadine Abbott Hoduski Founders Award (plaque). To recognize documents librarians who may not be known at the national level but who have made significant contributions to the field of state, international, local, or federal documents. *Winner:* Karen Lynn.

Readex/GODORT/ALA Catharine J. Reynolds Award ($2,000). Grants to documents librarians for travel and/or study in the field of documents librarianship or area of study benefiting performance as documents librarians. *Donor:* Readex Corporation. *Winner:* Irene Herold.

Intellectual Freedom Round Table (IFRT)

John Phillip Immroth Memorial Award for Intellectual Freedom ($500). For notable contribution to intellectual freedom fueled by personal courage. *Winner:* John Swan.

Eli M. Oboler Memorial Award ($1,500). Biennially, to an author of a published work in English, or in English translation, dealing with issues, events, questions, or controversies in the area of intellectual freedom. *Donor:* HBW Associates. *Winner:* "What Johnny Shouldn't Read: Textbook Censorship in America" by Joan DelFattore, sponsored by Providence Associates Inc.

State Program Award ($1,000). To a state library association intellectual freedom committee, state library media association intellectual freedom committee, or state intellectual freedom coalition, for the most successful and creative project during the calendar year. *Donor:* Social Issues Resources Series Inc. (SIRS). *Winner:* Freedom to Read Foundation.

International Relations Committee

Bogle International Library Travel Fund ($500). To ALA member(s) to attend first international conference. *Donor:* Bogle Memorial Fund. *Winner:* Dona J. Helmer.

John Ames Humphry/OCLC/Forest Press Award ($1,000). To an individual for significant contributions to international librarianship. *Donors:* OCLC/Forest Press *Winner:* Robert D. Stueart.

Library Administration and Management Association (LAMA)

Hugh C. Atkinson Memorial Award. *See under* American Library Association.

John Cotton Dana Library Public Relations Awards. To libraries or library organizations of all types for public relations programs or special projects ended during the preceding year. *Donor:* H. W. Wilson Company. *Winners:* (Annual Coordinated Public Relations Program) First United Methodist Church Library, Huntsville (TX); (New Identity with the Use of Graphics) Minneapolis (MN) Public Library; (Public Library Category) Atlanta (GA) Fulton Public Library System, Brown County Public Library, Green Bay (WI), Cuyahoga County Public Library, Parma (OH), Newark (NJ) Public Library, Richland County Public Library, Columbia

(SC), Signal Mountain (TN) Public Library; (College and University Category) The College of William and Mary, Earl Gregg Swem Library; (State Library Category) California State Library, Sacramento (FL) Division of Library Information Services, Bureau of Library Development, Tallahassee (FL); (Friends Category) Gustavus Library Associates, Gustavus Adolphus College, St. Peter (MN)

AIA/ALA–LAMA Library Buildings Award Program. For excellence in architectural design and planning. *Donors:* American Institute of Architects (AIA) and LAMA. Awards not given in 1994.

Library and Information Technology Association (LITA)

Hugh C. Atkinson Memorial Award. *See under* American Library Association.

LITA/CLSI Scholarship in Library and Information Technology ($2,500). *Winner:* To be announced.

LITA/Gaylord Award for Achievement in Library and Information Technology ($1,000). For achievement in library and information technology. *Donor:* Gaylord Bros., Inc. *Winner:* David McCarn.

LITA/*Library Hi Tech* Award ($1,000). To an individual or institution for a work that shows outstanding communication for continuing education in library and information technology. *Donor:* Pierian Press. *Winner:* Ching-chih Chen.

LITA/OCLC Minority Scholarship in Library and Information Technology ($2,500). To encourage a qualified member of a principal minority group, with a strong commitment to the use of automation in libraries, to enter library automation. *Donor:* OCLC. *Winner:* Joy M. Barron.

Library History Round Table (LHRT)

Phyllis Dain Library History Dissertation Award ($500). To the author of a dissertation treating the history of books, libraries, librarianship, or information science. Given every two years. *Winner:* Not awarded in 1994.

Justin Winsor Prize Essay ($500). To an author of an outstanding essay embodying original historical research on a significant subject of library history. *Winner:* Not awarded in 1994.

Library Research Round Table (LRRT)

Jesse H. Shera Award for Research ($500). For an outstanding and original paper reporting the results of research related to libraries. *Winner:* Judith Serebnick and Frank Quinn, "Measuring Diversity of Opinion in Collections in OCLC Libraries.

Map and Geography Round Table (MAGERT)

MAGERT Honors Award. *Winner:* Philip Hoehn.

National Library Week Committee

Grolier National Library Week Grant ($2,000). To libraries or library associations of all types for a public awareness campaign in connection with National Library Week in the year the grant is awarded. *Donor:* Grolier Educational Corporation. *Winner:* Dauphin County (PA) Library System.

New Members Round Table (NMRT)

NMRT EBSCO Scholarship ($1,000). To a U.S. or Canadian citizen to begin an MLS degree in an ALA-accredited program. Candidates must be members of NMRT. *Donor:* EBSCO Subscription Services. *Winner:* Patricia Curry.

Shirley Olofson Memorial Award. For individuals to attend their second ALA Annual Conference. *Winner:* Cathy Nelson Hartman.

3M/NMRT Professional Development Grant. To NMRT members to encourage professional development and participation in national ALA and NMRT activities. *Donor:* 3M. *Winners:* Pamela Moffett Padley, Nancy Louise Cummings, David C. D. Gansz.

Office for Library Personnel Resources

Louise Giles Minority Scholarship ($3,000). To a worthy U.S. or Canadian minority citizen to begin an MLS degree in an

ALA-accredited program. *Donor:* Scholarship endowment interest. *Winner:* Sherry Luna.

Public Library Association (PLA)

Excellence in Small and/or Rural Public Service Award. *Winner:* Decorah (IA) Public Library.

Library Video Award ($1,000). To a public library demonstrating excellence and innovation in library programming with video and the ability to market and promote the use of these services to library users. *Donor:* Baker & Taylor Video. *Winner:* Wichita (KS) Public Library.

Allie Beth Martin Award ($3,000). Honors a librarian who, in a public library setting, has demonstrated extraordinary range and depth of knowledge about books or other library materials and has distinguished ability to share that knowledge. *Donor:* Baker & Taylor Books. *Winner:* Carol G. Walters.

New Leaders Travel Grant (up to $1,500 each). To enhance the professional development and improve the expertise of public librarians by making their attendance at major professional development activities possible. *Donor:* GEAC Inc. *Winners:* Karen E. Brown, Mary E. Harper, Eileen Papile.

Leonard Wertheimer Multilingual Public Library Service Award ($1,000). To a person, group, or organization for work that enhances and promotes multilingual public library services. *Sponsor:* NTC Publishing Group. *Winners:* Dina Abramowicz, Sylva Manoogian.

Adult Lifelong Learning Section

Advancement of Literacy Award. Honors a publisher, bookseller, hardware and/or software dealer, foundation, or similar group that has made a significant contribution to the advancement of adult literacy. *Donor:* Library Journal. *Winner:* California State Library Foundation.

Publishing Committee

Carnegie Reading List Awards (amount varies). To ALA units for preparation and publication of reading lists, indexes, and other bibliographical and library aids useful in U.S. circulating libraries. *Donor:* Andrew Carnegie Fund. *Winners:* "Book Some Time Together," ALSC Task Force; "Reading List for Public Library Board," ALTA Task Force.

Whitney-Carnegie Awards ($5,000 maximum). For the preparation of bibliographic aids for research, with scholarly intent and general applicability. *Donor:* James Lyman Whitney and Andrew Carnegie Funds. *Winner:* Chestalene Pintossi for "Researching Global Change."

Reference and Adult Services Division (RASD)

Dartmouth Medal. For creating current reference works of outstanding quality and significance. *Donor:* Dartmouth College, Hanover, New Hampshire. *Winners: Black Women in America: An Historical Encyclopedia,* edited by Darlene Clark Hine; (honorable mention) *Encyclopedia of American Social History.*

Denali Press Award ($500). For creating reference works of outstanding quality and significance that provide information specifically about ethnic and minority groups in the United States. *Donor:* Denali Press. *Winner: Darlene Clark Hine for Black Women in America: An Historical Encyclopedia.*

Facts on File Grant ($2,000). To a library for imaginative programming that would make current affairs more meaningful to an adult audience. *Donor:* Facts on File Inc. *Winner:* Eastern Montana College, Billings.

Genealogical Publishing Company/History Section Award ($1,000 and citation). To encourage and commend professional achievement in historical reference and research librarianship. *Donor:* The Genealogical Publishing Company. *Winner:* J. Carlyle Parker.

Margaret E. Monroe Library Adult Services Award. To a librarian for impact on library service to adults. *Winner:* Elizabeth Ann Funk.

Isadore Gilbert Mudge Citation ($1,500). For distinguished contribution to reference librarianship. *Winner:* Anne Grodzins Lipow.

Reference Service Press Award ($1,000). To the author of the most outstanding article published in *RQ* during the preceding two volume years. *Donor:* Reference Service Press Inc. *Winner:* Sally W. Kalin.

John Sessions Memorial Award. To a library or library system in recognition of work with the labor community. *Donor:* AFL/CIO. *Winner:* Walter P. Reuther Library of Labor and Urban Affairs.

Louis Shores–Oryx Press Award ($1,000). To an individual, team, or organization to recognize excellence in reviewing of books and other materials for libraries. *Donor:* Oryx Press. *Winner:* Harold Robert Malinowsky.

Business Reference and Services Section (BRASS)

Disclosure Student Travel Award/BRASS ($1,000). To enable a student in an ALA-accredited master's program interested in a career as a business librarian to attend an ALA Annual Conference. *Donor:* Disclosure Inc. *Winner:* Lisa L. McClain.

Gale Research Award for Excellence in Business Librarianship/BRASS ($1,000). To an individual for distinguished activities in the field of business librarianship. *Donor:* Gale Research Inc. *Winner:* Judith M. Nixon.

Gale Research Award for Excellence in Reference and Adult Services ($1,000). To a library or library system for developing an imaginative and unique library resource to meet patrons' reference needs. *Donor:* Gale Research Inc. *Winner:* Wichita (KS) Public Library.

Social Responsibilities Round Table (SRRT)

Coretta Scott King Award. *See* "Literary Prizes, 1994" by Gary Ink.

SIRS/Peace Award ($500). To honor a library or librarian who has contributed to advancement of knowledge related to issues of international peace. *Donor:* Social Issues Resources Series Inc. (SIRS). *Winner:* Not awarded in 1994.

SRRT/Gay and Lesbian Task Force, Gay and Lesbian Book Awards. *Winners:* Leslie Feinberg (fiction), Phyllis Burke (nonfiction).

Young Adult Library Services Association (YALSA)

Baker & Taylor Conference Grants ($750). To young adult librarians in public or school libraries to attend an ALA Annual Conference for the first time. Candidates must be members of YALSA and have one to ten years of library experience. *Donor:* Baker & Taylor Books. *Winners:* Susan Wickenden Hunter, Myrna Kinkle.

Margaret A. Edwards Award ($1,000). To an author whose book or books have provided young adults with a window through which they can view their world and which will help them to grow and to understand themselves and their role in society. *Donor: School Library Journal. Winner:* Walter Dean Myers.

Frances Henne/YALSA/*Voice of Youth Advocates (VOYA)* Research Grant ($500). *Donor:* VOYA. *Winners:* Kathy Latrobe, Michael Havener.

YALSA/Econo-Clad Literature Program Award ($1,000). To a YALSA member for development and implementation of an outstanding program for children involving reading and the use of literature. *Donor:* Econo-Clad Books. *Winner:* Barbara Blosveren.

American Society for Information Science (ASIS)

ASIS Award of Merit. For an outstanding contribution to the field of information science. *Winner:* Harold Borko.

ASIS Best Information Science Book. *Winner:* William B. Green, *Introduction to Electronic Document Management Systems.*

ASIS Doctoral Forum Award (travel reimbursement to ASIS annual meeting, up to $250). *Winner:* Peiling Wang, "A Cognitive Model of Document Selection of Real Users in Information Retrieval."

ASIS Research in Information Science Award. For an outstanding research contribution in the field of information science that consists of a systematic program of research in a single study. *Winner:* Raya Fidel.

ASIS Outstanding Information Science Teacher Award ($500). *Winner:* Candy Schwartz.

Cretsos Leadership Award. *Winner:* Merri Beth Lavagnino.

ISI Information Science Doctoral Dissertation Scholarship ($1,000). *Donor:* Institute for Scientific Information (ISI). *Winner:* Corinne Jorgensen, "Image Attributes: An Investigation."

JASIS Paper Award. *Winner:* Ingrid Hsieh-Yee, "Effects of Search Experience and Subject Knowledge on the Search Tactics of Novice and Experienced Searchers."

Art Libraries Society of North America (ARLIS/NA)

Chadwyck-Healey Professional Development Award ($500). To encourage contribution to the society by participating as a moderator, panelist, or presenter of a paper at the ARLIS/NA annual conference. *Winner:* Judy Dyki.

Jim and Anna Emmett Travel Award ($600). To assist information professionals who are physically challenged to participate in the ARLIS/NA annual conference. *Winner:* Karen Genet.

G. K. Hall Conference Attendance Award ($400). To encourage attendance at the annual conference by ARLIS/NA committee members, chapter officers, and moderators. *Winner:* Jeanne Brown.

Howard Karno Travel Award ($500). To provide financial assistance to a professional art librarian from Mexico or Latin America to attend the ARLIS/NA annual conference. *CoSponsor:* Howard Karno Books. *Winner:* Martha Urrunaga.

Léonce Laget Travel Award ($1,000). To provide financial assistance for an art information professional from outside North America to attend the ARLIS/NA annual conference. *Cosponsor:* Librairie Léonce Laget. *Winner:* Gerard Regimbeau.

Fraiser McConnell Travel Award ($500). For members of an ethnic or cultural group underrepresented within ARLIS/NA. *Winner:* Mary Hernandez.

David Mirvish Books/Books on Art Travel Award ($500). To encourage art librarianship in Canada. *Winner:* Francoise Roux.

Norman Ross Travel Award. To encourage professional development through attendance at the ARLIS/NA annual conference. *Winner:* Tracey Lemon.

Association for Library and Information Science Education (ALISE)

ALISE Award for Professional Contribution to Library and Information Science Education. *Winner:* Not awarded in 1994.

ALISE Award for Teaching Excellence. *Winner:* David Carr.

ALISE Doctoral Students Dissertation Awards ($400). To promote the exchange of research ideas between doctoral students and established researchers. *Winner:* Rose Albritton, Françoise Hébert.

ALISE Research Award ($2,500). For a project that reflects ALISE goals and objectives. *Winner:* Norman Howden, Thomas Kochtanek, Nancy Zimmerman.

ALISE Research Paper Competition ($500). For a research paper concerning any aspect of librarianship or information studies by a member of ALISE. *Winners:* Patricia Dewdney, Catherine Sheldrick Ross.

ALISE Service Award. For outstanding contributions to the association. *Winner:* Not awarded in 1994.

Jane Anne Hannigan Research Award ($500). *Winner:* Louise S. Robbins.

Association of Jewish Libraries (AJL)

Fanny Goldstein Merit Award. *Winner:* Adaire Klein.

May K. Simon Scholarship ($500). For a student who intends to become a Judaica librarian. *Winners:* Dr. Raphael I. Panitz.

Sydney Taylor Manuscript Award ($1,000). To encourage outstanding new books with Jewish themes that have appeal to children everywhere. *Winner:* Faye Silton, *Of Heroes, Hooks and Heirlooms.*

Association of Records Managers and Administrators (ARMA)

ARMA International Scholarships ($750). To students pursuing an associate's degree, diploma program, or certification in information and records management at the professional/managerial level. *Winners:* Kim M. Mayberry, Dianna L. Oldaker, and Egils Abolins ($1,500 for work toward a bachelor degree).

Beta Phi Mu

Beta Phi Mu Award. *See under* American Library Association.

Harold Lancour Scholarship for Foreign Study ($1,000). For graduate study in a foreign country related to the applicant's work or schooling. *Winner:* Mary Graham.

Sarah Rebecca Reed Scholarship ($1,500). For study at an ALA-accredited library school. *Winners:* Andrea M. Chambers, Amy Melissa McAbee.

Frank B. Sessa Scholarship for Continuing Professional Education ($750). For continuing education for a Beta Phi Mu member. *Winners:* Maureen Delaney-Lehman, Deborah Pawlik.

Canadian Library Association (CLA)

CLA/Meckler Award for Innovative Technology. *Donor:* Meckler Corporation. *Winner:* National Library of Canada and Canadian Institute for Scientific and Technical Information (CISTI).

CLA Outstanding Service to Librarianship Award. *Donor:* Reed Reference Publishing/R. R. Bowker. *Winner:* Erik J. Spicer.

CLA Research and Development Grants ($1,000). *Winner:* Toni Samek.

Canadian Library Journal Student Article Award. *Winner:* Susan R. Fisher.

NFB/CLA Award for Outstanding Film or Video Librarian. *Donor:* National Film Board of Canada. *Winner:* Not awarded in 1994.

Award for the Advancement of Intellectual Freedom in Canada. *Winner:* Halifax (NS) City Regional Library Board.

Canadian Association of College and University Libraries (CACUL)

CACUL Award for Outstanding Academic Librarian. *Winner:* Ernie Ingles, University of Alberta.

CACUL Innovation Achievement Award ($1,500). *Winners:* University of Alberta, Edmonton, Alberta, and Queen's University, Kingston, Ontario.

CACUL Micromedia Award of Merit ($500). *Winner:* Barb Love.

Canadian Association of Public Libraries (CAPL)

CAPL Outstanding Public Library Service Award. *Winner:* Judith McAnanama.

CAPL Public Relations Award. *Donor:* Faxon Canada. *Winner:* Red Deer (AB) Public Library.

Canadian Association of Special Libraries and Information Services (CASLIS)

CASLIS Award for Special Librarianship in Canada. *Winner:* Marilyn Rennick, University of Ottawa.

Canadian Library Trustees Association (CLTA)

CLTA Achievement in Literacy Award. For an innovative literacy program by a public library board. *Donor:* ABC Canada. *Winner:* To be announced.

CLTA Merit Award for Distinguished Service as a Public Library Trustee. For outstanding leadership in the advancement of public library trusteeship and public library service in Canada. *Winner:* To be announced.

Canadian School Library Association (CSLA)

Canadian School Executive Award for Distinguished Service to School Libraries: *Winners:* E. A. (Ric) Hodgson, Principal, Oakridge Secondary School, London, Ontario; Gary Parkinson, Superintendent of Planning and Plant, Etobicoke (ON) Board of Education.

CANEBSCO School Library Media Periodical Award. *Winner: School Library News,* Barb Poustie, editor.

Grolier Award for Research in School Librarianship in Canada ($1,000). For theoretical or applied research that advances the field of school librarianship. *Winner:* Roy Doiron.

National Book Service Teacher-Librarian of the Year Award. *Winner:* Marilynne Earl, Saskatoon Public Board of Education.

Margaret B. Scott Award of Merit. For the development of school libraries in Canada. *Cosponsor:* Ontario Library Association. *Winner:* Dianne Oberg, University of Alberta.

Chinese-American Librarians Association (CALA)

CALA Distinguished Service Award. *Winner:* Julia W. Tung.

Sheila Suen Lai Scholarship ($500). To a student of Chinese nationality or descent pursuing full-time graduate studies for a master's degree in an ALA-accredited library school. *Winners:* Angela Gannousis, Hua Yi.

Church and Synagogue Library Association (CSLA)

CSLA Award for Outstanding Congregational Librarian. For distinguished service to the congregation and/or community through

devotion to the congregational library. *Winner:* Ruth Ridgway.
CSLA Award for Outstanding Congregational Library. For responding in creative and innovative ways to the library's mission of reaching and serving the congregation and/or the wider community. *Winner:* Steven Hill.
CSLA Award for Outstanding Contribution to Congregational Libraries. For providing inspiration, guidance, leadership, or resources to enrich the field of church or synagogue librarianship. *Winner:* Charles C. Brown.
Helen Keating Ott Award for Outstanding Contribution to Congregational Libraries. *Winner:* David A. Adler.

Council on Library Resources (CLR)

Grants. For a partial list of the recipients of CLR grants for the 1993–1994 academic year, see the report from the Council on Library Resources in Part 2.

Gale Research Company

ALTA/Gale Outstanding Trustee Conference Grant Award. *See under* American Library Association, American Library Trustee Association.
Gale/*Library Journal* Library of the Year Award ($5,000). *Winner:* Brown County Library, Green Bay, Wisconsin.
Gale Research Award for Excellence in Business Librarianship; and Gale Research Award for Excellence in Reference and Adult Services. *See under* American Library Association, Reference and Adult Services Division, Business Reference and Services Section.
Gale Research Financial Development Award. *See under* American Library Association.

Medical Library Association (MLA)

Estelle Brodman Award for the Academic Medical Librarian of the Year. To honor significant achievement, potential for leadership, and continuing excellence at mid-career in the area of academic health sciences librarianship. *Winner:* Not awarded in 1994.
Cunningham Memorial International Fellowship ($3,000). A six-month grant and travel expenses in the United States and Canada for a foreign librarian. *Winner:* Elena Ivanovna Korotkova.
Louise Darling Medal. For distinguished achievement in collection development in the health sciences. *Winner:* Nancy W. Zinn.
Janet Doe Lectureship ($250). *Winner:* Nina W. Matheson.
EBSCO/MLA Annual Meeting Grant ($1,000) *Winner:* Kenneth R. Nelson.
Ida and George Eliot Prize ($200). For an essay published in any journal in the preceding calendar year that has been judged most effective in furthering medical librarianship. *Donor:* Login Brothers Books. *Winner:* Jocelyn A. Rankin.
Murray Gottlieb Prize ($100). For the best unpublished essay submitted by a medical librarian on the history of some aspect of health sciences or a detailed description of a library exhibit. *Donor:* Ralph and Jo Grimes. *Winner:* Thomas A. Horrocks.
Joseph Leiter NLM/MLA Lectureship. *Winner:* M. R. C. Greenwood.
MLA Award for Distinguished Public Service. *Winner:* Edward M. Kennedy.
MLA Award for Excellence and Achievement in Hospital Librarianship. To a member of the MLA who has made significant contributions to the profession in the area of overall distinction or leadership in hospital librarianship. *Winner:* Linda G. Markwell.
MLA Doctoral Fellowship ($1,000). *Donor:* Institute for Scientific Information (ISI). *Winner:* Mary Moore.
MLA Scholarship ($2,000). For graduate study in medical librarianship at an ALA-accredited library school. *Winner:* Ronald A. Banks.
MLA Scholarship for Minority Students ($2,000). *Winner:* Hua Yi.
John P. McGovern Award Lectureship ($500). *Winner:* June E. Osborn.

Marcia C. Noyes Award. For an outstanding contribution to medical librarianship. The award is the highest professional distinction of MLA. *Winner:* Erika Love.

Rittenhouse Award ($500). For the best unpublished paper on medical librarianship submitted by a student enrolled in, or having been enrolled in, a course for credit in an ALA-accredited library school or a trainee in an internship program in medical librarianship. *Donor:* Rittenhouse Medical Bookstore. *Winner:* Mary Moore.

Frank Bradway Rogers Information Advancement Award ($500). For an outstanding contribution to knowledge of health science information delivery. *Donor:* Institute for Scientific Information (ISI). *Winner:* Nancy E. Start.

K. G. Saur (Munich, Germany)

Award for Best *College and Research Libraries* Article. *See under* American Library Association, Association of College and Research Libraries.

Hans-Peter Geh Grant. To enable a librarian from the former Soviet Union to attend a conference in Germany or elsewhere. *Winner:* Emilija Banionyte (Vilnius, Lithuania).

Gustav Hoffmann Study Grant. To allow a librarian in a country where librarianship is a newly developing profession to study an issue in one or more countries of Western Europe. *Winner:* Catherine Thunga Muyawala (Zambia).

Society of American Archivists (SAA)

C. F. W. Coker Prize for Finding Aids. *Winner:* Not awarded in 1994.

Colonial Dames Award. For archivists who have been in the field less than two years and who are working with holdings predating 1825, for a portion of the tuition, travel, and housing expenses at the Modern Archives Institute, Washington, D.C. *Winners:* Wayne Coleman, Tulane University; Maricel Cruz, University of Virginia.

Distinguished Service Award. Recognizes outstanding accomplishment. *Winner:* Research Libraries Group, Mountain View, California.

Fellows' Posner Prize. For the best article in the *American Archivist* journal. *Winner:* Not awarded in 1994.

J. Franklin Jameson Award for Archival Advocacy. Recognizes an organization that promotes greater public awareness of archival activities and programs. *Winner:* Hudson's Bay Company, Manitoba, Canada.

Philip M. Hamer–Elizabeth Hamer Kegan Award. For individuals and/or institutions that have increased the public awareness of a specific body of documents. *Winner:* American Heritage Center, University of Wyoming, for a two-part project, which includes an introductory videotape titled *The American Heritage Center,* and "Teaching History Through Documents," a series of educational packages.

Minority Student Award. Encourages minority students to consider careers in the archival profession and promotes minority participation in the Society of American Archivists with complimentary registration to the annual meeting. *Winner:* Kathryn Neal.

Preservation Publication Award. Recognizes the author of an outstanding work published in North America that advances the theory or the practice of preservation in archival institutions. *Winner:* Mary Lynn Ritzenthaler, *Preserving Archives and Manuscripts* (SAA).

Sister M. Claude Lane Award. For a significant contribution to the field of religious archives. *Winner:* Sister Emma Cecilia, O.S.U., of the Ursuline Sisters, Maple Mount, Kentucky.

Special Commendation. For writing of superior excellence in the field of preservation publications. *Winner:* Henry Wilhelm, *The Permanence and Care of Color Photographs* (Preservation Publishing).

SAA Fellows. Highest individual distinction awarded to a limited number of members for their outstanding contribution to the archival profession. *Honored:* Anne Van Camp, Hoover Institution, Stanford University; Roland Baumann, Oberlin College Archives.

Theodore Calvin Pease Award. For superior writing achievements by students enrolled in archival administration classes or engaged in formal archival internship programs. *Winner:* Anke Voss-Hubbard, School of Information Science and Policy, State University of New York at Albany, "No Documents—No History: Mary Ritter Beard and the Early History of Women's Archives."

Waldo Gifford Leland Prize. For writing of superior excellence and usefulness in the field of archival history, theory, or practice. *Winner:* F. Gerald Ham, *Selecting and Appraising Archives and Manuscripts* (SAA).

Special Libraries Association (SLA)

Mary Adeline Connor Professional Development Scholarship ($6,000). *Winner:* April Schwartz.

John Cotton Dana Award. For exceptional support and encouragement of special librarianship. *Winners:* Joan Gervino, Julia Peterson.

Steven I. Goldspiel Research Grant. *Sponsor:* Disclosure Inc. *Winners:* Raya Fidel, Michael Crandall.

Hall of Fame Award. To a member of the association at or near the end of an active professional career for an extended and sustained period of distinguished service to the association. *Winners:* Judith Genesen, Herbert S. White.

SLA Affirmative Action Scholarship ($6,000). *Winner:* Alicia Randolph.

SLA Fellows. *Winners:* Judith J. Field, Ellen Steininger Kuner, Dorothy McGarry.

SLA Meckler Award for Innovations in Technology. *Winners:* Pearl Alberts, Carl Braun, Barbara Butler, Wendy Diamond, Walt Howe, Sharyn Ladner, Barbara Mento, Ann Scholz, Hope Tillman, Jan Davis Tudor, Mel Westerman.

SLA President's Award. *Winner:* Nettie Seaberry.

SLA Professional Award. *Winner:* Not awarded in 1994.

SLA Scholarships ($6,000). For students with financial need who show potential for special librarianship. *Winners:* Julia Overstreet, Vinita Singh, Gaylene Sloane.

SLA H. W. Wilson Award. For the most outstanding article in the past year's *Special Libraries. Donor:* H. W. Wilson Company. *Winner:* To be announced.

Alphabetical List of Award Names

Individual award names are followed by a colon and the name of the awarding body; e.g., the Bound to Stay Bound Books Scholarship is given by ALA/Association for Library Service to Children. Consult the preceding list of "Library Scholarship and Award Recipients, 1994," which is alphabetically arranged by organization, to locate recipients and further information. Awards named for individuals are listed by surname.

AALL Scholarships: American Association of Law Libraries

AASL ABC/Clio Leadership Grant: ALA/American Association of School Librarians

AASL Distinguished School Administrator Award: ALA/American Association of School Librarians

AASL/Highsmith Research Grant: ALA/American Association of School Librarians

AASL Information Plus Continuing Education Scholarship: ALA/American Association of School Librarians

AASL Intellectual Freedom Award: ALA/American Association of School Librarians

AASL School Librarians Workshop Scholarship: ALA/American Association of School Librarians

ACRL Academic or Research Librarian of the Year Award: ALA/Association of College and Research Libraries

ACRL Doctoral Dissertation Fellowship: ALA/Association of College and Research Libraries

ACRL/EBSS Distinguished Education and Behavioral Sciences Librarian Award: ALA/Association of College and Research Libraries

AIA/ALA–LAMA Library Buildings Award Program: ALA/Library Administration and Management Association

ALA/Meckler Library of the Future Award: ALA

ALISE Award for Professional Contribution to Library and Information Science Education: Association for Library and Information Science Education

ALISE Award for Teaching Excellence: Association for Library and Information Science Education

ALISE Doctoral Students Dissertation Awards: Association for Library and Information Science Education

ALISE Methodology Paper Award: Association for Library and Information Science Education

ALISE Research Award: Association for Library and Information Science Education

ALISE Research Paper Competition: Association for Library and Information Science Education

ALISE Service Award: Association for Library and Information Science Education

ALSC/Book Wholesalers Summer Reading Program Grant: ALA/Association for Library Service to Children

ALSC/Econo-Clad Literature Program Award: ALA/Association for Library Service to Children

ALTA/Gale Outstanding Trustee Conference Grant Award: ALA/American Library Trustee Association

ALTA Major Benefactors Honor Awards ALA/American Library Trustee Association

ARMA International Scholarships: Association of Records Managers and Administrators

ASCLA Exceptional Service Award: ALA/Association of Specialized and Cooperative Library Agencies

ASCLA Leadership Achievement Award: ALA/Association of Specialized and Cooperative Library Agencies

ASCLA/National Organization on Disability Award: ALA/Association of Specialized and Cooperative Library Agencies

ASCLA Professional Achievement Award: ALA/Association of Specialized and Cooperative Library Agencies

ASCLA Service Award: ALA/Association of Specialized and Cooperative Library Agencies

ASIS Award of Merit: American Society for Information Science

ASIS Best Information Science Book: American Society for Information Science

ASIS Doctoral Forum Award: American Society for Information Science

ASIS Outstanding Information Science Teacher Award: American Society for Information Science

ASIS Research in Information Science Award: American Society for Information Science

Advancement of Literacy Award: ALA/Public Library Association, Adult Lifelong Learning Section

Joseph L. Andrews Bibliographical Award: American Association of Law Libraries

May Hill Arbuthnot Honor Lecturer: ALA/Association for Library Service to Children

Armed Forces Library Achievement Citation: ALA/Armed Forces Libraries Round Table

Armed Forces Library Certificate of Merit: ALA/Armed Forces Libraries Round Table

Armed Forces Library Newsbank Scholarship Award: ALA/Armed Forces Libraries Round Table

Hugh C. Atkinson Memorial Award: ALA

Award for the Advancement of Intellectual Freedom in Canada: Canadian Library Association

Carroll Preston Baber Research Grant: ALA

Baker & Taylor Conference Grants: ALA/Young Adult Library Services Association

Mildred L. Batchelder Award: ALA/Association for Library Service to Children

Best of "LRTS" Award: ALA/Association for Library Collections and Technical Services

Beta Phi Mu Award: ALA

Bibliographic Instruction Publication of the Year Award: ALA/Association of College and Research Libraries, Bibliographic Instruction Section

Blackwell/North America Scholarship Award: ALA/Association for Library Collections and Technical Services, Resources Section

Bogle International Library Travel Fund: ALA/International Relations Committee

Bound to Stay Bound Books Scholarship: ALA/Association for Library Service to Children

Bowker/Ulrich's Serials Librarianship Award: ALA/Association for Library Collections and Technical Services, Serials Section

Estelle Brodman Award for the Academic Medical Librarian of the Year: Medical Library Association

CACUL Award for Outstanding Academic Librarian: Canadian Association of College and University Libraries

CACUL Innovation Achievement Award: Canadian Association of College and University Libraries

CACUL Micromedia Award of Merit: Canadian Association of College and University Libraries

CALA Distinguished Service Award: Chinese-American Librarians Association

CALA President's Award: Chinese-American Librarians Association

CAPL Outstanding Public Library Service Award: Canadian Association of Public Libraries

CAPL Public Relations Award: Canadian Association of Public Libraries

CASLIS Award for Special Librarianship in Canada: Canadian Association of Special Libraries and Information Services

CIS/GODORT/ALA Documents to the People Award: ALA/Government Documents Round Table

CLA/Meckler Award for Innovative Technology: Canadian Library Association

CLA Outstanding Service to Librarianship Award: Canadian Library Association

CLA Research and Development Grants: Canadian Library Association

CLTA Achievement in Literacy Award: Canadian Library Trustees Association

CLTA Merit Award for Distinguished Service as a Public Library Trustee: Canadian Library Trustees Association

CSLA Award for Outstanding Congregational Librarian: Church and Synagogue Library Association

CSLA Award for Outstanding Congregational Library: Church and Synagogue Library Association

CSLA Award for Outstanding Contribution to Congregational Libraries: Church and Synagogue Library Association

Francis Joseph Campbell Citation: ALA/Association of Specialized and Cooperative Library Agencies, Section on Library Service to the Blind and Physically Handicapped

Canadian Library Journal Student Article Award: Canadian Library Association

Canadian School Executive Award for Distinguished Service to School Libraries: Canadian School Library Association

CANEBSCO School Library Media Periodical Award: Canadian School Library Association

Andrew Carnegie Medal: ALA/Association for Library Service to Children

Carnegie Reading List Awards: ALA/Publishing Committee

Chadwyck-Healey Professional Development Award: Art Libraries Society of North America

James Bennett Childs Award: ALA/Government Documents Round Table
David H. Clift Scholarship: ALA
C. F. W. Coker Prize for Finding Aids: Society of American Archivists
Colonial Dames Award: Society of American Archivists
Mary Adeline Connor Professional Development Scholarship: Special Libraries
Association
Cretsos Leadership Award: American Society for Information Science
Cunningham Memorial International Fellowship: Medical Library Association
Phyllis Dain Library History Dissertation Award: ALA/Library History Round Table
John Cotton Dana Award: Special Libraries Association
John Cotton Dana Library Public Relations Award: ALA/Library Administration
and Management Association
Louise Darling Medal: Medical Library Association
Dartmouth Medal: ALA/Reference and Adult Services Division
Denali Press Award: ALA/Reference and Adult Services Division
Melvil Dewey Medal: ALA/Reference and Adult Services Division
Disclosure Student Travel Award/BRASS: ALA/Reference and Adult Services
Division, Business Reference and Services Section
Distinguished School Administrators Award, AASL/SIRS: ALA/American
Association of School Librarians
Distinguished Service Award AASL/Baker & Taylor: ALA/American Association
of School Librarians
Distinguished Service Award: Society of American Archivists
Distinguished Service to ALSC Award: ALA/Association for Library Service to
Children
Janet Doe Lectureship: Medical Library Association
Tom and Roberta Drewes Scholarship: ALA
Miriam Dudley Bibliographic Instruction Librarian of the Year: ALA/
Association of College and Research Libraries, Bibliographic Instruction
Section
EBSCO ALA Conference Sponsorships: ALA
EBSCO Community College Learning Resources Achievement Awards:
ALA/Association of College and Research Libraries
EBSCO/MLA Annual Meeting Grant: Medical Library Association
Margaret A. Edwards Award: ALA/Young Adult Library Services Association
Ida and George Eliot Prize: Medical Library Association
Emergency Librarian Publication Award: ALA/American Association of School
Librarians
Jim and Anna Emmett Travel Award: Art Libraries Society of North America
Equality Award: ALA
Excellence in Small and/or Rural Public Service Award: ALA/Public Library
Association

Facts on File Grant: ALA/Reference and Adult Services Division

Federal Librarians Achievement Award: ALA/Federal Librarians Round Table

Fellows' Posner Prize: Society of American Archivists

First Step Award, Serials Section/Wiley Professional Development Grant: ALA/Association for Library Collections and Technical Services, Serials Section

Loleta D. Fyan Award: ALA

Gale/*Library Journal* Library of the Year Award: Gale Research Company

Gale Research Award for Excellence in Business Librarianship/BRASS: ALA/Reference and Adult Services Division, Business Reference and Services Section

Gale Research Award for Excellence in Reference and Adult Services: ALA/Reference and Adult Services Division, Business Reference and Services Section

Gale Research Financial Development Award: ALA

Marian Gould Gallagher Distinguished Service Award: American Association of Law Libraries

Hans-Peter Geh Grant: K. G. Saur

Genealogical Publishing Company/History Section Award: ALA/Reference and Adult Services Division

Louise Giles Minority Scholarship: ALA/Office for Library Personnel Resources

Steven I. Goldspiel Research Grant: Special Libraries Association

Fanny Goldstein Merit Award: Association of Jewish Libraries

Murray Gottlieb Prize: Medical Library Association

Grolier Award for Research in School Librarianship in Canada: Canadian School Library Association

Grolier Foundation Award: ALA

Grolier National Library Week Grant: ALA/National Library Week Committee

G. K. Hall Award for Library Literature: ALA

G. K. Hall Conference Attendance Award: Art Libraries Society of North America

Hall of Fame Award: Special Libraries Association

Philip M. Hamer–Elizabeth Hamer Kegan Award: Society of American Archivists

Jane Anne Hannigan Research Award: Association for Library and Information Science Education

Frances Henne Award: ALA/American Association of School Librarians

Frances Henne/YALSA/*Voice of Youth Advocates (VOYA)* Research Grant: ALA/Young Adult Library Services Association

Bernadine Abbott Hoduski Founders Award: ALA/Government Documents Round Table

Gustav Hoffmann Study Grant: K. G. Saur

Oliver Wendell Holmes Award: Society of American Archivists

Honorary ALA Membership: ALA

Miriam Hornback Minority Scholarship: ALA

John Ames Humphry/OCLC/Forest Press Award: ALA/International Relations Committee

ISI Information Science Doctoral Dissertation Scholarship: American Society for Information Science

John Phillip Immroth Memorial Award for Intellectual Freedom: ALA/ Intellectual Freedom Round Table

JASIS Paper Award: American Society for Information Science

J. Franklin Jameson Award for Archival Advocacy: Society of American Archivists

Howard Karno Travel Award: Art Libraries Society of North America

LITA/CLSI Scholarship in Library and Information Technology: ALA/Library and Information Technology Association

LITA/Gaylord Award for Achievement in Library and Information Technology: ALA/Library and Information Technology Association

LITA/*Library Hi Tech* Award: ALA/Library and Information Technology Association

LITA/OCLC Minority Scholarship in Library and Information Technology: ALA/Library and Information Technology Association

Léonce Laget Travel Award: Art Libraries Society of North America

Sheila Suen Lai Scholarship: Chinese-American Librarians Association

Harold Lancour Scholarship for Foreign Study: Beta Phi Mu

Sister M. Claude Lane Award: Society of American Archivists

Law Library Journal Article of the Year Award: American Association of Law Libraries

Law Library Publication Award: American Association of Law Libraries

Samuel Lazerow Fellowship for Research in Acquisitions or Technical Services: ALA/Association of College and Research Libraries

Katharine Kyes Leab and Daniel J. Leab *American Book Prices Current Exhibition Catalogue* Awards: ALA/Association of College and Research Libraries

Tony Leisner Scholarship: ALA

Joseph Leiter NLM/MLA Lectureship: Medical Library Association

Waldo Gifford Leland Prize: Society of American Archivists

Library Video Award: ALA/Public Library Association

Joseph W. Lippincott Award: ALA

Literacy Award: ALA/American Library Trustee Association

MAGERT Honors Award: ALA/Map and Geography Round Table

MLA Award for Distinguished Public Service: Medical Library Association

MLA Award for Excellence and Achievement in Hospital Librarianship: Medical Library Association

MLA Doctoral Fellowship: Medical Library Association

MLA Scholarship: Medical Library Association

MLA Scholarship for Minority Students: Medical Library Association

Fraiser McConnell Travel Award: Art Libraries Society of North America

John P. McGovern Award Lectureship: Medical Library Association

Margaret Mann Citation: ALA/Association for Library Collections and Technical Services

Allie Beth Martin Award: ALA/Public Library Association

Frederic G. Melcher Scholarship: ALA/Association for Library Service to Children

Microcomputer in the Media Center Award: ALA/American Association of School Librarians

Minority Student Award: Society of American Archivists

David Mirvish Books/Books on Art Travel Award: Art Libraries Society of North America

Margaret E. Monroe Library Adult Services Award: ALA/Reference and Adult Services Division

Bessie Boehm Moore Award: ALA

Isadore Gilbert Mudge Citation: ALA/Reference and Adult Services Division

NFB/CLA Award for Outstanding Film or Video Librarian: Canadian Library Association

NMRT EBSCO Scholarship: ALA/New Members Round Table

National Book Service Teacher-Librarian of the Year Award: Canadian School Library Association

National School Library Media Program of the Year Award: ALA/American Association of School Librarians

New Leaders Travel Grant: ALA/Public Library Association

Martinus Nijhoff International West European Specialist Study Grant: ALA/Association of College and Research Libraries

Marcia C. Noyes Award: Medical Library Association

Oberly Award for Bibliography in the Agricultural Sciences: ALA/Association of College and Research Libraries

Eli M. Oboler Memorial Award: ALA/Intellectual Freedom Round Table

Shirley Olofson Memorial Award: ALA/New Members Round Table

Helen Keating Ott Award for Outstanding Contribution to Congregational Libraries: Church and Synagogue Library Association

Theodore Calvin Pease Award: Society of American Archivists

Esther J. Piercy Award: ALA/Association for Library Collections and Technical Services

Preservation Publication Award: Society of American Archivists

Putnam and Grosset Book Group Awards: ALA/Association for Library Service to Children

Herbert W. Putnam Honor Award: ALA

Readex/GODORT/ALA Catharine J. Reynolds Award: ALA/Government Documents Round Table

Sarah Rebecca Reed Scholarship: Beta Phi Mu

Reference Service Press Award: ALA/Reference and Adult Services Division

Rittenhouse Award: Medical Library Association

Frank Bradway Rogers Information Advancement Award: Medical Library Association

Norman Ross Travel Award: Art Libraries Society of North America

SAA Distinguished Service Award: Society of American Archivists

SAA Fellows: Society of American Archivists

SIRS/Peace Award: ALA/Social Responsibilities Round Table

SRRT/Gay and Lesbian Task Force, Gay and Lesbian Book Awards: ALA/Social Responsibilities Round Table

SLA Affirmative Action Scholarship: Special Libraries Association

SLA Fellows: Special Libraries Association

SLA Meckler Award for Innovations in Technology: Special Libraries Association

SLA President's Award: Special Libraries Association

SLA Professional Award: Special Libraries Association

SLA Scholarships: Special Libraries Association

SLA H. W. Wilson Award: Special Libraries Association

K. G. Saur Award for Best *College and Research Libraries* Article: ALA/Association of College and Research Libraries

Margaret B. Scott Award of Merit: Canadian School Library Association

Frank B. Sessa Scholarship for Continuing Professional Education: Beta Phi Mu

John Sessions Memorial Award: ALA/Reference and Adult Services Division

Jesse H. Shera Award for Research: ALA/Library Research Round Table

Louis Shores-Oryx Press Award: ALA/Reference and Adult Services Division

May K. Simon Scholarship: Association of Jewish Libraries

Special Commendation: Society of American Archivists

State Program Award: ALA/Intellectual Freedom Round Table

Sydney Taylor Manuscript Award: Association of Jewish Libraries

3M/NMRT Professional Development Grant: ALA/New Members Round Table

Trustee Citations: ALA/American Library Trustee Association

Leonard Wertheimer Multilingual Public Library Service Award: ALA/Public Library Association

Whitney-Carnegie Awards: ALA/Publishing Committee

Laura Ingalls Wilder Award: ALA/Association for Library Service to Children

H. W. Wilson Library Periodical Award: ALA

H. W. Wilson Library Staff Development Grant: ALA

Justin Winsor Prize Essay: ALA/Library History Round Table

World Book–ALA Goal Awards: ALA

YALSA/Econo-Clad Literature Program Award: ALA/Young Adult Library Services Association

Part 4
Research and Statistics

Library Research and Statistics

Research on Libraries and Librarianship in 1994

Mary Jo Lynch

Director, Office for Research and Statistics, American Library Association

The largest U.S. Department of Education contract for research on libraries in many years was announced in late May and awarded in late September. An "Assessment of the Role of School and Public Libraries in Reaching the National Education Goals" will be conducted over a three-year period by Westat Inc., with assistance from the American Library Association (ALA). The department's Office of Library Programs will administer the $1.3 million contract, which is supported by dollars from the Secretary's Fund for Innovation in Education.

While school and public libraries have always viewed themselves as a basic and integral component of both formal and informal education in the United States, there has been no study conducted on a national level to determine how libraries support preschool and K–12 education. Ten years ago, the U.S. Department of Education's report *Alliance for Excellence: Librarians Respond to a Nation at Risk* called for the nation's school and public libraries to be "assessed for their ability to respond to the urgent proposals for excellence in education and lifelong learning."

The purpose of this study is to find out how school and public libraries are performing as education providers and how well they are responding to the coutry's urgent demands for school improvement. It is intended to inform researchers, policymakers, and practitioners on six key issues:

- To what extent are school and public libraries contributing to education reform and to what extent can they contribute?
- What programs and services are school and public libraries providing to meet the needs of preschool and elementary and secondary (K–12) education providers?
- How well do these services and programs meet the needs of preschool and K–12 education providers?
- Do school and public libraries have the capacity—human and information resources, technology, and facilities—to adequately respond to identified needs and support systemic reform?
- What new technologies are promoting student opportunity to learn by improving services and resources in school and public libraries?

- What can we learn from successful school and public library programs and services designed to support preschool and K–12 education? Can these programs serve as models for the improvement of all school and public libraries? What are the barriers to effective services and programs?

These questions will be answered by a combination of surveys, case studies, focus groups, and commissioned papers. The project will conclude with an invitational conference in the fall of 1997.

Digital Library Initiative

Last year this article began with a description of the Digital Library Initiative sponsored by the National Science Foundation (NSF), the National Aeronautics and Space Administration (NASA), and the Defense Department's Advanced Research Projects Agency (ARPA). The project would accelerate the development of a national, networked, distributed online system of linked digital libraries by funding research and development projects that address one or more of a long set of issues related to electronic libraries. In late September, six major grants were announced by university-led consortia that include libraries, museums, publishers, schools, and communications companies. Over the next four years these groups will spend $24.4 million to develop systems for collecting, storing, and organizing digital information and making it easily available to anyone who wishes to use it, from high school students to research scientists. Some of the consortia focus mainly on the problem of finding information scattered throughout cyberspace; others will concentrate on developing automated means to catalog new kinds of digital information, such as images and videos. At the end of the four years, each of the six teams should have created a working digital library that serves a large public while also acting as a testbed for further research and development.

The six lead institutions and the content of the projects are listed below:

- Carnegie Mellon University (digital video with math and science focus)
- University of California, Berkeley (environmental information)
- University of Michigan (multimedia with earth and space science focus)
- University of California, Santa Barbara (geographical information, including images and maps)
- Stanford University (technologies for a single, integrated virtual library)
- University of Illinois (engineering and science journals and magazines)

All of these projects were described succinctly in the October 7 issue of *Science* in an article on "Turning an Info-Glut Into a Library."

An interesting result of the competition that led to the six grants was a conference on "Digital Libraries '94" held in June at Texas A&M University. The first conference on the theory and practice of digital libraries drew most of its speakers from the many collaborative efforts to submit proposals under the digital library initiative jointly sponsored by NSF, ARPA, and NASA. The many hundreds of librarians, computer scientists, and social scientists who spent thousands of hours studying the issues of digital libraries brought their ideas to College Station for sharing in a conference sponsored by Texas A&M's Hypermedia Research Laboratory and the Washington University School of Medicine Library. Plans are already under way for "Digital Libraries '95" in San Antonio and a 1996 conference in St. Louis.

Reinventing the Office for Educational Research and Improvement

This article began by describing a large contract to be administered by the Office of Library Programs, which is part of the Department of Education's Office for Educational Research and Improvement (OERI). OERI was reorganized by the Educational Research, Development, Dissemination, and Improvement Act of 1994, which was added to the Goal 2000: Educate America Act signed into law on March 31, 1994, as PL 103-227. As before, the new OERI contains the Office of Library Programs and the National Center for Education Statistics (NCES). What is new is that the act calls for a National Library of Education [see article in Part 1—*Ed.*] and the establishment of five research institutes, each to focus on a specific topic. The five institutes are on:

- Student Achievement, Curriculum, and Assessment
- Education of At-Risk Students
- Early Childhood Development and Education
- Educational Governance, Finance, Policymaking, and Management
- Postsecondary Education, Libraries, and Lifelong Learning

Each institute will sponsor the following activities in its area of interest: national research and development center, fellowships and grants, directed research, field-initiated studies, and in-house research. Preliminary planning papers issued by OERI in the summer of 1994 contained very little about research related to libraries. The papers did describe research questions that could easily be applied to libraries, however, and several library agencies (among them ALA's Office for Research and Statistics and American Association of School Librarians, and the National Commission on Libraries and Information Service) wrote to suggest that this take place, in response to a request for comments on the OERI reorganization that appeared in the July 7 *Federal Register*. Given what has happened to the Higher Education Act (HEA) II-A and II-B (see below), the new institutes may be the only source of Department of Education funding for research about libraries.

Another article in this volume describes 1994 awards administered by the Office of Library Programs in their regular grant programs [see Part II—*Ed.*]. The Title II-B Library Research and Demonstration Program did not fund any research in 1994. Title II-A of the Act—College Library Technology and Cooperation Grants Program—gives awards in four categories, one of which is Research and Demonstration. Five new awards were made with 1994 funds in this category. Two will be described later in the section on academic libraries. In the Services to Institutions category, a grant to OCLC (Online Computer Library Center) for "Building a Catalog of Internet-Accessible Materials" has a strong research component. The project initiates a nationwide, coordinated effort among libraries and institutions of higher education to create, implement, test, and evaluate a searchable database of USMARC format bibliographic records, complete with electronic location and access information, for Internet-accessible materials. Records created in this effort will be accessible through the OCLC PRISM service and the FirstSearch WorldCat database. The collection of records also will be made available experimentally for general Internet access, and OCLC will test the technical feasibility of providing direct user access to remote materials based on encoded location and access information.

Late in 1994 Congress zeroed out the Title II-A College Library Technology Program and directed that the $6.5 million allocated to Title II-B Library Research and Demonstration Program be spent on two more statewide electronic library networks and a demonstration project on government information. Thus there will be no new dollars for research from the Office of Library Programs in 1995.

Academic Libraries

Two of the 1994 HEA II-A grants are for research in an academic library setting:

- University of California, Irvine; Rob Kling, Project Director; $122,000 for "Institutional and Organizational Dimensions of the Effective Use of Digital Libraries"

  The recent rapid growth of diverse digital library (DL) service raises questions about what conditions foster their effective use. This project examines how much university faculty and students use relevant DL resources, and the institutional and organizational practices that enhance their effective use. This is a multi-tiered study including (1) a comparative institutional analysis of eight university digital library and network information services; (2) an intensive field study of DL providers and 50 faculty and graduate students in five disciplines who use DL services at one institution; and (3) a mail survey of faculty and graduate students to learn patterns of DL usage in a broader population.

- Syracuse University; Cynthia L. Lopata, Assistant Professor, and Charles R. McClure, Professor; $140,834 for "Assessing the Impacts of Internet/NREN Networking on the Academic Institution"

  Despite the fact that many institutions of higher education have been connected to Internet and the evolving National Research and Education Network (NREN), there is little knowledge of how such connections have affected the institutions. This study will identify and describe the impacts of network access and use via exploratory, qualitative design, based on multiple data collection activities. Key components of the academic networked environment will be defined and indicators of the effects of networked information services and resources on academic institutions will be developed and operationalized.

Late in 1994 the National Center for Education Statistics (NCES) released 1992 statistics on academic libraries. In addition to statistical tables similar to those of earlier years, this report introduced something new: a series of ratios. Table 11 shows national average, lower quartile, median, and upper quartile for each of four "highest level of degree" categories and for private and public control on 11 variables. Six are ratios calculated "per FTE (full-time equivalent) student": total operating expenditures, expenditures for collections, expenditures for serials, volumes held, volumes added, and circulation. Total library staff is shown per 1,000 students. Total operating expenditures are shown as a percent of the institution's educational and general (E&G) expenditures. The final three ratios describe the library's budget: expenditures for collections as a percentage of total operating expenditures, expenditures for current serials as a percentage of total collection expenditures, and salaries and wages as a percentage of total operating expenditures.

The Association of Research Libraries (ARL) is expanding its statistical and measurement activities and in 1994 hired a new program officer, Martha Kyrillidou, to direct this work full time. The ARL Statistics and Measurement program will continue to collect basic statistical data on academic libraries and librarians. Analysis of existing data and new projects will aim at describing and measuring the performance of research libraries and their contribution to teaching, research, scholarship, and community service.

Public Libraries

Research on public libraries and Internet was prominent in 1994. February saw publication of an evaluation report prepared for NYSERNet Inc., *Connecting Rural Public Libraries to the Internet: Project GAIN—Global Access Information Network* by Charles R. McClure, et al. Project GAIN studied the concept that if rural librarians were given the tools and training to use networked information resources, they could do so effectively and thereby improve the quality of service they offered their patrons. The report describes a number of findings documenting the impacts of such connectivity on the library, the librarians, the local community, and the Internet community. The report also provides evaluation information that should be helpful for other public libraries considering opening a branch in cyberspace.

In June the final report of a survey funded by the National Commission on Libraries and Information Science (NCLIS) was published as *Public Libraries and the Internet: Study Results, Policy Issues, and Recommendations*. This report by Charles R. McClure, John Carlo Bertot, and Douglas L. Zweizig provides the first available statistical evidence of the extent to which public libraries are using Internet. Based on results of a questionnaire sent to a national sample of public libraries selected by NCES, the study describes several dimensions of Internet use by libraries serving all sizes of population (from under 5,000 to 1 million-plus). Seventy-nine figures display results on such topics as type of connection (e.g., VT100 terminal, E-mail gateway), use of Internet (e.g., E-mail, resource location, telnet/remote login, ftp), and barriers to Internet participation.

An October news release announced that the National Science Foundation will fund another study conducted by two of the authors of the NCLIS survey, McClure and Bertot. "Policy Issues in Assessing the Role of Public Libraries in the National Information Infrastructure (NII)" will expand on the NCLIS survey by using focus groups, interviews, and policy conferences with stakeholders to:

• Develop models that describe alternative roles and responsibilities (especially as they relate to public education and literacy) that public libraries might assume in NII
• Assess the impacts of these models in terms of criteria such as the promotion of universal access to networked information, costs, and training and personnel requirements
• Analyze the existing federal public library policy system to determine the degree to which that policy system might require modification to achieve administration policy objectives regarding public libraries in NII
• Offer policy recommendations to revise and extend the existing public library policy system to promote proposed policy objectives related to a new role for public libraries in NII

The project will conclude with a policy conference in May 1995 and a final report with specific recommendations regarding how current NII policy initiatives can best encourage public library participation in NII.

At the Public Library Association (PLA) National Conference in April, McClure and Zweizig presented preliminary results of the NCLIS survey. Also offered at that conference was a program titled "Centering on Research" that featured a panel of speakers from the four active "centers" doing public library research: the Library Research Service at the Colorado State Library, the Library Research Center at the University of Illinois, the Center for the Study of Rural Librarianship at Clarion University, and the now-defunct center at the School of Library and Information Studies at the University of Wisconsin at Madison.

School Libraries

Two important statistical reports on school libraries were published in 1994. Both partially update the 1985–1986 report *Statistics of Public and Private School Library Media Centers, 1985–86*. Neither, however, provides the detailed data that will be available when results are released from two surveys conducted by NCES in the fall of 1993–1994. Surveys on the school library media center and the school library media specialist were a part of the 1993–1994 Schools and Staffing Survey (SASS). Because it was known that results would not be available until late in 1995, and timely data were needed to support state reform efforts and national legislative efforts, NCLIS and ALA combined forces on a stop-gap measure. In the fall of 1993, ALA sent a three-page questionnaire to a random sample of public school librarians who are members of the American Association of School Librarians in 12 states selected to represent different regions and reform efforts. Results were published by NCLIS in May 1994 as *School Library Media Centers in 12 States*. From a research perspective, the report has many limitations. However, it does provide some current data and may be an early warning of what will be known when the 1993–1994 SASS data are released by NCES.

A limited amount of school library data was collected by NCES in the 1990–1991 SASS questionnaires sent to teachers and principals. Results were published by NCES in November 1994 as *School Library Media Centers in the United States: 1990–1991*. This report begins with a historical overview of the availability of school libraries and school librarians using NCES data going back as far as 1959. Next it describes the availability of school library media centers and staffing levels of school library media centers in different sectors of the school community (e.g., public/private, school level, school size). National figures are shown as well as data by state. The report also shows results of two questions asked on the teacher survey and one question on the principal survey. Teachers were asked if they planned with the librarian for the integration of the school library media centers into their teaching (29 percent did). They were also asked if library media center materials were adequate to their needs (35 percent said yes). Principals were asked if six different groups had a great deal of influence over establishing curriculum. Almost 16 percent of the principals said librarians and media specialists had such influence, ahead of parent associations at 7.7 percent, but well below school boards at 41.4 percent.

The November 1994 National Conference of the American Association of School Librarians was preceded by Treasure Mountain Research Retreat 5 held at the Abe Martin Lodge, Brown County State Park in Nashville, Indiana: This one-day conference, organized by Dan Barron, Bob Grover, and David Loertscher, featured a kickoff presentation by education futurist Jim Mecklenburger. During the rest of the day 14 papers were presented followed by discussion. The paper most talked about during the following conference in Indianapolis was one by Australian Ross J. Todd. His "What Will be Required to Lead and Support the Future Information Professional?" identifies two areas that have long-term ramifications for information practice in school—information literacy and developments in multimedia—and describes research needed in each area. In relation to information literacy, Todd briefly described a recent study he conducted. Details on that work have already been published in the Winter 1995 issue of *School Library Media Quarterly* as "Integrated Information Skills Instruction: Does It Make a Difference?" It is expected that all papers will be published in 1995 by Hi Willow Research and Publishing of Castle Rock, Colorado.

Awards That Support Research

Association for Library and Information Science Education

The first library and information science research awards of the year were presented in January at the annual meeting of the Association for Library and Information Science Education (ALISE), which preceded the 1994 ALA Midwinter Meeting in Los Angeles. The 1994 ALISE Research Grant ($2,500) was awarded to Norman Howden (North Texas), Thomas Kochtanek (Missouri-Columbia), and Nancy Zimmerman (Buffalo) for a project titled "Electronic Resources in ALA Accredited Schools." The 1994 Jane Anne Hannigan Research

Award ($500) was given to Louise S. Robbins (Wisconsin-Madison) for a study of "Anti-Communism, Racism, and Censorship in the McCarthy Era: The Case of Ruth Brown and the Bartlesville Public Library."

Library Acquisitions: Practice and Theory

In the spring, Library Acquisitions: Practice and Theory (LAPT) announced the recipients of its 1994 Research Award: Tina E. Chrzastowski and Karen A. Schmidt. Chrzastowski is Chemistry Librarian at the University of Illinois at Urbana-Champaign and Schmidt is Acquisitions Librarian at the same institution. Their proposal, "The Serials Cancellation Crisis: Determining Recent National Trends in Academic Library Serial Collections Through the Use of Commercial Vendor Subscription Records," will determine how recent rounds of serial cancellations have affected academic research collections nationwide. It will identify national trends in serial collections by analyzing serial cancellations and serial orders over three years (1991–1993) from ten academic research libraries located throughout the United States.

American Association of School Librarians

At the 1994 Annual Conference of ALA in Miami, winners of the American Association of School Librarians (AASL)/Highsmith Research Grants were announced. The grants, up to $2,500 for each project, are sponsored by the Highsmith Company Inc., of Fort Atkinson, Wisconsin, to enable school library media specialists, library educators, and library information science or education professors to conduct innovative research aimed at measuring and evaluating the impact of school library media programs on learning and education.

Two grants were made in 1994. Roberta Ponis, Dian Walster, and Lynda Welborn of Denver, Colorado, will study "Information Literacy Standards–Alternative Assessments." They will develop alternative assessment processes and tools for the Colorado Information Literacy Standards. Kathleen Garland of Ann Arbor, Michigan, will examine "The Information Search Process: A Study of Cognitive Strategies for Teaching Higher Level Thinking Skills." This project will examine the potential contribution of the library media specialist working cooperatively with teachers to teach higher-level thinking skills.

Association of College and Research Libraries

The $1,000 Samuel Lazerow Fellowship for Research in Acquisitions or Technical Services was presented at the Association of College and Research Libraries (ACRL) President's Program June 25 in Miami. Kuang-Hwei (Janet) Lee-Smeltzer, catalog librarian at Oregon State University in Corvallis, received the fellowship for a project titled "Library Automation in Taiwan: Exploring the Potential for Cooperative Cataloging of Chinese Language Materials on an International Basis." The project will investigate the development of library automation in the National Central Library and some of the major research and academic libraries in Taiwan. The goal is to provide information in this area that will foster future research and will serve as a basis and framework for establishing cooperative cataloging activities between research and academic libraries in the United States and Taiwan.

Stephen Lehmann, humanities bibliographer at the University of Pennsylvania in Philadelphia, is the 1994 recipient of ACRL's Martinus Nijhoff West European Specialists Study Grant. This grant, funded by Martinus Nijhoff International, is given to support research pertaining to West European studies, librarianship, or the book trade. Lehmann plans to examine and publish an article on the outstanding features of journal publishing in German academic librarianship. He will interview leading figures in German library journals to explore issues relating to editorial and financial policies, the relationship of the journals to the institutional structures of German librarianship, recruitment of authors, and other relevant issues.

Young Adult Library Services Association

Kathy Latrobe and Michael Havener, faculty members in the School of Library and Information Science at the University of Oklahoma in Norman, are the 1994 recipients of the Frances Henne/Voices of Youth Advocates (VOYA)/Young Adult Library Services Association (YALSA) Research Grant. The $500 grant, donated by VOYA, provides seed money for small-scale projects that will encourage significant research and that will have an influence on library services to young adults. Latrobe and Havener received the grant for their proposal titled 'An Exploratory Study of the Information Seeking Behavior of High School Honors Students." Their research will be conducted as a case study of a group of high school students in Norman, Oklahoma.

ALA Grants Not Awarded

Two ALA grants that support research were not made in 1994 due to lack of suitable proposals: ACRL's $1,000 Doctoral Dissertation Fellowship and ALA's $7,500 Carroll Preston Baber Research Grant.

Medical Library Association

At its 1994 Annual Meeting in San Antonio, the Medical Library Association (MLA) presented its 1994 Doctoral Fellowship ($1,000) to Mary Moore, doctoral student at the Graduate School of Library and Information Science, University of Texas at Austin. This year's fellowship will support Moore's research project, 'Characteristics of Early Adopters of Telemedicine Information Delivery Services." The project will examine the social, demographic, psychological, and communications characteristics of early adopters of telemedicine information technology services, focusing on factors critical to success. MLA did not award a Research, Development, and Demonstration Project Grant in 1994.

Special Libraries Association

The $15,000 Research Grant of the Special Libraries Association (SLA) was renamed the Stephen I. Goldspiel Memorial Research Grant. Goldspiel, who was president and chief executive officer of Disclosure Inc., a provider of public company information, died September 22, 1992. He was a good friend and long-time supporter of SLA.

The 1994 winners of the grant are Raya Fidel, associate professor, Graduate School of Library and Information Science, University of Washington, Seattle, and Michael Crandall, external systems requirements librarian, Boeing Technical Libraries, Boeing Corporation, Seattle. Their research will study methods that managers and engineers select to filter information from full-text electronic periodicals. Among the specific questions to be answered are:

• What factors do users perceive to be important in selecting a filtering method?

• What are the differences in how members of each of two groups— browsers and library users—seek information?

• What are the differences in information seeking between managers and engineers?

• What is the value added by the intermediary librarian?

Awards That Recognize Research

Association for Library and Information Science Education

The first awards for research well done were also made at the January 1994 Association for Library and Information Science Education (ALISE) conference in Los Angeles. Two $400 ALISE Doctoral Dissertation Awards were made in 1994. One went to Rose Albritton (University of Illinois, now of Wayne State University) for a dissertation on "Transformational Versus Transactional Leadership in University Libraries: A Test of the Model and Its Relationship to Perceived Library Organizational Effectiveness." Also winning an award was Françoise Hébert (University of Toronto) for her dissertation on "The Quality of Interlibrary Borrowing Service in Large Urban Public Libraries in Canada."

The 1994 ALISE Research Paper Award ($500) was won by Patricia Dewdney and Catherine Ross (both of Western Ontario) for a paper titled "Flying a Light Aircraft: Reference Services Evaluation from a User's Viewpoint." The paper was later published in the Winter 1994 issue of RQ.

American Library Association

The American Library Association (ALA) usually announces winners of two awards during the Joint Research Awards program at its Annual Conference—the Library Research Round Table (LRRT) Jesse H. Shera Award for Research and the Library History Round Table (LHRT) Justin Winsor Prize. The Justin Winsor Prize was not given this year. The 1994 Shera award was given to Judith Serebnick, associate professor in the School of Library and Information Science at Indiana University, Bloomington, and Frank Quinn, reference librarian and doctoral candidate at Indiana University. They received the award for a paper on "Measuring Diversity of Opinion in Collections in OCLC Public Libraries," which describes research supported by an Online Computer Library Center

(OCLC) Library and Information Science Research Grant. The paper was published in the January 1995 issue of *Library Quarterly*.

American Society for Information Science

In October, at its Annual Meeting in Arlington, Virginia, the American Society for Information Science (ASIS) announced awards to several researchers. The ASIS Research Award, which honors a systematic program of research in a single area at a level beyond the single study and recognizes outstanding research contributions in the field of information science was presented to Raya Fidel for her research on users' online searching behavior, including her adaptation of the case study method with controlled comparison from the social sciences to the field of information retrieval. Dr. Fidel has increased general awareness regarding the use of appropriate methodology in information science, especially with respect to capturing the complex behavior of interaction with technology.

The Best JASIS Paper Award went to Ingrid Hsieh-Yee, for her paper "Effects of Search Experience and Subject Knowledge on the Search Tactics of Novice and Experienced Searchers," investigating the differences in search tactics by novice and experienced searchers with and without subject knowledge. The award jury noted that this paper clearly describes the experiment in concise language, with the objectives and research questions well defined, based on an excellent literature review. The paper moves smoothly from hypotheses to conclusions, with appropriate discussion of variables and limitations of each method of data collection.

Winner of the ASIS Doctoral Forum Award presented for outstanding doctoral research done in the information field was Peiling Wang, a student at the University of Maryland, for "A Cognitive Model of Document Selection of Real Users in Information Retrieval." The 1994 Information Science Doctoral Dissertation Scholarship went to Corinne Jorgensen of Syracuse University for her proposal to conduct an exploratory study of the attributes people use to describe, sort, and search for images representing particular concepts. The results will inform a multitude of decisions that affect the design of image retrieval systems and ultimately affect access to images within these systems.

Library Association Activities

American Library Association

The 1994 Annual Conference of the American Library Association (ALA) in Miami included the usual set of research forums. The Library Research Round Table (LRRT) sponsored two such meetings and research forums were also sponsored by American Association of School Librarians (AASL), and by the Science and Technology Section of the Association of College and Research Libraries (ACRL). The conference also featured several programs where research was prominent. The Association for Library Collections and Technical Services (ALCTS) Research Committee's program on "Coping with Fluctuating Budgets" covered the design and execution of effective in-house studies both for the purpose of local decision making and for making worthwhile contributions to the research literature. The Public Library Association (PLA) sponsored a session titled "Does That Answer Your Question? Research Findings about Reference Effectiveness." The Reference and Adult Services Division (RASD) sponsored a program on "New Services, New Models: The Research/Experimental Approach to Introducing New Services" and RASD cooperated with the Library Administration and Management Association (LAMA) on a program on "The Truth about Reference: How to Find Out." The latter event featured four speakers followed by a poster session in an adjoining room where 13 projects were on display.

An important step for the future of research was taken in Miami when the ALA Council voted to adopt a Research and Statistics Policy Statement proposed by ALA's Committee on Research and Statistics (CORS). The following text will be placed in ALA's official Policy Manual along with similar policies on Intellectual Freedom, Legislation, Public Information, and Library Personnel:

> The American Library Association recognizes the need to continuously build and strengthen the knowledge base upon which library services and the library profession depend. Basic and applied research in the field of library and information studies, as well as research results in related disciplines will, in large measure, shape library and information services and the nature of the library profession in the future. Statistics are a necessary foundation for many kinds of research as well as for policy and planning. Through its Office for Research and Statistics (ORS), as well as through related groups in its membership units, ALA strives to reach the ALA's goals in the areas of research and statistics.
>
> In order to reach these goals:
>
> • ALA defines and identifies priority research areas
> • Stimulates and promotes the funding required to conduct research
> • Cooperates with library education research programs
> • Coordinates with other institutions and associations implementing the profession's research agenda
> • Stimulates discussion of research methodologies
> • Proposes programs designed to improve the quality, quantity, and impact of research
> • Promotes the role, importance, and necessity of research
>
> In addition, the association performs and supports research, and participates in cooperative research activities related to those research areas and topics identified as Association priorities.

Medical Library Association

The Medical Library Association (MLA) has had an Ad Hoc Task Force at work for over a year drafting a much more ambitious document for MLA. A preliminary draft of that group's work appeared in the September 1994 issue of *MLA News*. The final document, *Using Scientific Evidence to Improve Information Practice: The Research Policy Statement of the Medical Library Association*, was approved by the MLA board in January 1995.

This policy document "expresses the vision of the Medical Library Association (MLA) of research as a foundation for excellence in health information practice, for new and expanded roles for health sciences librarians, and for attracting excellent people to the profession." The document includes sections on "Role of Individual Health Science Librarians" and "Role of the Medical Library Association" along with an "Action Plan for the Medical Library Association" that includes paragraphs on education, research support, funding, dissemination, recognition, and measurement.

Special Libraries Association

The Special Libraries Association (SLA) has been without a research officer for several years, and SLA President Miriam Drake made the restoration of that position part of her campaign for a dues increase. The increase was passed and a research officer was hired; Lianna Sayer began work in January 1995 as director, research.

Activities of Other Agencies

Council on Library Resources

Another article in this volume describes the work of the Council on Library Resources (CLR) in 1994 and includes brief descriptions of several research projects [see Part II—*Ed.*]. Late in 1994 CLR announced a change in leadership. David W. Penniman, president of CLR for the last four years, resigned effective December 31, 1994, and Deanna B. Marcum was appointed president effective January 1, 1995. Marcum served as CLR vice president from 1984 to 1989. Since then she has been, first, dean of the School of Library and Information Science at Catholic University of America and most recently, director of public services and collection management at the Library of Congress.

OCLC

OCLC (Online Computer Library Center) has long held an important place on the library research scene because of the important research done at OCLC and because of the research OCLC sponsors elsewhere. A major change in leadership of the research effort at OCLC was announced in April 1994. Terry Noreault was appointed director of the newly formed research and special projects division (RSPD), which comprises the office of research, the electronic publishing solutions section, and the distributed systems section. He brings to the position practical and academic experience in information science, including nine years of research and product development at OCLC.

An article in the July/August 1994 issue of the *OCLC Newsletter* features a picture of the 18-member staff of the office of research (OR) next to an interview with Dr. Noreault about the office. His general view of the office is as follows:

> OR is a unique resource in the field of library-related research and represents OCLC's substantial commitment to research. This commitment is apparent in two important ways: OR fulfills both internal and external research needs, and OR applies its strengths to a set of opportunities that are an intersection of library science and computer science. This combination allows OR to take a leadership role in providing services for both constituencies. As a result, we will focus our investigations on those areas where we can make a difference. In short, OR's role is to create opportunities for OCLC, its membership and the library communi-

ty at large to explore ideas and provide knowledge that will allow OCLC to make informed decisions with respect to a multitude of options.

Noreault sees OR focusing on the following domains for the short term: database quality; networked information; and the analysis of data related to the Online Union Catalog (OLUC) and OCLC services. For the long term, he expects the same three areas to be important although he is also convinced that OR would change priorities "if a new means of information delivery appeared tomorrow."

Three grants for university-based research were announced by OCLC in November:

- Alexandra Dimitroff, Ph.D., assistant professor, and Dietmar Wolfram, Ph.D., assistant professor, University of Wisconsin–Milwaukee Graduate School: "Hypertext Bibliographic Retrieval: A Comparison of Linkage Environments." This research will investigate the effectiveness of different types of hypertext linkages in two hypertext-based information retrieval systems for bibliographic records. A user study comparing search effectiveness for novice and experienced searchers will be carried out for both systems. Results of the study will have applications in the design of bibliographic-based information retrieval systems by determining how the richness of linkage options and different types of linkages provide the searcher with the most effective search environment.

- Karen M. Drabenstott, Ph.D., associate professor, and Amy J. Warner, Ph.D., assistant professor, University of Michigan: "End-User Understanding of Subject Headings." The researchers will formulate questionnaires displaying subject headings in different contexts and forms, then recruit end users, catalogers, and reference librarians in public and academic libraries and ask them to provide the meaning of subject headings. The findings of the project will give direction for improving controlled vocabularies in the area of end-user understanding.

- Lei Zeng, Ph.D., assistant professor, Kent State University: "Developing Control Mechanisms for Intellectual Access for Discipline-Based Virtual Libraries—A Study of the Process." Control mechanisms for intellectual access in a virtual library environment are very important factors. This study proposes to identify basic and important considerations as part of the process of developing such control mechanisms, to explore new approaches in knowledge organization, and to present a model that demonstrates one of the approaches for developing such mechanisms. The research will focus on an examination of the mechanisms to access information sources in the client services area in a prototype Environmental Sciences Virtual Library. It will investigate approaches used by various sources, examine semantically cohesive categories in environmental sciences and related fields, and develop a broad scheme of concept categories. A draft model designed for virtual libraries will be revised and tested through an examination of the collected data.

New Journal

A posting on several listservs in December announced the start of a new journal for the publication of research. *Standpoints: The Electronic Journal of Information Contexts* was started because of the growing interest library educators have in acknowledging the urgent need for broader and more diversified approaches to library and information studies. This refereed electronic journal will be interdisciplinary, rather than disciplinary, and inclusive, rather than exclusive, in nature. It welcomes any sound research that deals with issues related to information contexts. The preference will be given to those studies taking nontraditional perspectives and/or approaches; to studies asking questions starting from lives of a wider variety of people; and to studies exhibiting interdisciplinarity. The editors explain that "some examples of the relationships we would like to see this journal support include: interpersonal communication in information contexts; gender studies in telecommunications; research in the communication of information about taboo subjects; intercultural communication of information; critical theory as applied to information systems design; information cultures and counter-cultures; analyses of contemporary technological responses to the 'information gap'; and building a conceptual framework for the organization of electronic information."

Agendas for the Future

It seems appropriate to end this year's article with some indication of what is likely to come in future years. One well-known organization and one well-known individual published research agendas in 1994. The American Society for Information Science (ASIS) research committee released preliminary work on a research agenda in the June/July issue of the *ASIS Bulletin*. The list of "Baby Grand Challenges in Information Science" includes 45 topics under nine broad headings: Public Interest, Technology, Databases, Indexing, Information Retrieval, Users (Human), Human–Computer Interaction, Standards, Research/ Evaluation. This is not a prioritized list. Based on further review and the comments of the ASIS membership, the research committee will prepare a "top ten" list of research needs most central to information science and with the greatest potential impact on the field.

A much more elaborate agenda by Frederick C. Lynden appeared in the Fall 1994 issue of *Publishing Research Quarterly*. Almost the entire issue was devoted to research agendas for different sectors of the publishing community. Topics and authors were as follows: "The Case for Reader Research" by John P. Dessauer; "Toward a History of the Book in America" by John B. Hench; "Politics and Publishing in a Democratic Society: Technical Breakthroughs and Research Agendas" by Irving Louis Horowitz and Mary E. Curtis; "Priorities for Publishing Research: A Multidisciplinary Agenda" by Beth Luey; "Bookselling Research: An Overview of the Past and Priorities for the Future" by Carol Miles; "Priorities for Publishing Research" by J. Kendrick Noble, Jr.; "Statistics, Standards, and Electronic Media" by Sandra K. Paul; and "Book History and Biography" by James L. W. West III.

Lynden's "A Research Agenda for Libraries" describes ten problem areas: rising costs, shrinking funding, electronic provision of services, deterioration of materials, use of document delivery services, changes in copyright and licensing, out-sourcing, staff training, organizational challenges, and redefining the library's role. The article explains major issues in each area and indicates what specific research is needed. It ends with a list of ten priority areas:

1 The causes for the unprecedented inflation in pricing of books and serials need to be examined and suggestions for alleviating the situation need to be proposed.

2 The costs of access versus acquisition need to be investigated. Further, successful programs—using primarily access rather than acquisitions—need to be studied and publicized.

3 Means for either meeting the funding crisis head-on, i.e., obtaining more funds, or developing alternative sources of information, e.g., national resource centers, should be researched.

4 The costs for substituting electronic sources for print ones need to be determined, and the barriers to such substitution need to be explored.

5 Research is required to make decisions on the most cost-effective and high-quality means for preserving publications, be it deacidification, microfilming, or digitization, or a combination of these methodologies. There should be an inventory of publishers still producing acidic papers, and steps should be taken to encourage them to use acid-free paper.

6 Questions should be raised about document delivery: should it be commercial or interlibrary loan; which sites have the most cost-effective and successful programs; should services be subsidized (i.e., fee, free, or a mixture); and can it be timely?

7 Copyright and licensing are issues that require cooperative research among publishers, vendors, and librarians. An ASCAP-type arrangement for payments for authors of articles sent via document delivery should be examined. Package prices for sets and/or serials, using licensing arrangements, can be beneficial to libraries and publishers. Research should go ahead on discovering the most profitable and user-friendly arrangements.

8 Research is needed on the costs of processing materials in libraries. This research will enable libraries, vendors, and publishers to select appropriate areas for out-sourcing, be it contract cataloging, table of contents services, or other processes. Out-sourcing could produce savings for libraries and translate into more sales, enabling publishers and vendors to offer more materials and services.

9 Libraries need to do research on the best means for educating and/or training staff for using the new technological advances as well as discovering which organizational structure promises the best service to the user.

10 Finally, research on the role of libraries, as part of the national information infrastructure in the new technological environment, needs to examine how libraries fit into the information discovery and knowledge production process.

Number of Libraries in the United States, Canada, and Mexico

Statistics are from the 47th edition of the *American Library Directory 1994–95 (ALD)* (R. R. Bowker, 1994). Data are exclusive of elementary and secondary school libraries.

Libraries in the United States

Public Libraries	15,346*
Public libraries, excluding branches	9,123†
Main public libraries that have branches	1,288
Public library branches	6,223
Academic Libraries	4,914*
Junior college	1,261
Departmental	101
Medical	7
Religious	3
University and college	3,653
Departmental	1,666
Law	178
Medical	213
Religious	104
Armed Forces Libraries	442*
Air Force	120
Medical	15
Army	177
Law	1
Medical	35
Navy	145
Law	1
Medical	18
Government Libraries	1,864*
Law	424
Medical	227
Special Libraries (excluding public, academic, armed forces, and government)	10,059*
Law	1,150
Medical	1,922
Religious	1,008
Total Special Libraries (including public, academic, armed forces, and government)	11,148
Total law	1,763
Total medical	2,443
Total religious	1,116
Total Libraries Counted(*)	32,625

Libraries in Regions Administered by the United States

Public Libraries	27*
Public libraries, excluding branches	12†
Main public libraries that have branches	3
Public library branches	15
Academic Libraries	51*
Junior college	7
University and college	44
Departmental	21
Law	2
Medical	1
Armed Forces Libraries	3*
Air Force	1
Army	1
Navy	1
Government Libraries	9*
Law	1
Medical	2
Special Libraries (excluding public, academic, armed forces, and government)	17*
Law	4
Medical	5
Religious	1
Total Special Libraries (including public, academic, armed forces, and government)	21
Total law	7
Total medical	8
Total religious	1
Total Libraries Counted(*)	107

Libraries in Canada

Public Libraries	1,743*
Public libraries, excluding branches	794†
Main public libraries that have branches	137
Public library branches	949
Academic Libraries	504*
Junior college	141
Departmental	46
Medical	1
Religious	3

University and college	363
Departmental	175
Law	18
Medical	17
Religious	18
Government Libraries	400*
Law	20
Medical	5
Special Libraries (excluding public, academic, armed forces, and government)	1,354*
Law	109
Medical	259
Religious	55
Total Special Libraries (including public, academic, and government)	1,471
Total law	147
Total medical	276
Total religious	73
Total Libraries Counted(*)	4,001

Libraries in Mexico

Public Libraries	20*
Public libraries, excluding branches	19†
Main public libraries that have branches	1
Public library branches	1
Academic Libraries	262*
Junior college	0
Departmental	0
Medical	0
Religious	0
University and college	262
Departmental	43
Law	1
Medical	1
Religious	0
Government Libraries	8*
Law	0
Medical	0
Special Libraries (excluding public, academic, armed forces, and government)	19*
Law	0

Medical	6
Religious	0
Total Special Libraries (including public, academic, and government)	28
Total law	17
Total medical	7
Total religious	0
Total Libraries Counted(*)	309

Summary

Total U.S. Libraries	32,625
Total Libraries Administered by the United States	107
Total Canadian Libraries	4,001
Total Mexican Libraries	309
Grand Total of Libraries Listed	37,042

Note: Numbers followed by an asterisk are added to find "Total libraries counted" for each of the four geographic areas (United States, U.S.-administered regions, Canada, and Mexico). The sum of the four totals is the "Grand total of libraries listed" in *ALD*. For details on the count of libraries, see the preface to the forty-seventh edition of *ALD—Ed.*

†Federal, state, and other statistical sources use this figure (libraries *excluding* branches) as the total for public libraries.

Highlights of NCES Surveys

Public Libraries

The following are highlights from *E.D. TABS Public Libraries in the United States: 1992*, released in May 1994.

Number of Libraries, Service Outlets, Governance

- 8,946 public libraries (administrative entities) were reported in the 50 states and the District of Columbia in 1992 (Table 1).
- Nearly 71 percent of the population of legally served areas in the United States was served by 957 (nearly 11 percent) public libraries. Each of these public libraries has a legal service area population of 50,000 or more (Tables 1A and 1B).
- 1,463 public libraries (over 16 percent) reported one or more branch library outlets, with a total of 7,035 branches. The total number of central library outlets reported was 8,837. The total number of stationary outlets reported (central library outlets and branch library outlets) was 15,872. Nearly 10 percent of reporting public libraries had one or more bookmobile outlets, with a total of 1,066 (Table 2).

- Over 81 percent of public libraries had only one service outlet (Table 17).
- Nearly 57 percent of public libraries were governed by a municipal government; almost 12 percent by a county/parish; nearly 10 percent by a nonprofit association or agency; over 6 percent by a library district; over 5 percent had multijurisdictional governance under an intergovernmental agreement; over 3 percent were governed by a school district; and over 1 percent by a combination of school/public or academic/public libraries. For over 5 percent of public libraries, their governance did not fit into any of these categories (Table 16).

Income, Expenditures, Staffing

- Public libraries reported that nearly 79 percent of total operating income of nearly $5.0 billion came from local sources, 12 percent from the state, 1 percent from federal sources, and over 8 percent from other sources, such as gifts and donations, service fees, and fines (Table 5).
- Per capita operating income from local sources was under $3 for over 14 percent of public libraries, $3 to $14.99 for nearly 54 percent and $15 or more for 32 percent. Per capita income from local sources varies considerably, with a percentage distribution of about 10 percent in each of 10 categories reported (Table 6).
- Total operating expenditures for public libraries were over $4.5 billion in 1992. Of this, nearly 65 percent was for paid full-time-equivalent (FTE) staff and over 15 percent for the library collection (Table 7). The average U.S. per capita operating expenditure was $18.73. The highest state average per capita operating expenditure was $35.81 and the lowest was $7.45 (Table 14).
- Over 42 percent of public libraries reported operating expenditures of less than $50,000 in 1992. Nearly 38 percent expended between $50,000 and $399,999, and over 20 percent exceeded $400,000 (Table 8).

Staffing, Collections

- Public libraries reported a total of 109,933 paid FTE staff (Table 3).
- Nationwide, public libraries reported over 642.6 million book and serial volumes in their collections, or 2.7 volumes per capita. By state, the number of volumes per capita ranged from 1.6 to 5.5 (Table 11).
- Nationwide, public libraries reported collections of over 22.6 million audio materials, about 532,000 films, and nearly 6.8 million video materials (Table 11).

Circulation, Interlibrary Loans

- Total nationwide circulation of library materials was over 1.5 billion or 6.4 per capita. Highest statewide circulation per capita was 11.7 and lowest was 3.2 (Table 15).
- Nationwide, nearly 6.8 million library materials were loaned by public libraries to other libraries (Table 15).

Academic Libraries

The following are highlights from *E.D. TABS Academic Libraries: 1992*, released in November 1994.

- In 1992, total operating expenditures for libraries at the 3,274 institutions of higher education totaled $3.6 billion (Table 1A).
- The three largest individual expenditure items for all academic libraries were salaries and wages, $1.9 billion (51.8 percent); current serial subscription expenditures, $639 million (17.5 percent); and print material expenditures, $421 million (11.5 percent) (Tables 2A and 3A).
- The libraries of the 500 doctoral-granting institutions (15.3 percent of the total institutions) accounted for $2.3 billion, or 62 percent of the total operating expenditure dollars at all college and university libraries. This included $1.1 billion for salaries and wages, $467 million current serial subscription expenditures, and $253 million print material expenditures (Tables 2B and 3B).
- The number of volumes held at all academic libraries at the end of FY 1992 totaled about 749 million (Table 5A).
- Libraries at institutions granting doctoral degrees held about 471 million volumes, or 63 percent of the total volumes held (Table 5B).
- The total number of full-time-equivalent (FTE) staff members in college and university libraries equaled about 96,000, including about 26,000 librarians and other professional staff, 40,000 other paid staff, 29,000 student assistants, and 404 staff who contributed their services (Table 4A).
- Libraries at institutions granting doctoral degrees accounted for 52,000, or half of all, FTE staff at all academic libraries. This included about 14,000 librarians and other professional staff, 24,000 other paid staff, 14,000 student assistants, and 128 staff who contributed their services (Table 4B).
- Academic libraries had 229 million circulation transactions; 78.8 percent from general collections, and 21.2 percent from reserve collections (Table 9A).
- Libraries at institutions granting doctoral degrees accounted for more than half of this total circulation with 129 million circulation transactions (Table 9B).

For further information about statistics collected by the National Center for Education Statistics, see the article in Part 1—*Ed.*

Library Acquisition Expenditures, 1993–1994: U.S. Public, Academic, Special, and Government Libraries

For more than two decades, the R. R. Bowker Company has compiled statistics on public and academic library acquisition expenditures (Tables 1 and 2) from information reported in the *American Library Directory (ALD)*. Since 1987, statistics also have been compiled for special and government libraries (Tables 3 and 4). The information in these tables is taken from the 47th edition of the directory (1994–1995). The total number of U.S. libraries listed in the 47th edition of *ALD* is 32,625, including 15,346 public libraries, 4,914 academic libraries, 10,059 special libraries, and 1,864 government libraries.

Understanding the Tables

Number of libraries includes only those U.S. libraries in *ALD* that reported annual acquisition expenditures (5,638 public libraries, 2,727 academic libraries, 2,031 special libraries, 511 government libraries). Libraries that reported annual income but not expenditures are not included in the count. Academic libraries include university, college, and junior college libraries. Special academic libraries, such as law and medical libraries, that reported acquisition expenditures separately from the institution's main library are counted as independent libraries.

The amount in the *total acquisition expenditures* column for a given state is generally greater than the sum of the categories of expenditures. This is because the total acquisition expenditures amount also includes the expenditures of libraries that did not itemize by category.

Figures in *categories of expenditure* columns represent only those libraries that itemized expenditures. Libraries that reported a total acquisition expenditure amount but did not itemize are only represented in the total acquisition expenditures column.

Unspecified includes monies reported as not specifically for books, periodicals, audiovisual materials and equipment, microform, preservation, other print materials, manuscripts and archives, machine-readable materials, or database fees (e.g., library materials). This column also includes monies reported for categories in combination—for example, audiovisual *and* microform. When libraries report only total acquisition expenditures without itemizing by category, the total amount is not reflected as unspecified.

Table 1 / Public Library Acquisition Expenditures

State	Number of Libraries	Total Acquisition Expenditures	Books	Other Print Materials	Periodicals	Manuscripts & Archives	AV Materials	AV Equipment	Microform	Machine-Readable Materials	Preservation	Database Fees	Unspecified
Alabama	72	5,893,542	2,965,919	320,418	422,146	—	367,074	19,653	362,186	76,141	15,029	61,927	391,434
Alaska	23	1,853,630	964,525	62,227	253,152	—	170,074	21,200	80,198	26,885	22,468	144,294	11,748
Arizona	54	10,331,771	6,888,249	29,590	1,336,169	168,500	271,305	23,974	325,319	476,140	132,747	108,098	22,623
Arkansas	31	2,449,079	1,178,185	1,941	280,073	6,500	32,977	13,688	53,919	5,850	17,898	59,525	10,641
California	168	87,285,732	34,762,170	868,846	25,470,880	136,979	4,009,096	36,571	3,731,272	384,205	424,008	1,595,177	1,853,068
Colorado	94	11,102,548	6,649,282	2,360	1,079,803	10,859	424,678	14,263	168,968	109,536	26,583	184,758	82,955
Connecticut	134	12,410,617	6,699,110	51,769	954,092	350	754,707	23,689	238,336	130,259	52,103	411,268	112,314
Delaware	20	2,301,794	672,187	1,000	95,834	—	45,269	9,805	16,740	20,810	—	33,912	—
District of Columbia	3	36,363,700	30,000	—	5,000	—	5,000	—	—	—	—	—	5,000
Florida	104	36,441,549	18,052,813	95,994	2,583,173	—	2,010,968	115,889	816,171	565,791	125,266	334,562	157,167
Georgia	52	12,400,239	5,375,891	57,051	622,742	—	534,702	12,133	225,939	19,033	24,532	13,383	32,482
Hawaii	2	3,138,414	2,150,717	—	857,048	—	39,600	18,000	69,049	—	—	4,000	—
Idaho	64	2,428,516	1,175,477	3,385	176,544	—	112,610	2,000	16,110	5,700	24,661	68,713	12,025
Illinois	366	48,762,109	24,045,361	230,958	3,559,646	3,010	2,700,264	244,336	725,630	348,268	88,086	711,373	384,027
Indiana	168	25,007,748	14,056,902	25,863	2,123,967	—	2,347,850	214,782	298,555	287,068	169,659	194,475	934,918
Iowa	293	7,860,556	4,908,973	73,200	708,778	259	456,599	53,625	63,518	116,900	13,654	74,494	49,885
Kansas	169	8,102,396	5,044,675	68,014	715,494	—	475,157	13,863	28,337	89,613	29,976	178,238	266,536
Kentucky	84	6,036,030	2,296,811	8,667	236,962	2,060	209,132	45,235	63,979	12,363	13,669	19,176	328,399
Louisiana	56	11,903,987	4,675,563	58,292	979,049	—	348,703	29,649	47,466	8,681	43,870	69,849	771,540
Maine	117	2,219,945	1,276,666	2,718	216,885	1,198	97,657	8,355	24,002	6,985	18,503	31,518	13,975
Maryland	26	15,761,210	7,007,153	16,800	630,184	718	1,844,529	4,567	11,560	189,550	2,914	41,786	35,835
Massachusetts	257	20,110,797	12,992,965	36,899	1,785,818	500	749,524	51,162	285,128	205,457	45,988	211,594	384,173
Michigan	263	30,385,507	11,644,451	273,409	1,965,982	1,950	1,773,044	40,748	402,598	135,188	36,329	317,143	629,750
Minnesota	101	15,127,116	9,041,129	145,599	1,050,692	—	1,000,303	27,306	97,529	88,548	42,775	819,861	15,531
Mississippi	42	3,415,489	1,929,166	17,672	307,305	2,963	129,750	7,530	47,789	27,132	10,286	11,830	14,456

Missouri	86	17,158,594	9,906,833	9,080	-,468,-57	2-9	1,280,818	27,883	604,569	190,555	77,250	109,523	757,663
Montana	46	1,314,054	551,539	300	133,-70	—	32,132	11,659	6,112	14,150	5,593	97,812	83,413
Nebraska	90	2,938,151	1,305,964	7,925	277,-71	—	83,482	6,343	18,815	20,510	19,820	41,822	1,100
Nevada	18	6,654,798	765,951	2,000	214,-96	—	22,320	10,585	21,298	1,000	4,341	34,712	3,500
New Hampshire	126	3,146,426	1,506,211	9,470	259,-84	—	111,503	18,350	57,323	21,133	18,960	5,111	13,184
New Jersey	235	31,022,135	16,538,848	130,580	3,024,-57	1,3-6	1,514,710	208,951	532,282	667,972	103,440	477,487	462,619
New Mexico	34	3,357,707	747,864	11,100	264,-58	—	53,297	6,750	12,610	3,275	6,500	142,379	—
New York	436	87,649,393	47,634,919	2,062,367	8,366,-10	26,300	3,-66,367	349,812	1,110,978	421,917	1,471,156	530,577	681,839
North Carolina	94	17,273,869	11,197,615	120,296	-,489,-58	2,100	1,-71,141	156,882	241,424	216,454	109,341	132,553	569,870
North Dakota	30	1,474,779	747,985	26,311	149,-84	—	49,268	8,920	30,117	36,702	4,405	56,025	4,503
Ohio	207	63,720,835	33,669,779	930,730	6,844,-20	4,032	6,456,955	114,614	1,124,499	589,499	1,062,681	762,070	276,034
Oklahoma	50	5,644,159	3,185,137	8,457	684,-08	—	318,558	41,461	32,725	20,655	26,004	174,961	274,977
Oregon	77	23,402,046	4,728,411	2,705	-,037,-17	—	611,671	5,335	31,964	62,226	55,531	61,599	31,236
Pennsylvania	317	19,210,485	10,585,881	92,813	2,093,-27	120	1,007,269	68,937	600,419	183,992	192,702	366,374	698,115
Rhode Island	34	2,198,695	1,330,311	—	229,-07	25,052	-34,841	3,647	44,225	83,403	38,279	64,561	3,229
South Carolina	40	8,137,688	5,265,271	29,971	922,-83	3,100	434,638	20,667	94,791	125,337	49,716	32,920	169,908
South Dakota	44	2,241,713	1,004,994	5,765	181,-73	—	-64,502	21,276	29,056	7,840	1,650	342,072	26,665
Tennessee	76	9,705,767	5,331,466	54,429	944,-52	250	632,299	19,105	179,742	17,100	73,465	145,377	1,746,032
Texas	261	32,022,762	16,944,065	124,011	3,964,-84	1,7-5	1,590,295	81,235	313,569	219,508	207,569	263,747	732,343
Utah	30	6,476,090	3,457,064	40,226	450,-53	—	352,734	31,523	42,776	310	19,941	38,900	14,491
Vermont	98	1,511,936	934,071	2,484	148,-69	—	39,092	2,024	10,223	1,779	8,360	1,687	5,266
Virginia	76	23,883,302	12,998,890	261,496	2,193,-49	54,750	805,433	24,984	442,174	183,610	100,340	137,927	546,184
Washington	57	21,939,706	8,949,550	157,942	2,297,-76	100	1,-38,320	4,210	371,112	140,356	40,812	298,356	121,837
West Virginia	54	2,658,707	1,057,949	2,050	141,-41	500	-03,867	7,300	11,776	5,445	12,839	12,816	80,234
Wisconsin	231	14,946,094	8,342,980	92,948	1,727,-14	145	1,053,175	55,703	125,309	93,995	46,285	286,038	710,864
Wyoming	23	1,572,041	643,338	5,094	97,-96	—	67,634	29,090	33,114	896	14,102	71,270	145,092
Pacific Islands	1	180,000	—	2,500	—	—	—	—	—	—	—	—	—
Puerto Rico	4	2,172,735	658,791	4,250	1,4C7,-41	—	—	—	—	200	85,724	8,029	8,000
Virgin Islands	—	—	—	—	—	—	—	—	—	—	—	—	—
Total	5,638	832,708,688	396,476,017	6,649,972	89,452,373	455,545	43,606,845	2,389,269	14 323,000	6,665,922	5,237,810	10,397,659	14,688,680
Estimated % of Acquisition Expenditures		67.16	1.13	1E.15	0.08	7.39	0.4	2.43	1.13	0.89	1.76		2.49

449

Table 2 / Academic Library Acquisition Expenditures

State	Number of Libraries	Total Acquisition Expenditures	Books	Other Print Materials	Periodicals	Manuscripts & Archives	AV Materials	AV Equipment	Microform	Machine-Readable Materials	Preservation	Database Fees	Unspecified
Alabama	50	18,492,159	5,922,661	97,114	9,872,272	3,750	157,802	146,662	337,678	67,913	570,001	150,165	282,967
Alaska	7	2,559,695	418,067	4,190	636,696	1,000	1,611	2,000	80,152	55,469	56,933	47,100	29,444
Arizona	25	20,460,555	2,159,744	37,990	3,098,558	—	89,283	55,237	105,460	182,501	104,729	119,167	712,002
Arkansas	26	10,665,956	2,620,343	60,062	4,597,586	2,673	206,786	33,440	311,801	203,382	154,085	526,597	53,385
California	210	118,726,714	27,435,694	2,464,531	44,665,479	34,541	905,484	682,948	2,137,751	1,223,091	4,316,330	1,142,877	7,048,478
Colorado	42	28,114,763	4,800,680	59,431	7,282,413	850	249,147	38,878	498,628	432,195	344,122	451,920	86,858
Connecticut	56	37,724,504	8,235,239	107,988	9,950,697	626,100	176,197	121,867	1,270,973	286,786	608,800	159,887	2,961,355
Delaware	5	4,669,614	2,142,098	20,000	2,264,708	45	12,100	10,370	18,254	1,000	2,700	44,178	150,888
District of Columbia	29	18,879,701	4,548,807	151,159	7,629,506	500	110,722	50,025	138,192	135,782	132,788	201,528	642,232
Florida	83	39,123,353	7,679,489	307,341	13,550,614	6,866	645,233	283,576	1,010,728	797,374	582,562	436,224	487,371
Georgia	61	28,304,738	7,109,059	1,010,839	13,301,082	30,000	276,858	243,931	1,271,302	555,147	246,773	846,270	506,941
Hawaii	13	5,929,623	2,001,171	600	2,611,319	—	70,197	19,000	56,084	60,330	254,489	37,580	163,825
Idaho	11	5,366,000	1,104,218	49,400	2,563,933	500	56,938	2,500	68,093	21,565	133,563	47,160	460,122
Illinois	105	60,614,914	16,328,506	466,532	23,348,642	8,815	722,788	703,807	1,059,300	803,705	951,568	686,761	791,299
Indiana	57	27,708,113	7,962,237	724,608	14,942,027	256,220	279,594	299,341	167,041	273,383	648,637	386,260	167,448
Iowa	44	18,755,435	3,555,131	25,182	5,907,056	1,200	168,623	121,409	64,951	124,979	133,389	104,932	278,475
Kansas	45	12,830,059	4,956,171	90,586	6,599,839	43,861	95,590	106,761	97,659	200,592	222,817	76,845	63,223
Kentucky	45	16,761,282	3,651,552	932,633	5,612,762	25,900	141,948	36,896	289,359	214,952	335,314	212,888	267,566
Louisiana	36	18,197,666	4,183,108	156,058	9,331,902	22,939	91,899	194,028	294,203	319,555	428,426	192,162	88,999
Maine	22	6,954,639	2,317,722	235,956	3,259,014	9,300	72,528	63,704	158,140	73,970	160,215	111,627	43,621
Maryland	48	21,170,695	6,565,714	299,794	10,348,672	—	205,109	221,298	323,062	292,980	279,797	269,621	799,454
Massachusetts	99	59,795,273	18,343,176	874,552	19,798,013	8,019	559,095	206,601	678,100	733,115	2,206,884	1,250,898	4,742,403
Michigan	98	51,438,889	10,172,105	463,315	19,874,914	10,448	429,895	259,724	589,250	523,857	910,759	609,008	1,289,772
Minnesota	48	22,330,964	7,088,891	134,905	9,590,367	2,855	795,304	290,895	108,686	142,606	844,735	216,340	696,169
Mississippi	26	8,913,477	1,557,195	27,902	5,812,181	500	130,455	85,579	244,363	130,812	230,978	48,394	265,306

Missouri	73	29,887,342	7,229,476	79,071	15,621,382	12,614	427,830	259,462	738,381	708,907	566,374	396,021	1,053,569
Montana	14	3,723,598	705,364	1,958	2,293,987	—	172,505	8,850	7,042	17,282	6,300	125,161	79,573
Nebraska	24	10,259,678	1,775,534	111,728	2,737,463	—	137,519	93,659	127,721	89,697	102,080	171,682	584,024
Nevada	7	6,088,646	2,391,770	—	2,701,095	—	121,573	36,941	194,403	117,975	177,117	14,780	110,158
New Hampshire	19	5,135,536	766,908	38,415	602,862	—	42,155	37,719	114,628	96,028	27,041	22,062	63,965
New Jersey	60	27,882,204	8,314,980	613,691	9,837,466	91,134	175,683	140,683	771,508	505,017	193,682	197,132	299,734
New Mexico	25	8,728,993	1,983,847	8,500	5,431,463	3,108	119,297	66,533	122,229	91,111	71,479	141,793	499,707
New York	203	98,648,778	21,195,882	2,181,823	33,416,814	15,614	1,018,893	535,844	1,981,853	1,659,682	1,828,434	1,520,377	5,181,565
North Carolina	96	54,155,540	11,318,277	169,749	17,469,998	7,970	805,411	677,332	1,060,997	1,114,809	606,326	529,948	421,503
North Dakota	15	4,130,000	1,022,322	19,357	2,389,696	—	37,609	34,884	74,450	17,713	64,932	60,472	33,920
Ohio	123	52,447,283	14,350,747	307,249	27,201,498	977	661,361	175,655	674,974	588,276	1,327,455	425,849	252,405
Oklahoma	38	14,253,974	2,944,440	112,235	7,585,793	470,800	100,619	111,049	195,089	175,720	323,582	180,102	188,408
Oregon	38	13,772,834	4,156,058	3,267	6,799,956	2,500	219,322	70,565	350,429	228,685	286,102	318,327	118,827
Pennsylvania	147	63,533,508	12,071,024	804,048	20,438,608	30,707	757,947	326,140	1,246,481	874,858	1,499,104	735,621	905,886
Rhode Island	12	13,247,287	652,303	16,000	821,717	2,797	51,379	33,210	88,093	56,739	42,470	18,338	235,496
South Carolina	46	13,814,795	3,765,385	482,358	6,166,302	3,270	253,806	61,269	335,177	244,382	284,704	221,295	309,660
South Dakota	17	4,276,444	883,700	—	2,018,929	500	37,565	49,621	38,230	24,076	70,152	43,806	211,305
Tennessee	58	26,120,053	6,458,695	596,280	3,177,533	41,550	336,034	195,677	396,725	343,743	396,437	289,319	1,202,069
Texas	147	78,967,381	20,242,034	761,175	34,858,664	46,157	1,580,897	782,669	1,787,860	1,485,951	1,524,338	1,793,171	1,493,840
Utah	9	7,247,175	2,427,425	8,898	3,383,231	14,611	81,905	83,125	11,049	143,083	236,977	81,772	6,313
Vermont	22	7,193,731	2,410,759	5,590	2,848,345	584	74,713	34,224	154,962	187,836	124,980	157,271	1,118,704
Virginia	70	39,350,299	11,300,207	496,558	18,295,456	4,200	587,885	134,699	1,266,189	1,062,420	784,988	361,001	1,131,074
Washington	43	22,919,604	6,391,280	225,727	12,919,106	—	359,125	381,961	326,437	245,199	187,564	303,589	172,428
West Virginia	28	7,054,657	1,719,992	71,192	3,548,033	—	69,165	152,704	207,197	96,502	87,313	166,164	457,911
Wisconsin	61	22,873,131	4,818,457	40,822	8,445,847	13,038	486,785	188,163	628,848	556,706	300,182	437,715	617,160
Wyoming	6	3,550,555	1,043,164	—	2,044,932	—	28,612	—	6,396	5,500	77,982	30,184	289,743
Pacific Islands	3	525,089	57,052	400	152,839	—	34,520	850	—	—	—	5,000	—
Puerto Rico	31	4,469,495	919,350	1,900	1,891,513	500	208,250	62,518	32,713	36,640	54,000	21,349	63,456
Virgin Islands	1	257,200	—	—	—	—	—	—	—	—	—	—	—
Total	2,727	1,309,003,591	316,175,210	15,960,659	521,427,900	1,859,513	15,649,551	9,016,483	24,319,271	18,631,578	26,114,139	17,145,690	40,182,006
Estimated % of Acquisition Expenditures		51.41	51.81	1.59	51.81	0.18	1.55	0.9	2.42	1.85	2.59	1.7	3.99

Table 3 / Special Library Acquisition Expenditures

State	Number of Libraries	Total Acquisition Expenditures	Books	Other Print Materials	Periodicals	Manuscripts & Archives	AV Materials	AV Equipment	Microform	Machine-Readable Materials	Preservation	Database Fees	Unspecified
Alabama	8	602,200	126,200	6,000	201,000	1,000	11,000	—	13,000	30,000	8,000	35,000	104,000
Alaska	6	82,200	20,600	3,000	15,300	800	—	1,700	—	16,100	2,700	17,000	—
Arizona	30	1,293,994	190,245	6,300	282,757	1,100	168,620	1,000	15,480	14,041	10,600	266,793	168,875
Arkansas	3	43,822	15,060	100	28,262	—	—	—	400	—	—	—	—
California	203	12,794,740	1,889,123	132,583	3,110,387	79,470	290,011	65,837	165,860	363,730	164,151	2,328,335	133,954
Colorado	37	2,710,927	314,007	12,000	1,035,225	36,400	71,048	14,480	85,311	71,550	18,628	302,840	109,380
Connecticut	51	3,482,747	603,242	120,999	847,141	31,250	35,445	19,400	22,070	39,709	114,381	163,853	34,247
Delaware	9	1,510,183	256,463	—	154,862	8,980	5,355	4,300	7,435	—	32,628	76,260	568,000
District of Columbia	64	11,303,957	1,635,025	358,850	2,217,859	8,800	7,150	12,700	46,664	33,700	213,317	320,672	37,000
Florida	58	2,640,881	626,711	4,885	884,387	10,200	45,143	17,618	62,706	59,096	41,431	353,265	54,135
Georgia	25	1,099,264	194,514	2,000	199,404	—	27,414	10,000	6,720	14,718	24,321	120,580	2,619
Hawaii	8	375,426	60,517	200	154,195	—	300	100	—	6,200	1,284	29,775	—
Idaho	7	232,635	67,000	—	98,435	—	1,000	—	—	12,000	—	19,200	—
Illinois	114	8,976,658	1,526,493	70,463	2,048,092	70,525	65,020	35,100	353,483	130,673	193,537	335,304	63,067
Indiana	48	1,560,919	254,295	114,300	486,531	602	29,628	30,578	30,020	93,475	3,850	247,588	9,367
Iowa	28	1,027,888	415,578	30,787	329,480	750	25,339	41,218	700	11,120	9,993	51,622	4,645
Kansas	17	248,646	64,573	3,900	85,517	—	5,531	7,375	12,250	—	4,275	6,172	275
Kentucky	14	458,707	107,075	—	124,507	10,000	8,500	5,300	19,500	7,500	4,700	3,025	—
Louisiana	7	336,115	66,960	2,425	211,559	2,000	6,251	2,480	3,500	5,000	5,330	30,610	—
Maine	22	691,099	74,557	3,200	323,609	200	19,288	5,887	40,000	1,000	54,400	62,244	4,565
Maryland	61	4,143,091	950,874	70,137	1,637,075	2,550	35,104	35,332	98,004	31,345	44,121	475,656	50,800
Massachusetts	96	9,279,826	3,047,188	40,765	2,347,272	20,300	80,682	14,268	49,754	185,650	112,828	940,244	80,626
Michigan	57	3,949,127	1,277,090	47,396	1,420,947	600	53,531	8,050	37,569	144,027	26,327	265,253	21,719
Minnesota	45	2,888,550	1,211,295	89,951	393,236	7,873	16,561	23,581	111,602	48,662	48,456	211,160	26,525
Mississippi	6	154,254	21,250	1,025	122,745	400	800	1,100	2,225	—	1,634	—	—

Missouri	46	3,234,072	563,601	75,052	791,421	12,010	43,938	4,820	12,534	12,720	156,786	541,650	154,711
Montana	11	160,440	41,682	4,030	77,440	5,600	14,444	735	10,683	600	3,111	550	—
Nebraska	17	244,223	53,279	400	60,693	2,000	2,420	—	39,102	300	1,250	2,445	10,927
Nevada	5	102,583	23,950	—	52,675	500	5,400	12,000	1,500	200	2,600	2,105	—
New Hampshire	14	1,035,524	274,620	8,000	393,948	4,000	525	631	315	46,500	25,000	12,385	—
New Jersey	61	4,712,286	1,570,721	30,675	1,080,212	1,500	25,247	26,453	71,600	23,923	12,625	200,940	57,821
New Mexico	25	2,554,171	586,395	3,900	1,510,573	430	7,150	2,500	2,450	3,742	9,250	18,000	3,861
New York	203	23,427,103	4,329,436	636,049	3,567,924	74,050	100,260	2,049,142	152,383	274,720	329,783	4,165,275	123,003
North Carolina	33	1,682,248	425,802	3,450	704,192	20	20,035	47,500	50,288	100,580	3,900	50,058	1,500
North Dakota	6	216,133	50,584	1,427	86,371	—	6,430	7,355	—	20,638	27,367	10,680	3,399
Ohio	100	7,983,193	2,073,272	322,635	1,971,301	1,750	115,464	39,314	99,169	39,680	103,270	340,884	74,266
Oklahoma	15	458,479	184,141	2,249	166,643	3,000	3,150	4,200	32,000	1,000	45,300	5,550	175
Oregon	21	767,982	94,052	5,125	200,874	—	1,823	582	4,125	13,485	866	72,150	—
Pennsylvania	131	7,732,255	1,005,916	148,354	2,000,234	57,507	63,413	37,289	128,636	478,507	176,261	252,185	157,628
Rhode Island	9	96,520	30,026	200	12,042	1,400	2,769	1,500	1,100	2,600	8,644	5,000	839
South Carolina	14	479,045	47,760	1,695	72,149	3,500	23,054	6,500	19,000	—	9,014	19,944	9,770
South Dakota	6	146,697	49,631	95	56,405	—	6,244	129	—	2,030	—	15,336	337
Tennessee	31	1,701,354	319,933	2,314	772,447	1,017	46,809	5,783	25,513	164,610	27,956	40,244	6,967
Texas	74	7,558,876	1,586,084	89,300	2,024,493	12,000	37,874	29,414	51,699	129,132	85,137	263,805	90,230
Utah	6	313,550	103,035	26,000	79,515	5,000	5,000	—	—	—	—	770	24,000
Vermont	12	112,907	16,000	169	12,590	1,595	—	200	—	—	6,729	5,690	6,823
Virginia	69	3,287,586	603,890	59,151	615,435	33,609	22,141	50,100	138,100	131,400	78,178	231,005	54,247
Washington	32	2,090,091	310,741	9,189	916,659	17,911	5,260	106,275	22,000	178,700	15,262	179,063	4,461
West Virginia	10	543,717	75,310	1,500	382,090	—	9,800	4,075	10,100	3,000	885	14,000	12,075
Wisconsin	46	1,716,718	612,140	49,215	403,565	6,166	17,595	18,000	12,160	16,558	14,123	131,262	96,258
Wyoming	7	52,850	18,000	1,150	5,200	—	300	—	200	—	4,200	600	2,200
Pacific Islands	—	—	—	—	—	—	—	—	—	—	—	—	—
Puerto Rico	3	192,558	162,437	—	10,390	—	8,492	—	5,000	—	2,739	—	3,500
Virgin Islands	—	—	—	—	—	—	—	—	—	—	—	—	—
** Total	2,031	144,491,017	30,228,373	2,602,590	36,787,265	533,335	1,603,758	2,811,901	2,073,910	2,963,921	2,290,828	13,244,027	2,372,797
Estimated % of Acquisition	31			2.67	37.73	0.55	1.64	2.88	2.13	3.04	2.35	13.58	2.43

453

Table 4 / Government Library Acquisition Expenditures

State	Number of Libraries	Total Acquisition Expenditures	Books	Other Print Materials	Periodicals	Manuscripts & Archives	AV Materials	AV Equipment	Microform	Machine-Readable Materials	Preservation	Database Fees	Unspecified
Alabama	5	237,442	88,172	1,277	16,856	—	3,000	—	3,000	2,150	3,720	5,670	5,645
Alaska	8	196,155	44,440	500	123,100	—	500	—	5,000	3,200	—	16,700	2,715
Arizona	13	1,123,170	96,900	4,500	94,200	1,000	6,300	100	2,500	3,500	3,500	11,600	14,000
Arkansas	3	130,990	55,815	2,878	52,369	—	8,928	—	—	500	—	5,203	5,297
California	58	9,440,133	2,160,649	651,830	3,409,159	—	200,062	35,238	89,204	33,850	94,315	374,071	121,620
Colorado	18	1,003,890	154,018	5,600	287,437	45,800	16,561	15,802	13,074	12,000	1,000	35,878	13,446
Connecticut	4	30,980	3,156	2,000	7,856	—	300	—	—	—	—	—	1,278
Delaware	2	108,073	86,873	1,500	7,100	—	1,000	3,000	4,700	—	950	—	2,950
District of Columbia	23	6,270,200	1,652,500	68,100	1,774,500	200	51,600	30,800	159,400	173,400	25,250	1,684,500	225,000
Florida	29	2,241,910	520,794	8,246	656,954	2,000	62,065	21,369	14,491	10,721	14,464	44,968	12,052
Georgia	3	155,700	80,900	5,700	61,100	—	1,000	—	—	7,500	500	—	—
Hawaii	2	771,888	160,990	480,120	20,000	—	4,000	—	56,000	—	—	1,000	49,778
Idaho	1	31,270	6,500	—	17,000	—	470	—	300	—	—	4,000	3,000
Illinois	13	4,619,897	1,036,795	—	398,022	—	7,300	3,000	49,958	700	86,500	16,000	15,512
Indiana	9	463,103	91,267	—	29,319	—	7,306	1,260	1,000	350	4,044	3,054	5,000
Iowa	6	147,643	30,725	500	89,250	20	1,900	400	3,000	2,000	—	6,200	5,000
Kansas	4	629,669	229,851	191,702	155,636	—	3,400	—	100	—	30,331	13,549	5,000
Kentucky	4	1,045,417	524,627	12,000	51,803	—	82,515	—	—	12,500	2,500	341,372	9,200
Louisiana	6	2,736,865	9,450	786	80,600	—	954	—	2,000	12,500	—	9,200	7,300
Maine	5	349,524	22,533	—	217,343	—	4,143	20,000	1,969	20,000	957	42,255	19,111
Maryland	14	10,434,367	1,365,119	2,000	4,118,556	25,000	155,000	20,100	10,000	37,000	1,137,728	499,536	135,505
Massachusetts	22	2,627,272	1,856,025	—	229,081	1,000	12,500	910	12,379	48,670	3,450	19,500	30,000
Michigan	14	999,187	199,023	14,050	264,732	—	32,777	—	24,359	6,820	2,820	21,812	5,514
Minnesota	11	1,892,593	89,718	212,650	736,626	3,000	9,600	18,400	35,000	30,500	11,500	83,474	9,675
Mississippi	3	212,610	11,800	—	34,052	—	4,495	—	—	—	494	4,924	9,675

State													
Missouri	7	448,711	28,218	11,700	45,777	—	7,000	16,500	750	21,220	2,000	3,300	—
Montana	5	273,521	10,222	35	19,581	—	150	3,803	3,900	5,200	—	1,881	1,400
Nebraska	4	121,609	16,399	—	39,590	—	52,570	8,000	—	50	—	1,000	4,000
Nevada	6	867,763	413,225	2,000	76,545	—	4,900	407	27,858	955	4,368	64,905	1,000
New Hampshire	2	55,500	2,000	5,000	18,000	—	1,000	—	29,500	—	—	—	—
New Jersey	9	412,665	101,212	5,000	109,653	3,000	—	—	2,000	—	1,000	89,000	7,000
New Mexico	7	489,977	110,533	187,342	72,802	—	10,300	3,500	13,800	12,000	10,500	40,000	—
New York	41	4,365,331	1,510,979	37,655	489,738	—	72,293	2,300	48,934	65,068	12,856	59,200	20,901
North Carolina	11	1,631,395	506,352	3,050	779,787	—	5,040	—	17,587	4,140	15,978	206,000	3,215
North Dakota	3	90,205	29,971	—	47,454	—	785	400	1,595	400	100	5,250	3,650
Ohio	16	1,173,285	278,170	14,700	521,480	—	16,030	1,000	3,585	4,600	2,500	15,991	30,655
Oklahoma	8	519,548	118,196	—	148,430	—	280	5,000	—	70	—	10,600	220
Oregon	6	490,439	115,200	—	181,300	—	—	—	3,500	151,300	—	10,439	—
Pennsylvania	23	1,740,194	723,476	36,250	109,256	—	6,488	4,808	9,000	—	27,100	14,000	42,497
Rhode Island	4	446,362	302,314	—	79,349	—	2,040	—	7,895	12,917	4,000	36,347	—
South Carolina	4	137,693	46,600	—	8,300	—	20,500	5,000	—	—	—	54,355	—
South Dakota	6	81,264	23,839	—	39,706	—	4,643	2,117	2,400	350	—	850	4,751
Tennessee	6	269,162	66,985	500	145,681	—	13,671	10,300	8,000	—	5,421	5,980	3,000
Texas	8	103,479	42,158	1,287	32,923	1,052	5,696	400	61,880	350	9,350	284	—
Utah	6	1,019,473	55,866	2,303	139,300	—	24,769	16,582	3,000	6,937	12,030	19,507	25,599
Vermont	3	70,818	19,850	1,500	300	1,200	200	—	1,000	5,000	5,000	200	—
Virginia	11	1,073,501	127,500	11,500	344,571	—	12,820	—	3,000	91,000	6,222	171,820	151,000
Washington	10	1,333,515	119,511	—	150,395	10,000	75,000	3,000	6,500	2,000	26,236	10,028	36,729
West Virginia	5	847,300	401,500	12,900	104,500	400	4,300	330	16,294	31,200	11,000	31,500	22,000
Wisconsin	12	603,714	378,692	—	128,728	—	8,500	—	8,000	6,595	500	56,219	5,936
Wyoming	5	259,249	170,592	1,000	55,600	—	—	10,000	—	—	—	5,057	—
Pacific Islands	—	—	—	—	—	—	—	—	—	—	—	—	—
Puerto Rico	3	737,490	208,990	—	525,500	—	—	500	—	—	—	—	4,500
Virgin Islands	—	—	—	—	—	—	—	—	—	—	—	—	—
Total	511	67,563,111	16,507,190	1,999,661	17,315,697	93,672	1,025,621	261,296	767,512	821,713	1,580,184	4,158,179	1,066,651
Estimated % of Acquisition Expenditures			36.21	4.39	57.97	0.21	2.25	0.57	1.68	1.8	3.47	9.12	2.34

Library Price Indexes for Colleges and Schools

Kent Halstead

Research Associates of Washington, 2605 Klingle Rd. N.W., Washington, DC 20008
202-966-3326

A rise in prices with the gradual loss of the dollar's buying power has been a continuing phenomenon in the U.S. economy. Libraries have been especially affected by the higher prices of books and periodicals. Price indexes are useful in documenting the impact of inflation. A measure of composite yearly price changes in the items libraries purchase can be projected to determine the additional funding required to maintain buying power. Price indexes can also be used to ascertain if spending has kept pace with inflation. A decline in constant dollars per user means a loss in real investment.

A price index compares the aggregate price level of a fixed market basket of goods and services in a given year with the price in the base year. To measure price change accurately, the *quality* and *quantity* of the items purchased must remain constant as defined in the base year. Weights attached to the importance of each item in the budget are changed infrequently—only when the relative *amount* of the various items purchased clearly shifts or when new items are introduced.

The indexes in Tables 1 through 6 are calculated with FY 1983 as the base year. This means that current prices are expressed as a percentage of prices for 1983. (Prices for library materials are generally quoted for the calendar year. They are reported here for the corresponding *fiscal year*—for example, calendar year 1985 prices are reported for FY 1985–1986.) An index of 110 means that prices have increased 10 percent since the base year. The indexes may be converted to any desired base period by dividing each index number by the value of the index for the selected base year.

Two composite library price indexes and their subcomponents are reported here for 1976–1992. For higher education, the academic library price index (ALPI) reports relative price levels affecting the *total operating budget* of college and university libraries. For elementary-secondary schools, price levels for *new acquisitions* are reported. Subsequent data are currently available from Research Associates of Washington.

Academic Library Price Index

The Academic Library Current Operations and Acquisitions Price Index (ALPI), together with its various subcomponents, is reported in Tables 2 through 5. The ALPI reflects the relative year-to-year price level of the goods and services purchased by college and university libraries for their current operations. Table 1 shows the composition of the library budget for pricing purposes and the 1982–1983 estimated national weighting structure. The priced components are organized in three major categories—personnel compensation; acquisitions; and contracted services, supplies, and materials. Because the size, responsibilities, and collections of academic libraries vary widely within the higher education

Table 1 / Budget Composition of College and University Library Operations by Object Category, FY 1983 Estimate

Category	Percent	Distribution
Personnel Compensation		
1.0 Salaries and wages		50.0
1.1 Administrators	15.0	
1.2 Librarians	30.0	
1.3 Other professionals	5.0	
1.4 Nonprofessional staff	40.0	
1.5 Students	10.0	
	100.0	
2.0 Fringe benefits		10.0
Acquisitions		
3.0 Books and periodicals		26.0
3.1a U.S. college books	20.0	
3.1b North American academic books	20.0	
3.2 Foreign books	10.0	
3.3 U.S. periodicals for academic libraries	40.0	
3.4 Foreign periodicals	10.0	
	100.0	
4.0 Other materials		2.0
4.1 Microfilm	50.0	
4.2 16-mm film	5.0	
4.3 Videocassettes	15.0	
4.4 Filmstrip	10.0	
4.5 Prerecorded cassette tape	10.0	
4.0 Machine readable, CD ROM	10.0	
	100.0	
Contracted Services, Supplies, Equipment		
5.0 Binding		1.2
6.0 Contracted services		5.4
7.0 Supplies and materials		3.0
8.0 Equipment		2.4
		100.0

Source: Derived from the National Center for Education Statistics, U.S. Department of Education, library budget data for 1985 and earlier years.

community, individual libraries may want to compile the price index for their own operations, using the price series in Tables 2 through 5 weighted by the composition of their local library budget. The tailoring procedure using a computer disk is outlined in *Inflation Measures for Schools, Colleges and Libraries: 1994 Update.*[1]

The ALPI reports inflation affecting a fixed market basket of goods and services and hence measures only the added funding necessary to buy the equivalent of last year's purchases. But library operations are seldom "business as usual." The collection acquisitions component in particular requires special attention.

(text continues on p. 465)

Table 2 / Academic Library Price Indexes for Major Components, FYs 1976–1992*

1983=100 Fiscal Year	Personnel Compensation		Acquisitions			Contracted Services, Supplies, and Materials			Library Price Index† ALPI
	Salaries and Wages (L1.0)	Fringe Benefits (L2.0)	Books and Periodicals (L3.0)	Other Acquisitions (L4.0)	Binding (L5.0)	Contracted Services (L6.0)	Supplies and Materials (L7.0)	Equipment (L8.0)	
1976	61.0	47.8	52.7	69.0	60.7	60.0	64.6	61.7	57.8
1977	64.2	52.8	57.8	70.9	64.7	63.5	67.8	64.8	61.6
1978	67.9	58.4	63.4	78.4	69.4	67.0	70.7	69.3	66.1
1979	73.1	64.5	70.9	79.5	75.2	71.0	75.2	74.7	71.8
1980	79.5	72.6	79.2	85.0	83.3	76.5	85.0	81.6	78.9
1981	86.5	81.8	89.7	83.7	89.7	85.3	92.9	89.6	87.0
1982	94.1	91.5	95.1	102.5	97.9	94.8	99.8	96.4	94.6
1983	100.0	100.0	100.0	100.0	100.0	100.0	100.0	100.0	100.0
1984	105.0	108.3	103.8	103.6	105.2	104.7	105.9	102.2	104.9
1985	110.4	117.7	108.7	104.8	106.8	109.2	112.1	104.8	110.4
1986	115.3	127.7	117.7	110.5	107.9	114.3	112.5	106.9	116.6
1987	119.5	137.4	131.7	101.2	111.6	117.8	118.8	108.8	123.6
1988	123.7	147.2	141.4	97.4	116.1	122.1	125.3	110.9	129.7
1989	130.3	158.8	153.1	99.8	124.0	129.0	137.9	115.8	138.2
1990	136.6	171.4	167.8	98.5	125.1	134.2	138.4	120.8	146.8
1991	142.7	184.5	183.6	107.3	126.8	140.2	138.6	123.4	155.9
1992*	147.6	193.9	195.3	105.6	125.6	144.6	133.0	125.9	162.4

*Data for 1993 and 1994 are available from Research Associates of Washington.

†1983 weights: LPI=50.0% salaries and wages + 10% fringe benefits + 26.0% books and periodicals + 2.0% other materials + 1.2% binding + 5.4% contracted services + 3.0% supplies and materials + 2.4% equipment.

Sources: Personnel compensation, see Table 3; acquisitions, see Tables 4 and 5; binding, Bureau of Labor Statistics (BLS), earnings in the printing and publishing industry; contract services, see *Inflation Measures for Schools, Colleges and Libraries: 1994 Update* (Research Associates of Washington); supplies and equipment, Producer Price Index components, BLS.

Table 3 / Academic Library Price Indexes for Personnel Compensation, FYs 1976–1992

1983=100 Fiscal Year		Salaries and Wages					Fringe Benefits (L2.0)
	Administrators (L1.1)	Librarians (L1.2)	Other Professionals (L1.3)	Non-Professionals (L1.4)	Students (L1.5)	Total* (L1.0)	
1976	62.7	62.7	63.9	59.0	60.0	61.0	47.8
1977	65.1	65.1	66.9	62.9	64.4	64.2	52.8
1978	67.6	67.6	70.4	67.7	69.2	67.9	58.4
1979	73.0	73.0	74.5	72.7	74.7	73.1	64.5
1980	78.6	78.6	79.8	79.6	82.2	79.5	72.6
1981	85.4	85.4	86.7	87.0	89.4	86.5	81.8
1982	93.7	93.7	93.9	94.3	95.5	94.1	91.5
1983	100.0	100.0	100.0	100.0	100.0	100.0	100.0
1984	104.9	104.9	104.7	105.6	103.6	105.0	108.3
1985	111.3	111.3	111.6	109.9	107.4	110.4	117.7
1986	117.6	116.8	118.4	114.2	110.3	115.3	127.7
1987	124.2	120.2	125.4	118.3	112.1	119.5	137.4
1988	127.6	123.1	131.6	123.5	116.5	123.7	147.1
1989	138.2	130.6	139.2	128.7	119.9	130.3	158.8
1990	146.0	136.8	147.7	134.5	124.5	136.6	171.4
1991	154.6	143.0	155.7	139.7	129.8	142.7	184.5
1992	156.5	149.2	161.1	144.9	133.8	147.6	193.9

*1983 weights: total salaries = 15% administrators + 30% librarians + 5% other professionals + 40% nonprofessionals + 10% students.

Sources: College and University Personnel Association, American Association of University Professors, and U.S. Bureau of Labor Statistics.

Table 4 / Academic Library Price Indexes for Books and Periodicals, FYs 1976–1992

1983=100 Fiscal Year	Hardcover Books U.S. College Books Price	Index (L3.1a)	North American Academic Books Price	Index (L3.1b)	Library of Congress Foreign Books Price	Index (L3.2)	Periodicals U.S. Academic Price	Index (L3.3)	Foreign (7 countries) Index (L3.4)	Books and Periodicals Index* (L3.0)
1976	$13.20	52.8	$14.00	47.2	$7.91	65.4	$38.94	49.9	62.0	52.7
1977	14.80	59.2	15.50	52.3	8.89	73.5	41.85	53.6	67.0	57.8
1978	16.50	66.0	17.60	59.4	9.41	77.8	45.14	57.8	74.0	63.4
1979	18.02	72.1	19.60	66.1	11.52	95.3	50.11	64.2	80.0	70.9
1980	19.70	78.8	21.98	74.2	13.05	107.9	57.23	73.3	84.5	79.2
1981	21.50	86.0	25.00	84.4	13.84	114.5	67.81	86.9	93.8	89.7
1982	23.10	92.4	27.87	94.1	11.91	98.5	73.89	94.7	100.8	95.1
1983	25.00	100.0	29.63	100.0	12.09	100.0	78.04	100.0	100.0	100.0
1984	27.00	108.0	30.34	102.4	11.78	97.4	82.47	105.7	97.0	103.8
1985	29.00	116.0	31.77	107.2	11.66	96.4	86.10	110.3	102.9	108.7
1986	31.00	124.0	33.60	113.4	13.52	111.8	92.32	118.3	116.9	117.7
1987	33.40	133.6	36.93	124.6	15.94	131.8	104.69	134.1	132.1	131.7
1988	35.07	140.3	39.14	132.1	14.59	120.7	117.75	150.9	144.6	141.4
1989	38.14	152.6	41.21	139.1	17.97	148.6	125.87	161.3	153.4	153.1
1990	40.52	162.1	44.19	149.1	20.15	166.7	139.75	179.1	172.7	167.8
1991	42.01	168.0	46.53	157.0	22.84	188.9	158.53	203.1	184.5	183.6
1992	44.55	178.2	49.53	167.2	22.61	187.0	170.93	219.0	198.7	195.3

Note: Prices of library materials are generally quoted for the calendar year, but they are reported here for the corresponding *fiscal year*, e.g., calendar year 1985 prices are reported for FY 1985–1986.

*1983 weights: books and periodicals = 20% U.S. college books + 20% North American academic books + 10% foreign books + 40% U.S. periodicals for academic libraries + 10% foreign periodicals.

Sources: U.S. College Books compiled by Donna Alsbury, Florida Center for Library Automation. North American Academic Books compiled by Stephen Bosch, University of Arizona.

Table 5 / Academic Library Price Index for Other Acquisitions Components, FYs 1976–1992

1983=100 Fiscal Year	Microfilm Price	Index (L4.1)	16-mm Film Price	Index (L4.2)	Videocassettes Price	Index (L4.3)	Filmstrip Price	Index (L4.4)	Prerecorded Cassette Tape Price	Index (L4.5)	Machine-Readable CD-ROM Price	Index (L4.6)	Other Acquisitions Index* (L4.0)
1976	$0.1190	54.5	$12.85	85.6	$—	—	$73.91	90.6	$10.32	96.1	$—	—	69.0
1977	0.1335	61.1	12.93	86.1	—	—	58.41	71.6	12.08	112.5	—	—	70.9
1978	0.1475	67.5	13.95	92.9	—	—	76.26	93.4	10.63	99.0	—	—	78.4
1979	0.1612	73.8	12.56	83.7	—	—	62.31	76.3	12.47	116.1	—	—	79.5
1980	0.1750	80.1	13.62	90.7	—	—	65.97	80.8	12.58	117.1	—	—	85.0
1981	0.1890	86.5	12.03	80.1	7.58	72.4	67.39	82.6	9.34	87.0	—	—	83.7
1982	0.2021	92.5	16.09	107.2	14.87	142.0	71.12	87.1	12.48	116.2	—	—	102.5
1983	0.2184	100.0	15.01	100.0	10.47	100.0	81.62	100.0	10.74	100.0	—	—	100.0
1984	0.2274	104.1	15.47	103.1	11.04	105.4	79.57	97.5	11.23	104.6	—	—	103.6
1985	0.2450	112.2	16.93	112.8	8.44	80.6	85.76	105.1	9.99	93.0	—	—	104.8
1986	0.2612	119.6	16.50	109.9	10.24	97.8	83.50	102.3	8.99	83.7	—	—	110.5
1987	0.2350	107.6	16.85	112.3	7.44	71.1	85.33	104.5	10.61	98.8	—	—	101.2
1988	0.2198	100.6	17.00	113.3	6.79	64.9	112.15	137.4	8.50	79.1	—	—	97.4
1989	0.2352	107.7	18.96	126.3	7.21	68.9	74.45	91.2	10.12	94.2	1,533	99.8	99.8
1990	0.2244	102.7	20.63	137.4	5.67	54.2	89.14	109.2	10.58	98.5	1,740	113.3	98.5
1991	0.2507	114.8	18.40	122.6	5.60	53.5	121.76	149.2	10.47	97.5	1,710	111.3	107.3
1992	0.2558	117.1	20.08	133.8	4.81	45.9	97.90	119.9	12.18	113.4	1,562	101.7	105.6

*1983 weights: other acquisition materials = 50% microfilm + 5% 16-mm film + 15% videocassettes + 10% filmstrip + 10% prerecorded cassette tape + 10% CD-ROM disks.

Sources: Microfilm compiled by Imre Jarmy, U.S. Library of Congress. 16-mm film, videocassettes, filmstrip, and prerecorded cassette tape compiled by Dana L. Alessi, Baker & Taylor; CD-ROM disks by Martha Kellogg and Theodore Kellogg, University of Rhode Island.

Table 6 / School Library Acquisitions Price Indexes, FYs 1976–1992

1983=100 Fiscal Year	Hardcover Books					Mass Market Paperback Books					
	Elementary*		Secondary		Total Index‡	Elementary		Secondary		Total Index§
	Average Price	Index	Average Price	Index		Average Price	Index	Average Price	Index	
1976	$5.82	65.6	$16.19	52.9	59.0	$1.07	53.0	$1.46	49.5	51.2
1977	5.87	66.2	17.20	56.2	61.0	1.22	60.4	1.60	54.2	57.3
1978	6.64	74.9	18.03	58.9	66.6	1.41	69.8	1.71	58.0	63.9
1979	6.59	74.3	20.10	65.7	69.8	1.47	72.8	1.91	64.7	68.8
1980	7.13	80.4	22.80	74.5	77.3	1.48	73.3	2.06	69.8	71.6
1981	8.21	92.6	23.57	77.1	84.5	1.65	81.7	2.50	84.7	83.2
1982	8.29	93.5	25.48	83.3	88.2	1.79	88.6	2.65	89.8	89.2
1983	8.87	100.0	30.59	100.0	100.0	2.02	100.0	2.95	100.0	100.0
1984	9.70	109.4	31.19	102.0	105.5	2.24	110.9	3.13	106.1	108.5
1985	10.11	114.0	29.82	97.5	105.4	2.28	112.9	3.38	114.6	113.7
1986	9.95	111.5	31.46	102.8	107.0	2.71	132.2	3.62	121.7	127.0
1987	10.64	118.5	32.43	105.9	112.0	2.71	134.2	3.86	131.2	132.7
1988	11.48	127.8	36.28	118.5	123.0	2.80	138.6	4.00	135.9	137.3
1989	11.79	131.3	39.00	127.4	129.3	3.18	157.4	4.55	154.6	156.0
1990	13.01	144.9	40.61	132.7	138.5	3.19	157.9	4.32	146.8	152.4
1991	13.07	145.6	42.12	137.6	141.4	3.56	176.2	4.57	155.3	165.8
1992†	16.64	185.3	44.17	144.3	163.9	3.38	167.3	5.08	172.6	170.0

*Juvenile books (age 8 or younger), fiction.

†Data for 1993 and 1994 are available from Research Associates of Washington.

‡Hardcover books total = 47.9% elementary + 52.1% secondary.

§Mass market paperback books total = 50.2% elementary + 49.8% secondary.

Note: Prices for library materials are generally quoted for the calendar year. They are reported here for the corresponding fiscal year, e.g., calendar year 1985 prices are reported for FY

Table 6 / School Library Acquisitions Price Indexes, FYs 1976–1992 (cont.)

| 1983=100 Fiscal Year | U.S. Periodicals | | | | | | Microfilm | | Audiovisual Materials | | | | | |
| | Elementary | | Secondary | | Total Index‖ | | | | 16-mm Film | | Videocassette | | Filmstrip | |
	Average Price	Index	Average Price	Index		Average Price	Index	Average Price	Index	Average Price	Index	Average Price	Index
1976	$4.69	47.4	$14.36	60.0	54.0	$0.1190	54.5	$12.85	85.6	$ —	—	$73.91	90.6
1977	5.32	53.7	15.24	63.7	58.9	0.1335	61.1	12.93	86.1	—	—	58.41	71.6
1978	5.82	58.8	16.19	67.7	63.4	0.1475	67.5	13.95	92.9	—	—	76.26	93.4
1979	6.34	64.0	17.26	72.1	68.3	0.1612	73.8	12.56	83.7	—	—	62.31	76.3
1980	6.70	67.7	18.28	76.4	72.2	0.1750	80.1	13.62	90.7	—	—	65.97	80.8
1981	7.85	79.3	19.87	83.0	81.2	0.1890	86.5	12.03	80.1	7.58	72.4	67.39	82.6
1982	8.56	86.5	21.83	91.2	88.9	0.2021	92.5	16.09	107.2	14.87	142.0	71.12	87.1
1983	9.90	100.0	23.93	100.0	100.0	0.2184	100.0	15.01	100.0	10.47	100.0	81.62	100.0
1984	11.49	116.1	26.43	110.4	113.1	0.2274	104.1	15.47	103.1	11.04	105.4	79.57	97.5
1985	12.21	123.3	27.90	116.6	119.8	0.2450	112.2	16.93	112.8	8.44	80.6	85.76	105.1
1986	13.31	134.4	26.41	110.4	121.9	0.2612	119.6	16.50	109.9	10.24	97.8	83.50	102.3
1987	13.76	139.0	26.95	112.6	125.3	0.2350	125.9	16.85	112.3	7.44	71.1	85.33	104.5
1988	15.19	153.4	27.79	116.1	134.0	0.2198	117.8	17.00	113.3	6.79	64.9	112.15	137.4
1989	16.39	165.6	28.29	118.2	140.9	0.2352	126.0	18.96	126.3	7.21	68.9	74.45	91.2
1990	16.95	171.2	29.69	124.1	146.7	0.2244	120.2	20.63	137.4	5.67	54.2	89.14	109.2
1991	17.51	176.9	31.24	130.5	152.7	0.2507	134.3	18.40	122.6	5.60	53.5	121.76	149.2
1992	18.38	185.7	32.25	134.8	159.1	0.2558	137.1	20.08	133.8	4.81	45.9	97.90	119.9

‖ U.S. periodicals total = 47.9% elementary + 52.1% secondary.

Table 6 / School Library Acquisitions Price Indexes, FYs 1976–1992 *(cont.)*

| 1983=100 Fiscal Year | Audiovisual Materials (cont.) | | | | | | Free Textbooks to Students | | | | | |
| | Prerecorded Cassette Tape | | Multimedia Kits | | Audiovisual Total Index** | Library Materials Index†† (7.1) | Hardbound | | Paperbound | | Total Index‡‡ (7.2) | Library Materials and Textbooks Index§§ (7.0) |
	Average Price	Index	Average Price	Index			Average Price	Index	Average Price	Index		
1976	$10.32	96.1	$140.25	n/a	89.5	64.5	$4.10	57.7	$2.08	58.4	57.8	60.6
1977	12.08	112.5	93.63	n/a	76.1	63.8	4.67	65.7	2.27	63.8	65.3	64.7
1978	10.63	99.0	93.65	n/a	93.0	71.7	5.23	73.6	2.40	67.4	72.4	72.1
1979	12.57	117.0	117.38	n/a	79.9	71.8	5.78	81.3	2.70	75.8	80.2	76.7
1980	12.58	117.1	85.70	n/a	84.3	78.1	6.12	86.1	2.87	80.6	85.0	82.1
1981	9.34	87.0	92.71	n/a	81.9	83.6	6.42	90.3	3.05	85.7	89.4	86.9
1982	12.48	116.2	46.99	n/a	95.4	89.9	6.64	93.4	3.23	90.7	92.9	91.6
1983	10.74	100.0	57.52	n/a	100.0	100.0	7.11	100.0	3.56	100.0	100.0	100.0
1984	11.23	104.6	Discontinued		99.2	105.1	7.80	109.7	3.75	105.3	108.9	107.3
1985	9.99	93.0			103.3	107.1	8.40	118.1	4.05	113.8	117.3	113.0
1986	8.99	83.7			101.7	108.6	9.12	128.1	4.98	139.9	130.4	121.2
1987	10.61	98.8			102.5	112.6	9.71	136.4	5.73	161.0	141.2	129.1
1988	8.50	79.1			125.0	125.1	11.82	156.1	5.62‖‖	175.0	159.8	145.2
1989	10.12	94.2			94.0	124.0	12.63	166.9	6.10	190.0	171.4	151.4
1990	10.58	98.5			107.7	133.0	15.41	203.6	7.15	222.4	207.3	175.9
1991	10.47	97.5			135.1	142.1	17.64	233.1	7.89	245.4	235.5	196.1
1992	12.18	113.4			115.4	152.7	18.87	249.3	8.41	261.6	251.7	209.9

**Total audiovisual = 12.3% 16-mm film + 7.9% videocassettes + 73.5% filmstrips + 6.3% prerecorded tapes.

††Library materials index = 61.2% hardcover books + 3.6% paperback books + 11.7% periodicals + 2.3% microfilm + 21.2% audiovisual.

‡‡Textbook index = 80.5% hardbound + 19.5% paperbound.

§§Library material and textbook index = 42.2% library materials + 57.8% textbooks.

‖‖Price source changed in FY 1988 and linked to previous series.

Sources: The following prices are published in Part 4 of the *Bowker Annual:* hardcover and paperback books; U.S. periodicals; 16-mm film, videocassettes, filmstrip, and prerecorded cassette tape; free textbooks, compiled from prices reported by the Association of American Publishers.

The acquisition budget should consist of three parts, each of which must be separately defended:

1 The basic acquisition budget is the amount required to maintain and update the collection; that is, sufficient funds to purchase annually the number of volumes that equals 5 percent of the collection (discounting older materials). The L3.0 and L4.0 components of the ALPI preserve the purchasing power of this basic acquisition budget.

2 Additional acquisition funding is the amount required annually to *extend* the collection in breadth and/or depth to satisfy changes in curriculum and other educational programs, changes in institutional level, or in faculty needs. The ALPI does not account for this funding.

3 Additional acquisition funding is the amount required annually to *upgrade* the overall rating of the collection by extending the quantity and price range of new acquisitions. This quality change is not accounted for by the ALPI. In the event that additional funding becomes a permanent part of the basic funding requirement, the purchasing power of the enlarged basic acquisition budget may be maintained by using the L3.0 and L4.0 price series as deflators.

L1.0 Salaries and Wages

For pricing purposes, library personnel are organized in five divisions. *Administrators (L1.1)* consists of the chief, deputy, associate, and assistant chief librarian—that is, staff members having administrative responsibilities for management of the library. L1.1 is based on the head librarian salary series reported by the College and University Personnel Association (CUPA). *Librarians (L1.2)* are all other professional library staff. Since 1984–1985, the L1.2 price series is based on the average median salary for circulation, acquisition, technical service, and public service librarians reported by CUPA. *Other professionals (L1.3)* includes personnel who are not librarians in positions normally requiring at least a bachelor's degree, including curators, archivists, computer specialists, budget officers, information and system specialists, subject bibliographers, and media specialists. The Higher Education Price Index (HEPI) faculty salary price series is used as a proxy. *Nonprofessional staff (L1.4)* includes technical assistants, secretaries, clerical, shipping, and storage personnel specifically assigned to the library and covered by the library budget, but excludes general custodial and maintenance workers and student employees. As the category is dominated by office workers, its wages are based on the HEPI clerical workers price series reported by the BLS (Bureau of Labor Statistics) Employment Cost Index. *Students (L1.5)* are usually employed part time for nearly minimum hourly wages. In some instances, wages are set by work-study program requirements of the institution's student financial aid office. The proxy price series used for student wages is the Employment Cost Index series for nonfarm laborers reported by the Bureau of Labor Statistics.

L2.0 Fringe Benefits

The price of fringe benefits is based on the HEPI fringe benefit price series for all college and university personnel.

L3.0 Books and Periodicals Acquisitions

The price of U.S. book acquisitions for smaller college libraries (L3.1a) is based on the U.S. college books price series, which is derived from the prices of approximately 6,000 titles reviewed in *Choice* during the calendar year. The prices of books acquired by larger university libraries (L3.1b) are based on the North American academic books price series, which is derived from data on approximately 85,000 titles in approval plans. (In this national ALPI the college and university price series have equal weight; however, in tailoring the ALPI to its own needs, a library should use the more suitable series.) The price of *foreign books (L3.2)* is based on Library of Congress data on appropriated funds for foreign books and titles purchased.[2] The price of *U.S. periodicals (L3.3)* is based on the U.S. periodicals for academic libraries price series compiled by the Faxon Institute. *Foreign periodicals (L3.4)* prices are based on a fixed weighted index of unit prices for seven major countries from data provided by the Faxon Institute.[3]

L4.0 Other Materials

The six other materials—microfilm, 16-mm film, videocassettes, filmstrip, prerecorded cassette tape, and machine-readable–CD-ROM—are representative of all collected library material other than books and periodicals. The largest estimated weight is assigned to microform used in the collection of government documents, newspapers, and preservation works. (Only the microfilm price is given; no price series for microfiche is available.) For the price sources, see Table 5.

L5.0 Binding

Binding is increasingly being contracted out at all but the largest libraries. As no wage series focuses exclusively on binding, L5.0 is based on the average weekly earnings of production or nonsupervisory workers in the printing and publishing industry (BLS, Employment and Earnings series).

L6.0 Contracted Services

Services contracted by libraries include communications, postal service, data processing, and printing and duplication. The L6.0 price is based on the HEPI contracted services subcomponent. (In this instance the data processing component generally represents the library's payment for use of a central campus computer service.) Libraries may also contract out such specialized activities as ongoing public access cataloging (OPAC), which are not given separate prices in the L6.0 component.

L7.0 Supplies and Materials

Prices of office supplies, which constitute the bulk of library supplies and materials, are based on the BLS Producer Price Indexes.

L8.0 Equipment

Equipment is limited to small, easily movable, relatively inexpensive and short-lived items, such as hand calculators, projectors, fans, cameras, tape recorders, and small televisions, which are not regarded as depreciable capital equipment. Prices are based on the HEPI equipment price series.

School Library Acquisitions Price Index

The School Library Acquisitions Price Index measures year-to-year price changes for a typical fixed market basket of books, periodicals, and other materials purchased by elementary-secondary school libraries. Table 6 shows the index and its subcomponents as well as prices paid by schools for students' textbooks. See the footnotes to Table 6 for a brief description of the various price series and sources.

Notes

1. *Inflation Measures for Schools, Colleges and Libraries: 1994 Update* (Research Associates of Washington, Washington, D.C., 1994) includes overall inflation measures for the higher education and school communities for 1976 through 1994.
2. The Library of Congress acquires much standard foreign material through exchange programs. Purchased foreign materials include exceptional monographs that would not normally be acquired by academic libraries.
3. Canada, Germany, France, Italy, Japan, the Netherlands, and the United Kingdom.

State Rankings of Selected Public Library Data, 1992

	Circulation Transactions per capita*	Reference Transactions per capita	Book and Serial Vols. per capita	Paid Librarians per 25,000 pop.	Operating Expenditures per capita	Local Income per capita
Alabama	49	38	47	32	47	44
Alaska	29	27	22	22	3	4
Arizona	25	14	43	39	30	22
Arkansas	47	41	39	51	51	48
California	35	6	44	43	21	17
Colorado	17	17	28	24	15	12
Connecticut	16	11	7	12	6	5
Delaware	43	37	46	42	44	45
D.C.	50	1	24	6	1	2
Florida	38	2	49	41	32	29
Georgia ·	41	30	38	50	40	41
Hawaii	31	9	26	26	14	51
Idaho	13	22	19	19	34	31
Illinois	20	7	20	11	7	1
Indiana	6	15	15	3	8	8
Iowa	9	32	11	4	31	26
Kansas	7	10	6	2	18	13
Kentucky	36	42	41	30	46	42
Louisiana	44	31	36	40	37	33
Maine	19	N/A†	2	5	26	34
Maryland	3	5	25	34	10	18
Massachusetts	24	N/A	4	9	16	19
Michigan	37	19	31	27	24	28
Minnesota	5	4	27	28	13	14
Mississippi	51	39	42	17	50	47
Missouri	18	35	10	48	28	21
Montana	33	34	23	8	45	38
Nebraska	15	N/A	12	13	27	23
Nevada	39	21	48	46	29	9
New Hampshire	4	18	1	1	11	6
New Jersey	32	20	14	20	5	3
New Mexico	26	N/A	13	25	33	30
New York	27	8	16	16	2	10
North Carolina	34	25	45	44	38	36
North Dakota	22	36	17	15	41	40
Ohio	1	3	18	10	4	49
Oklahoma	30	24	35	23	39	35
Oregon	8	N/A	34	33	22	16
Pennsylvania	42	28	37	37	36	43
Rhode Island	28	43	9	21	19	24
South Carolina	48	33	50	38	43	39
South Dakota	14	40	8	18	35	27
Tennessee	46	29	51	47	48	46
Texas	45	16	40	45	42	37
Utah	12	N/A	29	31	23	25
Vermont	23	N/A	3	7	25	32
Virginia	21	12	33	35	20	20
Washington	2	N/A	30	36	9	7
West Virginia	40	23	32	29	49	50
Wisconsin	11	13	21	14	17	15
Wyoming	10	26	5	49	12	11

The rankings were compiled by the National Data Resource Center of the National Center for Education Statistics using data submitted in July 1993 to NCES through the Federal State Cooperative System (FSCS) for public library data. A full report of these data was published as *Public Libraries in the U.S.: 1992*, and data are also available on diskette (for details, see the NCES article in Part 1).

The District of Columbia contributes to FSCS as do the 50 states and is therefore shown in the rankings. The reader is cautioned, however, that this library is probably more appropriately compared to libraries serving large urban areas rather than to states.

Source: National Center for Education Statistics, July 1993.

* Per capita calculations are based on libraries that reported the specific item and a nonzero value for population of legal service areas.

† N/A = not applicable.

Library Buildings 1994: Renovations—and Additions—on the Rise

Bette-Lee Fox

Managing Editor, *Library Journal*

Corinne O. Nelson

Editorial Assistant, *Library Journal*

Tax revolts and bond issue bashing notwithstanding, library buildings continued to be funded, to the tune of 273 projects in 1994. With only 108 projects, however, new public library buildings in 1994 (completed July 1, 1993 through June 30, 1994) were at their lowest number since 1988, while the 127 addition/renovations represented the highest number since that same benchmark year (101 and 142, respectively). Perhaps library boards and communities are beginning to adhere to that old adage: "If it ain't too broke, don't demolish it."

The figures for total project costs ($616,187,063) and funding reported in the Six-Year cost summary (table 3) appear to have jumped astronomically since 1993, but in reality they've been skewed upward by one huge project, the Central Library of the Los Angeles Public Library. At a cost of $215 million dollars, the 539,000-square-foot building makes financial data seem a bit too optimistic.

Omitting the L.A. project, the data aren't too far off from past years in terms of total dollars spent and funds raised. As always, local funding, at 82 percent, contributes the highest portion of total money. The most costly projects were the new Newport Beach Public Library, another California building, at $14.6 million, and the Hillyard Branch of the Spokane Public Library at $13.7 million. The largest addition/renovation projects were the Huntington Beach Central Library and Cultural Center (there's life in California libraries, yet) at $10 million and the Oshkosh Public Library, WI, at $10.8 million.

Surprisingly, there were considerably fewer academic projects in 1994 than in recent years, though the Science Library at the University of California–Irvine ($32 million) and the Washington University Library, Pullman ($36 million) are quite grand. We have data for 38 completed projects in 1994 vs. 51 projects in 1993 and 49 in 1992. Could this be a forecast of trouble ahead? *LJ* will keep a watch on this area in future Architectural Issues.

Note: Adapted from the December 1994 issue of *Library Journal*, which also lists architects' addresses.

Table 1 / New Public Library Buildings, 1994

Community	Pop. in M	Code	Project Cost	Const. Cost	Gross Sq.Ft.	Sq.Ft. Cost	Equip. Cost	Site Cost	Other Costs	Volumes	Reader Seats	Federal Funds	State Funds	Local Funds	Gift Funds	Architect
Alabama																
Birmingham	30	B	$1,553,939	$1,201,209	14,000	$85.80	$256,322	Owned	$96,408	50,000	80	$287,120	$0	$1,266,819	$0	Holley & Watson
Montgomery	220	StL	4,483,723	4,180,000	38,000	110.00	303,723	Owned	0	280,000	75	0	4,483,723	0	0	Lee Sims
Alaska																
Tuluksak	1	M	257,971	234,686	2,080	112.83	5,585	Owned	17,700	15,000	19	162,000	0	0	95,971	Gary Walters
Arizona																
Catalina	10	B	250,000	200,000	2,500	80.00	30,000	Leased	20,000	17,000	50	0	0	250,000	0	Sam Robison
Cottonwood	29	M	1,816,112	1,424,233	15,440	92.24	283,157	Owned	108,722	60,000	124	0	0	1,816,112	0	Lawrence Enyart
California																
Albany	17	B	3,538,430	2,359,680	15,200	155.24	190,233	482,000	506,517	50,000	122	0	2,639,340	678,190	220,900	Marquis Assocs.
Cameron Park	25	B	1,678,338	1,327,721	12,528	105.98	142,144	6,762	201,711	62,000	24	525,164	0	1,153,173	70,000	Peter Wolfe
Greenfield	9	B	1,548,572	960,050	7,152	134.24	117,275	330,000	141,247	21,100	65	0	1,006,572	536,000	6,000	Paul Davis
Newport Beach	68	MS	14,630,000	8,421,000	54,000	155.94	1,239,000	3,970,000	1,000,000	260,000	225	727,387	0	11,902,613	2,000,000	Simon Martin...
Perris	46	B	4,545,100	3,769,000	20,000	188.45	418,000	Leased	358,100	100,000	280	0	2,954,315	1,590,785	0	Thirtieth Street
San Diego	60	B	6,370,000	2,855,160	20,278	140.80	379,000	1,870,000	1,265,840	64,300	216	0	0	6,370,000	0	Bill Bocken
Colorado																
Denver	n/a	B	2,427,339	1,282,083	11,525	111.24	159,360	327,990	657,906	54,000	50	0	0	2,427,339	0	Barker-Rinker-Seacat
Evergreen	40	B	4,400,000	2,744,000	17,300	158.61	396,000	381,000	879,000	100,000	99	0	0	4,400,000	0	Cabell Childress
Delaware																
Bethany Beach	7	M	1,396,393	739,525	10,000	73.95	136,271	400,000	120,597	30,000	50	0	525,367	61,459	809,567	R.C. Clendaniel
Milford	18	M	1,800,000	960,000	13,000	73.85	60,000	255,000	525,000	56,000	70	0	565,000	0	1,235,000	Jennifer McCann
Wilmington	22	M	3,261,600	2,508,817	14,600	171.84	142,269	Owned	610,514	52,000	83	0	1,080,000	850,600	1,331,000	Cornerstone Partners
Florida																
Archer	4	B	421,701	287,963	3,900	73.84	19,354	34,509	79,875	13,000	18	0	0	419,701	2,000	Karl Thorne Assocs.
Coconut Creek	353	B	13,600,000	9,123,000	109,460	83.35	1,900,000	Owned	2,577,000	300,000	565	0	6,800,000	6,800,000	0	Oscar Vagi & Assocs.
Kissimmee	120	MS	2,984,950	2,292,950	43,000	53.32	524,000	Owned	168,000	200,000	125	0	0	2,984,950	0	Stottler Stagg
Newberry	4	B	387,895	296,841	3,960	74.96	19,283	12,553	59,218	13,000	18	0	0	387,895	0	Karl Thorne Assocs.

Symbol Code: B—Branch Library; BS—Branch & System Headquarters; M—Main Library; MS—Main & System Headquarters; S—System Headquarters; n/a—not available

Venice	40	B	1,826,000	1,552,106	12,500	124.17	173,394	Owned	100,000	50,000	78	0	0	1,826,000	0	Gaus & Tan
Georgia																
Adairsville	15	B	651,646	463,168	6,000	77.19	72,909	Owned	115,569	30,000	25	0	544,774	106,872	0	Kirkman Assocs.
Athens	90	MS	6,747,105	4,455,119	63,000	70.72	1,204,942	Owned	1,087,044	250,000	400	0	3,000,000	3,747,105	0	Nix Mann Viehman
Atlanta	748	B	10,369,909	5,113,020	50,000	102.26	826,927	3,732,041	667,921	50,000	97	0	2,887,000	7,482,909	0	Brown Design Assocs.
Atlanta	25	B	880,460	642,002	7,000	91.71	89,975	46,800	101,683	35,000	19	0	0	880,460	0	Harris & Partners
Canton	114	B	1,081,492	658,321	10,000	65.83	287,273	50,000	85,898	46,000	100	0	776,473	236,027	68,992	Sterling Pettefer
Centerville	8	B	486,348	297,102	4,000	74.28	78,985	Owned	110,261	25,000	30	0	360,000	126,348	0	Hollis Jelks McLees
Coolidge	1	B	251,700	198,500	2,140	92.76	40,000	Owned	13,200	10,000	26	0	225,068	26,632	0	Jinright, Ryan & Lynn
Meigs	1	B	252,000	200,000	2,140	93.46	40,000	Owned	12,000	10,000	26	0	225,068	26,932	0	Jinright, Ryan & Lynn
Summerville	22	MS	1,462,766	990,000	13,500	73.33	245,000	60,000	167,766	56,000	100	0	1,044,368	358,398	60,000	Page & Gauthreaux
Illinois																
Chicago	19	B	2,914,069	1,817,000	13,762	132.03	162,000	159,400	775,669	75,056	85	0	2,914,069	0	0	John Victor Frega
Chicago	78	B	3,010,721	1,930,454	13,611	141.83	172,136	115,000	793,131	90,000	93	0	3,000,721	10,000	0	City of Chicago
Chicago	13	B	3,756,558	2,335,000	14,132	165.23	210,000	250,000	951,558	75,000	73	0	3,746,558	10,000	0	Heitzman Architects
Lincolnshire	35	M	8,796,821	5,766,458	50,000	115.33	1,304,149	850,000	876,214	200,000	179	0	0	8,796,821	0	Yas/Fischel Ptnership.
Indiana																
Greensburg	24	M	2,430,000	1,796,530	21,000	85.55	354,480	75,000	203,990	100,000	100	229,125	0	2,200,875	0	Parke Randall
Lowell	15	M	3,225,702	2,051,970	24,000	85.50	399,265	97,500	676,967	100,000	139	300,000	0	2,915,000	10,702	David S. Nice
Schererville	40	B	2,798,323	2,298,953	26,500	86.75	338,878	Owned	160,492	68,000	178	0	0	2,798,323	0	Carras-Szany
Zionsville	12	M	3,862,728	3,053,181	25,411	120.15	423,810	160,000	225,737	60,000	127	0	0	3,730,458	132,270	K.R. Montgomery
Iowa																
Dike	1	M	236,500	200,000	3,374	59.76	17,000	Owned	19,500	10,575	30	42,000	0	0	194,500	Grimes, Port, Jones...
New Hampton	4	M	830,447	575,340	8,000	71.92	104,327	59,780	91,000	25,000	55	0	0	625,000	380,000	Durrant Architects
Kansas																
Leawood	19	B	2,790,941	1,434,428	10,800	132.82	837,484	310,628	208,401	40,000	63	0	0	2,790,941	0	Gould Evans
Kentucky																
Louisville	57	B	131,755	65,465	4,500	14.55	52,680	Leased	13,610	30,000	28	0	0	131,755	0	Noel Rueff
Louisville	45	B	120,528	n/a	9,400	n/a	75,528	Leased	n/a	75,000	53	0	0	119,018	1,510	Bardstown Rd....
St. Matthews	61	B	944,000	356,400	10,000	35.64	20,000	528,000	39,600	80,000	70	0	0	944,000	0	Presnell Assocs.

Symbol Code: B—Branch Library; BS—Branch & System Headquarters; M—Main Library; MS—Main & System Headquarters; S—System Headquarters; n/a—not available

Table 1 / New Public Library Buildings, 1994 (cont.)

Community	Pop. in M	Code	Project Cost	Const. Cost	Gross Sq.Ft.	Sq.Ft. Cost	Equip. Cost	Site Cost	Other Costs	Volumes	Reader Seats	Federal Funds	State Funds	Local Funds	Gift Funds	Architect
Walton	9	B	1,095,073	821,770	9,800	83.85	61,313	113,962	98,028	25,000	40	0	350,000	745,073	0	Robert Ehmet Hayes
Louisiana																
DeQuincy	3	B	358,308	261,650	3,331	78.55	34,027	Owned	62,631	16,236	35	0	0	358,308	0	Broussard/Moss
Maplewood	20	B	335,790	267,961	3,331	80.44	30,800	Owned	37,029	12,500	22	0	0	335,790	0	Broussard/Moss
Moss Bluff	8	B	1,332,284	994,835	11,528	86.30	115,877	120,000	101,572	20,252	56	0	0	1,332,284	0	William L. Patin
New Orleans	42	B	2,253,875	1,335,940	9,400	142.12	239,285	561,300	117,350	40,000	48	0	0	2,253,875	0	Imre Hegedus
St. Martinville	18	MS	1,505,910	1,016,631	14,200	71.59	267,898	145,000	76,381	70,000	65	279,200	0	1,091,710	135,000	Landry/Angelle
Sulphur	20	B	2,398,033	1,647,198	21,300	77.33	259,624	293,683	197,528	94,500	133	0	0	2,398,033	0	Ray Fugatt
Westlake	5	B	686,759	521,677	6,012	86.77	73,480	25,281	66,321	15,800	44	0	0	686,759	0	Broussard/Moss
Maryland																
Elkridge	30	B	4,858,000	2,730,000	15,500	176.13	715,000	1,040,000	373,000	60,000	120	0	0	4,858,000	0	Ronald Blomberg
Upper Marlboro	13	BS	5,875,265	872,500	51,146	17.06	363,165	4,500,000	139,600	125,000	n/a	0	0	5,875,265	0	Joe Lin & Assocs.
Michigan																
Carleton	10	B	651,037	486,781	6,350	76.66	81,350	29,773	53,133	30,000	35	0	0	651,037	0	Merritt McCallum…
Indian River	4	M	732,500	493,000	5,000	98.60	32,200	130,000	77,300	60,000	24	15,700	400,000	306,800	10,000	Wade-Trim/Granger
Saline	16	M	2,799,930	1,600,197	16,450	97.28	761,139	192,650	245,944	75,000	84	0	2,786,035	0	13,895	Michael Pogliano
Waldron	3	M	99,101	82,672	2,400	34.45	10,329	5,500	600	11,000	28	0	0	13,500	85,601	Perma Build Homes
Wixom	9	M	1,899,000	n/a	14,000	n/a	n/a	Owned	n/a	40,000	102	0	0	1,899,000	0	Minuro Yamasaki
Minnesota																
Butterfield	1	B	127,754	109,216	2,000	54.61	4,000	Owned	14,538	7,500	18	0	0	79,554	48,200	I & S Engineers
Roseville	33	M	4,800,000	3,500,000	43,000	81.40	377,000	530,000	393,000	200,000	150	0	0	4,500,000	300,000	Buetow & Assocs.
Missouri																
Kansas City	20	B	1,033,118	685,403	22,500	30.46	105,200	216,134	26,381	105,000	96	0	0	1,033,118	0	Tognascioli/Gross
Nevada																
Las Vegas	50	B	8,753,274	5,494,787	37,800	145.36	491,041	2,200,000	567,446	100,000	204	0	0	6,553,274	2,200,000	H.S.A. Architects
Las Vegas	75	B	9,254,894	7,081,386	40,165	176.31	470,801	980,000	722,707	150,000	120	0	0	8,797,996	507,801	Robert Fieden
Las Vegas	50	B	4,401,495	2,998,549	23,350	128.42	350,143	754,081	298,722	120,000	80	0	0	4,401,495	0	Homes & Sabitini

Symbol Code: B—Branch Library; BS—Branch & System Headquarters; M—Main Library; MS—Main & System Headquarters; S—System Headquarters; n/a—not available

Location																
Laughlin	9	B	2,850,250	2,021,259	15,600	129.57	216,358	386,000	226,333	65,000	106	0	0	2,850,250	0	Luchessi Galati
New Hampshire																
Madison	2	M	195,000	170,000	2,932	57.98	25,000	Owned	0	7,500	20	0	0	37,700	157,300	none
New York																
Bronx	23	B	1,338,477	1,131,713	6,910	163.78	87,243	Owned	119,521	16,500	24	0	31,910	1,012,830	325,534	David Prendergast
North Carolina																
Chapel Hill	42	M	5,442,000	2,900,000	27,315	106.17	853,400	1,050,000	635,600	125,000	125	63,000	0	4,090,000	1,289,000	Gurlitz & Giles
Franklinton	2	B	205,030	160,921	2,900	55.49	13,508	20,000	13,600	10,000	26	75,699	0	112,331	17,000	H.S. Annis
Leland	5	B	515,634	417,402	4,855	85.98	23,000	40,000	35,232	20,000	40	0	50,000	265,634	200,000	John Sawyer
Yaupon Beach	5	B	441,720	384,000	4,823	79.62	25,000	Owned	32,720	20,000	30	0	0	409,000	37,720	John Sawyer
Ohio																
Attica	6	M	866,867	734,165	7,440	98.68	48,630	10,000	74,072	31,000	45	416,096	0	364,840	85,931	Thomas Bodner
Avon	7	B	1,365,253	884,628	10,440	84.73	111,585	160,000	209,040	45,000	57	0	0	1,365,253	0	Clark & Post
Cincinnati	30	B	2,373,212	1,917,740	15,000	127.85	211,002	Owned	244,470	80,000	84	0	2,158,227	214,985	0	Harry Gaz
Columbus	40	B	1,900,000	1,256,000	12,000	104.67	188,200	284,200	171,600	60,000	97	0	950,000	950,000	0	Design Group
Elyria	70	B	3,476,784	2,616,682	30,444	85.95	250,974	285,000	324,128	109,000	166	0	0	3,476,784	0	not reported
Felicity	6	B	647,463	530,305	7,300	72.64	57,158	15,000	45,000	25,000	55	0	0	647,463	0	Gerald Harley
Lordstown	3	B	428,259	352,387	3,537	99.63	46,830	Leased	29,072	17,340	34	0	0	428,259	0	Baker, Bednar
Richmond Dale	5	B	177,555	128,800	1,260	102.22	20,255	15,000	13,500	9,000	10	0	0	177,555	0	Jack Harden
Sunbury	15	M	1,697,563	1,290,629	14,716	87.70	127,480	35,000	244,454	n/a	n/a	0	0	1,697,563	0	Schooley Caldwell
Twinsburg	12	M	2,911,706	2,295,408	25,000	91.82	162,169	157,000	297,129	85,000	104	0	0	2,911,706	0	Donald R. Spice
Oklahoma																
Atoka	15	B	259,200	217,600	5,000	43.52	38,000	Owned	3,600	15,000	32	125,000	0	38,000	96,200	Wes Brannon
Broken Arrow	29	B	785,813	426,405	6,100	69.90	61,521	53,282	244,605	27,000	48	0	0	785,813	0	Bates/LZW
Claremore	54	M	2,169,054	1,844,054	17,000	108.47	233,000	Owned	92,000	80,000	145	125,000	25,000	2,019,054	0	Beck Assocs.
Healdton	13	B	168,501	117,680	3,600	32.69	47,221	Owned	3,600	12,000	25	58,762	0	0	109,739	Wes Brannon
Pennsylvania																
Minersville	9	M	187,721	152,000	2,508	60.61	5,721	Owned	30,000	20,000	50	0	0	32,000	155,721	WJP Engineers
South Carolina																
Estill	4	B	180,000	155,000	2,000	77.50	20,000	Owned	5,000	10,000	24	124,000	30,000	6,000	20,000	Hussey, Gay, Bell…
Spartanburg	25	B	790,000	587,570	9,000	65.29	105,000	16,500	80,930	n/a	n/a	100,000	0	578,000	112,000	McMillan, Smith…

Symbol Code: B—Branch Library; BS—Branch & System Headquarters; M—Main Library; MS—Main & System Headquarters; S—System Headquarters; n/a—not available

Table 1 / New Public Library Buildings, 1994 *(cont.)*

Community	Pop. in M	Code	Project Cost	Const. Cost	Gross Sq.Ft.	Sq.Ft. Cost	Equip. Cost	Site Cost	Other Costs	Volumes	Reader Seats	Federal Funds	State Funds	Local Funds	Gift Funds	Architect
Spartanburg	9	B	569,470	402,079	5,600	71.80	75,914	10,000	81,477	n/a	n/a	0	0	495,470	74,000	Wayne Crocker
South Dakota																
Humboldt	1	B	56,703	34,738	725	47.91	19,480	Leased	2,485	5,525	8	21,644	0	26,895	8,164	Ellwyn Nohr
Texas																
Corroe	65	MS	6,081,232	3,204,028	50,000	64.08	562,500	2,000,000	314,704	111,125	300	0	0	4,081,232	2,000,000	Ray Bailey
Dallas	10	B	2,362,000	1,506,900	12,700	118.65	124,009	200,000	531,091	50,000	55	0	0	2,362,000	0	Jeff Bulla
San Marcos	40	M	2,619,300	2,095,000	27,000	77.59	272,300	Owned	252,000	190,000	232	300,000	0	2,285,300	34,000	Hidell Architects
The Woodlands	40	B	4,187,320	2,156,121	30,000	71.87	337,500	1,500,000	193,699	90,175	175	100,000	0	2,587,320	1,500,000	Ray Bailey
Virginia																
Manassas	40	B	4,200,000	2,654,898	25,000	106.19	772,631	Owned	772,471	120,000	132	0	0	4,200,000	0	Design Collaborative
Washington																
Elma	6	B	841,011	676,779	6,000	112.80	73,278	25,146	65,808	24,000	50	0	0	715,865	125,146	Lewis Architects
Freeland	12	B	555,722	413,150	3,500	118.04	40,659	46,299	55,614	13,000	24	202,266	0	150,000	203,456	Ray Johnston
North Bend	15	B	2,100,003	1,390,307	9,500	146.35	219,931	250,000	239,765	100,000	61	0	0	2,100,003	0	Bassetti Norton...
Pacific	9	B	1,592,350	1,098,665	5,250	209.27	135,250	139,045	219,390	50,000	34	0	0	1,562,350	30,000	Buffalo Design
Seattle	63	B	4,626,148	3,087,207	20,000	154.36	393,950	467,168	677,823	198,000	121	0	0	4,626,148	0	Portico Group
Spokane	40	B	1,296,133	893,528	8,234	108.52	209,997	Owned	192,608	42,000	56	0	0	1,296,133	0	J. Ronald Sims
Spokane	184	MS	13,769,987	10,133,709	116,885	86.70	1,481,255	Owned	2,155,023	320,000	350	0	0	13,769,987	0	Northwest; Hacker
Wisconsin																
Manawa	3	M	597,000	507,000	6,000	84.50	72,000	Owned	18,000	20,000	33	125,000	0	0	472,000	Richard Thern
Milwaukee	26	B	3,344,000	1,890,374	16,500	114.57	152,547	1,100,798	200,281	60,000	119	0	0	3,344,000	0	Joy Peot Shields
Somerset	3	M	264,629	201,679	3,500	57.62	33,790	Owned	29,160	9,000	25	79,629	0	0	185,000	Cedar Corp.
Waupaca	13	M	1,957,456	1,496,781	24,000	62.37	333,000	Owned	127,675	80,000	114	0	0	1,457,456	500,000	Durrant Group

Symbol Code: B—Branch Library; BS—Branch & System Headquarters; M—Main Library; MS—Main & System Headquarters; S—System Headquarters; n/a—not available

Table 2 / Public Library Buildings: Additions and Renovations, 1994

Community	Pop. in M	Code	Project Cost	Const. Cost	Gross Sq.Ft.	Sq.Ft. Cost	Equip. Cost	Site Cost	Other Costs	Volumes	Reader Seats	Federal Funds	State Funds	Local Funds	Gift Funds	Architect
Alabama																
Enterprise	21	M	$355,336	$280,548	11,500	$24.40	$48,336	Owned	$26,452	45,000	75	$91,224	$0	$100,000	$164,112	Wm. Wallace
Huntsville	15	B	228,000	204,000	3,000	68.00	10,000	Owned	14,000	30,000	16	0	0	228,000	0	Larrell D. Hughes
Russellville	15	M	62,150	25,750	3,500	7.36	1,400	35,000	0	16,000	35	0	0	19,650	42,500	none
Arizona																
Gilbert	45	MS	250,122	0	15,000	00.00	110,122	0	140,000	90,000	112	0	0	250,122	0	Zell Commercial
Kearny	5	M	100,560	92,060	761	120.97	0	Owned	8,500	20,000	24	0	96,260	0	4,300	Micou Design Group
Arkansas																
Mountain Home	32	M	221,675	177,175	3,024	58.59	36,000	Owned	8,500	100,000	105	63,000	0	25,000	133,675	Terry Cooper
California																
Coalinga	17	M	386,955	332,919	11,722	30.84	3,000	Owned	51,036	66,600	50	0	0	368,955	18,000	Dwayne Schults
Huntington Beach	189	M	10,000,000	9,095,000	43,000	160.00	80,000	Owned	325,000	80,000	250	0	0	6,000,000	4,000,000	Anthony & Langford
Lakeside	46	B	413,446	343,446	1,800	190.80	20,000	Owrred	50,000	25,000	45	390,000	0	3,446	20,000	Donald Schucard
Los Angeles	9000	M	215,000,000	135,000,000	539,000	250,000	26,000,000	9,000,000	43,300,000	4,000,000	1,487	0	0	215,000,000	0	Hardy Holzman Pfeiffer
Colorado																
Boulder	20	B	975,000	779,472	9,650	80.77	91,000	Owned	104,528	30,000	48	0	0	975,000	0	Peter Heinz
Denver	n/a	B	1,006,568	786,612	10,124	77.70	54,455	Owned	165,501	50,600	43	0	0	1,006,568	0	David Owen Tryba
Denver	n/a	B	1,056,336	852,153	10,026	84.99	61,059	Owned	143,124	50,780	45	0	0	1,056,336	0	David Owen Tryba
Denver	n/a	B	691,472	521,966	8,923	58.50	55,774	Owned	113,732	58,500	58	0	0	691,472	0	Roth Sheppard
Denver	n/a	B	399,070	286,558	11,410	25.12	49,907	Owned	62,605	58,000	50	0	0	399,070	0	Pouw & Assocs.
Denver	n/a	B	476,562	365,930	7,665	47.74	30,778	Owned	79,854	43,000	48	0	0	476,562	0	Pouw & Assocs.
Denver	n/a	B	749,967	627,457	4,690	133.79	34,952	Owned	87,558	26,000	26	0	0	749,967	0	David Owen Tryba
Connecticut																
Ansonia	18	M	108,454	94,392	1,098	86.00	3,226	Owned	10,836	n/a	35	0	33,576	28,678	46,200	Joan O'Riordan
Danielson	17	M	3,615,000	1,634,000	20,000	81.71	312,000	1,400,000	269,000	73,000	96	100,000	350,000	3,165,000	0	Chris Placo
Falls Church	1	M	418,817	330,476	5,115	64.61	29,895	Owned	58,446	30,000	40	0	106,500	226,071	86,246	King & Tuthill
Washington	4	M	2,222,500	1,750,000	15,575	112.36	80,000	Owned	392,500	44,100	113	47,205	350,000	50,000	1,775,295	King & Tuthill
Weston	9	M	1,041,740	801,265	6,600	121.40	29,122	Owned	211,352	55,000	56	0	300,570	548,000	193,170	Leonard Sussman
Delaware																
Dover	60	M	51,000	41,000	2,000	21	10,000	Owned	0	2,100	7	0	15,817	0	35,183	none

Symbol Code: B—Branch Library; BS—Branch & System Headquarters; M—Main Library; MS—Main & System Headquarters; S—System Headquarters; n/a—not available

Table 2 / Public Library Buildings: Additions and Renovations, 1994 *(cont.)*

Community	Pop. in M	Code	Project Cost	Const. Cost	Gross Sq.Ft.	Sq.Ft. Cost	Equip. Cost	Site Cost	Other Costs	Volumes	Reader Seats	Federal Funds	State Funds	Local Funds	Gift Funds	Architect
Florida																
Brocksville	65	B	578,132	480,915	14,700	32.72	55,428	Owned	41,789	59,500	76	0	250,000	328,132	0	William Henry
Daytona Beach	36	M	828,000	668,800	15,000	44.60	52,200	Owned	107,000	n/a	n/a	0	828,000	0	0	Dana M. Smith
Daytona Beach	65	M	691,804	650,481	38,058	17.09	0	Owned	41,323	135,000	186	248,982	0	392,822	50,000	Dana M. Smith
Fort Myers Beach	15	M	1,586,997	1,247,511	14,669	85.04	210,461	Owned	129,025	72,600	126	0	0	1,276,841	310,156	Gora McGahey
Miami	161	B	2,939,575	640,500	51,800	12.36	1,898,111	Owned	400,964	175,000	232	0	0	2,939,575	0	Pelayo Fraga
Miami	130	B	833,463		41,500	0	717,122	Leased	116,341	150,000	168	833,463	0	0	0	Arnold Gitten
Naples	35	B	660,587	479,299	7,000	68.47	68,458	Owned	112,830	40,000	60	0	0	616,587	44,000	Steve Davis
Plant City	23	M	1,468,725	1,035,350	20,000	51.77	257,725	85,000	90,650	110,000	n/a	0	0	1,000,000	468,725	Harvard Jolly Clees…
Sarasota	75	B	280,966	235,000	3,050	77.05	21,966	Owned	24,000	9,500	16	0	0	130,000	150,966	Carl Abbott
Venice	50	B	863,643	750,000	6,000	125.00	53,643	Owned	60,000	26,675	35	0	0	435,000	428,643	James F. Soller
Georgia																
Atlanta	748	MS	2,969,317	2,351,348	29,740	79.06	481,555	Owned	136,414	0	0	0	0	2,969,317	0	Stevens & Wilkinson
Bainbridge	42	BS	1,559,589	1,138,527	19,500	58.39	180,084	Owned	240,978	100,000	119	250,000	954,987	322,650	31,952	James. W. Buckley
Boston	1	B	251,000	220,000	3,000	73.33	18,500	Owned	12,500	10,000	30	0	224,830	26,170	0	Jinright, Ryan, & Lynn
Decatur	33	B	448,070	310,451	10,000	31.05	106,854	0	30,765	63,800	72	0	0	448,070	0	Milton Pate Assocs.
Louisville	18	MS	401,609	283,980	8,200	34.63	78,010	Owned	39,619	30,000	60	0	349,150	52,459	0	Bob Brown
Idaho																
Buhl	4	M	217,072	164,318	3,840	42.79	41,333	Owned	11,421	31,357	58	0	67,780	0	149,292	Russ Lively
Challis	1	M	44,000	34,914	3,800	9.19	6,364	Owned	2,722	12,500	20	20,000	4,000	20,000	0	Sundberg & Assocs.
Mullan	1	M	592,982	513,340	11,000	46.67	0	Owned	79,642	10,000	10	346,988	25,880	220,114	0	C.J. Bellamy
Illinois																
Chicago	11	B	4,880,900	n/a	4,287	n/a	98,839	0	n/a	13,838	60	0	0	4,880,900	0	Johnson & Lee
Chicago	33	B	2,190,379	1,478,160	14,000	105.58	176,000	Owned	536,219	75,000	81	0	2,190,379	0	0	City of Chicago
Chicago	25	B	2,274,396	1,538,220	10,900	141.12	114,000	Owned	622,176	71,000	60	0	2,274,396	0	0	Jack Train Assocs.
Glencoe	8	M	1,100,000	870,000	12,000	72.50	65,000	Owned	165,000	90,000	92	0	0	1,095,000	5,000	R. Scott Javore
Indiana																
Monon	3	M	1,087,618	828,184	8,140	101.74	125,356	Owned	134,078	25,992	53	114,563	0	973,055	0	H.L. Mohler
Iowa																
Manchester	9	M	839,033	694,200	8,600	80.72	28,421	66,912	49,500	35,000	55	0	0	633,000	206,033	Bradd A. Brown

Symbol Code: B—Branch Library; BS—Branch & System Headquarters; M—Main Library; MS—Main & System Headquarters; S—System Headquarters; n/a—not available

Kentucky																
Louisville	58	B	917,321	706,462	9,500	74.36	141,431	Owned	69,428	60,000	51	0	0	864,153	53,168	Tucker & Booker
Louisville	20	B	589,600	540,001	7,200	75.01	3,039	Owned	45,500	55,000	80	539,600	0	50,000	0	T. Dade Luckett
Whitesburg	27	M	1,013,794	194,167	21,600	8.99	59,535	Owned	51,122	70,000	120	300,574	265,000	33,616	414,604	Wm. Richardson
Louisiana																
Alexandria	55	S	132,000	n/a	2,700	n/a	11,500	Owned	n/a	0	0	0	0	10,000	132,000	none
Bell City	1	B	40,164	22,249	720	30.90	11,450	Leased	6,465	3,900	6	0	0	40,164	0	Randy Goodloe
Franklin	9	MS	244,000	193,000	4,200	45.95	30,000	Owned	21,000	52,000	40	0	0	240,500	3,500	Carl Blum
Harrisonburg	11	M	24,120	19,192	2,880	6.70	4,528	Owned	0	1,500	8	0	0	24,120	0	Terry, Inc.
Hayes	2	B	118,135	77,227	950	81.29	23,733	Owned	17,175	3,900	8	0	0	118,135	0	Randy Goodloe
Iowa	3	B	258,157	191,157	2,920	65.46	45,922	Owned	21,078	12,786	9	0	0	258,157	0	Randy Goodloe
Lake Charles	71	B	1,283,415	980,616	17,285	56.73	139,415	Owned	163,384	34,535	28	0	0	1,283,415	0	Pat Gallaugher
Lake Charles	71	B	186,719	131,015	3,775	34.70	30,147	Owned	25,557	15,000	58	0	0	186,719	0	Randy Goodloe
Logansport	25	B	182,023	143,436	4,029	35.60	23,374	Owned	15,213	20,000	23	75,000	0	107,023	0	Lester Haas
Starks	3	B	216,249	129,366	1,699	76.14	29,990	Owned	56,893	12,500	20	0	0	216,249	0	Broussard/Moss
Vinton	3	B	228,095	153,637	2,735	56.17	43,739	Owned	30,719	12,500	14	0	0	228,095	0	Broussard/Moss
Winnsboro	22	MS	530,155	451,305	14,500	31.12	0	Owned	78,850	50,000	35	250,000	0	269,730	10,425	Wm. Mattison
Massachusetts																
Attleboro	38	M	3,346,000	2,581,475	10,000	258.15	32,185	Owned	732,340	145,000	120	0	663,850	1,461,801	1,220,349	Anthony Tappe
Chilmark	1	M	267,027	190,313	1,220	155.99	9,500	Owned	67,214	25,000	30	0	0	92,800	174,227	Ben Moore
Millis	8	M	110,000	103,200	660	156.36	0	Owned	6,800	0	8	0	0	12,000	93,000	Leo MacCormack
Michigan																
Detroit	1000	M	212,360	202,550	36,000	5.63	0	Owned	9,810	n/a	n/a	0	0	212,360	0	Detroit Roofing
Detroit	1000	B	31,326	28,800	7,242	3.97	0	Owned	2,526	n/a	n/a	31,326	0	0	0	McCleer Architect
Dryden	3	M	156,000	143,000	1,900	75.26	0	Owned	13,000	20,000	28	0	0	156,000	0	Wm. Vogan
Harrison	10	M	150,787	142,187	6,247	22.76	0	Owned	8,600	50,000	30	45,000	0	105,787	0	David Riebschleger
Hartland	21	M	142,640	74,639	6,250	11.94	56,193	Owned	11,808	30,000	48	36,731	0	87,116	18,793	Wakely Assocs.
Midland	70	M	5,352,245	4,310,000	105,000	41.05	566,245	Owned	474,000	250,000	194	0	0	1,520,000	3,832,245	Dow-Howell-Gilmore
Missouri																
Huntsville	25	B	462,113	422,900	8,000	57.76	16,308	Owned	20,905	30,000	20	0	0	462,113	0	Frye Gillan Molinaro
Moberly	25	MS	1,381,015	1,113,300	20,000	69.05	153,088	Owned 20,000	94,627	100,000	80	0	0	1,381,015	0	Frye Gillan Molinaro
Montana																
Fort Benton	6	M	379,660	342,267	12,000	28.52	7,558	Owned	29,835	50,000	35	0	0	330,700	0	James Page
Nebraska																
Lincoln	89	B	2,571,099	1,886,011	31,000	60.84	362,284	Owned	322,804	151,862	130	0	0	2,571,099	0	Sinclair Hille

Symbol Code: B—Branch Library; BS—Branch & System Headquarters; M—Main Library; MS—Main & System Headquarters; S—System Headquarters; n/a—not available

Table 2 / Public Library Buildings: Additions and Renovations, 1994 *(cont.)*

Community	Pop. in M	Code	Project Cost	Const. Cost	Gross Sq.Ft.	Sq.Ft. Cost	Equip. Cost	Site Cost	Other Costs	Volumes	Reader Seats	Federal Funds	State Funds	Local Funds	Gift Funds	Architect
New Hampshire																
Enfield	4	M	248,460	n/a	10,386	n/a	n/a	Owned	n/a	23,000	20	12,000	0	236,460	0	Paul Trementozzi
Hollis	6	M	500,000	435,000	5,500	79.09	50,000	Owned	15,000	n/a	n/a	25,000	0	339,640	135,360	Galliher, Baier & Best
Raymond	9	M	345,000	270,000	4,600	58.70	18,000	Owned	16,000	25,000	24	23,000	0	306,000	16,000	Patricia Sherman
New Jersey																
Lake Hiawatha	19	B	385,826	309,244	9,900	31.23	43,275	Owned	33,307	55,000	69	0	0	385,826	0	Pasquale A. Fusco
South Plainfield	20	M	58,917	5,481	1,010	5.43	28,768	Owned	24,668	50,000	61	0	0	58,917	0	Globus Design
Succasunna	20	M	353,541	280,729	4,510	62.24	51,489	Owned	21,323	57,000	100	0	24,067	0	329,474	Stephen Bias
New York																
Auburn	35	B	530,000	470,109	3,000	156.70	14,000	Owned	45,891	n/a	n/a	0	0	0	530,000	Lawrence Liberatore
Bolton Landing	2	M	60,935	58,735	1,400	42.00	700	Owned	1,500	25,000	26	0	0	60,935	0	Douglas Lafferty
Bristol	2	M	52,700	51,649	12,000	4.30	50	1	1,000	6,000	14	0	5,200	42,000	5,500	Mark Mueller
Brooklyn	40	B	1,275,000	971,000	10,690	90.83	0	Owned	304,000	22,781	n/a	0	0	1,275,000	0	Wallace Kaminsky
Dundee	4	M	46,000	30,100	514	58.56	13,000	Owned	2,900	n/a	n/a	0	0	4,000	42,000	David Healy
Greenwich	1	M	122,000	107,000	3,100	39.36	0	Owned	15,000	20,000	12	36,750	19,267	0	65,983	Albert T. Squire
Lockport	55	M	3,643,825	2,890,000	34,300	84.26	409,825	Owned	344,000	145,000	244	0	25,000	3,300,000	318,825	Marlin Casker
Nyack	15	M	950,000	818,000	15,600	52.44	60,000	Owned	72,000	75,000	80	29,750	0	845,250	75,000	Michael Esmay
Plainview	31	B	943,677	703,821	28,996	32.55	173,237	Owned	66,619	10,623	89	0	1,073	0	942,604	CRC Collaborative
Rochester	29	M	42,628	36,190	142	254.86	4,208	Owned	2,230	n/a	n/a	14,920	9,045	6,589	12,074	Martha Gates
Rochester	40	B	1,400,000	816,000	12,000	68.00	76,500	300,000	207,500	40,000	70	0	0	1,209,413	0	City of Rochester
Somers	17	M	1,700,000	1,468,855	8,795	167.01	38,204	Owned	192,941	81,000	103	190,587	0	1,700,000	0	William Hall
North Carolina																
Cary	64	B	72,283	66,283	11,000	6.03	0	Leased	6,000	60,000	85	0	0	72,283	0	Sharon Crawford
Raleigh	8	B	42,747	7,557	2,550	2.96	35,190	Leased	0	15,000	29	0	0	42,747	0	none
Ohio																
Chillicothe	69	M	380,920	259,109	7,679	33.74	66,843	Owned	54,968	84,994	67	0	0	380,920	0	William Koster
Medina	30	MS	1,217,529	709,868	24,035	26.93	71,420	340,089	96,152	150,000	273	0	0	1,217,529	0	David Holzheimer
Ripley	31	M	180,286	151,000	1,400	107.86	9,286	Owned	20,000	n/a	n/a	0	0	160,286	20,000	McGill Smith Punshon
Rossford	15	M	702,635	614,836	13,622	45.14	4,811	Owned	82,988	50,000	100	0	0	702,635	0	Favorite Design Group
Shaker Heights	30	MS	4,988,107	4,241,742	60,800	69.77	406,205	Owned	340,160	92,000	258	0	0	4,988,107	0	Blunden Barclay
Steubenville	52	B	1,165,000	1,088,785	10,900	107.00	117,000	Owned	134,500	70,000	280	0	0	1,165,000	0	Michael Tabeling
Wapakoneta	16	MS	109,062	35,350	7,500	4.68	60,169	Owned	13,543	63,945	65	0	0	109,062	0	none

Symbol Code: B—Branch Library; BS—Branch & System Headquarters; M—Main Library; MS—Main & System Headquarters; S—System Headquarters; n/a—not available

Oklahoma

Community	No.	Code														Architect
Stillwater	37	M	4,771,516	3,643,313	50,400	72.29	773,683	34,500	320,020	100,000	163	0	0	4,769,243	2,273	Robert A. Wright
Pennsylvania																
Blue Bell	33	MS	3,029,000	960,242	22,500	42.68	185,408	1,776,324	107,026	105,000	124	0	0	2,502,637	526,363	Diseroad & Wolff
Saxonburg	16	M	387,520	167,045	4,000	41.76	24,992	173,000	22,483	24,000	28	0	12,500	0	375,020	none
Rhode Island																
Jamestown	5	M	1,388,172	1,217,172	7,316	166.37	31,000	Owned	140,000	45,000	40	0	694,086	694,086	694,086	Jay Litman
South Carolina																
Hartsville	23	B	1,467,874	996,623	16,520	60.32	178,503	175,000	117,748	46,000	106	1,292,874	694,086	175,000	0	W. Daniel Shelley
Tennessee																
Gray	32	B	466,332	43,751	6,000	7.29	54,000	350,000	18,581	40,000	42	99,075	0	314,257	53,000	Uwe Rothe
Memphis	n/a	B	150,000	100,000	6,500	15.38	50,000	Owned	0	40,000	40	0	0	150,000	0	Ed Howington
Memphis	n/a	B	135,000	100,000	6,600	15.15	25,000	Owned	10,000	35,300	40	0	0	135,000	0	Formus Architects
Somerville	26	M	336,067	260,323	7,310	35.61	1,045	55,000	19,699	59,600	20	99,075	35,000	193,172	8,820	Ronald M. McFarland
Texas																
Anahuac	8	MS	533,623	434,509	8,430	51.54	57,836	Owned	41,278	40,800	70	0	0	533,623	0	Busch, Hutchison
Carrollton	89	B	1,361,699	652,292	24,792	26.31	644,817	Leased	64,590	71,000	108	0	0	1,361,699	0	Jones McConnell Jr.
Friendswood	27	M	1,062,148	466,824	13,544	34.47	68,996	458,942	67,386	76,000	94	0	20,000	711,633	330,515	Hall/Merriman
Melissa	1	MS	15,000	10,000	1,000	10.00	5,000	Owned	0	10,000	8	0	0	11,000	4,000	Charles Fry
Midland	107	M	2,903,458	2,178,059	53,218	40.93	207,000	301,764	216,635	540,000	180	200,000	0	1,548,458	1,155,000	Connolly Architects
Waco	20	B	48,000	16,000	700	22.86	30,000	Leased	2,000	4,620	12	0	0	0	48,000	none
Utah																
Park City	20	B	n/a	600	2,400	00.43	n/a	Leased	n/a	10,000+	12	3,000	0	0	250	none
Salt Lake City	17	B	636,125	527,346	5,900	89.38	54,004	Owned	54,775	55,000	40	0	0	636,125	0	Brixen & Christopher
Salt Lake City	21	B	694,006	516,864	5,200	99.20	82,248	Owned	94,894	55,000	64	0	0	461,245	232,761	EDA Inc
Virginia																
Radford	16	M	351,171	325,171	13,654	23.82	0	Owned	26,000	82,241	86	121,959	0	175,000	54,212	Glenn Reynolds
Washington																
Lakewood	65	B	1,083,008	844,953	32,488	26.01	111,208	Owned	126,847	135,000	156	0	0	680,845	402,163	Lewis Architects
Wisconsin																
Mazomanie	2	M	452,617	344,371	3,600	95.66	48,739	29,772	29,735	15,000	19	121,500	75,000	56,070	200,047	CSG, Inc.
Milwaukee	52	B	436,807	289,794	22,548	25.09	73,730	Owned	73,233	60,000	92	0	0	436,807	0	Del Wilson
Milwaukee	59	B	523,857	356,206	14,739	24.18	64,520	83,131	83,131	75,000	93	0	0	523,857	0	Del Wilson
Oconto	10	M	598,980	520,003	10,675	48.71	-2,137	Owned	66,840	35,000	58	125,000	0	343,399	130,581	CPR Assocs.
Oshkosh	67	M	10,841,928	7,464,748	71,767	104.01	654,520	679,172	2,043,488	193,475	313	10,610	90,000	5,603,457	5,203,177	Frye Gillan; HNTB

Symbol Code: B—Branch Library; BS—Branch & System Headquarters; V—Main Library; MS—Main & System Headquarters; S—System Headquarters; n/a—not available

Table 3 / Public Library Buildings: Six-Year Cost Summary, 1989–1994

	Fiscal 1989	Fiscal 1990	Fiscal 1991	Fiscal 1992	Fiscal 1993	Fiscal 1994
No. of new buildings	111	127	120	118	113	108
No. of ARRs*	124	123	108	115	105	127
Sq. ft. new buildings	1,760,743	1,592,389	1,520,121	1,935,111	1,896,197	1,818,522
Sq. ft. ARRs	1,612,495	1,707,313	1,689,484	1,819,787	1,878,628	2,163,909
New Buildings						
Construction cost	$160,937,343	$128,175,181	$121,884,749	$188,143,273	$183,978,065	$176,678,555
Equipment cost	19,450,410	16,922,110	18,603,687	27,234,207	22,651,001	27,617,314
Site cost	14,191,713	13,147,809	14,504,740	21,011,768	28,353,201	34,696,765
Other cost	16,693,362	13,357,985	18,521,472	31,315,471	32,275,926	30,114,637
Total—Project cost	211,716,128	176,628,983	176,127,088	267,704,719	267,770,932	271,051,271
ARRs—Project cost	135,015,044	113,769,695	141,262,919	205,103,863	160,825,726	345,135,792
New and ARR project cost	$346,731,172	$290,398,678	$317,390,007	$472,808,582	$428,596,658	$616,187,063
Fund sources						
Federal, new buildings	$8,140,109	$10,593,149	$8,139,146	$9,851,065	$4,320,934	$4,483,792
Federal, ARRs	8,264,044	6,984,747	6,533,719	7,413,576	3,646,307	6,188,756
Federal, total	$16,404,153	$17,577,896	$14,672,865	$17,264,641	$7,967,241	$10,672,548
State, new buildings	$48,714,905	$29,450,257	$14,349,412	$10,753,499	$26,376,138	$45,559,588
State, ARRs	6,997,782	7,315,892	11,439,866	43,002,552	10,841,063	10,361,213
State, total	$55,712,687	$36,766,149	$25,789,278	$53,756,051	$37,217,201	$55,920,801
Local, new buildings	$137,650,121	$124,136,070	$138,176,957	$230,815,119	$208,363,930	$203,676,929
Local, ARRs	108,753,024	84,323,211	111,788,933	139,135,045	141,961,411	302,050,882
Local, total	$246,403,145	$208,459,281	$249,965,890	$369,950,164	$350,325,341	$505,727,811
Gift, new buildings	$17,428,326	$13,094,262	$15,810,151	$16,487,880	$28,878,559	$17,663,214
Gift, ARRs	11,219,980	15,928,366	11,561,261	15,849,230	4,389,236	26,614,547
Gift, total	$28,648,306	$29,022,628	$27,371,412	$32,337,110	$33,267,795	$44,277,761
Total Funds Used	$347,168,291	$291,825,954	$317,799,445	$473,307,966	$428,777,578	$616,598,921

*Additions, remodelings, and renovations.

Table 4 / New Academic Library Buildings, 1994

Institution	Project Cost	Gross Sq.Ft.	Sq.Ft. Cost	Construction Cost	Equipment Cost	Book Capacity	Seating Capacity	Architect
Science Library, University of California, Irvine	$32,226,000	189,570	$150.11	$28,457,000	$1,490,000	500,000	2,200	Wilford & Partners; IBI Group
Memphis State University	26,500,000	250,000	73.19	18,298,300	2,685,000	1,139,000	2,180	Pickering; Jones Mah Gaskill
California State University, Bakersfield	20,946,500	150,000	93.40	14,005,500	3,800,000	600,000	800	Esherick, Homsey, Dodge...
Seton Hall University, South Orange, N.J.	20,000,000	155,000	106.45	16,500,000	2,100,000	1,000,000	1,100	Skidmore, Owings...; Alfieri
Loyola University, Chicago	15,433,245	103,751	117.06	12,145,092	1,341,500	300,000	1,000	Holabird + Root
Eskind Biomedical Library, Vanderbilt University Medical Center, Nashville	13,500,000	78,000	150.40	11,731,000	553,000	217,000	239	Davis, Brody & Assocs.; Thomas Miller & Partners
Pennsylvania State University, Erie	11,157,000	97,000	97.68	9,476,000	1,100,000	225,000	825	L.D. Astorino
Sylvania Library, Portland Community College, Ore.	10,682,734	60,685	124.33	7,545,108	1,322,308	90,000	893	BOOR/A
Seattle Pacific University	9,000,000	62,000	104.84	6,500,000	1,000,000	400,000	650	Gabbert, Broweleit...
Jim Cherry Learning Resource Center, Dekalb College, Decatur, Ga.	8,850,097	107,000	79.33	8,488,522	756,800	300,000	1,250	Lord, Aeck, & Sargent
Bruno Business Library, University of Alabama, Tuscaloosa	8,400,000	65,996	n/a	n/a	336,000	200,000	787	PH&J Architects
West Campus Library, Texas A&M University, College Station	5,791,979	68,750	77.24	5,310,336	51,225	n/a	1,650	Ray Bailey Architects
Hendrix College, Conway, Ark.	n/a	63,138	81.48	5,144,250	349,000	275,000	450	Wittenberg, Delony...
Southwestern Adventist College, Keene, Tex.	3,351,000	45,000	72.78	3,275,231	75,769	167,280	302	Don Palmer
Hoole Special Collections Library, University of Alabama, Tuscaloosa	2,700,000	32,775	n/a	n/a	30,000	105,000	36	Garikes, Wilson & Assocs.
National College of Chiropractic, Lombard, Ill.	2,379,256	14,700	99.61	1,464,241	0	25,000	250	Daniel T. Roach
Baker College of Owosso, Mich.	1,000,000	14,800	54.05	800,000	200,000	45,000	175	Robert W. Giesey

Table 5 / Academic Library Buildings: Additions and Renovations, 1994

Institution	Status	Project Cost	Gross Sq.Ft.	Sq.Ft. Cost	Construction Cost	Equipment Cost	Book Capacity	Seating Capacity	Architect
Mississippi State University, Mississippi State	Total	$16,900,000	228,000	$60.97	$13,900,000	$2,000,000	1,600,000	1,600	Foil-Wyatt
	New	13,500,000	108,000	111.11	12,000,000	1,000,000	700,000	850	
	Renovated	3,400,000	120,000	15.83	1,900,000	1,000,000	900,000	750	
Alexander Library, Rutgers, the State University of New Jersey, New Brunswick	Total	14,834,570	90,000+	125.11	11,260,000	865,770	400,000	1,333	Hillier Group
	New	11,798,000	68,000	130.88	8,900,000	189,200	400,000	300	
	Renovated	3,036,570	22,000	107.27	2,360,000	676,570	0	1,033	
University of Rhode Island, Kingston	Total	13,500,000	237,500	n/a	n/a	n/a	1,500,000	1,300	Robinson Green Beretta
	New	n/a	89,000	n/a	n/a	n/a	700,000	190	
	Renovated	n/a	148,500	n/a	n/a	n/a	800,000	1,110	
University of Idaho, Moscow	Total	12,900,000	141,000	91.49	12,900,000	0	1,100,000	1,100	Ellis-Feeney; Integrus Architecture
	New	n/a	66,000	n/a	n/a	n/a	n/a	n/a	
	Renovated	n/a	75,000	n/a	n/a	n/a	n/a	n/a	
University of Wisconsin–au Claire	Total	8,300,000	77,000	81.82	6,300,000	1,200,000	700,092	1,970	Seymour Davis Seymour
	New	n/a	47,000	n/a	n/a	200,000	169,776	394	
	Renovated	n/a	30,000	n/a	n/a	1,000,000	530,316	1,576	
Dana Library, Rutgers, the State University of New Jersey, Newark	Total	7,380,000	47,388	123.96	5,874,000	631,000	252,800	1,072	Faridy Thorne Fraytak
	New	n/a	44,232	n/a	n/a	n/a	250,000	n/a	
	Renovated	n/a	3,156	n/a	n/a	n/a	2,800	n/a	
Montclair State University, Upper Montclair, N.J.	Total	5,623,023	107,560	45.72	4,917,123	705,900	480,300	718	H2L2 Architects
	New	4,498,418	42,816	88.58	3,792,518	705,900	202,600	356	
	Renovated	1,124,605	64,744	17.37	1,124,605	n/a	277,700	362	
Art Institute of Chicago	Total	4,000,000	27,430	103.20	2,830,643	494,650	364,000	60	V.O.A. Assocs; John Vinci Architects
	New	3,600,000	20,630	122.40	2,525,543	477,000	244,000	0	
	Renovated	400,000	6,800	44.86	305,100	17,650	120,000	60	

Table 6 / Academic Library Buildings: Additions Only, 1994

Institution	Project Cost	Gross Area	Sq.Ft. Cost	Construction Cost	Equipment Cost	Book Capacity	Seating Capacity	Architect
Washington State University, Pullman	$36,000,000	293,000	$100.34	$29,400,000	$3,114,000	n/a	674	ALSC; Zimmer Gunsul...
Arkansas State University, State University	10,976,369	119,667	87.55	10,476,369	500,000	490,000	1600	Brackett-Krennerich
Dwight Opperman Hall & Law Library, Drake University, Des Moines	8,123,066	71,110	98.40	6,997,066	456,000	225,434	345	Leonard Parker Assocs.
Cooley Science Library, Colgate University, Hamilton, N.Y.	350,000	3,000	104.00	312,000	0	10,000	44	T.W. Inglehart
Baker College of Flint, Mich.	300,000	3,000	78.33	235,000	65,000	15,000+	50+	Robert W. Giesey

Table 7 / Academic Library Buildings: Renovations Only, 1994

Institution	Project Cost	Gross Area	Sq.Ft. Cost	Construction Cost	Equipment Cost	Book Capacity	Seating Capacity	Architect
Johnson & Wales University, Providence	$3,000,000	43,685	$52.65	$2,300,000	$525,000	100,000	570	Robinson Green Beretta
Elmhurst College, Ill.	2,500,000	65,700	33.49	2,200,000	225,000	229,695	437	Balluff & Balluff
West Campus Library, Washington University, in St. Louis	1,700,000	43,000	32.56	1,400,000	3,200,000	140,000	35	Hastings & Chivetta/MDWR
Briar Cliff College, Sioux City, Iowa	1,043,310	17,200	57.79	721,798	321,332	110,000	250	Duffy, Ruble, Mamura...
North Park College & Theological Seminary, Chicago	251,395	2,580	33.66	86,850	164,545	66,000	54	Booth/Hansen Assocs.
University of Wisconsin–Madison	192,000	3,909	43.37	169,515	n/a	n/a	n/a	Strang, Inc.
Iowa State University, Ames	97,204	1,862	52.50	97,204	0	0	0	ISU Architects
Colorado Technical College, Colorado Springs	34,303	2,555	8.59	21,949	12,354	4,500+	75	Warren Keeler

Book Trade Research and Statistics

Prices of U.S. and Foreign Published Materials

Adrian W. Alexander
Chair, ALA ALCTS Library Materials Price Index Committee

In 1993, price increases for library materials, as studied by the ALCTS Library Materials Price Index Committee (LMPIC), moderated somewhat, as U.S. periodicals, serial services, and academic books experienced only slight increases, while hardcover trade book prices dropped dramatically. Only mass market and trade paperbacks showed any kind of significant increase (see chart below). For 1994, however, price changes were more varied. Periodicals returned to a more "typical" pattern, while hardcover trade books regained their pre-1993 price levels, but serial services and college books showed only moderate increases.

		Percent Change	
Index	1992	1993	1994
Consumer price index	2.9	1.3	2.7
Periodicals	12.2	5.5	9.6
Serial services	8.0	4.8	5.0
Hardcover books	2.0	-22.3	22.7*
Academic books	6.4	2.8	n.a.
College books	6.6	3.0	-2.0
Mass market paperbacks	2.8	11.5	-1.4*
Trade paperbacks	2.2	9.3	-2.5*

* preliminary; n.a. = not available

U.S. Published Materials

Tables 1 though 10 report average prices and price indexes for library materials published primarily in the United States. Categories include periodicals (Table 1), serial services (Table 2), hardcover books (Table 3), North American academic books (Table 4), college books (Table 5), mass market paperback books (Table 6), trade paperback books (Table 7), daily newspapers (Table 8), nonprint media (Table 9), and CD-ROMs (Table 10).

(text continues on p. 495)

Table 1 / U.S. Periodicals: Average Prices and Price Indexes, 1993–1995
(Index Base: 1977 = 100)

Subject Area	1977 Average Price	1993 Average Price	1993 Index	1994 Average Price	1994 Index	1995 Average Price	1995 Index
U.S. periodicals excluding Russian translations*	$24.59	$123.55	502.4	$135.37	550.5	$149.46	607.8
U.S. periodicals including Russian translations	33.42	165.25	494.5	179.53	537.2	196.57	588.2
Agriculture	11.58	53.17	459.2	57.05	492.7	62.07	536.0
Business and economics	18.62	81.33	436.8	88.10	473.1	94.37	506.8
Chemistry and physics	93.76	605.46	645.8	678.03	723.2	767.96	819.1
Children's periodicals	5.82	19.83	340.7	20.43	351.0	21.31	366.2
Education	17.54	70.48	401.8	74.76	426.2	80.87	451.1
Engineering	35.77	180.00	503.2	195.62	546.9	216.23	604.5
Fine and applied arts	13.72	42.08	306.7	44.92	327.4	46.74	340.7
General interest periodicals	16.19	35.73	220.7	37.39	230.9	38.45	237.5
History	12.64	42.46	335.9	44.99	355.9	47.83	378.4
Home economics	18.73	77.33	412.9	82.23	439.0	86.32	460.9
Industrial arts	14.37	74.66	519.6	78.78	548.2	82.49	574.0

Journalism and communications	16.97	447.2	80.14	472.2	86.06	507.1
Labor and industrial relations	11.24	649.0	78.42	697.7	81.59	725.9
Law	17.36	423.0	76.06	438.1	78.26	450.8
Library and information sciences	16.97	358.3	63.04	371.5	67.98	400.6
Literature and language	11.82	316.9	39.72	336.0	41.80	353.6
Mathematics, botany, geology, general science	47.13	511.2	271.68	576.4	308.79	655.2
Medicine	51.31	562.0	321.39	626.4	362.52	706.5
Philosophy and religion	10.89	347.5	40.25	369.6	42.86	393.6
Physical education and recreation	10.00	377.4	39.47	394.7	41.59	415.9
Political science	14.83	442.1	70.50	475.4	77.99	525.9
Psychology	31.74	493.8	171.80	541.3	190.58	600.4
Russian translations	175.41	516.7	964.13	549.6	1,033.65	589.3
Sociology and anthropology	19.68	493.1	106.28	540.0	115.77	588.3
Zoology	33.69	651.8	243.38	722.4	266.72	791.7
Total number of periodicals						
Excluding Russian translations	3,218	3,731	3,731	3,731		
Including Russian translations	3,418	3,942	3,941	3,941		

Compiled by Adrian W. Alexander and Kathryn Hammell Carpenter. For further comments see *American Libraries*, May 1993 and May 1994 issues. The price index is based on subscription price information supplied, compiled, and analyzed by the Faxon Company, and follows guidelines, definitions, and criteria established by the American National Standards Institute in *American National Standard for Library and Information Services and Related Publishing Practices—Library Materials—Criteria for Price Indexes* (ANSI Z39.20—1983).

* The category Russian Translations was added in 1986.

Table 2 / U.S. Serial Services: Average Prices and Price Indexes, 1993–1995*
(Index Base: 1977 = 100)

Subject Area	1977 Average Price	1993 Average Price	1993 Index	1994 Average Price	1994 Percent Increase	1994 Index	1995 Average Price	1995 Percent Increase	1995 Index
U.S. serial services**	$142.27	$466.57	327.9	$489.76	5	344.2	$522.01	6.6	366.9
Business	216.28	641.28	296.5	676.44	5.5	312.8	695.88	2.9	321.7
General and humanities	90.44	336.71	372.3	362.25	7.6	400.5	381.80	5.4	422.2
Law	126.74	490.44	387	504.86	2.9	398.3	542.73	7.5	428.2
Science and technology	141.16	560.45	397	593.73	5.9	420.6	640.14	7.8	453.5
Social sciences	145.50	448.88	308.5	466.86	4	320.9	487.16	4.3	334.8
U.S. documents	62.88	117.93	187.5	121.98	3.4	194	121.28	-0.6	192.9
Wilson Index	87.51	301.17	344.2	311.41	3.4	355.9	304.05	-2.4	347.4
Total number of services	1,432	1,308					1,299		

* 1994 and 1995 data compiled by Nancy J. Chaffin, Arizona State University (West); 1993 data compiled by Mark Sandler, University of Michigan, from data supplied by the Faxon Company, publishers' list prices, and library acquisition records. For further comments, see American Libraries, May 1995, "Serials Services 1995," by Nancy J. Chaffin, and American Libraries, May 1993, "Serials Services 1993," by Mark Sandler.

The definition of a serial service has been taken from American National Standard for Library and Information Services and Related Publishing Practices—Library Materials—Criteria for Price Indexes (ANSI Z39.20—1983).

** Excludes "Wilson Index"; excludes Russian Translations as of 1988.

Table 3 / U.S. Hardcover Books: Average Prices and Price Indexes, 1991–1994
(Index Base: 1977 = 100)

Subject Area	1977 Average Price	1977 Volumes	1991 Average Price	1991 Index	1992 Volumes	1992 Average Price	1992 Index	1993 Volumes	1993 Average Price	1993 Index	1994 (Preliminary) Volumes	1994 (Preliminary) Average Price	1994 (Preliminary) Index
Agriculture	$16.24	371	$57.73	355.5	359	$53.76	331.0	269	$41.84	257.6	226	$56.87	350.2
Art	21.24	717	44.99	211.8	815	44.59	209.9	812	39.99	188.3	654	39.70	186.9
Biography	15.34	1,416	27.52	179.4	1,359	30.41	198.2	1,290	28.37	198.0	1,102	29.78	194.1
Business	18.00	790	43.38	241.0	832	43.91	243.9	791	37.95	210.8	735	42.27	234.8
Education	12.95	556	41.26	318.5	653	48.77	376.6	574	38.60	298.1	445	50.43	389.4
Fiction	10.09	2,062	21.30	211.1	2,052	20.39	202.1	2,093	19.50	193.3	1,962	20.85	206.6
General works	30.99	1,071	51.74	167.0	1,160	56.29	181.6	882	45.41	146.5	760	55.54	179.2
History	17.12	1,442	39.87	232.9	1,533	39.19	223.9	1,429	40.78	238.2	1,159	39.86	232.8
Home economics	11.16	341	24.24	217.2	369	24.88	222.9	422	20.55	184.1	390	20.87	187.0
Juvenile	6.65	3,705	16.64	250.2	3,646	14.46	217.4	3,599	13.87	208.6	2,855	14.44	217.1
Language	14.96	240	51.72	345.7	362	49.68	332.1	308	34.02	227.4	246	54.23	362.5
Law	25.04	753	64.90	259.2	766	76.21	304.4	560	53.94	215.4	524	64.67	258.3
Literature	15.78	1,265	36.76	233.0	1,409	39.23	248.6	1,289	35.30	223.7	1,011	37.63	238.5
Medicine	24.00	2,078	71.44	297.7	2,277	75.22	313.4	1,360	49.78	207.4	1,476	76.22	317.6
Music	20.13	173	41.04	203.9	207	47.37	235.3	198	41.44	205.9	134	39.82	197.8
Philosophy and psychology	14.43	945	42.74	296.2	1,032	46.85	324.7	912	39.44	273.3	728	45.46	315.0
Poetry and drama	13.63	511	33.29	244.2	462	36.76	269.7	500	31.06	227.9	389	32.51	238.5
Religion	12.26	958	32.33	263.7	1,110	35.31	288.0	1,204	29.16	237.8	931	30.68	250.2
Science	24.88	1,818	80.14	322.1	1,955	81.95	329.4	1,261	52.71	211.9	1,294	77.50	311.5
Sociology and economics	29.88	4,306	48.43	162.1	4,861	45.53	152.4	4,300	41.32	138.3	3,559	49.85	166.8
Sports and recreation	12.28	440	30.68	249.8	465	34.62	231.9	462	32.28	262.9	349	33.03	269.0
Technology	23.61	1,620	76.40	323.6	1,621	82.18	348.1	981	56.31	238.5	822	79.12	335.1
Travel	18.44	156	32.43	175.9	182	33.28	180.5	159	26.22	142.2	129	35.41	192.0
Total	$19.22	27,734	$44.17	229.8	29,487	$45.05	234.4	25,665	$35.00	182.0	21,880	$42.96	223.5

Compiled by Adrian W. Alexander, Faxon Company, from data supplied by the R. R. Bowker Company. Price indexes on Tables 3 and 7 are based on books recorded in the R. R. Bowker Company's *Weekly Record* (cumulated in *American Book Publishing Record*). The 1994 preliminary figures include items listed during 1994 with an imprint date of 1994. Final data for previous years include items listed between January of that year and June of the following year with an imprint date of the specified year.

Table 4 / North American Academic Books: Average Prices and Price Indexes 1991–1993
(Index Base: 1989 = 100)

Subject Area	LC Class	1989		1991		1992		1993		
		No. of Titles	Average Price	No. of Titles	Average Price	No. of Titles	Average Price	No. of Titles	Average Price	% Change 1992–1993	Index
Agriculture	S	897	$45.13	781	$56.97	870	$52.63	682	$53.33	1.3	118.2
Anthropology	GN	406	32.81	400	35.34	487	35.07	463	36.75	4.8	112.0
Botany	QK	251	69.02	199	85.12	188	91.03	234	97.92	7.6	141.9
Business and economics	H	5,979	41.67	5,908	41.39	5,489	45.21	5,779	45.95	1.6	110.3
Chemistry	QD	577	110.61	544	110.63	520	127.47	544	127.30	-0.1	115.1
Education	L	1,685	29.61	1,692	35.55	1,802	36.10	1,844	37.62	4.2	127.1
Engineering and technology	T	4,569	64.94	4,563	70.67	4,615	75.70	4,659	76.48	1.0	117.8
Fine and applied arts	M-N	3,040	40.72	2,826	43.11	2,765	41.83	2,984	44.37	6.1	109.0
General works	A	333	134.65	129	41.42	119	38.09	90	47.29	24.2	35.1
Geography	G	396	47.34	384	50.44	458	54.40	548	50.64	-6.9	107.0
Geology	QE	303	63.49	209	71.51	202	76.40	251	78.72	3.0	124.0
History	C-D-E-F	5,549	31.34	5,545	37.04	5,638	32.29	5,662	34.05	5.5	108.6
Home economics	TX	535	27.10	510	28.64	556	27.66	614	29.60	7.0	109.2
Industrial arts	TT	175	23.89	159	30.25	172	24.26	173	22.68	-6.5	94.9
Law	K	1,252	51.10	1,414	54.62	1,406	59.67	1,555	62.04	4.0	121.4
Library and information science	Z	857	44.51	659	41.35	934	44.46	686	40.99	-7.8	92.1

Subject	LC Class										
Literature and language	P	10,812	24.99	10,804	30.02	10,469	27.62	11,066	27.83	0.8	111.4
Mathematics and computer science	QA	2,707	44.68	2,629	50.47	3,124	52.33	3,010	53.53	2.3	119.8
Medicine	R	5,028	58.38	5,244	63.58	5,109	65.99	4,889	67.01	1.5	114.8
Military and naval science	U-V	715	33.57	507	39.03	399	40.49	412	39.88	-1.5	118.8
Physical education and recreation	GV	814	20.38	644	35.14	726	33.69	777	22.61	-32.9	110.9
Philosophy and religion	B	3,518	29.06	3,672	25.15	3,534	22.77	3,734	34.22	50.3	117.8
Physics and astronomy	QB	1,219	64.59	1,236	82.90	1,222	83.78	1,180	87.75	4.7	135.9
Political science	J	1,650	36.76	1,376	49.25	1,479	42.11	1,524	43.03	2.2	117.1
Psychology	BF	890	31.97	933	36.61	896	38.52	813	39.03	1.3	122.1
Science (general)	Q	433	56.10	362	59.40	382	74.19	359	64.04	-13.7	114.2
Sociology	HM	2,742	29.36	2,906	36.07	3,085	34.64	2,997	35.19	1.6	119.9
Zoology	QH, L, P, R	1,967	71.28	1,985	79.20	1,789	78.76	1,853	82.43	4.7	115.6
Average for all subjects		59,299	$41.69	58,270	$45.84	58,435	$45.91	59,382	$47.17	2.8	113.1

Compiled by Stephen Bosch, University of Arizona from electronic data provided by Baker and Taylor; Blackwell/North America, Coutts Library Services, and Yankee Book Peddler. This table covers titles published or distributed in the United States and Canada during the calendar years listed.

Table 5 / U.S. College Books: Average Prices and Price Indexes, 1978, 1992, 1993, 1994
(Index Base for all years: 1978 = 100. 1993 also indexed to 1992; 1994 also indexed to 1993)

Subject Area	1978		1992			1993				1994			
	Number of Titles	Average Price per Title	Number of Titles	Average Price per Title	Prices Indexed to 1978	Number of Titles	Average Price per Title	Prices Indexed to 1978	Prices Indexed to 1992	Number of Titles	Average Price per Title	Prices Indexed to 1978	Prices Indexed to 1993
General	47	$15.25	12	$69.77	457.5	16	$54.45	357.0	78.0	8	$47.16	309.3	86.6
Humanities	92	16.14	20	35.48	219.8	15	40.41	250.4	113.9	18	39.46	244.5	97.6
Art and architecture	315	26.60	325	57.88	217.6	297	57.76	217.1	99.8	311	60.03	225.7	103.9
Photography[1]	—		16	53.18		16	48.92		92.0	0			
Communication	71	14.03	45	38.68	275.7	59	42.67	304.1	110.3	73	39.17	279.2	91.8
Language and literature	97	13.38	141	24.17	180.6	53	36.94	276.1	152.8	83	42.84	320.2	116.0
English and American	834	12.42	489	39.75	320.0	573	36.30	292.3	91.3	488	38.33	308.6	105.6
Germanic	51	12.35	55	32.92	266.6	49	34.25	277.3	104.0	44	35.57	288.0	103.8
Romance	101	12.27	100	42.39	345.5	91	34.82	283.8	82.1	124	33.16	270.2	95.2
Slavic	46	13.22	44	33.77	255.4	34	36.83	278.6	109.1	36	41.31	312.5	112.2
Non-European[4]	67	13.03	82	35.68	273.8	58	40.70	312.4	114.1	35	37.41	287.1	91.9
Performing arts	16	15.07	9	54.19	359.6	20	35.22	233.7	65.0	23	35.10	232.9	99.7
Dance	21	12.95	13	22.40	173.0	13	38.67	298.6	172.6	9	35.32	272.7	91.3
Film	80	15.70	70	38.89	247.7	87	39.68	252.7	102.0	104	38.47	245.0	97.0
Music	138	15.10	140	48.09	318.5	176	43.06	285.2	89.5	166	40.18	266.1	93.3
Theater	34	13.84	38	43.15	311.8	56	39.97	288.8	92.6	59	45.76	330.6	114.5
Philosophy	197	14.21	233	44.58	313.7	236	42.62	299.9	95.6	221	41.91	294.9	98.3
Religion	300	11.98	177	37.66	314.4	141	36.74	306.7	97.6	179	36.66	306.0	99.8
Total humanities[3]	2,500	$14.86	1,997	$42.24	284.3	1,974	$41.54	279.5	98.3	1,973	$42.22	284.1	101.6
Science and technology	102	$21.31	93	$44.29	207.8	89	$44.94	210.9	101.5	118	$40.76	191.3	90.7
History of science/technology	85	17.37	81	44.62	256.9	46	37.62	216.6	84.3	42	41.02	236.2	109.0
Astronautics/astronomy	22	23.78	43	47.91	201.5	51	51.36	216.0	107.2	38	35.51	149.3	69.1
Biology	231	23.67	138	53.66	226.7	122	53.50	226.0	99.7	107	54.22	229.1	101.4
Botany[1]	—	—	86	67.83	—	83	53.32		78.6	75	51.88		97.3
Zoology[1]	—	—	66	53.52	—	70	46.48		86.8	60	53.69		115.5
Chemistry	95	28.59	58	66.05	231.0	75	86.55	302.7	131.0	64	74.81	261.7	86.4
Earth science	84	29.99	65	63.09	210.4	49	71.57	238.6	113.4	48	65.90	219.8	92.1
Engineering	241	25.75	114	76.43	296.8	125	68.27	265.1	89.3	120	72.34	280.9	106.0
Health sciences	92	14.88	111	41.29	277.5	158	41.72	280.4	101.0	164	42.10	283.0	100.9
Information/computer science	53	20.37	83	42.57	209.0	60	46.54	228.5	109.3	78	45.56	223.7	97.9

Physics	47	28.77	53	58.40	203.0	57	56.11	195.0	96.1	47	52.04	180.9	92.8
Sports and physical education	73	10.32	21	39.55	383.2	30	38.29	371.0	96.8		30.74	297.8	80.3
Total sciences	1,195	$22.77	1,094	$54.09	237.5	1,089	$53.68	235.7	99.2	1,091	$51.26	225.1	95.5
Social/behavioral sciences	156	$16.37	31	$36.66	223.9	49	$43.46	265.5	118.5	38	$40.21	245.6	92.5
Anthropology	102	16.97	195	46.30	272.8	152	42.38	249.7	91.5	141	44.17	260.3	104.2
Business, management, labor	136	14.36	135	40.49	282.0	153	41.63	289.9	102.8	147	36.63	255.1	88.0
Economics	242	17.65	348	46.30	262.3	295	46.09	261.1	99.5	303	44.78	253.7	97.2
Education	129	12.48	92	40.66	325.8	113	47.18	378.0	116.0	114	40.10	321.3	85.0
History/geography/area studies	116	16.26	50	46.77	287.6	39	38.38	236.0	82.1	47	42.61	262.1	111.0
Africa	38	16.34	43	43.31	265.1	28	48.73	298.2	112.5	44	46.68	285.7	95.8
Asia and Oceania	78	19.03	87	42.83	225.1	55	47.09	247.5	109.9	79	53.50	281.1	113.6
Europe	308	16.52	354	50.42	305.2	336	47.95	290.3	95.1	276	47.64	288.4	99.4
Latin America and Caribbean	47	15.82	54	40.50	256.0	47	42.88	271.0	105.9	58	43.35	274.0	101.1
Middle East and North Africa	40	16.80	49	46.37	276.0	63	47.90	285.1	103.3	56	45.16	268.8	94.3
North America	275	16.08	380	33.01	205.3	400	36.37	226.2	110.2	371	36.99	230.0	101.7
Political science	281	14.74	12	55.80	378.6	30	40.21	272.8	72.1	18	40.73	276.3	101.3
Comparative politics[2]	—	—	162	41.82	—	171	44.48	—	106.4	202	44.81	—	100.7
International relations[2]	—	—	162	41.21	—	122	44.97	—	109.1	138	43.24	—	96.2
Political theory[2]	—	—	106	41.70	—	69	41.95	—	100.6	72	40.31	—	96.1
U.S. politics[2]	—	—	195	36.43	—	172	39.36	—	108.0	164	38.51	—	97.8
Psychology	142	15.39	146	41.02	266.5	153	44.56	289.5	108.6	149	39.33	255.6	88.3
Sociology	280	14.69	200	39.77	270.7	213	42.09	286.5	105.8	201	41.16	280.2	97.8
Total social/behavioral sciences	2,437	$15.98	2,801	$42.07	263.3	2,660	$43.14	270.0	102.5	2,618	$42.24	264.3	97.9
Total (excluding reference)[3]	6,179	$16.83	5,904	$44.41	263.9	5,739	$44.62	265.1	100.5	5,690	$43.97	261.3	98.5
Reference	453	$34.15	655	$75.13	220.0	720	$53.15	243.5	110.7	683	$80.91	236.9	97.3
Grand total (with reference)[3]	6,632	$18.02	6,559	$47.48	263.5	6,459	$48.92	271.5	103.0	6,373	$47.93	266.0	98.0

Compiled by Donna Alsbury, Florida Center for Library Automation, from book reviews appearing in Choice during the calendar year indicated. The cooperation of the Choice editorial staff is gratefully acknowledged. Additional information about these data appears in the April issue of Choice.
1 Began appearing as a separate section in September 1983.
2 Began appearing as a separate section in March 1988.
3 1978 totals include Linguistics (incorporated into Language and Literature in December 1985) and Classical Language and Literature and Ancient History (incorporated into Classical Studies in 1985).
4 Replaced Other in 1994.

Table 6 / U.S. Mass Market Paperback Books: Average Prices and Price Indexes, 1991–1994
(Index Base: 1981 = 100)

Subject Area	1981 Average Price	1981 Volumes	1991 Average Price	1991 Volumes	1991 Index	1992 Average Price	1992 Volumes	1992 Index	1993 Average Price	1993 Volumes	1993 Index	1994 (Preliminary) Average Price	1994 (Preliminary) Volumes	1994 (Preliminary) Index
Agriculture	$2.54	5	$5.00		196.9	$7.40	14	291.3	$6.48	23	255.1	$8.25	7	324.8
Art	5.49	7	10.13		184.5	10.33	3	188.2	14.47	14	263.6	11.04	9	201.1
Biography	3.82	76	6.18		161.8	6.18	92	161.8	6.23	89	163.1	7.75	36	202.9
Business	4.63	13	8.36		180.6	8.30	21	179.3	10.89	22	235.2	11.69	13	252.5
Education	3.96	5	5.98		151.0	9.96	15	251.5	4.55	45	114.9	13.07	17	330.1
Fiction	2.47	2,265	4.49		181.8	4.63	2,587	187.4	4.79	2,298	193.9	4.80	1,837	194.3
General works	3.63	52	7.48		206.1	7.25	65	199.7	12.79	61	352.3	9.32	37	256.7
History	3.53	28	8.37		237.1	7.14	43	202.3	8.79	17	249.0	10.60	9	300.3
Home economics	4.35	60	7.97		183.2	7.41	69	170.3	7.91	83	181.8	8.33	51	191.5
Juvenile	1.79	448	3.38		188.8	3.61	489	201.7	3.54	450	197.8	3.74	224	208.9
Language	3.42	9	7.26		212.3	6.26	11	183.0	8.32	9	243.3	15.30	3	447.4
Law	3.09	4	9.85		318.8	4.99	1	161.5	0.00	0	161.5	6.66	3	215.5
Literature	3.42	24	5.89		172.2	7.16	29	209.4	6.99	26	204.4	6.41	15	187.4
Medicine	3.66	32	5.88		160.7	9.02	21	246.4	10.23	25	279.5	8.48	7	231.7
Music	5.68	1	2.75		48.4	2.75	1	48.4	7.75	2	136.4	17.50	2	308.1
Philosophy and psychology	2.84	67	7.78		273.9	6.71	89	236.3	6.40	89	225.4	9.57	32	337.0
Poetry and drama	3.22	12	6.55		203.4	6.24	12	193.8	6.99	6	217.1	8.80	8	273.3
Religion	2.70	11	7.79		288.5	7.88	9	291.9	2.92	14	108.1	8.30	11	307.4
Science	4.45	15	8.27		185.8	8.16	9	183.4	7.30	10	164.0	11.54	7	259.3
Sociology and economics	3.43	42	7.56		220.4	6.48	59	188.9	8.83	55	257.4	8.92	38	260.1
Sports and recreation	3.05	139	7.50		245.9	6.84	142	224.3	7.93	144	260.0	9.15	90	300.0
Technology	4.20	29	25.58		609.0	31.18	40	742.4	30.47	73	725.5	25.20	39	600.0
Travel	3.23	26	10.95		339.0	9.10	5	281.7	10.10	9	312.7	13.46	4	416.7
Total	$2.65	3,370	$5.08		191.7	$5.22	3,826	197.0	$5.82	3,564	219.6	$5.74	2,499	216.6

Compiled by Adrian W. Alexander, Faxon Company, from data supplied by the R. R. Bowker Company. Average prices of mass market paperbacks are based on listings of mass market titles in *Paperbound Books in Print*.

Periodical and Serial Prices

LMPIC and the Faxon Company jointly produce the U.S. periodical price index. Subscription prices shown are publishers' list prices, and do not include publisher discounts or vendor service charges. This year's index includes data for 1993, 1994, and 1995. An expanded report, including subject breakdowns, LC-class comparisons, and rankings by rate of increase and average price, was published annually in the April 15 issue of *Library Journal* through 1992, and is now published in the May issue of *American Libraries*.

After a second consecutive double-digit increase in 1992 of 12.2 percent, the average U.S. periodical price (Table 1), excluding Russian translations, had dropped in 1993 to only 5.5 percent. In 1994, however, the average price rose once again, at a rate of 9.6 percent, to $135.37, a level more typical of the five-year period from 1986 to 1990. For 1995, moreover, this index moved more toward the higher increases experienced in 1991 and 1992 with an average price of $149.46, or an increase of 10.4 percent. Chemistry and physics titles continue to be much more expensive than all other subject categories surveyed, except for Russian translations, with an average price in 1995 of $767.96 (13.3 percent higher than in 1993). Mathematics, however, posted the highest rate of increase, with 13.7 percent, followed by chemistry and physics (13.3 percent), medicine (12.8 percent), and psychology (10.9 percent).

U.S. serial services have experienced moderate inflation over the period from 1993 to 1995. The overall average price for this group, excluding Wilson indexes, was $522.01, or 6.6 percent higher than in 1994. The previous increase from 1993 to 1994 was 5.0 percent. Two categories, U.S. documents and the Wilson indexes, experienced slight decreases in average price from 1994 to 1995. Expanded price index data and commentary for the U.S. serial services is also available in the May issue of *American Libraries*.

Book Prices

Based on preliminary data, the 1994 average price of U.S. hardcover books ($42.96) increased by 22.7 percent over the final 1993 average price of $35.00. It should be noted, however, that the preliminary price for 1993 as reported at this time last year was 4.0 percent lower than in 1992, and the final average price for 1993 was actually 22.3 percent lower than for 1992. This category had previously been characterized by low increases (less than 5 percent per annum over the previous four years). This index is compiled from information published in R. R. Bowker's *Weekly Record*.

Table 4 shows average prices and price indexes for North American academic books. As noted in last year's report, the methodology for compilation and analysis of this group has been changed. Data presented in Table 4 this year should be compared to data presented last year in Table 4, Figure 2. Data for this table covering calendar year 1994 were not available at press time. For 1993, academic books increased in average price by only 2.8 percent to $47.17.

U.S. college book prices (Table 5) averaged $47.93 in 1994, which was a 2.0 percent *decrease* from 1993. Humanities titles, as a group, increased slightly in price from 1993, but science titles dropped from $53.68 to $51.26. The social science group and reference titles also experienced slight decreases. Data for this index are compiled from *Choice* book reviews, and expanded data appear in the April 1995 issue of *Choice*.

U.S. mass market and trade paperbacks showed similar trends in 1993 and 1994. While preliminary 1993 figures reported last year were somewhat disparate, the final price increases reported by Bowker were closer together: 11.5 percent for the mass market group and 9.3 percent for the trade group. Similarly, the preliminary figures for 1994 indicate a 1.4 percent *decrease* for mass market paperbacks, and a 2.5 percent *decrease* for the trade group.

Newspaper Prices

This year marks the return of U.S. daily newspapers to this study. Table 8 covers 172 titles chosen from "The Top 100 Daily Newspapers in the United States According to Circulation" as listed in *The Editor and Publisher International Yearbook*, papers from large metropolitan areas listed in the *State and Metropolitan Area Databook* and the *Rand-McNally Commercial Atlas and Marketing Guide*, plus a newspaper from each state capital. Using 1990 as a base year, the 1995 version of the index shows an interesting "roller coaster" effect over the most recent five-year period, as price increases have risen and fallen from year to year. The 1994 increase, for example, was 13.9 percent, while the 1995 increase was only 3.2 percent, repeating a similar pattern in 1992 and 1993. Compilers Genevieve Owens and Wilba Swearingen note that the data seem to indicate pricing decisions made on an 18-month basis, rather than on an annual basis like other serials.

Prices of Other Media

The U.S. nonprint media index for 1994 (Table 9) continues the new methodology used to prepare the 1993 index. As with last year, the number of filmstrips and 16mm films continued to decline as other media such as video became more dominant. Only 19 filmstrips received citation mention in 1994 in *School Library Journal*, the only source that continues to review them. Similarly, only 18 16mm films were cited in sources this year, versus over 3,000 videocassettes. The purchase price per minute of video continues to decline, with an average price of only $2.11 in 1994 (as opposed to $15.05 per minute for 16mm film), down from $2.38 in 1993.

The CD-ROM price inventory (Table 10) covers the period 1992–1994. As in prior years, all prices listed are single-user (non-networked) prices, at the "highest level of service," meaning the most frequent interval plus all available archival discs. CD-ROM production continues to increase, from 806 titles listed in 1992 to 1,033 in 1994. The average price for 1994 increased over 1993 by only 2 percent, as compared to an 8 percent increase between 1992 and 1993. The subject area with the highest average cost per title was business, at $3,860, while the lowest cost was found in American history, at $523. The biggest price increase came in fine arts, which increased in cost by 53 percent between 1993 and 1994.

Foreign Prices

Indexes are included for British academic books (Table 11), German academic books (Table 12), German academic periodicals (Table 13), Dutch periodicals (Table 14), and Latin American periodicals (Table 15). The Dutch periodicals index and the Latin American periodicals tables are new for 1994. However, a previously published table for Latin American books does not appear this year, due to a lack of reliable data.

British Prices

Prices for British academic books (Table 11) are compiled from information supplied by B. H. Blackwell. The average price in 1994 was £35.44, which reflects an increase of only 0.1 percent over the 1993 average price of £35.39. This very nominal rise comes after a modest increase of only 2.5 percent in 1993. Compiler Curt Holleman notes also that British book production declined by 0.3 percent in 1994. Finally, the U.S. dollar did decline in strength against the pound in 1994, so the cost of British books for U.S. libraries rose by about 1.8 percent after a decline of 11.8 percent in 1993.

German Prices

The German academic book index (Table 12) is based on approval plan data provided by Otto Harrassowitz and covers only books published in Germany. Previously, some German-language imprints published in Austria and Switzerland were included here. The average price of books in Table 12 increased by 5.4 percent from 1993 to 1994, marking the second straight year of increases in excess of 5.0 percent, after an increase of less than 1 percent in 1992. The number of imprints increased significantly in 1994, from 15,670 in 1993 to 18,289. Compiler John Haar notes that increases in the number of business and law books were a significant factor in this trend.

German periodical prices (Table 13) rose in 1995 at a rate of 5.3 percent, over twice the rate of increase posted in 1994, from an average price in 1994 of DM283.04 to DM297.92. The largest increase in 1995 for a single subject category was in anthropology, with an unusual 156.0 percent. The number of titles in this category rose from 7 to 9, so one or both of the new titles must have been relatively high in price. More significantly for U.S. research libraries, chemistry rose by 25.5 percent. The only other category with an increase higher than 10 percent was zoology, at 12.7 percent.

Dutch Prices

Table 14 is a new index of English-language periodicals published in the Netherlands, which is a key publishing country for scientific, technical, and medical journals. Data for this index was provided by Martinus Nijhoff International and compiled by Frederick C. Lynden. The table covers 25 subject categories for 1993–1995, and prices are shown in Dutch guilders. The average price for this

(text continues on p. 499)

Table 7 / U.S. Trade (Higher Priced) Paperbook Books: Average Prices and Price Indexes, 1991–1994
(Index Base: 1977 = 100)

Subject Area	1977 Average Price	1991 No. of Books	1991 Average Price	1991 Index	1992 No. of Books	1992 Average Price	1992 Index	1993 No. of Books	1993 Average Price	1993 Index	1994 (Preliminary) No. of Books	1994 (Preliminary) Average Price	1994 (Preliminary) Index
Agriculture	$5.01	129	$14.90	297.4	179	$16.73	333.9	186	$18.32	365.7	116	$18.83	375.8
Art	6.27	509	19.11	304.8	549	19.52	311.3	596	19.98	318.7	352	19.81	315.9
Biography	4.91	536	13.38	272.5	516	13.59	276.8	555	15.75	320.8	438	15.28	311.2
Business	7.09	477	21.20	299.0	484	22.94	323.6	472	25.18	355.1	365	23.67	333.9
Education	5.72	453	23.30	407.3	480	23.25	406.5	502	23.06	403.1	396	21.78	380.8
Fiction	4.20	1,027	12.17	289.3	928	13.68	325.7	877	13.56	322.9	730	15.57	370.7
General works	6.18	650	34.74	562.1	868	29.20	472.5	693	31.19	504.7	621	33.15	536.4
History	5.81	717	16.99	292.4	724	17.42	299.8	730	21.20	364.9	555	19.60	337.3
Home economics	4.77	371	12.89	270.2	374	14.29	299.6	344	14.47	303.4	271	14.27	299.2
Juvenile	2.68	810	7.60	283.6	869	7.49	279.5	1,059	7.73	288.4	744	6.99	260.8
Language	7.79	250	16.83	216.0	230	17.61	226.1	279	42.93	551.1	203	22.55	289.5
Law	10.66	331	24.62	231.0	277	25.17	236.1	316	28.86	270.7	207	25.72	241.3
Literature	5.18	654	15.31	295.6	727	17.04	329.0	724	17.38	335.5	612	18.51	357.3
Medicine	7.63	702	24.20	317.2	855	26.16	342.9	842	29.66	388.7	573	25.95	340.1
Music	6.36	115	17.03	267.8	121	20.56	323.3	142	21.64	340.3	92	19.30	303.5
Philosophy and psychology	5.57	657	16.54	296.9	637	17.24	309.5	614	18.23	327.3	514	18.28	328.2
Poetry and drama	4.71	338	11.88	252.2	395	13.06	277.3	436	13.29	282.2	302	13.41	284.7
Religion	3.68	1,334	12.50	339.7	1,371	13.08	355.4	1,275	13.67	371.5	1,041	14.75	400.8
Science	8.81	567	28.31	321.3	640	27.98	317.6	602	31.79	360.8	499	34.71	394.0
Sociology and economics	6.03	2,294	19.68	326.4	2,354	19.72	327.0	2,508	22.42	371.8	2,004	22.09	366.3
Sports and recreation	4.87	449	15.03	308.6	490	15.64	321.1	504	15.82	324.8	366	15.93	327.1
Technology	7.97	586	33.39	418.9	589	28.75	360.7	557	30.04	376.9	393	25.57	320.8
Travel	5.21	301	14.06	269.9	276	14.75	283.1	297	15.90	305.2	186	15.97	306.5
Total	$5.93	14,257	$18.40	310.3	14,933	$18.81	317.2	15,110	$20.56	346.7	11,580	$20.05	338.1

Compiled by Adrian W. Alexander, Faxon Company, from data supplied by the R. R. Bowker Company. Price Indexes on Tables 3 and 7 are based on books recorded in R. R. Bowker Company's *Weekly Record* (circulated in *American Book Publishing Record*). The 1994 preliminary figures include items listed during 1994 with an imprint date of 1994. Final data for previous years include items listed between January of that year and June of the following year with an imprint date of the specified year.

Table 8 / U.S. Daily Newspapers, 1990–1995
(Index Base: 1990 = 100)

Year	No. Titles	Average Price	Percent Increase	Index
1990	165	$189.58	N/A	100
1991	166	198.13	4.5	104.5
1992	167	222.68	12.4	117.5
1993	171	229.92	3.3	121.3
1994	171	261.91	13.9	138.2
1995	172	$270.22	3.2	142.5

* Compiled by Genevieve S. Owens, University of Missouri, St. Louis, and Wilba Swearingen, Louisiana State University Medical Center, from data supplied by EBSCO Subscription Services.

group in 1995 was 1,452.52 Dfl., which reflects an increase of 11.7 percent over the 1994 average price of 1,300.66 Dfl. Comparatively, the rate of increase between 1993 and 1994 was 11.8 percent. Compiler Fred Lynden notes that these increases are consistent with a trend of double-digit inflation in guilders that began in 1991.

Latin American Prices

The Latin American Periodical Price Index (LAPPI) has been compiled for several years by Scott Van Jacob and appears as Table 15 of this study for the first time. This table includes price data on periodicals published in Central America, South America, and the Caribbean during the period 1992–1994. Data are shown in U.S. dollars.

Overall, Latin American periodicals increased in price in 1994 by 6.4 percent, from $58.81 to $62.58. Comparatively, the increase in 1993 was only 1.4 percent. Within the group, Guatemala posted the highest average price in 1994 at $162.70. The only other country exceeding $100 in price was Peru, at $100.96.

U.S. Purchasing Power Abroad

In 1994 the U.S. dollar lost much of the strength it had gained in 1993 against most key foreign currencies related to publishing. Against the important German and Dutch currencies in particular, the dollar dropped to near 1992 levels, while somewhat less erosion was experienced against the franc and the pound. Against the Japanese yen, however, the dollar dropped sharply in 1994. The following chart reports rates in currency per U.S. dollar based on quotations in the *Wall Street Journal*. Readers interested in quotations for earlier years should refer to previous volumes of the *Bowker Annual*.

	12/31/92	6/30/93	12/31/93	6/30/94	12/30/94
Canada	1.1955	1.2695	1.2820	1.3296	1.3835	1.4088
France	5.1035	5.5045	5.6835	5.8930	5.4260	5.3640
U.K.	0.5247	0.6614	0.6607	0.6774	0.6468	0.6412
Germany	1.5177	1.6160	1.6877	1.7353	1.5845	1.5525
Japan	125.45	124.60	106.32	111.83	98.69	99.65
Netherlands	1.7105	1.8156	1.8928	1.9385	1.7769	1.7391

Using the Price Indexes

Librarians are encouraged to monitor both trends in the publishing industry and changes in economic conditions when preparing budget projections. The ALA ALCTS Library Materials Price Index Committee endeavors to make information on publishing trends readily available by sponsoring the annual compilation and publication of the price data contained in Tables 1–15. The indexes cover newly published library materials and document prices and rates of price changes at the national level. They are useful benchmarks against which local costs may be compared, but because they reflect retail prices in the aggregate, they are not a substitute for cost data that reflect the collecting patterns of individual libraries.

In part, differences arise because the national indexes exclude discounts, service charges, shipping and handling fees, or other costs that libraries may bear. Discrepancies may also be related to subject focus, mix of current and retrospective materials, and the portion of total library acquisitions composed by foreign imprints. Such variables can affect the average price paid by a particular library although the library's rate of price increase may not significantly differ from national price indexes. LMPIC is interested in pursuing studies correlating a particular library's costs with national prices and would appreciate being informed of any planned or ongoing studies. The committee welcomes interested parties to its meeting at the ALA annual and midwinter conferences.

Current members of the Library Materials Price Index Committee are Adrian Alexander (chair), Donna Alsbury, Richard Brumley, Marifran Bustion, Gay Dannelly, Virginia Gilbert, Mollie Lawson (intern), Genevieve Owens, Andrew Shroyer, Eric Suess, and Wilba Swearingen. Consultants and other advisers who contributed to the preparation of the indexes are Dana Alessi, Stephen Bosch, Kathryn Hammel Carpenter, Nancy Chaffin, John Haar, Curt Holleman, Martha Kellogg, Frederick Lynden, Steven Thompson, and Scott Van Jacob.

Table 9 / U.S. Nonprint Media: Average Prices and Price Indexes, 1990–1994
(Index Base: 1980 = 100)

Category	1980 Average	1990 Average	1990 Index	1991 Average	1991 Index	1992 Average	1992 Index	1993 Average	1993 Index	1994 Average	1994 Index
16mm films											
Rental cost per minute	$1.41	$2.02	143.3	$2.46	174.5	$1.95	138.3	$1.97	139.7	$2.16	153.2
Purchase cost per minute	12.03	18.40	153.0	20.08	166.9	20.85	173.3	16.23	134.9	15.05	125.1
Cost of film	279.09	517.72	185.5	525.50	188.3	4'2.83	147.9	391.79	140.4	403.04	144.4
Length per film (min.)	23.2	28.1	—	26.2	—	19.8	—	24.1	—	26.78	—
Videocassettes											
Purchase cost per minute	7.58	5.60	73.9	4.81	63.5	3.23	42.6	2.38	31.4	2.11	27.9
Cost per video	271.93	215.34	79.2	199.67	73.4	112.92	41.5	93.22	34.3	84.19	27.9
Length per video (min.)	—	35.9	—	41.5	—	35.0	—	38.2	—	39.9	31.0
Filmstrips											
Cost of filmstrip	21.74	37.38	171.9	36.90	169.7	34.63	159.3	31.54	145.1	30.84	141.9
Cost of filmstrip set	67.39	121.76	108.7	97.90	145.3	81.73	121.3	81.06	120.3	58.6	113.0
No. of filmstrips per set	3.1	3.3	—	2.7	—	2.4	—	2.6	—	1.9	—
No. of frames per filmstrip	67.9	46.5	—	56.6	—	49.4	—	64.4	—	54.0	—
Sound recordings											
Cost per cassette	9.34	10.47	112.1	12.18	130.4	11.73	125.8	8.20	87.8	8.82	94.4
Cost per compact disc	—	—	—	—	—	—	—	13.36	—	14.80	107.8 *

* Base Year for compact discs = 1993
Compiled by Dana Alessi, Baker & Taylor, from data in *Booklist, Library Journal, School Library Journal,* and *Wilson Library Bulletin.*

Table 10 / CD-ROM Price Inventory 1992–1994: Average Costs by Subject Classification

Classification	LC Class	Number of Titles			Average Price per Title			Percent Change	
		1992	1993	1994	1992	1993	1994	1992–1993	1993–1994
General works	A	101	132	134	$1,717	$1,692	$1,688	-1	0
Philosophy, psychology, and religion	B	16	19	21	1,093	1,257	1,269	15	1
History: general & Old World	D	5	7	7	722	875	868	21	-1
History: America	E-F	16	18	19	595	553	523	-7	-5
Geography, anthropology, and recreation	G	30	35	37	1,643	1,524	1,700	-7	12
Social sciences	H	72	78	80	1,866	1,955	1,936	5	-1
Business	HB-HJ	50	76	86	3,825	4,117	3,860	8	-6
Political science	J	13	18	23	1,061	1,334	1,376	26	3
Law	K	16	20	25	2,289	2,179	2,149	-5	-1
Education	L	21	24	24	1,068	1,008	969	-7	-4
Music	M	11	12	13	400	831	890	108	7
Fine arts	N	31	33	34	1,175	1,122	1,712	-5	53
Language & literature	P	40	46	47	2,926	2,907	2,864	-1	-1
Science	Q	138	144	155	1,395	1,586	1,677	14	6
Medicine	R	94	126	131	1,377	1,457	1,528	6	5
Agriculture	S	22	32	37	2,464	2,982	3,048	21	2
Technology	T	38	55	58	2,822	2,338	2,374	-17	2
Military science	U-V	22	25	25	789	1,230	1,229	56	0
Bibliography, library science	Z	70	73	77	1,409	1,403	1,395	0	-1
Totals		806	973	1,033	$1,749	$1,883	$1,917	8	2

Compiled by Martha Kellogg and Theodore Kellogg, University of Rhode Island.

Table 11 / British Academic Books: Average Prices and Price Indexes, 1992–1994
(Index Base: 1985 = 100; prices listed are pounds sterling)

Subject Area	1985 No. of Titles	1985 Average Price	1992 No. of Titles	1992 Average Price	1992 Index	1993 No. of Titles	1993 Average Price	1993 Index	1994 No. of Titles	1994 Average Price	1994 Index
General works	29	£30.54	43	£47.79	156.5	30	£71.86	235.3	51	£42.75	140.0
Fine arts	329	21.70	400	32.00	147.5	411	34.28	158.0	408	30.99	142.8
Architecture	97	20.68	141	31.34	151.5	185	31.60	152.8	145	33.48	161.9
Music	136	17.01	146	33.73	198.3	127	29.89	175.7	123	25.86	152.0
Performing arts except music	110	13.30	138	22.60	169.9	164	24.93	187.4	118	24.44	183.8
Archaeology	146	18.80	143	30.01	159.6	141	32.55	173.1	126	33.28	177.0
Geography	60	22.74	64	37.62	165.4	62	32.69	143.8	56	37.21	163.6
History	1,123	16.92	1,381	28.65	169.3	1,282	30.42	179.8	1,361	32.37	191.3
Philosophy	127	18.41	154	42.84	232.7	182	37.12	201.6	156	39.20	212.9
Religion	328	10.40	291	22.24	213.8	408	21.43	206.1	362	24.62	236.7
Language	135	19.37	112	32.22	166.3	150	39.24	202.6	154	35.35	182.5
Miscellaneous humanities	59	21.71	54	30.00	138.2	59	25.37	116.9	63	29.59	136.3
Literary texts (excluding fiction)	570	9.31	501	14.09	151.3	431	18.91	203.1	493	14.91	160.2
Literary criticism	438	14.82	590	29.13	196.6	532	29.99	202.4	520	29.26	197.4
Law	188	24.64	236	52.77	214.2	285	47.96	194.6	298	45.72	185.6
Library science and book trade	78	18.69	85	33.40	178.7	80	42.42	227.0	83	36.04	192.8
Mass communications	38	14.20	106	25.70	181.0	107	24.12	169.9	84	24.68	173.8
Anthropology and ethnology	42	20.71	84	33.03	159.5	70	37.15	179.4	57	42.21	203.8
Sociology	136	15.24	190	35.55	233.3	180	34.93	229.2	187	42.19	276.8
Psychology	107	19.25	114	33.92	176.2	145	35.73	185.6	128	33.66	174.9
Economics	334	20.48	511	44.23	216.0	548	47.46	231.7	505	51.80	252.9
Political science, international relations	314	15.54	432	33.21	213.7	414	33.95	218.5	458	30.87	198.6
Miscellaneous social sciences	20	26.84	22	32.64	121.6	23	33.63	143.9	15	33.50	124.8
Military science	83	17.69	55	24.48	138.4	54	27.09	153.1	54	31.03	175.4

Table 11 / British Academic Books: Average Prices and Price Indexes, 1992–1994 *(cont.)*
(Index Base: 1985 = 100; prices listed are pounds sterling)

Subject Area	1985 No. of Titles	1985 Average Price	1992 No. of Titles	1992 Average Price	1992 Index	1993 No. of Titles	1993 Average Price	1993 Index	1994 No. of Titles	1994 Average Price	1994 Index
Sports and recreation	44	11.23	61	18.99	169.1	56	17.32	154.2	64	21.66	192.9
Social service	56	12.17	89	23.56	193.6	81	25.31	208.0	351	24.57	201.9
Education	295	12.22	302	24.95	204.2	328	25.17	206.0	536	26.50	216.9
Management and business administration	427	19.55	462	38.27	195.8	483	41.15	210.5	536	37.04	189.5
Miscellaneous applied social sciences	13	9.58	21	23.72	247.6	14	28.95	302.2	20	23.89	249.4
Criminology	45	11.45	66	25.88	226.0	54	24.64	215.2	62	35.83	312.9
Applied interdisciplinary social sciences	254	14.17	385	31.21	220.3	421	29.85	210.7	435	32.60	230.1
General science	43	13.73	33	34.18	248.9	31	37.10	270.2	42	39.29	286.2
Botany	55	30.54	52	38.77	126.9	49	41.25	135.1	36	63.06	206.5
Zoology	85	25.67	89	36.10	140.6	80	38.95	151.7	73	46.13	179.7
Human biology	35	28.91	17	40.38	139.1	42	45.07	155.9	36	45.21	156.4
Biochemistry	26	33.57	36	44.65	133.0	24	49.99	148.9	36	54.97	163.7
Miscellaneous biological sciences	152	26.64	158	42.64	160.1	150	36.31	136.3	160	41.92	157.4
Chemistry	109	48.84	108	67.34	137.9	91	72.40	148.2	124	66.53	136.2
Earth sciences	87	28.94	102	52.05	179.9	89	52.03	179.8	93	55.13	190.5
Astronomy	43	20.36	35	38.90	191.1	44	37.13	182.4	46	34.45	169.2
Physics	76	26.58	103	52.72	198.3	100	50.19	188.8	84	54.37	204.6
Mathematics	123	20.20	143	33.82	167.4	131	34.27	169.7	147	34.71	171.8
Computer sciences	150	20.14	248	32.73	162.5	259	29.85	148.2	211	31.11	154.5

Interdisciplinary technical fields	36	26.14	62	40.50	154.9	66	43.15	105.1	63	39.86	152.3
Civil engineering	134	28.68	153	59.51	207.5	151	61.38	214.0	150	50.39	175.7
Mechanical engineering	27	31.73	42	62.74	197.7	47	60.66	191.2	39	61.65	194.3
Electrical and electronic engineering	100	33.12	107	46.10	139.2	108	46.57	140.6	111	53.01	160.1
Materials science	54	37.93	105	79.82	210.4	93	81.76	215.6	98	78.88	208.0
Chemical engineering	24	40.48	31	62.73	155.0	46	64.55	159.5	32	78.48	193.9
Miscellaneous technology	217	36.33	268	54.87	151.0	247	60.09	165.4	219	51.30	141.2
Food and domestic science	38	23.75	54	57.06	240.3	42	58.12	244.7	56	57.41	241.7
Non-clinical medicine	97	18.19	125	29.93	164.5	144	29.79	163.8	134	28.45	156.4
General medicine	73	21.03	69	45.60	216.8	65	42.29	201.1	64	34.31	163.1
Internal medicine	163	27.30	182	50.99	186.8	186	48.24	176.7	194	44.76	164.0
Psychiatry and mental disorders	71	17.97	107	27.88	155.1	103	28.37	157.9	106	29.94	166.6
Surgery	50	29.37	54	59.96	204.2	53	62.88	214.1	63	70.14	238.8
Miscellaneous medicine	292	22.08	290	40.37	182.8	319	39.16	177.4	284	43.05	195.0
Dentistry	20	19.39	28	33.57	173.1	25	36.26	187.0	20	36.98	190.7
Nursing	71	8.00	56	14.90	186.3	56	15.71	196.4	90	15.64	195.5
Agriculture and forestry	78	23.69	95	39.68	167.5	95	40.61	171.4	78	45.42	191.7
Animal husbandry and veterinary medicine	34	20.92	48	32.32	154.5	53	41.90	200.3	52	42.70	204.1
Natural resources and conservation	58	22.88	58	43.32	189.3	50	39.38	172.1	40	45.24	197.7
Total, all books	9,049	£19.07	10,805	£34.51	181.0	10,925	£35.39	185.6	10,893	£35.44	185.8

Compiled by Curt Holleman, Southern Methodist University, from data supplied by B.H. Blackwell.

Table 12 / German Academic Books: Average Prices and Price Index, 1992–1994
(Index Base: 1989 = 100)

Subject Area	LC Class	1989 No. of Titles	1989 Average Price	1992 No. of Titles	1992 Average Price	1992 Percent Increase	1992 Index	1993 No. of Titles	1993 Average Price	1993 Percent Increase	1993 Index	1994 No. of Titles	1994 Average Price	1994 Percent Increase	1994 Index
Agriculture	S	171	DM59.14	200	DM62.74	1.9	106.1	293	60.01	-4.4	101.5	280	DM60.06	0.1	101.6
Anthropology	GN-GT	125	63.66	115	60.83	3.6	95.6	121	68.42	12.5	107.5	129	69.03	0.9	108.4
Botany	QK	66	87.88	68	96.86	1.6	110.2	86	93.61	-3.4	106.5	70	103.22	10.3	117.5
Business and economics	H-HJ	956	52.75	1,362	61.04	7.2	115.7	1,340	61.53	0.8	116.6	3,492	71.16	15.7	134.9
Chemistry	QD	59	103.06	101	97.95	-0.7	95.0	86	112.07	14.4	108.7	100	116.60	4.0	113.1
Education	L	200	45.20	319	39.98	1.6	88.5	304	44.31	10.8	98.0	301	43.99	-0.7	97.3
Engineering and technology	T	498	87.14	505	84.99	-3.4	97.5	532	102.92	21.1	118.1	398	97.02	-5.7	111.3
Fine and applied arts	M-N	1,557	51.98	1,757	58.40	4.8	112.4	1,914	61.61	5.5	118.5	2,010	62.19	0.9	119.6
General works	A	34	50.08	50	51.38	6.6	102.6	42	187.30	264.5	374.0	40	57.74	-69.2	115.3
Geography	G-GF	177	53.85	108	64.22	0.5	119.3	98	63.44	-1.2	117.8	109	68.47	7.9	127.2
Geology	QE	35	76.50	48	111.37	8.7	145.6	56	95.01	-14.7	124.2	44	88.46	-6.9	115.6
History	C,D,E,F	926	54.74	1,703	46.73	-0.7	85.4	1,797	52.48	12.3	95.9	1,647	55.13	5.1	100.7
Law	K	466	85.04	1,196	70.39	3.9	82.8	495	82.01	16.5	96.4	1,546	79.05	-3.6	93.0
Library and information science	Z	108	94.25	143	74.84	-26.9	79.4	125	92.13	23.1	97.7	129	91.01	-1.2	96.6
Literature and language	P	2,265	48.29	2,986	45.17	-3.8	93.6	3,230	48.64	7.7	100.7	3,072	50.75	4.3	105.1
Mathematics and computer science	QA	159	75.98	192	83.58	9.9	110.0	280	92.45	10.6	121.7	302	95.46	3.3	125.6
Medicine	R	1,087	74.17	1,447	72.61	-1.2	97.9	1,215	77.65	7.0	104.7	1,049	79.68	2.6	107.4
Military and naval science	U-V	67	58.90	57	84.62	78.7	143.7	54	65.76	-22.3	111.7	40	69.24	5.3	117.6
Natural history	QH	74	89.01	82	74.65	-1.8	83.9	97	75.07	0.6	84.3	110	100.62	34.0	113.0
Philosophy and religion	B	784	56.48	1,174	57.09	6.7	101.1	1,441	55.54	-2.7	98.3	1,342	60.40	8.8	106.9
Physical education and recreation	GV	86	37.07	67	41.60	18.0	112.2	76	38.23	-8.1	103.1	60	35.50	-7.1	95.8
Physics and astronomy	QB-QC	120	85.19	141	89.74	4.9	105.3	172	103.77	15.6	121.8	159	109.47	5.5	128.5
Physiology	QM-QR	121	105.14	117	91.98	-8.7	87.5	112	131.15	42.6	124.7	119	120.70	-8.0	114.8
Political science	J	445	42.53	399	48.67	8.6	114.4	420	43.60	-10.4	102.5	499	50.61	16.1	119.0
Psychology	BF	104	55.12	184	51.20	10.9	92.9	145	57.53	12.4	104.4	129	57.71	0.3	104.7
Science (general)	Q	67	57.83	110	63.57	7.5	109.9	161	81.39	28.0	140.8	89	84.02	3.2	145.3
Sociology	HM-HX	637	40.25	984	40.77	5.2	101.3	892	44.40	8.9	110.3	952	42.15	-5.1	104.7
Zoology	QL	43	80.33	27	132.43	32.0	164.9	86	86.07	-35.0	107.1	72	81.86	-4.9	101.9
Total		11,437	DM58.48	15,642	DM57.95	0.6	99.1	15,670	61.80	6.6	105.7	18,289	DM65.16	5.4	111.4

Compiled by John Haar, Vanderbilt University, from approval plan data supplied by Otto Harrassowitz. Data represent a selection of materials relevant to research and documentation published in Germany (see text for more information regarding the nature of the data).
Unclassified material as well as titles in home economics and industrial arts have been excluded.

Table 13 / German Academic Periodical Price Index, 1993–1995
(Index Base: 1990 = 100)

Subject Area	LC Class	1990 Average Price	1993 No. of Titles	1993 Average Price	1993 Percent Increase	1993 Index	1994 No. of Titles	1994 Average Price	1994 Percent Increase	1994 Index	1995 (Preliminary) No. of Titles	1995 Average Price	1995 Percent Increase	1995 Index
Agriculture	S	DM235.11	167	DM269.87	4.1	114.8	169	DM280.72	4.0	119.4	169	DM299.86	6.8	127.5
Anthropology	GN	112.88	7	162.97	30.8	144.4	7	169.22	3.8	149.9	9	433.23	156.0	383.8
Botany	QK	498.79	13	609.33	11.9	122.2	17	633.21	3.9	126.9	18	652.79	3.1	130.9
Business and economics	H-HJ	153.48	273	195.27	14.2	127.2	288	196.30	0.5	127.9	295	200.77	2.3	130.8
Chemistry	QD	553.06	47	696.32	-0.5	125.9	46	800.34	14.9	144.7	50	1,004.49	25.5	181.6
Education	L	70.86	62	74.69	4.8	105.4	60	84.26	12.8	118.9	61	87.30	3.6	123.2
Engineering and technology	T-TS	239.40	304	342.11	22.3	142.9	367	264.17	-22.8	110.3	376	271.83	2.9	113.5
Fine and applied arts	M-N	84.15	159	97.04	5.4	115.3	170	98.83	1.8	117.4	174	101.44	2.6	120.5
General works	A	349.37	89	348.32	-0.3	99.7	85	406.27	16.6	116.3	89	441.11	8.6	126.3
Geography	G	90.42	16	114.27	-0.7	126.4	15	146.64	28.3	162.2	15	149.17	1.7	165.0
Geology	QE	261.30	40	323.34	7.5	123.4	39	336.69	4.1	128.9	39	351.87	4.5	134.7
History	C,D,E,F	66.09	136	81.54	1.1	123.4	143	87.37	7.1	132.2	143	88.59	1.4	134.0
Law	K	193.88	142	250.69	4.2	129.3	151	258.05	2.9	133.1	154	270.68	4.9	139.6
Library and information science	Z	317.50	58	373.04	11.0	117.5	60	503.18	34.9	158.5	61	498.62	-0.9	157.0
Literature and language	P	102.69	168	119.74	-2.0	116.6	161	120.31	0.5	117.2	162	122.13	1.5	118.9
Mathematics and computer science	QA	1,064.62	36	1,138.83	-2.3	107.0	39	1,129.98	-0.8	106.1	39	1,170.18	3.6	109.9
Medicine	R	320.62	533	368.19	5.1	114.8	526	388.36	5.5	121.1	532	398.40	2.6	124.3
Military and naval science	U-V	86.38	23	100.51	11.6	116.4	22	97.05	-3.4	112.4	22	98.02	1.0	113.5
Natural history	QH	728.36	51	921.68	11.2	126.5	52	963.86	4.6	132.3	52	1,039.75	7.9	142.8
Philosophy and religion	B	65.00	185	89.32	19.8	137.4	189	98.72	10.5	151.9	192	98.26	-0.5	151.2
Physical education and recreation	GV	81.96	52	92.38	17.5	112.7	45	95.48	3.4	116.5	46	98.22	2.9	119.8
Physics and astronomy	QB-QC	684.40	53	945.91	9.4	138.2	52	917.83	-3.0	134.1	52	988.20	7.7	144.4
Physiology	QM-QR	962.83	8	1,378.18	20.9	143.1	9	1,379.91	0.1	143.3	10	1,380.70	0.1	143.4
Political science	J	80.67	140	87.46	-0.2	108.4	136	93.36	6.7	115.7	137	94.18	0.9	116.7
Psychology	BF	94.10	41	104.39	1.9	110.9	42	112.33	7.5	119.3	42	115.05	2.5	122.3
Science (general)	Q	310.54	33	396.33	16.1	127.6	33	406.51	2.6	130.9	33	442.54	8.9	142.5
Sociology	HM-HX	109.61	60	120.87	-0.7	110.3	58	131.69	9.0	120.1	58	133.92	1.7	122.2
Zoology	QL	161.02	32	211.86	-1.3	131.6	26	246.37	16.3	153.0	26	277.56	12.7	172.4
Total		DM228.40	2,953	DM277.58	4.4	121.5	3,007	DM283.04	2.0	123.9	3,056	DM297.92	5.3	130.4

Data, supplied by Otto Harrassowitz, represent periodical and newspaper titles published in German; prices listed in marks. Price information for 1995 is preliminary; price data are 84% complete. Index is compiled by Steven E. Thompson, Brown University Library.

Table 14 / Dutch (English Language) Periodicals Price Index, 1993–1995
(Index Base: 1993 = 100; currency Units: DFL)

Subject Area	LC Class	1993 No. of Titles	1993 Average Price	1994 No. of Titles	1994 Average Price	1994 Percent Increase	1994 Index	1995 No. of Titles	1995 Average Price	1995 Percent Increase	1995 Index
Agriculture	S	35	DFL869.10	35	DFL977.23	12.44	112.44	35	DFL1,109.06	13.49	127.6
Botany	QK	10	1,304.70	10	1,350.60	3.52	103.52	10	1,470.30	8.86	112.7
Business and economics	H-HJ	82	539.35	82	609.89	13.08	113.08	82	678.94	11.32	125.9
Chemistry	QD	35	3,060.63	35	3,464.77	13.20	113.20	35	3,836.81	10.74	125.4
Education	L	6	330.00	6	364.00	10.30	110.30	6	386.00	6.04	117.0
Engineering and technology	T-TS	71	1,112.22	71	1,286.14	15.64	115.64	71	1,458.27	13.38	131.1
Fine and applied arts	M-N	4	221.67	4	239.34	7.97	107.97	4	249.34	4.18	112.5
Geography	G	7	1,201.29	7	1,302.43	8.42	108.42	7	1,429.57	9.76	119.0
Geology	QE	24	1,100.47	24	1,275.41	15.90	115.90	24	1,433.07	12.36	130.2
History	D	9	220.78	9	223.78	1.36	101.36	9	236.25	5.57	107.0
Law	K	13	368.73	13	421.16	14.22	114.22	13	452.46	7.43	122.7
Library and information science	Z	6	235.50	6	243.17	3.26	103.26	6	254.33	4.59	108.0
Literature and language	P	33	291.67	33	311.42	6.77	106.77	33	336.55	8.07	115.4
Mathematics and computer science	QA	55	1,076.20	55	1,207.20	12.17	112.17	55	1,367.23	13.26	127.0
Medicine	R	60	963.54	60	1,059.57	9.97	109.97	60	1,214.67	14.64	126.1
Military and naval science	U-V	2	180.00	2	190.00	5.56	105.56	2	200.00	5.26	111.1
Natural history	QH	30	1,753.00	30	1,852.85	5.70	105.70	30	2,070.96	11.77	118.1
Philosophy and religion	B	31	324.14	31	349.19	7.73	107.73	31	384.29	10.05	118.6
Physics and astronomy	QB-QC	44	3,097.05	44	3,469.84	12.04	112.04	44	3,847.54	10.89	124.2
Physiology	QM-QR	16	2,529.25	16	2,837.81	12.20	112.20	16	3,149.88	11.00	124.5
Political science	J	3	402.00	3	444.50	10.57	110.57	3	467.67	5.21	116.3
Psychology	BF	4	720.00	4	763.00	5.97	105.97	4	810.25	6.19	112.5
Science (general)	Q	11	708.06	11	842.71	19.02	119.02	11	921.30	9.33	130.1
Sociology	HM	6	326.44	6	344.17	5.43	105.43	6	365.67	6.25	112.0
Zoology	QL	10	610.90	10	658.98	7.87	107.87	10	712.80	8.17	116.7
Total		607	DFL1,163.01	607	DFL1,300.66	11.84	111.84	607	DFL1,452.52	11.68	124.9

No data exist for Anthropology, General Works, and Physical Education.
Source: Martinus Nijhoff International

Table 15 / Latin American Periodicals, 1992–1994
(Index Base: 1992 = 100)

Country	1992 No. of Titles	1992 Average Price*	1993 No. of Titles	1993 Average Price*	1993 Index	1994 No. of Titles	1994 Average Price*	1994 Index
Argentina	153	$72.04	131	$83.30	115.60	128	$77.25	107.23
Bolivia	8	34.73	7	32.65	94.00	6	34.43	99.14
Brazil	120	74.14	204	54.68	73.80	223	53.01	71.50
Caribbean, Other	25	39.31	41	41.16	104.70	29	26.09	66.37
Chile	73	47.25	78	53.51	113.30	80	69.42	146.92
Colombia	67	46.63	62	54.02	115.90	64	48.63	104.29
Costa Rica	26	31.05	24	39.53	127.30	28	41.01	132.08
Cuba	21	38.06	4	28.91	76.00	10	52.48	137.89
Ecuador	15	33.02	15	35.45	107.40	13	39.22	118.78
El Salvador	6	15.47	4	20.86	134.80	7	31.87	206.01
Guatemala	14	87.19	15	95.57	109.60	11	162.70	186.60
Honduras	3	21.11	1	20.00	94.70	1	60.00	284.23
Jamaica	19	31.62	18	35.70	112.90	17	53.44	169.01
Mexico	184	57.08	194	62.00	108.60	198	66.41	116.35
Nicaragua	10	31.03	8	36.65	118.10	7	38.52	124.14
Panama	13	25.40	11	24.12	95.00	12	25.74	101.34
Paraguay	5	22.31	5	28.46	127.60	6	26.47	118.65
Peru	45	110.01	49	106.70	97.00	56	100.96	91.77
Uruguay	17	32.78	17	42.01	128.20	20	49.90	152.23
Venezuela	36	47.42	39	60.00	126.50	41	46.15	97.32
Region								
Caribbean	65	36.68	63	39.04	106.40	56	41.34	112.70
Central America	72	41.29	63	50.44	122.20	66	58.45	141.56
South America	539	64.68	607	64.54	99.80	637	63.86	98.73
Latin America	860	$57.98	927	$58.81	101.40	957	$62.58	107.93

* Average prices are weighted according to number of libraries with strong Latin American collections that hold that title.
Compiled by Scott Van Jacob, Dickinson College, from data supplied by the Library of Congress, the Faxon Company, and the University of Texas at Austin.

Book Title Output and Average Prices:
1993 Final and 1994 Preliminary Figures

Gary Ink
Research Librarian, *Publishers Weekly*

American book title production, which recorded a total of 49,757 titles in 1993, has clearly recovered from the low point reached in 1990. Although preliminary 1993 figures seemed to indicate that the recovery trend was slowing, final figures have proved this assumption incorrect. Final 1993 data, compiled for *Publishers Weekly* by R. R. Bowker, shows that title output increased by 481 titles over the 1992 final figure of 49,276 titles. Preliminary data for 1994 would appear to confirm that the peak title output of 56,027, reached in 1987, will not be equaled anytime soon.

Output by Category

Overall 1993 final category totals (Table 1) indicate that most categories recorded a modest increase over 1992. Categories showing noteworthy growth include: art, with an increase of 148 titles, and poetry and drama, with an increase of 105 titles. Several categories, however, show noticeable declines between 1992 and 1993: fiction declined by 271 titles, confirming the general sense among publishers that fiction publishing has declined; general works fell by 283 titles; medicine also declined by 140 titles. Children's books (Juveniles), which increased by only 33 titles between 1991 and 1992, rose by 325 titles in 1993. This would seem to run counter to the assumption that children's publishing is experiencing a slowdown.

Mass market output (Table 3), which appeared to show the beginning of an upward trend in 1992, now appears to signal the start of a decline. Total output for 1993 stands at 3,564 titles, a decline of 262 from the 1992 final total. The decline in fiction titles, which appeared to reverse itself in 1992, resumed with a drop of 289 titles in 1993. Children's books (Juveniles), which increased dramatically in 1992, declined again to 450 titles, the same level at which it stood in 1991. In the nonfiction categories, marked increases continue to be recorded in education and technology. Significant declines continue to be recorded in the categories of history and poetry.

Price Data Mixed

The final average price data for 1993 sends a mixed message. Figures shown here are derived from R. R. Bowker databases—*American Book Publishing Record* for hardcovers and trade paperbacks and *Paperbound Books in Print* for mass market paperbacks (Tables A–C). Overall prices for both mass market and trade paperback titles showed significantly larger increases than in 1992. The mass

Note: Adapted from *Publishers Weekly*, March 20, 1995.

market paperback price rose by 60 cents, while the trade paperback price rose by $1.75.

The more interesting, and certainly more controversial, data concerns the hardcover average prices. Preliminary 1993 figures indicated that hardcover average prices were declining. However, final data indicates that the overall average price for hardcover books in all subjects declined by a staggering $10.07 between 1992 and 1993. Average price declines were recorded in all categories except history, with especially large declines recorded in such technical categories as law, medicine, science, and technology. Fiction registered a decline of 89 cents to $19.50, bringing it once again below the $20 price unit.

Table 1 / American Book Title Production, 1992–1994

Category	1992 All Hard and Paper*	1993 Final Hard and Trade Paper Books	Editions	Totals	All Hard and Paper*	1994 Preliminary Hard and Trade Paper Books	Editions	Totals	All Hard and Paper*
Agriculture	565	434	101	535	558	318	76	394	401
Art	1,392	1,345	181	1,526	1,540	970	152	1,122	1,131
Biography	2,007	1,778	204	1,982	2,071	1,551	171	1,722	1,758
Business	1,367	1,088	332	1,420	1,442	1,005	276	1,281	1,294
Education	1,184	1,040	162	1,202	1,247	903	121	1,024	1,041
Fiction	5,690	3,014	107	3,121	5,419	2,772	156	2,928	4,765
General works	2,153	1,565	244	1,809	1,870	1,390	239	1,629	1,666
History	2,332	1,962	338	2,300	2,317	1,611	279	1,890	1,899
Home economics	826	684	114	798	881	618	99	717	768
Juveniles	5,144	4,796	223	5,019	5,469	3,872	175	4,047	4,271
Language	617	529	161	690	699	442	99	541	544
Law	1,066	807	336	1,143	1,143	570	263	833	836
Literature	2,227	1,919	224	2,143	2,169	1,626	213	1,839	1,854
Medicine	3,234	2,367	702	3,069	3,094	1,879	629	2,508	2,515
Music	346	312	63	375	377	208	61	269	271
Philosophy, psychology	1,806	1,466	209	1,675	1,764	1,243	170	1,413	1,445
Poetry, drama	899	948	50	998	1,004	720	38	758	766
Religion	2,540	2,247	372	2,619	2,633	1,894	243	2,137	2,148
Science	2,729	2,187	372	2,668	2,678	1,859	368	2,227	2,234
Sociology, economics	7,432	6,443	1,004	7,447	7,502	5,397	797	6,194	6,232
Sports, recreation	1,113	872	130	1,002	1,146	679	113	792	882
Technology	2,152	1,714	460	2,174	2,247	1,198	286	1,484	1,523
Travel	468	329	149	478	487	259	77	336	340
Total	49,276	39,846	6,347	46,193	49,757	32,984	5,101	38,085	40,584

* Includes mass market paperbacks (see Table 3).

Note: Figures for mass market paperbound book production are based on entries in R. R. Bowker's *Paperbound Books in Print*. Other figures are from the *Weekly Record* (American Book Publishing Record) database. Figures under "Books" and "Editions" designate new books and new editions.

Table 2 / Paperbacks (Excluding Mass Market), 1992–1994

Category	1992 Totals	1993 Final			1994 Preliminary		
		New Books	New Editions	Totals	New Books	New Editions	Totals
Fiction	495	375	121	496	303	85	388
Nonfiction	14,967	12,690	2,695	15,385	10,028	2,183	12,211
Total	15,462	13,065	2,816	15,881	10,331	2,268	12,599

Table 3 / Mass Market Paperbacks, 1991–1994

Category	1991 Final	1992 Final	1993 Final	1994 Preliminary
Agriculture	5	14	23	7
Art	7	3	14	9
Biography	76	92	89	36
Business	13	21	22	13
Education	5	15	45	17
Fiction	2,266	2,587	2,298	1,837
General works	52	65	61	37
History	28	43	17	9
Home economics	60	69	83	51
Juvenile	449	489	450	224
Language	9	11	9	3
Law	4	1	0	3
Literature	24	29	26	15
Medicine	32	21	25	7
Music	1	1	2	2
Philosophy, psychology	67	89	89	32
Poetry, drama	12	12	6	8
Religion	11	9	14	11
Science	15	9	10	7
Sociology, economics	42	59	55	38
Sports, recreation	139	142	144	90
Technology	29	40	73	39
Travel	29	5	9	4
Total	3,375	3,826	3,564	2,499

Table 4 / Imported Titles, 1992–1994
(Hard and Trade Paper Only)

Category	1992 Totals	1993 Final Books	1993 Final Editions	1993 Final Totals	1994 Preliminary Books	1994 Preliminary Editions	1994 Preliminary Totals
Agriculture	93	89	36	125	38	10	48
Art	156	211	14	225	80	14	94
Biography	124	123	13	136	77	7	84
Business	126	216	37	253	183	25	208
Education	232	225	21	246	197	7	204
Fiction	246	132	9	141	167	6	173
General works	313	280	28	308	211	23	234
History	348	333	40	373	270	32	302
Home economics	25	19	5	24	19	1	20
Juveniles	50	44	1	45	16	1	17
Language	164	150	22	172	120	21	141
Law	197	173	56	229	134	29	163
Literature	274	264	22	286	189	17	206
Medicine	514	447	85	532	328	84	412
Music	69	62	1	63	21	4	25
Philosophy, psychology	291	316	35	351	251	20	271
Poetry, drama	136	156	11	167	117	13	130
Religion	165	160	26	186	142	12	154
Science	840	741	127	868	604	80	684
Sociology, economics	1,521	1,505	147	1,652	1,275	131	1,406
Sports, recreation	112	130	14	144	51	12	63
Technology	458	399	77	476	290	47	337
Travel	52	46	7	53	33	9	42
Total	6,506	6,221	834	7,055	4,813	605	5,418

Table 5 / Translations into English, 1989–1994
(Hard and Trade Paper Only)

	1989 Final	1990 Final	1991 Final	1992 Final	1993 Final	1994 Prelim.
Arabic	45	26	24	26	23	15
Chinese	26	45	35	49	50	47
Danish	49	24	20	25	14	15
Dutch	33	40	30	30	35	31
Finnish	3	10	1	42	4	2
French	442	389	365	383	339	286
German	453	252	402	337	353	283
Hebrew	56	35	45	47	40	28
Italian	142	79	87	91	87	101
Japanese	84	82	83	70	59	38
Latin	38	51	49	10	55	38
Norwegian	12	7	8	62	2	4
Russian	251	185	168	146	133	117
Spanish	121	120	125	122	135	102
Swedish	36	30	25	25	27	8
Turkish	0	0	0	0	1	2
Yiddish	12	5	13	4	3	6
Total	1,803	1,380	1,480	1,469	1,360	1,123

Note: "Total" covers only the languages listed here.

Table A / Hardcover Average Per-Volume Prices, 1991–1994

Category	1991 Prices	1992 Prices	1993 Final Vols.	1993 Final $ Total	1993 Final Prices	1994 Preliminary Vols.	1994 Preliminary $ Total	1994 Preliminary Prices
Agriculture	$57.73	$53.76	269	$11,255.96	$41.84	226	$12,854.14	$56.87
Art	44.99	44.59	812	32,472.96	39.99	654	25,966.30	39.70
Biography	27.52	30.41	1,290	36,591.55	28.37	1,102	32,818.87	29.78
Business	43.38	43.91	791	30,021.41	37.95	735	31,073.48	42.27
Education	41.26	48.77	574	22,157.78	38.60	445	22,441.73	50.43
Fiction	21.30	20.39	2,093	40,813.33	19.50	1,962	40,909.91	20.85
General works	51.74	56.29	882	40,053.08	45.41	760	42,214.31	55.54
History	39.87	39.19	1,429	58,271.01	40.78	1,159	46,206.58	39.86
Home economics	24.23	24.88	422	8,671.79	20.55	390	8,141.50	20.87
Juveniles	16.64	14.46	3,599	49,920.42	13.87	2,855	41,252.28	14.44
Language	51.71	49.68	308	10,478.02	34.02	246	13,341.42	54.23
Law	64.89	76.21	560	30,208.71	53.94	524	33,888.90	64.67
Literature	36.76	39.23	1,289	45,495.34	35.30	1,011	38,048.44	37.63
Medicine	71.44	75.22	1,360	67,699.76	49.78	1,476	112,510.86	76.22
Music	41.04	47.37	198	8,204.82	41.44	134	5,336.05	39.82
Philosophy, psychology	42.74	46.85	912	35,966.56	39.44	728	33,101.87	45.46
Poetry, drama	33.29	36.76	500	15,531.75	31.06	389	12,648.79	32.51
Religion	32.33	35.31	1,204	35,110.27	29.16	931	28,569.89	30.68
Science	80.14	81.95	1,261	66,464.23	52.71	1,294	100,293.66	77.50
Sociology, economics	48.43	45.53	4,300	177,687.11	41.32	3,559	177,429.17	49.85
Sports, recreation	30.68	34.62	462	14,911.11	32.28	349	11,527.52	33.03
Technology	76.40	82.18	981	55,242.34	56.31	822	65,038.29	79.12
Travel	32.43	33.28	159	4,169.46	26.22	129	4,568.38	35.41
Total	$44.17	$45.05	25,655	$897,398.77	$34.98	21,880	$940,182.34	$42.97

Table A-1 / Hardcover Average Per-Volume Prices—Less Than $81, 1991–1994

Category	1991 Prices	1992 Prices	1993 Final Vols.	$ Total	Prices	1994 Preliminary Vols.	$ Total	Prices
Agriculture	$31.92	$35.13	257	$9,392	$36.54	186	$5,651.59	$30.38
Art	37.92	36.74	796	30,191	37.93	627	22,556.95	35.97
Biography	25.23	26.86	1,282	35,767	27.90	1,075	29,118.27	27.08
Business	38.01	39.58	779	28,344	36.39	697	26,293.98	37.72
Education	36.51	39.66	570	21,792	38.23	430	17,248.78	40.11
Fiction	19.55	19.71	2,092	40,568	19.39	1,953	39,458.01	20.20
General works	39.76	42.89	855	37,050	43.33	666	27,342.56	41.05
History	35.31	35.93	1,427	53,306	37.36	1,127	42,100.43	37.35
Home economics	23.89	23.21	422	8,672	20.55	389	8,051.55	20.69
Juveniles	13.37	13.85	3,599	49,920	13.87	2,854	41,168.28	14.42
Language	40.32	38.66	304	10,005	32.91	212	8,289.47	39.10
Law	41.31	43.27	504	21,872	43.39	410	18,216.65	44.43
Literature	33.64	35.22	1,286	45,165	35.12	981	34,188.59	34.85
Medicine	40.19	41.83	1,260	52,472	41.64	957	39,024.76	40.77
Music	38.17	39.81	194	7,273	37.49	132	5,166.05	39.13
Philosophy, psychology	36.75	39.00	900	33,928	37.70	676	26,196.22	38.75
Poetry, drama	31.32	32.12	500	15,532	31.06	379	11,365.94	29.98
Religion	29.70	31.02	1,199	34,451	28.73	898	25,559.34	28.46
Science	45.77	47.01	1,161	53,290	45.90	891	42,155.38	47.31
Sociology, economics	39.19	40.31	4,273	173,808	40.68	3,309	137,545.33	41.56
Sports, recreation	29.42	33.22	461	14,821	32.15	344	10,972.62	31.89
Technology	46.38	48.83	893	40,961	45.87	568	27,568.64	48.53
Travel	29.00	30.77	159	4,169	26.22	122	3,790.43	31.06
Total	$31.95	$33.55	25,173	$822,749	$32.68	19,883	$649,029.82	$32.64

Table B / Mass Market Paperbacks Average Per-Volume Prices, 1992–1994

Category	1992 Prices	1993 Final Vols.	$ Total	Prices	1994 Preliminary Vols.	$ Total	Prices
Agriculture	$7.40	23	$148.95	$6.48	7	$57.77	$8.25
Art	10.33	14	202.58	14.47	9	99.39	11.04
Biography	6.18	89	554.03	6.23	36	279.24	7.75
Business	8.30	22	239.67	10.89	13	151.97	11.69
Education	9.96	45	204.65	4.55	17	222.33	13.07
Fiction	4.63	2,298	11,012.72	4.79	1,837	8,832.91	4.80
General works	7.25	61	780.12	12.79	37	345.05	9.32
History	7.14	17	149.36	8.79	9	95.43	10.60
Home economics	7.41	83	656.47	7.91	51	425.00	8.33
Juveniles	3.61	450	1,592.29	3.54	224	838.12	3.74
Language	6.26	9	74.86	8.32	3	45.90	15.30
Law	4.99	0	0	0	3	19.98	6.66
Literature	7.16	26	181.65	6.99	15	96.20	6.41
Medicine	9.02	25	255.82	10.23	7	59.42	8.48
Music	2.75	2	15.50	7.75	2	35.00	17.50
Philosophy, psychology	6.71	89	569.88	6.40	32	306.27	9.57
Poetry, drama	6.24	6	41.95	6.99	8	70.42	8.80
Religion	7.88	14	40.88	2.92	11	91.38	8.30
Science	8.16	10	72.97	7.30	7	80.78	11.54
Sociology, economics	6.48	55	485.84	8.83	38	339.06	8.92
Sports, recreation	6.84	144	1,141.29	7.93	90	823.93	9.15
Technology	31.18	73	2,224.31	30.47	39	982.84	25.20
Travel	9.10	9	90.92	10.10	4	53.85	13.46
Total	$5.22	3,564	$20,736.40	$5.82	2,499	$14,352.24	$5.74

Table C / Trade Paperbacks Average Per-Volume Prices, 1991–1994

Category	1991 Prices	1992 Prices	1993 Final Vols.	$ Total	Prices	1994 Preliminary Vols.	$ Total	Prices
Agriculture	$14.90	$16.73	186	$3,406.99	$18.32	116	$2,185.14	$18.83
Art	19.11	19.52	596	11,910.17	19.98	352	6,973.45	19.81
Biography	13.38	13.59	555	8,741.34	15.75	438	6,693.55	15.28
Business	21.20	22.94	472	11,886.73	25.18	365	8,641.18	23.67
Education	23.30	23.25	502	11,576.44	23.06	396	8,625.77	21.78
Fiction	12.17	13.68	877	11,892.17	13.56	730	11,369.61	15.57
General works	34.74	29.20	693	21,615.78	31.19	621	20,590.44	33.15
History	16.99	17.42	730	15,474.33	21.20	555	10,879.42	19.60
Home economics	12.89	14.29	344	4,977.26	14.47	271	3,869.38	14.27
Juveniles	7.60	7.49	1,059	8,184.14	7.73	744	5,207.06	6.99
Language	16.83	17.61	279	11,978.09	42.93	203	4,579.24	22.55
Law	24.62	25.17	316	9,119.12	28.86	207	5,325.35	25.72
Literature	15.31	17.04	724	12,583.75	17.38	612	11,331.13	18.51
Medicine	24.20	26.16	842	24,976.24	29.66	573	14,871.27	25.95
Music	17.03	20.56	142	3,072.19	21.64	92	1,776.05	19.30
Philosophy, psychology	16.54	17.24	614	11,196.07	18.23	514	9,398.79	18.28
Poetry, drama	11.88	13.06	436	5,795.68	13.29	302	4,050.01	13.41
Religion	12.50	13.08	1,275	17,427.87	13.67	1,041	15,359.83	14.75
Science	28.31	27.98	602	19,137.12	31.79	499	17,322.78	34.71
Sociology, economics	19.68	19.72	2,508	56,219.06	22.42	2,004	44,282.40	22.09
Sports, recreation	15.03	15.64	504	7,973.53	15.82	366	5,833.35	15.93
Technology	33.39	28.75	557	16,734.74	30.04	393	10,049.30	25.57
Travel	14.06	14.75	297	4,721.59	15.90	186	2,971.24	15.97
Total	$18.40	$18.81	15,110	$310,600.40	$20.56	11,580	$232,185.74	$20.05

Book Sales Statistics, 1994:
AAP Preliminary Estimates

Association of American Publishers

The industry estimates shown in the following table are based on the U.S. Census of Manufactures. This census is conducted every fifth year—the most recent being the 1992 census.

Between censuses, the Association of American Publishers (AAP) estimates are "pushed forward" by the percentage changes that are reported to the AAP statistics program, and by other industry data that are available. Some AAP data are collected in a monthly statistics program, and it is largely this material that is shown in this preliminary estimate table. More detailed data are available from, and additional publishers report to, the AAP annual statistics program, and this

Table 1 / Estimated Book Publishing Industry Sales 1982, 1987, 1992–1994
(Millions of Dollars)

	1982 $	1987 $	1992 $	1993 $	% Change from 1992	1994 $	% Change from 1993	Compound Growth Rate (%) 1982–1994	1987–1994	1992–1994
Trade (total)	1,513.0	2,712.8	4,661.6	5,023.3	7.8	5,470.8	9.0	11.3	10.5	8.3
Adult hardbound	770.8	1,350.6	2,222.5	2,553.6	14.9	2,801.3	9.7	11.4	11.0	12.2
Adult paperbound	458.2	727.1	1,261.7	1,333.6	5.7	1,499.0	12.4	10.4	10.9	9.0
Juvenile hardbound	206.9	478.5	850.8	767.4	-9.8	751.3	-2.1	11.4	6.7	-6.0
Juvenile paperbound	77.1	156.6	326.6	368.7	12.9	419.2	13.7	15.2	15.1	13.3
Religious (total)	425.5	638.8	907.1	931.5	2.7	978.0	5.0	7.2	6.3	3.8
Bibles, testaments, hymnals, etc.	149.1	177.6	260.1	259.3	-0.3	275.6	6.3	5.3	6.5	2.9
Other religious	276.4	461.2	647.0	672.2	3.9	702.4	4.5	8.1	6.2	4.2
Professional (total)	1,536.4	2,207.3	3,106.7	3,320.5	6.9	3,606.1	8.6	7.4	7.3	7.7
Business	224.2	388.8	490.3	510.9	4.2	—	—	—	—	—
Law	560.9	780.0	1,128.1	1,177.7	4.4	—	—	—	—	—
Medical	287.2	406.5	622.7	707.4	13.6	—	—	—	—	—
Technical, scientific, other prof'l	464.1	632.0	865.6	924.5	6.8	—	—	—	—	—
Book clubs	522.9	678.7	742.3	804.7	8.4	873.9	8.6	4.4	3.7	8.5
Mail order publications	568.6	657.6	630.2	601.2	-4.6	557.3	-7.3	-0.2	-2.3	-6.0
Mass market paperback, rack-sized	703.4	913.7	1,263.8	1,359.8	7.6	1,392.4	2.4	5.9	6.2	5.0
University presses	125.4	170.9	280.1	292.9	4.6	325.7	11.2	8.3	9.6	7.8
Elementary and secondary text	1,108.2	1,695.6	2,080.9	2,318.1	11.4	2,155.8	-7.0	5.7	3.5	1.8
College text	1,206.1	1,549.5	2,084.1	2,140.4	2.7	2,176.8	1.7	5.0	5.0	2.2
Standardized tests	70.4	104.0	140.4	146.8	4.6	156.5	6.6	6.9	6.0	5.6
Subscription reference	306.9	437.6	572.3	602.0	5.2	641.3	6.5	6.3	5.6	5.9
Other sales (incl. AV)	310.1	423.8	449.0	452.5	0.8	457.2	1.0	3.3	1.1	0.9
Total	8,396.9	12,190.3	16,918.5	17,993.7	6.4	18,791.8	4.4	6.9	6.4	5.4

Source: Association of American Publishers.

additional data will be incorporated into Table S1, which will be published in the (forthcoming) AAP 1994 Industry Statistics.

Preliminary data from the 1992 U.S. Census of Manufactures are available at this time, but will be revised when the final report is issued later this spring (1995). When the final 1992 census is released, AAP industry estimates back to 1987 will then be adjusted accordingly. These revisions should be available for the AAP 1994 Industry Statistics.

Readers comparing the estimated data with census reports should recall that the U.S. Census of Manufactures does not include comprehensive data on most university presses or on other institutionally sponsored and not-for-profit publishing activities, or (under SIC 2731: Book Publishing) for the audiovisual and some other media materials that are included in this table. On the other hand, AAP estimates have traditionally excluded some "Sunday School" materials and certain pamphlets that are included in the census data.

It should be noted that the Other Sales category has been revised to include AV and certain other media, as well as incidental book sales, such as music, sheet sales (both domestic and export, except those to prebinders), and miscellaneous merchandise sales.

Estimates include domestic sales and export sales of U.S. product and do not cover indigenous activities of publishers' foreign subsidiaries.

Non-rack-size Mass Market Publishing is included in Trade—Paperbound. Prior to the 1988 AAP Annual Statistics, this was treated as Adult Trade Paperbound. It is recognized that part of this is Juvenile (1987 estimate: 20 percent), and adjustments have been made in this respect. AAP also notes that this area includes sales through traditional "mass market paperback channels" by publishers not generally recognized as being "mass market paperback."

United States Trade in Books: 1994

William S. Lofquist
Senior Analyst, U.S. Department of Commerce

U.S. trade in books is determined by a number of factors, including exchange rates, market demand, and market efficiencies: that is, a choice is made as to whether a market will be served by direct exports or through the sale of foreign rights and translations. No comprehensive data are available as to U.S. publishers' rights and translations activities, but the U.S. government has extensive statistics on exports and imports. This information is contained in Tables 1-6.

U.S. Book Exports

Since the early 1990s, a sluggish global economy has restrained foreign demand for U.S. books. As noted in Table 1, exports of U.S. books reached $1.7 billion in 1994, an increase over 1993 of just 2.3 percent in dollar value and 0.9 percent in

Table 1 / U.S. Exports of Books, 1994

	Value (millions of current $)	% Chg. 1993–1994	Units (millions of copies)	% Chg. 1993–1994
Dictionaries and thesauruses	$7.8	-18.7	2.3	-1.2
Encyclopedias	58.9	0.6	9.8	-6.9
Textbooks	303.0	8.3	47.8	11.3
Religious books	52.4	9.0	31.3	-14.9
Technical, scientific, and professional books	474.1	-3.1	88.4	4.4
Art and pictorial books	14.8	-30.0	10.1	-13.3
Hardcover books, n.e.s.	167.7	1.2	55.9	10.3
Mass market paperbound books	204.4	16.0	115.9	9.7
Children's picture and coloring books	22.9	-2.5	31.6	-10.3
Music books	21.2	10.5	4.0	2.5
Atlases	2.1	0.2	0.3	-12.8
All other books	368.3	0.7	457.3	-1.2
Total, all books	$1,697.5	2.3	854.6	0.9

Note: n.e.s.=not elsewhere specified. Individual shipments are excluded from the foreign trade data if valued under $2,500. Data for individual categories may not add to totals due to statistical rounding.
Source: U.S. Department of Commerce, Bureau of the Census.

number of copies shipped. Although U.S. exports of textbooks exceeded $300 million (a gain of 8.3 percent), foreign demand for U.S. technical, scientific, and professional books—traditionally the largest U.S. book export category—totaled just $474 million in 1994 (down 3 percent from 1993). In contrast, U.S. exports of mass market paperbound books surged in 1994, totaling $204 million in shipments on sales of 116 million copies.

Over 70 percent of U.S. book exports are destined for five countries: Canada, the United Kingdom, Australia, Japan, and Mexico. Table 2 shows U.S. book exports to the 35 largest foreign markets. Radical year-to-year changes in foreign demand for U.S. books are attributable to fluctuations in exchange rates, changes in foreign government expenditures for educational materials, and changes in foreign economies. Illustrative of these changes will be the combined impact of these factors on Mexico's book demand in 1995. Stimulated by the North American Free Trade Agreement (NAFTA), sales of U.S. books to Mexico jumped in the early 1990s and culminated in demand reaching $89 million in 1994. But Mexico's devalued peso and a restricted economy are expected to reduce significantly U.S. exports of all products—including books—in 1995.

Table 2 / U.S. Book Exports to Principal Countries, 1994

	Value (millions of current $)	% Chg. 1993–1994	Units (millions of copies)	% Chg. 1993–1994
Canada	$728.4	4.7	445.6	1.4
United Kingdom	182.0	-9.4	76.5	-19.7
Australia	135.6	8.4	69.2	21.1
Japan	98.2	4.8	36.6	25.1
Mexico	88.5	39.6	36.8	34.6
Germany	48.4	11.4	18.3	17.6
Netherlands	33.8	5.7	12.4	-13.4
Singapore	33.2	-10.3	12.5	-22.8
Taiwan	25.4	10.2	9.4	29.2
Hong Kong	22.3	-2.1	8.1	-7.1
Korea, Republic of	18.9	20.2	9.1	13.6
Philippines	18.1	-5.6	6.8	-14.3
South Africa, Republic of	18.0	-1.0	10.9	19.7
Brazil	17.1	-6.5	8.3	27.0
Denmark	17.0	2.9	2.6	-23.6
France	16.3	-14.4	6.6	-13.2
India	16.1	2.5	7.6	32.8
New Zealand	13.5	34.7	7.1	54.9
Spain	10.8	41.6	3.5	68.8
Switzerland	10.1	-42.8	3.1	-40.3
Argentina	9.8	-5.3	6.9	-9.9
Belgium	9.4	20.3	2.6	16.0
Ireland	8.5	-39.3	2.0	-34.8
Saudi Arabia	7.6	-18.8	2.4	-40.9
Thailand	7.3	14.3	2.3	1.4
Italy	7.3	-15.7	3.8	24.4
China	6.1	34.2	2.9	31.1
Sweden	5.8	49.6	2.4	74.6
Colombia	5.4	-3.9	2.2	-5.5
Israel	5.4	-6.6	2.1	-25.6
Malaysia	5.3	-6.9	2.2	0.3
Chile	4.3	-13.3	2.5	-18.0
Venezuela	3.8	-23.5	3.5	-37.3
Egypt	3.1	-19.8	0.9	27.6
United Arab Emirates	2.6	-31.2	1.4	-1.3
Total, all countries	$1,697.5	2.3	854.6	0.9

Notes: Individual shipments are excluded from the foreign trade data if valued under $2,500.
Source: U.S. Department of Commerce, Bureau of the Census

U.S. Book Imports

Despite a growing U.S. economy, U.S. demand for foreign books was generally held back in 1994—the result of a low-valued U.S. dollar and tightened public funds for the purchase of educational materials. U.S. book imports rose to $1.1 billion, a gain of 8.5 percent over 1993, but the value-diminished U.S. dollar kept unit sales even with shipments in 1993. Table 3 shows 1994 U.S. book imports, by subject category. In general, those book categories reflecting greatest U.S. demand—hardcover books, n.e.s., and children's picture and coloring books—are indicative not of foreign books purchased for their content, but rather of books whose foreign manufacture was contracted for by U.S. publishers.

Major foreign suppliers of books to the U.S. market appear in Table 4. Countries whose books are imported by the United States primarily on the basis of content showed mixed results in 1994. Imports from the United Kingdom,

Table 3 / U.S. Imports of Books, 1994

	Value (millions of current $)	% Chg. 1993–1994	Units (millions of copies)	% Chg. 1993–1994
Dictionaries and thesauruses	$8.6	26.5	1.9	5.0
Encyclopedias	5.4	10.6	0.9	0.8
Textbooks	97.6	-5.1	23.5	-6.7
Religious books	45.7	18.0	27.0	4
Technical, scientific, and professional books	136.3	2.6	28.5	-5.6
Art and pictorial books:				
valued under $5 each	14.0	-20.2	7.7	-40.3
valued at $5 or more	15.3	-9.5	1.4	-4.5
Hardcover books, n.e.s.	423.1	15.6	135.0	3.4
Mass market paperbound books	38.7	-16.4	29.0	-38.3
Children's picture and coloring books	138.5	28.3	138.2	22.3
Music books	2.6	-12.0	0.7	-3.5
Atlases	3.7	20.0	0.8	-33.0
All other books	163.3	1.8	82.7	-4.4
Total, all books	$1,092.80	8.5	477.3	-0.1

Notes: n.e.s.=not elsewhere specified. Individual shipments are excluded from the foreign trade data if valued under $1,250. Data for individual categories may not add to totals due to statistical rounding.
Source: U.S. Department of Commerce, Bureau of the Census.

France, and Australia surged, while shipments from Canada, Germany, and the Netherlands were either restrained or declined. Books whose U.S. import was primarily on the basis of attractive prices for color separations, printing, and binding also received mixed reviews in 1994. The low-valued U.S. dollar led to declining shipments from Hong Kong, Japan, and Taiwan. However, several major Far East printing companies have established a presence in China and are now serving U.S. publishers with books manufactured in that country.

Foreign/Domestic Book Trade

In virtually all of the years prior to World War II, the United States was a large net importer of books. This situation was at least partially encouraged by U.S. copyright law, which, beginning with the country's inception, protected U.S. authors but until the late 19th century failed to protect the works of foreigners. Since World War II, the trade situation reversed, with the United States establishing itself as a net book exporter. Table 5 compares U.S. book exports to book imports over the past quarter century. Exports of U.S. books have never reached twice the dollar level of the country's imports, regardless of the volume of foreign demand. Fluctuations in the value of exchange rates are a formidable trade factor: witness 1985, when a strong U.S. dollar discouraged exports and assisted imports.

The U.S. book publishing industry caters to the world's largest book market. The estimated apparent consumption of books by the United States (industry shipments - exports + imports) approached $18.8 billion in 1994. Although the large volume of U.S. book exports approaches that of Germany and the United Kingdom, Table 6 indicates that even 1994 exports of $1.7 billion account for less than 10 percent of total shipments of U.S. publishers. Through the remainder of this century, the ratio of direct exports to publishers' shipments is expected to continue on a downward trend—after reaching a peak of 9.3 percent in 1990. A combination of factors—including improved international copyright protection, satellite transmission of materials to offshore manufacturing facilities, enlarged markets for electronic products, and an expansion of rights and translations activities—are anticipated to make the choice of direct exports less appropriate. This should not, however, be taken as indicative of a withdrawal of U.S. publishers' interest in foreign markets. The works of U.S. publishers are expected to increase in international presence, irrespective of the means by which this presence is channeled.

Table 4 / U.S. Book Imports from Principal Countries, 1994

	Value (millions of current $)	% Chg. 1993–1994	Units (millions of copies)	% Chg. 1993–1994
United Kingdom	$247.8	19.3%	64.1	15.1%
Hong Kong	176.2	-2.4	93.0	1.6
Singapore	96.5	9.1	51.5	12.6
Canada	87.7	-1.2	77.6	-18.0
Italy	83.0	13.1	32.8	-8.3
Japan	82.8	-0.4	21.4	-14.2
Germany	57.1	-23.9	7.6	-61.5
China	42.5	51.1	34.8	31.9
Mexico	33.9	39.8	15.0	45.5
Spain	29.7	24.9	10.3	9.1
Korea, Republic of	19.4	16.0	10.0	7.5
France	16.7	28.1	3.3	-21.2
Colombia	16.3	0.1	10.6	9.6
Belgium	14.7	24.5	7.6	40.3
Netherlands	12.2	3.0	1.8	12.7
Australia	9.4	19.3	2.5	2.9
Taiwan	9.3	-4.0	8.2	34.5
Thailand	7.5	44.6	6.1	34.0
Israel	6.9	2.8	2.0	12.8
Switzerland	6.7	10.2	1.0	36.5
Sweden	3.8	33.8	0.8	36.4
Malaysia	3.6	34.8	1.5	13.5
Slovenia	3.1	86.3	0.8	39.7
Ireland	2.6	5.0	0.4	-20.6
Ecuador	2.6	126.5	1.0	27.3
Denmark	2.1	-36.0	0.4	-41.9
India	2.0	35.7	3.1	14.3
Portugal	1.7	-9.1	0.8	14.7
New Zealand	1.3	21.9	1.0	1.4
Argentina	1.2	21.2	0.4	-20.2
Russia	1.1	107.7	1.0	23.1
Indonesia	1.0	75.1	0.5	-88.5
Dominican Republic	0.9	51.9	0.5	100.9
Luxembourg	0.8	5,871.0	0.1	465.1
Austria	0.8	27.1	0.2	69.4
Total, all countries	$1,092.8	8.5	477.3	-0.1

Note: Individual shipments are excluded from the foreign trade data if valued under $1,250.
Source: U.S. Department of Commerce, Bureau of the Census.

Table 5 / U.S. Trade in Books, 1970–1994
(in millions of current dollars)

	U.S. Book Exports	U.S. Book Imports	Ratio, U.S. Book Exports/Imports
1994	$1,697.5	$1,092.8	1.55
1993	1,659.0	1,007.2	1.65
1990	1,428.0	845.1	1.69
1985	591.2	564.2	1.05
1980	518.9	306.5	1.69
1975	269.3	147.6	1.82
1970	174.9	92.0	1.90

Source: U.S. Department of Commerce, Bureau of the Census.

Table 6 / U.S. Book Industry Shipments Compared to U.S. Book Exports
(in millions of current dollars)

	Total Shipments U.S. Book Industry	U.S. Book Exports	Exports as % of Total Shipments
1994	$19,414.0 *	1,697.5	8.7
1993	18,246.0 *	1,659.0	9.1
1990	15,317.9	1,428.0	9.3
1985	10,196.2	591.2	5.8
1980	6,114.4	518.9	8.5
1975	3,536.5	269.3	7.6
1970	2,434.2	174.9	7.2

* Estimated by International Trade Administration, U.S. Department of Commerce.
Source: U.S. Department of Commerce, Bureau of the Census.

International Book Title Output

William S. Lofquist
Senior Analyst, U.S. Department of Commerce

Despite strong efforts by the world's authors and publishers, the international output of new titles and new editions each year remains below the 1 million mark. The international agency charged with collecting annual information on book title output—the United Nations Educational, Scientific, and Cultural Organization (Unesco)—reports that data for the most recent period (1990–1992) shows just 56 countries producing at least 1,000 new titles/editions. Over the period 1990–1992, combined output by publishers in these 56 countries averaged in the range of 700,000 new book titles/editions annually. The title statistics for these countries are listed in order of magnitude in the accompanying table.

The world's most prolific publishers are to be found in China, the United Kingdom, and Germany, with each of these countries having an annual title output of at least 60,000. A second tier of countries shows annual title production in the 35,000 to 50,000 range, and includes the United States, France, and Spain. A third tier with book title output in the 25,000 to 35,000 range consists of Italy, Russia, and the Republic of Korea. Unesco reports 17 countries with annual title output in the range of 5,000 to 15,000 and 30 countries whose publishers issue between 1,000 and 5,000 new titles/editions annually.

Collecting this information each year is no small feat, and the table reflects the difficulties faced by Unesco's staff. A listing of book title output by some major publishing countries has, for one reason or another, been omitted from the listing. Missing are book data from Australia, Brazil, Egypt, Israel, Japan, the Democratic People's Republic of Korea, New Zealand, and Singapore. In at least one case, Taiwan, the omission is deliberate. In addition, Unesco faces difficulties in achieving universal agreement as to what constitutes a book. The United States, for example, excludes from its title count the works of governmental agencies and university theses, among other items. This selective underreporting of a country's total book output may be uniform among the world's market economies, but less discernible among countries whose economies are more government controlled.

Statistics in this table are indicative not only of the difficulties of data uniformity and collection; the vicissitudes affecting a country's very existence are expressed in the data covering the former Yugoslavia, for example. Book title output is in many respects a cultural/commercial icon to which attention must be paid.

Table 1 / International Book Title Output, 1990–1992

	1990	1991	1992
China	73,923	90,156	n/a
United Kingdom	n/a	n/a	86,573
Germany	61,015	67,890	67,277
United States	46,743	48,146	49,276
France	41,720	43,682	45,379
Spain	36,239	39,082	41,816
Italy	25,068	27,751	29,351
Russia	n/a	34,050	28,716
Korea, Republic of	39,330	29,432	27,889
Switzerland	13,839	14,886	14,663
India	13,937	14,438	n/a
Belgium	12,157	13,913	n/a
Sweden	12,034	11,866	12,813
Netherlands	13,691	11,613	11,844
Denmark	11,082	10,198	11,761

Table 1 / International Book Title Output, 1990–1992 *(cont.)*

	1990	1991	1992
Finland	10,153	11,208	11,033
Poland	10,242	10,688	10,727
Canada	8,291	8,722	9,056
Hungary	8,322	8,133	8,536
Thailand	7,783	7,676	7,626
Czechoslovakia*	8,585	9,362	6,743
Turkey	6,291	6,365	6,549
Portugal	6,150	6,430	n/a
Indonesia	1,518	1,774	6,303
Argentina	4,915	6,092	5,628
Iran	n/a	5,018	n/a
Norway	3,712	3,884	4,881
Bulgaria	3,412	3,260	4,773
South Africa, Republic of	4,950	4,836	4,738
Ukraine	7,046	5,857	4,410
Sri Lanka	2,455	2,535	4,225
Greece	3,255	4,066	n/a
Venezuela	3,175	3,461	3,879
Austria	3,740	3,786	n/a
Malaysia	4,578	3,748	n/a
Romania	2,178	2,914	3,662
Slovakia	n/a	n/a	3,308
Afghanistan	2,795	n/a	n/a
Yugoslavia**	9,797	4,049	2,618
Mexico	2,608	n/a	n/a
Belarus	2,823	2,432	2,364
Lithuania	n/a	n/a	2,361
Croatia	2,239	n/a	n/a
Slovenia	1,851	2,459	2,136
Chile	n/a	1,966	1,820
Iceland	1,515	1,576	n/a
Nigeria	n/a	1,546	1,562
Estonia	1,628	1,654	1,557
Latvia	1,564	1,387	1,509
Colombia	n/a	1,481	n/a
Kazakhstan	n/a	n/a	1,226
Tunisia	n/a	181	1,165
Uruguay	n/a	1,143	n/a
Peru	894	1,063	n/a
Cuba	1,858	1,017	n/a
Philippines	1,112	825	n/a

Notes: n/a=not available.
* Title output for 1990 and 1991 refer to the former Czechoslovakia.
** Title output for 1990 refers to the former Yugoslavia.
Source: Unesco Statistical Yearbook, 1994, with the following exception: title output for Canada obtained from Statistics Canada, Ottawa.

Number of Book Outlets in the United States and Canada

The *American Book Trade Directory* has been published by R. R. Bowker since 1915. Revised annually, it features lists of booksellers, wholesalers, periodicals, reference tools, and other information about the U.S. and Canadian book markets. The data shown in Table 1, the most current available, are from the 1994–1995 edition of the directory.

The 30,650 stores of various types shown are located throughout the United States, Canada, and regions administered by the United States. "General" bookstores stock trade books and children's books in a general variety of subjects. "College" stores carry college-level textbooks. "Educational" outlets handle

Table 1 / Bookstores in the United States and Canada, 1994

Category	United States	Canada
Antiquarian general	1,344	96
Antiquarian mail order	620	16
Antiquarian specialized	276	9
Art supply store	78	1
College general	3,309	169
College specialized	161	12
Comics	294	31
Computer software	265	0
Cooking	126	9
Department store	2,577	91
Educational*	266	56
Federal sites†	309	1
Foreign language*	129	30
General	7,337	1,074
Gift shop	360	24
Juvenile*	472	54
Mail order general	418	21
Mail order specialized	186	8
Metaphysics and new age	293	23
Museum store and art gallery	591	35
Nature and natural history	152	8
Newsdealer	140	8
Office supply	68	17
Other‡	2,347	285
Paperback§	494	24
Religious*	3,971	251
Self help/development	81	11
Stationer	67	29
Toy store	102	9
Used*	1,304	111
Totals	28,137	2,513

* Includes mail order shops for this topic, which are not counted elsewhere in this survey.
† National historic sites, national monuments, and national parks.
‡ Includes mail order. Excludes used paperback bookstores, stationers, drugstores, or wholesalers handling paperbacks.
§ Stores specializing in subjects or services other than those covered in this survey.

school textbooks up to and including the high school level. "Mail order" outlets sell general trade books by mail and are not book clubs; all others operating by mail are classified according to the kinds of books carried. "Antiquarian" dealers sell old and rare books. Stores handling secondhand books are classified as "used." "Paperback" stores have more than 80 percent of their stock in paperbound books. Stores with paperback departments are listed under the appropriate major classification ("general," "department store," "stationer," etc.). Bookstores with at least 50 percent of their stock on a particular subject are classified by subject.

Book Review Media Statistics

Compiled by the staff of *The Bowker Annual.*

Number of Books Reviewed by Major Book-Reviewing Publications, 1993–1994

	Adult		Juvenile		Young Adult		Total	
	1993	1994	1993	1994	1993	1994	1993	1994
Booklist[1]	3,690	4,019	2,696	2,608	n/a	1,012	6,386	7,639
Bulletin of the Center for Children's Books	n/a	n/a	729	769	n/a	n/a	729	769
Chicago Sun Times	500	500	100	75	100	25	700	600
Chicago Tribune	730	750	55	60	n/a	n/a	785	810
Choice[2]	6,520	6,373	n/a	n/a	n/a	n/a	6,520	6,373
Horn Book Magazine[3]	n/a	n/a	500	400	n/a	n/a	500	400
Horn Book Guide[4]	n/a	n/a	3,750	3,700	n/a	n/a	3,750	3,700
Kirkus Services[5]	5,000	4,500	n/a	n/a	n/a	n/a	5,000	4,500
Library Journal[6]	5,500	5,300	n/a	n/a	n/a	n/a	5,500	5,300
Los Angeles Times	1,750	1,750	100	100	n/a	n/a	1,850	1,850
New York Review of Books	400	365	n/a	n/a	n/a	n/a	400	365
New York Times Sunday Book Review[7]	2,000	2,000	300	n/a	n/a	n/a	2,300	2,000
Publishers Weekly[8]	4,860	5,361	1,513	1,600	n/a	n/a	6,373	6,961
School Library Journal	n/a	n/a	3,256	3,460	366	240	3,622	3,700
Washington Post Book World	1,764	1,768	91	98	35	40	1,890	1,906
West Coast Review of Books (Rapport)	592	424	1	1	n/a	1	593	426

n/a = not applicable

[1] Figures are for a 12-month period from September 1 to August 31; 1994 figures are for September 1, 1993–August 31, 1994 (vol. 90). Some YA books are included in the juvenile total; the YA total includes reviews of adult books that are appropriate

[2] All figures are for a 12-month period beginning September and ending July/August; 1994 figures are for September 1993–July/August 1994.

[3] 1994 juvenile figures include young adult titles.

[4] 1994 juvenile figures include young adult titles.

[5] Adult figures include both adult and juvenile books.

[6] In addition, *LJ* reviewed 123 magazines in 18 issues; 408 audio books; 413 videos; 199 books in "round-ups"; 583 books in "Prepub Alert"; 360 in "Collection Development"; and 49 products in CD-ROM reviews.

[7] Juvenile figures include books reviewed in the "Bookshelf" column.

[8] Includes reviews of paperback originals and reprints.

Part 5
Reference Information

Ready Reference

Publishers' Toll-Free Telephone Numbers

Publishers' toll-free numbers continue to play an important role in ordering, verification, and customer service. This year's list comes from *Literary Market Place* (R. R. Bowker) and includes distributors and regional toll-free numbers, where applicable. The list is not comprehensive, and toll-free numbers are subject to change. Readers may want to call for toll-free directory assistance (800-555-1212).

Publisher/Distributor	Toll-Free No.
A-R Editions Inc, Madison, WI	800-736-0070
AACC Press, Washington, DC	800-892-1400
Abacus, Grand Rapids, MI	800-451-4319
Abbeville Publishing Group, New York, NY	800-ART-BOOK
Abbot, Foster & Hauserman Co, Spokane, WA	800-562-0025
ABC-CLIO, Santa Barbara, CA	800-422-2546
Abdo & Daughters Publishing, Minneapolis, MN	800-458-8399
Aberdeen Group, Addison, IL	800-323-3550
Abingdon Press, Nashville, TN	800-251-3320
Harry N Abrams Inc, New York, NY	800-345-1359
ACA Books, New York, NY	800-321-4510 ext 241
Academic Innovations, Santa Barbara, CA	800-967-8016
Academic Press Inc, San Diego, CA	(cust serv) 800-321-5068
Academic Therapy Publications, Novato, CA	800-422-7249
Academy Chicago Publishers, Chicago, IL	800-248-READ
The Academy of Producer Insurance Studies Inc, Austin, TX	800-526-2777
Accelerated Development Inc, Muncie, IN	800-222-1166
Acropolis Books Ltd, Washington, DC	800-451-7771
ACS Publications Inc, San Diego, CA	(orders) 800-888-9983
ACTA Publications, Chicago, IL	800-397-2282
Active Parenting Publishers Inc, Marietta, GA	800-825-0060
ACU Press, Abilene, TX	800-444-4228
Adams-Blake Publishing, Fair Oaks, CA	800-368-ADAM
Bob Adams Inc, Holbrook, MA	800-872-5627
ADAPT Publishing Co Inc, Austin, TX	800-333-8429

Publisher/Distributor	Toll-Free No.

Addison-Wesley Publishing Co Inc, Reading, MA   (school serv): 800-552-2259
  (college serv); 800-322-1377
  (college sales); 800-552-2499
  (trade & agency); 800-358-4566
  (corporate & govt); 800-822-6339

Adventure Publications, Cambridge, MN	800-678-7006
Aegean Park Press, Laguna Hills, CA	800-736-3587
The AEI Press, Washington, DC	800-223-2336
Aerofax Inc, Arlington, TX	800-733-2329
AGES (Ancestral Genealogical Endexing Schedules),	
Salt Lake City, UT	800-733-0844
Aglow Publications, Edmonds, WA	800-755-2456
Agora Inc, Baltimore, MD	800-433-1528
Ahsahta Press, Boise, ID	800-992-TEXT
AIHA Publications of America	
(ALPHA Publications of America Inc), Tucson, AZ	800-528-3494
Airmont Publishing Co Inc, New York, NY	800-223-5251
Alba House, Staten Island, NY	800-343-ALBA
The Alban Institute Inc, Bethesda, MD	800-436-1318
Alexander Books, Alexander, NC	800-472-0438
Alexander Hamilton Institute, Ramsey, NJ	800-879-2441
Alfred Publishing Co Inc, Van Nuys, CA	800-292-6122
Allworth Communications Inc, New York, NY	800-247-6553
Alpine Publications Inc, Loveland, CO	800-777-7257
AMACOM Books, New York, NY	(orders) 800-538-4761
Frank Amato Publications Inc, Portland, OR	800-541-9498
Amboy Associates, San Diego, CA	800-448-4023
America West Pubs, Bozeman, MT	800-729-4131
American Academy of Orthopaedic Surgeons, Rosemont, IL	800-626-6726
American Academy of Pediatrics, Elk Grove Village, IL	800-433-9016
American & World Geographic Publishing, Helena, MT	800-654-1105
American Association for Vocational Instructional Materials,	
Winterville, GA	800-228-4689
American Association of Cereal Chemists, St Paul, MN	800-328-7560
American Association of Engineering Societies, Washington, DC	800-658-8897
American Bible Society, New York, NY	800-543-8000
American Brain Tumor Association, Des Plaines, IL	800-886-2282
American Chemical Society, Washington, DC	800-227-5558
American College of Physician Executives, Tampa, FL	800-562-8088
American Correctional Association, Laurel, MD	800-825-2665
American Counseling Association,	
Alexandria, VA	800-545-2223; 800-347-6647
American Diabetes Association, Alexandria, VA	800-232-3472
American Education Publishing Co, Columbus, OH	800-542-7833
American Foundation for the Blind, New York, NY	800-232-5463
	(NY) 212-620-2147

Publisher/Distributor	Toll-Free No.
American Geophysical Union, Washington, DC	800-966-2481
American Guidance Service Inc, Circle Pines, MN	800-328-2560
American Health Publishing Co, Dallas, TX	800-736-7323
American Hospital Publishing Inc, Chicago, IL	800-621-6902
The American Institute of Architects Press, Washington, DC	(orders) 800-365-ARCH
American Law Institute, Philadelphia, PA	800-CLE-NEWS
American Library Association (ALA), Chicago, IL	800-545-2433
American Map Corp, Maspeth, NY	800-432-MAPS
American Mathematical Society, Providence, RI	800-321-4267
American Nurses Association, Washington, DC	800-637-0323
American Phytopathological Society, St Paul, MN	800-328-7560
American Printing House for the Blind Inc, Louisville, KY	800-223-1839
American Psychiatric Press Inc, Washington, DC	800-368-5777
American Society for Nondestructive Testing, Columbus, OH	800-222-2768
American Society of Civil Engineers, New York, NY	800-548-2723, (NY) 800-628-0041
American Society of Mechanical Engineers (ASME), New York, NY	800-843-2763
American Technical Publishers Inc, Homewood, IL	800-323-3471
Ameritype & Art Inc, Cleveland, OH	800-544-5314
The Analytic Press, Hillsdale, NJ	(orders) 800-926-6579
Ancestry Inc, Salt Lake City, UT	800-531-1790
Anderson Publishing Co, Cincinnati, OH	800-582-7295
Andrews & McMeel, Kansas City, MO	800-826-4216
Annabooks, San Diego, CA	800-462-1042
Annual Reviews Inc, Palo Alto, CA	800-523-8635
Antique Publications, Marietta, OH	800-533-3433
AOCS Press, Champaign, IL	800-336-AOCS
Aperture, New York, NY	800-929-2323
Aqua Quest Publications Inc, Locust Valley, NY	800-933-8989
The Archives Press, Los Altos, CA	800-373-1897
Ardis Publishers, Ann Arbor, MI	(orders) 800-877-7133
ARE Press, Virginia Beach, VA	800-723-1112
Ariel Press, Alpharetta, GA	800-336-7769
Jason Aronson Inc, Northvale, NJ	800-782-0015
Arrow Map Inc, Bridgewater, MA	800-343-7500
Artabras Inc, New York, NY	800-ART-BOOK
Arte Publico Press, Houston, TX	800-633-ARTE
Artech House Inc, Norwood, MA	800-225-9977
Artisan, New York, NY	800-722-7202
ASCP Press, Chicago, IL	800-621-4142
Ashgate Publishing Co, Brookfield, VT	800-535-9544
Aslan Publishing, Lower Lake, CA	800-275-2606
Aspen Books, Murray, UT	800-748-4850
Aspen Publishers Inc, Gaithersburg, MD	(orders) 800-638-8437

Publisher/Distributor	Toll-Free No.
Association for the Advancement of Medical Instrumentation, Arlington, VA	800-332-2264
Asylum Arts Publishing, Santa Maria, CA	(orders) 800-253-3605
ATL Press, Shrewsbury, MA	800-835-7543
ATLA Press, Washington, DC	800-424-2725
Atlantic Disk Publishers, Acworth, GA	800-808-9993
Augsburg Fortress Publishers: Publishing House of the Evangelical Lutheran Church in America, Minneapolis, MN	800-328-4648
August House Publishers Inc, Little Rock, AR	800-284-8784
Austin & Winfield Publishers Inc, San Francisco, CA	800-99-AUSTIN
Avalon Books, New York, NY	800-223-5251
Ave Maria Press, Notre Dame, IN	800-282-1865
Avery Publishing Group Inc, Wayne, NJ	800-548-5757
Avon Books, New York, NY	(orders) 800-238-0658
Ayer Company, Publishers Inc, North Stratford, NH	800-282-5413
B & B Publishing Inc, Walworth, WI	800-386-3228
Back to the Bible, Lincoln, NE	800-759-2425
Baha'i Publishing Trust, Wilmette, IL	800-999-9019
Baker Book House, Grand Rapids, MI	800-877-2665
Balcony Publishing Inc, Austin, TX	800-777-7949
Ballantine/Del Rey/Fawcett/Ivy Books, New York, NY	800-638-6460
Banks-Baldwin Law Publishing Co, Cleveland, OH	800-362-4500
Bantam Books, New York, NY	800-223-6834
Bantam Doubleday Dell Books for Young Readers, New York, NY	800-223-6834
Bantam Doubleday Dell Publishing Group Inc, New York, NY	800-223-6834
Baptist Spanish Publishing House, El Paso, TX	(cust serv) 800-755-5958
Barbour & Co Inc, Uhrichsville, OH	(orders) 800-852-8010
Barnes & Noble Books (Imports & Reprints), Lanham, MD	800-462-6420
Barron's Educational Series Inc, Hauppauge, NY	800-645-3476
Baskerville Publishers Inc, Dallas, TX	800-462-3568
Battelle Press, Columbus, OH	800-451-3543
Baywood Publishing Co Inc, Amityville, NY	800-638-7819
Beacham Publishing Inc, Washington, DC	800-466-9644
Beacon Hill Press of Kansas City, Kansas City, MO	800-877-0700
Bear & Co Inc, Santa Fe, NM	800-932-3277
Beautiful America Publishing Co, Wilsonville, OR	800-874-1233
Peter Bedrick Books Inc, New York, NY	800-788-3123
Beginning Press, Seattle, WA	800-831-4088
Behrman House Inc, West Orange, NJ	800-221-2755
Frederic C Beil Publisher Inc, Savannah, GA	800-829-8406
Bell Publishing Co, Raleigh, NC	800-544-2355
Bellerophon Books, Santa Barbara, CA	800-253-9943
Matthew Bender & Co Inc, New York, NY	(outside NY) 800-223-1940
	(NY) 800-422-2022

Publisher/Distributor	Toll-Free No.
John Benjamins North America Inc, Philadelphia, PA	800-562-5666
Robert Bentley Inc, Cambridge, MA	800-423-4595
Benziger Publishing Co, Mission Hills, CA	800-423-9534
Berkley Publishing Group, New York, NY	800-223-0510
Berkshire House Publishers, Stockbridge, MA	800-321-8526
Berlitz Publishing Co Inc, New York, NY	800-628-4808
Bernan Press, Lanham, MD	(US) 800-274-4447
Best Publishing Co, Flagstaff, AZ	800-468-1055
Bethany House Publishers, Minneapolis, MN	800-328-6109
Bethel Publishing Co, Elkhart, IN	800-348-7657
Betz Publishing Co Inc, Rockville, MD	800-634-4365
Beverage Marketing Corp, Mingo Junction, OH	800-332-6222
Beyond Words Publishing Inc, Hillsboro, OR	800-284-9673
Bhaktivedanta Book Publishing Inc, Los Angeles, CA	800-559-4455
Biblo & Tannen Booksellers & Publishers Inc, Cheshire, CT	(voice & fax) 800-272-8778
The Biosphere Press, Oracle, AZ	800-992-4603
Birkhauser Boston, Cambridge, MA	800-777-4643
George T Bisel Co, Philadelphia, PA	800-247-3526
Black Belt Press, Montgomery, AL	800-956-3245
Blackbirch Press Inc, Woodbridge, CT	800-831-9183
John F Blair, Publisher, Winston-Salem, NC	800-222-9796
Blake Books, San Luis Obispo, CA	800-727-8558
Blue Dolphin Publishing Inc, Nevada City, CA	800-643-0765
Blue Moon Books Inc, New York, NY	800-535-0007
Blue Mountain Press Inc, Boulder, CO	800-525-0642
Blue Note Publications, Cape Canaveral, FL	800-624-0401
Blue Poppy Press, Boulder, CO	800-487-9296
Bluestocking Press, Placerville, CA	800-959-8586
BNA Books, Washington, DC	800-372-1033
Bob Jones University Press, Greenville, SC	800-845-5731
Bonus Books Inc, Chicago, IL	800-225-3775
Book-Lab, New York, NY	800-654-4081
Book Lures Inc, O'Fallon, MO	800-844-0455
Book Publishing Co, Summertown, TN	800-695-2241
Book Sales Inc, Edison, NJ	800-526-7257
Don Bosco Multimedia, New Rochelle, NY	800-342-5850
R R Bowker, New Providence, NJ	(sales) 800-521-8110
Boyd & Fraser Publishing Co, Danvers, MA	800-225-3782
Boynton/Cook Publishers Inc, Portsmouth, NH	(orders) 800-541-2086
William K Bradford Publishing Co Inc, Acton, MA	800-421-2009
Branden Publishing Co Inc, Brookline Village, MA	(Mastercard & Visa sales) 800-537-7335
Breakthrough Publications, Ossining, NY	800-824-5000
Brethren Press, Elgin, IL	800-323-8039
Brick House Publishing Co, Amherst, NH	(orders) 800-446-8642

Publisher/Distributor	Toll-Free No.
Bridge Publications Inc, Los Angeles, CA	800-722-1733; (CA) 800-843-7389
E J Brill USA Inc, Kinderhook, NY	800-962-4406
Bristol Publishing Enterprises Inc, San Leandro, CA	800-346-4889
Broadman & Holman Publishers, Nashville, TN	800-251-3225
Broadway Press, Shelter Island, NY	800-869-6372
Paul H Brookes Publishing Co, Baltimore, MD	800-638-3775
The Brookings Institution, Washington, DC	800-275-1447
Brookline Books Inc, Cambridge, MA	800-666-2665
Brooks/Cole Publishing Co, Pacific Grove, CA	800-354-9706
Brown & Benchmark, Madison, WI	800-527-8198
Wm C Brown Communications Inc, Dubuque, IA	800-338-5578
Bruit Publishing Co Inc, Langley, WA	800-278-4893
Brunner/Mazel Inc, New York, NY	800-825-3089
Building News, Needham, MA	800-873-6397
Bull Publishing Co, Palo Alto, CA	800-676-2855
Business & Legal Reports Inc, Madison, CT	800-727-5257
Business News Publishing Co, Troy, MI	800-837-1037
Business Research Services Inc, Washington, DC	800-845-8420
Butterworth-Heinemann, Newton, MA	(orders, cust serv) 800-366-2665
Butterworth Legal Publishers, Salem, NH	800-548-4001
C & T Publishing, Martinez, CA	800-284-1114
Caddylak Systems Inc, Tonawanda, NY	800-523-8060
California College Press, National City, CA	800-221-7374
Cambridge Educational, Charleston, WV	800-468-4227
Cambridge Law Study Aids, Chicago, IL	800-628-1160
Cambridge University Press, New York, NY	800-221-4512
Camden House Inc, Columbia, SC	(orders) 800-723-9455
Camden House Publishing, Charlotte, VT	800-344-3350
Cameron & Co, San Francisco, CA	800-779-5582
The Career Press Inc, Hawthorne, NJ	800-CAREER-1
Career Publishing Inc, Orange, CA	800-854-4041
William Carey Library, Pasadena, CA	800-647-7466; 800-777-6371
Carlson Publishing Inc, Brooklyn, NY	800-336-7460
Carolrhoda Books Inc, Minneapolis, MN	800-328-4929
The Carroll Press, New York, NY	800-366-7086
CarTech Inc, North Branch, MN	800-551-4754
Castle Books Inc, Edison, NJ	(orders) 800-526-7257
CAT Publishing Co, Redding, CA	800-767-0511
Catholic News Publishing Co Inc, New Rochelle, NY	800-433-7771
The Caxton Printers Ltd, Caldwell, ID	800-657-6465
CEF Press, Warrenton, MO	800-748-7710
Celestial Arts, Berkeley, CA	800-841-BOOK
Center for Afro-American Studies Publications, Los Angeles, CA	800-206-CAAS
Center for Career Development Inc, Cincinnati, OH	800-992-4226

Publisher/Distributor	Toll-Free No.
Central Conference of American Rabbis/CCAR Press, New York, NY	800-935-CCAR
Chadwyck-Healey Inc, Alexandria, VA	800-752-0515
Chalice Press, St Louis, MO	800-366-3383
Chapman & Hall, New York, NY	(cust serv) 800-634-7064
Chariot Family Publishing, Elgin, IL	800-437-4337
Charlesbridge Publishing, Watertown, MA	800-225-3214
Chartwell Books Inc, Edison, NJ	(orders) 800-526-7257
Chelsea Green Publishing Co, Post Mills, VT	800-639-4099
Chess Combination Inc, Bridgeport, CT	800-354-4083
Chicago Review Press Inc, Chicago, IL	800-888-4741
Childrens Press, Chicago, IL	800-374-4329
Child's Play, West Orange, NJ	800-472-0099
Chilton Enterprises, Radnor, PA	800-695-1214
Chiron Publications, Wilmette, IL	(orders) 800-397-8109
Chivers North America Inc, Hampton, NH	800-621-0182
Chosen, Grand Rapids, MI	800-877-2665
Christendom Press, Front Royal, VA	800-877-5456
Christian Brothers Publications, Landover, MD	800-433-7593
Christian Classics Inc, Westminster, MD	800-888-3065
Christian Ed Publishers, La Jolla, CA	800-854-1531
Christian Literature Crusade Inc, Fort Washington, PA	800-659-1240
Christian Publications Inc, Camp Hill, PA	800-233-4443
Christian Schools International, Grand Rapids, MI	800-635-8288
Christopher Gordon Publishers Inc, Norwood, MA	800-934-8322
Chronicle Books, San Francisco, CA	(orders) 800-722-6657
Chronicle Guidance Publications Inc, Moravia, NY	800-622-7284
Chronimed Publishing, Minnetonka, MN	800-444-5951
Churchill Livingstone Inc, New York, NY	(IL) 800-553-5426
The Citizens Call Publishers	800-875-HEAL
Clarity Press Inc, Atlanta, GA	(COD or credit card orders) 800-247-6553
Clark City Press, Livingston, MT	800-835-0814
Cleaning Consultant Services Inc, Seattle, WA	800-622-4221
Clear Light Publishers, Santa Fe, NM	800-253-2747
Cliffs Notes Inc, Lincoln, NE	800-228-4078
Clinical Psychology Publishing Co Inc, Brandon, VT	800-433-8234
ClockWorks Press, Shingle Springs, CA	800-276-0701
Clothespin Fever Press, La Mesa, CA	800-231-8624
Clymer Publications, Overland Park, KS	800-654-6776
Cold Spring Harbor Laboratory Press, Cold Spring Harbor, NY	800-843-4388
Cole Group Inc, Santa Rosa, CA	800-959-2717
Collector Books, Paducah, KY	800-626-5420
Collectors Editions Inc, Canoga Park, CA	800-736-0001
College Press Publishing Co, Joplin, MO	800-289-3300
The Color Resource, San Francisco, CA	800-827-3311
Colorado Railroad Museum, Golden, CO	800-365-6263

Publisher/Distributor	Toll-Free No.
Colorado School of Mines Press, Golden, CO	800-446-9488
Columbia Publishing Co Inc, Baltimore, MD	800-544-0042
Columbia University Press, New York, NY	800-944-8648
Comex Systems Inc, Mendham, NJ	800-543-6959
Commerce Clearing House Inc (CCH), Riverwoods, IL	800-248-3248
Communication Publications & Resources, Blackwood, NJ	800-888-2086
Community Intervention Inc, Minneapolis, MN	800-328-0417
Compact Books, Hollywood, FL	800-771-3355
Comprehensive Health Education Foundation (CHEF), Seattle, WA	800-323-2433
Conari Press, Emeryville, CA	800-685-9595
Conciliar Press, Ben Lomond, CA	800-967-7377
Concordia Publishing House, St Louis, MO	800-325-3040
The Conference Board Inc, New York, NY	800-872-6273
Congressional Information Service Inc, Bethesda, MD	800-638-8380
Congressional Quarterly Books, Washington, DC	800-638-1710
Consulting Psychologists Press Inc, Palo Alto, CA	800-624-1765
The Continuum Publishing Group, New York, NY	800-937-5557
Cool Hand Communications Inc, Boca Raton, FL	800-428-0578
Copley Publishing Group, Acton, MA	800-562-2147
Cornell Maritime Press Inc, Centreville, MD	800-638-7641
Cornell University Press, Ithaca, NY (outside NY)	800-666-2211
CorpTech (Corporate Technology Information Services Inc), Woburn, MA	800-333-8036
Cortina Learning International Inc, Westport, CT	800-245-2145
Council Oak Publishing Co Inc, Tulsa, OK	800-247-8850
Council of State Governments, Lexington, KY	800-800-1910
Country Roads Press, Castine, ME	800-729-9179
The Countryman Press Inc, Woodstock, VT	800-245-4151
Countrysport Press, Traverse City, MI	800-367-4114
Course Technology Inc, Cambridge, MA	800-648-7450
Covered Bridge Press, North Attleboro, MA	800-752-3769
Cowley Publications, Boston, MA	800-225-1534
Crabtree Publishing Co, New York, NY	800-387-7650
Beverly Cracom Publications, Maryland Heights, MO	800-341-0880
Craftsman Book Co, Carlsbad, CA	800-829-8123
CRC Publications, Grand Rapids, MI	800-333-8300
Creative Arts Book Co, Berkeley, CA	800-848-7789
The Creative Co, Mankato, MN	800-445-6209
Creative Homeowner Press, Upper Saddle River, NJ	800-631-7795
Creative Publishing Co, College Station, TX	800-245-5841
Creative Teaching Press/Youngheart Music, Cypress, CA	800-444-4287
Cricket: The Magazine for Children, Mt Morris, IL (orders)	800-827-0227
Crisp Publications Inc, Menlo Park, CA	800-442-7477
Croner Publications Inc, Jericho, NY	800-441-4033
The Crossing Press, Freedom, CA	800-777-1048

Publisher/Distributor	Toll-Free No.
The Crossroad Publishing Co Inc, New York, NY	800-937-5557
Crossway Books, Wheaton, IL	800-323-3890
Crystal Clarity Publishers, Nevada City, CA	800-424-1055
Crystal Productions, Glenview, IL	800-255-8629
Cummings & Hathaway Publishers, East Rockaway, NY	800-344-7579
Cypress House, Fort Bragg, CA	800-773-7782
Da Capo Press Inc, New York, NY	800-221-9369
Dake Bible Sales, Lawrenceville, GA	800-241-1239
Dance Horizons, Pennington, NJ	800-220-7149
John Daniel & Co, Publishers, Santa Barbara, CA	800-662-8351
Dartnell Books, Chicago, IL	800-621-5463
DATA, Englewood, CO	800-447-4666
Data Research Inc, Eagan, MN	800-365-4900
F A Davis Co, Philadelphia, PA	800-523-4049
Davis Publications Inc, Worcester, MA	800-533-2847
DAW Books Inc, New York, NY	800-526-0275
Dawbert Press, Duxbury, MA	800-93-DAWBERT
The Dawn Horse Press, Middletown, CA	800-524-4941
Dawn Publications, Nevada City, CA	800-545-7475
DBI Books Inc, Northbrook, IL	800-767-6310
DDC Publishing, New York, NY	800-528-3897
DDL Books Inc, Miami, FL	800-635-4276
Cy De Cosse Inc, Minnetonka, MN	800-328-0590
De Vorss & Co Inc, Marina del Rey, CA	(CA) 800-331-4719
	(outside CA) 800-843-5743
Deaconess Press, Minneapolis, MN	800-544-8207
Ivan R Dee Inc, Chicago, IL	(orders) 800-634-0226
Marcel Dekker Inc, New York, NY	(outside NY) 800-228-1160
Dell Publishing, New York, NY	(outside NY) 800-223-6834
Delmar Publishers Inc, Albany, NY	(NY) 800-347-7707
Demos Publications, New York, NY	800-532-8663
T S Denison & Co Inc, Minneapolis, MN	800-328-3831
Derrydale Press Inc, Lyon, MS	800-443-6753
Deseret Book Co, Salt Lake City, UT	800-453-3876
Destiny Image, Shippensburg, PA	800-722-6774
Devyn Press, Louisville, KY	800-274-2221
DGC Associates Inc, Cedarhurst, NY	800-442-2342
Dharma Publishing, Berkeley, CA	800-873-4276
Dhyana Press, San Francisco, CA	800-549-0992
Digital Wisdom Inc, Tappahannock, VA	800-800-8560
Dimensions for Living, Nashville, TN	800-281-3320
Discipleship Resources, Nashville, TN	800-814-7833
Discovery Enterprises Ltd, Lowell, MA	800-729-1720
Discovery House Publishers, Grand Rapids, MI	800-653-8333
Distributed Art Publishers (DAP), New York, NY	800-338-2665
Diversity Press, Idabel, OK	800-642-0779

Publisher/Distributor	Toll-Free No.
Dominie Press Inc, San Diego, CA	800-232-4570
The Donning Co/Publishers, Virginia Beach, VA	800-296-8572
Doral Publishing, Portland, OR	800-858-9055
Dorset House Publishing Co Inc, New York, NY	800-DHBOOKS
Doubleday, New York, NY	800-223-6834
Douglas Charles Press,	
North Attleboro, MA	(New England) 800-752-3769
Dover Publications Inc, Mineola, NY	(orders) 800-223-3130
Down East Books, Camden, ME	800-766-1670
The Dramatic Publishing Co, Woodstock, IL	800-448-7469
The Dryden Press, Fort Worth, TX	800-323-7437
Dual Dolphin Publishing Inc, Norfolk, MA	800-336-5746
Duke Communications International, Loveland, CO	800-621-1544
Dun & Bradstreet Information Services, Murray Hill, NJ	800-526-0651
Duquesne University Press, Pittsburgh, PA	800-666-2211
Durkin Hayes Publishing, Niagara Falls, NY	800-962-5200
Dustbooks, Paradise, CA	800-477-6110
Eagle's View Publishing, Liberty, UT	(orders over $100) 800-547-3364
East Coast Publishing, Poughkeepsie, NY	800-327-4212; 800-405-1070
East View Publications, Minneapolis, MN	800-477-1005
Eastgate Systems Inc, Watertown, MA	800-562-1638
Eastland Press, Seattle, WA	800-453-3278
Eastwind Publishing, Dubuque, IA	800-636-2665
Eclipse Books, Forestville, CA	800-468-6828
EDC Publishing, Tulsa, OK	800-475-4522
Edition Q Inc, Carol Stream, IL	800-421-0387
Editorial Caribe, Miami, FL	800-633-6248
Editorial Unilit, Miami, FL	800-767-7726
EDL, Columbia, SC	800-227-1606
Education Systems, Sandy, UT	800-288-3987
Educational Impressions Inc, Hawthorne, NJ	800-451-7450
Educational Insights Inc, Dominguez Hills, CA	800-933-3277
Educational Ministries Inc, Prescott, AZ	800-221-0910
Educational Technology Publications,	
Englewood Cliffs, NJ	(orders, US & Canada) 800-952-BOOK
Educators Publishing Service Inc, Cambridge, MA	800-225-5750
Wm B Eerdmans Publishing Co, Grand Rapids, MI	800-253-7521
Elysium Growth Press, Los Angeles, CA	800-350-2020
Embassy Marine Publishing & Foremost Books,	
Old Saybrook, CT	800-999-1075
Embassy Publishing, Laguna Hills, CA	800-486-5012
EMC Corp, St Paul, MN	800-328-1452
Encyclopaedia Britannica Educational Corp, Chicago, IL	800-554-9862
Encyclopaedia Britannica Inc, Chicago, IL	800-323-1229
Engineering Information Inc, Hoboken, NJ	800-221-1044
EPM Publications Inc, McLean, VA	800-289-2339

Publisher/Distributor	Toll-Free No.
ERIC Clearinghouse on Reading, English & Communication, Bloomington, IN	800-759-4723
Lawrence Erlbaum Associates Inc, Hillsdale, NJ	(orders) 800-9-BOOKS-9
Essential Medical Information Systems Inc, Durant, OK	800-225-0694
ETC Publications, Palm Springs, CA	800-906-6666
ETR Associates, Santa Cruz, CA	800-321-4407
Evan-Moor Publishers, Monterey, CA	800-777-4362
Evangel Publishing House, Nappanee, IN	800-253-9315
The Evangelical Literature League, Jenison, MI	800-426-8255
Evanston Publishing Inc, Evanston, IL	800-594-5190
Everton Publishers Inc, Logan, UT	800-443-6325
Everyday Learning Corp, Evanston, IL	800-382-7670
Exley Giftbooks, New York, NY	800-423-9539
Explorers Guide Publishing, Rhinelander, WI	800-497-6029
Faber & Faber Inc, Winchester, MA	(outside NY) 800-666-2211
Facts on File Inc, New York, NY	800-322-8755
Fairchild Books & Visuals, New York, NY	800-247-6622
Falcon Press Publishing Co Inc, Helena, MT	800-582-2665
Fantagraphics Books, Seattle, WA	800-657-1100
W D Farmer Residence Designer Inc, Atlanta, GA	800-225-7526
	(GA) 800-221-7526
FASA Corp, Chicago, IL	800-424-FASA
The Faxon Co, Westwood, MA	800-999-3594 ext 292
Fearon Teacher Aids, Carthage, IL	800-242-7272
Philip Feldheim Inc, Spring Valley, NY	800-237-7149
Fell Publishers, Hollywood, FL	800-771-FELL
Fire Engineering Books & Videos, Saddle Brook, NJ	800-752-9768
First Teacher Press, Weston, MA	(orders) 800-677-6644
	(cust serv) 800-825-0061
Fisher Books, Tucson, AZ	800-255-1514
The Fisherman Library, Point Pleasant, NJ	800-553-4745
Fitzroy Dearborn Publishers, Chicago, IL	800-850-8102
Five Corners Publications Ltd, Plymouth, VT	800-972-3868
J Flores Publications Inc, Miami, FL	800-472-2388
Flower Valley Press Inc, Gaithersburg, MD	800-735-5197
Focus Information Group Inc, Newburyport, MA	(orders) 800-848-7236
Focus on the Family Publishing, Colorado Springs, CO	800-232-6459
Fodor's Travel Publications Inc, New York, NY	800-733-3000
Foghorn Press, San Francisco, CA	(CA) 800-FOGHORN
Fondo de Cultura Economica USA Inc, San Diego, CA	800-532-3872
Food First Books, Oakland, CA	800-888-3314
Fordham University Press, Bronx, NY	800-247-6553
Foreign Policy Association, New York, NY	(orders) 800-477-5836
Forest House Publishing Co Inc, Lake Forest, IL	800-394-READ
Fort Dearborn Press, Chicago, IL	(book orders) 800-247-6553

Publisher/Distributor	Toll-Free No.
Forward Movement Publications, Cincinnati, OH	800-543-1813
The Foundation Center, New York, NY	800-424-9836
Franciscan University Press, Steubenville, OH	800-783-6357
The Free Press, New York, NY	(cust serv) 800-257-5755;
	(orders) 800-323-7445
Free Spirit Publishing Inc, Minneapolis, MN	800-735-7323
Friends United Press, Richmond, IN	800-537-8838
Fromm International Publishing Corp, New York, NY	800-688-3766
Front Row Experience, Byron, CA	(voice & fax) 800-524-9091
Fulcrum Publishing Inc, Golden, CO	800-992-2908
Fulcrum Publishing Inc, Washington, DC	800-525-3444
Futura Publishing Co Inc, Armonk, NY	800-877-8761
P Gaines Co, Oak Park, IL	800-578-3853
Gale Research Inc, Detroit, MI	(cust serv) 800-877-GALE
	(edit) 800-347-GALE
Gallaudet University Press, Washington, DC	800-451-1073
Gallopade Publishing Group, Atlanta, GA	800-536-2GET
Gardner Press Inc, Lake Worth, FL	800-756-8534
Garrett Educational Corp, Ada, OK	800-654-9366
Garrett Publishing Inc, Deerfield Beach, FL	800-638-7571
Gateway Books, Oakland, CA	(credit card orders) 800-669-0773
Wm W Gaunt & Sons Inc, Holmes Beach, FL	800-942-8683
Thomas Geale Publications Inc, Montara, CA	800-554-5457
Genealogical Publishing Co Inc, Baltimore, MD	800-296-6687
General Publications Group, Boston, MA	800-228-7090
General Publishing Group Inc, Santa Monica, CA	800-745-9000
Geological Society of America (GSA), Boulder, CO	800-472-1988
Gessler Publishing Co Inc, New York, NY	800-456-5825
The C R Gibson Co, Norwalk, CT	800-243-6004
Gleim Publications Inc, Gainesville, FL	800-87-GLEIM
Glen Abbey Books Inc, Seattle, WA	(cust serv) 800-782-2239
Glencoe, Westerville, OH	800-848-1567
Peter Glenn Publications Ltd, New York, NY	800-223-1254
Global Professional Publications, Englewood, CO	800-854-7179
Global Travel Publishers Inc, Pompano Beach, FL	800-882-9453
The Globe Pequot Press Inc, Old Saybrook, CT	800-243-0495;
	(CT) 800-962-0973
The Gold Book, Atlanta, GA	800-842-6848
Gold Horse Publishing Inc, Annapolis, MD	800-966-DOLL
Gold 'N' Honey Books, Sisters, OR	800-929-0910
Golden Aura Publishing, Philadelphia, PA	800-979-8642
Golden Educational Center, Redding, CA	800-800-1791
Golf Gifts & Gallery Inc, Lombard, IL	800-552-4430
Good Books, Intercourse, PA	800-762-7171
Goodheart-Willcox Co, South Holland, IL	800-323-0440
Gordon & Breach Publishers Inc, Newark, NJ	800-545-8398

Publisher/Distributor	Toll-Free No.
Gospel Publishing House, Springfield, MO	800-641-4310
Gould Publications Inc, Longwood, FL	800-847-6502
Government Research Service, Topeka, KS	800-346-6898
Grapevine Publications Inc, Corvallis, OR	800-338-4331
Graphic Arts Center Publishing Co, Portland, OR	800-452-3032
Graphic Learning, Waterbury, CT	800-874-0029
Grayson Bernard Publishers, Bloomington, IN	800-925-7853
Great Quotations Inc, Glendale Heights, IL	800-354-4889
Green Hill Publishers Inc, Ottawa, IL	800-426-1357
Warren H Green Inc, St Louis, MO	800-537-0655
Greenberg Publishing Co Inc, Waukesha, WI	800-533-6644
Greenhaven Press Inc, San Diego, CA	800-231-5163
Greenwillow Books, New York, NY	800-631-1199
Greenwood Publishing Group Inc, Westport, CT	(orders) 800-225-5800
Grey House Publishing Inc, Lakeville, CT	800-562-2139
Group Publishing Inc, Loveland, CO	800-447-1070
Grove/Atlantic Inc, New York, NY	800-521-0178
Grove's Dictionaries Inc, New York, NY	800-221-2123
Gryphon Editions, New York, NY	800-633-8911
Gryphon House Inc, Beltsville, MD	800-638-0928
The Guilford Press, New York, NY	(orders) 800-365-7006
Gulf Publishing Co, Book Division, Houston, TX	(TX) 800-392-4390
(all other except AK & HI) 800-231-6275	
GW Medical Inc, St Louis, MO	800-600-0330
Hagstrom Map Co Inc, Maspeth, NY	800-432-MAPS
Hambleton Hill Publishing Inc, Nashville, TN	800-327-5113
Hammond Inc, Maplewood, NJ	800-526-4953
Hampton-Brown Co Inc, Carmel, CA	800-933-3510
Hampton Roads Publishing Co Inc, Norfolk, VA	800-766-8009
Hanley & Belfus Inc, Philadelphia, PA	800-962-1892
Hannibal Books, Hannibal, MO	800-747-0738
Hanser-Gardner Publications, Cincinnati, OH	800-950-8977
Harbinger House, Tucson, AZ	800-759-9945
Harbor House (West) Publishers Inc, Summerland, CA	800-423-8811
Harcourt Brace & Company, Orlando, FL	(cust serv) 800-225-5425
Harcourt Brace College Publishers, Fort Worth, TX	(cust serv) 800-782-4479
Harcourt Brace Professional Publishing, San Diego, CA	800-543-1918
Harcourt Brace Trade Division, San Diego, CA	(cust serv) 800-543-1918
HarperCollins Publishers, New York, NY	800-242-7737
(PA) 800-982-4377	
The Harrington Park Press, Binghamton, NY	800-342-9678
800-3-HAWORTH	
Harris Media/Newspower, Northfield, MA	800-346-8330
Harris Publishing Co, Twinsburg, OH	800-888-5900
Harrison House Publishers, Tulsa, OK	800-888-4126
Harvard Business School Press, Boston, MA	800-545-7685

Publisher/Distributor	Toll-Free No.
Harvard University Press, Cambridge, MA (orders, US & Canada)	800-448-2242
Harvest House Publishers Inc, Eugene, OR	800-547-8979
The Haworth Press Inc, Binghamton, NY	800-342-9678
Hay House Inc, Carson, CA (orders)	800-654-5126
Haynes Publications Inc, Newbury Park, CA	800-442-9637
Hazelden Publishing Group, Center City, MN	800-328-9000
HCIA Inc, Baltimore, MD	800-568-3282
Health Communications Inc, Deerfield Beach, FL (cust serv)	800-851-9100
Health for Life, Marina del Rey, CA	800-874-5339
Health Leadership Associates Inc, Potomac, MD	800-435-4775
Health Press, Santa Fe, NM	800-643-BOOK
Health Science, Santa Barbara, CA	800-446-1990
Heartland Samplers Inc, Edina, MN	800-999-2233
D C Heath & Co, Lexington, MA	800-235-3565
William S Hein & Co Inc, Buffalo, NY	800-828-7571
Heinemann, Portsmouth, NH	800-541-2086
Heinle & Heinle Publishers, Boston, MA	800-237-0053
Hemingway Western Studies Series, Boise, ID	800-992-TEXT
Hendrickson Publishers Inc, Peabody, MA	800-358-3111
Virgil Hensley Publishing, Tulsa, OK	800-288-8520
Herald House, Independence, MO	800-767-8181
Herald Press, Scottdale, PA	800-245-7894
Heritage Books Inc, Bowie, MD	800-398-7709
Heritage House, Indianapolis, IN	800-419-0200
Hi-Time Publishing Corp, Milwaukee, WI	800-558-2292
Marilyn Hickey Ministries, Denver, CO	800-743-1324
Highsmith Press LLC, Fort Atkinson, WI	800-558-2110
Hill & Wang, New York, NY (orders, cust serv)	800-631-8571
Lawrence Hill Books, New York, NY (orders)	800-888-4741
Hillcrest Press Inc, Santa Ana, CA	800-248-8057
Hillsdale College Press, Hillsdale, MI	800-437-2268
Himalayan Publishers, Honesdale, PA	800-822-4547
Hive Publishing Co, Easton, PA	800-355-HIVE
Peg Hoenack's MusicWorks, Bethesda, MD	800-466-8668
Hogrefe & Huber Publishers, Kirkland, WA	800-228-3749
Holmes & Meier Publishers Inc, New York, NY (orders)	800-698-7781
Henry Holt & Co Inc, New York, NY	800-488-5233
Holt, Rinehart and Winston, Inc, Orlando, FL (cust serv)	800-782-4479
Home Builder Press, Washington, DC	800-223-2665
Home Planners Inc, Tucson, AZ	800-521-6797
Homestyles Publishing & Marketing Inc, Minneapolis, MN	800-547-5570
Hope Publishing Co, Carol Stream, IL	800-323-1049
Hope Publishing House, Pasadena, CA (orders)	800-326-2671
Horizon House Publishers, Camp Hill, PA	800-233-4443
Horizon Publishers & Distributors Inc, Bountiful, UT	800-453-0812

Publisher/Distributor	Toll-Free No.
Houghton Mifflin Co, Boston, MA	(trade books) 800-225-3362
	(textbooks) 800-257-9107
	(college texts) 800-225-1464
Howard University Press, Washington, DC	800-441-1303
Howell Press Inc, Charlottesville, VA	800-868-4512
Human Kinetics Inc, Champaign, IL	800-747-4457
Human Resource Development Press, Amherst, MA	800-822-2801
Humanics Ltd, Atlanta, GA	800-874-8844
Huntington House Publishers, Lafayette, LA	800-749-4009
Hyperion, New York, NY	(orders) 800-343-9204
IAP Inc, Casper, WY	800-443-9250
IBC USA (Publications) Inc, Ashland, MA	800-343-5413
Ican Press Publishers Inc, Chula Vista, CA	800-869-1531
ICP, Indianapolis, IN	800-428-6179
ICS Books Inc, Merrillville, IN	800-541-7323
ICS Press, San Francisco, CA	800-326-0263
Ideals Publications Inc, Nashville, TN	800-558-4383
IDG Books Worldwide Inc, San Mateo, CA	800-762-2974
IEEE Computer Society Press, Los Alamitos, CA	800-272-6657
IFSTA/Fire Protection Publications, Stillwater, OK	800-654-4055
Igaku-Shoin Medical Publishers Inc, New York, NY	800-765-0800
Ignatius Press, San Francisco, CA	(orders) 800-651-1531
Illuminated Way Publishing Inc, Golden Valley, MN	800-457-9063
IllumiNet Press, Lilburn, GA	800-236-INET
Imaginart Press, Bisbee, AZ	800-828-1376
Imagine Inc, Pittsburgh, PA	800-926-6653
Impressions Ink, Memphis, TN	800-388-5382
Incentive Publications Inc, Nashville, TN	800-421-2830
Index Publishing Group Inc, San Diego, CA	800-546-6707
Indiana University Press, Bloomington, IN	(orders) 800-842-6796
Infinity Publications, Sedona, AZ	800-530-5303
InfoBooks, Santa Monica, CA	800-669-0409
Information Guides, Hermosa Beach, CA	800-347-3257
Information Plus, Wylie, TX	800-313-INFO
Information Resources Press, Arlington, VA	800-451-7363
Inner Traditions International Ltd, Rochester, VT	800-488-2665
	(VT call collect) 802-878-0315
Institute for Language Study, Westport, CT	800-245-2145
Institute for Palestine Studies, Washington, DC	800-874-3614
Interarts Ltd, Cambridge, MA	800-626-4655
Interchange Inc, St Louis Park, MN	800-669-6208
Intern Guild of Occult Sciences Research Society, Palm Springs, CA	800-395-4467
The International Center for Creative Thinking, Larchmont, NY	800-328-4465
International Information Associates Inc, Morrisville, PA	800-645-6973
International Library-Book Publishers Inc, Gaithersburg, MD	800-359-3349

Publisher/Distributor	Toll-Free No.
International Linguistics Corp, Kansas City, MO	800-237-1830
International Specialized Book Services, Portland, OR	800-944-6190
International Wealth Success, Merrick, NY	800-323-0548
Interstate Publishers Inc, Danville, IL	800-843-4774
Intertec Publishing Corp, Overland Park, KS	800-262-1954:
	(orders) 800-453-9620
Interurban Press, Pasadena, CA	(continental US) 800-899-8722
InterVarsity Press, Downers Grove, IL	800-843-7225
Iowa State University Press, Ames, IA	(orders) 800-862-6657
IPS Publishing Inc, Vancouver, WA	800-933-8378
Richard D Irwin Inc, Burr Ridge, IL	(orders) 800-634-3961
Ishiyaku EuroAmerica Inc, St Louis, MO	800-633-1921
Island Press, Washington, DC	800-828-1302
ITP School Publishing Co, Cincinnati, OH	800-543-0487
Ivory Tower Publishing Co Inc, Watertown, MA	800-322-5016
J & B Editions, Norfolk, VA	800-266-5480
J-Mart Press, Virginia Beach, VA	800-487-4060
Jalmar Press, Torrance, CA	800-662-9662
Jamestown Publishers, Providence, RI	800-USA-READ
Jane's Information Group Inc, Alexandria, VA	800-243-3852
Janson Publications Inc, Dedham, MA	800-322-MATH
January Productions Inc, Hawthorne, NJ	800-451-7450
Jewish Lights Publishing, Woodstock, VT	800-962-4544
Jewish Publication Society, Philadelphia, PA	800-234-3151
JIST Works Inc, Indianapolis, IN	800-648-5478
The Johns Hopkins University Press, Baltimore, MD	800-537-5487
Johnson Institute, Minneapolis, MN	800-231-5165
Jones & Bartlett Publishers Inc, Boston, MA	800-832-0034
Joy Publishing, Fountain Valley, CA	800-783-6265
JSA Publications Inc, Farmington Hills, MI	800-345-0096
Judson Press, Valley Forge, PA	800-331-1053
Justice Systems Press, Port Angeles, WA	800-553-1903
Kalmbach Publishing Co, Waukesha, WI	800-558-1544
Kar-Ben Copies Inc, Rockville, MD	800-4-KARBEN
KC Publications Inc, Las Vegas, NV	800-626-9673
Keats Publishing Inc, New Canaan, CT	800-858-7014
Kendall/Hunt Publishing Co, Dubuque, IA	(orders) 800-228-0810
Kennedy Publications, Fitzwilliam, NH	800-531-0007
Kent State University Press, Kent, OH	(orders) 800-247-6553
Key Curriculum Press, Berkeley, CA	800-338-7638
Kirkbride Bible Co Inc, Indianapolis, IN	800-428-4385
Neil A Kjos Music Co, San Diego, CA	800-854-1592
The S Klein Library on Computer Graphics, Norwell, MA	800-874-9980
Alfred A Knopf Inc, New York, NY	800-638-6460
Knopf Publishing Group, New York, NY	800-638-6460
Knowledge Ideas & Trends Inc, Manchester, CT	800-826-0529

Publisher/Distributor	Toll-Free No.
Knowledge Industry Publications Inc, White Plains, NY	800-800-5474
Knowledge Systems Inc, Indianapolis, IN	800-999-8517
Kodansha America Inc, New York, NY	800-788-6262
Kraus International Publications, Millwood, NY	800-223-8323
Kraus Reprint, Millwood, NY	800-223-8323
Kraus Sikes Inc, Madison, WI	800-969-1556
Kregel Publications, Grand Rapids, MI	(orders) 800-733-2607
Kumarian Press Inc, West Hartford, CT	(orders) 800-289-2664
Ladybird Books Inc, Auburn, ME	800-523-9247
Ladybug: The Magazine for Children, Mt Morris, IL	(orders) 800-827-0227
Laffing Cow Press, Saratoga, NY	800-722-6932
Lakewood Publications, Minneapolis, MN	800-328-4329
Veronica Lane Books, Santa Monica, CA	800-651-1001
Langenscheidt Publishers Inc, Maspeth, NY	800-432-MAPS
LangMarc Publishing, San Antonio, TX	800-864-1648
Laredo Publishing Co Inc, Torrance, CA	800-547-5113
Larousse Kingfisher Chambers Inc, New York, NY	800-497-1657
Lawyers Cooperative Publishing, Rochester, NY	800-527-0430
Leading Edge Reports, Cleveland, OH	800-866-4648
Learning Links Inc, New Hyde Park, NY	800-724-2616
Learning Publications Inc, Holmes Beach, FL	(orders) 800-222-1525
Learning Resources Network (LERN), Manhattan, KS	(orders) 800-678-5376
The Learning Works Inc, Santa Barbara, CA	800-235-5767
Lectorum Publications Inc, New York, NY	800-345-5946
Legacy Publishing Group, Clinton, MA	800-322-3866
Legend Productions, Fort Worth, TX	800-286-3167
Lerner Publications Co, Minneapolis, MN	800-328-4929
Lexington Books, New York, NY	(cust serv) 800-257-5755
	(orders) 800-323-7445
Libraries Unlimited Inc, Englewood, CO	800-237-6124
Life Action Press, Los Angeles, CA	800-367-2246
Lifetime Books Inc, Hollywood, FL	800-771-3355
Liguori Publications, Liguori, MO	800-464-2555
Lincoln Institute of Land Policy, Cambridge, MA	800-LAND-USE
LinguiSystems Inc, East Moline, IL	800-PRO-IDEA
Linton Day Publishing Co, Stone Mountain, GA	800-927-0409
Lion Publishing, Elgin, IL	800-447-5466
J B Lippincott Co, Philadelphia, PA	(MD) 800-638-3030
Literary Works Publishers, Queens Village, NY	800-647-4232, 4286
Little, Brown and Co Inc, Boston, MA	800-343-9204
Littlefield, Adams Quality Paperbacks, Lanham, MD	800-462-6420
The Liturgical Press, Collegeville, MN	800-858-5450
Liturgy Training Publications, Chicago, IL	800-933-1800
Llewellyn Publications, St Paul, MN	800-843-6666
Lloyds of London Press Inc, New York, NY	800-955-6937

Publisher/Distributor	Toll-Free No.
Loizeaux Brothers Inc, Neptune, NJ	800-526-2796
Lone Eagle Publishing Co, Los Angeles, CA	800-345-6257
Lonely Planet Publications, Oakland, CA	(orders) 800-275-8555
Longmeadow Press, Stamford, CT	(orders) 800-937-5557
Longstreet Press, Marietta, GA	800-927-1488
Lothrop, Lee & Shepard Books, New York, NY	800-843-9389
Lotus Light Publications, Twin Lakes, WI	(orders) 800-824-6396
Loyola University Press, Chicago, IL	800-621-1008
Lucent Books Inc, San Diego, CA	800-231-5163
LuraMedia Inc, San Diego, CA	800-367-5872
M & H Publishing Co Inc, LaGrange, TX	800-521-9950
McClanahan Publishing House Inc, Kuttawa, KY	800-544-6959
McCormack's Guides, Martinez, CA	800-222-3602
McCutchan Publishing Corp, Berkeley, CA	800-227-1540
The McDonald & Woodward Publishing Co, Blacksburg, VA	800-233-8787
McGraw-Hill Healthcare Management Group, New York, NY	800-544-8168
Madison Books Inc, Lanham, MD	800-462-6420
Mage Publishers Inc, Washington, DC	800-962-0922
Magna Publications Inc, Madison, WI	800-433-0499
Maharishi International University Press, Fairfield, IA	800-831-6523
Mancorp Publishing Inc, Tampa, FL	800-853-3888
Many Cultures Publishing, San Francisco, CA	800-484-4173 ext 1073
MARC Publications, Monrovia, CA	(US) 800-777-7752
Mariposa Publishing Co, St Paul, MN	800-442-1419
Market Data Retrieval Inc, Shelton, CT	800-333-8802
Marketcom Inc, Fenton, MO	800-325-3884
Marlor Press Inc, St Paul, MN	800-669-4908
Marshall Cavendish Corp, North Bellmore, NY	800-821-9881
MarshMedia, Kansas City, MO	800-821-3303
Marsilio Publishers Corp, New York, NY	800-992-9685
Master Books, Colorado Springs, CO	800-999-3777
MasterMedia Ltd, New York, NY	800-334-8232
Masters Press Inc, Indianapolis, IN	800-722-2677
The Mathematical Association of America, Washington, DC	800-331-1622
Maverick Publications Inc, Bend, OR	800-800-4831
Mayfair Games Inc, Niles, IL	800-432-4376
Mayfield Publishing Co, Mountain View, CA	800-433-1279
Mayhaven Publishing, Mahomet, IL	800-230-4273
Meadowbrook Press Inc, Deephaven, MN	800-338-2232
R S Means Co Inc, Kingston, MA	800-448-8182
Mecklermedia, Westport, CT	800-632-5537
Med Index Publications, Salt Lake City, UT	800-999-4600
Medbooks, Houston, TX	800-443-7397
Media & Methods, Philadelphia, PA	800-523-4540
Media Publishing, Kansas City, MO	800-347-2665
Medical Physics Publishing Corp, Madison, WI	800-442-5778

Publisher/Distributor	Toll-Free No.
The Russell Meerdink Co Ltd, Neenah, WI	800-635-6499
Mel Bay Publications Inc, Pacific, MO	800-863-5229
Melius Publishing Inc, Pierre, SD	800-882-5171
Menasha Ridge Press Inc, Birmingham, AL	800-247-9437
Mercer University Press, Macon, GA	800-637-2378; 800-342-0841
Mercury House Inc, San Francisco, CA	800-998-9129
Meriwether Publishing Ltd/Contemporary Drama Service, Colorado Springs, CO	800-93PLAYS
Merryant Publishers Inc, Vashon, WA	800-228-8958
Mesorah Publications Ltd, Brooklyn, NY	800-637-6724
Metal Bulletin Inc, New York, NY	800-METAL-25
Metamorphous Press, Inc, Portland, OR	800-937-7771
Michelin Travel Publications, Greenville, SC	800-423-0485; 800-223-0987
The Michie Co, Charlottesville, VA	800-446-3410
Microsoft Press, Redmond, WA	800-MSPRESS
MidWest Plan Service, Ames, IA	800-562-3618
Milady Publishing Co, Albany, NY	800-836-5239
The Millbrook Press Inc, Brookfield, CT	800-462-4703
Miller Freeman Inc, San Francisco, CA	(orders) 800-848-5594
Milliken Publishing Co, St Louis, MO	800-325-4136
Mills & Sanderson, Publishers, Bedford, MA	(orders) 800-441-6224
The Minerals, Metals & Materials Society (TMS), Warrendale, PA	800-759-4867
Minnesota Historical Society Press, St Paul, MN	800-647-7827
MIS: Press, Inc, New York, NY	800-488-5233
The MIT Press, Cambridge, MA	(orders) 800-356-0343
MMB Music Inc, St Louis, MO	800-543-3771
Mockingbird Books, Marietta, GA	800-497-6663
Modern Learning Press/Programs for Education, Rosemont, NJ	800-627-5867
Momentum Books Ltd, Troy, MI	800-758-1870
Monday Morning Books Inc, Palo Alto, CA	800-777-4489
Money Market Directories Inc, Charlottesville, VA	800-446-2810
Moody Press, Chicago, IL	800-678-8812
Moon Publications Inc, Chico, CA	800-345-5473
Moonbeam Publications Inc, Traverse City, MI	800-445-2391
More Than a Card Inc, New Orleans, LA	800-635-9672
Morehouse Publishing Co, Harrisburg, PA	(cust serv) 800-877-0012
Morgan Kaufmann Publishers Inc, San Francisco, CA	800-745-7323
Morgan Quitno Corp, Lawrence, KS	800-457-0742
Morgan-Rand Inc, Huntingdon Valley, PA	800-677-3839
Morningside Bookshop, Dayton, OH	800-648-9710
Morrow Junior Books, New York, NY	800-843-9389
William Morrow & Co Inc, New York, NY	800-843-9389
Mosaic Press Miniature Books, Cincinnati, OH	800-932-4044
C V Mosby Co, St Louis, MO	800-325-4177

Publisher/Distributor	Toll-Free No.
Motorbooks International Publishers & Wholesalers Inc, Osceola, WI	800-458-0454
Mountain n' Air Books, Tujunga, CA	800-446-9696
Mountain Press Publishing Co, Missoula, MT	800-234-5308
Mountaineers Books, Seattle, WA	800-553-4453
John Muir Publications Inc, Santa Fe, NM	800-888-7504
Mulberry Books, New York, NY	800-843-9389
Multnomah Books, Sisters, OR	800-929-0910
Municipal Analysis Services Inc, Austin, TX	800-488-3932
Mike Murach & Associates Inc, Fresno, CA	800-221-5528
MUSA Video Publishing, Dallas, TX	800-933-6872
Music Sales Corp, New York, NY	800-431-7187
NADJA Publishing, Lake Forest, CA	800-795-9750
NAFSA: Association of International Educators, Washington, DC	800-836-4994
The Naiad Press Inc, Tallahassee, FL	(orders) 800-533-1973
NAPSAC Reproductions, Marble Hill, MO	800-758-8629
National Academy Press, Washington, DC	800-624-6242
National Association of Broadcasters, Washington, DC	800-368-5644
National Association of Secondary School Principals, Reston, VA	800-253-7746
National Association of Social Workers (NASW), Washington, DC	800-638-8799
National Council of Teachers of English (NCTE), Urbana, IL	800-369-6283
National Council on Radiation Protection & Measurements, Bethesda, MD	800-229-2652
National Geographic Society, Washington, DC	800-638-4077
National Institute for Trial Advocacy, Notre Dame, IN	800-225-6482
National Learning Corp, Syosset, NY	800-645-6337
National Museum of Women in the Arts, Washington, DC	800-222-7270
National Practice Institute, Minneapolis, MN	800-328-4444
National Press Books Inc, Bethesda, MD	800-275-8888
National Science Teachers Association (NSTA), Arlington, VA	(orders) 800-722-NSTA
National Textbook Co (NTC), Lincolnwood, IL	(orders) 800-323-4900
Naturegraph Publishers Inc, Happy Camp, CA	800-390-5353
Naval Institute Press, Annapolis, MD	800-233-8764
NavPress Publishing Group, Colorado Springs, CO	800-366-7788
Nelson Publications, Port Chester, NY	800-333-6357
Thomas Nelson Inc, Nashville, TN	800-251-4000
Net Research, Aurora, CO	800-455-5340
New Amsterdam Books, Franklin, NY	800-944-4040
New City Press, Hyde Park, NY	(orders) 800-462-5980
New Creation Publishing Group, Philipsburg, MT	800-875-HEAL
New Dimensions in Education, Waterbury, CT	800-227-9120
New Directions Publishing Corp, New York, NY	(PA) 800-233-4830
New Harbinger Publications Inc, Oakland, CA	(orders) 800-748-6273

Publisher/Distributor	Toll-Free No.
New Horizon Press, Far Hills, NJ	(orders) 800-533-7978
New Leaf Press Inc, Green Forest, AR	800-643-9535
New Life Foundation, Pine, AZ	800-293-3377
New Readers Press, Syracuse, NY	800-448-8878
New Society Publishers, Philadelphia, PA	800-333-9093
New Victoria Publishers, Norwich, VT	800-326-5297
New World Library, San Rafael, CA	(retail orders) 800-227-3900
New York Academy of Sciences, New York, NY	800-THE-NYAS
Newcastle Publishing Co Inc, North Hollywood, CA	800-932-4809
Nightshade Press, Troy, ME	(book orders) 800-497-9258
Nippan Publications, Carson, CA	800-562-1410
The Noble Press Inc, Chicago, IL	800-486-7737
Nolo Press, Berkeley, CA	800-992-6656
Norman Publishing, San Francisco, CA	800-544-9359
North River Press Inc, Great Barrington, MA	800-486-2665
North-South Books Inc, New York, NY	800-282-8257
Northland Publishing Co, Flagstaff, AZ	800-346-3257
Northmont Publishing Co, West Bloomfield, MI	800-472-3485
Northwest Publishing Inc, Salt Lake City, UT	800-398-2102
Northwind Press, Sandpoint, ID	800-235-7756
NorthWord Press Inc, Minocqua, WI	(orders) 800-336-6398
Jeffrey Norton Publishers Inc, Guilford, CT	800-243-1234
W W Norton & Co Inc, New York, NY	(orders, cust serv) 800-233-4830
Nucleus Publications, Willow Springs, MO	800-762-6595
Nutrinfo Corp, Watertown, MA	800-676-6686
Nystrom, Chicago, IL	800-621-8086
The Oasis Press, Grants Pass, OR	800-228-2275
Odonian Press, Berkeley, CA	800-732-5786
Official Airline Guides, Oak Brook, IL	800-323-3537
Ohara Publications Inc, Valencia, CA	800-423-2874
Ohio University Press, Athens, OH	800-621-2736
Oldbuck Press Inc, Conway, AR	800-884-8184
Oliver-Nelson Books, Nashville, TN	800-251-4000
Oliver Wight Ltd Publications Inc, Essex Junction, VT	800-343-0625
Omnigraphics Inc, Detroit, MI	800-234-1340
The One-Off CD Shop Washington Inc, White Plains, MD	800-678-8760
One On One, Computer Training, Addison, IL	800-242-8668
Online Press Inc, Bellevue, WA	800-854-3344
Open Court Publishing Co, Peru, IL	800-435-6850
Open Horizons Publishing Co, Fairfield, IA	800-796-6130
Optical Society of America, Washington, DC	800-582-0416
Orbis Books, Maryknoll, NY	(orders) 800-258-5838
Orchard Books, New York, NY	800-433-3411
O'Reilly & Associates Inc, Sebastopol, CA	800-998-9938
Organization for Economic Cooperation & Development, Washington, DC	800-456-6323

Publisher/Distributor	Toll-Free No.
Orion Research Corp, Scottsdale, AZ	800-844-0759
The Oryx Press, Phoenix, AZ	800-279-6799
Osborne/McGraw-Hill, Berkeley, CA	800-227-0900
Our Sunday Visitor Publishing, Huntington, IN	(orders) 800-348-2440
The Overmountain Press, Johnson City, TN	800-992-2691
Richard C Owen Publishers Inc, Katonah, NY	800-262-0787
Oxbridge Communications Inc, New York, NY	800-955-0231
Oxford University Press Inc, New York, NY	(cust serv) 800-451-7556
Oxmoor House Inc, Birmingham, AL	800-366-4712
Pacific Press Publishing Association, Boise, ID	800-447-7377
Paladin Press, Boulder, CO	800-835-2246 ext 21
Palindrome Press, Washington, DC	800-843-5990
Panel Publishers, New York, NY	800-638-8437
Panoptic Enterprises, Burke, VA	800-594-4766
Pantheon Books/Schocken Books, New York, NY	800-638-6460
Papier-Mache Press, Watsonville, CA	800-776-1956
PAR Publishers, Burr Ridge, IL	800-634-3961
Para Publishing Co, Santa Barbara, CA	800-PARAPUB
Paraclete Press, Orleans, MA	800-451-5006
Paragon House, New York, NY	800-937-5557
Parenting Press Inc, Seattle, WA	800-99-BOOKS
Parker Publications, Carlsbad, CA	800-452-9873
Passport Books, Lincolnwood, IL	(orders) 800-323-4900
Pathway Book Service, Gilsum, NH	800-345-6665
Patrick's Press Inc, Columbus, GA	800-654-1052
PBC International Inc, Glen Cove, NY	800-527-2826
Peachpit Press Inc, Berkeley, CA	800-283-9444
Peachtree Publishers Ltd, Atlanta, GA	800-241-0113
Pelican Publishing Co Inc, Gretna, LA	800-843-1724
The Pennsylvania State University Press, University Park, PA	800-326-9180
PennWell Books, Tulsa, OK	800-752-9764
Penton Overseas Inc, Carlsbad, CA	800-748-5804
Per Annum Inc, New York, NY	800-548-1108
The Perfection Learning Corp, Des Moines, IA	800-762-2999
Performance Dimensions Publishing, Powers Lake, WI	800-877-7413
Peter Pauper Press Inc, White Plains, NY	800-833-2311
Peterson's Guides Inc, Princeton, NJ	800-338-3282
Pfeifer-Hamilton Publishers, Duluth, MN	800-247-6789
Phi Delta Kappa Educational Foundation, Bloomington, IN	800-766-1156
Philosophy Documentation Center, Bowling Green, OH	800-444-2419
Phoenix Learning Resources, New York, NY	800-221-1274
Picket Fence Press, Dallas, TX	800-742-5381
Picton Press, Camden, ME	(credit card orders) 800-742-8667
Pictorial Histories Publishing Co Inc, Missoula, MT	800-638-6873
Pieces of Learning, Beavercreek, OH	800-729-5137
The Pierian Press, Ann Arbor, MI	800-678-2435

Publisher/Distributor	Toll-Free No.
The Pilgrim Press/United Church Press, Cleveland, OH	800-537-3394
The Pilgrim's Path, Ojai, CA	800-284-5864 ext H
PJS Publications Inc, Peoria, IL	800-521-2885
Planning/Communications, River Forest, IL	800-829-5220
Pleasant Co Publications Inc, Middleton, WI	800-233-0264
Plenum Publishing Corp, New York, NY	800-221-9369
PMA Publishing Corp, Dana Point, CA	800-654-4425
PMD Publishers Group Inc, Winter Park, FL	800-438-5911
Pomegranate Artbooks Inc, Rohnert Park, CA	800-227-1428
Popular Culture Ink, Ann Arbor, MI	800-678-8828
Clarkson Potter Publishers, New York, NY	800-526-4264
Praeger Publishers, Westport, CT	(orders) 800-225-5800
Prairie House Inc, Fargo, ND	800-866-BOOK
Prakken Publications Inc, Ann Arbor, MI	(orders) 800-530-9673
Precept Press, Chicago, IL	800-225-3775
Prep Publishing, Fayetteville, NC	800-533-2814
Presbyterian & Reformed Publishing Co, Phillipsburg, NJ	800-631-0094
Preservation Press, Washington, DC	800-766-6847
Presidio Press, Novato, CA	800-966-5179
Presscott Publishing Co, Maryville, MO	800-528-5197
Princeton Architectural Press, New York, NY	800-458-1131
Princeton Book Co Publishers, Pennington, NJ	800-220-7149
Princeton University Press, Princeton, NJ	800-777-4726
The Printers Shopper, Chula Vista, CA	800-854-2911
Pro Lingua Associates, Brattleboro, VT	800-366-4775
Probus Publishing Co, Chicago, IL	800-PROBUS-1
Productivity Press Inc, Portland, OR	800-394-6868
The Professional Education Group Inc, Minnetonka, MN	800-229-2531
Professional Publications Inc, Belmont, CA	800-426-1178
Professional Publishing, Burr Ridge, IL	800-634-3966
Professional Resource Exchange Inc, Sarasota, FL	800-443-3364
Prometheus Books, Buffalo, NY	800-421-0351
Prompt Publications, Indianapolis, IN	800-428-7267
ProStar Publications Ltd, Los Angeles, CA	800-292-6657
Pruett Publishing Co, Boulder, CO	800-247-8224
Psychological Assessment Resources Inc (PAR), Lutz, FL	800-331-8378
The Psychological Corp, San Antonio, TX	(cust serv) 800-228-0752
Public Utilities Reports Inc, Arlington, VA	800-368-5001
Purdue University Press, West Lafayette, IN	800-933-9637
Purple Mountain Press Ltd, Fleischmanns, NY	800-325-2665
The Putnam Berkley Group Inc, New York, NY	800-631-8571
QED Press, Fort Bragg, CA	800-773-7782
Quail Ridge Press, Brandon, MS	800-343-1583
Quality Education Data, Denver, CO	800-525-5811
Quality Medical Publishing Inc, St Louis, MO	800-423-6865
Quality Press, Milwaukee, WI	800-248-1946

Publisher/Distributor	Toll-Free No
Quality Resources, White Plains, NY	800-247-851ᶜ
Quintessence Publishing Co Inc, Carol Stream, IL	800-621-038ᴉ
Quixote Press, Fort Madison, IA	800-571-BOOK
Rainbow Books Inc, Highland City, FL	(book orders) 800-356-931ᶜ
Raintree/Steck-Vaughn Publishers, Austin, TX	800-531-501ᶜ
RAM Research Corp, Frederick, MD	800-874-899ᶜ
Rand McNally, Skokie, IL	800-333-013ᶜ
Random House Inc, New York, NY	800-726-060ᶜ
Ransom Hill Press, Ramona, CA	800-423-062ᶜ
Rapha Resources, Houston, TX	800-383-467ᶜ
Reader's Digest Association Inc, Pleasantville, NY	800-431-172ᶜ
Reader's Digest USA, Pleasantville, NY	800-431-172ᶜ
Reader's Digest USA Condensed Books, Pleasantville, NY	800-431-172ᶜ
Recovery Publications Inc, San Diego, CA	800-873-838ᴉ
Recruiting & Search Report, Panama City Beach, FL	800-634-454ᴉ
Red Crane Books, Santa Fe, NM	800-922-339ᶻ
Redleaf Press, St Paul, MN	800-423-830ᶜ
Thomas Reed Publications Inc, Boston, MA	800-995-499ᶜ
The Reference Press Inc, Austin, TX	(orders) 800-486-866ᶜ
Regal Books, Ventura, CA	800-235-341ᶜ
Regnery Publishing Inc, Washington, DC	800-462-642ᶜ
Regular Baptist Press, Schaumburg, IL	(orders) 800-727-444ᶜ
Rei America Inc, Miami, FL	800-726-533ᴉ
REPAIRMASTER, West Jordan, UT	800-347-5163
Research Periodicals & Books Publishing House, Houston, TX	800-521-0061
Research Publications International, Woodbridge, CT	800-444-079ᶜ
Resource Media, Huntingdon Valley, PA	800-677-383ᶜ
Resurrection Press Ltd, Williston Park, NY	800-892-665ᴉ
Retail Reporting Corp, New York, NY	800-251-454ᶜ
Fleming H Revell Co, Grand Rapids, MI	800-877-266ᶜ
Review & Herald Publishing Association, Hagerstown, MD	800-234-7630
Rip Off Press Inc, Auburn, CA	800-468-266ᶜ
The Riverside Publishing Co, Chicago, IL	(general) 800-656-842ᶜ
	(orders) 800-767-3378
Rizzoli International Publications Inc, New York, NY	(orders, cust serv) 800-221-794ᶜ
Roberts Rinehart Publishers, Niwot, CO	800-352-198ᶜ
Rockbridge Publishing Co, Berryville, VA	800-473-394ᶜ
Rockwell Publishing, Bellevue, WA	800-221-934ᴉ
Rodale Press Inc, Emmaus, PA	800-441-7761
Roper Press Inc, Dallas, TX	800-284-015ᶜ
The Rosen Publishing Group Inc, New York, NY	800-237-9932
Ross Books, Berkeley, CA	800-367-0930
Norman Ross Publishing Inc, New York, NY	800-648-8850
Roth Publishing Inc, Great Neck, NY	800-899-ROTH
Fred B Rothman & Co, Littleton, CO	800-457-1986

Publisher/Distributor	Toll-Free No.
Rowman & Littlefield Publishers Inc, Lanham, MD	800-462-6420
Rudi Publishing, Iowa City, IA	(orders) 800-999-6901
Rudra Press, Portland, OR	800-876-7798
Running Press Book Publishers, Philadelphia, PA	(orders) 800-345-5359
Russell Sage Foundation, New York, NY	800-666-2211
Rutgers University Press, New Brunswick, NJ	(orders) 800-446-9323
Rutledge Hill Press, Nashville, TN	800-234-4234
William H Sadlier Inc, New York, NY	800-221-5175
Sagamore Publishing Inc, Champaign, IL	(orders) 800-327-5557
St Anthony Messenger Press, Cincinnati, OH	800-488-0488
Saint Anthony Publishing Inc, Reston, VA	800-632-0123
St James Press, Detroit, MI	800-345-0392 ext 1326
St Martin's Press Inc, New York, NY	800-221-7945
St Martin's Press, Scholarly & Reference Div, New York, NY	800-817-2525
Saint Mary's Press, Winona, MN	800-533-8095
Saint Nectarios Press, Seattle, WA	800-643-4233
St Paul Books & Media, Boston, MA	800-876-4463
Salem Press Inc, Englewood Cliffs, NJ	800-221-1592
Sandlapper Publishing Inc, Orangeburg, SC	800-849-7263
Santillana Publishing Co Inc, Compton, CA	800-245-8584
Sasquatch Books, Seattle, WA	800-775-0817
W B Saunders Co, Philadelphia, PA	(cust serv) 800-545-2522
K G Saur, New Providence, NJ	(orders) 800-521-8110
Scarborough House, Lanham, MD	800-462-6420
Scarecrow Press Inc, Metuchen, NJ	800-537-7107
Scepter Publishers, Princeton, NJ	800-322-8773
Schaffer Frank Publications Inc, Torrance, CA	800-421-5565
Scholarly Publications, Houston, TX	800-275-7825
Scholarly Resources Inc, Wilmington, DE	800-772-8937
Scholars Press, Atlanta, GA	(cust serv) 800-437-6692
Scholastic Inc, New York, NY	800-392-2179
Scholastic Professional Books, New York, NY	800-325-6149
School Zone Publishing Co, Grand Haven, MI	800 253-0564
Arthur Schwartz & Co Inc, Woodstock, NY	800-669-9080
Science & Behavior Books, Palo Alto, CA	800-547-9982
Scientific American Medicine, New York, NY	800-545-0554
Scott & Daughters Publishing Inc, Los Angeles, CA	800-547-2688
Scott, Foresman & Co, Glenview, IL	(orders) 800-782-2665
Scott Publications, Livonia, MI	800-458-8237
Scott Publishing Co, Sidney, OH	800-572-6885
The Seedsowers, Beaumont, TX	800-228-2665
Self-Counsel Press Inc, Bellingham, WA	800-663-3007
Servant Publications, Ann Arbor, MI	(US orders) 800-458-8505
	(MI orders) 800-533-8505
Seven Locks Press Inc, Arlington, VA	800-354-5348
Dale Seymour Publications Inc, Palo Alto, CA	800-872-1100

Publisher/Distributor	Toll-Free No.
M E Sharpe Inc, Armonk, NY	800-541-6563
Harold Shaw Publishers, Wheaton, IL	800-SHAW-PUB
Sheed & Ward, Kansas City, MO	(cust serv) 800-333-7373
	800-444-8910
Sheep Meadow Press, Bronx, NY	800-972-4491
Signature Books Inc, Salt Lake City, UT	800-356-5687
Sigo Press, Boston, MA	800-338-0446
Simon & Schuster, New York, NY	(cust serv) 800-223-2348
	(orders) 800-223-2336
Singular Publishing Group Inc, San Diego, CA	800-521-8545
SIRS Inc, Boca Raton, FL	800-232-7477
Skidmore-Roth Publishing Inc, El Paso, TX	800-825-3150
Skill Check Inc, Winchester, MA	800-648-3166
Skillpath Publications Inc, Mission, KS	800-873-7545
Sky Publishing Corp, Cambridge, MA	800-253-0245
Slack Inc, Thorofare, NJ	800-257-8290
Smith & Kraus Inc Publishers, Lyme, NH	800-862-5423
M Lee Smith Publishers & Printers, North Nashville, TN	800-274-6774
Smithmark Publishers Inc, New York, NY	800-645-9990
Smithsonian Institution Press, Washington, DC	800-678-2675
Smyth & Helwys Publishing Inc, Macon, GA	(US) 800-747-3016
	(Canada) 800-568-1248
Snow Lion Publications Inc, Ithaca, NY	800-950-0313
Society for Industrial & Applied Mathematics, Philadelphia, PA	800-447-SIAM
Society of Manufacturing Engineers, Dearborn, MI	800-733-4SME
Sophia Institute Press, Manchester, NH	800-888-9344
Sopris West Inc, Longmont, CO	800-547-6747
Soundprints, Norwalk, CT	800-228-7839
Source Books, Trabuco Canyon, CA	800-695-4237
South Carolina Bar, Columbia, SC	(SC) 800-768-7787
Southern Institute Press, Indian Rocks Beach, FL	800-633-4891
Specialty Press Publishers & Wholesalers, North Branch, MN	800-895-4585
Sphinx Publishing, Clearwater, FL	800-226-5291
Spider, Mt Morris, IL	(orders) 800-827-0227
Spirit Dance Publishing, Sorrento, FL	800-223-5333
Spoken Arts Inc, St Petersburg, FL	800-726-4090
Springer-Verlag New York Inc, New York, NY	800-SPRINGER
Springhouse Corp, Springhouse, PA	800-346-7844
SRA Technology Training Co, Chicago, IL	(orders) 800-772-1277
ST Publications Book Division, Cincinnati, OH	800-925-1110
Stackpole Books, Mechanicsburg, PA	800-732-3669
Stalsby-Wilson Press, Houston, TX	800-642-3228
Standard Publishing Co, Cincinnati, OH	800-543-1301
Standard Publishing Corp, Boston, MA	800-682-5759
Starlite Inc, St Petersburg, FL	800-577-2929

Publisher/Distributor	Toll-Free No.
State University of New York Press, Albany, NY	800-666-2211
Statesman Examiner Inc, Colville, WA	800-488-5676
Steck-Vaughn Co, Austin, TX	800-531-5015
Stenhouse Publishers, York, ME	(orders) 800-874-8816
Sterling Publishing Co Inc, New York, NY	800-367-9692
Gareth Stevens Inc, Milwaukee, WI	800-341-3569
Stewart, Tabori & Chang, Publishers, New York, NY	800-722-7202
Stillpoint Publishing International Inc, Walpole, NH	800-847-4014
Stockton Press, New York, NY	800-221-2123
Stoeger Publishing Co, South Hackensack, NJ	800-631-0722
Stone Bridge Press, Berkeley, CA	800-947-7271
Storey Publishing/Garden Way Publishing, Pownal, VT	800-359-7436
Strang Communications Co/Creation House, Altamonte Springs, FL	800-451-4598
Studio Press, Soulsbyville, CA	800-445-7160
Success Advertising & Publishing, Palm Beach Gardens, FL	800-330-4643
Sulzburger & Graham Publishing Co Ltd, New York, NY	800-366-7086
Summers Press Inc, Bedford, TX	800-743-6491
The Summit Group, Fort Worth, TX	800-875-3346
Summit Publications, Indianapolis, IN	800-419-0200
Summit University Press, Livingston, MT	800-323-5228
SunCity Publishing, Tri-Cities, WA	800-831-5208
Sundance Publishers, Littleton, MA	800-343-8204
Sunrise River Press Inc, North Branch, MN	800-895-4585
Sunset Books, Menlo Park, CA	800-227-7346
	(CA) 800-321-0372
Sunstone Publications, Cooperstown, NY	800-327-0306
Surrey Books Inc, Chicago, IL	800-326-4430
Swedenborg Foundation Inc, West Chester, PA	(cust serv) 800-355-3222
SYBEX Inc, Alameda, CA	800-227-2346
Syracuse University Press, Syracuse, NY	800-365-8929
Tabor Publishing, Allen, TX	800-527-5030
Tambourine Books, New York, NY	800-843-9389
Tapestry Press Ltd, Acton, MA	800-535-2007
The Taunton Press Inc, Newtown, CT	800-283-7252
	(orders) 800-888-8286
Taylor & Francis Publishers Inc, Bristol, PA	800-821-8312
Taylor Publishing Co, Dallas, TX	(voice & fax) 800-677-2800
te Neues Publishing Co, New York, NY	800-352-0305
TEACH Services, Brushton, NY	800-367-1844
Teacher Ideas Press, Englewood, CO	800-237-6124
Teachers Friend Publications Inc, Riverside, CA	800-343-9680
Teachers Press Publications, Ventura, CA	800-423-8943
Technical Association of the Pulp & Paper Industry (TAPPI), Atlanta, GA	800-332-8686
Technical Insights Inc, Fort Lee, NJ	800-245-6217

Publisher/Distributor	Toll-Free No.
Technomic Publishing Co Inc, Lancaster, PA	800-233-9936
Techware Corp, Altamonte Springs, FL	800-34-REACH
Telecom Library Inc, New York, NY	800-542-7279
Temple University Press, Philadelphia, PA	800-447-1656
Templegate Publishers, Springfield, IL	800-367-4844
Ten Speed Press, Berkeley, CA	800-841-BOOK
Test Corp of America	800-347-BOOK
Tetra Press, Blacksburg, VA	800-526-0650
Texas A & M University Press, College Station, TX	(orders) 800-826-8911
Texas Instruments Inc Data Book Marketing, Dallas, TX	800-336-5236
Texas Tech University Press, Lubbock, TX	800-832-4042
Texas Western Press, El Paso, TX	800-488-3789
TFH Publications Inc, Neptune, NJ	800-631-2188
Thames and Hudson Inc, New York, NY	800-233-4830
That Patchwork Place Inc, Bothell, WA	800-426-3126
Theosophical Publishing House, Wheaton, IL	800-669-9425
Thieme Medical Publishers Inc, New York, NY	800-782-3488
Thinkers Press, Davenport, IA	800-397-7117
Thinking Publications, Eau Claire, WI	800-225-4769
Charles C Thomas, Publisher, Springfield, IL	800-258-8980
William A Thomas Braille Bookstore, Stuart, FL	800-336-3142
Thomasson-Grant Publishers, Charlottesville, VA	800-999-1780
Thomson Financial Publishing, Skokie, IL	800-444-0064
Tidewater Publishers, Centreville, MD	800-638-7641
Time Being Books-Poetry in Sight & Sound, St Louis, MO	800-331-6605
Time Life Inc, Alexandria, VA	800-621-7026
Times Books, New York, NY	800-733-3000
Todd Publications, West Nyack, NY	800-747-1056
TODTRI Productions Ltd, New York, NY	800-241-4477
Tor Books, New York, NY	(cust serv) 800-221-7945
Torah Aura Productions, Los Angeles, CA	800-238-6724
The Touchstones Project (CZM Press), Annapolis, MD	800-456-6542
Tower Publishing Co, Standish, ME	800-287-7323
Traders Press Inc, Greenville, SC	800-927-8222
Tradery House, Memphis, TN	800-727-1034
Trails Illustrated, Evergreen, CO	800-962-1643
Trakker Maps Inc, Miami, FL	800-432-1730
Transnational Juris Publications Inc, Irvington-on-Hudson, NY	(orders) 800-914-8186
Traveler's Tales Inc, Sebastopol, CA	800-998-9938
Treasure Chest Publications Inc, Tucson, AZ	800-969-9558
Tree by the River Publishing, Carson City, NV	(orders) 800-487-6610
Tree of Life Publications, Joshua Tree, CA	(orders) 800-247-6553
Treehaus Communications Inc, Loveland, OH	(orders) 800-638-4287
Trinity Press International, Valley Forge, PA	800-421-8874
TripBuilder Inc, New York, NY	800-525-9745

Publisher/Distributor	Toll-Free No.
Troll Associates, Mahwah, NJ	800-526-5289
TrueSpeech Productions, Middletown, CA	800-432-7729
Trumpet Club, New York, NY	800-223-6834
Tself/Editorial CLIE, Fort Lauderdale, FL	800-327-7933
TSR Inc, Lake Geneva, WI	800-DRAGONS
Charles E Tuttle Co Inc, Boston, MA	800-526-2778
21st Century Education Inc, Kingston, NY	800-866-5559
Twenty-Third Publications Inc, Mystic, CT	800-321-0411
Tyndale House Publishers Inc, Wheaton, IL	800-323-9400
Type & Temperament Inc, Gladwyne, PA	800-IHS-TYPE
ULI-The Urban Land Institute, Washington, DC	800-462-1254
UMI Publications Inc, Charlotte, NC	800-462-5831
Unarius Academy of Science Publications, El Cajon, CA	800-842-2725
Unique Publications Books & Videos, Burbank, CA	800-332-3330
The United Methodist Publishing House, Nashville, TN	800-251-3320
United Nations Publications, New York, NY	800-253-9646
United States Institute of Peace, Washington, DC	(cust serv) 800-537-9359
United States Pharmacopeial Convention Inc, Rockville, MD	800-227-8772
United States Tennis Association, White Plains, NY	800-223-0456
University Microfilms International (UMI), Ann Arbor, MI	800-521-0600
	(Canada) 800-343-5299
The University of Arizona Press, Tucson, AZ	(orders) 800-426-3797
The University of Arkansas Press, Fayetteville, AR	800-525-1823
University of California Press, Berkeley, CA	800-822-6657
University of Chicago Press, Chicago, IL	(orders) 800-621-2736
University of Denver Center for Teaching International Relations Publications, Denver, CO	800-967-2847
University of Hawaii Press, Honolulu, HI	800-956-2840
University of Illinois Press, Champaign, IL	(orders) 800-545-4703
University of Iowa Press, Iowa City, IA	(orders) 800-235-2665
University of Minnesota Press, Minneapolis, MN	800-388-3863
University of Missouri Press, Columbia, MO	800-828-1894
University of Nebraska at Omaha Center for Public Affairs Research, Omaha, NE	800-227-4533
University of Nebraska Press, Lincoln, NE	(orders) 800-755-1105
University of New Mexico Press, Albuquerque, NM	(orders) 800-249-7737
The University of North Carolina Press, Chapel Hill, NC	(orders) 800-848-6224
University of Notre Dame Press, Notre Dame, IN	(orders) 800-621-2736
University of Oklahoma Press, Norman, OK	(orders) 800-627-7377
University of Oregon ERIC Clearinghouse on Educational Management, Eugene, OR	800-438-8841
University of Pennsylvania Press, Philadelphia, PA	(orders, cust service) 800-445-9880
University of Pittsburgh Press, Pittsburgh, PA	800-666-2211

Publisher/Distributor	Toll-Free No
University of South Carolina Press, Columbia, SC	(editorial) 800-763-0089
	(orders) 800-768-2500
University of Tennessee Press, Knoxville, TN (warehouse, continental US except IL)	800-621-2736
University of the South Press, Sewanee, TN	800-367-1179
University of Utah Press, Salt Lake City, UT	800-444-8638 ext 6771
University of Washington Press, Seattle, WA	800-441-4115
University Press of America Inc, Lanham, MD	800-462-6420
University Press of Florida, Gainesville, FL	(orders) 800-226-3822
The University Press of Kentucky, Lexington, KY	800-666-2211
University Press of Mississippi, Jackson, MS	800-737-7788
University Press of New England, Hanover, NH	800-421-1561
University Publications of America, Bethesda, MD	800-692-6300
University Publishing Group, Frederick, MD	800-654-8188
Upstart Publishing Co Inc, Dover, NH	800-235-8866
Upward Way Publications Inc, Hermitage, TN	800-367-2665
US Catholic Conference, Washington, DC	800-235-8722
US Games Systems Inc, Stamford, CT	800-544-2637; 800-54GAMES
Van Patten Publishing, Portland, OR	800-626-4330
VanDam Inc, New York, NY	800-UNFOLDS
Vanderbilt University Press, Nashville, TN	(orders) 800-937-5557
VCH Publishers Inc, New York, NY	800-367-8249
Ventana Press, Chapel Hill, NC	(orders) 800-743-5369
VGM Career Horizons, Lincolnwood, IL	(orders) 800-323-4900
Victor Books, Wheaton, IL	800-323-9409
Visible Ink Press, Detroit, MI	800-776-6265
Vision Books International, Santa Rosa, CA	800-377-3431
Vista Publishing Inc, Long Branch, NJ	800-634-2498
Visual Education Association, Springfield, OH	(USA) 800-243-7070
Vitesse Press, Brattleboro, VT	800-848-3747
Volcano Press Inc, Volcano, CA	800-879-9636
Voyageur Press, Stillwater, MN	800-888-9653
Waite Group Press, Corte Madera, CA	800-368-9369
J Weston Walch Publisher, Portland, ME	800-341-6094
Walker & Co, New York, NY	800-AT-WALKER
Walker's Western Research Co, San Mateo, CA	800-258-5737
Wallace Homestead Book Co, Radnor, PA	800-695-1214
Warren, Gorham & Lamont, New York, NY	800-922-0066
Warren Publishing House Inc, Everett, WA	800-334-4769
Washington State University Press, Pullman, WA	800-354-7360
Waterfront Books, Burlington, VT	(orders) 800-639-6063
Watson-Guptill Publications, New York, NY	800-451-1741
Franklin Watts Inc, New York, NY	(cust serv) 800-621-1115
Weatherhill Inc, New York, NY	800-788-7323
Webster International Inc, Brentwood, TN	800-727-6833

Publisher/Distributor	Toll-Free No.
Samuel Weiser Inc, York Beach, ME	800-423-7087
Weka Publishing, Shelton, CT	800-222-9352
Wellspring, York, PA	800-533-3561
Wesleyan University Press, Middletown, CT	800-421-1561
West Publishing Co, St Paul, MN	(orders) 800-328-9352
Westchester Publishing, Los Altos, CA	800-950-4095
Westcliffe Publishers Inc, Englewood, CO	800-523-3692
Western Psychological Services, Los Angeles, CA	(US & Canada) 800-648-8857
Western Publishing Co Inc, Racine, WI	(ordering & shipping) 800-558-5972
The Westminster Press/John Knox Press, Louisville, KY	800-395-7234
Westport Publishers Inc, Kansas City, MO	800-347-BOOK
WH&O International, Wellesley, MA	800-553-6678
Whispering Coyote Press, Danvers, MA	800-929-6104
Whitaker House, Springdale, PA	800-444-4484
White Cliffs Media Inc, Tempe, AZ	(orders) 800-359-3210
Whitehorse Press, Boston, MA	800-531-1133
Albert Whitman & Co, Morton Grove, IL	800-255-7675
The Whitney Library of Design, New York, NY	800-526-3641
Whole Person Associates Inc, Duluth, MN	800-247-6789
Wide World of Maps Inc, Phoenix, AZ	800-279-7654
Wilderness Press, Berkeley, CA	800-443-7227
John Wiley & Sons Inc, New York, NY	(orders) 800-CALL WILEY
Wiley-QED Publishing, Wellesley, MA	800-225-5945
Williams & Wilkins, Baltimore, MD	800-638-0672
Williamson Publishing Co, Charlotte, VT	800-234-8791
H W Wilson Co, Bronx, NY	800-367-6770
The Wimmer Companies Inc, Memphis, TN	800-727-1034
Win Publications!, Tulsa, OK	800-749-4597
Windward Publishing Inc, Miami, FL	800-330-6232
The Wine Appreciation Guild Ltd, San Francisco, CA	800-242-9462
Winston-Derek Publishers Group Inc, Nashville, TN	800-826-1888
Wintergreen Orchard House Inc, New Orleans, LA	800-321-9479
Wisdom Publications, Boston, MA	800-272-4050
WJ Fantasy Inc, Bridgeport, CT	800-ABC-PLAY
Wolfe Publishing Co, Prescott, AZ	800-899-7810
Kaye Wood Publishing, West Branch, MI	800-248-KAYE
Woodbine House, Bethesda, MD	800-843-7323
Woodbridge Press Publishing Co, Santa Barbara, CA	800-237-6053
Woodland Books, Pleasant Grove, UT	800-777-2665
Word Inc, Dallas, TX	800-933-9673
Word Publishing, Dallas, TX	800-933-9673
Wordware Publishing Inc, Plano, TX	800-229-4949
Workman Publishing Co, New York, NY	800-722-7202
World Bible Publishers Inc, Iowa Falls, IA	800-247-5111

Publisher/Distributor	Toll-Free No.
World Book Direct Marketing, Evanston, IL	800-874-0520
World Book Educational Products, Elk Grove Village, IL	800-433-6580
World Book Inc, Chicago, IL	(cust serv) 800-621-8202
World Book Publishing, Chicago, IL	800-255-1750
World Citizens, Mill Valley, CA	(orders) 800-247-6553
World Eagle Inc, Littleton, MA	800-854-8273
World Information Technologies Inc, Northport, NY	800-WORLD-INFO
World Resources Institute, Washington, DC	800-822-0504
World Scientific Publishing Co Inc, River Edge, NJ	800-227-7562
Worldtariff, San Francisco, CA	800-556-9334
Worth Publishers Inc, New York, NY	(orders, inquiries) 800-321-9299
	(mktg) 800-223-1715
The Wright Group, Bothell, WA	(training dept) 800-523-2371
	800-345-6073
Write Source Educational Publishing House, Burlington, WI	800-445-8613
Writer's Digest Books, Cincinnati, OH	800-289-0963
WRS Publishing, Waco, TX	800-299-3366 ext 291
Wyrick & Co, Charleston, SC	800-227-5898
YMAA Publication Center, Jamaica Plain, MA	800-669-8892
Young Discovery Library, Ossining, NY	800-343-7854
Yucca Tree Press, Las Cruces, NM	800-383-6183
Zagat Survey, New York, NY	800-333-3421
Zaner-Bloser Inc, Columbus, OH	800-421-3018
Zebra Books, New York, NY	800-221-2647
Ziff-Davis Press, Emeryville, CA	800-688-0448
Zino Press Children's Books, Middleton, WI	800-356-2303
Zondervan Publishing House, Grand Rapids, MI	(cust serv) 800-727-1309

How to Obtain an ISBN

Emery Koltay

Director
United States ISBN Agency

The International Standard Book Numbering (ISBN) system was introduced into the United Kingdom by J. Whitaker & Sons Ltd., in 1967 and into the United States in 1968 by the R. R. Bowker Company. The Technical Committee on Documentation of the International Organization for Standardization (ISO TC 46) defines the scope of the standard as follows:

> . . . the purpose of this standard is to coordinate and standardize the use of identifying numbers so that each ISBN is unique to a title, edition of a book, or monographic publication published, or produced, by a specific publisher, or producer. Also, the standard specifies the construction of the ISBN and the location of the printing on the publication.

Books and other monographic publications may include printed books and pamphlets (in various bindings), mixed media publications, other similar media including educational films/videos and transparencies, books on cassettes, microcomputer software, electronic publications, microform publications, braille publications and maps. Serial publications and music sound recordings are specifically excluded, as they are covered by other identification systems. [ISO Standard 2108]

The ISBN is used by publishers, distributors, wholesalers, bookstores, and libraries, among others, in 90 countries to expedite such operations as order fulfillment, electronic point-of-sale checkout, inventory control, returns processing, circulation/location control, file maintenance and update, library union lists, and royalty payments.

Construction of an ISBN

An ISBN consists of 10 digits separated into the following parts:

1. Group identifier: national, geographic, language, or other convenient group
2. Publisher or producer identifier
3. Title identifier
4. Check digit

When an ISBN is written or printed, it should be preceded by the letters *ISBN*, and each part should be separated by a space or hyphen. In the United States, the hyphen is used for separation, as in the following example: ISBN 1-879500-01-9. In this example, 1 is the group identifier, 879500 is the publisher identifier, 01 is the title identifier, and 9 is the check digit. The group of English-speaking countries, which includes the United States, Australia, Canada, New Zealand, and the United Kingdom, uses the group identifiers 0 and 1.

The ISBN Organization

The administration of the ISBN system is carried out at three levels—through the International ISBN Agency in Berlin, Germany; the national agencies; and the publishing houses themselves. Responsible for assigning country prefixes and for coordinating the worldwide implementation of the system, the International ISBN Agency in Berlin has an advisory panel that represents the International Organization for Standardization (ISO), publishers, and libraries. The International ISBN Agency publishes the *ISBN System User's Manual*—the basic guide for all national agencies—and the *Publishers International ISBN Directory,* which is distributed in the United States by R. R. Bowker. As the publisher of *Books in Print,* with its extensive and varied database of publishers' addresses, R. R. Bowker was the obvious place to initiate the ISBN system and to provide the service to the U.S. publishing industry. To date, the U.S. ISBN Agency has entered more than 82,000 publishers into the system.

ISBN Assignment Procedure

Assignment of ISBNs is a shared endeavor between the U.S. ISBN Agency and the publisher. The publisher is provided with an application form, an Advance Book Information (ABI) form, and an instruction sheet. After an application is received and verified by the agency, an ISBN publisher prefix is assigned, along with a computer-generated block of ISBNs. The publisher then has the responsibility to assign an ISBN to each title, to keep an accurate record of the numbers assigned by entering each title in the ISBN Log Book, and to report each title to the *Books in Print* database. One of the responsibilities of the ISBN Agency is to validate assigned ISBNs and to retain a record of all ISBNs in circulation.

ISBN implementation is very much market-driven. Wholesalers and distributors, such as Baker & Taylor, Brodart, and Ingram, as well as such large retail chains as Waldenbooks and B. Dalton recognize and enforce the ISBN system by requiring all new publishers to register with the ISBN Agency before accepting their books for sale. Also, the ISBN is a mandatory bibliographic element in the International Standard Bibliographical Description (ISBD). The Library of Congress Cataloging in Publication (CIP) Division directs publishers to the agency to obtain their ISBN prefixes.

Location and Display of the ISBN

On books, pamphlets, and other printed material, the ISBN shall be on the verso of the title leaf or, if this is not possible, at the foot of the title leaf itself. It should also appear at the foot of the outside back cover if practicable and at the foot of the back of the jacket if the book has one (the lower right-hand corner is recommended). If neither of these alternatives is possible, then the number shall be printed in some other prominent position on the outside. The ISBN shall also appear on any accompanying promotional materials following the provisions for location according to the format of the material.

On other monographic publications, the ISBN shall appear on the title or credit frames and any labels permanently affixed to the publication. If the publication is issued in a container that is an integral part of the publication, the ISBN shall be displayed on the label. If it is not possible to place the ISBN on the item or its label, then the number should be displayed on the bottom or the back of the container, box, sleeve, or frame. It should also appear on any accompanying material, including each component of a multitype publication.

Printing of ISBN in Machine-Readable Coding

In the last few years, much work has been done on machine-readable representations of the ISBN, and now all books should carry ISBNs in bar code. The rapid worldwide extension of bar code scanning has brought into prominence the 1980 agreement between the International Article Numbering, formerly the European Article Numbering (EAN), Association and the International ISBN Agency that translates the ISBN into an ISBN Bookland EAN bar code.

All ISBN Bookland EAN bar codes start with a national identifier (00–09 representing the United States), *except* those on books and periodicals. The greement replaces the usual national identifier with a special "ISBN Bookland" identifier represented by the digits 978 for books (see Figure 1) and 977 for periodicals. The 978 ISBN Bookland/EAN prefix is followed by the first nine digits of the ISBN. The check digit of the ISBN is dropped and replaced by a check digit calculated according to the EAN rules.

Figure 1 / Printing the ISBN in Bookland/EAN Symbology

The following is an example of the conversion of the ISBN to ISBN Bookland/EAN:

ISBN	1-879500-01-9
ISBN without check digit	1-879500-01
Adding EAN flag	978187950001
EAN with EAN check digit	9781879500013

Five-Digit Add-On Code

In the United States, a five-digit add-on code is used for additional information. In the publishing industry, this code can be used for price information or some other specific coding. The lead digit of the five-digit add-on has been designated a currency identifier, when the add-on is used for price. Number 5 is the code for the U.S. dollar; 6 denotes the Canadian dollar; 1 the British pound; 3 the Australian dollar; and 4 the New Zealand dollar. Publishers that do not want to indicate price in the add-on should print the code 90000 (see Figure 2).

Figure 2 / Printing the ISBN Bookland/EAN Number in Bar Code with the Five-Digit Add-On Code

978 = ISBN Bookland/EAN prefix
5 + Code for U.S. $
0995 = $9.95

90000 means no information
in the add-on code

Reporting the Title and the ISBN

After the publisher reports a title to the ISBN Agency, the number is validated and the title is listed in the many R. R. Bowker hard-copy and electronic publica tions, including *Books in Print, Forthcoming Books, Paperbound Books in Print Books in Print Supplement, Books Out of Print, Books in Print Online, Books in Print Plus-CD ROM, Children's Books in Print, Subject Guide to Children's Books in Print, On Cassette: A Comprehensive Bibliography of Spoken Word Audiocassettes, Variety's Complete Home Video Directory, Software En cyclopedia, Software for Schools,* and other specialized publications.

For an ISBN application form and additional information, write to United States ISBN Agency, R. R. Bowker Company, 121 Chanlon Rd., New Pro vidence, NJ 07974, or call 908-665-6770.

How to Obtain an ISSN

National Serials Data Program
Library of Congress

Two decades ago, the rapid increase in the production and dissemination of infor mation and an intensified desire to exchange information about serials in comput erized form among different systems and organizations made it increasingly clea: that a means to identify serial publications at an international level was needed The International Standard Serial Number (ISSN) was developed and has become the internationally accepted code for identifying serial publications. The number itself has no significance other than as a brief, unique, and unambiguous identifi er. It is an international standard, ISO 3297, as well as a U.S. standard ANSI/NISO Z39.9. The ISSN consists of eight digits in arabic numerals 0 to 9 except for the last, or check, digit, which can be an X. The numbers appear a: two groups of four digits separated by a hyphen and preceded by the letters ISSN—for example, ISSN 1234-5679.

The ISSN is not self-assigned by publishers. Administration of the ISSN i coordinated through the ISSN Network, an intergovernmental organization with in the UNESCO/UNISIST program. The network consists of national and region al centers, coordinated by the ISSN International Centre. Centers have the responsibility to register serials published in their respective countries.

Because serials are generally known and cited by title, assignment of the ISSN is inseparably linked to the key title, a standardized form of the title derived from information in the serial issue. Only one ISSN can be assigned to a title; if the title changes, a new ISSN must be assigned. Centers responsible for assigning ISSNs also construct the key title and create an associated bibliograph ic record.

The ISSN International Centre handles ISSN assignments for internationa organizations and for countries that do not have a national center. It also main tains and distributes the collective ISSN database that contains bibliographic records corresponding to each ISSN assignment as reported by the rest of the network. The database contains more than 600,000 ISSNs.

In the United States, the National Serials Data Program at the Library of Congress is responsible for assigning and maintaining the ISSNs for all U.S. serial titles. Publishers wishing to have an ISSN assigned can either request an application form from or send a current issue of the publication to the program and ask for an assignment. Assignment of the ISSN is free, and there is no charge for its use.

The ISSN is used all over the world by serial publishers to distinguish similar titles from each other. It is used by subscription services and libraries to manage files for orders, claims, and back issues. It is used in automated check-in systems by libraries that wish to process receipts more quickly. Copyright centers use the ISSN as a means to collect and disseminate royalties. It is also used as an identification code by postal services and legal deposit services. The ISSN is included as a verification element in interlibrary lending activities and for union catalogs as a collocating device. In recent years, the ISSN has been incorporated into bar codes for optical recognition of serial publications and into the standards for the identification of issues and articles in serial publications.

For further information about the ISSN or the ISSN network, U.S. libraries and publishers should contact the National Serials Data Program, Library of Congress, Washington, DC 20540-4160 (202-707-6452; FAX 202-707-6333; Internet: issn@loc.gov). Non-U.S. parties should contact the ISSN International Centre, 20 rue Bachaumont, 75002 Paris, France (telephone: (33 1) 44-88-22-20; FAX (33 1) 40-26-32-43; Internet: issnic@well.com).

ISSN application forms and instructions for obtaining an ISSN are also available via the Library of Congress Internet gopher site, LC MARVEL. Point your gopher client to marvel.loc.gov (use port 70), or telnet to marvel.loc.gov and log in as marvel. The application form is also available via the Library of Congress World-Wide Web Site, URL http://lcweb.loc.gov/homepage/lchp.html.

Distinguished Books

Best Books of 1994

This is the 48th year in which the Notable Books Council of the Reference and Adult Services Division of the American Library Association has issued its list of "Notable Books" for adults.

Fiction

Alvarez, Julia. *In the Time of the Butterflies*. $21.95. Algonquin. ISBN 1-56512-038-8.

Bainbridge, Beryl. *The Birthday Boys*. $18.95. Carroll & Graf. ISBN 0-7867-0071-8.

Betts, Doris. *Souls Raised from the Dead*. $23. Knopf. ISBN 0-679-42621-3.

Drury, Tom. *The End of Vandalism*. $21.95. Houghton. ISBN 0-395-62151-8.

Ignatieff, Michael. *Scar Tissue*. $21. Farrar. ISBN 0-374-25428-1.

Maitland, Sara. *Ancestral Truths*. $22.50. Holt. ISBN 0-8050-2536-7.

Munro, Alice. *Open Secrets*. $23. Knopf. ISBN 0-679-43575-1.

Norman, Howard. *The Bird Artist*. $20. Farrar. ISBN 0-374-11330-0.

O'Brien, Tim. *In the Lake of the Woods*. $21.95. Houghton. ISBN 0-395-48889-3.

Paley, Grace. *The Collected Stories*. $27.50. Farrar. ISBN 0-374-12636-4.

Power, Susan. *The Grass Dancer*. $22.95. Putnam. ISBN 0-399-13911-7.

Schulman, Audrey. *The Cage*. $17.95. Algonquin. ISBN 1-56512-035-3.

Poetry

Bierds, Linda. *The Ghost Trio*. $19.95. Holt. ISBN 0-8050-3485-4.

Clampitt, Amy. *A Silence Opens*. $20. Knopf. ISBN 0-679-42997-2.

Nonfiction

Bealbs, Melba. *Warriors Don't Cry*. $22. Pocket. ISBN 0-671-86638-9.

Chaikin, Andrew. *A Man on the Moon*. $24.95. Viking. ISBN 0-670-81446-6.

Cohen, Leah Hager. *Train Go Sorry*. $22.95. Houghton. ISBN 0-395-63625-6.

Gates, Henry L., Jr. *Colored People*. $22. Knopf. ISBN 0-679-42179-3.

Gilmore, Mikal. *Shot in the Heart*. $25. Doubleday. ISBN 0-385-42293-8.

Goodwin, Doris. *No Ordinary Time*. $30. Simon & Schuster. ISBN 0-671-64240-5.

Martin, Russell. *Out of Silence*. $22.50. Holt. ISBN 0-8050-1998-7.

Nuland, Sherwin. *How We Die*. $24. Knopf. ISBN 0-679-41461-4.

Price, Reynolds. *A Whole New Life*. $20. Atheneum. ISBN 0-689-12197-0.

Weiner, Jonathan. *The Beak of the Finch*. $25. Knopf. ISBN 0-679-40003-6.

Winerip, Michael. *9 Highland Rd*. $25. Pantheon. ISBN 0-679-40724-3.

Wolff, Tobias. *In Pharaoh's Army*. $23. Knopf. ISBN 0-679-40217-9.

Best Young Adult Books of 1994

In January each year a committee of the Young Adult Library Services Association of the American Library Association (ALA) compiles a list of best books published for young adults in the last 16 months, selected for their proven or potential appeal to the personal reading taste of the young adult. *School Library Journal (SLJ)* also provides a list of best books for young adults. Books on the 1994 list, which was published in the December 1994 issue of the journal, all meet one or a combination of criteria including topical appeal to young adults and outstanding literary quality. The following list combines the titles selected for both lists. The notation "ALA" or "*SLJ*" following the ISBN indicates the source of each selection.

Alvarez, Julia. *In the Time of the Butterflies.* $21.95. Algonquin. ISBN 1-56512-038-8. ALA

Bachrach, Susan D. *Tell Them We Remember: The Story of the Holocaust.* $19.95. Little, Brown. ISBN 0-316-69264-6. ALA

Bauer, Marion Dane, ed. *Am I Blue? Coming Out from the Silence.* $15. HarperCollins. ISBN 0-06-024253-1. ALA

Beake, Lesley. *The Song of Be.* $14.95. Henry Holt. ISBN 0-8050-2905-2. ALA

Bennett, James. *Dakota Dream.* $14.95. Scholastic. ISBN 0-590-46680-1. ALA

Bode, Janet, and Stan Mack. *Heartbreak and Roses: Real-Life Stories of Troubled Love.* $15.95. Delacorte. ISBN 0-385-32068-X. ALA

Bonner, Cindy. *Looking After Lily.* $18.95. Algonquin. ISBN 1-56512-045-0. ALA

Bosse, Malcolm. *The Examination.* $17. Farrar. ISBN 0-374-32234-1. ALA

Brooks, Martha. *Traveling on into the Light: And Other Stories.* $14.95. Orchard. ISBN 0-531-06863-3. ALA, *SLJ*

Brown, Mary. *Pigs Don't Fly.* $5.99. Baen. ISBN 0-671-87601-5. ALA

Bull, Emma. *Finder: A Novel of the Borderlands.* $21.95. Tor. ISBN 0-312-85418-8. ALA

Butler, Octavia E. *Parable of the Sower.* $19.95. Four Walls Eight Windows. ISBN 0-941423-99-9. ALA

Carlson, Lori M., ed. *Cool Salsa.* $14.95. Henry Holt. ISBN 0-8050-3135-9. ALA, *SLJ*

Casey, Maude. *Over the Water.* $14.95. Henry Holt. ISBN 0-8050-3276-2. *SLJ*

Cooney, Caroline B. *Driver's Ed.* $15.95. Delacorte. ISBN 0-385-32087-6. ALA

Coville, Bruce. *Oddly Enough.* $15.95. Harcourt. ISBN 0-15-200093-3. ALA

Creech, Sharon. *Walk Two Moons.* $16. HarperCollins. ISBN 0-06-023334-6. ALA, *SLJ*

Cushman, Karen. *Catherine, Called Birdy.* $14.95. Clarion. ISBN 0-395-68186-3. ALA, *SLJ*

Derby, Pat. *Grams, Her Boyfriend, My Family, and Me.* $16. Farrar. ISBN 0-374-38131-3. *SLJ*

Farmer, Nancy. *The Ear, the Eye, and the Arm.* $16.95. Orchard. ISBN 0-531-06829-3. ALA

Fine, Anne. *Flour Babies.* $14.95. Little, Brown. ISBN 0-316-28319-3. ALA, *SLJ*

Fletcher, Ralph. *I Am Wings: Poems about Love.* $12.95. Bradbury. ISBN 0-02-735395-8. *SLJ*

Fletcher, Susan. *Flight of the Dragon Kyn.* $15.95. Atheneum. ISBN 0-689-31880-4. ALA

Freedman, Russell. *Kids at Work: Lewis Hine and the Crusade Against Child Labor.* $16.95. Clarion. ISBN 0-395-58703-4. ALA, *SLJ*

French, Albert. *Billy.* $20. Viking. ISBN 0-670-85013-6. ALA

Hambly, Barbara. *Stranger at the Wedding.* $5.99. Del Rey. ISBN 0-345-38097-5. ALA

Harris, Robie H. *It's Perfectly Normal: A Book about Changing Bodies, Growing Up, Sex and Sexual Health.* $19.95. Illus. by Michael Emberley. Candlewick. ISBN 1-56402-199-8. *SLJ*

Hayes, Daniel. *No Effect.* $15.95. Godine. ISBN 0-87923-989-1. ALA

Hesse, Karen. *Phoenix Rising.* $15.95. Holt. ISBN 0-8050-3108-1. ALA, *SLJ*

Hite, Sid. *It's Nothing to a Mountain.* $15.95. Henry Holt. ISBN 0-8050-2769-6. ALA

Johnston, Julie. *Adam and Eve and Pinch-Me.* $14.95. Little, Brown. ISBN 0-316-46990-4. ALA, *SLJ*

Jones, Maurice K. *Say It Loud! The Story of Rap Music.* $19.90 Millbrook. ISBN 1-56294-386-3. ALA

Jordan, Sherryl. *Wolf-Woman.* $13.95. Houghton. ISBN 0-395-70932-6. ALA

Kerr, M. E. *Deliver Us from Evie.* $15. HarperCollins. ISBN 0-06-024475-5. ALA, *SLJ*

Kindl, Patrice. *Owl in Love.* $13.95. Houghton. ISBN 0-395-66162-5. ALA

King, Laurie R. *The Beekeeper's Apprentice.* $21.95. St. Martin's. ISBN 0-312-10423-5. ALA

Klass, David. *California Blue.* $13.95. Scholastic. ISBN 0-590-46688-7. *SLJ*

Koebner, Linda. *Zoo Book: The Evolution of Wildlife Conservation Centers.* $29.95. Forge. ISBN 0-312-85322-X. ALA

Koertge, Ron. *Tiger, Tiger Burning Bright.* $14.95. Orchard. ISBN 0-531-06840-4. ALA

Krisher, Trudy. *Spite Fences.* $14.95. Delacorte. ISBN 0-385-32088-4. ALA

Kuklin, Susan. *After a Suicide: Young People Speak Up.* $15.95. Putnam. ISBN 0-399-22605-2. ALA

Lasky, Kathryn. *Beyond the Burning Time.* $13.95. Scholastic. ISBN 0-590-47331-X. ALA

Lawlor, Laurie. *Shadow Catcher: The Life and Work of Edward S. Curtis.* $16.95. Walker. ISBN 0-8027-8288-4. ALA

Levitin, Sonia. *Escape from Egypt.* $16.95. Little, Brown. ISBN 0-316-52273-2. ALA

Lynch, Chris. *Gypsy Davey.* $14. HarperCollins. ISBN 0-06-023586-1. ALA

———. *Iceman.* $15. HarperCollins. ISBN 0-06-023340-0. ALA

McCall, Nathan. *Makes Me Wanna Holler.* $23. Random. ISBN 0-679-41268-9. ALA

Marrin, Albert. *Unconditional Surrender: U. S. Grant and the Civil War.* $19.95. Atheneum. ISBN 0-689-31837-5. ALA, *SLJ*

Marsden, John. *Letters from the Inside.* $13.95. Houghton. ISBN 0-395-68985-6. ALA, *SLJ*

Myers, Walter Dean. *The Glory Field.* $14.95. Scholastic. ISBN 0-590-45897-3. ALA

Naythons, Matthew. *Sarajevo: A Portrait of the Siege.* $29.95. Warner. ISBN 0-446-51824-7. ALA

Nelson, Theresa. *Earthshine.* $15.95. Orchard. ISBN 0-531-06867-6. ALA, *SLJ*

Nichols, Michael. *The Great Apes: Between Two Worlds.* $34.95. ISBN 0-87044-947-8. ALA

O'Donohoe, Nick. *The Magic and the Healing.* $5.99. Ace. ISBN 0-441-00053-3. ALA

Panzer, Nora, ed. *Celebrate America: In Poetry and Art.* $18.95. Hyperion. ISBN 1-56282-665-4. ALA, *SLJ*

Paulsen, Gary. *Winterdance: The Fine Madness of Running the Iditarod.* $21.95. Harcourt. ISBN 0-15-126227-6. ALA

Porte, Barbara Ann. *Something Terrible Happened.* $16.95. Orchard. ISBN 0-531-06869-2. ALA

Power, Susan. *The Grass Dancer.* $22.95. Putnam. ISBN 0-399-13911-7. ALA

Qualey, Marsha. *Come in from the Cold.* $15.95. Houghton. ISBN 0-395-68986-4. ALA

Rapp, Adam. *Missing the Piano.* $14.99. Viking. ISBN 0-670-85340-2. ALA

Reaver, Chap. *Bill.* $14.95. Delacorte. ISBN 0-385-31175-3. *SLJ*

Reuter, Bjarne. *The Boys from St. Petri.* $14.99. Dutton. ISBN 0-525-45121-8. ALA

Reynolds, Marilyn. *Too Soon for Jeff.* $15.95. Morning Glory. ISBN 0-930934-90-3. ALA

Rivers, Glenn, and Bruce Brooks. *Those Who Love the Game: Glenn "Doc" Rivers on Life in the NBA and Elsewhere.* $15.95. Henry Holt. ISBN 0-8050-2822-6. ALA

Rodowsky, Colby. *Hannah in Between.* $15. Farrar. ISBN 0-374-32837-4. ALA

Ross, Stewart. *Shakespeare and Macbeth: The Story Behind the Play.* $16.99. Viking. ISBN 0-670-85629-0. ALA

Roybal, Laura. *Billy.* $14.95. Houghton. ISBN 0-395-67649-5. ALA

Rylant, Cynthia, and Walker Evans. *Something Permanent.* $16.95. Harcourt. ISBN 0-15-277090-9. ALA

Salisbury, Graham. *Under the Blood-Red Sun.* $15.95. Delacorte. ISBN 0-385-32099-X. ALA

Schulman, Audrey. *The Cage.* $17.95 Algonquin. ISBN 1-56512-035-3. ALA

Sebestyen, Ouida. *Out of Nowhere.* $15.95. Orchard. ISBN 0-531-06839-0. *SLJ*

Shoup, Barbara. *Wish You Were Here.* $16.95. Hyperion. ISBN 0-7868-0028-3. ALA

Sinclair, April. *Coffee Will Make You Black.* $19.95. Hyperion. ISBN 1-56282-796-0. ALA

Springer, Nancy. *Toughing It.* $10.95. Harcourt. ISBN 0-15-200008-9. ALA

Stanley, Jerry. *I Am an American: A True Story of Japanese Internment.* $15. Crown. ISBN 0-517-59786-1. *SLJ*

Stolz, Mary. *Cezanne Pinto.* $15. Knopf. ISBN 0-679-84917-3. ALA

Sutton, Roger. *Hearing Us Out: Voices from the Gay and Lesbian Community.* $16.95. Little, Brown. ISBN 0-316-82326-0. ALA

Sweeney, Joyce. *Shadow.* $15.95. Delacorte. ISBN 0-385-32051-5. ALA

Temple, Frances. *The Ramsay Scallop.* $15.95. Orchard. ISBN 0-531-06836-6. ALA

Voigt, Cynthia. *When She Hollers.* $13.95. Scholastic. ISBN 0-590-46714-X. ALA, *SLJ*

Watkins, Yoko Kawashima. *My Brother, My Sister, and I.* $16.95. Bradbury. ISBN 0-02-792526-9. ALA

Wilson, Elizabeth B. *Bibles and Bestiaries: A Guide to Illuminated Manuscripts.* $25. Farrar. ISBN 0-374-30685-0. *SLJ*

Wilson, Robert Charles. *Mysterium.* $11.95. Bantam. ISBN 0-553-37365-X. ALA

Wolf, Sylvia. *Focus: Five Women Photographers.* $18.95. Albert Whitman. ISBN 0-8075-2531-6. ALA

Wood, June Rae. *A Share of Freedom.* $15.95. Putnam. ISBN 0-399-22767-9. *SLJ*

Woodson, Jacqueline. *I Hadn't Meant to Tell You This.* $14.95. Delacorte. ISBN 0-385-32031-0. ALA

Best Children's Books of 1994

A list of notable children's books is selected each year by the Notable Children's Books Committee of the Association for Library Service to Children of the American Library Association (ALA). The committee is aided by suggestions from school and public children's librarians throughout the United States. The book review editors of *School Library Journal (SLJ)* also compile a list each year, with full notations, of best books for children. The following list is a combination of ALA's 1995 choices and *SLJ*'s "Best Books of 1994," published in the December 1994 issue of *SLJ*. The source of each selection is indicated by the notation "ALA" or "*SLJ*" following each entry. [See "Literary Prizes, 1994" later in Part 5 for Newbery, Caldecott, and other award winners—*Ed.*]

Aardema, Verna. *Misoso.* $18. Knopf. ISBN 0-679-83430-3. ALA

Arnosky, Jim. *All About Alligators.* Illus. by the author. $14.95. Scholastic. ISBN 0-590-46788-3. *SLJ*

Avi. *The Barn.* $13.95. Orchard. ISBN 0-531-06861-7. ALA

Baker, Barbara. *One Saturday Morning.* Illus. by Kate Duke. $12.99. Dutton. ISBN 0-525-45262-1. *SLJ*

Bash, Barbara. *Ancient Ones: The World of the Old-Growth Douglas Fir.* Illus. by the author. $16.95. Sierra Club. ISBN 0-87156-561-7. *SLJ*

Bauer, Marion Dane. *A Question of Trust.* $13.95. Scholastic. ISBN 0-590-47915-6. *SLJ*

Binch, Caroline. *Gregory Cool.* Illus. by the author. $14.99. Dial. ISBN 0-8037-1577-3. *SLJ*

Bonners, Susan. *Hunter in the Snow: The Lynx.* Illus. by the author. $14.95. Little, Brown. ISBN 0-316-10201-6. *SLJ*

Brust, Beth Wagner. *The Amazing Paper Cuttings of Hans Christian Andersen.* $15.95. Ticknor & Fields. ISBN 0-395-66787-9. ALA

Bunting, Eve. *Night of the Gargoyles.* Illus. by David Wiesner. $14.95. Clarion. ISBN 0-395-66553-1. *SLJ*

———. *Smoky Night.* Illus. by David Diaz. $14.95. Harcourt. ISBN 0-15-269954-6. ALA, *SLJ*

Byars, Betsy. *The Golly Sisters Ride Again.* $14. HarperCollins. ISBN 0-06-021563-1. ALA

Christiansen, C. B. *I See the Moon.* $14.95. Atheneum. ISBN 0-689-31928-2. ALA

Cooper, Floyd. *Coming Home.* $15.95. Putnam. ISBN 0-399-22682-6. ALA

Dalakoy, Vedat. *Sister Shako and Kolo the Goat.* $13. Lothrop. ISBN 0-688-13271-5. ALA

Dewey, Jennifer Owings. *Wildlife Rescue: The Work of Dr. Kathleen Ramsay.* Photos by Don MacCarter. $16.95. Caroline House/Boyds Mills. ISBN 1-56397-045-7. *SLJ*

Dorris, Michael. *Guests.* $13.95. Hyperion. ISBN 0-7868-0047-X. ALA

Facklam, Margery. *The Big Bug Book.* Illus. by Paul Facklam. $15.95. Little, Brown. ISBN 0-316-27389-9. ALA, *SLJ*

———. *What Does the Crow Know? The Mysteries of Animal Intelligence.* Illus. by Pamela Johnson. $15.95. Sierra Club. ISBN 0-87156-544-7. *SLJ*

Fleming, Denise. *Barnyard Banter.* $15.95. Henry Holt. ISBN 0-8050-1957-X. ALA

Florian, Douglas. *Beast Feast.* $14.95. Harcourt. ISBN 0-15-295178-4. ALA

Foreman, Michael. *War Game.* $16.95. Arcade. ISBN 1-55970-242-7. ALA

Fox, Mem. *Tough Boris.* $13.95. Harcourt. ISBN 0-15-289612-0. ALA

Goldin, Barbara Diamond. *The Passover Journey.* $15.99. Viking. ISBN 0-670-82421-6. ALA

Graham, Joan Bransfield. *Splish Splash.* Illus. by Steve Scott. $13.95. Ticknor & Fields. ISBN 0-395-70128-7. *SLJ*

Grimes, Nikki. *Meet Danitra Brown.* $15. Lothrop. ISBN 0-688-12073-3. ALA

Helldorfer, M. C. *Gather Up, Gather In: A Book of Seasons.* Illus. by Judy Pedersen. $14.99. Viking. ISBN 0-670-84752-6. *SLJ*

Hesse, Karen. *Sable.* Illus. by Marcia Sewell. $14.95. Holt. ISBN 0-8050-2416-6. *SLJ*

Hughes, Langston. *Sweet and Sour Animal Book.* $15.95. Oxford. ISBN 0-19-509185-X. ALA

Isaacs, Anne. *Swamp Angel.* Illus. by Paul O. Zelinsky. $14.99. Dutton. ISBN 0-525-45271-0. ALA, *SLJ*

James, Betsy. *Mary Ann.* Illus. by the author. $13.99. Dutton. ISBN 0-525-45077-7. *SLJ*

Johnson, James Weldon. *The Creation.* $15.95. Holiday House. ISBN 0-8234-1069-2. ALA

Kendall, Russ. *Russian Girl.* $14.95. Scholastic. ISBN 0-590-45789-6. ALA

Kimmel, Eric. *The Three Princes.* $15.95. Holiday House. ISBN 0-8234-1115-X. ALA

King-Smith, Dick. *Three Terrible Trins.* $15. Crown. ISBN 0 517-59828-0. ALA

Krull, Kathleen. *Lives of the Writers: Comedies, Tragedies (and What the Neighbors Thought).* Illus. by Kathryn Hewitt. $18.95. Harcourt. ISBN 0-15-248009-9. *SLJ*

Lasky, Kathryn. *The Librarian Who Measured the Earth.* Illus. by Kevin Hawkes. $16.95. Little, Brown. ISBN 0-316-51526-4. *SLJ*

Lavies, Bianca. *Mangrove Wilderness: Nature's Nursery.* Photos by the author. $15.99. Dutton. ISBN 0-525-45186-2. *SLJ*

Lester, Julius. *John Henry.* $16.99. Dial. ISBN 0-8037-1606-0. ALA

Lionni, Leo. *An Extraordinary Egg.* Illus. by the author. $15. Knopf. ISBN 0-679-85840-1. *SLJ*

McCully, Emily Arnold. *My Real Family.* $13.95. Illus. by the author. Harcourt. ISBN 0-15-277698-2. *SLJ*

McDermott, Gerald. *Coyote.* $14.95. Harcourt. ISBN 0-15-220724-4. ALA

McEwan, Ian. *The Daydreamer.* Illus. by Anthony Browne. $14. HarperCollins. ISBN 0-06-024426-7. *SLJ*

Maguire, Gregory. *Seven Spiders Spinning.* $13.95. Houghton. ISBN 0-395-68965-1. ALA

Mahy, Margaret. *The Rattlebang Picnic.* Illus. by Steven Kellogg. $14.99. Dial. ISBN 0-8037-1318-5. ALA, *SLJ*

Markle, Sandra. *Outside and Inside Birds.* $15.95. Macmillan. ISBN 0-02-762312-2. ALA

Mayne, William. *Hob and the Goblins.* Illus. by Norman Messenger. $12.95. Dorling Kindersley. ISBN 1-56458-713-4. ALA, *SLJ*

Meddaugh, Susan. *Martha Calling.* Illus. by the author. $14.95. Houghton. ISBN 0-395-69825-1. *SLJ*

Monceaux, Morgan. *Jazz.* $18. Knopf. ISBN 0-679-86518-7. ALA

Nolen, Jerdine. *Harvey Potter's Balloon Farm.* $15. Lothrop. ISBN 0-688-07887-7. ALA

Novak, Matt. *Mouse TV.* Illus. by the author. $14.95. Orchard. ISBN 0-531-06856-0. *SLJ*

Nye, Naomi Shihab. *Sitti's Secrets.* Illus. by Nancy Carpenter. $15.95. Four Winds. ISBN 0-02-768460-1. *SLJ*

Oppenheim, Shulamith. *Iblis.* $15.95. Harcourt. ISBN 0-15-238016-7. ALA

Orozco, Jose Luis. *De Colores and Other Latin American Folk Songs for Children.* $16.99. Dutton. ISBN 0-525-45260-5. ALA

Paterson, Katherine. *Flip-Flop Girl.* $13.99. Lodestar. ISBN 0-525-67480-2. ALA, *SLJ*

Polacco, Patricia. *My Rotten Redheaded Older Brother.* Illus. by the author. $15. Simon & Schuster. ISBN 0-671-72751-6. ALA, *SLJ*

————. *Pink and Say.* Illus. by the author. $15.95. Putnam. ISBN 0-399-22671-0. ALA, *SLJ*

Priceman, Marjorie. *How to Make an Apple Pie and See the World.* $15. Knopf. ISBN 0-679-83705-1. ALA

Purdy, Carol. *Mrs. Merriwether's Musical Cat.* Illus. by Petra Mathers. $15.95. Putnam. ISBN 0-399-22543-9. *SLJ*

Rathmann, Peggy. *Good Night, Gorilla.* $12.95. Putnam. ISBN 0-399-22445-9. ALA

Rattigan, Jama Kim. *Truman's Aunt Farm.* Illus. by G. Brian Karas. $13.95. Houghton. ISBN 0-395-65661-3. *SLJ*

Reiser, Lynn. *The Surprise Family.* $14. Greenwillow. ISBN 0-688-11671-X. ALA

Rogasky, Barbara. *Winter Poems.* Illus. by Trina Schart Hyman. $15.95. Scholastic. ISBN 0-590-42872-1. ALA, *SLJ*

Rohmann, Eric. *Time Flies.* $15. Crown. ISBN 0-517-59598-2. ALA

Rylant, Cynthia. *Henry and Mudge and the Careful Cousin.* Illus. by Suçie Stevenson. $13.95. Bradbury. ISBN 0-02-778021-X. *SLJ*

Sabuda, Robert. *The Christmas Alphabet.* $19.95. Orchard. ISBN 0-531-06857-9. ALA

Schertle, Alice. *How Now, Brown Cow?* $14.95. Harcourt. ISBN 0-15-276648-0. ALA

Scott, Ann Herbert. *Hi!* $14.95. Putnam. ISBN 0-399-21964-1. ALA

Silverman, Erica. *Don't Fidget a Feather.* $14.95. Macmillan. ISBN 0-02-782685-6. ALA

Snyder, Zilpha Keatley. *Cat Running.* $14.95. Delacorte. ISBN 0-385-31056-0. *SLJ*

Stanley, Diane, and Peter Vennema. *Cleopatra.* $15. Morrow. ISBN 0-688-10413-4. ALA

Steig, William. *Zeke Pippin.* Illus. by the author. $15. HarperCollins. ISBN 0-06-205076-1. *SLJ*

Stoeke, Janet Morgan. *A Hat for Minerva Louise.* Illus. by the author. $12.99. Dutton. ISBN 0-525-45328-8. ALA, *SLJ*

Turnbull, Ann. *Too Tired.* $13.95. Harcourt. ISBN 0-15-200549-8. ALA

Wild, Margaret. *Going Home.* $14.95. Scholastic. ISBN 0-590-47958-X. ALA

————. *Our Granny.* $13.95. Ticknor & Fields. ISBN 0-395-67023-3. ALA

Bestsellers of 1994: The Long-Running Hits

Daisy Maryles

Executive Editor, *Publishers Weekly*

The top sellers of 1994 continued some of the trends we noted back in 1993, most notably the favorable impact that the media coverage and tie-ins can have on a book's success. But at the midpoint of the 20th century's final decade, a new trend is gaining strength that will have an even more remarkable effect on the book marketplace.

For enlightenment, consider the following:

- In the previous two years (1992 and 1993) Rush Limbaugh dominated the charts and was the nonfiction top seller during the height of the holiday season. In 1994 it was Pope John Paul II. His book, *Crossing the Threshold of Hope*, had about 1.6 million copies in print after two months on sale.

- In the previous two years love stories penned by Robert James Waller were the favored fiction stocking stuffers; in 1994 a book on politically correct bedtime stories by James Finn Garner and James Redfield's *Celestine Prophecy*, a tale of a psychological New Age quest, headed the fiction list. Both books suffered numerous publisher rejections on their way to success. Redfield's book is now up to 2.1 million copies in print, and Garner's *Politically Correct Bedtime Stories*, which started with a 40,000 first printing, has passed the 1 million mark.

- In the latter half of 1994 *The Catechism of the Catholic Church* sold about 2 million copies, at least half of that through the book retail marketplace. And having an angel as part of one's book title proved to be a definite sales go-getter (a recent Gallup poll found that more than half of all American adults believe in angels and one in seven claims to have met one). Also, the trade paper list finished off the year with "soul" as the subject of three books.

- William Bennett's *Book of Virtues: A Treasury of Great Moral Stories* was a top seller in general and religious bookstores and made *PW*'s charts 49 out of 51 weeks. John Gray's *Men Are from Mars, Women Are from Venus*, on improving understanding and communications between men and women, never missed a week. And Betty J. Eadie's *Embraced by the Light*, about her communications with Jesus Christ during her near-death experience, went from the top of the hardcover chart to the top of the mass market chart without skipping a beat.

- Last year Barbara Bush and Dan Quayle published more successful autobiographies than Marlon Brando and Lauren Bacall. And the most successful thespians' books on the list were by comics Tim Allen and Paul

Note: Adapted from *Publishers Weekly*, January 2, 1995.

Reiser; instead of tell-alls, they gave advice on relationships. Both titles had more than 1 million copies in print before the year was out.

• In the countdown days before Christmas, the hottest new book was *Illuminata: Prayers for Everyday Living* by Marianne Williamson.

These examples—and there are more—all point to the very clear direction of many 1994 bestsellers. Books with inspirational and spiritual themes, as well as those espousing or discussing issues of morality and values, seem to be hitting a nerve among U.S. consumers. Perhaps it's the approaching millennium or the aging baby boomers. Perhaps it's a reaction to the excesses of the 1980s, or to the veil of corruption that seems to encircle our elected officials. Perhaps it's the endless headlines about murder and abuse or the many diseases and plagues that continue to take too big a toll on humankind. Whatever the reason, this trend toward looking for books that offer insight, solace, and inspiration is certain to continue for the next several years. Close observers of the themes of the top sellers were probably less surprised than others on the turn that the 1994 elections took.

The Media's Clout Continues

In 1993 we noted that TV, radio, and movies were the catalysts for getting books to the top of the bestseller charts. And comedian-turned-author continued, as noted earlier, to be a winning combination. But the one name that continues to have publishers checking their in-stock sheets is a confirmation of an appearance on Oprah. She is one of the strongest influences on a book's salability.

Oprah alone added major dollars to many publishers' coffers in the course of the year, but the biggest windfall was Knopf's. At one time, it had counted on a yet-to-be-finished manuscript from the TV talk-show empress, but there were few complaints since Oprah's cook came through with a sizzler. *In the Kitchen with Rosie: Oprah's Favorite Recipes* was published in mid-April with a 400,000-copy first printing. The book set some staggering new sales records. Knopf booked around-the-clock press time at two printers and was shipping up to 350,000 copies for several weeks after Daley's appearance on *Oprah* on April 28. A combined sales total at the two major chains during the week leading up to Mother's Day was a record 140,000 copies. To date, after 30 back-to-press trips, copies in print now total 5.6 million. Yes, Oprah's cook sets a new record for the fastest-selling book of all time.

Movie Tie-in Fever

Perhaps it was Daley's success, but more probably it was the strength of movie tie-ins that inspired another bestselling cookbook in 1994. Winston Groom's book *Forrest Gump* had a major paperback run following the release of the popular Tom Hanks movie, and Oxmoor House packaged (what else?) *The Bubba Gump Shrimp Co. Cookbook*, which debuted in the fall with a 700,000-copy first printing (the largest ever for a hardcover cookbook). Sales have been brisk, particularly at the chains.

Movie tie-ins this year continued to break new sales ground. *Schindler's List* had a long run on the trade paper list; the print figure for the Thomas Kenneally book passed the 1 million mark in 1994. With the release of the film version of *Interview with the Vampire*, Ballantine got two Anne Rice titles on the mass market list at the end of 1994, with several other Rice books hovering below the top 15—an impressive feat considering that the movie got mixed reviews. And Michael Crichton's *Disclosure* moved back to the top of the charts as soon as the film hit the screen.

Assessing the Numbers

There was more opportunity for a book to get on a bestseller list last year than in the previous four years. During the course of 1994, 310 new books made it onto *PW*'s four lists; in this decade, only 1990 had a better record, when 319 new books hit the charts. Most of the gain was in the mass market category, where 115 books made the lists, up from the 1993 tally of 99. The hardcover fiction list had 80 newcomers but only one first novel—Little, Brown's *The Day After Tomorrow* by Allan Folsom—had any list presence, racking up 14 weeks on that chart. Hopeful contenders for the nonfiction hardcover and the trade paperback lists had a tougher time getting on last year. Nonfiction had only 60 new titles, the lowest score yet; the previous low was 64 in 1993. In trade paper, 55 books made the grade in 1994, compared to 60 the previous year.

Getting to No. 1

The lead spot on the list was also a mixed bag of opportunity. Eleven novels had a run in the No. 1 slot but the only one that garnered that coveted spot for double-digit time was *The Celestine Prophecy*—13 weeks in the top spot. *The Chamber* had an eight-week run and *Disclosure, Accident,* and *Debt of Honor* enjoyed five weeks each. In 1993 Robert James Waller hogged the top of the fiction list, with *The Bridges of Madison County* and *Slow Waltz at Cedar Bend* holding 40 of the 51 opportunities.

In nonfiction, eight books made it to the top of the list. Two, *In the Kitchen with Rosie* and *Embraced by the Light*, dominated, with 19 and 15 weeks in the lead, respectively. *Men Are from Mars, Women Are from Venus* had a seven-week run and *Crossing the Threshold of Hope* had a six-week run. All others had to be satisfied with one week each.

In mass market, 14 titles made it to the top but only one, *The Client* by John Grisham, had a double-digit run, 13 weeks. The next highest was Michael Crichton's *Disclosure*, with eight weeks on the list. In 1993 opportunity for writers not named Grisham or Crichton was scarce; those two men had a book at the head of the list for a total of 36 weeks.

While six trade paperbacks enjoyed the top spot, two books of high quality dominated. Thomas Keneally's *Schindler's List* was No. 1 for 17 straight weeks and E. Annie Proulx's award-winning (National Book Award and Pulitzer) *The Shipping News* spent 18 weeks on the top of the list.

In tracking the leading publishing players in mass market, we count the best-sellers under individual imprints. The tally for the entire Ballantine/Fawcett/Del Rey/Ivy group is 22 books and a total of 116 weeks, slightly ahead of Bantam's 21 books and 107 weeks on the list. Berkley Jove's total would be 19 books and 118 weeks on the list. The top five mass market groups were Ballantine and its imprints; Bantam, Berkley Jove, Pocket Books, and Dell.

Publishers in Control

While an author's reputation or a high profile outside the book industry is often the key to admittance to the bestseller club, another factor is the publisher. Judging by the accompanying chart, clearly a writer's best shot at the charts is getting one of the top conglomerates to issue his or her book. Adding up the figures on the charts, the top eight account for 83.9 percent of all the available hardcover positions on the list throughout the course of the year, and 85 percent of all the paperback positions.

The next six publishers bring the share to 92.6 percent for hardcovers and 94 percent for paperbacks. That doesn't leave much room for the rest of the hundreds—or thousands, counting smaller independent houses—of publishing players.

Last year was the first time we did these calculations and it's interesting to see which publishers gained or lost bestseller real estate share. The big winners were Simon & Schuster, Time Warner, and Putnam Berkley. The gain for S&S was 7.4 percent, impressive even after you factor in its purchase of Macmillan (whose 1993 share for hardcover and paper totaled 2.6 percent). Time Warner's share in 1994 increased by 5.5 percent; Putnam Berkley's by 3.9 percent. Much of these gains seemed to be at the expense of Random Inc., whose share dropped by 9 percent (most of the share loss was from Ballantine, which in 1993 had *Women Who Run with the Wolves* on the list for 47 weeks plus four Michael Crichton titles that added up to 123 weeks), and Penguin, where the 1994 share was 5.3 percent lower than the year earlier.

It will be interesting to see what bestseller trends will define the century's final years, particularly with the increasing numbers of households wiring up for electronic information. But in a year that saw more million-copy-plus hardcover bestsellers than ever before, the bestseller business seems to be flourishing. And with angels, popes, and other celestial influences in the driver's seat; Oprah taking good care of herself; and powerful Republicans seeking bestselling status, projections can only be for even larger sales in 1995.

Spotlight 1994: The Fall of Snyder, and Other Major Moves

The departure of Richard Snyder, ousted from the leadership of Simon & Schuster by his new corporate bosses at Viacom, had to be the sensation of the year, but there were many other significant shifts in the perpetual reshaping of the book business.

William Shinker, out for a while from Harper, was given a division of his own at Bantam Doubleday Dell, to take shape next year—and wife Susan Moldow also left Harper, for a top spot at Scribner; that house also picked up Nan Graham from Viking, which in turn acquired Scribner's former publisher Barbara Grossman.

Noted departures included veteran editor Cork Smith, abandoned in Harcourt's downsizing of its trade operation; Howard Kaminsky, who departed struggling Hearst Books; small press guru Scott Walker, who gave up Graywolf; Roger Straus III, who left not only the family firm, Farrar Straus & Giroux, but also Aperture (inspiring his father to sell the company to Germany's Holtzbrinck group); Rebecca Sinkler, who retired as editor of the influential *New York Times Book Review* (to be succeeded by Charles McGrath of *The* New Yorker*);* and Erwin Glikes, who left the Free Press for Penguin, but died (in May) before he could really begin anew. Charles Cumello was a casualty of changing priorities at Borders-Walden.

Morrow, rebuilding, brought aboard Greg Euson from Random, Elizabeth Perle McKenna from Addison-Wesley, Anne Freedgood from Harcourt, and Henry Ferris from Times Books. Villard, on the other hand, lost key staffers Diane Reverand (to Harper) and Doug Stumpf (to Vanity Fair). Even Knopf, known for the longevity of its editors, lost two, with the departures of longtime staffers Corona Machemer and Gordon Lish.

Perhaps as a harbinger of things to come, a major religion publishing figure, Bruce Barbour, moved from a religion house (Nelson) to launch a Christian imprint, Moorings, at Ballantine.

PW's 1994 Longest-Running Hardcover Bestsellers

These titles achieved the No. 1 spot during their presence on *PW's* bestseller lists. Numbers in parentheses show how many weeks the book was on *PW's* lists in 1993.

Fiction

1. *The Bridges of Madison County* by Robert James Waller. Warner/(51) 51
2. *The Celestine Prophecy* by James Redfield. Warner/43
3. *Like Water for Chocolate* by Laura Esquivel. Doubleday/(37) 26
4. *The Alienist* by Caleb Carr. Random House/25
5. *Politically Correct Bedtime Stories* by James Finn Garner. Macmillan/24
6. *Slow Waltz at Cedar Bend* by Robert James Waller. Warner/(8) 21
7. *Disclosure* by Michael Crichton. Knopf/20
8. *The Chamber* by John Grisham. Doubleday/19
9. *Debt of Honor* by Tom Clancy. Putnam/17
10. *Accident* by Danielle Steel. Delacorte/15

Nonfiction

1. *Men Are from Mars, Women Are from Venus* by John Gray. HarperCollins/(36) 51
2. *The Book of Virtues* by William J. Bennett. Simon & Schuster/(1) 48

3. *Embraced by the Light* by Betty J. Eadie. Gold Leaf Press/(31) 39
4. *Midnight in the Garden of Good and Evil* by John Berendt. Random House/36
5. *In the Kitchen with Rosie* by Rosie Daley. Knopf/35
6. *Magic Eye* by Thomas Baccei. Andrews & McMeel/32
7. *Magic Eye II* by Thomas Baccei. Andrews & McMeel/22
8. *Soul Mates* by Thomas Moore. HarperCollins/21
9. *Ageless Body, Timeless Mind* by Deepak Chopra, M.D. Harmony/(21) 17
10. *Stop the Insanity* by Susan Powter. Simon & Schuster/(12) 17
11. *Couplehood* by Paul Reiser. Bantam/16
12. *Having Our Say* by Sarah and A. Elizabeth Delany with Amy Hearth. Kodansha/(4) 15
13. *Barbara Bush: A Memoir* by Barbara Bush. Scribner/15

PW's 1994 Longest-Running Paperback Bestsellers

These titles achieved the No. 1 spot during their presence on *PW*'s bestseller lists. Numbers in parentheses show how many weeks the book was on *PW*'s lists in 1993.

Mass Market

1. *The Client* by John Grisham. Dell/31
2. *Without Remorse* by Tom Clancy. Berkley/24
3. *Smilla's Sense of Snow* by Peter Hoeg. Dell/18
4. *A Case of Need* by Michael Crichton. Signet/16
5. *Degree of Guilt* by Richard N. Patterson. Ballantine/15
6. *Forrest Gump* by Winston Groom. Pocket/15
7. *I'll Be Seeing You* by Mary Higgins Clark. Pocket/15
8. *Like Water for Chocolate* by Laura Esquivel. Doubleday/Anchor/15
9. *Disclosure* by Michael Crichton. Ballantine/25

Trade

1. *The Road Less Traveled* by M. Scott Peck, M.D. S&S/Touchstone/(21) 51
2. *7 Habits of Highly Effective People* by Stephen R. Covey. S&S/Fireside/ (51) 51
3. *Care of the Soul* by Thomas Moore. HarperPerennial/50
4. *What to Expect When You're Expecting* by Eisenberg, Murkoff, and Hathway. Workman/(23) 45
5. *Where Angels Walk* by Joan W. Anderson. Ballantine/36
6. *The Shipping News* by E. Annie Proulx. S&S/Touchstone/30
7. *T-Factor Fat-Gram Counter* by Jamie Pope-Cordle and Martin Katahn. Norton/(48) 27

8. *All the Pretty Horses* by Cormac McCarthy. Vintage/(20) 23
9. *Schindler's List* by Thomas Keneally. S&S/Touchstone/23
10. *Chicken Soup for the Soul* by Jack Canfield and Mark Hansen. Health Communications/22
11. *Mama Makes Up Her Mind* by Bailey White. Vintage/20
12. *Pigs in Heaven* by Barbara Kingsolver. HarperPerennial/(19) 19
13. *Listening to Prozac* by Peter Kramer, M.D. Penguin/18
14. *A History of God* by Karen Armstrong. Ballantine/17
15. *Reengineering the Corporation* by Michael Hammer and James Champy. HarperBusiness/16

Ranking the Houses: How the Divisions and Imprints Competed in 1994

	No. of Books	No. of Weeks
Hardcover		
Putnam	19	136
Random House	14	145.5
Knopf	12	123
Bantam	12	82
HarperCollins	11	127
Delacorte	9	53
Pocket Books	9	32
Warner	6	135
Doubleday	6	55
Viking	5	37
Little, Brown	5	37
Villard	4	24
Houghton Mifflin	4	22
Andrews & McMeel	3	67
Hyperion	3	19
Scribner	2	26
St. Martin's	2	15
Morrow	2	14
Holt	2	13
Crown	2	9
Harper San Francisco	2	7
Ballantine	2	4
Gold Leaf	1	39
Macmillan	1	24
Harmony	1	17
Kodansha	1	15
Free Press	1	8
Pantheon	1	5
Tor	1	5
Del Rey	1	4
HarperBusiness	1	1

	No. of Books	No. of Weeks
Mass Market		
Bantam	21	107
Pocket Books	17	102
Ballantine	13	81
Dell	12	116
Berkley	12	78
Signet	9	55
Warner	9	54
Jove	7	40
Avon	7	28
Harper Paperbacks	6	38
Fawcett	4	23
Ivy	4	8
St. Martin's	2	10
Pinnacle	2	2
Doubleday/Anchor	1	15
Del Rey	1	4
Little, Brown	1	2
Topaz	1	1
Tor	1	1
Trade		
HarperPerennial	10	98
Vintage	10	93
Andrews & McMeel	6	31
S&S/Touchstone	5	107
Ballantine	4	67
Workman	4	63
Pocket	4	25
S&S/Fireside	3	68
Warner	3	35
Penguin	2	22
World Almanac	2	13
Houghton Mifflin	2	6
Berkley	2	5
Norton	1	27
Health Communications	1	22
HarperBusiness	1	16
Wiley	1	13
Rutledge Hill	1	10
Cadence Books	1	9
Collins San Francisco	1	5
Satori	1	5
Ten Speed	1	5
Rand McNally	1	4
Little, Brown	1	3
M.M. & Co.	1	3
Washington Sq. Press	1	2
Yankee	1	2
Prentice Hall	1	2

	No. of Books	No. of Weeks
Plume	1	1
Delta	1	1
Harcourt Brace	1	1
Liguori	1	1

Bestsellers by Corporation: How the Large Companies Fared on *PW*'s 1994 Charts

	Hardcover			Paperback		
	No. of Books	No. of Weeks	Percent Share*	No. of Books	No. of Weeks	Percent Share*
Random Inc.	37	331.5	21.7	36	276	18
Simon & Schuster	32	269.5	17.6	31	306	20
Bantam Doubleday Dell	27	190	12.4	35	239	15.6
HarperCollins	14	135	8.8	18	157	10.3
Time Warner	11	172	11.2	14	94	6.1
Putnam Berkley	19	136	8.9	21	123	8
Penguin USA	5	37	2.4	13	79	5.2
Hearst	2	14	.9	7	28	1.8
Andrews & McMeel	3	67	4.4	6	31	2
Workman	—	—	—	4	63	4.1
Norton	1	6	.4	1	27	1.8
St. Martin's	3	20	1.3	3	11	0.7
Houghton Mifflin	4	22	1.4	2	6	0.4
Hyperion	3	19	1.2	—	—	—

*This figure represents the publisher's share of the 1,530 hardcover or 1,530 paperback bestseller positions during 1994.

Bestsellers: The Rankings

Daisy Maryles
Executive Editor, *Publishers Weekly*

The big news about the 1994 hardcover bestsellers is the numbers. At every level of sales, new records were set and often the high tallies were considerably ahead of previous years' numbers. Just the fact that 17 books went over the million-copy mark demonstrates why publishers are often willing to pay (perhaps overpay) vast sums when they sense a winner. Getting that level of "shipped and billed" in a calendar year can do wonders for the bottom line, not to mention corporate morale. Even when one considers that the numbers in this feature are gross and not net, it seems reasonable to state that in 1994, more books were sold

Note: Adapted from *Publishers Weekly*, March 20, 1995.

at retail—discount and full-price—than ever before. A large percentage of these increased sales were made in the superstore and/or discount environment. Just the 1994 sales figures for the big 3—Barnes & Noble, Borders/Waldenbooks, and Crown—show a 15 percent increase over 1993; their total retail sales for the year reached $3.4 billion. These are the outlets that provide a large portion of the increased sales units of bestseller titles; their growth is clearly a major factor in the thus far unprecedented sales levels for last year's most visible titles.

And just how big were these sales figures? Consider the following sales records set in 1994:

Four of the 17 million-plus megasellers sold multiple millions, and the sales leader of the year, *In the Kitchen with Rosie*, racked up sales of almost 5.5 million from May to December, making it one of the fastest-selling books in publishing history. The previous million-copy-plus record for a given year was set in 1993, when nine books hit seven figures. And it took just a year to knock *The Bridges of Madison County* off its perch as all-time fastest-selling book (it still holds that record for fiction).

The top-15 for both fiction and nonfiction peaked at the highest level ever— 575,000+ and 650,000+, respectively. Two years earlier (before the superstore explosion), both lists peaked with figures under 300,000.

The number of fiction and nonfiction titles with reported sales of 100,000 or more handily broke the 1993 record of 157 books. The new record is 183 books (not counting many of the religion bestsellers). Fiction's total (89) was four ahead of the 1993 record; nonfiction's 94 titles beat the record set in 1989, when the number was 78. It's easy to see how tough it is these days to get a book onto the weekly charts (remember many books on the list for short runs don't even hit the six-figure point). In 1994, 80 novels and 60 works of nonfiction debuted on the weekly charts.

New records were also set at every sales level. The impressive 17 books that went over the million mark beat out the 1993 record of nine books. Here are more 1994 tallies: 36 books sold more than 500,000; 47 books sold more than 400,000; 55 books sold more than 300,000; and 100 books sold more than 200,000. These can be compared to the 1993 records: 26 books with sales of 500,000+; 38 books with sales of 400,000+; 48 books with sales of 300,000+; and 81 with sales of 200,000+.

The Gross/Net Conundrum

As in previous years, all our calculations are based on shipped-and-billed figures supplied by publishers for new books issued in 1994 and 1993 (a few titles published in 1992 that continued their bestselling trek into 1994 are also included). These figures reflect only 1994 domestic trade sales—publishers were requested not to include book club and overseas transactions. Also, while publishers were instructed to take into account returns through the end of January 1995, most returns—especially for books published in the latter half of the year—come back later in the year.

The number of books with sales of 100,000 or more that did not show on *PW*'s weekly charts or only went on for a week or two also increased significant-

y. Clearly, the competition for the weekly slots is sometimes so fierce that many books with more than respectable sales never make the grade. But there are also more sales venues, particularly discount outlets, for some of the name megasellers. That was certainly true for *The Bubba Gump Shrimp Co. Cookbook.* Its strongest sales were at the discounters and national chains. The publisher reports less than 3 percent returns on that title so far, and with the Paramount video for *Forrest Gump* set at the 10-million-unit level (each carrying promo for the cookbook), it could be one of the books where the numbers for gross sales and net sales are a close match.

What's New in Blockbusters?

It's the same old story for books that set the sales records. In fiction, the name of the game is the name. A newcomer has almost no chance of winning when up against John Grisham (his newest set a sales record for him), Danielle Steel (with three titles amongst the top 15), Mary Higgins Clark (she took two spots), and Robert James Waller (his *Bridges* is still on the weekly charts after more than two and a half years). And there are also the veterans of these year-end lists like Tom Clancy, Stephen King, Michael Crichton, Sidney Sheldon, Dean Koontz, and Anne Rice. There were two curiosities that had more to do with the zeitgeist: *The Celestine Prophecy* for all those seeking some level of new age spirituality and *Politically Correct Bedtime Stories,* a natural for PC followers as well as detractors. Each of these had the advantage of being the first of its kind. Nonfiction is almost a more eclectic list, but the power of the media continues to be the influence for getting to the top 15: well-known personalities accounted for about half of the list. The year's curiosity—3-D illustrations with a hidden picture—accounted for three slots. The O.J. Simpson murder trial spawned its first bestseller even before the opening statements. While it's not clear yet if Faye Resnick's inside skinny on Nicole Brown Simpson will benefit the defense or prosecution team, it gave its publisher, Dove Books, a national bestseller for its first published book.

Another record in 1994 was the number of markdowns by publishers of major books in the marketplace that were not moving according to expectations. It may be too soon to ascertain whether these price adjustments will stem the flow of massive returns for some of the books. What is clear is that for one, *Dolly,* it truly worked. A price reduction from $25 to $14.99 about a month after publication seemed to be the right ticket to best sellerdom.

Fiction Top 15

1. *The Chamber* by John Grisham. Doubleday (6/94); 3,189,893
2. *Debt of Honor* by Tom Clancy. Putnam (8/94); 2,302,529
3. *The Celestine Prophesy* by James Redfield. Warner (3/94); 2,092,526
*4. *The Gift* by Danielle Steel. Delacorte (7/94); **1,500,000
5. *Insomnia* by Stephen King. Viking (10/94); 1,398,213

6. *Politically Correct Bedtime Stories* by James Finn Garner. Macmillan (4/94); 1,300,000

*7. *Wings* by Danielle Steel. Delacorte (11/94); **1,225,000

*8. *Accident* by Danielle Steel. Delacorte (2/94); **1,150,000

9. *The Bridges of Madison County* by Robert James Waller. Warner (4/92) 844,574 (5.3 million since pub.)

10. *Disclosure* by Michael Crichton. Knopf (1/94); 764,599

11. *Nothing Lasts Forever* by Sidney Sheldon. Morrow (9/94); 764,000

12. *Taltos* by Anne Rice. Knopf (9/94); 706,145

13. *Dark Rivers of the Heart* by Dean Koontz. Knopf (11/94); 652,860

*14. *The Lottery Winner* by Mary Higgins Clark. Simon & Schuster (11/94) **625,000

*15. *Remember Me* by Mary Higgins Clark. Simon & Schuster (5/94) **575,000

Nonfiction

1. *In the Kitchen with Rosie* by Rosie Daley. Knopf (5/94); 5,487,369

2. *Men Are from Mars, Women Are from Venus* by John Gray. HarperCollins (6/92); 1,853,000 (2.9 million since pub.)

3. *Crossing the Threshold of Hope* by John Paul II. Knopf (10/94); 1,625,883

4. *Magic Eye* by N.E. Thing Enterprises. Andrews & McMeel (10/93) 1,589,882

*5. *The Book of Virtues* edited by William J. Bennett. Simon & Schuster (11/93); **1,550,000

6. *Magic Eye II* by N.E. Thing Enterprises. Andrews & McMeel (4/94) 1,383,339

7. *Embraced by the Light* by Betty J. Eadie with Curtis Taylor. Gold Leaf Press (11/92); 1,224,074 (2.2 million since pub.)

8. *Don't Stand Too Close to a Naked Man* by Tim Allen. Hyperion (10/94) 1,125,282

9. *Couplehood* by Paul Reiser. Bantam (9/94); 1,000,003

10. *Magic Eye III* by N.E. Thing Enterprises. Andrews & McMeel (8/94) 964,288

†11. *Dolly* by Dolly Parton. HarperCollins (9/94); 870,000

Note: Rankings are determined by sales figures provided by the publishers; the numbers generally reflect reports of copies "shipped and billed" in calendar year 1994 and take into account some early returns through the end of January 1994. Publishers do not at that time know what their total returns will be—indeed, the majority of returns occur later in the year—so none of these figures should be regarded as final net sales.

*Sales figures were submitted to *PW* in confidence, for use in placing the title on the list.

**Numbers shown are rounded down to the nearest 25,000 to indicate relationships to sales figures that are printed.

†Book was remaindered in place shortly after its on-sale date.

12. *James Herriott's Cat Stories* by James Herriott. St. Martin's (10/94); 829,724
13. *Barbara Bush* by Barbara Bush. Scribner (9/94); 725,000
14. *Nicole Brown Simpson* by Faye D. Resnick. Dove Books (10/94); 700,000
15. *The Bubba Gump Shrimp Co. Cookbook.* Oxmoor House/Leisure Arts (9/94); 651,652

The Fiction Runners-Up

This was the first time that a book with sales of 500,000 and more did not make a top-15 list. The majority of these books spent between two and three months on the 1994 list (*The Alienist* had the best record, with 25 weeks). Here too (also in the nonfiction runners-up), books with double stars by the sales figures indicate that the number was rounded down to the nearest 25,000 to indicate its relationship to the other top-sellers.

16. *The Body Farm* by Patricia Cornwell (Scribner, 570,000)
17. *"K" Is for Killer* by Sue Grafton (Holt, 488,000)
18. *Everything to Gain* by Barbara Taylor Bradford (HarperCollins, 480,859)
19. *Spencerville* by Nelson DeMille (Warner, 454,431)
20. *Wild Horses* by Dick Francis (Putnam, 417,992)
21. *Inca Gold* by Clive Cussler (Simon & Schuster, **400,000)
22. *Mutant Message Down Under* by Marlo Morgan (HarperCollins, 393,218)
23. *Lord of Chaos* by Robert Jordan (Tor, 336,000)
24. *Fatal Cure* by Robin Cook (Putnam, 320,557)
25. *Family Blessings* by LaVyrle Spencer (Putnam, 310,533)
26. *Star Wars: The Crystal Star* by Vonda McIntyre (Bantam, **300,000)
27. *God's Other Son* by Don Imus (Simon & Schuster)
28. *The Alienist* by Caleb Carr (Random House, 274,442)
29. *Lovers* by Judith Krantz (Crown, 266,927)
30. *A Tangled Web* by Judith Michael (Simon & Schuster)

Higher Numbers, Lower Ranks

Back in 1993, we were astounded by the record number of fiction titles with reported sales of 200,000+ that did not even make a top-30 list—14 in 1993 compared with the previous record of six titles set in 1992. One year later, a new record is set with 23 novels that shipped and billed more than 200,000 copies. Some did not make *PW*'s weekly charts, including books by Herman Wouk, Barbara De Angelis, Jude Deveraux, and Stephen Coonts.

The 23 with 200,000+ sales are: *Hollywood Kids* by Jackie Collins (Simon & Schuster); *Day After Tomorrow* by Alan Folsom (Little, Brown); *Until You* by Judith McNaught (Pocket); *Star Wars: The Courtship of Princess Leia* by Dave Wolverton (Bantam); *Charade* by Sandra Brown (Warner); *The Fist of God* by

Frederick Forsyth (Bantam); *The Glory* by Herman Wouk (Little, Brown); *Undue Influence* by Steve Martini (Putnam); *A Son of the Circus* by John Irving (Random House); *Star Trek: Generations* by J.M. Dillard (Pocket); *Brothers and Sisters* by Bebe Moore Campbell (Putnam); *Real Moments* by Barbara De Angelis (Delacorte); *Bad Love* by Jonathan Kellerman (Bantam); *Night Prey* by John Sandford (Putnam); *Honor Bound* by W.E.B. Griffin (Putnam); *Remembrance* by Jude Deveraux (Pocket); *Star Trek: Federation* by Judith and Garfield Reeves Stevens (Pocket); *Storming Heaven* by Dale Brown (Putnam); *On Dangerous Ground* by Jack Higgins (Putnam); *Star Trek: All Good Things* by Michael Jan Friedman (Pocket); *The Crossing* by Cormac McCarthy (Knopf); *The Intruders* by Stephen Coonts (Pocket); and *Daybreak* by Belva Plain (Delacorte).

More No-Shows for High Tallies

The number of books with reported sales of 150,000+ that didn't make a top-30 list in 1994 is down from last year's record of 16. Here, the list of books that did not make a weekly chart is fairly hefty.

The 11 titles are: Tom Robbins's *Half Asleep in Frog Pajamas* (Bantam); John Saul's *The Homing* (Fawcett); James Michener's *Recessional* (Random House); Lawrence Sanders's *McNally's Caper* (Putnam); Terry Brooks's *The Tangle Box* (Del Rey); *Rogue Warrior: Red Cell* by Richard Marcinko and John Weisman (Pocket); David Eddings's *The Hidden City* (Del Rey); Robert Parker's *All Our Yesterdays* (Delacorte); Peter David's *Star Trek: The Next Generation: Q-Squared* (Pocket); and Anne McCaffrey's *The Dolphins of Pern* (Del Rey).

The 1994 total for 125,000+ "shipped and billed" is 11, down just 1 for the dozen for 1993; the all-time high for this tally was in 1992 with 15.

Two books with these reported sales have yet to make *PW*'s weekly charts or the *New York Times* list. They are Peter Benchley's *White Shark* (Random House) and Connie Briscoe's *Sisters and Lovers* (HarperCollins). For the other nine, performances on *PW*'s charts for books published last year varies. *One True Thing, Walking Shadow*, and *Tunnel Vision* spent nine, seven, and five weeks respectively; most of the others between one and three weeks.

The nine novels are Sara Paretsky's *Tunnel Vision* (Delacorte); Robert B. Parker's *Walking Shadow* (Putnam); Jayne Ann Krentz's *Grand Passion* (Pocket); Laura Esquivel's *Like Water for Chocolate* (Doubleday); Joseph Heller's *Closing Time* (Simon & Schuster); Ann Crispin's *Star Trek: Sarek* (Pocket); Amanda Quick's *Mistress* (Bantam); Robert James Waller's *Slow Waltz in Cedar Bend* (Warner); and Anna Quindlen's *One True Thing* (Random House).

There were 14 more fiction books in 1994 with sales of more than 100,000 (same number as in 1993), six of which made it on to the weekly charts. E.L. Doctorow's *The Waterworks* (Random House) enjoyed the longest tenure (10 weeks), while Lilian Jackson Braun's *The Cat Who Came to Breakfast* (Putnam) and James Lee Burke's *Dixie City Jam* (Hyperion) stayed on for nine and eight weeks,respectively. Shorter stays of three to six weeks were enjoyed by Anne Rivers Siddons's *Downtown* (HarperCollins), Walter Mosley's *Black Betty* (Norton), and Wilbur Smith's *River God* (St. Martin's).

The other eight have yet to make an appearance. They are: *The Proud and the Free* by Janet Dailey (Little Brown), *The Nightingale Legacy* by Catherine Coulter (Putnam), *Seasons of Her Life* by Fern Michaels (Ballantine), *Twelve Red Herrings* by Jeffrey Archer (HarperCollins), *Everville* by Clive Barker (HarperCollins), *Faith* by Len Deighton (HarperCollins), *Desperate Measures* by David Morrell (HarperCollins), and *Shadow Song* by Terry Kay (Pocket).

Nonfiction Runners-Up

Two years earlier, most of these titles would have been assured of a top-15 slot. Many were strong performers and *Midnight in the Garden of Good and Evil, Soul Mates, Stop the Insanity, Hot Zone,* and *Standing Firm* all had double-digit runs on the list. John Gray, a fixture on the 1994 chart for *Men Are from Mars,* never made the weeklies for *What Your Mother Couldn't Tell You.* The publisher still expects a good sell through.

16. *The Agenda* by Bob Woodward (Simon & Schuster, **600,000)
17. *What Your Mother Couldn't Tell You and Your Father Didn't Know* by John Gray (HarperCollins, 560,000)
18. *Reba: My Story* by Reba McIntire (Bantam, **525,000)
19. *Standing Firm* by Dan Quayle (HarperCollins, 512,822)
20. *The Weight Watchers Complete Cookbook and Program Basics* (Macmillan, 500,000)
21. *Old Songs in a New Cafe* by Robert James Waller (Warner, 468,151)
22. *Baseball* by Ken Burns and Geoffrey C. Ward (Knopf, 436,393)
23. *First Things First* by Stephen R. Covey and A. Roger Merrill (Simon & Schuster, 432,288)
24. *The Hot Zone* by Richard Preston (Random House, 430,880)
25. *Midnight in the Garden of Good and Evil* by John Berendt (Random House, 406,490)
26. *The Bell Curve* by Richard J. Herrnstein and Charles Murray (Free Press, 400,000)
27. *Illuminata* by Marianne Williamson (Random House, 358,660)
28. *Soul Mates* by Thomas Moore (HarperCollins, 351,360)
29. *Disney's Magic Eye* by N.E. Thing Enterprises (Hyperion, 313,454)
30. *Stop the Insanity* by Susan Powter (Simon & Schuster, **275,000)

17 More 200,000+ No Shows

The number of books with reported sales of more than 200,000 that didn't make a top-30 list was astoundingly high—17 books. That number easily broke the 1993 record of seven books. How strong the final net sales might be for some of these books is still uncertain. Six have yet to make *PW*'s weekly charts, including titles by the Delany sisters, James Champy, William Shatner, Martha Stewart,

J.M. Dillard, and Anne Pasternak. Others like *How We Die* and *Motherless Daughters* enjoyed double-digit tenures. *See, I Told You So, SeinLanguage,* and *Ageless Body, Timeless Mind* were amongst the top five bestsellers of 1993 and went on to sell 200,000+ last year.

In ranked "shipped and billed" order, the 200,000+ group is: *The Delany Sisters' Book of Everyday Wisdom* by Sarah Delany and A. Elizabeth Delany with Amy Hill Hearth (Kodansha); *Reengineering Management* by James Champy (HarperCollins); *Brando: Songs My Mother Taught Me* by Marlon Brando (Random House); *How We Die* by Sherwin Nuland (Knopf); *Star Trek Movie Memories* by William Shatner (HarperCollins); Martha Stewart's *Menus for Entertaining* (Crown); *See, I Told You So* by Rush Limbaugh (Pocket); *Moon Shot* by Alan Shephard and Deke Slayton (Turner); *Smart Exercise* by Covert Bailey (Houghton Mifflin); *SeinLanguage* by Jerry Seinfeld (Bantam); *Star Trek: Where No Man Has Gone Before* by J.M. Dillard (Pocket); *Ageless Body, Timeless Mind* by Deepak Chopra (Crown); *Motherless Daughters* by Hope Edelman (Addison-Wesley); *Ann-Margret* by Ann-Margret with Todd Gold (Putnam); *Mary's Message to the World* by Annie Kirkwood (Putnam); *Saved by the Light* by Dannion Brinkley (Villard); and *Princess in Love* by Anna Pasternak (Dutton).

Record Higher Figures

Records continued to be broken in 1994. A huge group—20—with sales of 150,000 and more didn't make the 1994 list of top 30; that handily broke the 1993 record of 11. Back in 1992 there were only five 150,000+ sellers that didn't make a top-30 list. There were only four books that never made it on to a *PW* chart. They are: *Saturday Night Live* edited by Michael Cader (Houghton Mifflin); *Talking from 9 to 5* by Deborah Tannen (Morrow); *To the Stars* by George Takei (Pocket); and *Macmillan's Betty Crocker's New Choices Cookbook* (brand-name cookbooks seldom get reported on the charts no matter how strong the sales).

The 16 other books over the 150,000 mark are: *Zlata's Diary* by Zlata Filipovic (Viking); *The Warren Buffett Way* by Robert G. Hagstrom Jr. (Wiley); *Guns, Crime, and Freedom* by Wayne LaPierre (Regnery); *Running from Safety* by Richard Bach (Morrow); *All's Fair* by Mary Matalin and James Carville (Random House/Simon & Schuster); *Angels* edited by Rex Hauck (Ballantine); *D-Day* by Stephen Ambrose (Simon & Schuster); *Makes Me Wanna Holler* by Nathan McCall (Random House); *Beyond Peace* by Richard M. Nixon (Random House); *All the Trouble in the World* by P.J. O'Rourke (Atlantic Monthly Press); *I Could Do Anything . . .* by Barbara Shear (Delacorte); *October 1964* by David Halberstam (Villard); *An Angel to Watch Over Me* by Joan Wester Anderson (Ballantine); *No Ordinary Time* by Doris Kearns Goodwin (Simon & Schuster); *The Haldeman Diaries* (Putnam); and *The Tribe of Tiger* by Elizabeth Marshall Thomas (Simon & Schuster).

Eleven titles had sales between 125,000 and 149,000 in 1993 and, except for Harvey Penick's book, a 1993 top-15 seller, none of these titles made their way onto *PW*'s hardcover charts. (A few have hit the 1995 trade paper list.) The 11 are: *Long Walk to Freedom* by Nelson Mandela (Little, Brown); *Meditations* by Thomas Moore (HarperCollins); *New Joy of Sex* by Alex Comfort (Crown); *Diplomacy* by Henry Kissinger (Simon & Schuster); *And If You Play Golf, You're My Friend* by Harvey Penick with Bud Shrake (Simon & Schuster); *The Prince of Wales* by Jonathan Dimbleby (Morrow); *It Wasn't Always Easy But I Sure Had Fun* by Lewis Grizzard (Villard); *Driven to Distraction* by Edward M. Hallowell, M.D. and John J. Ratey, M.D. (Pantheon); *Ten Stupid Things Women Do to Mess Up Their Lives* by Laura Schlessinger (Villard); *Entertaining with Regis & Kathie Lee* (Hyperion); and *75 Seasons* by Will McDonough et al. (Turner).

There were 16 nonfiction titles with reported sales of 100,000 or more, four more than in 1993 and five less than in 1992. Seven of these made it on to *PW*'s charts, usually just for a few weeks. Two exceptions were Michael Jordan's *I Can't Accept Not Trying* (HSF), which had a six-week run, and Maya Angelou's *Wouldn't Take Nothing for My Journey Now* (Random House), which was #14 on 1993's annual list and was on the 1994 charts for 13 weeks. The five other bestsellers were: *Wherever You Go, There You Are* by Jon Kabat-Zinn (Hyperion); *Strange Justice* by Jill Mayer and Jill Abramson (Houghton Mifflin); *Dave Barry's Not Making This Up* by Dave Barry (Crown); *Prayers and Devotions* by John Paul II (Viking); and *Fear of Fifty* by Erica Jong (HarperCollins).

The nine that didn't get a shot at our weekly charts include: *Grace* by Robert Lacey (Putnam); *The Lessons of Love* by Melody Beattie (Harper San Francisco); *Dave Barry's Gift Guide to End All Gift Guides* (Crown); *To Be Loved* by Berry Gordy (Warner); Mary Engelbreit's *Mother's Journal* (Andrews & McMeel); *Pale Blue Dot* by Carl Sagan (Random House); *All I Really Need to Know I Learned from Watching Star Trek* by Dave Marinaccio (Crown); *How I Got This Way* by Patrick McManus (Holt); and *Oprah Winfrey* by George Mair (Carol).

Paperback Bestsellers: Delineating a Decade

Maria Simson
Paperback Editor, *Publishers Weekly*

In order to get a wider view on trends, we compared the 1994 trade paperback lists not only with lists from the last couple of years but with those of a decade ago. Not surprisingly many things remain the same: comic books and self-help are perpetual staples. The little oddities that might serve to distinguish one year's tastes from another are merely replaced by different but equally frivolous fare: 1984's *How to Kazoo* has been transformed, in 1994, into *The Duct Tape Book*; and the noxious *Who F*rted* became the obnoxious *Beavis and Butthead's Ensucklopedia*.

Health is a mainstay of both lists but there has been a slight shift. The num-ber of bestselling childcare titles in 1994 was half of that in 1984—six to three—while the number of general health titles has increased from two to six, figures that may reflect new preoccupations of aging baby boomers.

More dramatic are the changes in nutrition and cookbooks. While only one book could really be described as a nutrition title in 1984, there were five in 1994. The biggest shift of all remains in cookbooks. Of the 11 that made it to the list a decade ago, only two specifically addressed diet or health. Of the 12 that made it this past year, 9 were of the low-fat, heart-healthy ilk.

There are some other, even bigger changes, none of which would bear out gloomy predictions of creeping illiteracy. From *The Magic of Michael Jackson* (961,000 copies) to *Tough and Tender: The Story of Mr. T* (59,200) there were seven celebrity biographies (eight if you count George Carlin's autobiography) in 1984 and one celebrity beauty book (remember Morgan Fairchild?). This year either stars (or readers) decided they were too busy—not one celebrity book made it.

What has replaced them? To some extent fiction and nonfiction works of lit-erary value. Yes, 1984 saw Alice Walker's *The Color Purple*, Russell Baker's *Growing Up*, David Shipler's *Russia*, two books from William Kennedy and one each from Ferrol Sams, Michael Ende, and Robert Mason, as well as successful reissues of *Passage to India* and *The Sun Also Rises*. But depending on exactly how broad your criteria, the number hovers at around an even dozen. In 1994, books by David Halberstam, Gabriel García Márquez, Cormac McCarthy, Cornel West, Dorothy Allison, Ernest Gaines, Isabel Allende, and Tony Kushner made the trade paper list, as did the reissues of Toni Morrison's *The Bluest Eye* and Richard Wright's *Native Son* and *Black Boy* and tie-in editions of *Schindler's List* and Armistead Maupin's *Tales of the City*. All tolled, books of literary quali-ty in 1994 outnumbered those of 1984 almost two to one.

Then there's *The Shipping News* by E. Annie Proulx, and what news it is. With 750,000 copies to its credit, it is the first literary book to clear the 500,000 mark without the benefit of a movie or TV tie-in since *The Color Purple* did it in 1983 (two years before the Spielberg movie) with 564,000.

Trade paperback figures reflect originals, reprints, or dual editions published in 1993 or 1994 for which publishers have billed and shipped at least 50,000 copies in 1994. They do not always reflect net sales.

Mass Markets

With 69 titles this year, it may seem that numbers of titles have declined for mass markets as well, considering that here were 105 and 117 in 1992 and 1993, respectively. But that figure is in keeping with the 78 titles on last year's list, the first affected by refinements in our determination of what makes a mass market bestseller.

What is there really to say about the makeup of the list? There are a few new(ish) names like Laura Esquivel, Peter Hoeg, and Scott Smith, and a few non-fiction: Nellie Bly's *Oprah!*, Jerry Seinfeld's *SeinLanguage*, Betty J. Eadie's *Embraced by the Light*, and Rush Limbaugh's *See, I Told You So*.

But for the most part it consists of the usual suspects: the scary—Dean Koontz (three books), Stephen King (two), Anne Rice (two), V.C. Andrews (two); the adventurous—Michael Crichton (two), Tom Clancy (two), Lawrence Sanders (two), Stephen Coonts, Jack Higgins; the litigious—John Grisham, Scott Turow, Nancy Taylor Rosenberg; the mysterious—Mary Higgins Clark, Patricia D. Cornwell (twice), John le Carré, Tony Hillerman, Sue Grafton; the romantic—Danielle Steel, and, with two books apiece, Johanna Lindsey, Catherine Coulter, Nora Roberts, Julie Garwood, and Sandra Brown.

A comparison with the mass market lists of 1984 doesn't show the kind of change apparent in trade paper. Many of the names are exactly the same and where they are not, their replacements are treading precisely in the same footsteps, making for a list with no dint of the evolution shown by the trade paperback entries. But perhaps, by definition, products directed toward the "mass market" do not so much reflect change as they do broad, enduring consensus.

Trade Paperbacks

Schindler's List. Thomas Keneally. Reprint. Touchstone (1,115,000)

Homicidal Psycho Jungle Cat. Bill Watterson. Original. Andrews & McMeel (1,169,708)

Chicken Soup for the Soul. Jack Canfield and Mark Victor Hansen. Health Communications (1,000,000)

The T-Factor Fat Gram Counter. Jamie Pope-Cordle and Martin Katahn. Reprint. Norton

Care of the Soul. Thomas Moore. Harper Perennial (833,793)

The Curse of Madame "C". Gary Larson. Original. Andrews & McMeel (830,775)

The Shipping News. E. Annie Proulx. Reprint. Touchstone (750,000)

Butter Busters: The Cookbook. Pam Mycoskie. Reprint. Warner (623,597)

Gumpisms. Winston Groom. Original. Pocket (599,800)

Magic Eye Poster Book. N.E. Thing Enterprises. Original. Andrews & McMeel (532,372)

Magic Eye Book of Postcards. N.E. Thing Enterprises. Original. Andrews & McMeel (503,917)

Lasher. Anne Rice. Reprint. Ballantine (420,914)

Beavis & Butthead's Ensucklopedia. Mike Judge. Original. Pocket (433,100)

The Pocket Powter. Susan Powter. Original. Fireside (425,000)

Pigs in Heaven. Barbara Kingsolver. Reprint. HarperPerennial (424,623)

The Little Book of Christmas Joys. H. Jackson Brown, Jr. Original. Rutledge Hill (417,737)

Reengineering the Corporation. Michael Hammer and James Champy. Reprint. HarperPerennial (406,474)

Eat More Weigh Less. Dean Ornish. Reprint. HarperPerennial (404,808)

Dianetics. L. Ron Hubbard. Reprint. Bridge (387,624)

Do You See What I See. N.E. Thing Enterprises. Original. Andrews & McMeel (371,300)

What to Expect the Toddler Years. Arlene Eisenberg, Heidi Murkoff, and Sandee Hathaway. Original. Workman (361,625)

Star Trek: Encyclopedia. Michael Okuda. Original. Pocket (354,200)

Life's Little Instruction Book, Vol. 2. H. Jackson Brown, Jr. Original. Rutledge Hill (334,623)

Shoppers Guide to Fat in Your Food. Karen J. Bellerson. Original. Avery (319,000)

All Around the World Cookbook. Sheila Lukins. Original. Workman (300,454)

Armored Cav. Tom Clancy. Original. Berkley (300,000)

* *Note:* Titles marked by an asterisk were published in 1993. Sales figures for some books were submitted in confidence, for use only in positioning titles.

Soul Mates. Thomas Moore. Reprint. Harper-Perennial (292,755)

*Bottoms Up! Joyce L. Vedral. Original. Warner (254,690)

Money Doesn't Grow on Trees. Neale S. Godfrey. Original. (250,000)

Wall Street Journal Guide to Understanding Money and Investing. Kenneth M. Morris and Allan M. Siegel. Original. Fireside (250,000)

A Woman's Worth. Marianne Williamson. Reprint. Ballantine (248,166)

Secrets of Fat-Free Baking. Sandra Woodruff. Original. Avery (247,000)

*The Te of Piglet. Benjamin Hoff. Reprint. Penguin (230,000)

Further Along the Road Less Traveled. M. Scott Peck. Reprint. Touchstone (220,000)

Contract with America. Newt Gingrich. Original. Times (219,204)

Listening to Prozac. Peter Kramer. Reprint. Penguin (202,000)

*Acts of Faith. Iyanla Vanzant. Original. Fireside (200,000)

Beating the Street. Peter Lynch. Reprint. Fireside (200,000)

Daily Reflections for Highly Effective People. Stephen R. Covey. Original. Fireside (200,000)

Mama Makes Up Her Mind. Bailey White. Reprint. Vintage (200,000)

*All the Pretty Horses. Cormac McCarthy. Reprint. Vintage (200,000)

*The Anatomy Coloring Book, 2nd ed. Wynn Kapit and Lawrence Elson. Reprint. Harper-Reference (184,755)

Garfield Pulls His Weight. Jim Davis. Original. Ballantine (179,681)

Why Cats Paint. Heather Busch and Burton Silver. Ten Speed (179,000)

The Low-Fat Good Food Cookbook. Martin and Terry Katahn. Original. Norton

Leaving Cold Sassy. Olive Ann Burns. Reprint. Dell (176,000)

*A Return to Love. Marianne Williamson. Reprint. HarperPerennial (171,790)

*The Days Are Just Packed. Bill Watterson. Original. Andrews & McMeel (167,451)

His Kisses Are Dreamy. Berke Breathed. Original. Little, Brown (166,855)

Winner Within. Pat Riley. Reprint. Berkley (166,000)

Einstein's Dreams. Alan Lightman. Reprint Warner (162,974)

The Celestine Prophecy: An Experientia Guide. James Redfield and Carol Adrienne. Original. Warner (156,323)

Creating Love. John Bradshaw. Reprint. Bantam

The Internet Yellow Pages. Harley Hahn and Rick Stout. Original. Osborne/McGraw-Hill (154,000)

*Random Acts of Kindness. Editors of Conari Press. Original. Conari (154,000)

Giant Steps. Tony Robbins. Original. Fireside (150,000)

Moosewood Restaurant Cooks at Home. The Moosewood Restaurant Collective. Original. Fireside (150,000)

The Whole Internet User's Guide & Catalog. Ed Krol. Reprint. O'Reilly (150,000)

The Tom Peters' Seminar. Tom Peters. Reprint. Vintage (150,000)

Girl, Interrupted. Susanna Kaysen. Reprint. Vintage (150,000)

*Far Side Gallery TV. Gary Larson. Original. Andrews & McMeel (147,685)

Touchpoints. T. Berry Brazelton. Reprint. Addison-Wesley (142,000)

In Search of Angels. David Connolly. Original. Berkley (141,000)

Race Matters. Cornel West. Reprint. Vintage (135,000)

How to Study, 3rd ed. Ron Fry. Original. Career Press (132,400)

*Men, Women and Relationships. John Gray. Beyond Words (130,521)

*The Low-Fat Supermarket Fat Gram Counter. Jamie Pope-Cordle and Martin Katahn. Original. Norton

Best Cat Ever. Cleveland Amory. Reprint. Little, Brown (125,549)

Food, Your Miracle Medicine. Jean Carper. Reprint. HarperPerennial (125,134)

Holidays: The Best of Martha Stewart Living. The Editors of Martha Stewart Living. Original. Crown (121,549)

*The Chickens Are Restless. Gary Larson. Original. Andrews & McMeel (121,245)

Betty Crocker's Cookbook, 7th ed. Betty Crocker editors. Reprint. Macmillan (120,000)

The New Fit or Fat. Covert Bailey. Houghton Mifflin (117,806)

101 Great Answers to the Toughest Interview Questions, 2nd ed. Ron Fry. Original. Career Press (115,860)

The Internet Complete Reference. Harley Hahn and Rick Stout. Original. Osborne/McGraw-Hill (115,000)

The Fifties. David Halberstam. Reprint. Fawcett (112,714)

Live Your Dreams. Les Brown. Original. Avon (112,107)

Simplify Your Life. Elaine St. James. Original. Hyperion (110,443)

A Guide to the Star Wars Universe. William Slaviceek. Original. Ballantine (110,188)

More Random Acts of Kindness. Editors of Conari Press. Original. Conari (110,000)

Hotel Pastis. Peter Mayle. Reprint. Vintage (110,000)

The Angels Within Us. John R. Price. Original. Fawcett (107,685)

The Millennium Whole Earth Catalog. Edited by Howard Rheingold. Original Harper-SanFrancisco (107,198)

Starless Night. R.A. Salvatore. Reprint. TSR (106,000)

The Low-Fat Fast Food Guide. Jamie Pope-Cordle and Martin Katahn. Original. Norton

The Millennium Whole Earth Catalog. Edited by Howard Rheingold. Dual. HarperSan Francisco (105,655)

The Fifth Discipline Fieldbook. Peter Senge, et al. Original. Currency/Doubleday (104,888)

Beyond Fair Chase. Jim Posewitz. Original. Falcon (103,000)

Black Boy. Richard Wright. Reprint. HarperPerennial (102,889)

More Low-Fat Recipes. Sunset Editors. Original. Sunset (101,100)

There's An Angel on Your Shoulder. Kelsey Tyler. Original. Berkley (100,000)

Graham Kerr's Creative Choices Cookbook. Graham Kerr. Reprint. Berkley (100,000)

Vamps & Tramps. Camille Paglia. Original. Vintage (100,000)

Young Men and Fire. Norman Maclean. Reprint. Univ. of Chicago (97,714)

The Book of Guys. Garrison Keillor. Reprint. Penguin (97,000)

Chaos Curse. R.A. Salvatore. Original. TSR (97,000)

World Record Airplane Book. Ken Blackburn and Jeff Lammers. Original. Workman (96,425)

1001 Ways to Reward Employees. Bob Nelson. Original. Workman (96,145)

Snaps. James Percelay, Monteria Ivy and Stephan Dweck. Original. Morrow (95,998)

The English Patient. Michael Ondaatje. Reprint. Vintage (85,000)

Love, Remember Me. Bertrice Small. Original. Ballantine (93,190)

The Duct Tape Book. Jim Berg and Tim Nyberg. Original. Pfeifer-Hamilton (91,184)

Born for Love. Leo F. Buscaglia. Reprint. Fawcett (90,553)

The Making of Deep Space Nine. Judith and Garfield Reeves-Stevens. Original. Pocket (90,200)

Excess Baggage. Judith Sills. Reprint. Penguin (90,000)

I Am Becoming the Woman I've Wanted. Sandra Haldeman Martz. Original. Papier-Mache (86,381)

Dragons of Krynn. Edited by Margaret Weis and Tracy Hickman. Original. TSR (86,000)

In the Spirit. Susan L. Taylor. Reprint. HarperPerennial (85,784)

Monster. Sanyika Shakur. Reprint. Penguin (85,000)

Net Guide. Michael Wolff & Co. Original. Random House Electronic (85,000)

Dakota. Kathleen Norris. Reprint. Houghton Mifflin (84,926)

Never Confuse a Memo with Reality. Richard A. Moran. Original. HarperPerennial (84,858)

Tibetan Book of Living and Dying. Sogyal Rinpoche. Reprint. HarperSanFrancisco (84,453)

A World Waiting to Be Born. M. Scott Peck. Reprint. Bantam

Deepest Thoughts. Jack Handey. Original. Hyperion (83,911)

Black Pearls. Eric Copage. Original. Morrow (83,200)

Liberation Management. Tom Peters. Reprint. Fawcett (82,548)

PDR Family Guide to Women's Health & Prescription Drugs. PDR Staff. Original. Medical Economics (81,100)

The Wisdom of Teams. Jon Katzenbach. Reprint. HarperPerennial(81,010)

American Heritage Dictionary. Reprint. Dell (81,000)

The Infinite Plan. Isabel Allende. Reprint. HarperPerennial (80,178)

Nitpicker's Guide for Next Generation Trekkers. Phil Ferrand. Original. Dell (79,000)

Crown of Fire. Ed Greenwood. Original. TSR (78,000)

In the Name of the Father. Gerry Conlon. Original. Plume (76,428)

Native Son. Richard Wright. Reprint. HarperPerennial (78,192)

The Path of Transformation. Shakti Gawain. Original. Nataraj (75,552)

Low-Fat Mexican Cook Book. Sunset Editors. Sunset (73,900)

Dance of Deception. Harriet Goldhor Lerner. Reprint. HarperPerennial (73,308)

Garfield Hits the Big Time #25. Jim Davis. Original. Ballantine (73,138)

It's the Thought That Counts. Lynn Johnston. Original. Andrews & McMeel (72,126)

Everyday Wisdom. Wayne Dyer. Original. Hay House (72,000)

Your Blues Ain't Like Mine. Bebe Moore Campbell. Ballantine (71,856)

A Wife's Little Instruction Book. Diane Jordan and Paul Seaborn. Original. Avon (70,721)

The Great Whitewater Fiasco. Martin Gross. Original. Ballantine (70,617)

Unbelievably Good Deals & Great Adventures That You Absolutely Can't Get Unless You Are Over 50. Joan Rattner Heilman. Original. Contemporary (70,113)

Black Holes and Baby Universes. Stephen Hawking. Reprint. Bantam

Don't Eat Your Heart Out Cookbook (Revised). Joe Piscatella. Original. Workman (69,030)

Raising a Daughter. Jeanne and Don Elium. Original. Ten Speed (69,000)

The New Router Handbook. Patrick Spielman. Original. Sterling (68,751)

Images. Robert James Waller. Original. Warner (68,727)

Cheap Advice. Calvert DeForest. Original. Warner (67,677)

Thinking Out Loud. Anna Quindlen. Reprint. Fawcett (67,573)

Shave the Whales. Scott Adams. Original. Andrews & McMeel (67,509)

Bringers of the Dawn: Teachings from the Pleiadians. Barbara Marciniak. Original. Bear & Co. (67,500)

Nutribase Nutrition Facts Desk Reference. Art Ulene. Original. Avery (67,000)

Jazz. Toni Morrison. Reprint. Plume (67,255)

Night of the Eye. Mary Kirchoff. Original. TSR (67,000)

Caring for Your Baby and Young Child. Stephen P. Shelov. Reprint. Bantam

Bluest Eye. Toni Morrison. Reprint. Plume (65,192)

Challenging Lateral Thinking Puzzles. Paul Sloane. Original. Sterling (64,376)

Elfsong. Elaine Cunningham. Original. TSR (64,000)

Angels in America, Part Two: Perestroika. Tony Kushner. Original. Theatre Communications (63,690)

Nobody Nowhere. Donna Williams. Original. Avon (63,083)

Teaching Your Children Responsibility. Richard and Linda Eyre. Original. Fireside (63,000)

Angel Wisdom. Terry Lynn Taylor and Mary Beth Crain. Original. HarperSanFrancisco (62,967)

Bonsai Basics. Christian Pessey and Remy Samson. Original. Sterling (62,935)

Control Your Destiny or Someone Else Will. Noel Tichy. Reprint. HarperPerennial (62,411)

NPR Guide to Building a Classical CD Collection. Ted Libbey. Original. Workman (62,133)

Anger Kills. Redford Williams. Reprint. HarperPerennial (61,525)

Beware of Those Who Ask for Feedback. Richard A. Moran. Original. HarperPerennial (61,039)

366 Low-Fat Brand-Name Recipes in Minutes. M.J. Smith. Original. Chronimed (61,000)

More Tales of the City. Armistead Maupin.
Reprint. HarperPerennial (60,787)
How to Make Money in Stocks. William
O'Neil. Reprint edition. McGraw-Hill
(60,337)
Happiness Is a Choice. Barry Neil Kaufman.
Fawcett (60,160)
Mrs. Webster's Dictionary. Pacific North-
west. Original. Great Quotations (60,000)
A Lesson Before Dying. Ernest Gaines.
Reprint. Vintage (60,000)
Nobody's Fool. Richard Russo. Reprint. Vin-
tage (60,000)
Job Survival Instruction Book. Karin Ireland.
Original. Career Press (59,225)
May the Force Be With Us. Bill Amend.
Original. Andrews & McMeel (58,762)
Breads. Sunset Editors. Reprint. Sunset
(58,200)
We Were Soldiers Once and Young. Harold
Moore. Reprint. HarperPerennial (58,038)
SAT Success. Joan Carris, with Michael R.
Crystal and William R. McQuade. Peter-
son's (58,000)
The Couple's Companion. Harville Hendrix.
Original. Pocket (57,600)
Never Ask a Man the Size of His Spread.
Gladiola Montana. Original. Gibbs Smith
(57,599)
Bastard Out of Carolina. Dorothy Allison.
Reprint. Plume (57,499)
Tales of the City. Armistead Maupin. Reprint.
HarperPerennial (56,832)
*Rationalizations for Women Who Do Too
Much While Running with the Wolves.*
Allison McCune. Original. Adams (56,748)
The Home Brewer's Companion. Charlie
Papazian. Original. Avon (56,320)
Incredible Fishing Stories. Shaun Morey.
Original. Workman (56,044)
Still Life With Menu. Mollie Katzen. Origi-
nal. Ten Speed (56,000)
Don't Know Much About History. Ken
Davis. Reprint. Avon (55,782)
The Art of Dreaming. Carlos Castaneda.
Reprint. HarperPerennial (55,235)
Strange Pilgrims. Gabriel García Márquez.
Reprint. Penguin (55,000)
Tell Me the Truth About Dying. W.H. Auden.
Original. Vintage (55,000)

Mass Market

The Client. John Grisham. Reprint/Movie tie-
in edition. Dell (8,100,000)
Disclosure. Michael Crichton. Reprint/Movie
tie-in edition. Ballantine (4,013,998)
Without Remorse. Tom Clancy. Reprint.
Berkley (3,300,000)
Vanished. Danielle Steel. Reprint. Dell
(3,000,000)
I'll Be Seeing You. Mary Higgins Clark.
Reprint. Pocket (2,272,000)
Interview with the Vampire. Anne Rice.
Reprint. Ballantine (2,687,308)
Nightmares & Dreamscapes. Stephen King.
Reprint. Signet (2,600,636)
A Case of Need. Michael Crichton. Reprint.
Signet (2,500,206)
Winter Moon. Dean Koontz. Reprint. Ballan-
tine (2,338,731)
Pleading Guilty. Scott Turow. Reprint.
Warner (2,227,175)
The Door to December. Dean Koontz. Reprint.
Signet (2,200,512)
Mr. Murder. Dean Koontz. Reprint. Berkley
(2,100,000)
Ruby. V.C. Andrews. Original. Pocket
(2,033,400)
Pearl in the Mist. V.C. Andrews. Original.
Pocket (1,882,200)
Slow Waltz in Cedar Bend. Robert James
Waller. Reprint. Warner (1,853,628)
Dangerous Fortune. Ken Follett. Reprint.
Dell (1,702,000)
November of the Heart. LaVyrle Spencer.
Reprint. Berkley (1,700,000)
Clear and Present Danger. Tom Clancy.
Reprint/Movie tie-in. Berkley (1,700,000)
The Scorpio Illusion. Robert Ludlum.
Reprint. Bantam
See, I Told You So. Rush Limbaugh. Reprint.
Pocket (1,578,300)
Whispers. Belva Plain. Reprint. Dell
(1,575,000)
You Belong to Me. Johanna Lindsey. Origi-
nal. Avon (1,563,329)
Surrender My Love. Johanna Lindsey. Origi-
nal. Avon (1,538,764)
Cruel and Unusual. Patricia D. Cornwell.
Reprint. Avon (1,533,779)
Forrest Gump. Winston Groom. Reprint.
Pocket (1,465,200)

All That Remains. Patricia D. Cornwell. Reprint. Avon (1,440,579)

SeinLanguage. Jerry Seinfeld. Reprint. Bantam

Honor Among Thieves. Jeffrey Archer. Reprint. HarperCollins (1,403,500)

Pot of Gold. Judith Michael. Reprint. Pocket (1,392,500)

The Guardian. John Saul. Reprint. Fawcett (1,325,093)

Mexico. James Michener. Reprint. Fawcett (1,301,167)

The Throat. Peter Straub. Reprint. Signet (1,300,087)

McNally's Risk. Lawrence Sanders. Reprint. Berkley (1,300,000)

Winter Prey. John Sandford. Reprint. Berkley (1,300,000)

Prime Witness. Steve Martini. Reprint. Berkley (1,300,000)

Terminal. Robin Cook. Reprint. Berkley (1,300,000)

Private Pleasures. Lawrence Sanders. Reprint. Berkley (1,300,000)

Streets of Laredo. Larry McMurtry. Reprint. Pocket (1,299,300)

Perfect. Julie Garwood. Reprint. Pocket (1,297,800)

"J" Is for Judgment. Sue Grafton. Reprint. Fawcett (1,240,105)

Sacred Clowns. Tony Hillerman. Reprint. HarperCollins (1,236,000)

Christy. Catherine Marshall. Reprint/TV tie-in. Avon (1,229,701)

Interest of Justice. Nancy Taylor Rosenberg. Reprint. Signet (1,200,449)

Where There's Smoke. Sandra Brown. Reprint. Warner (1,200,113)

Lord of Raven's Peak. Catherine Coulter. Original. Berkley (1,200,000)

Wyndham Legacy. Catherine Coulter. Reprint. Berkley (1,200,000)

Gone, But Not Forgotten. Philip Margolin. Reprint. Bantam

Texas Sunrise. Fern Michaels. Original. Ballantine (1,123,443)

Like Water for Chocolate. Laura Esquivel. Reprint. Anchor/Doubleday (1,111,248)

The Stand. Stephen King. Reprint/TV tie-in. Signet (1,100,131)

Vampire Lestat. Anne Rice. Reprint. Ballantine (1,114,947)

Bad Love. Jonathan Kellerman. Reprint. Bantam

Hilltowns. Anne Rivers Siddons. Reprint HarperCollins (1,102,000)

Born in Fire. Nora Roberts. Original. Berkley (1,100,000)

A Simple Plan. Scott Smith. Reprint. St. Martin's (1,100,000)

Gai Jin. James Clavell. Reprint. Del (1,100,000)

Smilla's Sense of Snow. Peter Hoeg. Reprint Dell (1,100,000)

Saving Grace. Julie Garwood. Reprint. Pocket (1,091,000)

The Red Horseman. Stephen Coonts. Reprint Pocket (1,087,400)

Natural Causes. Michael Palmer. Reprint Bantam

The Night Manager. John le Carré. Reprint Ballantine (1,039,821)

Rebel Bride. Catherine Coulter. Original Topaz (1,000,445)

Finnegan's Week. Joseph Wambaugh Reprint. Bantam

The Pelican Brief. John Grisham. Reprint Movie tie-in edition. Dell (1,000,000)

Oprah! Up Close and Down Home. Nellie Bly. Original. Pinnacle (1,000,000)

Chase the Wind. Janelle Taylor. Reprint Zebra (1,000,000)

In the Presence of Enemies. William Coughlin. Reprint. St. Martin's (1,000,000)

Hidden Fires. Sandra Brown. Reprint. Warner (1,000,000)

Thunder Point. Jack Higgins. Reprint. Berkley (1,000,000)

Private Scandals. Nora Roberts. Reprint Berkley (1,000,000)

Almanacs, Atlases, and Annuals

The World Almanac and Book of Facts, 1995 Edited by Robert Famighetti. Original World Almanac (1,965,000)

The World Almanac and Book of Facts 1994. Edited by Robert Famighetti. Original. World Almanac (1,830,000)

J.K. Lasser's Your Income Tax 1995. The J Lasser Institute. Original. Macmillan (595,000)

The 1994 Information Please Almanac Original. Houghton Mifflin (302,463)

*The Ernst & Young Tax Guide 1994. Ernst & Young. Original. Wiley (265,692)

The Old Farmer's Almanac 1995 Edition. Edited by Judson D. Hale. Original. Random House (207,533)

The 1994 Christmas Ideals. Ideals Editors. Ideals (152,135)

1995 Sports Almanac. Sports Illustrated. Original. Little, Brown (126,925)

The 1995 Official Price Guide to Baseball Cards, 14th Edition. James Beckett. Original. House of Collectibles (112,714)

*The 1994 Information Please Sports Almanac. Original. Houghton Mifflin (104,421)

Peterson's Guide to Four-Year Colleges 1995. Original. Peterson's (102,000)

The Complete Guide to Prescription and Non-Prescription Drugs 1995. H. Winter Griffith. Original. Berkley (101,000)

H&R Block Income Tax Guide. H&R Block. Original. Fireside (100,000)

*The 1994 What Color Is Your Parachute. Richard Nelson Bolles. Original. Ten Speed (97,000)

Birnbaum's Walt Disney World: The Official 1995 Guide. Birnbaum Travel Guides. Original. Hyperion (96,585)

Kovels' Antiques and Collectibles Price List 1994. Ralph and Terry Kovel. Original. Crown (94,426)

Best American Short Stories 1994. Edited by Tobias Wolff. Original. Houghton Mifflin (89,059)

*Knock 'em Dead, 1994 Edition. Martin Yate. Adams (88,444)

People Entertainment Almanac. Editors at People. Original. Little, Brown (81,839)

The 1995 Official Blackbook Price Guide of U.S. Coins. Marc Rudgeons, Jr. Original. House of Collectibles (78,417)

*The 1994 Complete Guide to Prescription and Non-Prescription Drugs. H. Winter Griffith. Original. Berkley (78,000)

The 1995 Essential Guide to Prescription Drugs. James W. Long and James J. Rybacki. Original. HarperReference (76,097)

Hugh Johnson's Pocket Encyclopedia of Wine '95. Hugh Johnson. Original. Fireside (55,000)

Children's Books: Lion King Roars, Goosebumps Soar

Diane Roback
Children's Book Editor, Publishers Weekly

Lions and rangers and goosebumps, oh my! As this year's figures attest, nothing sells a children's book faster than a Hollywood or TV tie-in—that is, unless the cover has the word "Goosebumps" on it. And since a Goosebumps TV show is scheduled to debut in fall 1995, the series certainly won't be heading to the graveyard anytime soon.

For this roundup, publishers supplied sales figures for frontlist hardcovers that sold more than 75,000 copies in 1994; frontlist paperbacks and backlist hardcovers that sold more than 100,000 copies; and backlist paperbacks that sold more than 125,000 copies. We asked publishers to supply trade sales figures only, reflecting returns as of February 1. Since figures do not include total returns, they consequently do not necessarily represent net sales. Some books appear without sales figures; these were submitted to PW in confidence, for use only in ranking the titles.

An Improving Picture

The good news: hardcover sales are up. In 1994, 59 new hardcovers sold more than 75,000 copies, compared to 48 titles in 1993. And in backlist, 75 hardcovers sold more than 100,000 copies, compared with only 47 titles that performed that well in 1993. Granted, that doesn't constitute a hardcover explosion, but in light of recent flat or decreasing results, the rise in numbers is a welcome sign.

Paperback sales were also up: 130 new paperbacks sold in excess of 100,000 copies last year, compared with 90 titles that did that well in 1993. Paperback backlist remained about the same, with 106 titles selling more than 125,000 copies, compared with 101 titles in 1993.

The year's big winner has to be Scholastic, whose white-hot Goosebumps series by R.L. Stine has hit the paperback jackpot. Goosebumps titles nabbed 13 of the top 15 paperback frontlist spots, and 13 of the top 15 paperback backlist spots as well. In 1994, there were 13 new Goosebumps titles released; each sold more than 500,000 copies, or 8,180,000 copies in total. Goosebumps titles from 1993 (the year of their debut) sold 5,700,000 copies in 1994, for a grand Goosebumps total of 13,880,000 copies sold. Spooktacular!

The only other phenomenon that approached those kinds of numbers were the tie-in editions to *The Lion King*, 1994's top-grossing movie—hardcovers and paperbacks combined for just under 10 million copies sold. Titles from older Disney movies are still going strong, and TV's Barney and Mighty Morphin Power Rangers chalked up remarkable numbers as well.

R.L. Stine's other series, Fear Street, sold just under three million frontlist copies in total, plus more than a million backlist copies. And Christopher Pike is no piker, either, with more than one million assorted paperback frontlist titles sold.

The Baby-sitters Club, while selling slower than during its heyday a few years ago, still turned in respectable numbers, as did a few other series aimed at girls, including Sweet Valley University and American Girls. And to prove the endurance of the series genre, in hardcover backlist you can find the first Hardy Boys and first Nancy Drew titles (from 1927 and 1930)—still popular more than 60 years later.

Elsewhere on the lists, the tried and true prevail: Dr. Seuss books, Newbery titles in paperback, familiar authors like Jan Brett, Margaret Wise Brown, and Shel Silverstein. It's good to see hardcover hits of recent years show their staying power, such as *Stellaluna* and *Mama, Do You Love Me?* Two new hardcovers by first-timers made the list: *Ship of Dreams* and *Miss Spider's Tea Party*, as did Dolly Parton's first effort for children, *Coat of Many Colors*. And *The Rainbow Fish* continues its extraordinary run, with 469,900 copies sold of the 1992 title (its 1994 followup, *Dazzle the Dinosaur*, sold 135,520 copies as well).

Looking at 1994 in review, publishers can take heart. Though the industry has experienced a seemingly downtrodden mood in recent months, this year's compilation of figures contains several bright spots that hopefully point to continued success.

Hardcover Frontlist Bestsellers

200,000+

1. *The Lion King* (Classic). Disney/Mouse Works (3,094,450)
2. *The Lion King* (Little Golden Book). Justine Korman, illus. by D. Williams and H.R. Russell. Golden (2,635,900)

3. *The Lion King* (Big Golden Book). Justine Korman, illus. by H.R. Russell. Golden (533,900)

4. *Simba Roars!* Disney/Mouse Works (455,629)

5. *Aladdin's Magic Carpet Ride.* T. Slater Margulies. Golden (351,700)

6. *The Christmas Bunny.* Arnold Rabin, illus. by Carolyn Ewing. Golden (348,500)

7. *The Lion King Illustrated Classic.* Illus. by Michael Humphries and Marshall Toomey. Disney (324,450)

8. *The Lion King* (Sturdy Shape). Mary Packard, illus. by Darrell Baker. Golden (307,800)

9. *The Sorcerer's Apprentice.* Don Ferguson. Golden (261,300)

10. *The Very Hungry Caterpillar Board Book.* Eric Carle. Philomel (255,864)

11. *The Lion King* (Little Library). Disney/Mouse Works (233,600)

12. *The Fox and the Hound.* (Classic) Disney/Mouse Works (219,133)

13. *A Day with Barney.* Mary Ann Dudko and Margie Larsen. Lyons/Barney (212,711)

100,000+

14. *I Spy Fantasy.* Jean Marzollo, photos by Walter Wick. Cartwheel (196,000)

15. *Winnie the Pooh and the Honey Tree.* Mary Packard. Golden (194,600)

16. *The Flintstones Movie Storybook.* Wendy Larson. Grosset & Dunlap (178,174)

17. *The Magic School Bus in the Time of the Dinosaurs.* Joanna Cole, illus. by Bruce Degen. Scholastic (155,000)

18. *Find Simba.* Disney/Mouse Works (151,593)

19. *Town Mouse Country Mouse.* Jan Brett. Putnam (147,142)

20. *The Lion King* (Interlocking). Disney/Mouse Works (143,926)

21. *Barney's Imagination Island.* Adapted by Stephen White. Lyons/Barney (143,066)

22. *Coat of Many Colors.* Dolly Parton, illus. by Judith Sutton. HarperCollins (142,189)

23. *Winnie the Pooh* (Classic). Disney/Mouse Works (140,094)

24. *Dazzle the Dinosaur.* Marcus Pfister. North-South (135,520)

25. *Baby Bop's Foods.* Mary Ann Dudko and Margie Larsen. Lyons/Barney (130,176)

26. *Alpha Bugs.* David A. Carter. Little Simon (129,912)

27. *Ship of Dreams.* Dean Morrissey. Abrams (129,000)

28. *Barnyard Dance.* Sandra Boynton. Workman (122,578)

29. *Frosty the Snowman.* Rebecca Bondor, illus. by Josie Yee. Golden (121,200)

30. *Squeak Abu!* Disney/Mouse Works (120,655)

31. *Simba's New Home.* Disney/Mouse Works (113,847)

32. *The Children's Illustrated Bible*. Retold by Selina Hastings, illus. by Eric Thomas. Dorling Kindersley (108,300)
33. *The Lion King Pop-Up Book*. Illus. by Philippe Harchy. Disney (106,105)
34. *Winnie the Pooh: All Year Long*. Walt Disney. Golden (103,600)
35. *Barney's Wonderful Winter Day*. Stephen White. Lyons/Barney (103,260)
36. *Red Ranger Came Calling*. Berkeley Breathed. Little, Brown (102,223)
37. *American Heritage Dictionary*. Houghton Mifflin (100,832)
38. *The Cat Next Door*. Elizabeth Koda-Callen. Workman (100,206)

75,000+

39. *Peter Pan* (Classic). Disney/Mouse Works (97,119)
40. *Stephen Biesty's Cross-Sections: Castle*. Richard Plat, illus. by Stephen Biesty. Dorling Kindersley (96,000)
41. *Oh My, Oh My, Oh Dinosaurs*. Sandra Boynton. Workman (95,996)
42. *The Very Hungry Caterpillar 25th Anniversary Edition*. Eric Carle. Philomel (95,538)
43. *Uh, Oh Dopey!* Disney/Mouse Works (95,448)
44. *Barney and Baby Bop Follow That Cat!* Stephen White. Lyons/Barney (95,384)
45. *Baby Bop Goes to School*. Mark Bernthal. Lyons/Barney (91,717)
46. *The Lion King: Morning at Pride Rock*. Teddy Slater. Disney (89,735)
47. *What Can It Be? Stephen White*. Lyons/Barney (89,171)
48. *Time for Bed*. Mem Fox, illus. by Jane Dyer. Harcourt Brace (89,000)
49. *The Baby-sitters Club Secret Santa*. Ann M. Martin. Scholastic (87,000)
50. *Simba's Adventure*. Disney/Mouse Works (85,121)
51. *One, Two, Three!* Sandra Boynton. Workman (82,027)
52. *Morphin Power*. Disney/Fun Works (81,866)
53. *The Most Amazing Science Pop-Up Book*. Jay Young. HarperCollins (79,584)
54. *The Story of Christmas Story Book Set & Advent Calendar*. Workman (78,402)
55. *Carl Pops Up*. Alexandra Day. Little Simon (77,929)
56. *The Book That Jack Wrote*. Jon Scieszka, illus. by Dan Adel. Viking (77,770)
57. *Miss Spider's Tea Party*. David Kirk. Scholastic (76,000)
58. *Magic Merry Christmas*. Amye Rosenberg. Grosset & Dunlap (75,192)
59. *Polar the Titanic Bear*. Daisy Corning Stone Spedden, illus. by Laurie McGaw. Little, Brown (75,134)

Paperback Frontlist Bestsellers

200,000+

1. *The Lion King* (Look-Look Book). Margo Hover, illus. by Judy Barnes and Robbin Cuddy. Golden (1,576,900)
2. *Deep Trouble* (Goosebumps #19). R.L. Stine. Scholastic (734,000)
3. *One Day at Horror Land* (GB #16). R.L. Stine. Scholastic (723,000)
4. *The Scarecrow Walks at Midnight* (GB #20). R.L. Stine. Scholastic (702,000)
5. *Monster Blood II* (GB #18). R.L. Stine. Scholastic (691,000)
6. *Ghost Beach* (GB #22). R.L. Stine. Scholastic (677,000)
7. *Go Eat Worms!* (GB #21). R.L. Stine. Scholastic (625,000)
8. *Why I'm Afraid of Bees* (GB #17). R.L. Stine. Scholastic (622,000)
9. *Phantom of the Auditorium* (GB #24). R.L. Stine. Scholastic (611,000)
10. *My Hairiest Adventure* (GB #26). R.L. Stine. Scholastic (592,000)
11. *Return of the Mummy* (GB #23). R.L. Stine. Scholastic (579,000)
12. *Attack of the Mutant* (GB #25). R.L. Stine. Scholastic (559,000)
13. *The Werewolf of Fever Swamp* (GB #14). R.L. Stine. Scholastic (553,000)
14. *You Can't Scare Me!* (GB #15) R.L. Stine. Scholastic (512,000)
15. *Mighty Morphin Power Rangers: Megazord to the Rescue.* Cathy East Dubowski. Grosset & Dunlap (465,718)
16. *Mighty Morphin Power Rangers: Rita's Revenge.* Rusty Hailock. Grosset & Dunlap (459,189)
17. *Mighty Morphin Power Rangers: Terror Toad.* Jean Waricha. Grosset & Dunlap (456,437)
18. *Mighty Morphin Power Rangers: It's Morphin Time.* William McCay. Grosset & Dunlap (454,698)
19. *The Lion King Jr. Novel.* Gina Ingoglia. Disney (343,962)
20. *The Cheerleaders: The New Evil* (Fear Street Super Chiller). R.L. Stine. Pocket/Archway
21. *Enter the X-Men.* Marvel Comics. Random House (293,288)
22. *Remember Me 2.* Christopher Pike. Pocket/Archway
23. *Happy Birthday, Addy!* Connie Porter, illus. by Bradford Brown. Pleasant Co. (272,843)
24. *House of Evil: The Third Horror* (99 Fear Street). R.L. Stine. Pocket/Archway
25. *Addy Saves the Day.* Connie Porter, illus. by Bradford Brown. Pleasant Co. (261,030)
26. *Here's to You, Rachel Robinson.* Judy Blume. Dell (249,041)
27. *The Midnight Club.* Christopher Pike. Pocket/Archway
28. *House of Evil: The Second Horror* (99 Fear Street). R.L. Stine. Pocket/Archway

29. *The Giver*. Lois Lowry. Dell (243,747)
30. *Wrong Number 2* (Fear Street). R.L. Stine. Pocket/Archway
31. *Morlock Madness*. Marvel Comics. Random House (240,313)
32. *Silent Night 2* (Fear Street Super Chiller). R.L. Stine. Pocket/Archway
33. *Barney Says "Please and Thank You."* Stephen White. Lyons/Barney (228,523)
34. *The Baby-sitters Remember* (Baby-sitters Club Super Special #11). Ann M. Martin. Scholastic (228,000)
35. *House of Evil: The First Horror* (99 Fear Street). R.L. Stine. Pocket/ Archway
36. *The Mind Reader* (Fear Street). R.L. Stine. Pocket/Archway
37. *The Dead Lifeguard* (Fear Street Super Chiller). R.L. Stine. Pocket/Archway
38. *Bad Dreams* (Fear Street). R.L. Stine. Pocket/Archway
39. *The Beast*. R.L. Stine. Pocket/Archway
40. *The Last Vampire*. Christopher Pike. Pocket/Archway
41. *The Last Vampire 2*. Christopher Pike. Pocket/Archway
42. *One Evil Summer* (Fear Street). R.L. Stine. Pocket/Archway
43. *Call Waiting*. R.L. Stine. Scholastic (214,000)
44. *Double Date* (Fear Street). R.L. Stine. Pocket/Archway
45. *The Thrill Club* (Fear Street). R.L. Stine. Pocket/Archway
46. *Mighty Morphin Power Rangers: Super Zords*. Jean Waricha. Grosset & Dunlap (211,826)
47. *Mighty Morphin Power Rangers: Bad Dream Machine*. Cathy East Dubowski. Grosset & Dunlap (210,073)
48. *Mighty Morphin Power Rangers: Bumble Beast*. Harriet Gray. Grosset & Dunlap (209,763)
49. *Mighty Morphin Power Rangers: Putty Attack*. Francine Hughes. Grosset & Dunlap (209,147)
50. *The Lion, the Witch and the Wardrobe*. C.S. Lewis. HarperCollins (207,957)
51. *The Dare* (Fear Street). R.L. Stine. Pocket/Archway
52. *The New Boy* (Fear Street). R.L. Stine. Pocket/Archway
53. *The Mystery of the Cupboard*. Lynne Reid Banks. Avon/Camelot (203,810)
54. *The Wicked Heart*. Christopher Pike. Pocket/Archway
55. *Changes for Addy*. Connie Porter, illus. by Bradford Brown. Pleasant Co. (198,388)
56. *I Saw You That Night!* R.L. Stine. Scholastic (198,000)
57. *Baby Bop Pretends*. Mary Ann Dudko and Margie Larsen. Lyons/Barney (180,348)
58. *The Berenstain Bears' New Neighbors*. Stan and Jan Berenstain. Random House (178,109)
59. *What Your Parents Don't Know* (Sweet Valley University #3). Francine Pascal. Bantam (171,165)

60. *Anything for Love* (SVU #4). Francine Pascal. Bantam (170,859)
61. *Mary Anne and Miss Priss* (BSC #73). Ann M. Martin. Scholastic (160,000)
62. *Night of Sentinels.* Marvel Comics. Random House (158,799)
63. *Stacey's Lie* (BSC #76). Ann M. Martin. Scholastic (158,000)
64. *The Flintstones: Big Time in Bedrock.* Wendy Larson. Grosset &Dunlap (157,177)
65. *Elmo's Big Lift & Look Book.* Random House (157,021)
66. *The Flintstones: Yabba Dabba Doo.* Wendy Larson. Grosset & Dunlap (156,124)
67. *To Stop a Juggernaut.* Marvel Comics. Random House (154,749
68. *Halloween Night II.* R.L. Stine. Scholastic (153,000)
69. *Kristy and the Copycat* (BSC #74). Ann M. Martin. Scholastic (153,000)
70. *Jessi's Horrible Prank* (BSC #75). Ann M. Martin. Scholastic (152,000)
71. *The Magic School Bus on the Ocean Floor.* Joanna Cole, illus. by Bruce Degen. Scholastic (152,000)
72. *Stacey and the Mystery at the Mall* (BSC Mystery #14). Ann M. Martin. Scholastic (152,000)
73. *Where's Spot?* Eric Hill. Puffin (150,177)
74. *Poky's Busy Counting Book.* Rita Balducci. Golden (149,000)
75. *Here Come the Bridesmaids!* (BSC Super Special #12) Ann M. Martin. Scholastic (148,000)
76. *Just Me & My Mom.* Mercer Mayer. Golden (146,600)
77. *Dawn and the We Love Kids Club* (BSC #72). Ann M. Martin. Scholastic (146,000)
78. *Kristy and the Vampires* (BSC Mystery #15). Ann M. Martin. Scholastic (142,000)
79. *Just Me in the Tub.* Mercer Mayer. Golden (140,800)
80. *The Love of Her Life* (SVU #6). Francine Pascal. Bantam (139,616)
81. *The Flintstones: The Novelization.* Francine Hughes. Grosset & Dunlap (138,440)
82. *Tales to Give You Goosebumps* (book and light set). R.L. Stine. Scholastic (136,000)
83. *Almost Married* (Sweet Valley High #102). Francine Pascal. Bantam (135,448)
84. *It Happened to Nancy.* Anonymous. Avon/Flare (135,224)
85. *Beware of the Wolfman.* Francine Pascal. Bantam (135,053)
86. *Mallory Pike, #1 Fan* (BSC #80). Ann M. Martin. Scholastic (134,000)
87. *Mary Anne and the Library Mystery* (BSC Mystery #13). Ann M. Martin. Scholastic (134,000)
88. *A Married Woman* (SVU #5). Francine Pascal. Bantam (132,023)
89. *Claudia and Crazy Peaches* (BSC #78). Scholastic (132,000)
90. *Karen's Lucky Penny* (BSLS #50). Ann M. Martin. Scholastic (131,000)

91. *Stacey and the Mystery at the Empty House* (BSC Mystery #18). Ann M. Martin. Scholastic (131,000)

92. *Left at the Altar* (SVH #108). Francine Pascal. Bantam (130,397)

93. *Dawn and Whitney, Friends Forever* (BSC #77). Ann M. Martin. Scholastic (129,000)

94. *Mary Anne Breaks the Rules* (BSC #79). Ann M. Martin. Scholastic (129,000)

95. *A Deadly Christmas* (SVH #111). Francine Pascal. Bantam (128,932)

96. *Home for Christmas* (SVU #8). Francine Pascal. Bantam (128,292)

97. *Little Women*. Laurie Lawlor. Pocket/Minstrel

98. *Operation Love Match* (SVH #103). Francine Pascal. Bantam (126,630)

99. *Clifford's First Christmas*. Norman Bridwell. Scholastic (126,000)

100. *Clifford's Happy Easter*. Norman Bridwell. Scholastic (126,000)

101. *Claudia and the Clue in the Photograph* (BSC Mystery #16). Ann M. Martin. Scholastic (123,000)

102. *Love and Death in London* (SVH #104). Francine Pascal. Bantam (122,873)

103. *Aliens Ate My Homework*. Bruce Coville, illus. by Katherine Coville. Pocket/Minstrel

104. *The Berenstain Bears and the Bully*. Stan and Jan Berenstain. Random House (119,661)

105. *The Bones & Skeleton Game Book*. Karen Anderson & Stephen Cumbaa. Workman (116,846)

106. *Good-Bye to Love* (SVU #7). Francine Pascal. Bantam (115,975)

107. *Jessica's Secret Love* (SVH #107). Francine Pascal. Bantam (115,297)

108. *The Magician's Nephew*. C.S. Lewis. HarperCollins (115,037)

109. *A Date with a Werewolf* (SVH #105). Francine Pascal. Bantam (114,586)

110. *Dawn and the Halloween Mystery* (BSC Mystery #17). Ann M. Martin. Scholastic (113,000)

111. *Horrors of the Haunted Museum* (Twist-a-Plot). R.L. Stine. Scholastic (113,000)

112. *Mighty Morphin: Ultimate Play Set*. Michi Fujimoto, illus. by Greg Winter. Price Stern Sloan (112,461)

113. *Karen's Kite* (BSLS #47). Ann M. Martin. Scholastic (112,000)

114. *Where's Waldo? The Dazzling Deep-Sea Divers Sticker Book*. Martin Handford.Candlewick (110,780)

115. *Karen's Stepmother* (BSLS #49). Ann M. Martin. Scholastic (109,000)

116. *Shannon's Story* (BSC Special Edition). Ann M. Martin. Scholastic (109,000)

117. *Elizabeth's Secret Diary* (SVH). Francine Pascal. Bantam (107,698)

118. *Dear Mr. Henshaw*. Beverly Cleary. Avon/Camelot (106,513)

119. *Enter Magneto*. Marvel Comics. Random House (105,815)

120. *Todd Runs Away* (Sweet Valley Twins #77). Francine Pascal. Bantam (103,997)
121. *101 Dalmatians* (Look-Look Book). Mary Fulton. Golden (103,700)
122. *Little Farm in the Ozarks*. Roger MacBride. HarperCollins (103,640)
123. *Jessica's Secret Diary* (SVH). Francine Pascal. Bantam (103,519)
124. *Stacey's Book* (BSC Portrait Collection). Ann M. Martin. Scholastic (103,000)
125. *Death Threat* (SVH #110). Francine Pascal. Bantam (102,137)
126. *Clifford the Firehouse Dog*. Norman Bridwell. Scholastic (102,000)
127. *Karen's Two Families* (BSLS #48). Ann M. Martin. Scholastic (102,000)
128. *Days of Future Past*. Marvel Comics. Random House (101,715)
129. *Timothy of the Cay*. Theodore Taylor. Avon/Flare (100,611)
130. *Where's Waldo? The Fabulous Flying Carpets Sticker Book*. Martin Handford. Candlewick (100,363)

Hardcover Backlist Bestsellers

200,000+

1. *The Poky Little Puppy's First Christmas*. Justine Korman, illus. by Jean Chandler. Golden, 1993 (477,200)
2. *The Rainbow Fish*. Marcus Pfister. North-South, 1992 (469,900)
3. *Aladdin*. Karen Kreider, illus. by Darrell Baker. Golden, 1992 (460,800)
4. *Snow White and the Seven Dwarfs*. Walt Disney. Golden, 1984 (458,400)
5. *Green Eggs & Ham*. Dr. Seuss. Random House, 1966 (446,755)
6. *Barney Goes to the Zoo*. Linda Cress Dowdy. Lyons/Barney, 1993 (420,417)
7. *Snow White and the Seven Dwarfs* (Classic). Disney/Mouse Works, 1990 (391,367)
8. *Oh, the Places You'll Go*. Dr. Seuss. Random House, 1990 (385,785)
9. *Barney's Favorite Mother Goose Rhymes, Vol. 2*. Stephen White. Lyons/Barney, 1993 (384,211)
10. *Barney's Favorite Mother Goose Rhymes, Vol.1*. Stephen White. Lyons/Barney, 1993 (380,430)
11. *One Fish, Two Fish*. Dr. Seuss. Random House, 1966 (363,021)
12. *The Cat in the Hat*. Dr. Seuss. Random House, 1966 (352,820)
13. *Barney's Color Surprise*. Mary Ann Dudko and Margie Larsen. Lyons/Barney, 1993 (346,159)
14. *Dr. Seuss ABC Book*. Dr. Seuss. Random House, 1966 (286,770)
15. *Goodnight Moon* (board book). Margaret Wise Brown, illus. by Clement Hurd. HarperCollins, 1991 (283,792)
16. *The Teapot's Tale*. Justine Korman. Golden, 1993 (275,100)
17. *Where the Sidewalk Ends*. Shel Silverstein. HarperCollins, 1974 (274,568)
18. *101 Dalmatians*. Justine Korman. Golden, 1991 (274,300)

19. *Hop on Pop. Dr.* Seuss. Random House, 1966 (274,073)
20. *The Jungle Book.* Rudyard Kipling, illus. by Walt Disney. Golden, 1967 (265,500)
21. *The Giving Tree.* Shel Silverstein. HarperCollins, 1964 (255,865)
22. *Prayers for Children.* Illus. by Eloise Wilkin. Golden, 1952 (253,100)
23. *Baby Bop's Counting Book.* Mary Ann Dudko and Margie Larsen. Lyons/Barney, 1993 (248,343)
24. *Are You My Mother?* P.D. Eastman. Random House, 1960 (236,823)
25. *Happy, Sad, Grouchy, and Glad.* Constance Allen. Golden, 1992 (231,600)
26. *Pat the Bunny.* Dorothy and Edith Kunhardt. Golden, 1993 (230,000)
27. *My First Counting Book.* Lilian Moore, illus. by Garth Williams. Golden, 1956 (220,900)
28. *Barney's Farm Animals.* Kimberly Kearns and Marie O'Brien. Lyons/Barney, 1993 (218,087)
29. *The Cat in the Hat Comes Back.* Dr. Seuss. Random House, 1966 (217,237)
30. *The Polar Express.* Chris Van Allsburg. Houghton Mifflin, 1985 (211,056)
31. *Chip the Teacup.* Betty Birney, illus. by Mones and Edward Gutierrez. Golden, 1992 (200,100)

100,000+

32. *Go, Dog, Go!* P.D. Eastman. Random House, 1966 (198,199)
33. *Light in the Attic.* Shel Silverstein. HarperCollins, 1981 (193,246)
34. *The Little Mermaid.* Michael Teitelbaum, illus. by Sue DiCicco. Golden, 1992 (185,600)
35. *Fox in Socks.* Dr. Seuss. Random House, 1966 (185,342)
36. *Beauty and the Beast* (Classic). Disney/Mouse Works, 1991 (181,796)
37. *Snuggle Up with Winnie the Pooh.* Disney/Mouse Works, 1993 (181,478)
38. *Baby Bop Discovers Shapes.* Stephen White. Lyons/Barney, 1993 (180,543)
39. *Aladdin* (Classic). Disney/Mouse Works, 1992 (177,511)
40. *The Velveteen Rabbit.* Margery Williams, illus. by Judith Sutton. Golden, 1992 (175,100)
41. *The Poky Little Puppy.* Janette Sebring Lowrey, illus. by Gustaf Tenggren. Golden, 1942 (158,600)
42. *Thomas the Tank Engine and the Freight Train.* Rev. W. Awdry. Random House, 1991 (154,358)
43. *Stellaluna.* Janell Cannon. Harcourt Brace, 1993 (150,000)
44. *Jack and the Beanstalk.* Rita Balducci, illus. by Richard Walz. Golden, 1992 (149,800)
45. *If You Give a Mouse a Cookie.* Laura Numeroff, illus. by Felicia Bond. HarperCollins, 1985 (145,199)
46. *The Little Engine That Could* (original edition). Watty Piper, illus. by George and Doris Hauman. Platt & Munk, 1978 (142,282)

47. *Runaway Bunny* (board book). Margaret Wise Brown. HarperCollins, 1991 (141,297)

48. *The Giver.* Lois Lowry. Houghton Mifflin, 1993 (136,151)

49. *The Little Mermaid* (Classic). Disney/Mouse Works, 1991 (135,956)

50. *Follow That Squeak with Mickey Mouse.* Disney/Mouse Works, 1993 (134,217)

51. *Put Me in the Zoo.* Robert Lopshire. Random House, 1960 (128,594)

52. *I Can Read with My Eyes Shut.* Dr. Seuss. Random House, 1978 (126,362)

53. *Mama, Do You Love Me?* Barbara Joosse, illus. by Barbara Lavellee. Chronicle, 1991 (126,155)

54. *Grandfather's Journey.* Allen Say. Houghton Mifflin, 1993 (123,861)

55. *I Spy Christmas.* Jean Marzollo, photos by Walter Wick. Cartwheel, 1992 (123,000)

56. *101 Dalmatians* (Classic). Disney/Mouse Works, 1991 (122,465)

57. *Baby Bop's Toys.* Kimberly Kearns and Marie O'Brien. Lyons/Barney, 1993 (120,770)

58. *The Tower Treasure* (Hardy Boys #1). Franklin W. Dixon. Grosset & Dunlap, 1927 (120,286)

59. *The Secret of the Old Clock* (Nancy Drew #1). Carolyn Keene. Grosset & Dunlap, 1930 (118,025)

60. *The Jungle Book* (Classic). Disney/Mouse Works, 1990 (117,912)

61. *Thomas Gets Tricked.* Rev. W. Awdry. Random House, 1989 (116,151)

62. *The Stinky Cheese Man.* Jon Scieszka, illus. by Lane Smith. Viking, 1992 (115,769)

63. *Thomas's Noisy Trip.* Rev. W. Awdry. Random House, 1989 (114,517)

64. *How the Grinch Stole Christmas.* Dr. Seuss. Random House, 1966 (111,895)

65. *Cinderella* (Classic). Disney/Mouse Works, 1991 (110,411)

66. *The Hidden Staircase* (Nancy Drew #2). Carolyn Keene. Grosset & Dunlap, 1930 (110,068)

67. *Oh, the Thinks You Can Think!* Dr. Seuss. Random House, 1975 (109,181)

68. *Old Turtle.* Douglas Wood, illus. by Cheng-Khee Chee. Pfeifer-Hamilton, 1991 (107,181)

69. *The House on the Cliff* (Hardy Boys #2). Franklin W. Dixon, Grosset & Dunlap, 1927 (106,051)

70. *Pinocchio* (Classic). Disney/Mouse Works, 1992 (102,030)

71. *Oh, Say Can You Say?* Dr. Seuss. Random House, 1979 (101,807)

72. *I Spy.* Jean Marzollo, photos by Walter Wick. Cartwheel, 1992 (101,000)

73. *The Magic Locket.* Elizabeth Koda-Callen. Workman, 1988 (100,057)

74. *Elmo's Guessing Game.* Constance Allen. Golden, 1993 (100,000)

75. *The Rainbabies.* Laura Krauss Melmed, illus. by Jim LaMarche. Morrow, 1992 (100,000)

Paperback Backlist Bestsellers

200,000+

1. *Say Cheese and Die* (Goosebumps #4). R.L. Stine. Scholastic, 1992 (642,000)
2. *Welcome to Dead House* (GB #1). R.L. Stine. Scholastic, 1992 (635,000)
3. *Tent Too Full.* Stephen White. Lyons/Barney, 1993 (625,763)
4. *Monster Blood.* (GB #3) R.L. Stine. Scholastic, 1992 (590,000)
5. *Stay Out of the Basement* (GB #2). R.L. Stine. Scholastic, 1992 (573,000)
6. *Curse of the Mummy's Tomb* (GB #5). R.L. Stine. Scholastic, 1993 (539,000)
7. *Welcome to Camp Nightmare* (GB #9). R.L. Stine. Scholastic, 1993 (513,000)
8. *Piano Lessons Can Be Murder* (GB #13). R.L. Stine. Scholastic, 1993 (502,000)
9. *The Ghost Next Door* (GB #10). R.L. Stine. Scholastic, 1993 (485,000)
10. *Let's Get Invisible!* (GB #6) R.L. Stine. Scholastic, 1993 (479,000)
11. *Baby Bop's ABCs.* Mark Bernthal. Lyons/Barney, 1993 (470,838)
12. *Be Careful What You Wish For* (GB #12). R.L. Stine. Scholastic, 1993 (468,000)
13. *The Haunted Mask* (GB #11). R.L. Stine. Scholastic, 1993 (443,000)
14. *The Girl Who Cried Monster* (GB #8). R.L. Stine. Scholastic, 1993 (425,000)
15. *Night of the Living Dummy* (GB #7). R.L. Stine. Scholastic, 1993 (410,000)
16. *Meet Addy.* Connie Porter, illus. by Melodye Rosales. Pleasant Co., 1993 (333,977)
17. *Addy Learns a Lesson.* Connie Porter, illus. by Melodye Rosales. Pleasant Co., 1993 (304,262)
18. *Addy's Surprise.* Connie Porter, illus. by Melodye Rosales. Pleasant Co., 1993 (289,069)
19. *The Outsiders.* S.E. Hinton. Dell, 1968 (288,556)
20. *Charlotte's Web.* E.B. White, illus. by Garth Williams. HarperCollins, 1974 (282,462)
21. *Merry Christmas, Mom & Dad.* Mercer Mayer. Golden, 1982 (273,500)
22. *The Indian in the Cupboard.* Lynne Reid Banks. Avon/Camelot, 1982 (238,291)
23. *Bridge to Terabithia.* Katherine Paterson. HarperCollins, 1987 (234,631)
24. *Island of the Blue Dolphins.* Scott O'Dell. Dell, 1987 (232,913)
25. *Number the Stars.* Lois Lowry. Dell, 1990 (231,097)
26. *Roll of Thunder, Hear My Cry.* Mildred Taylor. Puffin, 1991 (229,355)
27. *Just Me & My Dad.* Mercer Mayer. Golden, 1977 (226,400)
28. *Sarah, Plain and Tall.* Patricia MacLachlan. HarperCollins, 1987 (223,413)
29. *Where the Red Fern Grows.* Wilson Rawls. Bantam, 1984 (221,873)

30. *Snow White and the Seven Dwarfs.* Rita Balducci, illus. by Don Williams. Golden, 1992 (219,900)
31. *Where the Wild Things Are.* Maurice Sendak. HarperCollins, 1988 (213,814)
32. *Sesame Street: Merry Christmas, Everybody.* Constance Allen, illus. by David Prebenna. Golden (213,100)
33. *Meet Kirsten.* Janet Shaw, illus. by Renee Graef. Pleasant Co., 1986 (212,072)
34. *Meet Samantha.* Susan Adler, illus. by Nancy Niles. Pleasant Co., 1986 (211,437)
35. *The Bones Book & Skeleton.* Stephen Cumbaa. Workman, 1993 (207,587)
36. *The Sign of the Beaver.* Elizabeth Speare. Dell, 1983 (207,409)
37. *Amelia Bedelia.* Peggy Parish, illus. by Fritz Seibel. HarperCollins, 1992 (206,180)
38. *The Boxcar Children.* Gertrude Chandler Warner. Albert Whitman, 1989 (206,128)
39. *Little House on the Prairie.* Laura Ingalls Wilder, illus. by Garth Williams. HarperCollins, 1971 (206,043)
40. *The Genie's Tale.* Karen Kreider. Golden, 1993 (201,600)

150,000+

41. *Hatchet.* Gary Paulsen. Puffin, 1988 (191,303)
42. *Barney's Hats.* Mary Ann Dudko & Margie Larsen. Lyons/Barney, 1993 (190,944)
43. *Goodnight Moon.* Margaret Wise Brown, illus. by Clement Hurd. HarperCollins, 1977 (180,353)
44. *A Wrinkle in Time.* Madeleine L'Engle. Dell, 1973 (177,517)
45. *Stone Fox.* John Reynolds Gardiner, illus. by Marcia Sewall. HarperCollins, 1983 (171,650)
46. *Merry Christmas Mystery.* Betty Birney, illus. by Nancy Stevenson. Golden, 1993 (170,800)
47. *The Zoo Book.* Jan Pfloog. Golden, 1967 (170,700)
48. *Meet Felicity.* Valerie Tripp, illus. by Dan Andreasen. Pleasant Co., 1991 (168,912)
49. *Samantha Learns a Lesson.* Susan Adler, illus. by Nancy Niles and Robert Grace. Pleasant Co., 1986 (168,736)
50. *I Was So Mad.* Mercer Mayer. Golden, 1985 (165,600)
51. *Samantha's Surprise.* Maxine Rose Schur, illus. by Nancy Niles and Robert Grace. Pleasant Co., 1986 (163,550)
52. *Shiloh.* Phyllis Reynolds Naylor. Dell, 1992 (163,314)
53. *The Berenstain Bears Learn About Strangers.* Stan and Jan Berenstain. Random House, 1985 (162,995)
54. *Christmas Carol.* Jim Henson Productions. Golden, 1993 (162,500)

55. *Where Are My Shoes?* Mary Ann Dudko and Margie Larsen. Lyons/Barney, 1993 (162,264)
56. *The Berenstain Bears Forget Their Manners.* Stan and Jan Berenstain. Random House, 1985 (161,706)
57. *The Berenstain Bears' New Baby.* Stan and Jan Berenstain. Random House, 1974 (160,515)
58. *Kirsten Learns a Lesson.* Janet Shaw, illus. by Renee Graef. Pleasant Co., 1986 (159,814)
59. *The New Baby.* Mercer Mayer. Golden, 1983 (158,700)
60. *Kirsten's Surprise.* Janet Shaw, illus. by Renee Graef. Pleasant Co., 1986 (158,663)
61. *Happy Birthday, Samantha.* Valerie Tripp, illus. by Robert Grace and Nancy Niles. Pleasant Co., 1987 (157,986)
62. *The Pigman.* Paul Zindel. Bantam, 1983 (157,139)
63. *Beauty and the Beast.* Rita Balducci. Golden, 1992 (156,200)
64. *Tales of a Fourth Grade Nothing.* Judy Blume. Dell, 1976 (154,341)
65. *Happy Birthday, Kirsten!* Janet Shaw, illus. by Renee Graef. Pleasant Co., 1987 (154,279)
66. *Snow White.* Teddy Slater. Golden, 1993 (153,500)
67. *The Berenstain Bears and the Bad Dream.* Stan and Jan Berenstain. Random House, 1988 (153,457)
68. *Samantha Saves the Day.* Valerie Tripp, illus. by Robert Grace and Nancy Niles. Pleasant Co., 1988 (152,326)
69. *Kirsten Saves the Day.* Janet Shaw, illus. by Renee Graef. Pleasant Co., 1988 (152,313)
70. *The Berenstain Bears and the Truth.* Stan and Jan Berenstain. Random House, 1983 (150,340)
71. *Changes for Samantha.* Valerie Tripp, illus. by Luann Roberts. Pleasant Co., 1988 (150,122)
72. *Scary Stories to Tell in the Dark.* Alvin Schwartz, illus. by Stephen Gammell. HarperCollins, 1986 (150,074)

125,000+

73. *The Book of Cards for Kids.* Gail MacColl. Workman, 1992 (149,803)
74. *Julie of the Wolves.* Jean Craighead George. HarperCollins, 1974 (149,632)
75. *The Farm Book.* Jan Pfloog. Golden, 1964 (148,500)
76. *Scary Stories 3: More Tales to Chill Your Bones.* Alvin Schwartz, illus. by Stephen Gammell. HarperCollins, 1991 (147,982)
77. *James and the Giant Peach.* Roald Dahl. Puffin, 1988 (147,748)
78. *Farm Animals Work Book.* Hans Helweg. Random House, 1984 (145,428)

79. *Ramona Quimby, Age 8.* Beverly Cleary. Avon/Camelot, 1992 (145,375)
80. *Meet Molly.* Valerie Tripp, illus. by Nick Backes. Pleasant Co., 1986 (145,291)
81. *The Truck Book.* Bill Gere, illus. by Tom LaPadula. Golden, 1987 (144,500)
82. *Knot Now.* Margaret Hartelius. Grosset & Dunlap, 1992 (144,328)
83. *Just Shopping with Mom.* Mercer Mayer. Golden, 1989 (144,100)
84. *Danny and the Dinosaur.* Syd Hoff. HarperCollins, 1978 (143,925)
85. *More Scary Stories to Tell in the Dark.* Alvin Schwartz, illus. by Stephen Gammell. HarperCollins, 1986 (143,785)
86. *The Berenstain Bears and the Messy Room.* Stan and Jan Berenstain. Random House, 1983 (142,655)
87. *Changes for Kirsten.* Janet Shaw, illus. by Renee Graef. Pleasant Co., 1988 (142,280)
88. *Sesame Street: Sleep Tight.* Constance Allen, illus. by David Prebenna. Golden, 1991 (141,300)
89. *Maniac Magee.* Jerry Spinelli. HarperCollins, 1992 (140,825)
90. *The Magic School Bus Lost in the Solar System.* Joanna Cole, illus. by Bruce Degen. Scholastic, 1992 (140,000)
91. *Noah's Ark.* Linda Hayward, illus. by Amy Flynn. Random House, 1993 (137,251)
92. *The Return of the Indian.* Lynne Reid Banks. Avon/Camelot, 1987 (136,748)
93. *Little Critter Trick or Treat.* Mercer Mayer. Golden, 1993 (133,500)
94. *Little House in the Big Woods.* Laura Ingalls Wilder, illus. by Garth Williams. HarperCollins, 1971 (132,726)
95. *Just Go to Bed.* Mercer Mayer. Golden, 1983 (131,900)
96. *My Side of the Mountain.* Jean Craighead George. Puffin, 1991 (131,396)
97. *Wonderful World—Precious Moments.* Illus. by John Kurtz. Golden, 1992 (130,800)
98. *The Berenstain Bears Go Out for the Team.* Stan and Jan Berenstain. Random House, 1987 (130,690)
99. *The True Confessions of Charlotte Doyle.* Avi. Avon/Flare, 1992 (130,151)
100. *A Cow on the Line.* Rev. W. Awdry. Random House, 1992 (129,442)
101. *Tuck Everlasting.* Natalie Babbitt. FSG, 1985 (129,436)
102. *Surprise Island* (Boxcar Children #2). Gertrude Chandler Warner. Albert Whitman, 1989 (129,257)
103. *Aladdin.* Ann Braybrooks, illus. by Phil Oritz and Serge Michaels. Golden, 1992 (128,900)
104. *Wrong Number* (Fear Street). R.L. Stine. Pocket/Archway, 1990
105. *The Baby-sitter.* R.L. Stine. Scholastic, 1989 (128,000)
106. *The Magic School Bus Inside the Human Body.* Joanna Cole, illus. by Bruce Degen. Scholastic, 1990 (126,000)

Literary Prizes, 1994

Gary Ink

Research Librarian, *Publishers Weekly*

ABBY Awards. To honor titles that members have most enjoyed hand-selling in the past year. *Offered by:* American Booksellers Association. *Winners:* (adult) Laura Esquivel for *Like Water for Chocolate* (Anchor Books); (children's) Janell Cannon for *Stellaluna* (Harcourt Brace).

Academy of American Poets Fellowship Award. For distinguished poetic achievement. *Offered by:* Academy of American Poets. *Winner:* David Ferry.

J. R. Ackerley Award (Great Britain). For autobiography. *Offered by:* PEN (UK). *Winner:* Blake Morrison for *And When Did You Last See Your Father?* (Granta).

American Academy of Arts and Letters Awards in Literature. *Offered by:* American Academy of Arts and Letters. *Winners:* (poetry) Marvin Bell, Chase Twichell; (fiction) Stuart Dybek, Mary Lee Settle, Geoffrey Wolff.

Hans Christian Andersen Awards. *Offered by:* International Board on Books for Young People (IBBY). *Winners:* (author) Michio Mado (Japan); (illustrator) Jorg Muller (Switzerland).

Bancroft Prizes. For books of exceptional merit and distinction in American history, American diplomacy, and the international relations of the United States. *Offered by:* Columbia University. *Winners:* Stanley Elkins and Eric McKitrick for *The Age of Federalism* (Oxford); Winthrop D. Jordan for *Tumult and Silence at Second Creek* (Louisiana State Univ. Press); David Levering Lewis for *W. E. B. Du Bois: The Biography of a Race, 1868–1919* (Henry Holt).

Mildred L. Batchelder Award. For an American publisher of a children's book originally published in a foreign language in a foreign country and subsequently published in English in the United States. *Offered by:* ALA Association for Library Service to Children. *Winner:* Farrar, Straus & Giroux for *The Apprentice*, by Pilar Molina.

James Beard Awards. For cookbooks. *Offered by:* James Beard Foundation. *Winners:* (cookbook of the year) Madhur Jaffrey for *Madhur Jaffrey's A Taste of the Far East* (Crown); (international) Madhur Jaffrey for *Madhur Jaffrey's A Taste of the Far East* (Crown); (entertaining and special occasions) Joe Famularo for *Celebrations* (Barron's) and Chuck Williams and Joyce Goldstein for *Festive Occasions Cookbook* (Weldon Owen); (convenience) Linda Gassenheimer for *Dinner in Minutes* (Chapters); (fruits, vegetables, and grains) Faye Levy for *Faye Levy's International Vegetable Cookbook* (Warner Books); (writings on food) Cathy Luchetti for *Home on the Range* (Villard Books); (Italian) Carol Field for *Italy in Small Bites* (Morrow); (healthy focus) Bonnie Sanders Polin and Frances Tower Giedt for *The Joselin Diabetes Gourmet Cookbook* (Bantam); (general) Rozanne Gold for *Little Meals* (Villard Books); (photography) Kathryn Kleinman and Christopher Idone for *Lemons: A Country Garden Cookbook* (Collins); (Americana) Nathalie Dupree for *Nathalie Dupree's Southern Memories* (Clarkson Potter); (single subject) Mel London and Sheryl London for *Seafood Celebration* (Simon & Schuster); (baking and desserts) George Greenstein for *Secrets of a Jewish Baker* (Crossing Press).

Curtis Benjamin Award for Creative Publishing. *Offered by:* Association of American Publishers. *Winner:* Margaret K. McElderry.

Helen B. Bernstein Award for Excellence in Journalism. *Offered by:* New York Public Library. *Winner:* David Remnick for *Lenin's Tomb: The Last Days of the Soviet Empire* (Random House).

James Tait Black Memorial Prizes (Great Britain). For the best biography and the best novel of the year. *Offered by:* University of Edinburgh. *Winners:* (fiction) Caryl

Phillips for *Crossing the River* (Blooms-bury); (biography) Richard Holmes for *Dr. Johnson and Mr. Savage* (Hodder).

Rebekah Johnson Bobbitt National Prize for Poetry. *Offered by:* Library of Congress. *Winner:* A. R. Ammons for *Garbage* (Norton).

Booker Prize for Fiction (Great Britain). *Offered by:* Book Trust. *Winner:* James Kelman for *How Late It Was, How Late* (Secker & Warburg).

Boston Globe-Horn Book Awards. For excellence in text and illustration. *Winners:* (fiction) James Berry for *Ajeemah and His Son* (HarperCollins); (nonfiction) Patricia McKissack and Fredrick McKissack for *Sojourner Truth: Ain't I a Woman?* (Scholastic); (picture book) Lloyd Alexander for *The Fortune Tellers,* illus. by Trina Schart Hyman (Dutton).

British Book Awards (Great Britain). *Offered by:* Publishing News. *Winners:* (author of the year) Roddy Doyle; (publisher of the year) Transworld.

Witter Bynner Prize for Poetry. To support the work of a young poet. *Offered by:* American Academy of Arts and Letters. *Winner:* Rosanna Warren.

Caldecott Medal. For the artist of the most distinguished picture book. *Offered by:* R. R. Bowker Company. *Winner:* Allen Say for *Grandfather's Journey* (Houghton Mifflin).

John W. Campbell Memorial Award. For outstanding science fiction writing. *Offered by:* Center for the Study of Science Fiction. *Winner:* Amy Thomson.

Carnegie Medal (Great Britain). For the outstanding children's book of the year. *Offered by:* The Library Association. *Winner:* Robert Swindells for *Stone Cold* (Hamish Hamilton).

Children's Book Award (Great Britain). To recognize the achievement of authors and illustrators. *Offered by:* Federation of Children's Book Groups. *Winner:* Ian Strachan for *The Boy in the Bubble* (Methuen).

Cholmondeley Awards (Great Britain). For contributions to poetry. *Offered by:* Society of Authors. *Winners:* Ruth Fainlight; Gwen Harwood; Elizabeth Jennings; John Mole.

Christopher Book Awards. For books that affirm the highest values of the human spirit. *Offered by:* The Christophers. *Winners:* (adult) Luis Alberto Urrea for *Across the Wire* (Anchor Books); Helen Prejean for *Dead Man Walking* (Random House); Ronald Takaki for *A Different Mirror* (Little, Brown); Brian Keenan for *An Evil Cradling* (Viking); Gilbert M. Gaul for *Giant Steps* (St. Martin's); Sarah Delany and Elizabeth Delany with Amy Hill for *Having Our Say* (Kodansha); Doris Donnelly for *Spiritual Fitness* (HarperSF); Kay Mills for *This Little Light of Mine* (Dutton); (children's) Gerda Marie Scheidl, illus. by Nathalie Duroussy, tr. by Rosemary Lanning, for *The Crystal Ball* (North-South Books); Phillip Hoose for *It's Our World, Too!* (Little, Brown); Ruud van der Rol and Rian Verhoeven, tr. by Tony Langham, for *Anne Frank: Beyond the Diary* (Viking).

Arthur C. Clarke Award (Great Britain). For the best science fiction novel of the year. *Offered by:* British Science Fiction Association. *Winner:* Jeff Noon for *Vurt* (Ringpull).

Commonwealth Club of California Book Awards. For books of exceptional literary merit by authors who are legal residents of California. *Winners: Gold Medal:* (nonfiction) John Diizikes for *Opera in America* (Yale Univ. Press); *Silver Medals:* (nonfiction) Allan Temko for *How to Build a Ballpark and Other Irreverent Essays on Architecture* (Chronicle Books); (Californiana) Gerald Haslam, Stephen Johnson, and Robert Dawson for *The Great Valley: California's Heartland* (Univ. of California Press); (poetry) Terry Ehret for *Lost Body* (Copper Canyon Press); (first novel) W. Glasgow Phillips for *Tuscaloosa* (Morrow); (notable contribution to publishing) *The Arts and Crafts Movement in California* (Oakland Museum); (juvenile, age 10 and under) Allen Say for *Grandfather's Journey* (Houghton Mifflin); (juvenile, ages 11–16) Laurence Yep for *Dragon's Gate* (HarperCollins); (juvenile, ages 11–16) Paul Fleischman for *Bull Run* (HarperCollins).

Commonwealth Writers Prize (Great Britain). *Offered by:* Commonwealth Institute. *Win-*

ners: Vikram Seth for *A Suitable Boy* (Orion); (first work) Keith Oakley for *The Case of Emily V* (Secker & Warburg).

Thomas Cook Travel and Guide Book Awards (Great Britain). *Offered by:* Book Trust. *Winners:* (travel) William Dalrymple for *City of Djinns* (HarperCollins); (guide book) Eleanor Berman for *Eyewitness Guide to New York* (Dorling Kindersley).

John Creasey Award (Great Britain). For outstanding mystery writing. *Offered by:* Crime Writers' Association. *Winner:* Doug Swanson for *Big Town* (Little, Brown).

Crime Writers' Association/Agatha Christie Dagger Awards (Great Britain). For mystery, detective, and crime writing. *Offered by:* Crime Writers' Association. *Winners:* (Diamond Dagger for outstanding achievement) Reginald Hill; (Gold Dagger) Minette Walters for *The Scold's Bridle* (Macmillan); (Silver Dagger) Peter Hoeg for *Miss Smilla's Feeling for Snow* (Harvill); (last laugh award) Simon Shaw for *The Villain of the Earth* (Gollancz).

Alice Fay Di Castagnola Award. For a work-in-progress to recognize a poet at a crucial stage in his or her work. *Offered by:* Poetry Society of America. *Winner:* David Mason for *The Country I Remember* (work-in-progress).

T. S. Eliot Prize (Great Britain). For poetry. *Offered by:* Poetry Book Society. *Winner:* Ciaran Carson for *First Language* (Gallery Books).

Encore Award (Great Britain). For a second novel. *Offered by:* Society of Authors. *Winner:* Amit Chaudhuri for *Afternoon Raag* (Heinemann).

Esquire/Volvo/Waterstone's Non-Fiction Award (Great Britain). To give greater prominence to good general nonfiction. *Winner:* Tobias Wolff for *In Pharaoh's Army* (Bloomsbury).

Norma Faber First Book Award. For a first book of poetry. *Offered by:* Poetry Society of America. *Winner:* Susan Wheeler for *Bag O' Diamonds* (Univ. of Georgia).

Faulkner Award for Fiction. To honor the best work of fiction published by an American writer. *Offered by:* PEN American Center. *Winner:* Philip Roth for *Operation Shylock* (Simon & Schuster).

E. M. Forster Award in Literature. To a young writer from England, Ireland, Scotland, or Wales for a stay in the United States. *Offered by:* American Academy of Arts and Letters. *Winner:* Janice Galloway.

Forward Poetry Prize (Great Britain). *Offered by: The Forward. Winners:* (main prize) Alan Jenkins for *Harm* (Chatto); (first collection) Kwame Dawes for *Progeny of Air* (Peepal Tree).

French-American Foundation Translation Prize. For an outstanding translation into English of a French prose work, fiction, or nonfiction. *Offered by:* French-American Foundation. *Winner:* Joachim Neugroschel for *With Downcast Eyes* (Little, Brown).

Frost Silver Medal. To a person who has shown lifelong dedication and achievement in poetry. *Offered by:* Poetry Society of America. *Winner:* A. R. Ammons.

Lionel Gelber Literary Prize (Canada). For the year's best book on international relations available in English. *Offered by:* Lionel Gelber Foundation. *Winner:* Michael Ignatieff for *Blood and Belonging* (BBC/Vintage).

Tony Godwin Award. For an American or British editor (in alternate years) to spend six weeks working at a publishing house in the other's country. *Offered by:* Harcourt Brace. *Winner:* Diane Wachtell.

Golden Kite Awards. For outstanding children's books. *Offered by:* Society of Children's Book Writers and Illustrators. *Winners:* (fiction) Virginia Euwer Wolff for *Make Lemonade* (Henry Holt); (nonfiction) Russell Freedman for *Eleanor Roosevelt* (Clarion); (illustration) Kevin Hawkes for *By the Light of the Halloween Moon*, written by Caroline Stutson (Lothrop, Lee & Shepard).

Kate Greenaway Medal (Great Britian). For children's book illustration. *Offered by:* The Library Association. *Winner:* Alan Lee for *Black Ships Before Troy*, by Rosemary Sutcliff (Frances Lincoln).

Eric Gregory Trust Awards (Great Britain). For poets under the age of 30. *Offered by:* Society of Authors. *Winners:* Steven Blyth; Kate Clanchy; Julia Copus; Giles Goodland; Alice Oswald.

Guardian Children's Fiction Prize (Great Britain). To discover fresh writing and to salute established excellence. *Offered by:* The Guardian. *Winner:* Sylvia Waugh for *The Mennyms* (Julia MacRae).

Guardian Fiction Prize (Great Britain). For recognition of a novel by a British or Commonwealth writer. *Winner:* Candia McWilliam for *Debatable Land* (Bloomsbury).

Guggenheim Fellowships. *Offered by:* Guggenheim Memorial Foundation. *Winners:* (fiction) Jeffrey Eugenides, Christina Garcia, Thom Jones, Randall Kenan, Dale Peck, Jonathan Wilson; (poetry) Mark Doty, Eamon Grennan, Brenda Hillman, Karl Kirchwey, Elizabeth Macklin, James McManus.

R. R. Hawkins Award. For the most outstanding professional, reference, or scholarly work of the year. *Offered by:* Association of American Publishers, Professional/Scholarly Publishing Division. *Winner:* Oxford University Press for *Buildings of the United States.*

Drue Heinz Literature Prize. To recognize and encourage the writing of short fiction. *Offered by:* Drue Heinz Foundation and University of Pittsburgh Press. *Winner:* Jennifer C. Cornell for *Departures and Other Stories* (Univ. of Pittsburgh Press).

Ernest Hemingway Foundation Award. For a work of first fiction by an American. *Offered by:* PEN American Center. *Winner:* Dagoberto Gilb for *The Magic of Blood* (Univ. of New Mexico Press).

David Higham Prize for Fiction (Great Britain). For recognition of a first novel or book of short stories written in English. *Offered by:* Book Trust. *Winner:* Fred D'Aguiar for *The Longest Memory* (Chatto).

Independent Award for Fiction (Great Britain). *Offered by:* The Independent. *Winner:* Bao Ninh for *The Sorrow of War* (Secker & Warburg).

Sue Kaufman Prize for First Fiction. *Offered by:* American Academy of Arts and Letters. *Winner:* Emile Capouya for *In the Sparrow Hills* (Algonquin Books).

Sir Peter Kent Conservation Book Prizes (Great Britain). For books that most imaginatively promote nature conservation.

Offered by: Book Trust. *Winners:* (adult) Edward O. Wilson for *The Diversity of Life* (Penguin); (children's) Jo Readman for *Muck and Magic* (Search Press).

Coretta Scott King Awards. For works that promote the cause of peace and brotherhood. *Offered by:* American Library Association, Social Responsibilities Round Table. *Winners:* (author) Angela Johnson for *Toning the Sweep* (Orchard/Jackson); (illustrator) Tom Feelings for *Soul Looks Back in Wonder* (Dial).

Roger Klein Award for Editing. For an outstanding record of recognizing talent and helping authors to realize their potential. *Offered by:* Roger Klein Foundation and PEN American Center. *Winner:* Faith Sale, Putnam.

Gregory Kolovakos Award. For a sustained contribution over time to Hispanic literature in English translation. *Offered by:* PEN American Center. *Winner:* Helen R. Lane.

Gregory Kolovakos Award for AIDS Writing. *Offered by:* Words Project for AIDS. *Winner:* Bo Huston for *The Listener* (St. Martin's).

Lamont Poetry Selection. *Offered by:* Academy of American Poets. *Winner:* Brigit Pegeen Kelly.

Harold Morton Landon Translation Award. For a book of verse translated into English by a single translator. *Offered by:* Academy of American Poets. *Winner:* Rosemarie Waldrop for *The Book of Margins* by Edmond Jabes (Univ. of Chicago Press).

Lannan Literary Awards. *Offered by:* Lannan Foundation. *Winners:* (poetry) Simon Armitage, Eavan Boland, Jack Gilbert, Linda Hogan, Richard Kenney; (fiction) Edward P. Jones, Steven Millhauser, Caryl Phillips, Stephen Wright; (nonfiction) Jonathan Kozol.

Ruth Lilly Poetry Prize. *Offered by:* American Council for the Arts and Modern Poetry Association. *Winner:* Donald Hall.

Locus Awards. For science fiction writing. *Offered by:* Locus Publications. *Winners:* (best novel) Kim Stanley Robinson for *Green Mars* (Bantam); (best fantasy novel) Peter S. Beagle for *The Innkeeper's Daughter* (Roc); (best horror novel) Lucius Shepard for *The Golden* (Bantam); (best first novel) Patricia Anthony for *Cold Allies* (Harcourt Brace); (best nonfiction) John Clute and Peter Nicholls, eds., for *The Encyclopedia of Science Fiction* (St. Martin's); (best art book) Michael Whelan for *The Art of Michael Whelan* (Bantam); (best collection) Connie Willis for *Impossible Things* (Bantam); (best anthology) Gardner Dozois, ed., for *The Year's Best Science Fiction: Tenth Annual Collection* (St. Martin's); (best publisher) Tor Books.

Los Angeles Times Book Prizes. To honor literary excellence. *Winners:* (fiction) David Malouf for *Remembering Babylon* (Pantheon); (biography) Mikal Gilmore for *Shot in the Heart* (Doubleday); (history) George Chauncey for *Gay New York* (Basic Books); (poetry) Carolyn Forche for *The Angel of History* (HarperCollins); (current interest) Henry A. Kissinger for *Diplomacy* (Simon & Schuster); (science and technology) Jonathan Weiner for *The Beak of the Finch* (Knopf); (Art Seidenbaum Award for First Fiction) Martin M. Simecka for *The Year of the Frog* (Louisiana State Univ. Press).

McKitterick Prize (Great Britain). For a first novel by a writer over the age of 40. *Offered by:* Society of Authors. *Winner:* Helen Dunmore for *Zennor in Darkness* (Viking).

McVittie's Prize (Great Britain). For the Scottish writer of the year. *Winner:* Janice Galloway for *Foreign Parts* (Cape).

Ralph Manheim Medal for Translation. To a literary translator of extraordinary achievement. *Offered by:* PEN American Center. *Winner:* Richard Wilbur.

Lenore Marshall/*The Nation* Poetry Prize. For an outstanding book of poems published in the United States. *Offered by: The Nation* and New Hope Foundation. *Winner:* W. S. Merwin for *Unframed Originals* (Henry Holt).

Kurt Maschler Award (Great Britain). For a children's book in which text and illustrations are both excellent and perfectly harmonious. *Offered by:* Book Trust. *Winner:* Trish Cooke and Helen Oxenbury for *So Much* (Walker Books).

Somerset Maugham Awards (Great Britain). For young British writers to gain experience in foreign countries. *Offered by:* Society of Authors. *Winners:* Jackie Kay A. L. Kennedy; Philip Marsden.

Milton Center Prize. To recognize significant contributions to Christian arts and letters *Offered by:* Milton Center, Kansas Newman College. *Winner:* Annie Dillard.

Eric Mitchell Prize for the History of Art (Great Britain). For recognition of contributions to the history of art. *Offered by:* Royal Academy of Arts. *Winner:* John Gage for *Colour and Culture* (Thames & Hudson).

NCR Book Award (Great Britain). For nonfiction. *Winner:* John Campbell for *Edward Heath: A Biography* (Cape).

National Arts Club Medal of Honor for Literature. *Offered by:* National Arts Club. *Winner:* Maya Angelou.

National Book Awards. *Offered by:* National Book Foundation. *Winners:* (fiction) William Gaddis for *A Frolic of His Own* (Poseidon Press); (nonfiction) Sherwin B. Nuland for *How We Die* (Knopf); (poetry) James Tate for *Worshipful Company of Fletchers* (Ecco Press).

National Book Critics Circle Awards. *Offered by:* National Book Critics Circle. *Winners:* (fiction) Ernest J. Gaines for *A Lesson Before Dying* (Knopf); (general nonfiction) Alan Lomax for *The Land Where the Blues Began* (Pantheon); (biography/autobiography) Edmund White for *Genet* (Knopf); (criticism) John Dizikes for *Opera in America* (Yale Univ. Press); (poetry) Mark Doty for *My Alexandria* (Univ. of Illinois Univ. Press).

National Book Foundation Medal for Distinguished Contribution to American Letters. *Offered by:* National Book Foundation. *Winner:* Gwendolyn Brooks.

Nebula Awards. *Offered by:* Science Fiction Writers of America. *Winners:* (novel) Kim Stanley Robinson for *Red Mars* (Bantam).

Neustadt International Prize for Literature. *Offered by: World Literature Today* and the University of Oklahoma. *Winner:* Edward Kamau Brathwaite.

John Newbery Medal. For the most distinguished contribution to literature for children. *Donor:* American Library Association, Association for Library Service to Children. *Medal Contributed by:* Daniel Melcher. *Winner:* Lois Lowry for *The Giver* (Houghton Mifflin).

Charles H. and N. Mildred Nilon Excellence in Minority Fiction Award. *Offered by:* University of Colorado Press/Fiction Collective Two. *Winner:* Ivan Webster for *The Cares of the Day* (Univ. of Colorado Press/Fiction Collective Two).

Nobel Prize in Literature. For the total literary output of a distinguished writer. *Offered by:* Swedish Academy. *Winner:* Kenzaburo Oe.

Flannery O'Connor Award for Short Fiction. *Offered by:* University of Georgia Press. *Winners:* Carol Lee Lorenzo for *The Murderer's Daughter* (Univ. of Georgia Press); Alyce Miller for *The Nature of Longing* (Univ. of Georgia Press).

Scott O'Dell Award for Historical Fiction. *Offered by: Bulletin of the Center for Children's Books,* Univ. of Chicago. *Winner:* Paul Fleischman for *Bull Run* (Harper-Collins).

PEN/Book-of-the-Month Club Translation Prize. *Offered by:* PEN American Center. *Winner:* Bill Zavatsky and Zack Rogow for *Earthlight* by André Breton (Sun & Moon Press).

Edgar Allan Poe Awards. For outstanding mystery, crime, and suspense writing. *Offered by:* Mystery Writers of America. *Winners:* (novel) Minette Walters for *The Sculptress* (St. Martin's); (first novel) Laurie King for *A Grave Talent* (St. Martin's); (original paperback) Steven Womack for *Dead Folk's Blues* (Ballantine); (fact crime) Bella Stumbo for *Until the Twelfth of Never* (Pocket Books); (critical/biographical) Burl Barer for *The Saint: A Complete History* (McFarland); (young adult) Joan Lowery Nixon for *The Name of the Game Was Murder* (Delacorte); (juvenile) Barbara Brooks for *The Twin in the Tavern* (Atheneum); (Grand Master) Lawrence Block.

Renato Poggioli Translation Award. For an outstanding translation. *Offered by:* PEN American Center. *Winner:* Moira Madden for *Commentary on His Sonnets* by Lorenzo de Medici (work-in-progress).

Prix de la Littérature Etrangère (France). Awarded to a foreign writer for an entire body of work. *Offered by:* Salon du Livre. *Winner:* John McGahern.

Prix Goncourt (France). For a work of imagination, preferably a novel, exemplifying youth, originality, esprit, and form. *Winner:* Didier van Cauwelaert for *Un Aller Simple* (Albin Michel).

Pulitzer Prizes in Letters. To honor distinguished work by American writers, dealing preferably with American themes. *Offered by:* Columbia University, Graduate School of Journalism. *Winners:* (fiction) E. Annie Proulx for *The Shipping News* (Scribner); (history) no award given; (biography) David Levering Lewis for *W. E. B. Du Bois: Biography of a Race, 1868–1919* (Henry Holt); (poetry) Yusef Komunyakaa for *Neon Vernacular* (Wesleyan Univ. Press); (general nonfiction) David Remnick for *Lenin's Tomb: The Last Days of the Soviet Empire* (Random House).

Rea Award for the Short Story. To honor a living writer who has made a significant contribution to the short story as an art form. *Offered by:* American Academy of Arts and Letters and Philip Morris Companies. *Winner:* Tillie Olsen.

Revson Foundation Fellowship. For a poet age 35 or under, to recognize a young writer whose published works or work in progress shows exceptional promise. *Offered by:* PEN American Center. *Winner:* James Harms.

John Llewellyn Rhys Memorial Award (Great Britain). *Offered by: Mail on Sunday. Winner:* Jason Goodwin for *On Foot to the Golden Horn* (Chatto).

Romance Novelists Award (Great Britain). For the best romance novel of the year. *Offered by:* Romance Novelists Association. *Winner:* Elizabeth Buchan for *Consider the Lily* (Macmillan).

Rome Fellowship in Literature. For a one-year residence at the American Academy in Rome. *Offered by:* American Academy of Arts and Letters and Philip Morris Companies. *Winner:* Karl Kirchwey.

Richard and Hinda Rosenthal Foundation Award. For a work of fiction that is a considerable literary achievement though not necessarily a commercial success. *Offered by:* American Academy of Arts and Letters. *Winner:* Janet Peery for *Alligator Dance* (Southern Methodist Univ. Press).

Runcimann Award (Great Britain). For a book about Greece. *Offered by:* Anglo-Hellenic League. *Winner:* Paul Magdalino for *The Empire of Manuel I Komnenos, 1143–1180* (Cambridge Univ. Press).

Sagittarius Prize (Great Britain). For a first novel by a writer over the age of 60. *Offered by:* Society of Authors. *Winner:* G. B. Hummer for *Red Branch* (Sinclair-Stevenson).

Shelley Memorial Award. To a poet living in the United States who is chosen on the basis of genius and need. *Offered by:* Poetry Society of America. *Winner:* Kenneth Koch.

Smarties Book Prizes (Great Britain). To encourage high standards and to stimulate interest in books for children. *Offered by:* Book Trust. *Winners:* (overall and ages 9–11) Hilary McKay for *The Exiles at Home* (Gollancz); (ages 0–5) Trish Cook and Helen Oxenbury for *So Much* (Walker Books); (ages 6–8) Henrietta Branford for *Dimanche Diller* (Collins).

W. H. Smith Literary Award (Great Britain). For a significant contribution to literature. *Offered by:* W. H. Smith. *Winner:* Vikram Seth for *A Suitable Boy* (Orion).

Jean Stein Award for Nonfiction. *Offered by:* American Academy of Arts and Letters. *Winner:* Chris Offutt.

Bram Stoker Awards. For best horror writing of the year. *Offered by:* Horror Writers of America. *Winners:* (novel) Peter Straub for *The Throat* (Dutton); (first novel) Nina Kiriki Hoffman for *The Thread That Binds the Bones* (Avon); (collection) Ramsey Campbell for *Alone with the Horrors* (Arkham House); (nonfiction) Robert Bloch for *Once Around the Bloch* (Tor Books); (lifetime achievement) Joyce Carol Oates.

Sunday Express Book of the Year Award (Great Britain). *Offered by: Sunday Express. Winner:* William Trevor for *Felicia's Journey* (Viking).

Sunday Times Small Publisher of the Year Award (Great Britain). *Offered by: Sunday Times. Winner:* Nick Hern Books.

Sunday Times Young Writer of the Year Award (Great Britain). *Offered by: Sunday Times. Winner:* William Dalrymple for *City of Djinns* (HarperCollins).

Sunday Times Writer of the Year Award (Great Britain). *Offered by: Sunday Times. Winner:* Margaret Atwood.

Templeton Prize for Progress in Religion. *Offered by:* Templeton Foundation. *Winner:* Michael Novak for *The Catholic Ethic and the Spirit of Capitalism* (Free Press).

Betty Trask Awards (Great Britain). For works of a romantic or traditional nature by writers under the age of 35. *Offered by:* Society of Authors. *Winners:* Colin Bateman for *Divorcing Jack* (HarperCollins); Nadeem Aslam for *Season of the Rainbirds* (Deutsch); Guy Burt for *After the Hole* (Black Swan); Frances Liardet for *The Game* (Macmillan); Jonathan Rix for *Some Hope* (Deutsch).

Kate Frost Tufts Discovery Award for Poetry. For a first book of poetry that exhibits excellence in substance and style. *Offered by:* American Academy of Arts and Letters. *Winner:* Catherine Bowman for *1-800-HOT-RIBS* (Peregrine Smith).

Kingsley Tufts Poetry Award. *Offered by:* Claremont Graduate School. *Winner:* Yusef Komunyakaa for *Neon Vernacular* (Wesleyan Univ. Press).

Voelcker Award for Poetry. For a U.S. poet whose body of work represents a notable and accomplished presence in American literature. *Offered by:* PEN American Center. *Winner:* Jane Kenyon.

Harold D. Vursell Memorial Award in Literature. *Offered by:* American Academy of Arts and Letters. *Winner:* Darryl Pinckney.

Lila Wallace–Reader's Digest Fund Writer's Awards. *Offered by:* Lila Wallace Foundation. *Winners:* Sherman Alexie; Christopher Durang; Ian Frazier; Jessica Hagendorn; June Jordan; W. S. Merwin; David Mura; Lee Smith; Wakako Yamuchi.

Whitbread Book of the Year (Great Britain). *Offered by:* Booksellers Association of

Great Britain. *Winner:* Joan Brady for *Theory of War* (Deutsch).

Whitbread Literary Awards (Great Britain). For literature of merit that is readable on a wide scale. *Offered by:* Booksellers Association of Great Britain. *Winners:* (novel) William Trevor for *Felicia's Journey* (Viking); (first novel) Fred D'Aguiar for *The Longest Memory* (Chatto); (biography) Brenda Maddox for *A Married Man: A Life of D. H. Lawrence* (Sinclair-Stevenson); (poetry) James Fenton for *Out of Danger* (Penguin); (children's novel) Geraldine McCaughrean for *Gold Dust* (Oxford Univ. Press).

William Allen White Children's Book Award. *Offered by:* Emporia State University. *Winner:* Phyllis Reynolds Naylor for *Shiloh* (Atheneum).

Whiting Writers Awards. *Offered by:* Mrs. Giles Whiting Foundation. *Winners:* Mark Doty; Louis Edwards; Kennedy Fraser; Mary Hood; Randall Kenan; Wayne Koestenbaum; Rosemary Mahoney; Claudia Roth Pierpont; Mary Swander; Kate Wheeler.

Walt Whitman Award. For poetry. *Offered by:* Academy of American Poets. *Winner:* Jan Richman for *Because the Brain Can Be Talked Into Anything* (Louisiana State Univ. Press).

William Carlos Williams Award. For the best book of poetry published by a small, non-profit, or university press. *Offered by:* Poetry Society of America. *Winner:* David Ray for *Wool Highways* (Helicon Nine Editions).

Robert H. Winner Memorial Award. For a poem or sequence of poems characterized by a delight in language and the possibilities of ordinary life. *Offered by:* Poetry Society of America. *Winner:* Natalie S. Reciputi.

L. L. Winship Book Award. To an author who has written the best book with a connection to New England. *Offered by:* Boston Globe. *Winner:* Jack Beatty for *The Rascal King* (Addison-Wesley).

World Fantasy Convention Awards. For outstanding fantasy writing. *Offered by:* World Fantasy Convention. *Winners:* (novel) Lewis Shiner for *Glimpses* (Morrow); (best collection) Ramsey Campbell for *Alone with the Horrors* (Arkham House); (best anthology) Lou Aronica, Amy Stout, and Betsy Mitchell, eds., for *Full Spectrum 4* (Bantam); (life achievement) Jack Williamson.

World Science Fiction Convention Hugo Awards. For outstanding science fiction writing. *Winners:* (fiction) Kim Stanley Morrison for *Green Mars* (Bantam); (nonfiction) John Clute and Peter Nicholls, eds. for *The Encyclopedia of Science Fiction* (St. Martin's).

Part 6
Directory of Organizations

Directory of Library and Related Organizations

Networks, Consortia, and Other Cooperative Library Organizations

This list is taken from the 1994-1995 edition of *American Library Directory* (R. R. Bowker), which includes additional information on member libraries and primary functions of each organization.

United States

Alabama

Alabama Health Libraries Association Inc. (ALHeLa), Mobile Infirmary Medical Center, Box 2144, Mobile 36652. SAN 372-8218. Tel. 205-431-3134. FAX 205-431-2529. *Pres.* Joy H. Harriman; *V.P.* Sondra Pfieffer.

Jefferson County Hospital Librarians Association, Medical Lib., AMI, Brookwood Medical Center, 2010 Brookwood Dr., Birmingham 35209. SAN 371-2168. Tel. 205-877-1131. FAX 205-877-1189. *Coord.* Lucy Moor.

Library Management Network Inc., 915 Monroe St., Box 443, Huntsville 35804. SAN 322-3906. Tel. 205-532-5963. FAX 205-532-5994. *System Coord.* Charlotte Moncrief.

Marine Environmental Sciences Consortium, Dauphin Island Sea Lab, Box 369-370, Dauphin Island 36528. SAN 322-0001. Tel. 205-861-2141. FAX 205-861-4646. *Dir.* George Crozier; *Libn.* Connie Mallon.

Network of Alabama Academic Libraries, c/o Alabama Commission on Higher Education, 3465 Norman Bridge Rd., Montgomery 36105-2310. SAN 322-4570. Tel. 205-281-1921. FAX 205-240-3349. *Dir.* Sue O. Medina.

Alaska

Alaska Library Network (ALN), 344 W. Third Ave., Suite 125, Anchorage 99501. SAN 371-0688. Tel. 907-261-2976. FAX 907-272-8484. *Coord.* Judy Monroe.

Arizona

Central Arizona Biomedical Librarians (CABL), c/o Maricopa County Medical Society Lib., 326 E. Coronado, No. 104, Phoenix 85004. SAN 370-7598. Tel. 602-252-2451. FAX 602-251-3224. *Chair* Joe Esposito; *Program Chair, Chair-Elect* Lenore Schmaitman.

Maricopa County Community College District, Lib. Technical Services, 2411 W. 14 St., Tempe 85281-6941. SAN 322-0060. Tel. 602-731-8774. FAX 602-731-8787. *Coord., Acquisitions* Randi Sher; *Coord., Technical Services* Kathy A. Lynch; *Dir.* Gilbert Gonzales.

Arkansas

Arkansas Area Health Education Center Consortium (AHEC), Sparks Regional Medical Center, 1311 S. I St., Box 17006, Fort Smith 72917-7006. SAN 329-3734. Tel. 501-441-5337. FAX 501-441-5339. *Regional Health Science Libn.* Grace Anderson.

Independent College Fund of Arkansas, Twin City Bank Bldg., Suite 610, One Riverfront Place, North Little Rock 72114. SAN 322-0079. Tel. 501-378-0843. FAX 501-374-1523. *Pres.* E. Kearney Dietz.

Northeast Arkansas Hospital Library Consortium, 223 E. Jackson, Jonesboro 72401. SAN 329-529X. Tel. 501-972-1290. FAX 501-931-0839. *Dir.* Peggy Blair.

South Arkansas Film Coop, 202 E. Third, Malvern 72104. SAN 321-5938. Tel. 501-332-5442. FAX 501-332-6679. *Coord.* Tammy Lackey; *Project Dir.* Mary Cheatham.

California

Area Wide Library Network (AWLNET), 2420 Mariposa St., Fresno 93721. SAN 322-0087. Tel. 209-488-3229. *Dir. Info. Services* Sharon Vandercook.

Asian Shared Information and Access (ASIA), 2225 W. Commonwealth Ave., Alhambra 91803. SAN 371-5086. Tel. 818-284-7744. FAX 818-284-1475. *Project Dir.* Kate Seifert.

Bay Area Library and Information Network (BAYNET), California Academy of Science, M. W. Malliard Lib., Golden Gate Pk., San Francisco 94118. SAN 371-0610. Tel. 415-750-7101. *Pres.* Barbara Kornstein; *Treas.* Ann Patterson.

Central Association of Libraries (CAL), 605 N. El Dorado, Stockton 95202. SAN 322-0125. Tel. 209-944-8649. FAX 209-944-8292. *Chair* Susan Walsh.

Chiropractic Library Consortium (CLIBCON), Cleveland Chiropractic College, 590 N. Vermont Ave., Los Angeles 90004-2196. SAN 328-8218. Tel. 213-660-6166. FAX 213-665-1931. *Chair* Marian Hicks.

Consumer Health Information Program & Services (CHIPS), County of Los Angeles Public Lib., 151 E. Carson St., Carson 90745. SAN 372-8110. Tel. 310-830-0909. FAX 310-830-6181. *Libn.* Ellen Mulkern.

Cooperating Libraries in Claremont (CLIC), c/o Honnold Lib., Claremont Colleges, 800 Dartmouth Ave., Claremont 91711. SAN 322-3949. Tel. 909-621-8045. *Dir.* Bonnie J. Clemens.

Cooperative Library Agency for Systems and Services (CLASS), 1415 Koll Circle, Suite 101, San Jose 95112-4698. SAN 322-0117. Tel. 408-453-0444. FAX 408-453-5379. *Exec. Dir.* Robert A. Drescher *Chair* Dennis E. Smith.

Dialog Information Services Inc., 3460 Hillview Ave., Palo Alto 94304. SAN 322-0176. Tel. 415-858-3785. FAX 415-858-7069. *Pres.* Patrick Tierney.

Health Information Providers, El Camino Hospital, 2500 Grant Rd., Mountain View 94039. SAN 322-0184. Tel. 415-940-7210. *Medical Libn.* Soma Bradley.

Health Information to Community Hospitals (HITCH), c/o Norris Medical Lib., Univ. of Southern California, 2003 Zonal Ave., Los Angeles 90033-4582. SAN 322-4066. Tel. 213-342-1967. FAX 213-221-1235. *Dir.* Nelson J. Gilman; *Coord.* William Clintworth.

Inland Empire Academic Libraries Cooperative, Wilson Lib., Univ. of LaVerne, 2040 Third St., LaVerne 91750. SAN 322-015X. Tel. 909-593-6251. *Coord.* Marlin Heckman.

Inland Empire Medical Library Cooperative (IEMLC), c/o Kaiser Foundation Hospital, 9961 Sierra Ave., Fontana 92335. SAN 371-8980. Tel. 909-353-3658. FAX 909-353-3262. *Chair* Ilga Pubilus.

Kaiser Permanente Library System–Southern California Region (KPLS), Health Sciences Lib., 4647 Zion Ave., San Diego 92120. SAN 372-8153. Tel. 714-978-4714. *Dir.* Donna Neves.

Learning Resources Cooperative, c/o County Office of Education, 6401 Linda Vista Rd., San Diego 92111. SAN 371-0785. Tel. 619-292-3608. FAX 619-467-1549. *Dir.* Marvin Barbula.

Los Angeles County Health Sciences Library Consortium, c/o Rancho Los Amigos Medical Center, Health Sciences Lib., 7601 E. Imperial Hwy., Downey 90242. SAN 322-4317. Tel. 310-940-7696. *Coord.* Evelyn Marks.

Metropolitan Cooperative Library System (MCLS), 2235 N. Lake Ave., Suite 106, Altadena 91001. SAN 371-3865. Tel. 818-798-1146. *System Dir.* Linda Katsouleas.

National Network of Libraries of Medicine–Pacific Southwest Region (PSRML), Louise Darling Biomedical Lib., 10833 Leconte

Ave., Los Angeles 90024-1798. SAN 372-8234. Tel. 310-825-1200. FAX 310-825-5389. *Dir.* Alison Bunting.

Northern California and Nevada Medical Library Group, 2140 Shattuck Ave., Box 2105, Berkeley 94704. SAN 329-4617. *Pres.* Peggy Tahir.

Northern California Association of Law Libraries (NOCALL), 1800 Market St., Box 109, San Francisco 94102. SAN 323-5777. Tel. 415-622-2854. *Pres.* Lauri Flynn.

Northern California Consortium of Psychology Libraries (NCCPL), Pacific Grad. School of Psychology Lib., 935 E. Meadow Dr., Palo Alto 94303. SAN 371-9006. Tel. 415-494-7477, Ext. 11. FAX 415-856-6734. *Co-Chairs* Christine Dassoff, Peter Hirose.

Northern California Telecommunications Consortium, 2595 Capitol Oaks Dr., Sacramento 95833. SAN 329-4412. Tel. 916-565-0188. FAX 916-565-0189. *Exec. Dir.* Jerome Thompson; *Operations Supv.* Sandra Scott-Smith.

OCLC Pacific, 9227 Haven Ave., Suite 260, Rancho Cucamonga 91730. SAN 370-0747. Tel. 909-941-4220. FAX 909-948-9803. *Dir.* Irene Hoffman.

Pacific Southwest Regional Medical Library (PSRML), c/o Louise Darling Biomedical Lib., 10833 Le Conte Ave., Los Angeles 90024-1798. SAN 322-0192. Tel. 310-825-1200. FAX 310-825-5389. *Dir.* Alison Bunting.

Peninsula Libraries Automated Network (PLAN), 25 Tower Rd., San Mateo 94402-4000. SAN 371-5035. Tel. 415-571-6798. FAX 415-349-5089. *Project Dir.* Lois Kershner.

Performing Arts Libraries Network of Greater Los Angeles (PALNET), Academy of Motion Picture Arts and Sciences, Margaret Herrick Lib., 333 S. La Cienega Blvd., Beverly Hills 90211. SAN 371-3997. Tel. 310-247-3000. FAX 310-657-5193. *Chair* Linda Mehr.

Research Libraries Group Inc. (RLG), 1200 Villa St., Mountain View 94041-1100 (see also under National Library and Information Industry Associations). SAN 322-0206.

Tel. 415-962-9951. FAX 415-964-0943. *Pres.* James P. Michalko.

Sacramento Area Health Sciences Librarians, Memorial Hospital, 1700 Coffee Dr., Modesto 95355-2869. SAN 322-4007. Tel. 209-526-4500, Ext. 6653. *Pres.* Nancy Mangum.

San Bernardino, Inyo, Riverside Counties United Library Services, 3581 Seventh St., Box 468, Riverside 92502. SAN 322-0222. Tel. 909-369-7995. FAX 909-784-1158. *Exec. Dir.* Kathleen F. Aaron.

San Francisco Biomedical Library Group, California College of Pediatric Medicine, 1210 Scotts St., San Francisco 94115. SAN 371-2125. Tel. 415-292-0409. *Coord.* Tilly Roche.

San Francisco Consortium, 513 Parnassus Ave., Box 0400, San Francisco 94143. SAN 322-0249. Tel. 415-476-9155. *Exec. Dir.* Malcolm S. M. Watts.

Santa Clarita Interlibrary Network (SCIL-NET), 24700 McBean Pkwy., Santa Clarita 91355. SAN 371-8964. Tel. 805-253-7885. FAX 805-254-4561. *Pres.* Josefina Reyes; *Recorder* Robin Wallace.

Serra Cooperative Library System, 5555 Overland Ave., Bldg. 15, San Diego 92123. SAN 372-8129. Tel. 619-694-3600. *System Coord.* Susan Swisher.

The SMERC Library, 101 Twin Dolphin Dr., Redwood City 94065-1064. SAN 322-0265. Tel. 415-802-5650. *Educational Services Mgr.* Karol Thomas; *Reference Coord.* Mary Moray.

SOUTHNET, c/o South Bay Cooperative Lib. System, 180 W. San Carlos St., San Jose 95113. SAN 322-4260. Tel. 408-294-2345. FAX 408-295-7388. *Asst. Systems Dir.* Susan Holmer.

State of California Answering Network (SCAN), c/o Los Angeles Public Lib., 630 W. Fifth St., Los Angeles 90071-2097. SAN 322-029X. Tel. 213-228-7520. FAX 213-228-7522. *Dir.* Evelyn Greenwald.

Substance Abuse Librarians and Information Specialists (SALIS), Box 9513, Berkeley 94709-0513. SAN 372-4042. Tel. 510-642-5208. FAX 510-642-7175. *Dir. SALIS Institutional Home* Andrea Mitchell; *Chair* Jill Austin.

Total Interlibrary Exchange (TIE), 5755 Valentine Rd., Suite 210, Ventura 93003-7441. SAN 322-0311. Tel. 805-650-7732. FAX 805-642-9095. *Pres.* John Murray.

Colorado

Arkansas Valley Regional Library Service System (AVRLSS), 635 W. Corona, Suite 113, Pueblo 81004. SAN 371-5094. Tel. 719-542-2156. FAX 719-542-3155. *Dir.* Donna Jones Morris; *Chair* Chuck Rose.

Bibliographical Center for Research, Rocky Mountain Region Inc., 14394 E. Evans Ave., Aurora 80014-1478. SAN 322-0338. Tel. 303-751-6277. FAX 303-751-9787. *Exec. Dir.* David H. Brunell.

Central Colorado Library System (CCLS), 4350 Wadsworth Blvd., Suite 340, Wheat Ridge 80033-4638. SAN 371-3970. Tel. 303-422-1150. FAX 303-431-9752. *Dir.* Gordon C. Barhydt.

Colorado Alliance of Research Libraries (CARL), 3801 E. Florida Ave., Bldg. D, Suite 370, Denver 80210. SAN 322-3760. Tel. 303-758-3030. *Exec. Dir.* Alan Charnes.

Colorado Association of Law Libraries, Box 13363, Denver 80201. SAN 322-4325. Tel. 303-492-2705. FAX 303-492-2707. *Pres.* Jane Thompson.

Colorado Council of Medical Librarians (CCML), Fitzsimmons Army Medical Center, HSHG-ZBM (Coldren), Aurora 80045-5000. SAN 370-0755. Tel. 303-361-3407. FAX 303-340-0528. *Pres.* Sue Coldren.

Colorado Resource Sharing Network, c/o Colorado State Lib., 201 E. Colfax, Denver 80203-1799. SAN 322-3868. Tel. 303-866-6900. FAX 303-830-0793. *Coord.* Susan Fayad.

High Plains Regional Library Service System, 800 Eighth Ave., Suite 341, Greeley 80631. SAN 371-0505. Tel. 303-356-4357. FAX 303-353-4355. *Dir.* Nancy Knepel; *Chair* Patty Everett.

Irving Library Network, c/o Jefferson County Public Lib., 10200 W. 20 Ave., Lakewood 80215. SAN 325-321X. Tel. 303-232-7114. *Network Mgr.* Carol Lehman.

Peaks and Valleys Library Consortium, c/o Arkansas Valley Regional Lib. Service System, 635 W. Corona Ave., Suite 113,

Pueblo 81004. SAN 328-8684. Tel. 719-542-2156. *Pres.* Dick Maxwell.

Pueblo Library System Software Users-Group, 300 N. Adams, Loveland 80537. SAN 322-4635. Tel. 303-962-2400. FAX 303-962-2905. *Pres.* Ted Schmidt.

Southwest Regional Library Service System (SWRLSS), Drawer B, Durango 81302. SAN 371-0815. Tel. 303-247-4782. FAX 303-247-5087. *Technical Services Resource Sharing Mgr.* Judith M. Griffiths.

Connecticut

Capitol Area Health Consortium, 183 E. Cedar St., Newington 06111. SAN 322-0370. Tel. 203-666-3304, Ext. 302. FAX 203-666-8110. *Dir.* Robert Boardman.

Capitol Region Library Council, 599 Matianuck Ave., Windsor 06095-3567. SAN 322-0389. Tel. 203-549-0404. FAX 203-728-0135. *Exec. Dir.* Dency Sargent.

Connecticut Association of Health Sciences Libraries (CAHSL), Rockville General Hospital, 31 Union St., Rockville 06066. SAN 322-0397. Tel. 203-872-5277. FAX 203-872-5169. *Pres.* Laurie Fornes.

Council of State Library Agencies in the Northeast (COSLINE), Connecticut State Lib., 231 Capitol Ave., Hartford 06106. SAN 322-0451. Tel. 203-566-4301. FAX 203-566-8940. *Pres.* Sara Parker.

CTW Library Consortium, Olin Memorial Lib., Wesleyan Univ., Middletown 06457-6065. SAN 329-4587. Tel. 203-347-9411, Ext. 3143. FAX 203-344-7969. *Dir.* Alan E. Hagyard.

Eastern Connecticut Libraries (ECL), 74 W. Main St., Norwich 06360-5654. SAN 322-0478. Tel. 203-885-2760. FAX 203-885-2757. *Dirs.* Marietta Johnson, Patricia Holloway.

Hartford Consortium for Higher Education, 260 Girard Ave., Hartford 06105. SAN 322-0443. Tel. 203-236-1203. *Exec. Dir.* Kimberly Burris.

LEAP (Library Exchange Aids Patrons), 2901 Dixwell Ave., Hamden 06518. SAN 322-4082. Tel. 203-281-7498. FAX 203-288-4052. *Exec. Dir.* Richard J. Dionne; *Chair* Lois Baldini.

Libraries Online Inc. (LION), 123 Broad St., Middletown 06457. SAN 322-3922. Tel.

203-347-1704. FAX 203-347-4048. *Pres.* Marie Shaw; *Exec. Dir.* William F. Edge, Jr.

National Network of Libraries of Medicine, New England Region, NN-LM NE Region, Univ. of Connecticut Health Center, 263 Farmington Ave., Farmington 06030-5370. SAN 372-5448. Tel. 203-679-4500. FAX 203-679-1305. *Dir.* Ralph D. Arcari.

Northwestern Connecticut Health Science Libraries, 50 Hospital Hill Rd., Sharon 06069. SAN 329-5257. Tel. 203-364-4095. FAX 203-364-4003. *Libn.* Michael Schott; *Coord.* Jackie Rourke.

Southern Connecticut Library Council, 2405 Whitney Ave., Suite 3, Hamden 06518. SAN 322-0486. Tel. 203-288-5757. FAX 203-287-0757. *Dir.* Susan Carlquist Muro.

Western Connecticut Library Council Inc., 530 Middlebury Rd., Suite 210B, Middlebury 06762. SAN 322-0494. Tel. 203-577-4010. FAX 203-577-4015. *Exec. Dir.* Thomas A. Lawrence.

Delaware

Central Delaware Library Consortium, Dover Public Lib., 45 S. State St., Dover 19901. SAN 329-3696. Tel. 302-736-7030. FAX 302-736-0985. *Dir.* Robert S. Wetherall.

Delaware Library Consortium, Delaware Academy of Medicine, 1925 Lovering Ave., Wilmington 19806. SAN 329-3718. Tel. 302-656-6398. FAX 302-656-0470. *Pres.* Gail P. Gill.

Kent Library Network, 412 N. Governor's Ave., Dover 19901. SAN 371-2214. Tel. 302-736-6184. *Pres.* Richard Krueger.

Libraries in the New Castle County System (LINCS), Univ. of Delaware, Newark 19717-5267. SAN 329-4889. Tel. 302-831-2455. *Pres.* Paul Anderson.

Sussex Help Organization for Resources Exchange (SHORE), 109 E. Laurel, Georgetown 19947-1442. SAN 322-4333. Tel. 302-846-9894. *Pres.* Diana McDonnell.

Wilmington Area Biomedical Library Consortium (WABLC), 1925 Lovering Ave., Wilmington 19806. SAN 322-0508. Tel. 302-656-6398. FAX 302-656-0470. *Pres.* Gail P. Gill.

District of Columbia

American Association of Zoological Parks and Aquariums–Librarians Special Interest Group (AAZPA–LSIG), Nat. Zoological Pk., Washington 20008. SAN 373-0891. Tel. 202-673-4771. FAX 202-673-4900. *Chair* Kay Kenyon.

CAPCON Library Network, 1320 19th St. N.W., Suite 400, Washington 20036. SAN 321-5954. Tel. 202-331-5771. FAX 202-797-7719. *Pres.* Dennis Reynolds.

Christian College Coalition, 329 Eighth St. N.E., Washington 20002. SAN 322-0524. Tel. 202-546-8713. FAX 202-546-8913. *Pres.* Myron S. Augsburger.

Cluster of Independent Theological Schools, 391 Michigan Ave. N.E., Washington 20017. SAN 322-0532. Tel. 202-529-5244. *Chair* Richard Murphy.

Educational Resources Information Center (ERIC), U.S. Dept. of Educ., 555 New Jersey Ave. N.W., Washington 20208-5720. SAN 322-0567. Tel. 202-219-2289. FAX 202-219-1817. *Dir.* Robert Stonehill.

ERIC Clearinghouses

—ERIC Clearinghouse for Community Colleges, Univ. of California, Math-Sciences Bldg., Rm. 8118, 405 Hilgard Ave., Los Angeles, CA 90024-1564. SAN 322-0648. Tel. 310-825-3931. FAX 310-206-8095. *Dir.* Art Cohen.

—ERIC Clearinghouse for Science, Mathematics and Environmental Education, Ohio State Univ., 1929 Kenny Rd., Columbus, OH 43210-1080. SAN 322-0680. Tel. 614-292-6717. FAX 614-292-0263. *Dir.* David Haury.

—ERIC Clearinghouse for Social Studies–Social Science Education, Indiana Univ., Social Studies Development Center, 2805 E. Tenth St., Bloomington, IN 47408-2698. SAN 322-0699. Tel. 812-855-3838. FAX 812-855-0455. *Dir.* John Patrick.

—ERIC Clearinghouse on Adult, Career, and Vocational Education, Center on Education and Training for Employment, 1900 Kenny Rd., Columbus, OH 43210-1090. SAN 322-0575. Tel. 614-292-4353. FAX 614-292-1260. *Dir.* Susan Imel.

—ERIC Clearinghouse on Assessment and Evaluation, Catholic Univ. of America, 210 O'Boyle Hall, Washington, DC

20064-4035. SAN 322-0710. Tel. 202-319-5120. FAX 202-319-6692. *Dir.* Lawrence Rudner.

—ERIC Clearinghouse on Counseling and Student Services, Univ. of North Carolina at Greensboro, School of Education, Greensboro, NC 27412-5001. SAN 322-0583. Tel. 919-334-4114. FAX 919-334-4116. *Dir.* Garry Walz.

—ERIC Clearinghouse on Disabilities and Gifted Education, Council for Exceptional Children, 1920 Association Dr., Reston, VA 22091-1589. SAN 322-0613. Tel. 703-264-8474. FAX 703-264-9494. *Dir.* Fred Weintraub.

—ERIC Clearinghouse on Educational Management, Univ. of Oregon, 1787 Agate St., Eugene, OR 97403-5207. SAN 322-0605. Tel. 503-346-5043. FAX 503-346-2334. *Dir.* Phil Piele.

—ERIC Clearinghouse on Elementary and Early Childhood Education, College of Education, Univ. of Illinois, 805 W. Pennsylvania Ave., Urbana, IL 61801-4897. SAN 322-0591. Tel. 217-333-1386. FAX 217-333-3767. *Dir.* Lilian Katz.

—ERIC Clearinghouse on Higher Education, George Washington Univ., One Dupont Circle, Suite 630, Washington, DC 20036-1183. SAN 322-0621. Tel. 202-296-2597. FAX 202-296-8379. *Dir.* Jon Fife.

—ERIC Clearinghouse on Information and Technology, Syracuse Univ., Center for Science and Technology, 4th fl., Rm. 194, Syracuse, NY 13244-4100. SAN 322-063X. Tel. 315-443-3640. FAX 315-443-5448. *Dir.* Michael B. Eisenberg.

—ERIC Clearinghouse on Languages and Linguistics, Center for Applied Linguistics, 1118 22nd St. N.W., Washington, DC 20037-0037. SAN 322-0656. Tel. 202-429-9292. FAX 202-659-5641. *Dir.* Charles Stansfield.

—ERIC Clearinghouse on Reading, English, and Communication, Indiana Univ., Smith Research Center, Bloomington, IN 47408-2698. SAN 322-0664. Tel. 812-855-5847. FAX 812-855-4220. *Dir.* Carl Smith.

—ERIC Clearinghouse on Rural Education and Small Schools, Appalachia Educational Laboratory, 1031 Quarrier St., Box 1348, Charleston, WV 25325-1348. SAN 322-0672. Tel. 304-347-0465. FAX 304-347-0487. *Dir.* Craig B. Howley.

—ERIC Clearinghouse on Teaching and Teacher Education, American Assn. of Colleges for Teacher Education, One Dupont Circle N.W., Suite 610, Washington, DC 20036-1186. SAN 322-0702. Tel. 202-293-2450. FAX 202-457-8095. *Dir.* Mary Dilworth.

—ERIC Clearinghouse on Urban Education, Teachers College, Columbia Univ., 525 W. 120 St., Box 40, New York, NY 10027-9998. SAN 322-0729. Tel. 212-678-3433. FAX 212-678-4048. *Dir.* Erwin Flaxman.

EDUCOM, 1112 16th St. N.W., Suite 600, Washington 20036. SAN 371-487X. Tel. 202-872-4200. *Pres.* Robert Heteric; *Publications Mgr.* John Gehl.

FEDLINK (Federal Library and Information Network), c/o Federal Lib. and Info. Center Committee, Lib. of Congress, Washington 20540-5110. SAN 322-0761. Tel. 202-707-4800. FAX 202-707-4818. *Acting Dir.* Joseph W. Price; *Network Coord.* Milton McGee.

Forest Service Information Network, USDA Forest Service, Rm. 809, RPE, Box 96090, Washington 20090-6090. SAN 322-032X. Tel. 703-235-1042. FAX 703-235-1767. *Mgr.* Seung Ja Sinatra.

NASA Library Network, ARIN (Aerospace Research Information Network), NASA Headquarters, Code JTT, Washington 20546. SAN 322-0788. Tel. 202-358-1388. FAX 202-358-3063. *Program Mgr.* Barbara Bauldock; *Project Dir.* Roland Ridgeway.

National Education Medical School Consortium, c/o Dahlgren Memorial Lib.–Georgetown Univ. Medical Center, 3900 Reservoir Rd. N.W., Washington 20007. SAN 371-067X. Tel. 202-687-1176. FAX 202-687-1862. *Libn.* Naomi C. Broering.

National Library Service for the Blind and Physically Handicapped, Lib. of Congress, 1291 Taylor St. N.W., Washington 20542. SAN 370-5870. Tel. 202-707-5100. FAX 202-707-0712. *Dir.* Frank Kurt Cylke.

Transportation Research Information Services (TRIS), 2101 Constitution Ave. N.W., TRB, 2133-307, Washington 20418.

SAN 370-582X. Tel. 202-334-3250. FAX 202-334-3495. *Dir.* Jerome T. Maddock.
Veterans Affairs Library Network (VALNET), Lib. Div. Programs Office, 810 Vermont Ave. N.W., Washington 20420. SAN 322-0834. Tel. 202-535-7521. FAX 202-535-7539. *Dir. Lib. Programs* Wendy N. Carter.
Washington Theological Consortium, 487 Michigan Ave. N.E., Washington 20017-1585. SAN 322-0842. Tel. 202-832-2675. FAX 202-526-0818. *Exec. Dir.* David Trickett.

Florida

Central Florida Library Consortium (CFLC), 431 E. Horatio Ave., Suite 230, Maitland 32751. SAN 371-9014. Tel. 407-644-9050. FAX 407-644-9081. *Exec. Dir.* Marta Westall.
Consortium of Southern Biomedical Libraries (CONBLS), Univ. of Florida Health Science Center Lib., Box 100206, Gainesville 37614. SAN 370-7717. Tel. 904-392-4017. FAX 904-392-6803. *Pres.* Ted F. Sryglen.
Florida Library Information Network, c/o Bureau of Lib. and Network Services, State Lib. of Florida, R. A. Gray Bldg., Tallahassee 32399-0250. SAN 322-0869. Tel. 904-487-2651. FAX 904-922-3678. *Chief, Lib. and Technical Services Bureau* Linda Tepp Fuchs.
Miami Health Sciences Library Consortium (MHSLC), c/o Mercy Hospital Lib., 3663 S. Miami Ave., Miami 33133. SAN 371-0734. Tel. 305-285-2160. FAX 305-285-2128. *Chair* Karen L. Kinsey; *Contact* Dolores Farooqui.
Palm Beach Health Sciences Library Consortium (PBHSLC), c/o Good Samaritan Medical Center, Medical Lib., Box 3166, West Palm Beach 33402. SAN 370-0380. Tel. 407-650-6315. FAX 407-650-6417. *Chair* Linda Kressal.
Panhandle Library Access Network (PLAN), 5 Miracle Strip Loop, Suite 2, Panama City Beach 32407. SAN 370-047X. Tel. 904-233-9051. FAX 904-235-2286. *Dir.* Selma K. Jaskowski.
Southeast Florida Library Information Network Inc. (SEFLIN), 100 S. Andrews Ave., Fort Lauderdale 33301. SAN 370-0666. Tel. 305-357-7318. FAX 305-357-6998. *Exec. Dir.* Elizabeth Curry; *Pres.* Samuel F. Morrison.
Tampa Bay Library Consortium Inc., 10002 Princess Palm Ave., Suite 124, Tampa 33619. SAN 322-371X. Tel. 813-622-8252. FAX 813-628-4425. *Pres.* Betty Stidham; *Exec. Dir.* Barbara J. Stites.
Tampa Bay Medical Library Network (TABAMLN), Box 527, Bay Pines 33504. SAN 322-0885. Tel. 813-953-1730. FAX 813-953-1218. *Pres.* Barbara Hartman.

Georgia

Association of Southeastern Research Libraries, Pullen Lib., Georgia State Univ., 100 Decatur St. S.E., Atlanta 30303-3018. SAN 322-1555. Tel. 404-651-2172. FAX 404-651-2508. *Chair* Ralph E. Russell.
Atlanta Health Science Libraries Consortium, Medical Lib., Egleston Children's Hospital, 1405 Clifton Ave., Atlanta 30322. SAN 322-0893. Tel. 404-325-6438. FAX 404-325-6463. *Pres.* Mamie Bell.
Emory Medical Television Network, 1440 Clifton Rd. N.E., Rm. 110, Atlanta 30322. SAN 322-0931. Tel. 404-727-9797. FAX 404-727-9799. *Dir.* Dan Joiner; *Business Mgr. & Producer* Julie S. Budnik.
Georgia Health Sciences Library Association (GHSLA), Hughston Sports Medicine Foundation Lib., 6262 Hamilton Rd., Columbus 31908. SAN 372-8307. Tel. 706-576-3390. *Chair* Elaine G. Powers.
Georgia Interactive Network for Medical Information (GaIN), c/o Medical Lib., School of Medicine, Mercer Univ., 1550 College St., Macon 31207. SAN 370-0577. Tel. 912-752-2515. FAX 912-752-2051. *Dir.* Jocelyn A. Rankin.
Georgia Online Database (GOLD), c/o Div. of Public Lib. Services, 156 Trinity Ave. S.W., 1st fl., Atlanta 30303-3692. SAN 322-094X. Tel. 404-656-2461. FAX 404-656-7297. *Dir.* Joe Forsee; *Coord.* Jo Ellen Ostendorf.
Health Science Libraries of Central Georgia (HSLCG), c/o J. Rankin Medical Lib., Mercer Univ. School of Medicine, 1550 College St., Macon 31207. SAN 371-5051.

Tel. 912-752-2515. FAX 912-752-2051. *In Charge* Michael Shadix.

South Georgia Associated Libraries, 208 Gloucester St., Brunswick 31523-0901. SAN 322-0966. Tel. 912-267-1212. FAX 912-267-9597. *Pres.* Betty Frazier; *Secy.-Treas.* Jim Darby.

Southeast Georgia Health Sciences Libraries (SEGHSL), Memorial Medical Center, Box 23089, Savannah 31413. SAN 373-0867. Tel. 912-350-8619. *Chair* Karen Waters.

Southeastern Library Network (SOLINET), 1438 W. Peachtree St. N.W., Suite 200, Atlanta 30309-2955. SAN 322-0974. Tel. 404-892-0943. FAX 404-892-7879.

Southwest Georgia Health Sciences Library Consortium (SWGHSLC), Health Sciences Lib., Colquitt Regional Medical Center, Moultrie 31776. SAN 372-8072. Tel. 912-890-3460. FAX 912-890-2396. *Med. Libn.* Susan Staton.

University Center in Georgia Inc., 50 Hurt Plaza, Suite 465, Atlanta 30303-2923. SAN 322-0990. Tel. 404-651-2668. FAX 404-656-0757. *Exec. Dir.* Charles B. Bedford.

Hawaii

Medical Library Group of Hawaii (MLGH), 1221 Punch Bowl St., Honolulu 96817. SAN 371-3946. Tel. 808-536-9302. *Chair* Marlene Oshia.

Idaho

Boise Valley Health Sciences Library Consortium (BVHSLC), Health Sciences Lib., Saint Alphonsus Regional Medical Center, Boise 83706. SAN 371-0807. Tel. 208-378-2271. FAX 208-378-2702. *Contact* Judy Balcerzak.

Cooperative Information Network (CIN), 8385 N. Government Way, Hayden Lake 83835. SAN 323-7656. Tel. 208-772-7648. FAX 208-772-2498. *Contact* John Hartung.

Eastern Idaho System, 457 Broadway, Idaho Falls 83402. SAN 323-7699. Tel. 208-529-1450. FAX 208-529-1464. *Contact* Paul Holland.

Health Information Retrieval Center, Saint Luke's Regional Medical Center, 190 E. Bannock St., Boise 83712. SAN 322-1008. Tel. 208-386-2277. FAX 208-384-0254. *Dir.* Pamela Spickelmier.

Idaho Health Information Association (IHIA), c/o Medical Lib., Magic Valley Regional Medical Center, Box 409, Twin Falls 83301. SAN 371-5078. Tel. 208-737-2133. FAX 208-737-2769. *Pres.* Nola Rheams-Higley.

VALNET, Eighth Ave. and Sixth St., Lewiston 83501. SAN 323-7672. Tel. 208-799-2227. FAX 208-799-2831. *Contact* Paul Krause.

Illinois

American Theological Library Association (ATLA), 820 Church St., Suite 300, Evanston 60201-5603. SAN 371-9022. Tel. 708-869-7788. FAX 708-869-8513. *Dir. Memb. Services* Madeline Gray.

Areawide Hospital Library Consortium of Southwestern Illinois (AHLC), c/o Memorial Hospital, 4500 Memorial Dr., Belleville 62223. SAN 322-1016. Tel. 618-233-7750, Ext. 5343. FAX 618-233-7750, Ext. 5658. *Coord.* Barbara Grout.

Association of Chicago Theological Schools (ACTS), c/o Mundelein Seminary, Mundelein 60060-1174. SAN 370-0658. Tel. 708-566-6401. FAX 708-566-7330. *Pres.* Gerald F. Kicanas.

Capital Area Consortium, Brookins Lib., Interlibrary Loans, Sangamon State Univ., Springfield 62794-0251. SAN 322-1024. Tel. 217-786-6601. FAX 217-786-6597. *Coord.* Nancy Stump.

Center for Research Libraries, 6050 S. Kenwood, Chicago 60637-2804. SAN 322-1032. Tel. 312-955-4545. FAX 312-955-4339. *Pres.* Donald B. Simpson.

Chicago and South Consortium, La Grange Memorial Hospital, La Grange 60525. SAN 322-1067. Tel. 708-579-4040. FAX 708-352-6072. *Coord.* Pat Grundke.

Chicago Library System (CLS), 400 State St., 10th fl., Chicago 60605. SAN 372-8188. Tel. 312-747-4013. FAX 312-747-4035. *Exec. Dir.* Alice Calabrese.

Consortium of Museum Libraries in the Chicago Area, John G. Shedd Aquarium

Lib., 1200 S. Lake Shore Dr., Chicago 60605. SAN 371-392X. Tel. 312-986-2289. *Dir.* Janet E. Powers; *Chair* Laura Jenkins.

Council of Directors of State University Librarians of Illinois (CODSULI), Univ. Lib., Univ. of Illinois at Chicago, Chicago 60680. SAN 322-1083. Tel. 312-996-2716. FAX 312-413-0424. *Chair* Sharon A. Hogan.

East Central Illinois Consortium, Medical Lib., Sarah Bush Lincoln H.C., Box 372, Mattoon 61938. SAN 322-1040. Tel. 217-258-2262. FAX 217-258-2288. *Coord.* Nina Pals.

Fox Valley Health Science Library Consortium, Edward Hospital, 801 S. Washington St., Naperville 60566-7060. SAN 329-3831. Tel. 708-527-3939. FAX 708-355-9703. *Coord.* Donna Roginski.

Heart of Illinois Library Consortium, College of Nursing Lib., Saint Francis Medical Center, 211 Greenleaf St., Peoria 61603. SAN 322-1113. Tel. 309-655-2180. FAX 309-655-6997. *Dir.* Joyce Hexdall.

Illinois Department of Mental Health and Developmental Disabilities Library Services Network (LISN), Elgin Mental Health Center, 750 S. State St., Elgin 60120. SAN 322-1121. Tel. 708-742-1040, Ext. 2660. *Chair* Jennifer Ford.

Illinois Health Libraries Consortium, c/o Meat Industry Info. Center, National Livestock and Meat Board, 444 N. Michigan Ave., Chicago 60611. SAN 322-113X. Tel. 312-467-5520, Ext. 272. *Coord.* William D. Siarny, Jr.

Illinois Library and Information Network (ILLINET), c/o Illinois State Lib., 300 S. Second St., Springfield 62701-1796. SAN 322-1148. Tel. 217-782-2994. FAX 217-785-4326. *Dir.* Bridget L. Lamont.

Illinois Library Computer Systems Office (ILCSO), Univ. of Illinois, 205 Johnstowne Centre, 502 E. John St., Champaign 61820. SAN 322-3736. Tel. 217-244-7593. FAX 217-244-7596. *Dir.* Kristine Hammerstrand.

Illinois State Curriculum Center–East Central Network (ISCC), Sangamon State Univ., F-2, Springfield 62794-9423. SAN 371-5108. Tel. 217-786-6375. FAX 217-786-

6036. *Dir.* Rebecca Douglass; *Libn.* Susie Shackleton.

Illinois Valley Library System (IVLS), 845 Brenkman Dr., Pekin 61554. SAN 371-0637. Tel. 309-353-4110. FAX 309-353-8281. *Exec. Dir.* Valerie J. Wilford.

Judaica Library Network of Metropolitan Chicago (JLNMC), c/o Asher Lib., Spertus College of Judaica, 618 S. Michigan Ave., Chicago 60605. SAN 370-0615. Tel. 312-922-8248. FAX 312-922-6406. *Pres.* Cheryl Banks.

Libras Inc., North Central College, Naperville 60540. SAN 322-1172. Tel. 708-420-3400. *Pres.* Rayonia Babel.

Metropolitan Consortium of Chicago, V.A. Westside Medical Center Lib., 820 S. Damen Ave., Chicago 60612. SAN 322-1180. Tel. 312-663-2116. *Coord.* Ina Ostertag.

National Network of Libraries of Medicine, Greater Midwest Region, c/o Lib. of the Health Sciences, Univ. of Illinois at Chicago, 1750 W. Polk St., Box 7509, Chicago 60680-7509. SAN 322-1202. Tel. 312-996-2464. FAX 312-996-2226. *Dir.* Elaine Martin.

Northern Illinois Learning Resources Cooperative (NILRC), 91 Sugar Lane, Suite 4, Box 509, Sugar Grove 60554. SAN 329-5583. Tel. 708-466-4848. FAX 708-466-4895. *Exec. Dir.* Donald E. Drake.

Private Academic Libraries of Illinois (PALI), c/o North Park College Lib., 3225 W. Foster Ave., Chicago 60625. SAN 370-050X. Tel. 312-583-2700, Ext. 4080. FAX 312-463-0570. *Pres.* Dorothy-Ellen Gross.

Quad Cities Libraries in Cooperation (QUAD-LINC), 220 W. 23 Ave., Coal Valley 61240. SAN 373-093X. Tel. 309-799-3155. FAX 309-799-7916. *Dir.* Robert McKay.

River Bend Library System (RBLS), Box 125, Coal Valley 61240. SAN 371-0653. Tel. 309-799-3155. FAX 309-799-7916. *Coord.* Mary Root.

Sangamon Valley Academic Library Consortium, c/o Illinois College, Schewe Lib., 1101 W. College Ave., Jacksonville 62650. SAN 322-4406. Tel. 217-245-3020. FAX 217-243-2520. *Chair* Martin Gallas.

Shabbona Consortium, c/o Illinois Valley Community Hospital, 925 West St., Peru 61354. SAN 329-5133. Tel. 815-223-3300, Ext. 494. FAX 815-223-3394. *Dir.* Linda Maciejewski.

Upstate Consortium, Health Sciences Lib., CGH Medical Center, 100 E. LeFeure Rd., Sterling 61081-1279. SAN 329-3793. Tel. 815-625-0400, Ext. 4416. FAX 815-625-0203. *Coord.* Nancy Gebhardt.

USA Toy Library Association, 2530 Crawford Ave., Suite 111, Evanston 60201. SAN 371-215X. Tel. 708-864-3330. *Exec. Dir.* Judith Q. Iacuzzi.

Indiana

Area Library Services Authority, Region 2, 209 Lincolnway E., Mishawaka 46544-2084. SAN 322-1210. Tel. 219-255-5262. FAX 219-255-8489. *Exec. Dir.* Shirleen R. Martens.

Area Library Services Authority, Region 3 (TRI-ALSA), 629 South St., Lafayette 47901-1470. SAN 322-1229. Tel. 317-429-0250. FAX 317-429-0223. *Coord.* Dennis Lawson.

Central Indiana Area Library Services Authority, 1100 W. 42 St., Suite 305, Indianapolis 46208-3302. SAN 322-1237. Tel. 317-926-6561. FAX 317-923-3658. *Acting Dir.* Tim Holt.

Central Indiana Health Science Libraries Consortium, Methodist Hospital Lib., Box 1367, Indianapolis 46206. SAN 322-1245. Tel. 317-929-8021. FAX 317-929-8397. *Coord.* Christine Bockrath.

Collegiate Consortium Western Indiana, c/o Cunningham Memorial Lib., Indiana State Univ., Terre Haute 47809. SAN 329-4439. Tel. 812-237-3700. FAX 812-237-2567. *Dean* Ronald G. Leach.

Eastern Indiana Area Library Services Authority, 111 E. 12 St., Anderson 46016. SAN 322-1253. Tel. 317-641-2471. FAX 317-641-2468, 747-8221. *Admin.* Jan Gillespie.

Evansville Area Library Consortium, 3700 Washington Ave., Evansville 47750. SAN 322-1261. Tel. 812-479-4151. FAX 812-473-7564. *Coord.* E. Jane Saltzman.

Four Rivers Area Library Services Authority, Old Vanderburgh County Court House, 201 N.W. Fourth St., Rm. 5, Evansville

47708. SAN 322-127X. Tel. 812-425-1946. FAX 812-425-1969. *Exec. Dir.* Ida L. McDowell.

Indiana Cooperative Library Services Authority (INCOLSA), 5929 Lakeside Blvd., Indianapolis 46278-1996. SAN 322-1296. Tel. 317-298-6570. FAX 317-328-2380. *Exec. Dir.* Barbara Evans Markuson.

—INCOLSA Processing Center, 5929 Lakeside Blvd., Indianapolis 46278-1996. SAN 322-130X. Tel. 317-298-6570. FAX 317-328-2380.

Indiana State Data Center, Indiana State Lib., 140 N. Senate Ave., Indianapolis 46204-2296. SAN 322-1318. Tel. 317-232-3733. FAX 317-232-3728. *Dir..* Laurence E. Hathaway.

Northeast Indiana Health Science Libraries Consortium (NEIHSL), Caylor-Nickel Clinic, Lutheran Center for Health Services, 3024 Fairfield Ave., Fort Wayne 46807. SAN 373-1383. Tel. 219-458-2277. *Provisional Coord.* Lauralee Aven.

Northwest Indiana Area Library Services Authority (NIALSA), 1919 W. 81 Ave., Merrillville 46410. SAN 322-1342. Tel. 219-736-0631. FAX 219-736-0633. *Pres.* Catherine Salyers; *Admin.* Barbara Topp.

Northwest Indiana Health Science Library Consortium, c/o Northwest Center for Medical Education, Indiana Univ. School of Medicine, 3400 Broadway, Gary 46408-1197. SAN 322-1350. Tel. 219-980-6852. FAX 219-980-6566. *Coord.* Rachel Feldman.

Society of Indiana Archivists, c/o Indiana State Archives, 140 N. Senate Ave., Indianapolis 46204. SAN 329-5508. Tel. 317-232-3660. *Pres.* Wesley Wilson; *Secy.-Treas.* Stephen E. Towne.

Southeastern Indiana Area Library Services Authority (SIALSA), 128 W. Spring St., New Albany 47150-3639. SAN 322-1369. Tel. 812-948-8639. FAX 812-948-0293. *Exec. Dir.* Sue Stultz.

Stone Hills Library Network, 112 N. Walnut, Suite 500, Bloomington 47408-3367. SAN 322-1377. Tel. 812-334-8347. FAX 812-334-8378. *Coord.* Sara G. Laughlin.

Wabash Valley Health Science Library Consortium, Indiana State Univ., Cunningham Memorial Lib., Terre Haute 47809. SAN

371-3903. Tel. 812-237-2540. FAX 812-237-8028. *Dir.* Ronald G. Leach; *Coord.* Evelyn J. Birkey.
Wabash Valley Library Network, 629 South St., Lafayette 47901. SAN 322-1385. Tel. 317-429-0250. FAX 317-429-0223. *Admin.* Dennis Lawson; *Reference Libn.* Becky Marthey.

Iowa

Bi-State Academic Libraries (BI-SAL), c/o Teikyo Marycrest Univ., Davenport 52804. SAN 322-1393. Tel. 319-326-9255. *Chair* Sister Joan Sheil.
Consortium of College and University Media Centers, Media Research, Iowa State Univ., 121 Pearson Hall, Ames 50011. SAN 322-1091. Tel. 515-294-1811. FAX 515-294-8089. *Exec. Dir.* Don A. Rieck.
Dubuque (Iowa) Area Library Information Consortium, 360 W. 11 St., Dubuque 52001-4697. SAN 322-1407. Tel. 319-589-4225. FAX 319-589-4217. *Pres.* Nicky Stanke.
Iowa Online Users Group, Iowa Dept. of Educ., Grimes State Office Bldg., Des Moines 50319-0146. SAN 322-3728. Tel. 515-281-5286. FAX 515-242-5988. *Chair* Mary Jo Bruett.
Iowa Private Academic Library Consortium (IPAL), Luther College Lib., Decorah 52101-1060. SAN 329-5311. Tel. 319-387-1190. *Chair* Norma Hervey.
Iowa Resource and Information Sharing (IRIS), State Lib. of Iowa, E. 12 and Grand, Des Moines 50319. SAN 322-1415. Tel. 515-281-4105. FAX 515-281-6191. *State Libn.* Sharman B. Smith.
Linn County Library Consortium, 500 Third Ave. S.E., Cedar Rapids 52406. SAN 322-4597. Tel. 319-398-8328. *Pres.* Bridget Janus; *V.P.* Margaret White.
Polk County Biomedical Consortium, Broadlawns Medical Center, 18 and Hickman Rd., Des Moines 50314. SAN 322-1431. Tel. 515-282-2394. *Coord.* Phyllis Anderson.
Quad City Area Biomedical Consortium, Mercy Hospital, Medical Lib., W. Central Pk., Davenport 52804. SAN 322-435X. Tel. 319-383-1067. FAX 319-383-1068. *Coord.* Mary Vickrey.

Sioux City Library Cooperative (SCLC), c/o Sioux City Public Lib., 529 Pierce St., Sioux City 51101-1203. SAN 329-4722. Tel. 712-252-5669. *Agent* Janus F. Olsen.
Tri-College Cooperative Effort, c/o Loras College, Wahlert Memorial Lib., 1450 Alta Vista, Dubuque 52004-0178. SAN 322-1466. Tel. 319-588-7125. FAX 319-588-7292. *Dirs.* Paul Roberts, Joel Samuels, Robert Klein.

Kansas

Associated Colleges of Central Kansas, 105 E. Kansas, McPherson 67460. SAN 322-1474. Tel. 316-241-5150. FAX 316-241-5153. *Libn.* Donna Zerger.
Dodge City Library Consortium, 905 Central Ave., Dodge City 67801. SAN 322-4368. Tel. 316-227-6532. *Chair* Marlene Trenkle.
Kansas Library Network Board, State Capitol, 3rd fl., Topeka 66612-1593. SAN 329-5621. Tel. 913-296-3296. FAX 913-296-6650. *Exec. Dir.* Michael Piper.
Kansas State Audiovisual Center, 223 S. Main, Wichita 67202. SAN 322-1482. Tel. 316-262-0611. FAX 316-262-4540. *Dir.* Sondra B. Koontz.

Kentucky

Bluegrass Medical Librarians (BML), 1740 Nicholasville Rd., Lexington 40503. SAN 371-3881. Tel. 606-275-6297. *Pres.* Luann Matthews; *Secy.-Treas.* Carol Dellapina.
Council of Independent Kentucky Colleges and Universities, Box 668, Danville 40423-0668. SAN 322-1490. Tel. 606-236-3533. FAX 606-236-3534. *Exec. Dir.* John W. Frazer; *Dir. Lib. Consortium* Christie Robinson.
Eastern Kentucky Health Science Information Network (EKHSIN), c/o Camden-Carroll Lib., Morehead State Univ., Morehead 40351. SAN 370-0631. Tel. 606-783-2610. FAX 606-784-3788. *Coord.* William J. DeBord.
Kentuckiana Metroversity Inc., 3113 Lexington Rd., Louisville 40206. SAN 322-1504. Tel. 502-897-3374. FAX 502-895-1647. *Exec. Dir.* Thomas Diener.

Kentucky Health Science Libraries Consortium, Alliant Health System, Box 35070, Louisville 40232-5070. SAN 370-0623. Tel. 502-629-3191. FAX 502-629-8138. *Pres.* Leslie Pancratz.

Kentucky Library Information Center, c/o Western Kentucky Univ., Helm Lib., Office 101, Bowling Green 42101-3576. SAN 322-1512. Tel. 502-745-6118. FAX 502-745-5943. *Dean of Libs.* Michael Binder.

Kentucky Library Network Inc., 300 Coffee Tree Rd., Box 537, Frankfort 40602. SAN 371-2184. Tel. 502-875-7000. FAX 502-564-5773. *Pres.* Brenda Macy.

State Assisted Academic Library Council of Kentucky (SAALCK), c/o Steely Lib., Northern Kentucky Univ., Highland Heights 41099. SAN 371-2222. Tel. 606-572-5483. *Chair and Pres.* Marian C. Winner.

Theological Education Association of Mid America (TEAM-A), c/o Southern Baptist Theological Seminary, 2825 Lexington Rd., Louisville 40280-0294. SAN 322-1547. Tel. 502-897-4807. *Dir.* Ronald F. Deering.

Louisiana

Baton Rouge Hospital Library Consortium, Baton Rouge General Hospital, Box 2511, Baton Rouge 70821. SAN 329-4714. Tel. 504-387-7012. FAX 504-336-2914. *Dir.* Vince Owry.

Lasernet, State Lib. of Louisiana, Box 131, Baton Rouge 70821. SAN 371-6880. Tel. 504-342-4923. FAX 504-342-3547. *Deputy State Libn.* Michael R. McKann.

Louisiana Government Information Network (LaGIN), c/o State Lib. of Louisiana, Box 131, Baton Rouge 70821. SAN 329-5036. Tel. 504-342-4920. FAX 504-342-3547. *Coord., User Services* Blanche Cretini.

New Orleans Educational Telecommunications Consortium, 1215 Prytamia Ave., Suite 205, New Orleans 70130. SAN 329-5214. Tel. 504-523-5737. FAX 504-523-5736. *Chair* Gregory O'Brien; *Exec. Dir.* Robert J. Lucas.

Maine

Health Science Library Information Consortium (HSLIC), Westbrook College, Abplanalp Lib., 716 Stevens Ave., Portland 04103. SAN 322-1601. Tel. 207-797-7261, Ext. 330. *Chair* Elaine Rigby.

North Atlantic Health Sciences Libraries Inc. (NAHSL), Maine Medical Center, 22 Bramhall St., Portland 04102. SAN 371-0599. *Chair* Robin Rand.

Maryland

Cooperating Libraries of Central Maryland (CLCM), 5 Harry S. Truman Pkwy., Annapolis 21601. SAN 322-3914. Tel./FAX 410-222-7288. *Exec. Dir.* Cecy Keller.

Criminal Justice Information Exchange Group, c/o National Inst. of Justice/NCJRS, 1600 Research Blvd., Rockville 20850. SAN 329-580X. FAX 301-251-5212.

District of Columbia Health Sciences Information Network (DOCHSIN), see under District of Columbia.

ERIC Processing and Reference Facility, 1301 Piccard Dr., Suite 300, Rockville 20850-4305. SAN 322-161X. Tel. 301-258-5500. FAX 301-948-3695. *Dir.* Ted Brandhorst.

Interlibrary Users Association (IUA), c/o ComSat Corp., 22300 ComSat Dr., Clarksburg 20871. SAN 322-1628. Tel. 301-428-4512. FAX 301-428-7747. *Pres.* Merilee Worsey; *V.P.* Charles Gallagher.

Maryland Interlibrary Organization (MILO), c/o Enoch Pratt Free Lib., 400 Cathedral St., Baltimore 21201-4484. SAN 343-8600. Tel. 410-396-5498. FAX 410-396-5837. *Admin.* Mary Anne Hodel; *Head* Elizabeth Ruffin.

Metropolitan Area Collection Development Consortium (MCDAC), c/o Arlington County Dept. of Libs., 1015 N. Quincy St., Arlington 22201. SAN 323-9748. Tel. 703-358-5981. FAX 703-358-5962. *Chief, Materials Management Div.* Eleanor K. Pourron.

National Clearinghouse for Alcohol and Drug Information (NCADI), Box 2345, Rockville 20847-2345. SAN 371-9162. Tel. 301-468-2600. FAX 301-468-6433. *Project Dir.* David Rowden.

National Library of Medicine, Medical Literature Analysis and Retrieval System (MEDLARS), 8600 Rockville Pike, Bethesda 20894. SAN 322-1652. FAX 301-496-0822. *Head MEDLARS Management Section* Carolyn Tilley.
—AIDSDRUGS. SAN 323-7427.
—AIDSLINE. SAN 323-7443.
—AIDSTRIALS. SAN 323-746X.
—AVLINE. SAN 326-7180.
—BIOETHICSLINE. SAN 326-7202.
—CANCERLIT. SAN 326-7229.
—CATLINE. SAN 326-7261.
—CCRIS (Chemical Carcinogenesis Information System). SAN 328-8560.
—ChemID. SAN 371-4772.
—CHEMLINE. SAN 322-1679.
—DART (Development and Reproduction Toxicology). SAN 371-4780.
—DENTALPROJ. SAN 323-7508.
—DIRLINE. SAN 326-730X.
—DOCUSER. SAN 323-7524.
—EMICBACK (Environmental Mutagen Information BACKfile). SAN 371-4799.
—ETICBACK (Environmental Teratology Information Center BACKfile). SAN 371-4802.
—GENETOX. SAN 371-4756.
—HISTLINE. SAN 326-6796.
—HSDD (Hazardous Substances Data Bank). SAN 326-6818.
—IRIS (Integrated Risk Information System). SAN 371-4764.
—MEDLINE. SAN 322-1695.
—MESH Vocabulary File. SAN 326-6893.
—Name Authority File. SAN 326-6915. *In Charge* Carolyn Tilley.
—PDQ (Physician Data Query). SAN 326-6931.
—POPLINE. SAN 326-6958.
—Registry of Toxic Effects of Chemical Substances (RTECS). SAN 322-1709.
—SDILINE. SAN 326-6974.
—SERLINE. SAN 326-6990.
—TOXLINE. SAN 322-1660.
—TOXLIT. SAN 323-7540.
—TRI (Toxic Chemical Release Inventory). SAN 323-7567.
National Network of Libraries of Medicine, Southeastern-Atlantic Region, Univ. of Maryland Health Sciences Lib., 111 S. Greene St., Baltimore 21201-1583. SAN

322-1644. Tel. 410-706-2855. FAX 410-706-0099. *Exec. Dir.* Faith A. Meakin.
National Network of Libraries of Medicine (NN-LM), National Lib. of Medicine, 8600 Rockville Pike, Rm. B1E03, Bethesda 20894. SAN 373-0905. Tel. 301-496-4777. FAX 301-480-1467. *Head* Becky Lyon.
Washington Research Library Consortium (WRLC), 4207 Forbes Blvd., Lanham 20706. SAN 322-0540. Tel. 301-390-2000. FAX 301-390-2013. *Exec. Dir.* Lizanne Payne.

Massachusetts

Boston Area Music Libraries (BAML), Music Lib., Morse Memorial Lib., 771 Commonwealth Ave., Boston 02215. SAN 322-4392. Tel. 617-353-3705. FAX 617-353-2084. *Coord.* Holy E. Mockovak.
Boston Biomedical Library Consortium (BBLC), Malden Hospital, 100 Hospital Rd., Malden 02148-3591. SAN 322-1725. Tel. 617-322-2221, Ext. 5307. *Chair* Elizabeth Fitzpayne.
Boston Library Consortium, c/o Boston Public Lib., 666 Boylston St., Rm. 317, Boston 02117. SAN 322-1733. Tel. 617-262-0380. FAX 617-236-4306. *Exec. Dir.* Hannah M. Stevens.
Boston Theological Institute Library Program, 45 Francis Ave., Cambridge 02138. SAN 322-1741. Tel. 617-495-5780, 527-4880. *Lib. Coord.* Clifford Putney.
Cape Libraries Automated Materials Sharing (CLAMS), 60 Benjamin Franklin Way, Unit E, Hyannis 02601. SAN 370-579X. Tel. 508-790-4399. *Pres.* Ann L. Morris.
Central Massachusetts Consortium of Health Related Libraries (CMCHRL), c/o Estate Mutual Co., 440 Lincoln St., Worcester 01605. SAN 371-2133. Tel. 508-855-2557. FAX 508-853-6332. *Pres.* Tim Rivard.
Consortium for Information Resources, Emerson Hospital, Old Rd. to Nine Acre Corner, Concord 02083. SAN 322-4503. Tel. 508-369-1400. FAX 508-369-7655. *Pres.* Nancy Caloander.
Cooperating Libraries of Greater Springfield (CLGS), c/o Springfield Technical Community College, Armory Sq., Springfield

01101-9000. SAN 322-1768. Tel. 413-781-7822, Ext. 3302. FAX 413-781-5805. *Chair* Tamson Ely.

C W Mars (Central Western Massachusetts Automated Resource Sharing), One Sunset Lane, Paxton 01612-1197. SAN 322-3973. Tel. 508-755-3323. FAX 508-755-3721. *Mgr.* David T. Sheehan; *Supv. User Services* Gale E. Eckerson.

Digital Library Network (DLN), 30 Porter Rd., LJ02/I4, Littleton 01460-1446. SAN 370-0534. Tel. 508-486-2300. FAX 508-486-2302. *Mgr.* Jillian Hamer.

Essex County Cooperating Libraries, Beverly Public Lib., 32 Essex St., Beverly 01915. SAN 322-1776. Tel. 508-921-6062. *Pres.* Suzanne Nickelson-Wonson.

Fenway Libraries Online (FLO), Wentworth Inst. of Technology, 550 Huntington Ave., Boston 02115. SAN 373-9112. Tel. 617-442-2384. *Network Dir.* Jamie Ingram.

Fenway Library Consortium, Simmons College, Boston 02115-5898. SAN 327-9766. Tel. 617-521-2741. *Coord.* Artemis G. Kirk.

HILC Inc. (Hampshire Interlibrary Center), Box 740, Amherst 01004. SAN 322-1806. Tel. 413-256-8316. *Admin. Asst.* Dora Tudryn; *Business Mgr.* Jean Stabell.

Libraries and Information for Nursing Consortium (LINC), c/o School of Nursing Lib., Saint Elizabeth's Hospital, 159 Washington St., Brighton 02135. SAN 371-0580. Tel. 617-789-2304. *Coord.* Robert L. Loud.

Merrimac Interlibrary Cooperative, Hemingway Lib., Bradford College, 320 S. Main St., Haverhill 01835. SAN 329-4234. Tel. 508-372-7161, Ext. 387. *Chair* Ruth Hooten.

Merrimack Valley Library Consortium, c/o Chelmsford Public Lib., 25 Boston, Chelmsford 01824. SAN 322-4384. Tel. 508-256-2344. FAX 508-256-4368. *Chair* Mary Mahoney; *Dir.* Evelyn Kuo.

Minuteman Library Network, 49 Lexington St., Framingham 01701. SAN 322-4252. Tel. 508-879-8575. FAX 508-879-5470. *Exec. Dir.* Joan Kuklinski.

NELINET Inc., 2 Newton Executive Pk., Newton 02162. SAN 322-1822. Tel. 617-969-0400. FAX 617-332-9634. *Exec. Dir.* Marshall Keys.

New England Law Library Consortium Inc. Harvard Law School Lib., Langdell Hall Cambridge 02138. SAN 322-4244. Tel 617-495-9918. FAX 617-496-2666. *Exec Dir.* Martha Berglund Crane.

North of Boston Library Exchange Inc (NOBLE), 112 Sohier Rd., Suite 117, Beverly 01915. SAN 322-4023. Tel. 508-927-5050. FAX 508-927-7939. *Exec. Dir* Ronald A. Gagnon; *Database Mgr.* Elizabeth B. Thomsen.

Northeast Consortium of Colleges and Universities in Massachusetts (NECCUM), c/c Middlesex Community College, Spring Rd., Bedford 01730. SAN 371-0602. Tel 617-275-8910. *Coord.* Caryl Dundurf.

Northeastern Consortium for Health Information (NECHI), Beverly Hospital, Heather and Herrick Sts., Beverly 01915. SAN 322-1857. Tel. 508-922-3000, Ext. 2920 FAX 508-922-3011. *Pres.* Ann Tomes.

Southeastern Automated Libraries Inc. (SEAL) 732 Dartmouth St., South Dartmouth 02748. SAN 371-5000. Tel. 508-996-8700 FAX 508-992-9914. *Network Admin.* Deborah K. Conrad; *Systems Admin.* Barbara Bonville.

Southeastern Massachusetts Consortium of Health Science Libraries (SEMCO), Shattuck Hospital, 170 Morton St., Jamaica Plain 02130. SAN 322-1873. Tel. 617-522-8110, Ext. 307. *Pres.* Anne Lima.

Southeastern Massachusetts Cooperating Libraries (SMCL), c/o Cushing-Martin Lib., Stonehill College, North Easton 02357-4015. SAN 322-1865. Tel. 508-230-1111. FAX 508-238-9253. *Chair* Edward Hynes.

Wellesley–Lexington Area Cooperative Libraries (WELEXACOL), c/o Solomon R. Baker Lib., Bentley College, 175 Forest St., Waltham 02154-4705. SAN 370-5978. Tel. 617-891-2231. *Pres.* Sherman Hayes; *Treas.* Marion Slack.

West of Boston Network (WEBNET), Horn Lib., Babson College, Babson Park 02157. SAN 371-5019. Tel. 617-239-4308. FAX 617-239-5226. *System Admin.* Orley J. Jones; *Network Pres.* Hope N. Tillman.

Western Massachusetts Health Information Consortium, Shriners Hospital Medical Lib., 516 Carew St., Springfield 01104.

SAN 329-4579. Tel. 413-787-2053. *Chair* Susan LaForte.

Worcester Area Cooperating Libraries, c/o Worcester State College Learning, Resources Center, Rm. 221, 486 Chandler St., Worcester 01602-2597. SAN 322-1881. Tel. 508-754-3964, 793-8000, Ext. 8544. FAX 508-793-8083. *Coord.* Gladys Wood.

Michigan

Berrien Library Consortium, Andrews Univ. Campus, Berrien Springs 49104. SAN 322-4678. Tel. 616-926-6139. FAX 616-982-3710. *Pres.* Fred Kirby.

Capital Area Library Network (CALNET), 407 N. Cedar St., Mason 48854. SAN 370-5927. Tel. 517-676-2008. FAX 517-676-9646. *Contact* Kathleen M. Vera; *Chair* David Keddle.

Cloverland Processing Center, c/o Bay de Noc Community College, Learning Resource Center, 2001 N. Lincoln Rd., Escanaba 49829-2511. SAN 322-189X. Tel. 906-786-5802, Ext. 122. FAX 906-786-5802, Ext. 244. *Dean* Christian Holmes.

Detroit Area Consortium of Catholic Colleges, c/o Sacred Heart Seminary, 2701 Chicago Blvd., Detroit 48206. SAN 329-482X. Tel. 313-883-8500. FAX 313-868-6440. *Chair* John Nienstedt.

Detroit Associated Libraries Region of Cooperation (DALROC), Detroit Public Lib., 5201 Woodward Ave., Detroit 48202. SAN 371-0831. Tel. 313-833-4036. FAX 313-832-0877. *Chair* Robert Holley; *Contact* James Lawrence.

Flint Area Health Science Libraries Network, c/o Flint Osteopathic Hospital, Medical Lib., 3921 Beecher Rd., Flint 48532-3699. SAN 329-4757. Tel. 313-762-4587. *Chair* Ria Lukes; *Dir.* Doris Blauet.

Kalamazoo Consortium for Higher Education (KCHE), Kalamazoo College, 1200 Academy St., Kalamazoo 49007. SAN 329-4994. Tel. 616-337-7220. FAX 616-337-7305. *Pres.* Lawrence Bryan; *Coord.* Margie Flynn.

Lakeland Area Library Network (LAKENET), 60 Library Plaza N.E., Grand Rapids 49503. SAN 371-0696. Tel. 616-454-0272. *Coord.* Harriet Field.

Library Cooperative of Macomb (LCM), Macomb County Lib., 16480 Hall Rd., Clinton Township 48038. SAN 373-9082. Tel. 286-6660. *Dir.* Susan Hill.

Michigan Health Sciences Libraries Association (MHSLA), MCMC, Pennsylvania Campus, 2727 S. Pennsylvania, Lansing 48910-3490. SAN 323-987X. Tel. 517-377-8389. FAX 517-372-0341. *Pres.* Judith A. Barnes.

Michigan Library Consortium (MLC), 6810 S. Cedar St., Suite 8, Lansing 48911. SAN 322-192X. Tel. 517-694-4242. FAX 517-694-9303. *Exec. Dir.* Kevin C. Flaherty.

Northland Interlibrary System (NILS), 316 E. Chisholm St., Alpena 49707. SAN 329-4773. Tel. 517-356-1622. FAX 517-354-3939. *Dir.* Rebecca E. Cawley.

Sault Area International Library Association, c/o Lake Superior State Univ. Lib., Sault Sainte Marie 49783. SAN 322-1946. Tel. 906-635-2402. FAX 906-635-2193. *Chairs* Ruth Neveu, Brian Ingram.

Southeastern Michigan League of Libraries (SEMLOL), c/o Kresge Lib., Oakland Univ., Rochester 48309. SAN 322-4481. Tel. 313-370-2486. FAX 313-370-2458. *Chair* Indra David.

Southern Michigan Region of Cooperation (SMROC), 415 S. Superior, Suite A, Albion 49224-2135. SAN 371-3857. Tel. 517-629-9469. FAX 517-628-3812. *Fiscal Agent* James C. Seidl.

Southwest Michigan Library Cooperative (SMLC), 200 S. Kalamazoo St., Paw Paw 49079. SAN 371-5027. Tel. 616-657-4698. FAX 616-657-4494. *Dir.* Alida L. Geppert.

State Council of Michigan Health Science Libraries, 401 W. Greenlawn Ave., Lansing 48910-2819. SAN 329-4633. Tel. 517-334-2270. FAX 517-334-2551. *Pres.* Barbara Kormelink; *Mid-West Rep.* David Keddle.

Upper Peninsula of Michigan Health Science Library Consortium, c/o Marquette General Hospital, 420 W. Magnetic, Marquette 49855. SAN 329-4803. Tel. 906-225-3429. FAX 906-225-3524. *Chair* Kenneth Nelson.

Upper Peninsula Region Library Cooperation Inc., 1615 Presque Isle Ave., Marquette

49855. SAN 329-5540. Tel. 906-228-7697. FAX 906-228-5627. *Pres.* Phyllis Johnson; *Treas.* Suzanne Dees.

Wayne Oakland Library Federation (WOLF), 33030 Van Born Rd., Wayne 48184. SAN 370-596X. Tel. 313-326-8910. FAX 313-326-3035. *Dir.* Harry Courtright.

Minnesota

Arrowhead Health Sciences Library Network, Tilderquist Memorial Medical Lib., 502 E. Second St., Duluth 55805-1982. SAN 322-1954. Tel. 218-720-1362. FAX 218-720-1397. *Coord.* Annelie Sober.

Catholic Library Association, Saint Mary's College of Minnesota, 700 Terrace Heights, Winona 55987-1399. SAN 329-1030. Tel. 507-457-6935. FAX 507-457-1565. *Pres.* Paul Ostendorf.

Central Minnesota Libraries Exchange (CMLE), c/o Learning Resources, Rm. 61, Saint Cloud State Univ., Saint Cloud 56301-4498. SAN 322-3779. Tel. 612-255-2950. FAX 612-654-5131. *Dir.* Patricia E. Peterson.

Community Health Science Library, c/o Saint Francis Medical Center, 415 Oak St., Breckenridge 56520. SAN 370-0585. Tel. 218-643-7507. *Dir.* Geralyn Mategcek.

Cooperating Libraries in Consortium (CLIC), 1619 Dayton Ave., Suite 204A, Saint Paul 55104. SAN 322-1970. Tel. 612-644-3878. FAX 612-644-6258. *Exec. Dir.* David Barton.

METRONET, 226 Metro Sq. Bldg., Seventh and Robert Sts., Saint Paul 55101. SAN 322-1989. Tel. 612-224-4801. FAX 612-224-4827. *Dir.* Mary Treacy Birmingham.

Metropolitan Library Service Agency (MELSA), 570 Asbury St., Suite 201, Saint Paul 55104-1849. SAN 371-5124. Tel. 612-645-5731. FAX 612-649-3169. *Exec. Dir.* William M. Duncan; *Program Officer* Tzvee Morris.

Minitex Library Information Network, c/o S-33 Wilson Lib., Univ. of Minnesota, 309 19th Ave. S., Minneapolis 55455-0414. SAN 322-1997. Tel. 612-624-4002. FAX 612-624-4508. *Dir.* William DeJohn.

Minnesota Department of Human Services Library Consortium, DHS Lib. and Resource Center, 444 Lafayette, Saint Paul

55155-3821. SAN 371-0750. Tel. 612-297-8708. *Dir. and Coord.* Pat Loehlein.

Minnesota Theological Library Association, c/o Luther Northwestern Theological Seminary Lib., 2375 Como Ave., Saint Paul 55108. SAN 322-1962. Tel. 612-641-3202. FAX 612-641-3280. *Database Admin.* Tom Walker.

North Country Library Cooperative, Olcott Plaza, Suite 110, 820 Ninth St. N., Virginia 55792-2298. SAN 322-3795. Tel. 218-741-1907. FAX 218-741-1907. *Coord.* Sandra L. Romans.

Northern Lights Library Network, 318 17th Ave. E., Box 845, Alexandria 56308-0845. SAN 322-2004. Tel. 612-762-1032. FAX 612-762-1032. *Dir.* Joan B. Larson.

SMILE (Southcentral Minnesota Inter-Library Exchange), Box 3031, Mankato 56002-3031. SAN 321-3358. Tel. 507-625-4049. FAX 507-625-4049. *Dir.* Lucy Lowry; *Smiline I & R Dir.* Kate Tohal.

Southeast Library System (SELS), 107 W. Frontage Rd., Hwy. 52 N., Rochester 55901. SAN 322-3981. Tel. 507-288-5513. FAX 507-288-8697. *Multitype Libn.* Roger M. Leachman.

Southwest Area Multi-County Multi-Type Interlibrary Exchange (SAMMIE), Southwest State Univ. Lib., Marshall 56258. SAN 322-2039. Tel. 507-532-9013. FAX 507-532-2039. *Dir.* Mary Ann Hagemeyer.

Twin Cities Biomedical Consortium, c/o College of Saint Catherine's Lib., Saint Mary's Campus, 2500 S. Sixth St., Minneapolis 55454. SAN 322-2055. Tel. 612-690-7780. *Chair* Rocky Ralebipi.

Waseca Interlibrary Resource Exchange (WIRE), Janesville-Waldorf-Pemberton Public Schools, 110 E. Third St., Box 389, Janesville 56048-0389. SAN 370-0593. Tel. 507-234-5181. *Dir.* Pauline Fenelon.

Westlaw, 610 Opperman Dr., Box 64526, Saint Paul 55164-0526. SAN 322-4031. Tel. 612-687-7000. *Mgr.* Thomas McLeod.

Mississippi

Central Mississippi Consortium of Medical Libraries (CMCML), Medical Center, U.S. Dept. of Veterans Affairs, 1500 E. Woodrow Wilson Dr., Jackson 39216. SAN 372-

8099. Tel. 601-362-4471, Ext. 1703. *Chair* Rose Anne Tucker.

Central Mississippi Library Council (CMLC), c/o McLendon Lib., Hinds Community College, Raymond 39154. SAN 372-8250. Tel. 601-857-3378. *Chair* Wayne Woodward.

Gulf Coast Biomedical Library Consortium, c/o Memorial Hospital, Box 1810, Gulfport 39502-1810. SAN 322-2063. Tel. 601-865-3159. *Chair* Connie Keel.

Mississippi Biomedical Library Consortium, c/o Northern Mississippi Medical Center, Resource Center, 830 S. Gloster, Tupelo 38801. SAN 371-070X. Tel. 601-841-4399. FAX 601-841-3552. *Pres.* Mary Lillian Randle.

Missouri

Kansas City Library Network Inc., Univ. of Missouri Dental Lib., 650 E. 25 St., Kansas City 64108. SAN 322-2098. Tel. 816-235-2030.

Kansas City Metropolitan Library Network, 15624 E. 24 Hwy., Independence 64050. SAN 322-2101. Tel. 816-521-7257. FAX 816-521-7253. *Office Mgr.* Susan Burton.

Kansas City Regional Council for Higher Education, 9140 Ward Pkwy., Kansas City 64114. SAN 322-211X. Tel. 816-444-3500. FAX 816-444-0330. *Pres.* Frederick Baus.

Missouri Libraries Film Cooperative (MLFC), 15616 E. Hwy. 24, Independence 64050. SAN 371-4993. Tel. 816-836-5200. FAX 816-836-5200. *Admin.* Billy F. Windes; *Pres.* John Mertens.

Missouri Library Network Corporation, 10332 Old Olive St. Rd., Saint Louis 63141. SAN 322-466X. Tel. 314-567-3799. FAX 314-567-3798. *Dir.* Susan Singleton.

Municipal Library Cooperative, 140 E. Jefferson, Kirkwood 63122. SAN 322-2152. Tel. 314-966-5568. FAX 314-822-3755. *ILL* Barbara Leevy.

PHILSOM-PHILNET-BACS Network, c/o Washington Univ., Medical Lib. and Biomedical Communications Center, 660 S. Euclid Ave., Saint Louis 63110. SAN 322-2187. Tel. 314-362-2788. FAX 314-367-9547. *Dir.* Loretta Stucki.

Saint Louis Regional Library Network, 9425 Big Bend, Saint Louis 63119. SAN 322-2209. Tel. 314-965-1305. FAX 314-965-4443. *Admin.* Bernyce Christiansen.

Montana

Helena Area Health Science Libraries Consortium (HAHSLC), Corette Lib., Carroll College, Helena 59625. SAN 371-2192. Tel. 406-447-4341. FAX 406-447-4525. *Chair* Lois Fitzpatrick.

Nebraska

Eastern Library System (ELS), 11902 Elm St., Suite 6A, Omaha 68144. SAN 371-506X. Tel./FAX 402-330-7884. *Admin.* Kathleen Tooker; *Pres.* Matthew Rodhe.

Lincoln Health Sciences Library Group (LHSLG), Learning Resource Center, Southeast Community College, 8800 O St., Lincoln 68520. SAN 329-5001. Tel. 402-437-2588. FAX 402-437-2404. *Chair* Susan M. Dunn.

Meridian Library System, 2022 Ave. A, Suite 14, Kearney 68847. SAN 325-3554. Tel./FAX 308-234-2087. *Pres.* Judy Henning; *Admin.* Sharon Osenga.

Metro Omaha Health Information Consortium (ICON), Lib., Clarkson College, 101 S. 42 St., Omaha 68131-2715. SAN 372-8102. Tel. 402-552-2058. *Pres.* Dorothy Willis.

National Network of Libraries of Medicine–Midcontinental Region (NN-LM-MR), c/o McGoogan Lib. of Medicine, Univ. of Nebraska Medical Center, 600 S. 42 St., Box 686706, Omaha 68198-6706. SAN 322-225X. Tel. 402-559-4326. FAX 402-559-5482. *Dir.* Nancy N. Woelfl.

NEBASE, c/o Nebraska Lib. Commission, 1200 N St., Suite 12D, Lincoln 68508-2023. SAN 322-2268. Tel. 402-471-2045. FAX 402-471-2083. *Coord.* Paul Seth Hoffman.

Northeast Library System, 2813 13th St., Columbus 68601. SAN 329-5524. Tel. 402-564-1586. *Admin.* Carol Speicher.

Southeast Nebraska Library System, Union College Lib., 3800 S. 48 St., Lincoln 68506. SAN 322-4732. Tel. 402-486-2555. FAX 402-486-2557. *Admin.* Kate Marek.

Nevada

Information Nevada, Interlibrary Loan Dept., Nevada State Lib. and Archives, Capitol Complex, Carson City 89710-0001. SAN 322-2276. Tel. 702-687-8325. FAX 702-687-8330.

Nevada Cooperative Medical Library, 2040 W. Charleston Blvd., Suite 500, Las Vegas 89102. SAN 321-5962. Tel. 702-383-2368. FAX 702-383-2369. *Dir. Lib. Services* Aldona Jonynas.

Nevada Medical Library Group (NMLG), c/o Medical Lib., Dept. of Veterans Affairs, 1000 Locust St., Reno 89520. SAN 370-0445. Tel. 702-328-1470. FAX 702-328-1732. *Chair* Christine Simpson.

Western Council of State Libraries Inc., Nevada State Lib., Capitol Complex, Carson City 89710. SAN 322-2314. Tel. 702-687-8315. *Pres.* Joan Kerschner.

New Hampshire

Bearcamp Neighborhood Library Association, Box 209, Madison 03849. SAN 371-8999. Tel. 603-367-8048. *Secy.* Nancy H. Dannies.

Hillstown Cooperative, 3 Meetinghouse Rd., Bedford 03110. SAN 371-3873. Tel. 603-472-2300. *Chair* Frances M. Wiggin.

Librarians of the Upper Valley Coop (LUV Coop), c/o Cass Memorial Lib., Box 89, Springfield 03284-0089. SAN 371-6856. Tel. 603-763-4381. FAX 603-763-4381. *Secy.* Celeste Klein.

Merri-Hill-Rock Library Cooperative, Sandown Public Lib., 305 Main St., Sandown 03873-0580. SAN 329-5338. Tel. 603-887-3428. *Chair* Barbara LaChance.

New Hampshire College and University Council, Libs. Committee, 116 S. River Rd., D4, Bedford 03110. SAN 322-2322. Tel. 603-669-3432. FAX 603-623-8182. *Exec. Dir.* Thomas R. Horgan.

North Country Consortium (NCC), Gale Medical Lib., Littleton Regional Hospital, 107 Cottage St., Littleton 03561. SAN 370-0410. Tel. 603-444-7731, Ext. 164. *Coord.* Linda L. Ford.

Nubanusit Library Cooperative, c/o Peterborough Town Lib., Main St. and Concord, Peterborough 03458. SAN 322-4600. Tel. 603-924-6401. *Contact* Ann Geisel.

Scrooge and Marley Cooperative, 310 Central St., Franklin 03235. SAN 329-515X. Tel. 603-934-2911. *Chair* Randy Brough.

Seacoast Coop Libraries, North Hampton Public Lib., 235 Atlantic Ave., Box 628, North Hampton 03862. SAN 322-4619. Tel. 603-964-6326. *Contact* Pam Schwatzer.

New Jersey

AT&T Library Network, 600 Mountain Ave., Rm. 6A-311, Murray Hill 07974. SAN 329-5400. Tel. 908-582-4361. FAX 908-582-3146. *Business Development Mgr.* Ronnye Schreiber.

Bergen County Cooperative Library System, 810 Main St., Hackensack 07601. SAN 322-4546. Tel. 201-489-1904. FAX 201-489-4215. *Exec. Dir.* Robert W. White.

Bergen Passaic Health Sciences Library Consortium, c/o Englewood Hospital and Medical Center, 350 Engle St., Englewood 07631. SAN 371-0904. Tel. 201-894-3145. FAX 201-894-9049. *Pres.* Lia Sabbagh.

Central Jersey Health Science Libraries Association, Saint Francis Medical Center Medical Lib., 601 Hamilton Ave., Trenton 08629. SAN 370-0712. Tel. 609-599-5068. FAX 609-599-5773. *Dir.* Donna Barlow; *Technical Info. Specialist* Eileen Monroe.

Central Jersey Regional Library Cooperatives–Region V, 55 Schanck Rd., Suite B-15, Freehold 07728-2942. SAN 370-5102. Tel. 908-409-6484. FAX 908-409-6492. *Exec. Dir.* Dottie Hiebing.

Cosmopolitan Biomedical Library Consortium, c/o Elizabeth General Medical Center, 925 E. Jersey St., Elizabeth 07201. SAN 322-4414. Tel. 908-558-8092. FAX 908-820-8974. *Pres.* Catherine Boss.

County of Essex Cooperating Libraries System (CECLS), Maplewood Memorial Lib., 51 Baker St., Maplewood 07040. SAN 322-4562. Tel./FAX 201-762-0762. *Pres.* William R. Swinson.

Dow Jones News Retrieval, Box 300, Princeton 08543-0300. SAN 322-404X. Tel. 609-452-1511. FAX 609-520-4775. *Sr. Marketing Coord.* Maggie Landis.

Essex-Hudson Regional Library Cooperative–Region Three, 350 Scotland Rd., Suite 201, Orange 07050. SAN 329-5117. Tel. 201-673-6373. FAX 201-673-6121. *Exec. Dir.* Sue Bausghman.

Health Sciences Library Association of New Jersey (HSLANJ), Rutgers Univ. Center for Alcohol Studies, Bush Campus, Piscataway 08855-0969. SAN 370-0488. Tel. 908-932-4442. FAX 908-932-5944. *Pres.* Catherine Weglarz.

Highlands Regional Library Cooperative, 31 Fairmount Ave., Box 486, Chester 07930. SAN 329-4609. Tel. 908-879-2442. FAX 908-879-8812. *Exec. Dir.* Diane Macht Solomon; *Program Coord.* Joyce L. Wemer.

Infolink Eastern New Jersey Regional Library Cooperative Inc., 44 Stelton Rd., Suite 330, Piscataway 08854. SAN 371-5116. Tel. 908-752-7720. FAX 908-752-7785. *Exec. Dir.* Gail L. Rosenberg; *Program and Services Coord.* Cheryl O'Connor.

LMX Automation Consortium, c/o MCC Lib., 155 Mill Rd., Edison 08818-3050. SAN 329-448X. Tel. 908-750-2525. *Exec. Dir.* Ellen Parravano. *Database Mgr.* Ann MacDonald.

Monmouth-Ocean Biomedical Information Consortium (MOBIC), Community Medical Center, 99 Hwy. 37 W., Toms River 08755. SAN 329-5389. Tel. 908-240-8117. FAX 908-341-8093. *Dir.* Reina Reisler.

Morris Automated Information Network (MAIN), County College of Morris LRC, 214 Center Grove Rd., Randolph 07869. SAN 322-4058. Tel. 201-328-5321. FAX 201-328-2370. *Coord. Network Services* Pam Sahr.

Morris-Union Federation, 214 Main St., Chatham 07928. SAN 310-2629. Tel. 201-635-0603. *Contact* Diane O'Brien.

New Jersey Academic Library Network, c/o Kean College, Nancy Thompson Lib., Union 07083. SAN 329-4927. Tel. 908-527-2017. FAX 908-527-2365. *Chair* Barbara Simpson.

New Jersey Health Sciences Library Network (NJHSN), c/o Rutgers Univ. Center for Alcohol Studies Lib., Smithers Hall, Busch Campus, Piscataway 08855-0969.

SAN 371-4829. Tel. 908-932-4442. FAX 908-932-5944. *Chair* Catherine Weglarz.

New Jersey Library Network, Lib. Development Bureau, 185 W. State St., CN 520, Trenton 08625-0520. SAN 372-8161. Tel. 609-984-3293. *Service Coord.* Marilyn R. Veldof.

Pinelands Consortium for Health Information, c/o Kennedy Memorial Hospital, Washington Township Div. Medical Lib., 435 Huffville-Cross Keys Rds., Turnersville 08012. SAN 370-4874. Tel. 609-582-2675. FAX 609-582-3190. *Coord.* William Dobkowski.

Society for Cooperative Healthcare and Related Education (SCHARE), Union County College, 1033 Springfield Ave., Cranford 07016. SAN 371-0718. Tel. 908-276-5710. *Chair* Geri Farina. *Coord.* Anne Calhoun.

South Jersey Regional Library Cooperative, Paint Works Corporate Center, 10 Foster Ave., Suite F-3, Gibbsboro 08026. SAN 329-4625. Tel. 609-346-1222. FAX 609-346-2839. *Exec. Dir.* Karen Hyman; *Program Development Coord.* Katherine Schalk-Greene.

New Mexico

New Mexico Consortium of Academic Libraries, Miller Lib., Western New Mexico Univ., Box 680, Silver City 88062. SAN 371-6872. Tel. 505-538-6358. FAX 505-538-6178. *Pres.* Ben Wakashige; *Pres.-Elect* Harris Richards.

New Mexico Consortium of Biomedical and Hospital Libraries, c/o Lovelace Medical Lib., 5400 Gibson Blvd. S.E., Albuquerque 87108. SAN 322-449X. Tel. 505-262-7158. *Permanent Contact* Sarah Morley.

New York

Academic Libraries of Brooklyn, 175 Willoughby St., Suite 15C, Brooklyn 11201. SAN 322-2411. Tel. 718-260-3626. FAX 718-260-3756. *Pres.* Aline Locascio.

Associated Colleges of the Saint Lawrence Valley, Satterlee Hall, State Univ. of New York, Potsdam 13676-2299. SAN 322-242X. Tel. 315-267-3331. FAX 315-267-2771. *Exec. Dir.* Susan M. Cypert.

Brooklyn–Queens–Staten Island Health Sciences Librarians (BQSI), College of Staten Island Lib., 2800 Victory Blvd., Staten Island 10314. SAN 370-0828. Tel. 718-982-4016. *Pres.* Raja Jayatilleke.

Capital District Library Council for Reference and Research Resources, 28 Essex St., Albany 12206. SAN 322-2446. Tel. 518-438-2500. FAX 518-438-2872. *Exec. Dir.* Charles D. Custer; *Admin. Secy.* Carolyn Houlihan.

Central New York Library Resources Council, 763 Butternut, Syracuse 13208. SAN 322-2454. Tel. 315-478-6080. FAX 315-478-0512. *Exec. Dir.* Keith E. Washburn.

Consortium of Foundation Libraries, c/o International Planned Parenthood Foundation, Western Hemisphere Region, 902 Broadway, New York 10017. SAN 322-2462. Tel. 212-995-8800. FAX 212-995-8853. *Chair* Abigail Hourwich.

Council of Archives and Research Libraries in Jewish Studies (CARLJS), 330 Seventh Ave., 21st fl., New York 10001. SAN 371-053X. Tel. 212-629-0500. FAX 212-629-0508. *Exec. Dir.* Richard Siegel; *Pres.* Sandra Weiner.

Educational Film Library Association, c/o AV Resource Center, Cornell Univ., Business and Technology Pk., Ithaca 14850. SAN 371-0874. Tel. 607-255-2090. FAX 607-255-9946. *AV Coord.* Rich Gray; *AV Sales* Liz Powers; *AV Technology* Gerry Kalk.

Health Information Libraries of Westchester (HILOW), c/o New York Medical College, Medical Lib., Basic Sciences Bldg., Valhalla 10595. SAN 371-0823. Tel. 914-993-4204. *Pres.* Christine Breglia.

Library Consortium of Health Institutions in Buffalo, c/o Info. Dissemination Service, Health Sciences Lib., Univ. at Buffalo, Buffalo 14214. SAN 329-367X. Tel. 716-829-3351. *Dir.* Cynthia Bertuca.

Long Island Library Resources Council, Melville Lib. Bldg., Suite E5310, Stony Brook 11794-3399. SAN 322-2489. Tel. 516-632-6650. FAX 516-632-6662. *Dir.* Herbert Biblo.

Manhattan-Bronx Health Sciences Libraries Group, c/o NCI Lib., 41 Madison Ave., New York 10010. SAN 322-2465. Tel.

212-684-0909. FAX 212-213-4694. *Pres.* Judy Lee.

Medical and Scientific Libraries of Long Island (MEDLI), c/o Palmer School of Lib. and Info. Science, C. W. Post Campus, Long Island Univ., Brookville 11548. SAN 322-4309. Tel. 516-299-2866. FAX 516-626-2665. *Pres.* William F. Casey.

Medical Library Center of New York, 5 E. 102 St., New York 10029. SAN 322-3957. Tel. 212-427-1630. FAX 212-860-3496. *Dir.* Lois Weinstein.

Middle Atlantic Region National Network of Libraries of Medicine, New York Academy of Medicine, 2 E. 103 St., New York 10029-5293. SAN 322-2497. Tel. 212-876-8763. FAX 212-534-7042. *Dir.* Arthur Downing.

New York Metropolitan Reference and Research Library Agency (METRO), 57 E. 11 St., New York 10003. SAN 322-2500. Tel. 212-228-2320. FAX 212-228-2598. *Dir.* Joan Neumann; *Coord. of Programs and Services* Alar Kruus.

New York State Interlibrary Loan Network (NYSILL), c/o New York State Lib., Albany 12230. SAN 322-2519. Tel. 518-474-5383. FAX 518-474-5786. *State Libn.* Joseph F. Shubert; *Dir.* Jerome Yavarkovsky; *Principal Libn.* J. Van der veer Judd.

North Country Reference and Research Resources Council, 7 Commerce Lane, Canton 13617. SAN 322-2527. Tel. 315-386-4569. FAX 315-379-9553. *Exec. Dir.* John J. Hammond.

Research Library Association of South Manhattan, Bobst Lib., New York Univ., 70 Washington Square S., New York 10012. SAN 372-8080. Tel. 212-998-2566. *Coord.* Joan Grant.

Rochester Regional Library Council (RRLC), 390 Packetts Landing, Box 66160, Fairport 14450. SAN 322-2535. Tel. 716-223-7570. FAX 716-223-7712. *Dir.* Janet M. Welch.

South Central Research Library Council, 215 N. Cayuga St., Ithaca 14850. SAN 322-2543. Tel. 607-273-9106. FAX 607-272-0740. *Acting Dir.* Jean Currie.

Southeastern New York Library Resources Council, 220 Rte. 299, Box 879, Highland 12528. SAN 322-2551. Tel. 914-691-

2734. FAX 914-691-6987. *Exec. Dir.* John L. Shaloiko.

State University of New York–OCLC Library Network (SUNY–OCLC), Central Administration, State Univ. of New York, State Univ. Plaza, Albany 12246. SAN 322-256X. Tel. 518-443-5444. FAX 518-432-4346. *Dir.* Glyn T. Evans.

Western New York Library Resources Council, 180 Oak St., Buffalo 14203. SAN 322-2578. Tel. 716-852-3844. FAX 716-852-0276. *Exec. Dir.* Mary W. Ghikas.

North Carolina

Cape Fear Health Sciences Information Consortium, c/o Cape Fear Valley Medical Center, Box 2000, Fayetteville 28302. SAN 322-3930. Tel. 919-609-6601. FAX 919-433-7710. *Chair* Pat Hammond.

Microcomputer Users Group for Libraries in North Carolina, Health Sciences Lib., Univ. of North Carolina, Chapel Hill 27599-7585. SAN 322-4449. Tel. 919-962-0700. FAX 919-966-1537. *Pres.* Julia Shaw-Kolcot.

Mid-Carolina Academic Library Network (MID-CAL), 400 N. ACC Dr., Wilson 27893. SAN 371-3989. Tel. 919-399-6501. *Chair* Marty Smith; *Project Dir.* Ted Waller.

NC Area Health Education Centers, Health Sciences Lib., CB 7585, Univ. of North Carolina, Chapel Hill 27599-7585. SAN 323-9950. Tel. 919-962-0700. FAX 919-966-1537. *Network Coord.* Diana C. McDuffee.

North Carolina Department of Community Colleges, Institutional Services, 200 W. Jones St., Raleigh 27603-1337. SAN 322-2594. Tel. 919-733-7051, Ext. 634. FAX 919-733-0680. *Dir.* Major Boyd.

North Carolina Information Network, 109 E. Jones St., Raleigh 27601-2807. SAN 329-3092. Tel. 919-733-2570. FAX 919-733-8748. *Dir.* Diana Young.

Northwest AHEC Library at Salisbury, c/o Rowan Memorial Hospital, 612 Mocksville Ave., Salisbury 28144. SAN 322-4589. Tel. 704-638-1081. FAX 704-636-5050. *Dir.* James Leist.

Northwest AHEC Library Information Network, Northwest Area Health Education Center, Bowman Gray School of Medicine, Medical Center Blvd., Winston-Salem 27157-1060. SAN 322-4716. Tel. 919-716-9210. *Coord.* Phyllis Gillikin.

Resources for Health Information Consortium (ReHI), Box 14465, Raleigh 27620-4465. SAN 329-3777. Tel. 919-250-8529. *Dir.* Karen Grandage.

Triangle Research Libraries Network, Wilson Lib., CB 3940, Chapel Hill 27599-3940. SAN 329-5362. Tel. 919-962-8022. FAX 919-962-0484. *Exec. Dir.* David H. Carlson.

Unifour Consortium of Health Care and Educational Institutions, c/o Northwest AHEC Lib. at Hickory, Catawba Memorial Hospital, 810 Fair Grove Church, Hickory 28602. SAN 322-4708. Tel. 704-326-3662. FAX 704-322-2921. *Dir.* Phyllis Gillikin.

North Dakota

American Indian Higher Education Consortium (AIHEC), c/o UTTC, 3315 University Dr., Bismarck 58501. SAN 329-4056. Tel. 701 255-3285. *Pres.* David Gipp.

Central Dakota Cooperating Libraries (CDCL), 515 N. Fifth St., Bismarck 58501. SAN 373-1391. Tel. 701-222-6410. FAX 701-221-6854. *Chair* Thomas T. Jones; *Secy.-Treas.* Cheryl Bailey.

North Dakota Network for Knowledge, c/o North Dakota State Lib., Liberty Memorial Bldg., Capitol Grounds, 604 E. Blvd. Ave., Bismarck 58505-0800. SAN 322-2616. Tel. 701-224-2492. FAX 701-224-2040. *State Libn.* William Strader.

Tri-College University Libraries Consortium, c/o North Dakota State Univ., 306 Ceres Hall, Fargo 58105. SAN 322-2047. Tel. 701-237-8170. FAX 701-237-7205. *Coord.* John W. Beecher; *Provost, Tri-College Univ.* William C. Nelson.

Valley Medical Network, 720 N. Fourth St., Fargo 58122. SAN 329-4730. Tel. 701-234-5837. FAX 701-234-5927. *Pres.* Margaret Wagner.

Ohio

Central Ohio Hospital Library Consortium, Medical Lib., Riverside Methodist Hospital, 3535 Olentangy River Rd., Columbus 43214. SAN 371-084X. Tel. 614-566-5230. FAX 614-265-2437. *Archival Records* Jo Yeoh.

Cleveland Area Metropolitan Library System (CAMLS), 20600 Chagrin Blvd., Suite 500, Shaker Heights 44122-5334. SAN 322-2632. Tel. 216-921-3900. FAX 216-921-7220. *Dir.* Jacqueline Mundell.

Columbus Area Library and Information Council of Ohio (CALICO), c/o Westerville Public Lib., 126 S. State St., Westerville 43081. SAN 371-683X. Tel. 614-882-7277, Ext. 156. *Pres.* Lois Szudy.

Consortium of Popular Culture Collections in the Midwest (CPCCM), c/o Popular Culture Lib., Bowling Green State Univ., Bowling Green 43403-0600. SAN 370-5811. Tel. 419-372-2450. FAX 419-372-7996.

Greater Cincinnati Library Consortium, 3333 Vine St., Suite 605, Cincinnati 45220-2214. SAN 322-2675. Tel. 513-751-4422. FAX 513-751-0463. *Exec. Dir.* Martha J. McDonald.

Miami Valley Libraries (MVL), c/o Tipp City Public Lib., 11 E. Main St., Tipp City 45371. SAN 322-2691. Tel. 513-667-3826. FAX 513-667-7968. *Pres.* Patricia Liening.

NEOUCOM Council of Associated Hospital Librarians, Ocasek Regional Medical Info. Center, Box 95, Rootstown 44272-0095. SAN 370-0526. Tel. 216-325-2511, Ext. 542. FAX 216-325-0522. *Chair* Jean Williams Sayre.

NOLA Regional Library System, 4445 Mahoning Ave. N.W., Warren 44483. SAN 322-2713. Tel. 216-847-7744. FAX 216-847-7704. *Dir.* Holly C. Carroll.

North Central Library Cooperative, 27 N. Main St., Mansfield 44902-1703. SAN 322-2683. Tel. 419-526-1337. FAX 419-526-2145. *Dir.* Jennifer J. Davis.

Northeastern Ohio Major Academic and Research Libraries (NEOMARL), c/o College of Wooster, Andrews Lib., Wooster 44691-2364. SAN 322-4236. Tel. 216-263-2152. FAX 216-263-2253. *Chair* Damon D. Hickey.

Northwest Library District (NORWELD), 251 N. Main St., Bowling Green 43402.

SAN 322-273X. Tel. 419-352-2903. FAX 419-354-0405. *Dir.* Allan Gray.

OCLC (Online Computer Library Center) Inc., 6565 Frantz Rd., Dublin 43017-3395. SAN 322-2748. Tel. 614-764-6000. FAX 614-764-6096. *Pres.* K. Wayne Smith.

Ohio-Kentucky Coop Libraries, c/o Cedarville College, Box 647, Cedarville 45314. SAN 325-3570. Tel. 513-766-7842. FAX 513-766-2337. *Eds.* Patti Ashby, Janice Bosma.

Ohio Network of American History Research Centers, Ohio Historical Society Archives/ Lib., 1982 Velma Ave., Columbus 43211-2497. SAN 323-9624. Tel. 614-297-2510. FAX 614-297-2546. *Archivist* George Parkinson.

Ohio Regional Consortium of Law Libraries (ORCLL), Ohio State Univ. Law Lib., 1659 High St., Columbus 43210-1391. SAN 371-3954. Tel. 614-292-3202. *Pres.* Katherine Carrick.

Ohio Valley Area Libraries (OVAL), 252 W. 13 St., Wellston 45692-2299. SAN 322-2756. Tel. 614-384-2103. FAX 614-384-2106. *Dir.* Eric S. Anderson.

OHIONET, 1500 W. Lane Ave., Columbus 43221-3975. SAN 322-2764. Tel. 614-486-2966. FAX 614-486-1527. *Exec. Dir.* Michael P. Butler.

Southwest Ohio Regional Library System (SWORL), 505 Kathryn Dr., Wilmington 45177-2274. SAN 322-2780. Tel. 513-382-2503. FAX 513-382-2504. *Dir.* Corinne Johnson.

Southwestern Ohio Council for Higher Education, 3171 Research Blvd., Suite 141, Dayton 45420-4014. SAN 322-2659. Tel. 513-259-1370. FAX 513-259-1380. *Dir.* Tamara Yeager; *Chair Lib. Div.* Lynn Brock.

Oklahoma

Greater Oklahoma Area Health Sciences Library Consortium, Box 60918, Oklahoma City 73146. SAN 329-3858. *Pres.* Cheryl Suttles.

Metropolitan Libraries Network of Central Oklahoma Inc. (MetroNetwork), Box 250, Oklahoma City 73101-0250. SAN 372-8137. Tel. 405-235-0571, Ext. 198. *Chair* Habib Tabatabai.

Mid-America Law School Library Consortium (MALSLC), c/o College of Law Lib., Univ. of Tulsa, 3120 E. Fourth Place, Tulsa 74104-3189. SAN 371-6813. Tel. 918-631-2459. FAX 918-631-3556. *Chair* Richard E. Ducey.

Midwest Curriculum Coordination Center, 1500 W. Seventh Ave., Stillwater 74074-4364. SAN 329-3874. Tel. 405-377-2000. FAX 405-743-5142. *Dir.* Mary Ann Houston.

Oklahoma Telecommunications Interlibrary System (OTIS), 200 N.E. 18 St., Oklahoma City 73105-3298. SAN 322-2810. Tel. 405-521-2502. FAX 405-525-7804. *Head* Mary Hardin.

Tulsa Area Library Cooperative, 400 Civic Center, Tulsa 74103. SAN 321-6489. Tel. 918-596-7893. FAX 918-596-7895. *Coord.* Paula Emmons.

Oregon

Association of Visual Science Librarians (AVSL), c/o Good Samaritan Hospital and Medical Center, 1015 N.W. 22 Ave., Portland 97210. SAN 370-0569. Tel. 503-229-7711. *Chair* Madelyn Hall.

Chemeketa Cooperative Regional Library Service, c/o Chemeketa Community College, Box 14007, Salem 97309-7070. SAN 322-2837. Tel. 503-399-5105. FAX 503-399-5214. *Coord.* Linda Cochrane.

Coos County Library Service District, Extended Service Office, Tioga 107, 1988 Newmark, Coos Bay 97420. SAN 322-4279. Tel. 503-888-7260. FAX 503-888-7285. *Ext. Services Coord.* Mary Jane Fisher.

Library Information Network of Clackamas County, 16239 S.E. McLoughlin Blvd., Suite 208, Oak Grove 97267. SAN 322-2845. Tel. 503-655-8550. FAX 503-655-8555. *Network Admin.* Joanna Rood.

Oregon Health Information Network, Oregon Health Sciences Univ. Lib., Box 573, Portland 97207-0573. SAN 322-4287. Tel. 503-494-3444. FAX 503-494-5241. *Coord.* Steve Teich.

Oregon Health Sciences Libraries Association (OHSLA), c/o Willamette Falls Hospital, 1500 Division St., Oregon City 97045. SAN 371-2176. Tel. 503-650-

6757. FAX 503-650-6836. *Chair* Katherine R. Martin.

Portland Area Health Sciences Librarians, c/o Oregon Geriatric Education Center, Portland State Univ., Box 751, Portland 97207. SAN 371-0912. Tel. 503-725-5149. FAX 503-725-5199. *Secy.* Jennifer Gregorio.

Southern Oregon Library Federation, c/o Jackson County Public Lib. System, Medford Lib. Branch, 413 W. Main St., Medford 97501. SAN 322-2861. Tel. 503-776-7281. FAX 503-776-7290. *Pres.* Bob Wilson.

Washington County Cooperative Library Services, 17880 S.W. Blanton St., Box 5129, Aloha 97006. SAN 322-287X. Tel. 503-642-1544. FAX 503-591-0445. *Mgr.* Peggy Forcier.

Pennsylvania

Associated College Libraries of Central Pennsylvania, c/o Dickinson College, Carlisle 10713. SAN 322-2888. Tel. 717-245-1396. *Chair* John Stachacz.

Basic Health Sciences Library Network, c/o Consortium for Health Information, One Medical Center Blvd., Upland 19013. SAN 371-4888. Tel. 215-447-6163. FAX 215-447-6164. *Chair* Kathleen Kell.

Berks County Library Association (BCLA), R.D. 1, Box 1343, Hamburg 19526. SAN 371-0866. Tel. 215-655-6355. *Treas.* Pamela Hehr.

Berks County Public Library System (BCPLS), Agricultural Center, Box 520, Leesport 19533. SAN 371-8972. Tel. 215-378-5260. FAX 215-378-1525. *Admin.* Julie Rinehart.

Can-Do Consortium, Dauphin County Lib. System, 101 Walnut St., Harrisburg 17101. SAN 372-8196. Tel. 717-234-4961. *Dir.* Rich Bowra; *Dist. Coord.* James Hollinger.

Central Pennsylvania Consortium, c/o Franklin and Marshall College, Box 3003, Lancaster 17604-3003. SAN 322-2896. Tel. 717-291-3919. FAX 717-291-3969. *Dir.* Marigrace Bellart.

Confederation of State and State Related Institutions, Somerset State Hospital Staff Lib., Box 631, Somerset 15501. SAN 323-9829. Tel. 814-443-0216. FAX 814-443-0217. *Dir. Lib. Services* Eve Kline.

Consortium for Health Information and Library Services, One Medical Center Blvd., Upland 19013-3995. SAN 322-290X. Tel. 215-447-6163. FAX 215-447-6164. *Exec. Dir.* Kathleen Vick Kell.

Cooperating Hospital Libraries of the Lehigh Valley Area, Saint Joseph Hospital, 12 and Walnut Sts., Reading 19603. SAN 371-0858. Tel. 215-378-2393. FAX 215-378-2390. *Libn.* Kathleen Mazurek.

Delaware Valley Information Consortium, Abington Memorial Hospital, 1200 York Rd., Abington 19001. SAN 329-3912. Tel. 215-576-2096. *Coord.* Marion Chayes.

Eastern Mennonite Associated Libraries and Archives (EMALA), 2215 Millstream Rd., Lancaster 17602. SAN 372-8226. Tel. 717-393-9745. *Chair* Ray K. Hacker. *Secy.* Lloyd Zeager.

Erie Area Health Information Library Cooperative (EAHILC), Warren State Hospital, 33 Main St., North Warren 16365-5099. SAN 371-0564. Tel. 814-723-5500, Ext. 223. FAX 814-726-4562. *Chair* Helen Sweitzer.

Film Library Intercollege Cooperative of Pennsylvania (FLIC), c/o Delaware County Community College, Rte. 252, Media Line Rd., Media 19063. SAN 322-2926. Tel. 215-359-5156. *Pres.* Kate Hickey.

Greater Philadelphia Law Library Association (GPLLA), Box 335, Philadelphia 19105. SAN 373-1375. Tel. 215-592-5697. *Pres.* Kathleen A. Caron.

Health Information Library Network of Northeastern Pennsylvania, c/o Community Medical Center, Doctor's Lib., 1800 Mulberry St., Scranton 18510. SAN 322-2934. Tel. 717-969-8197. *Chair* Corrine McNabb.

Health Sciences Libraries Consortium, 3600 Market St., Suite 550, Philadelphia 19104-2646. SAN 323-9780. Tel. 215-222-1532. FAX 215-222-0416. *Exec. Dir.* Joseph C. Scorza.

Interlibrary Delivery Service of Pennsylvania, 471 Park Lane, State College 16803-3208. SAN 322-2942. Tel. 814-238-0254. FAX 814-238-9686. *Admin. Dir.* Janet C. Phillips.

Laurel Highlands Health Sciences Library Consortium, Owen Lib., Rm. 209, Univ. of Pittsburgh at Johnstown, Johnstown 15904. SAN 322-2950. Tel. 814-269-7280. FAX 814-266-8230. *Dir.* Heather W. Brice.

Lehigh Valley Association of Independent Colleges Inc., Moravian College, 1200 Main St., Bethlehem 18018-6650. SAN 322-2969. Tel. 215-882-5275. FAX 215-882-5515. *Dir.* Galen C. Godbey.

Mid-Atlantic Law Library Cooperative (MALLCO), c/o Allegheny County Law Lib., 921 City/County Bldg., Pittsburgh 15219. SAN 371-0645. Tel. 412-355-5353. FAX 412-355-5889. *Dir.* Joel Fishman; *Coord.* Frank Liu.

NEIU Consortium, 1300 Old Plank Rd., Mayfield 18433. SAN 372-817X. Tel. 717-282-9268. *IMS Dir.* Robert Carpenter; *Program Coord.* Rose Bennett.

Northeastern Pennsylvania Bibliographic Center, c/o Learning Resources Center, Marywood College, Scranton 18509-1598. SAN 322-2993. Tel. 717-348-6211, Ext. 546. FAX 717-348-1817. *Dir.* Catherine H. Schappert.

Northwest Interlibrary Cooperative of Pennsylvania (NICOP), Penn State at Erie, Behrend College Lib., Station Rd., Erie 16563. SAN 370-5862. Tel. 814-898-6106. FAX 814-898-6350. *Chair* Elizabeth Smith.

Oakland Library Consortium (OLC), Carnegie Mellon Univ., Hunt Lib., Rm. 302, Pittsburgh 15213-3890. SAN 370-5803. Tel. 412-268-2890. FAX 412-268-6944. *Board Pres.* Charles B. Lowry; *Secy.* Staci Quakenbush.

PALINET and Union Library Catalogue of Pennsylvania (PALINET), 3401 Market St., Suite 262, Philadelphia 19104. SAN 322-3000. Tel. 215-382-7031. FAX 215-382-0022. *Exec. Dir.* James E. Rush; *Mgr. OCLC Services* Meryl Cinnamon; *Mgr. Microcomputer Services* Clifford Coughlin; *Mgr. Admin. Services* Donna Wright.

Pennsylvania Citizens for Better Libraries (PCBL), 806 West St., Homestead 15120. SAN 372-8285. Tel. 412-461-1322. FAX 412-461-1399. *Pres.* Rocco J. Longo.

Pennsylvania Community College Library Consortium, c/o Bucks County Community College, Swamp Rd., Newtown 18940. SAN 329-3939. Tel. 215-968-8055. *Pres.* John Bradley.

Pennsylvania Library Association, 1919 N. Front St., Harrisburg 17102. SAN 372-8145. Tel. 717-233-3113. FAX 717-233-3121. *Exec. Dir.* Margaret S. Bauer; *Pres.* Christine Roysdon.

Philadelphia Area Consortium of Special Collections Libraries (PACSCL). SAN 370-7504. Tel. 215-561-6050. FAX 215-561-6477. *Chair Exec. Committee* Thomas Horrocks.

Pittsburgh Council on Higher Education (PCHE), 3814 Forbes Ave., Pittsburgh 15213-3506. SAN 322-3019. Tel. 412-683-7905. FAX 412-648-1492. *Exec. Dir.* Betty K. Hunter.

Pittsburgh-East Hospital Library Cooperative, Saint Francis Medical Center, 400 45th St., Pittsburgh 15201. SAN 322-3027. Tel. 412-622-4110. *Pres.* Pam Sgalio.

Pittsburgh Regional Library Center (PRLC), 103 Yost Blvd., Pittsburgh 15221-4833. SAN 322-3035. Tel. 412-825-0600. FAX 412-825-0762. *Exec. Dir.* Christina Russell.

Somerset–Bedford County Medical Library Consortium, Box 631, Somerset 15501-0631. SAN 322-3043. Tel. 814-445-6501, Ext. 216. FAX 814-443-0217. *Dir.* Eve Kline; *Libn.* Kathy Plaso.

Southeast Pittsburgh Library Consortium (SEPLC), Uniontown Hospital, Professional Lib., 500 W. Berkeley St., Uniontown 15401. SAN 371-5132. Tel. 412-430-5178. FAX 412-430-3349. *Chair* Marilyn Miller.

Southeastern Pennsylvania Theological Library Association (SEPTLA), c/o Saint Charles Borromeo Seminary, Ryan Memorial Lib., 1000 E. Wynnewood Rd., Overbrook 19096-3012. SAN 371-0793. Tel. 610-667-3394, Ext. 280. FAX 610-664-7913. *Pres.* Lorena Boylan.

State System of Higher Education Libraries Council (SSHELCO), c/o Rohrbach Lib., Kutztown Univ., Kutztown 19530-0730. SAN 322-2918. Tel. 610-683-4480. FAX 610-683-4483. *Chair* Margaret K. Devlin.

Susquehanna Library Cooperative, c/o Stevenson Lib., Lock Haven Univ., Lock Haven 17745. SAN 322-3051. Tel. 717-893-2309. FAX 717-893-2506. *Pres.* Robert Bravard.

Tri-State College Library Cooperative (TCLC), c/o Rosemont College Lib., Rosemont 19010. SAN 322-3078. Tel. 215-525-0796. FAX 215-525-1939. *Coord.* Ellen Gasiewski.

Rhode Island

Association of Rhode Island Health Sciences Librarians (ARIHSL), c/o Isaac Ray Medical Lib., Butler Hospital, 345 Blackstone Blvd., Providence 02906. SAN 371-0742. Tel. 401-455-6249. *Pres.* Ruth Ann Gildea.

Consortium of Rhode Island Academic and Research Libraries (CRIARL), Box 40041, Providence 02940-0041. SAN 322-3086. Tel. 401-454-6278. *Pres.* Carol S. Terry.

Cooperating Libraries Automated Network (CLAN), c/o Providence Public Lib., 225 Washington St., Providence 02903. SAN 329-4560. Tel. 401-455-8044. FAX 401-455-8080. *Chair* Susan Reed. *Exec. Dir.* Virginia Taken.

Rhode Island Library Network (RHILINET), 300 Richmond St., Providence 02903-4222. SAN 371-6821. Tel. 401-277-2726. FAX 401-831-1131. *Dir.* Barbara Weaver.

South Carolina

Catawba-Wateree Area Health Education Consortium, 1020 W. Meeting St., Box 2049, Lancaster 29721. SAN 329-3971. Tel. 803-286-4121. FAX 803-286-4165. *Libn.* Penny Welling.

Charleston Academic Libraries Consortium, College of Charleston, Robert Scott Small Lib., Charleston 29424. SAN 371-0769. Tel. 803-953-5530. *Chair* David Cohen.

Columbia Area Medical Librarians' Association (CAMLA), Professional Lib., Box 202, Columbia 29202. SAN 372-9400. Tel. 803-734-7136. FAX 803-734-7087. *Coord.* Neeta N. Shah.

South Carolina AHEC Consortium (AHEC), 171 Ashley Ave., Charleston 29425. SAN 329-3998. Tel. 803-792-4431. FAX 803-792-4430. *Acting Dir.* Sabra Slaughter.

South Carolina State Library, South Carolina Library Network, 1500 Senate St., Box 11469, Columbia 29211-1469. SAN 322-4198. Tel. 803-734-8666. FAX 803-734-8676. *State Libn.* James B. Johnson, Jr.

Upper Savannah AHEC, Medical Lib., Self Memorial Hospital, 1325 Spring St., Greenwood 29646. SAN 329-4110. Tel. 803-227-4851. FAX 803-227-4838. *Libn.* Thomas Hill.

South Dakota

Colleges of Mid-America Inc. (CMA), c/o Mount Marty College, 1105 W. Eighth St., Yankton 57058. SAN 322-3132. Tel. 605-668-1548. *Dir.* Mary C. Miller.

South Dakota Library Network (SDLN), Box 9672, Univ. Sta., Spearfish 57799-9672. SAN 371-2117. Tel. 605-642-6835. FAX 605-642-6298. *Operating Dir.* Gary Johnson.

Tennessee

Association of Memphis Area Health Science Libraries (AMAHSL), c/o Univ. of Tennessee Health Science Lib., 877 Madison Ave., Memphis 38163. SAN 323-9802. Tel. 901-448-5168. *Pres.* Glenda Mendina.

Knoxville Area Health Sciences Library Consortium (KAHSLC), c/o Univ. of Tennessee Medical Center, Preston Medical Lib., 1924 Alcoa Hwy., Knoxville 37920. SAN 371-0556. Tel. 615-544-9525. *Pres.* Doris Prichard.

Mid-Tennessee Health Science Librarians Consortium, Saint Thomas Hospital, Box 380, Nashville 37202. SAN 329-5028. Tel. 615-386-6658. FAX 615-386-6659. *Pres.* Alice Lovvern.

Tennessee Health Science Library Association (THeSLA), Vanderbilt Univ. Medical Center Lib., Nashville 37232-2340. SAN 371-0726. Tel. 615-322-2291. FAX 615-343-6454. *Pres.* Evelyn Forbes.

Tri-Cities Area Health Sciences Libraries Consortium, East Tennessee State Univ., James H. Quillen College of Medicine, Medical Lib., Box 70693, Johnson City 37614-0693. SAN 329-4099. Tel. 615-929-6252. FAX 615-461-7025. *Dir.* Janet S. Fisher.

West Tennessee Academic Library Consortium, c/o Jackson State Community College Lib., 2046 N. Parkway, Jackson 38301. SAN 322-3175. Tel. 901-425-2615. FAX 901-425-2647. *Chair* Scott Cohen.

Texas

Abilene Library Consortium, Box 8177, Abilene Christian Univ. Sta., Abilene 79699-8177. SAN 322-4694. Tel. 915-674-2434. FAX 915-674-2202. *System Mgr.* Robert Gillette.

Alliance for Higher Education, 17103 Preston Rd., Suite 250, LB 107, Dallas 75248-1373. SAN 322-3337. Tel. 214-713-8170. FAX 214-713-8209. *Pres.* Allan Watson; *Exec. Dir. Education Info.* Mary M. Huston.

Amigos Bibliographic Council Inc., 12200 Park Central Dr., Suite 500, Dallas 75251. SAN 322-3191. Tel. 214-851-8000. FAX 214-991-6061. *Exec. Dir.* Bonnie Juergens.

APLIC International Census Network, c/o Population Research Center, 1800 Main Bldg., Univ. of Texas, Austin 78713. SAN 370-0690. Tel. 512-471-5514. FAX 512-471-4886. *Dir.* Gera Draaijer; *Libn.* Diane Fisher.

Council of Research and Academic Libraries (CORAL), Box 290236, San Antonio 78280-1636. SAN 322-3213. Tel. 210-341-1366. *Pres.* Cliff Dawdy.

—Circulation and Interlibrary Loan Group (CIRCILL), c/o San Antonio College, 1001 Howard St., San Antonio 78212. SAN 322-323X. Tel. 210-733-2489. *Chair* John Deosdade.

—Coral Periodicals-Serials Librarians Group (CORPSE), Inst. of Texan Cultures, Box 1226, San Antonio 78294. SAN 322-3248. Tel. 210-226-7651. *Chair* Diane Bruce.

—Documents Users Group (DOCS), c/o San Antonio College, 1001 Howard St., San Antonio 78212. SAN 322-3256. Tel. 210-733-2598. *Chair* Christine Petimezas.

—Instructional Media Services Group (IMS), Our Lady of the Lake Univ., 411 S.W. St., San Antonio 78207-4689. SAN 322-3221. Tel. 210-434-6711. *Pres.* Jean Thornblom.

—Special Collections Interest Group (SCIG), Trinity Univ., 715 Stadium Dr., San Antonio 78212. SAN 324-2986. Tel. 210-736-7344. *Pres.* Craig Likness.

—Technical Services Interest Group (TSIG), Southwest Research Inst., 6220 Culebra Rd., San Antonio 78228-0510. SAN 322-3272. Tel. 210-522-2126. *Pres.* Rowland Craig.

Del Norte Biosciences Library Consortium, c/o Reference Dept. Lib., Univ. of Texas at El Paso, El Paso 79968-0582. SAN 322-3302. Tel. 915-747-5643. FAX 915-747-5327. *Pres.* Esperanza A. Moreno.

Harrington Library Consortium, Box 447, Amarillo 79178. SAN 329-546X. Tel. 806-371-5135. FAX 806-371-5370. *Exec. Dir.* Roseann Perez.

Health Library Information Network, c/o Texas College of Osteopathic Medicine, Health Science Lib., 2500 Camp Bowie Blvd., Fort Worth 76107. SAN 322-3299. Tel. 817-735-2588. *Chair* Regina Lee.

Health Oriented Libraries of San Antonio (HOLSA), Briscoe Lib., Univ. of Texas Health Science Center, 7703 Floyd Curl Dr., San Antonio 78284. SAN 373-5907. Tel. 210-567-2425. *Pres.* Janna Lawrence.

Houston Area Research Library Consortium (HARLiC), c/o Rice Univ., Fondren Lib., 6100 S. Main St., Houston 77005. SAN 322-3329. Tel. 713-527-4021. *Pres.* Beth Shapiro.

National Network of Libraries of Medicine–South Central Region, c/o HAM-TMC Lib., 1133 M. D. Anderson Blvd., Houston 77030-2809. SAN 322-3353. Tel. 713-790-7053. FAX 713-790-7030. *Contact* Mary Ryan.

Northeast Texas Library System (NETLS), 625 Austin, Garland 75040-6365. SAN 370-5943. Tel. 214-205-2566. FAX 214-205-2523. *Dir.* Lowell Lindsey; *Coord.* Elizabeth Crabb.

Piasano Consortium, Victoria College, Univ. of Houston at Victoria, 2602 N. Ben Jordan, Victoria 77901-5699. SAN 329-4943. Tel. 512-573-3291, 576-3151. FAX 512-573-4401. *Coord.* Joe F. Dahlstrom.

Regional Information and Communication Exchange, Fondren Lib., Rice Univ., Box 1892, Houston 77251-1892. SAN 322-3345. Tel. 713-528-3553. FAX 713-523-4117. *Dir.* Una Gourlay.

South Central Academic Medical Libraries Consortium (SCAMEL), Lewis Health Science Lib., Univ. of North Texas Health Science Center, 3500 Camp Bowie Blvd., Fort Worth 76107. SAN 372-8269. Tel. 817-735-2380. FAX 817-735-2283. *Chair* James Pat Craig.

Texas Council of State University Librarians, Southwest Texas State Univ., San Marcos 78666-4604. SAN 322-337X. Tel. 512-245-2133. FAX 512-245-3002. *Chair* Joan Heath.

TEXNET, Box 12927, Austin 78711. SAN 322-3396. Tel. 512-463-5465. FAX 512-463-5436. *Mgr.* Rebecca Linton.

USDA Southwest Regional Document Delivery System, c/o Texas A&M Univ. Lib., Interlib. Loan Service, College Station 77843-5000. SAN 322-340X. Tel. 409-845-5641. FAX 409-845-4512. *ILL Head* Susan Raschke.

Utah

Utah College Library Council (UCLC), c/o Brigham Young Univ., 1354 HBLL, Provo 84602. SAN 322-3418. Tel. 801-378-4482. FAX 801-378-6347. *Secy.* Terry Dahlin.

Utah Health Sciences Library Consortium (UHSLC), c/o Saint Benedict Hospital, 5475 S. 500 E., Ogden 84405. SAN 370-5900. Tel. 801-479-2055. *Chair* Sandy Eckersley.

Vermont

Health Science Libraries of New Hampshire and Vermont (HSL-NH-VT), Health Sciences Lib., Rutland Regional Medical Center, 160 Allen St., Rutland 05701. SAN 371-6864. Tel. 802-747-3777. FAX 802-747-1620. *Pres.* Daphne Pringle.

Vermont Resource Sharing Network, c/o Vermont Dept. of Libraries, 109 State St., Montpelier 05609-0601. SAN 322-3426. Tel. 802-828-3261. FAX 802-828-2199. *Contact* Marjorie Zunder.

Virginia

American Gas Association, Library Services (AGA-LSC), 1515 Wilson Blvd., Arlington 22209. SAN 371-0890. Tel. 703-841-8400. FAX 703-841-8406. *Dir.* Steven Dorner.

Defense Technical Information Center, Cameron Sta., Bldg. 5, Alexandria 22304-6145. SAN 322-3442. Tel. 703-274-3848. FAX 703-274-9274. *Admin.* Kurt N. Molholm.

Infopro Technologies, 8000 Westpark Dr., McLean 22102. SAN 322-2438. Tel. 703-442-0900. FAX 703-893-4632. *Pres.* Andrew Gregory.

Lynchburg Area Library Cooperative, Lipscomb Lib., Randolph-Mason Woman's College, Lynchburg 24503. SAN 322-3450. Tel. 804-947-8133. FAX 804-947-8134. *Pres.* Patricia DeMars.

Richmond Academic Library Consortium (RALC), VCU Libs., Box 2033, Richmond 23284-2033. SAN 371-3938. Tel. 804-367-1107. *Pres.* Barbara Ford.

Richmond Area Film-Video Cooperative, c/o Virginia Commonwealth Univ., James Branch Cabell Learning Resource Center, Richmond 23284-2033. SAN 322-3469. Tel. 804-367-1088. FAX 804-367-0151. *Dir.* Barbara Ford.

Southside Virginia Library Network (SVLN), Longwood College, 201 High St., Farmville 23909-1897. SAN 372-8242. Tel. 804-395-2433. *Dir.* Calvin J. Boyer.

Southwestern Virginia Health Information Librarians (SWVAHILI), c/o Southwestern Virginia Mental Health Inst., Marion 24354. SAN 323-9527. Tel. 703-783-1200, Ext. 161. FAX 703-783-9712. *Chair* Alice Hurlebaus; *Secy.-Treas.* Mary Horner.

Tidewater Health Sciences Libraries (THSL), c/o Eastern Virginia Medical School Lib., Box 1980, Norfolk 23501-1980. SAN 317-3658. Tel. 804-446-5840. *Dir.* Anne Cramer.

U.S. Army Training and Doctrine Command (TRADOC), Lib. and Info. Network (TRALINET) Center, ATBO-N, Bldg. 117, Fort Monroe 23651-5117. SAN 322-418X. Tel. 804-727-4491. FAX 804-727-2750. *Dir.* Janet Scheitle; *Systems Libn.* Edwin Burgess.

Virginia Library and Information Network (VLIN), c/o Virginia State Lib. and Archives, 11 St. at Capitol Sq., Richmond 23219-3491. SAN 373-0921. Tel. 804-786-2320. FAX 804-225-4608. *State Libn.* John C. Tyson; *Dir. Lib. Development and Networking* Anthony Yankus.

Virginia Tidewater Consortium for Higher Education, Health Science Bldg., Rm. 129, 5215 Hampton Blvd., Norfolk 23529-0293. SAN 329-5486. Tel. 804-683-3183. FAX 804-683-4515. *Pers.* Lawrence G. Dotolo.

Washington

Central Washington Hospital Consortium, Box 1887, Wenatchee 98807. SAN 329-3750. Tel. 509-662-1511. *Coord.* Susan Marshall.

Consortium for Automated Library Services, Evergreen State College Lib., Rm. L2300, Olympia 98505. SAN 329-4528. Tel. 206-866-6000, Ext. 6260. FAX 206-866-6790. *Systems Mgr.* Steven A. Metcalf.

Council on Botanical Horticultural Libraries, Lawrence Pierce Lib., Rhododendron Species Federation, 2525 S. 336 St., Box 3798, Federal Way 98063-3798. SAN 371-0521. Tel. 206-927-6960. FAX 206-838-4686. *Chair* Mrs. George Harrison.

Inland Northwest Health Sciences Libraries (INWHSL), Box 10283, Spokane 99209-0283. SAN 370-5099. Tel. 509-325-6139. FAX 509-325-7163. *Chair* Robert Pringle.

National Network of Libraries of Medicine–Pacific Northwest Region, Univ. of Washington, SB-55, Seattle 98195. SAN 322-3485. Tel. 206-543-8262. FAX 206-543-2469. *Dir.* Sherrilynne S. Fuller.

Seattle Area Hospital Library Consortium, Valley Medical Center Lib., Seattle 98055. SAN 329-3815. Tel. 206-228-3450, Ext. 5632. *Dir.* Nancy Turntine.

Spokane Cooperative Library Information System (SCOLIS), E12004 Main, Spokane 99206-5193. SAN 322-3892. Tel. 509-922-1371. FAX 509-926-7139. *Mgr.* Linda Dunham.

WLN, Box 3888, Lacey 98503-0888. SAN 322-3507. Tel. 206-923-4000. FAX 206-923-4009. *Pres.* Ronald F. Miller; *Mgr. Customer Service and Sales* Gwen Culp.

West Virginia

Consortium of South Eastern Law Libraries (COSELL), c/o West Virginia Univ., College of Law Lib., Law Center Dr., Box 6135, Morgantown 26506-6135. SAN 372-8277. Tel. 304-293-7641. FAX 304-293-6020. *Chair* Camille Riley; *Pres.* Thomas Steele.

East Central Colleges, c/o Bethany College, Box AJ, Bethany 26032-1434. SAN 322-2667. Tel. 304-829-7812. FAX 304-829-7546. *Exec. Dir.* Dennis Landon.

Huntington Health Science Library Consortium, Marshall Univ. Health Science Libs., Huntington 25755-9210. SAN 322-4295. Tel. 304-696-3170. *Chair* Edward Dzierzak.

Mountain States Consortium, c/o Alderson Broaddus College, Philippi 26416. SAN 329-4765. Tel. 304-457-1700. *Treas.* Leonard Lobello.

Southern West Virginia Library Automation Corporation, 221 N. Kanawha St., Box 1876, Beckley 25802. SAN 322-421X. Tel. 304-255-0511, Ext. 19. FAX 304-255-0516. *Systems Mgr.* Margaret Williamson.

Wisconsin

Council of Wisconsin Libraries Inc. (COWL), 728 State St., Rm. 464, Madison 53706-1494. SAN 322-3523. Tel. 608-263-4962. FAX 608-263-3684. *Dir.* Kathryn Schneider Michaelis.

Fox River Valley Area Library Consortium, Theda Clark Regional Medical Center, Box 2021, Neenah 54957-2021. SAN 322-3531. Tel. 414-729-2190. FAX 414-729-2321. *Coord.* Mary Horan.

Fox Valley Library Council (FVLC), c/o Outagamie/Wayaaca Lib. Council, 225 N. Oneida St., Appleton 54911. SAN 323-9640. Tel. 414-832-6190. *Pres.* Dennis Parks.

Library Council of Metropolitan Milwaukee Inc., 814 W. Wisconsin Ave., Milwaukee 53233. SAN 322-354X. Tel. 414-271-8470. FAX 414-286-2794. *Exec. Dir.* Corliss Rice.

North East Wisconsin Intertype Libraries Inc. (NEWIL), c/o Nicolet Federated Lib. System, 515 Pine St., Green Bay 54301. SAN 322-3574. Tel. 414-448-4412. FAX 414-448-4420. *Coord.* Terrie Howe.

Northwestern Wisconsin Hospital Library Consortium, c/o Health Sciences Lib., Saint Michael's Hospital, 900 Illinois Ave., Stevens Point 54481. SAN 322-3604. Tel. 715-346-5091. FAX 715-346-5077. *Dir.* Jan Kraus.

South Central Wisconsin Health Science Library Cooperative, Meriter Hospital, 202 S. Park St., Madison 53715. SAN 322-4686. Tel. 608-267-6234. FAX 608-267-6288. *Coord.* JoAnne Meulenbach.

Southeastern Wisconsin Health Science Library Consortium, c/o Sinai-Samaritan Medical Center, Hurwitz Memorial Lib., Box 0342, Milwaukee 53201-0342. SAN 322-3582. Tel. 414-283-6710. *Contact* Mary Jo Baertschy.

Southeastern Wisconsin Information Technology Exchange Inc. (SWITCH), 6801 N. Yates Rd., Milwaukee 53217-3985. SAN 371-3962. Tel. 414-351-2423. FAX 414-352-6062. *Exec. Dir.* David Weinberg-Kinsey.

Wisconsin Area Research Center Network, ARC Network, 816 State St., Madison 53706. SAN 373-0875. Tel. 608-264-6480. *State Archivist* Peter Gottlieb.

Wisconsin Interlibrary Services (WILS), 728 State St., Rm. 464, Madison 53706-1494. SAN 322-3612. Tel. 608-263-4962, 263-5051. FAX 608-263-3684. *Dir.* Kathryn Schneider Michaelis.

Wisconsin Valley Library Service (WVLS), 400 First St., Wausau 54403. SAN 371-3911. Tel. 715-847-5535. FAX 715-845-4270. *Dir.* Heather Ann Eldred.

Wyoming

Health Sciences Information Network (HSIN), c/o Science and Technology Lib., Univ. of Wyoming, Box 262, Laramie 82071-3262. SAN 371-4861. Tel. 307-766-4263. FAX 307-766-3611. *Coord.* Janice Gahagan.

Northeastern Wyoming Medical Library Consortium, Campbell County Memorial Hospital, Box 3011, Gillette 82716. SAN 370-484X. Tel. 307-682-8811, Ext. 183. FAX 307-687-5182. *Chair* Dorothy O'Brien.

Wyoming Library Network, c/o Wyoming State Lib., Supreme Court and State Lib. Bldg., Cheyenne 82002. SAN 371-0661. Tel. 307-777-7281. FAX 307-777-6289. *Deputy State Libn.* Jerry Krois.

Virgin Islands

VILINET (Virgin Islands Library and Information Network), c/o Division of Libs., Museums and Archives, 23 Dronningens Gade, Saint Thomas 00802. SAN 322-3639. Tel. 809-774-3407, 774-3725. *Chair* Jeanette Allis Bastian.

Canada

Alberta

Alberta Association of College Librarians (AACL), Medicine Hat College, 299 College Dr. S.E., Medicine Hat T1A 3Y6. SAN 370-0763. Tel. 403-529-3867. FAX 403-529-2437. *Chair* Susan Brayford.

Alberta Government Libraries Council (AGLC), c/o Alberta Public Safety Service Lib., 10320 146th St., Edmonton T5N 3A2. SAN 370-0372. Tel. 403-451-7178. *Chair* Teresa Richey.

Alberta Occupational Health and Safety (AEOH), Alberta Occupational Health Lib. Services, 10709 Jasper Ave., 6th fl., Edmonton T5J 3N3. SAN 370-0801. Tel. 403-427-3530. FAX 403-427-5698. *Public Services Libn. and Mgr.* Peggy Yeh.

Northern Alberta Health Libraries Association (NAHLA), c/o Peter Wilcock Lib., Charles Camsell Hospital, 2804 114th Ave., Edmonton T5M 3A4. SAN 370-5951. Tel. 403-453-5581. FAX 403-453-6565. *Pres.* Gail Moores.

British Columbia

British Columbia College and Institute Library Services, Clearinghouse for the Print Impaired (CILS), Vancouver Community College, Langara Campus Lib., 100 W. 49 Ave., Vancouver V5Y 2Z6. SAN 329-6970. Tel. 604-324-5237. FAX 604-324-5544. *Contact* Phyllis Mason.

British Columbia Post-Secondary Interlibrary Loan Network (NET), Univ. of British Columbia, Box 2139, Vancouver V6B 3T1. SAN 322-4724. Tel. 604-822-4430. FAX 604-822-6465. *Head ILL* Margaret Friesen.

Central Vancouver Librarian Group (CVLG), c/o Lib. Processing Centre–Serials, Univ. of British Columbia, 2206 E. Mall, Vancouver V6T 1Z8. SAN 323-9543. Tel. 604-822-4578. FAX 604-822-3201. *Chair* Kat McGrath.

Media Exchange Cooperative (MEC), Capilano College, 2055 Purcell Way, North Vancouver V7J 3H5. SAN 329-6954. Tel. 604-984-4943. FAX 604-984-1728. *Pres.* Frieda Wiebe.

Manitoba

Manitoba Government Libraries Council (MGLC), 1329 Niakwa Rd. E., Winnipeg R2J 3T4. SAN 371-6848. Tel. 204-945-1413. FAX 204-945-1784. *Chair* Betty Dearth.

Manitoba Library Consortium Inc. (MLCI), c/o Aikins, MacAulay and Thorvaldson, Community Exchange Tower, 360 Main St., Winnipeg R3C 4G1. SAN 372-820X. Tel. 304-632-2232. *Chairs* Patricia Bozyk, Kathy Thornborough.

New Brunswick

LINK–Library Information Network, c/o Ward Chipman Lib., Univ. of New Brunswick, Box 5050, Saint John E2L 4L5. SAN 370-0798. Tel. 506-648-5704. FAX 506-648-5701. *Coord.* Susan Collins.

Maritimes Health Libraries Association (MHLA/ABSM), Saint John Regional Hospital, Health Sciences Lib., Box 2100, Saint John E2L 4L2. SAN 370-0836. Tel. 506-648-6763. *Pres.* Anne Kilfoil.

Nova Scotia

Council of Metropolitan University Librarians (COMUL), Technical Univ. of Nova Scotia, Box 1000, Halifax B3J 2X4. SAN 370-0704. Tel. 902-420-7700. FAX 902-420-7551. *Chair* Donna Richardson.

Novanet, 1379 Seymour St., Halifax B3H 3J5. SAN 372-4050. Tel. 902-494-1785. FAX 902-494-1536. *System Mgr.* Leslie A. Foster.

Ontario

Bibliocentre, 80 Cowdray Ct., Scarborough M1S 4N1. SAN 322-3663. Tel. 416-754-6600. FAX 416-299-0902. *Dir.* Doug Wentzel.

Canadian Association of Research Libraries (CARL/ABRC), Univ. of Ottawa, Morisset Hall, Rm. 602, 65 University St., Ottawa K1N 9A5. SAN 323-9721. Tel. 613-564-5864. FAX 613-564-5871. *Exec. Dir.* David L. McCallum.

Canadian Health Libraries Association (CHLA/ABSC), Office of Secretariat, 3332 Yonge St., Box 94038, Toronto M4N 3R1. SAN

370-0720. Tel./FAX 416-485-0377. *Contact* Dorothy Davey; *Pres.* Beverly Brown.
•Canadian Heritage Information Network (CHIN), 365 Laurier Ave. W., Journal Tower S., 12th fl., Ottawa K1A 0C8. SAN 329-3076. Tel. 613-992-3333, Ext. 186. FAX 613-952-2318. *Dir. Gen.* L. Eliott Sherwood; *Coord.* Merridy Bradley.
•County and Regional Municipal Library (CARML), c/o Lennox and Addington County Lib., 37 Dundas St. W., Napanee K7R 1Z5. SAN 323-9705. Tel. 613-354-2585. FAX 613-354-7527. *Chair* Sam Coghlan; *Secy.* Mary Anne Evans.
Disability Resource Library Network (DRLN), c/o Hugh McMillan Rehabilitation Center, Health Science Lib., 350 Rumsey Rd., Toronto M4G 1R8. SAN 323-9837. Tel. 416-425-6220, Ext. 517. *Chair* Pui-Ying Wong.
Education Libraries Sharing of Resources–A Network (ELSOR), 45 York Mills Rd., Willowdale M2P 1B6. SAN 370-0399. Tel. 416-397-2523. FAX 416-397-2640. *Chair* Martha E. Murphy.
Hamilton and District Health Library Network, c/o Health Sciences Lib., McMaster Univ., Hamilton L8N 3Z5. SAN 370-5846. Tel. 902-525-9110, Ext. 22322. FAX 902-528-3733. *Network Coord.* Dorothy Fitzgerald.
Health Science Information Consortium of Toronto, Univ. of Toronto, 7 King's College Circle, Toronto M5S 1A5. SAN 370-5080. Tel. 416-978-6359. FAX 416-978-7666. *Exec. Dir.* Joan L. Leishman.
Hi-Tech Libraries Network, c/o Cal Corp., 1050 Morrison Dr., Ottawa K2H 8K7. SAN 323-9586. Tel. 613-820-8280. FAX 613-820-8314. *Contact* Sandra Spence.
Information Network for Ontario, Ministry of Culture, Tourism and Recreation, Libs. and Community Info. Branch, 77 Bloor St. W., 3rd fl., Toronto M7A 2R9. SAN 329-5605. Tel. 416-314-7611. FAX 416-314-7635. *Dir.* Barbara Clubb.
Kingston Area Health Libraries Association (KAHLA), c/o Staff Lib., Brockville Psychiatric Hospital, Box 1050, Brockville K6V 5W7. SAN 370-0674. Tel. 613-345-1461. *Pres.* Michelle Lamarche.

Ontario Council of University Libraries (OCUL), Univ. of Ottawa, 65 Univ., Ottawa K1N 9A5. SAN 371-9413. Tel. 613-564-6892. FAX 613-564-9886. *Chair* Richard Greene.
Ontario Hospital Libraries Association, Region 9 (OHLAR9), c/o Rideau Regional Centre Lib., Box 2000, Smith Falls K7A 4T7. SAN 370-0550. Tel. 613-284-0123, Ext. 225. FAX 613-283-3463. *Chair* Janet Joyce; *Pres.* Pat Kiteley.
Ontario Hospital Libraries Association, c/o Victoria Hospital Lib. Services, Box 5375, London N6A 4G5. SAN 370-0739. Tel. 519-685-8500, Ext. 7717. FAX 519-667-6794. *Dir.* Jan Greenwood.
Ottawa Hull Health Libraries Association (OHHLA), c/o Canadian Medical Association Lib., 1867 Alta Vista Dr., Ottawa K1G 0G8. SAN 370-0844. Tel. 613-731-9331, Ext. 2144. FAX 613-731-9013. *Pres.* Kathleen Beaudoin; *Secy.-Treas.* Judith Bosschart.
QL Systems Limited, One Gore St., Box 2080, Kingston K7L 5J8. SAN 322-368X. Tel. 613-549-4611. FAX 613-548-4260. *Pres.* Hugh Lawford.
—Calgary Branch, 505 Third St. S.W., Suite 1010, Calgary, AB T2P 3E6. SAN 322-3817. Tel. 403-262-6505. FAX 403-264-7193. *Marketing Mgr.* Anita Manley.
—Halifax Branch, 1819 Granville St., Suite 300, Halifax, NS B3J 1X8. SAN 325-4194. Tel. 902-420-1666. FAX 902-422-3016. *Mgr.* Ruth Rintoul.
—Ottawa Branch, 901 Saint Andrews Tower, 275 Sparks, Ottawa, ON K1R 7X9. SAN 322-3825. Tel. 613-238-3499. FAX 613-238-7594. *V.P. Marketing* Adrienne Herron; *Mgr.* Alan Dingle.
—Toronto Branch, 411 Richmond St. E., Suite 101, Toronto, ON M5A 3S5. SAN 322-3833. Tel. 416-862-7656. FAX 416-862-8073. *Mgr.* Tim Outhit.
—Vancouver Branch, 355 Burrard St., Suite 920, Vancouver, BC V6C 2G8. SAN 322-3841. Tel. 604-684-1462. FAX 604-684-5581. *Mgr.* Joan Honeywell.
Shared Library Services (SLS), South Huron Hospital Shared Lib. Services, 24 Huron St. W., Exeter N0M 1S2. SAN 323-9500.

Tel. 519-235-2700, Ext. 49. FAX 519-235-3405. *Dir.* Linda Wilcox.

Sheridan Park Association, Library and Information Science Committee (SPA-LISC), 2275 Speakman Dr., Mississauga L5K 1B1. SAN 370-0437. Tel. 905-823-6160. *Chair* Carolyne Sidey; *SPA Mgr.* E. Gordon.

Southern Ontario Library Service–Hamilton (SOLS), 1133 Central Ave., Hamilton L8K 1N7. SAN 371-0629. Tel. 416-544-2780. *Dir.* L. Irvine.

Toronto Health Libraries Association (THLA), Box 94056, Toronto M4N 3R1. SAN 323-9853. Tel. 416-978-2872. *Pres.* Sylvia Newman.

Toronto School of Theology, c/o Knox College, 59 Saint George St., Toronto M5S 2E6. SAN 322-452X. Tel. 416-978-4504. FAX 416-971-2133. *Secy. Lib. Commission* Chris Tucker.

Wellington Waterloo Dufferin (WWD) Health Library Network, c/o Medical Lib., Saint Mary's General Hospital, 911 Queens Blvd., Kitchener N2M 1B2. SAN 370-0496. Tel. 519-742-3611, Ext. 2235. *Coord.* Elaine Baldwin.

Quebec

Association des Bibliothèques de la Santé Affiliées à l'Université de Montréal (ABSAUM), c/o Health Lib., Univ. of Montreal, Montreal H3C 3J7. SAN 370-5838. Tel. 514-343-6826. FAX 514-343-2550. *Secy.* Bernard Bedard.

Montreal Health Libraries Association (MHLA), 4565 Queen Mary Rd., Montreal H3W 1W5. SAN 323-9608. Tel. 514-340-1424, Ext. 3266. FAX 514-340-2807. *Pres.* Louise Bourbonais.

Montreal Medical Online Users Group (MMOUG), McGill Health Sciences Lib., 3655 Drummond St., Montreal H3G 1Y6. SAN 370-0771. Tel. 514-398-4757. FAX 514-398-3890. *Coord.* Angella Lambrou.

Saskatchewan

Saskatchewan Government Libraries Council (SGLC), c/o Saskatchewan Agriculture and Food Lib., 3085 Albert St., Regina S4S 0B1. SAN 323-956X. Tel. 306-787-5151. FAX 306-787-0216. *Chair* Helene Stewart.

National Library and Information-Industry Associations, United States and Canada

American Association of Law Libraries

Executive Director, Roger Parent
53 W. Jackson Blvd., Chicago, IL 60604
312-939-4764, FAX 312-431-1097
Internet: lawrhp@orion.depaul.edu

Object

The American Association of Law Libraries (AALL) is established for educational and scientific purposes. It shall be conducted as a nonprofit corporation to promote and enhance the value of law libraries to the public, the legal community, and the world; to foster the profession of law librarianship; to provide leadership in the field of legal information; and to foster a spirit of cooperation among the members of the profession. Established 1906.

Membership

Memb. 4,800. Persons officially connected with a law library or with a law section of a state or general library, separately maintained. Associate membership available for others. Dues (Indiv.) $118; (Inst.) two or fewer professional libns., $236; more than two, $115 times the number of professionals; (Indiv. Assoc.) $118; (Inst. Assoc.) $227 times the number of members; (Retired) $32.50; (Student) $26; (SIS Memb.) $12 each per year. Year. July 1 to June 30.

Officers (July 1994–June 1995)

Pres. Carol D. Billings, Dir., Law Lib. of Louisiana, Supreme Ct. Bldg., Rm. 100, 301 Loyola Ave., New Orleans, LA 70112. Tel. 504-568-5706, FAX 504-568-5069, cbilli@nomvs.lsumc.edu; *V.P./Pres.-Elect* Patrick E. Kehoe, Dir., Washington College of Law Lib., American Univ., 4400 Massachusetts Ave. N.W., Washington, DC 20016-8087. Tel. 202-885-2674, FAX 202-885-2703, pkehoe@american.edu; *Past Pres.* Kay M. Todd, Paul Hastings Janofsky and Walker, 133 Peachtree St. N.E., 42nd fl., Atlanta, GA 30303. Tel. 404-527-8241, FAX 404-523-1542; *Secy.* Gale Edelman Webb, Riverside County Law Lib., 3989 Lemon St., Riverside, CA 92501. Tel. 909-275-6395, FAX 909-275-6394; *Treas.* Judith Meadows, State Law Libn., State Law Lib. of Montana, Justice Bldg., 215 N. Sanders, Helena, MT 59620-3004. Tel. 406-444-3660, FAX 406-444-3603, mtlawjm@class.org.

Executive Board (1994–1995)

Margaret Maes Axtmann, Patricia Patterson, Ann Puckett, Thomas H. Reynolds, Patricia G. Strougal, Victoria K. Trotta.

Committee Chairpersons

Awards. Bettie Scott.
Call for Papers. Susan Catterall.
Constitution and Bylaws. Nicholas Triffin.
Copyright. David J. Ensign.
Diversity. Grace M. Mills.
Education. James S. Heller.
Government Relations. Susan Dow.
Grants. Beverly G. Rubenstein.
Index to Foreign Legal Periodicals. Amber Lee Smith.

Indexing Periodical Literature. Kathy Carlson.
Law Library Journal and Newsletter. Scott Pagel.
Mentoring and Retention. Rhea A.-L. Ballard.
National Legal Resources. John Howland.
Nominations. Charlie Colokathis.
Placement. Gregory L. Ivy.
Preservation. Katherine I. Hedin.
Public Relations. Merle J. Slyhoff.
Publications Policy. Mary Lu Linnane.
Publications Review. Nathan Aaron Rosen.
Recruitment. Carol Alpert.
Relations with Information Vendors. Betty Kern.
Research. Kathy Shimpock-Vieweg.
Scholarships. Ruth Bridges.
Statistics. Claire Engel.

Special-Interest Section Chairpersons

SIS Council. Phyllis Post.
Academic Law Libraries. Barbara A. Bintliff.
Automation and Scientific Development. Gary Gott.
Foreign, Comparative, and International Law. Lyonette Louis-Jacques.
Government Documents. Carol Moody.
Legal History and Rare Books. Mary Cooper Gilliam.
Legal Information Services to the Public. Maria E. Protti.
Micrographics and Audiovisual. John W. Pedini.
Online Bibliographic Services. Mary Chapman.
Private Law Libraries. Alvin Podboy.
Reader Services. Roberta (Bobbie) Studwell.
Social Responsibilities. James Milles.
State Court and County Law Libraries. Marvin Anderson.
Technical Services. Katherine Tooley.

American Library Association

Executive Director, Elizabeth Martinez
50 E. Huron St., Chicago, IL 60611-2795
312-944-6780, 800-545-2433

Object

The mission of the American Library Association (ALA) is to provide leadership for the development, promotion, and improvement of library and information services and the profession of librarianship in order to enhance learning and ensure access to information for all. Founded 1876.

Membership

Memb. (Indiv.) 52,567; (Inst.) 2,789; (Total) 55,356. Any person, library, or other organization interested in library service and librarians. Dues (Indiv.) 1st year, $38; renewing memb., $75; (Nonsalaried Libn.) $26; (Trustee and Assoc. Memb.) $34; (Student) $19; (Foreign Indiv.) $45; (Inst.) $70 and up, depending on operating expenses of institution.

Officers (1994–1995)

Pres. Arthur Curley, Dir. and Libn., Boston Public Lib., Copley Sq., Boston, MA 02117; *Pres.-Elect* Betty J. Turock, Dir. and Chair, Lib. & Info. Studies, Rutgers SCILS, 4 Huntington St., New Brunswick, NJ 08903. Tel. 908-932-7917, FAX 908-932-6916, turock@zodiac.rutgers.edu; *Treas.* Ann K. Symons, Juneau Douglas H.S. Lib., 10014 Crazy Horse Dr., Juneau, AK 99801; *Exec. Dir.* Elizabeth Martinez, ALA Headquarters, 50 E. Huron St., Chicago, IL 60611.

Executive Board

Hardy Franklin (*Past Pres.*); Charles E. Beard (1997); Betty J. Blackman (1995); Nancy M. Bolt (1995); Cesar Caballero (1996); Bruce E. Daniels (1996); Nancy C. Kranich (1998); Mary R. Somerville (1997); Eric Wilson-Lingbloom (1998).

Endowment Trustees

Bernard A. Margolis (1995); Gerald Garbacz (1997); Patricia Glass Schuman (1996); *Exec. Board Liaison* Ann K. Symons; *Staff Liaison* Elizabeth Martinez.

Divisions

See the separate entries that follow: American Assn. of School Libns.; American Lib. Trustee Assn.; Assn. for Lib. Collections and Technical Services; Assn. for Lib. Service to Children; Assn. of College and Research Libs.; Assn. of Specialized and Cooperative Lib. Agencies; Lib. Admin. and Management Assn.; Lib. and Info. Technology Assn.; Public Lib. Assn.; Reference and Adult Services Div.; Young Adult Lib. Services Assn.

Publications

ALA Handbook of Organization and Membership Directory 1994–1995 (ann.).
American Libraries (11 per year; membs.; organizations $60; foreign $70; single copy $6).
Book Links (6 per year; U.S. $20; foreign $22; single copy $3.50).
Booklist (22 per year; U.S. and possessions $65; foreign $85; single copy $4.50).
Choice (11 per year; U.S. $165; foreign $187; single copy $20).

Round Table Chairpersons

(ALA staff liaison is given in parentheses.)
Armed Forces Libraries. Wendy E. Davis (Patricia A. Muir).
Continuing Library Education Network and Exchange. Duncan F. Smith (Margaret Myers).
Ethnic Materials and Information Exchange. Bosiljka Stevanovic (Mattye L. Nelson).

Exhibits. John Ison (Paul Graller).

Federal Librarians. S. Lynn McDonald (Patricia A. Muir).

Government Documents. Mary Redmond (Patricia A. Muir).

Independent Librarians Exchange. Murray S. Martin (Margaret Myers).

Intellectual Freedom. Paul C. Vermouth, Jr. (Anne Penway).

International Relations. Beverly P. Lynch (Robert Doyle).

Library History. James V. Carmichael, Jr. (Charles T. Harmon).

Library Instruction. Charlotte J. Files (Jeniece Guy).

Library Research. Carol Kuhlthau (Mary Jo Lynch).

Map and Geography. Nancy J. Butkovich (Judy Hambrick).

New Members. Elizabeth M. Fordon (Judy Hambrick).

Social Responsibilities. Stephen J. Stillwell (Mattye L. Nelson).

Staff Organizations. Linda L. Wiler (Jeniece Guy).

Support Staff Interests. Betty F. Smith (Margaret Myers).

Video. Kristine R. Brancolini (Irene P. Wood).

Committee Chairpersons

Accreditation (Standing). Carla D. Hayden (Prudence W. Dalrymple).

ALA Self-Study (Special). F. William Summers (Emily Melton).

American Libraries (Advisory). Irene B. Hoadley (Thomas M. Gaughan).

Appointments (Advisory). Betty J. Turock (Emily Melton).

Awards. Robert S. Smith (Peggy Barber).

Chapter Relations (Standing). Margaret L. Crist (Gerald G. Hodges).

Committee on Committees (Elected Council Committee). Betty J. Turock (Emily Melton).

Conference Program (Standing), Chicago (1995). Arthur Curley (Peggy Barber).

Conference Program Procedures and Policies Review (Special). Kay A. Cassell (Paul Graller).

Constitution and Bylaws (Standing). Pamela Gay Bonnell (Emily Melton).

Council Orientation (Special). Kay A. Cassell (Lois Ann Gregory-Wood).

Development (Advisory). Albert W. Daub (Patricia Martin).

Intellectual Freedom (Standing, Council). Candace D. Morgan (Judith F. Krug).

International Relations (Standing, Council). E. J. Josey (Robert P. Doyle).

Legislation (Standing, Council). Patricia Glass Schuman (Eileen D. Cooke).

Library Education (Standing, Council). Margaret M. Kimmel (Margaret Myers).

Library Outreach Services, Office for (Standing, Advisory). Kathleen de la Pena McCook (Mattye L. Nelson).

Library Personnel Resources, Office for (Standing, Advisory). Barbara J. Ford (Margaret Myers).

Membership (Standing). Kay A. Cassell (Gerald G. Hodges).

Minority Concerns and Cultural Diversity (Standing, Council). Gloria J. Leonard (Mattye L. Nelson).

Nominating, 1995 Election (Special). Norman Horrocks (Emily Melton).

Organization (Standing, Council). Sarah M. Pritchard (Charles Harmon).

Pay Equity (Standing, Council). Penelope S. Jeffrey (Margaret Myers).

Planning (Standing, Council). Gail P. Warner (to be appointed).

Policy Monitoring (Council). Charles A. Bunge (Lois Ann Gregory-Wood).

Professional Ethics (Standing, Council). Jeanne M. Isacco (Judith Krug).

Program Evaluation and Support (Standing, Council). Joseph A. Boisse (Gregory Calloway).

Public Information (Standing, Advisory). Fred E. Goodman (Linda K. Wallace).

Publishing (Standing, Council). Elizabeth Futas (Donald Chatham).

Research and Statistics (Standing). Barbara F. Immroth (Mary Jo Lynch).

Resolutions (Standing, Council). Judith R. Farley (Emily Melton).

Standards (Standing). Keith C. Wright (Mary Jo Lynch).

User Instruction for Information Literacy (Standing). Charles T. Townley (Jeniece N. Guy).

Women in Librarianship, Status of (Standing, Council). Lois Winkel (Margaret Myers).

Joint Committee Chairpersons

American Association of Law Libraries/ American Correctional Association–ASCLA Committee on Institution Libraries (joint). Thea Chesley (ACA); Timothy Brown (ASCLA).

American Federation of Labor/Congress of Industrial Organizations–ALA, Library Service to Labor Groups, RASD. Andrew W. Lee (ALA); Anthony Sarmiento (AFL/CIO).

Anglo-American Cataloguing Rules Common Revision Fund. Elizabeth Martinez (ALA); Karen S. Adams (Canadian Lib. Assn.); Ross Shimmon (Library Assn.).

Anglo-American Cataloguing Rules, Joint Steering Committee for Revision of. Janet Swan Hill (ALA).

Association for Educational Communications and Technology–AASL. Frances M. McDonald (AASL); Janis H. Bruwelheide (AECT).

Association for Educational Communications and Technology–ACRL. Marilyn McDonald; Gretchen H. Neill.

Association of American Publishers–ALA. Arthur Curley (ALA); to be appointed (AAP).

Association of American Publishers–ALCTS. Joseph W. Raker (ALCTS); Audrey D. Melkin (AAP).

Children's Book Council–ALA. Kay E. Vandergrift (ALA); Jazan Higgins (CBC).

Society of American Archivists–ALA (Joint Committee on Library–Archives Relationships). Karma A. Beal (ALA); Nicholas Burckel (SAA).

American Library Association
American Association of School Librarians

Executive Director, Ann Carlson Weeks
50 E. Huron St., Chicago, IL 60611-2795
312-944-6780, 800-545-2433, FAX 312-664-7459

Object

The American Association of School Librarians (AASL) is interested in the general improvement and extension of library media services for children and young people. AASL has specific responsibility for planning a program of study and service for the improvement and extension of library media services in elementary and secondary schools as a means of strengthening the educational program; evaluation, selection, interpretation, and utilization of media as they are used in the context of the school program; stimulation of continuous study and research in the library field and establishing criteria of evaluation; synthesis of the activities of all units of the American Library Association in areas of mutual concern; representation and interpretation of the need for the function of school libraries to other educational and lay groups; stimulation of professional growth, improvement of the status of school librarians, and encouragement of participation by members in appropriate type-of-activity divisions; conducting activities and projects for improvement and extension of service in the school library when such projects are beyond the scope of type-of-activity divisions, after specific approval by the ALA Council. Established in 1951 as a separate division of ALA.

Membership

Memb. 7,585. Open to all libraries, school library media specialists, interested individuals, and business firms with requisite membership in ALA.

Officers (1994–1995)

Pres. Jacqueline C. Mancall (1996); David V. Loertscher (1997); *Treas./Financial Officer* Helen R. Adams (1996); *Secy.* Susan D. Ballard 1995); *Past Pres.* E. Blanche Woolls (1995).

Board of Directors

Officers; Regional Dirs. Veda J. Arteaga (1997); Frances B. Bradburn (1996); Susan M. Bryan (1997); Donna Gilliland (1997); Marybeth Green (1995); M. Ellen Jay (1995); Marjorie L. Pappas (1996); Gail K. Dickinson (1995); Michael B. Eisenberg (1996); Jody Gehrig (1995); Frances M. McDonald (1995); Joie L. Taylor (1995); Barbara H. Weathers (1997); *Ex officio* Judith M. King (1998), Ann C. Weeks.

Publications

AASL Presidential Hotline/CONNECTIONS (q.; memb. not available by subscription). *School Library Media Quarterly* (q.; memb.; nonmemb. $40). *Ed.* Mary Kay Biagini, SLIS, Univ. of Pittsburgh, 135 N. Bellefield Ave., Pittsburgh, PA 15260.

Committee Chairpersons

Unit I: Organizational Maintenance

Unit Head. Phyllis Heroy.
Budget. Jane Klasing.
Bylaws and Organizations. Mary Alice Hunt.
Leadership Enhancement. Daniel Van Gesen.
Long-Range Planning. Julie I. Tallman.
Membership. Italia A. Negroni.
Nominating (1994). Elizabeth Reardon.
Revisit AASL Structure. Ken Haycock.

Unit II: Organizational Relationships

Unit Head. Elizabeth Day.
AECT/AASL Joint Committee. Francis McDonald.

American University Press Services Publication Selection. Raymond Barber.
Certification Competencies for Educators. Carolyn Markuson, Barbara Weaver.
International Relations. Carolyn Markuson.
Legislation. Thomas Hart.
National Council for the Accreditation of Teacher Education. Frank Birmingham.
School Library Statistics Program. Evelyn Daniel.

Unit III: Library Media Personnel Development

Unit Head. Margaret Tassia.
Annual Conference Local Arrangements. Lois Farrell Fisher, Barbara Inbody.
Annual Conference Program Planning. Margaret Tassia.
Continuing Education. Robert Grover.
General Conference, Portland, John McGinnis.
Professional Development Coordinating. Robert Grover.
Publications Advisory. M. Elspeth Goodin, Hilda Wrisberg.
Publications Coordinating. M. Elspeth Goodin, Hilda Wrisberg.
SLMQ Editorial Board. Mary Kay Biagini.

Unit IV: Library Media Program Development

Unit Head. Drucilla Raines.
Count on Reading. Brenda White.
Intellectual Freedom. Pat Scales.
National Guidelines—Implementation. Barbara Jeffus.
National Guidelines—Vision. Elizabeth Marcoux.
National Guidelines for Library Programs. Marilyn Miller.
Replication of Lance Study. Yvonne B. Carter.
Research. M. Susan Easun.
Resource-Based Teaching. Margaret Tassia.
Technology. Patricia Wilson Berger.

Unit V: Public Information

Unit Head. Diane C. Pozar.
Awards. Darlene Shiverdecker Basone.
Award Subcommittees. Distinguished School Administrator's Award, AASL/SIRS, Lucille Thomas; Distinguished Service Award, AASL/Baker and Taylor, Sheila Salmon; *Emergency Librarian* Periodical Award, Charles R. White; Frances Henne Award, Karen Winsor; Highsmith Research, Mary Jane McNally; Information Plus Continuing Education Award, John Emerick; Intellectual Freedom Award, AASL/ SIRS, Constance Champlin; Leadership Development Award, ABC/CLIO, Barbara Jeffus; Microcomputer in the Media Center Award, AASL/Follett Software, Thoma Hart; National School Library Media Pro gram of the Year Award, Follett Library Resources, Carol Kroll; School Librarian Workshop Award, Carolyn Marcato. National School Library Media Month Celeste Nalwasky.
Public Awareness. Harriet LaPointe.

Section Chairpersons

Educators of Library Media Specialist (ELMSS). Kenneth Pengelly.
Independent Schools Section (ISS). Nancy Higher.
Supervisors (SPVS). Jody Gehrig.

American Library Association
American Library Trustee Association

Executive Director, Susan Roman
50 E. Huron St., Chicago, IL 60611-2795
312-280-2161, 800-545-2433 Ext. 2161, FAX 312-440-9374

Object

The American Library Trustee Association (ALTA) is interested in the development of effective library service for all people in all types of communities and in all types of libraries; it follows that its members are concerned, as policymakers, with organizational patterns of service, with the development of competent personnel, the provision of adequate financing, the passage of suitable legislation, and the encouragement of citizen support for libraries. ALTA recognizes that responsibility for professional action in these fields has been assigned to other divisions of ALA; its specific responsibilities as a division, therefore, are:

1. A continuing and comprehensive educational program to enable library trustees to discharge their grave responsibilities in a manner best fitted to benefit the public and the libraries they represent.

2. Continuous study and review of the activities of library trustees.

3. Cooperation with other units within ALA concerning their activities relating to trustees.

4. Encouraging participation of trustees in other appropriate divisions of ALA.

5. Representation and interpretation of the activities of library trustees in contacts outside the library profession, particularly with national organizations and governmental agencies.

6. Promotion of strong state and regional trustee organizations.

7. Efforts to secure and support adequate library funding.

8. Promulgation and dissemination of recommended library policy.

9. Assuring equal access of information to all segments of the population.

10. Encouraging participation of trustees in trustee/library activities, at local, state, regional, and national levels.

Organized 1890. Became an ALA division in 1961.

Membership

Memb. 1,532. Open to all interested persons and organizations. For dues and membership year, see ALA entry.

Officers (1994–1995)

Pres. Sharon A. Saulmon (1996); *1st V.P./ Pres.-Elect* Wayne Coco (1997); *2nd V.P.* Virginia M. McCurdy (1995); *Past Pres.* Ann L. Donoghue (1995); *Parliamentarian* Ira B. Harkavy (1994); *Councillor* Terri C. Jacobs (1995).

Board of Directors

Officers; *Council Administrators* Shirley A. Barrett (1995); Denise E. Botto (1995), Clifford Dittrich (1995); Ira B. Harkavy (1995), Patricia F. Turner (1995); *ALTA Newsletter Ed.* James C. Baughman (1997); *Regional V.P.s* Gloria F. Aguilar (1995), Floy Johnson (1995), J. A. Killian (1995), Ruth Newell (1995), E. McKenney Pepin (1995); Barbara S. Prentice (1995), Jack T. Short (1995), Julie Silvers (1995), Lucille C. Thomas (1995), 3 to be appointed; *PLA Rep.* William T. Balcom (1995); *Ex officio* Susan Roman.

Staff

Exec. Dir. Susan Roman; *Deputy Exec. Dir.* Lorelle R. Swader.

Publication

ALTA Newsletter (6 per year; memb.). *Ed.* James C. Baughman.

Committee Chairpersons

Action Development. Ann L. Donoghue.
ALTA WILL (Task Force). Jack Cole.
Awards. Paulette H. Holahan.
Budget. Wayne Coco.
Common Concerns, ALTA/PLA (Interdivisional). William T. Balcom, Helen S. Kohlman.
Conference Program and Evaluation. Gail Dysleski.
Corporate Funding/Financial Development. Wayne Coco.
Editorial Advisory Board. Sharon A. Saulmon.
Education of Trustees. Nicholas G. Spillios.
Intellectual Freedom. Lillian Broad.
Legislation. Robert D. Terry.
Membership. Patricia F. Turner.
Nominating. Carol K. Vogelman.
Preconference. Shirley A. Barrett.
President's Program. Carol K. Vogelman.
Publications. Patricia H. Fisher.
Resolutions. Ira B. Harkavy.
Speakers Bureau. Wynne E. Weiss.
Special Functions. William G. Murphy.
Specialized Outreach Services. Suzine Har-Nicolescu.
Trustee Citations, Jury on. Virginia G. Young.
White House Conference Implementation (Subcommittee). Robert J. McCullough, Lila Milford.

American Library Association
Association for Library Collections and Technical Services

Executive Director, Karen Muller
50 E. Huron St., Chicago, IL 60611-2795
800-545-2433 Ext. 5031, FAX 312-280-3257
Bitnet: U19466@UICVM; Internet: u19466@uicvm.uic.edu

Object

The Association for Library Collections and Technical Services is responsible for the following activities: acquisition, identification, cataloging, classification, and preservation of library materials; the development and coordination of the country's library resources; and those areas of selection and evaluation involved in the acquisition of library materials and pertinent to the development of library resources. ALCTS has specific responsibility for:

1. Continuous study and review of the activities assigned to the division.
2. Conduct of activities and projects within its area of responsibility.
3. Syntheses of activities of all units within ALA that have a bearing on the type of activity represented.
4. Representation and interpretation of its type of activity in contacts outside the profession.
5. Stimulation of the development of librarians engaged in its type of activity, and stimulation of participation by members in appropriate type-of-library divisions.
6. Planning and development of programs of study and research for the type of activity for the total profession.

ALCTS will provide its members, other ALA divisions and members, and the library and information community with leadership and a program for action on the access to, and identification, acquisition, description, organization, preservation, and dissemination of information resources in a dynamic collaborative environment. In addition, ALCTS provides forums for discussion, research, and development, and opportunities for learning in all of these areas. To achieve this mission,

ALCTS has the following organizational goals:

1. To promote the role of the library and information science in an information society.
2. To provide its members with opportunities for information exchange.
3. To promote innovative and effective library education and training, to foster the recruitment of individuals with diverse qualities to library work, and to provide continuing education for librarians and library practitioners.
4. To develop, support, review, and promote standards to meet library and information needs.
5. To provide opportunities for members to participate through research and publications and professional growth.
6. To manage the association effectively and efficiently.

Established 1957; renamed 1988.

Membership

Memb. 5,364. Any member of the American Library Association may elect membership in this division according to the provisions of the bylaws.

Officers (1994–1995)

Pres. Robert P. Holley, 106 Kresge Lib., Wayne State Univ., Detroit, MI 48202; *V.P.* David Farrell, 1285 Brighton Ave., Albany, CA 94706.

Address correspondence to the executive director.

Directors

Officers; *Exec. Dir.* Karen Muller; *Past Pres.* Jennifer Younger; *Dirs.-at-Large* Marjorie E. Bloss (term expires 1995); Barbara B. Tillett (1997); *ALCTS Councillor* Jean Farrington (1995); *Council of Regional Groups Chair* Ann Denton (1995); *LRTS Ed.* Richard P. Smiraglia (1996); *ALCTS Newsletter Ed.* Dale Swensen (1999); *ALCTS Planning Committee Chair* John P. Webb (1995); *ALCTS Budget and Finance Chair* Shirley Leung (1994).

Publications

ALCTS Network News (irreg.; free). *Ed.* Karen Whittlesey. Available on Bitnet and Internet; subscribe via listserv@uicvm.bitnet.

ALCTS Newsletter (6 per year; memb.; non-memb. $25). *Ed.* Dale Swensen, Lee Library, Brigham Young Univ., Provo, UT 84602.

Library Resources & Technical Services (q.; memb.; nonmemb. $55). *Ed.* Richard P. Smiraglia, Palmer School of Lib. and Info. Science, Long Island Univ., Brookville, NY 11548. Tel. 516-299-2866.

Section Chairpersons

Acquisitions. Christian M. Bolssonnas.
Cataloging and Classification. John K. Duke.
Collection Management and Development. Barbara Van Deventer.
Preservation and Reformatting. Robert L. DeCandido, Robert B. Harriman.
Serials. Julia C. Blixrud.

Committee Chairpersons

Association of American Publishers/ALCTS Joint Committee. Joseph W. Raker, Audrey Melkin.
Audiovisual. Sheila A. Smyth.
Best of *LRTS*. Tschera H. Connell.
Blackwell North America Scholarship Award. Frederick C. Lynden.
Budget and Finance. Shirley W. Leung.

Catalog Form and Function. Catherine S. Herlihy.
Commercial Technical Services. J. Randolph Call.
Conference Program, Chicago (1995). Robert P. Holley.
Continuing Education Needs of Paraprofessionals (Task Force). Barry Baker.
Duplicates Exchange Union. Douglas A. DeLong.
Education. Barbara J. Strauss.
International Relations. Cecily A. Johns.
Legislation. John R. James.
Library Materials Price Index. Adrian W. Alexander.
LRTS Editorial Board. Richard P. Smiraglia.
MARBI. Priscilla L. Caplan.
Membership. Frank A. D'Andraia.
Nominating. Jean Acker Wright.
Organization and Bylaws. Jennifer A. Younger.
Esther J. Piercy Award Jury. Wanda V. Dole.
Planning. John P. Webb.
Publications. Suzanne H. Freeman.
Publisher/Vendor Library Relations. Joseph W. Barker.
Research and Statistics. Sharon E. Clark.
Scholarly Communication. Paul J. Kobulnicky.
Technical Services Measurements. Kathleen Brown.

Discussion Groups

Automated Acquisitions/In-Process Control Systems. Jeri Van Goethem.
Computer Files. Ann M. Sandberg-Fox.
Creative Ideas in Technical Services. Christa Hoffmann, Susan M. Mueller.
Electronic Publishing. Jean S. Callaghan.
LITA/ALCTS Authority Control in the Online Environment (Interest Group). Karen S. Calhoun.
LITA/ALCTS Innovative Microcomputer Support of Technical Services (Interest Group). Michael Kaplan.
LITA/ALCTS MARC Holdings (Interest Group). Diane I. Hillmann.
LITA/ALCTS Retrospective Conversion (Interest Group). Cynthia M. Whitacre (ALCTS), Judith W. Wild (LITA).
LITA/ALCTS Serials Automation (Interest Group). Karen H. Wilhoit.

Newspaper. Donnell L. Ruthenberg.
Out of Print. Marilyn Ng.
Pre-Order and Pre-Catalog Searching. Mary S. Konkel.

Role of the Professional in Academic Research Technical Services Departments. Helen Miller.

Technical Services Administrators of Medium-Sized Research Libraries. Colleen Hyslop.

Technical Services Directors of Large Research Libraries. Brian E. Schottlaender.

Technical Services in Public Libraries. Elisabeth A. Konrad.

American Library Association
Association for Library Service to Children

Executive Director, Susan Roman
50 E. Huron St., Chicago, IL 60611-2795
312-280-2163, 800-545-2433

Object

Interested in the improvement and extension of library services to children in all types of libraries. Responsible for the evaluation and selection of book and nonbook materials for, and the improvement of techniques of, library services to children from preschool through the eighth grade or junior high school age, when such materials or techniques are intended for use in more than one type of library. Founded 1901.

Membership

Memb. 3,475. Open to anyone interested in library services to children. For information on dues, see ALA entry.

Officers

Pres. Virginia McKee; Pres.-Elect Therese G. Bigelow; Past Pres. Ellen M. Stepanian.

Address correspondence to the executive director.

Directors

Rita Auerbach, Oralia Garza Cortes, Ellen G. Fader, Carole Fiore, Leslie Edmonds Holt, Sara L. Miller, Virginia A. Walter, Gretchen M. Wronka; Councillor Frances V. Sedney; Staff Liaison Susan Roman.

Publications

ALSC Newsletter (q.; memb.). Ed. Anitra T. Steele.

Journal of Youth Services in Libraries (q.; memb.; nonmemb. $40; foreign $50). Eds. Donald J. Kenney, Virginia Polytechnic Institute, Box 90001, Blacksburg, VA 24062-9001; Linda J. Wilson, Dept. of Educational Studies, 206A Russell Hall, Radford Univ., Radford, VA 24142.

Committee Chairpersons

Priority Group I: Child Advocacy

Consultant. Cynthia K. Richey.
Boy Scouts of America (Advisory).
Legislation.
Liaison with Mass Media.
Liaison with National Organizations Serving the Child.

Priority Group II: Evaluation of Media

Consultant. Margaret A. Bush, Grad. School of Lib. and Info. Science, Simmons College, 300 The Fenway, Boston, MA 02115.
Computer Software Evaluation.
Film and Video Evaluation.
Notable Children's Books.
Recording Evaluation.
Selection of Children's Books from Various Cultures.

Priority Group III: Professional Development

Consultant. Patsy Weeks, Box 15, Bangs, TX 76823.
Arbuthnot Honor Lecture.
(Louise Seaman) Bechtel Fellowship.
Distinguished Service Award.
Econo-Clad Literature Program Award.
Education.
Managing Children's Services (Committee and Discussion Group).
Putnam and Grosset Group Awards.
Scholarships: Melcher and Bound to Stay Bound.
Teachers of Children's Literature (Discussion Group).

Priority Group IV: Social Responsibilities

Consultant. Eliza T. Dresang, 440 Virginia Terr., Madison, WI 53705.
Intellectual Freedom.
International Relations.
Library Service to Children with Special Needs.
Preschool Services (Discussion Group).
Preschool Services and Parent Education.
Social Issues (Discussion Group).
Social Issues in Relation to Materials and Services for Children (Committee).

Priority Group V: Planning and Research

Consultant. Kathryn McClelland.
Caldecott Medal Calendar.
Collections of Children's Books for Adult Research (Discussion Group).
Grants.
Local Arrangements.
Membership.
National Planning of Special Collections.
National Reading Program.
Nominating.
Oral Record Project Advisory Committee.
Organization and Bylaws.
Planning and Budget.
Preconference Planning.
Publications.
Research and Development.
Storytelling (Discussion Group).

Priority Group VI: Award Committees

Consultant. Ruth I. Gordon, 225 N. Foothill Blvd., Cloverdale, CA 95425-3115.
(Mildred L.) Batchelder Award Selection.
Caldecott Award.
Carnegie Award.
Newbery Award.
Wilder Award.

American Library Association
Association of College and Research Libraries

Executive Director, Althea H. Jenkins
50 E. Huron St., Chicago, IL 60611-2795
312-280-3248, 800-545-2433 Ext. 2521, FAX 312-280-2520
E-mail: u55385@uicvm.uic.edu

Object

The mission of the Association of College and Research Libraries (ACRL) is to foster the profession of academic and research librarianship and to enhance the ability of academic and research libraries to serve effectively the library and information needs of current and potential library users. This includes all types of academic libraries— community and junior college, college, and university—as well as comprehensive and specialized research libraries and their professional staffs. Founded 1938.

Membership

Memb. 10,500. For information on dues, see ALA entry.

Officers

Pres. Susan K. Martin, Univ. Libn., Lauinger Lib., Georgetown Univ., 37 and O Sts. N.W., Washington, DC 20057-1006. Tel. 202-687-7425, FAX 202-687-7501; *Pres.-Elect* Patricia Senn Breivik, Assoc. V.P. for Info. Resources, Towson State Univ., Towson, MD 21204-7097. Tel. 410-830-2498, FAX 410-830-3760; *Past Pres.* Thomas Kirk, College Libn., Lilly Lib., Earlham College, Richmond, IN 47374. Tel. 317-983-1360, FAX 317-983-1304; *Budget and Finance Chair* Helen Spalding, Assoc. Dir. of Libs., Univ. of Missouri–Kansas City, 5100 Rockhill Rd., Kansas City, MO 64110-2446. Tel. 816-235-1558, FAX 816-333-5584; *ACRL Councilor,* W. Lee Hisle, Dir., Learning Resource Services, Austin Community College Dist., 1212 Rio Grande Ave., Austin, TX 78701. Tel. 512-495-7197, FAX 512-495-7200; *Exec. Dir. (ex officio)* Althea H. Jenkins, ALA, 50 E. Huron St., Chicago, IL 60611-2795. Tel. 312-280-3248, FAX 312-280-2520.

Board of Directors

Officers; Jill B. Fatzer, Bernard Fradkin, Frances J. Maloy, Ray E. Metz, Victoria A. Montovan, Linda L. Phillips, Mary Reichel; *Planning Committee Chair (ex officio)* Sandra Ready.

Publications

ACRL Publications in Librarianship (formerly ACRL Monograph Series) (irreg.). *Ed.* Stephen E. Wiberly, Jr., Univ. of Illinois at Chicago, Chicago, IL 60680.

Choice (11 per year; $165; foreign $187). *Choice Reviews-on-Cards* ($253; foreign $275). *Ed.* Francine L. Graf, 100 Riverview Center, Middletown, CT 06457-3401.

College and Research Libraries (6 per year; memb.; nonmemb. $50). *Ed.* Gloriana St. Clair, Pennsylvania State Univ., University Park, PA 16802.

College and Research Libraries News (11 per year; memb.; nonmemb. $35). *Ed.* Mary Ellen Kyger Davis, ACRL, ALA, 50 E. Huron St., Chicago, IL 60611-2795.

Rare Books and Manuscripts Librarianship (s. ann.; $30). *Ed.* Sidney E. Berger, Special Collections, Univ. of California, Riverside, CA 92517-5900.

List of other ACRL publications available through the ACRL office, ALA, 50 E. Huron St., Chicago, IL 60611-2795, or call 312-280-2521.

Committee and Task Force Chairpersons

Academic Libraries Brochure Task Force. Connie Vinita Dowell.

Academic Library Statistics. Elizabeth Salzer.

Academic or Research Librarian of the Year Award. Carla J. Stoffle.

Academic Status. Janice C. Fennell.

Access Policy Guidelines Task Force. Kathleen Gunning.

Appointments (1994) and Nominations (1995). Suzanne H. Calpestri.

Appointments (1995) and Nominations (1996). Maxine H. Reneker.

(Hugh C.) Atkinson Memorial Award. Thomas W. Leonhardt.

Budget and Finance. Helen H. Spalding.

Certification for Library and Information Professionals Task Force. Deborah J. Leather.

Choice Editorial Board. Norma G. Kobzina.

Colleagues. Joseph A. Boisse.

College and Research Libraries Editorial Board. Gloriana St. Clair.

College and Research Libraries News Editorial Board. Pamela Snelson.

Conference Program Planning, Chicago (1995). Susan K. Martin.

Conference Program Planning, Orlando (1996). Patricia Senn Breivik.

Constitution and Bylaws. Nicholas C. Burckel.

Copyright. Sarah E. Cox.

Doctoral Dissertation Fellowship. Lawrence J. McCrank.

Government Relations. Nancy M. Koller.

Image Enhancement. Anne K. Beaubien.

Intellectual Freedom. Barbara M. Jones.

International Relations. David L. Easterbrook.

(Samuel) Lazerow Fellowship for Research in Acquisition or Technical Services. Julia A. Gammon.

Media Resources. Stephen D. Fitt.

Membership. Mary Ann Griffin.

New Publications Advisory Board. Paula Murphy.

Orientation. Thomas Kirk.

Pittsburgh National Conference Executive Committee. Joanne R. Euster.

Planning. Sandra Ready.

President's Program Planning, Orlando, 1996. Melvin R. George.

Professional Education. Richard E. Sapon-White.

Professional Liaison. William Miller.

Publications. Richard Hume Werking.

Racial and Ethnic Diversity. Patrick J. Dawson, Rhonda A. Rios Kravitz.

Rare Books and Manuscripts Librarianship Editorial Board. Sidney E. Berger.

Registration Fee Task Force. Nora J. Quinlan.

Research. Maxine H. Reneker.

(K. G.) Saur Award for Best *College and Research Libraries* Article. James F. Williams II.

Standards and Accreditation. Carolyn Dusenbury.

Standards Study Task Force. Edward D. Garten.

Discussion Group Chairpersons

Academic Librarians' Associations. Roberta J. Kramer.

Australian Studies. Noelene P. Martin.

Canadian Studies. Linda DiBiase.

Electronic Library Development in Academic Libraries. Craig Mulder.

Electronic Text Centers. Marianne I. Gaunt.

Exhibits and Displays. Michael M. Miller.

Fee-Based Information Service Centers in Academic Libraries. Pamela J. MacKintosh.

Fundraising and Development. John D. Haskell.

Heads of Public/Readers Services. Anita K. Evans.

Home Economics/Human Ecology Librarians. Linda Stein.

Librarians of Library Science Collections. Patricia Stinson Switzer.

Medium-Sized Libraries. David B. Walch.

MLA International Bibliography in Academic Libraries. Elaine A. Franco.

Personnel Administrators and Staff Development Officers. Marie E. Marsh, Wendy L. Scott.

Philosophical, Religious, and Theological Studies. Blake Landor.

Popular Culture and Libraries. Nancy L. Buchanan.

Public Relations in Academic Libraries. Helen B. Josephine.

Research. Darrell L. Jenkins.

Undergraduate Librarians. Linda K. Ter Haar.

Section Chairpersons

Afro-American Studies Librarians. Michael C. Walker.

Anthropology and Sociology. Margaret R. Dittemore.

Arts. Lynn Barstis Williams.

Asian, African and Middle Eastern. Brenda E. Bickett.

Bibliographic Instruction. Katherine Anne Branch.

College Libraries. Susan McCarthy Campbell.

Community and Junior College Libraries. Susan M. Maltese.

Education and Behavioral Sciences. Nancy P. O'Brien.

English and American Literature. Michaelyn Burnette.

Extended Campus Library Services. Kathleen M. O'Connor.

Law and Political Science. Ronald J. Heckart.

Rare Books and Manuscripts. Lisa M. Browar.

Science and Technology. Katherine E. Clark.

Slavic and East European. Alan P. Pollard.

University Libraries. Nancy L. Baker.

Western European Specialists. Tom D. Kilton.

Women's Studies. Lori A. Goetsch.

American Library Association
Association of Specialized and Cooperative Library Agencies

Executive Director, Cathleen Bourdon
50 E. Huron St., Chicago, IL 60611-2795
312-280-4395, 800-545-2433 Ext. 4396, FAX 312-944-8085

Object

To represent state library agencies, specialized library agencies, and multitype library cooperatives. Within the interest of these types of library organizations, the Association of Specialized and Cooperative Library Agencies (ASCLA) has specific responsibility for:

1. Development and evaluation of goals and plans for state library agencies, specialized library agencies, and multitype library cooperatives to facilitate the implementation, improvement, and extension of library activities designed to foster improved user services, coordinating such activities with other appropriate ALA units.

2. Representation and interpretation of the role, functions, and services of state library agencies, specialized library agencies, and multitype library cooperatives within and outside the profession, including contact with national organizations and government agencies.

3. Development of policies, studies, and activities in matters affecting state library agencies, specialized library agencies, and multitype library cooperatives relating to (a) state and local library legislation, (b) state grants-in-aid and appropriations, and (c) relationships among state, federal, regional, and local governments, coordinating such activities with other appropriate ALA units.

4. Establishment, evaluation, and promotion of standards and service guidelines relating to the concerns of this association.

5. Identifying the interests and needs of all persons, encouraging the creation of services to meet these needs within the areas of concern of the association, and promoting the use of these services provided by state library agencies, specialized library agencies, and multitype library cooperatives.

6. Stimulating the professional growth and promoting the specialized training and continuing education of library personnel at all levels of concern of this association and encouraging membership participation in appropriate type-of-activity divisions within ALA.

7. Assisting in the coordination of activities of other units within ALA that have a bearing on the concerns of this association.

8. Granting recognition for outstanding library service within the areas of concern of this association.

9. Acting as a clearinghouse for the exchange of information and encouraging the development of materials, publications, and research within the areas of concern of this association.

Membership

Memb. 1,420.

Board of Directors (1994–1995)

Pres. Amy Owen (1996), Dir., Utah State Lib. Div., 2150 S. 300 W., Suite 16, Salt Lake City, UT 84115-2579. Tel. 801-466-5888, FAX 801-533-4657, amy@usl.gov, send mail to: 7453 Lost Canyon Circle, Salt Lake City, UT 84121-4624; *V.P.* Leslie Burger (1997), Lib. Development Solutions, 64 Princeton-Hightstown Rd., Princeton Junction, NJ 08550. Tel. 609-275-4821, FAX 609-275-4784; *Past Pres.* Barbara L. Perkis (1995), Asst. Dir., Illinois Regional Lib. for the Blind and Physically Handicapped, 1055

W. Roosevelt Rd., Chicago, IL 60608. Tel. 312-746-9217, FAX 312-746-9192; *Dirs.-at-Large* Elizabeth Curry (1996), Joan Neumann (1995), Ruth O'Donnell (1996), Barbara Will (1995); *Div. Councillor* Lorraine S. Summers (1997); *Section Reps.* Thea B. Chesley, Vibeke Lehmann, Linda Tepp Fuchs, Jack C. Mulkey (all 1995); *"Interface" Ed. (ex officio)* Thomas J. Dorst (1995); *Organization and Bylaws Committee Chair (ex officio)* Rod Wagner (1995).

Executive Staff

Exec. Dir. Cathleen Bourdon; *Deputy Exec. Dir.* Joanne Crispen.

Publication

Interface (q.; memb.; nonmemb. $15). *Ed.* Thomas J. Dorst, Illinois State Lib., 300 S. Second St., Springfield, IL 62701-1796. Tel. 217-782-5012, FAX 217-785-4326.

Committees

American Correctional Association/ASCLA Joint Committee on Institution Libraries. Thea Chesley, Tim Brown.
Awards. Bridget Lamont.
Budget and Finance. Leslie Burger.
Conference Program Coordination. Kate Nevins.
Legislation. Sandra Stephan.
Library Personnel and Education. Amy Kellerstrass.
Membership Promotion. Donna Pontau.
Organization and Bylaws. Rod Wagner.
Planning. Leslie Burger.
Publications. Marlene Deuel.
Research. Jeannette Smithee.
Serials Advisory. Leslie Burger.
Standards Review. Rhea Rubin; Guidelines for Library Service for People with Developmental Disabilities, Marilyn Irwin, Ruth O'Donnell; Revision of Standards for Library Service to the Blind and Physically Handicapped, Donna Dziedzic.

American Library Association
Library Administration and Management Association

Executive Director, Karen Muller
50 E. Huron St., Chicago, IL 60611-2795
312-280-5031, 800-545-2433 Ext. 5031, FAX 312-280-3257

Object

The Library Administration and Management Association (LAMA) provides an organizational framework for encouraging the study of administrative theory, for improving the practice of administration in libraries, and for identifying and fostering administrative skill. Toward these ends, the division is responsible for all elements of general administration that are common to more than one type of library. These may include organizational structure, financial administration, personnel management and training, buildings and equipment, and public relations. LAMA meets this responsibility in the following ways:

1. Study and review of activities assigned to the division with due regard for changing developments in these activities.

2. Initiating and overseeing activities and projects appropriate to the division, including activities involving bibliography compilation, publication, study, and review of professional literature within the scope of the division.

3. Synthesis of those activities of other ALA units that have a bearing upon the responsibilities or work of the division.

4. Representation and interpretation of library administrative activities in contacts outside the library profession.

5. Aiding the professional development of librarians engaged in administration and encouragement of their participation in appropriate type-of-library divisions.

6. Planning and development of those programs of study and research in library administrative problems that are most needed by the profession.

Established 1957.

Membership

Memb. 5,131.

Officers (1994–1995)

Pres. Donald E. Riggs, Dean, Univ. Lib., Univ. of Michigan, 818 Hatcher Grad. Lib., Ann Arbor, MI 48109-1205. Tel. 313-764-9356, FAX 313-763-5080; *V.P./Pres.-Elect* John J. Vasi, Assoc. Univ. Libn., 3589 Lib., Univ. of California, Santa Barbara, CA 93106. Tel. 805-893-2674, FAX 805-893-7010, vasi@library.ucsb.edu; *Past Pres.* Carol F. L. Liu, Exec. Asst. to Dir., Queens Borough Public Lib., 162-20 Ninth Ave., Apt. 9C, Whitestone, NY 11357. Tel. 718-990-0890, FAX 718-291-8936; *Councillor* Malcolm K. Hill, Dir., Mid-York Lib. System, 463 Ernst Rd., Clinton, NY 13323. Tel. 315-735-8328, FAX 315-735-0943, hill@midyork.lib.ny.us; *Exec. Dir.* Karen Muller, 50 E. Huron St., Chicago, IL 60611. Tel. 312-280-5031, FAX 312-280-3257.

Board of Directors

Dirs. Charles E. Beard, Deborah Carver, Joyce N. Davis, Joan R. Giesecke, Susan F. Gregory, Elizabeth C. Habich, Susanne Henderson, Ronald P. Naylor, Gene Rollins, Thomas L. Wilding; *Dirs.-at-Large* Judith A. Adams, Kriza A. Jennings; *Ex officio* Kathleen R. T. Imhoff, Charles E. Kratz, Jr., Sharon A. Lincoln, Nancy Lee Meyers, Cathy C. Miesse, Kathryn Page, Dorothy M. Persson.

Publication

Library Administration and Management (q.; memb.; nonmemb. $50; foreign $60). *Ed.* Joan R. Giesecke, Univ. of Nebraska–Lincoln, 106 Love Lib., Lincoln, NE 68588-0410. Tel. 402-472-2526, FAX 402-472-5131, joang@unllib.unl.edu.

Committee Chairpersons

Budget and Finance. Ronald P. Naylor.
Governmental Affairs. Bernadette R. Storck.
Membership. Robert A. Daugherty.
Organization. Susanne Henderson.
Orientation. Joan Reyes.
Program. Rebecca R. Martin.
Publication. John Lubans, Jr.
Recognition of Achievement. William G. Jones.
Small Libraries Publications Series. Larayne J. Dallas.
Special Conferences and Programs. Kathryn J. Deiss.

Section Chairpersons

Buildings and Equipment. Elizabeth C. Habich.
Fund Raising and Financial Development. Susan F. Gregory.
Library Organization and Management. Thomas L. Wilding.
Personnel Administration. Deborah Carver.
Public Relations. Charles E. Beard.
Statistics. Gene Rollins.
Systems and Services. Joyce N. Davis.

American Library Association
Library and Information Technology Association

Executive Director, Linda J. Knutson
50 E. Huron St., Chicago, IL 60611-2795
312-280-4270, 800-545-2433

Object

The Library and Information Technology Association (LITA) envisions a world in which the complete spectrum of information technology is available to everyone. People in all their diversity will have access to a wealth of information technology in libraries, at work, and at home. In this world, everybody can realize their full potential with the help of information technology. The very boundaries of human relations will expand beyond the limitations of time and space we experience today. The outer limits are still unknown; what is known is that the exploration will be challenging.

LITA provides its members, other ALA divisions and members, and the library and information science field as a whole with a forum for discussion, an environment for learning, and a program for action on the design, development, and implementation of automated and technological systems in the library and information science field.

LITA is concerned with the planning, development, design, application, and integration of technologies within the library and information environment, with the impact of emerging technologies on library service, and with the effect of automated technologies on people. Its major focus is on the interdisciplinary issues and emerging technologies. LITA disseminates information, provides educational opportunities for learning about information technologies and forums for the discussion of common concerns, monitors new technologies with potential applications in information science, encourages and fosters research, promotes the development of technical standards, and examines the effects of library systems and networks.

LITA's strategic planning goals are to provide opportunities for professional growth and performance in areas of information technology; to influence national- and international-level initiatives relating to information and access; to promote, participate in, and influence the development of technical standards related to the storage, dissemination, and delivery of information, and to strengthen the association and assure its continued success.

Membership

Memb. 5,460.

Officers (1994–1995)

Pres. Nancy K. Roderer (1996); *Pres.-Elect* R. Bruce Miller (1997); *Past Pres.* Tamara J. Miller (1995).

Directors

Officers; Pamela Q. J. Andre (1997); Betty G. Bengtson (1996), Michele I. Dalehite (1995); Barbara B. Higginbotham (1997); Elizabeth Lane Lawley (1997); Jean Armour Polly (1995); Craig A. Summerhill (1996); *Div. Councillor* Carol A. Parkhurst (1997); *Ex officio* David R. McDonald (1995); *Exec. Dir.* Linda J. Knutson.

Publications

Information Technology and Libraries (q.; memb.; nonmemb. $50; single copy $15). *Ed.* Thomas W. Leonhardt, Dir. of Technical Services, Univ. Of Oklahoma Lib., 401 W. Brooks St., Norman, OK 73019-0528. For information or to send manuscripts, contact the editor.

LITA Newsletter (q.; memb.; nonmemb. $25; single copy $8). *Ed.* Gail Junion-Metz.

Committee Chairpersons

Hugh C. Atkinson Memorial Award. Thomas W. Leonhardt.
Budget Review. Tamara J. Miller.
Bylaws and Organization. David R. McDonald.
Education. William P. Kane and Dayna E. Buck.
Executive. Nancy K. Roderer.
Information Technology and Libraries Editorial Board. Thomas J. Leonhardt.
International Relations. Elaine Hartman.
Internet Room Steering. Gail Clement, Gretchen Whitney.
Leadership Development. George Rickerson.
Legislation and Regulation. Patrick Flannery.
LITA/Geac Scholarship (Subcommittee). Jerry D. Saye.
LITA/OCLC and LITA/LSSI Minority Scholarship (Subcommittee). Francis Miksa.
LITA/Gaylord Award. Edward A. Warro.
LITA/*Library Hi Tech* Award. Michele I. Dalehite.
LITA Newsletter (Subcommittee). Gail Junion-Metz.
Machine-Readable Form of Bibliographic Information (MARBI), ALCTS/RASD. Priscilla L. Caplan.
Membership. Kathleen A. Wakefield.
National Conference 1996 Steering (LAMA/LITA). Dennis Reynolds, Terri Tomchyshyn.
Nominating. Victor Rosenberg.
Program Planning. Pamela R. Mason.
Publications. George S. Machovec.
Regional Institutes Task Force. Gail M. Persky.
Research. William Gray Potter.
Technical Standards for Library Automation (TESLA). Phyllis H. Johnson.
Technology and Access. Mary Alice Ball.
Telecommunications Electronic Reviews Board. Thomas C. Wilson.

Interest Group Chairpersons

Interest Group Coordinator. Colby M. Riggs.
Adaptive Technologies. Dennis A. Norlin.
Artificial Intelligence/Expert Systems. Martin Kesselman.
Authority Control in the Online Environment, LITA/ALCTS. Daniel V. Pitti.
Customized Applications for Library Microcomputers. Andy Boze.
Desktop Publishing. Xiao-Yan (Cheyenne) Shen.
Distributed Systems and Networks. Joan Latta Konecky.
Electronic Mail/Electronic Bulletin Boards. Ray E. Metz.
Emerging Technologies. Roberta Rand.
Geographic Information Systems. Joan Maier McKean.
Human/Machine Interface. Tim Cole.
Imagineering. Carolyn Meanley.
Library Consortia/Automated Systems. Gregory J. Zuck.
MARC Holdings, LITA/ALCTS. Diane I. Hillmann.
Microcomputer Support of Technical Services, LITA/ALCTS. Michael Kaplan.
Microcomputer Users. Robert B. McGeachin.
Online Catalogs. Laurie Preston.
Optical Information Systems. David Billick.
Programmer/Analyst. Mark Needleman.
Retrospective Conversion, LITA/ALCTS. Judith W. Wild.
Serials Automation, LITA/ALCTS. Karen H. Wilhoit.
Small Integrated Library System. Carl E. Bengston, Robert Bocher.
Technology and the Arts. Howard Besser.
Telecommunications. Beth Sandore.
Vendor/User. Barbara J. Ritchie

American Library Association
Public Library Association

Executive Director, George Needham
50 E. Huron St., Chicago, IL 60611-2795
800-545-2433 Ext. 5025, FAX 312-280-5029

Object

The Public Library Association (PLA) will advance the development and effectiveness of public library service and public librarians. PLA has specific responsibility for:

1. Conducting and sponsoring research about how the public library can respond to changing social needs and technical developments.

2. Developing and disseminating materials useful to public libraries in interpreting public library services and needs.

3. Conducting continuing education for public librarians by programming at national and regional conferences, by publications such as the newsletter, and by other delivery means.

4. Establishing, evaluating, and promoting goals, guidelines, and standards for public libraries.

5. Maintaining liaison with relevant national agencies and organizations engaged in public administration and human services, such as the National Association of Counties, Municipal League, and Commission on Post-Secondary Education.

6. Maintaining liaison with other divisions and units of ALA and other library organizations, such as the Association of American Library Schools and the Urban Libraries Council.

7. Defining the role of the public library in service to a wide range of user and potential user groups.

8. Promoting and interpreting the public library to a changing society through legislative programs and other appropriate means.

9. Identifying legislation to improve and to equalize support of public libraries.

PLA exists to provide a diverse program of communication, publication, advocacy, and continuing education. The program priorities are determined by PLA members and may include some areas or concerns also identified as priorities by ALA. The primary staff program responsibility is to facilitate members' activities and initiatives by providing coordination and support.

As a division, we are effective when we:

1. Provide leadership for the improvement of public libraries.

2. Provide an effective forum for discussing issues of concern to public librarians.

3. Provide relevant, high-quality continuing education through publications, workshops, and programs.

4. Provide opportunities for developing and enhancing individual professional networks.

5. Develop and disseminate policy statements on matters affecting public libraries.

6. Communicate effectively with the nonlibrary world about matters impacting public library service.

7. Maintain a stable membership and financial base.

PLA's priority concerns are adequate funding for public libraries; improved management of public libraries; recognition of the importance of all library staff in providing quality public service; recruitment, education, training, and compensation of public librarians; effective use of technology; intellectual freedom; improved access to library resources; and effective communication with the nonlibrary world. Organized 1944.

Membership

Memb. 7,600+. Open to all ALA members interested in the improvement and expansion of public library services to all ages in various types of communities.

Officers (1994–1995)

Pres. Judith A. Drescher, Memphis-Shelby County Public Lib., 1850 Peabody Ave., Memphis, TN 38104, Tel. 901-725-8855, FAX 901-725-8883, dresher@sol1.solinet.net; *V.P./Pres.-Elect* LaDonna T. Kienitz, Newport Beach Public Lib., 3300 Newport Blvd., Newport Beach, CA 92658-9815, Tel. 714-644-3157, FAX 714-644-3155, E-mail: nbplijk@class.org; *Past Pres.* Pat A. Woodrum, Tulsa City-County Lib., 400 Civic Center, Tulsa, OK 74103. Tel. 918-596-7897, FAX 918-596-2641.

Board of Directors (1994–1995)

Officers; Dirs.-at-Large Rick Ashton, Marilyn Boria, John D. Hales, Jr., Donald J. Napoli, Donna Barrett Schremser, Carol Starr; *Section Reps.:* Joseph H. Green (MPLSS, 1995); Annette M. Milliron (SMLS, 1997), Marlys H. O'Brien (CIS, 1995); Kathryn M. Panares (ALLS, 1995); Kay K. Runge (PPPLS, 1996); Lamar Veatch (MLS, 1995); Diana D. Young (PLSS, 1995); other reps.: Lorraine Sano Jackson (PLAN, 1995); Helen S. Kohlman (ALTA, 1995); councilor, Linda P. Elliott (1998); *Ex officio* George M. Needham; Patrick O'Brien (Budget and Finance ch., 1995).

Publication

Public Libraries (bi-mo.; memb.; nonmemb. $50; foreign $60; single copy $10). *Feature Ed.* Ellen Altman, 1936 E. Belmont Dr., Tempe, AZ 85284; *Managing Ed.* Sandra Causey Garrison, PLA, 50 E. Huron St., Chicago, IL 60611.

Section Presidents

Adult Lifelong Learning. Virginia L. Fore. Community Information. Beth E. Wladis. Marketing of Public Library Services. Joseph H. Green. Metropolitan Libraries. Lamar Veatch. Planning, Measurement, and Evaluation. Kathleen S. Reif. Public Library Systems. Diana D. Young. Public Policy for Public Libraries. Fran C. Freimarck. Small and Medium-Sized Libraries. Vickie L. Novak.

Committee Chairpersons

Audiovisual. James E. Massey.
Awards. Robert S. Smith.
Budget and Finance. Patrick O'Brien.
Business Council. Susan J. Strehl.
Bylaws and Organization. Catherine A. O'Connell.
Cataloging Needs of Public Libraries. Rita Hamilton.
Children, Service to. Penny S. Markey.
Children's Services Statistics, ALSC/PLA. Neel Parikh.
Common Concerns, ALTA/PLA. William T. Balcom.
Conference Program Coordinating (1995). Harriet Henderson.
Conference Program Coordinating (1996). Clara N. Bohrer.
Intellectual Freedom. Sara T. Behrman.
Leadership Development (1995). Donna Mancini.
Leadership Development (1996). Sandra S. Nelson.
Legislation. Susan S. Goldberg.
Library Video Award. Scott Parsons.
LSCA Ad Hoc (Special). Sarah A. Long.
Allie Beth Martin Award. Ann Barnett Hutton.
Membership. Ross W. McLachlan.
Multilingual Materials and Library Service. Susan K. Soy.
National Achievement Citation. Kay K. Runge.

National Conference (1996). June M. Garcia; National Conference Exhibitors Advisory. (vacant); National Conference Local Arrangements. Ginnie Cooper; National Conference Program. Christine L. Hage. New Leaders Travel Grant. S'ann Freeman. Nominating (1995). Ronald A. Dubberly. Nominating (1996). June M. Garcia. PLA Partners. Ronald S. Kozlowski. Planning Off-Site Delivery of Library Services (Special). Ernest DiMattia. President's Program/Hot Topics (1995). Marilyn Boria.

President's Program/Hot Topics (1996). Tom Phelps. *Public Libraries* Advisory Board. Claudia B. Sumler. Public Library History. Donald J. Sager. Public Library Services to the Homeless. Mary Johnson. Publications. Thomas C. Phelps. Research and Statistics. Thomas A. Childers. Retail Outlets in Public Libraries. Jennifer D'Oliveira. Technology in Public Libraries. William H. Ptacek. Leonard Wertheimer Multilingual Award. Tamiye M. Trejo-Meehan.

American Library Association
Reference and Adult Services Division

Executive Director, Cathleen Bourdon
50 E. Huron St., Chicago, IL 60611-2795
312-944-6780, 800-545-2433, FAX 312-644-7459

Object

The Reference and Adult Services Division (RASD) is responsible for stimulating and supporting in every type of library the delivery of reference/information services to all groups, regardless of age, and of general library services and materials of adults. This involves facilitating the development and conduct of direct service to library users, the development of programs and guidelines for service to meet the needs of these users, and assisting libraries in reaching potential users. The specific responsibilities of RASD are:

1. Conduct of activities and projects within the division's areas of responsibility.
2. Encouragement of the development of librarians engaged in these activities, and stimulation of participation by members of appropriate type-of-library divisions.
3. Synthesis of the activities of all units within the American Library Association that have a bearing on the type of activities represented by the division.
4. Representation and interpretation of the division's activities in contacts outside the profession.
5. Planning and development of programs of study and research in these areas for the total profession.
6. Continuous study and review of the division's activities.

Membership

Memb. 5,399. For information on dues, see ALA entry.

Officers (June 1994–June 1995)

Pres. David Kohl; *Pres.-Elect* Mary Lou Goodyear; *Secy.* Julia Rholes.

Directors and Other Members

Daniel Barthell, Linda Friend, Mary E. Jackson, Mark Leggett, Margaret Ann Reinert, Beth Woodard; *Councillor* Gail Schlachter;

Past Pres. Charles Gilreath; *Ed. RASD Update* Jane Kleiner; *Eds. RQ* Connie Van Fleet, Danny Wallace; *Ed. Round-up* John Hepner; *Exec. Dir.* Cathleen Bourdon. Address correspondence to the executive director.

Publications

RASD Update (memb.; nonmemb. $15). *Ed.* Jane Kleiner, Middleton Lib., Louisiana State Univ., Baton Rouge, LA 70803-7010.

Round-up: Newsletter of the RASD Council of State and Regional Groups (s. ann.). *Ed.* John C. Hepner, Box 507, Denton, TX 76202-0507.

RQ (q.; memb; nonmemb. $42). *Eds.* Connie Van Fleet and Danny Wallace, Louisiana State Univ., 267 Coates, Baton Rouge, LA 70803-7010.

RQ Occasional Papers (irreg.). *Ed.* Nancy Huling, Suzallo Lib., FM-25, Univ. of Washington, Seattle, WA 98195.

Section Chairpersons

Business Reference and Services. Theodora Haynes.
Collection Development and Evaluation. Ferne Hyman.
History. Ruth Carr.
Machine-Assisted Reference. Peggy Seiden.
Management and Operation of Public Service. William D. Michel.
Services to User Populations. Edward Erazo.

Committee Chairpersons

Access to Information. Pat Timberlake.
AFL/CIO Joint Committee on Library Services to Labor Groups. Andrew Lee.
Awards Coordinating. Dana Rooks.
Conference Program. Peter Watson.
Conference Program Coordinating. Kelly Janousek.
Dartmouth Medal. Diane Zabel.
Denali Press Award. Leslie Canterbury.
Executive. David Kohl.
Facts on File Grant. Ree DeDonato.
Finance. Charles Gilreath.
Gale Research Award for Excellence in Reference and Adult Services. Michael Golrick.
Legislation. Jim Rettig.
Membership. Linda Simons.
Margaret E. Monroe Library Adult Services Award. Patricia M. Hogan.
Isadore Gilbert Mudge/R. R. Bowker Award. Danuta Nitecki.
Nominating (1995). Bonnie Macewan.
Organization. Karen Chapman.
Publications. Nancy Huling.
Reference Services Press Award. Glenda Neely.
RQ Editorial Advisory Board. Connie Van Fleet, Danny Wallace.
John Sessions Memorial Award. Art Meyers.
Louis Shores/Oryx Press Award. Ilene Rockman.
Standards and Guidelines. Larayne Dallas.

American Library Association
Young Adult Library Services Association

Executive Director, Ann Carlson Weeks
50 E. Huron St., Chicago, IL 60611-2795
312-944-6780, 800-545-2433 Ext. 4388, FAX 312-664-7459

Object

In every library in the nation, quality library service to young adults is provided by a staff that understands and respects the unique informational, educational, and recreational needs of teenagers. Equal access to information, services, and materals is recognized as a right not a privilege. Young adults are actively involved in the library decision-making process. The library staff collaborates and cooperates with other youth-serving agencies to provide a holistic, community-wide network of activities and services that support healthy youth development.

To ensure that this vision becomes a reality, the Young Adult Library Services Association (YALSA), a division of the American Library Association (ALA)

1. Advocates extensive and developmentally appropriate library and information services for young adults, ages 12 to 18.
2. Promotes reading and supports the literacy movement.
3. Advocates the use of information and communications technologies to provide effective library service.
4. Supports equality of access to the full range of library materials and services, including existing and emerging information and communications technologies, for young adults.
5. Provides education and professional development to enable its members to serve as effective advocates for young people.
6. Fosters collaboration and partnerships among its individual members with the library community and other groups involved in providing library and information services to young adults.

7. Influences public policy by demonstrating the importance of providing library and information services that meet the unique needs and interests of young adults.
8. Encourages research and is in the vanguard of new thinking concerning the provision of library and information services for youth.

Membership

Memb. 2,200. Open to anyone interested in library services and materials for young adults. For information on dues, see ALA entry.

Officers (July 1994–July 1995)

Pres. Jennifer Jung Gallant, 482 Dover Center, Bay Village, OH 44140. Tel. 216-623-6955, FAX 216-623-6957; *V.P./Pres.-Elect* Patricia Muller, 14425 Coachway Drive, Centreville, VA 22020. Tel. 703-358-5951, FAX 703-358-5962; *Past Pres.* Judith Druse, Washburn Univ., 1700 College Ave., Topeka, KS 66621. Tel. 913-231-1000 Ext. 1277, FAX 913-357-1240; *Councillor* Pamela Klipsch, 117 E. Bodley Ave., Kirkwood, MO 63122. Tel. 618-462-0651, FAX 618-462-0665.

Directors

Officers; Elizabeth Elam (term expires 1995), Amy Oxley (1995), Lesley Farmer (1996), Patrick Jones (1996), Michael Cart (1997), Joel Shoemaker (1997); *Ex officio Chair, Budget and Finance* Gayle Keresey; *Ex offi-*

cio Chair, Long-Range Planning Pamela Spencer; *Ex officio Chair, Organization and Bylaws* Helen Vandersluis.

Publication

Journal of Youth Services in Libraries (q.; memb.; nonmemb. $40; foreign $50). *Eds.* Donald J. Kenney, Director's Office, Virginia Polytechnic Inst., Box 90001, Blacksburg, VA 24062-9001. Tel. 703-231-5595, FAX 703-231-9263; Linda J. Wilson, Dept. of Educational Studies, Radford Univ., 206A Russell Hall, Radford, VA 24142. Tel. 703-831-544, FAX 703-831-5302.

Committee Chairpersons

ALSC/YALSA JOYS Editorial Advisory. Donald Kenny, Linda J. Wilson.

ALSC/YALSA JOYS Evaluation Refereed Journal (Ad Hoc). Joan Atkinson.

Baker and Taylor Conference Grant. Susan Meck.

Best Books for Young Adults (1995). Audra Caplan.

Book Wholesalers, Inc./YALSA Collection Development Grant. Amy Oxley.

Budget and Finance. Gayle Keresey.

CRC/YALSA Joint Task Force on Teenage Library Association. Mary Elizabeth Wendt.

Division Promotion. Elizabeth Reed.

Econo-Clad Program Award for Young Adult Reading or Literature Program. Karlan Sick.

Education. Betty Carter.

Margaret A. Edwards Award (1995). JoAnn Mondowney.

Margaret A. Edwards Award (1996). Marilee Foglesong.

Executive. Jennifer Jung Gallant.

Genre List Coordinator. Michael Cart.

Genre List—Fantasy (1996). Paulette Goodman.

Genre List—Humor (1996). Mary Huebscher.

Genre List—Romance (1996). Judy Sasges.

Genre List—Sports(1966). Mary Arnold.

Genre Marketing (Task Force). Candace Conklin.

Intellectual Freedom. Susan Uebelacker.

Legislation. Gary Morrison.

Local Arrangements (1995). Deborah Mason.

Long-Range Planning. Pamela Spencer.

Media Selection and Usage. Stephen Crowley.

National Organizations Serving the Young Adult (Liaison). Judy Nelson.

Nominating (1995). Mike Printz.

Organization and Bylaws. Helen Vandersluis.

Outreach. James Cook.

Oversight. Pamela Spencer.

PLA/YALSA Output Measures Implementation. Jody Stefansson.

Preconference, Chicago (1995). Keith Swigger.

Program Planning Clearinghouse and Evaluation. Jana Fine.

Publications. Patrick Jones.

Publishers' Liaison. Juanita Foster.

Recommended Books for Reluctant Young Adult Reader (1995). Peter Butts.

Recommended Books for the Reluctant Young Adult Reader Policies and Procedures (Ad Hoc). Nellie Ward.

Research. Keith Swigger.

Selected Films and Videos for Young Adults (1995). Catherine Clancy.

Selected Films and Videos for Young Adults Policies and Procedures (Task Force). Stephen Crowley.

Special Needs, Library Service to Young Adults with. Stella Baker.

Technology for Young Adults. Catherine Birdseye.

Amelia Elizabeth Walden Award (Ad Hoc). Caryn Sipos.

Young Adult Literature (Discussion Group). Susan Rosenzweig.

Youth Participation. Constance Lawson.

American Merchant Marine Library Association

(An affiliate of United Seamen's Service)
Executive Director, Roger T. Korner
One World Trade Center, Suite 2161, New York, NY 10048
212-775-1038

Object

Provides ship and shore library service for American-flag merchant vessels, the Military Sealift Command, the U.S. Coast Guard, and other waterborne operations of the U.S. government. Established 1921.

Officers (1994–1995)

Honorary Chair Adm. Albert J. Harbenger; *Pres.* Talmage E. Simpkins; *Chair, Exec. Committee* Arthur W. Friedberg; *V.P.s* Joel Bern, John M. Bowers, Capt. Timothy E. Brown, James Capo, Ernest Corrado, John Halas, Lane Kirkland, George E. Murphy, S. Nakanishi, Capt. Gregorio Oca, Luis Parise, Michael Sacco; *Secy.* Lillian Rabins; *Treas.* William D. Potts; *Exec. Dir.* Roger T. Korner.

American Society for Information Science

Executive Director, Richard B. Hill
8720 Georgia Ave., Suite 501, Silver Spring, MD 20910
301-495-0900, FAX 301-495-0810
E-mail: asis@cni.org

Object

The American Society for Information Science (ASIS) provides a forum for the discussion, publication, and critical analysis of work dealing with the design, management, and use of information, information systems, and information technology.

Membership

Memb. (Indiv.) 3,700; (Student) 600; (Inst.) 115. Dues (Indiv.) $95; (Student) $25; (Inst.) $350 and $550.

Officers

Pres. James E. Rush, Palinet, 3401 Market St., Suite 262, Philadelphia, PA 19104; *Pres.-Elect* Clifford Lynch, Univ. of California, 6400 Christie No. 5406, Emeryville, CA 94608; *Treas.* Anne M. Buck, Calif. Inst. of Technology; *Past Pres.* Marjorie M. K. Hlava, Access Innovations, 4314 Mesa Grande S.E., Box 40130, Albuquerque, NM 87196.

Board of Directors

Chapter Assembly Dir. Judith E. Watson; *SIG Cabinet Dir.* Karla Petersen; *Dirs.-at-Large* Joseph A. Busch, Paula L. Galbraith, Barbara H. Kwasnik, Elisabeth L. Logan, Jane K. Starnes, Carol Tenopir.

Publications

Advances in Classification Research. Vols. 1–3. *Eds.* Barbara Kwasnik and Raya Fidel. Available from Learned Information, 143 Old Marlton Pike, Medford, NJ 08055.

Annual Review of Information Science and Technology. Available from Learned Information, 143 Old Marlton Pike, Medford, NJ 08055.

ASIS Thesaurus of Information Science and Librarianship. Available from Learned Information, 143 Old Marlton Pike, Medford, NJ 08055.

Bulletin of the American Society for Information Science. Available from ASIS.

Challenges in Indexing Electronic Texts and Images. Eds. Raya Fidel, Trudi Bellardo (Hahn), Edie M. Rasmussen, and Philip J. Smith. Available from Learned Information, 143 Old Marlton Pike, Medford, NJ 08055.

Interfaces for Information Retrieval and Online Systems: The State of the Art. Ed. Martin Dillon. Available from Greenwood Press, 88 Post Rd. W., Westport, CT 06881.

Journal of the American Society for Information Science. Available from John Wiley and Sons, 605 Third Ave., New York, NY 10016.

Networking, Telecommunications and the Networked Information Revolution. Proceedings of the 1992 ASIS Mid-Year. Available from ASIS.

Proceedings of the ASIS Annual Meetings. Available from Learned Information, 143 Old Marlton Pike, Medford, NJ 08055.

Studies in Multimedia. Eds. Susan Stone and Michael Buckland. Based on the Proceedings of the 1991 ASIS Mid-Year Meeting. Available from Learned Information, 143 Old Marlton Pike, Medford, NJ 08050.

Committee Chairpersons

Awards and Honors. Gregory Newby.
Budget and Finance. Anne Buck.
Career Development. Maurica Fedors.
Conferences and Meetings. Ann Dodson.
Constitution and Bylaws. Nancy Blase.
Continuing Education. Samantha Hastings.
Executive Committee. James Rush.
Information Policy. Ann Prentice.
Information Science Education. Joseph Fitzsimmons.
Leadership Development. Helen Manning.
Membership. Thomas Kinney.
Nominations. Marjorie Hlava.
Publications. Nancy Roderer.
Standards. Mark Needleman.

American Theological Library Association

820 Church St., Suite 300, Evanston, IL 60201-5603
708-869-7788, FAX 708-869-8513

Object

To bring its members into close working relationships with each other, to support theological and religious librarianship, to improve theological libraries, and to interpret the role of such libraries in theological education, developing and implementing standards of library service, promoting research and experimental projects, encouraging cooperative programs that make resources more available, publishing and disseminating literature and research tools and aids, cooperating with organizations having similar aims, and otherwise supporting and aiding theological education. Founded 1947.

Membership

Memb. (Inst.) 185; (Indiv.) 500. Membership is open to persons engaged in professional library or bibliographical work in theological or religious fields and others who are interested in the work of theological librarianship. Dues (Inst.) $75 to $500, based on total library expenditure; (Indiv.) $15 to $100, based on salary. Year. Sept. 1–Aug. 31.

Officers (July 1994–June 1995)

Pres. Roger L. Loyd, Duke Divinity School Lib., Duke Univ., Durham, NC 27708-0972. Tel. 919-660-3452, FAX 510-649-1417; *V.P.* Linda Corman, Trinity College Lib., 6 Hoskin Ave., Toronto, ON M5S 1H8, Canada. Tel. 416-978-2653, FAX 416-978-2797; *Secy.* Marti S. Alt, Ohio State Univ. Libs., 1858 Neil Ave. Mall, Columbus, OH 43210-1282. Tel. 614-292-3035, FAX 614-294-7895.

Board of Directors

Officers; Christopher Brennan, Richard R. Berg, Lorena A. Boylan, Alan D. Krieger, Diane Choquette, M. Patrick Graham, Valerie R. Hotchkiss, Mitzi M. Jarrett Budde, Mary Williams; *Exec. Dir.* Albert E. Hurd; *Dir. of Finance* Patricia Adamek; *Dir. of Development* John Bollier; *Rec. Secy.* Joyce L. Farris.

Publications

ATLA Religion Database on CD-ROM, 1949–.
ETHICS Index on CD-ROM, 1990–.
Index to Book Reviews in Religion (ann.).
Newsletter (q.; memb.; nonmemb. $10). *Ed.* Melody Chartier.
Proceedings (ann.; memb.; nonmemb. $20). *Ed. Dir. of Member Services.*
Religion Index One: Periodicals (s. ann.).
Religion Index Two: Multi-Author Works (ann.).
Religion Indexes: RIO/RIT/IBRR, 1975– on CD-ROM.

Research in Ministry: An Index to Doctor of Ministry Project Reports (ann.).

Committee Chairpersons and Other Officials

Annual Conference. Christine Wenderoth.
Archivist. Boyd Reese.
Automation and Technology. Cassandra Brush.
Collection Evaluation and Development. Bruce Eldevik.
College and University. Judy Clarence.
Education. René House.
NISO Representative. Myron Chace.
Nominating. Cait Kokolus.
OCLC Theological User Group. Linda Umoh.
Online Reference Resource. Charles Willard.
Oral History. Alice Kendrick.
Public Services. Andrew Kadel.
Publication. Rev. George C. Papademetriou.
Special Collections. Sara Myers.
Statistician. Dir. of Member Services.
Technical Services. Chris W. Cullnane.

Archivists and Librarians in the History of the Health Sciences

(formerly the Association of Librarians in the History of the Health Sciences)
President, Barbara Smith Irwin
University of Medicine and Dentistry of New Jersey Libraries
30 12th Ave., Newark, NJ 07103-2754
201-982-6293, FAX 201-982-7474
Internet: irwin@umdnj.edu

Object

This association is established exclusively for educational purposes to serve the professional interests of librarians, archivists, and other specialists actively engaged in the librarianship of the history of the health sciences by promoting the exchange of information and by improving the standards of service.

Membership

Memb. (Voting) 180.

Officers (May 1994–May 1995)

Pres. Barbara Smith Irwin, Univ. of Medicine and Dentistry of New Jersey Libs., 30 12th Ave., Newark, NJ 07103-2754. Tel. 201-982-6293; *Secy.-Treas.* Susan Rushworth, American College of Obstetrics and Gynecology, 409 12th St. S.W., Washington, DC 20024-2188. Tel. 202-638-5577; *Eds.* Jodi Koste, Special Collections and Archives, Medical College of Virginia, MCV Box 582, Richmond, VA 23113-0582; and Joan Echtenkamp Klein, Historical Collections, Univ. of Virginia Health Sciences Center, Box 234, Charlottesville, VA 22908.

Steering Committee

Officers; Adele Lerner, Medical Archives, New York Hospital–Cornell Medical Center, 1300 York Ave., New York, NY 10021; Billie Broaddus, Historical, Archival and Museum Services, Univ. of Cincinnati, 231 Bethesda, Cincinnati, OH 45267-0574.

Committees

Archives. Phyllis Kauffman, Center for Health Sciences Lib., 1305 Linden Dr., Madison, WI 53706.
Awards. Christopher Hoolihan, Miner Lib., Univ. of Rochester, 601 Elmwood Ave., Rochester, NY 14642.

Nominating. Katherine E. S. Donahue, Biomedical Lib., UCLA, 10833 Leconte Ave., Los Angeles, CA 90024.
Program. Jonathon Erlen, 123 Northview Dr., Pittsburgh, PA 15261.

Publication

Watermark (q.; memb.; nonmemb. $15). *Eds.* Jodi Koste, Special Collections and Archives, Medical College of Virginia, MCV Box 582, Richmond, VA 23113-0582; and Joan Echtenkamp Klein, Historical Collections, Univ. of Virginia Health Sciences Center, Box 234, Charlottesville, VA 22908.

ARMA International
(Association of Records Managers and Administrators)

Executive Director, James P. Souders
4200 Somerset Dr., Suite 215, Prairie Village, KS 66208
913-341-3808, FAX 913-341-3742

Object

To promote a scientific interest in records and information management; to provide a forum for research and the exchange of ideas and knowledge; to foster professionalism; to develop and promulgate workable standards and practices; and to furnish source of records and information management guidance through education and publication.

Membership

Membership application is available through ARMA headquarters. Annual dues are $100 for international affiliation. Chapter dues vary from city to city. Membership categories are chapter member ($100 plus chapter dues), student member ($15), and unaffiliated member.

Officers (1994–1995)

Pres. Tyrone G. Butler, TransNational Records and Info. Services, 498 Saint Paul's Ave., Staten Island, NY 10304. Tel. 718-442-2658, FAX 718-442-2204; *Immediate Past Pres. and Chair of the Board* James Allin Spokes, Records Management, Manitoba Hydro, Box 815, Winnipeg, MB R3C 2P4, Canada. Tel. 204-474-3295, FAX 204-475-9044; *Pres.-Elect* Richard Weinholdt, National Archives, 201 Weston St., Winnipeg, MB R3E 3H4, Canada. Tel. 204-983-8845, FAX 204-983-4649; *Secy.-Treas.* Michael P. Flanagan, Union Pacific Railroad Co., 1416 Dodge St., Rm. 830, Omaha, NE 68179. Tel. 402-271-3072, FAX 402-271-5610; *Region V.P.s Region I* Robert Nawrocki; *Region II* Julie A. Gee; *Region III* J. Michael Pemberton; *Region IV* Karen Shaw; *Region V* Douglas P. Allen; *Region VI* Linda L. Masquefa; *Region VII* Gifford Salisbury; *Region VIII* Susan A. Dalati; *Region IX* Susan Eichinger; *Region X* Carole Guy Blowers; *Region XI* Kenneth Hopkins; *Region XII* Christine M. Ardern.

Publication

Records Management Quarterly. Ed. Ira Penn, Box 4580, Silver Spring, MD 20914.

Committee Chairpersons

Awards. James Allin Spokes, Records Management, Manitoba Hydro, Box 815, Winnipeg, MB R3C 2P4, Canada. Tel. 204-474-3295, FAX 204-475-9044; Pat Dixon, Southland Corp., Box 711, Dallas, TX 75221. Tel. 214-828-5503, FAX 214-841-6672.

Education Development. Juanita M. Skillman, Corporate Services, American Honda Motor Co., 1919 Torrance Blvd., MS 540, Torrance, CA 90501-2746. Tel. 310-781-4365, FAX 310-781-4343.

Financial Planning/Management Audit. Michael P. Flanagan, Union Pacific Railroad Co., 1416 Dodge St., Rm. 830, Omaha, NE 68179. Tel. 402-271-3072, FAX 402-271-5610.

IAC Assistants. Nyoakee B. Salway, Occidental Petroleum Corp., 10889 Wilshire Blvd., Suite 920, Los Angeles, CA 90024. Tel. 310-443-6219, FAX 310-443-6340; Lee G. Webster, School Dist. of Philadelphia, 734 Schuylkill Ave., Rm. 234, Philadelphia, PA 19146-397. Tel. 215-875-3932, FAX 215-875-5780.

Industry Action. Timothy W. Hughes, Madison Gas and Electric Co., Box 1231, Madison, WI 53701-1231. Tel. 608-252-4799, FAX 608-252-7098.

Legislative and Regulatory Affairs (Canada). Raphaël A. Thierrin, 208, 4515 45th St. S.W., Calgary, AB T3E 6K7, Canada. Tel./FAX 403-686-3310.

Nominating. James Allin Spokes, Records Management, Manitoba Hydro, Box 815, Winnipeg, MB R3C 2P4, Canada. Tel. 204-474-3295, FAX 204-475-9044.

Organizational Outreach. Tad C. Howington, County of Tarrant, Dept. of Records and Microfilm, 401 W. Belknap, UO17, Fort Worth, TX 76196-0135. Tel. 817-884-1726, FAX 817-884-3363.

Program Chairman (1995). Marilyn J. Brozovic, Wm. Beaumont Hospital, 1350 Stephenson Hwy., Troy, MI 48083-1188. Tel. 313-597-2710, FAX 313-589-9196.

Public Relations, Marketing, and Membership. Karen L. Harris, 4557 N. O'Connor, Apt. 1287, Irving, TX 75062. Tel. 713-374-2172, FAX 713-374-0686.

Publications Coordination. Susan K. Goodman, Infoflow Consulting, 2482 Wickfield Rd., West Bloomfield, MI 48323. Tel./FAX 810-932-3806.

Publications Coordination: Publications Research Development (Subcommittee). Jean K. Brown, Univ. Archives, Univ. of Delaware, 002 Pearson Hall, Newark, DE 19716. Tel. 302-831-2750, FAX 302-831-6903.

Publications Coordination: Standards Advisory and Development (Subcommittee). Marti Fischer, DataLOK Co., 500 Valley Dr., Brisbane, CA 94005. Tel. 415-467-2700, FAX 415-467-2524.

Technology Investigations and Studies. John T. Phillips, 1803 Nantasket Rd., Knoxville, TN 37922. Tel. 615-574-0328, FAX 615-574-1761.

U.S. Government Relations. Andrea D. Lentz, Ohio Dept. of Human Services, Info. Mgt. Section, 2098 Integrity Dr. N., Columbus, OH 43209. Tel. 614-443-5800, FAX 614-443-2822.

Art Libraries Society of North America

Executive Director, Penney De Pas
4101 Lake Boone Trail, Suite 201, Raleigh, NC 27607
919-787-5181, FAX 919-787-4916

Object

To foster excellence in art librarianship and visual resources curatorship for the advancement of the visual arts. Established 1972.

Membership

Memb. 1,325. Dues (Inst.) $80; (Indiv.) $65; (Business Affiliate) $100; (Student/Retired/Unemployed) $40; (Sustaining) $200; (Sponsor) $500; (Overseas) $80. Year. Jan. 1–Dec. 31. Membership is open and encouraged for all those interested in visual librarianship, whether they be professional librarians, students, library assistants, art book publishers, art book dealers, art historians, archivists, architects, slide and photograph curators, or retired associates in these fields.

Officers (Feb. 1994–March 1995)

Pres. Janis Ekdahl; *V.P./Pres.-Elect* Edward Teague; *Secy.* Sherman Clarke; *Treas.* Barbara Sykes-Austin; *Exec. Dir.* Penny DePas; *Past Pres.* Deirdre C. Stam.

Address correspondence to the executive director.

Executive Board

President, past president, president-elect, secretary, treasurer, and five regional representatives (Northeast, Midwest, South, West, and Canada).

Publications

ARLIS/NA Update (bi-mo.; memb.).
Art Documentation (q.; memb.).
Handbook and List of Members (ann.; memb.).
Occasional Papers (price varies).
Topical Papers (price varies).
Miscellaneous others (request current list from headquarters).

Committees

AAT Advisory.
Cataloging Advisory.
Collection Development.
Conference.
Cultural Diversity.
Development.
International Relations.
Membership.
Gerd Muehsam Award.
Nominating.
Professional Development.
Publications.
Research.
Standards.
Technology.
Travel Award.
George Wittenborn Award.

Chapters

Arizona; Central Plains; DC-Maryland-Virginia; Delaware Valley; Kentucky-Tennessee-West Virginia; Michigan; Midstates; Montreal-Ottawa-Quebec; New England; New Jersey; New York; Northern California; Northwest; Ohio; Ontario; Southeast; Southern California; Texas; Twin Cities; Western New York.

Asian/Pacific American Librarians Association

President, Erlinda J. Regner
Business Reference Librarian, Chicago Public Library
Harold Washington Library Center
400 S. State St., Chicago, IL 60605
312-747-4414, FAX 312-747-4975

Object

To provide a forum for discussing problems and concerns of Asian/Pacific American librarians; to provide a forum for the exchange of ideas by Asian/Pacific American librarians and other librarians; to support and encourage library services to the Asian/Pacific American communities; to recruit and support Asian/Pacific American librarians in the library/information science professions; to seek funding for scholarships in library/information science schools for Asian/Pacific Americans; and to provide a vehicle whereby Asian/Pacific American librarians can cooperate with other associations and organizations having similar or allied interests. Founded 1980; incorporated 1981; affiliated with ALA 1982.

Membership

Open to all librarians and information specialists of Asian/Pacific descent working in U.S. libraries and information centers and other related organizations and to others who support the goals and purposes of APALA. Asian/Pacific Americans are defined as those who consider themselves Asian/Pacific Americans. They may be Americans of Asian/Pacific descent, Asian/Pacific people with the status of permanent residency, or Asian/Pacific people living in the United States. Dues (Inst.) $25; (Indiv.) $10 (Students/Unemployed Librarians) $5.

Officers (July 1994–June 1995)

Pres. Erlinda J. Regner, Business Reference Libn., Chicago Public Lib., Harold Washington Lib. Center, 400 S. State St., Chicago, IL 60605. Tel. 312-747-4414, FAX 312-747-4975; *V.P./Pres.-Elect* Amy Seetoo, Michigan Initiative for Women's Health, Univ. of Michigan, Ann Arbor, MI 48109-0482. Tel. 313-747-0472; *Secy.* Susan G. Shiroma, New York Univ. Lib., 70 Washington Sq. S., New York, NY 10012. Tel. 212-998-2602; *Treas.* Wilfred W. Fong, Univ. of Wisconsin–Milwaukee, Milwaukee, WI 53211. Tel. 414-229-5421.

Advisory Committee

President, immediate past president, vice president/president-elect, secretary, treasurer, chairpersons of regional chapters, and an elected representative of the standing committees.

Publications

APALA Newsletter. Ed. Feng-Hwa Wang-Schaefer, Univ. Lib., M/C 234, Univ. of Illinois–Chicago, 801 S. Morgan, Box 8198, Chicago, IL 60680. Tel. 312-996-2728.

Committee Chairpersons

Awards. Sushila Shah.
Constitution and Bylaws. Sharad Karkhanis.
Finance. Henry Chang.
Local Arrangements. Linda Hack, Nita Salutillo, Paula Epstein, Tamije Trejo-Meehan.
Membership. Kyosik Oh.
Newsletter. Feng-Hwa Wang-Schaefer.
Nominations. Lourdes Y. Collantes.
Publicity and Program. Cynthia Hsieh.
Recruitment and Scholarship. Amy Seeto.

Association for Information and Image Management

President, Sue Wolk
1100 Wayne Ave. Suite 1100, Silver Spring, MD 20910
301-587-8202, FAX 301-587-2711

Object

The mission of the Association for Information and Image Management is to be the world's leading association for information industry users and providers.

The purpose of the association is to create value for users and providers of information content, products, and services through promotion and advocacy; education and professional development; knowledge exchange; standards development; professional relationships; and recognition of achievements.

Officers

Chair Paul M. Carman, Eastman Kodak Co., 901 Elmgrove Rd., Rochester, NY 14653-6320; *V.Chair* David F. Liddell, IBM Corp., Rte. 100, MD 1335, Somers, NY 10589; *Treas.* David A. Mindel, Xerox Corp., 800 Salt Rd., 843-16S, Webster, NY 14580.

Publications

INFORM (10 per year; memb.). *Ed.* John Harney.

Association for Library and Information Science Education

Executive Director, Penney De Pas
4101 Lake Boone Trail, Suite 201, Raleigh, NC 27607
919-787-5181, FAX 919-787-4916
E-mail: omg@ruby.ils.unc.edu

Object

The Association for Library and Information Science Education (ALISE) is devoted to the advancement of knowledge and learning in the interdisciplinary field of information studies. Established 1915.

Membership

Memb. 680. Dues (Inst.) for ALA-accredited programs $250; all others $150; (International Affiliate Inst.) $75; (Indiv.) $25 or $60. Year. Sept.–Aug. Any library/information science school with a program accredited by the ALA Committee on Accreditation may become an institutional member. Any school that offers a graduate degree in librarianship or a cognate field but whose program is not accredited by the ALA Committee on Accreditation may become an institutional member at the lower rate. Any school outside the United States and Canada offering a program comparable to that of institutional membership may become an international affiliate institutional member. Any faculty member, administrator, librarian, researcher, or other individual employed full time may become a personal member. Any retired or part-time faculty member, student, or other individual employed less than full time may become a personal member at the lower rate.

Officers (1995–1996)

Pres. June Lester, Univ. of Oklahoma; *V.P./Pres.-Elect* Joan Durrance, Univ. of Michigan; *Past Pres.* Charles Curran, Univ. of South Carolina; *Secy.-Treas.* Carl Orgren, Univ. of Iowa.

Directors

Officers; Elfreda Chatman (term expires 1998); Martha Hale (1997); Margaret Mary Kimmel (1996); *Ed.* Rosemary R. DuMont; *Exec. Dir.* Penney De Pas; Parliamentarians Charles A. Bunge, Norman Horrocks.

Publications

ALISE Library and Information Science Education Statistical Report (ann.; $32; foreign $34).
Journal of Education for Library and Information Science (4 per year; $60; foreign $70).
Membership Directory (ann.; $34).

Association of Academic Health Sciences Library Directors

Administrator, Shirley Bishop
2033 Sixth Ave., Suite 804, Seattle, WA 98121
206-441-6020, FAX 206-441-8262

Object

To promote—in cooperation with educational institutions, other educational associations, government agencies, and other nonprofit organizations—the common interests of academic health sciences libraries located in the United States and elsewhere, through publications, research, and discussion of problems of mutual interest and concern, and to advance the efficient and effective operation of academic health sciences libraries for the benefit of faculty, students, administrators, and practitioners.

Membership

Dues (Inst.) $500; (Assoc. Inst.) $200. Regular membership is available to nonprofit educational institutions operating a school of health sciences that has full or provisional accreditation by the Association of American Medical Colleges. Regular members shall be represented by the chief administrative officer of the member institution's health sciences library. Associate membership (and nonvoting representation) is available to organizations having an interest in the purposes and activities of the association.

Officers

Pres. Karen Brewer; *Pres.-Elect* David Curry.

Board of Directors

J. Michael Homan, Brett A. Kirkpatrick; Patricia Michelson.

Association of Jewish Libraries

c/o National Foundation for Jewish Culture
Room 1034, 15 E. 26 St., New York, NY 10010
212-678-8092

Object

To promote the improvement of library services and professional standards in all Jewish libraries and collections of Judaica; to serve as a center of dissemination of Jewish library information and guidance; to encourage the establishment of Jewish libraries and collections of Judaica; to promote publication of literature that will be of assistance to Jewish librarianship; and to encourage people to enter the field of librarianship. Organized in 1965 from the merger of the Jewish Librarians Association and the Jewish Library Association.

Membership

Memb. 1,100. Dues (Inst.) $30; (Student/Retired) $18. Year. July 1–June 30.

Officers (June 1994–June 1996)

Pres. Zachary Baker, Lib., Yivo Inst. for Jewish Research, 555 W. 57 St., New York, NY 10019; *V.P./Pres.-Elect* Esther Nussbaum, Upper School Lib., 60 E. 78 St., New York, NY 10021; *Past Pres.* Ralph R. Simon, Sindell Lib., Temple Emanu-El, 2200 S. Green Rd., University Heights, OH 44121; *V.P. Memb.* Phyllis Roberts, Richter Lib., Univ. of Miami, Box 248214, Coral Gables,

FL 33124; *Treas.* Salome Cory, Temple Emanu-El, 1 E. 65 St., New York, NY 10021-6596; *Rec. Secy.* Merrily E. Hart, Aaron Gerber Lib., Cleveland College of Jewish Studies, 26500 Shaker Blvd., Beachwood, OH 44122; *Corresponding Secy.* Rita Lifton, Lib., Jewish Theological Seminary of America, 3080 Broadway, New York, NY 10027; *Publications V.P.* Beverly Newman, 11808 High Drive, Leawood, KS 66211.

Address correspondence to the association.

Publications

AJL Newsletter (q.). *Eds.* Irene S. Levin-Wixman, Judaica Lib., Temple Emanu-El, 190 N. County Rd., Palm Beach, FL 33480; Hazel Karp, Hebrew Academy of Atlanta Lib., 5200 Northland Dr., Atlanta, GA 30342.

Judaica Librarianship (irreg.). *Eds.* Marcia Posner; Bella Hass Weinberg, Yivo Lib., 1048 Fifth Ave., New York, NY 10028.

Miscellaneous (request current list from Beverly Newman, 11808 High Drive, Leawood, KS 66211).

Division Presidents

Research and Special Library. David Gilner.
Synagogue, School, and Center Libraries. Toby Rossner.

Association of Research Libraries

Executive Director, Duane E. Webster
21 Dupont Circle N.W., Suite 800, Washington, DC 20036
202-296-2296

Object

The mission of the Association of Research Libraries (ARL) is to shape and influence forces affecting the future of research libraries in the process of scholarly communication. ARL programs and services promote equitable access to and effective use of recorded knowledge in support of teaching, research, scholarship, and community service. The Association articulates the concerns of research libraries and their institutions, forges coalitions, influences information policy development, and supports innovation and improvement in research library operations. ARL is a not-for-profit membership organization comprising the libraries of North American research institutions and operates as a forum for the exchange of ideas and as an agent for collective action.

Membership

Membership is institutional. Memb. 119.

Officers (Oct. 1994–Oct. 1995)

Pres. Jerry D. Campbell, Univ. Libn., Duke Univ. Libs., Durham, NC; *Pres.-Elect* Nancy Cline, Dean of Univ. Libs., Pennsylvania State Univ., University Park, PA; *Past Pres.* John Black, Chief Libn., Univ. of Guelph Lib., Guelph, ON, Canada.

Board of Directors

John Black, Univ. of Guelph; Jerry D. Campbell, Duke Univ.; Dale B. Canelas, Univ. of Florida; Nancy Cline, Pennsylvania State Univ.; Nancy Eaton, Iowa State Univ.; Kent Hendrickson, Univ. of Nebraska–Lincoln; James G. Neal, Indiana Univ.; George W. Shipman, Univ. of Oregon; David H. Stam, Syracuse Univ.; Barbara von Wahlde, SUNY

Buffalo; Gloria Werner, UCLA; James F. Williams, Univ. of Colorado.

Publications

ARL: A Bimonthly Newsletter of Research Libraries Issues and Actions ($50; memb. $25).
ARL Annual Salary Survey ($65; memb. $25).
ARL Preservation Statistics (ann.; $65; memb. $25).
ARL Statistics (ann.; $65; memb. $25).
Directory of Electronic Journals, Newsletters, and Academic Discussion Lists (ann.; $54; memb. $36).
Proceedings of the ARL Membership Meetings (2 issues per yr.; $70; memb. $45).
Subject Index to SPEC Kits in Print (ann.; $10; memb. $7.50).
Systems and Procedures Exchange Center (SPEC) *Kits and Flyers* (10 issues per yr.; kits $280; memb. $18; flyers $50).

Committee Chairpersons

Access to Information Resources. Nancy Eaton, Iowa State Univ.
Information Policies. James Neal, Indiana Univ.
Management of Research Library Resources. Kent Hendrickson, Univ. of Nebraska–Lincoln.
Minority Recruitment and Retention. Joan Chambers, Colorado State Univ.
Nominations. Jerry D. Campbell, Duke Univ.
Preservation of Research Library Materials. Betty G. Bengtson, Univ. of Washington.
Research Collections. Dale B. Canelas, Univ. of Florida.
Scholarly Communication. Donald Koepp, Princeton Univ.
Statistics and Measurement. William J. Crowe, Univ. of Kansas.

Units

Coalition for Networked Information. Formed by ARL, Cause, and EDUCOM in March 1990 to advance scholarship and intellectual productivity by promoting the provision of information resources on existing and future telecommunications networks, and the linkage of research libraries to these networks and to their respective constituencies.

Office of Management Services. Provides consulting, training, and publishing services on the management of human and material resources in libraries.

Office of Research and Development. To pursue the ARL research agenda through the identification and development of projects in support of the research library community's mission.

Office of Scientific and Academic Publishing. Established in 1990 to identify and influence the forces affecting the production, dissemination, and use of scholarly and scientific information.

ARL Membership

Nonuniversity Libraries

Boston Public Lib., Canada Institute for Scientific and Technical Info., Center for Research Libs., Linda Hall Lib., Lib. of Congress, National Agricultural Lib., National Lib. of Canada, National Lib. of Medicine, New York Public Lib., New York State Lib., Smithsonian Institution Libs.

University Libraries

Alabama, Alberta, Arizona, Arizona State, Auburn, Boston, Brigham Young, British Columbia, Brown, California (Berkeley), California (Davis), California (Irvine), California (Los Angeles), California (Riverside), California (San Diego), California (Santa Barbara), Case Western Reserve, Chicago, Cincinnati, Colorado, Colorado State, Columbia, Connecticut, Cornell, Dartmouth, Delaware, Duke, Emory, Florida, Florida State, Georgetown, Georgia, Georgia Institute of Technology, Guelph, Harvard, Hawaii, Houston, Howard, Illinois (Chicago), Illinois (Urbana), Indiana, Iowa, Iowa State, Johns Hopkins, Kansas, Kent State, Kentucky, Laval, Louisiana State, McGill, McMaster, Manitoba, Maryland, Massachusetts, Massachusetts Institute of Technology, Miami, Michigan, Michigan State, Minnesota, Missouri, Nebraska (Lincoln), New Mexico, New York, North Carolina, North Carolina State, Northwestern, Notre Dame, Ohio State, Oklahoma, Oklahoma State, Oregon, Pennsylvania, Pennsylvania State, Pittsburgh, Princeton, Purdue, Queen's (Kingston, Canada), Rice, Rochester, Rutgers, Saskatchewan, South Carolina, Southern California, Southern Illinois, Stanford, SUNY (Albany), SUNY (Buffalo), SUNY (Stony Brook), Syracuse, Temple, Tennessee, Texas, Texas A & M, Toronto, Tulane, Utah, Vanderbilt, Virginia, Virginia Polytechnic, Washington (Seattle), Washington (Saint Louis), Washington State, Waterloo, Wayne State, Western Ontario, Wisconsin, Yale, York.

Association of Visual Science Librarians

c/o Good Samaritan Hospital and Medical Center, 1040 N.W. 22 Ave., Portland, OR 97210
503-229-7678, FAX 503-790-1201

Object

To foster collective and individual acquisition and dissemination of visual science information, to improve services for all persons seeking such information, and to develop standards for libraries to which members are attached. Founded 1968.

Membership

Memb. (U.S.) 55; (Foreign) 13.

Publications

Opening Day Book Collection—Visual Science.
PhD Theses in Physiological Optics (irreg.).
Standards for Visual Science Libraries.
Union List of Vision-Related Serials (irreg.).

Meetings

Annual meeting held in December in connection with the American Academy of Optometry; midyear mini-meeting with the Medical Library Association.

Beta Phi Mu
(International Library and Information Science Honor Society)

Executive Secretary, Blanche Woolls
School of Library and Information Science, University of Pittsburgh, Pittsburgh, PA 15260
412-624-9435, FAX 412-648-7001

Object

To recognize high scholarship in the study of librarianship and to sponsor appropriate professional and scholarly projects. Founded at the University of Illinois in 1948.

Membership

Memb. 25,000. Open to graduates of library school programs accredited by the American Library Association who fulfill the following requirements: complete the course requirements leading to a fifth year or other advanced degree in librarianship with a scholastic average of 3.75 where A equals 4 points (this provision shall also apply to planned programs of advanced study beyond the fifth year that do not culminate in a degree but that require full-time study for one or more academic years); receive a letter of recommendation from their respective library schools attesting

to their demonstrated fitness for successful professional careers. Former graduates of accredited library schools are also eligible on the same basis.

Officers

Pres. Elfreda A. Chatman (1995), School of Lib. and Info. Science, Univ. of North Carolina, Chapel Hill, NC 27599-3360. Tel. 919-962-8366, FAX 919-962-8071; *V.P./Pres.-Elect* Mary Biggs, West Lib., Trenton State College, Hillwood Lakes, CN 4700, Trenton, NJ 08650-4700; *Past Pres.* Norman Horrocks, V.P., Editorial, Scarecrow Press, Box 4167, Metuchen, NJ 08840; *Treas.* Dennis K. Lambert, Head of Collection Management, Falvey Memorial Lib., Villanova Univ., Villanova, PA 19085-1699; *Exec. Secy.* Blanche Woolls, School of Lib. and Info. Science, Univ. of Pittsburgh, Pittsburgh, PA 15260.

Directors

Mary E. Donor (1995), Carol S. Robinson (1995), Zary M. Shafa (1996), Rhonda Marker (1996), W. Michael Havener (1997), Arthur C. Gunn (1997); *Dir.-at-Large* Nancy P. Zimmerman.

Publications

Beta Phi Mu Monograph Series. Book-length scholarly works based on original research in subjects of interest to library and information professionals. Available from Greenwood Press, 88 Post Rd. W., Box 5007, Westport, CT 06881-9990.
Chapbook Series. Limited editions on topics of interest to information professionals. Call Beta Phi Mu for availability.
Newsletter. Ed. William Scheeren.

Chapters

Alpha. Univ. of Illinois, Grad. School of Lib. and Info. Science, Urbana, IL 61801; *Beta.* Univ. of Southern California, School of Lib. Science, Univ. Pk., Los Angeles, CA 90007; *Gamma.* Florida State Univ., School of Lib. Science, Tallahassee, FL 32306; *Delta* (Inactive). Loughborough College of Further Education, School of Libnshp., Loughborough, England; *Epsilon.* Univ. of North Carolina, School of Lib. Science, Chapel Hill, NC 27514; *Zeta.* Atlanta Univ., School of Lib. and Info. Studies, Atlanta, GA 30314; *Theta.* Pratt Institute, Grad. School of Lib. and Info. Science, Brooklyn, NY 11205; *Iota.* Catholic Univ. of America, School of Lib. and Info. Science, Washington, DC 20064; Univ. of Maryland, College of Lib. and Info. Services, College Park, MD 20742; *Kappa.* Western Michigan Univ., School of Libnshp., Kalamazoo, MI 49008; *Lambda.* Univ. of Oklahoma, School of Lib. Science, Norman, OK 73019; *Mu.* Univ. of Michigan, School of Lib. Science, Ann Arbor, MI 48109; *Nu* (Inactive); *Xi.* Univ. of Hawaii, Grad. School of Lib. Studies, Honolulu, HI 96822; *Omicron.* Rutgers Univ., Grad. School of Lib. and Info. Studies, New Brunswick, NJ 08903; *Pi.* Univ. of Pittsburgh, School of Lib. and Info. Science, Pittsburgh, PA 15260; *Rho.* Kent State Univ., School of Lib. Science, Kent, OH 44242; *Sigma.* Drexel Univ., School of Lib. and Info. Science, Philadelphia, PA 19104; *Tau* (Inactive). State Univ. of New York at Geneseo, School of Lib. and Info. Science, Geneseo, NY 14454; *Upsilon.* Univ. of Kentucky, College of Lib. Science, Lexington, KY 40506; *Phi* (Inactive). Univ. of Denver, Grad. School of Libnshp. and Info. Mgt., Denver, CO 80208; *Chi.* Indiana Univ., School of Lib. and Info. Science, Bloomington, IN 47401; *Psi.* Univ. of Missouri at Columbia, School of Lib. and Info. Sciences, Columbia, MO 65211; *Omega* (Inactive). San Jose State Univ., Div. of Lib. Science, San Jose, CA 95192; *Beta Alpha.* Queens College, City College of New York, Grad. School of Lib. and Info. Studies, Flushing, NY 11367; *Beta Beta.* Simmons College, Grad. School of Lib. and Info. Science, Boston, MA 02115; *Beta Delta.* State Univ. of New York at Buffalo, School of Info. and Lib. Studies, Buffalo, NY 14260; *Beta Epsilon.* Emporia State Univ., School of Lib. Science, Emporia, KS 66801; *Beta Zeta.* Louisiana State Univ., Grad. School of Lib. Science, Baton Rouge, LA 70803; *Beta Eta.* Univ. of Texas at Austin, Grad. School of Lib. and Info. Science, Austin, TX 78712; *Beta Theta.* Brigham Young Univ., School of Lib. and Info. Science, Provo, UT 84602; *Beta Iota.* Univ. of Rhode Island, Grad. Lib. School, Kingston, RI 02881; *Beta Kappa.* Univ. of Alabama, Grad. School of Lib. Service, University, AL 35486; *Beta Lambda.* North Texas State Univ., School of Lib. and Info. Science, Denton, TX 76203; Texas Woman's Univ., School of Lib. Science, Denton, TX 76204; *Beta Mu.* Long Island Univ., Palmer Grad. Lib. School, C. W. Post Center, Greenvale, NY 11548; *Beta Nu.* Saint John's Univ., Div. of Lib. and Info. Science,

Jamaica, NY 11439; *Beta Xi.* North Carolina Central Univ., School of Lib. Science, Durham, NC 27707; *Beta Omicron.* Univ. of Tennessee at Knoxville, Grad. School of Lib. and Info. Science, Knoxville, TN 37916; *Beta Pi.* Univ. of Arizona, Grad. Lib. School, Tucson, AZ 85721; *Beta Rho.* Univ. of Wisconsin at Milwaukee, School of Lib. Science, Milwaukee, WI 53201; *Beta Sigma.* Clarion State College, School of Lib. Science, Clarion, PA 16214; *Beta Tau.* Wayne State Univ., Div. of Lib. Science, Detroit, MI 48202; *Beta Upsilon* (Inactive). Alabama A & M Univ., School of Lib. Media, Normal, AL 35762; *Beta Phi.* Univ. of South Florida, Grad. Dept. of Lib., Media, and Info. Studies, Tampa, FL 33620; *Beta Psi.* Univ. of Southern Mississippi, School of Lib. Service, Hattiesburg, MS 39406; *Beta Omega.* Univ. of South Carolina, College of Libnshp., Columbia, SC 29208; *Beta Beta Alpha.* Univ. of California at Los Angeles, Grad. School of Lib. and Info. Science, Los Angeles, CA 90024; *Beta Beta Gamma.* Rosary College, Grad. School of Lib. and Info. Science, River Forest, IL 60305; *Beta Beta Delta.* Univ. of Cologne, Germany; *Beta Beta Epsilon.* Univ. of Wisconsin at Madison, Lib. School, Madison, WI 53706; *Beta Beta Zeta.* Univ. of North Carolina at Greensboro, Dept. of Lib. Science and Educational Technology, Greensboro, NC 27412; *Beta Beta Theta.* Univ. of Iowa, School of Lib. and Info. Science, Iowa City, IA 52242; *Pi Lambda Sigma.* Syracuse Univ., School of Info. Studies, Syracuse, NY 13210.

Bibliographical Society of America

Executive Secretary, Marjory Zaik
Box 397, Grand Central Station, New York, NY 10163
212-647-9171

Object

To promote bibliographical research and to issue bibliographical publications. Organized 1904.

Membership

Memb. 1,250. Dues $40. Year. Jan.–Dec.

Officers (Jan. 1994–Jan. 1996)

Pres. William P. Barlow, Jr.; *V.P.* David Vander Meulen; *Treas.* R. Dyke Benjamin; *Secy.* Hope Mayo.

Council

Sandra Alston, John Lancaster, Fred Schreiber, Alice Schreyer (1995); James N. Green, Alexandra Mason, Leslie Morris, James E. Walsh (1996); Robert H. Hirst, Trevor Howard-Hill, Katharine Leab, Paul Needham (1997).

Publication

Papers (q.; memb.). *Ed.* Trevor Howard-Hill, Dept. of English, Univ. of South Carolina, Columbia, SC 29208.

Committee Chairpersons

Fellowship Program. Richard Landon.
Publications. Katharine Leab.
Bibliographical Projects. Roger E. Stoddard.
Finance. Paul Gourary.

Canadian Association for Information Science
(Association Canadienne des Sciences de l'Information)

140 Saint George St., Toronto, ON M5S 1A1, Canada
416-978-8876

Object

To bring together individuals and organizations concerned with the production, manipulation, storage, retrieval, and dissemination of information with emphasis on the application of modern technologies in these areas. The Canadian Association for information Science (CAIS) is dedicated to enhancing the activity of the information transfer process, utilizing the vehicles of research, development, application, and education, and serving as a forum for dialogue and exchange of ideas concerned with the theory and practice of all factors involved in the communication of information.

Membership

Institutions and individuals interested in information science and involved in the gathering, organization, and dissemination of information (computer scientists, documentalists, information scientists, librarians, journalists, sociologists, psychologists, linguists, administrators, etc.) can become members of CAIS. Dues (Inst.) $165; (Personal) $75; (Student) $40.

Board of Directors

Pres. Charles T. Meadow, Faculty of Info. Studies, Univ. of Toronto, 140 Saint George St., Toronto, ON M5S 1A1. Tel. 416-978-4665, FAX 416-971-1399; *Pres.-Elect* Kent Weaver, Univ. of Toronto Lib., 130 Saint George St., Toronto, ON M5S 1A1. Tel. 416-

978-7292; *Past Pres.* David LaFranchise, Foreign Affairs and International Trade, Lester B. Pearson Bldg., 125 Sussex Dr., Ottawa, ON K1A 0G2. Tel. 613-992-6032; *Treas.* Maggie Weaver, Micromedia, 20 Victoria St., Toronto, ON M5C 2N8. Tel. 416-362-5211, FAX 416-362-6161; *Publications Dir.* Michael J. Nelson, Grad. School of Lib. and Info. Science, Univ. of Western Ontario, London, ON N6G 1H1. Tel. 519-679-2111, FAX 519-661-3506; *Journal Ed.* Joan Cherry, Faculty of Info. Studies, Univ. of Toronto, 140 Saint George St., Toronto, ON M5S 1A1. Tel. 416-978-4663; *Secy.* Mary Nash, Nash Info. Services, 1975 Bel Air Dr., Ottawa, ON K2C 0X1; *Dirs.* Bernd Frohmann, Grad. School of Lib. and Info. Science, Univ. of Western Ontario, London, ON N6G 1H1. Tel. 519-679-2111, FAX 519-661-3506; Lynne Howarth, Faculty of Info. Studies, Univ. of Toronto, 140 Saint George St., Toronto, ON M5S 1A1. Tel. 416-978-152, FAX 416-971-1399; Margaret E. Gross, Spar Aerospace, 21025 Trans Canada Hwy., Sainte Anne-de-Bellevue, PQ H9X 3R2. Tel. 514-457-2150.

Chapters

CAIS West. Jocelyn Godolphin. Ottawa. Pat Johnston.

Publication

Canadian Journal of Information and Library Science (q.; $95; outside Canada $110).

Canadian Library Association

Executive Director, Karen Adams
200 Elgin St., Ottawa, ON K2P 1L5, Canada
613-232-9625, FAX 613-563-9895

Object

To provide leadership in the promotion, development, and support of library and information services in Canada for the benefit of association members, the profession, and Canadian society. Offers library school scholarship and book awards; carries on international liaison with other library associations; makes representation to government and official commissions; offers professional development programs; and supports intellectual freedom. Founded in 1946, CLA is a nonprofit voluntary organization governed by an elected executive council.

Membership

Memb. (Indiv.) 4,000; (Inst.) 1,000. Open to individuals, institutions, and groups interested in librarianship and in library and information services. Dues (Indiv.) $55 to $175, depending on salary; (Inst.) from $175 up, graduated on budget basis. Year. Anniversary date renewal.

Officers (1994–1995)

Pres. Patricia Cavill, 651 Willow Brook Dr. S.E., Calgary, AB T2J 1N6. Tel. 403-278-1630, FAX 403-278-1630, pcavill@acs.ucalgary.ca; *V.P./Pres.-Elect* Penny Marshall, Univ. Libn., Univ. College of Cape Breton, Sydney, NS B1P 6L2. Tel. 902-539-5300 Ext. 338, FAX 902-562-6949, pmarshall@capcr2.uccb.ns.ca; *Treas.* Deborah deBruijn, Univ. of Calgary Libs., 2500 Univ. Dr. N.W., Calgary, AB T2N 1N4. Tel. 403-220-3461, FAX 403-282-6837, debruijn@acs.ucalgary.ca; *Past Pres.* Françoise Hébert, 7 Thornwood Rd., Suite 302, Toronto, ON M4W 2R8. Tel. 416-926-8048, FAX 416-962-0293, hebert@flis.utoronto.ca.

Executive Council

Table officers, divisional presidents, and councillors-at-large.

Publications

CM: Canadian Materials for Schools and Libraries (6 per year; $42).
Feliciter (10 per year; newsletter).

Division Representatives

Canadian Association of College and University Libraries. Judith Head, Univ. of Lethbridge, 4401 Univ. Dr., Lethbridge, AB T1K 3M4. Tel. 403-329-2261, FAX 403-329-2022, lib_head@hg.uleth.ca.
Canadian Association of Public Libraries. Virginia Van Vliet, Brentwood Lib., 36 Brentwood Rd. N., Etobicoke, ON M8X 2B5. Tel. 416-394-5245, FAX 416-394-5257.
Canadian Association of Special Libraries and Information Services. Margo Young, Science and Technology Libn., Cameron Lib., Univ. of Alberta, Edmonton, AB T6G 2J8. Tel. 403-492-7918, FAX 403-492-2721, myoung@library.ualberta.ca.
Canadian Library Trustees Association. Hazel Thornton-Lazier, 2012-49 Thorncliffe Pk. Dr., Toronto, ON M4H 1J6. Tel. 416-423-7177, FAX 416-423-4212.
Canadian School Library Association. Jane Thornley, Supv., Lib. and Info. Services, Halifax County, Bedford Dist. School Board, 946 Main St., Westphal, NS B2W 3V3. Tel. 902-435-6616, FAX 902-434-3402, jthornle@fox.nstn.ns.ca.

Catholic Library Association

President, Jean R. Bostley, SSJ, St. Joseph Central High School, 22 Maplewood Ave.,
Pittsfield, MA 01201-4780
413-447-9121
E-mail: jbostley@k12.ucs.umass.edu

Object

The promotion and encouragement of Catholic literature and library work through cooperation, publications, education, and information. Founded 1921.

Membership

Memb. 1,300. Dues $45–$500. Year. July–June.

Officers (1995–1997)

Pres. Jean R. Bostley, SSJ, St. Joseph Central High School, 22 Maplewood Ave., Pittsfield, MA 01201-4780. Tel. 413-447-9121; *V.P./ Pres.-Elect* Lauretta McCusker, OP, Rosary College GSLIS, 7900 W. Division St., River Forest, IL 60305; *Past Pres.* Paul J. Ostendorf, FSC, Saint Mary's College of Minnesota, 700 Terrace Heights, Winona, MN 55987. Address correspondence to the president.

Executive Board

Officers; Tina-Karen Forman, UCLA Research Lib., 405 Hilgard Ave., Los Angeles, CA 90024 (term expires 1997); Nicholas Falco, 1256 Pelham Pkwy., Bronx, NY 10461 (1999); Mary E. Gallagher, SSJ, College of Our Lady of the Elms, 291 Springfield St., Chicopee, MA 01013 (1999); Julanne Good, 5005 Jamieson, Saint Louis, MO 63109 (2001); Bonaventure Hayes, OFM, Christ the King Seminary, East Aurora, NY 14052-0607 (1997); Anne Kilpatrick, RSM, Saint Bernard Academy, 2020 24th Ave. S., Nashville, TN 37212-404 (2001).

Publications

Catholic Library World (4 per year; memb.; nonmemb. $60). *Ed.* Allen Gruenke.
Catholic Periodical and Literature Index (q.; $400 for college and university libraries, seminaries, public libraries, and publishers; $200 for school and parish libraries; abridged ed. $100). *Ed.* Dana Cernaianu.

Section Chairpersons

Academic Libraries. Priscilla Berthiaume.
Archives. Mary E. Gallagher.
Children's Libraries. Sandra Duplessis.
High School Libraries. Father Joseph Kromenaker.
Parish/Community Libraries. Gloria Ann Griffin.

Round Table Chairpersons

Bibliographic Instruction. Sister Margaret Ruddy.
Cataloging and Classification. Tina-Karen Forman.

Chapters

Acadiana (LA); Bishop Byrne (Houston, TX); Brooklyn/Long Island; Greater Cincinnati; Metropolitan Catholic Colleges (NYC area); Michigan; Midwestern; Neumann (PA); New England; Greater New Orleans; Greater New York; Northern Illinois; Northern New Jersey; Northern Ohio; Northern Virginia; Greater Saint Louis; San Antonio; Southern California; Southwestern Pennsylvania; Washington, DC/ Maryland; Western New York; Wisconsin.

Chief Officers of State Library Agencies

167 W. Main St., Suite 600, Lexington, KY 40507
606-231-1925, FAX 606-231-1928

Object

To provide a means of cooperative action among its state and territorial members to strengthen the work of the respective state and territorial agencies, and to provide a continuing mechanism for dealing with the problems faced by the heads of these agencies, which are responsible for state and territorial library development.

Membership

The Chief Officers of State Library Agencies (COSLA) is an independent organization of the men and women who head the state and territorial agencies responsible for library development. Its membership consists solely of the top library officers of the 50 states, the District of Columbia, and the territories, variously designated as state librarian, director, commissioner, or executive secretary.

Officers (1994–1996)

Pres. J. Maurice Travillian, Asst. State Superintendent for Libs., Maryland State Dept. of Educ., 200 W. Baltimore St., Baltimore, MD 21201-2595. Tel. 410-333-2113, FAX 410-333-2507; *V.P./Pres.-Elect* Sara Parker, Commissioner of Libs., Pennsylvania Dept. of Educ., Commonwealth Libs., Box 1601, Harrisburg, PA 17105-1601. Tel. 717-787-2646, FAX 717-772-3265; *Secy.* James B. Johnson, Jr., Dir., South Carolina State Lib., Box 11469, Columbia, SC 29211. Tel. 803-734-8666, FAX 803-734-8676; *Treas.* Bridget L. Lamont, Dir., Illinois State Lib., 300 S. Second St., Springfield, IL 62701-1796. Tel. 217-782-2992, FAX 217-785-4326.

Directors

Officers; *Immediate Past Pres.* Nancy L. Zussy, State Libn., Washington State Lib., Box 42460, Olympia, WA 98504-2460. Tel. 206-753-2915, FAX 206-586-7575; *Dirs.* Amy Owen, Dir., Utah State Lib.; Jane Kolbe, State Libn., South Dakota.

Chinese-American Librarians Association

Executive Director, Sheila S. Lai
c/o California State University at Sacramento,
2000 Jed Smith Dr., Sacramento, CA 95819-6039
916-278-6201, FAX 916-363-0868
Internet: sheilalai@csus.edu

Object

To enhance communications among Chinese-American librarians as well as between Chinese-American librarians and other librarians; to serve as a forum for discussion of mutual problems and professional concerns among Chinese-American librarians; to promote Sino-American librarianship and library services; and to provide a vehicle whereby Chinese-American librarians may cooperate with other associations and organizations having similar or allied interest.

Membership

Memb. 770. Open to everyone who is interested in the association's goals and activities. Dues (Regular) $15; (Student/Nonsalaried) $7.50; (Inst.) $45; (Permanent) $200.

Officers (July 1994–June 1995)

Pres. Linda Tse; *V.P./Pres.-Elect* Wilfred W. Fong; *Exec. Dir.* Sheila S. Lai; *Treas.* Peter Wang.

Publications

Journal of Library and Information Science (2 per year; memb.; nonmemb. $15).
Membership Directory (memb.).
Newsletter (3 per year; memb.; nonmemb. $10).

Committee Chairpersons

Awards. Marjorie H. Li.
Constitution and Bylaws. Eugenia Tang.
Finance. Peter Wang.
Local Arrangements. Anna McElroy.
Membership. Diana Shih, Nancy Sun Hershoff.
Nomination. Betty L. Tsai.
Program Book Editor. Carl Chan.
Program Planning. Wilfred W. Fong.
Public Relations. Eveline Yang.
Publications. Bor-Sheng Tsai.
Scholarship. Ling-Hwey Jeng.

Task Force (Ad Hoc Committee) Chairpersons

CALA/APALA Relations. Ling-Hwey Jeng.
Cultural Studies. Marjorie Li.
International Relations. Wei-ling Dai.
Professional Development. Christina Hyun.
Services to Chinese Populations. Linda Tse.

Chapter Presidents

California. Mengxiong Liu.
Greater Mid-Atlantic. Michelle S. Lee.
Midwest. Pei-Ling Wu.
Northeast. Linna Yu.
Southwest. Connie C. Wang.

Journal Officers

Newsletter Eds. Emilly Fang, Lib. and Center for Knowledge Management, Univ. of California at San Francisco, 530 Parnassus Ave., San Francisco, CA 94143. Tel. 415-376-3397, FAX 415-476-4653, fang@library.ucsf.edu; Vicki Toy-Smith, Reno Getchell Lib. Rm. 322, Univ. of Nevada, Reno, NV 89577. Tel. 702-784-4692, FAX 702-784-1751, vicki@e2quinox.unr.edu.

Church and Synagogue Library Association

Box 19357, Portland, OR 97280-0357
503-244-6919

Object

To act as a unifying core for the many existing church and synagogue libraries; to provide the opportunity for a mutual sharing of practices and problems; to inspire and encourage a sense of purpose and mission among church and synagogue librarians; to study and guide the development of church and synagogue librarianship toward recognition as a formal branch of the library profession. Founded 1967.

Membership

Memb. 1,900. Dues (Inst.) $125; (Affiliated) $60; (Church/Synagogue) $35; (Indiv.) $20. Year. July–June.

Officers (July 1994–June 1995)

Pres. Russell L. Newburn, 9493 Moulin Ave., Alliance, OH 44601; *Exec. Secy.* Judith Janzen; *Publications Ed.* Sarah T. Moore;

Book Review Ed. Charles Snyder; *1st V.P.* Joyce S. Allen, 3815 N. Bolton Ave., Indianapolis, IN 46226; *2nd V.P.* Cheri Grout, 132 Foxwood Dr., Brownsburg, IN 46112; *Treas.* J. Robert Waggoner, 413 Robindale Ave., Dearborn, MI 48128; *Past Pres.* William Gentz, 300 E. 34 St., New York, NY 10016.

Executive Board

Officers; committee chairpersons.

Publications

Bibliographies (1–6; price varies).

Church and Synagogue Libraries (bi-mo.; memb.; nonmemb. $25; Canada $35). *Ed.* Sarah T. Moore.
CSLA Guides (1–16; price varies).

Committee Chairpersons

Awards. Lillian Koppin.
Chapters. Gail Waggoner.
Conference. Ruth Butler.
Continuing Education. Marilyn Demeter.
Finance and Fund Raising. Emil Hirsch.
Library Services. Jane Parke.
Nominations and Elections. Maryann Dotts.
Personnel. Bill Gentz.
Publications. Carol Campbell.

Council of National Library and Information Associations

1700 18th St. N.W., Washington, DC 20009

Object

To provide a central agency for cooperation among library/information associations and other professional organizations of the United States and Canada in promoting matters of common interest.

Membership

Open to national library/information associations and organizations with related interests of the United States and Canada. American Assn. of Law Libs.; American Lib. Assn.; American Society of Indexers; American Theological Lib. Assn.; Art Libs. Society of North America; Assn. of Christian Libns.; Assn. of Jewish Libs.; Catholic Lib. Assn.; Chinese-American Libns. Assn.; Church and Synagogue Lib. Assn.; Council of Planning Libns.; Lib. Binding Inst.; Lutheran Church Lib. Assn.; Medical Lib. Assn.; Music Lib. Assn.; National Libns. Assn.; Society of American Archivists; Special Libs. Assn.; Theatre Lib. Assn.

Officers (July 1994–June 1995)

Chair Donald Vorp, Collection Development Libn., Speer Lib., Princeton Theological Seminary, Box 111, Princeton, NJ 08542-0803, *V.Chair/Chair-Elect* Emmet Corry, OSF, St. Francis Monastery, 135 Remsen St., Brooklyn, NY 11201; *Past Chair* Madeline Taylor, 36 Park Pl., Brooklyn, NY 11217; *Secy./Treas.* Marie F. Melton, RSM, Saint John's Univ. Lib., Rm. 322, 8000 Utopia Pkwy., Jamaica, NY 11439. Tel. 718-990-6735, FAX 718-380-0353.

Directors

Linda Beck (term expires 1996), Norma Yueh (1995).

Council of Planning Librarians

Deborah Thompson-Wise, Editor
552 Hodges Library, University of Tennessee, Knoxville, TN 37996-1000
615-974-0033, FAX 615-974-2708

Object

To provide a special interest group in the field of city and regional planning for libraries and librarians, faculty, professional planners, university, government, and private planning organizations; to provide an opportunity for exchange among those interested in problems of library organization and research and in the dissemination of information about city and regional planning; to sponsor programs of service to the planning profession and librarianship; to advise on library organization for new planning programs; and to aid and support administrators, faculty, and librarians in their efforts to educate the public and their appointed or elected representatives to the necessity for strong library programs in support of planning. Founded 1960.

Membership

Memb. 100. Open to any individual or institution that supports the purpose of the council, upon written application and payment of dues to the treasurer. Dues (Inst.) $55; (Indiv.) $35; (Student) $15. Year. July 1–June 30.

Officers and Board (1994–1995)

Pres. Elizabeth Douthitt Byrne, Environmental Design Lib., 210 Wurster Hall, Univ. of California, Berkeley, CA 94720. Tel. 510-643-7323; *V.P./Pres.-Elect* Debbie Fowler, City of Toronto Planning and Development Dept., City Hall, 19th fl., Toronto, ON M5H 2N2. Tel. 416-392-1526; *Past Pres.* Jane McMaster, Science and Engineering Lib., Ohio State Univ., Columbus, OH 43210. Tel. 614-292-3053; *Treas.* Gretchen Beal, Knoxville–Knox County Metropolitan Planning Commission, 400 Main Ave., Knoxville, TN 37902; *Secy.* Joan Friedman, MTC/ABAG Lib., 101 8th St., Oakland, CA 94607-4700. Tel. 510-464-7833; *Newsletter Editor* Thelma Helyar, Inst. for Public Policy and Business Research, 607 Blake Hall, Univ. of Kansas, Lawrence, KS 66045-2960; Tel. 913-864-3701; *Editor, CPL Bibliographies* Deborah Thompson-Wise, 552 Hodges Lib., Univ. of Tennessee, Knoxville 37996-1000.

Publications

CPL Bibliographies may be purchased on standing order or by individual issue. Catalog sent upon request.

CPL Newsletter. 10–12 issues a year. Available to members.

Council on Library Resources

1400 16th St. N.W., Suite 510, Washington, DC 20036-2217
202-483-7474, FAX 202-483-6410
Internet: clr@cni.org

Object

A private operating foundation, the council seeks to assist in finding solutions to the problems of libraries, particularly academic and research libraries. In pursuit of this aim, the council conducts its own projects, makes grants to and contracts with other organizations and individuals, and calls upon many others for advice and assistance with its work. The council was established in 1956 by the Ford Foundation, and it now receives support from a number of private foundations and other sources. Current program emphases include human resources, access and processing, economics of libraries, and infrastructure.

Membership

The council's membership and board of directors are limited to 25.

Officers

Chair Martin M. Cummings; *V.Chair* William N. Hubbard, Jr.; *Pres.* Deanna B. Marcum; *Secy.-Treas.* Mary Agnes Thompson.
Address correspondence to headquarters.

Publications

Annual Report.
CLR Reports (newsletter).

Federal Library and Information Center Committee

Executive Director, Susan M. Tarr
Library of Congress, Washington, DC 20540-5100
202-707-4800

Object

The committee makes recommendations on federal library and information policies, programs, and procedures to federal agencies and to others concerned with libraries and information centers.

The committee coordinates cooperative activities and services among federal libraries and information centers and serves as a forum to consider issues and policies that affect federal libraries and information centers, needs and priorities in providing information services to the government and to the nation at large, and efficient and cost-effective use of federal library and information resources and services.

Furthermore, the committee promotes improved access to information, continued development and use of the Federal Library and Information Network (FEDLINK), research and development in the application of new technologies to federal libraries and information centers, improvements in the management of federal libraries and information centers, and relevant education opportunities. Founded 1965.

Membership

Libn. of Congress, Dir. of the National Agricultural Lib., Dir. of the National Lib. of Medicine, representatives from each of the other executive departments, and representatives from each of the following agencies: National Aeronautics and Space Admin., National Science Foundation, Smithsonian Institution, U.S. Supreme Court, U.S. Info. Agency, National Archives and Records Admin., Admin. Offices of the U.S. Courts, Defense Technical Info. Center, Government Printing Office, National Technical Info. Service, and Office of Scientific and Technical

Info. (Dept. of Energy), Exec. Office of the President, Dept. of the Army, Dept. of the Navy, Dept. of the Air Force, and chairperson of the FEDLINK Advisory Council. Fifteen additional voting member agencies shall be selected on a rotating basis by the voting members of FEDLINK and nine rotating members through selection by the permanent members of the committee. These rotating members will serve three terms. One representative from each of the following agencies is invited as an observer to committee meetings: General Accounting Office, General Services Admin., Joint Committee on Printing, National Commission on Libs. and Info. Science, Office of Mgt. and Budget, Office of Personnel Mgt., and Lib. of Congress Financial Services Directorate.

Officers

Chair James H. Billington, Libn. of Congress; Chair Designate Donald C. Curran, Assoc. Libn. for Constituent Services, Lib. of Congress; Exec. Dir. Susan M. Tarr, Federal Lib. and Info. Center Committee, Lib. of Congress, Washington, DC 20540-5100.

Address correspondence to the executive director.

Publications

Annual FLICC Forum on Federal Information Policies (summary and papers).
Annual Report.
FLICC Newsletter (q.).

Federal Publishers Committee

Chairperson, John Weiner
Energy Information Administration, EI-23, Mail Sta. BG-057,
1000 Independence Ave. S.W., Washington, DC 20585
202-586-6537, FAX 202-586-0114

Object

To foster and promote effective management of data development and dissemination in the federal government through exchange of information, and to act as a focal point for federal agency publishing.

represented are the Joint Committee on Printing, Government Printing Office, National Technical Information Service, National Commission on Libraries and Information Science, and the Library of Congress. Meetings are held monthly during business hours.

Membership

Memb. 700. Membership is available to persons involved in publishing and dissemination in federal government departments, agencies, and corporations, as well as independent organizations concerned with federal government publishing and dissemination. Some key federal government organizations

Officers

Chair John Weiner; Secy. Marilyn Marbrook.

Committee Chairpersons

Programs. Sandra Smith.
Roundtable Activity. June Malina.

Information Industry Association

555 New Jersey Ave. N.W., Suite 800, Washington, DC 20001
202-639-8262, FAX 202-638-4403

Membership

Memb. 500+ companies. Open to companies involved in the creation, distribution, and use of information products, services, and technologies. For details on membership and dues, write to the association headquarters.

Staff

Pres. Kenneth B. Allen; *V.P.* Emily G. Pilk; *V.P. and General Counsel* Steven J. Metalitz; *V.P. Memb.* Judith Angerman; *Dir., Industry Relations* Michael I. Atkin; *Dir., Meetings* Carol Madden; *Dir., Global Issues Council and Optical Publishing Div.* Robert Vitro; *Dir., Small and Emerging Business Council and Voice Info. Services Div.* Terri L. Lageman.

Board of Directors

Chair Hugh Yarrington, Commerce Clearing House Inc.; *Chair-Elect* Andrew Prozes, Southam Info. and Technology Group; *Past Chair* John Hockenberry, Washington Post; *Treas.* Paul Wojcik, Bureau of National Affairs Inc.; *Secy.* W. Leo McBlain, ADP Brokerage Info. Services; *V.Chairs* James E. Coane, Telebase Systems Inc.; Linda J. Laskowski, U S WEST Communications; Paul P. Massa, Congressional Info. Service; *Membs.* Kathleen Bingham, Find/SVP Inc.; Steven Graham, AT&T Microelectronics; Michael Jabara, Jabara and Co.; Natalie S. Lang, Oryx Press; Richard Levine, Dow Jones and Co.; Thomas McClain, Dun and Bradstreet Info. Services; J. Edward McEntire, Info. Handling Services; Thomas J. McLeod, West Publishing; Barbara A. Munder, McGraw-Hill; Joseph Rhyne, Mead Data Central; Peter Simon, Reed Reference Publishing; Patrick J. Tierney, Dialog Info. Services; Lawrence Wills, IBM Corp.

Division Chairpersons

Directory. Russell Perkins, Morgan-Rand Inc.
Electronic Information Services. Huw Morgan, Southam Info. and Technology Group.
Financial Information Services. W. Leo McBlain, ADP Brokerage Info. Services.
Optical Publishing. Paul Earl, Emerging Technology Applications.
Voice Information Services. Thomas Pace, Dow Jones and Co.

Council Chairpersons

Global Issues. Andrew Prozes, Southam Info. and Technology Group.
Public Policy and Government Relations. Cynthia Braddon, McGraw-Hill.
Small and Emerging Business. H. Donald Wilson, Conquest Software.

Publication

Information Sources (annual; memb. $55; nonmemb. $95).

Lutheran Church Library Association

Executive Director, Leanna D. Kloempken
122 W. Franklin Ave., Minneapolis, MN 55404
612-870-3623

Object

To promote the growth of church libraries by publishing a quarterly journal, *Lutheran Libraries;* furnishing booklists; assisting member libraries with technical problems; and providing meetings for mutual encouragement, assistance, and exchange of ideas among members. Founded 1958.

Membership

Memb. 1,800. Dues $25, $37.50, $50, $75, $100, $500, $1,000. Year. Jan.–Jan.

Officers (Jan. 1995–Jan. 1996)

Pres. Charles R. Mann, 21512 Maple Ave., Rogers, MN 55374; *V.P.* Vernita Kennen, 5 Beswick Court, Pleasant Hill, CA 94523; *Secy.* Evelyn Pearson, 9550 Collegeview Rd., No. 330, Bloomington, MN 55437; *Treas.* Marilyn Anderson, 5328 51st Ave. N., Minneapolis, MN 55429.

Address correspondence to the executive director.

Directors

Hazel Arndt, Odella Baak, Judy Casserberg, Viola Gering, Elaine King, Marilyn Miller.

Publication

Lutheran Libraries (q.; memb.; nonmemb. $25).

Board Chairpersons

Advisory. Rev. Rolf Aaseng.
Council of National Library and Information Associations. Chuck Mann, Linda Beck.
Finance. L. Edwin Wang.
Library Services. Betty LeDell.
Membership. Erwin John (interim).
Publications. Rod Olson.

Medical Library Association

Executive Director, Carla Funk
6 N. Michigan Ave., Suite 300, Chicago, IL 60602
312-419-9094, FAX 312-419-8950

Object

The major purposes of the Medical Library Association (MLA) are to foster medical and allied scientific libraries, to promote the educational and professional growth of health science librarians, and to exchange medical literature among the members. Through its programs and publications, MLA encourages professional development of its membership, whose foremost concern is dissemination of health sciences information for those in research, education, and patient care. Founded 1898; incorporated 1934.

Membership

Memb. (Inst.) 1,300; (Indiv.) 3,700. Institutional members are medical and allied scientific libraries. Individual members are people who are (or were at the time membership was established) engaged in professional library or bibliographic work in medical and allied scientific libraries or people who are interested in medical or allied scientific libraries. Dues (Student) $25; (Emeritus) $40; (Intro.) $75; (Indiv.) $110; (Sustaining) $345; and (Inst.) $175–$410, based on the number of the libraries periodical subscriptions. Members may be affiliated with one or more of MLA's 24 special-interest sections and 14 regional chapters.

Officers

Pres. Fred W. Roper, College of Lib. and Info. Science, Univ. of South Carolina, Columbia, SC 29208; *Pres.-Elect* Jana Bradley, School of Lib. and Info. Science, Indiana Univ. at Indianapolis, 755 W. Michigan, UL11OD, Indianapolis, IN 46202-5195; *Past Pres.* June H. Fulton, Medical Documentation Service, Institute for Scientific Info., 3501 Market St., Philadelphia, PA 19104.

Directors

Dottie Eakin (1997), Janet S. Fisher (1996), Carole M. Gilbert (1996), Kathryn J. Hoffman (1995), Christiane J. Jones (1996), Joanne G. Marshall (1997), Daniel T. Richards (1996), Ada M. Seltzer (1995), M. Sandra Wood (1995).

Publications

Bulletin of the Medical Library Association (q.; $136).
Directory of the Medical Library Association, 1994/95 ($150).
MLA News (10 per year; $48.50).
Miscellaneous (request current list from association headquarters).

Committee Chairpersons

Awards. Camilla B. Reid.
Books (Panel). Beverly R. Renford.
Books Editor. J. Michael Homan.
Bulletin Consulting Editor (Panel). Naomi C. Broering.
Bylaws. Jill Mayer.
Centennial Coordinating. Frances Groen.
Continuing Education. Susan B. Case.
  Instructor Approval. Rochelle L. Minchow.
  Instructional Development. Laurie L. Thompson.

Credentialing. Jo Ann Bell.
Exchange (Advisory). Barbara A. Carlson.
Governmental Relations. Sara Jean Jackson.
Grants and Scholarships. Jean W. Sayre.
Health Sciences Library Technicians. Rajia C. Tobia.
Hospital Libraries. Rosalind F. Dudden.
Joseph Leiter NLM/MLA Lectureship. Lois Ann Colaianni.
Membership. Janis Glover.
National Program (1995). Linda A. Watson.
National Program (1996). Jacqueline D. Doyle.
Professional Recognition (Review Panel). Patricia M. Rodgers.
Publications. Jeanette C. McCray.
Publishing and Information Industries Relations. Marion N. Sabella.
SEICC. Lynne A. Silvers.

Juries

Continuing Education Grant. Tracy E. Powell
Cunningham Memorial International. Lenny Rhine.
EBSCO/MLA Annual Meeting. Grant. Janice Swiatek.
MLA Doctoral Fellowship. Walter P. Wilkins.
MLA Research Grant. Alexandra Dimitroff.
MLA Scholarship. Marsha Gelman-Kmec.
MLA Scholarship for Minority. Kellie N. Kaneshiro.

Ad Hoc Committee Chairpersons

Centennial Coordinating. Frances Groen.
Committee to Establish Cunningham Endowment. Robert G. Cheshier.
Executive. Fred W. Roper.
Joint MLA/AAHSLD Legislative (Task Force). June Glaser.
MLA/NLM Collaboration (Task Force). Susan Lessick Russell.
Nominating. Jacqueline D. Bastille.
Platform for Change Implementation (Task Force). Mary M. Horres.
Research (Task Force). Prudence W. Dalrymple.

Music Library Association

Box 487, Canton, MA 02021
617-828-8450, FAX 617-828-8915

Object

To promote the establishment, growth, and use of music libraries; to encourage the collection of music and musical literature in libraries; to further studies in musical bibliography; to increase efficiency in music library service and administration; and to promote the profession of music librarianship. Founded 1931.

Membership

Memb. 1,900. Dues (Inst.) $78; (Indiv.) $65; (Student) $35. Year. Sept. 1–Aug. 31.

Officers

Pres. Michael Ochs, 115 E. 78 St., Apt. 26A, New York, NY 10128; *V.P./Pres.-Elect* Jane Gottlieb, Juilliard School, 60 Lincoln Center Plaza, New York, NY 10023-6588; *Rec. Secy.* Laura Snyder, 132 Amsterdam Rd., Rochester, NY 14610-1008; *Exec. Secy.* Richard Griscom, Anderson Music Lib., Univ. of Louisville, Louisville, KY 40292.

Members-at-Large

Elizabeth Davis, Columbia Univ.; David Hunter, Univ. of Texas at Austin; Jerry L. McBride, Middlebury College; Paula Matthews, Bates College; John Shepard, NY Public Lib. for the Performing Arts; Judy Tsou, Univ. of California at Berkeley.

Special Officers

Business Mgr. James S. P. Henderson, Box 487, Canton, MA 02021.
Convention Mgr. Joseph Fuchs, Glendale Public Lib., 222 E. Harvard St., Glendale, CA 91205.

Placement. Elizabeth Rebman, Music Lib., 240 Morrison Hall, Univ. of California at Berkeley, CA 94720.
Publicity. Richard E. Jones, 1904 Sandlewood Dr., Greencastle, IN 46135-9214.

Publications

MLA Index Series (irreg.; price varies).
MLA Newsletter (q.; memb.).
MLA Technical Reports (irreg.; price varies).
Music Cataloging Bulletin (mo.; $25).
Notes (q.; indiv. $60; inst. $71).

Committee Chairpersons

Administration. Charles P. Coldwell, Seattle Public Lib.
Bibliographic Control. Jennifer Bowen, Eastman School of Music.
Development. Linda Solow Blotner, Univ. of Hartford.
Education. Roberta Chodaclei, East Carolina Univ.
Finance. Elizabeth Davis, Columbia Univ.
Walter Gerboth Award. Joseph Boonin, NYPL.
Legislation. Donna J. Boettcher, Bowling Green State Univ.
Preservation. John Shepard, New York Public Lib. Tel. 212-870-1654.
Program (1995 meeting). Jean Purnell, Univ. of the Pacific.
Program (1996 meeting). James P. Cassaro, Cornell Univ.
Public Libraries. Carolyn Dow, Lincoln (NE) City Libs.
Publications. Ruth Henderson, City Univ. of New York. Tel. 212-650-7271.
Publications Awards. Lenore Coral, Cornell Univ.
Reference and Public Service. Leslie Troutman, Univ. of Illinois, Urbana.
Resource Sharing and Collection Development. Elizabeth Davis, Columbia Univ.

National Association of Government Archives and Records Administrators

Executive Director, Bruce W. Dearstyne
48 Howard St., Albany, NY 12207
518-473-8037

Object

Founded in 1984, the association is successor to the National Association of State Archives and Records Administrators, which had been established in 1974. NAGARA is a growing nationwide association of local, state, and federal archivists and records administrators, and others interested in improved care and management of government records. NAGARA promotes public awareness of government records and archives management programs, encourages interchange of information among government archives and records management agencies, develops and implements professional standards of government records and archival administration, and encourages study and research into records management problems and issues.

Membership

State archival and records management agencies are NAGARA's sustaining members, but individual membership is open to local governments, federal agencies, and to any individual or organization interested in improved government records programs.

Officers

Pres. David Hoober, Arizona Dept. of Lib. Archives and Public Records; *V.P.* Cathryn Hammond Baker, Archives of the Commonwealth, Massachusetts; *Secy.* Gerald Newborg, Florida Bureau of Archives and Records Management; *Treas.* Jim Berberich, State Historical Society of North Dakota.

Publications

Clearinghouse (q.; memb.).
Government Records Issues (series).
Information Clearinghouse Needs of the Archival Profession (report).
Local Government Records.
Preservation Needs in State Archives (report).
Program Reporting Guidelines for Government Records Programs.
Technical Publications (series).

National Federation of Abstracting and Information Services

Executive Director, Richard T. Kaser
1518 Walnut St., Philadelphia, PA 19102
215-893-1561, FAX 215-893-1564

Object

NFAIS is an international, not-for-profit membership organization comprising leading information producers, distributors, and corporate users of secondary information. Its purpose is to serve the information community through education, research, and publication. Founded 1958.

Membership

Memb. 70+. Full membership (regular and government) is open to organizations that, as a substantial part of their activity, produce secondary information services for external use. Secondary information products are compilations containing printed or electronic summaries of, or references to, multiple sources of publicly available information. For example, organizations that assemble bibliographic citations, abstracts, indexes, and data are all secondary information services.

Associate membership is available to organizations that operate or manage online information services, networks, in-house information centers, and libraries; conduct research or development work in information science or systems; are otherwise involved in the generation, promotion, or distribution of secondary information products under contract; or publish primary information sources.

Members pay dues annually based on the fiscal year of July 1–June 30. Dues are assessed based on the member's revenue derived from information-related activities.

Officers (1994–1995)

Pres. Dennis Auld; *Past Pres.* Kurt Molholm; *Secy.* Bonnie Maxwell; *Treas.* Jim Ashling.

Directors

John Anderson, Gladys Cotter, Phyllis Franklin, Sheldon Kotzin, Taissa Kusma, John Regazzi, Linda Sacks, Ralph Ubico.

Staff

Exec. Dir. Richard T. Kaser; *Publications Coord.* Wendy Wicks; *Promotions Coord.*

Anthony Tripido; *Financial Asst.* Wendy Carter; *Admin. Asst.* Antoinette Dennis.

Publications

Automated Support to Indexing (1992; memb. $80; nonmemb. $100).

CD-ROM for Information Distribution (1992; memb. $80; nonmemb. $100).

Changing Roles in Information Distribution (1994; memb. $50; nonmemb. $60).

Customer Services and User Training (1991; memb. $40; nonmemb. $50).

Developing New Markets for Information Products (1993; memb. $50; nonmemb. $60).

Flexible Workstyles in the Information Industry (1993; memb. $50; nonmemb. $60).

Government Information and Policy: Changing Roles in a New Administration (1994; memb. $50; nonmemb. $60).

Guide to Careers in Abstracting and Indexing (1992; memb. $20; nonmemb. $25).

Guide to Database Distribution, 2nd ed. (1994; memb. $140; nonmemb. $175).

Multimedia in the Information Industry (1992; memb. $80; nonmemb. $100).

NFAIS Newsletter (mo.; North America $110; elsewhere, $125).

Recognition Technology in the Information Industry (1992; memb. $80; nonmemb. $100).

Three Views of the Internet (1993; memb. $50; nonmemb. $60).

National Information Standards Organization

Executive Director, Patricia Harris
Box 1056, Bethesda, MD 20827
301-975-2814, FAX 301-869-8071
Internet: niso@enh.nist.gov

Object

To develop technical standards used in libraries, publishing, and information services. Experts from the information field volunteer to lend their expertise in the development and writing of NISO standards. The standards are approved by the consensus of

NISO's voting membership, which consists of 57 voting members representing libraries, government, associations, and private businesses and organizations. NISO is supported by its membership and corporate grants. Formerly a committee of the American national Standards Institute (ANSI), NISO, formed in 1939, was incorporated in 1983 as a nonprofit educational organization. NISO is accredited by ANSI and serves as the U.S. Technical Advisory Group to ISO/TC 46.

Membership

Memb. 57. Open to any organization, association, government agency, or company—national in scope—willing to participate in and having substantial concern for the development of NISO standards.

Officers

Chair Michael J. Mellinger, Pres., Data Research Assocs., 1276 N. Warson Rd., Box 8495, Saint Louis, MO 63132-1806; *V.Chair/Chair-Elect* Michael J. McGill, Chief Info. Officer, Univ. of Michigan Medical Center, 1500 E. Medical Center Dr., TCB 1240-0308, Ann Arbor, MI 48019-0308; *Past Chair* James Rush, Exec. Dir., PALINET, 3401 Market St., Suite 262, Philadelphia, PA

19104-3374; *Treas.* Joel Baron, Chief Publications Officer, Faxon Co., 15 Southwest Pk., Westwood, MA 02090; *Exec. Dir./Secy.* Patricia Harris, NISO, Box 1056, Bethesda, MD 20827; *Dirs.* Bob Badger, Springer Verlag, New York, NY; Marjorie Hlava, Access Innovations, Albuquerque, NM; John Kolman, NOTIS Systems, Evanston, IL; Rebecca Lenzini, CARL Corp., Denver, CO; Clifford Lynch, Univ. of California, Oakland, CA; Nolan Pope, Univ. of Wisconsin, Madison, WI; Lennie Stovel, Research Libs. Group, Mountain View, CA; Vinod Chachra, VTLS, Blacksburg, VA; Elizabeth Bole Eddison, Inmagic, Woburn, MA.

Publications

Information Standards Quarterly (q.; $65; foreign $85). *Ed.* Pat Ensor.
NISO published standards are available from NISO Press, Box 338, Oxon Hill, MD 20750-0338. Tel. 301-567-9522, 800-282-6476, FAX 301-567-9553.

National Librarians Association

Executive Secretary, Peter Dollard
Box 486, Alma, MI 48801
FAX 517-463-8694

Object

To promote librarianship, to develop and increase the usefulness of libraries, to cultivate the science of librarianship, to protect the interest of professionally qualified librarians, and to perform other functions necessary for the betterment of the profession of librarians, rather than as an association of libraries. Established 1975.

Membership

Memb. 200. Dues $20/year; $35/2 years; (Students, Retired, and Unemployed Libns.) $10. Floating membership year. Any person interested in librarianship and libraries who holds a graduate degree in library science

may become a member upon election by the executive board and payment of the annual dues. The executive board may authorize exceptions to the degree requirements for applicants who present evidence of outstanding contributions to the profession. Student membership is available to those graduate students enrolled full time at any ALA-accredited library school.

Officers

Pres. Carol Meyer, Cincinnati, OH. Tel. 513-632-8372; *V.P./Pres.-Elect* Don Barlow, Westerville, OH. Tel. 614-882-7277; *Secy.-Treas.* Peter Kaatrude, Port Arthur, TX. Tel. 409-983-4921.

Executive Board

Officers; *Past Pres.* Matthew Kubiak; *Members-at-Large* Lawrence Auld, Alvin Bailey, Don Barlow, Joseph Harzbecker, Don Tipka, Hope Waller.

Publication

National Librarian (q.; $15). *Ed.* Peter Dollard.

REFORMA
(National Association to Promote Library Services to the Spanish Speaking)

President, Gilda Baeza Ortego
Sul Ross State University Lib., Alpine, TX 79832
915-837-8121, FAX 915-837-8400

Object

To promote the development of library collections to include Spanish-language and Hispanic-oriented materials; the recruitment of more bilingual and bicultural professionals and support staff; the development of library services and programs that meet the needs of the Hispanic community; the establishment of a national network among individuals who share our goals; the education of the U.S. Hispanic population in regard to the availability and types of library services; and lobbying efforts to preserve existing library resource centers serving the interest of Hispanics.

Membership

Memb. 700. Any person who is supportive of the goals and objectives of REFORMA.

Officers

Pres. Gilda Baeza Ortego, Sul Ross State Univ. Lib., Alpine, TX 79832. Tel. 915-837-8121, FAX 915-837-8400; *V.P./Pres.-Elect* Judith Castiano, San Diego Public Lib., Tierra Santa Branch, 4985 La Cuenta Dr., San Diego, CA 92124. Tel. 619-573-1385, FAX 619-236-5878; *Past Pres.* Camila Alire, Auraria Lib., Lawrence at 11th, Denver, CO 80204. Tel. 303-556-3526, FAX 303-556-3528; *Treas.* Rene Amaya, 1750 Coolidge Ave., Altadena, CA 91001; *Secy.* Ivonne

Jimenez, El Paso Public Lib., 501 N. Oregon St., El Paso, TX 79901. Tel. 915-543-5418, FAX 915-543-5410; *Newsletter Ed.* Felipe de Ortego y Gasca, Sul Ross State Univ., Educ. Dept., Box 6031, Alpine, TX 79832. Tel. 915-837-8275, FAX 915-837-8400; *Archivist/Historian* Salvador Guerena, Univ. Lib.-CEMA, Univ. of California, Santa Barbara, CA 93106. Tel. 805-893-8563, FAX 805-893-4676.

Publication

REFORMA Newsletter (q.; memb.). *Ed.* Felipe de Ortego y Gasca, Sul Ross State Univ., Alpine, TX 79832. Tel. 915-837-8375, FAX 915-837-8400.

Committees

Book Awards. Sandra Balderrama.
Children's Services. Oralia Garza de Cortez.
Membership. Al Milo.
Nominations. Ramiro Salazar.
Organizational Development. Linda Chavez.
Public Relations. Edward Erazo.
Scholarship. Luis Chapparo.

Meetings

All meetings take place at the American Library Association's Midwinter meeting and annual conference.

Research Libraries Group Inc.

Director of Corporate Communications, Jennifer Hartzell
1200 Villa St., Mountain View, CA 94041-1100
415-691-2207
E-mail: bl.jhl@rlg.stanford.edu

Object

The Research Libraries Group Inc. (RLG) is a not-for-profit membership corporation of nearly 150 universities, archives, historical societies, museums, and other institutions devoted to improving access to information that supports research and learning. RLG exists to support its members in containing costs, improving local services, and contributing to the nation's collective access to scholarly materials. For its members, RLG develops and operates cooperative programs to manage, preserve, and extend access to research library, museum, and archival holdings. For both its members and for nonmember institutions and individuals worldwide, RLG develops and operates databases and software to serve an array of information access and management needs. Aril®, CitaDel®, CJK®, Eureka™, RLG Conspectus®, RLIN®, and Zephyr™ are trademarks and service marks of the Research Libraries Group Inc.

Membership

Memb. 148+. Membership is open to any nonprofit institution with an educational, cultural, or scientific mission. There are two membership categories: general and special. General members are institutions that serve a clientele of more than 5,000 faculty, academic staff, research staff, professional staff, students, fellows, or members. Special members serve a similar clientele of 5,000 or fewer.

Directors

RLG has a 19-member Board of Directors, comprising 12 directors elected from and by RLG's member institutions, 6 at-large directors elected by the board itself, and the president. Theirs is the overall responsibility for the organization's governance and for ensuring that it faithfully fulfills its purpose and goals. Annual board elections are held in the spring. The board's chair for 1994–1995 is Paul H. Mosher, vice provost and director of libraries, Univ. of Pennsylvania.

Staff

Pres. James Michalko; *V.P., Planning and Research Resources* John Haeger; *Acting Dir., Member Services* Nancy Elkington; *Dir., Lib. and Bibliographic Services* Karen Smith-Yoshimura; *Dir., Access Services* Wayne Davison; *Dir., Customer and Operations Support* Jack Grantham; *Dir., Computer Development* David Richards; *Dir., Finance and Administration* Molly Singer; *Dir., Sales and Marketing* Kristin Tague; *Dir., Corporate Communications* Jennifer Hartzell.

Publications

Digital Imaging Technology for Preservation (symposium proceedings).

Electronic Access to Information: A New Service Paradigm (symposium proceedings).

The Research Libraries Group News (3 per year).

RLG Archives Microfilming Manual (RLG-developed guidelines and practice).

RLIN Focus (bi-mo.; 8-page user services newsletter).

RLG Preservation Microfilming Handbook (RLG-developed guidelines and practice).

Society for Scholarly Publishing

Executive Director, Francine Butler
c/o Resource Center for Associations, 10200 W. 44 Ave., Suite 304, Wheat Ridge, CO 80033
303-422-3914

Object

To draw together individuals involved in the process of scholarly publishing. This process requires successful interaction of the many functions performed within the scholarly community. The Society for Scholarly Publishing (SSP) provides the leadership for such interaction by creating opportunities for the exchange of information and opinions among scholars, editors, publishers, librarians, printers, booksellers, and all others engaged in scholarly publishing.

Membership

Open to all with an interest in scholarly publishing and information dissemination. There are four categories of membership: individual, $50; contributing, $250; sustaining, $500; and sponsoring, $1,500. Year. Jan. 1–Dec. 31.

Executive Committee

Pres. Christine Lamb, 105 Hill St., Concord, MA 01742; *Past Pres.* Robert Shirrell, Univ. of Chicago Press, 5720 S. Woodlawn Ave., Chicago, IL 60637. Tel. 312-702-8785; *V.P.* Margaret Foti; *Secy.-Treas.* Patricia E. Sabosik; *Assoc. Dir. for Operation*, Michael Leonard, MIT Press, 55 Hayward St., Cambridge, MA 02142.

Directors

Executive Committee; Czeslaw Jan Grycz, Univ. of California, 300 Lakeside Dr., 8th fl.,

Oakland, CA 94612-3550; Cynthia Smith, Aspen Publishers, 200 Orchard Ridge Dr., Gaithersburg, MD 20878; Phyllis Hall, IEEE, 345 E. 47 St., New York, NY 10017-2394; Isabella L. Hinds, Copyright Clearance Center, 27 Congress St., Salem, MA 01970; Karen Hunter, Elsevier Science Publishing, 655 Sixth Ave., New York, NY 10010; Stephen Prudhomme, National Research Council–Canada, Sussex Dr., Rm. 1011, Ottawa, ON K1A 0R6, Canada; Robert H. Mars, Dir., Publications Div., American Chemical Society, 1155 16th St. N.W., Washington, DC 20036; Nina Matheson, Dir., Welsh Lib., Johns Hopkins Univ., 1900 E. Monument St., Baltimore, MD 21205; *Exec. Dir.* Francine Butler, 10200 W. 44 Ave., Suite 304, Wheat Ridge, CO 80033; *Assoc. Dir.* Jerry Bowman, 10200 W. 44 Ave., Suite 304, Wheat Ridge, CO 80033.

Committee Chairpersons

Annual Meeting (Vacant.)
Education. Norma Brennan.
Executive. Christine Lamb.
Investment. Mike Leonard.
Membership. Ron Akie, Diane Appleton.
Newsletter. Ed Barnas.

Meetings

An annual meeting is conducted in either May or June. The location changes each year. Additionally, SSP conducts several seminars throughout the year.

Society of American Archivists

Executive Director, Susan E. Fox
600 S. Federal St., Suite 504, Chicago, IL 60605
312-922-0140, FAX 312-347-1452

Object

To promote sound principles of archival economy and to facilitate cooperation among archivists and archival agencies. Founded 1936.

Council

Karen Benedict, Susan Davis, Luciana Duranti, Tim Ericson, Margaret Hedstrom, Steve Hensen, Tom Hickerson, Sharon Thibodeau, Elizabeth Yakel.

Membership

Memb. 4,800. Dues (Indiv.) $65–$170, graduated according to salary; (Assoc.) $65, domestic; (Student) $40, with a two-year maximum on membership; (Inst.) $210; (Sustaining) $410.

Staff

Exec. Dir. Susan E. Fox; *Memb. Asst.* Bernice E. Brack; *Managing Ed.* Teresa Brinati; *Publications Asst.* Troy Sturdivant; *Bookkeeper* Carroll Dendler; *Sr. Archivist* Jane Kenamore; *Meeting Planner* Debra Mills.

Officers (1994–1995)

Pres. Maygene Daniels; *V.P.* Brenda Banks; *Treas.* Lee Stout.

Publications

American Archivist (q.; $75; foreign $90). *Ed.* Richard Cox; *Managing Ed.* Teresa Brinati. Books for review and related correspondence should be addressed to the managing editor.
Archival Outlook (bi-mo.; memb.). *Ed.* Teresa Brinati.

Special Libraries Association

Executive Director, David R. Bender
1700 18th St. N.W., Washington, DC 20009-2508
202-234-4700, FAX 202-265-9317
Internet: slal@capcon.net

Object

To advance the leadership role of special librarians in putting knowledge to work in the information society.

Membership

Memb. 14,000. Dues (Sustaining) $400; (Indiv.) $105; (Student) $30. Year. Jan.–Dec. or July–June.

Officers (July 1994–June 1995)

Pres. Didi Pancake, 100 Montvue Dr., Charlottesville, VA 22901-2021. Tel. 804-295-0419, FAX 804-984-0566, ehp@virginia.edu; *Pres.-Elect* Jane Dysart, Dysart and Jones Assocs., 47 Rose Pk. Dr., Toronto, ON M4T 1R2, Canada; *Past Pres.* Miriam A. Drake, Price Gilbert Memorial Lib., Georgia Inst. of Technology, Atlanta, GA 30332-0900. Tel. 404-894-4510, FAX 404-894-6084; *Treas.* Donna W. Scheeder, U.S. Lib. of Congress, Congressional Reference Div., Rm. LM219,

First and Independence Aves. S.E., Washington, DC 20504. Tel. 202-707-8939, FAX 202-707-1833; *Chapter Cabinet Chair* Bill Fisher, School of Lib. and Info. Science, San Jose State Univ., One Washington Sq., San Jose, CA 95192-0029. Tel. 408-924-2494, FAX 408-924-2476; *Chapter Cabinet Chair-Elect* Susan DiMattia, Business Info. Consultants, 44 Chatham Rd., Stamford, CT 06903. Tel. 203-322-9055, FAX 203-968-9396; *Div. Cabinet Chair* Monica Ertel, Apple Lib. and Info. Services, Apple Computer, 4 Infinite Loop, MS304-2A, Cupertino, CA 95014. Tel. 408-974-2552, FAX 408-725-8502; *Div. Cabinet Chair-Elect* Barbara Spiegelman, Westinghouse Electric Corp., Power Systems, Box 355, Pittsburgh, PA 15230. Tel. 412-374-4816, FAX 412-374-5744.

Directors

Officers; Charlene Baldwin (1997); Billie M. Connor (1995); Richard Geiger (1996); Judy Macfarlane (1995); Ethel Salonen (1996); Hope Tillman (1997).

Publications

Special Libraries (q.) and *SpeciaList* (mo.). Cannot be ordered separately ($60 for both; foreign $65). *Ed.* Gail Repsher.

Committee Chairpersons

Affirmative Action. Frank Domingo Lopez.
Association Office Operations. Didi Pancake.
Awards and Honors. Catherine D. "Kitty" Scott.
Bylaws. James B. Tchobanoff.
Cataloging. Lillian R. Mesner.
Committee on Committees. Roger K. Haley.
Conference Program, Montreal (1995). Karen Holloway.
Conference Program, Boston (1996). Ellen S. Kuner.
Consultation Service. Margaret A. Miller.
Copyright Law Implementation. Sarah K. Wiant.
Finance. Donna W. Scheeder.
Government Relations. Barbara J. Walker.
International Relations. Melvin E. Westerman.
Networking. Doris Small Helfer.
Nominating, 1995 Elections. Helen Manning.
Nominating, 1996 Elections. Richard Hulser.
Professional Development. Mary E. Dickerson.
Public Relations. Anne K. Abate.
Publications. Open.
Publisher Relations. Connie Kelley.
Research. Eileen M. Curtin.
SLA Scholarship. Kathleen Eisenbeis.
Strategic Planning. Richard Geiger.
Student Affairs. Marion Paris.
Technical Standards. Marjorie Hlava.
Tellers. Lyle W. Minter.

Theatre Library Association

Secretary-Treasurer, Richard M. Buck
New York Public Library for the Performing Arts
111 Amsterdam Ave., New York, NY 10023-7498
212-870-1644, 212-870-1670

Object

To further the interests of collecting, preserving, and using theatre, cinema, and performing arts materials in libraries, museums, and private collections. Founded 1937.

Membership

Memb. 500. Dues (Indiv.) $20; (Inst.) $25. Year. Jan. 1–Dec. 31.

Officers (1994–1995)

Pres. Geraldine Duclow; *V.P.* Bob Taylor, Curator, Billy Rose Theatre Collection, New

York Public Lib. for the Performing Arts, 111 Amsterdam Ave., New York, NY 10023-7498; *Secy.-Treas.* Richard M. Buck, Asst. to the Exec. Dir., New York Public Lib. for the Performing Arts, 111 Amsterdam Ave., New York, NY 10023-7498.

Executive Board

Susan Brady, Lauren Bufferd, Nena Couch, Rosemary Cullen, Steven Higgins, Catherine Johnson, Paul Newman, Louis A. Rachow, Dorothy Swerdlove, Richard Wall, Walter Zvonchenko; *Ex officio* Madeleine Nichols, Alan J. Pally, Barbara Naomi Cohen-Stratyner, Maryann Chach; *Honorary* Paul Myers; *Historian* Louis A. Rachow.

Publications

Broadside (q.; memb.). *Ed.* Maryann Chach, Catherine Johnson.
Performing Arts Resources (ann.; memb.). *Ed.* Barbara Naomi Cohen-Stratyner.

Committee Chairpersons

Awards. Steven Vallillo.
Collection Resources. Walter Zvonchenko.
Long-Range Planning. To be appointed.
Membership. Geraldine Duclow.
Nominations. Richard Wall.
Program and Special Events. Richard M. Buck, Bob Taylor.
Publications. Maryann Chach, Catherine Johnson.

Urban Libraries Council

President, Eleanor Jo (Joey) Rodger
1603 Orrington Ave., Suite 1080, Evanston, IL 60201
708-866-9999, FAX 708-866-9989

Object

To identify and make known the problems relating to urban libraries serving cities of 50,000 or more individuals, located in a Standard Metropolitan Statistical Area; to provide information on state and federal legislation affecting urban library programs and systems; to facilitate the exchange of ideas and programs of member libraries and other libraries; to develop programs that enable libraries to act as a focus of community development and to supply the informational needs of the new urban populations; to conduct research and educational programs that will benefit urban libraries and to solicit and accept grants, contributions, and donations essential to their implementation.

ULC currently receives all of its funding from membership dues. Future projects will involve the solicitation of grant funding. ULC is a 501(c)(3) not-for-profit corporation based in the state of Illinois.

Membership

Membership is open to public libraries and library systems serving populations of 50,000 or more located in a Standard Metropolitan Statistical Area. Dues are based on the size of the organization's operating budget, according to the following schedule: under $2 million, $700; $2 million to $5 million, $1,000; $5 million to $10 million, $1,250; $10 million to $15 million, $1,500; over $15 million, $2,000. In addition, ULC member libraries may choose Sustaining or Contributing status (Sustaining, $1,000; Contributing, $3,000 to $9,000). Corporate memberships are also available.

Officers (1994–1995)

Chair James R. Dawe, 750 B St., Suite 2100, San Diego, CA 92101; *V.Chair* Lawrence A. Kane, Jr., Dinsmore and Shohl, 1900 Chemed Center, Cincinnati, OH 45202; *Secy.* Sally Frazier, 7204 Sleepy Hollow Rd., Tulsa, OK

74136; *Treas.* Esther W. Lopato, 1231 E. 21 St., Brooklyn, NY 11210. Officers and members of the executive board serve two-year terms. New officers are elected and take office at the summer annual meeting of the Council.

Officers

Pres. Eleanor Jo Rodger; *V.P., Admin. and Program* Bridget A. Bradley; *Secy.* Joan Roe; *Project Dir.* Marybeth Schroeder.

Executive Board

Andrew Blau, Ginnie Cooper, Robert B. Croneberger, Carla Hayden, G. Victor Johnson, Susan Goldberg Kent, Roslyn S. Kurland, Charles W. Robinson, Michael A. Schott, Elliot L. Shelkrot, Reginald W. Williams.

Publications

Balancing the Books: Financing American Public Library Service (1992).
Frequent Fast Facts Surveys: *Fees Survey Results* (1993); *Fund Raising and Financial Development Survey Results* (1993); *Staffing Survey Results* (1993); *Collection Development Survey Results* (1994); *Library Security Survey Results* (1994); *Public Libraries and Private Fund Raising: Opportunities and Issues* (1994).
Keeping the Books: Public Library Financial Practices (1992).
Large Urban Libraries: Their Roles, Responsibilities and Contributions (1991).
Urban Libraries Exchange (mo.; memb.).

State, Provincial, and Regional Library Associations

The associations in this section are organized under three headings: United States, Canada, and Regional. Both the United States and Canada are represented under Regional associations.

United States

Alabama

Memb. 1,200. Term of Office. Apr. 1994–Apr. 1995. Publication. *The Alabama Librarian* (q.).
Pres. Margaret Blake. Tel. 205-690-8377; *Exec. Dir.* Barbara Black, 400 S. Union St., Suite 255, Montgomery 36104. Tel. 205-262-5210.
Address correspondence to the executive director.

Alaska

Memb. 482. Term of Office. Mar. 1994–Mar. 1995. Publication. *Newspoke* (bi-m.).
Pres. Rita Dursi Johnson, Egan Lib., 11120 Glacier Hwy., Juneau 99801-8676. Tel. 907-465-6466, E-mail jfrdj@acad1.alaska.edu; *V.P.* Greg Hill, Wien Lib., 1215 Cowles St., Fairbanks 99701. Tel. 907-459- 1020, E-mail gregh1@muskox.alaska.edu; *Secy.* Beth Odsen, Anchorage Law Lib., 303 K St., Anchorage 99501. Tel. 907-264-0587, FAX 907-264-0587, E-mail betho@muskox. alaska.edu; *Treas.* Betty Galbraith, Biblioda-ta, Box 80782, Fairbanks 99708. Tel. 907-479-5196, E-mail ffbjg@aurora.alaska.edu.
Address correspondence to the secretary.

Arizona

Memb. 1,241. Term of Office. Nov. 1994–Nov. 1995. Publication. *AzLA Newsletter* (mo.). Articles for the newsletter should be sent to the attention of the newsletter editor.
Pres. Jean Collins, Northern Arizona Univ., Cline Lib., Box 6022, Flagstaff 86011-6022. Tel. 602-523-6802; *Treas.* Bill Pillow, Scottsdale Public Lib., 3839 Civic Center Blvd., Scottsdale 85251. Tel. 602-994-2474; *Exec. Secy.* Jim Johnson, 14449 N. 73 St., Scottsdale 85260-3133. Tel. 602-998-1954.

Address correspondence to the executive secretary.

Arkansas

Memb. 800. Term of Office. Jan.–Dec. 1995. Publication. *Arkansas Libraries* (bi-mo.). *Pres.* Jenelle Stephens, Deputy Dir., Arkansas State Lib., One Capitol Mall, Little Rock 72201. Tel. 501-682-2550, FAX 501-682-1529; *Exec. Dir.* Sherry Walker, Arkansas Lib. Assn., 1100 N. Univ. Ave., Suite 109, Little Rock 72207. Tel. 501-661-1127, FAX 501-663-1218.

Address correspondence to the executive director.

California

Memb. 2,600. Term of Office. Nov. 1994–Nov. 1995. Publication. *California Libraries*. *Pres.* Mary Jo Levy, Palo Alto Public Lib.; *V.P./Pres.-Elect* David Price, Sonoma County Public Lib.; *Exec. Dir.* Mary Sue Ferrell, California Lib. Assn., 717 K St., Suite 300, Sacramento 95814. Tel. 916-447-8541, FAX 916-447-8394.

Address correspondence to the executive director.

Colorado

Memb. 863. Term of Office. Oct. 1994–Oct. 1995. Publication. *Colorado Libraries* (q.). *Ed.* Nancy Carter, Univ. of Colorado, Campus Box 184, Boulder 80309. *Pres.* Margaret Owens, Jefferson County Public Lib., 10200 W. 20 Ave., Lakewood 80215; *Treas.* Vicki Nichols, Jefferson County Public Lib., 4305 Brentwood St., Wheat Ridge 80033.

Address correspondence to the association, Box 489, Pinecliffe 80471. Tel. 303-642-0203, FAX 303-642-0201.

Connecticut

Memb. 1,100. Term of Office. July 1994–June 1995. Publication. *Connecticut Libraries* (11 per year). *Ed.* David Kapp, 4 Llynwood Dr., Bolton 06040. Tel. 203-647-0697. *Pres.* Janet V. Day, Woodbridge Town Lib., 10 Newton Rd., Woodbridge 06525. Tel. 203-389-3435. *Pres.-Elect* Maxine Blei-

weis, Lucy Robbins Welles Lib., 95 Cedar St., Newington 06111. Tel. 203-665-8700; *Treas.* Joan Schneider, 20 Lantern Lane, Niantic 06357. Tel. 203-445-5577; *Administrator* Karen Zoller, Connecticut Lib. Assn., Box 1046, Norwich 06360-1046. Tel. 203-885-2758.

Address correspondence to the administrator.

Delaware

Memb. 300. Term of Office. Apr. 1994–Apr. 1995. Publication. *DLA Bulletin* (3 per year). *Pres.* Jonathan B. Jeffery, Morris Lib., Univ. of Delaware, Newark 19717-5267. Tel. 302-831-6945, FAX 302-831-1046; *V.P./Pres.-Elect* Patricia Woods, Sussex Technical H.S., Benjamin Franklin Info. Center, Rte. 9, Box 351, Georgetown 19947-0351. Tel. 302-856-0961, FAX 302-856-7875; *Acting Secy.* Donna Noble, Corbit-Calloway Memorial Lib., 115 High St., Odessa 19730. Tel. 302-378-8838, FAX 302-378-7803; *Treas.* Janet D. Shaw, Newark H.S., E. Delaware Ave., Newark 19711. Tel. 302-454-2254.

Address correspondence to the association, Box 816, Dover 19903-0816.

District of Columbia

Memb. 900. Term of Office. Sept. 1994–Aug. 1995. Publication. *INTERCOM* (mo.). *Pres.* Trellis C. Wright, Lib. of Congress, Copyright Office, Dept. 17, Washington 20540. Tel. 202-707-2441; *V.P./Pres.-Elect* Dan Clemmer, U.S. Dept. of State Lib., 2201 C St. N.W., Washington 20520. Tel. 202-647-3602; *Secy.* Rita Thompson-Joyner, D.C. Public Lib., 901 G St. N.W., Washington 20001. Tel. 202-727-1101; *Treas.* Denise Davis, Univ. of Maryland, CARS Office, McKeldin Lib., College Park, MD 20742.

Address correspondence to the association, Box 14177, Benjamin Franklin Station, Washington 20044.

Florida

Memb. (Indiv.) 1,071; (In-state Inst.) 98. Term of Office. July 1994–June 1995. *Pres.* Holen Moeller, Leon County Public Lib. Tel. 904-487-2665; *V.P./Pres.-Elect* Elizabeth Curry, SEFLIN. Tel. 305-357-

7318; *Secy.* Betty D. Johnson, duPont-Ball Lib., Stetson Univ. Tel. 904-822-7178; *Treas.* Kathleen McCook, USF. Tel. 813-974-3520; *Exec. Secy.* Marjorie Stealey, Florida Lib. Assn., 1133 W. Morse Blvd., Suite 201, Winter Park 32789. Tel. 407-647-8839.

Address correspondence to the executive secretary.

Georgia

Memb. 1,055. Term of Office. Oct. 1993–Oct. 1995. Publication. *Georgia Librarian.* *Ed.* Bill Richards, North Georgia College, Dahlonega 30597. Tel. 706-864-1518.

Pres. Donna D. Mancini, DeKalb County Public Lib., 215 Sycamore St., Decatur 30030. Tel. 404-370-8450; *1st V.P./Pres.-Elect* Sue Hatfield, Dir., Lib. Services, DeKalb College, 555 N. Indian Creek Rd., Clarkston 30021. Tel. 404-294-3491; *2nd V.P.* Grace McLeod, Chattahoochee Technical Institute, Resource Center, 980 S. Cobb Dr. S.E., Marietta 30060. Tel. 404-528-4536; *Secy.* David Searcy, Community Extension Services, Atlanta Fulton Public Lib., Bldg. B, Suite 105, 3645 Southside Industrial Pkwy., Atlanta 30354. Tel. 404-366-0710; *Treas.* Alan Kaye, Dir., Roddenbery Memorial Lib., 320 N. Board St., Cairo 31728. Tel. 912-377-3632.

Address correspondence to the president.

Hawaii

Memb. 450. Publications. *HLA Newsletter* (q.); *HLA Journal* (ann.); *HLA Membership Directory* (ann.).

Pres. Jean Ehrhorn, 507 Koko Isle Circle, Honolulu 96822. Tel. 808-956-2472; *Pres.-Elect/Conference Chair* Diane Eddy, 4823 Kolohala St., Honolulu 96816. Tel. 808-689-8392.

Address correspondence to the association, Box 4441, Honolulu 96812-4441.

Idaho

Memb. 500. Term of Office. Oct. 1994–Oct. 1995. Publication. *Idaho Librarian* (q.). *Ed.* Mary Bolin, Univ. of Idaho Lib., Moscow 83844-2363. Tel. 208-885-7737.

Pres. Karen Strege, 633 E. 25 Ave., Spokane, WA 99203; *1st V.P./Pres.-Elect* Vivian Wells, 3219 E. 3600 N., Kimberly 83341. Tel. 208-733-6551; *2nd V.P./Pres.-Elect* Mary Carr, NIC Lib., Coeur d'Alene 83814. Tel. 208-769-3215; *Treas.* Tim Brown, Boise State Univ. Lib., 1910 Univ. Dr., Boise 83725. Tel. 208-385-1234; *Secy.* Joe Reiss, Post Falls Public Lib., Post Falls. Tel. 208-465-2263; *Conference Exhibits Coord.* Donna M. Hanson, Idaho Lib. Assn., Box 8533, Moscow 83843. Tel. 208-885-2505.

Address conference exhibits correspondence to the exhibits coordinator. Address all other correspondence to the president.

Illinois

Memb. 4,100. Term of Office. July 1994–June 1995. Publication. *ILA Reporter* (10 per year).

Pres. Lee Logan, Alliance Lib. System, 845 Brenkman, Pekin 61554-1522; *V.P./Pres.-Elect* Sue Stroyan, Illinois Wesleyan Univ., Box 2899, Bloomington 61702-2900; *Treas.* Denise Zielinski, Helen Plum Memorial Lib., 110 W. Maple, Lombard 60148; *Exec. Dir.* Jane Getty, ILA, 33 W. Grand Ave., Suite 301, Chicago 60610. Tel. 312-644-1896, FAX 312-644-1899.

Address correspondence to the executive director.

Indiana

Memb. (Indiv.) 1,000; (Inst.) 300. Term of Office. May 1994–May 1995. Publications. *Focus on Indiana Libraries* (11 per year), *Ed.* Raquel M. Ravinet; *Indiana Libraries* (2 per year), *Ed.* Raquel M. Ravinet.

Pres. Diane Bever, 6160 N. Forest Ave., Forest 46039. Tel. 317-455-9511, FAX 317-455-9276, E-mail bever@ucs.indiana.edu; *1st V.P.* Laura G. Johnson, 4129 Cranbrook Dr., Indianapolis 46250. Tel. 317-269-1850; *2nd V.P.* Sally Otte, 5251 N. Delaware St., Indianapolis 46220. Tel. 317-257-5800; *Secy.* Cheryl Blevens, Vigo County Public Lib., 1800 E. Fort Harrison Rd., No. 5, Terre Haute 47804-1492; *Treas.* Jan Preusz, Vigo County Public Lib., One Library Square, Terre Haute 47807.

Address correspondence to the Indiana Lib. Federation, 6408 Carrollton Ave., Indianapolis 46220. Tel. 317-257-2040, FAX 317-257-1393.

Iowa

Memb. 1,805. Term of Office. Jan.–Dec. 1995. Publication. *The Catalyst* (bi-mo.). *Ed.* Naomi Stovall.

Pres. Catherine Rod, Grinnell College, Grinnell 50112.

Address correspondence to the association, 823 Insurance Exchange Bldg., 505 Fifth Ave., Des Moines 50309. Tel. 515-243-2172, FAX 515-243-0614.

Kansas

Memb. 1,100. Term of Office. July 1994–June 1995. Publications. *KLA Newsletter* (q.); *KLA Membership Directory* (ann.).

Pres. Rowena Olsen, Miller Lib., McPherson College, McPherson 67460; Tel. 316-241-0731 Ext. 1213, E-mail millerlib@ink.org; *Pres.-Elect* Susan Willis, Chanute Public Lib., 111 N. Lincoln, Chanute 66720. Tel. 316-431-2820, E-mail chanulib@ink.org; *Exec. Secy.* Leroy Gattin, South Central Kansas Lib. System, 901 N. Main St., Hutchinson 67501. Tel. 316-663-5441, Ext. 110, FAX 316-663-1215, E-mail lgatt@class.org; *Secy.* Marianne Eichelberger, Newton Public Lib., 720 N. Oak, Newton 67114. Tel. 316-283-2890, FAX 316-283-2916; *Treas.* Marcella Ratzlaff, Hutchinson Public Lib., 901 N. Main St., Hutchinson 67501. Tel. 316-663-5441.

Address correspondence to the executive secretary.

Kentucky

Memb. 1,900. Term of Office. Oct. 1994–Oct. 1995. Publication. *Kentucky Libraries* (q.).

Pres. June Martin. Tel. 606-622-6176; *V.P./Pres.-Elect* Lucinda Brown. Tel. 606-371-6227; *Secy.* Elaine Steinberg; *Exec. Secy.* John Underwood, 1501 Twilight Trail, Frankfort 40601. Tel. 502-223-5322.

Address correspondence to the executive secretary.

Louisiana

Memb. (Indiv.) 1,500; (Inst.) 60. Term of Office. July 1994–June 1995. Publication. *LLA Bulletin* (q.). *Ed.* Florence Jumonville, 7911 Birch St., New Orleans 70118. Tel. 504-523-4662.

Pres. Walter W. Wicker, 5027 Stow Creek, Ruston 71270. Tel. 318-257-2577; *1st V.P./ Pres.-Elect* Marvene Dearman, 1471 Chevelle Dr., Baton Rouge 70806. Tel. 504-357-6464; *2nd V.P.* Emma B. Perry, 6145 Stratford Ave., Baton Rouge 70808. Tel. 504-771-4991; *Secy.* Angelle M. Deshautelles, 1908 N. Amelia Ave., Gonzales 70737. Tel. 504-473-8052; *Parliamentarian* Kevin D. Cuccia, 1009 Nelson Ave., Ruston 71270. Tel. 318-257-4357; *Past Pres.* Grace G. Moore, 4554 Whitehaven St., Baton Rouge 70808. Tel. 504-342-4929; *ALA Councilor* Joy Lowe; *SELA Rep.* Sybil Boudreaux; *LLA Admin. Officer* Carol McMahan.

Address correspondence to the association, Box 3058, Baton Rouge 70821. Tel. 504-342-4928, FAX 504-342-3547.

Maine

Memb. 1,100. Term of Office. (Pres., V.P.) Spring 1994–Spring 1996. Publications. *Maine Entry* (4 per year); *Maine Memo* (mo.).

Pres. Valerie Osborne, Old Town Public Lib., Old Town 04468; *V.P.* Karen Reilly, Eastern Maine Technical College, Bangor 04401; *Secy.* Nancy Crowell, Scarborough Public Lib., Scarborough 04074; *Treas.* Jean Oplinger, Farmington Public Lib., Farmington 04938.

Address correspondence to the association, 60 Community Dr., Augusta 04330. Tel. 207-623-8428, FAX 207-626-5947.

Maryland

Memb. 1,200. Term of Office. July 1994–June 1995. Publication. *The Crab.*

Pres. William G. Wilson, Univ. of Maryland, College of Lib. and Info. Services, College Park 20742. Tel. 301-405-2067. *V.P.* K. Lynn Wheeler, Baltimore County Public Lib., 320 York Rd., Towson 21204. Tel. 410-887-6177; *Secy.* Cynthia K. Steinhoff, Anne

Arundel Community College, 101 College Pkwy., Arnold 21012. Tel. 410-541-2534; *Treas.* Hampton M. Auld.

Address correspondence to the association, 400 Cathedral St., 3rd fl., Baltimore 21201. Tel. 410-727-7422, FAX 410-625-9594, E-mail mla@epfl1.epflbalto.org.

Massachusetts

Memb. (Indiv.) 950; (Inst.) 100. Term of Office. July 1994–June 1995. Publication. *Bay State Librarian* (10 per year).

Pres. Ellen Rainville, Fletcher Lib., 50 Main St., Westford 01886. Tel. 508-692-5557, FAX 508-692-0287; *V.P.* Ellen Rauch, EMRLS, Boston Public Lib., Copley Sq., Box 286, Boston 02117. Tel. 800-287-4065, FAX 617-267-0364; *Secy.* Brian Donoghue, Massachusetts Board of Lib. Commissioners, 648 Beacon St., Boston 02215. Tel. 800-952-7403, 617-267-9400, FAX 617-421-9833; *Treas.* Dodie Gaudet, WMRLS, 58 Main St., Hatfield 01038. Tel. 800-282-7755, 413-247-9306, FAX 413-247-9740; *Exec. Secy.* Barry Blaisdell, Massachusetts Lib. Assn., Countryside Offices, 707 Turnpike St., North Andover 01845. Tel. 508-686-8543.

Address correspondence to the executive secretary.

Michigan

Memb. (Indiv.) 2,200; (Inst.) 300. Term of Office. June 1994–June 1995. Publication. *Michigan Librarian Newsletter* (10 per year).

Pres. Sandra Scherba, Cromaine Lib., 3688 N. Hartland Rd., Hartland 48353-0950; *Treas.* Marney Cooley, Brighton District Lib., 200 N. First St., Brighton 48116-1593; *Exec. Dir.* Marianne Hartzell, Michigan Lib. Assn., 1000 Long Blvd., Suite 1, Lansing 48911. Tel. 517-694-6615.

Address correspondence to the executive director.

Minnesota

Memb. 1,016. Term of Office. (Pres., Pres.-Elect) Jan.–Dec. 1995; (Treas.) Jan. 1994–

Dec. 1995; (Secy.) Jan. 1995–Dec. 1996. Publication. *MLA Newsletter* (10 per year).

Pres. Linda DeBeau-Melting, 499 Wilson Lib., Univ. of Minnesota, Minneapolis 55406; *Pres.-Elect* Mark Ranum, East Central Regional Lib., 244 S. Birch, Cambridge 55008; *ALA Chapter Councillor* Janice Feye-Stukas, Lib. Development and Services, 440 Capitol Sq., 500 Cedar St., Saint Paul 55101; *Secy.* Lucy Lowry, SMILE, Box 3031, Mankato 56001; *Treas.* Deborah Struzyk, Minneapolis Public Lib., 300 Nicollet Mall, Minneapolis 55401; *Exec. Dir.* Deborah K. Sales, Minnesota Lib. Assn., 1315 Lowry Ave. N., Minneapolis 55411-1398. Tel./FAX 612-529-5503.

Address correspondence to the executive director.

Mississippi

Memb. 1,100. Term of Office. Jan.–Dec. 1995. Publication. *Mississippi Libraries* (q.).

Pres. Charline Longino; *V.P./Pres.-Elect* Glenda Segars; *Treas.* Carol Cubberley; *Secy.* Charlotte Moman. Tel. 601-352-3917.

Address correspondence to the secretary.

Missouri

Memb. 1,000. Term of Office. Oct. 1994–Oct. 1995. Publication. *MO INFO* (6 per year). *Ed.* Jean Ann McCartney.

Pres. Elizabeth Eckles, Wolffner Lib. for the Blind and Physically Handicapped, Box 387, Jefferson City 65102. Tel. 314-751-8720. *V.P./Pres.-Elect* Nick Niederlander, Richmond Heights Memorial Lib. Tel. 314-645-6202; *Secy.* Rebecca Kiel, Cottey College. Tel. 417-667-8181; *Treas.* Don Gaertner; *Exec. Dir.* Jean Ann McCartney, Missouri Lib. Assn., 1306 Business 63 S., Suite B, Columbia 65201. Tel. 314-449-4627.

Address correspondence to the executive director.

Montana

Memb. 650. Term of Office. July 1994–June 1995. Publication. *Montana Library Focus* (4 per year). *Ed.* Greg Notess, Renne Lib., Montana State Univ., Bozeman 59717-0332. Tel.

406-994-6563, FAX 406-994-2851, E-mail align@montana.edu.

Pres. Susan Nissen, Montana Power Co. Law Lib., 40 E. Broadway, Butte 59701. Tel. 406-723-5454 Ext. 72111, FAX 406-496-5051, E-mail mpclaw@wln.com; *V.P./Pres.-Elect* Mary Bushing, Montana State Univ. Libs., Bozeman 59717. Tel. 406-994-4994, FAX 406-994-2851, E-mail alimb@msu. pscs.montana.edu; *Secy./Treas.* Terri Dood, Bozeman Public Lib., 220 E. Lamme, Bozeman 59715. Tel. 406-586-4788, FAX 406-587-7785; *Admin. Asst.* John Thomas, Box 505, Helena 59624. Tel. 406-442-9446, FAX 406-447-4525.

Address correspondence to the administrative assistant.

Nebraska

Memb. 1,000. Term of Office. Oct. 1994–Oct. 1995. Publication. *NLA Quarterly.*

Pres. Rod Wagner, Nebraska Lib. Commission, Suite 120, 1200 N St., Lincoln 68508-2006. Tel. 800-307-2665, FAX 404-471-2083; *Secy.* Carol Reed, Kearney Public Lib., 2020 First Ave., Kearney 68847; *Treas.* Tracy Bicknell, 216N Love Lib., Lincoln 68588-0410; *Exec. Dir.* Ken Oyer, 5302 S. 75 St., Ralston 68127-3903. Tel. 402-398-6092, FAX 402-398-6923.

Address correspondence to the executive director.

Nevada

Memb. 400. Term of Office. Jan.–Dec. 1995. Publication. *Highroller* (4 per year).

Pres. Karen Albrethson, Spring Creek Elementary School, Elko, 89801. Tel. 702-753-6881; *Treas.* Elizabeth Bradt, Washoe County Lib., Reno. Tel. 702-785-4503; *Exec. Secy.* Yolanda Flores, W. Charleston Libs., 6301 W. Charleston, Las Vegas 89102. Tel. 702-878-3682.

Address correspondence to the president.

New Hampshire

Memb. 700. Term of Office. June 1994–May 1995. Publication. *NHLA Newsletter* (bi-mo.).

Pres. Randy Brough; *Secy.* Ginny Foose, Tracy Memorial Lib., Box 1919, New London 03257; *Treas.* Pamela Schwotzer, North Hampton Public Lib., 235 Atlantic Ave., North Hampton 03862.

Address correspondence to the association, Box 2332, Concord 03302-2332.

New Jersey

Memb. 1,700. Term of Office. May 1994–Apr. 1995. Publications. *New Jersey Libraries* (q.); *New Jersey Libraries Newsletter* (mo.).

Pres. Mary Louise Abrams, Paramus Public Lib., E. 116 Century Rd., Paramus 07652. Tel. 201-599-1300; *V.P./Pres.-Elect* Timothy Murphy, Maurice M. Pine Lib., 10-01 Fair Lawn, Fair Lawn 07410. Tel. 201-796-3400; *Treas.* Joseph Keenan, Elizabeth Public Lib., 11 S. Broad St., Elizabeth 07202; *Exec. Dir.* Patricia Tumulty, New Jersey Lib. Assn., 4 W. Lafayette St., Trenton 08608. Tel. 609-394-8032.

Address correspondence to the executive director, Box 1534, Trenton 08607.

New Mexico

Memb. 550. Term of Office. Apr. 1995–Apr. 1996. Publication. *New Mexico Library Association Newsletter* (q.). *Ed.* Donnic Curtis, Box 3358, Las Cruces 88003. Tel. 505-646-6926, FAX 505-646-4335.

Pres. Kathy Flanary, New Mexico School for the Visually Handicapped, 1900 N. White Sands Blvd., Alamogordo 88310. Tel. 505-437-7851 Ext. 129, E-mail schlnmsvhl@technet.nm.org; *1st V.P.* Jennifer Minter, 1090 Crossley, Las Cruces 88005. Tel. 505-527-7556, FAX 505-527-7515.

Address correspondence to the association, Suite 8, El Dorado Sq., 11200 Montgomery N.E., Albuquerque 87111.

New York

Memb. 3,000. Term of Office. Oct. 1994–Nov. 1995. Publication. *NYLA Bulletin* (10 per year). *Eds.* Paul and Christine Girsdansky. *Pres.* Rhonna Goodman, New York Academy of Medicine Lib., 2 E. 103 St., New York 10029; *V.P./Pres.-Elect* Betsy Sywetz, Delaware Chenango BOCES-SLS, R.R. 3, Box 307, Norwich 13815; *Treas.* J. Robert Verbesey, Mastic Moriches-Shirley Community Lib., William Floyd Pkwy., Shirley 11967; *Exec. Dir.* Susan Lehman Keitel, New York Lib. Assn., 252 Hudson Ave., Albany 12210. Tel. 518-432-6952; *Asst. Dir.* Gail Ghazzawi.

Address correspondence to the executive director.

North Carolina

Memb. 2,200. Term of Office. Oct 1993–Oct. 1995. Publication. *North Carolina Libraries* (q.). *Ed.* Frances Bradburn, Media and Technology, N.C. Dept. of Public Instruction, 301 N. Wilmington St., Raleigh, 27601-2825. *Pres.* Gwen G. Jackson, S.E. Technical Assistance Center, 2013 Lejeune Blvd., Jacksonville 28546. Tel. 919-577-8920, FAX 919-577-1427; *V.P./Pres.-Elect* David Fergusson, Forsyth County Public Lib., 660 W. Fifth St., Winston-Salem 27101. Tel. 919-727-2556, FAX 919-727-2549; *Secy.* Judy LeCroy, Davidson County Schools, Box 2057, Lexington 27293-2057. Tel. 704-249-8181, FAX 704-249-1062; *Treas.* Wanda Brown Cason, Reynolds Lib., Wake Forest Univ., Box 7777, Reynolda Sta., Winston-Salem 27109-7777. Tel. 919-759-5094, FAX 919-759-9831.

Address correspondence to the secretary.

North Dakota

Memb. (Indiv.) 404; (Inst.) 19. Term of Office. Oct. 1994–Sept. 1995. Publication. *The Good Stuff* (q.). *Ed.* Dan Koper, Mildred Johnson Lib., NDSCS, Wahpeton 58076. *Pres.* Kathy Waldera, Bismarck Public Lib., 515 N. Fifth St., Bismarck 58501; *V.P./Pres.-Elect* Thom Hendricks, Mandan Public Lib., 108 First St. N.W., Mandan

58554; *Secy.* Barbara Knight, Angus Cameron Medical Lib., 20 Burdick Expressway, Minot 58701; *Treas.* Neil Price, Dept. of Lib. Science, Univ. of North Dakota, Box 8174, Grand Forks 58202.

Address correspondence to the president.

Ohio

Memb. 2,940. Term of Office. Jan.–Dec. 1995. Publications. *Access* (mo.); *Ohio Libraries* (4 per year).

Chair Dave Miller, 300 E. Poe Rd., Bowling Green 43402. Tel. 419-352-4611; *Vice Chair* Jeannine Wilbarger, Toledo-Lucas County Public Lib., 325 Michigan, Toledo 43624. Tel. 419-259-5278; *Secy.* Susan Hanlon, 545 Park Meadows Ct., Wadsworth 44281. Tel. 216-972-7685; *Treas.* Julia Brandow, Kirtland Public Lib., 9267 Chillicothe Rd., Kirtland 44094. Tel. 216-256-3747.

Address correspondence to the association, 35 E. Gay St., Suite 305, Columbus 43215. Tel. 614-221-9057.

Oklahoma

Memb. (Indiv.) 1,050; (Inst.) 60. Term of Office. July 1994–June 1995. Publication. *Oklahoma Librarian* (bi-mo.).

Pres. Robert Swisher; *V.P./Pres.-Elect* Jan Sanders; *Secy.* Denyvetta Davis; *Treas.* Ken Bierman; *Exec. Dir.* Kay Boies, 300 Hardy Dr., Edmond 73013. Tel./FAX 405-348-0506.

Address correspondence to the executive director.

Oregon

Memb. (Indiv.) 1,000. Term of Office. Sept. 1994–Aug. 1995. Publications. *OLA Hotline* (bi-w.), *OLA Quarterly.*

Pres. Anne Billeter, Jackson County Lib., 413 W. Main St., Medford 97501. Tel. 503-776-7285, FAX 503-776-7295; *V.P./Pres.-Elect* Deborah Carver, Knight Lib., Univ. of Oregon, Eugene 97403. Tel. 503-346-1892; *Secy.* Linda Lybecker, Washington County Cooperative Lib. Services, Box 5129, Aloha 97006. Tel. 503-642-1544; *Treas.* Michael

Gaston, Siuslaw Public Lib., Box A, Florence 97439.
Address correspondence to the secretary.

Pennsylvania

Memb. 1,750. Term of Office. Jan.–Dec. 1995. Publication. *PLA Bulletin* (mo.).
Pres. Kathy K. Kennedy, Monroeville Public Lib., 2615 Mosside Blvd., Monroeville 15146-3381. Tel. 412-372-0500; *V.P.* Mary Anne Fedrick, 211 Haverford Dr., Laflin 18702. Tel. 717-961-4728; *Interim Exec. Dir.* Lois K. Albrecht, Pennsylvania Lib. Assn., 1919 N. Front St., Harrisburg 17102. Tel. 717-233-3113.
Address correspondence to the executive director.

Rhode Island

Memb. (Indiv.) 359; (Inst.) 59. Term of Office. Nov. 1994–Nov. 1995. Publication. *Rhode Island Library Association Bulletin. Ed.* Mattie Gustafson.
Pres. James T. Giles, Cranston Public Lib., 140 Sockanosset Cross Rd., Cranston 02920. Tel. 401-943-9080; *V.P./Pres.-Elect* Donna Dufault, North Kingstown Free Lib., 100 Boone St., North Kingstown 02852. Tel. 401-294-3306; *Secy.* Patience Bliss, Coventry Public Lib., 1672 Flat River Rd., Coventry 02816. Tel. 401-822-9100; *Treas.* Christopher La Roux, Greenville Public Lib., 573 Putnam Pike, Greenville 02828. Tel. 401-949-3630; *ALA Councillor* Frank Iacono, Dept. of State Lib. Services, 300 Richmond St., Providence 02903. Tel. 401-277-2726; *NELA Councillor* Shirley Long, Providence Public Lib., 225 Washington St., Providence 02903. Tel. 401-455-8020.
Address correspondence to the secretary.

South Carolina

Memb. 800. Term of Office. Feb. 1995–Dec. 1995; Publication. *News and Views of the South Carolina Library Association.*
Pres. Debby Coleman, Barnwell Elementary School, Barnwell. Tel. 803-541-1342, FAX 803-541-1313, E-mail dcoleman@ blackville.sc.fred.org; *V.P./Pres.-Elect* Felita

Green, Richland County Lib., Columbia. Tel. 803-799-9084, FAX 803-929-3439; *Exec. Secy.* Drucie Raines, South Carolina Lib. Assn., Box 219, Goose Creek 29445. Tel. 803-764-3668, FAX 803-824-2690, E-mail rainesd@citadel.edu.
Address correspondence to the executive secretary.

South Dakota

Memb. (Indiv.) 482; (Inst.) 71. Term of Office. Oct. 1994–Oct. 1995. Publication. *Book Marks* (bi-mo.).
Pres. Elvita A. Landau, Brookings Public Lib., 515 Third St., Brookings 57006-2077. Tel. 605-692-9407, FAX 605-692-9386; *V.P./Pres.-Elect* Bonnie Baumann Harrison, Douglas School System, 1 Patriot Dr., Ellsworth AFB 57706. Tel. 605-923-1882, FAX 605-923-6387. *Secy.* Nancy D. Sabbe, Madison Public Lib., 209 E. Center, Madison 57042-2998. Tel. 605-256-7525; *Treas.* Cathy R. Enlow, Brookings Public Lib., 515 Third St., Brookings 57006-2077. Tel. 605-692-9407, FAX 605-692-9386; *ALA Councillor* Ethelle Bean, Karl E. Mundt Lib., Dakota State Univ., Madison 57042; *MPLA Rep.* Mary Caspers, Box 2115, Brookings 57007.
Address correspondence to the association, Box 673, Pierre 57501.

Tennessee

Memb. 1,239. Term of Office. July 1994–July 1995. Publications. *Tennessee Librarian* (q.), *TLA Newsletter* (bi-m.).
Pres. John E. Evans, Memphis State Univ. Libs., Memphis 38152. Tel. 901-678-4485, FAX 901-678-2511; *V.P./Pres.-Elect* Lynette Sloan, Dir., Blue Grass Regional Lib., 104 E. Sixth St., Columbia 38401. Tel. 800-331-8487, FAX 615-388-1762; *Treas.* Kathryn E. Pagles, Blount County Public Lib., 801 McGhee, Maryville 37801. Tel. 615-982-0981; *Past Pres.* Carolyn Daniel, McGavock H.S., Nashville 37214. Tel. 615-885-8881; *Exec. Secy.* Betty Nance, Box 158417, Nashville 37215-8417. Tel. 615-297-8316, FAX 615-269-1807.
Address correspondence to the executive secretary.

Texas

Memb. 5,800. Term of Office. Apr. 1994–Apr. 1995. Publications. *Texas Library Journal* (q.); *TLAcast* (9 per year).
Pres. Ruth Dahlstrom, Goliad ISD Lib., Box 830, Goliad 77963; Tel. 512-645-3257; *Exec. Dir.* Patricia Smith, TLA Office, 3355 Bee Cave Rd., Suite 401, Austin 78746-6763. Tel. 512-328-1518, FAX 512-328-8852.
Address correspondence to the executive director.

Utah

Memb. 650. Term of Office. May 1994–Feb. 1995. Publication. *UTAH Libraries News* (bimo.).
Pres. Pete Giacoma, 365 Emery, Salt Lake City 84104. Tel. 801-451-2322; *Treas./Exec. Secy.* Chris Anderson. Tel. 801-581-8771.
Address correspondence to the association, 2150 S. 300 W., Suite 16, Salt Lake City 84115.

Vermont

Memb. 450. Term of Office. May 1994–May 1995. Publication. *VLA News* (10 per year).
Pres. Nancy Wilson, Lawrence Memorial Lib., 40 North St., Bristol 05443. Tel. 802-453-2366; *Secy.* Paula Arnold, Gary Lib., Vermont College, Montpelier 05602. Tel. 802-828-8747; *Treas.* Kip Roberson, Ilsley Lib., Middlebury 05753. Tel. 802-388-4095; *ALA Councillor* Melissa Malcolm, Mount Abraham Union H.S., 7 Airport Dr., Bristol 05443. Tel. 802-453-2333; *NELA Rep.* Russell Moore, Springfield Town Lib., 43 Main St., Springfield 05156. Tel. 802-885-3108.
Address correspondence to the president.

Virginia

Memb. 1,400. Term of Office. Jan.–Dec. 1995. Publications. *Virginia Librarian* (q.), *Eds.* Lucretia McCulley and Daniel Ream, Boatwright Lib., Univ. of Richmond, Richmond 23173; *VLA Newsletter* (10 per year), *Ed.* Sue Trask, College of William and Mary, Williamsburg 23187.

Pres. Linda Farynk, Radford Univ., McConnell Lib., Radford 24142. Tel. 703-831-5471, FAX 703-831-6104; *V.P./Pres.-Elect* Caroline Parr, Central Rappahannock Regional Lib., 1201 Caroline St., Fredericksburg 22401. Tel. 703-372-1160; *2nd V.P.* Suzanne Freeman, Virginia Commonwealth Univ., Cabell Lib., Box 2033, Richmond 23284. Tel. 804-367-1112; *Secy.* Patsy Hansel, Williamsburg Regional Lib., 515 Scotland St., Williamsburg 23185. Tel. 804-220-9214; *Treas.* Diana Granger, Fairfax County Public Lib., 13135 Lee Jackson Hwy., Fairfax 22033. Tel. 703-222-3179, FAX 703-222-3193; *Exec. Dir.* Deborah Trocchi, Virginia Lib. Assn., 669 S. Washington St., Alexandria 22314. Tel. 703-519-7853, FAX 703-519-7732.
Address correspondence to the executive director.

Washington

Memb. 1,350. Term of Office. Aug. 1993–July 1995. Publications. *ALKI* (3 per year); *WLA Link* (5 per year).
Pres. Sharon Hammer, Fort Vancouver Regional Lib., 1007 E. Mill Plain Blvd., Vancouver 98663. Tel. 206-695-1561.
Address correspondence to the association, 4016 First Ave. N.E., Seattle 98105-6502. Tel. 206-545-1529, FAX 206-545-1543.

West Virginia

Memb. 600. Term of Office. Dec. 1994–Nov. 1995. Publication. *West Virginia Libraries.* *Ed.* Yvonne Farley, Kanawha County Public Lib.
Pres. Charles A. Julian, 148 Edgewood St., Apt. C, Wheeling 26003. Tel. 304-242-7377; *Past Pres.* J. D. Waggoner, West Virginia Lib. Commission, 1900 Kanawha Blvd. E., Charleston 25305. Tel. 304-558-2531; *V.P./Pres.-Elect* Jo Ann Calzonetti, Wise Lib., West Virginia Univ., Box 6069, Morgantown 26506-6069. Tel. 304-293-3051; *2nd V.P.* Linda Heddinger, South Charleston Public Lib., 312 Fourth Ave., South Charleston 25303. Tel. 304-744-6561; *Treas.* David

Childers, West Virginia Lib. Commission, 1900 Kanawha Blvd. E., Charleston 25305. Tel. 304-558-2041; *Secy.* Myra Ziegler, Summers County Public Lib., 201 Temple St., Hinton 25951. Tel. 304-466-4490; *ALA Councillor* Tom Brown, Box 901, Athens 24712. Tel. 304-384-5366.
Address correspondence to the president.

Wisconsin

Memb. 2,000. Term of Office. Jan.–Dec. 1995. Publication. *WLA Newsletter* (6 per year).
Pres. Venora McKinney, 4785 Hayes Rd., Madison 53704-7364; Tel. 414-286-3025; *Pres.-Elect* Dale Bartkowiak, 4785 Hayes Rd., Madison 53704-7364. Tel. 715-387-8494; *Exec. Dir.* Larry J. Martin, 4785 Hayes Rd., Madison 53704-7364. Tel. 608-242-2040, FAX 608-242-2050.
Address correspondence to the executive director.

Wyoming

Memb. (Indiv.) 450; (Inst.) 21; (Subscribers) 24. Term of Office. Oct. 1994–Oct. 1995.
Pres. Kathy Carlson, State Law Lib., Supreme Court Bldg., Cheyenne 82002. Tel. 307-777-7509; *V.P./Pres.-Elect* Lucie Osborn, Laramie County Public Lib., 2800 Central Ave., Cheyenne 82001. Tel. 307-635-1032; *Exec. Secy.* Laura Grott, Box 1387, Cheyenne 82001. Tel. 307-632-7622, FAX 307-638-3469.
Address correspondence to the executive secretary.

Guam

Memb. 75. Publication. *Guam Library Association News* (mo. during school year).
Pres. Mark Goniwiecha, Robert F. Kennedy Memorial Lib., Univ of Guam, Mangilao 96923. Tel. 671-734-9332; *V.P. Programs* Sheryl Nixt; *V.P. Memb. and Newsletter* Harry Uyehara, College of Ed., Univ. of Guam, Mangilao 96923. Tel. 671-734-9519; *Secy.* Beth McClure; *Treas.* Rick Castro; *ALA Councillor* Mark Goniwiecha.

Address correspondence to the association, Robert F. Kennedy Memorial Lib., Univ. of Guam, Mangilao 96923.

Canada

Alberta

Memb. 700. Term of Office. May 1994–Apr. 1995. Publication. *Letter of the L.A.A.* (5 per year).
Pres. Linda C. Cook, Yellowhead Regional Lib., 433 King St., Box 400, Spruce Grove T7X 2Y1. Tel. 403-962-2003, FAX 403-962-2770; *Exec. Dir.* Christine Sheppard, 80 Baker Crescent N.W., Calgary T2L 1R4. Tel. 403-284-5818, FAX 403-282-6646.
Address correspondence to the association, 5512 Fourth St. N.W., Box 64197, Calgary T2K 6J1. Tel. 403-284-5818, FAX 403-282-6646.

British Columbia

Memb. 940. Term of Office. Apr.–May. Publication. *BCLA Reporter.* Ed. Susan Fafyam.
Pres. Leonora Crema; *V.P./Pres.-Elect* Lee Teal.
Address correspondence to the association, 110-6545 Bonsor Ave., Burnaby V5H 1H3. Tel. 604-430-9633, FAX 604-430-8595.

Manitoba

Memb. 462. Term of Office. Spring 1994–Spring 1995. Publication. *Newsline* (mo.).
Pres. John Tooth; *V.P.* Ganga Dakshinamurti; *Office Mgr.* Jeannette Dankewych.
Address correspondence to the association, 208-100 Arthur St., Winnipeg R3B 1H3. Tel. 204-943-4567, FAX 204-942-1555.

Ontario

Memb. Over 3,750. Term of Office. Nov. 1994–Nov. 1995. Publications. *Inside OLA* (bi-mo.); *The Teaching Librarian* (q.); *Access* (3 per year).
Pres. Jane Horrocks, Richmond Hill Public Lib. Tel. 905-770-1310; *Treas.* Lenny

Goldberg, Vaughan Public Libs. Tel. 905-477-5733.
Address correspondence to the association, 100 Lombard St., Suite 303, Toronto M5C 1M3. Tel. 416-363-3388, FAX 416-941-9581.

Quebec

Memb. (Indiv.) 170; (Inst.) 42; (Commercial) 7. Term of Office. May 1994–May 1995. Publications. *ABQ/QLA Bulletin* (3 per year); *QASL Newsletter* (3 per year).
Pres. Maria Varvarikos, Lower Canada College, 4090 Royal Ave., Montreal H4A 2M5; *Exec. Secy.* Marie Eberlin, Quebec Lib. Assn., Box 1095, Pointe Claire H9S 4H9. Tel. 514-630-4875.
Address correspondence to the executive secretary.

Saskatchewan

Memb. 300. Term of Office. July 1995–June 1996. Publication. *Saskatchewan Library Association Forum* (5 per year).
Pres. Todd Mundle; *Exec. Dir.* Kate Fisher, Box 3388, Regina S4P 3H1. Tel. 306-780-9413, FAX 306-757-4422.
Address correspondence to the executive director.

Regional

Atlantic Provinces: N.B., Nfld., N.S., P.E.I.

Memb. (Indiv.) 392; (Inst.) 44. Term of Office. May 1994–May 1995. Publications. *APLA Bulletin* (bi-mo.), *Ed.* Edith Haliburton; *Membership Directory and Handbook* (ann.).
Pres. Charles Cameron; *V.P./Pres.-Elect* Susan Libby; *V.P. Nova Scotia* Mark Leggott; *V.P. Prince Edward Island* Nichola Cleaveland; *V.P. New Brunswick* Jocelyne Thompson; *V.P. Newfoundland* Karen Lippold; *V.P. Memb.* Kelly Campbell; *Secy.* Elizabeth Browne. Tel. 709-737-7433; *Treas.* Caren Mofford.
Address correspondence to Atlantic Provinces Lib. Assn., c/o School of Lib. and

Info. Studies, Dalhousie Univ., Halifax, NS B3H 4H8.

Middle Atlantic: Del., D.C., Md., Va., W.Va.

Term of Office. June 1994–July 1995.
Pres. Ernest Kallay, Jr., Lib. Dir., Clarksburg Harrison Public Lib., 404 W. Pike St., Clarksburg, WV 26301. Tel. 304-624-4411; *Treas.* Darrell Lemke, 9207 Chanute Dr., Bethesda, MD 20814.
Address correspondence to the president.

Midwest: Ill., Ind., Minn., Ohio

Term of Office. 1992–1995.
Pres. Patricia Llerandi, Schaumburg Township Lib., 32 W. Library Lane, Schaumburg 60194. Tel. 708-885-3373, Ext. 150; *V.P./Pres.-Elect* Kathy East. Tel. 419-352-5104; *Secys.* Diane Bever, Tel. 317-455-9265, Linda Kolb, Tel. 317-257-2040.
Address correspondence to the president, Midwest Federation of Lib. Assns.

Mountain Plains: Ariz., Colo., Kans., Mont., Neb., Nev., N.Dak., Okla., S.Dak., Utah, Wyo.

Memb. 920. Term of Office. One year. Publications. *MPLA Newsletter* (bi-mo.), *Ed. and Adv. Mgr.* Jim Dertien, Sioux Falls Public Lib., 201 N. Main Ave., Sioux Falls, SD 57102. Tel. 605-339-7115; *Membership Directory* (ann.).
Pres. Blaine H. Hall, Brigham Young Univ. Lib., Provo, UT 84602. Tel. 801-378-6117, E-mail bhh@hbll1.byu.edu; *V.P./Pres.-Elect* Doug Hindmarsh, Utah State Lib., 2150 S. 300 W., Salt Lake City, UT 84115. Tel. 801-466-5888; *Exec. Secy.* Joe Edelen, Weeks Lib., Univ. of South Dakota, Vermillion, SD 57069. Tel. 605-677-6082, E-mail jedelen@charlie.usd.edu.
Address correspondence to the executive secretary, Mountain Plains Lib. Assn.

New England: Conn., Maine, Mass., N.H., R.I., Vt.

Memb. (Indiv.) 1,200; (Inst.) 100. Term of Office. One year (Treas., Dirs., two years). Publication. *New England Libraries* (6 per

year). *Ed.* Cara Barlow, Massachusetts Board of Libs. Commission, 648 Beacon St., Boston, MA 02115. Tel. 617-267-9400.
Pres. Krista McLeod, Nevins Memorial Lib., 305 Broad Way, Methuen, MA 01844. Tel. 508-686-4080; *V.P./Pres.-Elect* Carolyn Noah, Central Massachusetts Regional Lib. System, Salem Square, Worcester, MA 01603. Tel. 508-799-1728; *Secy.* Pamela Turner, Baxter Memorial Lib., 71 South St., Gorham, ME 04038. Tel. 207-839-5031; *Treas.* Lucy Gangone, Somers Public Lib., Somers, CT 06071. Tel. 203-763-3501; *Exec. Secy.* Barry Blaisdell, New England Lib. Assn., 707 Turnpike St., North Andover, MA 01845. Tel. 508-685-5966.

Address correspondence to the executive secretary.

Pacific Northwest: Alaska, Idaho, Mont., Oreg., Wash., Alberta, B.C.

Memb. (Active) 725; (Subscribers) 160. Term of Office. Oct. 1994–Sept. 1995. Publication. *PNLA Quarterly. Ed.* Katherine G. Eaton, 1631 E. 24 Ave., Eugene, OR 97403. Tel. 503-344-2027, FAX 503-341-5898.

Pres. Ann Haley, Walla Walla Public Lib., 238 E. Alder St., Walla Walla, WA 99362-1967. Tel. 509-545-6549, FAX 509-527-3748; *1st V.P./Pres.-Elect* Carol Otteson, Wm. Eagan Lib., Univ. of Alaska Southeast, 11120 Glacier Hwy., Juneau, AK 99801. Tel. 907-465-6440, FAX 907-465-6249. *2nd V.P.* Terry Heyer, Pocatello Public Lib., 812 E. Clark St., Pocatello, ID 83201-9266. Tel. 208-232-1263, FAX 208-232-9266; *Secy.* Marg Anderson, SAIT, Communicative Arts, 1301 16th Ave. N.W., Calgary, AB T2M OL4. Tel. 403-284-7016, FAX 403-284-7121; *Treas.* Paul E. Jensen, Des Moines Lib., King County Lib. System, 21620 11th Ave. S., Des Moines, WA 98198. Tel. 206-824-6083, FAX 206-296-5047.

Address correspondence to the president, Pacific Northwest Lib. Assn.

Southeastern: Ala., Ark., Fla., Ga., Ky., La., Miss., N.C., S.C., Tenn., Va., W. Va.

Memb. 1,650. Term of Office. Oct. 1994–Oct. 1996. Publication. *The Southeastern Librarian* (q.).
Pres. Joe Forsee, Dir., Div. of Public Lib. Services, 156 Trinity Ave. S.W., Atlanta, GA

State and Provincial Library Agencies

The state library administrative agency in each of the U.S. states will have the latest information on its state plan for the use of federal funds under the Library Services and Construction Act. The directors and addresses of these state agencies are listed below.

Alabama

Patricia L. Harris, Dir., Alabama Public Lib. Service, 6030 Monticello Dr., Montgomery 36130-2001. Tel. 205-213-3900, FAX 205-272-9419.

Alaska

Karen R. Crane, Dir., Div. of State Libs., Archives, and Museums, Alaska Dept. of Educ., Box 110571, Juneau 99811-0571. Tel. 907-465-2910, FAX 907-465-2151.

Arizona

Arlene Bansal, Dir., Dept. of Lib., Archives, and Public Records, State Capitol, 1700 W. Washington, Suite 200, Phoenix 85007-2896. Tel. 602-542-4035, FAX 602-542-4972.

Arkansas

John A. (Pat) Murphey, Jr., State Libn., Arkansas State Lib., One Capitol Mall, Little Rock 72201-1081. Tel. 501-682-1526, 682-2848, FAX 501-682-1529.

California

Kevin Starr, State Libn., California State Lib., Box 942837, Sacramento 94237-0001. Tel. 916-654-0174, FAX 916-654-0064.

Colorado

Nancy M. Bolt, Asst. Commissioner, Colorado State Lib., 201 E. Colfax Ave., Denver 80203. Tel. 303-866-6733, FAX 303-830-0793.

Connecticut

Richard G. Akeroyd, Jr., State Libn., Connecticut State Lib., 231 Capitol Ave., Hartford 06106. Tel. 203-566-4301, FAX 203-566-8940.

Delaware

George J. Coyle, Asst. Secy. of State, Dept. of State, Townsend Bldg., Box 1401, Dover 19903-1401. Tel. 302-739-4711, FAX 302-739-3811; Tom Sloan, State Libn. and Div. Dir., Div. of Libs., 43 S. DuPont Hwy., Dover 19901. Tel. 302-739-4748, FAX 302-739-6787.

District of Columbia

Hardy R. Franklin, Dir., Dist. of Columbia Public Lib., 901 G St. N.W., Washington 20001. Tel. 202-727-1101, FAX 202-727-1129.

Florida

Barratt Wilkins, State Libn., State Lib. of Florida, R. A. Gray Bldg., Tallahassee 32399-0250. Tel. 904-487-2651, FAX 904-488-2746.

Georgia

Joe B. Forsee, Dir., Div. of Public Lib. Services, 156 Trinity Ave. S.W., Atlanta 30303-3692. Tel. 404-656-2461, FAX 404-656-9447.

Hawaii

Bartholomew A. Kane, State Libn., Hawaii State Public Lib. System, 465 S. King St., Rm. B1, Honolulu 96813. Tel. 808-586-3704, FAX 808-586-3715.

Idaho

Charles A. Bolles, State Libn., Idaho State Lib., 325 W. State St., Boise 83702-6072. Tel. 208-334-5124, FAX 208-334-4016.

Illinois

Bridget L. Lamont, Dir., Illinois State Lib., 300 S. Second St., Springfield 62701-1796. Tel. 217-782-2994, FAX 217-785-4326.

Indiana

C. Ray Ewick, Dir., Indiana State Lib., 140 N. Senate Ave., Indianapolis 46204-2296. Tel. 317-232-3692, FAX 317-232-0002.

Iowa

Sharman B. Smith, Dir., State Lib. of Iowa, Dept. of Education, E. 12 and Grand, Des Moines 50319. Tel. 515-281-4105, FAX 515-281-3384.

Kansas

Duane F. Johnson, State Libn., Kansas State Lib., State Capitol, 3rd fl., Topeka 66612-1593. Tel. 913-296-3296, FAX 913-296-6650.

Kentucky

James A. Nelson, State Libn./Commissioner, Kentucky Dept. for Libs. and Archives, 300 Coffee Tree Rd., Box 537, Frankfort 40602-0537. Tel. 502-875-7000, FAX 502-564-5773.

Louisiana

Thomas F. Jaques, State Libn., State Lib. of Louisiana, Box 131, Baton Rouge 70821-0131. Tel. 504-342-4923, FAX 504-342-3547.

Maine

J. Gary Nichols, State Libn., Maine State Lib., LMA Bldg., State House Sta. 64,

Augusta 04333-0064. Tel. 207-287-5620, FAX 207-287-0933.

Maryland

J. Maurice Travillian, Asst. State Superintendent for Libs., Div. of Lib. Development and Services, Maryland State Dept. of Educ., 200 W. Baltimore St., Baltimore 21201-2595. Tel. 410-333-2113, FAX 410-333-2507.

Massachusetts

Keith M. Fiels, Dir., Massachusetts Board of Lib. Commissioners, 648 Beacon St., Boston 02215. Tel. 617-267-9400, FAX 617-421-9833.

Michigan

Jeffrey P. Johnson, Deputy State Libn., Lib. of Michigan, 717 Allegan St., Box 30007, Lansing 48909-9945. Tel. 517-373-1580, FAX 517-373-5700.

Minnesota

William G. Asp, Dir., Office of Lib. Development and Services, Minnesota Dept. of Educ., 440 Capitol Sq. Bldg., 550 Cedar St., Saint Paul 55101. Tel. 612-296-2821, FAX 612-296-3272.

Mississippi

Mary Ellen Pellington, Exec. Dir., Mississippi Lib. Commission, 1221 Ellis Ave., Box 10700, Jackson 39289-0700. Tel. 601-359-1036, FAX 601-354-4181.

Missouri

Monteria Hightower, Assoc. Commissioner for Libs./State Libn., Missouri State Lib., 600 W. Main, Box 387, Jefferson City 65102-0387. Tel. 314-751-2751, FAX 314-751-3612.

Montana

Richard T. Miller, Jr., State Libn., Montana State Lib., 1515 E. Sixth Ave., Helena 59620-1800. Tel. 406-444-3115, FAX 406-444-5612.

Nebraska

Rod Wagner, Dir., Nebraska Lib. Commission, The Atrium, 1200 N St., Suite 120, Lincoln 68505-2006. Tel. 402-471-2045, FAX 402-471-2083.

Nevada

Joan G. Kerschner, Dir., Museums, Lib. and Arts, Nevada State Lib. and Archives, Capitol Complex, Carson City 89710. Tel. 702-687-8315, FAX 702-687-8311.

New Hampshire

Kendall F. Wiggin, State Libn., New Hampshire State Lib., 20 Park St., Concord 03301-6303. Tel. 603-271-2392, FAX 603-271-2205.

New Jersey

Louise Minervino, State Libn., New Jersey State Lib., Dept. of Educ., 185 W. State St., CN520, Trenton 08625-0520. Tel. 609-292-6200, FAX 609-292-2746.

New Mexico

Karen J. Watkins, State Libn., New Mexico State Lib., 325 Don Gaspar St., Santa Fe 87503. Tel. 505-827-3804, FAX 505-827-3888.

New York

Joseph F. Shubert, State Libn./Asst. Commissioner for Libs., New York State Lib., C.E.C., Rm. 10C34, Empire State Plaza, Albany 12230. Tel. 518-474-5930, FAX 518-474-2718.

North Carolina

Sandra M. Cooper, Dir./State Libn., North Carolina State Lib., Dept. of Cultural Resources, 109 E. Jones St., Raleigh 27601-2807. Tel. 919-733-2570, FAX 919-733-8748.

North Dakota

William R. Strader, State Libn., North Dakota State Lib., Liberty Memorial Bldg., Capitol Grounds, 604 E. Blvd. Ave., Bismarck 58505-0800. Tel. 701-224-2492, FAX 701-224-2040.

Ohio

Richard M. Cheski, Dir., State Lib. of Ohio, 65 S. Front St., Columbus 43266-0334. Tel. 614-644-6845, FAX 614-466-3584.

Oklahoma

Robert L. Clark, Jr., State Libn., Oklahoma Dept. of Libs., 200 N.E. 18 St., Oklahoma City 73105-3298. Tel. 405-521-2502, FAX 405-525-7804.

Oregon

Jim Scheppke, State Libn., Oregon State Lib., State Lib. Bldg., Salem 97310-0640. Tel. 503-378-4367, FAX 503-588-7119.

Pennsylvania

Sara Parker, Commissioner of Libs., State Lib. of Pennsylvania, Box 1601, Harrisburg 17105. Tel. 717-787-2646, FAX 717-783-2070.

Rhode Island

Barbara Weaver, Dir., Rhode Island Dept. of State Lib. Services, 300 Richmond St., Providence 02903-4222. Tel. 401-277-2726, FAX 401-831-1131.

South Carolina

James B. Johnson, Jr., Dir., South Carolina State Lib., 1500 Senate St., Box 11469, Columbia 29211. Tel. 803-734-8666, FAX 803-734-8676.

South Dakota

Jane Kolbe, State Libn., South Dakota State Lib., 800 Governors Dr., Pierre 57501-2294. Tel. 605-773-3131, FAX 605-773-4950.

Tennessee

Riley C. Darnell, Secy. of State, G-13 John Sevier Bldg., Nashville 37243-0305. Tel. 615-741-2816; Edwin Gleaves, State Libn./Archivist, Tennessee State Lib. and Archives, 403 Seventh Ave. N., Nashville 37243-0315. Tel. 615-741-7996, FAX 615-741-6471.

Texas

William D. Gooch, Dir./State Libn., Texas State Lib., 1201 Brazos St., Box 12927, Capitol Sta., Austin 78711-2927. Tel. 512-463-5460, FAX 512-463-5436.

Utah

Amy Owen, Dir., State Lib. Div., 2150 S. 300 W., Suite 16, Salt Lake City 84115-2579. Tel. 801-466-5888, FAX 801-533-4657.

Vermont

Patricia E. Klinck, State Libn., Vermont Dept. of Libs., c/o State Office Bldg. P.O., Montpelier 05609-0601. Tel. 802-828-3265, FAX 802-828-2199.

Virginia

Nolan T. Yelich, Acting State Libn., Virginia State Lib. and Archives, 11 St. at Capitol Sq., Richmond 23219-3491. Tel. 804-786-2332, FAX 804-786-5855.

Washington

Nancy L. Zussy, State Libn., Washington State Lib., Box 42460, Olympia 98504-2460. Tel. 206-753-2915, FAX 206-586-7575.

West Virginia

Frederic J. Glazer, Dir., West Virginia Lib. Commission, Cultural Center, Charleston 25305. Tel. 304-558-2041, FAX 304-558-2044.

Wisconsin

William J. Wilson, Asst. Superintendent, Div. for Libs. and Community Learning, Dept. of Public Instruction, 125 S. Webster St., Box 7841, Madison 53707-7841. Tel. 608-266-2205, FAX 608-267-1052.

Wyoming

Helen Meadors Maul, State Libn., Wyoming State Lib., Supreme Court and State Lib. Bldg., Cheyenne 82002-0060. Tel.307-777-7281, FAX 307-777-6289.

American Samoa

Emma F. C. Penn, Program Dir., Office of Lib. Services, Box 1329, Pago Pago 96799. Tel. 011-684-633-1181 or 1182.

Guam

Carmen Kaneshi, Acting Territorial Libn., Nieves M. Flores Memorial Lib., 254 Martyr St., Agana 96910. Tel. 671-477-6913, 472-6417, FAX 671-477-9777.

Northern Mariana Islands

Susan Grant, Acting Dir., Joeten-Kiyu Public Lib., Box 1092, Commonwealth of the Northern Mariana Islands, Saipan 96950. Tel. 670-235-7322, FAX 670-235-7550; William Matson, Federal Programs Coord., Dept. of Educ., Commonwealth of the Northern Mariana Islands, Saipan 96950. Tel. 670-322-6405, FAX 670-322-5873; DC Contact, Pete A. Torres or Luis A. Benavente. Tel. 202-673-5869, FAX 202-673-5873.

Palau (Republic of)

Masa-Aki N. Emesiochl, Federal Grants Coord., Bureau of Educ., Box 189, Koror 96940. Washington Office, Tel. 202-624-7793, FAX 202-624-7795; Fermina Salvador, Libn., Palau Public Lib., Box 189, Koror 96940. Tel. 680-488-2973.

Puerto Rico

Anabel Casey, Secy., Dept. of Educ., Apartado 759, Box 11496, Hato Rey 00919. Tel. 809-754-5972, FAX 809-754-0843; Consuelo Figuera, Special Asst. for Library Matters, Tel. 809-754-5972, FAX 809-754-0843.

Virgin Islands

Jeannette Allis Bastian, Dir. and Territorial Libn., Div. of Libs., Archives and Museums, 23 Dronningens Gade, Saint Thomas 00802. Tel. 809-774-3407, FAX 809-775-1887.

Canada

Alberta

Lucy Pana, Dir., Alberta Community Development Libs. Branch, 901 Standard Life Center, 10405 Jasper Ave., Edmonton T5J 4R7. Tel. 403-427-2556, FAX 403-427-0263.

British Columbia

Barbara Greeniaus, Dir., Lib. Services Branch, Ministry of Municipal Affairs, 800 Johnson St., Victoria V8V 1X4. Tel. 604-356-1791, FAX 604-387-4048.

Manitoba

Sylvia Nicholson, Dir., Manitoba Culture, Heritage, and Citizenship, Public Lib. Services, Unit 200, 1525 First St., Brandon R7A 7A1. Tel. 204-726-6864, FAX 204-726-6868.

Newfoundland

David Gale, Provincial Dir., Public Libs. Service, Arts and Culture Centre, Allandale Rd., Saint John's A1B 3A3. Tel. 709-737-3964, FAX 709-737-3009.

New Brunswick

Jocelyne LeBel, Dir., New Brunswick Lib. Service, Box 6000, Fredericton E3B 5H1. Tel. 506-453-2354, FAX 506-453-2416.

Northwest Territories

Xuliang Feng, Dir., Northwest Territories Public Lib. Services, Government of the Northwest Territories, Box 1100, Hay River X0E 0R0. Tel. 403-874-6531, FAX 403-874-3321.

Nova Scotia

Marion L. Pape, Provincial Libn., Nova Scotia Provincial Lib., 3770 Kempt Rd., Halifax B3K 4X8. Tel. 902-424-2456, FAX 902-424-0633. E-mail: mpape@nshpl.library.ns.ca.

Ontario

Barbara Clubb, Dir., Libs. and Community Info. Branch, Ministry of Culture and Communications, 77 Bloor St. W., 3rd fl., Toronto M7A 2R9. Tel. 416-314-7611, FAX 416-314-7635.

Prince Edward Island

Harry Holman, Provincial Libn., P.E.I. Provincial Lib., Red Head Rd., Box 7500, Morell C0A 1S0. Tel. 902-961-3200.

Quebec

Odette Blouin-Cliche, Dir., Direction des arts, des lettres, et des bibliothèques publiques, Ministère de la Culture et de la Communication, 225 Grande Allée E., Bloc A, 3 étage, Quebec G1R 5G5. Tel. 418-644-7206, FAX 418-644-0380.

Saskatchewan

Maureen Woods, Provincial Libn., Saskatchewan Provincial Lib., 1352 Winnipeg St., Regina S4P 3V7. Tel. 306-787-2972, FAX 306-787-8866.

Yukon Territory

Linda R. Johnson, Dir., Dept. of Educ., Libs., and Archives, Box 2703, Whitehorse Y1A 2C6. Tel. 403-667-5309, FAX 403-667-4253.

State School Library Media Associations

Alabama

Children's and School Libns. Div., Alabama Lib. Assn. Memb. 450. Publication. *The Alabama Librarian* (q.).
Exec. Dir. Barbara Black, 400 S. Union St., Suite 255, Montgomery 36104.
Address correspondence to the executive director.

Arizona

School Lib. Media Div., Arizona Lib. Assn. Memb. 500. Term of Office. Dec. 1994–Nov. 1995. Publication. *ASLA Newsletter*.
Pres. Mary Morris, Show Low H.S., 11350 N. Central, Show Low 85901. Tel. 602-537-2901; *Pres.-Elect* Susan Garvin, Conchos Elementary School, 1718 W. Vineyard, Phoenix 85041. Tel. 602-243-4928.
Address correspondence to the president.

Arkansas

Arkansas Assn. of School Libns. and Media Educators. Term of Office. Jan.–Dec. 1995.
Chair Linda Taylor, Benton H.S., 2900 Breckenridge Rd., Benton 72015. Tel. 501-778-5767, FAX 501-776-5783; *Chair-Elect* Sylvia Chudy, Arkansas School for Math & Science, Rte. 1, Box 299, Bismarck 71929. Tel 501-865-3887; *Secy.-Treas.* Rachel

Shankles, Lakeside H.S., 202 Stonehenge Ct., Hot Springs 71901. Tel. 501-624-7138.
Address correspondence to the chairperson.

California

California Media and Lib. Educators Assn. Memb. 1,800. Term of Office. June 1994–May 1995. Publication. *CMLEA Journal.* Ed. Barbara Jeffus. Job Hotline 415-697-8832.
Pres. John McGinnis, Cerritos Community College, 11110 Alondra Blvd., Norwalk 90650; *Pres.-Elect* Bonnie O'Brian, LA Unif. School District, 1320 W. Third St., Los Angeles 90017; *Secy.* Hilda Wiens, Kerman Unif. School District, 151 S. First St., Kerman 93630; *Treas.* Betty D. Silva, Fairfield H.S., 205 E. Atlantic, Fairfield 94533; *Business Office Secy.* Nancy D. Kohn, CMLEA, 1499 Old Bayshore Hwy., Suite 142, Burlingame 94010. Tel. 415-692-2350.
Address correspondence to the business office secretary.

Colorado

Colorado Educational Media Assn. Memb. 650. Term of Office. Feb. 1994–Feb. 1995.
Pres.-Elect Lorena Mitchell; *Secy.* Debra Phillips; *Exec. Secy.* Mary Anne Strasser.
Address correspondence to the executive secretary, Box 22814, Wellshire Sta., Denver 80222. Tel. 303-777-9122.

Connecticut

Connecticut Educational Media Assn. Term of Office. May 1994–May 1995. Publications. *CEMA Update Quarterly; CEMA Gram Monthly;* CEMA videotape "The School Library Media Specialist—A Continuing Story," available in 1/2" ($35); *Resource Guide* ($14).
Pres. Tally Negroni, 53 Blueberry Hill, Weston 06883. Tel. 203-227-8044; *V.P.* Eileen Skruck, 38 Flint St., Trumbull 06611. Tel. 203-268-0525; *Secy.* Susan Wargo, 86 Wilsonville Rd., North Grosvenordale 06255. Tel. 203-935-5581; *Treas.* Michael Quigley, 3 Dittmar Rd., Bethel 06801. Tel. 203-744-3250; *Admin. Secy.* Anne Weimann, 25 Elm-

wood Ave., Trumbull 06611. Tel. 203-372-2260.
Address correspondence to the administrative secretary.

Delaware

Delaware School Lib. Media Assn., Div. of Delaware Lib. Assn. Memb. 100. Term of Office. Apr. 1994–Apr. 1995. Publications. *DSLMA Newsletter* (irreg.); column in *DLA Bulletin* (3 per year).
Pres. Susan Cushwa, Middletown H.S. Appoquinimink, 504 S. Broad St., Middletown. Tel. 302-378-5000.
Address correspondence to the president.

District of Columbia

District of Columbia Assn. of School Libns. Memb. 93. Term of Office. Aug. 1993–July 1995. Publication. *Newsletter* (4 per year).
Pres. Anita Drayton; *V.P.* Lydia Jenkins; *Rec. Secy.* Olivia Hardison; *Treas.* Mary Minnis; *Financial Secy.* Connie Lawson; *Corres. Secy.* Sharon Sorrels, Banneker H.S., 800 Euclid St. N.W., Washington 20001.
Address correspondence to the association, Box 90488, Washington 20090-0488.

Florida

Florida Assn. for Media in Education. Memb. 1,450. Term of Office. Oct. 1994–Oct. 1995. Publication. *Florida Media Quarterly.* Ed. Pat Conlon, Rte. 4, Box 461, Hawthorne 32640. Tel. 904-620-7587.
Pres. Linda Schroeder, 4249 N.W. 56 Way, Gainesville 32606. Tel. 904-955-6702; *Pres.-Elect* Sherie Bargar, 4377 Weeping Willow Circle, Casselberry 32707. Tel. 407-623-1462; *V.P.* Helen Tallman, 7601 S.W. 94 Ave., Miami 33173. Tel. 305-365-6278, FAX 305-361-0996; *Secy.* Susan Manalli, 1116 Alcala, Saint Augustine 32086. Tel. 904-824-5548; *Treas.* Vic Burke, 1105 N.E. 8 St., Ocala 34470. Tel. 904-620-7751; *FAME Office Correspondent* Mary Margaret Rogers, Box 13119, Tallahassee 32317. Tel. 904-668-7606.
Address correspondence to the office correspondent.

Georgia

School Lib. Media Div., Georgia Lib. Assn. Term of Office. Oct. 1993–Oct. 1995. *Chair* Jane D. Bennett, Morgan Rd. Middle School, 3635 Hiers Blvd., Hephzibah 30815. Tel. 706-796-4992; *Pres.* Donna Mancini, DeKalb County Public Lib., 215 Sycamore St., Decatur 30030. Tel 404-370-8450, FAX 404-370-8469; *Secy.* David Searcy, Atlanta Fulton Public Lib., Community Extension Services, 3645 Southside Ind. Pkway., Bldg 8, Suite 105, Atlanta 30354. Tel. 404-366-0710, FAX 404-363-0174.

Address correspondence to the association, Box 39, Young Harris 30582. Tel. 706-379-4313, FAX 706-379-4314.

Hawaii

Hawaii Assn. of School Libns. Memb. 299. Term of Office. June 1994–May 1995. Publications. *HASL Newsletter* (1 per semester); *Golden Key Journal* (1 every 5 years).

Pres. Katherine Kiyabu. Tel. 808-373-2136, FAX 808-373-5196; *1st V.P.* Julie Tomomitsu; *2nd V.P.* Irmalee Choo; *Rec. Secy.* Linda Reser; *Corres. Secy.* Beverly Ono; *Treas.* Dianne Sugihara; *Dirs.* Faith Ishihara, Betsy Young.

Address correspondence to the association, Box 23019, Honolulu 96822.

Idaho

Educational Media Div., Idaho Lib. Assn. Memb. 125. Term of Office. Oct. 1994–Oct. 1995. Publication. Column in *The Idaho Librarian* (q.).

Chair Larry Gold, School District Office, 3115 Poline Rd., Pocatello 83201. Tel. 208-253-3222; *Chair-Elect* Barbara Barrett, Hillside Jr. H.S., 6806 Fernwood, Boise 83709. Tel. 208-376-7180; *Secy.* Sue Crofts, 33 Purdue Ave., Pocatello 83204.

Address correspondence to the chairperson.

Illinois

Illinois School Lib. Media Assn. Memb. 850. Term of Office. July 1994–July 1995. Publications. *ISLMA News* (6 per year), *ISLMA Membership Directory* (ann.).

Pres. Sondra Miller, 29 Providence Lane, Springfield 62707. Tel. 217-546-0907; *Pres.-Elect* Carol J. Fox, 721 Tamarack Lane, Rockford 61107. Tel. 815-398-2949; *Exec. Secy.* Kay Maynard, Box 598, Canton 61520. Tel. 309-649-0911, FAX 309-647-0140, E-mail: cant@darkstar.rsa.lib.il.us.

Address correspondence to the executive secretary.

Indiana

Assn. for Indiana Media Educators. Memb. 1,025. Term of Office. May 1994–Apr. 1995. Publications. *AIME News* (mo.); *Indiana Media Journal* (q.).

Pres. Bonnie Grimble, Carmel H.S., 520 E. Main St., Carmel 46032. Tel. 317-846-7721, FAX 317-571-4066; *Pres.-Elect* Dennis LeLoup, Indiana Dept. of Education, Learning Resources Unit, Rm. 229 State House, Indianapolis 46204. Tel. 317-232-9119, FAX 317-232-9121; *Management Consultant* Karen G. Burch, 1908 E. 64 St., South Dr., Indianapolis 46220. Tel. 317-257-8558, FAX 317-259-4191.

Address correspondence to the management consultant.

Iowa

Iowa Educational Media Assn. Memb. 500. Term of Office. Mar. 1994–Mar. 1995. Publication. *Iowa Media Message* (5 per year). *Ed.* Arletta Dawson, Western Hills AEA, 1520 Morningside Ave., Sioux City 51106.

Pres. Lucille Lettow; *Pres.-Elect* Kay Rewerts; *Secy.* Mary Ann Emerick; *Treas.* Rick Maehl; *Exec. Secy.* Paula Behrendt, 2306 Sixth, Harlan 51537. Tel./FAX 712-755-5918.

Address correspondence to the executive secretary.

Kansas

Kansas Assn. of School Libns. Memb. 700. Term of Office. July 1994–June 1995. Publication. *KASL Newsletter* (s. ann.).

Pres. Roma McConkey, 75 W. 106, No. 315, Overland Park 66212. Tel. 913-681-4475; *V.P./Pres.-Elect* Sharon Coatney, Box

38, Linwood 66052. Tel. 913-681-4325; *Exec. Secy.* Dannette Schmidt, 2092 Norton, Salina 67401. Tel. 913-827-4018.

Address correspondence to the executive secretary.

Kentucky

Kentucky School Media Assn. Memb. 695. Term of Office. Oct. 1994–Oct. 1995. Publication. *KSMA Newsletter* (q.).

Pres. Donna Hornsby, Beechwood Independent School, Beechwood Rd., Fort Mitchell 41017. Tel. 606-331-1220, FAX 606-331-5595; *Pres.-Elect* Earlene Arnold, Cold Hill Elementary School, 4012 W. Laurel, London 40741-9709. Tel. 606-878-6195; *Secy.* Sandra Wood, Taylor Elementary School, Gibson Dr., Rte. 1, Box 4, Brooksville 41004. Tel. 606-735-2169; *Treas.* Diane Culbertson, Paul Lawrence Dunbar H.S., 1600 Man o' War Blvd., Lexington 40356. Tel. 606-224-3140, FAX 606-224-4385.

Address correspondence to the president.

Louisiana

Louisiana Assn. of School Libns. Memb. 500. Term of Office. July 1994–June 1995.

Pres. Mary Ellen Shiflett, 5 Country Club, LaPlace 70068. Tel. 504-758-2116; *1st V.P./Pres.-Elect* Claudia Fisher, 23990 Reames Rd., Zachary 70791; *2nd V.P.* Andrea Laborde, 508 E. Charles St., Hammond 70401. Tel. 504-549-2206; *Secy.* Melissa Elrod, 255 Stuart St., Shreveport, LA 71105. Tel. 318-227-9211.

Address correspondence to the association, c/o Louisiana Lib. Assn., Box 3058, Baton Rouge 70821.

Maine

Maine Educational Media Assn. Memb. 350. Term of Office. May 1993–May 1995. Publication. *Maine Entry* (with the Maine Lib. Assn.).

Pres. David W. Anderson, Thornton Academy, 438 Main St., Saco 04072. Tel. 207-282-3361; *1st V.P.* Linda Lord, Maine State Lib., State House Sta. 64, Augusta 04333; *2nd V.P.* Susan Allison, Lewiston H.S., 156

East Ave., Lewiston 04240; *Secy.* Carol King, Wells Jr. H.S., Box 310, Wells 04090; *Treas.* Suzan Nelson, Portland H.S., 284 Cumberland Ave., Portland 04101.

Address correspondence to the president.

Maryland

Maryland Educational Media Organization. Term of Office. July 1994–June 1995. Publication. *MEMORANDOM.*

Contact Karen Ohlrich, 6537 Overheart Lane, Columbia 21045.

Address correspondence to the association, Box 21127, Baltimore 21228.

Massachusetts

Massachusetts School Lib. Media Assn. Memb. 700. Term of Office. June 1994–May 1995. Publication. *Media Forum* (q.).

Pres. Bonnie Shapland; *Secy.* Kathy Lowe; *Admin. Asst.* Sue Rebello, MSLMA, 18 Sasur St., Three Rivers 01080-1031. Tel./FAX 413-283-6675.

Address correspondence to the administrative assistant.

Michigan

Michigan Assn. for Media in Education. Memb. 1,400. Term of Office. Jan.–Dec. 1995. Publications. *Media Spectrum* (4 per year); *MAME Newsletter* (5 per year).

Pres. Sue Schwartz, REMC 13, Ingham ISD, 210 State St., Mason 48854. Tel. 517-676-9726; *Pres.-Elect* Terence Madden, Ann Arbor Public Schools, 601 W. Stadium Blvd., Ann Arbor 48104. Tel. 313-999-2160; *Treas.* LaRene Klink, Genesee School Dist., 7347 N. Genesee Rd., Genesee 48437. Tel. 313-640-3111; *V.P. for Regions* Diane Nye, St. Joseph Public Schools, 2214 S. State St., Saint Joseph 49085; *Secy.* Linda Arbogast, Lewiston Schools, Box 417, Lewiston 49756. Tel. 517-786-2253; *Exec. Dir.* Burton H. Brooks, 6810 S. Cedar St., Suite 8, Lansing 48911. Tel. 517-699-1717, 616-842-9195, FAX 616-842-9195, E-mail: bhbrooks@aol.com.

Address correspondence to the executive director.

Minnesota

Minnesota Educational Media Organization. Memb. 840. Term of Office. (Pres.) Aug. 1994–Aug. 1995 (other offices 2 years in alternating years). Publications. *Minnesota Media* (3 per year); *ImMEDIAte; MEMOrandom* (mo.). *Pres.* Fran McDonald, Rte.1, Box 173, Kasota 56050. Tel. 507-389-5211, FAX 507-389-5751, E-mail: fmcdonald@vax1.mankato.msus.edu; *Pres.-Elect* Phyllis Lacroix, 1700 11th Ave. S.E., Saint Cloud 56301. Tel. 612-255-2062, E-mail: lacroix@tigger.stcloud.msus.edu; *Secy.* Mary Childs, 826 Stevens Circle, Park Rapids 56470. Tel. 218-732-3333, E-mail: 0309prms@informns.k12.mn.us; *Treas.* Charlie (Linda) Lindberg, R.R. 1, Box 37, Kennedy 56733. Tel. 218-842-3682, E-mail: 2359kcsh@informmnsk12.mn.us; *Admin. Secy.* Al Lundquist, 264 Queenan Ave. S., Lakeland 55043. Tel. 612-458-6225.

Mississippi

School Section, Mississippi Lib. Assn. Memb. 1,300. Term of Office. Jan.–Dec. 1995. *Chair* Iris Collins; *Secy.* Becky Dailey. Address correspondence to the association, c/o Mississippi Lib. Assn., Box 20448, Jackson 39289-1448.

Missouri

Missouri Assn. of School Libns. Memb. 900. Term of Office. June 1994–May 1995. *Pres.* Rita Linck, Parkway South H.S., Ballwin 63021. Tel. 314-394-8354, FAX 314-394-8353; *Pres.-Elect* Beth Cobb, Northwest H.S., House Springs 63051. Tel. 314-671-3470. Address correspondence to the association, 8049 Hwy. E, Bonne Terre 63628-3771.

Montana

Montana School Lib. Media Div., Montana Lib. Assn. Memb. 225. Term of Office. July 1994–June 1995. Publication. *Montana Library Focus* (published by Montana Lib. Assn.) (q.). *Chair* Polly Taggart, 2515 Silver Blvd., Billings 59102. Tel. 406-652-6692, E-mail: x_taggart@vino.emcmt.edu; *V.P./Chair-*

Elect Vicki Gale, 319 N. Cody Ave., Hardin 59034. Tel. 406-665-3079. Address correspondence to the chairperson.

Nebraska

Nebraska Educational Media. Assn. Memb. 350. Term of Office. July 1994–June 1995. Publication. *NEMA News* (4 per year). *Pres.* Steve Davis, Kearney Public Schools, Whittier Education Center, 310 W. 24 St., Kearney 68847. Tel. 308-237-6032, FAX 308-237-6014; *Pres.-Elect* Barbara Hansen, 801 17th St., Box 957, Stanton 68779. Tel. 402-439-5025; *Secy.* Terry Zimmers, 388 Eighth St., Box 94, Syracuse 68446. Tel. 402-269-2994; *Treas.* Marilyn Scahill, 323 North Shore Dr., Hastings 68901. Tel. 402-461-3888. Address correspondence to the president.

Nevada

Nevada School and Children's Lib. Section, Nevada Lib. Assn. Memb. 120. Term of Office. Jan.–Dec. 1995. *Pres.* Dorothy Neely, Battle Mountain Jr. H.S., Box 1360, Battle Mountain 89820. Tel. 702-635-2415.

New Hampshire

New Hampshire Educational Media Assn., Box 418, Concord 03302-0418. Memb. 265. Term of Office. June 1994–June 1995. Publications. *Online* (5 per year); *Taproot* (s. ann.). *Pres.* Deirdre Angwin, McKelvie Middle School, 108 Liberty Hill Rd., Bedford 03110. Tel. 603-472-3729, FAX 603-472-4503; *Pres.-Elect* Kim Carter, Souhegan H.S., 412 Boston Post Rd., Amherst 03031. FAX 603-672-1786; *V.P.* Albert (Duke) Southard, Kennett Jr./Sr. H. S., Main St., Conway 03818. Tel. 603-447-6364; *Treas.* Jeffrey Kent, Broken Ground School, Portsmouth St., Concord 03301. Tel. 603-225-0825; *Rec. Secy.* Marion (Mimi) Crowley, Charlotte Elementary School, Nashua 03062. Tel. 603-594-4334; *Corres. Secy.* Linda Mack, Bartlett/Maple School, Goffstown 03045. Tel. 603-497-3330. Address correspondence to the president.

New Jersey

Educational Media Assn. of New Jersey. Memb. 1,100. Term of Office. June 1994–May 1995. Publications. *Signal Tab* (mo.); *Emanations* (2 per year).
Pres. Pam Chesky, 135 Midwood Way, Colonia 07067; *Pres.-Elect* Dagmar Finkle, 81 Lisa Dr., Chatham 07928; *V.P.* Suzanne Manczuk, 114 Mine Rd., Pennington 08534; *Rec. Secy.* Nina Kemps, 647 Guilford Rd., Cherry Hill 08003; *Corres. Secy.* Judy Dursema, 19 Strong St., Mahwah 07430; *Treas.* Jackie Gould, 1089 Tristram Circle, Mantua 08501.
Address correspondence to the president.

New Mexico

School Libs. Children and Young Adult Services Div., New Mexico Lib. Assn. Memb. 240. Term of Office. Apr. 1994–Apr. 1995.
Chair Jerry Klopfer, Paul Horgan Lib., New Mexico Military Academy, 100 W. College, Roswell 88201-5173. Tel. 505-624-8382; *Chair-Elect* Dianah Jentgen.
Address correspondence to the chairperson.

New York

School Lib. Media Section, New York Lib. Assn., 252 Hudson St., Albany 12210. Tel. 518-432-6952, 800-252 6952. Memb. 950. Term of Office. Oct. 1994–Oct. 1995. Publications. *SLMSGram* (q.); participates in *NYLA Bulletin* (mo. except July and Aug.).
Pres. Gail K. Dickinson, Union-Endicott Central School District, Endicott 13760. Tel. 607-757-2187; *V.P., Communications* Judy Busch, Norwich H.S., Midland Dr., Norwich 13815; *V.P., Conferences* Kristine Littrell, Pittsford Mendon H.S., Mendon Rd., Pittsford 14534. Tel. 716-385-4138; *Secy.* Suzanne Shearman, Barclay School, Brockport Central School District, 40 Allen St., Brockport, NY 19420; *Treas.* Connie Wright, Southwestern Central School, 600 Hunt Rd., Jamestown 14701. Tel. 716-664-6273; *Bureau of School Lib. Media Programs* Robert Barron, State Educ. Dept., Education Bldg. Annex, Rm. 676, Albany 12234. Tel. 518 474-2468; *Div. of Lib. Development* Joseph Mattie, New York State Lib., CED, Rm. 10B41, Albany 12230. Tel. 518-474-7890.
Address correspondence to the president or secretary.

North Carolina

North Carolina Assn. of School Libns. Memb. 1,000. Term of Office. Oct. 1993–Oct. 1995.
Chair Augie Beasley, East Mecklenburg H.S., 6800 Monroe Rd., Charlotte 28212. Tel. 704-343-6430; *Chair-Elect* Karen Perry, High Point Central H.S., 801 Ferndale Dr., High Point 27262. Tel. 919-819-2852.
Address correspondence to the chairperson.

North Dakota

School Lib. and Youth Services Section, North Dakota Lib. Assn. Memb. 108. Term of Office. Sept. 1994–Sept. 1995. Publication. *The Good Stuff* (q).
Pres. Patricia M. Adams, South H.S., 1840 15th Ave. S., Fargo 58103. Tel. 701-241-4747, FAX 701-241-6080, E-mail: adams@sendit.nodak.edu; *V.P.* Patricia Sandness, Hughes Jr. H.S., Bismarck 58501. Tel. 701-221-3566; *Secy.* Nancy Hancy, Mandan Sr. H.S., Mandan 58554. Tel. 701-663-9532, FAX 701-663-0471.
Address correspondence to the president.

Ohio

Ohio Educational Lib. Media Assn. Memb. 1,300. Term of Office. Jan.–Dec. 1995. Publication. *Ohio Media Spectrum.*
Pres. Kimberley Miller-Smith, Columbus City Schools, Columbus. *Exec. Dir.* Ann Hanning, 1631 N.W. Professional Plaza, Columbus 43220. Tel. 614-326-1460, FAX 614-459-2087.
Address correspondence to the executive director.

Oklahoma

Oklahoma Assn. of School Lib. Media Specialists. Memb. 225. Term of Office. July 1994–June 1995. Publication. *Information Powerline.*
Chair Phil Woolverton, McLoud H.S., Box 40, McLoud, 74851-0040. Tel. 405-964-3352, FAX 405-964-2801; *Chair-Elect* Pat

Davis, Enid H.S., 500 S. Independence, Enid 73701-5693. Tel. 405-249-4593, FAX 405-249-3565; *Secy.* Paulette LaGasse, Bennett Elementary School, 108 W. Fifth, Broken Bow 74728-2912. Tel. 405-584-2046, FAX 405-584-3306; *Treas.* JoAnne Hope, State Dept. of Educ., 2500 N. Lincoln Blvd., Suite 215, Oklahoma City 73105-4599. Tel. 405-521-2956, FAX 405-521-6205.

Address correspondence to the chairperson.

Oregon

Oregon Educational Media Assn. Memb. 700. Term of Office. Oct. 1994–Sept. 1995. Publication. *INTERCHANGE.*

Pres. Diane Claus-Smith; *Pres.-Elect* Jim Hayden; *Exec. Secy.* Sherry Hevland, 16695 S.W. Rosa Rd., Beaverton 97007. Tel. 503-649-5764.

Address correspondence to the executive secretary.

Pennsylvania

Pennsylvania School Libns. Assn. Term of Office. July 1994–June 1996. Publication. *Learning and Media* (4 per year).

Pres. Rebecca Frost, 2422 Riverview Ave., Bloomsburg 17815. FAX 717-784-6856.

Address correspondence to the president.

Rhode Island

Rhode Island Educational Media Assn. Memb. 350. Term of Office. June 1994–May 1995. Publication. *RIEMA Newsletter* (5 per year). *Ed.* Bette G. Dion, 8 Evelyn Dr., Bristol 02809. Tel. 401-253-9345.

Pres. Paul Venancio, Middletown School Dept., Aquidenck Ave., Middletown 02842. Tel. 401-846-6395; *V.P.* Karen M. Shore, 27 Nancy St., Pawtucket 02860. Tel. 401-722-2108.; *Secy.* Patricia Menoche, Tiverton Middle School, 10 Quintal Dr., Tiverton 02878. Tel. 401-624-6668; *Treas.* Livia Giroux, West Warwick H.S., Webster Knight Dr., West Warwick 02893. Tel. 401-828-6596; *Memb. Chair* Michael Mello, 486 Water St., Portsmouth 02871. Tel. 401-683-4499, FAX 401-683-5204.

Address correspondence to the association, Box 762, Portsmouth 02871.

South Carolina

South Carolina Assn. of School Libns. Memb. 1,128. Term of Office. June 1994–May 1995. Publication. *Media Center Messenger* (5 per year).

Pres. Elisabeth Hall, Arden Elementary School, 1300 Ashley St., Columbia 29203. Tel. 803-735-3400; *Pres.-Elect* Anne Shaver, Greenville County Schools, Box 2848, Greenville. 29602. Tel. 803-241-3530; *Exec. Secy.* David Cobb, Box 2442, Columbia 29202. Tel. 803-822-5640.

Address correspondence to the executive secretary.

South Dakota

South Dakota School Lib. Media Assn., Section of the South Dakota Lib. Assn. and South Dakota Education Assn. Term of Office. Oct. 1994–Oct. 1995.

Pres. Maritta Brown; *Pres.-Elect* Kitty Kringen; *Secy.-Treas.* Rosalie Aslesen, Spearfish H.S., Spearfish 57783. Tel. 605-642-2612, FAX 605-642-8816.

Address correspondence to the secretary-treasurer.

Tennessee

Tennessee Assn. of School Libns., Tennessee Education Assn. Memb. 450. Term of Office. Nov. 1993–July 1995. Publication. *Footnotes* (q.).

Pres. Donna Garrett, 1784 Old Mill Rd., Germantown 38138; *V.P./Pres.-Elect* Yuvonne Joslin, 3900 Kings Rd., Nashville 37218; *Secy.* Cathy Cathay, Rte. 13, Box 39, Crossville 38555; *Treas.* Patty Williams, 2601 Brighton, Kingsport 37660.

Address correspondence to the president.

Texas

Texas Assn. of School Libns. Memb. 2,905. Term of Office. Apr. 1994–Apr. 1995. Publication. *Media Matters* (3 per year).

Chair Marian R. Staton, 6007 Rutgers St., Amarillo 79109. Tel. 806-622-0293.

Address correspondence to an officer or to the association, 3355 Bee Cave Rd., Suite 401, Austin 78746. Tel. 512-328-1518.

Utah

Utah Educational Lib. Media Assn. Memb. 351. Term of Office. Mar. 1995–Feb. 1996. Publication. *UELMA Newsletter* (5 per year). *Pres.* Carolyn Derricott, West Jordan H.S., 8136 S. 2700 W., West Jordan 84088. Tel. 801-565-7576; *1st V.P.* Richard Siddoway, Electronic High School—USOE, 250 E. 500 South, Salt Lake City 84111. Tel. 801-538-7500; *2nd V.P.* Gary Temple, Fairfield Jr. H.S., 951 N. Fairfield Rd., Kaysville 84037. Tel. 801-546-7370; *Exec. Secy.* Larry Jeppesen, Box 117, Wellsville 84339. Tel. 801-245-6008. *Secy.* Dennis Morgan, Riverview Jr. H.S., 751 W. Tripp Lane, Murray 84123. Tel. 801-264-7406; *Treas.* Jan Staheli, Canyon Crest Elementary, 4664 N. Canyon Rd., Provo 84604. Tel. 801-221-9873.

Address correspondence to the executive secretary.

Vermont

Vermont Educational Media Assn. Memb. 203. Term of Office. May 1994–May 1995. Publication. *VEMA News* (q.).
Pres. Mary Prior, Barnet Elementary School, W. Barnet Rd., Barnet, VT 05821. Tel. 802-633-4978; *Pres.-Elect* Holly Kruse, Cabot School, Cabot 05647. Tel. 802-563-2289; *Secy.* Dianne Wyllie, Teacher Learning Center, 7 Cherry St., Saint Johnsbury 05819. Tel. 802-748-4569; *Treas.* Patricia Nelson, Berlin Elementary School, R.D. 4, Box 2060, Montpelier 05602. Tel. 802-223-2796.

Address correspondence to the president.

Virginia

Virginia Educational Media Assn. Memb. 1,100. Term of Office. Oct. 1994–Oct. 1995. Publications. *Mediagram* (q.); *VEMA Journal* (s. ann.).
Pres. Verley Dotson, Box 163, Wolford, VA 24658. Tel. 703-566-8334, FAX 703-566-7738; *Pres.-Elect* Arline Schmidt, 6051 Clerkenwell Ct., Burke 22015. Tel. 703-978-8699, FAX 703-978-6728; *Secy.* Melinda Younger; *Treas.* Ann Martin.

Address correspondence to the president.

Washington

Washington Lib. Media Assn. Memb. 1,200. Term of Office. Oct. 1994–Oct. 1995. Publications. *The Medium* (3 per year); *The Message* (s.ann.). *Ed.* Mary Lou Gregory, 711 Spruce St., Hoquiam 98550. Tel. 206-533-4897.
Pres. Joanne Sheely, 1312 Dayton Ave. N.E., Renton 98056. Tel. 206-271-1690; *Pres.-Elect* Eve Datisman, Box 1965, Forks 98331. Tel. 360-374-6895; *V.P.* Paul Christensen, Box 50, Indianaola 98342. Tel. 360-297-2965; *Secy.* JoAnn Ekstrom, Box 322, Newman Lake 99025. Tel. 509-328-0663; *Treas.* Barbara Baker, Box 1413, Bothell 98041. Tel. 206-823-0836.

Address correspondence to the president.

West Virginia

West Virginia Educational Media Assn. Memb. 150. Term of Office. Apr. 1994–Apr. 1995. Publication. *WVEMA Focus.*
Pres. Martha Danzig, North County H.S., Learning Resource Center, Rte. 2, Box 86, Weston 26452. Tel. 304-269-8315, Ext. 127.

Address correspondence to the president.

Wisconsin

Wisconsin Educational Media Assn. Memb. 968. Term of Office. Apr. 1994–Apr. 1996. Publications. *Dispatch* (6 per year); *Wisconsin Ideas in Media* (ann.).
Pres. Terri Iverson, 1835 Ridgeview Acres, Platteville 53818. Tel. 608-822-3276, FAX 608-822-3828; *Pres.-Elect* Helen Adams, 7743 Hwy. 66, Rosholt 54473. Tel. 715-592-4614, FAX 715-677-3543.

Address correspondence to the president.

Wyoming

Section of School Library Media Personnel, Wyoming Lib. Assn. Memb. 80. Term of Office. Oct. 1994–Oct. 1995.
Chair Rod Knudson, Hulett School, Box 127, Hulett 82720. Tel. 307-467-5947, FAX 307-467-5280.

Address correspondence to the chairperson.

International Library Associations

Inter-American Association of Agricultural Librarians and Documentalists—AIBDA

c/o IICA-CIDIA, Apdo. 55, 2200 Coronado, Costa Rica
(506) 229-0222, FAX 229-4741/229-2659

Object

To serve as liaison among the agricultural librarians and documentalists of the Americas and other parts of the world; to stimulate the exchange of information and experiences through technical publications and meetings; to promote the improvement of library services in the field of agriculture and related sciences; to seek the professional improvement of the agricultural librarians and documentalists of Latin America and the Caribbean.

Officers

Exec. Secy. Ghislaine Poitevien.

Publications

AIBDA Actualidades (irreg.).
Boletín Especial (irreg.).
Boletín Informativo (3 per year).
Revista AIBDA (2 per year).

International Association of Agricultural Information Specialists

c/o J. van der Burg, President
CIRAD/CIDARC, B.P. 5035, 34032 Montpellier Cedex 1, France
67-61-58-00, FAX 67-61-58-20

Object

The association shall, internationally and nationally, promote agricultural library science and documentation as well as the professional interest of agricultural librarians and documentalists. Founded 1955.

Membership

Memb. 600+. Dues (Inst.) $80; (Indiv.) $30.

Officers

Pres. J. van der Burg, CIRAD/CIDARC, B.P. 5035, 34032 Montpellier Cedex 1, France.

Publications

Quarterly Bulletin of the IAALD (memb.).
World Directory of Agricultural Information Resource Centres.

International Association of Law Libraries

c/o Covington & Burling, 1201 Pennsylvania Ave. N.W., Washington, DC 20044-7566
202-662-6152, FAX 202-662-6291

Object

IALL is a worldwide organization of librarians, libraries, and other persons or institutions concerned with the acquisition and use of legal information emanating from sources other than their jurisdictions, and from multinational and international organizations. IALL's basic purpose is to facilitate the work of librarians who must acquire, process, organize, and provide access to foreign legal materials. IALL has no local chapters but maintains liaison with national law library associations in many countries and regions of the world.

Membership

Over 500 members in more than 50 countries on five continents.

Officers

Pres. Katalin Balazs-Veredy (Hungary); *1st V P* Larry Wenger (USA); *2nd V.P.* Jurgen Godan (Germany); *Secy.* Roberta Shaffer (USA); *Treas.* Marie-Louise Bernal (USA).

Board Members

Bruitt Kjolstad (Switzerland); June Renie (Trinidad); Adolf Sprudzs (USA); Raimund-Ekkhard Walter (Germany); Jacqueline Elliott (Australia); Joachim Schwietzke (Germany); Josep Sort Tico (Spain).

Publications

International Journal of Legal Information (3 per year; US$55 for individuals; $80 for institutions).

Committee Chairpersons

Constitution and Bylaws. Jurgen Godan (Germany).

Nominations. Larry Wenger (USA).

International Association of Metropolitan City Libraries

c/o Charles W. Hunsberger, Secretary-Treasurer
Box 73221, Las Vegas, NV 89170-3221

Object

INTAMEL is a platform for professional communication and information for libraries of cities with 400,000 or more inhabitants.

Membership

More than 100 members in approximately 40 countries.

Officers (1993–1995)

Pres. Edwin S. Holmgren, New York Public Lib., 455 Fifth Ave., New York, NY 10016; *Secy.-Treas.* Charles W. Hunsberger, Box 73221, Las Vegas, NV 89170-3221.

Publications

Annual International Statistics of City Libraries (INTAMEL).
INTAMEL Newsletter.
Various lecture papers.

International Association of Music Libraries, Archives and Documentation Centres (IAML)

c/o Alison Hall, Secretary-General
Cataloging Dept., Carleton University Library
1125 Colonel By Drive, Ottawa, Ont. K15 5B6, Canada
FAX 1-613-788-2750

Object

To promote the activities of music libraries, archives, and documentation centers and to strengthen the cooperation among them; to promote the availability of all publications and documents relating to music and further their bibliographical control; to encourage the development of standards in all areas that concern the association; and to support the protection and preservation of musical documents of the past and the present.

Membership

Memb. 1,900.

Board Members (1992–1995)

Pres. Don L. Roberts, Music Lib., Northwestern Univ., Evanston, IL 60208; *Past*

Pres. Catherine Massip, Dir., Département de la Musique, Bibliothèque Nationale, 58 Rue Richelieu, F-75084 Paris Cedex 02, France; *V.P.s* Hugh Cobbe, Music Libn., British Lib., Great Russell St., London WC1B 3DG, England; Lenore Coral, 1309 E. State St., Ithaca, NY 14850; Wolfgang Krueger, Heumadener Str. 23, D-73760 Ostfildern 4 (Kemnat), Germany; *Secy.-Gen.* Veslemöy Heintz, Svenskt Musikhistoriskt Arkiv, Box 16326, S-103 26 Stockholm, Sweden; *Treas.* Pamela Thompson, Head Libn., Royal College of Music, Prince Consort Rd., London SW7 2BS, England.

Publication

Fontes Artis Musicae (4 per year; memb.). *Ed.* Susan T. Sommer, New York Public Lib. for the Performing Arts, 111 Amsterdam Ave., New York, NY 10023-7498.

Professional Branches

Archives and Music Documentation Centres Branch. Inger Enquist, Svensk Musikhistoriskt Arkiv, Box 16326, S-103 26 Stockholm, Sweden.

Broadcasting and Orchestra Libraries. Helen Faulkner, 26 Vere Rd., Brighton, Sussex BN1 4NR, England.

Libraries in Music Teaching Institutions. Michèle Lancelin, Bibliothèque du Conservatoire National de Région, 22 Rue de la Belle Feuille, F-92100 Boulogne, France.

Public Libraries. Heikki Poroila, Vantaa City Lib., Box 20, SF-01301 Vantaa, Finland.

Research Libraries. Hugh Cobbe, Music Libn., British Lib., Great Russell St., London WC1B 3DG, England.

International Association of Orientalist Librarians

c/o Kenneth Klein, Secretary-Treasurer
East Asia Library, University of Southern California
University Park, Los Angeles, CA 90089-0182
213-740-1772

Object

To promote better communication among Orientalist librarians and libraries, and others in related fields, throughout the world; to provide a forum for the discussion of problems of common interest; to improve international cooperation among institutions holding research resources for Oriental Studies. The term *Orient* specifies the Middle East, East Asia, and the South and Southeast Asia regions.

Founded in 1967 at the 27th International Congress of Orientalists (ICO) in Ann Arbor, Michigan. Affiliated with the International Federation of Library Associations and Institutions (IFLA) and International Congress for Asian and North African Studies (formerly ICO).

Officers

Pres. William S. Wong; *Secy.-Treas.* Kenneth Klein; *Ed.* Raymond D. Lum.

Publication

International Association of Orientalist Librarians Bulletin (s. ann.; memb.).

International Association of School Librarianship

c/o Jean Lowrie, Executive Secretary
Box 19586, Kalamazoo, MI 49019

Object

To encourage the development of school libraries and library programs throughout all countries; to promote the professional preparation of school librarians; to bring about close collaboration among school libraries in all countries, including the loan and exchange of literature; to initiate and coordinate activities, conferences, and other projects in the field of school librarianship. Founded 1971.

Membership

Memb. (Indiv.) 800; (Assn.) 41.

Officers and Executive Board

Pres. Lucille C. Thomas, USA; *V.P.* Gerald R. Brown, Canada; *Treas.* Donald Adcock, USA; *Exec. Secy.* Jean Lowrie, USA; *Dirs.* Beatrice Anderson, Jamaica; Kenneth Haycock, Canada; David Elaturoti,Nigeria; Gloria Hall, Bolivia; Anne Taylor, N. Ireland; Mieko Nagakura, Japan; Paul Lupton, Australia; Melvin Rainey, Fiji; Felix Tawete, Swaziland.

Publications

Books and Borrowers.
Connections: School Library Associations and Contact People Worldwide.

IASL Conference Proceedings (ann.).
IASL Monograph Series.
School Libraries Worldwide (s-ann.).

U.S. Members

American Assn. of School Libs.; Assn. de Bibliotecarios Escolares de Puerto Rico; Educational Media Assn. of New Jersey; Hawaii School Lib. Assn.; Illinois Assn. for Media in Education; Louisiana Assn. of School Libns.; Maryland Educational Media Organization; Michigan Assn. for Media in Education; Oregon Educational Media Assn.; Virginia Educational Media Assn.; Washington Lib. Media Assn.

International Association of Technological University Libraries

c/o President, Gerard A. J. S. van Marle
Twente University of Technology Library
Box 217, 7500 AE Enschede, Netherlands
31-53-892057, FAX 31-53-341578
E-mail: marlevan@utwente.nl

Object

To provide a forum where library directors can meet to exchange views on matters of current significance in the libraries of universities of science and technology. Research projects identified as being of sufficient interest may be followed through by working parties or study groups.

Membership

Ordinary, official observer, sustaining, and nonvoting associate. Membership fee is 550 kroner per year (1,450 kroner for 3 years, 2,300 kroner for 5 years). Memb. 187 (in 40 countries).

Officers and Executives

Pres. Gerard A. J. S. van Marle, Central Lib., Twente Univ., Box 217, 7500 AE Enschede, Netherlands; *Secy.* Michael Breaks, Libn., Heriot-Watt Univ., Riccarton, Edinburgh EH14 4AS, Scotland. E-mail: libmlb@vaxb. hw.ac.uk; *Treas.* Annette Winkel Schwarz, National Technological Lib. of Denmark, Anker Engelundsvej 1, DK-2800 Lyngby, Denmark; *1st V.P.* Nancy Fjällbrant, Sweden; *Membs.* Tom Cochrane, Australia; Dietmar Brandes, Germany; Sinikka Koskiala, Finland; *North American Regional Group Chair* Jay K. Lucker, USA; *Ed.* Nancy Fjällbrant, Sweden.

Publications

IATUL News (irreg.).
IATUL Proceedings (ann.).

International Council on Archives

Charles Kesckeméti, Secretary General
60 Rue des Francs-Bourgeois, F-75003 Paris, France

Object

To establish, maintain, and strengthen relations among archivists of all lands, and among all professional and other agencies or institutions concerned with the custody, organization, or administration of archives, public or private, wherever located. Established 1948.

Membership

Memb. 1,300 (representing 150 countries and territories). Dues (Indiv.) $80 or $120; (Inst.) $120; (Archives Assns.) $120 or $200; (Central Archives Directorates) $250 or $125 minimum, computed on the basis of GNP per capita.

Officers

Secy.-Gen. Charles Kesckeméti.

Publications

Archivum (ann.; memb. or subscription to K. G. Saur Verlag, Ortlerstr. 8, Postfach 70 16 20, W-8000 Munich 70, Germany).
Guide to the Sources of the History of Nations (Latin American Series, 12 vols. pub.; African Series, 14 vols. pub.; Asian Series, 13 vols. pub.).
ICA Bulletin (s. ann.; memb.).
Janus (s. ann.; memb.)
List of other publications available from the secretary general.

International Federation for Information and Documentation (FID)

Executive Director, Ben G. Goedegebuure
Box 90402, 2509 LK The Hague, Netherlands
3140671, FAX 3140667; Internet: fid-geo2.geomail.org

Object

To promote, through international cooperation, research in and development of information science, information management, and documentation, which includes inter alia the organization, storage, retrieval, repackaging, dissemination, value adding, and evaluation of information, however recorded, in the fields of science, technology, industry, social sciences, arts, and humanities.

Program

FID devotes much of its attention to corporate information; industrial, business, and finance information; information policy research; the application of information technology; information service management; the marketing of information systems and services; content analysis, for example, in the design of database systems; linking information and human resources; and the repackaging of information for specific user audiences. The following commissions, committees, and groups have been established to execute FID's program of activities: *Regional Commissions:* Commission for Western, Eastern and Southern Africa (FID/CAF), Commission for Asia and Oceania (FID/CAO), Commission for Latin America (FID/CLA), Commission for the Caribbean and North America (FID/CNA), Commission for Northern Africa and the Near East (FID/NANE), Regional Organization for Europe (FID/ROE); *Committees:* Classification Research, Education and Training, Fundamental Theory of Information, Information for Industry, Information Policies and Programmes, Intellectual Property Issues, Social Sciences Documentation and Information, Universal Decimal Classification; *Special Interest Groups:* Advisory Services for Small and Medium-Sized Enterprises; Archives and Records Management; Banking, Finance, and Insurance Information; Environmental Information; Executive Information Systems; Information for Public Administration; Quality Issues in the Information Sector; Roles, Careers, and Development of the Modern Information Professional; Marketing Systems and Services; Safety Control and Risk Management.

Publications

FID Annual Report (ann.).
FID Directory (bienn.).
FID News Bulletin (mo.) with quarterly inserts *Document Delivery Survey* and *ET Newsletter.*
FID Publications List (irreg.).
International Forum on Information and Documentation (q.).
Newsletter on Education and Training Programmes for Information Personnel (q.).
Proceedings of congresses; Universal Decimal Classification editions; manuals; directories; bibliographies on information science, documentation, mechanization, linguistics, training, and classification.

International Federation of Film Archives (FIAF)

Secretariat, 190 rue Franz Merjay, B-1180 Brussels, Belgium
32-2-343-06-91, FAX 32-2-343-76-22

Object

To facilitate communication and cooperation between its members, and to promote the exchange of films and information; to maintain a code of archive practice calculated to satisfy all national film industries, and to encourage industries to assist in the work of the federation's members; to advise its members on all matters of interest to them, especially the preservation and study of films; to give every possible assistance and encouragement to new film archives and to those interested in creating them. Founded in Paris, 1938. Affiliates: 93 (in 60 countries).

Officers

Pres. Robert Daudelin, Canada; *V.P.*s Hoos Blotkamp, Netherlands; Vladimir Opela, Czech Republic; Ivan Trujillo Bolio, Mexico; *Secy.-Gen.* Eva Orbanz, Germany; *Treas.* Clyde Jeavons, England.

Address correspondence to B. van der Elst, executive secretary, c/o the Secretariat.

Executive Committee

Officers; Hoos Blotkamp, Netherlands; José Manuel Costa, Portugal; Jan-Christopher Horak, USA; Jorge Nieto, Colombia; Vladimir Opela, Czech Republic; José Maria Prado, Spain; Guy-Claude Rochemont, France; Steven Rice, USA; Roger Smither, UK; Ivan Trujillo Bolio, Mexico.

Publications

Annual Bibliography of FIAF Members' Publications.

Bibliography of National Filmographies.

Evaluating Computer Cataloguing Systems, by Roger Smither (a guide for film archivists).

FIAF Cataloguing Rules for Film Archives.

FIAF Journal of Film Preservation.

Glossary of Filmographic Terms in English, French, German, Spanish, and Russian (a second version in 12 languages).

Handbook for Film Archives (available in English or French).

International Directory to Film & TV Documentation Sources.

International Index to Film Periodicals (cumulative volumes).

International Index to Film and Television Periodicals (microfiche service and available on CD-ROM).

International Index to Television Periodicals (cumulative volumes).

Study on the Usage of Computers for Film Cataloguing.

Technical Manual of the FIAF Preservation Commission.

International Federation of Library Associations and Institutions (IFLA)

c/o The Royal Library, Box 95312, 2509 CH The Hague, Netherlands

Object

To promote international understanding, cooperation, discussion, research, and development in all fields of library activity, including bibliography, information services, and the education of library personnel, and to provide a body through which librarianship can be represented in matters of international interest. Founded 1927.

Membership

Memb. (Lib. Assns.) 137; (Inst.) 907; (Aff.) 189; 130 countries, Sponsors: 30; 10 from USA.

Officers and Executive Board

Pres. Robert Wedgeworth, Univ. of Illinois, Urbana-Champaign; *1st V.P.* Russell Bowden, Lib. Assn., London, England; *2nd V.P.* Marta Terry, Biblioteca Nacional, Havana, Cuba; *Treas.* Warren Horton, National Lib. of Australia, Canberra, Australia; *Exec. Board* Ekaterina Genieva, Lib. for Foreign Literature, Moscow, Russia; Robert D. Stueart, GSLIS, Simmons College, Boston, Mass.; Eeva-Maija Tammekann, Lib. of Parliament, Helsinki, Finland; Sun Beixin, China Soc. of Lib. Science, Beijing, China; *Ex officio memb.* Ian M. Johnson, SLIS, Robert Gordon Inst. of Technology, Aberdeen, Scotland; *Secy.-Gen.* Leo Voogt; *Coord. Professional Activities* Winston Roberts; *IFLA Office for Universal Bibliographic Control and International MARC Program Dir.* Kurt Nowak; *Program Officer* Marie-France Plassard, c/o Deutsche Bibliothek, Frankfurt/ Main, Germany; *IFLA International Program for UAP Program Dir.* David Bradbury; *Program Officer* Graham Cornish, c/o British Lib. Document Supply Centre, Boston Spa,

Wetherby, West Yorkshire, England; *IFLA Office for Preservation and Conservation Program Dir.* M. T. Varlamoff, c/o Bibliothèque Nationale de France, Paris; *IFLA Office for University Dataflow and Telecommunications Program Dir.* Leigh Swain; *Program Officer* Paula Tallim, c/o National Lib. of Canada, Ottawa, Canada; *IFLA Office for the Advancement of Librarianship in the Third World Program Dir.* Birgitta Bergdahl, c/o Uppsala Univ. Lib., Uppsala, Sweden; *IFLA Office for International Lending Dir.* David Bradbury.

Publications

IFLA Annual.
IFLA Directory (bienn.).
IFLA Journal (q.).
IFLA Professional Reports.
IFLA Publications Series.
International Cataloguing and Bibliographic Control (q.).
PAC Newsletter.
UAP Newsletter (s. ann.).
UDT Newsletter.

American Membership

American Assn. of Law Libs.; American Lib. Assn.; Art Libs. Society of North America; Assn. for Lib. and Info. Science Education; Assn. for Population Planning/Family Planning Libs.; Assn. of Research Libs.; International Assn. of Law Libs.; International Assn. of Orientalist Libns.; International Assn. of School Libns.; Medical Lib. Assn.; Special Libs. Assn. *Institutional Membs.* There are 127 libraries and related institutions that are institutional members or affiliates of IFLA in the United States (out of a total of 907), and 60 personal affiliates (out of a total of 189).

International Organization for Standardization (ISO)

ISO Central Secretariat
1 rue de Varembé, Case Postale 56, CH-1211 Geneva 20, Switzerland

Object

To promote the development of standardization and related activities in the world with a view to facilitating international exchange of goods and services, and to developing cooperation in the sphere of intellectual, scientific, technological, and economic activity.

Officers

Pres. Eberhard Möllmann, Germany; *V.P.* B. Vaucelle, France; *Secy.-Gen.* L. D. Eicher.

Technical Work

The technical work of ISO is carried out by over 200 technical committees. These include:

ISO/TC 46—Information and documentation (Secretariat, Deutsches Institut für Normung, Burggrafenstr. 6, Postfach 1107, 1000 Berlin 30, Germany. Scope: Standardization of practices relating to libraries, documentation and information centers, indexing and abstracting services, archives, information science, and publishing.

ISO/TC 37—Terminology (principles and coordination) (Secretariat, Österreiches Normungsinstitut, Heinestr. 38, Postfach 130, A-1021 Vienna, Austria). Scope: Standardization of methods for creating, compiling, and coordinating terminologies.

ISO/IEC JTC 1 (Joint technical committee for information technology) (Secretariat, American National Standards Institute, 11 W. 42 St., 13th fl., New York, NY 10036). Scope: Standardization in the field of information technology.

Publications

Bulletin (mo.).
Catalogue (ann.).
ISO 9000 News (bi-mo.).
Memento (ann.).

Foreign Library Associations

The following list of regional and national library associations around the world is a selective one. A more complete list can be found in *International Literary Market Place* (R. R. Bowker).

Regional

Africa

Standing Conference of African Univ. Libs., c/o E. Bejide Bankole, Editor, African Journal of Academic Librarianship, Box 46, Univ. of Lagos, Yaba, Lagos, Nigeria.

The Americas

Asociación de Bibliotecas Universitarias, de Investigación e Institucionales del Caribe (Assn. of Caribbean Univ., Research and Institutional Libs.), Box S, University Station, San Juan 00931, Puerto Rico. *Exec. Secy.* Oneida R. Ortiz.

Seminar on the Acquisition of Latin American Lib. Materials, c/o *Exec. Secy.* Sharon Moynahan, General Lib., Univ. of New Mexico, Albuquerque, NM 87131-1466.

Asia

Congress of Southeast Asian Libns. IV, c/o Serafin N. Quiason, National Lib. of the Philippines, T. M. Kalaw St., 100 Ermita, Box 2926, Manila, Philippines.

The Commonwealth

Commonwealth Lib. Assn., c/o *Hon. Exec. Secy.* Norma Y. Amenu-Kpodo, Box 144, Mona, Kingston 7, Jamaica.

Standing Conference on Lib. Materials on Africa, Records Branch, Foreign and Commonwealth Office, Hanslope Park, Milton Keynes MK19 7BH, England.

Europe

LIBER–Ligue des Bibliothèques Européennes de Recherche (Assn. of European Research Libs.), c/o H.-A. Koch, Staats- und Universitätsbibliothek, Postfach 330440, 28334 Bremen, Germany.

National

Argentina

Asociación de Bibliotecarios Graduados de la República Argentina (Assn. of Graduate Libns. of Argentina), Corrientes 1642, 1° piso, Of. 22-2° cuerpo, 1042 Buenos Aires. *Pres.* Roberto Jorge Servidio; *Exec. Secy.* Ana María Peruchena Zimmermann.

Australia

Australian Council of Libs. and Info. Services, Box E202, Queen Victoria Terrace, Canberra, ACT 2600. *Pres.* Tom Cochrane; *Exec. Officer* Gordon Bower.

Australian Lib. and Info. Assn., Box E441, Queen Victoria Terrace, Canberra, ACT 2600. *Exec. Dir.* Virginia Walsh.

Australian Society of Archivists, Box 83, O'Connor, ACT 2601. *Pres.* Chris Coggin; *Secy.* Jennifer Davidson.

Council of Australian State Libs., c/o State Lib. of Queensland, Queensland Cultural Centre, South Brisbane, Qld. *Chair* D. H. Stephens.

Austria

Büchereiverband Österreichs (Assn. of Austrian Public Libs. and Libns.), *Chair* Franz Pscher; *Secy.* Heinz Buchmüller, Lange Gasse 37, A-1080 Vienna.

Österreichische Gesellschaft für Dokumentation und Information (Austrian Society for Documentation and Info.), c/o Österreichisches Normungsinstitut, Heinestrasse 38, A-1021 Vienna.

Vereinigung Österreichischer Bibliothekare (Assn. of Austrian Libns.), Innrain 50, A-6010 Innsbruck. *Pres.* Walter Neuhauser; *Secy.* Mag Eva Ramminger.

Bangladesh

Lib. Assn. of Bangladesh, c/o Lib. Training Inst., Bangladesh Central Public Lib., Shahbagh, Ramna, Dacca 1000. *Pres.* A. K. M. Abdur Nur; *Gen. Secy.* M. Shamsul Islam Khan.

Barbados

Lib. Assn. of Barbados, Box 827E, Bridgetown. *Pres.* Shirley Yearwood; *Secy.* Hazelyn Devonish.

Belgium

Archives et Bibliothèques de Belgique/ Archief- en Bibliotheekwezen in België (Archives and Libs. of Belgium), 4 Blvd. de l'Empereur, 1000 Brussels. FAX 02-519-5533. *Gen. Secy.* Tony Verschaffel.

Association Belge de Documentation/Belgische Vereniging voor Documentatie (Belgian Assn. for Documentation), Blvd. L. Schmidt-Iaan 119, B. 3, B-1040 Brussels. *Pres.* Jean-Louis Janssens; *Secy.* Philippe Laurent.

Association Professionnelle des Bibliothécaires et Documentalistes, B.P. 31, B-1070 Brussels. *Pres.* Michel Gilles; *Secy.* Georges Lecocq.

Institut d'Enseignement Supérieur Social de la Communauté Française de Belgique, Section Bibliothécaires-Documentalistes-Gradués (State Inst. of Higher Social Education, Libn., and Documentalist Section), Rue de l'Abbaye 26, B-1050 Brussels. *Dir.* Roselyne Simon-Saint-Hubert.

Vlaamse Vereniging voor Bibliotheek-, Archief-, en Documentatiewezen (Flemish Assn. of Libns., Archivists, and Documentalists), Goudbloemstraat 10-12, B-2060 Antwerp. *Pres.* Erwin Pairon; *Gen. Secy.* Relinde Raedmaekers.

Belize

Belize Lib. Assn., c/o Central Lib., Bliss Inst., Box 287, Belize City. *Pres.* H. W. Young; *Secy.* Robert Hulse.

Bolivia

Asociación Boliviana de Bibliotecarios (Bolivian Lib. Assn.), c/o Biblioteca y Archivo Nacional, Calle Bolívar, Sucre.

Bosnia and Herzegovina

Društvo bibliotekara Bosne i Hercegovine (Libns. Society of Bosnia and Herzegovina), Obala v Stepe 42, 7100 Sarajevo. *Pres.* Neda Cukac.

Botswana

Botswana Lib. Assn., Box 1310, Gaborone. *Chair* Amos P. Thapisa; *Secy.* Edwin Qabose.

Brazil

Associação dos Arquivistas Brasileiros (Assn. of Brazilian Archivists), 9-sala 1004, Rio de Janeiro 20091-020. Tel./FAX 21-233-7142. *Pres.* Lia Temporal Malcher; *Secy.* Laura Regina Xavier.

Brunei

Persatuan Perpustakaan Kebangsaan Negara Brunei (National Lib. Assn. of Brunei), c/o Language and Literature Bureau Lib., Jalan Elizabeth II, Bandar Seri Begawan.

Bulgaria

Sâjuz na Bibliotechnite i Informazionnite Rabotnitzi (Union of Libns. and Info. Officers), Box 269, Sofia 1000. *Pres.* Tatyana Yanakieva.

Cameroon

Association des Bibliothécaires, Archivistes, Documentalistes et Muséographes du Cameroon (Assn. of Libns., Archivists, Documentalists and Museum Curators of Cameroon), Université de Yaounde, Bibliothèque Universitaire, B.P. 337, Yaounde.

Canada

Bibliographical Society of Canada/La Société Bibliographique du Canada, Box 575, Postal Sta. P, Toronto, ON M5S 2T1. *Secy.* Anne Dondertman.

Canadian Assn. for Info. Science/Association Canadienne de Science de l'Information, Univ. of Toronto, 140 Saint George St., Toronto, ON M5S 1A1.

Canadian Council of Lib. Schools/Conseil Canadien des Ecoles de Bibliothéconomie, c/o *Pres.* Adele M. Fasick, Faculty of Lib. and Info. Science, Univ. of Toronto, 140 Saint George St., Toronto, ON M5S 1A1.

Canadian Lib. Assn., c/o *Exec. Dir.* Karen Adams, 200 Elgin St., Suite 602, Ottawa, ON K2P 1L5. (For detailed information on the Canadian Lib. Assn. and its divisions, see "National Library and Information-Industry Associations, United States and Canada;" for information on the library associations of the provinces of Canada, see "State, Provincial, and Regional Library Associations.")

Chile

Colegio de Bibliotecarios de Chile AG (Chilean Lib. Assn.), Diagonal Paraguay 383, Torre II, Santiago. *Pres.* Esmerelda Ramos Ramos; *Secy.* Mónica Núñez Navarrete.

China

Chinese Society of Lib. Science, 39 Bai Shi Qiao Rd., Beijing 100081. FAX 1-841-2971. *Pres.* Liu Deyou.

Colombia

Asociación Colombiana de Bibliotecarios (Colombian Lib. Assn.), Calle 10, No. 3-16, Apdo. Aéreo 30883, Bogota.

Costa Rica

Asociación Costarricense de Bibliotecarios (Costa Rican Assn. of Libns.), Apdo. 3308, San Jose. *Secy.-Gen.* Nelly Kopper.

Croatia

Hrvatsko Bibliotekarsko Društvo (Croation Lib. Assn.), National and Univ. Lib., Marulićev trg 21, 41000 Zagreb. FAX 41-426-676. *Pres.* Aleksandra Horvat; *Secy.* Daniela Živković.
Lib. Assn. of Cuba, Biblioteca Nacional José Martí, Ave. de Independencia e 20 de Mayo y Aranguren, Plaza de la Revolución José Martií, Apdo. 6881, Havana. *Pres.* Marta Terry González.

Cyprus

Kypriakos Synthesmos Vivliothicarion (Lib. Assn. of Cyprus), Box 1039, Nicosia. *Pres.* Costas D. Stephanon; *Secy.* Paris G. Rossos.

Czech Republic

Svaz Knihovníkía Informačních Pracovníkù Ceské Republiky (Assn. of Lib. and Info. Professionals of the Czech Republic), Klementinum 190, 110 01 Prague 1. FAX 2-261-775.
Ústřední Knihovnická Rada ČR (Central Lib. Council of the Czech Republic), Valdštejnské Nám. 4, Prague 1. FAX 2-532-185. *Pres.* Jaroslav Vyčichio; *Secy.* Adolf Knoll.

Denmark

Arkivforeningen (Archives Society), Rigsarkivet, Rigsdagsgarden 9, DK-1218 Copenhagen K. FAX 3315-3239. *Pres.* Tyge Krogh; *Secy.* Charlotte Steinmark.
Bibliotekarforbundet (Union of Libns.), Lindevangs Allé 2, DK-2000 Frederiksberg. FAX 3888-3206. *Pres.* Elsebeth Tank.
Danmarks Biblioteksforening (Danish Lib. Assn.), Telegrafvej 5, DK-2750 Ballerup. FAX 4468-1103. *Dir.* F. Ettrup.
Danmarks Forskningsbiblioteksforening (Danish Research Lib. Assn.), Danmarks Tekniske Bibliotek, Anker Engelundsvej 1, DK-2800 Lyngby. *Pres.* Lars Bjørnshauge; *Secy.* Aase Lindahl.
Danmarks Skolebiblioteksforening (Assn. of Danish School Libns.), Vesterbrogade 20, DK-1620 Copenhagen V. FAX 3325-3223. *Chief Exec.* Bente Frost.

Dominican Republic

Asociación Dominicana de Bibliotecarios (Dominican Assn. of Libns.), c/o Biblioteca Nacional, Plaza de la Cultura, Cesar Nicolás Penson 91, Santo Domingo. *Pres.* Prospero J. Mella-Chavier; *Secy.-Gen.* V. Regús.

Ecuador

Asociación Ecuatoriana de Bibliotecarios (Ecuadoran Lib. Assn.), Casa de la Cultura Ecuatoriana "Benjamin Carrión," Apdo. 67, Avda. 6 de Diciembre 794, Quito. *Pres.* Eulalia Galarza.

Egypt

Egyptian Assn. for Lib. and Info. Science, c/o Dept. of Archives, Librarianship and Info. Science, Faculty of Arts, Univ. of Cairo, Cairo. *Pres.* M. El-Shenity; *Secy.* Hamed Diab.

El Salvador

Asociación de Bibliotecarios de El Salvador (El Salvador Lib. Assn.), c/o Biblioteca Nacional, 8A Avda. Norte y Calle Delgado, San Salvador.
Asociación General de Archivistas de El Salvador (Assn. of Archivists of El Salvador), Archivo General de la Nación, Palacio Nacional, San Salvador.

Ethiopia

Ye Ethiopia Betemetshaft Serategnoch Mahber (Ethiopian Lib. Assn.), Box 30530, Addis Ababa. *Pres.* Adhana Mengsteab; *Secy.* Befekadu Debela.

Fiji

Fiji Lib. Assn., Govt. Bldgs., Box 2292, Suva. FAX 300-830. *Secy.* Ilisapeci Gukilau Kuruvoli.

Finland

Suomen Kirjastoseura/Finlands Biblioteksförening (Finnish Lib. Assn.), Museokatu 18-A-5, SF-00100 Helsinki. FAX 90-441-345. *Pres.* Mirja Ryyanen; *Secy.-Gen.* Tuula Haavisto.

Tietopalveluseura/Samfundet för Informationstjänst i Finland (Finnish Society for Info. Services), Harakantie 2, SF-02600 Espoo.

France

Association des Archivistes Français (Assn. of French Archivists), 60 Rue des Francs-Bourgeois, F-75141 Paris Cedex 03. *Pres.* Jean-Luc Eichenlaub; *Secy.* Jean LePottier.

Association des Bibliothécaires Français (Assn. of French Libns.), 7 Rue des Lions-Saint-Paul, F-75004 Paris. FAX 4887-9713. *Pres.* F. Danset.

Association des Professionnels de l'Information et de la Documentation (French Assn. of Info. and Documentation Professionals), 25 Rue Claude Tillier, F-75012 Paris. *Pres.* Jean Michel; *Gen. Secy.* Eric Sutter.

Germany

Arbeitsgemeinschaft der Spezialbibliotheken (Assn. of Special Libs.), c/o M. Schwarzer, Kekulé-Bibliothek, Bayer AG, 51373 Leverkusen-Bayerwerk. *Chair* Wolfrudolf Laux; *Secretariat Dir.* Marianne Schwarzer.

Deutsche Gesellschaft für Dokumentation (German Society for Documentation), Hanauer Landstr. 126-128, 6000 Frankfurt-am-Main 1. FAX 69-490-9096. *Pres.* Arnoud de Kemp.

Deutscher Bibliotheksverband (German Lib. Assn.), Bundesallee 184-185, 10717 Berlin. FAX 30-850-5100. *Pres.* Jochen Dieckmann.

Verein der Bibliothekare an Öffentlichen Bibliotheken (Assn. of Libns. at Public Libs.), Postfach 1324, 72703 Reutlingen. FAX 7121-300-433. *Pres.* Konrad Umlauf; *Secy.* Katharina Boulanger.

Verein der Diplom-Bibliothekare an Wissenschaftlichen Bibliotheken (Assn. of Certified Libns. at Academic Libs.), c/o *Chair* Marianne Saule, Universitätsbibliothek, Universitätsstr. 31, 93053 Regensburg.

Verein Deutscher Archivare (Assn. of German Archivists), Westphälisches Archivamt, 48133 Munster. FAX 251-591-269. *Chair* Norbert Reimann.

Verein Deutscher Bibliothekare (Assn. of German Libns.), Postfach 4020, 55030 Mainz. FAX 6131-393-822. *Pres.* Andreas Anderhub; *Secy.* Monika Hagenmaier-Farnbauer.

Ghana

Ghana Lib. Assn., Box 4105, Accra. *Pres.* E. S. Asiedo; *Secy.* P. S. Hughes.

Great Britain

See United Kingdom.

Greece

Enosis Hellinon Bibliothekarion (Greek Lib. Assn.), Skouleniou 4, 10561 Athens. *Pres.* K. Xatzopoulou; *Gen. Secy.* A. Solomou.

Guatemala

Asociación Bibliotecológica de Guatemala (Lib. Assn. of Guatemala), c/o Dir., Biblioteca Nacional de Guatemala, 5 Ave. 7-26, Zona 1, Guatemala City. *Dir.* Flory de Borja.

Guyana

Guyana Lib. Assn., c/o National Lib., 76-77 Main St., Box 10240, Georgetown. *Pres.* Hetty London; *Secy.* William Daly.

Honduras

Asociación de Bibliotecarios y Archiveros de Honduras (Assn. of Libns. and Archivists of Honduras), 11a Calle, 1 y 2a Avdas. No. 105, Comayagüela DC, Tegucigalpa. *Pres.* Fransisca de Escoto Espinoza; *Secy.-Gen.* Juan Angel R. Ayes.

Hong Kong

Hong Kong Lib. Assn., GPO 10095, Hong Kong. *Pres.* Mary Leong; *Hon. Secy.* Edward Spodick.

Hungary

Magyar Könyvtárosok Egyesülete (Assn. of Hungarian Libns.), Szabó Ervin tér 1, H-1088 Budapest. Tel./FAX 1-118-2050. *Pres.* Tibor Horváth; *Secy.* István Papp.

Iceland

Bókavardafélag Islands (Icelandic Lib. Assn.), Box 1497, 121 Reykjavik. *Pres.* Hildur Gudrun Eythordóttir; *Secy.* E. R. Gudmundsdóttir.

India

Indian Assn. of Special Libs. and Info. Centres, P-291, CIT Scheme 6M, Kankurgachi, Calcutta 700054.
Indian Lib. Assn., Dr. Mukerjee Nagar, A/40-41, Flat 201, Ansal Bldg., Delhi 110009. *Pres.* C. P. Vashishth; *Gen. Secy.* A. P. Gakhar.

Indonesia

Ikatan Pustakawan Indonesia (Indonesian Lib. Assn.), Jl Imam Bonjol 7, Box 3624, Jakarta 10002. FAX 21-310-3554. *Pres.* M. H. Prakoso.

Iraq

Iraqi Lib. Assn., c/o National Lib., Bab-el-Muaddum, Baghdad. *Dir.* Abdul Hameed Al-Alawehi.

Ireland

Cumann Leabharlann Na h-Eireann (Lib. Assn. of Ireland), 53 Upper Mount St., Dublin 2. FAX 1-761-628. *Pres.* B. Doran; *Hon. Secy.* B. Teeling.

Israel

Israel Lib. Assn., Box 303, Tel Aviv 61002. *Chair* Awaham Vilner; *Secy.* R. Eidelstein.
Israel Society of Special Libs. and Info. Centers, Box 43074, Tel Aviv 61430. *Chair* Liliane Frenkiel.

Italy

Associazione Italiana Biblioteche (Italian Lib. Assn.), C.P. 2461, I-00100 Rome AD. Tel./FAX 6-446-3532. *Chair* Rossella Caffo; *Secy.* Luca Bellingeri.

Ivory Coast

Association pour le Développement de la Documentation des Bibliothèques et Archives de la Côte d'Ivoire (Assn. for the Development of Documentation Libs. and Archives of the Ivory Coast), c/o Bibliothèque Nationale, B.P. V180, Abidjan. *Dir.* Ambroise Agnero; *Secy.-Gen.* Cangah Guy.

Jamaica

Jamaica Lib. Assn., Box 58, Kingston 5. *Pres.* A. Jefferson; *Secy.* G. Greene.

Japan

Joho Kagaku Gijutsu Kyôkai (Info. Science and Technology Assn.), Sasaki Bldg., 5-7 Koisikawa, 2-chome, Bunkyo-ku, Tokyo 112. FAX 3-3813-3793. *Pres.* Takuya Gondoh; *Gen. Mgr.* Yukio Ichikawa
Nihon Toshokan Kyôkai (Japan Lib. Assn.), c/o *Secy.-Gen.* Reiko Sakagawa, 1-10 Taishido, 1-chome, Setagaya-ku, Tokyo 154. FAX 3-3421-7588.
Senmon Toshokan Kyôgikai (Japan Special Libs. Assn.), c/o National Diet Lib., 10-1 Nagata-cho, 1-chome, Chiyoda-ku, Tokyo

100. FAX 3-3597-9104. *Pres.* Rokuro Ishikawa; *Exec. Dir.* Naotake Ito.

Jordan

Jordan Lib. Assn., Box 6289, Amman. *Pres.* Anwar Akroush; *Secy.* Yousra Abu Ajamich.

Kenya

Kenya Lib. Assn., Box 46031, Nairobi. FAX 254-336-885. *Chair* Peter S. Weche; *Secy.* Damaris Ng'ang'a.

Korea (Democratic People's Republic of)

Lib. Assn. of the Democratic People's Republic of Korea, Box 200, Central District, Pyongyang. *Exec. Secy.* Li Geug.

Korea (Republic of)

Korean Lib. Assn., c/o *Exec. Dir.* Dae Kwon Park, 60-1 Panpo 2 Dong, Box 2041, Seo-cho-ku, Seoul. *Pres.* Ilyo-Soon Song.

Laos

Association des Bibliothécaires Laotiens (Assn. of Laotian Libns.), c/o Direction de la Bibliothèque Nationale, Ministry of Education, B.P. 704, Vientiane. *Dir.* Somthong.

Latvia

Lib. Assn. of Latvia, Latvian National Lib., Kr. Baronaiela 14, 1423 Riga. Tel./FAX 132-280-851. *Pres.* Aldis Ábele.

Lebanon

Lebanese Lib. Assn., c/o American Univ. of Beirut, Univ. Lib./Gifts and Exchange, Box 113/5367, Beirut. *Pres.* Ma'rouf Rafi'.

Lesotho

Lesotho Lib. Assn., Private Bag A26, Maseru 100. *Chair* E. M. Nthunya; *Secy.* M. M. Moshoeshoe.

Malawi

Malawi Lib. Assn., Box 429, Zomba. *Chair* Ralph Masanjika; *Secy.* Flossie A. Matenje.

Malaysia

Persatuan Perpustakaan Malaysia (Lib. Assn. of Malaysia), Box 12545, 50782 Kuala Lumpur. *Pres.* Chew Wing Foong; *Secy.* Leni Abdul Latif.

Mali

Association Malienne des Bibliothécaires, Archivistes et Documentalistes (Mali Assn. of Libns., Archivists, and Documentalists), c/o Bibliothèque Nationale du Mali, Ave. Kasse Keïta, B.P. 159, Bamako. *Dir.* Mamadou Konoba Keita.

Malta

Ghaqda Bibljotekarji/Lib. Assn. (Valletta), c/o Public Lib., Florianna. *Chair* Joe Grima; *Secy.* Joseph Debattista.

Mauritania

Association Mauritanienne des Bibliothécaires, Archivistes et Documentalistes (Mauritanian Assn. of Libns., Archivists, and Documentalists), c/o Bibliothèque Nationale, B.P. 20, Nouakchott. *Pres.* O. Diouwara; *Secy.* Sid' Ahmed Fall dit Dah.

Mauritius

Mauritius Lib. Assn., c/o The British Council, Royal Rd., Box 11, Rose Hill. FAX 549-553. *Pres.* K. Appadoo; *Secy.* S. Rughoo.

Mexico

Asociación Mexicana de Bibliotecarios (Mexican Assn. of Libns.), Apdo. 27-651, Admin. de Correos 27, 06760 Mexico, D.F. *Pres.* Estela Morales; *Secy.* Elías Cid Ramírez.

Nepal

Nepal Lib. Assn., c/o National Lib., Pulchowk, Lalitpur. *Libn.* Shusila Dwivedi.

The Netherlands

Nederlandse Vereniging van Bibliothecarissen, Documentalisten en Literatuur Onderzoekers (Netherlands Libns. Society), Verenigingsbureau, Plompetorengracht 11, NL-3512 CA Utrecht. FAX 30-311-830. *Pres.* A. C. Klugkist; *Secy.* A. C. G. M. Eyffinger.

UKB–Samenwerkingsverband van de Universiteitsbibliotheken, de Koninklijke Bibliotheek en de Bibliotheek van de Koninklijke Nederlandse Akademie van Wetenschappen (Assn. of the Univ. Libs., the Royal Lib., and the Lib. of the Royal Netherlands Academy of Arts and Sciences), c/o *Exec. Secy.* J. H. de Swart, Bibliotheek Vrije Universiteit, De Boelelaan 1103, NL-1081 HV Amsterdam.

New Zealand

New Zealand Lib. and Info. Assn., c/o *Exec. Dir.* Lydia Klimovitch, Box 12-212, Wellington. FAX 4-499-1480.

Nicaragua

Asociación Nicaraguense de Bibliotecarios y Profesionales a Fines (Nicaraguan Assn. of Libns.), Apdo. postal 3257, Calle F. Guzman Bolanos, Altamira del Est, Casa 120, Managua. *Exec. Secy.* Susana Morales Hernández.

Nigeria

Nigerian Lib. Assn., c/o Polytechnic Lib., PMB 22, UI P.O., Ibadan. *Pres.* Jacob Oluwafemi Fasanya; *Secy.* L. I. Ehigiator.

Norway

Arkivarforeningen (Assn. of Archivists), Postboks 10, N-0807 Oslo. FAX 22-237-489.

Norsk Bibliotekforening (Norwegian Lib. Assn.), Malerhaugveien 20, N-0661 Oslo.

Norsk Fagbibliotekforening (Norwegian Assn. of Special Libs.), Malerhaugveien 20, N-0661 Oslo. FAX 22-672-368. *Chair* Else-Margrethe Bredland.

Pakistan

Pakistan Lib. Assn., c/o Pakistan Inst. of Development Economics, Univ. Campus, Box 1091, Islamabad. *Pres.* Jameel Jalibi; *Secy.-Gen.* Sadiq Ali Shan.

Panama

Asociación Panameña de Bibliotecarios (Panama Lib. Assn.), c/o Biblioteca Interamericana Simón Bolívar, Estafeta Universitaria, Panama City. *Pres.* Bexie Rodríguez de León.

Paraguay

Asociación de Bibliotecarios del Paraguay (Assn. of Paraguayan Libns.), Casilla de Correo 1505, Asuncion. *Secy.* Mafalda Cabrerar.

Peru

Asociación Peruana de Archiveros (Peruvian Assn. of Archivists), Archivo General de la Nación, Calle Manuel Cuadros s/n, Palacio de Justicia, Apdo. 3124, Lima.

Asociación Peruana de Bibliotecarios, Bellavista 561 Miraflores, Apdo. 995, Lima 18. *Pres.* Martha Fernandez de Lopez; *Secy.* Luzmila Tello de Medina.

Philippines

Assn. of Special Libs. of the Philippines, College of Public Admin. Lib., Univ. of the Philippines, Box 474, Manila D-406. *Pres.* Filamena C. Mercado; *Secy.* Edna P. Ortiz.

Bibliographical Society of the Philippines, National Lib. of the Philippines, T. M. Kalaw St., 1000 Ermita, Box 2926, Manila.

Philippine Libns. Assn., c/o National Lib. of the Philippines, Rm. 301, T. M. Kalaw St., Manila. *Pres.* Salvación M. Arlante; *Secy.* Elizabeth R. Peralejo.

Poland

Stowarzyszenie Bibliotekarzy Polskich (Polish Libns. Assn.), Ul. Konopczyńskiego 5-7, 00-953 Warsaw. *Chair* Stanislaw Czajka; *Secy.-Gen.* Dariusz Kuźmiński.

Portugal

Associaçao Portuguesa de Bibliotecários, Arquivistas e Documentalistas (Portuguese Assn. of Libns., Archivists, and Documentalists), Campo Grande 83, 1751 Lisbon. FAX 1-815-4508. *Pres.* António José Pina Falcão.

Puerto Rico

Sociedad de Bibliotecarios de Puerto Rico (Society of Libns. of Puerto Rico), Apdo. 22898, Universidad de Puerto Rico Sta., Rio Piedras 00931. *Pres.* Aura Jiménez de Panepinto; *Secy.* Olga L. Hernández.

Romania

Asociatia Bibliotecarilor din Bibliotecile Publice din România (Assn. of Public Libns. of Romania), Bibloteca National, Str. Ion Ghica 4, Bucharest. FAX 0-312-3381. *Pres.* Gheorghe-Iosif Bercan; *Secy.* Georgeta Clinca.

Russia

Lib. Council, Lenin State Lib., Prospect Kalinina 3, Moscow 101000.

Senegal

Association Sénégalaise des Bibliothécaires, Archivistes et Documentalistes (Senegalese Assn. of Libns., Archivists and Documentalists), B.P. 3252, Dakar. FAX 242-379. *Pres.* Mariétou Diongue Diop; *Secy.* Emmanuel Kabou.

Sierra Leone

Sierra Leone Assn. of Archivists, Libns., and Info. Scientists, c/o Sierra Leone Lib. Board, Box 326, Freetown. *Pres.* Deanna Thomas.

Singapore

Lib. Assn. of Singapore, c/o Branch Lib., Bukit Merah Central, Box 0693, Singapore 9115. *Hon. Secy.* Glenda Gwee.

Slovenia

Zveza Bibliotekarskih Društev Slovenije (Lib. Assn. of Slovenia), Turjaška 1, 61000 Ljubljana. FAX 61-125-0134. *Pres.* Ivan Kanic; *Exec. Sec.* Lili Hubej.

South Africa

African Lib. Assn. of South Africa, c/o Lib., Univ. of the North, Private Bag X1106, Sovenga 0727. *Secy.* Mrs. A. N. Kambule.

Spain

Asociación Española de Archiveros, Bibliotecarios, Museólogos y Documentalistas (Spanish Assn. of Archivists, Libns., Curators and Documentalists), Apdo. 14281, 28001 Madrid. *Pres.* Alonso Vicenta Cortés; *Secy.* Martín Carmen Cayetano.

Sri Lanka

Sri Lanka Lib. Assn., Professional Center, 275/75 Bauddhaloka Mawatha, Colombo 7. *Pres.* N. U. Yapa; *Secy.* Wilfred Ranasinghe.

Swaziland

Swaziland Lib. Assn., Box 2309, Mbabane. *Chair* M. R. Mavuso; *Secy.* F. K. Tawete.

Sweden

Svenska Arkivsamfundet (Swedish Assn. of Archivists), c/o Riksarkivet, Fyrverkarbacken 13-17, Box 12541, S-102 29 Stockholm. FAX 8-737-6474. *Pres.* Erik Norbert.
Svenska Bibliotekariesamfundet (Swedish Assn. of Univ. and Research Libs.), c/o Univ. College of Borås, Box 874, S-501 15 Boras. FAX 33-114-839. *Exec. Secy.* Staffan Lööf.
Sveriges Allmänna Biblioteksförening (Swedish Lib. Assn.), Box 3127, S-103 62 Stockholm. FAX 8-723-0038. *Contact* Christina Stenberg.

Switzerland

Association des Bibliothèques et Bibliothécaires Suisses/ Vereinigung Schweizerischer Bibliothekare/Associazione dei Bibliotecari Svizzeri (Assn. of Swiss Libns.), Effingerstr. 35, CH-3008 Berne. FAX 31-382-4648. *Secy.* Myriam Boussina Mercille.

Schweizerische Vereinigung für Dokumentation/Association Suisse de Documentation (Swiss Assn. of Documentation), Postfach 200, CH-3605 Thun. FAX 33-284-247. *Pres.* E. Wyss; *Secy.* Th. Brenzikofer.

Vereinigung Schweizerischer Archivare (Assn. of Swiss Archivists), Archivstr. 24, CH-3003 Berne. *Secy.* Bernard Truffer.

Taiwan

Lib. Assn. of China, c/o National Central Lib., 20 Chungshan S. Rd., Taipei. FAX 2-382-0747. *Pres.* Chen-ku Wang; *Secy.-Gen.* Teresa Wang Chang.

Tanzania

Tanzania Lib. Assn., Box 2645, Dar es Salaam. *Chair* T. E. Mlaki; *Secy.* M. Ngaiza.

Thailand

Thai Lib. Assn., 273 Vibhavadee Rangsit Rd., Phayathai, Bangkok 10400. *Pres.* M. Chavalit; *Secy.* Karnmanee Suckcharoen.

Trinidad and Tobago

Lib. Assn. of Trinidad and Tobago, Box 1275, Port of Spain. *Pres.* Jennifer Joseph; *Secy.* Jewel Matheson-Stewart.

Tunisia

Association Tunisienne des Documentalistes, Bibliothécaires et Archivistes (Tunisian Assn. of Documentalists, Libns., and Archivists), B.P. 380, R.P. Tunis. *Pres.* Ahmed Ksibi.

Turkey

Türk Küüphaneciler Derneği (Turkish Libns. Assn.), Elgün Sok-8/8, 06440 Yenisehir,
Ankara. *Pres.* Necmeddin Sefercioglu; *Gen. Secy.* S. Gürbüz.

Uganda

Uganda Lib. Assn., Box 5894, Kampala. *Chair* P. Birungi; *Secy.* L. M. Ssengero.

United Kingdom

ASLIB (The Assn. for Info. Management), Information House, 20-24 Old St., London EC1V 9AP, England. FAX 71-430-0514. *Dir.* Roger Bowes; *Contact* R. Turner.

Bibliographical Society, c/o British Lib., Great Russell St., London WC1B 3DG, England. *Hon. Secy.* Mirjam Foot.

The Lib. Assn., 7 Ridgmount St., London WC1E 7AE, England. FAX 71-436-7218. *Chief Exec.* Ross Shimmon.

Private Libs. Assn., c/o *Hon. Secy.* Frank Broomhead, 16 Brampton Grove, Kenton, Harrow, Middlesex HA3 8LG, England.

School Lib. Assn., Liden Lib., Barrington Close, Liden, Swindon, Wiltshire SN3 6HF, England. *Pres.* Frank N. Hogg; *Exec. Secy.* Valerie Fea.

Scottish Lib. Assn., Motherwell Business Centre, Coursington Rd., Motherwell ML1 1PW, Scotland. FAX 698-252-057. *Dir.* Robert Craig.

Society of Archivists, Information House, 20-24 Old St., London, EC1V 9AP, England. FAX 71-253-3942. *Exec. Secy.* P. S. Cleary.

Standing Conference of National and Univ. Libs., 102 Euston St., London NW1 2HA. FAX 71-383-3197. *Exec. Secy.* G. M. Pentelow.

Welsh Lib. Assn., c/o Publications Office, Public Lib., Dew St., Haverfordwest, Dyfed SA61 1SU, Wales. *Exec. Officer* Glyn Collins.

Uruguay

Agrupación Bibliotecológica del Uruguay (Uruguayan Lib. and Archive Science Assn.), Cerro Largo 1666, 11200 Montevideo. *Pres.* Luis Alberto Musso.

Asociación de Bibliocólogos del Uruguay, Eduardo u Haedo 2255, CC 1315, 11200 Montevideo.

Vatican City

Biblioteca Apostolica Vaticana, 00120 Vatican City, Rome. FAX 6-698-4795. *Prefect* Leonard E. Boyle

Venezuela

Colegio de Bibliotecólogos y Archivólogos de Venezuela (Assn. of Venezuelan Libns. and Archivists), Apdo. 6283, Caracas. *Pres.* O. Ruiz LaScalea.

Vietnam

Hôi Thu-Viên Viet Nam (Vietnamese Lib. Assn.), National Lib. of Viet Nam, 31 Trang Thi, 1000 Hanoi.

Zaire

Association Zairoise des Archivistes, Bibliothécaires et Documentalistes (Zaire Assn. of Archivists, Librarians, and Documentalists), B.P. 805, Kinshasa X1. *Exec. Secy.* E. Kabeba-Bangasa.

Zambia

Zambia Lib. Assn., Box 33129, Lusaka. *Chair* V. Chifwepa; *Hon. Secy.* E. M. Msadabwe.

Zimbabwe

Zimbabwe Lib. Assn., Box 3133, Harare. *Chair* A. L. Ngwenya; *Hon. Secy.* Driden Kunaka.

Directory of Book Trade and Related Organizations

Book Trade Associations, United States and Canada

For more extensive information on the associations listed in this section, see the annual edition of *Literary Market Place* (R. R. Bowker).

American Booksellers Assn. Inc., 828 S. Broadway, Tarrytown, NY 10591. Tel. 914-591-2665. *Pres.* Avin Mark Domnitz, Harry W. Schwartz Bookshops, Milwaukee, WI 53217; *V.P.* Barbara Bonds Thomas, Toad Hall, Austin, TX 78705; *Secy.* Linda Brummett, BYU Bookstore, Provo, UT 84602; *Treas.* Richard Howorth, Square Books, Oxford, MS 38655; *Publications Dir.* Dan Cullen.

American Institute of Graphic Arts, 164 Fifth Ave., New York, NY 10010. Tel. 212-807-1990, FAX 212-807-1799. *Pres.* William Drenttel; *Assoc. Dir.* Irene Bareis.

American Medical Publishers Assn. *Pres.* Mary K. Cowell, Raven Press, 1185 Ave. of the Americas, New York, NY 10036. Tel. 212-930-9500; *Secy.-Treas.* Joan Blumberg, W. B. Saunders Co., Curtis Bldg., Philadelphia, PA 19106. Tel. 215-238-7860; *Exec. Dir.* Jill Rudansky. Tel./FAX 516-423-0075.

American Printing History Assn., Box 4922, Grand Central Sta., New York, NY 10163-1005. *Pres.* Martin W. Hunter; *V.P. Programs* Anne Anninger; *V.P. Publications* Michael Peich; *V.P. Memb.* James R. Kelly; *Treas.* John Hench; *Ed., Printing History* David Pankow; *Exec. Secy.* Stephen Crook.

American Society of Indexers Inc., Box 386, Port Aransas, TX 78373. Tel. 512-749-4052, FAX 512-749-6334. *Pres.* Carolyn McGovern, 2957 Filbert Dr., Walnut Creek, CA 94598; *V.P.* Elinor Lindheimer,

Box 902, Mendocino, CA 95460-0902; *Secy.* Barbara Cohen, 1708 Ridgeland Dr., Champaign, IL 61821; *Treas.* Frances Lennie, Box 18609, Rochester, NY 14618-0609; *Contact Person* Bobbie Reeves.

American Society of Journalists and Authors, 1501 Broadway, Suite 302, New York, NY 10036. Tel. 212-997-0947, FAX 212-768-7414. *Exec. Dir.* Alexandra Cantor.

American Society of Media Photographers, 14 Washington Rd., Suite 502, Princeton Junction, NJ 08550-1033. Tel. 609-799-8300, FAX 609-799-2233. *Pres.* Matt Herron; *Exec. Dir.* Richard Weisgrau.

American Society of Picture Professionals Inc., c/o *Memb. Chair* Mindy Klarman, Macmillan/McGraw-Hill School Div., 1221 Ave. of the Americas, 15th fl., New York, NY 10020. Tel. 212-512-4326; *National Pres.* Larry Levin, Nation's Business, 1615 H St. N.W., Washington, DC 20062. Tel. 202-463-5447; *National Secy.* Judy Mason, Music St., Box 869, West Tisbury, MA 02575. Tel. 508-696-8716.

American Translators Assn., 1735 Jefferson Davis Hwy., Suite 903, Arlington, VA 22202. Tel. 703-412-1500, FAX 703-412-1501. *Pres.* Edith F. Losa; *Secy.* Anne Cordero; *Treas.* Seth Reames; *Exec. Dir.* Walter W. Bacak, Jr.

Antiquarian Booksellers Assn. of America, 50 Rockefeller Plaza, New York, NY 10020. Tel. 212-757-9395, FAX 212-459-0307. *Pres.* Robert Rulon-Miller, Jr.; *V.P.* Jennifer S. Larson; *Secy.* Jeffrey Marks;

Treas. Robert Fleck; *Exec. Dir.* Liane Wood-Thomas. Address correspondence to the executive director.

Assn. of American Publishers, 71 Fifth Ave., New York, NY 10003. Tel. 212-255-0200. *Pres.* Nicholas Veliotes; *Exec. V.P.* Thomas McKee; *V.P.s* James Lichtenberg, Roger Rogalin; *Dirs.* Barbara Meredith, Roberta Plutzik; *Washington Office* 1718 Connecticut Ave. N.W., Washington, DC 20009. Tel. 202-232-3335; *V.P.s* Michael Klipper, Carol Risher; *Dirs.* Judith Platt, Diane Rennert; *Chair* Jack Hoeft, Bantam Doubleday Dell Publishing Group; *V.Chair* Richard Robinson, Scholastic; *Treas.* Lawrence E. Levinson, Simon & Schuster; *Secy.* Alberto Vitale, Random House.

Assn. of American Univ. Presses, 584 Broadway, Suite 410, New York, NY 10012. Tel. 212-941-6610. *Pres.* Bruce Wilcox, Univ. of Massachusetts Press; *Exec. Dir.* Peter Grenquist; *Assoc. Exec. Dir.* Hollis Holmes. Address correspondence to the executive director.

Assn. of Authors' Representatives Inc., 10 Astor Place, 3rd fl., New York, NY 10003. Tel. 212-353-3709. *Pres.* Perry Knowlton; *Admin. Secy.* Ginger Knowlton.

Assn. of Book Travelers, Box 1795, New York, NY 10185. Tel. 212-206-7715. *Pres.* Paul Drougas. Address correspondence to the president.

Assn. of Canadian Publishers, 2 Gloucester St., Suite 301, Toronto, ON M4Y 1L5, Canada. Tel. 416-413-4929, FAX 416-413-4920. *Exec. Dir.* Garry Neil; *Exec. Secy.* Boa Burns. Address correspondence to the executive director.

Assn. of Jewish Book Publishers, 838 Fifth Ave., New York, NY 10021. *Pres.* Rabbi Elliot Stevens. Address correspondence to the president.

Assn. of the Graphic Arts, 330 Seventh Ave., New York, NY 10001. Tel. 212-279-2100, FAX 212-279-2104. *Pres.* William Dirzulaitis; *Dir. Ed.* Molly Connolly; *Dir. Exhibits* Carl Gessman.

Book Industry Study Group Inc., 160 Fifth Ave., New York, NY 10010. Tel. 212-929-1393, FAX 212-989-7542. *Chair* Laura Conley; *V.Chair* Richard Mathies; *Treas.* Seymour Turk; *Secy.* Robert Bell; *Managing Agent* SKP Assocs. Address correspondence to William Raggio.

Book Manufacturers Institute, 45 William St., Suite 245, Wellesley, MA 02181-4007. Tel. 617-239-0103. *Pres.* Carl Carlson, Mid-City Lithographers; *Exec. V.P.* Stephen P. Snyder. Address correspondence to the executive vice president.

Book Publicists of Southern California, 6464 Sunset Blvd., Suite 580, Hollywood, CA 90028. Tel. 213-461-3921, FAX 213-461-0917. *Pres.* Irwin Zucker; *V.P.* Sol Marshall; *Secy.* Joe Sorrentino; *Treas.* Nina Mills.

Book Week Headquarters, Children's Book Council Inc., 568 Broadway, New York, NY 10012. Tel. 212-966-1990. *Pres.* Paula Quint; *Asst. V.P.* Maria Juarez; *Chair* Louise Howton, Harcourt Brace, 525 B St., San Diego, CA 92101. Tel. 619-699-6810.

Bookbinders' Guild of New York, c/o *Secy.* Tracy Cabanis, Alfred Knopf, 201 E. 50 St., New York, NY 10022. Tel. 212-572-2004; *Pres.* Sheila Anderson, W. H. Freeman, 41 Madison Ave., New York, NY 10010. Tel. 212-576-9484; *V.P.* Linda Palladino, William Morrow and Co., 1350 Ave. of the Americas, New York, NY 10019. Tel. 212-261-6675; *Treas.* Irwin Wolf, Graphic Design Studio, 108 John St., North Massapequa, NY 11758; *Financial Secy.* Patti Froehlich, Macmillan/McGraw-Hill, 10 Union Sq. E., New York, NY 10003. Tel. 212-512-6575.

Bookbuilders of Boston Inc., 27 Wellington Dr., Westwood, MA 02090. Tel. 617-461-0298, FAX 617-326-2975. *Pres.* Ann Kimball.

Bookbuilders West, Box 7046, San Francisco, CA 94120-9727. *Pres.* Barbara Redman, Color Tech Corp., 121 Second St., 2nd fl., San Francisco, CA 94105. Tel. 415-546-4991.

Canadian Book Publishers' Council, 250 Merton St., Suite 203, Toronto, ON M4S 1B1, Canada. Tel. 416-322-7011, FAX 416-322-6999. *Pres.* Gordon S. Bain, Random House of Canada; *1st V.P.* Brian O'Donnell, Irwin Publishing; *Treas.* Andrew Nopper, Distican; *Exec. Dir.* Jacqueline Hushion; *Special Interest Groups* The

School Group, The College Group, The Trade Group.

Canadian Booksellers Assn., 301 Donlands Ave., Toronto, ON M4J 3R8, Canada. Tel. 416-467-7883, FAX 416-467-7886. *Exec. Dir.* John J. Finlay.

Catholic Book Publishers Assn. Inc., 333 Glen Head Rd., Old Brookville, NY 11545. Tel. 516-671-9342, FAX 516-759-4227; *Pres.* Peter Dwyer; *V.P.* John Thomas; *Treas.* Emilie Cerar; *Exec. Secy.* Charles A. Roth; Barbara Curran.

Chicago Book Clinic, 11 S. LaSalle St., Suite 1400, Chicago, IL 60603-1210. Tel. 312-553-2200. *Exec. Dir.* Cindy Clark; *Pres.* Sue Nisson; *Pres.-Elect* Joe Erl; *Secy.* Mark Pattis; *Treas.* Mark Tiberi.

Children's Book Council Inc., 568 Broadway, New York, NY 10012. Tel. 212-966-1990. *Pres.* Paula Quint; *Asst. V.P.* Maria Juarez; *Chair* Barbara Marcus, Scholastic, 555 Broadway, New York, NY 10012. Tel. 212-343-6100.

Christian Booksellers Assn., Box 200, Colorado Springs, CO 80901. Tel. 719-576-7880. *Pres.* William Anderson.

Copyright Society of the U.S.A., 1133 Ave. of the Americas, 33rd fl., New York, NY 10036. Tel. 212-354-6401, FAX 212-354-2847. *Pres.* Eugene L. Girden; *Administrator* Barbara Pannone.

Educational Paperback Assn., c/o *Exec. Secy.* Marilyn Abel, Box 1399, East Hampton, NY 11937. Tel. 212-879-6850. *Pres.* Sanford Jaffe, The Booksource, Saint Louis, MO 63108. Tel. 800-525-4862.

Evangelical Christian Publishers Assn., 3225 S. Hardy Dr., Suite 101, Tempe, AZ 85282. Tel. 602-966-3998, FAX 602-966-1944. *Exec. Dir.* Doug Ross.

Friendship Press, 475 Riverside Dr., New York, NY 10115-0050. Tel. 212-870-2495, FAX 212-870-2550. *Exec. Dir.* Audrey Miller; *Board of Mgrs. Pres.* Sandra Rooney.

Graphic Artists Guild Inc., 11 W. 20 St., 8th fl., New York, NY 10011-3704. Tel. 212-463-7730. *Natl. Exec. Dir.* Paul Basista; *Pres.* Karen Guancione. Address correspondence to the national executive director.

Great Lakes Booksellers Assn., c/o *Exec. Dir.* Jim Dana, Box 901, 509 Lafayette, Grand Haven, MI 49417. Tel. 616-847-2460, FAX 616-842-0051. *Pres.* Greg Wybel, Wybel Marketing, Box 970353, Ypsilanti, MI 48197; *V.P.* Susan Schenone, The Book Bag, 2600 Roosevelt Rd., Valparaiso, IN 46383.

Guild of Book Workers, 201 E. Capitol St. S.E., Washington, DC 20003. Tel. 202-544-4600. *Pres.* Franklin Mowery.

International Assn. of Printing House Craftsmen Inc., 7042 Brooklyn Blvd., Minneapolis, MN 55429-1370. Tel. 612-560-1620. *Exec. Dir.* Kevin Keane.

International Copyright Information Center, c/o Assn. of American Publishers, 1718 Connecticut Ave. N.W., 7th fl., Washington, DC 20009-1148. Tel. 202-232-3335, FAX 202-745-0694. *Dir.* Carol Risher.

International Standard Book Numbering U.S. Agency, 121 Chanlon Rd., New Providence, NJ 07974. Tel. 908-665-6700, FAX 908-665-2895. *Dir.* Emery Koltay; *Officers* Lynn Sahner, Diana Fumando, Bill McCahery, Don Riseborough, Albert Simmonds, Peter Simon.

Jewish Book Council, 15 E. 26 St., New York, NY 10010. Tel. 212-532-4949 Ext. 297, FAX 212-481-4174. *Pres.* Arthur Kurzweil; *Exec. Dir.* Carolyn Starman Hessel.

Library Binding Institute, 7401 Metro Blvd., Suite 325, Edina, MN 55439. *Exec. Dir.* Sally Grauer.

Magazine and Paperback Marketing Institute, 4000 Coolidge Ave., Baltimore, MD 21229. Tel. 410-525-3355. *Exec. V.P.* Don DeVito.

Metropolitan Lithographers Assn., 950 Third Ave., Suite 1500, New York, NY 10022. Tel. 212-838-8480. *Pres.* Frank Stillo; *Exec. Dir.* Jane Bernd.

Mid-America Publishers Assn., c/o *Exec. Dir.* Jerry Kromberg, Box 30242, Lincoln, NE 68503-0242. Tel. 402-466-9665, FAX 402-466-9093. *Pres.* Karen Adler, Two Lane Press, Kansas City, MO 64111. Tel. 816-531-3129, FAX 816-531-6113.

Mid-Atlantic Booksellers Assn., 108 S. 13 St., Philadelphia, PA 19107. Tel. 215-735-9598. *Exec. Dir.* Larry Robin.

Midwest Independent Publishers Assn., 9561 Woodridge Circle, Eden Prairie, MN 55347-2744. Tel. 612-941-5053; E-mail patjbell@aol.com; *Exec. Secy.* Pat Bell.

Miniature Book Society Inc., c/o *Pres.* Rev. Joseph L. Curran, 770 Mount Auburn St., Watertown, MA 02172. Tel. 617-924-9110; *V.P.* Arthur Keir, 506 Buell Ave., Joliet, IL 60435. Tel. 815-726-1286; *Secy.* Doris Selmer, 55 E. Arthur Ave., Arcadia, CA 91006; *Treas.* Loretta Gentile, 10 Albert St., Waltham, MA 02154.

Minnesota Book Publishers Roundtable. *Pres.* Teresa Bonner, Milkweed Editions, 430 First Ave. N., Suite 400, Minneapolis, MN 55401; *V.P.* Richard Wick, Burgess International Group, 7110 Ohms Lane, Edina, MN 55439; *Secy.-Treas.* Brad Vogt, Liturgical Press, Collegeville, MN 56321. Tel. 612-363-2538. Address correspondence to the secretary-treasurer.

Mountains and Plains Booksellers Assn., 805 LaPorte Ave., Fort Collins, CO 80521. Tel./FAX 303-484-5856. *Exec. Dir.* Lisa Knudsen; *Pres.* Kasha Songer; *V.P.* Patricia Nelson; *Secy.* Patrick Ewing; *Treas.* Lynn Mezzano.

National Assn. of College Stores, 500 E. Lorain St., Oberlin, OH 44074-1294. Tel. 216-775-7777, FAX 216-775-4769. *Pres./Treas.* Richard McDaniel; *Pres.-Elect/Secy.* Tommye Miller; *Public Relations Coord.* Jerry L. Buchs. Address correspondence to the public relations coordinator.

New England Booksellers Assn., 847 Massachusetts Ave., Cambridge, MA 02139. Tel. 617-576-3070, FAX 617-576-3091. *Pres.* Carole Horne; *Exec. Dir.* Wayne Drugan.

New Mexico Book League, 8632 Horacio Place N.E., Albuquerque, NM 87111. Tel. 505-299-8940. *Exec. Dir.* Dwight A. Myers; *Pres.* Robert R. White; *V.P.* Martha Liebert; *Treas.* C. Rittenhouse; *Ed.* Carol Myers.

New York Rights and Permissions Group, c/o *Chair* Jeanne Gough, Gale Research Inc., 835 Penobscot Bldg., Detroit, MI 48226. Tel. 313-961-6813.

Northern California Independent Booksellers Assn., 5643 Paradise Dr., Suite 12, Corte Madera, CA 94925. Tel. 415-927-3937, FAX 415-927-3971. *Exec. Dir.* Ginie Thorp.

Optical Publishing Assn., Box 21268, Columbus, OH 43221. Tel. 614-442-8805, FAX 614-442-8815, Internet: 71333,1114@ compuserve.com. *Exec. Dir.* Richard A. Bowers.

Pacific Northwest Booksellers Assn., 1510 Mill St., Eugene, OR 97401-4258. Tel. 503-683-4363. *Pres.* Marilyn Newman; *Exec. Dir.* Thom Chambliss.

Periodical and Book Assn. of America Inc., 120 E. 34 St., Suite 7K, New York, NY 10016. Tel. 212-689-4952, FAX 212-545-8328. *Pres.* Mary C. McEvoy, Lang Communications; *V.P.s* Keith Furman, New York Times Womens' Group; Will Michalopoulos, Consumer Reports; Robert Cermak, Playboy Enterprises; *Treas.* Edward Handi, Flynt Publications; *Secy.* Kathi Robold, Scientific American; *Exec. Dir.* Michael Morse; *Legal Counsel* Lee Feltman; *Advisers to the Pres.* Irwin Billman, Norman Jacobs, Adrian Lopez, Michael McCarthy, Robert Woltersdorf.

Periodical Marketers of Canada, 2 Berkeley St., Suite 503, Toronto, ON M5A 2W3, Canada. Tel. 416-363-4549, FAX 416-363-4791. *Pres.* John Seebach, Great Pacific News, 2500 Vauxhall Place, Richmond, BC V6V 1Y8, Canada. Tel. 604-278-4841, FAX 604-278-5642; *Secy.-Treas.* Steve Shepherd, Ottawa Valley News Co., Box 157, Arnprior, ON K7S 3H4, Canada. Tel. 613-623-3197; *Asst. Exec. Dir.* Janette Hatcher.

Philadelphia Book Clinic, c/o *Secy.-Treas.* Thomas Colaiezzi, 136 Chester Ave., Yeadon, PA 19050-3831. Tel. 610-259-7022.

Publishers Advertising and Marketing Assn., c/o *V.P.* Judy Murphy, Bon Appetit. Tel. 212-880-8058; *Pres.* Lee Wiggins. Tel. 212-754-2575; *Treas.* Mary Ann Petyak, Warner Books, 1271 Ave. of the Americas, New York, NY 10022. Tel. 212-522-2951.

Publishers' Publicity Assn., c/o *Pres.* Patricia Eisemann, Macmillan Publishing Co., 866 Third Ave., New York, NY 10022. Tel. 212-702-6757; *V.P.* Beth Davey, Little, Brown and Co., 1271 Ave. of the Americas, New York, NY 10020. Tel. 212-522-8063; *Secy.* Ben Petrone, Carol Publishing Group, 600 Madison Ave., New York, NY 10022. Tel. 212-418-4090; *Treas.* Lottchen Shivers, Henry Holt and Co., 115 W. 18 St., New York, NY 10011. Tel. 212-886-9269.

Religion Publishing Group, c/o *Secy.* Hargis Thomas, Oxford Univ. Press, 200 Madison Ave., New York, NY 10016. Tel. 212-679-7300 Ext. 7235. *Pres.* Elizabeth Gold, Guideposts Books, 16 E. 34 St., New York, NY 10016. Tel. 212-251-8130.

Research and Engineering Council of the Graphic Arts Industry Inc., Box 639, Chadds Ford, PA 19317. Tel. 610-388-7394, FAX 610-388-2708. *Pres.* Robert Peters; *Exec. V.P./Secy.* Brian Chapman; *Exec. V.P./Treas.* Bernard Knox; *Managing Dir.* Fred Rogers.

Southern California Booksellers Assn., Box 4176, Culver City, CA 90231-4176. *Pres.* Lise Friedman, Dutton's Brentwood Books, 11975 San Vicente Blvd., Los Angeles, CA 90049. Tel. 310-476-6263, FAX 310-471-0399.

Technical Assn. of the Pulp and Paper Industry, Technology Pk./Atlanta, Box 105113, Atlanta, GA 30348-5113. Tel. 404-446-1400. *Pres.* Jack E. Chinn; *V.P.* Dale Dill; *Exec. Dir./Treas.* W. L. Cullison.

West Coast Book People Assn., 27 McNear Dr., San Rafael, CA 94901. *Secy.* Frank Goodall. Tel. 415-459-1227, FAX 415-459-1227.

Women's National Book Assn., 160 Fifth Ave., New York, NY 10010. Tel. 212-675-7805, FAX 212-989-7542. *Pres.* Sue MacLaurin, 3554 Crownridge Dr., Sherman Oaks, CA 91403. Tel. 818-501-3925; *V.P.* Donna Paz, 212 Sloan Rd., Nashville, TN 37209, Tel. 615-298-2303; *Secy.* Joanne MacKenzie, 256 Market St., Suite 2, Brighton, MA 02135. Tel. 617-661-3330; *Treas.* Margaret Auer, Univ. of Detroit Mercy, Box 19900, Detroit, MI 48219-0900. Tel. 313-993-1090; *Chapter Pres.*: *Atlanta* Ann Braziel, 1616 Isham Dr., Lawrenceville, GA 30245. Tel. 404-962-5231; *Binghamton* Dorothea Seargent, 277 Nowlan Rd., Binghamton, NY 13904. Tel. 607-724-6253; *Boston* Dorothy O'Connor, 192 Howard St., Melrose, MA 02176. Tel. 617-665-5005; *Dallas* Judy Searles, SMU Box 750153, Dallas, TX 75275-0153. Tel. 214-768-3225; *Detroit* Joanne Johnson, Box 46523, Mount Clements, MI 48046. Tel. 313-935-3434; *Los Angeles* Pearl Barber, 2332 S. Bentley Ave., Suite 204, Los Angeles, CA 90064. Tel. 310-479-8974; *Nashville* Lee Fairbend, 210 Brittain Ct., Brentwood, TN 37027. Tel. 615-834-7323; *New York* Lucy Kenyon, 226 E. 3rd St., Suite 2B, New York, NY 10009. Tel. 212-995-5579; *San Francisco* Andrea Brown, Box 1137, Montara, CA 94037. Tel. 415-728-1783; *Washington, D.C.* Lynn Page Whittaker, 427 Old Town Ct., Alexandria, VA 22314. Tel. 703-519-9197.

International and Foreign Book Trade Associations

For Canadian book trade associations, see the preceding section, "Book Trade Associations, United States and Canada." For a more extensive list of book trade organizations outside the United States and Canada, with more detailed information, consult *International Literary Market Place* (R. R. Bowker), which also provides extensive lists of major bookstores and publishers in each country.

International

Afro-Asian Book Council, 4835/24 Ansari Rd., New Delhi 110-002, India. Tel. 11-326-1487, FAX 11-326-7437. *Chair.* S. Bissoondoyal; *Secy.-Gen.* Asang Machwe; *Dir. Secretariat* Abul Hasan.

Centre Régional pour la Promotion du Livre en Afrique (Regional Center for Book Promotion in Africa), Box 1646, Yaoundé, Cameroon. Tel. 022-4782/2936. *Secy.* William Moutchia.

Centro Regional para el Fomento del Libro en América Latina y el Caribe (CERLALC) (Regional Center for Book Promotion in Latin America and the Caribbean), Calle 70, No. 9-52, Apdo. Aéreo 57348, Bogota 2, Colombia. Tel. 01-249-5141, 01-255-4594, FAX 01-255-4614. *Dir.* Jorge Salazar.

Federation of European Publishers, 92 Ave. de Tervuren, B-1040 Brussels, Belgium. Tel. 2-736-36-16, FAX 2-736-19-87. *Pres.* Volker Schwarz; *Dir.* Paul Cerf.

Group of Booksellers Assns. in the EEC, Blvd. Lambermont, LN-140-B-1, B-1030 Brussels, Belgium. *Pres.* John Hitchin; *Gen. Secy.* Christiane Vuidar.

International Board on Books for Young People (IBBY), Nonnenweg 12, Postfach, CH-4003 Basel, Switzerland. Tel. 061-272-29-17, FAX 061-272-27-57. *Dir.* Leena Maissen.

International Booksellers Federation, c/o Börsenverein des Deutscher Buchhandels, Grosser Hirschgraben, Frankfurt, Germany. *Gen. Secy.* Jochen Grönke.

International League of Antiquarian Booksellers, c/o *Pres.* Anton Gerits, Delilaan 5, NL-1217 HJ Hilversum, The Netherlands. *Secy.* Helen Kahn, Box 323, Victoria Sta., Montreal, PQ H3Z 2V8, Canada.

International Publishers Assn. (Union Internationale des Editeurs), Ave. Miremont 3, CH-1206 Geneva, Switzerland. Tel. 22-346-3018, FAX 22-347-5717. *Secy.-Gen.* J. Alexis Koutchoumow.

National

Argentina

Cámara Argentina de Publicaciones (Argentine Publications Assn.), Lavalle 437 6to, Dto D, 6° piso, 1063 Buenos Aires. Tel.1-361-5537, 8778. *Pres.* Manuel J. Rodriguez.

Cámara Argentina del Libro (Argentine Book Assn.), Avda. Belgrano 1580, 6° piso, 1093 Buenos Aires. Tel. 1-381-8383, 9277, FAX 1-381-9253. *Dir.* Norberto J. Pou.

Australia

Australian and New Zealand Assn. of Antiquarian Booksellers, 161 Commercial Rd., South Yarra, Vic. 3141. Tel. 3-826-1779, FAX 3-521-3412. *Sec.* Nicholas Dawes.

Australian Book Publishers Assn., 89 Jones St., Ultimo, Sydney, N.S.W. 2007. Tel. 2-281-9788, FAX 2-281-1073. *Dir.* Susan Blackwell.

Australian Booksellers Assn., Box 173, North Carlton, Vic. 3054. *Pres.* Tony Horgan; *Exec. Dir.* Celia Pollock.

National Book Council, Suite 3, 21 Drummond Pl., Carlton, Vic. 3053. Tel. 3-663-8655, FAX 3-663-8658. *Pres.* Michael G. Zifcak; *Exec. Dir.* Thomas Shapcott.

Austria

Hauptverband des Österreichischen Buchhandels (Austrian Publishers and Booksellers

Assn.), Grünangergasse 4, A-1010 Vienna. Tel. 222-512-1535, FAX 222-512-1535-21. *Pres. and Secy.* Otto Mang.

Österreichischer Buchhändlerverband (Austrian Booksellers Assn.), Grünangergasse 4, A-1010 Vienna. Tel. 222-512-1535-16, FAX 222-512-1535-21.*Pres.* Michael Kernstock; *Secy.* Otto Mang.

Österreichischer Verlegerverband (Assn. of Austrian Publishers), Grünangergasse 4, A-1010 Vienna. Tel. 222-512-1535, FAX 222-512-1535-21. *Secy.-Gen.* Otto Mang.

Verband der Antiquare Österreichs (Austrian Antiquarian Booksellers Assn.), Grünangergasse 4, A-1010 Vienna. Tel. 222-512-1535, FAX 222-512-1535-21. *Pres.* Hansjörg Krug; *Secy.-Gen.* Otto Mang.

Belgium

Vereniging ter Bevordering van het Vlaamse Boekwezen (Assn. for the Promotion of Dutch Language Books/Books from Flanders), Hof ter Schrieclaan 17, B-2600 Berchem/Antwerp. Tel. 3-230-8923, FAX 3-281-2240. *Secy.* Wim de Mont.

Vlaamse Boekverkopersbond (Flemish Booksellers Assn.), Hof ter Schrieclaan 17, B-2600 Berchem/Antwerp. Tel. 3-230-8923, FAX 3-281-2240. *Pres.* Yvonne Steinberger; *Gen. Secy.* Wim De Mont.

Bolivia

Cámara Boliviana del Libro (Bolivian Booksellers Assn.), Casilla 682, Edif. Las Palmas, Avda. 20 de Octubre 2005, Planta Baja, La Paz. Tel. 2-327-039, FAX 2-391-817. *Pres.* Rolando S. Condori.

Brazil

Associação Brasileira de Livreiros Antiquarios (Brazilian Assn. of Antiquarian Booksellers), Rua do Rosario 155 Centro, 20041 Rio de Janeiro. Tel. 21-224-8616, FAX 21-221-4582.

Câmara Brasileira do Livro (Brazilian Book Assn.), Av. Ipiranga 1267, 10° andar, 01039-000 Sao Paulo. Tel. 11-229-7855, FAX 11-229-7463. *Gen. Mgr.* Aloysio T. Costa.

Sindicato Nacional dos Editores de Livros (Brazilian Book Publishers Assn.), Av. Río Branco 37, 15° andar, Salas 1503/6 e, 1510/12, 20090-003 Rio de Janeiro. Tel. 21-233-6481, FAX 21-253-8502. *Pres.* Sérgio Abreu da Cruz Machado; *Exec. Secy.* Henrique Maltese.

Bulgaria

Dăržavno Sdruženie Bălgarska Kniga i Petčat (Central Board of Press and Book Publishing), pl. Slavejkov 11, Sofia. Tel. 2-87-011. *Pres.* Slav Todorov.

Chile

Cámara Chilena del Libro (Chilean Assn. of Publishers, Distributors and Booksellers), Avda. Libertador Bernardo O'Higgins 1370, Of. 501, 13526 Santiago. Tel. 2-698-9519, FAX 2-698-9226. *Exec. Secy.* Carlos Franz.

Colombia

Cámara Colombiana del Libro (Colombian Book Assn.), Carrera 17A, No. 37-27, Apdo. 8998, Bogota. Tel. 1-288-6188, 245-1940, FAX 1-287-3320. *Pres.* Jairo Camacho Cuellar; *Exec. Dir.* Miguel Laverde Espejo.

Czech Republic

Svaz Českých Nakladatelůa Knihkupců(Czech Publishers and Booksellers Assn.), Karlovo nám. 5, Box 85, 12800 Prague 2. Tel./FAX 2-299-643. *Pres.* Ivo Železný

Denmark

Danske Antikvarboghandlerforening (Danish Antiquarian Booksellers Assn.), Postboks 2028, DK-1012 Copenhagen K. *Chair.* Poul Jan Poulsen.

Danske Boghandlerforening (Danish Booksellers Assn.), Siljangade 6, DK-2300 Copenhagen S. Tel. 3-154-2255, FAX 3-157-2422.

Danske Forlaeggerforening (Danish Publishers Assn.), Købmagergade 11/13, DK-1150 Copenhagen K. Tel. 3-315-6688, FAX 3-315-6588. *Dir.* Erik V. Krustrup.

Ecuador

Cámara Ecuatoriana del Libro, Guayaquil 1629, 4° piso, Casilla 17-01-3329, Quito. Tel. 2-322-1226, FAX 2-325-6634. *Pres.* Claudio Mena Villamar; *Secy.* Luis Mora Ortega.

Egypt

General Egyptian Book Organization, Box 1660, Corniche El-Nile, Boulac, Cairo. Tel. 2-77-549, 77-500, FAX 2-754-213.

Estonia

Estonian Publishers Assn., Parnu mnt 10, EE-0090 Tallinn. Tel. 142-666-925, FAX 142-445-720. *Dir.* Ants Sild.

Finland

Kirja-ja Paperikauppojen Liittory (Finnish Booksellers and Stationers Assn.), Eerikinkatu 15-17 D 43-44, SF-00100 Helsinki. Tel. 694-4899, FAX 694-4900. *Chief Exec.* Olli Eräkivi.

Suomen Kustannusyhdistys ry (Finnish Book Publishers Assn.), Box 177, SF-00121 Helsinki. *Secy.-Gen.* Veikko Sonninen.

France

Cercle de la Librairie (Circle of Professionals of the Book Trade), 35 Rue Grégoire-de-Tours, F-75006 Paris. Tel. 1-43-29-10-00, FAX 1-43-29-68-95. *Pres.* Marc Friedel.

Fédération Française des Syndicats de Libraires (French Booksellers Assn.), 43 Rue de Châteaudun, F-75009 Paris. Tel. 1-42-82-00-03, FAX 1-42-82-10-51. *Pres.* Jean-Luc Dewas.

France Edition, 35 Rue Grégoire-de-Tours, F-75006 Paris. Tel. 1-44-41-13-13, FAX 1-46-34-63-83. *Chair.* Bernard Foulon; *Pres.* Patrick C. Dubs. New York Branch: French Publishers Agency, 853 Broadway, New York, NY 10003-4703. Tel. 212-254-4520, FAX 212-979-6229.

Syndicat National de la Librairie Ancienne et Moderne (National Assn. of Antiquarians and Modern Booksellers), 4 Rue Gît-le-Coeur, F-75006 Paris. Tel. 1-43-29-46-38, FAX 1-43-25-41-63. *Pres.* Dominique Courvoisier.

Syndicat National de l'Edition (National Union of Publishers), 35 Rue Grégoire-de-Tours, F-75006 Paris. Tel. 1-43-29-75-75, FAX 1-43-25-35-01. *Pres.* Serge Eyrolles; *Sec.* Alain Roland Kirsch.

Union des Libraires de France, 40 Rue Grégoire-de-Tours, F-75006 Paris. Tel. 1-43-29-88-79, FAX 1-46-33-65-29. *Pres.* Eric Hardin; *Gen. Delegate* Marie-Dominique Doumenc.

Germany

Börsenverein des Deutschen Buchhandels e.V. (Stock Exchange of German Booksellers), Postfach 100442, 60549 Frankfurt-am-Main. Tel. 69-130-60, FAX 69-130-6201; Gerichtsweg 26, 07010 Leipzig. Tel. 341-29-3851; Dahlmannstr. 20, 5300 Bonn 1. Tel. 228-22-1078. *Gen. Mgr.* Hans-Karl von Kupsch.

Bundesverband der Deutschen Versandbuchhändler e.V. (National Federation of German Mail-Order Booksellers), An der Ringkirche 6, 65197 Wiesbaden. Tel. 6121-44-9091. *Mgrs.* Stefan Rutkowsky, Kornelia Wahl.

Verband Deutscher Antiquare e.V. (German Antiquarian Booksellers Assn.), Braubachstr. 34, 60311 Frankfurt-am-Main. Tel. 69-28-8166, FAX 69-29-6682 *Pres.* Christine Pressler; *V.P.* Edmund Brumme.

Ghana

Ghana Book Publishers Assn., Box M430, Accra. Tel. 21-22-9178, FAX 21-22-0271. *Exec. Sec.* Peter Kokol.

Great Britain

See United Kingdom

Greece

Hellenic Federation of Publishers and Booksellers, 73 Themistocleous St., GR-10683 Athens. Tel. 1-330-0924, FAX 1-330-0926. *Pres.* D. Pandeleskos.

Syllogos Ekdoton Bibliopolon Athinon (Publishers and Booksellers Assn. of Athens), 54 Themistocleous St., GR-10681 Athens.

Tel. 1-363-0029, FAX 1-322-3222. *Pres.* Thomasis Kastaniotis.

Hungary

Magyar Könyvkiadók és Könyvterjesztök Egyesülése (Assn. of Hungarian Publishers and Booksellers), Vörösmarty tér 1, H-1051 Budapest. Tel. 1-117-6222. *Pres.* István Bart; *Secy.-Gen.* Péter Zentai.

Iceland

Félag Íslenskra Bókaútgefenda (Icelandic Publishers Assn.), Sudurlandsbraut 4A, IS-108 Reykjavik. Tel. 1-38-020, FAX 1-888-668. *Gen. Mgr.* Vilborg Hardardóttir.

India

Federation of Indian Publishers, Federation House, 18/1-C, Institutional Area, JNU Rd., Aruna Asaf Ali Marg, New Delhi 110067. Tel. 11-654-847, FAX 11-686-4054. *Pres.* S. K. Sachdeva; *Exec. Secy.* P. K. Arora.

Indonesia

Ikatan Penerbit Indonesia (Assn. of Indonesian Book Publishers), Jl. Kalipasir 32, Jakarta 10330. Tel. 21-321-907, FAX 21-314-6050. *Secy.-Gen.* Setia Dharma Majid; *Head, Foreign Relations* Aida Joesoef Ahmad.

Ireland

Booksellers Assn. of Great Britain and Ireland, Book House Ireland, 65 Middle Abbey St., Dublin 1. Tel. 1-730-108, FAX 1-730-620. *Admin.* Cecily Golden.

CLÉ: The Irish Book Publishers' Assn., The Writers' Centre, 19 Pannell Sq., Dublin 1. Tel. 1-872-9090, FAX 1-872-2035. *Contact* Hilary Kennedy.

Israel

Book and Printing Center, Israel Export Institute, Industry House, 29 Hamered St., Box 50084, Tel Aviv 68125. Tel. 3-514-2895, FAX 3-514-2881. *Dir.* Corine Knafo.

Book Publishers Assn. of Israel, 29 Carlebach St., Box 20123, Tel Aviv 67132. Tel. 3-561-4121, FAX 3-561-1996. *Managing Dir.* Amnon Ben Shmuel

Italy

Associazione Italiana Editori (Italian Publishers Assn.), Via delle Erbe 2, I-20121 Milan. Tel. 2-86-46-3091, FAX 2-89-01-0863.

Associazione Librai Antiquari d'Italia (Antiquarian Booksellers Assn. of Italy), Via Jacopo Nardi 6, I-50132 Florence. Tel./FAX 55-24-3253. *Pres.* Vittorio Soave.

Associazione Librai Italiani (Italian Booksellers Assn.), Corso Venezia 49, I-20121 Milan. Tel. 2-775-0216, FAX 2-775-0470.

Jamaica

Booksellers Assn. of Jamaica, c/o Sangster's Book Stores Ltd., 97 Harbour St., Box 366, Kingston. Tel. 809-922-3648, FAX 809-922-3813. *Contact Norman* Marshall.

Japan

Japan Book Importers Assn., Chiyoda Kaikan 21-4, Nihonbashi 1-chome, Chuo-ku, Tokyo 103. Tel. 3-32-71-6901, FAX 3-32-71-6920, *Secy.* Shunji Kanda

Japan Book Publishers Assn., 6 Fukuro-machi, Shinjuku-ku, Tokyo 162. Tel. 3-32-68-1301, FAX 3-32-68-1196. *Pres.* Toshiyuki Hattori; *Exec. Dir.* Toshikazu Gomi.

Kenya

Kenya Publishers Assn., Kitau House, Box 18650, Parklands, Nairobi. Tel. 2-22-3262, FAX 2-22-2309. *Secy.* Stanley Irura.

Korea (Republic of)

Korean Publishers Assn., 105-2 Sagan-dong, Chongno-ku, Seoul 110-190. Tel. 2-734-0790, FAX 2-738-5414. *Pres.* Nak-Joon Kim; *Secy.-Gen.* Jong-Jin Jung.

Latvia

Latvian Book Publishers Assn., Aspazijas Bulvaris 24, LV-1050 Riga.

Lithuania

Lithuanian Publishers Assn., K. Sirvydo 6, 2600 Vilnius. Tel. 3702-628-945, FAX 3702-619-696. *Pres.* Vincas Akelis.

Mexico

Cámara Nacional de la Industria Editorial Mexicana, Holanda No. 13, CP 04120 Mexico 21. Tel. 5-688-2011, FAX 5-604-3147. *Secy.-Gen.* R. Servin.

The Netherlands

Koninklijke Nederlandse Uitgeversbond (Royal Dutch Publishers Assn.), Keizersgracht 391, 1016 EJ Amsterdam. Tel. 20-626-7736, FAX 20-620-3859. *Pres.* Karel Leeflang; *Secy.* R. M. Vrij.

Koninklijke Vereeniging ter Bevordering van de Belangen des Boekhandels (Royal Dutch Book Trade Assn.), Postbus 15007, 1001 MA Amsterdam. Tel. 20-240-212, FAX 20-208-871. *Secy.* M. van Vollenhoven-Nagel.

Nederlandsche Vereeniging van Antiquaren (Netherlands Assn. of Antiquarian Booksellers), Postbus 664, 1000 AR Amsterdam. Tel. 20-627-2285, FAX 20-625-8970. *Secy.* A. Gerits.

Nederlandse Boekverkopersbond (Dutch Booksellers Assn.), Waalsdorperweg 119, Postbus 90731, 2509 LS The Hague. Tel. 70-324-4395, FAX 70-324-4411. *Pres.* W. Karssen; *Exec. Secy.* A. C. Doeser.

New Zealand

Book Publishers Assn. of New Zealand, Box 386, Auckland 1. Tel. 9-309-2561, FAX 9-309-7798. *Pres.* Tony Harkins.

Booksellers New Zealand, Box 11-377, Wellington. Tel. 4-472-8678, FAX 4-472-8628. *Chair.* Joan MacKenzie; *Pres.* Tony Harkins; *Chief Exec.* Jo Breese.

Nigeria

Nigerian Publishers Assn., 14 Awosika Ave., Off Oshunto Kun Ave., Old Bodija, Box 3541, Dugbie, Ibadan. Tel. 22-411-557. *Pres.* Azed Echebiri.

Norway

Norske Bokhandlerforening (Norwegian Booksellers Assn.), Øvre Vollgate 15, N-0158 Oslo 1. Tel. 2-410-760, FAX 2-333-269.

Norske Forleggerforening (Norwegian Publishers Assn.), Øvre Vollgate 15, N-0158 Oslo 1. Tel. 2-242-1355, FAX 2-233-3830. *Dir.* Paul Martens Røthe.

Pakistan

National Book Council of Pakistan, 1st fl., Block 14D, Al-Markaz F-8, Islamabad. Tel. 51-850-892. *Dir.-Gen.* Rafiq Ahmad.

Paraguay

Cámara Paraguaya de Editores, Libreros y Asociados (Paraguayan Publishers Assn.), Caballero 270, Asunción. Tel. 21-496-991, FAX 21-448-721. *Dir.* Alejandro Gatti.

Peru

Cámara Peruana del Libro (Peruvian Publishers Assn.), Jirón Washington 1206, Of. 507-508, Apdo. 10253, Lima 1. Tel. 14-325-694. *Pres.* Julio Cesar Flores Rodriguez; *Exec. Dir.* Celia E. Acurio Ismodes.

Philippines

Book Development Assn. of the Philippines, 40 Valencia St., New Manila, Quezon City 3008. Tel. 2-783-976, FAX 2-721-8782.

Philippine Educational Publishers' Assn., 927 Quezon Ave., 1104 Quezon City. Tel. 2-985-171, FAX 2-921-3788. *Pres.* J. Ernesto Sibal.

Poland

Polskie Towarzystwo Wydawców Książek (Polish Society of Book Editors), ul. Mazowiecka 2/4, 00-048 Warsaw. Tel. 22-260-735. *Pres.* Andrzej Karpowicz; *Gen. Secy.* Donat Chruscicki.

Stowarzyszenie Ksiegarzy Polskich (Assn. of Polish Booksellers), ul. Mokotowska 4/6, 00-641 Warsaw. Tel. 22-252-874. *Pres.* Tadeusz Hussak.

Romania

Societa Ziaristilor din România, Piata Presei Libere 1, R-71341 Bucharest. Tel. 0-617-1591, FAX 0-312-8266. *Deputy Gen. Dir.* Victor Mircea.

Russia

All-Union Book Chamber, Kremlevskaya nab 1/9, 121019 Moscow G-19.Tel. 95-203-5608, FAX 95-202-3992. *Dir.-Gen.* Yuri Torsuev.
Publishers Assn., Hertsen Str. 44B, 121069 Moscow. Tel. 95-202-1174, FAX 95-202-3989. *Contact* M. Shishigin.

Singapore

Singapore Book Publishers Assn., B1K 86, Marine Parade Central 03-213, Singapore 1544. Tel. 344-7801, FAX 447-0897. *Pres.* N. T. S. Chopra. Tel. 344-1495, FAX 344-0180; *Honorary Secy.* Wu Cheng Tan.

Slovenia

Zdruzenje Zaloznikov in Knjigotrzcev Slovenije Gospodarska Zbornica Slovenije (Assn. of Publishers and Booksellers of Slovenia), Dimičeva 9, 61000 Ljubljana. Tel. 61-102-008, FAX 61-342-398. *Contact* Joze Korinsek.

South Africa

Associated Booksellers of Southern Africa, Box 870, Bellville 7530. Tel. 21-951-2194, FAX 21-951-4903. *Pres.* M. Margraves; *Sec.* W. D. Fuchs.
Publishers Assn. of South Africa, Private Bag 91932, Auckland Park 2006. Tel. 11-726-7470, FAX 11-482-3409. *Chair.* Mike Peacock.

Spain

Federación de Gremios de Editores de España (Federation of Spanish Publishers Assns.), 45 Juan Ramón Jiménez, 9° piso, Izda. 28036 Madrid. Tel. 1-350-9105, FAX 1-345-4351. *Pres.* Fermín Vargas; *Secy.* Ana Moltó.

Gremi d'Editors de Catalunya (Assn. of Catalonian Publishers), Valencia 279, First Planta, Barcelona 08009. Tel. 3-215-5091, FAX 3-215-5273. *Pres.* P. Vicens i Rahola.
Gremio de Libreros de Barcelona i Catalunya (Booksellers Assn. of Barcelona and Catalonia), Mallorca 274, 08037 Barcelona. Tel. 3-215-4254.

Sri Lanka

Sri Lanka Assn. of Publishers, 112 S. Mahinda Mawatha, Colombo 10. Tel. 1-695-773, FAX 1-696-653. *Pres.* Dayawansa Jayakody.

Sudan

Sudanese Publishers Assn., H. Q. Al Ikhwa Bldg., Flat 7, 7th fl., Box 2771, Khartoum. Tel. 249-117-5051.

Suriname

Publishers Assn. Suriname, Domineestr. 26, Box 1841, Paramaribo.Tel. 472-545, FAX 410-563. *Mgr.* E. Hogenboom.

Sweden

Lettura AB (Swedish Booksellers Assn.), Karlsrogatan 2, Box 1308, 17125 Solna. Tel. 8-850-300, FAX 8-660-0666. *Man. Dir.* Thomas Rönström.
Svenska Antikvariatforeningen (Swedish Antiquarian Booksellers Assn.), Box 22549, S-10422 Stockholm. Tel. 8-411-9136, FAX 8-20-9308.
Svenska Bokförläggareföreningen (Swedish Publishers Assn.), Drottninggatan 97, 2 tr, S-11360 Stockholm. Tel. 8-736-1940, FAX 8-736-1944. *Dir.* Kent Muldin.
Svenska Bokhandlareföreningen (Swedish Booksellers Assn.), Skeppargatan 27, S-11452 Stockholm. *Managing Dir.* Thomas Rönström.

Switzerland

Schweizerischer Buchhändler- und Verleger-Verband (Swiss German-Language Booksellers and Publishers Assn.), Baumackerstr. 42, Postfach 9045, CH-8050 Zurich. Tel. 1-318-6400, FAX 1-318-6462. *Secy.* Egon Räz.

Società Editori della Svizzera Italiana (Publishers Assn. for the Italian-Speaking Part of Switzerland), C.P. 2600, Viale Portone 4, CH-6501 Bellinzona.

Société des Libraires et Editeurs de la Suisse Romande (Assn. of Swiss French-Language Booksellers and Publishers), 2 Ave. Agassiz, CH-1001 Lausanne. Tel. 21-319-7111, FAX 21-319-7910. *Dir.* Robert Junod.

Tanzania

Publishers Assn. of Tanzania, Box 1408, Dar es Salaam. Tel. 51-512-7608. *Exec. Sec.* Thomas A. R. Kamigisha.

Thailand

Publishers and Booksellers Assn. of Thailand, 323 Mul Soi Thiraphat, Pracha-u-thit Rd., Bangkok 10140. Tel. 2-427-5709, FAX 2-427-1703.

United Kingdom

Antiquarian Booksellers Assn., 154 Buckingham Palace Rd., London SW1. Tel. 71-730-9273, FAX 71-497-2114. *Sec.* Jacqueline White.

Assn. of Learned and Professional Society Publishers, 48 Kelsey Lane, Beckenham, Kent BR3 3NE, England. Tel. 81-658-0459, FAX 81-663-3583. *Secy.* B. T. Donovan.

Book Trust, 45 E. Hill, Wandsworth, London SW18 2QZ, England. Tel. 81-870-9055, FAX 81-874-4790.

Book Trust Scotland, Scottish Book Centre, 137 Dundee St.,Edinburgh EH11 1BG, Scotland. Tel. 31-229-3663, FAX 31-228-4293. *Exec. Dir.* Lindsey Fraser.

Booksellers Assn. of Great Britain and Ireland, Minster House, 272 Vauxhall Bridge Rd., London SW1V 1BA, England. Tel. 71-834-5477, FAX 71-834-8812. *Chief Exec.* Tim Godfray.

Educational Publishers Council, 19 Bedford Sq., London WC1B 3HJ, England. Tel. 71-580-6321, FAX 71-636-5375. *Dir.* John R. M. Davies.

Publishers Assn., 19 Bedford Sq., London WC1B 3HJ, England. Tel. 71-580-6321, FAX 71-636-5375. *Pres.* Nicholas Chapman; *Chief Exec.* Clive Bradley; *Secy.* Marian Donne.

Scottish Publishers Assn., Fountainbridge Library, 137 Dundee St., 1st fl., Edinburgh EH11 1BG, Scotland. Tel. 31-228-6866, FAX 31-228-3220. *Dir.* Lorraine Fannin; *Chair.* Steven Mair.

Welsh Books Council (Cyngor Llyfrau Cymraeg), Castell Brychan, Aberystwyth, Dyfed SY23 2JB, Wales. Tel. 970-624-151, FAX 970-625-385. *Dir.* Gwerfyl Pierce Jones.

Welsh Publishers Union (Undeb Cyhoeddwyr Cymru), Gwasg Gomer, Llandysul, Dyfed. Tel. 559-322-371, FAX 559-363-758. *Chair.* Huw Lewis.

Uruguay

Cámara Uruguaya del Libro (Uruguayan Publishers Assn.), Juan D. Jackson 1118, 11200 Montevideo. Tel. 2-241-5732, FAX 2-241-1860. *Sr. Pres.* Vincente Porcelli; *Secy.* A. Medone.

Venezuela

Cámara Venezolana del Libro (Venezuelan Publishers Assn.), Ave. Andrés Bello, Torre Oeste, 11° piso, Of. 112-0, Apdo. 51858, Caracas 1050-A. Tel. 2-793-1347, FAX 2-793-1368. *Sec.* M. P. Vargas.

Zambia

Booksellers and Publishers Assn. of Zambia, Box 32664, Lusaka. Tel. 1-218-612. *Exec. Dir.* Basil Mbewe.

Zimbabwe

Zimbabwe Book Publishers Assn., 1179 Causeway, Box CY, Harare. Tel. 4-739-681, FAX 4-751-202.

National Information Standards Organization (NISO) Standards

Book Production and Publishing

Z39.4-1984*	Basic Criteria for Indexes
Z39.5-1985*	Abbreviation of Titles of Publications
Z39.14-1987*	Writing Abstracts
Z39.21-1988	Book Numbering (ISBN)
Z39.22-1989	Proof Corrections
Z39.41-1990	Printed Information on Spines
Z39.43-1993	Standard Address Number for the Publishing Industry (SAN)
Z39.48-1992	Permanence of Paper for Printed Publications and Documents in Libraries and Archives
Z39.66-1992	Durable Hardcover Binding for Books

Codes and Numbering Systems

Z39.9-1992	International Standard Serial Numbering (ISSN)
Z39.21-1988	Book Numbering (ISBN)
Z39.23-1990*	Standard Technical Report Number (STRN), Format, and Creation
Z39.43-1993	Standard Address Number for the Publishing Industry
Z39.47-1993	Extended Latin Alphabet Coded Character Set for Bibliographic Use
Z39.53-1994	Codes for the Representation of Languages for Information Interchange
Z39.56-1991*	Serial Item and Contribution Identifier
Z39.64-1989*	East Asian Character Code
ANSI/NISO/ISO 3166	Codes for the Representation of Names of Countries

Indexes, Thesauri, and Database Development

Z39.4-1984*	Basic Criteria for Indexes
Z39.19-1993	Guidelines for the Construction, Format, and Management of Monolingual Thesauri

Microforms

Z39.62-1993   Eye Legible Information on Microfilm Leader Send Trailers and on Containers of Processed Microfilm on Open Reels

Technical Reports and Papers

Z39.18-1995   Scientific and Technical Reports–Elements, Organization, and Design

Z39.23-1990*   Standard Technical Report Number (STRN), Format and Creation

Serial Publications

Z39.5-1985*   Abbreviation of Titles of Publications

Z39.9-1992   International Standard Serial Numbering (ISSN)

Z39.44-1986*   Serials Holding Statements

Z39.48-1992   Permanence of Paper for Printed Publications

Z39.56-1991*   Serial Item and Contribution Identifiers

Automation and Electronic Publishing

Z39.2-1994   Information Interchange Format

Z39.44-1986*   Serials Holding Statements

Z39.47-1993   Extended Latin Alphabet Coded Character Set for Bibliographic Use (ANSEL)

Z39.50-1995   Information Retrieval Application Service Definition and Protocol Specification for Open Systems

Z39.57-1989*   Holding Statements for Non-Serial Items

Z39.58-1992   Common Command Language for Interactive Information Retrieval

Z39.63-1989*   Interlibrary Loan Data Elements

Z39.67-1993   Computer Software Description

NISO/ANSI/ISO 3166   Codes for the Representation of Names of Countries

NISO/ANSI/ISO 9660   Volume and File Structure of CD-ROM for Information Interchange

NISO/ANSI/ISO 12083   Electronic Manuscript Preparation and Markup

Library Equipment

Z39.73-1994   Single-Tier Steel Bracket Library Shelving

Standards Committees

SC Q   Periodicals–Format and Arrangement

SC LL   Record Format for Patron Records, Circulation Transaction Format

SC MM	Environmental Conditions for the Exhibition of Library and Archival Materials
SC SS	Information to Be Included in Ads [etc.] for Products Used for the Storage, Binding, or Repair of Library Materials
SC ZZ	Library Binding
SC AC	Guides to Microform Sets
SC OO	Revision of Z39.29-1977 Bibliographic References
SC UU	Revision of Z39.7-1983 Library Statistics
SC YY	Revision of Z39.4-1989 Basic Criteria for Indexes
SC AE	Format for the Submission of Data for Multimedia CD-ROM Mastering
SC AG	Writing Abstracts
SC AJ	Standard Format for Downloading Records from Bibliographic and Abstracting Indexing Databases
SC AK	Sorting of Alphanumeric Characters and Other Symbols
SC AL	Holding Statements for Bibliographic Items
SC AM	S.I.C.I. (Revision of Z39.56-1991)
SC AN	Revision of Z39.23 S.T.R.N.
SC AO	Title Page Information for Conference Proceedings

Other Standards in Development

Z39.76-199X	Data Elements for Binding of Library Materials
Z39.32-199X	Information on Microfiche Headers

*This standard is being reviewed by NISO's Standards Development Committee or is under revision. For further information please contact NISO, Box 1056, Bethesda, MD 20827; Tel. 301-654-2512; FAX 301-654-1721.

Calendar 1995–1997

The list below contains information on association meetings or promotional events that are, for the most part, national or international in scope. State and regional library association meetings are also included. To confirm the starting or ending date of a meeting, which may change after the *Bowker Annual* has gone to press, contact the association directly. Addresses of library and book trade associations are listed in Part 6 of this volume. For information on additional book trade and promotional events, see the *Exhibits Directory*, published annually by the Association of American Publishers; *Chase's Annual Events*, published by Contemporary Books, 180 N. Michigan Ave., Chicago, IL 60601; *Literary Market Place* and *International Literary Market Place*, published by R. R. Bowker; and the "Calendar" section in each issue of *Publishers Weekly* and *Library Journal*.

1995

May

1-3	Massachusetts Library Association	Sturbridge, MA
2-4	New Jersey Library Association	Atlantic City, NJ
2-6	Illinois Library Association	Peoria, IL
4-6	New York Library Association, School Library Media Section	Kiamesha Lake, NY
5-11	Medical Library Association	Washington, DC
11	Archivists and Librarians in the History of the Health Sciences	Pittsburgh, PA
11-13	Quebec Library Association	Montreal, PQ, Canada
16-19	Prague International Book Fair and Writers Festival	Prague, Czech Republic
17-18	Vermont Library Association	Burlington, VT
17-22	Warsaw International Book Fair	Warsaw, Poland
21-23	Maine Educational Media Association	Orono, ME
24-25	New Hampshire Library Association	Dixville Notch, NH
25-28	Atlantic Provinces Library Association	Charlottetown, PE, Canada
*	Turin National Book Fair	Turin, Italy

June

1-2	Publishers Marketing Association	Chicago, IL

*To Be Determined

June 1995 *(cont.)*

3-5	Periodical Marketers of Canada	Winnipeg, MB, Canada
3-6	Association for Information and Image Management	Chicago, IL
7-10	Canadian Association for Information Science	Edmonton, AB, Canada
8-10	Research and Engineering Council of the Graphic Arts Industries	Williamsburg, VA
9-10	American Society of Indexers	Montreal, PQ, Canada
10-15	Special Libraries Association	Montreal, PQ, Canada
12-17	Canadian Booksellers Association	Toronto, ON, Canada
13-16	Association of Christian Librarians	Lakeland, FL
14-17	American Theological Library Association	Nashville, TN
14-18	Canadian Library Association	Calgary, AB, Canada
17-20	American Booksellers Association	Chicago, IL
17-20	Association of American University Presses	Nashville, TN
18-23	International Association of Music Libraries Archives and Documentation Centres	Helsingor, Denmark
22-29	American Library Association	Chicago, IL
23-27	Church and Synagogue Library Association	Houghton, NY
25-26	Asian/Pacific American Librarians Association	Chicago, IL
*	UK Library Association	Manchester, England

July

8-12	International Association of Technological University Libraries	Irvine, CA
15	Evangelical Christian Publishers Association	Denver, CO
15-20	American Association of Law Libraries	Pittsburgh, PA
15-20	Christian Booksellers Association	Denver, CO
17-22	International Association of School Librarianship	Dorchester, England
20-22	Tennessee Association of School Librarians	Memphis, TN
20-24	Hong Kong Book Fair	Wanchai, Hong Kong

August

2-6	Zimbabwe International Book Fair	Harare, Zimbabwe
5-8	International Association of Printing House Craftsmen	Jacksonville, FL
9-13	Pacific Northwest Library Association	Whistler, BC, Canada

*To Be Determined

August 1995 *(cont.)*

18-28	Edinburgh Book Festival	Edinburgh, Scotland
20-26	International Federation of Library Associations and Institutions	Istanbul, Turkey
30-9/3	Society of American Archivists	Washington, DC
*	Associated Booksellers of South Africa	Johannesburg, South Africa

September

1-4	Miniature Book Society	Los Angeles, CA
3-7	Society of American Archivists	Chicago, IL
15-17	Great Lakes Booksellers Association	Grand Rapids, MI
15-17	Pacific Northwest Booksellers Association	Bellevue, WA
16	Antiquarian Book Fair	Sturbridge, MA
22-24	Mountains and Plains Booksellers Association	Denver, CO
22-24	Northern California Booksellers Association	Oakland, CA
28-29	Publishers Association of the South	Atlanta, GA
28-10/1	American Institute of Graphic Arts National Design Conference	Seattle, WA
28-10/2	Association of Directory Publishers	San Diego, CA
28-10/2	Colorado Library Association	Snowmass, CO
29-10/3	Pennsylvania Library Association	Pittsburgh, PA
30-10/1	New England Booksellers Association	Boston, MA
*	International Hispanic Book Fair	California
*	Moscow International Book Fair	Moscow, Russia
*	Worddidac	Mexico

October

1-2	Mid-Atlantic Booksellers Association	Atlantic City, NJ
1-3	New England Library Association	Providence, RI
1-7	Distripress	Istanbul, Turkey
3-6	Florida Association for Media in Education	Daytona Beach, FL
4-7	Mountain Plains Library Association/ South Dakota Library Association/ North Dakota Library Association	Sioux Falls, SD
5-7	Minnesota Educational Media Organization	St. Cloud, MN
6-8	Northern California Independent Booksellers	Oakland, CA
11-13	Minnesota Library Association	Mankato, MN
11-16	Frankfurt Book Fair	Frankfurt, Germany

*To Be Determined

October 1995 *(cont.)*

12-14	Oregon Educational Media Association/ Washington Library Media Assn.	Portland, OR
13-16	Arkansas Library Association	Fort Smith, AR
17-20	Michigan Library Association	Lansing, MI
18-20	Iowa Library Association	Des Moines, IA
18-20	Ohio Educational Library Media Association	Dayton, OH
18-27	Muscat International Book Fiar	Muscat, Oman
22-26	Association of Records Managers and Administrators	Nashville, TN
22-26	Southeast Library Association/Kentucky Library Association	Lexington, KY
24-27	Mississippi Library Association	Jackson, MS
24-27	Wisconsin Library Association	Appleton, WI
25-27	Nebraska Library Association/Nebraska Educational Media Association	Kearney, NE
25-29	New York Library Association	Rochester, NY
26-28	Georgia Council of Media Organizations (Georgia Library Association)	Jekyll Island, GA
26-28	Illinois School Library Media Association	Decatur, IL
29-11/1	Book Manufacturers Institute	Palm Beach, FL
*	Children's Book Week	London, England
*	International Council on Archives	Washington, DC
*	ISBN Advisory Board	Athens, Greece

November

4-5	San Francisco Book Council	San Francisco, CA
4-12	Istanbul Book Fair	Istanbul, Turkey
8-12	American Translators Association	Nashville, TN
9-10	Connecticut Educational Media Association	*
11	Missouri Association of School Librarians	Jefferson City, MO
11-14	California Library Association	Santa Clara, CA
11-14	Periodical Marketers of Canada	Toronto, ON, Canada
13-19	National Children's Book Week	USA
16-18	Arizona Library Association	Phoenix, AZ
16-21	Montreal Book Show	Montreal, PQ, Canada
24-12/7	Cairo International Book Fair	Cairo, Egypt

December

4-5	Electronic Books Conference	New York, NY
27-30	Modern Language Association of America	Chicago, IL

*To Be Determined

1996

January

19-25	American Library Association	San Antonio, TX

February

14-17	Music Library Association	Seattle, WA
14-18	Association for Educational Communications and Technology/ Association for Indiana Media Educators	Indianapolis, IN

March

19-22	Louisiana Library Association	Alexandria, LA
24-25	Oregon Library Association	Portland, OR

April

9-12	Catholic Library Association	Philadelphia, PA
13-17	National Association of College Stores	San Diego, CA
14-17	Association for Information and Image Management	New York, NY
16-19	Alabama Library Association	Mobile, AL
23-27	Texas Library Association	Houston, TX
24-27	Montana Library Association	Helena, MT
25-27	Pennsylvania School Librarians Association	Hershey, PA
*	Archivists and Librarians in the History of the Health Sciences	*

May

2-5	Alberta Library Association	Jasper, AB, Canada
14-17	Illinois Library Association	Chicago, IL
31-6/6	Medical Library Association	Kansas City, MO

June

6-9	Canadian Library Association	Halifax, NS, Canada
17-20	Association for Information and Image Management	Chicago, IL
21-25	American Theological Library Association	Denver, CO
30-7/4	International Association of Technological University Libraries	Trondheim, Norway

*To Be Determined

July 1996 *(cont.)*
July

4-10	American Library Association	New York, NY
6-11	American Association of Law Libraries	Indianapolis, IN
*	International Association of School Librarianship	Ocho Rios, Jamaica

August

16-18	Colorado Library Association/Colorado Educational Media Association	Denver, CO
25-31	International Federation of Library Associations and Institutions	Beijing, China
28-9/1	Society of American Archivists	San Diego, CA
*	Alaska Library Association	Fairbanks, AK
*	International Association of Printing House Craftsmen	Montreal, PQ, Canada

September

20-22	Great Lakes Booksellers Association	Toledo, OH
26-28	North Dakota Library Association	Bismarck, ND
*	International Council on Archives	Beijing, China

October

2-4	Idaho Library Association	Nampa, ID
6-8	New England Library Association	Manchester, NH
6-9	Pennsylvania Library Association	Lancaster, PA
8-10	Florida Association for Media in Education	Daytona Beach, FL
8-10	Iowa Library Association	Waterloo, IA
9-12	South Dakota Library Association	Spearfish, SD
13-16	Library and Information Technology Association/Library Administration and Management Association	Pittsburgh, PA
14-17	Association of Records Managers and Administrators	Denver, CO
14-18	Michigan Library Association	Dearborn, MI
22-26	Southeastern Library Association	Lexington, KY
22-27	New York Library Association	Saratoga Springs, NY
23-25	North Carolina Association of School Librarians	Raleigh, NC
24	Minnesota Library Association	St. Cloud, MN
30-11/3	American Translators Association	Colorado Springs, CO
31-11/2	Illinois School Library Media Association	Lincolnshire, IL
*	ISBN Advisory Board	Berlin, Germany

*To Be Determined

November

| 11-14 | Wisconsin Library Association | Middleton, WI |

1997

February

| 14-20 | American Library Association | Washington, DC |

March

| 16-18 | Louisiana Library Association | Kenner, LA |

April

1-4	Catholic Library Association	Minneapolis, MN
2-6	American Association of School Librarians	Portland, OR
8-12	Texas Library Association	Fort Worth, TX
11-14	Association of College and Research Libraries	Nashville, TN
17-19	Pennsylvania School Librarians Association	Hershey, PA
24-27	Alberta Library Association	Jasper, AB, Canada

May

| 23-29 | Medical Library Association | Seattle, WA |

June

| 19-22 | Canadian Library Association | Ottawa, ON, Canada |
| * | American Theological Library Association | Boston, MA |

July

| * | International Association of School Librarianship | Vancouver, BC, Canada |

August

| 31-9/5 | International Federation of Library Associations and Institutions | Copenhagen, Denmark |
| * | International Association of Printing House Craftsmen | Seattle, WA |

September

| 25-27 | North Dakota Library Association | Minot, ND |
| 25-28 | Pennsylvania Library Association | Philadelphia, PA |

*To Be Determined

October 1997

1-4	South Dakota Library Association	Huron, SD
8-10	Iowa Library Association	Sioux City, IA
20-23	Association of Records Managers and Administrators	Chicago, IL
22-25	Michigan Library Association	Lansing, MI
23-25	Illinois School Library Media Association	Springfield, IL
*	Colorado Library Association	Copper Mountain, CO
*	ISBN Advisory Board	Stockholm, Sweden

November

4-7	Wisconsin Library Association	Milwaukee, WI
5-9	American Translators Association	San Francisco, CA

*To Be Determined

Authors and Contributors

Alexander, Adrian W.
Anderson, Nancy D.
Baker, John F.
Bearman, Toni Carbo
Biden, Francis W.
Brandhorst, Ted
Chute, Adrienne
Cole, John Y.
Curley, Arthur
Dalrymple, Prudence W.
Fox, Bette–Lee
Fry, Ray M.
Halstead, Kent
Haycock, Ken
Heanue, Anne H.
Henderson, Carol C.
Hilts, Paul
Ink, Gary
King, Thomas N.
Koltay, Emery
Kott, Katherine
Lamolinara, Guy
Lisowski, Lori A.
Lofquist, William S.
Lottman, Herbert R.

Lynch, Mary Jo
Maryles, Daisy
Mehnert, Robert
Miles, Carol
Molz, R. Kathleen
Montgomery, Judy
Mutter, John
Myers, Margaret
Nelson, Corinne O.
Norris, Brian
Olson, Renée
Phelps, Thomas C.
Platt, Judith
Roback, Diane
St. Lifer, Evan
Segal, JoAn S.
Serepca, Mark S.
Simson, Maria
Tarr, Susan M.
Taylor, Sally
Timmer, Ellen B.
Wallace, David A.
Webster, Duane E.
Williams, Jane
Zipkowitz, Fay

Acronyms

CD-ROM. Compact Disc Read-Only Memory

CIC. Committee on Inter-Institutional Cooperation

CIES. Council for International Exchange of Scholars

CIP. Cataloging and classification, Cataloging in Publication

CIPS. National Archives and Records Administration, Centers Information Processing System

CLA. Canadian Library Association; Catholic Library Association

CLASE. Citas Latinoamericanas en Ciencias Sociales y Humanidades

CLR. Council on Library Resources

CNI. Center for Networked Information; Coalition for Networked Information

CNLIA. Council of National Library and Information Associations

COPA. Council on Postsecondary Accreditation

COSLA. Chief Officers of State Library Agencies

CPL. Council of Planning Librarians

CRS. Congressional Research Service

CSLA. Canadian School Library Association; Church and Synagogue Library Association

CTP. Publishers and publishing, computer-to- plate (CTP) production systems

CWEIS. Community-Wide Education and Information Services

CYFERNET. CYFERNET (Child, Youth and Family Education and Research Network)

D

DDA. R. R. Donnelly, Donnelley Digital Architecture (DDA) system

DOE. Education, U.S. Department of

DOL. Labor, U.S. Department of

E

EAN. Bookland EAN

EDRS. Educational Resources Information Center, ERIC Document Reproduction Service

EIDS. Government Printing Office, Electronic Information Dissemination Services

ENAL. Egyptian National Agricultural Library

ERIC. Educational Resources Information Center

F

FAME. Awards, FAME (Federal Applications Medal for Excellence)

FDA. Food and Drug Administration

FDLP. Government Printing Office, Federal Depository Library Program

FIAF. International Federation of Film Archives

FID. International Federation for Information and Documentation

FLICC. Federal Library and Information Center Committee

FLRT. American Library Association, Federal Librarians Round Table

FPC. Federal Publishers Committee

FSCS. Federal-State Cooperative System (FSCS) for Public Library Data

G

GATT. General Agreement on Tariffs and Trade

GILS. Government Information Locator Service

GLIN. Global Legal Information Network

GODORT. American Library Association, Government Documents Round Table

GPO. Government Printing Office

H

HBCUs. Colleges and research libraries, black colleges, historically black colleges and universities

HEA. Higher Education Act

HEDBIB. International Bibliography of Higher Education

HPCC. High Performance Computing and Communication (HPCC) Coordination Office

HTML. Hypertext Markup Language

I

IALL. International Association of Law Libraries

IAML. International Association of Music Libraries, Archives and Documentation Centres

IAOL. International Association of Orientalist Librarians

IASL. International Association of School Librarianship

IATUL. International Association of Technological University Libraries

ICSECA. International Contributions for Scientific, Educational and Cultural Activities

IFLA. International Federation of Library Associations and Institutions

IFRT. American Library Association, Intellectual Freedom Round Table

IIA. Information Industry Association

IIPA. International Intellectual Property Alliance

IITF. Information Infrastructure Task Force

ILL. Interlibrary loan

INTAMEL. International Association of Metropolitan City Libraries

IPA. International Publishers Association

ISBN. International Standard Book Number

ISIS. ISIS (Integrated System for Information Services)

ISO. International Organization for Standardization

ISSN. International Standard Serial Number

L

LAMA. Library Administration and Management Association

LAPPI. Latin America, Latin American Periodicals Price Index

LAPT. *Library Acquisitions: Practice and Theory*

LARS. FEDLINK, Library Automation Resource Service

LHRT. American Library Association, Library History Round Table

LIS. Library/information science

LITA. Library and Information Technology Association

LJ. *Library Journal*

LRRT. American Library Association, Library Research Round Table

LSCA. Library Services and Construction Act

LSP. National Center for Education Statistics, Library Statistics Program

M

MAGERT. American Library Association, Map and Geography Round Table

MARC. Cataloging and classification, MARC (machine-readable cataloging)

Marvel. Library of Congress, Machine-Assisted Realization of the Virtual Electronic Library

MLA. Medical Library Association; Music Library Association

MLC. Michigan Library Consortium

MLNC. Missouri Library Network Corporation

MPAA. Motion Picture Association of America

MSUS/PALS. Minnesota State University System's Project for Automated Library Systems

MURLs. Major Urban Resource Libraries

N

NAFTA. North American Free Trade Agreement

NAGARA. National Association of Government Archives and Records Administrators

NAILDD. North American Interlibrary Loan and Document Delivery (NAILDD) Project

NAL. National Agricultural Library

NALIS. Nevada Academic Libraries Information System

NARA. National Archives and Records Administration

NATDP. National Agricultural Library, National Agricultural Text Digitizing Project

NCCP. National Coordinated Cataloging Program

NCES. National Center for Education Statistics

NCLIS. National Commission on Libraries and Information Science

NEH. National Endowment for the Humanities

NEII. National Engineering Information Initiative

NFAIS. National Federation of Abstracting and Information Services

NFSMI. National Food Service Management Institute

NII. National information instructure

NISO. National Information Standards Organization

NLA. National Librarians Association; National Library of Australia

NLC. National Library of Canada

NLE. National Library of Education

NLM. National Library of Medicine

NMRT. American Library Association, New Members Round Table

NPIN. National Parent Information Network

NPTN. National Public Telecomputing Network

NSF. National Science Foundation

NTIA. National Telecommunications and Information Administration

NTIS. National Technical Information Service

O

OCLC. OCLC (Online Computer Library Center)

OERI. Education, U.S. Department of, Office of Educational Research and Improvement

OERR. Environmental Protection Agency, Office of Emergency and Remedial Response

ORION. ORION (Ozark Regional Information On-Line Network)

OSAP. Association of Research Libraries, Scientific and Academic Publishing, Office of

P

PDQ. United States Information Agency, library programs, Public Diplomacy Query (PDQ) database

PEN. PEN (Public Electronic Network)

PGD. Plant Genome Database

PLA. Public Library Association

PRLC. PRLC (Pittsburgh Regional Library Center)

PTW. Playing to Win

PW. Publishers Weekly

R

RASD. American Library Association, Reference and Adult Services Division

RBOCs. Regional Bell Operating Companies

RINET. Rhode Island Network

RLG. Research Libraries Group

RTSD. American Library Association, Resources and Technical Services Division. *see new name* Association for Library Collections and Technical Services

S

SAA. Society of American Archivists

SASS. National Center for Education Statistics, Schools and Staffing Survey

SGML. Standard Generalized Markup Language

SLA. Special Libraries Association

SLJ. School Library Journal

SRRT. American Library Association, Social Responsibilities Round Table

SSP. Society for Scholarly Publishing

STM. Scientific, Technical and Medical Publishers

T

TAR. Teachers as Readers
TERCS. National Archives and Records
 Administration, Technology to Enhance
 Reference Customer Satisfaction
TIIAP. Telecommunications and Information
 Infrastructure Assistance Program
TLA. Theatre Library Association
TPR. Telecommunications Policy Roundtable
TPR-NE. Telecommunications Policy
 Roundtable-Northeast
TRIPS. Trade Related Intellectual Property
 Rights

U

ULC. Urban Libraries Council
USDA. Agriculture, United States Depart-
 ment of
USIA. United States Information Agency

USIS. United States Information Service,
 overseas name for United States Information Agency
USPS. Postal Service, U.S.

V

VALS. Vermont Automated Library System

W

WILS. Wisconsin InterLibrary Services
WLN. WLN Washington Library Network;
 Western Library Network
WTO. World Trade Organization

Y

YALSA. Young Adult Library Services
 Association
YDIC. National Agricultural Library, Youth
 Development Information Center

Index of Organizations

Please note that this index includes cross-references to the Subject Index. Many additional organizations can be found in Part 6 under the following headings: Networks, Consortia, and Cooperative Library Organizations; National Library and Information-Industry Associations, United States and Canada; State, Provincial, and Regional Library Associations; State and Provincial Library Agencies; State School Library Media Associations; International Library Associations; Foreign Library Associations; Book Trade Associations, United States and Canada; International and Foreign Book Trade Associations.

A

ACLIN (Access Colorado Library and Information Network), 54
Advanced Information Management, 359-360
Advanced Marketing Services (AMS), 24
Advanced Research Projects Agency (ARPA), 28
Advisory Commission on Textbook Specifications (ACTS), 236
AGRICOLA (AGRICultural OnLine Access), 156-157, 160, 162-163
Agriculture, U.S. Department of, 157, 158, 162
  See also AGRICOLA; ISIS; National Agricultural Library; Plant Genome Database
Alliance of Libraries, Archive and Records Management (ALARM), 97-98
American Association of Law Libraries (AALL), 658-659
  awards, 399
  career hotline, 360
American Association of School Librarians (AASL), 126, 198, 431, 662-624
  awards, 400-401, 432
American Booksellers Association (ABA), 238-247

antitrust suit, 26
awards, 241
Booksellers Order Service (BOS), 246-247
convention and trade exhibit, 26, 239, 240-241
education and professional development, 242-243
government affairs, 242
headquarters, new, 26, 238-239
membership, 240
publications, 243-244
publisher relations, 246
research, 244-246
seminar, 246
standardization committee, 247
American Booksellers Foundation for Free Expression (ABFFE), 241-242
American Forest & Paper Association (AFPA), 20-22
American Library Association (ALA), 197-205, 660-682
  Accreditation, Committee on, 72-76
  ALA Goal 2000, 205
  Armed Forces Libraries Round Table awards, 401-402
  awards, 399-408, 433, 434
  Banned Books Week, 201
  conferences, 48, 197-198

Subject Index

Please note that many cross-references refer to entries listed in the Index of Organizations.

A

Academic books, prices and price indexes, 460(table)
British averages, 1992-1994, 503-505(table)
German averages, 1992-1994, 506(table)
North American averages, 1991-1993, 490-491(table)
U.S. college books, averages, 1978, 1992, 1993, 1994, 492-493(table)
See also Association of American Publishers, Professional and Scholarly Publishing Division; Society for Scholarly Publishing
Academic libraries, *see* College and research libraries; Academic Libraries Survey
Academic Libraries Survey (ALS), 125-126, 128
Accreditation, 70-72, 73-74
master's programs in LIS studies, 393-395
regulating accrediting bodies, 74-75
See also Council on Postsecondary Accreditation
Acquisitions
electronics, 42
expenditures, 447-455
academic libraries, 450-451(table)
government libraries, 454-455(table)
public libraries, 448-449(table)
special libraries, 452-453(table)
research award, 432
See also Association of Research Libraries, collections services program *and* specific types of libraries, i.e., Public libraries; *Library Acquisitions: Practice and Theory*
Adults, services for, *see* American Library Association, Reference and Adult Services Division; Literacy programs; Senior citizens, library services for
Aerospace engineering information, 287
African Americans
colleges and universities
historically black colleges and universities (HBCUs), 170
NAL ties to, 157-158
See also Coretta Scott King Awards; Minorities
Agencies, library, *see* Library associations and agencies
Agricultural libraries, *see* Agriculture, U.S. Department of; Inter-American Association of Agricultural Librarians and Documentalists; International Association of Agricultural Librarians and Documentalists; National Agricultural Library
AIDS/HIV information services, 167, 169-170
Alabama
LJ report, 8, 9, 10
networks and cooperative library organizations, 627
SLJ news report, 13
Alaska; networks and cooperative library organizations, 627
Allen, Tim, 577
Almanacs, bestselling, 600-601
American Booksellers Book of the Year (ABBY), 241
American Geophysical Union v. Texaco, 208, 223, 255-256
American Historical Association et al. v. Peterson, 256
American Libraries as placement source, 360
American Technology Preeminence Act (ATPA), 108

Mississippi
LJ report, 6-7, 9
networks and cooperative library
organizations, 642-643
Missouri
LJ report, 7, 10
networks and networking, 643
civic, 32-33
SLJ news report, 12, 16
Moldea, Dan, 226
Montana
LJ report, 7, 8, 9
networks and networking, 29, 31, 643
Movies, and bestselling books, 578-579, 587,
601-602
Multimedia; joint ventures, 23
Music libraries, *see* International Association
of Music Libraries, Archives and Doc-
umentation Centres; Music Library
Association

N

National Book Week, 231, 238
National Engineering Information Initiative
(NEII), 287
National Film Preservation Act of 1992, 135
National Independent Bookstore Week, 247
National information infrastructure (NII), 27,
57, 58-59, 65-69, 259-260
AAP activities, 224, 225
Advisory Council, 67-69, 260
electronic access, 69
members, 68-69
ALA activities, 198-199, 265
ALA support for, 262, 265
defined, 65-66
grants, 36
intellectual property issue, 211, 270
libraries and, 288
NCLIS activities, 101-102
outreach, 67-68
principles and goals, 66
school/library connections, 265
SLA activities, 207
task force, *see* Information Infrastructure
Task Force
telecommunications policy
See also Internet

National Library Week, 200, 202, 208-209,
406
International Special Librarians Day, 208-
209
"Libraries Change Lives", 202, 203
Library Legislative Day, 208, 252
National Technical Information Act of 1988,
110
Native Americans, library and information
services to
LSCA Title IV, 309-311
basic grant awards, FY 1994, 311(table)
special projects awards, FY 1994,
312(table)
Nebraska
LJ report, 9, 10
networks and cooperative library
organizations, 643
The Netherlands; periodical prices and price
indexes, 497, 499
Dutch (English Language), 1993-1995,
508(table)
Networks and networking, 11
book sales, 24
bulletin board systems, 28
campus networks, 38-45
children and young adults, 161-162, 177-
178
civic, *see* Civic networks
community, *see* Civic networks
cooperative library organizations, 627-656
defined, 59
financial aspects, 57
future of, 59-61
grants, 32, 298(table)
health services, 28
image transfer, 43, 164-165, 167, 291
international, *see* Internet
key issues, 55-58
libraries and, 46-61, 627-656
LSCA funding, 350-352
NAL activities, 163
national, 46-50, 56
NCLIS activities, 101-102
NLM enhancements, 167
origins of, 28-29
reference services, 40
regional, 50, 51(table), 52-53, 56, 57-58
security issues, 53-54
state, 53-54, 56

Q

R

Reiser, Paul, 577-578
Religious libraries, *see* American Theological Library Association; Association of Jewish Libraries; Catholic Library Association; Church and Synagogue Library Association; Lutheran Church Library Association
Research libraries, *see* College and research libraries
Rhode Island
LJ report, 6, 7
networks and networking, 651
civic, 32
Rice, Anne, 579
Rushdie, Salman, 90, 227, 241-242
Russia; LC exhibit, 134

S

Safire, William, 11
Salaries, 380-392, 465
AAP survey, 236
1993 U.S. graduates
by school, 385-386(table)
summary by region, 381(table)
average salary index, starting library positions, 382, 391(table)
comparisons by type of library, 392(table)
library price indexes for personnel compensation, FYs, 1976-1992, 459(table)
LJ report, 5, 8
Sarajevo, 228
Scholarly books, *see* Academic books, prices and price indexes; Association of American Publishers, Professional and Scholarly Publishing Division; Textbooks
Scholarships and fellowships
award recipients, 399-421
HEA programs, 300-302(tables)
library scholarship sources, 395-398
USIA Library Fellows Program, 121, 204, 373-374
Robert Vosper IFLA Fellows Program, 288, 290
School libraries
acquisitions price indexes, FYs 1976-1992, 462-464(table)
NII, connection to, 265
placement for librarians, 372, 383-384(table)

research, 430-431
salaries compared by type of library, 1993, 392(table)
See also American Association of School Librarians; International Association of School Librarianship; School library media centers and services
School Library Journal (SLJ)
best books lists, 572-576
news report, 10-16
School library media centers and services, 265-266
Canadian, 97-98
NCES survey, 103, 126-127
SLJ news report, 16
statistics, 102-103, 430
See also American Association of School Librarians; International Association of School Librarianship; School libraries
Security issues, networks and networking, 53-54
Seminars, *see* Conferences and seminars
Senior citizens, library services for LSCA
funding, 337-338
expenditures, 339(table)
See also American Library Association, Reference and Adult Services Division
Serials, *see* Periodicals and serials
Sheldon, Sidney, 202
Simon, Jeanne Hurley, 99, 100
O.J. Simpson murder trial, 587
Smokey the Bear, 165
Snyder, Richard, 580
Sound recordings, *see* Audiovisual materials; CD-ROM (Compact disc Read-Only Memory)
South Africa; LC reception, 134-135
South Carolina
LJ report, 7
networks and cooperative library organizations, 651-652
South Dakota
LJ report, 9
networks and cooperative library organizations, 652
SLJ news report, 13
South Korea, 228
pirated books, 233